Oxford Handbook of Anxiety and Related Disorders

OXFORD LIBRARY OF PSYCHOLOGY

Editor-in-Chief
Peter E. Nathan

Oxford Handbook of Anxiety and Related Disorders

Edited by

Martin M. Antony

Murray B. Stein

OXFORD
UNIVERSITY PRESS

2009

OXFORD
UNIVERSITY PRESS

Oxford University Press, Inc., publishes works that further
Oxford University's objective of excellence
in research, scholarship, and education.

Oxford   New York
Auckland   Cape Town   Dar es Salaam   Hong Kong   Karachi
Kuala Lumpur   Madrid   Melbourne   Mexico City   Nairobi
New Delhi   Shanghai   Taipei   Toronto

With offices in
Argentina   Austria   Brazil   Chile   Czech Republic   France   Greece
Guatemala   Hungary   Italy   Japan   Poland   Portugal   Singapore
South Korea   Switzerland   Thailand   Turkey   Ukraine   Vietnam

Published by Oxford University Press, Inc.
198 Madison Avenue, New York, New York 10016

www.oup.com

Oxford is a registered trademark of Oxford University Press.

Library of Congress Cataloging-in-Publication Data
Oxford handbook of anxiety and related disorders / edited by Martin M. Antony, Murray B. Stein.
p. ; cm. — (Oxford library of psychology)
Includes bibliographical references and index.
ISBN: 978-0-19-530703-0
1. Anxiety—Handbooks, manuals, etc.
[DNLM: 1. Anxiety Disorders.   WM 172 O98 2008]   I. Title: Handbook of anxiety and
related disorders.   II. Antony, Martin M.   III. Stein, Murray B., 1959–   IV. Series.
RC531.O94 2008
616.85'22—dc22   2007050112

9 8 7 6 5 4 3 2 1

Printed in the United States of America
on acid-free paper

CONTENTS

Contributors ix

Part One • Overview and Introduction

1. Overview and Introduction to Anxiety Disorders   3
   Martin M. Antony, Anita Federici, and Murray B. Stein

Part Two • Phenomenology and Epidemiology of Anxiety Disorders

2. Epidemiology of Anxiety Disorders   19
   Ronald C. Kessler, Ayelet Meron Ruscio, Katherine Shear, and Hans-Ulrich Wittchen
3. Phenomenology of Panic and Phobic Disorders   34
   Stefan G. Hofmann, Georg W. Alpers, and Paul Pauli
4. Phenomenology of Generalized Anxiety Disorder   47
   Holly Hazlett-Stevens, Larry D. Pruitt, and Angela Collins
5. Phenomenology of Obsessive-Compulsive Disorder   56
   Carol A. Mathews
6. Phenomenology of Posttraumatic Stress Disorder and Acute Stress Disorder   65
   Matthew J. Friedman

Part Three • Approaches to Understanding Anxiety Disorders

7. Preclinical Approaches to Understanding Anxiety Disorders   75
   Victoria B. Risbrough and Mark A. Geyer
8. Heritability and Genetics of Anxiety Disorders   87
   Joel Gelernter and Murray B. Stein
9. Neuroanatomy and Neuroimaging of Anxiety Disorders   97
   Jennifer C. Britton and Scott L. Rauch
10. Neuroendocrinology of Anxiety Disorders   111
    Samir Khan, Anthony P. King, James L. Abelson, and Israel Liberzon
11. Developmental Approaches to Understanding Anxiety Disorders   123
    Richie Poulton, Jessica R. Grisham, and Gavin Andrews
12. Information-Processing Approaches to Understanding Anxiety Disorders   136
    Richard J. McNally and Hannah E. Reese

13. Understanding Anxiety Disorders from a "Triple Vulnerability"
    Framework   153
    Liza M. Suárez, Shannon M. Bennett, Clark R. Goldstein, and David H. Barlow
14. Familial and Social Environments in the Etiology and Maintenance
    of Anxiety Disorders   173
    Jennifer L. Hudson and Ronald M. Rapee
15. Personality Factors in the Anxiety Disorders   190
    Jina Pagura, Brian J. Cox, and Murray W. Enns
16. Psychological Models of Phobic Disorders and Panic   209
    Sheila R. Woody and Elizabeth Nosen
17. Psychological Models of Worry and Generalized Anxiety Disorder   225
    Peter L. Fisher and Adrian Wells
18. Psychological Approaches to Understanding Obsessive-Compulsive
    Disorder   238
    Christine Purdon
19. Psychological Models of Posttraumatic Stress Disorder and
    Acute Stress Disorder   250
    Lori A. Zoellner, Afsoon Eftekhari, and Michele Bedard-Gilligan

Part Four • Classification and Assessment
20. Classification and Boundaries Among Anxiety-Related Problems   265
    Amy E. Lawrence and Timothy A. Brown
21. Assessment of Anxiety Disorders   277
    Jennifer L. Harrington and Martin M. Antony

Part Five • Treatment of Anxiety Disorders
22. Pharmacotherapy for Panic Disorder and Agoraphobia   295
    Mark H. Pollack and Naomi M. Simon
23. Psychological Treatment of Panic Disorder and Agoraphobia   308
    Randi E. McCabe and Shannon Gifford
24. Pharmacotherapy for Social Anxiety Disorder and
    Specific Phobia   321
    Michael Van Ameringen, Catherine Mancini, and Beth Patterson
25. Psychological Treatment of Social Anxiety Disorder
    and Specific Phobia   334
    Leanne Magee, Brigette A. Erwin, and Richard G. Heimberg
26. Pharmacotherapy for Generalized Anxiety Disorder   350
    Sanjay J. Mathew and Ellen J. Hoffman
27. Psychological Treatment of Generalized Anxiety Disorder   364
    Melisa Robichaud and Michel J. Dugas
28. Biological Treatment for Obsessive-Compulsive Disorder   375
    S. Evelyn Stewart, Eric Jenike, and Michael A. Jenike
29. Psychological Treatment of Obsessive-Compulsive Disorder   391
    *Jonathan S. Abramowitz, Autumn E. Braddock,
    and Elizabeth L. Moore*

30. Pharmacotherapy for Posttraumatic Stress Disorder and
    Other Trauma-Related Disorders   405
    Mary F. Dent and J. Douglas Bremner
31. Psychological Treatment of Posttraumatic Stress Disorder and
    Acute Stress Disorder   417
    David S. Riggs and Edna B. Foa
32. Combining Pharmacological and Cognitive Behavioral Therapy
    in the Treatment of Anxiety Disorders   429
    *Michael W. Otto, Evelyn Behar, Jasper A. J. Smits, and
    Stefan G. Hofmann*
33. Integrated Psychological Treatment of Multiple Anxiety Disorders   441
    Peter J. Norton
34. Complementary and Alternative Approaches to Treating
    Anxiety Disorders   451
    Kathryn M. Connor and Sandeep Vaishnavi
35. Exposure-Based Treatments for Anxiety Disorders:
    Theory and Process   461
    David A. Moscovitch, Martin M. Antony, and Richard P. Swinson
36. Mindfulness and Acceptance-Based Treatments for
    Anxiety Disorders   476
    Lizabeth Roemer, Shannon M. Erisman, and Susan M. Orsillo
37. Self-Help Treatments for Anxiety Disorders   488
    John R. Walker, Norah Vincent, and Patricia Furer
38. Prevention of Child and Youth Anxiety and Anxiety Disorders   497
    Paula Barrett and Lara Farrell
39. Managing Anxiety in Primary Care   512
    Denise A. Chavira, Murray B. Stein, and Peter Roy-Byrne

Part Six · Other Anxiety-Based Conditions
40. Hypochondriasis and Health Anxiety   525
    Steven Taylor and Gordon J. G. Asmundson
41. Body Dysmorphic Disorder   541
    David Veale
42. Fear of Pain   551
    Gordon J. G. Asmundson and R. Nicholas Carleton

**Part Seven · Comorbidity and Relationships With
              Other Conditions**
43. Anxiety Disorders and Substance Use Disorder Comorbidity   565
    Marc Zahradnik and Sherry H. Stewart
44. Anxiety Disorders and Depression Comorbidity   576
    Jonathan D. Huppert
45. Anxiety Disorders and Personality Disorders Comorbidity   587
    Mina Brandes and O. Joseph Bienvenu

46. Anxiety Disorders and Physical Comorbidity   596
    Shay-Lee Belik, Jitender Sareen, and Murray B. Stein
47. Anxiety and Sleep   611
    Allison G. Harvey, Ilana S. Hairston, June Gruber, and Anda Gershon

Part Eight · Anxiety in Specific Populations

48. Anxiety Disorders and Hoarding in Older Adults   625
    Catherine R. Ayers, Steven R. Thorp, and
    Julie Loebach Wetherell
49. Anxiety Disorders in Children and Adolescents   636
    Jami M. Furr, Shilpee Tiwari,
    Cynthia Suveg, and Philip C. Kendall
50. Anxiety and Culture   657
    Laila Asmal and Dan J. Stein

Part Nine · Future Directions

51. Future Directions in Anxiety Disorders Research   667
    Martin M. Antony and Murray B. Stein

Index   679

CONTRIBUTORS

James L. Abelson
Anxiety Disorders Clinic
Department of Psychiatry
University of Michigan
Ann Arbor, MI

Jonathan S. Abramowitz
Department of Psychology
University of North Carolina at
Chapel Hill
Chapel Hill, NC

Georg W. Alpers
Department of Psychology, Biological
Psychology, Clinical Psychology, and
Psychotherapy
University of Würzburg
Würzburg, Germany

Gavin Andrews
University of New South Wales, and
Clinical Research Unit for Anxiety and
Depression (CRUfAD)
School of Psychiatry
Sydney, Australia

Martin M. Antony
Department of Psychology
Ryerson University
Toronto, Canada and
Anxiety Treatment and Research Centre
St. Joseph's Healthcare
Hamilton, Canada

Laila Asmal
Department of Psychiatry and
Mental Health
University of Cape Town
Cape Town, South Africa

Gordon J. G. Asmundson
Faculty of Kinesiology and
Health Studies
University of Regina
Regina, Canada

Catherine R. Ayers
Sharp Mesa Vista Hospital, and
Veterans Affairs San Diego Healthcare
System
San Diego, CA

David H. Barlow
Center for Anxiety and Related Disorders
Boston University
Boston, MA

Paula Barrett
School of Education
The University of Queensland, and
Pathways Health and Research Centre
West End, Australia

Michele Bedard-Gilligan
Department of Psychology
University of Washington
Seattle, WA

Evelyn Behar
Department of Psychology
University of Illinois at Chicago
Chicago, IL

Shay-Lee Belik
Department of Psychiatry, and
Department of Community Health Sciences
University of Manitoba
Winnipeg, Canada

Shannon M. Bennett
Center for Anxiety and Related Disorders
Department of Psychology
Boston University
Boston, MA

O. Joseph Bienvenu
Johns Hopkins Anxiety Disorders Clinic
Department of Psychiatry and Behavioral
Sciences
Johns Hopkins University School of
Medicine
Baltimore, MD

Autumn E. Braddock
Anxiety Disorders Clinic
Department of Psychiatry and
Psychology
Mayo Clinic
Rochester, MN

Mina Brandes
Department of Psychiatry and
Behavioral Sciences
Johns Hopkins University School
of Medicine
Baltimore, MD

J. Douglas Bremner
Emory Center for Positron Emission
Tomography
Emory University School of Medicine
Atlanta, GA

Jennifer C. Britton
Department of Psychiatry
Massachusetts General Hospital
Charlestown, MA

Timothy A. Brown
Center for Anxiety and Related
Disorders
Department of Psychology
Boston University
Boston, MA

R. Nicholas Carleton
Department of Psychology
University of Regina
Regina, Canada

Denise A. Chavira
Department of Psychiatry
University of California at San Diego
San Diego, CA

Angela Collins
Department of Psychology
University of Nevada at Reno
Reno, NV

Kathryn M. Connor
Clinical Neuroscience
Merck Research Laboratories
North Wales, PA

Brian J. Cox
Department of Psychiatry, Department
of Psychology, and Department of
Community Health Sciences
University of Manitoba
Winnipeg, Canada

Mary F. Dent
Emory Clinical Neurosciences
Research Unit
Emory University
Atlanta, GA

Michel J. Dugas
Department of Psychology
Concordia University
Montreal, Canada

Afsoon Eftekhari
Department of Psychology
University of Washington
Seattle, WA

Murray W. Enns
Department of Psychiatry, and
Department of Community
Health Sciences
University of Manitoba
Winnipeg, Canada

Shannon M. Erisman
Department of Psychology
University of Massachusetts at Boston
Boston, MA

Brigette A. Erwin
Adult Anxiety Clinic
Department of Psychology
Temple University
Philadelphia, PA

Lara Farrell
School of Psychology
The University of Queensland
St Lucia, Australia

Anita Federici
Anxiety Treatment and
Research Centre
St. Joseph's Healthcare
Hamilton, Canada

Peter L. Fisher
Division of Clinical
Psychology
University of Liverpool
Liverpool, United Kingdom

Edna B. Foa
Center for the Study and
Treatment of Anxiety
Department of Psychiatry
University of Pennsylvania
School of Medicine
Philadelphia, PA

Matthew J. Friedman
National Center for Posttraumatic
Stress Disorder
Veterans Affairs Medical Center
White River Junction, VT, and
Departments of Psychiatry,
Pharmacology and Toxicology
Dartmouth Medical School
Hanover, NH

Patricia Furer
Department of Clinical Health Psychology,
and Anxiety Disorders Program
St. Boniface General Hospital
University of Manitoba
Winnipeg, Canada

Jami M. Furr
Child and Adolescent Anxiety
Disorders Clinic
Department of Psychology
Temple University
Philadelphia, PA

Joel Gelernter
Genetics and Neurobiology
Yale University School of Medicine
New Haven, CT

Anda Gershon
Sleep and Psychological
Disorders Lab
Psychology Department
University of California at Berkeley
Berkeley, CA

Mark A. Geyer
Department of Psychiatry
University of California at San Diego
La Jolla, CA

Shannon Gifford
Operational Stress Injury Clinic
Parkwood Hospital
St. Joseph's Health Care
London, Canada

Clark R. Goldstein
Center for Anxiety and Related Disorders
Department of Psychology
Boston University
Boston, MA

Jessica R. Grisham
School of Psychology
University of New South Wales
Sydney, Australia

June Gruber
Sleep and Psychological Disorders Lab
Psychology Department
University of California at Berkeley
Berkeley, CA

Ilana S. Hairston
Sleep and Psychological Disorders Lab
Psychology Department
University of California at Berkeley
Berkeley, CA

Jennifer L. Harrington
Department of Psychology
University of Waterloo
Waterloo, ON, and
Anxiety Treatment and Research Centre
St. Joseph's Healthcare
Hamilton, Canada

Allison G. Harvey
Sleep and Psychological Disorders Lab
Psychology Department
University of California at Berkeley
Berkeley, CA

Holly Hazlett-Stevens
Department of Psychology
University of Nevada at Reno
Reno, NV

Richard G. Heimberg
Department of Psychology, and
Adult Anxiety Clinic
Temple University
Philadelphia, PA

Ellen J. Hoffman
Department of Psychiatry
Mount Sinai School of Medicine
New York, NY

Stefan G. Hofmann
Department of Psychology
Center for Anxiety and
Related Disorders
Boston University
Boston, MA

Jennifer L. Hudson
Department of Psychology
Macquarie University
Sydney, Australia

Jonathan D. Huppert
Department of Psychology
The Hebrew University of Jerusalem
Jerusalem, Israel

Eric Jenike
Psychiatric and Neurodevelopmental
Genetics Unit
Massachusetts General Hospital
Boston, MA

Michael A. Jenike
Harvard Medical School
Massachusetts General Hospital
Boston, MA

Philip C. Kendall
Child and Adolescent Anxiety Disorders Clinic
Department of Psychology
Temple University
Philadelphia, PA

Ronald C. Kessler
Department of Health Care Policy
Harvard Medical School
Boston, MA

Samir Khan
Department of Psychiatry
University of Michigan
Ann Arbor, MI

Anthony P. King
Department of Psychiatry
University of Michigan
Ann Arbor, MI

Amy E. Lawrence
Center for Anxiety and Related Disorders
Department of Psychology
Boston University
Boston, MA

Israel Liberzon
Department of Psychiatry and
Neuroscience
University of Michigan
Ann Arbor, MI

Leanne Magee
Adult Anxiety Clinic
Department of Psychology
Temple University
Philadelphia, PA

Catherine Mancini
Department of Psychiatry and
Behavioural Neurosciences
McMaster University, and
Anxiety Disorders Clinic
McMaster University Medical Centre
Hamilton Health Sciences
Hamilton, Canada

Sanjay J. Mathew
Department of Psychiatry
Mount Sinai School of Medicine
New York, NY

Carol A. Mathews
Department of Psychiatry
University of California at San Francisco
San Francisco, CA

Randi E. McCabe
Department of Psychiatry and Behavioural
Neurosciences
McMaster University, and
Anxiety Treatment and Research Centre
St. Joseph's Healthcare
Hamilton, Canada

Richard J. McNally
Department of Psychology
Harvard University
Cambridge, MA

Elizabeth L. Moore
OCD/Anxiety Disorders Program
Mayo Clinic
Rochester, MN

David A. Moscovitch
Department of Psychology
University of Waterloo
Waterloo, Canada

Peter J. Norton
Department of Psychology, and
Anxiety Disorder Clinic
University of Houston
Houston, TX

Elizabeth Nosen
Department of Psychology
University of British Columbia
Vancouver, Canada

Susan M. Orsillo
Psychology Department
Suffolk University
Boston, MA

Michael W. Otto
Center for Anxiety and Related Disorders
Boston University
Boston, MA

Jina Pagura
Department of Psychology, and
Department of Psychiatry
University of Manitoba
Winnipeg, Canada

Beth Patterson
Anxiety Disorders Clinic
Hamilton Health Sciences
McMaster University Medical Centre
Hamilton, Canada

Paul Pauli
Department of Psychology, Biological
Psychology, Clinical Psychology, and
Psychotherapy
University of Würzburg
Würzburg, Germany

Mark H. Pollack
Center for Anxiety and Traumatic
Stress Disorders
Massachusetts General Hospital, and
Department of Psychiatry
Harvard Medical School
Boston, MA

Richie Poulton
Dunedin Multidisciplinary Health and
Development
Research Unit
Dunedin School of Medicine
University of Otago
Dunedin, New Zealand

Larry D. Pruitt
Department of Psychology
University of Nevada at Reno
Reno, NV

Christine Purdon
Department of Psychology
University of Waterloo
Waterloo, Canada

Ronald M. Rapee
Center for Emotional Health
Department of Psychology
Macquarie University
Sydney, Australia

Scott L. Rauch
Department of Psychiatry
Harvard Medical School,
Boston, MA, and
Partners Psychiatry and Mental Health
McLean Hospital
Belmont, MA

Hannah E. Reese
Department of Psychology
Harvard University
Cambridge, MA

David S. Riggs
Center for Deployment Psychology, and
Department of Medical and Clinical
Psychology
Uniformed Services University
Bethesda, MD

Victoria B. Risbrough
Department of Psychiatry
University of California at San Diego
La Jolla, CA

Melisa Robichaud
Anxiety Disorders Clinic
University of British Columbia
Hospital
Vancouver, Canada

Lizabeth Roemer
Department of Psychology
University of Massachusetts at Boston
Boston, MA

Peter Roy-Byrne
Department of Psychiatry and
Behavioral Sciences
University of Washington at Harborview
Medical Center
Seattle, WA

Ayelet Meron Ruscio
Department of Psychology
University of Pennsylvania
Philadelphia, PA

Jitender Sareen
Department of Psychiatry, and
Department of Community
Health Sciences
University of Manitoba
Winnipeg, Canada

Katherine Shear
Department of Psychiatry
Columbia University School of
Social Work
New York, NY

Naomi M. Simon
Center for Anxiety and Traumatic
Stress Disorders
Massachusetts General Hospital
Boston, MA

Jasper A. J. Smits
Department of Psychology
Southern Methodist University
Dallas, TX

Dan J. Stein
Department of Psychiatry and
Mental Health
University of Cape Town
Cape Town, South Africa

Murray B. Stein
Department of Psychiatry, and
Anxiety and Traumatic Stress Program
University of California at San Diego,
and Veterans Affairs San Diego
Healthcare System
La Jolla, CA

Evelyn Stewart
Harvard Medical School
Department of Psychiatry
Massachusetts General Hospital
Boston, MA

Sherry H. Stewart
Department of Psychology, and
Department of Psychiatry
Dalhousie University
Halifax, Canada

Liza M. Suárez
Institute for Juvenile Research
Department of Psychiatry
University of Illinois at Chicago
Chicago, IL

Cynthia Suveg
Department of Psychology
University of Georgia
Athens, GA

Richard P. Swinson
Department of Psychiatry and
Behavioural Neurosciences
McMaster University, and Anxiety
Treatment and Research Centre
St. Joseph's Healthcare
Hamilton, Canada

Steven Taylor
Department of Psychiatry
University of British Columbia
Vancouver, Canada

Steven R. Thorp
Department of Psychiatry
University of California at San Diego, and
PTSD Clinical Team
Veterans Affairs San Diego
Healthcare System
San Diego, CA

Shilpee Tiwari
Child and Adolescent Anxiety
Disorders Clinic
Department of Psychology
Temple University
Philadelphia, PA

Sandeep Vaishnavi
Johns Hopkins University School of
Medicine
Baltimore, MD

Michael Van Ameringen
Department of Psychiatry and Behavioural
Neurosciences
McMaster University, and
Anxiety Disorders Clinic
Hamilton Health Sciences
McMaster University Medical Centre
Hamilton, Canada

David Veale
Institute of Psychiatry
King's College London
London, United Kingdom

Norah Vincent
Department of Clinical
Health Psychology
University of Manitoba
Health Sciences Centre
Winnipeg, Canada

John R. Walker
Department of Clinical Health Psychology
University of Manitoba, and
Anxiety Disorders Program
St. Boniface General Hospital
Winnipeg, Canada

Adrian Wells
Academic Division of
Clinical Psychology
University of Manchester
Manchester, United Kingdom

Julie Loebach Wetherell
Department of Psychiatry
Veterans Affairs San Diego
Healthcare System
San Diego, CA

Hans-Ulrich Wittchen
Institute of Clinical Psychology and
Psychotherapy
Technische Universitaet Dresden
Dresden, Germany

Sheila R. Woody
Department of Psychology
University of British Columbia
Vancouver, Canada

Marc Zahradnik
Department of Psychology
Dalhousie University
Halifax, Canada

Lori A. Zoellner
Department of Psychology
University of Washington
Seattle, WA

PART 1

Overview and Introduction

Overview and Introduction to Anxiety Disorders

Martin M. Antony, Anita Federici *and* Murray B. Stein

Abstract

This chapter provides an overview of the *Oxford Handbook of Anxiety and Related Disorders*, and an introduction to the nature and treatment of anxiety and related disorders. With 51 chapters, this handbook covers a wide range of topics related to anxiety disorders, including phenomenology, etiology, assessment, and treatment. Key features of panic attacks and of each of the major anxiety disorders (e.g., panic disorder and agoraphobia, social phobia, specific phobia, generalized anxiety disorder, obsessive-compulsive disorder, and posttraumatic stress disorder) are reviewed. Etiological factors such as genetics, biological processes, learning, information processing, cultural factors, and personality are considered. The chapter concludes with a review of effective treatments (e.g., pharmacotherapy, psychological interventions, and combined approaches).

Keywords: anxiety disorders, etiology, treatment

Orientation to the Handbook

As the fields of psychology, psychiatry, and related disciplines evolve, it is important for researchers and clinicians to remain up-to-date with the latest empirical findings, theoretical perspectives, and trends that subsequently guide their practices. In the area of anxiety research, significant gains have been made in recent years with respect to our conceptualization of anxiety disorders and the development of evidence-based treatments. While traditional theories and approaches remain highly influential, health professionals are continually searching for strategies and interventions to enhance existing therapies.

The primary goal in developing this text was to create a comprehensive and up-to-date handbook that would detail the various research and clinical developments in the field of anxiety. From phenomenology and classification to treatment and comorbidity, the reader is provided with extensive descriptive information, empirical findings, areas of controversy, and suggested future directions.

The balance between breadth and depth and the integration of both traditional and contemporary theories will appeal to clinicians, researchers, educators, and students alike. Each topic was chosen to reflect clinical and theoretical approaches that currently inform our understanding of the development and treatment of anxiety disorders. Furthermore, in order to incorporate multiple approaches and perspectives, chapters were written by authors from a variety of academic disciplines and clinical backgrounds (e.g., psychology, psychiatry, nursing, social work).

The first part of the book includes this overview and introduction. Part Two provides a descriptive review of each of the main anxiety disorders: panic disorder, social phobia, and specific phobia (Chapter 3), generalized anxiety disorder (GAD) (Chapter 4), obsessive-compulsive disorder (OCD) (Chapter 5), and posttraumatic stress disorder (PTSD) (Chapter 6). In addition to a review of diagnostic criteria, prevalence rates, and comorbidity, each chapter highlights current conceptual, methodological, and clinical issues in the field. For example, suicide risk, health care utilization, and functional impairment across the anxiety disorders are discussed in Chapter 2. Hazlett-Stevens, Pruitt, and Collins (Chapter 4) add clarity to the term *worry* in GAD by differentiating it from obsessive thoughts, depressive ruminations, and "normal" levels of worry in the general population. In her review of OCD, Mathews (Chapter 5) discusses the pros and cons of various subtyping approaches and highlights current diagnostic and conceptual issues between OCD and other comorbid conditions.

Part Three focuses on empirically supported neurobiological and psychological approaches to understanding anxiety disorders. Chapters 7 through 10 describe advances in animal research (Chapter 7), genetic research (Chapter 8), and neuoranatomical models (Chapter 9) that have contributed to our evolving understanding of the biological processes involved in decision making, detection of threat, and emotional responding. Chapters 11 through 19 offer detailed descriptions of the most influential psychological models in the field of anxiety. While some chapters provide details on well-established theoretical models (e.g., learning theories, cognitive behavioral models), other chapters present more contemporary and integrative theories (e.g., Barlow's "triple vulnerability" model in Chapter 13; emotional dysregulation and intolerance of uncertainty models of GAD in Chapter 17). This section is strengthened by the addition of several chapters that focus on developmental theories, early prevention (Chapter 11), the impact of family and social relationships (Chapter 14), and the role of personality (Chapter 15) in the development and maintenance of anxiety disorders.

Part Four presents current issues in classification and assessment. Establishing accurate diagnoses, determining predominant conditions, and ruling out additional disorders is a challenging and complex skill. Given that diagnoses have important implications for case conceptualization and treatment planning, a thorough and up-to-date understanding of issues that may complicate assessment (e.g., differential diagnoses, comorbidity) is essential. Lawrence and Brown (Chapter 20) address concerns regarding diagnostic overlap between syndromes and draw attention to the limitations of the primarily categorical approach adopted in the current edition of the *Diagnostic and Statistical Manual of Mental Disorders* (*DSM–IV–TR*; American Psychiatric Association [APA], 2000). The following chapter on

assessment strategies (Chapter 21) reviews the functions of assessment and provides a useful framework for selecting various empirically supported assessment measures.

Part Five represents the largest section of this book and focuses specifically on treatment approaches. For each of the major anxiety disorders, detailed discussions of both pharmacological and psychological approaches are provided. In addition to reviewing empirical data on traditional and well-recognized interventions, these chapters also highlight innovative and alternative treatment approaches. For example, chapters include information on the use of virtual reality (Chapter 25), transdiagnostic protocols (Chapter 33), the use of herbal products and complementary treatments (Chapter 34), acceptance and mindfulness-based approaches (Chapter 36), and self-help treatments (Chapter 37). In addition, unique issues such as treating nocturnal panic attacks (Chapter 22), eye movement desensitization reprocessing techniques in PTSD (Chapter 31), the use of surgical procedures to treat OCD (Chapter 28), prevention of anxiety in children (Chapter 38), and treating anxiety in primary care settings (Chapter 39) are also discussed in detail.

The attention to breadth and depth is also apparent in the next three sections of the book where in-depth information is provided about other anxiety-based conditions, (e.g., hypochondriasis, body dysmorphic disorder), special topics related to comorbid substance use, cultural issues, and the impact of anxiety disorders in specific populations (e.g., children, older adults). Additionally, the inclusion of such topics as the fear of pain (Chapter 42) and the relationship between anxiety and sleep (Chapter 47) further expand our scope of understanding. The final part of the book (Chapter 51) provides an overview of future directions in anxiety disorders research.

In the remainder to this introductory chapter, a brief introduction to the diagnostic features of the anxiety disorders will be provided, followed by a general summary of issues pertaining to etiology and treatment. The purpose of this section is to offer a concise review of the major themes, concepts, and approaches that will be discussed in subsequent chapters.

General Introduction to the Anxiety Disorders

The anxiety disorders are among the most common and debilitating of the psychological disorders. Often chronic in nature, anxiety disorders are associated with severe impairments across interpersonal and occupational domains. The purpose of this section is to provide a general introduction to the main anxiety disorders outlined in the *DSM–IV–TR*. Specific attention is given to diagnostic features, prevalence rates, comorbidity, and issues in assessment.

Panic Attacks

The *DSM–IV–TR* defines a panic attack as a period of intense fear or discomfort in which the individual experiences at least four of the following symptoms (peaking in intensity within 10 minutes or less): racing or pounding heart, sweating, trembling, shortness of breath, choking sensations, chest pain or tightness, nausea or stomach upset, dizziness, derealization or depersonalization, fear of losing control or going crazy, fear of dying, numbness or tingling sensations, and chills or hot flushes. The term *limited symptom attack* is used to describe an attack in which fewer than four symptoms are present. Panic attacks are not specific to any one anxiety disorder. For example, individuals with panic disorder, specific phobia, and social phobia may experience panic attacks during the course of their illness. In order to provide greater diagnostic and descriptive clarity, there are three main types of panic attacks. *Unexpected or "uncued" attacks* are those that occur in situations or places in which the individual normally feels safe. Often, people report that they occur "out of the blue" and are not associated with any specific trigger or cue. *Situationally bound or "cued" attacks* are those that occur almost always in response to a feared stimulus (e.g., a person with a specific phobia of driving experiences a panic attack when riding in a car). *Situationally predisposed attacks* are those that are more likely to occur in particular types of situations, but do not always occur (e.g., a person with panic disorder with agoraphobia who often has panic attacks in public places).

Panic Disorder

Diagnostic criteria for panic disorder require that an individual experience recurrent and unexpected panic attacks that are followed by a period of at least 1 month of marked worry about having additional attacks, anxiety about the implications of the attacks (e.g., having a heart attack, going crazy), and/or a significant change in behavior. Although they frequently co-occur, panic disorder may or may not be associated with *agoraphobia,* or the intentional avoidance of situations/places from which it might be difficult to escape or receive help in the event of a panic attack (e.g., being away from home, crowds, public transportation, shopping malls). For individuals whose symptoms have never met full criteria for panic disorder but who endorse significant avoidance and fear of panic-like symptoms (e.g., diarrhea, dizziness), a diagnosis of agoraphobia without a history of panic disorder may be warranted. Lifetime prevalence rates of panic disorder (with or without agoraphobia) in the general population are estimated to be at about 4.5%, whereas agoraphobia without history of panic disorder has been found to occur in 1.4% of the population (Kessler, Berglund, Demler, Jin, & Walters, 2005). This condition is more common among women than men. Symptoms typically develop in late adolescence or early adulthood and tend to vary in frequency and intensity across the lifespan.

Social Phobia

The essential feature of social phobia (or social anxiety disorder) is marked fear and anxiety about being negatively evaluated in social or performance-based situations (e.g., public speaking, meeting strangers, maintaining conversations). Fearful of being judged, criticized, or embarrassed, individuals with social phobia often avoid social situations or endure them with considerable distress. For individuals whose fears are related to multiple situations (e.g., formal speaking, eating in front of others, dating situations, etc.), the diagnostic specifier *generalized type* may be added. Common in the general population (lifetime prevalence rates range from 7% to 13%) (Furmark, 2002; Ruscio et al., 2008), the disorder typically begins in early adolescence (APA, 2000). In addition, it is not uncommon for social phobia to be associated with substance use, bulimia nervosa, and to occur within the context of a mood disorder or other anxiety disorders. Currently, an area of debate and an issue of diagnostic specificity is the significant symptom overlap between social phobia on Axis I and avoidant personality disorder on Axis II (see Chapter 3).

Specific Phobia

The *DSM–IV–TR* describes specific phobia as clinically significant anxiety and disproportionate fear of specific objects or situations. The five main types of specific phobia in *DSM–IV–TR* include *animal type* (e.g., fear of snakes, spiders, dogs), *natural environment type* (e.g., fear of heights, storms, water), *blood-injection-injury type* (e.g., fear of blood, needles, surgery), *situational type* (e.g., fear of enclosed places, driving, flying), and *other type* (e.g., fear of vomiting, choking, or other specific objects or situations). Despite awareness that their fear is excessive, individuals with specific phobia typically avoid the feared object or situation. Although specific phobia is among the most commonly occurring anxiety disorders, with a recent lifetime prevalence estimate of 12.5% (Kessler et al., 2005), only a small proportion of sufferers (12% to 30%) are estimated to seek treatment for their symptoms (APA, 2000). Often, specific phobias are diagnosed as additional disorders in people suffering from other anxiety disorders or depression. In these cases, the other disorder is usually the prominent focus of attention. Among the anxiety disorders, specific phobias are the most responsive to treatment. As discussed in greater detail in Chapter 25, significant improvements have been observed after a single session of exposure treatment. With regard to assessment, it is important for clinicians to be aware of diagnostic similarities between specific phobia and other psychological disorders such as hypochondriasis (fear of illness or disease), panic disorder (fear of physical sensations), and eating disorders (fear of food or weight gain).

Obsessive-Compulsive Disorder

Obsessive-compulsive disorder (OCD) is characterized by persistent and intrusive obsessions and/or compulsive behaviors. Obsessions may take the form of thoughts, images, or impulses and often surround themes such as contamination, doubting, aggression, accidental harm, religion, or thoughts of a sexual nature. Unlike a delusional or psychotic disorder, individuals with OCD recognize that their obsessions are a product of their own mind (APA, 2000). Compulsions are ritualistic behaviors that an individual feels compelled to perform in order to reduce feelings of anxiety and discomfort brought on by the obsession. Compulsive behaviors may include repeated hand-washing, checking, counting, hoarding, or a need for symmetry. In order to meet diagnostic criteria for OCD, the obsessions and compulsions must either be time-consuming or cause clinically significant distress. Prevalence rates for OCD have been estimated to be approximately 1.6% in community samples (Kessler et al., 2005) and the disorder appears to be about equally distributed among males and females (APA, 2000). Accurate assessment of OCD is complicated by the need to differentiate obsessions from delusional beliefs, depressive ruminations in major depressive disorder, and excessive worries about real-world concerns in generalized anxiety disorder (see Chapter 4). A key

area of current interest among researchers and clinicians is the relationship between OCD and disorders that have similar obsessive and compulsive traits. Sometimes referred to as the obsessive-compulsive spectrum disorders, some researchers hypothesize that conditions such as Tourette's syndrome, body dysmorphic disorder, trichotillomania, eating disorders, hypochondriasis, and obsessive-compulsive personality disorder may be etiologically similar to OCD.

Posttraumatic Stress Disorder

Posttraumatic stress disorder (PTSD) describes a set of characteristic somatic and cognitive symptoms, lasting at least 1 month, that occur in response to a highly traumatic event. As outlined in the *DSM–IV–TR*, the individual must experience or witness a traumatic event involving physical threat to the self or other (e.g., serious car accident, rape, combat). The criteria also specify that the person's response to the event must be one of intense fear, helplessness, or horror. In addition, individuals must demonstrate clinically significant and distressing symptoms from three distinct clusters: *reexperiencing symptoms* (e.g., recurrent nightmares, intrusive thoughts, flashbacks), *increased arousal* (e.g., irritability, hypervigilance), and *avoidance/numbing symptoms* (e.g., feelings of detachment, avoidance of people or places connected to the trauma). Posttraumatic stress disorder can be acute (>3 months duration), chronic (<3 months duration), or with delayed onset (symptoms develop 6 months after traumatic event). In the general population, PTSD has a lifetime prevalence rate of approximately 8% (APA, 2000); however, rates are significantly greater among victims of abuse, crime, and war. Chapter 6 provides a review of epidemiological data, risk factors, and prominent psychological models of PTSD.

Acute Stress Disorder

Introduced with the publication of *DSM–IV* (APA, 1994), acute stress disorder (ASD) is a relatively new diagnostic entity. The term is used to describe the development following exposure to a traumatic event of time-limited symptoms that are similar to those in PTSD (e.g., reexperiencing, avoidant, and arousal symptoms). However, ASD differs from PTSD in that it must occur within 1 month of the traumatic event and may not last longer than 4 consecutive weeks (beyond which a diagnosis of PTSD might be made). In addition, there is greater emphasis on dissociative symptoms in ASD (e.g., depersonalization, numbing, derealization, dissociative amnesia). The exact prevalence of ASD is not presently known, although estimates ranging from 14% to 33% in the aftermath of traumatic events have been described in the literature (APA, 2000). For more information on ASD and other stress-based responses (e.g., complex PTSD, disorders of extreme stress), see Chapter 6.

Generalized Anxiety Disorder

The hallmark of generalized anxiety disorder (GAD) is excessive and pervasive worry about a variety of topics such as minor matters (e.g., punctuality, small repairs), job security, finances, health of loved ones, future events. Worries in GAD are distinguished from nonpathological worry by their unrealistic and uncontrollable nature. In GAD, the worry is frequent (occurring more days than not) and chronic (lasting at least 6 months), though individuals with GAD often report that they have worried in this manner for the majority of their life. The criteria for GAD also require that individuals report at least three of the following symptoms: restlessness, fatigue, difficulty concentrating, irritability, muscle tension, and difficulty sleeping. Lifetime prevalence rates for GAD have been estimated to be 5.7% (Kessler et al., 2005), and GAD is more common among women than men (APA, 2000). Similar to the patterns observed in other anxiety disorders, individuals with GAD often have additional psychological disorders, the two most common being major depressive disorder and panic disorder (Campbell & Brown, 2002). More information about the features of GAD can be found in Chapter 4. It is also notable that, as GAD has evolved diagnostically over the past two decades, pharmacological and psychological treatments for GAD have also advanced. A review of the empirical data and a discussion on more contemporary approaches to treatment are described in Chapters 26 and 27.

Etiology of Anxiety Disorders

Most theorists agree that a single etiological cause in not sufficient to explain the developmental complexity and heterogeneity that characterize the anxiety disorders. Whereas early theoretical accounts tended to emphasize the independent and exclusive role of either nature (e.g., biology, including genetics) or nurture (e.g., learning, environment), contemporary theories of the development and maintenance of anxiety are based on more sophisticated, biopsychosocial models that include cognitive, behavioral, genetic, and environmental

elements. Over the past 20 years, these multidimensional approaches have greatly enhanced the way clinicians understand and treat these disorders. The following section will provide a brief introduction to the predominate approaches that currently guide research and treatment protocols.

Biological Processes

A great many biological processes have been implicated in risk for anxiety disorders, as well as in expression of anxiety disorders. In the past decade, biochemical theories of anxiety—which, it should be noted, overlap substantially with biochemical theories of depression—have focused on neurotransmitter systems that use serotonin (5-HT) or corticotropin-releasing factor (CRF), though numerous other neurotransmitters and neurohormones have also been implicated (see Chapters 7 and 10). More recently, there has been some convergence of theory (and supporting evidence) that risk for many (though perhaps not all of the) anxiety disorders may overlap substantially with biological factors that influence anxiety-related personality traits (e.g., the confluence of high neurosis and low extraversion, sometimes referred to as "neurotic introversion") (Bienvenu, Hettema, Neale, Prescott, & Kendler, 2007). What types of biological factors fit this mold?

There is evidence from animal studies that variation in the serotonin transporter promoter (5-HTTLPR) is relevant to our understanding of the relationship between personality and anxiety (and depressive) disorders. Mice with loss of serotonin transporter function due to genetic knockout have increased anxiety-like behaviors and exaggerated stress responses (Holmes, Murphy, & Crawley, 2003). In addition, Barr et al. (2004) assessed stress responsivity in infant rhesus macaques reared either with their mothers or in peer-only groups. At 6 months of age, adrenocorticotropic hormone (ACTH) responses and cortisol levels were measured at baseline and during a period of separation. Serotonin transporter genotype was also measured, and animals were characterized as either being homozygous for the long form of the serotonin transporter ("l/l") or having one copy of the long form and one copy of the short form ("l/s"). It was found that ACTH and cortisol levels increased during separation, consistent with the stressful nature of this experience. There was also an interaction between rearing experience and 5-HTLLPR genotype such that l/s animals had higher ACTH levels during separation than did l/l animals. This study is an example in nonhuman primates of how early life experience and genetics may interact to yield alterations in stress responsiveness and, by inference, risk for anxiety and mood disorders. The observation— now oft-replicated—that human variation in this polymorphism (5-HTTLPR) is associated with risk for adverse mental health outcomes (e.g., depression) in the context of life stress has resulted in 5-HTTLPR becoming the *gene celebre* of anxiety and depression research. More important, however, it has taken discussion of biopsychosocial models from the realm of the philosophical to the level of systems neuroscience (Caspi & Moffitt, 2006), ushering in an era of testable theories about genes and environment and their interaction. Though much of this work to date has focused on gene-environment interactions relevant to understanding depression, evidence is accruing that these relationships may be equally—or more—important for understanding risk for anxiety and related disorders (Stein, Schork, & Gelernter, in press). The role of genetic factors in anxiety and related disorders is covered in Chapter 8.

The notion of differential susceptibility to stress is certain to influence our thinking about the etiology of anxiety for years to come. In fact, measures of psychological resilience have been developed and validated (Campbell-Sills & Stein, in press; Connor & Davidson, 2003), and are likely to feature more prominently in research studies. Furthermore, the concept of resilience to stress is now being considered from a neuroscience perspective, yielding many candidate systems—above and beyond those involving serotonin—whose further study will undoubtedly help us ascertain individual differences that determine how the human psyche can so often thrive in the face of great adversity (Charney, 2004).

Brain imaging has provided another window into the biology of anxiety and related disorders, and is the focus of Chapter 9. Having evolved from studies of symptom provocation to the use of various types of emotion-processing tasks (e.g., the viewing of emotional faces), investigators have identified neural circuits that seem to function differently in patients with anxiety disorders. Two brain regions that have been consistently observed in patients with anxiety disorders to exhibit increased responsiveness in these types of paradigms are the amygdala and insula (Etkin & Wager, 2007). Moreover, hyperactivity in these regions has also been seen in individuals with high levels of traits such as neuroticism or anxiety sensitivity that can be considered to characterize them as anxiety-prone (Stein, Simmons, Feinstein, & Paulus, 2007), therein extending the possibility that this represents a "core" biological feature of these disorders. Notably, however, not all anxiety disorders share all these functional neuroimaging features (e.g., OCD), and it is these differences that may ultimately support the kind of biologically based classification system discussed earlier in this chapter.

Psychological Processes

Psychological theories of anxiety have predominately focused on the role of cognitive processes and behavioral responses to describe the acquisition and maintenance of anxiety disorders. Behavioral models include both classical and operant conditioning theories, highlighting the role of learning and the reinforcing nature of maladaptive responses to objects or situations. Classical conditioning models posit that fear and phobias develop as a result of the pairing between a neutral stimulus (e.g., dog) and an aversive experience (e.g., being bitten by a dog). While this model offered insight into the etiology of anxiety disorders, it did not account for the persistence and generalization of the fear response (e.g., fearing all dogs). To address this shortcoming, Mowrer (1960) proposed a two-factor theory of fear acquisition. Drawing from the pioneering work of Pavlov, Watson, and Skinner, he theorized that fears were established through principles of classical conditioning and maintained as a function of operant conditioning. In other words, while the avoidant and escape behaviors commonly observed among anxiety sufferers reduce distress and suffering in the short-term, they ultimately perpetuate anxiety in the long-term through negative reinforcement. In this way, the natural course of extinction is prevented and the fear is maintained. Several chapters include information on the influence of traditional and present-day learning theories among the anxiety disorders including posttraumatic stress disorder (Chapter 19), panic and phobias (Chapter 16), and generalized anxiety disorder (Chapter 17).

While conditioning models were highly influential, several important limitations were identified. For instance, they are unable to explain why some people develop phobias and others do not, after exposure to the same aversive or distressing stimulus. They also fail to explain how some individuals develop anxiety disorders in the absence of a personally aversive experience (e.g., developing a fear of flying, without having ever been on a plane). It was also unclear why certain stimuli (e.g., snakes, spiders, heights) were more likely to establish a fear response than others (e.g., electrical outlets, guns). The criticisms concerning the behavioral theories prompted clinicians and researchers to develop more sophisticated and inclusive models to explain anxiety, and to acknowledge the importance of observational learning, learning through the verbal transmission of information, emotional processing, and biological constraints on learning (e.g., Craske, Hermans & Vansteenwegen, 2006; Otto, 2002; Rachman, 1976; Rothbaum, 2006).

Some of the most influential work to emerge in the field of anxiety disorders was based on cognitive theories and approaches. Beck's (1976) cognitive theory of anxiety and depression was particularly important in providing a conceptual framework for anxiety. He proposed that emotions were largely determined by dysfunctional thoughts, beliefs, and attitudes. For example, a person with social phobia may believe that he or she will be ridiculed and rejected by others and consequently begins to experience anxiety and fear. In turn, these beliefs lead to avoidant behaviors, which, as previously noted, serve to maintain fear by prohibiting the individual from learning how to successfully cope with an anxiety-provoking situation. In addition, research has shown that maladaptive thoughts and beliefs significantly impact other cognitive domains such as memory, attention, and information processing. For instance, individuals with anxiety disorders are more likely to selectively recall and attend to fear-congruent objects or situations in their environments, and to process ambiguous stimuli as threatening (Mathews & MacLeod, 1994). McNally and Reese (Chapter 12) provide a comprehensive review of this area.

The specific meanings that people attach to their thoughts and experiences have also received increased attention in recent years. David Clark's (1986) influential theory proposed that one of the key variables that determined the maintenance of panic disorder was the misinterpretation of physical sensations (see Chapter 16). For example, a person with panic disorder may sense uncomfortable physical sensations during a panic attack (e.g., increased heart rate, shaking) and interpret these sensations as a sign of impending danger ("I'm having a heart attack"; "I will die or lose control if this continues"). Also drawing from the cognitive theories, Paul Salkovskis (2002) has emphasized the role of beliefs about personal responsibility and a sense of inflated importance that individuals with OCD attribute to their obsessional thoughts (see Chapter 18). Concepts such as *thought-action fusion* (e.g., believing that having a thought increases the likelihood of a particular outcome) and the tendency for individuals with OCD to believe that their intrusive and disturbing thoughts are a reflection of their underlying moral character are additional examples of how beliefs and perceptions shape and maintain anxiety (see Chapter 18).

Developmental Processes

Developmental theories that contribute to current understandings of the anxiety disorders emphasize the role of childhood temperament, parenting styles, family relationships, and aversive experiences in early childhood. As outlined by Hudson and Rapee (Chapter 14), one area that has received much attention is the impact of parenting styles on the development and maintenance of anxiety. Research has fairly consistently demonstrated a strong relationship between the development of an anxiety disorder and parents who are described as controlling, and overprotective. Furthermore, anxiety disorders are more common among offspring of parents who support avoidant behaviors and who fail to adequately encourage independence in their children. Though more research is needed, there may be a relationship between anxiety disorders and parents who exhibit greater levels of rejection and indifference toward their children. With regard to the broader family in general, the degree of cohesion, warmth, and support between parents, children, and among siblings appears to increase risk for developing an anxiety disorder. The consequences of these factors on parent-child attachment are discussed in greater detail in Chapter 14.

In addition to these findings, it is also widely acknowledged that childhood temperament likely plays a significant role in the parent-child relationship. For instance, children who are shy, inhibited, anxious, or depressed may elicit overprotective behaviors in parents. Researchers have suggested that such parenting styles tend to increase a child's overall vulnerability to anxiety disorders by decreasing self-confidence, self-efficacy, and autonomy. Childhood temperament has also been associated with the development of specific anxiety disorders. In Chapter 11, Poulton, Grisham, and Andrews review research demonstrating a relationship between childhood hyperactivity, antisocial behavior, trauma exposure, and the subsequent development of PTSD. These data suggest that difficulties with emotion regulation in childhood may increase vulnerability to posttraumatic stress reactions as the individual may not be able to adequately process, integrate, and psychologically cope with aversive or traumatic experiences over his or her lifetime. Other types of aversive childhood experiences that tend to increase the risk of developing anxiety disorders include marital conflict and divorce, death of a parent, sexual abuse, mental health problems within the immediate family, and other psychosocial stressors such as financial strain and low socioeconomic status (for more information on these topics, see Chapters 11, 14, and 49).

Other prominent areas of study within the developmental framework include the evaluation of parental and extrafamilial modeling and the role of social and peer relationships. With regard to the former, there is some evidence to suggest that anxiety-related information may be transmitted to children through the behaviors and beliefs of their parents or from individuals in their social environments (see Chapter 14). For example, anxious parents may directly or indirectly communicate and reinforce avoidant behaviors in their children as a result of their own fears and phobias. In terms of social relationships, researchers are beginning to focus more attention on the role of peer victimization, social acceptance, and the quality of friendships as important variables in both the development and maintenance of anxiety disorders. Hudson and Rapee (Chapter 14) discuss the impact of social rejection, teasing, and bullying on anxiety and also provide information on including family members in treatment.

Cultural Influences

Researchers from a variety of clinical, theoretical, and international backgrounds have begun to explore the way in which cultural variables influence the development and expression of anxiety disorders. To date, the majority of research in this area has focused on differences in the presentation and prevalence rates of pathological anxiety between Eastern and Western societies. These data demonstrate that the anxiety disorders appear to be represented relatively consistently across cultures, although their manifestations may be markedly different. For example, obsessional thoughts in individuals with OCD tend to be culturally relevant (e.g., thoughts of witchcraft versus thoughts of sexually abusing a child). Asmal and Stein (Chapter 50) discuss how anxiety disorders vary across cultures and discuss similarities between various "culture-bound" syndromes. Though research in this area is still in its infancy, investigators hypothesize that the religious beliefs, norms, gender expectations, and illness perceptions of the dominant culture greatly shape the presentation of the anxiety disorders. Hudson and Rapee (Chapter 14) also describe briefly how specific cultural beliefs may shape reported prevalence rates.

Personality Traits and Disorders

One of the ways researchers have attempted to differentiate and further understand the anxiety disorders has been to evaluate the presence of specific personality traits among sufferers. The most consistent finding to date is that neuroticism occurs frequently across anxiety disorders. Other factors, however, have emerged that have become differentially associated with specific anxiety presentations. Pagura, Cox, and Enns (Chapter 15) discuss the unique relationships between anxiety sensitivity and panic disorder, perfectionism and OCD, antisocial behaviors and PTSD, and shyness/self-criticism in social phobia.

With regard to specific Axis II comorbidity, cluster C disorders (anxious/avoidant type) are most common among individuals with anxiety disorders. Rates of avoidant personality disorder, dependent personality disorder, and obsessive-compulsive personality disorder are particularly high among patients with social phobia, panic disorder, and OCD, respectively. The co-occurrence of these disorders presents unique challenges in the domains of assessment and treatment. As reviewed by Brandes and Bienvenu (Chapter 45), comorbid personality and anxiety disorders are associated with a more protracted clinical course, greater impairment and distress, increased suicidal ideation or attempts, and an overall poor response to treatment. A current area of debate involves the significant overlap between the diagnostic criteria for social phobia and avoidant personality disorder. Sharing many key features, some argue that the two disorders essentially capture the same construct at varying levels of intensity and functional impairment, with avoidant personality disorder corresponding to a more severe variant of social phobia. Further discussion regarding categorical versus dimensional classification approaches can be found in Chapter 20.

While the precise nature of the relationship between personality and anxiety is unclear, competing theories have been proposed to explain how they might interact and influence one another. For example, some researchers argue that personality traits and temperament are inherent factors that place an individual at greater risk for the subsequent development of an anxiety disorder. Others contend that the presence of chronic anxiety precedes and shapes the expression of specific personality traits. Still others propose that the co-occurring disorders share a common underlying cause and are, therefore, etiologically related. Relevant empirical data for these theoretical models and related treatment implications are presented in Chapter 45.

Treatment of Anxiety and Related Disorders

In recent years, a number of practice guidelines have been published on the treatment of anxiety disorders. These include guidelines from the Canadian Psychiatric Association on the treatment of all anxiety disorders (Swinson et al., 2006), as well as practice guidelines from the American Psychiatric Association on the treatment of particular anxiety disorders, including ASD and PTSD (APA, 2004), OCD (APA, 2007), and panic disorder (APA, 1998; Campbell-Sills & Stein, 2006) (note that the American Psychiatric Association's practice guideline for panic disorder is currently being revised). These are welcome updates to older guidelines published by New Zealand's National Health Committee (1998), as well as Expert Consensus Guidelines for treating OCD (March, Frances, Kahn, & Carpenter, 1997) and PTSD (Foa, Davidson, & Frances, 1999), developed by Expert Knowledge Systems.

Recommendations from across these guidelines are fairly consistent. They confirm that anxiety disorders are responsive to intervention, and that effective treatments include pharmacological approaches, psychological approaches (particularly cognitive and behavioral treatments), and combinations of these treatments. Part Five of this book provides a detailed review of these strategies for treating anxiety disorders. In this section, we provide a brief overview of effective treatments.

Biological Treatments

Comprehensive reviews of pharmacological treatments for anxiety disorders may be found in Swinson et al. (2006), as well as in Chapters 22, 24, 26, 28, and 30 of this volume. Effective medications exist for each of the anxiety disorders, with the exception of specific phobias, where the treatment of choice is almost always behavioral (in particular, exposure to feared situations and objects), though as-needed (p.r.n.) benzodiazepines may have a role for occasional use only. Generally, most first-line pharmacological treatments are antidepressants. For example, there is broad support for the use of selective serotonin reuptake inhibitors (SSRIs; e.g., citalopram, escitalopram, fluoxetine, fluvoxamine, parox-

etine, sertraline) for all of the anxiety disorders, except for specific phobia. Serotonin-norepinephrine reuptake inhibitors (SNRIs) such as venlafaxine extended-release (and more recently, duloxetine) are also effective for many of the anxiety disorders. Newer antidepressants such as mirtazapine (a noradrenergic/specific serotonergic antidepressant or NaSSA) and reboxetine (a norepinephrine reuptake inhibitor) also show promise for treating several of the anxiety disorders, but much more research is needed. However, older antidepressants, such as tricyclic antidepressants and monoamine oxidase inhibitors (MAOIs), are used less frequently now than they were in the past because they tend to be more difficult to tolerate and are more dangerous in overdose.

Benzodiazepines (e.g., alprazolam, clonazepam, lorazepam, diazepam), typically introduced as a second-line treatment, primarily because of the risk of dependence, are still widely used—though oft-disparaged—in the treatment of anxiety disorders. There is now emerging evidence supporting the use of several anticonvulsants (e.g., gabapentin, pregabalin) for certain anxiety disorders, though further research is needed. Combining atypical antipsychotics (e.g., risperidone, olanzapine) with antidepressants may lead to improved outcomes for some patients with anxiety disorders such as OCD or PTSD. There is also evidence supporting the use of buspirone for GAD, and beta-adrenergic blockers (taken on a p.r.n. basis) may have a role in the treatment of discrete performance fears (e.g., fears of public speaking), though these medications are not supported for the treatment of generalized social anxiety disorder.

For treatment refractory cases of OCD, there is preliminary evidence from large case series supporting the use of specific neurosurgical procedures (e.g., cingulotomy, bilateral anterior capsulotomy) as a last option, though controlled studies are lacking (see Chapter 28). Finally, there is preliminary evidence supporting the use of several herbal products and other alternative treatments for particular anxiety disorders (see Chapter 34).

Psychological Treatments

Although there are a few preliminary studies supporting the use of client-centered psychotherapy, brief psychodynamic psychotherapy, and interpersonal psychotherapy for particular anxiety disorders (e.g., Lipsitz, Markowitz, Cherry, & Fyer, 1999; Milrod et al., 2007; Teusch, Böhme, & Gastpar, 1997), almost all research on psychological treatments for anxiety-based problems has focused on cognitive and behavioral approaches (for a review, see Swinson et al., 2006, as well as Chapters 23, 25, 27, 29, 31, 33, 35, 36, and 37 in this volume). Furthermore, some studies have found cognitive behavioral therapy (CBT) to be more effective for treating anxiety disorders than other approaches, such as supportive psychotherapy (e.g., Heimberg et al., 1990).

Cognitive behavioral therapy is not a single approach to treatment, but rather one that involves a wide variety of strategies that often differ across patients and across disorders. Although investigators have begun to study transdiagnostic approaches to treating anxiety disorders (see Chapter 33), most studies have tended to focus on the treatment of a single anxiety disorder. Evidence-based cognitive and behavioral strategies for anxiety disorders include psychoeducation (e.g., presenting a cognitive model of anxiety; discussing treatment options, etc.), in vivo exposure (i.e., exposure to feared situations and objects), exposure in imagination (e.g., to feared thoughts, images, and impulses), interoceptive exposure (i.e., exposure to feared physical sensations), prevention of compulsive rituals and other safety behaviors, cognitive restructuring (e.g., evaluating the evidence for anxiety-provoking beliefs), relaxation training, mindfulness and acceptance-based approaches, and skills training (e.g., social skills training, problem-solving training).

Variations on these approaches have also been studied. For example, *applied tension* is an effective treatment for blood and injection phobias. This treatment combines exposure (for reducing fear) with muscle tension exercises (for increasing blood pressure, thereby preventing fainting) (Öst, Fellenius, & Sterner, 1991). Exposure-based treatments have also been developed using virtual reality technology, and preliminary studies suggest that computer-generated, virtual reality exposures may be as effective as in vivo exposure for certain phobias (Emmelkamp, Bruynzeel, Drost, & van der Mast, 2001). Finally, eye movement desensitization and reprocessing (EMDR; a treatment that combines imaginal exposure with bilateral eye movements, as well as other strategies) has been studied for a number of anxiety disorders, though most of this work has been in the area of PTSD. Although research supports the effectiveness of EMDR for PTSD, there is no evidence that the eye movements add anything to the treatment, and critics have observed that the essential elements of EMDR are similar to those of other evidence-based psychological treatments, including exposure, for example (Lohr, Tolin, & Lilienfeld, 1998).

Table 1 lists well-supported psychological treatment strategies for each of the main anxiety disorders, as well as strategies for which support is preliminary, mixed, or tentative.

Combination Treatments

Large trials comparing medication, CBT, and their combination have been conducted for several anxiety disorders, including panic disorder (Barlow, Gorman, Shear, & Woods, 2000), social phobia (Davidson et al., 2004), and OCD (Foa et al., 2005). Preliminary evidence regarding combined treatments also exists for GAD (Bond, Wingrove, Curran, & Lader, 2002) and PTSD (Cohen, Mannarino, Perel, & Staron, 2007). Although a few studies have found combined treatments to be superior to either medication or CBT alone, most studies across the anxiety disorders have found combined treatments to be equivalent to monotherapies immediately following treatment (Black, 2006; Chapter 32, this volume). However, there is evidence that over the long term (once treatment has been discontinued), CBT alone leads to superior outcomes for the treatment of panic disorder, relative to those following medication alone or the combination of medication and CBT (Barlow et al., 2000). The long-term effects of treatment on other anxiety disorders remain to be studied. Also, most studies on combined treatment have studied the effects of beginning CBT and pharmacotherapy concurrently. Additional research on the sequential introduction of CBT and pharmacotherapy is needed.

Conclusion

Anxiety disorders include a diverse group of conditions that share a number of common features, such as a predominance of anxiety and fear, avoidance of feared situations and experiences, and reliance on safety behaviors designed to reduce perceived threat. There is strong evidence supporting the role of biological, psychological, and environmental factors in the cause and maintenance of anxiety disorders. Although anxiety disorders are often chronic conditions, most individuals experience a reduction in symptoms following treatment with medications, cognitive behavioral therapy, or a combination of these approaches. The remainder of this handbook provides detailed reviews on the phenomenology, etiology, assessment, and treatment of each of the main anxiety disorders, as well as for several related conditions.

Table 1. Summary of Psychological Treatment Strategies

Anxiety Disorder	Well-Established Strategies[a]	Strategies with Preliminary Support or Mixed Support
Panic Disorder and Agoraphobia	• Psychoeducation • Cognitive restructuring • Interoceptive exposure • In vivo exposure (for agoraphobia)	• Breathing retraining[b] • Psychodynamic psychotherapy[c] • Experiential psychotherapy[c]
Social Anxiety Disorder	• Psychoeducation • Cognitive restructuring • In vivo exposure • Simulated exposures (role plays) • Social skills training	• Applied relaxation training[d] • Virtual reality exposure[e] • Interpersonal Psychotherapy[e]
Specific Phobia	• In vivo exposure • Applied tension (for blood and injection phobias)	• Applied relaxation[f] • Virtual reality exposure[g]
Generalized Anxiety Disorder	• Cognitive restructuring • Progressive muscle relaxation	• Mindfulness and acceptance-based strategies[h] • Exposure to worry-related imagery[i] • Problem-solving training[i] • Prevention of worry behaviors[i] • Stimulus control strategies (e.g., scheduling times to worry)[i]
Obsessive-Compulsive Disorder	• Exposure and ritual prevention • Cognitive restructuring	• Exposure in imagination[j]
Posttraumatic Stress Disorder	• In vivo exposure • Exposure in imagination • Cognitive restructuring • Progressive muscle relaxation	• Eye movement desensitization and reprocessing (EMDR)[k] • Virtual reality exposure[l]

[a]Support for well-established treatment strategies can be found in Swinson et al., 2006, as well as in Chapters 23, 25, 27, 29, 31, 33, 35, 36, and 37 in this volume. [b]Although this strategy is often included in treatment protocols for panic disorder, there is little evidence that it adds to treatment outcome overall (Schmidt et al., 2000). [c]Support is still very preliminary, based on a very small number of studies (e.g., Milrod et al., 2007; Teusch, Böhme, & Gastpar, 1997). [d]This strategy involves combining relaxation training with exposure. Although preliminary studies suggest it is effective for reducing social anxiety (e.g., Öst, Jerremalm, & Johansson, 1981), there is no evidence that it is any more effective than exposure alone, and one study found that it is less effective than cognitive therapy (Clark et al., 2006). [e]Success has been reported in a small number of trials using virtual reality for public speaking fears (Anderson, Zimand, Hodges, & Rothbaum, 2005; Klinger et al., 2005) and interpersonal psychotherapy (Lipsitz, Markowitz, Cherry, & Fyer, 1999). [f]This strategy involves combining relaxation training with exposure. Although preliminary studies suggest it is effective for reducing phobic fear (e.g., in claustrophobia; Öst, Johansson, & Jerremalm, 1982), there is no evidence that it is any more effective than exposure alone. [g]A number of studies support the use of virtual reality for height phobias, flying phobias, and other specific phobias. A small number of studies have compared virtual exposure to live exposure, finding few differences (e.g., Emmelkamp, Bruynzeel, Drost, & van der Mast, 2001), though more comparative studies are needed. [h]Success has been reported in a small number of uncontrolled trials (e.g., Roemer & Orsillo, 2007). [i]These strategies have been included in a number of trials of CBT for GAD. However, dismantling studies are needed to determine whether they add any specific benefits beyond the other strategies included in standard treatments. [j]This strategy has been included in a number of trials on the treatment of OCD. However, dismantling studies are needed to determine whether it adds any specific benefit beyond in vivo exposure and ritual prevention. [k]Numerous studies support the use of EMDR for treating PTSD, though this treatment appears to be no more effective than other established treatments (Davidson & Parker, 2001). There is little evidence that the eye movements contribute to the effectiveness of EMDR, and outcomes are probably related to the effects of exposure and other treatment components (Davidson & Parker, 2001; Lohr, Tolin, & Lilienfeld, 1998). [l]Support has been based primarily on small uncontrolled studies and case reports (e.g., Ready, Pollack, Rothbaum, & Alarcon, 2006; Rothbaum, Hodges, Ready, Graap, & Alarcon, 2001).

References

American Psychiatric Association. (1994). *Diagnostic and statistical manual of mental disorders* (4th ed.). Washington, DC: Author.

American Psychiatric Association. (1998). Practice guideline for the treatment of patients with panic disorder. *American Journal of Psychiatry, 155*(Suppl. 5), 1–34.

American Psychiatric Association. (2000). *Diagnostic and statistical manual of mental disorders* (4th ed., text revision). Washington, DC: Author.

American Psychiatric Association. (2004). *Practice guideline for the treatment of patients with acute stress disorder and posttraumatic stress disorder.* Arlington, VA: Author. Available online at http://www.psych.org/psych_pract/treatg/pg/prac_guide.cfm

American Psychiatric Association. (2007). *Practice guideline for the treatment of patients with obsessive-compulsive disorder.* Arlington, VA: Author. Available online at http//www.psych.org/psych_pract/treatg/pg/prac_ guide.cfm

Anderson, P. L., Zimand, E., Hodges, L. F., & Rothbaum, B. O. (2005). Cognitive behavioral therapy for public-speaking anxiety using virtual reality for exposure. *Depression and Anxiety, 22,* 156–158.

Barlow, D. H., Gorman, J. M., Shear, M. K., & Woods, S. W. (2000). Cognitive-behavioral therapy, imipramine, or their combination for panic disorder: A randomized controlled trial. *Journal of the American Medical Association, 283,* 2529–2536.

Barr, C. S., Newman, T. K., Shannon, C., Parker, C., Dvoskin, R. L., Becker, M. L., et al. (2004). Rearing condition and rh5-HTTLPR interact to influence limbic-hypothalamic-pituitary-adrenal axis response to stress in infant macaques. *Biological Psychiatry, 55,* 733–738.

Beck, A. T. (1976). *Cognitive therapy and the emotional disorders.* New York: International Universities Press.

Bienvenu, O. J., Hettema, J. M., Neale, M. C., Prescott, C. A., & Kendler, K. S. (2007). Low extraversion and high neuroticism as indices of genetic and environmental risk for social phobia, agoraphobia, and animal phobia. *American Journal of Psychiatry, 164,* 1714–1721.

Black, D. W. (2006). Efficacy of combined pharmacotherapy and psychotherapy versus monotherapy in the treatment of anxiety disorders. *CNS Spectrums, 11,* 29–33.

Bond, A. J., Wingrove, J., Curran, H. V., & Lader, M. H. (2002). Treatment of generalised anxiety disorder with a short course of psychological therapy, combined with buspirone or placebo. *Journal of Affective Disorders, 72,* 267–271.

Campbell, L. A., & Brown, T. A. (2002). Generalized anxiety disorder. In M. M. Antony & D. H. Barlow (Eds.), *Handbook of assessment and treatment planning for psychological disorders* (pp. 147–181). New York: Guilford.

Campbell-Sills, L., & Stein, M. B. (2006). *Guideline watch: Practice guideline for the treatment of patients with panic disorder.* Arlington, VA: American Psychiatric Association. Available online at http://www.psych.org/psych_pract/treatg/pg/prac_guide.cfm

Campbell-Sills, L., & Stein, M. B. (in press). Psychometric analysis and refinement of the Connor Davidson Resilience Scale (CD-RISC): Validation of a 10-item measure of resilience. *Journal of Traumatic Stress.*

Caspi, A., & Moffitt, T. E. (2006). Gene-environment interactions in psychiatry: Joining forces with neuroscience. *Nature Reviews: Neuroscience, 7,* 583–590.

Charney, D. S. (2004). Psychobiological mechanisms of resilience and vulnerability: Implications for successful adaptation to extreme stress. *American Journal of Psychiatry, 161,* 195–216.

Clark, D. M. (1986). A cognitive approach to panic. *Behaviour Research and Therapy, 24,* 461–470.

Clark, D. M., Ehlers, A., Hackman, A., McManus, F., Fennell, M., Grey, N., et al. (2006). Cognitive therapy versus exposure plus applied relaxation in social phobia: A randomized controlled trial. *Journal of Consulting and Clinical Psychology, 74,* 568–578.

Cohen, J. A., Mannarino, A. P., Perel, J. M., & Staron, V. (2007). A pilot randomized controlled trial of combined trauma-focused CBT and sertraline for childhood PSTD symptoms. *Journal of the American Academy of Child and Adolescent Psychiatry, 46,* 811–819.

Connor, K. M., & Davidson, J. R. (2003). Development of a new resilience scale: The Connor-Davidson Resilience Scale (CD-RISC). *Depression and Anxiety, 18,* 76–82.

Craske, M. G., Hermans, D., & Vansteenwegen, D. (2006). *Fear and learning: From basic processes to clinical implications.* Washington, DC: American Psychological Association.

Davidson, J.R.T., Foa, E. B., Huppert, J. D., Keefe, F. J., Franklin, M. E., Compton, J. S., et al. (2004). Fluoxetine, comprehensive cognitive behavioral therapy, and placebo in generalized social phobia. *Archives of General Psychiatry, 61,* 1005–1013.

Davidson, P. R., & Parker, K.C.H. (2001). Eye movement desensitization and reprocessing (EMDR): A meta-analysis. *Journal of Consulting and Clinical Psychology, 69,* 305–316.

Emmelkamp, P. M., Bruynzeel, M., Drost, L., & van der Mast, C. A. (2001). Virtual reality treatment in acrophobia: A comparison with exposure in vivo. *Cyberpsychology and Behavior, 4,* 335–339.

Etkin, A., & Wager, T. D. (2007). Functional neuroimaging of anxiety: A meta-analysis of emotional processing in PTSD, social anxiety disorder, and specific phobia. *American Journal of Psychiatry, 164,* 1476–1488.

Foa, E. B., Davidson, J.R.T., & Frances, A. (Eds.). (1999). The Expert Consensus Guidelines™: Treatment of posttraumatic stress disorder. *Journal of Clinical Psychiatry, 60*(Suppl. 16), 1–76.

Foa, E. B., Liebowitz, M. R., Kozak, M. J., Davies, S., Campeas, R., Franklin, M. E., et al. (2005). Randomized, placebo-controlled trial of exposure and ritual prevention, clomipramine, and their combination in the treatment of obsessive-compulsive disorder. *American Journal of Psychiatry, 162,* 151–161.

Furmark, T. (2002). Social phobia: Overview of community surveys. *Acta Psychiatrica Scandinavica, 105,* 84–93.

Heimberg, R. G., Dodge, C. S., Hope, D. A., Kennedy, C. R., Zollo, L., & Becker, R. E. (1990). Cognitive-behavioral group treatment of social phobia: Comparison to a credible placebo control. *Cognitive Therapy and Research, 14,* 1–23.

Holmes, A., Murphy, D. L., & Crawley, J. N. (2003). Abnormal behavioral phenotypes of serotonin transporter knockout mice: Parallels with human anxiety and depression. *Biological Psychiatry, 54,* 953–959.

Kessler, R. C., Berglund, P., Demler, O., Jin, R., & Walters, E. E. (2005). Lifetime prevalence and age-of-onset distributions of *DSM–IV* disorders in the National Comorbidity Survey Replication. *Archives of General Psychiatry, 62,* 593–602.

Klinger, E., Bouchard, S., Légeron, P., Roy, S., Lauer, F., Chemin, I., et al. (2005). Virtual reality therapy versus cognitive behavior therapy for social phobia: A preliminary controlled study. *Cyberpsychology and Behavior, 8,* 76–88.

Lipsitz, J. D., Markowitz, J. C., Cherry, S., & Fyer, A. J. (1999). Open trial of interpersonal psychotherapy for the treatment of social phobia. *American Journal of Psychiatry, 156,* 1814–1816.

Lohr, J. M., Tolin, D. F., & Lilienfeld, S. O. (1998). Efficacy of Eye Movement Desensitization and Reprocessing: Implications for behavior therapy. *Behavior Therapy, 29,* 123–156.

March, J. S., Frances, A., Kahn, D. A., & Carpenter, D. (Eds.). (1997). The Expert Consensus Guidelines™: Treatment of obsessive-compulsive disorder. *Journal of Clinical Psychiatry, 58*(Suppl. 4), 1–72.

Mathews, A., & MacLeod, C. (1994). Cognitive approaches to emotion and emotional disorders. *Annual Review of Psychology, 45,* 25–50.

Milrod, B., Leon, A. C., Busch, F., Rudden, M., Schwalberg, M., Clarkin, J., et al. (2007). A randomized controlled clinical trial of psychoanalytic psychotherapy for panic disorder. *American Journal of Psychiatry, 164,* 265–272.

Mowrer, O. H. (1960). *Learning theory and behavior.* New York: Wiley.

National Health Committee. (1998). *Guidelines for assessing and treating anxiety disorders.* Wellington, New Zealand: National Health Committee. Available online at http://www.nzgg.org.nz/guidelines/dsp_guideline_popup.cfm?&guidelineID=38

Öst, L.-G., Fellenius, J., & Sterner, U. (1991). Applied tension, exposure *in vivo,* and tension-only in the treatment of blood phobia. *Behaviour Research and Therapy, 29,* 561–574.

Öst, L.-G., Jerremalm, A., & Johansson, J. (1981). Individual response patterns and the effects of different behavioral methods in the treatment of social phobia. *Behaviour Research and Therapy, 19,* 1–16.

Öst, L.-G., Johansson, J., & Jerremalm, A. (1982). Individual response patterns and the effects of different behavioral methods in the treatment of claustrophobia. *Behavior Research and Therapy, 20,* 445–460.

Otto, M. W. (2002). Learning and "unlearning" fears: Preparedness, neural pathways, and patients. *Biological Psychiatry, 52,* 917–920.

Rachman, S. (1976). The passing of the two-stage theory of fear and avoidance: Fresh possibilities. *Behaviour Research and Therapy, 14,* 125–131.

Ready, D. J., Pollack, S., Rothbaum, B. O., & Alarcon, R. D. (2006). Virtual reality exposure for veterans with posttraumatic stress disorder. *Journal of Aggression, Maltreatment, and Trauma, 12,* 199–220.

Roemer, L., & Orsillo, S. M. (2007). An open trial of an acceptance-based behavior therapy for generalized anxiety disorder. *Behavior Therapy, 38,* 72–85.

Rothbaum, B. O. (Ed.). (2006). *Pathological anxiety: Emotional processing in etiology and treatment.* New York: Guilford.

Rothbaum, B. O., Hodges, L. F., Ready, D., Graap, K., & Alarcon, R. D. (2001). Virtual reality exposure therapy for Vietnam veterans with posttraumatic stress disorder. *Journal of Clinical Psychiatry, 62,* 617–622.

Ruscio, A. M., Brown, T. A., Chiu, W. T., Sareen, J., Stein, M. B., & Kessler, R. C. (2008). Social fears and social phobia in the USA: Results from the National Comorbidity Survey Replication. *Psychological Medicine, 38,* 15–28.

Salkovskis, P. M. (2002). Understanding and treating obsessive-compulsive disorder. *Behaviour Research and Therapy, 37,* S29–S52.

Schmidt, N. B., Woolaway-Bickel, K., Trakowski, J., Santiago, H., Storey, J., Koselka, M., et al. (2000). Dismantling cognitive-behavioral treatment for panic disorder: Questioning the utility of breathing retraining. *Journal of Consulting and Clinical Psychology, 68,* 417–424.

Stein, M. B., Schork, N. J., & Gelernter, J. (in press). Gene-by-environment (serotonin transporter and childhood maltreatment) interaction for anxiety sensitivity, an intermediate phenotype for anxiety disorders. *Neuropsychopharmacology.*

Stein, M. B., Simmons, A., Feinstein, J. S., & Paulus, M. P. (2007). Increased amygdala and insula activation during emotion processing in anxiety-prone subjects. *American Journal of Psychiatry, 164,* 318–327.

Swinson, R. P., Antony, M. M., Bleau, P., Chokka, P., Craven, M., Fallu, A., et al. (2006). Clinical practice guidelines: Management of anxiety disorders. *Canadian Journal of Psychiatry, 51*(Suppl. 2), 1S–92S.

Teusch, L., Böhme, H., & Gastpar, M. (1997). The benefit of an insight-oriented and experiential approach on panic and agoraphobia symptoms: Results of a controlled comparison of client-centered therapy alone and in combination with behavioral exposure. *Psychotherapy and Psychosomatics, 66,* 293–301.

PART 2

Phenomenology and Epidemiology of Anxiety Disorders

2

Epidemiology of Anxiety Disorders

Ronald C. Kessler, Ayelet Meron Ruscio, Katherine Shear
and Hans-Ulrich Wittchen

Abstract

This chapter reviews the results of community epidemiological surveys concerning the descriptive epidemiology of anxiety disorders, with a focus on lifetime prevalence, age-of-onset, persistence, and comorbidity. Anxiety disorders are found to be very common despite current *DSM* and *ICD* criteria underestimating many clinically significant cases. Anxiety disorders often have early age-of-onset and high comorbidity. They typically are temporally primary to the disorders with which they are comorbid. Young people with anxiety disorders seldom receive treatment prior to the onset of secondary conditions. The chapter closes with a discussion of the importance of long-term studies to determine whether early treatment of primary anxiety disorders would influence the subsequent onset and course of secondary disorders.

Keywords: agoraphobia, anxiety disorder, epidemiology, generalized anxiety disorder, obsessive-compulsive disorder, panic disorder, phobia, posttraumatic stress disorder, separation anxiety disorder, World Mental Health (WMH) surveys

This chapter presents an overview of the descriptive epidemiology of anxiety disorders, with an emphasis on lifetime prevalence, age-of-onset distributions, persistence, subtypes, and comorbidity. The disorders considered include panic disorder, agoraphobia, specific phobia, social phobia, generalized anxiety disorder (GAD), posttraumatic stress disorder (PTSD), obsessive-compulsive disorder (OCD), and separation anxiety disorder (SEPAD). Mixed disorders (e.g., mixed anxiety-depression), acute stress disorder, and adjustment disorder with anxious mood are not considered based on the scant epidemiological data available on them. We focus largely on evidence obtained in general population surveys, although some findings are also reported from clinical epidemiological studies with regard to subtyping. In light of the fact that *Diagnostic and Statistical Manual of Mental Disorders (DSM)* criteria have been used more widely

than *International Classification of Diseases (ICD)* criteria in epidemiological studies, we focus largely on disorders defined by the *DSM* system, although a few important differences with *ICD* disorders are highlighted.

Assessment of Mental Disorders in Epidemiological Surveys

Data on the epidemiology of anxiety disorders have proliferated over the past two decades due to the development of diagnostic criteria in the *DSM* and *ICD* systems that are amenable to operationalization and the subsequent development of fully structured research diagnostic interviews based on these criteria. The first such interview was the Diagnostic Interview Schedule (DIS) (Robins, Helzer, Croughan, & Ratcliff, 1981), which was developed for use in a large community epidemiological survey in the United States (Robins & Regier, 1991) and subsequently used in similar surveys in other parts of the world. The DIS was based on *DSM–III* criteria (Horwath & Weissman, 2000).

The World Health Organization (WHO) subsequently developed the Composite International Diagnostic Interview (CIDI) (Robins et al., 1988), which was based on the DIS, in order to have an instrument that operationalized *ICD–10* as well as *DSM* criteria and that could be used reliably in many different cultures (Wittchen, 1994). As general population surveys were carried out in a number of countries with the first version of CIDI, WHO developed a cross-national research consortium to carry out systematic comparisons of CIDI survey results (Kessler, 1999).

Results based on these comparisons led to the expansion and refinement of the CIDI and to a new generation of cross-national CIDI surveys in the WHO World Mental Health (WMH) Survey Initiative. The latter is an initiative to carry out parallel CIDI surveys in 28 countries throughout the world (www.hcp.med.harvard.edu/wmh). Some preliminary cross-national comparative results have been reported for the first half of participating WMH countries (The WHO World Mental Health Survey Consortium, 2004). However, the full set of baseline WMH surveys has not yet been completed, which means that WMH results are currently available largely in country-specific reports (e.g., Bromet et al., 2005; Karam et al., 2006; Shen et al., 2006).

Other instruments besides the CIDI have been used to carry out recent community epidemiological surveys in various parts of the world (Grant et al., 2004; Jenkins et al., 2003). However, the CIDI is so predominant that a few words need to be said about CIDI validity. Clinical reappraisal studies of the original version of CIDI were quite mixed, some showing concordance of anxiety disorder diagnoses with clinical diagnoses to be low (Brugha, Jenkins, Taub, Meltzer, & Bebbington, 2001) and others moderate to good (Wittchen, Kessler, Zhao, & Abelson, 1995). Concordance has been considerably better for more recent versions of CIDI in clinical reappraisal studies carried out in Western countries (Haro et al., 2006; Kessler et al., 1998; Wittchen et al., 1995; Wittchen, Zhao, Abelson, Abelson, & Kessler, 1996).

This evidence for clinical relevance of CIDI diagnoses applies much more to Western than non-Western countries, as prevalence estimates in CIDI surveys in some non-Western countries are implausibly low (Gureje, Lasebikan, Kola, & Makanjuola, 2006; Shen et al., 2006). Methodological studies that debriefed respondents in these surveys discovered that some respondents are uneasy admitting emotional problems to strangers, with underestimation of disorder prevalence varying geographically and sociodemographically as a function of variation in this reluctance. There also appear to be instances in which some CIDI questions are confusing to respondents in certain countries. Innovative methods have been developed to address these problems and to make post hoc corrections based on recalibration of CIDI diagnoses with diagnoses based on independent clinical reappraisal interviews (Kessler, Abelson et al., 2004). However, no results based on these methods have yet been published for anxiety disorders. As a result, data on the epidemiology of anxiety disorders in less developed countries need to be interpreted with caution.

Three cautions must to be kept in mind when considering estimates of the lifetime prevalence, age-of-onset (AOO), and course of anxiety disorders. The first two apply largely to estimates of lifetime prevalence. First, differences in diagnostic criteria across *DSM–III–R*, *DSM–IV*, and *ICD–10*, even if they seem small, can influence prevalence estimates substantially. Second, differences in survey characteristics and populations can introduce variation in prevalence estimates even when the same interview schedule and diagnostic system are used. Based solely on these two factors, we should expect variation in lifetime prevalence estimates across studies.

The third caution is that estimates of lifetime prevalence, AOO, and course in epidemiological studies are generally based on retrospective reports made by survey respondents who are asked to review their entire life and report if they ever experienced particular syndromes, when they started, and how long they persisted. Lifetime review questions are extremely difficult to answer and are prone to a number of problems, such as underreporting bias with regard to occurrence and "telescoping" bias (i.e., bias in the direction of thinking things happened more recently than they really did) in AOO reports. These biases are especially likely for older people, who have more years of life to review than younger people and might have reduced cognitive capacity to carry out such a review with accuracy (Kessler, Wittchen, Abelson, & Zhao, 2000).

It is noteworthy in light of the considerations in the last paragraph that most community epidemiological surveys find that lifetime anxiety disorder prevalence estimates are lower for older than younger people, although AOO distributions are generally the same among older as younger respondents (International Consortium in Psychiatric Epidemiology, 2000). A number of methodological factors could account for this finding, such as that people living in institutions (including nursing homes and other assisted living facilities) are often excluded from general population surveys and that people who die early are excluded, resulting in the elderly survey participants being especially healthy. It is noteworthy in this regard that anxiety disorders have been shown in prospective research to be significant risk factors for early mortality (M. L. Bruce, Leaf, Rozal, Florio, & Hoff, 1994). It is also important to consider the possibility that the lower reported lifetime prevalence of anxiety disorders among older respondents might be due to a genuine cohort effect. Based on the plausibility of both methodological and substantive interpretations, it is impossible to draw a firm conclusion about the relative importance of methodological and substantive factors in the lower lifetime prevalence estimates of anxiety disorders in community surveys. Whichever is more important, though, both sets of explanations agree that the lifetime prevalence estimates found in community surveys should be considered lower bound on the true prevalence of recent cohorts.

Lifetime Prevalence, Age-of-Onset, and Persistence

With these cautions as a backdrop, we now consider estimates of lifetime prevalence, AOO, and course of anxiety disorders reported in recent community epidemiological surveys. Several literature reviews have recently been published that present detailed summary tables of prevalence estimates for individual anxiety disorders across many epidemiological surveys (Fehm, Pelissolo, Furmark, & Wittchen, 2005; Goodwin et al., 2005; Lepine, 2002; Lieb, 2005; Lieb, Becker, & Altamura, 2005; Wittchen & Jacobi, 2005). Rather than reproduce these tables, we refer the reader to those reviews for detailed estimates and present only summary results here.

A number of patterns in the lifetime prevalence data are quite consistent. The three most striking are that anxiety disorders overall are consistently more prevalent than any other class of mental disorders; that specific phobia is consistently the most prevalent lifetime anxiety disorder, with estimates usually in the 6%–12% range; and that OCD is consistently the least prevalent lifetime anxiety disorder, with estimates always less than 3%. Prevalence estimates of other anxiety disorders fall within these

extremes. However, as detailed in the remainder of this section, uncertainties exist about diagnostic boundaries for the anxiety disorders, and prevalence estimates could become considerably higher based on future revisions of diagnostic criteria.

Although fewer published data exist on retrospectively reported AOO distributions of anxiety disorders (Burke, Burke, Regier, & Rae, 1990; Christie et al., 1988; Jacobi et al., 2004; Kessler, Berglund, Demler, Jin, & Walters, 2005), a number of noteworthy patterns can be seen in these data. Specific phobia is always found to have a modal AOO in childhood, with the vast majority of lifetime cases having onsets by early adulthood. Social phobia and OCD are always found to have a modal AOO in adolescence or early adulthood, with the vast majority of cases beginning by the start of mid-life. Panic disorder, agoraphobia, and GAD are always found to have later and more widely dispersed AOO distributions, with median AOO in the early to mid-20s and an interquartile range of up to two decades. Finally, PTSD is generally found to have the latest and most variable AOO distribution, presumably reflecting the fact that trauma exposure can occur at any time in the life course. Somewhat earlier AOO estimates are generally found in prospective-longitudinal studies than in retrospective AOO reports (Wittchen, Lieb, Schuster, & Oldehinkel, 1999).

This early onset, coupled with the fact that significant associations exist between early-onset anxiety disorders and the subsequent first onset of other mental and substance use disorders (Zimmermann et al., 2003), has led some commentators to suggest that aggressive treatment of child-adolescent anxiety disorders might be effective in preventing the onset of the secondary mental and substance disorders that are associated with the vast majority of people with serious mental illness (Kendall & Kessler, 2002). It is noteworthy in this regard that despite their generally early ages of onset, first treatment of anxiety disorders usually does not occur until adulthood, often more than a decade after onset of the disorder (Christiana et al., 2000).

Course of illness has been less well studied in epidemiological studies of anxiety disorders than either prevalence or AOO. However, estimates of recent prevalence (variously reported for the year, 6 months, or 1 month before interview) are often reported in these surveys in parallel with estimates of lifetime prevalence. Indirect information about chronicity can be obtained by computing recent-to-lifetime prevalence ratios. The 12-month to lifetime prevalence ratios for anxiety disorders are typically in the range 0.4–0.6, with the highest ratios usually found for specific phobia and the lowest for generalized anxiety disorder (Bijl, Ravelli, & van Zessen, 1998; Kringlen, Torgersen, & Cramer, 2001). Ratios as high as these strongly imply that anxiety disorders are quite persistent throughout the life course. More detailed analyses of these ratios could be carried out by breaking them down separately for subsamples defined by age at interview or by time since first onset, but we are unaware of any published research that has reported such analyses. Our own preliminary analyses of this sort in the WMH data suggest, as one might expect, that the 12-month to lifetime prevalence ratios decline with increasing age. The more striking result, though, is that this decline is fairly modest, suggesting that anxiety disorders are often equally persistent over the life course. The few long-term longitudinal studies that exist in representative samples of people with anxiety disorders show that this persistence is usually due to a recurrent-intermittent course that often features waxing and waning episodes of different comorbid anxiety disorders (Angst & Vollrath, 1991; Bruce et al., 2005; Hasler et al., 2005; Perkonigg et al., 2005; Yonkers, Bruce, Dyck, & Keller, 2003).

Panic Disorder

The lifetime prevalence of panic disorder is consistently found to be in the range 2%–5% in general population epidemiological surveys (Hoyer, Beesdo, Bittner, & Wittchen, 2003). A much higher proportion of respondents in most of these surveys report having one or more panic attacks in their life (Wittchen, Reed, & Kessler, 1998). In the U.S. National Comorbidity Survey Replication (NCS-R), respondents with a history of panic attacks were divided into four subgroups: history of one or more attacks in the absence of both panic and agoraphobia, attacks in the absence of panic disorder but with agoraphobia, panic disorder without agoraphobia, and panic disorder with agoraphobia. Persistence, number of lifetime attacks, number of years with attacks, clinical severity, and comorbidity were all found to increase monotonically across these four subgroups. These results could be interpreted as suggesting that panic exists along a continuum in which panic attacks and panic disorder differ in degree rather than in kind. It would be premature to conclude from these results that the boundary between panic attacks and panic disorder is arbitrary, as a generally similar sort of pattern can be found for subthreshold symptoms of virtually any disorder. However, given the high prevalence and

negative outcomes associated with panic attacks in the absence of panic disorder, there is a need for further research to improve differentiation of pathological and normal panic experiences.

A complicating factor in this line of thinking is that panic attacks are so common and so often found to be precursors of a wide range of other mental disorders that it might make more sense to think of isolated panic attacks as a core psychopathological marker for psychopathology than as a subthreshold manifestation of panic disorder (Goodwin et al., 2005). This possibility broadens the continuum concept to include the consideration of comorbidity among syndromes as well as levels of symptom severity and duration within a single syndrome. We postpone the discussion of this broader consideration of comorbidity among the anxiety disorders and of anxiety disorders with other mental disorders to a later section in the chapter.

Specific Phobia

The lifetime prevalence of specific phobia is as high as 11% in some community epidemiological surveys (Magee, Eaton, Wittchen, McGonagle, & Kessler, 1996). Systematic variation exists in AOO distributions and symptom profiles of specific phobia subtypes (Antony, Brown, & Barlow, 1997; Lipsitz, Barlow, Mannuzza, Hofmann, & Fyer, 2002). Blood-injury phobia is particularly distinct in this regard (Bienvenu & Eaton, 1998). However, other research suggests that the number of specific fears is more important for course than type of fears. In particular, data from a large epidemiological survey showed that the number of fears with avoidance reported by people with specific phobia is strongly related to persistence and severity of overall phobia (Curtis, Magee, Eaton, Wittchen, & Kessler, 1998). We are unaware of any attempt to replicate this finding in other epidemiological surveys. This is not to say that some people who report only one specific fear never have persistent or severe specific phobia, as such cases do exist even though they are considerably less common than persistent-severe specific phobia with a number of specific fears. However, it could be that the former are distinct from the latter in some way that has implications for diagnosis. One possibility is that persistent-severe specific phobia with only one specific fear is more likely to be caused by a trauma, such as being attacked by a dog as a child leading to a dog phobia. If so, then further research to elucidate this distinction might lead to downward revision of current lifetime prevalence estimates for specific phobia by differentiating a generalized subtype that does not require trauma exposure and a pure type that does require trauma exposure.

Agoraphobia Without Panic Disorder

Agoraphobia without a history of panic disorder is another type of phobia that has been the source of controversy regarding prevalence. Agoraphobia is considered by many experts (especially in the United States) to be a response to panic (Klein & Gorman, 1987), which means that agoraphobia without panic disorder would only occur when the agoraphobia was caused by a fear of recurrence of paniclike symptoms rather than by a fear of recurrence of panic attacks. *DSM–III–R* was revised to embody this perspective, requiring fear of either panic attacks or paniclike symptoms as the precipitating factor for a diagnosis of agoraphobia. The *ICD* system, in comparison, allows for the possibility that agoraphobia is caused by broader fears about being trapped or about safety when outside the home, such as fear of assault. Many experts outside the United States hold to this broader view of agoraphobia. Consistent with the *ICD* perspective, community epidemiological surveys consistently find that agoraphobia without a history of prior panic attacks or paniclike symptoms is as common as, if not more common than, agoraphobia with a history of prior panic (Andrews & Slade, 2002; Wittchen, Reed et al., 1998).

This inconsistency was first addressed empirically in a clinical reappraisal study carried out in a subsample of 22 respondents from a large U.S. epidemiological survey who were diagnosed by the Diagnostic Interview Schedule (Robins et al., 1981), the fully structured diagnostic interview that was the basis for the later development of the CIDI, as having agoraphobia without panic disorder (Horwath, Lish, Johnson, Hornig, & Weissman, 1993). Diagnoses were based on *DSM–III* criteria, which have a broader definition of agoraphobia without panic disorder than either later *DSM* editions or the *ICD–10*. The researchers concluded that 19 of the 22 respondents actually had a specific phobia rather than agoraphobia, one had panic disorder with agoraphobia, and that the remaining two had agoraphobia with paniclike symptoms. In other words, the high estimated prevalence of agoraphobia without panic disorder in the original version of the CIDI seemed to be due to measurement error—a confusion of specific phobia with agoraphobia. The story does not end here. A subsequent version of CIDI was created that expanded the assessment of specific phobia in

an effort to address the problem of confusing specific phobia for agoraphobia. A survey carried out using that version of the instrument found that a substantial proportion of the people originally classified as having agoraphobia without a history of panic actually had specific phobia rather than agoraphobia (Wittchen, Reed et al., 1998). However, the study also found that the number of respondents who genuinely had agoraphobia without a history of panic was quite large even after clinical review of cases—3.5% of the sample. This estimate stands in sharp contrast to the 0.2% lifetime prevalence of *DSM–IV* agoraphobia without panic disorder reported in a very large recent national survey of the United States (Grant et al., 2006).

Whether the high prevalence of agoraphobia in the absence of any prior paniclike symptoms holds up in future epidemiological investigations is an issue of considerable importance in light of the apparent severity of the syndrome in the recent surveys where it has been rigorously evaluated (Andrews & Slade, 2002; Wittchen, Reed et al., 1998). The WMH surveys have taken this as a topic of central importance and to this end have expanded the number of questions asked about agoraphobic fears and expanded the probes about the focus of fear in the assessment of agoraphobia. For example, adult separation anxiety disorder (SEPAD) is one possible basis for the fear of being out alone and separated from loved ones. This disorder was not assessed in any of the previous CIDI surveys that documented a high prevalence of agoraphobia without any prior paniclike symptoms, but it is assessed in the WMH surveys. Adult separation anxiety disorder as a focus of agoraphobic fears is included in the WMH assessment of agoraphobia along with parallel assessments of such things as fear of crime and fear of an attack of an episodic illness such as asthma or epilepsy. In consequence, although our current understanding is so incomplete that we cannot say whether the lifetime prevalence of independent agoraphobia is vanishingly small or as high as 3%–5%, we can anticipate a reduction in this uncertainty based on analysis of the WMH survey data that should be completed in the near future.

A related issue concerns the temporal priority between panic and agoraphobia. As noted above, the thinking on which the *DSM–IV* definition is based assumes that agoraphobia occurs as a result of panic rather than the reverse. However, a recent follow-up of the original ECA sample in Baltimore that was reinterviewed 13 years after the baseline survey found that this was not the case (Bienvenu et al., 2006).

Psychiatrist follow-up evaluations in this sample documented not only the existence of agoraphobia in the absence of a history of spontaneous panic attacks, but also showed that this type of independent agoraphobia at baseline predicted the subsequent first onset of panic disorder with about the same strength that baseline panic disorder predicted the subsequent first onset of agoraphobia. Such a pattern of equal-sized cross-lagged associations is more consistent with a common causes model (i.e., that panic and agoraphobia are both indicators of a common diathesis) than with a one-way causal model in which panic leads to agoraphobia but agoraphobia does not lead to panic.

Social Phobia

Prevalence estimates of social phobia in recent epidemiological surveys have varied more than those of specific phobia or agoraphobia. Two recent nationally representative surveys of the United States, for example, reported widely differing lifetime prevalence estimates of *DSM–IV* social phobia: 12.8% in a survey based on the CIDI (Kessler, Berglund et al., 2005) and 5.0% in a survey based on a less widely used fully structured diagnostic interview (Grant et al., 2005). It is noteworthy that a clinical reappraisal study in the CIDI sample, where a probability sample of respondents was blindly administered a follow-up semistructured diagnostic interview by a clinician, confirmed the high prevalence of social phobia suggested by the CIDI. No clinical reappraisal study was carried out in conjunction with the survey that found the lower prevalence estimate. Nonetheless, even in recent CIDI surveys, the estimated prevalence of social phobia has varied between less than 3% (ESEMeD/MHEDEA 2000 Investigators, 2004) and nearly 14% (DeWit, Ogborne, Offord, & MacDonald, 1999).

It is not clear why such large differences in prevalence estimates should exist. Most methodological explanations are excluded by the fact that the same instrument was used in studies that found both high prevalence and those that found low prevalence. It is noteworthy that the highest prevalence estimates were obtained independently in CIDI surveys carried out in the United States and Canada (DeWit et al., 1999; Kessler, Berglund et al., 2005) and that consistently lower prevalence estimates were found in a coordinated series of surveys using an identical version of the CIDI in six Western European countries (ESEMeD/MHEDEA 2000 Investigators, 2004; DeWit et al., 1999). Is it possible that the true prevalence of social phobia is markedly higher in North America than in Europe? As noted above, a clinical reappraisal study carried out in conjunction with the U.S. CIDI survey confirmed the estimated prevalence of *DSM–IV* social phobia as being greater than 12%. At least a dozen independent epidemiological surveys in Europe, in comparison, have estimated a much lower prevalence of *DSM–IV* social phobia, with a median lifetime prevalence (6.6%) only about half as high as in the North American studies (Fehm et al., 2005). Based on these results, the most plausible conclusion is that the prevalence of social phobia is genuinely higher in North America than Europe, although direct comparisons with parallel clinical reappraisal studies would be needed to resolve this question definitively.

Separation Anxiety Disorder

We noted above in the discussion of agoraphobia without panic that one hypothesis regarding overdiagnosis is that people with separation anxiety disorder (SEPAD) might be misdiagnosed as having agoraphobia without panic. In *DSM–IV–TR,* SEPAD is described as a childhood disorder that seldom persists into adulthood. Epidemiological studies have found that 2%–6% of children and adolescents have a lifetime history of SEPAD (Jurbergs & Ledley, 2005). However, empirical studies in clinical samples argue that adult SEPAD is more common than suggested by *DSM–IV–TR* (Diener & Kim, 2004). This could be due to either of two possibilities. First, a higher proportion of childhood-onset cases might persist into adulthood than assumed in *DSM–IV–TR.* Second, at least some first onsets might occur in adulthood.

Only a few short-term follow-up studies of clinical samples have evaluated the first possibility (Foley, Pickles, Maes, Silberg, & Eaves, 2004). While these studies showed that the vast majority of childhood cases remit before adulthood, they did not follow cases long enough to determine whether an adult form of the disorder subsequently reemerged in conjunction with the development of adult attachment relationships. A few studies of adult SEPAD have evaluated the second possibility (Cyranowski et al., 2002). These studies consistently found a number of adults with SEPAD who reported never having childhood SEPAD. However, as these studies were all based on small and unrepresentative samples, no generalizations can be made from them about prevalence or correlates of adult-onset SEPAD.

The WMH surveys are the only community epidemiological surveys of which we are aware that assessed adult SEPAD. Only one WMH report has appeared so far on SEPAD (Shear, Jin, Ruscio, Walters, & Kessler, 2006). This report is based on the nationally representative CIDI survey carried out in the United States. Lifetime prevalence estimates of childhood and adult SEPAD in this survey were 4.1% and 6.6%, respectively. Approximately one-third (36.1%) of respondents classified as childhood cases were found to persist into adulthood, while the majority (77.5%) of respondents classified as adult cases were found to have first onsets in adulthood.

In interpreting these results, it needs to be noted that adult SEPAD was found to be highly comorbid with other mental disorders. This is especially important in light of the fact that the *DSM* gives little guidance on diagnosis of SEPAD among adults. This underscores the need for further exploration of the boundaries between normal response to loss of an attachment figure, separation anxiety as an adjustment reaction, and syndromal separation anxiety disorder in order to arrive at a clear and principled set of criteria for adult SEPAD in future editions of *DSM* and *ICD*.

Generalized Anxiety Disorder

Prevalence estimates of GAD have varied widely in community epidemiological surveys over the years due to the fact that the criteria for a diagnosis of GAD have changed substantially in the various editions of the *DSM* as well as the fact that the *DSM* system requires worry to be "excessive" but the *ICD* system does not and that the *DSM* includes a hypervigilance syndrome that does not exist in the *ICD* definition (Kessler, Keller, & Wittchen, 2001). Lifetime prevalence estimates of *DSM–IV* GAD in recent epidemiological surveys have been in the range 1%–6% (Kessler, Brandenburg et al., 2005). However, recent research has shown that variation in the key assumptions of duration and excessiveness has a marked effect on these estimates (Ruscio et al., 2005).

The minimum duration requirement for GAD was 1 month when GAD was introduced in *DSM–III* (American Psychiatric Association [APA], 1980). However, clinical studies found that *DSM–III* GAD seldom occurred in the absence of other comorbid anxiety or mood disorders in clinical samples (Breslau & Davis, 1985b), suggesting that GAD might better be conceptualized as a prodrome, residual, or severity marker than an independent disorder.

Based on clinical evidence that comorbidity substantially decreased with episode duration (Breslau & Davis, 1985a), GAD was retained in *DSM–III–R* (APA, 1987) with an increased duration requirement

of 6 months. This change also addressed the problem of distinguishing short episodes of GAD from situational stress reactions (Barlow & Wincze, 1998). A requirement that "unrealistic, hard to control worry" be present was also included in *DSM–III–R* to sharpen the distinction between GAD and nonspecific distress associated with other anxiety and mood disorders (Barlow, Blanchard, Vermilyea, Vermilyea, & DiNardo, 1986). The *ICD–10* criteria for research also require a 6-month duration (World Health Organization, 1993), but the *ICD–10* criteria for clinical practice take a middle position on duration by requiring GAD to last "several months" (World Health Organization, 1992).

This variation in required duration could dramatically influence the number of people classified with GAD. Contrary to the motivation for increasing the *DSM–III–R* duration requirement, epidemiological data have subsequently shown that GAD is not more comorbid than most other anxiety or mood disorders (Kessler et al., 2001; Kessler, Walters, & Wittchen, 2004) and that the extremely high comorbidity of GAD in early clinical studies was due to a help-seeking bias (Wittchen, Zhao, Kessler, & Eaton, 1994). The 6-month duration requirement was nonetheless retained in *DSM–IV* (APA, 1994), which means that episodes of shorter duration receive no diagnosis even if they recur over many years. It has been suggested that such "orphaned" cases of GAD are substantial in number (Rickels & Rynn, 2001).

Several large community epidemiological studies have examined whether episodes of GAD with durations less than 6 months might be either less impairing or less comorbid with other *DSM* disorders than episodes lasting 6 months or longer. No significant differences were found in any of these studies. In the largest and most comprehensive of these studies (Kessler, Brandenburg et al., 2005), the lifetime prevalence estimate of *DSM–IV* GAD more than doubled (from 6.1% to 12.7%) when the duration requirement was changed from 6 months to 1 month. Cases with episodes of 1–5 months were found not to differ greatly from those with episodes of 6 or more months in onset, persistence, impairment, comorbidity, parental GAD, or sociodemographic correlates. These results support the view that a large number of people exist with a clinically significant GAD-like syndrome that is characterized by episodes of less than 6 months duration (Rickels & Rynn, 2001). In saying this, the issue of recurrence is one of obvious importance. Cases with exclusively short episodes typically were found to recur over a number of years, with the average number of years with an episode equal to that of cases with episodes that last 6–11 months, raising the possibility that it might be useful for future studies to consider whether episode recurrence should play a more important part than it currently does as a defining feature of GAD among cases with exclusively short episodes.

A question can be raised whether reverting to a 1-month duration requirement would make sense clinically in that treatment might not be necessary for cases with such short durations. However, as noted in the last paragraph, these cases typically have high recurrence that might be prevented through effective treatment. It is not clear from existing trials whether currently available treatments would be effective in preventing recurrence of cases with short episode durations, as psychotherapy outcome studies and maintenance pharmacotherapy trials have been carried out almost exclusively with cases of longer duration (Pollack, Meoni, Otto, Simon, & Hackett, 2003). However, even if currently available therapies are not effective in this way, it could be argued that this failure should not be reified by defining the problem out of existence by excluding cases with short-recurrent episodes from a diagnosis.

The excessiveness criterion poses many of the same assessment challenges that led to the removal in DSM–IV of the requirement that worry must be "unrealistic" (Abel & Borkovec, 1995; Barlow & Wincze, 1998). For example, there is considerable confusion over what makes worry "excessive" as well as uncertainty over who should determine whether worry is excessive. There is also the question of what leads individuals to appraise their worry as excessive and whether this appraisal corresponds to objective characteristics of the worry experience. It is perhaps not surprising in light of these considerations that one study of DSM–III–R GAD found excessiveness to be the criterion on which assessors most often disagreed, with its elimination leading to a dramatic rise in interrater reliability of diagnosis (Wittchen et al., 1995).

In addition to these problems of conceptual confusion, concerns can be raised about the implications of the excessiveness criterion for diagnostic validity. In particular, critics have noted that the excessiveness requirement excludes from the GAD diagnosis individuals who develop clinically significant generalized anxiety in the context of chronic, objectively stressful situations (Kessler & Wittchen, 2002). Importantly, community epidemiological

research has shown that a sizable number of individuals exist who are diagnosed with GAD by ICD–10, but not by DSM–IV, solely because they fail to meet the excessiveness criterion (Slade & Andrews, 2001). Little is known about these individuals or their likely impact on estimates of the prevalence, severity, or correlates of GAD.

An epidemiological study based on a nationally representative U.S. sample found that the estimated lifetime prevalence of DSM–IV GAD increased by approximately 40% when the excessiveness requirement was removed (Ruscio et al., 2005). It also found that GAD with excessive worry begins earlier in life than GAD without excessive worry, that the former has a more chronic course than the latter and is associated with greater symptom severity and psychiatric comorbidity than the latter. However, GAD without excessive worry was nonetheless found to have substantial persistence and impairment and significantly elevated comorbidity compared to respondents without GAD. Nonexcessive cases also were found to have sociodemographic characteristics comparable to excessive cases and, importantly, were found to have the same familial aggregation of GAD as excessive cases assessed with modified family history RDC interviews of respondents.

Posttraumatic Stress Disorder

Prevalence estimates of PTSD are more difficult to estimate than those of other anxiety disorders because the prevalence of PTSD is a joint function of the prevalence of particular types of trauma exposure and the conditional prevalence of PTSD among people exposed to these traumas. An additional complication is that conditional risk of PTSD among people exposed to trauma varies greatly by type of trauma (Kessler, 2000). Most research on the epidemiology of PTSD has focused on the second of these two prevalence estimates by studying victims of specific traumas such as physical assault (Kilpatrick & Resnick, 1992), sexual assault (Pynoos & Nader, 1988), natural disaster (Koopman, Classen, & Spiegel, 1994), and military combat (Solomon, Neria, Ohry, Waysman, & Ginzburg, 1994). Less is known about the total population prevalence of trauma exposure or PTSD. However, it is possible to piece together such a portrait by combining the results of general population surveys on the prevalence of trauma exposure with the results of more in-depth studies carried out in trauma samples on the conditional prevalence of PTSD among people exposed to trauma.

The largest body of general population data on the prevalence of trauma exposure comes from the United States, where recent surveys have shown that trauma exposure is highly prevalent (Breslau, Davis, Andreski, & Peterson, 1991). A national survey of the U.S. household population found that 60.7% of men and 51.2% of women reported exposure to at least one lifetime traumatic event, with the majority of respondents who reported trauma saying that they experienced more than one type of trauma (Kessler, Sonnega, Bromet, Hughes, & Nelson, 1995).

It is unclear whether these U.S. results generalize to other developed countries. The fact that crime statistics for extreme forms of assaultive violence such as murder and rape are considerably higher in the United States than in other developed countries (Langan & Farrington, 1998) means that exposure to traumatic interpersonal violence is likely to be lower in other developed countries than in the United States. However, rates of exposure to natural disasters and life-threatening accidents, two of the most commonly reported traumas in the U.S. surveys, presumably are comparable in other developed countries. The situation is almost certainly quite different in less developed countries, where we know that exposure to traumatic events involving interpersonal violence is much more common. To take but one of many examples in the literature, Husain et al. (1998) evaluated a sample of 791 Bosnian school children aged 7–15 in Sarajevo at the end of the city's siege in 1994. These children reported that during the previous year, 85% had been shot at by snipers, 66% had lost a family member, and between 10% and 48% had experienced various types of physical deprivation, such as water shortage and lack of shelter.

Turning to the conditional risk of PTSD given trauma exposure, comparison of results across epidemiological studies of particular traumatic stressors shows that conditional risk of PTSD among trauma victims varies enormously depending on the type of trauma under investigation. The general pattern is that PTSD risk is much greater after exposure to trauma involving assaultive violence than after other forms of traumas (Breslau et al., 1998) and that the probability of PTSD is associated with the number of preexisting traumas, exposure severity, and exposure duration as well as with the occurrence of secondary stressors (Stein et al., 2002). A meta-analysis of epidemiological surveys in populations directly exposed to terrorism found the prevalence of PTSD to be in the range 12%–16% (DiMaggio & Galea,

2006). Prevalence has usually been considerably lower in surveys of populations exposed to natural disasters (Galea, Nandi, & Vlahov, 2005). The only report from an epidemiological survey to generate a comprehensive list of traumas and to evaluate risk of PTSD for one randomly selected trauma from each respondent was based on a representative sample of young adults (ages 18–44) in a metropolitan area of the United States (Breslau et al., 1998). Conditional risk of PTSD after a representative trauma was 9.2%, while the highest conditional risk (20.9%) was associated with traumas characterized by assaultive violence. In particularly traumatic situations, though, conditional risk can be higher. In the study of Bosnian school children mentioned in the last paragraph, for example, the prevalence of PTSD was greater than 40%.

It is difficult to combine the estimates of the unconditional prevalence of trauma exposure with the estimates of conditional risk of PTSD after trauma exposure into an overall estimate of population-wide PTSD prevalence due to the complexities associated with many people being exposed to multiple lifetime traumas that vary in prevalence as well as in conditional risk of PTSD. An added complication is that some evidence suggests that conditional risk of PTSD associated with a particular trauma varies as a function of prior exposure to other traumas (Breslau, Chilcoat, Kessler, Peterson, & Lucia, 1999). The only nationally representative estimate of lifetime PTSD prevalence in the United States, which is based on DSM–III–R criteria, is 7.8% (Kessler, Berglund et al., 2005).

Lifetime prevalence estimates of PTSD in the general populations of Western European countries are substantially lower than in the United States. The six Western European countries in the WMH survey series estimated that 1.9% of their populations had PTSD at some time in their lives (ESEMeD/MHEDEA 2000 Investigators, 2004). Other recent Western European surveys had estimates between less than 1% and 2% (Hoyer et al., 2003). As with social phobia, where a similar difference exists between the results of surveys carried out in North America and Western Europe, the most plausible conclusion is that the prevalence of PTSD is genuinely higher in the United States, although direct comparisons involving identical lists with all kind of traumatic events in line with DSM–IV and studies with parallel clinical reappraisal would be needed to resolve this question definitively. While comparable surveys have not been carried out in less developed countries, it is likely that PTSD is considerably more prevalent in the subset of those countries that have experienced prolonged sectarian violence.

Obsessive-Compulsive Disorder

As noted in the introduction, epidemiological surveys find that OCD is one of the least prevalent anxiety disorders, with lifetime prevalence estimates consistently less than 3% (Horwath & Weissman, 2000). There is considerable interest, though, in the possibility that a number of other disorders are part of an OCD spectrum that might be far more prevalent than OCD itself (Goldsmith, Shapiro, Phillips, & McElroy, 1998). Conditions thought to be part of the OCD spectrum include tic disorders, body dysmorphic disorder, eating disorders, trichotillomania and related self-harm disorders, and possibly even hypochondriasis. The argument for the existence of this hypothesized spectrum is based on similarities across the different disorders in a subjective sense of compulsion, in difficulty inhibiting repetitive behaviors, in age of onset, in course of illness, in patterns of comorbidity, in family history, and in specificity of treatment response (Neziroglu, Henricksen, & Yaryura-Tobias, 2006).

Although some controversy exists about the range of conditions that fall within the OCD spectrum (Richter, Summerfeldt, Antony, & Swinson, 2003), the notion that there exists such a spectrum is now widely enough accepted that it has been proposed that spectrum disorders should be reclassified in the *ICD* and *DSM* systems as subtypes of OCD (Yaryura-Tobias et al., 2000). Needless to say, if this happens, the estimated prevalence of OCD could increase substantially. As far as we know, no large-scale community epidemiological research exists on the prevalence of OCD spectrum disorders, so it is difficult to know how high the prevalence estimate might become if OCD spectrum disorders are eventually redefined as subtypes of OCD. A complication is that other research has documented heterogeneity within OCD (Watson, Wu, & Cutshall, 2004), such as a clear distinction between OCD with and without hoarding (Grisham, Brown, Liverant, & Campbell-Sills, 2005). It is currently unclear how this evidence of within-disorder heterogeneity is related to evidence of an OCD spectrum.

Comorbidity Among the Anxiety Disorders

Comorbidity among anxiety disorders is quite common, with up to one-third of people with a lifetime anxiety disorder in some surveys meeting criteria for two or more such disorders (Kessler, 1995).

Furthermore, there is some evidence that anxiety disorders are more highly comorbid than other mental disorders both with each other and with other mental and physical disorders (Toft et al., 2005). Factor analytic studies of diagnostic comorbidity consistently document separate internalizing and externalizing factors in which anxiety and mood disorders have high factor loadings on the internalizing dimension, while most impulse-control disorders and substance use disorders have high factor loadings on the externalizing dimension (Kendler, Prescott, Myers, & Neale, 2003). The internalizing disorders, furthermore, have secondary dimensions of fear disorders (panic, phobia) and distress disorders (depression, dysthymia, GAD) (Watson, 2005). The locations of OCD and PTSD in this two-dimensional space are less distinct; the former appears to be more related to the fear dimension (Watson, 2005) and the latter more related to the distress dimension (Cox, Clara, & Enns, 2002), although neither is strongly indicated by either of these dimensions. Social phobia additionally appears to be somewhat more strongly related to the distress dimension than are the other phobias. Separation anxiety disorder has not been included in factor analytic studies to date.

These results have recently been used by Watson (2005) to call into question the codification of anxiety disorders as a distinct class of disorders in the *DSM* and *ICD* systems and to suggest that a more useful organizing scheme in the upcoming *DSM–V* would be one that distinguished between fear disorders and distress disorders, with the latter including not only GAD and possibly PTSD but also unipolar depression and dysthymia. The argument for a class of fear disorders has the stronger support of the two in neurobiological research based on extensive investigation of fear brain circuitry (Knight, Nguyen, & Bandettini, 2005). The possibility also exists that future research might lead to OCD being distinguished from either fear disorders or distress disorders as part of a spectrum of impulse-control disorders based both on evidence of differential comorbidity and differences in brain circuitry (Whiteside, Port, & Abramowitz, 2004).

Studies of multivariate disorder profiles confirm the complexity of the comorbidity that exists among anxiety disorders. The most comprehensive of these analyses was carried out in the U.S. National Comorbidity Survey Replication (Kessler & Merikangas, 2004) by examining the multivariate profiles among 19 separate *DSM–IV* disorders (Kessler, Chiu, Demler, Merikangas, & Walters,

2005). Of the 524,288 (2^{19}) logically possible multivariate disorder profiles among these disorders, 433 were observed. Nearly 80% of them involved highly comorbid cases (three or more disorders), accounting for 27.0% of all respondents with a disorder and 55.9% of all instances of these disorders.

Importantly, the distribution of comorbidity was found to be significantly different from the distribution one would expect to find if the multivariate structure among the disorders was due entirely to the two-way associations that are the focus of factor analysis, suggesting that the more typical factor analytic studies of comorbidity fail to detect important structure. Based on this result, latent class analysis (LCA) was used to study nonadditive comorbid profiles. A seven-class LCA model provided the best fit to the data, with four classes featuring anxiety disorders prominently.

Results as complex as these clearly need to be replicated before they are taken seriously, but even if accepted as no more than preliminary, they suggest that understanding comorbidity in the anxiety disorders will require considerably more in-depth analysis than has previously been used to study these associations. A dynamic perspective might be useful here in building in information about AOO distributions that allows an investigation of the temporal unfolding of comorbidity. This type of dynamic analysis is currently being used to investigate lifetime comorbidity among anxiety, mood, and impulse-control disorders in the cross-national WMH surveys as well as in a multiwave 10-year prospective analysis of a large cohort of adolescents and young adults (Wittchen, Perkonigg, Lachner, & Nelson, 1998).

The Societal Costs of Anxiety Disorders

We noted earlier in the chapter, but did not emphasize, that early-onset anxiety disorders are powerful predictors of the subsequent onset and persistence of other mental and substance use disorders. It is important to note that these predictive associations are part of a larger pattern of associations that have been documented between anxiety disorders and a much wider array of adverse life course outcomes that might be conceptualized as societal costs of these disorders, including reduced educational attainment, early marriage, marital instability, and low occupational and financial status (Lepine, 2002). A considerable amount of research has been carried out to quantify the magnitude of the short-term societal costs of anxiety disorders in terms of health care expenditures, impaired functioning, and

reduced longevity (Marciniak, Lage, Landbloom, Dunayevich, & Bowman, 2004). The magnitude of the cost estimates in these studies is staggering. For example, Greenberg et al. (1999) estimated that the annual total societal costs of active anxiety disorders in the United States over the decade of the 1990s exceeded $42 billion. This estimate excludes the indirect costs of early-onset anxiety disorders through adverse life course outcomes (e.g., the documented effects of child-adolescent anxiety disorders in predicting low educational attainment and consequent long-term effects on lower income) and through increased risk of other disorders (e.g., anxiety disorders predicting the subsequent onset of cardiovascular disorder).

Summary and Conclusions

The results summarized here document that anxiety disorders are commonly occurring in the general population, often have an early age of onset, and are characterized by frequent comorbidity with each other as well as with other mental disorders. We reviewed evidence to suggest that the current *DSM* and *ICD* definitions of anxiety disorders might substantially underestimate the proportion of the population with a clinically significant anxiety condition. It is noteworthy that research on comorbidity among anxiety disorders generally ignores the existence of anxiety spectrum conditions, a failing that should be rectified in future research.

Based on these results, along with results regarding the societal costs of anxiety disorders, we can safely conclude that anxiety disorders are common and consequential problems that are deeply interwoven with a wide range of other physical, mental, and broader personal difficulties in the general population. As early-onset conditions, anxiety disorders typically begin prior to the vast majority of the other problems with which they are subsequently associated. Yet, as noted earlier in the chapter, young people with early-onset anxiety disorders seldom receive treatment. This is a situation that has to change if we are to be effective in addressing the enormous public health burden created by anxiety disorders throughout the world. To do this will require a level of political will that has heretofore been lacking in even the most progressive countries in the world. One can but hope that future research focused on the long-term costs of illness and the cost-effectiveness of early effective treatment will correct this situation by demonstrating the wisdom of overcoming the current neglect of this extremely prevalent and important class of disorders.

Note

The authors appreciate the helpful comments on earlier drafts by Kathleen Merikangas and T. Bedirhan Üstün.

References

Abel, J. L., & Borkovec, T. D. (1995). Generalizability of *DSM–III–R* generalized anxiety disorder to proposed *DSM–IV* criteria and cross-validation of proposed changes. *Journal of Anxiety Disorders, 9*, 303–315.

American Psychiatric Association. (1980). *Diagnostic and statistical manual of mental disorders* (3rd ed.). Washington, DC: Author.

American Psychiatric Association. (1987). *Diagnostic and statistical manual of mental disorders* (3rd ed. revised). Washington, DC: Author.

American Psychiatric Association. (1994). *Diagnostic and statistical manual of mental disorders* (4th ed.). Washington, DC: Author.

Andrews, G., & Slade, T. (2002). Agoraphobia without a history of panic disorder may be part of the panic disorder syndrome. *Journal of Nervous and Mental Disease, 190*, 624–630.

Angst, J., & Vollrath, M. (1991). The natural history of anxiety disorders. *Acta Psychiatrica Scandinavica, 84*, 446–452.

Antony, M. M., Brown, T. A., & Barlow, D. H. (1997). Heterogeneity among specific phobia types in *DSM–IV. Behavioral Research Therapy; 35*, 1089–1100.

Barlow, D. H., Blanchard, E. B., Vermilyea, J. A., Vermilyea, B. B., & DiNardo, P. A. (1986). Generalized anxiety and generalized anxiety disorder: Description and reconceptualization. *American Journal of Psychiatry; 143*, 40–44.

Barlow, D. H., & Wincze, J. (1998). *DSM–IV* and beyond: What is generalized anxiety disorder? *Acta Psychiatrica Scandinavica, 98*(Suppl. 393), 23–29.

Bienvenu, O. J., & Eaton, W. W. (1998). The epidemiology of blood-injection-injury phobia. *Psychological Medicine, 28*, 1129–1136.

Bienvenu, O. J., Onyike, C. U., Stein, M. B., Chen, L. S., Samuels, J., Nestadt, G., et al. (2006). Agoraphobia in adults: Incidence and longitudinal relationship with panic. *British Journal of Psychiatry; 188*, 432–438.

Bijl, R. V., Ravelli, A., & van Zessen, G. (1998). Prevalence of psychiatric disorder in the general population: Results of the Netherlands Mental Health Survey and Incidence Study (NEMESIS). *Social Psychiatry and Psychiatric Epidemiology; 33*, 587–595.

Breslau, N., Chilcoat, H. D., Kessler, R. C., Peterson, E. L., & Lucia, V. C. (1999). Vulnerability to assaultive violence: Further specification of the sex difference in post-traumatic stress disorder. *Psychological Medicine, 29*, 813–821.

Breslau, N., & Davis, G. C. (1985a). *DSM–III* generalized anxiety disorder: An empirical investigation of more stringent criteria. *Psychiatry Research, 15*, 231–238.

Breslau, N., & Davis, G. C. (1985b). Further evidence on the doubtful validity of generalized anxiety disorder. *Psychiatry Research, 16*, 177–179.

Breslau, N., Davis, G. C., Andreski, P., & Peterson, E. (1991). Traumatic events and posttraumatic stress disorder in an urban population of young adults. *Archives of General Psychiatry; 48*, 216–222.

Breslau, N., Kessler, R. C., Chilcoat, H. D., Schultz, L. R., Davis, G. C., & Andreski, P. (1998). Trauma and posttraumatic stress disorder in the community: The 1996 Detroit Area Survey of Trauma. *Archives of General Psychiatry; 55*, 626–632.

Bromet, E. J., Gluzman, S. F., Paniotto, V. I., Webb, C. P., Tintle, N. L., Zakhozha, V., et al. (2005). Epidemiology of psychiatric and alcohol disorders in Ukraine: Findings from the Ukraine World Mental Health Survey. *Social Psychiatry and Psychiatric Epidemiology; 40*, 681–690.

Bruce, M. L., Leaf, P. J., Rozal, G. P., Florio, L., & Hoff, R. A. (1994). Psychiatric status and 9-year mortality data in the New Haven Epidemiologic Catchment Area Study. *American Journal of Psychiatry; 151*, 716–721.

Bruce, S. E., Yonkers, K. A., Otto, M. W., Eisen, J. L., Weisberg, R. B., Pagano, M., et al. (2005). Influence of psychiatric comorbidity on recovery and recurrence in generalized anxiety disorder, social phobia, and panic disorder: A 12-year prospective study. *American Journal of Psychiatry; 162*, 1179–1187.

Brugha, T. S., Jenkins, R., Taub, N., Meltzer, H., & Bebbington, P. E. (2001). A general population comparison of the Composite International Diagnostic Interview (CIDI) and the Schedules for Clinical Assessment in Neuropsychiatry (SCAN). *Psychological Medicine, 31*, 1001–1013.

Burke, K. C., Burke, J. D., Jr., Regier, D. A., & Rae, D. S. (1990). Age at onset of selected mental disorders in five community populations. *Archives of General Psychiatry; 47*, 511–518.

Christiana, J. M., Gilman, S. E., Guardino, M., Mickelson, K., Morselli, P. L., Olfson, M., et al. (2000). Duration between onset and time of obtaining initial treatment among people with anxiety and mood disorders: An international survey of members of mental health patient advocate groups. *Psychological Medicine, 30*, 693–703.

Christie, K. A., Burke, J. D. J., Regier, D. A., Rae, D. S., Boyd, J. H., & Locke, B. Z. (1988). Epidemiologic evidence for early onset of mental disorders and higher risk of drug-abuse in young-adults. *American Journal of Psychiatry; 145*, 971–975.

Cox, B. J., Clara, I. P., & Enns, M. W. (2002). Posttraumatic stress disorder and the structure of common mental disorders. *Depression and Anxiety; 15*, 168–171.

Curtis, G. C., Magee, W. J., Eaton, W. W., Wittchen, H.-U., & Kessler, R. C. (1998). Specific fears and phobias: Epidemiology and classification. *British Journal of Psychiatry; 173*, 212–217.

Cyranowski, J. M., Shear, M. K., Rucci, P., Fagiolini, A., Frank, E., Grochocinski, V. J., et al. (2002). Adult separation anxiety: Psychometric properties of a new structured clinical interview. *Journal of Psychiatric Research, 36*, 77–86.

DeWit, D. J., Ogborne, A., Offord, D. R., & MacDonald, K. (1999). Antecedents of the risk of recovery from *DSM–III–R* social phobia. *Psychological Medicine, 29*, 569–582.

Diener, M. L., & Kim, D.-Y. (2004). Maternal and child predictors of preschool children's social competence. *Journal of Applied Developmental Psychology; 25*, 3–24.

DiMaggio, C., & Galea, S. (2006). The behavioral consequences of terrorism: A meta-analysis. *Academy of Emergency Medicine, 13*, 559–566.

ESEMeD/MHEDEA 2000 Investigators. (2004). Prevalence of mental disorders in Europe: Results from the European Study of the Epidemiology of Mental Disorders (ESEMeD) project. *Acta Psychiatrica Scandinavica, 109*(Suppl. 420), 21–27.

Fehm, L., Pelissolo, A., Furmark, T., & Wittchen, H.-U. (2005). Size and burden of social phobia in Europe. *European Neuropsychopharmacology; 15*, 453–462.

Foley, D. L., Pickles, A., Maes, H. M., Silberg, J. L., & Eaves, L. J. (2004). Course and short-term outcomes of separation anxiety disorder in a community sample of twins. *Journal of the American Academy of Child and Adolescent Psychiatry; 43,* 1107–1114.

Galea, S., Nandi, A., & Vlahov, D. (2005). The epidemiology of post-traumatic stress disorder after disasters. *Epidemiological Reviews, 27,* 78–91.

Goldsmith, T., Shapiro, M. A., Phillips, K. A., & McElroy, S. L. (1998). Conceptual foundations of obsessive-compulsive spectrum disorders. In R. P. Swinson, M. M. Anthony, S. Rachman, & M. A. Richter (Eds.), *Obsessive-compulsive disorder: Theory; research, and treatment* (pp. 397–425). New York: Guilford Press.

Goodwin, R. D., Faravelli, C., Rosi, S., Cosci, F., Truglia, E., de Graaf, R., et al. (2005). The epidemiology of panic disorder and agoraphobia in Europe. *European Neuropsychopharmacology; 15,* 435–443.

Grant, B. F., Hasin, D. S., Blanco, C., Stinson, F. S., Chou, S. P., Goldstein, R. B., et al. (2005). The epidemiology of social anxiety disorder in the United States: Results from the National Epidemiologic Survey on Alcohol and Related Conditions. *Journal of Clinical Psychiatry; 66,* 1351–1361.

Grant, B. F., Hasin, D. S., Stinson, F. S., Dawson, D. A., Goldstein, R. B., Smith, S., et al. (2006). The epidemiology of *DSM–IV* panic disorder and agoraphobia in the United States: Results from the National Epidemiologic Survey on Alcohol and Related Conditions. *Journal of Clinical Psychiatry; 67,* 363–374.

Grant, B. F., Stinson, F. S., Dawson, D. A., Chou, S. P., Dufour, M. C., Compton, W., et al. (2004). Prevalence and co-occurrence of substance use disorders and independent mood and anxiety disorders: Results from the National Epidemiologic Survey on Alcohol and Related Conditions. *Archives of General Psychiatry; 61,* 807–816.

Greenberg, P. E., Sisitsky, T., Kessler, R. C., Finkelstein, S. N., Berndt, E. R., Davidson, J. R., et al. (1999). The economic burden of anxiety disorders in the 1990s. *Journal of Clinical Psychiatry; 60,* 427–435.

Grisham, J. R., Brown, T. A., Liverant, G. I., & Campbell-Sills, L. (2005). The distinctiveness of compulsive hoarding from obsessive-compulsive disorder. *Journal of Anxiety Disorders, 19,* 767–779.

Gureje, O., Lasebikan, V. O., Kola, L., & Makanjuola, V. A. (2006). Lifetime and 12-month prevalence of mental disorders in the Nigerian Survey of Mental Health and Well-Being. *British Journal of Psychiatry; 188,* 465–471.

Haro, J. M., Arbazadeh-Bouchez, S., Brugha, T. S., de Girolamo, G., Guyer, M. E., Jin, R., et al. (2006). Concordance of the Composite International Diagnostic Interview Version 3.0 (CIDI 3.0) with standardized clinical assessments in the WHO World Mental Health Surveys. *International Journal of Methods in Psychiatric Research, 15,* 167–180.

Hasler, G., Gergen, P. J., Kleinbaum, D. G., Ajdacic, V., Gamma, A., Eich, D., et al. (2005). Asthma and panic in young adults: A 20-year prospective community study. *American Journal of Respiratory and Critical Care Medicine, 171,* 1224–1230.

Horwath, E., Lish, J. D., Johnson, J., Hornig, C. D., & Weissman, M. M. (1993). Agoraphobia without panic: Clinical reappraisal of an epidemiologic finding. *American Journal of Psychiatry; 150,* 1496–1501.

Horwath, E., & Weissman, M. M. (2000). The epidemiology and cross-national presentation of obsessive-compulsive disorder. *Psychiatric Clinics of North America, 23,* 493–507.

Hoyer, J., Beesdo, K., Bittner, A., & Wittchen, H.-U. (2003). Epidemiologia dei Disturbi d'Ansia [Epidemiology of anxiety disorders]. In A. C. Altamura (Ed.), *Ansia generalizzata e comorbidità con i disturbi dell'umore [Comorbidity of generalized anxiety disorder and mood disorders]* (pp. 44–83). Pisa: Pacini Editore.

Husain, S. A., Nair, J., Holcomb, W., Reid, J. C., Vargas, V., & Nair, S. S. (1998). Stress reactions of children and adolescents in war and siege conditions. *American Journal of Psychiatry; 155,* 1718–1719.

International Consortium in Psychiatric Epidemiology. (2000). Cross-national comparisons of the prevalences and correlates of mental disorders. WHO International Consortium in Psychiatric Epidemiology. *Bulletin of the World Health Organization, 78,* 413–426.

Jacobi, F., Wittchen, H.-U., Holting, C., Hofler, M., Pfister, H., Muller, N., et al. (2004). Prevalence, co-morbidity and correlates of mental disorders in the general population: Results from the German Health Interview and Examination Survey (GHS). *Psychological Medicine, 34,* 597–611.

Jenkins, R., Lewis, G., Bebbington, P., Brugha, T., Farrell, M., Gill, B., et al. (2003). The National Psychiatric Morbidity Surveys of Great Britain—initial findings from the household survey. *International Review of Psychiatry; 15,* 29–42.

Jurbergs, N., & Ledley, D. R. (2005). Separation anxiety disorder. *Pediatric Annals, 34,* 108–115.

Karam, E. G., Mneimneh, Z. N., Karam, A. N., Fayyad, J. A., Nasser, S. C., Chatterji, S., et al. (2006). Prevalence and treatment of mental disorders in Lebanon: A national epidemiological survey. *Lancet, 367,* 1000–1006.

Kendall, P. C., & Kessler, R. C. (2002). The impact of childhood psychopathology interventions on subsequent substance abuse: Policy implications, comments, and recommendations. *Journal of Consulting and Clinical Psychology; 70,* 1303–1306.

Kendler, K. S., Prescott, C. A., Myers, J., & Neale, M. C. (2003). The structure of genetic and environmental risk factors for common psychiatric and substance use disorders in men and women. *Archives of General Psychiatry; 60,* 929–937.

Kessler, R. C. (1995). Epidemiology of psychiatric comorbidity. In M. T. Tsuang, M. Tohen, & G.E.P. Zahner (Eds.), *Textbook in psychiatric epidemiology* (pp. 179–197). New York: Wiley.

Kessler, R. C. (1999). The World Health Organization International Consortium in Psychiatric Epidemiology (ICPE): Initial work and future directions—the NAPE Lecture 1998. Nordic Association for Psychiatric Epidemiology. *Acta Psychiatrica Scandinavica, 99,* 2–9.

Kessler, R. C. (2000). Posttraumatic stress disorder: The burden to the individual and to society. *Journal of Clinical Psychiatry; 61*(Suppl. 5), 4–12; discussion 13–14.

Kessler, R. C., Abelson, J., Demler, O., Escobar, J. I., Gibbon, M., Guyer, M. E., et al. (2004). Clinical calibration of *DSM–IV* diagnoses in the World Mental Health (WMH) version of the World Health Organization (WHO) Composite International Diagnostic Interview (WMH-CIDI). *International Journal of Methods in Psychiatric Research, 13,* 122–139.

Kessler, R. C., Berglund, P., Demler, O., Jin, R., & Walters, E. E. (2005). Lifetime prevalence and age-of-onset distributions of *DSM–IV* disorders in the National Comorbidity Survey Replication. *Archives of General Psychiatry; 62,* 593–602.

Kessler, R. C., Brandenburg, N., Lane, M., Roy-Byrne, P., Stang, P. D., Stein, D. J., et al. (2005). Rethinking the duration requirement for generalized anxiety disorder: Evidence from the National Comorbidity Survey Replication. *Psychological Medicine, 35,* 1073–1082.

Kessler, R. C., Chiu, W. T., Demler, O., Merikangas, K. R., & Walters, E. E. (2005). Prevalence, severity, and comorbidity of 12-month *DSM–IV* disorders in the National Comorbidity Survey Replication. *Archives of General Psychiatry; 62,* 617–627.

Kessler, R. C., Keller, M. B., & Wittchen, H.-U. (2001). The epidemiology of generalized anxiety disorder. *Psychiatric Clinics of North America, 24,* 19–39.

Kessler, R. C., & Merikangas, K. R. (2004). The National Comorbidity Survey Replication (NCS-R): Background and aims. *International Journal of Methods in Psychiatric Research, 13,* 60–68.

Kessler, R. C., Sonnega, A., Bromet, E., Hughes, M., & Nelson, C. B. (1995). Posttraumatic stress disorder in the National Comorbidity Survey. *Archives of General Psychiatry; 52,* 1048–1060.

Kessler, R. C., Walters, E. E., & Wittchen, H.-U. (2004). Epidemiology. In R. G. Heimberg, C. L. Turk, & D. S. Mennin (Eds.), *Generalized anxiety disorder: Advances in research and practice* (pp. 29–50). New York: Guilford Press.

Kessler, R. C., & Wittchen, H.-U. (2002). Patterns and correlates of generalized anxiety disorder in community samples. *Journal of Clinical Psychiatry; 63*(Suppl. 8), 4–10.

Kessler, R. C., Wittchen, H.-U., Abelson, J. M., McGonagle, K. A., Schwarz, N., Kendler, K. S., et al. (1998). Methodological studies of the Composite International Diagnostic Interview (CIDI) in the U.S. National Comorbidity Survey. *International Journal of Methods in Psychiatric Research, 7,* 33–55.

Kessler, R. C., Wittchen, H.-U., Abelson, J. M., & Zhao, S. (2000). Methodological issues in assessing psychiatric disorder with self-reports. In A. A. Stone, J. S. Turrkan, C. A. Bachrach, J. B. Jobe, H. S. Kurtzman, & V. S. Cain (Eds.), *The science of self-report: Implications for research and practice* (pp. 229–255). Mahwah, NJ: Erlbaum.

Kilpatrick, D., & Resnick, H. (1992). Posttraumatic stress disorder associated with exposure to criminal victimization in clinical and community populations. In J. Davidson & E. Foa (Eds.), *Posttraumatic stress disorder: DSM–IV and beyond* (pp. 113–143). Washington, DC: American Psychiatric Press.

Klein, D. F., & Gorman, J. M. (1987). A model of panic and agoraphobic development. *Acta Psychiatrica Scandinavica, 76*(Suppl. 335), 87–95.

Knight, D. C., Nguyen, H. T., & Bandettini, P. A. (2005). The role of the human amygdala in the production of conditioned fear responses. *Neuroimage, 26,* 1193–1200.

Koopman, C., Classen, C., & Spiegel, D. (1994). Predictors of posttraumatic stress symptoms among survivors of the Oakland/Berkeley, Calif., firestorm. *American Journal of Psychiatry; 151,* 888–894.

Kringlen, E., Torgersen, S., & Cramer, V. (2001). A Norwegian psychiatric epidemiological study. *American Journal of Psychiatry; 158,* 1091–1098.

Langan, P. A., & Farrington, D. P. (1998). *Crime and justice in the United States and in England and Wales, 1981–96.* Washington, DC: United States Department of Justice, Office of Justice Programs, Bureau of Justice Statistics.

Lepine, J. P. (2002). The epidemiology of anxiety disorders: Prevalence and societal costs. *Journal of Clinical Psychiatry; 63*(Suppl. 14), 4–8.

Lieb, R. (2005). Anxiety disorders: Clinical presentation and epidemiology. *Handbook of Experimental Pharmacology; 169,* 405–432.

Lieb, R., Becker, E., & Altamura, C. (2005). The epidemiology of generalized anxiety disorder in Europe. *European Neuropsychopharmacology; 15,* 445–452.

Lipsitz, J. D., Barlow, D. H., Mannuzza, S., Hofmann, S. G., & Fyer, A. J. (2002). Clinical features of four *DSM–IV*–specific phobia subtypes. *Journal of Nervous and Mental Disease, 190,* 471–478.

Magee, W. J., Eaton, W. W., Wittchen, H.-U., McGonagle, K. A., & Kessler, R. C. (1996). Agoraphobia, simple phobia, and social phobia in the National Comorbidity Survey. *Archives of General Psychiatry; 53,* 159–168.

Marciniak, M., Lage, M. J., Landbloom, R. P., Dunayevich, E., & Bowman, L. (2004). Medical and productivity costs of anxiety disorders: Case control study. *Depression and Anxiety; 19,* 112–120.

Neziroglu, F., Henricksen, J., & Yaryura-Tobias, J. A. (2006). Psychotherapy of obsessive-compulsive disorder and spectrum: Established facts and advances, 1995–2005. *Psychiatric Clinics of North America, 29,* 585–604.

Perkonigg, A., Pfister, H., Stein, M. B., Hofler, M., Lieb, R., Maercker, A., et al. (2005). Longitudinal course of posttraumatic stress disorder and posttraumatic stress disorder symptoms in a community sample of adolescents and young adults. *American Journal of Psychiatry; 162,* 1320–1327.

Pollack, M. H., Meoni, P., Otto, M. W., Simon, N., & Hackett, D. (2003). Predictors of outcome following venlafaxine extended-release treatment of *DSM–IV* generalized anxiety disorder: A pooled analysis of short- and long-term studies. *Journal of Clinical Psychopharmacology; 23,* 250–259.

Pynoos, R. S., & Nader, K. (1988). Children who witness the sexual assaults of their mothers. *Journal of the American Academy of Child and Adolescent Psychiatry; 27,* 567–572.

Richter, M. A., Summerfeldt, L. J., Antony, M. M., & Swinson, R. P. (2003). Obsessive-compulsive spectrum conditions in obsessive-compulsive disorder and other anxiety disorders. *Depression and Anxiety; 18,* 118–127.

Rickels, K., & Rynn, M. (2001). Overview and clinical presentation of generalized anxiety disorder. *Psychiatric Clinics of North America, 24,* 1–17.

Robins, L. N., Helzer, J. E., Croughan, J. L., & Ratcliff, K. S. (1981). National Institute of Mental Health Diagnostic Interview Schedule: Its history, characteristics and validity. *Archives of General Psychiatry; 38,* 381–389.

Robins, L. N., & Regier, D. A. (1991). An overview of psychiatric disorders in America. In L. N. Robins & D. A. Regier (Eds.), *Psychiatric disorders in America: The Epidemiologic Catchment Area Study* (pp. 328–366). New York: Free Press.

Robins, L. N., Wing, J., Wittchen, H.-U., Helzer, J. E., Babor, T. F., Burke, J., et al. (1988). The Composite International Diagnostic Interview. An epidemiologic instrument suitable for use in conjunction with different diagnostic systems and in different cultures. *Archives of General Psychiatry; 45,* 1069–1077.

Ruscio, A. M., Lane, M., Roy-Byrne, P., Stang, P. E., Stein, D. J., Wittchen, H.-U., et al. (2005). Should excessive worry be required for a diagnosis of generalized anxiety disorder? Results from the U.S. National Comorbidity Survey Replication. *Psychological Medicine, 35,* 1761–1772.

Shear, K., Jin, R., Ruscio, A. M., Walters, E. E., & Kessler, R. C. (2006). Prevalence and correlates of estimated *DSM–IV* child and adult separation anxiety disorder in the National Comorbidity Survey Replication. *American Journal of Psychiatry; 163,* 1074–1083.

Shen, Y. C., Zhang, M. Y., Huang, Y. Q., He, Y. L., Liu, Z. R., Cheng, H., et al. (2006). Twelve-month prevalence, severity, and unmet need for treatment of mental disorders in metropolitan China. *Psychological Medicine, 36,* 257–267.

Slade, T., & Andrews, G. (2001). *DSM–IV* and *ICD–10* generalized anxiety disorder: Discrepant diagnoses and associated disability. *Social Psychiatry and Psychiatric Epidemiology; 36,* 45–51.

Solomon, Z., Neria, Y., Ohry, A., Waysman, M., & Ginzburg, K. (1994). PTSD among Israeli former prisoners of war and soldiers with combat stress reaction: A longitudinal study. *American Journal of Psychiatry; 151,* 554–559.

Stein, M. B., Hofler, M., Perkonigg, A., Lieb, R., Pfister, H., Maercker, A., et al. (2002). Patterns of incidence and psychiatric risk factors for traumatic events. *International Journal of Methods in Psychiatric Research, 11,* 143–153.

Toft, T., Fink, P., Oernboel, E., Christensen, K., Frostholm, L., & Olesen, F. (2005). Mental disorders in primary care: Prevalence and co-morbidity among disorders: Results from the functional illness in primary care (FIP) study. *Psychological Medicine, 35,* 1175–1184.

Watson, D. (2005). Rethinking the mood and anxiety disorders: A quantitative hierarchical model for *DSM–V. Journal of Abnormal Psychology , 114,* 522–536.

Watson, D., Wu, K. D., & Cutshall, C. (2004). Symptom subtypes of obsessive-compulsive disorder and their relation to dissociation. *Journal of Anxiety Disorders, 18,* 435–458.

Whiteside, S. P., Port, J. D., & Abramowitz, J. S. (2004). A meta-analysis of functional neuroimaging in obsessive-compulsive disorder. *Psychiatry Research, 132,* 69–79.

The WHO World Mental Health Survey Consortium. (2004). Prevalence, severity, and unmet need for treatment of mental disorders in the World Health Organization World Mental Health Surveys. *Journal of the American Medical Association, 291,* 2581–2590.

Wittchen, H.-U. (1994). Reliability and validity studies of the WHO—Composite International Diagnostic Interview (CIDI): A critical review. *Journal of Psychiatric Research, 28,* 57–84.

Wittchen, H.-U., & Jacobi, F. (2005). Size and burden of mental disorders in Europe—a critical review and appraisal of 27 studies. *European Neuropsychopharmacology; 15,* 357–376.

Wittchen, H.-U., Kessler, R. C., Zhao, S., & Abelson, J. (1995). Reliability and clinical validity of UM-CIDI *DSM–III–R* generalized anxiety disorder. *Journal of Psychiatric Research, 29,* 95–110.

Wittchen, H.-U., Lieb, R., Schuster, P., & Oldehinkel, A. J. (1999). When is onset? Investigations into early developmental stages of anxiety and depressive disorders. In J. L. Rapoport (Ed.), *Childhood onset of adult psychopathology. Clinical and research advances* (pp. 259–302). Washington, DC: American Psychiatric Press.

Wittchen, H.-U., Perkonigg, A., Lachner, G., & Nelson, C. B. (1998). Early developmental stages of psychopathology study (EDSP): Objectives and design. *European Addiction Research, 4,* 18–27.

Wittchen, H.-U., Reed, V., & Kessler, R. C. (1998). The relationship of agoraphobia and panic in a community sample of adolescents and young adults. *Archives of General Psychiatry; 55,* 1017–1024.

Wittchen, H.-U., Zhao, S., Abelson, J. M., Abelson, J. L., & Kessler, R. C. (1996). Reliability and procedural validity of UM-CIDI *DSM–III–R* phobic disorders. *Psychological Medicine, 26,* 1169–1177.

Wittchen, H.-U., Zhao, S., Kessler, R. C., & Eaton, W. W. (1994). *DSM–III–R* generalized anxiety disorder in the National Comorbidity Survey. *Archives of General Psychiatry; 51,* 355–364.

World Health Organization. (1992). *The ICD–10 Classification of Mental and Behavioral Disorders: Clinical descriptions and diagnostic guidelines.* Geneva: Author.

World Health Organization. (1993). *The ICD–10 Classification of Mental and Behavioral Disorders: Diagnostic criteria for research.* Geneva: Author.

Yaryura-Tobias, J. A., Grunes, M. S., Todaro, J., McKay, D., Neziroglu, F. A., & Stockman, R. (2000). Nosological insertion of Axis I disorders in the etiology of obsessive-compulsive disorder. *Journal of Anxiety Disorders, 14,* 19–30.

Yonkers, K. A., Bruce, S. E., Dyck, I. R., & Keller, M. B. (2003). Chronicity, relapse, and illness—course of panic disorder, social phobia, and generalized anxiety disorder: Findings in men and women from 8 years of follow-up. *Depression and Anxiety; 17,* 173–179.

Zimmermann, P., Wittchen, H.-U., Hofler, M., Pfister, H., Kessler, R. C., & Lieb, R. (2003). Primary anxiety disorders and the development of subsequent alcohol use disorders: A 4-year community study of adolescents and young adults. *Psychological Medicine, 33,* 1211–1222.

CHAPTER

3

Phenomenology of Panic and Phobic Disorders

Stefan G. Hofmann, Georg W. Alpers *and* Paul Pauli

Abstract

Panic and phobic disorders are common and serious psychiatric conditions. The first part of this chapter presents the commonalities and unique characteristics of the diagnostic definitions, phenomenology, and associated features of panic disorder, agoraphobia, social anxiety disorder (social phobia), and specific phobia. The second part discusses some of the specific and common psychological factors that maintain the disorder, including panic attacks and dysfunctional cognitions. Biological models and psychological theories are discussed. It is concluded that the challenge of the upcoming new edition of the *DSM* is to address the complexities of the relationship between these diagnostic categories within the framework of a parsimonious classification system.

Keywords: agoraphobia, cognitions, diagnostic, maintaining factors, nosology, panic attack, panic disorder, phenomenology, phobia, social anxiety disorder

Diagnostic Features and Description

The creation of the *DSM* anxiety disorder categories was partly the result of studies that were aimed at distinguishing two types of anxiety disorder patients based on their pharmacological treatment response (Klein, 1964). Specifically, Klein and his colleagues observed that imipramine, a tricyclic antidepressant, was effective for spontaneous panic attacks, but not for chronic and anticipatory anxiety. Klein concluded that panic and anticipatory anxiety reflect two qualitatively different underlying biological processes.

Epidemiological studies of adult community samples (e.g., Kessler, Berglund, Demler, Jin, & Walters, 2005; Kessler, Chiu, Demler, & Walters, 2005) indicate that anxiety disorders are among the most commonly occurring forms of psychological disturbances but the rate at which they are diagnosed varies between countries (Demyttenaere et al., 2004). Anxiety disorders are also highly comorbid, as suggested by a large study of outpatients in a mood and anxiety disorder clinic

(Brown, Campbell, Lehman, Grisham, & Mancill, 2001). Based on clinical interviews of 1,127 individuals to assess for *DSM–IV* diagnoses, this study reported that 55% of patients with a principal anxiety or mood disorder had at least one additional anxiety or depressive disorder at time of the assessment. When examining lifetime diagnoses, this rate increased to 76%.

This chapter will review the diagnostic definitions, phenomenology, and associated features of panic disorder, social anxiety disorder (also known as social phobia), and specific phobia. The first part of this chapter will present the commonalities and unique characteristics. In the second part, we will then discuss some of the specific and common psychological factors that maintain the disorder, including panic attacks and dysfunctional cognitions.

Panic Disorder and Agoraphobia
Definition

Although anxiety attacks were well described in early case reports (e.g., Freud, 1895), panic disorder did not become an important diagnostic category until the arrival of *DSM–III* (American Psychiatric Association [APA], 1980). To meet *DSM–IV* (APA, 1994) criteria for panic disorder (with or without agoraphobia) a person must experience at least one unexpected (or uncued) panic attack and develop substantial anxiety over the possibility of having another attack or its implications. The *DSM–IV* defines a panic attack as a discrete period of intense fear that is accompanied by at least 4 of 13 somatic (e.g., palpitations, shortness of breath) or cognitive (e.g., fear of dying) symptoms. The typical attack has a sudden onset, which builds rapidly to a peak and is accompanied by a sense of imminent danger or impending doom and an urge to escape. Importantly, panic attacks are not restricted to panic disorder; they also occur in specific phobia or social phobia, however, in these cases, they have recognizable external triggers (i.e., cued panic attacks).

Although all panic disorder patients did experience at least one uncued panic attack, some also may have experienced cued panic attacks. As a consequence, panic disorder with agoraphobia may develop. It is characterized by an avoidance of many situations in which having a panic attack could be dangerous or embarrassing or in which it may be difficult to get help. However, agoraphobia can also occur without panic disorder. These patients either experience no panic attacks at all, only cued panic attacks, or isolated attacks that do not meet full criteria for panic disorder. In contrast to specific phobia, agoraphobia involves the fear of clusters of situations, which are most often related to being alone, being in crowded spaces, or traveling far from home. Finally, people who experience isolated panic attacks but otherwise do not meet criteria of panic disorder or agoraphobia have an elevated risk to develop panic disorder or other psychopathologies.

Phenomenology and Associated Features

Findings from the National Comorbity Survey-Replication (NCS-R) indicate that the 12-month prevalence rate of panic disorder is 2.7%, for agoraphobia without panic, 0.8% (Kessler, Berglund et al., 2005; Kessler, Chiu, et al., 2005; Kessler et al., 2006). This is consistent across a large number of societies (Weissman et al., 1997). While panic disorder with agoraphobia is approximately three to four times as common in women as in men, panic disorder without agoraphobia is only about 1.3 times more frequent in women than in

men. Panic attacks without the full diagnosis of panic disorder are clearly more prevalent. The lifetime prevalence is 22.7% for panic attacks without agoraphobia and 0.8% for panic attacks with agoraphobia without panic disorder (Kessler et al., 2006).

Anxiety disorders in general are chronic conditions in the majority of men and women. However, compared to panic disorder with agoraphobia and other forms of anxiety disorders, panic disorder without agoraphobia is associated with higher recovery rates, suggesting that the presence of agoraphobia is associated with poor long-term outcome (Bruce et al., 2005; Yonkers, Bruce, Dyck, & Keller, 2003). This view was confirmed by a recent study of Kessler et al. (2006) that used the NCS-R data (n = 9,282) to compare four mutually exclusive groups: panic attacks only without panic disorder or agoraphobia (22.7% of the sample), panic attacks without panic disorder but with agoraphobia (0.8%), panic disorder without agoraphobia (3.7%), and panic disorder with agoraphobia (1.1%). This study revealed monotonic increases for number of attacks, comorbidity, clinical severity, role impairment, and treatment-seeking with lowest values for respondents with panic attacks only, intermediate values for agoraphobia without panic disorder and panic disorder without agoraphobia, and highest values for panic disorder with agoraphobia. The authors suggest that agoraphobia might be a severity marker of panic or might have a direct effect on impairment. Considerable research focused on panic attacks as the main characteristic of panic disorder. The typical panic attack is characterized by three symptoms, most frequently, palpitations, dizziness, and dyspnea. However, retrospective distortions are likely since the number of symptoms was highest if assessed with a retrospective questionnaire and lowest if assessed with a diary completed immediately after the attack (Margraf, Taylor, Ehlers, & Roth, 1987). Although uncued panic attacks are important for the differential diagnosis, it is notable that they are not clearly different from cued attacks in physiological characteristics. Moreover, cued panic attacks are more common than uncued attacks, even in panic disorder patients; therefore, the distinction between cued and uncued panic attacks might be called into question (Kessler et al., 2006).

About 80% of the panic patients retrospectively report that the disorder started with a sudden initial panic attack (Öst, 1987). However, the high prevalence of people experiencing panic attacks without meeting criteria of any anxiety disorder (22.7%; Kessler et al., 2006) are not only at risk to develop later in life panic disorder, but also other anxiety disorders or other psychopathologies, especially major depressive disorder (MDD), somatoform disorders, or alcohol or drug abuse (Kessler et al., 1994, 2006).

The *DSM–IV* implies that agoraphobia is typically preceded by spontaneous panic attacks (APA, 1994). This is in large part due to the low prevalence of agoraphobia without history of panic disorder (see above). However, recent longitudinal data show that while a baseline diagnosis of panic disorder is the strongest predictor of the onset of agoraphobia, a baseline diagnosis of agoraphobia without spontaneous panic attacks also predicts the onset of panic disorder (Bienvenu et al., 2006). These data confirm the importance of agoraphobia as a separate diagnosis and suggest reconsidering the implicitly assumed one-way causal relationship from panic to agoraphobia. In addition, clinicians should be aware that panic attacks increase treatment-seeking and this may be the reason why agoraphobic patients without panic disorder are less likely to receive appropriate treatment.

Panic patients are characterized by enhanced anxiety sensitivity that can be assessed as a dispositional variable with the Anxiety Sensitivity Index (ASI) (Reiss, Peterson, Gursky, & McNally, 1986) and refers to fear of anxiety-related sensations. Especially interesting are longitudinal prospective studies showing that high ASI scores constitute a risk for panic attacks, panic disorder, and avoidance behavior (see review by McNally, 2002; Wilson & Hayward, 2006). For example, Schmidt, Lerew, & Jackson (1997, 1999) observed that about 6% of a cohort of cadets entering the U.S. Air Force Academy experience panic attacks during the 5-week basic training. Most important, ASI scores assessed before training predicted panic even after controlling for several moderating variables. However, the explained variance was only modest, indicating the importance of other variables.

Although some panic attacks are associated with intense fear and anxiety, the majority of attacks only reach an intensity level of 6 on a scale ranging from 1 to 10 (Margraf et al., 1987). Ambulatory monitoring of heart rate and blood pressure changes revealed in the average only moderate physiological changes during attack, although few attacks might be associated with considerable physiological changes (Cohen, Barlow, & Blanchard, 1985). The average attack is characterized by heart rates around 90 bpm, an increase of around 7 bpm compared to control periods 24 hours later, and moderate increases in systolic and diastolic blood pressure. Comparable physiological changes frequently occur during daily activities (Margraf et al., 1987; White & Baker, 1987). However, panic attacks not only happen during the daytime. Nocturnal panic occurs in 18% to 45% of panic disorder patients and refers to waking from sleep in a state of panic without a period of waking time before panicking and without any obvious trigger (e.g., absence of nightmares as triggers). Panic patients with and without nocturnal panic are equally avoidant and distressed, but individuals with nocturnal panic report daytime panic and general somatic sensations more frequently and were found to be more distressed during a relaxation task (Craske, Lang, Tsao, Mystkowski, & Rowe, 2001).

Biological models of panic disorder were founded on the observation that pharmacological agents (e.g., sodium lactate, CO_2, Yohimbin) trigger panic attacks in panic patients far more often than in healthy volunteers (e.g., Gorman et al., 1984, 1994). Some studies even demonstrated that lactate infusions during sleep trigger greater heart rate increases in panic patients than in healthy volunteers (Koenigsberg, Pollak, Fine, & Kakuma, 1994). However, the diversity of substances shown to elicit panic in patients with panic disorder suggests that it is not a specific pharmacological effect but rather a common nonspecific effect (e.g., the elicitation of feared physical sensations) that triggers panic attacks. In addition, several studies indicate that the effects of the pharmacological manipulations greatly depend on cognitive factors, for example, expectation and attribution of symptoms as well as social support (e.g., Carter, Hollon, Carson, & Shelton, 1995; Craske et al., 2002; van der Molen, van den Hout, Vroemen, Lousberg, & Griez, 1986).

Psychological theories (e.g., Bouton, Mineka, & Barlow, 2001; Barlow, 2002; Clark, 1986) of panic disorder focus on the role of bodily symptoms as triggers for panic attacks. For example, Pauli et al. (1991) using an ambulatory field approach found that panic patients reported anxiety after approximately two-thirds of their cardiac perceptions while healthy controls never reported anxiety responses. Most important, panic patients and healthy controls showed a comparable heart rate increase preceding the cardiac perception, but only panic patients exhibited a further heart rate increase after the perception. Controlled laboratory studies mainly used external stimuli associated with bodily sensations to examine the panic patients' responses to these stimuli. For example, a simulated heart rate increase within a false heart rate feedback paradigm caused increased fear accompanied by heart rate, blood pressure, and skin conductance increases in patients with panic disorder but not in control participants (Ehlers, Margraf, Roth, Taylor, & Birbaumer, 1988). Panic patients were also found to have a lowered perception threshold for body-related words (Lundh, Wikström, Westerlund, & Öst, 1999; Pauli et al., 1997), and this word category compared to neutral words triggers enhanced event-related brain potentials in panic patients but not in healthy participants, indicating an enhanced cortical involvement (Pauli et al., 1997; Pauli, Amrhein, Mühlberger, Dengler, & Wiedemann, 2005). Since these differences in event-related brain potentials were found as early as 300 ms after stimulus presentation, a rather automatic processing bias has to be assumed (Pauli, Amrhein, et al., 2005). Panic patients are also characterized by an attentional bias and an implicit and explicit memory bias for body-related stimuli (e.g., Pauli, Dengler, & Wiedemann, 2005); interestingly, most other anxiety patients only show an implicit memory bias (Coles & Heimberg, 2002). Finally, panic patients expect aversive consequences after stimuli depicting bodily harm (e.g., pictures depicting medical emergency situations). Experimental studies revealed for panic patients and participants with high agoraphobia scores an expectancy as well as a covariation bias (Pauli, Montoya, & Martz, 1996, 2001; Wiedemann, Pauli, & Dengler, 2001), the latter being also reflected in an enhanced slow wave potential between stimulus and the expected consequence (Amrhein, Pauli, Dengler, & Wiedemann, 2005). Fear-relevant stimuli also trigger an asymmetric frontal brain activity in panic patients with an enhanced left frontal activity that may be indicative of an active avoidance-withdrawal system (Wiedemann et al., 1999).

Social Anxiety Disorder
Definition

Social phobia (social anxiety disorder, SAD) is characterized by excessive fear, self-consciousness, and avoidance of social situations due to the possibility of embarrassment or humiliation. The definition of the disorder as we know it today dates back only to 1966 when Marks and Gelder (1966) described a condition in which a person becomes very anxious when subject to scrutiny by others while performing a specific task. While some individuals with SAD fear mostly performance-oriented situations such as public speaking, others show a more generalized fear of interacting socially. Panic attacks with marked physical symptoms can occur during exposure to the feared situation. The most common situation of this type to which most people can relate is public speaking. But other types of situations also meet the definitional criteria, such as eating at a lunch counter or in any public restaurant; writing one's signature in front of a bank clerk; or, for males, urinating in a crowded men's room.

The concept of SAD was elaborated over the years by Isaac Marks (e.g., Marks, 1969) and was adopted within the category of anxiety disorders in DSM–III (APA, 1980) as a "phobic disorder" together with agoraphobia and "simple phobia," to which it was closely related conceptually. It was further assumed that an individual, typically, only fears one particular social situation. Interestingly, the fear of social interaction was not part of the definition, and the diagnosis of SAD was ruled out if the person met criteria for avoidant personality disorder (APD). These diagnostic criteria underwent some changes in the DSM–III–R (APA, 1987), which remained unchanged in DSM–IV (APA, 1994). There is now a "generalized subtype" of SAD if an individual fears "most social situations." Furthermore, a person can be diagnosed with both APD and SAD.

The operational definition of "most social situations" varies considerably within the SAD literature (see Hofmann, Heinrichs, & Moscovitch, 2004, for a review). There is also a large and inconsistent literature on the issue of SAD subtypes (Brown, Heimberg, & Juster, 1995; Heimberg, Hope, Dodge, & Becker, 1990; Herbert, Hope, & Bellack, 1992; Hofmann, Newman, Ehlers, & Roth, 1995; Hofmann & Roth, 1996; Holt, Heimberg, Hope, & Liebowitz, 1992; Levin, et al., 1993; McNeil et al., 1995; Stein, Walker, & Forde, 1996). One of the most significant problems is the unclear definition of SAD subtypes. Holt et al. (1992) identified four different domains—formal speaking/interaction, informal speaking/interaction, assertive interaction, and observation by others. Recent studies suggest that this schema can be useful for subtyping social phobic individuals (Hofmann & Roth, 1996; Hofmann et al., 1999). However, it still remains uncertain whether the SAD subtypes based on the number of feared social situations are indeed meaningful diagnostic categories or whether a dimensional system is a more meaningful way to capture the heterogeneity of the SAD (Hofmann, Heinrichs et al., 2004).

Another problem with the current diagnostic system is the high overlap between the generalized subtype of SAD on Axis I and APD on Axis II (e.g., Heimberg, 1996; Schneier, Spitzer, Gibbon, Fyer, & Liebowitz, 1991). This is not overly surprising, given that 6 of the 7 diagnostic criteria for APD include a social interactional component. Thus, many researchers have questioned the utility of maintaining two diagnostic categories on two separate *DSM–IV* axes, especially since both diagnoses (the generalized subtype of SAD and APD) are associated with a high level of social anxiety, poor overall psychosocial functioning, greater overall psychopathology, high trait anxiety, and depression (e.g., Boone et al., 1999; Brown et al., 1995; Herbert et al., 1992; Holt et al., 1992; Tran & Chambless, 1995; Turner, Beidel, & Townsley, 1992). It has, therefore, been suggested that these diagnoses may simply represent different points on the social anxiety continuum of increasing severity from specific (nongeneralized) SAD to generalized SAD without APD, and to generalized SAD with APD (McNeil, 2000).

On the other hand, other studies suggest that not all differences in these diagnostic groupings can simply be explained by differences in the level of social anxiety. Some studies showed subgroup differences in age and mode of onset (Brown et al., 1995; Mannuzza et al., 1995; Stemberger, Turner, Beidel, & Calhoun, 1995), cognitive processing (Hofmann, Gerlach, Wender, & Roth, 1997; McNeil et al., 1995), and psychophysiological response during exposure (Boone et al., 1999; Heimberg, Hope et al., 1990; Hofmann et al., 1995; Levin et al., 1993). These findings are consistent with the notion that individuals with generalized SAD (and those with the additional diagnosis of APD) experience more of an *anxiety* response, whereas people with nongeneralized SAD (and also those without APD) experience more of a *fear* reaction (i.e., a response that is physiologically more robust and closely tied to specific stimulus situations) during social threat (Hofmann & Barlow, 2002). It might also be possible that the subtype distinction is linked to embarrassment and shame, which might be more closely related to APD and the generalized subtype of SAD (Hofmann, Heinrichs et al., 2004).

Phenomenology and Associated Features

A recent review surveyed 43 epidemiological studies from 1980 to the present and found that the lifetime prevalence of SAD in Western countries ranges between 7% and 13% (Furmark, 2002). Results from the National Comorbidity Survey indicate that the lifetime prevalence rate of SAD is 12.1% (Kessler, Berglund et al., 2005). The average

gender ratio (female:male) in community studies ranges between 1:1 (Moutier & Stein, 1999) and 3:2 (Kessler et al., 1994). The discrepancy in the gender ratios might be due to differences in study procedures, sample characteristics, and so on. In most treatment settings, however, the sexes are either equally represented, or the majority of social phobic patients is male (APA, 1994).

SAD often begins in the mid-teens, but can also occur in early childhood. During childhood, SAD is commonly associated with overanxious disorder, mutism, school refusal, separation anxiety, behavioral inhibition, and shyness. If untreated, the disorder typically follows a chronic, unremitting course, leading to substantial impairments in vocational and social functioning (Davidson, Hughes, George, & Blazer, 1993; Liebowitz, Gorman, Fyer, & Klein, 1985; Schneier, Johnson, Hornig, Liebowitz, & Weissman, 1992; Schneier et al., 1994; Stein & Kean, 2001; Stein, Torgrud, & Walker, 2000; Stein et al., 1996).

There is a considerable degree of variance among individuals with SAD in the number and type of situations they fear, as well as in a number of other characteristics, which will be outlined in more detail below. The most commonly feared social situation is public speaking (e.g., Pollard & Henderson, 1988). Other feared performance situations include eating, writing, or urinating in public, while commonly feared social interaction situations include initiating or maintaining conversations, going to parties, dating, and meeting strangers.

Early theorists assumed that SAD is due to a deficit in social skills (e.g., Stravynski & Greenberg, 1989). Although it is questionable whether socially anxious individuals are, in fact, deficient in any of their social skills (Glasgow & Arkowitz, 1975; Halford & Foddy, 1982; Hofmann et al., 1997; Rapee & Lim, 1992; Stopa & Clark, 1993), they do tend to appraise their own performance in social situations more negatively than nonanxious individuals, even when actual differences in performance are accounted for (Alden & Wallace, 1995; Glasgow & Arkowitz, 1975; Rapee & Lim, 1992; Stopa & Clark, 1993). Furthermore, socially anxious people tend to interact with others in an "innocuously" social manner, which involves polite smiling, agreeableness, and increased head nodding (Leary, 1983; Leary, Knight, & Johnson, 1987; Patterson & Ritts, 1997). They also make greater use of excuses and apologies (Edelman, 1987; Schlenker, 1987), exhibit fewer behaviors of social cooperativeness and dominance than do nonanxious controls (Trower &

Gilbert, 1989; Walters & Hope, 1998), and they tend to avoid emotional faces, as indicated by eye-movement data (Mühlberger, Wieser, & Pauli, in press) and electrophysiological data (Santesso et al., in press). Other studies have shown that socially anxious individuals frequently doubt their ability to create desired impressions on others (Alden & Wallace, 1995), and they expect their performance to fall short of other people's expectations of them (Alden & Wallace, 1995; Wallace & Alden, 1991, 1997). Therefore, it has been suggested that social anxiety arises when people desire to make a particular impression on others, but doubt that they will be able to do so (Leary & Kowalski, 1994). Negative self-focused cognitions increase anxiety when anticipating social threat (Schulz, Alpers, & Hofmann, 2008). A comprehensive model of these cognitive factors is presented elsewhere (Hofmann, 2007).

The disorder is common around the world. Interestingly, however, there are certain forms of social concerns that seem to be culturally specific, including *taijin kyofusho* (TKS), an emotional disorder that is believed to be particularly prevalent in the Japanese and Korean culture. Similar to individuals suffering from SAD, patients with TKS are concerned about being observed and, consequently, avoid a variety of social situations. The major difference from SAD, however, is that a person with TKS is concerned about doing something, or presenting an appearance, that will offend or embarrass *others*. In contrast, SAD is defined as the fear of embarrassing *oneself* (Kirmayer, 1991; Takahashi, 1989).

Specific Phobia
Definition

Specific phobia is characterized by intense and persistent fear cued by exposure to or anticipation of a clearly discernible and circumscribed object or situation such as certain animals or insects, blood/injury/injection, natural environmental events (e.g., thunder), or other stimuli (e.g., vomiting, contracting an illness, etc). While adults with phobias realize that these fears are irrational, they avoid confrontation in order to avoid triggering panic or severe anxiety. The fear experienced if the confrontation with threatening situations cannot be avoided is accompanied with extreme discomfort and strong bodily symptoms that are reflected in profound bodily responses in the autonomic nervous, respiratory, and endocrine systems (Alpers, Abelson, Wilhelm, & Roth, 2003; Alpers, Wilhelm, & Roth, 2005, Alpers & Sell, 2008). Some symptoms are very specific to certain fears, such as body sway, which is closely associated with fear of heights (Alpers & Adolph, 2008).

In his seminal book on phobias, Marks (1969) differentiated between agoraphobia, SAD, animal phobias, and other specific phobias. Correspondingly, the *DSM–III* (APA, 1987) listed them together in one category labeled as phobic disorders. Phobias related to specific objects or situations were then called "simple phobias," which was later dropped because it may misleadingly imply that these phobias are less severe. Since the introduction of *DSM–IV* (APA, 1994), they are listed under the preferable term *specific phobias*.

The *DSM–IV* (APA, 1994) now lists six discrete subtypes of specific phobias: (1) animal type: if the fear is cued by animals or insects; (2) natural environment type: if the fear is cued by objects in the natural environment, such as storms, heights, or water; (3) blood-injection-injury type: if the fear is cued by seeing blood or an injury or by receiving an injection or other invasive medical procedure; (4) situational type: if the fear is cued by a specific situation such as public transportation, tunnels, bridges, elevators, flying, driving, or enclosed places; and (5) other type: if the fear is cued by other stimuli (including choking, vomiting, or contracting an illness, fear of falling, and children's fears of loud sounds or costumed characters).

Although most subtypes of phobic disorder can be diagnosed reliably (Fyer et al., 1989), a major difficulty is the diagnostic distinction of phobias and panic disorder. With the exception of phobias of the animal type, panic disorder patients—especially those with marked agoraphobia—often fear typical phobic cues such as heights, invasive medical procedures, public transportation, or contracting illness. Moreover, specific phobias often co-occur (Hofmann, Lehman, & Barlow, 1997), and patients with specific phobias often experience panic attacks with marked physical symptoms during exposure to the feared situation (e.g., during exposure to driving or flying) (Alpers, et al., 2005; Ehlers, Hofmann, Herda, & Roth, 1994; Hofmann, Ehlers, & Roth, 1995; Wilhelm & Roth, 1997). Symptoms of these situational panic attacks markedly overlap with typical symptoms experienced by panic disorder patients (Craske, 1991); for example, the symptom profile of the phobic fear of enclosed places is most similar to that of panic disorder and the fear of enclosed places is frequent in panic disorder patients. A further complication arises because the phobias trace back to a spontaneous panic attack in many patients (Himle, Crystal, Curtis, & Fluent, 1991).

In spite of these similarities, phobic fear and panic disorder are clearly distinguished by most theoretical accounts. One of the strongest arguments for this view is not so much descriptive but based on the differential effects of pharmacological interventions on uncued (i.e., as seen in panic disorder) and cued (i.e., as seen in specific phobia) panic attacks (Klein, 1964).

Although the characteristic emotional experience in phobias is fear upon exposure to the phobic cue, some cues may also elicit the distinct emotion disgust (Davey, 1994; Woody, McLean, & Klassen, 2005), which seems to change with therapy on different gradients (Smits, Telch, & Randall, 2002).

Phenomenology and Associated Features

Previous studies estimated the lifetime-prevalence of specific phobias to be between 1% and 19% of the population. More recent data suggest that the lifetime and 12-month prevalence rates of specific phobia are 12.5% and 8.7%, respectively (Kessler, Berglund et al., 2005; Kessler, Chiu et al., 2005). These data suggest that specific phobia is the most common form of anxiety disorder. Prevalence rates are generally higher in women than in men (ratios vary between 2:1 and 4:1 from study to study) with much variance between subtypes of phobias (Curtis, Magee, Eaton, Wittchen, & Kessler, 1998; Fredrikson, Annas, Fischer, & Wik, 1996). The highest prevalence rates have been found for specific animal phobias in women and claustrophobia in men (Curtis, et al., 1998). Prevalence rates also differ with ethnicity; the rates of specific phobias being almost twice as high in African American individuals, with African American men having the same rates as White women (Eaton, Dryman, & Weissman, 1991). Much variation in prevalence rates can be found between cultures worldwide (Good & Kleinman, 1985).

Phobias of animals, of the natural environment, and blood-injection-injury type often start in childhood while most situational phobias usually start in early adulthood (e.g., Lipsitz, Barlow, Mannuzza, Hofmann, & Fyer, 2002). Typical childhood fears (darkness or medical treatment) often go away without specific interventions. However, phobias are usually very persistent in adults; in the prospective Munich Follow-up Study 93% of patients still met criteria for the same diagnosis after 7 years (Wittchen, 1988).

Rachman (1977) suggested that there are three routes to develop a phobia: First, by classical conditioning due to a traumatic experience in a specific situation or in the presence of a specific object; second, by vicarious learning; and third, by instruction (usually the parents) or information (e.g., the media). Empirical data suggest that specific phobia develops following a traumatic experience in 36% of the cases, the observation of fearful behavior or observation of a trauma to others in 8%, and the instruction by others in 8%. This means that about 50% of the phobic patients do not recall how or why they developed the phobia (Kendler, Myers, & Prescott, 2002).

Although these data show that some phobias date back to aversive experiences, this does not explain why certain classes of typical cues (e.g., spiders and snakes) often elicit phobic reactions although they rarely inflict harm, while others often inflict harm (e.g., knives) but are rarely feared. This seeming paradox can be explained if one assumes that the typical phobic cues are prepared fear stimuli (Seligman, 1971).

Indeed, several experiments consistently confirmed that fear responses conditioned to typical fear cues are more resistant to extinction (Mineka & Öhman, 2002). Also, vicarious learning of fear responses that has been documented for laboratory-reared monkeys who learned to avoid snakes from a model (Mineka, Davidson, Cook, & Keir, 1984) seems to be prepared for evolutionary relevant fear cues (Cook & Mineka, 1989). In humans it has also been demonstrated that children avoid a novel object (e.g., a plastic snake) after they have observed their mothers avoid it (Gerull & Rapee, 2002). The premise of the preparedness theory—that preparedness helps to protect humans from dangerous predators—has been questioned (Gerdes, Uhl, Alpers, in press; Hofmann, Moscovitch, & Heinrichs, 2002) and it has been shown that mere instruction can elicit substantial fear in children (Field & Lawson, 2003). Being read a story about an animal unknown to the child not only elicited higher self-rated fear and overt avoidance behavior, but also induced a negative attitude measurable in an implicit association test. This highlights the importance of cognitions in fear acquisition (Hofmann, 2008).

Beyond the three routes described by Rachman (1977) it is evident that there are certain fears in animals and humans that are inborn, for example, most monkeys react with fear when exposed to a snake (Nelson, Shelton, & Kalin, 2003), but these fears in general extinguish relatively quickly. In humans it has also been shown that the experience with certain inborn fear-eliciting situations such as heights is needed to unlearn the fear (Poulton & Menzies, 2002).

Theoretically, the characteristic avoidance behavior phobic patients display can be explained by the two-factor model (Mowrer, 1947). This model assumes that classically conditioned fear stimuli elicit a fear response that is then reduced or ameliorated by the instrumental avoidance behavior. The conclusion that this dysfunctional avoidance helps to maintain the fear response can be extended to fears acquired through other routes than classical conditioning.

Impairment has been found to strongly correlate with the number of phobic symptoms a patient experiences (Curtis, et al., 1998). In addition to the high prevalence of multiple phobias, comorbidity with other mental disorders is high: 84% of all phobic patients have one or more comorbid disorders. Aside from other anxiety disorders, affective disorders and substance-related disorders are common. The phobia more often preceded the comorbid disorder (57%) (Magee et al., 1996).

Phobic patients display several cognitive biases (for an introduction and overview see Williams, Watts, MacLeod, & Mathews, 1997). Theoretically, this is based on an adaptive conservatism (Mineka & Öhman, 2002) helping the organism to protect itself from potential threat and survival risks but bearing the disadvantage of frequent responses to false alarms. These false alarms may lead to the unpleasant experience of fear but do not affect the organism's survival. Cognitive biases have been documented to occur in attention, memory, as well as expectancy or contingency estimations. For example, patients with a fear of flying exhibit a covariation bias and overestimated the contingency between aversive flying-related slides (e.g., of a plane crash) and aversive electric stimuli in spite of an objectively random relationship between slide categories and outcome (illusory correlation) (Pauli, Wiedemann, & Montoya, 1998; Mühlberger, Herrmann, Wiedemann, & Pauli, 2006). In contrast to several theoretical accounts, there is little evidence that attentional engagement to phobic cues occurs automatically (Alpers et al., in press). Instead, patients with a spider phobia seem to have a deficit in disengaging their attention from spider cues (Gerdes, Alpers, & Pauli, 2008).

It has been shown that the induction of such processing biases can have causal effects on anxiety (MacLeod, Rutherford, Campbell, Ebsworthy, & Holker, 2002). In an extensive learning phase of close to 600 trials one group of participants learned

to turn their attention to fear-relevant stimuli that were always followed by the target dot-probe to which the participant had to respond. This induced a typical attentional bias to fear-relevant cues that remained even though the contingency of fear-relevant stimuli and target was absent in subsequent trials. Most interestingly, the participants who were trained to attend to negative cues responded more strongly to a stressful task following the dot-probe test.

Maintaining Factors
Panic Attacks

In earlier editions of the *DSM*, panic attacks were defined as discrete periods of intense fear (or discomfort) unique to the diagnosis of panic disorder. The current fourth edition of the *DSM*, however, assumes that panic attacks can occur in the context of several different anxiety disorders, such as specific phobias, SAD, or even posttraumatic stress disorder (PTSD). This is consistent with Barlow's (2002) notion that there is no indication that panic attacks are qualitatively different from episodes of intense fear. In fact, panic attacks are not unique to any particular group of anxiety disorders and are commonly found in the general population (see Kessler et al., 2006). The only distinguishing feature between clinical and nonclinical panic appears to be that nonclinical panic is less intense and less frequent than the attacks reported by individuals with panic disorder. Because these attacks appear to be an expression of the body's *fight or flight* response system in the absence of any actual danger, Barlow (2002) refers to them as *false alarms*. False alarms that are associated with neutral objects or conditioned stimuli can become *learned alarms*. If alarms occur in the presence of actual danger, they are referred to as *true alarms*.

These three forms of alarms constitute different pathways for the etiology of panic and phobias. For example, some individuals who experience a false alarm followed by the development of anxious apprehension over the next panic attack may develop panic disorder given the presence of specific vulnerabilities. Other people may experience true alarms and consequently develop specific phobias as a result of learned alarms. Other anxiety disorders, such as SAD, may reflect a combination of the occurrence of false alarms, true alarms, and learned alarms and the development of anxious apprehension. For example, a person with SAD may experience a false alarm in social and evaluative situations following a stressful event. As a result this person then focuses attention inward, on the anxiety response, and other possible threatening aspects of the situations (e.g., being observed by others), which further perpetuates anxious apprehension and thereby further increases the likelihood for developing more panic attacks in social situations.

Cognitions

Although maladaptive cognitions are not always considered to be a central defining feature of each of the anxiety disorders, cognitive processes (e.g., attributions, predictions) are typically seen as essential to the development of these disorders. For example, in the case of panic disorder, the cognitive model (e.g., Clark, 1986) assumes that panic attacks result from the catastrophic misinterpretation of certain bodily sensations, such as palpitations, breathlessness, dizziness, and so on. Similar negative predictions are common in individuals with other anxiety disorders. In cases of SAD, for example, the focus is usually placed upon the consequence of public scrutiny and subsequent negative evaluation ("Nobody is going to like me"; "I'm going to make a fool of myself"). Individuals with agoraphobia without a history of panic disorder feel distress if they are unable to escape or get help in case they develop certain symptoms (e.g., dizziness, diarrhea) in a variety of situations (e.g., shopping, crowds).

Although some of the cognitions typically associated with each diagnosis may be disorder-specific, there are a number of commonalities of cognitions across the anxiety disorders. First, the maladaptive cognitions associated with the anxiety disorders tend to be future-oriented perceptions of danger or threat (e.g., what is about to happen, what will happen). This sense of danger may involve either physical (e.g., having a heart attack) or psychological (e.g., anxiety focused on embarrassment) threat. In addition, these cognitions tend to focus upon a sense of uncontrollability over the situation or symptoms of anxiety.

Summary and Conclusions

Panic disorder, agoraphobia, SAD, and specific phobia are common mental health problems. This chapter presented the definition, phenomenology, and associated features of these disorders. Many of the commonalities and unique characteristics of these syndromes are related to the role of panic attacks and cognitions that contribute to the maintenance of these conditions. The challenge of the upcoming new edition of the *DSM* is to address the complexities of the relationship between these diagnostic categories within the framework of a parsimonious classification system.

References

Alpers, G. W., Abelson, J. L., Wilhelm, F. H., & Roth, W. T. (2003). Salivary cortisol response during exposure treatment in driving phobics. *Psychosomatic Medicine, 65,* 679–687.

Alpers, G. W., & Adolph, D. (2008). Exposure to heights in a theme park: Fear, dizziness, and body sway. *Journal of Anxiety Disorders, 22,* 591–601.

Alpers, G. W., Gerdes, A., Lagarie, B., Tabbert, K., Vaitl, D., & Stark, R. (in press). Attention and amygdala activity: An fMRI study with spider pictures in spider phobia. *Journal of Neural Transmission.*

Alpers, G. W., & Sell, R. (in press). And yet they correlate: Psychophysiological measures predict the outcome of exposure therapy in claustrophobia. *Journal of Anxiety Disorders, 22.*

Alpers, G. W., Wilhelm, F. H., & Roth, W. T. (2005). Psychophysiological assessment during exposure in driving phobic patients. *Journal of Abnormal Psychology, 114,* 126–139.

Alden, L. E., & Wallace, S. T. (1995). Social phobia and social appraisal in successful and unsuccessful social interactions. *Behaviour Research and Therapy, 33,* 497–505.

American Psychiatric Association. (1980). *Diagnostic and statistical manual of mental disorders* (3rd ed.). Washington, DC: Author.

American Psychiatric Association. (1987). *Diagnostic and statistical manual for mental disorders* (3rd ed. revised). Washington, DC: Author.

American Psychiatric Association. (1994). *Diagnostic and statistical manual for mental disorders* (4th ed.). Washington, DC: Author.

Amrhein, C., Pauli, P., Dengler, W., & Wiedemann, G. (2005). Covariation bias and its physiological correlates in panic disorder patients. *Journal of Anxiety Disorders, 19,* 177–191.

Barlow, D. H. (2002). *Anxiety and its disorders.* New York: Guilford Press.

Bienvenu, O. J., Onyike, C. U., Stein, M. B., Chen, L.-S., Samuels, J., Nestadt, G., et al. (2006). Agoraphobia in adults: Incidence and longitudinal relationship with panic. *British Journal of Psychiatry, 188,* 432–438.

Boone, M. L., McNeil, D. W., Masia, C. L., Turk, C. L., Carter, L. E., Ries, B. J., et al. (1999). Multimodal comparisons of social phobia subtypes and avoidant personality disorder. *Journal of Anxiety Disorders, 13,* 271–292.

Bouton, M. E., Mineka, S., & Barlow, D. H. (2001). A modern learning theory perspective on the etiology of panic disorder. *Psychological Review, 108,* 4–32.

Brown, E. J., Heimberg, R. G., & Juster, H. R. (1995). Social phobia subtype and avoidant personality disorder: Effect on severity of social phobia, impairment, and outcome of cognitive behavioral treatment. *Behavior Therapy, 26,* 467–489.

Brown, T. A., Campbell, L. A., Lehman, C. L., Grisham, J. R., & Mancill, R. B. (2001). Current and lifetime comorbidity of the *DSM–IV* anxiety and mood disorders in a large clinical sample. *Journal of Abnormal Psychology, 110,* 49–58.

Bruce, S. E., Yonkers, K. A., Otto, M. W., Eisen, J. L., Weisberg, R. B., Pagano, M., et al. (2005). Influence of psychiatric comorbidity on recovery and recurrence in generalized anxiety disorder, social phobia, and panic disorder: A 12-year prospective study. *American Journal of Psychiatry, 162,* 1179–1187.

Carter, M. M., Hollon, S. D., Carson, R., & Shelton, R. C. (1995). Effects of a safe person on induced distress following a biological challenge in panic disorder with agoraphobia. *Journal of Abnormal Psychology, 104,* 156–163.

Clark, D. M. (1986). A cognitive approach to panic. *Behaviour Research and Therapy, 24,* 461–470.

Cohen, A. S., Barlow, D. H., & Blanchard, E. B. (1985). Psychophysiology of relaxation-associated panic attacks. *Journal of Abnormal Psychology, 94,* 96–101.

Coles, M. E., & Heimberg, R. G. (2002). Memory biases in the anxiety disorders: Current status. *Clinical Psychology Review, 22,* 587–627.

Cook, M., & Mineka, S. (1989). Observational conditioning of fear to fear-relevant versus fear-irrelevant stimuli in rhesus monkeys. *Journal of Abnormal Psychology, 98,* 448–459.

Craske, M. G. (1991). Phobic fear and panic attacks: The same emotional states triggered by different cues? *Clinical Psychology Review, 11,* 599–620.

Craske, M. G., Lang, A. J., Rowe, M., DeCola, J. P., Simmons, J., Mann, C., et al. (2002). Presleep attributions about arousal during sleep: Nocturnal panic. *Journal of Abnormal Psychology, 111,* 53–62.

Craske, M. G., Lang, A. J., Tsao, J., Mystkowski, J. L., & Rowe, M. (2001). Reactivity to interoceptive cues in nocturnal panic. *Journal of Behavior Therapy and Experimental Psychiatry, 32,* 173–190.

Curtis, G. C., Magee, W. J., Eaton, W. W., Wittchen, H.-U., & Kessler, R. C. (1998). Specific fears and phobias: Epidemiology and classification. *British Journal of Psychiatry, 173,* 212–217.

Davey, G.C.L. (1994). The "disgusting" spider: The role of disease and illness in the perpetuation of fear of spiders. *Society & Animals, 2,* 17–25.

Davidson, J.R.T., Hughes, D. L., George, L. K., & Blazer, D. G. (1993). The epidemiology of social phobia: Findings from the Duke Epidemiological Catchment Area Study. *Psychological Medicine, 23,* 709–718.

Demyttenaere, K., Bruffaerts, R., Posada-Villa, J., Gasquet, I., Kovess, V., Lepine, J. P., et al. (2004). Prevalence, severity, and unmet need for treatment of mental disorders in the World Health Organization World Mental Health Surveys. *Journal of the American Medical Association, 291,* 2581–2590.

Eaton, W. W., Dryman, A., & Weissman, M. M. (1991). Panic and phobia. In L. N. Robins & D. A. Regier (Eds.), *Psychiatric disorders in America: The Epidemiologic Catchment Area Study* (pp. 155–179). New York: Free Press.

Edelman, R. J. (1987). *The psychology of embarrassment.* Chichester, UK: Wiley.

Ehlers, A., Hofmann, S. G., Herda, C. A., & Roth, W. T. (1994). Clinical characteristics of driving phobia. *Journal of Anxiety Disorders, 8,* 323–339.

Ehlers, A., Margraf, J., Roth, W. T., Taylor, C. B., & Birbaumer, N. (1988). Anxiety induced by false heart rate feedback in patients with panic disorder. *Behaviour Research and Therapy, 26,* 1–11.

Field, A. P., & Lawson, J. (2003). Fear information and the development of fears during childhood: Effects on implicit fear responses and behavioural avoidance. *Behaviour Research and Therapy, 41,* 1277–1293.

Fredrikson, M., Annas, P., Fischer, H., & Wik, G. (1996). Gender and age differences in the prevalence of specific fears and phobias. *Behaviour Research and Therapy, 34,* 33–39.

Freud, S. (1895). Über die Berechtiung, von der Neurasthenie einen bestimmten Symptomenkomplex als "Angstneurose" abzutrennen. Neurologisches Zentralblatt, 2. In S. Freud (1947). *Gesammelte Werke.* Band 1. London: Imago.

Furmark, T. (2002). Social phobia: Overview of community surveys. *Acta Psychiatrica Scandinavica, 105,* 84–93.

Fyer, A. J., Mannuzza, S., Martin, L. Y., Gallops, M. S., Endicott, J., Schleyer, B., et al. (1989). Reliability of anxiety assessment. II. Symptom agreement. *Archives of General Psychiatry, 46,* 1102–1110.

Gerdes, A. B. M., Alpers, G. W., & Pauli, P. (2008). When spiders appear suddenly: Spider phobic patients are distracted by task-irrelevant spiders. *Behaviour Research and Therapy, 46,* 174–187.

Gerdes, A. B. M., Uhl, G., & Alpers, G. W. (in press). Spiders are special: Harmfulness does not explain why they are feared. *Evolution and Human Behavior.*

Gerull, F. C., & Rapee, R. M. (2002). Mother knows best: The effects of maternal modelling on the acquisition of fear and avoidance behaviour in toddlers. *Behaviour Research and Therapy, 40,* 279–287.

Glasgow, R. E., & Arkowitz, H. (1975). The behavioral assessment of male and female social competence in dyadic interactions. *Behavior Therapy, 6,* 488–498.

Good, B. J., & Kleinman, A. M. (1985). Culture and anxiety: Cross-cultural evidence for the patterning of anxiety disorders. In A. H. Tuma & J. D. Maser (Eds.), *Anxiety and the anxiety disorders* (pp. 297–323). Hillsdale, NJ: Erlbaum.

Gorman, J. M., Askanazi, J., Liebowitz, M. R., Fyer, A. J., Stein, J., Kinney, J. M., et al. (1984). Response to hyperventilation in a group of patients with panic disorder. *American Journal of Psychiatry, 141,* 857–861.

Gorman, J. M., Papp, L. A., Coplan, J. D., Martinez, J. M., Lennon, S., Goetz, R. R., et al. (1994). Anxiogenic effects of CO_2 and hyperventilation with panic disorder. *American Journal of Psychiatry, 151,* 547–553.

Halford, K., & Foddy, M. (1982). Cognitive and social skills correlates of social anxiety. *British Journal of Clinical Psychology, 21,* 17–28.

Heimberg, R. G. (1996). Social phobia, avoidant personality disorder and the multiaxial conceptualization of interpersonal anxiety. In P. M. Salkovskis (Ed.), *Trends in cognitive and behavioural therapies* (pp. 43–61). New York: Wiley.

Heimberg, R. G., Hope, D. A., Dodge, C. S., & Becker, R. E. (1990). *DSM–III–R* subtypes of social phobia: Comparison of generalized social phobics and public speaking phobics. *Journal of Nervous and Mental Disease, 178,* 172–179.

Herbert, J. D., Hope, D. A., & Bellack, A. S. (1992). Validity of the distinction between generalized social phobia and avoidant personality disorder. *Journal of Abnormal Psychology, 101,* 332–339.

Himle, J. A., Crystal, D., Curtis, G. C., & Fluent, T. E. (1991). Mode of onset of simple phobia subtypes: Further evidence of heterogeneity. *Psychiatry Research, 36,* 37–43.

Hofmann, S. G. (2007). Cognitive factors that maintain social anxiety disorder: A comprehensive model and its treatment implications. *Cognitive Behaviour Therapy, 36,* 195–209.

Hofmann, S. G. (2008). Cognitive processes during fear acquisition and extinction in animals and humans: Implications for exposure therapy of anxiety disorders. *Clinical Psychology Review, 28,* 200–211.

Hofmann, S. G., Albano, A. M., Heimberg, R. G., Tracey, S., Chorpita, B. F., & Barlow, D. H. (1999). Subtypes of social phobia in adolescents. *Depression and Anxiety, 9,* 15–18.

Hofmann, S. G., & Barlow, D. H. (2002). Social phobia (social anxiety disorder). In D. H. Barlow (Ed.), *Anxiety and its disorders: The nature and treatment of anxiety and panic* (2nd ed., pp. 454–476). New York: Guilford Press.

Hofmann, S. G., Ehlers, A., & Roth, W. T. (1995). Conditioning theory: A model for the etiology of public speaking anxiety? *Behaviour Research and Therapy, 33,* 567–571.

Hofmann, S. G., Gerlach, A., Wender, A., & Roth, W. T. (1997). Speech disturbances and gaze behavior during public speaking in subtypes of social phobia. *Journal of Anxiety Disorders, 11,* 573–585.

Hofmann, S. G., Heinrichs, N., & Moscovitch, D. A. (2004). The nature and expression of social phobia: Toward a new classification. *Clinical Psychology Review, 24,* 769–797.

Hofmann, S. G., Lehman, C. L., & Barlow, D. H. (1997). How specific are specific phobias? *Journal of Behavior Therapy and Experimental Psychiatry, 28,* 233–240.

Hofmann, S. G., Moscovitch, D. M., & Heinrichs, N. (2002). Evolutionary mechanisms of fear and anxiety. *Journal of Cognitive Psychotherapy, 16,* 317–330.

Hofmann, S. G., Newman, M. G., Ehlers, A., & Roth, W. T. (1995). Psychophysiological differences between subtypes of social phobia. *Journal of Abnormal Psychology, 104,* 224–231.

Hofmann, S. G., & Roth, W. T. (1996). Issues related to social anxiety among controls in social phobia research. *Behavior Therapy, 27,* 79–91.

Holt, C. S., Heimberg, R. G., Hope, D. A., & Liebowitz, M. R. (1992). Situational domains of social phobia. *Journal of Anxiety Disorders, 6,* 63–77.

Kendler, K. S., Myers, J., & Prescott, C. A. (2002). The etiology of phobias: An evaluation of the stress-diathesis model. *Archives of General Psychiatry, 59,* 242–248.

Kessler, R. C., Berglund, P., Demler, O., Jin, R., & Walters, E. (2005). Lifetime prevalence and age-of-onset distributions of *DSM–IV* disorders in the National Comorbidity Survey Replication. *Archives of General Psychiatry, 62,* 593–602.

Kessler, R. C., Chiu, W. T., Demler, O., & Walters, E. E. (2005). Prevalence, severity, comorbidity, and 12-month *DSM–IV* disorders in the National Comorbidity Survey Replication. *Archives of General Psychiatry, 62,* 617–627.

Kessler, R. C., Chiu, W. T., Jin, R., Ruscio, A. M., Shear, K., & Walters, E. E. (2006). The epidemiology of panic attacks, panic disorder, and agoraphobia in the National Comorbidity Survey Replication. *Archives of General Psychiatry, 63,* 415–424.

Kessler, R. C., McGonagle, K. A., Shanyang, Z., Nelson, C. B., Hughes, M., Eshleman, S., et al. (1994). Lifetime and 12-month prevalence of *DSM–III–R* psychiatric disorders in the United States. *Archives of General Psychiatry, 51,* 8–19.

Kirmayer, L. (1991). The place of culture in psychiatric nosology: Taijin kyofusho and *DSM–III–R. Journal of Nervous and Mental Disease, 179,* 19–28.

Klein, D. F. (1964). Delineation of two drug-responsive anxiety syndromes. *Psychopharmacologia, 5,* 397–408.

Koenigsberg, H. W., Pollak, C. P., Fine, J., & Kakuma, T. (1994). Cardiac and respiratory activity in panic disorder: Effects of sleep and sleep lactate infusions. *American Journal of Psychiatry, 151,* 1148–1152.

Leary, M. R. (1983). Social anxiousness: The construct and its measurement. *Journal of Personality Assessment, 47,* 66–75.

Leary, M. R., Knight, P. D., & Johnson, K. A. (1987). Social anxiety and dyadic conversation: A verbal response analysis. *Journal of Social and Clinical Psychology, 5,* 34–50.

Leary, M. R., & Kowalski, R. M. (1994). *Social anxiety.* New York: Guilford Press.

Levin, A. P., Saoud, J. B., Strauman, T., Gorman, J. M., Fyer, A., Crawford, R., et al. (1993). Responses of generalized and discrete social phobics during public speaking. *Journal of Anxiety Disorders, 7,* 207–221.

Liebowitz, M. R., Gorman, J. M., Fyer, A. J., & Klein, D. F. (1985). Social phobia: Review of a neglected anxiety disorder. *Archives of General Psychiatry, 42,* 729–736.

Lipsitz, J. D., Barlow, D. H., Mannuzza, S., Hofmann, S. G., & Fyer, A. J. (2002). Clinical features of four *DSM–IV* specific phobia subtypes. *Journal of Nervous and Mental Disease, 190,* 471–478.

Lundh, L.-G., Wikström, J., Westerlund, J., & Öst, L.-G. (1999). Preattentive bias for emotional information in panic disorder with agoraphobia. *Journal of Abnormal Psychology, 108,* 222–232.

MacLeod, C., Rutherford, E., Campbell, L., Ebsworthy, G., & Holker, L. (2002). Selective attention and emotional vulnerability: Assessing the causal basis of their association through the experimental manipulation of attentional bias. *Journal of Abnormal Psychology, 111,* 107–123.

Magee, W. J., Eaton, W. W., Wittchen, H. U., McGonagle, K. A., & Kessler, R. C. (1996). Agoraphobia, simple phobia, and social phobia in the National Comorbidity Survey. *Archives of General Psychiatry, 53,* 159–168.

Mannuzza, S., Schneier, F. R., Chapman, T. F., Liebowitz, M. R., Klein, D. F., & Fyer, A. J. (1995). Generalized social phobia: Reliability and validity. *Archives of General Psychiatry, 52,* 230–237.

Margraf, J., Taylor, C. B., Ehlers, A., & Roth, W. T. (1987). Panic attacks in the natural environment. *Journal of Nervous & Mental Disease, 175,* 558–565.

Marks, I. M. (1969). *Fears and phobias.* London: Academic Press.

Marks, I. M., & Gelder, M. G. (1966). Different ages of onset in varieties of phobias. *American Journal of Psychiatry, 123,* 218–221.

McNally, R. J. (2002). Anxiety sensitivity and panic disorder. *Biological Psychiatry, 52,* 938–946.

McNeil, D. W. (2000). Terminology and evolution of the constructs. In S. G. Hofmann & P. M. DiBartolo (Eds.), *From social anxiety to social phobia: Multiple perspectives* (pp. 8–19). Needham Heights, MA: Allyn & Bacon.

McNeil, D. W., Ries, B. J., Taylor, L. J., Boone, M. L., Carter, L. E., Turk, C. L., et al. (1995). Comparison of social phobia subtypes using Stroop tests. *Journal of Anxiety Disorders, 9,* 47–57.

Mineka, S., Davidson, M., Cook, M., & Keir, R. (1984). Observational conditioning of snake fear in rhesus monkeys. *Journal of Abnormal Psychology, 93,* 355–372.

Mineka, S., & Öhman, A. (2002). Phobias and preparedness: The selective, automatic, and encapsulated nature of fear. *Biological Psychiatry, 52,* 927–937.

Moutier, C. Y., & Stein M. B. (1999). The history, epidemiology, and differential diagnosis of social anxiety disorder. *Journal of Clinical Psychiatry, 60,* 4–8.

Mowrer, O. H. (1947). On the dual nature of learning—a reinterpretation of "conditioning" and "problem-solving." *Harvard Educational Review, 17,* 102–148.

Mühlberger, A., Herrmann, M. J., Wiedemann, G., & Pauli, P. (2006). Phylo- and ontogenetic fears and the expectation of danger: Differences between spider and flight phobics in cognitive and physiological responses to disorder specific stimuli. *Journal of Abnormal Psychology, 115,* 580–589.

Mühlberger, A., Wieser, M., & Pauli, P. (in press). Visual attention during virtual social situations depends on social anxiety. *CyberPsychology & Behavior.*

Nelson, E. E., Shelton, S. E., & Kalin, N. H. (2003). Individual differences in the responses of naieve rhesus monkeys to snakes. *Emotion, 3,* 3–11.

Öst, L.-G. (1987). Age of onset in different phobias. *Journal of Abnormal Psychology, 96,* 223–229.

Patterson, M. L., & Ritts, V. (1997). Social and communicative anxiety: A review and meta-analysis. In B. R. Burleson (Ed.), *Communication yearbook 20* (pp. 263–303). Thousand Oaks, CA: Sage.

Pauli, P., Amrhein, C., Mühlberger, A., Dengler, W., & Wiedemann, G. (2005a). Electrocortical evidence for an early abnormal processing of panic-related words in panic disorder patients. *International Journal of Psychophysiology, 57,* 33–41.

Pauli, P., Dengler, W., & Wiedemann, G. (2005b). Implicit and explicit memory processes in panic patients as reflected in behavioral and electrophysiological measures. *Journal of Behavior Therapy and Experimental Psychiatry, 36,* 111–127.

Pauli, P., Dengler, W., Wiedemann, G., Montoya, P., Flor, H., Birbaumer, N., et al. (1997). Behavioral and neurophysiological evidence for altered processing of anxiety-related words in panic disorder. *Journal of Abnormal Psychology, 106,* 213–220.

Pauli, P., Marquardt, C., Hartl, L., Nutzinger, D. O., Hölzl, R., & Strian, F. (1991). Anxiety induced by cardiac perceptions in patients with panic attacks: A field study. *Behaviour Research and Therapy, 29,* 137–145.

Pauli, P., Montoya, P., & Martz, G.-E. (1996). Covariation bias in panic-prone subjects. *Journal of Abnormal Psychology, 105,* 658–662.

Pauli, P., Montoya, P., & Martz, G.-E. (2001). On-line and a posteriori covariation estimates in panic-prone individuals: Effects of a high contingency of shocks following fear-irrelevant stimuli. *Cognitive Therapy and Research, 25,* 103–116.

Pauli, P., Wiedemann, G., & Montoya, P. (1998). Covariation bias in flight phobics. *Journal of Anxiety Disorders, 12,* 555–565.

Pollard, C. A., & Henderson, J. G. (1988). Four types of social phobia in a community sample. *Journal of Nervous and Mental Disorders, 176,* 440–445.

Poulton, R., & Menzies, R. G. (2002). Non-associative fear acquisition: A review of the evidence from retrospective and longitudinal research. *Behaviour Research and Therapy, 40,* 127–149.

Rachman, S. (1977). The conditioning theory of fear-acquisition: A critical examination. *Behaviour Research and Therapy, 15,* 375–387.

Rapee, R. M., & Lim, L. (1992). Discrepancy between self- and observer ratings of performance in social phobics. *Journal of Abnormal Psychology, 101,* 728–731.

Reiss, S., Peterson, R. A., Gursky, D. M., & McNally, R. J. (1986). Anxiety sensitivity, anxiety frequency and the prediction of fearfulness. *Behaviour Research and Therapy, 24,* 1–8.

Santesso, D. L., Meuret, A. E., Hofmann, S. G., Mueller, E. M., Ratner, K. G., Roesch, E. B., et al. (in press). Electrophysiological correlates of spatial orienting towards angry faces: A source localization study. *Neuropsychologia.*

Schlenker, B. R. (1987). Threats to identity: Self-identification and social stress. In C. R. Snyder & C. Ford (Eds.), *Coping with negative life events: Clinical and social psychology perspectives* (pp. 273–321). New York: Plenum Press.

Schmidt, N. B., Lerew, D. R., & Jackson, R. J. (1997). The role of anxiety sensitivity in the pathogenesis of panic: Prospective evaluation of spontaneous panic attacks during acute stress. *Journal of Abnormal Psychology, 106,* 355–364.

Schmidt, N. B., Lerew, D. R., & Jackson, R. J. (1999). Prospective evaluation of anxiety sensitivity in the pathogenesis of panic: Replication and extension. *Journal of Abnormal Psychology, 108,* 532–537.

Schneier, F. R., Heckelman, L. R., Garfinkel, R., Campeas, R., Fallon, B., Gitow, A., et al. (1994). Functional impairment in social phobia. *Journal of Clinical Psychiatry, 55,* 322–331.

Schneier, F. R., Johnson, J., Hornig, C. D., Liebowitz, M. R., & Weissman, M. M. (1992). Social phobia: Comorbidity and morbidity in an epidemiological sample. *Archives of General Psychiatry, 49,* 282–288.

Schneier, F. R., Spitzer, R. L., Gibbon, M., Fyer, A. J., & Liebowitz, M. R. (1991). The relationship of social phobia subtypes and avoidant personality disorder. *Comprehensive Psychiatry, 32,* 496–502.

Schulz, S. M., Alpers, G. W., & Hofman, S. G. (2008). Negative self-focused cognitions mediate the effect of trait social anxiety on state anxiety. *Behaviour Research and Therapy, 46,* 438–449.

Seligman, M. (1971). Phobias and preparedness. *Behavior Therapy, 2,* 307–320.

Smits, J. A., Telch, M. J., & Randall, P. K. (2002). An examination of the decline in fear and disgust during exposure-based treatment. *Behaviour Research and Therapy, 40,* 1243–1253.

Stein, M. B., & Kean, Y. M. (2001). Disability and quality of life in social phobia: Epidemiologic findings. *American Journal of Psychiatry, 157,* 1606–1613.

Stein, M. B., Torgrud, L. J., & Walker, J. (2000). Social phobia symptoms, subtypes, and severity. *Archives of General Psychiatry, 57,* 1046–1052.

Stein, M. B., Walker, J. R., & Forde, D. R. (1996). Public speaking fears in a community sample: Prevalence, impact on functioning, and diagnostic classification. *Archives of General Psychiatry, 53,* 169–174.

Stemberger, R. T., Turner, S. M., Beidel, D.C., & Calhoun, K. S. (1995). Social phobia: An analysis of possible developmental factors. *Journal of Abnormal Psychology, 104,* 526–531.

Stopa, L., & Clark, D. M. (1993). Cognitive processes in social phobia. *Behaviour Research and Therapy, 31,* 255–267.

Stravynski, A., & Greenberg, D. (1989). Behavioural psychotherapy for social phobia and dysfunction. *International Review of Psychiatry, 1,* 207–218.

Takahashi, T. (1989). Social phobia syndrome in Japan. *Comprehensive Psychiatry, 30,* 45–52.

Tran, G. Q., & Chambless, D. L. (1995). Psychopathology of social phobia: Effects of subtype and of avoidant personality disorder. *Journal of Anxiety Disorders, 9,* 489–501.

Trower, P., & Gilbert, P. (1989). New theoretical conceptions of social anxiety and social phobia. *Clinical Psychology Review, 9,* 19–35.

Turner, S. M., Beidel, D. C., & Townsley, R. M. (1992). Social phobia: A comparison of specific and generalized subtypes and avoidant personality disorder. *Journal of Abnormal Psychology, 101,* 326–331.

Van der Molen, G. M., van den Hout, M. A., Vroemen, J., Lousberg, H., & Griez, E. (1986). Cognitive determinants of lactate-induced anxiety. *Behaviour Research and Therapy, 24,* 677–680.

Wallace, S. T., & Alden, L. E. (1991). A comparison of social standards and perceived ability in anxious and nonanxious men. *Cognitive Therapy and Research, 15,* 237–254.

Wallace, S. T., & Alden, L. E. (1997). Social phobia and positive social events: The price of success. *Journal of Abnormal Psychology, 106,* 416–424.

Walters, K. S., & Hope, D. A. (1998). Analysis of social behavior in individuals with social phobia and nonanxious participants using a psychobiological model. *Behavior Therapy, 29,* 387–407.

Weissman, M. M., Bland, R. C., Canino, G. J., Faravelli, C., Greenwald, S., Hwu, H. G., et al. (1997). The cross-national epidemiology of panic disorder. *Archives of General Psychiatry, 54,* 305–309.

White, W. B., & Baker, L. H. (1987). Ambulatory blood pressure monitoring in patients with panic disorder. *Archives of Internal Medicine, 147,* 1973–1975.

Wiedemann, G., Pauli, P., & Dengler, W. (2001). A priori expectancy bias in patients with panic disorder. *Journal of Anxiety Disorders, 15,* 401–412.

Wiedemann, G., Pauli, P., Dengler, W., Lutzenberger, W., Birbaumer, N., & Buchkremer, G. (1999). Frontal brain asymmetry as a biological substrate of emotions in panic patients. *Archives of General Psychiatry, 56,* 78–84.

Wilhelm, F. H., & Roth, W. T. (1997). Clinical characteristics of flight phobia. *Journal of Anxiety Disorders, 11,* 241–261.

Williams, J.M.G., Watts, F. N., MacLeod, C., & Mathews, A. M. (1997). *Cognitive psychology and emotional disorders* (2nd ed.). Chichester, England: Wiley.

Wilson, K. A., & Hayward, C. (2006). Unique contributions of anxiety sensitivity to avoidance: A prospective study in adolescents. *Behaviour, Research and Therapy, 44,* 601–609.

Wittchen, H.-U. (1988). Natural course and spontaneous remission of untreated anxiety disorders: Results of the Munich Follow-up Study (MFS). In I. Hand & H.-U. Wittchen (Eds.), *Panic and phobias* (pp. 3–17). Berlin, Germany: Springer.

Woody, S. R., McLean, C., & Klassen, T. (2005). Disgust as a motivator of avoidance of spiders. *Journal of Anxiety Disorders, 19,* 461–475.

Yonkers, K. A., Bruce, S. E., Dyck, I. R., & Keller, M. B. (2003). Chronicity, relapse, and illness-course of panic disorder, social phobia, and generalized anxiety disorder: Findings in men and women from 8 years of follow-up. *Depression and Anxiety 17,* 173–179.

CHAPTER

4

Phenomenology of Generalized Anxiety Disorder

Holly Hazlett-Stevens, Larry D. Pruitt *and* Angela Collins

Abstract

Generalized anxiety disorder (GAD) involves excessive and uncontrollable worry as well as chronic somatic anxiety symptoms. The lifetime prevalence is estimated at 5.7%, suggesting that GAD is a pervasive problem in the United States. GAD disproportionately affects women compared to men. Worry typically involves verbal-linguistic thought instead of imagery and tends to be vague and abstract rather than concrete. Worry appears to suppress physiological activation and may interfere with emotional processing following exposure to stressful stimuli. GAD is characterized by autonomic inflexibility and chronic muscle tension rather than autonomic hyperactivity. Individuals with GAD tend to report worry about minor topics more often than nonanxious individuals. GAD may be maintained by meta-cognitive beliefs about the functions and consequences of worry. These topics along with differences between worry, obsessions, and depressive rumination are examined in the chapter.

Keywords: clinical features, depressive rumination, diagnosis, epidemiology, generalized anxiety disorder, OCD, worry

Over the past 20 years, great strides have been made in the diagnosis and treatment of generalized anxiety disorder (GAD). Recent advances are largely due to our increased understanding of the core phenomenon underlying GAD: chronic worry. This chapter begins with a brief review of diagnostic features and presentation of up-to-date epidemiological information. Basic research examining the nature and function of worry is discussed within the context of GAD and pathological worry. Finally, comparisons between worry and other types of intrusive thought are made.

Diagnosis and Clinical Features

In this section, the history of GAD diagnosis and current diagnostic criteria are presented and discussed. Recent epidemiological data and common comorbid conditions are also described.

History of GAD Diagnosis

GAD first appeared in the third edition of the *Diagnostic and Statistical Manual of Mental Disorders* (*DSM–III;* American Psychiatric Association [APA], 1980). At that time, GAD was considered only a residual diagnosis, reserved for individuals who failed to meet diagnostic criteria for other *DSM–III* anxiety disorders. In 1987, GAD diagnostic criteria were largely revised (*DSM–III–R;* APA, 1987). Importantly, GAD became recognized as an independent diagnosis rather than a residual one. *DSM–III–R* criteria included excessive or unrealistic worry about at least two life domains and a minimum of 6 somatic symptoms from a list of 18 possible symptoms. The required duration of worry and somatic symptoms was 6 months, and this duration criterion was retained in the most recent *DSM* edition (*DSM–IV;* APA, 1994).

Other GAD diagnostic criteria were updated in the *DSM–IV*. Research showed that reports of uncontrollable worry distinguished individuals with GAD from individuals in nonanxious control conditions (Craske, Rapee, Jackel, & Barlow, 1989) but reports of unrealistic worry did not (Abel & Borkovec, 1995). Consistent with such research findings, the requirement that worry be perceived as uncontrollable remained in the *DSM–IV* while the "unrealistic" worry criterion was dropped. The presence of worry about two or more life spheres changed to worry that is excessive and "about a number of events or activities." Major changes were also made to the list of somatic symptoms required for diagnosis. Based on findings that many of the autonomic nervous system arousal symptoms contained in the *DSM–III–R* list were not frequently endorsed by individuals with GAD (Marten et al., 1993) and were not observed in laboratory studies (Hoehn-Saric, McLeod, & Zimmerli, 1989), these symptoms were dropped. *DSM–IV* diagnosis instead requires at least three of six anxiety symptoms reflecting general tension and vigilance.

Current DSM–IV–TR Diagnostic Criteria

Diagnosis of GAD currently requires at least 6 months of excessive anxiety and worry about a number of events or activities such as work or school performance (*DSM–IV–TR;* APA, 2000). The worry is perceived as difficult to control and is accompanied by a minimum of three chronic anxiety symptoms. These associated symptoms include restlessness, fatigue, difficulty concentrating, irritability, muscle tension, and sleep disturbance. The anxiety and worry are not limited to features of another Axis I disorder and are not due to the direct physiological effects of a substance or general medical condition. Finally, the symptoms must cause clinically significant distress or functional impairment.

Although these changes in *DSM* criteria led to improved diagnostic reliability (Turk, Heimberg, & Mennin, 2004), some concerns remain. First, discrimination between GAD and mood disorders is often difficult, as many GAD symptoms overlap with symptoms of depression (Brown, Marten, & Barlow, 1995). Second, others have questioned the utility of the 6-month duration requirement. Kessler, Brandenburg, et al. (2005) compared *DSM–IV* GAD prevalence estimates when the duration requirement was changed from 6 months to various durations ranging from 1 to 12 months. Many cases with episodes ranging from 1 to 5 months were found. Moreover, these individuals did not significantly differ from

individuals meeting the 6-month duration criterion on sociodemographic variables or measures of onset, chronicity, impairment, comorbidity, and parental GAD. Finally, this same group of experts challenged the *DSM–IV* excessive worry criterion. Recognizing that the *International Classification of Diseases,* 10th edition *(ICD–10)* does not require excessive worry for GAD diagnosis, Ruscio et al. (2005) found that elimination of this criterion increased the estimated lifetime prevalence by approximately 40%. Individuals meeting the excessive worry criterion exhibited earlier onset, more chronic course, greater symptom severity, and higher comorbidity than individuals with GAD who failed to meet this *DSM* criterion. However, individuals with GAD who did not experience excessive worry reported elevated impairment, chronicity, treatment-seeking, and comorbidity compared to survey respondents without GAD. Furthermore, the two GAD groups were comparable on sociodemographic variables and familial aggregation of GAD.

Prevalence and Related Statistics

Often-cited prevalence estimates for GAD were collected from the National Comorbidity Survey (NCS), a large epidemiology survey study conducted in the United States using *DSM–III–R* diagnostic criteria. The original NCS estimated current prevalence at 1.6%, 1-year prevalence at 3.1%, and a lifetime prevalence rate of 5.1% (Kessler et al., 1994). Kessler and colleagues recently completed a NCS replication study, collecting epidemiological survey data from 9,282 respondents in the United States using *DSM–IV* diagnostic criteria. Estimated prevalence rates for GAD were quite comparable to those found in the original NCS: the lifetime prevalence rate was estimated at 5.7% (Kessler, Berglund, et al., 2005) and the 1-year prevalence rate was again estimated at 3.1% (Kessler, Chiu, Demler, & Walters, 2005). This 1-year prevalence rate is noticeably higher than the 0.4% 1-year prevalence estimate found in a Mexican urban sample (Medina-Mora et al., 2005). GAD prevalence rates within primary care medical settings are markedly higher than those found in community survey research. In a recent review of this literature, Roy-Byrne and Wagner (2004) found that rates of GAD varied between 2.8% and 8.5% within the primary care setting, approximately twice the rate reported in the original NCS.

GAD appears to affect women at disproportionately greater rates than men. The original NCS study found that approximately two-thirds of respondents with GAD were women (Wittchen, Zhao, Kessler, & Eaton, 1994). A similar gender distribution has been reported in clinical treatment-seeking samples (Woodman, Noyes, Black, Schlosser, & Yagla, 1999). However, it is unclear how well these findings generalize to non-American cultures. Epidemiological research conducted in South Africa found a higher prevalence of GAD in men compared to women (Bhagwanjee, Parekh, Paruk, Petersen, & Subedar, 1998). GAD is associated with a chronic course and an early age of onset. In one clinical sample, 64% reported onset before the age of 19 (Hoehn-Saric, Hazlett, & McLeod, 1993). While the symptoms of GAD might seem less dramatic than some of the other anxiety disorders, GAD often results in significant functional impairment (Wittchen et al., 1994). GAD has recently been associated with low life satisfaction and poor perceived well-being, even after controlling for the independent effects of co-occurring depression (Stein & Heimberg, 2004).

Comorbidity

Comorbid psychological disorders are quite common among individuals with GAD; a majority of these patients also meet diagnostic criteria for other *DSM* diagnoses (e.g., Sanderson & Barlow, 1990). Among the other anxiety disorders, social anxiety disorder appears to be the most common: up to 59% of individuals with GAD also meet diagnostic criteria for this additional diagnosis (Sanderson, Di Nardo, Rapee, & Barlow, 1990). Depressive disorders are also frequent additional diagnoses. In a clinical sample diagnosed with dysthymia, more than 65% also met diagnostic criteria for GAD (Pini et al., 1997). Along similar lines, 42% of a GAD patient sample reported a history of major depression (Brawman-Mintzer et al., 1993). Almost half (49%) of GAD patients appear to suffer from a comorbid Axis II disorder (Sanderson, Wetzler, Beck, & Betz, 1994), with avoidant and dependent personality disorders most often diagnosed (Sanderson & Wetzler, 1991).

Comorbid medical conditions are often seen in GAD patients as well. This is not surprising, given the tendency of GAD patients to present in primary care medical settings, their high utilization of medical services, and the chronic somatic complaints associated with GAD diagnosis (Roy-Byrne & Wagner, 2004). Physical symptoms involving the gastrointestinal system appear particularly problematic for individuals with GAD. Gastrointestinal problems such as ulcers and stomach distress were linked to GAD more so than other medical conditions were (Sareen, Cox, Clara, & Asmundson, 2005). GAD patients sought treatment from gastroenterologists more often than any other medical specialty (Kennedy & Schwab, 1997). Individuals who suffer from GAD also appear prone to irritable bowel syndrome (IBS). Among a clinical sample of GAD patients, 37% also met diagnostic criteria for IBS (Tollefson et al., 1991). In addition, 34% of a sample of IBS patients also had a lifetime history of GAD (Lydiard, 1992). A high degree of comorbidity between GAD and IBS was also found in an unselected college student sample (Hazlett-Stevens, Craske, Mayer, Chang, & Naliboff, 2003).

The Nature of Worry in GAD

Experimental study of worry began in the 1970s within the context of test anxiety. Investigations in the early 1980s identified worry as a cognitive process common during states of anxiety. This line of research evolved into the systematic study of chronic or pathological worry and empirical comparisons between nonanxious and GAD or chronically worried individuals.

Definitions of Worry

Borkovec and colleagues (Borkovec, Robinson, Pruzinsky, & DePree, 1983) offered one of the earliest definitions of worry found in the empirical literature:

> Worry is a chain of thoughts and images, negatively affect-laden and relatively uncontrollable. The worry process represents an attempt to engage in mental problem-solving on an issue whose outcome is uncertain but contains the possibility of one or more negative outcomes. Consequently, worry relates closely to fear process. (p. 10)

Their initial self-report research revealed that worry is characterized by concerns about the future rather than the present and is associated with feelings of anxiety, apprehension, and general tension. Participants reporting high levels of worry also demonstrated more uncontrollable cognitive intrusions, poorer ability to focus attention on an experimental task, and greater subjective anxiety than participants who self-identified as "nonworriers."

Evidence exists for considering worry a unique psychological process. Davey, Hampton, Farrell, and Davidson (1992) found that measures of worry and trait anxiety were independent yet related constructs, with each contributing unique sources of variance. While trait anxiety was associated with expected maladaptive psychological processes, worry was linked to adaptive problem-solving and information-seeking cognitive strategies. Davey and colleagues therefore proposed that worry is typically a normal, adaptive process that facilitates problem solving. Anxiety only results and becomes detrimental when this adaptive process becomes thwarted or when worry is attempted during other negative psychological states such as poor perceived personal control. Davey (1994) demonstrated that chronic worry relates to poor confidence and poor perception of control in situations that require problem solving independent of the actual ability to solve problems.

Although the worry process contains both verbal-linguistic thought and imagery, the former type of mental activity is predominant (Borkovec & Inz, 1990). This verbal-linguistic thought process may be especially characteristic of worry among individuals reporting excessive worry (Freeston, Dugas, & Ladouceur, 1996). Worry content also tends to be vague and abstract, a property of worry that may function to minimize the impact of the thoughts and images experienced during worry (Stöber, 1998). Worries that are not concrete would therefore result in thoughts and images that are lackluster, slow to develop, difficult to access, and not personally relevant. In short, the full emotional impact of the worry content could be avoided by switching from topic to topic before vivid imagery develops.

Effects of Worry

Anxiety is the predominant affect during worry, accompanied by increased negative thought intrusions (Borkovec et al., 1983). In laboratory studies, subjective anxiety was maintained while worry reduced physiological arousal in response to phobic imagery (Borkovec & Hu, 1990; Borkovec, Lyonfields, Wiser, & Deihl, 1993). However, suppressed physiological arousal following worry was not demonstrated in a study utilizing in vivo exposure (Hazlett-Stevens & Borkovec, 2001), and worry may ultimately be an unsuccessful way to avoid the physiology associated with emotional processing (Peasly-Miklus & Vrana, 2000). Worry *after* exposure to stressful stimuli might interfere with subsequent emotional processing as evidenced by increased negative thought intrusions (Butler, Wells, & Dewick, 1995; Wells & Papageorgiou, 1995).

Several other physiological effects have been identified. For both nonanxious individuals and individuals with GAD, laboratory worry inductions reduced heart rate variability, a measure of cardiac vagal tone associated with parasympathetic nervous system activity (Lyonfields, Borkovec, & Thayer, 1995; Thayer, Friedman, & Borkovec, 1996). These investigations also found deficits in parasympathetic tone among individuals with GAD during baseline rest and relaxation states. Thus, the primary physiological correlate of GAD appears to be autonomic inflexibility rather than autonomic hyperactivity. States of worry have also been linked to left cortical EEG activation (Carter, Johnson, & Borkovec, 1986), and chronic worriers exhibited suppressed immune system responses compared to low worriers (Segerstrom, Glover, Craske, & Fahey, 1999; Segerstrom, Solomon, Kemeny, & Fahey, 1998). In EMG studies, individuals with GAD exhibited increased muscle tension compared to nonanxious participants (Hazlett, McLeod, & Hoehn-Saric, 1994; Hoehn-Saric et al., 1989).

Normal Versus Pathological Worry

A number of studies have compared the content and nature of worry between GAD or chronically worried individuals and nonanxious control groups. Worry content research has revealed few differences except that individuals with GAD report worry about minor, miscellaneous topics more often than nonanxious control groups (Craske et al., 1989; Roemer, Molina, & Borkovec, 1997) and more often than individuals with panic disorder (Breitholtz, Johansson, & Öst, 1999). Individuals with GAD also reported a greater breadth of worry content (Roemer et al., 1997) and worried more about the future (Dugas et al., 1998) than individuals in a control group. An investigation of worry beliefs revealed that individuals with GAD endorsed the belief that worry serves to distract them from "more emotional topics" more strongly than participants without GAD (Borkovec & Roemer, 1995). Individuals endorsing both positive and negative worry beliefs scored higher on psychopathology measures than those only endorsing negative worry consequences (Davey, Tallis, & Capuzzo, 1996).

The process of worry may distinguish chronic worriers from nonworriers. Vasey and Borkovec (1992) administered a catastrophizing interview similar to the cognitive therapy intervention of decatastrophizing. Compared to nonworriers, chronic worriers generated more catastrophizing steps, rated the events described in those steps as more likely to occur, and experienced increased subjective distress over the course of the interview. Provencher, Freeston, Dugas, and Ladouceur (2000) also found that high worriers rated these feared consequences as more likely than low worriers did. High worriers also reported more severe ultimate outcomes and less variability in these ultimate outcomes compared to low worriers. The catastrophizing worry chain has been characterized as more perseverative and more often associated with themes of inadequacy and failure among chronically worried individuals and individuals with GAD relative to nonanxious individuals (Davey & Levy, 1998; Hazlett-Stevens & Craske, 2003). Thus, the worry among individuals with GAD may be uniquely characterized by underlying fears of failure, inadequacy, or incompetence.

Recent research has further suggested that worry may function as an emotion regulation strategy for individuals with GAD. Mennin, Heimberg, Turk, and Fresco (2005) found that scores on a battery of emotion dysregulation measures predicted GAD in both student and clinical populations. GAD participants also reported increased physiological arousal in response to emotionally evocative music and displayed greater difficulty with their emotional responses when compared to nonanxious control participants. Individuals with GAD have also endorsed elevated levels of experiential avoidance, a variable that correlated with levels of stress, anxiety, and fear of emotional responding (Roemer, Salters, Raffa, & Orsillo, 2005).

Worry and Related Cognitive Phenomena

Worry is a cognitive process common during periods of anxiety and negative affect. However, other types of unwanted thought activity associated with dysphoria appear similar to worry. From a conceptual and clinical standpoint, it is important to distinguish worry from similar constructs. In this section, we briefly review the available empirical literature comparing and contrasting worry, obsessions, and depressive rumination.

Worry and Obsessions

Obsessions are typically linked to a diagnosis of obsessive-compulsive disorder (OCD). The DSM–IV–TR (APA, 2000; p. 462) defines obsessions as "recurrent and persistent thoughts, impulses, or images that are experienced, at some time during the disturbance, as intrusive and inappropriate and that cause marked anxiety or distress." Individuals with OCD most often realize and acknowledge that their obsessions are unreasonable and/or excessive, and the obsessions are experienced as foreign to the individual. Obsession content can vary greatly, although common examples include repeated thoughts about contamination, needing to have things in a specific

order, recurring doubts, sexual imagery, and violent or horrendous impulses. DSM–IV–TR explicitly states that the thoughts, images, or impulses associated with obsessions "are not simply excessive worries about real-life problems and are unlikely to be related to a real-life problem."

As discussed earlier, worry is a core characteristic of GAD. Individuals with GAD typically experience worry as excessive and uncontrollable, much as individuals with OCD suffer from an excessive frequency of obsessions also perceived as difficult to control. However, the DSM–IV–TR primarily distinguishes worry from obsessions on the basis of content. Worry associated with GAD is usually about mundane everyday life situations, such as work or financial responsibilities, health of family members, safety of children, or household responsibilities. In contrast, the DSM–IV–TR describes the content of obsessions as "ego-dystonic," reflecting that the obsession is experienced as alien to the individual and unlike the type of mental content the person expects to have.

Turner, Beidel, and Stanley (1992) identified a number of similarities as well as differences between obsessions and worry in their review of these empirical literatures. Both worry and obsessions can be found among clinical and nonanxious populations, and both types of mental activity have been linked to negative mood states. Similar to the finding that worry content does not typically differentiate normal from clinical individuals, the content of obsessions does not appear to distinguish OCD patients from normal control groups. As expected, both obsessions and worry were more severe for clinical individuals than for nonclinical individuals. Both types of thought activity occurred at greater frequencies and with more perceptions of the thoughts or images as out of control in the clinical populations.

Turner et al. (1992) also identified a number of important differences between worry and obsessions. Worry is more often triggered by an external or internal event that the individual is able to identify. Content differences proposed by the DSM–IV–TR were also found: worries were more often related to mundane events whereas obsessions consisted of themes associated with contamination, sex, and aggression. Unlike obsessions, the content of worries was not typically perceived as unacceptable. Worry and obsessions also differed in form: worry is usually experienced as verbal-linguistic thought, while obsessions often include images and impulses.

A handful of empirical investigations has compared worry and obsessions directly. Wells and Morrison (1994) compared the worries and obsessions of 30 nonclinical undergraduate and graduate student volunteer participants. As predicted, worry contained more verbal content and obsessions consisted of more imagery. Worry was also rated as longer lasting, less involuntary, more distracting, and more realistic than obsessions. Interestingly, worry was also associated with greater compulsions to act. Worries and obsessions did not differ in ratings of intrusiveness or the extent to which they were resisted. In a similar study with an unselected college student sample, Clark and Claybourn (1997) found that participants rated their experience of worry as more distressing, contributing to greater focus on the negative consequence of an event, causing more worry about feeling distressed, causing more interference with day-to-day living, and as having a greater association with checking behaviors than obsessionlike intrusive thoughts. Clark and Claybourn also found that the perceived consequences of the mental activity differentiated worry from obsessions. Perceived negative outcomes of events predicted worry, whereas the perceived meaning of having the thought predicted obsessionlike activity.

Langlois, Freeston, and Ladouceur (2000a) further found that their nonclinical student sample reported greater responsibility for obsessions than for worry. Even though obsessional content was considered less likely to occur, the consequence was perceived as more serious if it did. This finding is consistent with "thought-action fusion" research, in which obsessions were uniquely associated with the belief that thoughts can influence outside events or are equivalent to action (Coles, Mennin, & Heimberg, 2001). In contrast, thought-action fusion correlated weakly with worry (i.e., all bivariate correlation coefficients fell below .2) and was not predictive of GAD status after controlling for worry (Hazlett-Stevens, Zucker, & Craske, 2002). In their follow-up study, Langlois, Freeston, and Ladouceur (2000b) compared the factor structure of worry and obsessions. Obsessions were characterized by their upsetting thought content, whereas worry was characterized by intrusiveness and causing disturbance. The factor structure of coping strategies used in response to worries and obsessions was similar. An important limitation of each investigation directly comparing worry to obsessions is the use of unselected college student samples. Empirical comparisons of worry and obsessions among GAD, OCD, and other anxiety disordered individuals are sorely lacking.

Worry and Depressive Rumination

Rumination has been defined as repetitive negative thinking and is associated with depression and a host of detrimental psychological outcomes (see Papageorgiou & Siegle, 2003 for a review). However, only a couple of research investigations have examined the relationship between worry and rumination. Fresco, Frankel, Mennin, Turk, and Heimberg (2002) administered a battery of self-report measures to a large sample of undergraduate college students. Factor analysis results demonstrated that although worry and rumination were distinct processes, both were equally related to measures of anxiety and depression. In a similar study, Segerstrom, Tsao, Alden, and Craske (2000) found that measures of worry and rumination both loaded on a higher-order factor labeled "repetitive thought," a factor that predicted both anxiety and depression. Clearly, more empirical work delineating these two types of cognitive activity and their relationships to GAD and depressive disorders is needed.

Summary and Conclusions

GAD is characterized by excessive and uncontrollable worry coupled with impairing chronic anxiety symptoms. Frequent comorbid psychological disorders include social anxiety and unipolar depressive disorders, and medical conditions such as IBS are not uncommon. Worry has been associated with a number of psychological and physiological effects for nonanxious individuals as well as individuals with GAD. However, individuals with GAD report worry about minor topics, endorse that worry serves to distract from more emotional topics, and exhibit signs of emotional dysregulation more than nonanxious control groups. Worry among individuals with GAD may also be characterized by fears of failure to a greater degree than among nonanxious individuals. A great deal more research is needed to clarify similarities and differences between worry, obsessions, and depressive rumination.

References

Abel, J. L., & Borkovec, T. D. (1995). Generalizability of *DSM–III–R* generalized anxiety disorders to proposed *DSM–IV* criteria and cross-validation of proposed changes. *Journal of Anxiety Disorders, 9,* 303–315.

American Psychiatric Association. (1980). *Diagnostic and statistical manual of mental disorders* (3rd ed.). Washington, DC: Author.

American Psychiatric Association. (1987). *Diagnostic and statistical manual of mental disorders* (3rd ed. revised). Washington, DC: Author.

American Psychiatric Association. (1994). *Diagnostic and statistical manual of mental disorders* (4th ed.). Washington, DC: Author.

American Psychiatric Association. (2000). *Diagnostic and statistical manual of mental disorders* (4th ed. text revision.). Washington, DC: Author.

Bhagwanjee, A., Parekh, A., Paruk, Z., Petersen, I., & Subedar, H. (1998). Prevalence of minor psychiatric disorders in an adult African rural community in South Africa. *Psychological Medicine, 28,* 1137–1147.

Borkovec, T. D., & Hu, S. (1990). The effect of worry on cardiovascular response to phobic imagery. *Behaviour Research and Therapy, 28,* 69–73.

Borkovec, T. D., & Inz, J. (1990). The nature of worry in generalized anxiety disorder: A predominance of thought activity. *Behaviour Research and Therapy, 28,* 153–158.

Borkovec, T. D., Lyonfields, J. D., Wiser, S. L., & Deihl, L. (1993). The role of worrisome thinking in the suppression of cardiovascular response to phobic imagery. *Behaviour Research and Therapy, 31,* 321–324.

Borkovec, T. D., Robinson, E., Pruzinsky, T., & DePree, J. A. (1983). Preliminary exploration of worry: Some characteristics and processes. *Behaviour Research and Therapy, 21,* 9–16.

Borkovec, T. D., & Roemer, L. (1995). Perceived functions of worry among generalized anxiety disorder subjects: Distraction from more emotionally distressing topics? *Journal of Behavior Therapy and Experimental Psychiatry, 26,* 25–30.

Brawman-Mintzer, O., Lydiard, R. B., Emmanuel, N., Payeur, R., Johnson, M., Roberts, J., et al. (1993). Psychiatric comorbidity in patients with generalized anxiety disorder. *American Journal of Psychiatry, 150,* 1216–1218.

Breitholtz, E., Johansson, B., & Öst, L. G. (1999). Cognitions in generalized anxiety disorder and panic disorder patients: A prospective approach. *Behaviour Research and Therapy, 7,* 533–544.

Brown, T. A., Marten, P. A., & Barlow, D. H. (1995). Discriminant validity of the symptoms constituting the *DSM–III–R* and *DSM–IV* associated symptom criterion of generalized anxiety disorder. *Journal of Anxiety Disorders, 9,* 317–328.

Butler, G., Wells, A., & Dewick, H. (1995). Differential effects of worry and imagery after exposure to a stressful stimulus: A pilot study. *Behavioural and Cognitive Psychotherapy, 23,* 45–56.

Carter, W. R., Johnson, M. C., & Borkovec, T. D. (1986). Worry: An electrocortical analysis. *Advances in Behaviour Research and Therapy, 8,* 193–204.

Clark, D. A., & Claybourn, M. (1997). Process characteristics of worry and obsessive intrusive thoughts. *Behaviour Research and Therapy, 35,* 1139–1141.

Coles, M. E., Mennin, D. S., & Heimberg, R. G. (2001). Distinguishing obsessive features and worries: The role of thought-action fusion. *Behaviour Research and Therapy, 39,* 947–959.

Craske, M. G., Rapee, R. M., Jackel, L., & Barlow, D. H. (1989). Qualitative dimensions of worry in *DSM–III–R* generalized anxiety disorder subjects and nonanxious controls. *Behaviour Research and Therapy, 27,* 397–402.

Davey, G.C.L. (1994). Worrying, social problem-solving abilities, and social problem-solving confidence. *Behaviour Research and Therapy, 32,* 327–330.

Davey, G.C.L., Hampton, J., Farrell, J., & Davidson, S. (1992). Some characteristics of worrying: Evidence for worrying and anxiety as separate constructs. *Personality and Individual Differences, 13,* 133–147.

Davey, G.C.L., & Levy, S. (1998). Catastrophic worrying: Personal inadequacy and a perseverative iterative style as features of the catastrophizing process. *Journal of Abnormal Psychology, 107,* 576–586.

Davey, G.C.L., Tallis, F., & Capuzzo, N. (1996). Beliefs about the consequences of worrying. *Cognitive Therapy and Research, 20,* 499–520.

Dugas, M. J., Freeston, M. H., Ladouceur, R., Rhéaume, J., Provencher, M., & Boisvert, J. (1998). Worry themes in primary GAD, secondary GAD, and other anxiety disorders. *Journal of Anxiety Disorders, 12,* 253–261.

Freeston, M. H., Dugas, M. J., & Ladouceur, R. (1996). Thoughts, images, worry, and anxiety. *Cognitive Therapy and Research, 20,* 265–273.

Fresco, D. M., Frankel, A. N., Mennin, D. S., Turk, C. L., & Heimberg, R. G. (2002). Distinct and overlapping features of rumination and worry: The relationship of cognitive production to negative affective states. *Cognitive Therapy and Research, 26,* 179–188.

Hazlett, R. L., McLeod, D. R., & Hoehn-Saric, R. (1994). Muscle tension in generalized anxiety disorder: Elevated muscle tonus or agitated movement? *Psychophysiology, 31,* 189–195.

Hazlett-Stevens, H., & Borkovec, T. D. (2001). Effects of worry and progressive relaxation on the reduction of fear in speech phobia: An investigation of situational exposure. *Behavior Therapy, 32,* 503–517.

Hazlett-Stevens, H., & Craske, M. G. (2003). The catastrophizing worry process in generalized anxiety disorder: A preliminary investigation of an analog population. *Behavioural and Cognitive Psychotherapy, 31,* 387–401.

Hazlett-Stevens, H., Craske, M. G., Mayer, E. A., Chang, L., & Naliboff, B. D. (2003). Prevalence of irritable bowel syndrome among university students: The roles of worry, neuroticism, anxiety sensitivity, and visceral anxiety. *Journal of Psychosomatic Research, 55,* 501–505.

Hazlett-Stevens, H., Zucker, B., & Craske, M. G. (2002). The relationship of thought-action fusion to pathological worry and generalized anxiety disorder. *Behaviour Research and Therapy, 40,* 1199–1204.

Hoehn-Saric, R., Hazlett, R. L., & McLeod, D. R. (1993). Generalized anxiety disorder with early and late onset of anxiety symptoms. *Comprehensive Psychiatry, 34,* 291–298.

Hoehn-Saric, R., McLeod, D. R., & Zimmerli, W. D. (1989). Symptoms and treatment responses of generalized anxiety disorder patients with high versus low levels of cardiovascular complaints. *American Journal of Psychiatry, 146,* 854–859.

Kennedy, B. L., & Schwab, J. J. (1997). Utilization of medical specialists by anxiety disorder patients. *Psychosomatics, 38,* 109–112.

Kessler, R. C., Berglund, P., Demler, O., Jin, R., Merikangas, K. R., & Walters, E. E. (2005). Lifetime prevalence of age-of-onset distributions of *DSM–IV* disorders in the National Comorbidity Survey Replication. *Archives of General Psychiatry, 62,* 593–602.

Kessler, R. C., Brandenburg, N., Lane, M., Roy-Byrne, P., Stang, P. D., Stein, D. J., et al. (2005). Rethinking the duration requirement for generalized anxiety disorder: Evidence from the National Comorbidity Survey Replication. *Psychological Medicine, 35,* 1073–1082.

Kessler, R. C., Chiu, W. T., Demler, O., & Walters, E. E. (2005). Prevalence, severity, and comorbidity of 12-month *DSM–IV* disorders in the National Comorbidity Survey Replication. *Archives of General Psychiatry, 62,* 617–627.

Kessler, R. C., McGonagle, K. A., Zhao, S., Nelson, C. B., Hughes, M., Eshleman, S., et al. (1994). Lifetime and 12-month prevalence of *DSM–III–R* psychiatric disorders in the United States: Results from the National Comorbidity Study. *Archives of General Psychiatry, 51,* 8–19.

Langlois, F., Freeston, M. H., & Ladouceur, R. (2000a). Differences and similarities between obsessive intrusive thoughts and worry in a non-clinical population: Study 1. *Behaviour Research and Therapy, 38,* 157–173.

Langlois, F., Freeston, M. H., & Ladouceur, R. (2000b). Differences and similarities between obsessive intrusive thoughts and worry in a non-clinical population: Study 2. *Behaviour Research and Therapy, 38,* 175–189.

Lydiard, R. B. (1992). Anxiety and the irritable bowel syndrome. *Psychiatric Annals, 22,* 612–618.

Lyonfields, J. D., Borkovec, T. D., & Thayer, J. F. (1995). Vagal tone in generalized anxiety disorder and the effects of aversive imagery and worrisome thinking. *Behavior Therapy, 26,* 457–466.

Marten, P. A., Brown, T. A., Barlow, D. H., Borkovec, T. D., Shear, M. K., & Lydiard, R. B. (1993). Evaluation of the ratings comprising the associated symptom criterion of *DSM–III–R* generalized anxiety disorder. *Journal of Nervous and Mental Disease, 181,* 676–682.

Medina-Mora, M. E., Borges, G., Lara, C., Benjet, C., Blanco, J., Feliz, C., et al. (2005). Prevalence, service use, and demographic correlates of 12-month *DSM–IV* psychiatric disorders in Mexico: Results from the Mexican National Comorbidity Survey. *Psychological Medicine, 35,* 1–11.

Mennin, D. S., Heimberg, R. G., Turk, C. L., & Fresco, D. M. (2005). Preliminary evidence for an emotion dysregulation model of generalized anxiety disorder. *Behaviour Research and Therapy, 43,* 1281–1310.

Papageorgiou, C., & Siegle, G. J. (2003). Rumination and depression: Advances in theory and research. *Cognitive Therapy and Research, 27,* 243–245.

Peasley-Miklus, C., & Vrana, S. R. (2000). Effect of worrisome and relaxing thinking on fearful emotional processing. *Behaviour Research and Therapy, 38,* 129–144.

Pini, S., Cassano, G. B., Simonini, E., Savino, M., Russo, A., & Montomery, S. A. (1997). Prevalence of anxiety disorders comorbidity in bipolar depression, unipolar depression and dysthymia. *Journal of Affective Disorders, 42,* 145–153.

Provencher, M. D., Freeston, M. H., Dugas, M. J., & Ladouceur, R. (2000). Catastrophizing assessment of worry and threat schemata among worriers. *Behavioural and Cognitive Psychotherapy, 28,* 211–224.

Roemer, L., Molina, S., & Borkovec, T. D. (1997). An investigation of worry content among generally anxious individuals. *Journal of Nervous and Mental Disease, 185,* 314–319.

Roemer, L., Salters, K., Raffa, S. D., & Orsillo, S. M. (2005). Fear and avoidance of internal experiences in GAD: Preliminary tests of a conceptual model. *Cognitive Therapy and Research, 29,* 71–88.

Roy-Byrne, P. P., & Wagner, A. (2004). Primary care perspectives on generalized anxiety disorder. *Journal of Clinical Psychiatry, 65,* 20–26.

Ruscio, A. M., Lane, M., Roy-Byrne, P., Stang, P. E., Stein, D. J., Wittchen, H., et al. (2005). Should excessive worry be required for a diagnosis of generalized anxiety disorder? Results from the U.S. National Comorbidity Survey Replication. *Psychological Medicine, 35,* 1–12.

Sanderson, W. C., & Barlow, D. H. (1990). A description of patients diagnosed with *DSM–III–R* generalized anxiety disorder. *Journal of Nervous and Mental Disease, 178,* 588–591.

Sanderson, W. C., Di Nardo, P. A., Rapee, R. M., & Barlow, D. H. (1990). Syndrome comorbidity in patients diagnosed with a *DSM–III–R* anxiety disorder. *Journal of Abnormal Psychology, 99,* 308–312.

Sanderson, W. C., & Wetzler, S. (1991). Chronic anxiety and generalized anxiety disorder: Issues in comorbidity. In R. M. Rapee & D. H. Barlow (Eds.), *Chronic anxiety: Generalized anxiety disorder and mixed anxiety-depression* (pp. 119–135). New York: Guilford Press.

Sanderson, W. C., Wetzler, S., Beck, A. T., & Betz, F. (1994). Prevalence of personality disorders among patients with anxiety disorders. *Psychiatry Research, 51,* 167–174.

Sareen, J., Cox, B. J., Clara, I., & Asmundson, G. J. G. (2005). The relationship between anxiety disorders and physical disorders in the U.S. National Comorbidity Survey. *Depression and Anxiety, 21,* 193–202.

Segerstrom, S. C., Glover, D. A., Craske, M. G., & Fahey, J. L. (1999). Worry affects the immune response to phobic fear. *Brain, Behavior and Immunity, 13,* 80–92.

Segerstrom, S. C., Solomon, G. F., Kemeny, M. E., & Fahey, J. L. (1998). Relationship of worry to immune sequelae of the Northridge earthquake. *Journal of Behavioral Medicine, 21,* 433–450.

Segerstrom, S. C., Tsao, J.C.I., Alden, L. E., & Craske, M. G. (2000). Worry and rumination: Repetitive thought as a concomitant and predictor of negative mood. *Cognitive Therapy and Research, 24,* 671–688.

Stein, M. B., & Heimberg, R. G. (2004). Well-being and life satisfaction in generalized anxiety disorder: Comparison to major depressive disorder in a community sample. *Journal of Affective Disorders, 79,* 161–166.

Stöber, J. (1998). Worry, problem elaboration and suppression of imagery: The role of concreteness. *Behaviour Research and Therapy, 36,* 751–756.

Thayer, J. F., Friedman, B. H., & Borkovec, T. D. (1996). Autonomic characteristics of generalized anxiety disorder and worry. *Biological Psychiatry, 39,* 255–266.

Tollefson, G. D., Tollefson, S. L., Pederson, M., Luxenberg, M., & Dunsmore, G. (1991). Comorbid irritable bowel syndrome in patients with generalized anxiety and major depression. *Annals of Clinical Psychiatry, 3,* 215–222.

Turk, C. L., Heimberg, R. G., & Mennin, D. S. (2004). Assessment. In R. G. Heimberg, C. L. Turk, & D. S. Mennin (Eds.), *Generalized anxiety disorder: Advances in research and practice* (pp. 219–247). New York: Guilford Press.

Turner, S. M., Beidel, D. C., & Stanley, M. A. (1992). Are obsessional thoughts and worry different cognitive phenomena? *Clinical Psychology Review, 12,* 257–270.

Vasey, M. W., & Borkovec, T. D. (1992). A catastrophizing assessment of worrisome thoughts. *Cognitive Therapy and Research, 16,* 505–520.

Wells, A., & Morrison, A. P. (1994). Qualitative dimensions of normal worry and normal obsessions: A comparative study. *Behaviour Research and Therapy, 32,* 867–870.

Wells, A., & Papageorgiou, C. (1995). Worry and the incubation of intrusive images following stress. *Behaviour Research and Therapy, 33,* 579–583.

Wittchen, H., Zhao, S., Kessler, R. C., & Eaton, W. W. (1994). *DSM–III–R* generalized anxiety disorder in the National Comorbidity Survey. *Archives of General Psychiatry, 51,* 355–364.

Woodman, C. L., Noyes, R., Black, D. W., Schlosser, S., & Yagla, S. J. (1999). A 5-year follow-up study of generalized anxiety disorder and panic disorder. *Journal of Nervous and Mental Disease, 187,* 3–9.

Phenomenology of Obsessive-Compulsive Disorder

Carol A. Mathews

Abstract

This chapter focuses on the phenomenology of obsessive-compulsive disorder (OCD), which is an anxiety disorder whose key features are recurrent, distressing, intrusive obsessions and/or compulsions. Obsessive-compulsive symptoms (OCS) occur along a continuum; mild or moderate symptoms are normal or adaptive in some circumstances, but can develop into a clinically significant disorder if they persist or cause substantial distress or impairment. OCD is heterogeneous, with multiple symptom subtypes (e.g., contamination fears, aggressive or sexual obsessions, hoarding) that may have different etiologies and treatment response patterns. OCD is also frequently comorbid with other psychiatric disorders, including tic, eating, mood, and other anxiety disorders. Although the phenomenology of OCD is well elucidated, the relationship between normal OCS and OCD, and their relationships to other neuropsychiatric disorders is less well understood.

Keywords: avoidance behavior, compulsion, obsession, obsessive-compulsive disorder, OCD diagnostic, OCD phenomenology, obsessive-compulsive spectrum, phenotype, rumination, symptom subtype, threat domain

Obsessive-compulsive disorder (OCD) is an anxiety disorder characterized by intrusive, distressing thoughts, urges, or images (obsessions), and repetitive, ritualized actions aimed at reducing anxiety or distress (compulsions) (American Psychiatric Association [APA], 2000; Stein, 2002). It affects 2%–3% of the population worldwide, and according to the World Health Organization (WHO), is among the top 20 disorders causing significant disability among 18- to 44-year-olds (WHO, 2001). In spite of its prevalence and high cost burden to society, OCD is underdiagnosed and undertreated, with an average of 9 years from onset of OCD symptoms to appropriate diagnosis and treatment (Hollander, 1997). Fortunately, as research into the presentation and etiology of OCD and related disorders expands, recognition and treatment of this disorder is improving. This chapter discusses the phenomenology of OCD, including diagnostic features, symptom subtypes, and the relationship of OCD with other frequently comorbid disorders, including obsessive-compulsive spectrum disorders (OCSD).

Definitions and Diagnostic Features of OCD

According to the *DSM–IV–TR,* the key features of OCD are recurrent obsessions or compulsions that are severe enough to be time-consuming (taking at least an hour a day), to cause marked distress, or to cause significant impairment (APA, 2000). *Obsessions* are defined as persistent, recurrent, and distressing thoughts, images, impulses, or fears that are experienced as inappropriate and intrusive. Common examples of obsessions include contamination fears, fears or urges to behave aggressively toward others or oneself, worry about causing harm by not being careful enough, superstitious fears or magical thinking, and a need for things to be symmetrical, exact or "just right" (see Table 1). In contrast to ruminations, which are persistent, recurrent thoughts or fears about real life or everyday worries that commonly occur in anxiety and mood disorders, obsessions are ego-dystonic; that is, they are perceived as alien, outside of the individual's control, and not the type of thoughts that the individual experiencing them would expect to have (APA, 2000; Hong, 2007). *Compulsions* are repetitive or ritualized behaviors or mental acts that an individual feels compelled to perform in order to reduce anxiety or distress or to prevent some dreaded event from happening (APA, 2000). They are often, but not always, performed in response to obsessions. Common examples of compulsions include excessive or ritualized hand washing or showering; repeated checking; mental rituals such as thinking or saying a certain word, phrase, or prayer over and over again; counting; and repeating rituals (see Table 1). Compulsions, like obsessions, are ego-dystonic, and seen as unreasonable and excessive by the individual experiencing them. They differ from routines, which are repeated behaviors that the individual enjoys or that serve a particular purpose, and also from stereotypes, which are repetitive, unvarying behaviors that have no apparent goal or function.

Pathological doubt and avoidance behaviors are also common features of OCD, which, while not required for a diagnosis, can have a substantial impact on the course and treatment of OCD. Pathological doubt is most prominent in individuals with checking compulsions or repeating rituals who will often report uncertainty about whether they have performed a task correctly or completely or, in extreme cases, whether they have performed it at all, even in the face of objective sensory evidence (e.g., being uncertain if the door is locked completely, even when it can be seen that the lock is engaged). Avoidance behaviors, like compulsions, are aimed at reducing the anxiety and distress caused by obsessions, and include avoiding activities of daily living such as showering or cooking to avoid triggering contamination fears or to avoid lengthy washing rituals, avoiding particular places or people that are associated with superstitious fears or, in extreme cases, staying in bed or in a particular room in the house for most of the day to avoid triggering obsessions or compulsions. Although avoidance can also be seen in many other neuropsychiatric disorders, including panic disorder, agoraphobia, and depression, pathological doubt is more specific to OCD, and may be related in part to an emotional inability to tolerate uncertainty or to decreased confidence in one's own memory (Tolin et al., 2001; Tolin, Abramowitz, Brigidi, & Foa, 2003).

Table 1. Common Symptom Subtypes in OCD and Examples of Associated Obsessions and Compulsions

Symptom Subtype	Obsession	Compulsion
Cleaning/contamination	• Germ fears • Fears of environmental contaminants	• Repetitive or excessive washing, showering • Using gloves, masks to do daily tasks
Aggressive/sexual/religious	• Fears, urges to harm self or others • Fears of offending God	• Avoidance of sharp objects • Repeated requests for reassurance
Hoarding	• Fears of throwing away useless objects such as candy wrappers	• Collecting/saving objects with little or no actual or sentimental value such as old newspapers
Symmetry/exactness/"just right"	• Needing things to be symmetrical/ aligned just so • Urges to do things over and over until they feel "just right"	• Lining things up • Repeating rituals
Miscellaneous/global	• Superstitious fears	• Checking

Nonclinical Obsessions and Compulsions

Although obsessive-compulsive symptoms are most commonly thought of in the context of dysfunction, they are present at low levels throughout life in many normal individuals, and are adaptive at several stages of development. The presence of substantial rates of obsessive and/or compulsive symptoms begins in early childhood, and persist into early adulthood (Feygin, Swain, & Leckman, 2006). Developmentally normal ritualistic or compulsive behaviors generally appear between 2 and 5 years of age, and include compulsive behaviors associated with lining things up, need for symmetry, and bedtime or eating rituals (Evans, Gray, & Leckman, 1999; Zohar & Felz, 2001). These behaviors, which usually diminish around age 5 or 6, are thought to be important both in the development of behavioral and cognitive control, including mastery of the environment, ability to regulate emotion, and awareness of the concept that there is or can be a "way that things ought to be," and as an adaptive reaction to common childhood fears and anxieties (Evans et al., 1999; Franzblau, 1997; Zohar & Felz, 2001). Ritualistic and repetitive behaviors are nearly ubiquitous among children in this age group; on average, such behaviors are reported by parents in approximately 60%–70% of children at any given time, with some behaviors, such as repeating rituals, reported in more than 80% (Evans et al., 1999, 1997). Ritualistic and compulsive behaviors are also common in older children, adolescents, and young adults, when low levels of obsessionality may help with organization, sense of control, and self-efficacy during a time of separation/individuation from parents and other authority figures (Franzblau, 1997; Zohar & Felz, 2001). Feygin et al. (2006) have suggested that there are four categories of obsessive-compulsive fears and behaviors that are associated with particular types of threat, or threat domains, which occur in different manifestations throughout the lifespan, and can be explained from an evolutionary perspective. These include the *aggressive* threat domain, which concerns fears about one's well-being and that of loved ones, and includes intrusive thoughts about separation and loss; the *physical security* threat domain, which relates to the immediate home environment, and includes checking, symmetry, and "just right" symptoms; the *environmental cleanliness* threat domain, which relates to personal hygiene and cleanliness, and includes contamination fears and washing and cleaning rituals; and the *privation* threat domain, which relates to concerns about essential resources, and includes hoarding behaviors, magical thinking, and rituals (Feygin et al., 2006).

These categories roughly correspond to obsessive-compulsive symptom subtypes that have been observed both among individuals with OCD and in nonclinical samples of adolescents and young adults, suggesting that there may be some inherent underlying structure to the type and manifestation of obsessive-compulsive symptoms that has evolutionary and/or etiological relevance.

OCD Symptom Subtypes

Although the *DSM–IV–TR* considers OCD to be a single diagnostic entity, it is clearly a heterogeneous disorder. In an attempt to better understand OCD from both a clinical and an etiological perspective, efforts are ongoing to further classify OCD into subtypes based on a variety of factors, including age of onset, presence or absence of comorbid traits such as tics, symptom type, or comorbid features such as comorbid obsessive-compulsive spectrum disorders (Bienvenu et al., 2000; Lochner & Stein, 2006; Mataix-Cols, 2006). These efforts, while not entirely satisfactory, have provided some additional insight into the complexity of this disorder. For example, subgrouping by age of onset has suggested that individuals with an onset of symptoms prior to 18 years appear to have a more heritable form of OCD than do those with a later age of onset, as well as being more likely to have comorbid tics and to be male, suggesting that early- and late-onset OCD may be etiologically distinct (Delorme et al., 2005; Hemmings et al., 2004).

The most common form of subtyping OCD is based on categorizing specific symptoms such as contamination obsessions and cleaning and washing compulsions into subgroups using factor analytic approaches. These analyses have consistently identified between three and five symptom factors, both in clinical and nonclinical populations, with the majority of analyses pointing to four primary factors (Mataix-Cols, 2006; Mataix-Cols, Rosario-Campos, & Leckman, 2005; Miguel et al., 2005). The most commonly identified factors are contamination and cleaning; hoarding; symmetry and ordering; and aggressive, sexual, and religious obsessions (Hasler et al., 2005). Other common obsessive-compulsive symptoms such as checking, repeating rituals, mental rituals, superstitious obsessions, and miscellaneous symptoms load variably on each of these factors or form additional factors, depending on the study population, the approach used, and the instrument assessed. Although remarkably consistent at the population level, the meaning and utility of these symptom subgroups is somewhat less clear at the individual level. Symptom expression waxes and wanes over the course of the illness, with many individuals experiencing symptoms from several or all of the symptom subgroups at some time in their lives (Delorme et al., 2006; Leonard et al., 1993; Mataix-Cols et al., 2002; Rufer, Grothusen, Mass, Peter, & Hand, 2005). Children in particular show little stability in symptom expression, although adults with OCD have more stable symptom expression patterns (Delorme et al., 2006; Leonard et al., 1993).

One weakness of the symptom subtype approach to reducing the heterogeneity of OCD is that, of the identified factors, only hoarding has been consistently associated with specific clinical, etiological, and neuroanatomic features such as treatment response, brain regions activated in neuroimaging studies, and likely genetic etiology (Husted, Shapira, & Goodman, 2006; Lochner, Kinnear et al., 2005; Mataix-Cols, Rauch, Manzo, Jenike, & Baer, 1999; Mataix-Cols et al., 2004; Samuels et al., 2002). Studies examining the clinical and etiological correlates of the other three to four factors have been somewhat less consistent, and no clear pattern has yet emerged (Alsobrook, Leckman, Goodman, Rasmussen, & Pauls, 1999; Cavallini, Di Bella, Siliprandi, Malchiodi, & Bellodi, 2002; Mataix-Cols et al., 1999).

Obsessive-Compulsive Spectrum Disorders

Another approach to reducing the heterogeneity of OCD is to create subtypes based on comorbid obsessive-compulsive spectrum disorders (OCSD). The OCSD are neuropsychiatric disorders that overlap with OCD clinically, phenomenologically, or neurobiologically, and are hypothesized to have a shared pathogenesis (Hollander et al., 1996; Jaisoorya, Reddy, & Srinath, 2003; Phillips, 2002). In addition to compulsive behaviors, many of the OCSD are also characterized by impulsive behaviors, which are driven by a need to maximize pleasure or stimulation rather than to decrease anxiety or discomfort (APA, 2000). Although different in their underlying drives, disorders of compulsivity and impulsivity can be thought of as sharing an inability to delay or inhibit repetitive behaviors, and thus have been hypothesized to have underlying etiological features in common (Hollander, Friedberg, Wasserman, Yeh, & Iyengar, 2005).

Despite the similarities between them, the relationships between disorders of impulsivity and disorders of compulsivity have not been fully elucidated. Tourette Syndrome, trichotillomania, pathological skin picking, body dysmorphic disorder, hypochondriasis, and eating disorders (anorexia nervosa and bulimia nervosa) are generally considered to be the core OCSD, as they show consistently increased comorbidity or evidence of an etiological relationship with OCD (Bienvenu et al., 2000; Jaisoorya et al., 2003; Richter, Summerfeldt, Antony, & Swinson, 2003). Although there is an increase in comorbidity between OCD and the other putative OCSD, which include pathological gambling, compulsive shopping, kleptomania, sexual compulsive behavior (and in some formulations autism, self-injurious behavior, depersonalization, and other disorders displaying impulsive features), there is less evidence to support an etiological relationship between them (Hollander et al., 2005; Richter et al., 2003).

In the OCSD subtyping system, individuals with OCD are grouped according to the presence or absence of OCSD using cluster analyses (Lochner, Hemmings et al., 2005; Lochner & Stein, 2006). This approach has identified three primary clusters: a *reward deficiency* cluster, which includes trichotillomania, Tourette Syndrome, pathological gambling, and hypersexual disorder; an *impulsivity* cluster, which includes eating disorders, compulsive shopping, kleptomania, self-injury, and intermittent explosive disorder; and a *somatic* cluster, which includes body dysmorphic disorder and hypochondriasis (Lochner, Hemmings et al., 2005). As with the subtypes based on symptom groupings, attempts have been made to correlate the OCSD clusters with other relevant variables such as age of onset, symptom type, gender, and treatment response (Lochner, Hemmings et al., 2005). The OCSD cluster approach is still preliminary, and as with the symptom clusters, the meaning and utility of the identified clusters is still to be determined.

Categorical Versus Dimensional Approaches to Subtyping OCD

From a phenomenological perspective, approaches to reducing the heterogeneity of OCD have been very successful in capturing the variety of ways that the disorder can be expressed within an individual or group. From a practical perspective, however, these attempts have been somewhat less useful, as they have not yet led to insights about the etiology or treatment of OCD, sparking heated debate about the best way to understand this complex disorder. On one side of the debate are those who believe that OCD is likely to ultimately consist of distinct categories, each with separate etiologies (Hemmings et al., 2004). On the other side are those who believe that although heterogeneous, OCD is likely to be a dimensional disorder, with multiple etiological factors contributing jointly to its development (McKay et al., 2004). A third position, one being increasingly adopted by OCD researchers, combines the dimensional and categorical approaches. This position argues that OCD consists of a hierarchy of dimensions or factors, with one higher-order factor common to all OCD, and additional factors (based on symptom groups, comorbidities, or other variables) present in subsets of individuals or to varying degrees within an individual or family (Leckman, Mataix-Cols, & do Rosario-Campos, 2005a; Taylor, 2005). There is some empirical evidence to support this idea. Twin and family studies have identified a unidimensional higher-order factor that is common to individuals with OCD, is heritable, and does not overlap with the symptom-based categories that can also be identified (Mathews et al., 2007; van Grootheest, Boomsma, Hettema, & Kendler, 2007). In general, this unidimensional factor consists of symptoms reflecting pathological doubt, checking behaviors, and avoidance—features that are common to all of the previously identified symptom subtypes, as well as being common to many of the spectrum disorders. A variation on this argument proposes that both categorical subtyping (e.g., early onset, OCD plus tics) and dimensional subtyping will help to identify underlying genetic or other etiological factors for OCD, the first by identifying susceptibility genes for specific subgroups of individuals, and the other by leading to endophenotypes for OCD (Leckman et al., 2005a, 2005b).

Relationship of OCD to Other Neuropsychiatric Disorders

The lifetime prevalence of comorbid Axis I and II disorders in OCD is quite high, between 50%–60%, making comorbidity the rule rather than the exception for this disorder (Denys, Tenney, van Megen, de Geus, & Westenberg, 2004). In addition to the OCSD, OCD commonly co-occurs with a variety of other neuropsychiatric disorders, including mood and anxiety disorders, psychotic disorders, and personality disorders. Although less extensive than work on the OCSD, some attempt has been made to subgroup individuals with OCD on the basis of comorbidity with these disorders. These

analyses suggest that in some cases (e.g., depressive disorders), OCD is the primary disorder and the comorbid disorder is a secondary phenomenon, while in other cases, the OCD symptoms develop after the occurrence of the comorbidity, and are thought to be a secondary manifestation of the primary disorder (e.g., schizophrenia, bipolar disorder).

Mood and Anxiety Disorders

Major depression is the disorder most commonly reported to be comorbid with OCD, with 25%–50% of individuals with OCD reporting at least one major depressive episode in their lifetime (Carter, Pollock, Suvak, & Pauls, 2004). Children with OCD tend to have a lower rate of depressive disorders than do adults with OCD, and in many adults, the onset of obsessive-compulsive symptoms precedes the onset of depressive symptoms, suggesting that depressive symptoms may develop as a secondary response to OCD symptoms. Family studies suggest that major depression is elevated in relatives of OCD probands only when the relatives themselves have OCD, providing further evidence that depressive symptoms may represent secondary phenomena (Carter et al., 2004; Nestadt et al., 2001). Whether primary or secondary, the presence of a comorbid depressive disorder has a substantial impact on the prognosis and course of treatment of OCD, and is associated with higher rates of anxiety, poorer response to pharmacotherapy, and higher rates of disability (Shetti et al., 2005; Tukel, Meteris, Koyuncu, Tecer, & Yazici, 2006).

Bipolar disorder is also highly comorbid with OCD, although the relationship between them is more complex. Comorbidity estimates show a substantially increased risk of bipolar II disorder (11%–18%) in individuals with OCD compared to the population prevalence (1%), but somewhat less evidence for an increased risk for bipolar I disorder (1%–4%) (Hantouche et al., 2002; Nestadt et al., 2001). Conversely, the risk of OCD in individuals with BP I or II is between two and ten times greater than would be expected by chance. Family studies show no increase in risk of either disorder for relatives, however, suggesting that OCD and bipolar disorder are not genetically related (Lapalme, Hodgins, & LaRoche, 1997; Nestadt et al., 2001). Instead, given the comorbidity patterns, obsessive-compulsive symptoms may represent secondary phenomena in bipolar disorder, perhaps developing in response to manic or hypomanic symptoms, an idea that is supported by the observation that individuals with OCD plus bipolar disorder have a more episodic course of illness and generally better insight than do individuals with OCD alone or than those with OCD plus major depression (Centorrino et al., 2006; Tukel et al., 2006).

Overall rates of anxiety disorders are also elevated in individuals with OCD, with generalized anxiety disorder (GAD), panic disorder, and agoraphobia showing the most consistent patterns. Rates of panic disorder and/or agoraphobia are from two to ten times higher in individuals with OCD, while rates of GAD are from four to seven times higher (Carter et al., 2004; Denys et al., 2004; Nestadt et al., 2003). Family studies and latent class analyses show moderate evidence for an etiological relationship between OCD and GAD, and somewhat weaker evidence for a relationship between OCD and panic/agoraphobia, suggesting that OCD, panic/agoraphobia, and GAD may all be alternate expressions of an underlying susceptibility to anxiety (Carter et al., 2004).

Schizo-Obsessive Disorder

Current *DSM–IV–TR* criteria for OCD require that the individual must at some point in the illness recognize that the obsessions and compulsions are excessive and unreasonable (APA, 2000). However, the degree of insight varies widely with age (the insight requirement does not hold for children, who may not have the needed cognitive capacity to understand that their fears are not rational) and with severity of illness. Individuals who do not recognize their symptoms as excessive or unreasonable most of the time are said to have a *poor insight* form of OCD, or schizo-obsessive disorder, a concept that refers to a spectrum of disorders characterized by both obsessive-compulsive symptoms and psychotic spectrum symptoms, and basically encompasses three subgroups: OCD with schizotypal features, OCD with loss of insight or delusional symptoms, and schizophrenia with comorbid OCD (Eisen, Phillips, & Rasmussen, 1999).

The best studied of these subgroups is OCD plus schizophrenia. Although only 3%–4% of individuals with primary OCD will go on to develop schizophrenia, between 10% and 25% of individuals with schizophrenia will develop OCD or significant obsessive-compulsive symptoms (Eisen et al., 1999; Eisen & Rasmussen, 1993; Tibbo & Warneke, 1999). The presence of significant OCD symptoms in the context of schizophrenia occurs more often in males, and is associated with a more deteriorating course and a poorer long-term outcome than is seen in schizophrenia alone (Eisen

et al., 1999; Tibbo, Kroetsch, Chue, & Warneke, 2000). In OCD with schizotypal features, individuals have soft psychotic symptoms, including ideas of reference, magical thinking or odd beliefs, and prominent suspiciousness (Eisen et al., 1999; Stanley, Turner, & Borden, 1990). Between 3% and 8% of individuals with OCD have been found to meet *DSM–IV* criteria for schizotypal personality disorder and 25%–50% have subclinical schizotypal symptoms (Sobin, Blundell, & Karayiorgou, 2000; Stanley et al., 1990). Schizotypal symptoms, even if mild, are associated with an earlier age of onset of OCD symptoms and a higher number of comorbid psychiatric diagnoses, including learning disabilities (Sobin, Blundell, Weiller, Gavigan, Haiman, & Karayiorgou, 2000). The category of OCD with delusional symptoms is the hardest to assess, in part because it can be defined in a variety of ways. About 5% of individuals with OCD are clearly delusional at some point during the course of their illness, that is, they have complete conviction about the reasonableness of their obsessions (Eisen et al., 1999; Eisen & Rasmussen, 1993). Another 10%–25% have what would be considered to be OCD with poor insight; that is, they have varying degrees of certainty about the reasonableness of their obsessions or think that there may reasonably be consequences (other than anxiety) for not performing a compulsion (Eisen et al., 1999). Adults with the delusional or poor insight form of OCD are more likely to have a poor treatment response, both to pharmacotherapy and to behavior therapy, and a poor prognosis relative to OCD with good insight (Lochner & Stein, 2006). Family studies show no evidence of a genetic relationship between OCD and schizophrenia or psychosis, despite the high comorbidity rates seen between the disorders (Kendler, McGuire, Gruenberg, & Walsh, 1994; Nestadt et al., 2000). Instead, the data suggest that the syndromes with milder psychotic symptoms (i.e., delusional OCD, OCD with poor insight, and OCD with schizotypal features) represent a more severe form of OCD, while schizophrenia plus OCD represents a variant form of schizophrenia.

Personality Disorders

In addition to high comorbidity with Axis I disorders, OCD shows substantial comorbidity with personality disorders as well; between 20%–40% of individuals with OCD meet criteria for a comorbid personality disorder. All of the personality disorders have been variably reported to be elevated in OCD, but the most consistent finding is an increase in cluster C disorders (avoidant, dependent, and obsessive-compulsive personality disorders). Not unexpectedly, the overlap is highest with obsessive-compulsive personality disorder (OCPD), with up to 30% of individuals with OCD also meeting criteria for OCPD (Denys et al., 2004; Samuels et al., 2000). OCPD is also more common than would be expected by chance in family members of individuals with OCD, suggesting that they may be etiologically related (Samuels et al., 2000). Part, although not all, of this increase is probably due to an overlap in symptoms between the two disorders, most specifically, perfectionism and a reluctance to throw out useless or worn-out objects; not surprisingly, hoarding is the symptom subtype most commonly comorbid with OCPD (Samuels et al., 2002, 2000). In addition to personality disorders, the prevalence of personality traits such as neuroticism and low excitement seeking are substantially higher in individuals with OCD and their relatives, suggesting that underlying personality characteristics may predispose to the development of OCD, or share etiological features in common (Samuels et al., 2000).

Summary and Conclusions

OCD is an extremely heterogeneous disorder, with multiple frequently comorbid conditions and an enormous variety of symptom presentations. It is associated with significant functional impairment, and is a leading cause of disability worldwide. In recent years, substantial progress has been made in the attempt to further understand this complex disorder from a phenomenological perspective. Similar progress has been made in our understanding of the adaptive nature and potential evolutionary role of obsessive and compulsive traits in the general population. Somewhat less well understood are the relationships between normal adaptive obsessive-compulsive traits and OCD, the etiology of both normal and maladaptive obsessionality, and their relationships to other neuropsychiatric disorders. Work to improve our understanding of the pathogenesis of obsessionality, OCD, and related disorders is ongoing, and will eventually allow for the further refinement of the OCD phenotype, as well as leading to further advances in diagnosis and treatment of this common disorder.

References

Alsobrook, I. J., Leckman, J. F., Goodman, W. K., Rasmussen, S. A., & Pauls, D. L. (1999). Segregation analysis of obsessive-compulsive disorder using symptom-based factor scores. *American Journal of Medical Genetics, 88,* 669–675.

American Psychiatric Association. (2000). *Diagnostic and statistical manual of mental disorders* (4th ed. text revision). Washington, DC: Author.

Bienvenu, O. J., Samuels, J. F., Riddle, M. A., Hoehn-Saric, R., Liang, K. Y., Cullen, B. A., et al. (2000). The relationship of obsessive-compulsive disorder to possible spectrum disorders: Results from a family study. *Biological Psychiatry, 48,* 287–293.

Carter, A. S., Pollock, R. A., Suvak, M. K., & Pauls, D. L. (2004). Anxiety and major depression comorbidity in a family study of obsessive-compulsive disorder. *Depression and Anxiety, 20,* 165–174.

Cavallini, M. C., Di Bella, D., Siliprandi, F., Malchiodi, F., & Bellodi, L. (2002). Exploratory factor analysis of obsessive-compulsive patients and association with 5-HTTLPR polymorphism. *American Journal of Medical Genetics, 114,* 347–353.

Centorrino, F., Hennen, J., Mallya, G., Egli, S., Clark, T., & Baldessarini, R. J. (2006). Clinical outcome in patients with bipolar I disorder, obsessive compulsive disorder or both. *Human Psychopharmacology, 21,* 189–193.

Delorme, R., Bille, A., Betancur, C., Mathieu, F., Chabane, N., Mouren-Simeoni, M. C., et al. (2006). Exploratory analysis of obsessive compulsive symptom dimensions in children and adolescents: A prospective follow-up study. *BMC Psychiatry, 6,* 1.

Delorme, R., Golmard, J. L., Chabane, N., Millet, B., Krebs, M. O., Mouren-Simeoni, M. C., et al. (2005). Admixture analysis of age at onset in obsessive-compulsive disorder. *Psychological Medicine, 35,* 237–243.

Denys, D., Tenney, N., van Megen, H. J., de Geus, F., & Westenberg, H. G. (2004). Axis I and II comorbidity in a large sample of patients with obsessive-compulsive disorder. *Journal of Affective Disorders, 80,* 155–162.

Eisen, J. L., Phillips, K. A., & Rasmussen, S. A. (1999). Obsessions and delusions: The relationship between obsessive-compulsive disorder and the psychotic disorders. *Psychiatric Annals, 29,* 515–522.

Eisen, J. L., & Rasmussen, S. A. (1993). Obsessive compulsive disorder with psychotic features. *Journal of Clinical Psychiatry, 54,* 373–379.

Evans, D. W., Gray, F. L., & Leckman, J. F. (1999). The rituals, fears and phobias of young children: Insights from development, psychopathology and neurobiology. *Child Psychiatry and Human Development, 29,* 261–276.

Evans, D. W., Leckman, J. F., Carter, A., Reznick, J. S., Henshaw, D., King, R. A., et al. (1997). Ritual, habit, and perfectionism: The prevalence and development of compulsive-like behavior in normal young children. *Child Development, 68,* 58–68.

Feygin, D. L., Swain, J. E., & Leckman, J. F. (2006). The normalcy of neurosis: Evolutionary origins of obsessive-compulsive disorder and related behaviors. *Progress in Neuropsychopharmacology and Biological Psychiatry, 30,* 854–864.

Franzblau, S. H. (1997). The phenomenology of ritualized and repeated behaviors in nonclinical populations in the United States. *Cultural Diversity and Mental Health, 3,* 259–272.

Hantouche, E. G., Kochman, F., Demonfaucon, C., Barrot, I., Millet, B., Lancrenon, S., et al. (2002). Bipolar obsessive-compulsive disorder: Confirmation of results of the "ABC-OCD" survey in 2 populations of patient members versus non-members of an association. *L'Encéphale, 28,* 21–28.

Hasler, G., LaSalle-Ricci, V. H., Ronquillo, J. G., Crawley, S. A., Cochran, L. W., Kazuba, D., et al. (2005). Obsessive-compulsive disorder symptom dimensions show specific relationships to psychiatric comorbidity. *Psychiatry Research, 135,* 121–132.

Hemmings, S. M., Kinnear, C. J., Lochner, C., Niehaus, D. J., Knowles, J. A., Moolman-Smook, J. C., et al. (2004). Early-versus late-onset obsessive-compulsive disorder: Investigating genetic and clinical correlates. *Psychiatry Research, 128,* 175–182.

Hollander, E. (1997). Obsessive-compulsive disorder: The hidden epidemic. *Journal of Clinical Psychiatry, 58*(Suppl. 12), 3–6.

Hollander, E., Friedberg, J. P., Wasserman, S., Yeh, C.-C., & Iyengar, R. (2005). The case for the OCD spectrum. In J. S. Abramowitz & A. C. Houts (Eds.), *Concepts and controversies in obsessive-compulsive disorder* (pp. 95–116). New York: Springer.

Hollander, E., Kwon, J. H., Stein, D. J., Broatch, J., Rowland, C. T., & Himelein, C. A. (1996). Obsessive-compulsive and spectrum disorders: Overview and quality of life issues. *Journal of Clinical Psychiatry, 57*(Suppl. 8), 3–6.

Hong, R. Y. (2007). Worry and rumination: Differential associations with anxious and depressive symptoms and coping behavior. *Behaviour Research and Therapy, 2,* 277–290.

Husted, D. S., Shapira, N. A., & Goodman, W. K. (2006). The neurocircuitry of obsessive-compulsive disorder and disgust. *Progress in Neuropsychopharmacology and Biological Psychiatry, 30,* 389–399.

Jaisoorya, T. S., Reddy, Y. C., & Srinath, S. (2003). The relationship of obsessive-compulsive disorder to putative spectrum disorders: Results from an Indian study. *Comprehensive Psychiatry, 44,* 317–323.

Kendler, K. S., McGuire, M., Gruenberg, A. M., & Walsh, D. (1994). Clinical heterogeneity in schizophrenia and the pattern of psychopathology in relatives: Results from an epidemiologically based family study. *Acta Psychiatrica Scandinavica, 89,* 294–300.

Lapalme, M., Hodgins, S., & LaRoche, C. (1997). Children of parents with bipolar disorder: A meta-analysis of risk for mental disorders. *Canadian Journal of Psychiatry, 42,* 623–631.

Leckman, J. F., Mataix-Cols, D., & do Rosario-Campos, M. C. (2005a). Combined dimensional and categorical perspectives as an integrative approach to OCD. In J. S. Abramowitz & A. C. Houts (Eds.), *Concepts and controversies in obsessive-compulsive disorder* (pp. 43–47). New York: Springer.

Leckman, J. F., Mataix-Cols, D., & do Rosario-Campos, M. C. (2005b). Symptom dimensions in OCD: Developmental and evolutionary perspectives. In J. S. Abramowitz & A. C. Houts (Eds.), *Concepts and controversies in obsessive-compulsive disorder* (pp. 3–25). New York: Springer.

Leonard, H. L., Swedo, S. E., Lenane, M. C., Rettew, D. C., Hamburger, S. D., Bartko, J. J., et al. (1993). A 2- to 7-year follow-up study of 54 obsessive-compulsive children and adolescents. *Archives of General Psychiatry, 50,* 429–439.

Lochner, C., Hemmings, S. M., Kinnear, C. J., Niehaus, D. J., Nel, D. G., Corfield, V. A., et al. (2005). Cluster analysis of obsessive-compulsive spectrum disorders in patients with obsessive-compulsive disorder: Clinical and genetic correlates. *Comprehensive Psychiatry, 46,* 14–19.

Lochner, C., Kinnear, C. J., Hemmings, S. M., Seller, C., Niehaus, D. J., Knowles, J. A., et al. (2005). Hoarding in obsessive-compulsive disorder: Clinical and genetic correlates. *Journal of Clinical Psychiatry, 66,* 1155–1160.

Lochner, C., & Stein, D. J. (2006). Does work on obsessive-compulsive spectrum disorders contribute to understanding the heterogeneity of obsessive-compulsive disorder? *Progress in Neuropsychopharmacology and Biological Psychiatry, 30,* 353–361.

Mataix-Cols, D. (2006). Deconstructing obsessive-compulsive disorder: A multidimensional perspective. *Current Opinion in Psychiatry, 19,* 84–89.

Mataix-Cols, D., Rauch, S. L., Baer, L., Eisen, J. L., Shera, D. M., Goodman, W. K., et al. (2002). Symptom stability in adult obsessive-compulsive disorder: Data from a naturalistic two-year follow-up study. *American Journal of Psychiatry, 159,* 263–268.

Mataix-Cols, D., Rauch, S. L., Manzo, P. A., Jenike, M. A., & Baer, L. (1999). Use of factor-analyzed symptom dimensions to predict outcome with serotonin reuptake inhibitors and placebo in the treatment of obsessive-compulsive disorder. *American Journal of Psychiatry, 156,* 1409–1416.

Mataix-Cols, D., Rosario-Campos, M. C., & Leckman, J. F. (2005). A multidimensional model of obsessive-compulsive disorder. *American Journal of Psychiatry, 162,* 228–238.

Mataix-Cols, D., Wooderson, S., Lawrence, N., Brammer, M. J., Speckens, A., & Phillips, M. L. (2004). Distinct neural correlates of washing, checking, and hoarding symptom dimensions in obsessive-compulsive disorder. *Archives of General Psychiatry, 61,* 564–576.

Mathews, C. A., Greenwood, T., Wessel, J., Azzam, A., Garrido, H., Chavira, D. A., et al. (2007). Evidence for a heritable unidimensional symptom factor underlying obsessionality. *American Journal of Medical Genetics Part B: Neuropsychiatric Genetics.* Retrieved May 28, 2008, from http://www3.interscience.wiley.com/journal/11781068/abstract.

McKay, D., Abramowitz, J. S., Calamari, J. E., Kyrios, M., Radomsky, A., Sookman, D., et al. (2004). A critical evaluation of obsessive-compulsive disorder subtypes: Symptoms versus mechanisms. *Clinical Psychology Review, 24,* 283–313.

Miguel, E. C., Leckman, J. F., Rauch, S., do Rosario-Campos, M. C., Hounie, A. G., Mercadante, M. T., et al. (2005). Obsessive-compulsive disorder phenotypes: Implications for genetic studies. *Molecular Psychiatry, 10,* 258–275.

Nestadt, G., Addington, A., Samuels, J., Liang, K. Y., Bienvenu, O. J., Riddle, M., et al. (2003). The identification of OCD-related subgroups based on comorbidity. *Biological Psychiatry, 53,* 914–920.

Nestadt, G., Samuels, J., Riddle, M., Bienvenu, O. J., Liang, K. Y., LaBuda, M., et al. (2000). A family study of obsessive-compulsive disorder. *Archives of General Psychiatry, 57,* 358–363.

Nestadt, G., Samuels, J., Riddle, M. A., Liang, K. Y., Bienvenu, O. J., Hoehn-Saric, R., et al. (2001). The relationship between obsessive-compulsive disorder and anxiety and affective disorders: Results from the Johns Hopkins OCD Family Study. *Psychological Medicine, 31,* 481–487.

Phillips, K. A. (2002). The obsessive-compulsive spectrums. *Psychiatric Clinics of North America, 25,* 791–809.

Richter, M. A., Summerfeldt, L. J., Antony, M. M., & Swinson, R. P. (2003). Obsessive-compulsive spectrum conditions in obsessive-compulsive disorder and other anxiety disorders. *Depression and Anxiety, 18,* 118–127.

Rufer, M., Grothusen, A., Mass, R., Peter, H., & Hand, I. (2005). Temporal stability of symptom dimensions in adult patients with obsessive-compulsive disorder. *Journal of Affective Disorders, 88,* 99–102.

Samuels, J., Bienvenu, O. J., Riddle, M. A., Cullen, B. A., Grados, M. A., Liang, K. Y., et al. (2002). Hoarding in obsessive compulsive disorder: Results from a case-control study. *Behaviour Research and Therapy, 40,* 517–528.

Samuels, J., Nestadt, G., Bienvenu, O. J., Costa, P. T., Jr., Riddle, M. A., Liang, K. Y., et al. (2000). Personality disorders and normal personality dimensions in obsessive-compulsive disorder. *British Journal of Psychiatry, 177,* 457–462.

Shetti, C. N., Reddy, Y. C., Kandavel, T., Kashyap, K., Singisetti, S., Hiremath, A. S., et al. (2005). Clinical predictors of drug nonresponse in obsessive-compulsive disorder. *Journal of Clinical Psychiatry, 66,* 1517–1523.

Sobin, C., Blundell, M. L., & Karayiorgou, M. (2000). Phenotypic differences in early- and late-onset obsessive-compulsive disorder. *Comprehensive Psychiatry, 41,* 373–379.

Sobin, C., Blundell, M. L., Weiller, F., Gavigan, C., Haiman, C., & Karayiorgou, M. (2000). Evidence of a schizotypy subtype in OCD. *Journal of Psychiatric Research, 34,* 15–24.

Stanley, M. A., Turner, S. M., & Borden, J. W. (1990). Schizotypal features in obsessive-compulsive disorder. *Comprehensive Psychiatry, 31,* 511–518.

Stein, D. J. (2002). Obsessive-compulsive disorder. *Lancet, 360,* 397–405.

Taylor, S. (2005). Putting the Symptom Dimension Model to the test. In J. S. Abramowitz & A. C. Houts (Eds.), *Concepts and controversies in obsessive-compulsive disorder* (pp. 49–52). New York: Springer.

Tibbo, P., Kroetsch, M., Chue, P., & Warneke, L. (2000). Obsessive-compulsive disorder in schizophrenia. *Journal of Psychiatric Research, 34,* 139–146.

Tibbo, P., & Warneke, L. (1999). Obsessive-compulsive disorder in schizophrenia: Epidemiologic and biologic overlap. *Journal of Psychiatry and Neuroscience, 24,* 15–24.

Tolin, D. F., Abramowitz, J. S., Brigidi, B. D., Amir, N., Street, G. P., & Foa, E. B. (2001). Memory and memory confidence in obsessive-compulsive disorder. *Behaviour Research and Therapy, 39,* 913–927.

Tolin, D. F., Abramowitz, J. S., Brigidi, B. D., & Foa, E. B. (2003). Intolerance of uncertainty in obsessive-compulsive disorder. *Journal of Anxiety Disorders, 17,* 233–242.

Tukel, R., Meteris, H., Koyuncu, A., Tecer, A., & Yazici, O. (2006). The clinical impact of mood disorder comorbidity on obsessive-compulsive disorder. *European Archives of Psychiatry and Clinical Neuroscience, 256,* 240–245.

van Grootheest, D. S., Boomsma, D. I., Hettema, J. M., & Kendler, K. S. (2007). Heritability of obsessive-compulsive symptom dimensions. *American Journal of Medical Genetics Part B: Neuropsychiatric Genetics.* Retrieved May 28, 2008, from http://www3.interscience.wiley.com/journal/117864807/abstract.

World Health Organization. (2001). *World Health Report 2001.* Geneva: Author.

Zohar, A. H., & Felz, L. (2001). Ritualistic behavior in young children. *Journal of Abnormal Child Psychology, 29,* 121–128.

Phenomenology of Posttraumatic Stress Disorder and Acute Stress Disorder

Matthew J. Friedman

Abstract

This chapter reviews how fear-conditioning models of posttraumatic stress disorder (PTSD) have been bolstered by our growing understanding of neurocircuitry involving the amygdala, hippocampus, and prefrontal cortex. It describes the reexperiencing, avoidant/numbing, and hyperarousal symptom clusters as well as other PTSD diagnostic criteria with specific reference to *DSM–IV*'s changes in the A (A_1 and A_2) stressor criterion. Associated symptoms (e.g., danger to self or others, intolerance of ongoing stressors, capacity to acquire social support, and risk of reactivation and relapse) are briefly discussed. Longitudinal course, comorbidity, epidemiology, risk factors, and cross-cultural issues are also addressed. Other posttraumatic syndromes described include acute stress disorder, partial/subsyndromal PTSD, and complex PTSD. Finally, clinical issues in assessment are considered.

Keywords: A criterion, acute stress disorder, avoidant symptoms, clinical issues, epidemiology, flashback, hyperarousal symptoms, numbing symptoms, altered neurocircuitry, PTSD diagnostic criteria, posttraumatic syndromes, psychological models, risk factors, trauma

Introduction of posttraumatic stress disorder (PTSD) by the American Psychiatric Association in the third edition of its *Diagnostic and Statistical Manual (DSM–III)* in 1980 (American Psychiatric Association [APA], 1980) was an important milestone. By officially recognizing the deleterious impact of traumatic stress, the PTSD diagnosis provided a conceptual tool that validated the clinical phenomenology exhibited by patients who had become psychiatrically incapacitated by overwhelming, uncontrollable, and unpredictable events such as rape, war, genocide, torture, motor vehicle accidents, natural disasters, and the like.

Overview

Before describing the specific symptoms that constitute PTSD diagnostic criteria, it is important to emphasize that this is primarily a disorder of reactivity rather than of an altered baseline state as in major depressive disorder, general anxiety disorder, or obsessive-compulsive disorder. Posttraumatic stress disorder originates during exposure to a traumatic event and its psychopathology is characteristically expressed during interactions with the interpersonal or physical environment. People with PTSD are consumed by concerns about personal safety. They persistently scan the environment for dangerous stimuli. When in doubt, they are more likely to assume that a threat is present and will react accordingly. The avoidant and hyperarousal symptoms, to be described subsequently, can be understood within this context. The primacy of traumatic over other memories (e.g., the reexperiencing symptoms) can also be understood as a pathological exaggeration of the normal human response to dangerous encounters.

The sustained anxiety about potential threats to life and limb, pervasive and an uncontrollable sense of danger, and preoccupation with concerns about the personal safety of oneself and one's family can be explicated in terms of psychological models such as classic Pavlovian fear conditioning (Kolb, 1987), two-factor theory (Keane, Zimering, & Caddell, 1985), or emotional processing theory (Foa & Kozak, 1986). The traumatic (unconditioned) stimulus (the rape, assault, disaster, etc.) automatically evokes the posttraumatic (unconditioned) emotional response (fear, helplessness, and/or horror). The intensity of this emotional reaction provokes avoidant or protective behaviors that reduce the emotional impact of the stimulus. Stimuli reminiscent of such traumatic events (conditioned stimuli) (e.g., seeing someone who resembles the original assailant, confronting war zone reminders, or exposure to high winds or torrential downpours reminiscent of a hurricane, etc.) evoke similar conditioned responses manifested as fear-induced avoidant and protective behaviors.

Such psychological models can also be explicated within the context of neurocircuitry that mediates the processing of threatening or fearful stimuli. In short, traumatic stimuli activate the amygdala, which in turn produces outputs to the hippocampus, medial prefrontal cortex, locus coeruleus, thalamus, hypothalamus, and dorsal/ventral striatum (Charney, 2004; Davis & Whalen, 2001). In PTSD, the normal restraint on the amygdala exerted by the medial prefrontal cortex, especially the anterior cingulate gyrus and orbitofrontal cortex, has been severely disrupted. Such disinhibition of the amygdala creates an abnormal psychobiological state of hypervigilance in which innocuous or ambiguous stimuli are more likely to be misinterpreted as threatening. In a dangerous situation, it is adaptive to be hypervigilant. To remain so after the danger has passed is not.

Fear conditioning models help to understand many PTSD symptoms such as intrusive recollections (e.g., nightmares and psychological/physiological reactions to traumatic reminders), avoidant behaviors, or hypervigilence. Emotional numbing is another important manifestation of PTSD that does not conform to a fear-conditioning model, which is potentially even more disruptive and disturbing to the affected individual and loved ones. It may produce an insurmountable emotional barrier between the PTSD patient and his or her family. Such individuals are unable to experience loving feelings or to reciprocate those of partners and children. As a result, they isolate themselves and become emotionally inaccessible to loved ones to whom they had previously been very close. They also cut themselves off from friends. Finally, there are symptoms that jeopardize the capacity to function effectively at work such as diminished ability to concentrate, irritability, and loss of interest in work or school. In short, there is a perceived discontinuity between the pre- and posttraumatic self. People with PTSD see themselves as altered by their traumatic experience. They feel as if they have been drastically and irrevocably changed by this encounter. Others have described this discontinuity as a "broken connection" with the past (Lifton, 1967); or "shattered assumptions" about oneself and one's world (Janoff-Bulman, 1992).

Diagnostic Criteria
Trauma Defined—The A Criterion

When *trauma* was first introduced in the *DSM–III,* it was defined as a catastrophic stressor that "would evoke significant symptoms of distress in most people." Trauma was thought to be a rare and overwhelming event—"generally outside the range of usual human experience"—that differed qualitatively from "common experiences such as bereavement, chronic illness, business losses or marital conflict." Traumatic events cited in *DSM–III* included: rape, assault, torture, incarceration in a death camp, military combat, natural disasters, industrial/vehicular accidents, or exposure to war/civil/domestic violence. We have learned during the past 26 years that catastrophic events are not rare, but are experienced by 60.7% and 51.2% of American men and women, respectively (Kessler, Sonnega, Bromet, Hughes, & Nelson, 1995). In nations or regions torn by war, genocide, internal conflict, and so forth, exposure to trauma is much higher. For example, in Algeria it is 92% (de Jong et al., 2001).

The *DSM–III* defined trauma exclusively in terms of an external event that happened to an individual who was in the wrong place at the wrong time. According to this definition, anyone who had been exposed to war, rape, torture, natural disaster, and so on, had been "traumatized" (APA, 1980). This was changed in the 1994 *DSM–IV* (APA, 1994) and retained in the 2000 *DSM–IV–TR* (APA, 2000a) because most people exposed to catastrophic events do not develop PTSD. Although exposure to catastrophic stress is a necessary condition, it is not sufficient by itself to "traumatize" an individual. What also matters is the emotional response of the person exposed to such an event. If the rape or accident produced an intense emotional response (characterized in *DSM–IV* as "fear, helplessness, or horror"), the event is "traumatic." If an intense emotional response is not experienced, then the event is not considered a "traumatic event"; therefore, by *DSM* definition, the event cannot cause PTSD.

In other words, the *DSM–IV* redefined *DSM–III*'s unitary concept of trauma, a catastrophic stressor that "would evoke significant symptoms of distress in most people," into a two-component construct: A_1 (external) and A_2 (internal) diagnostic criteria.

The acceptable list of A_1 events that qualified as traumatic stressors was expanded not only to include people who had experienced or witnessed an extremely stressful experience but also people who had "been confronted" by such events. Therefore, people who had learned that a loved one had been tortured or executed by paramilitary forces but had neither been in personal danger themselves, nor had witnessed such an occurrence, now met the *DSM–IV* criterion. Expansion of the original *DSM–III* A to the *DSM–IV* A_1 criterion has been criticized for having lowered the threshold for a traumatic stressor much too much. Others have argued that what really matters is expression of the B, C, and D symptoms of PTSD and that it would make no difference if the A (A_1 and A_2) criterion was eliminated entirely (see Friedman & Karam, 2008).

The A_2 criterion has also been criticized because it has not served its anticipated gatekeeper function. The presence of A_2 does not predict the subsequent development of PTSD. Several studies suggest, however, that the presence of A_2 does predict PTSD severity and that the absence of A_2 predicts that PTSD is unlikely to develop. Despite these current concerns, it is not at all apparent that expansion of A_1 and inclusion of A_2 in the *DSM–IV* has significantly altered PTSD prevalence estimates (see Friedman & Karam, 2008). It is also not apparent that *DSM–IV*'s two-component stressor criterion has either improved our conceptual understanding of traumatic stress or improved diagnostic precision.

Reexperiencing Symptoms

These symptoms reflect the persistence of thoughts, feelings, and behaviors specifically related to the traumatic event. Such recollections are intrusive because they are not only unwanted, but are also powerful enough to negate consideration of anything else. Daytime recollections and traumatic nightmares often evoke panic, terror, dread, grief, or despair.

Consistent with conditioning models, traumatic stimuli can evoke intolerable trauma-related emotions such as fear, anger, guilt, and shame. They can also elicit physiological reactions such as racing pulse, rapid breathing, or sweating. Researchers can take advantage of this unique stimulus-driven aspect of PTSD in laboratory paradigms that measure cognitive, autonomic, muscular, and cerebral reactivity to traumatic reminders.

Sometimes when people with PTSD are exposed to traumatic stimuli they are suddenly thrust into a psychological state—the PTSD flashback—in which they relive the traumatic experience, losing all connection with the present. This acute dissociative state unfolds as an episode in which they actually behave as if they must fight for their lives, as was the case during exposure to the initial trauma. It appears that PTSD flashbacks are an expression of an extremely heightened level of arousal associated with excessive adrenergic activity since they can be evoked by yohimbine, which promotes increased presynaptic release of norepinephrine (Southwick et al., 1993).

Avoidant/Numbing Symptoms

These symptoms can be understood as behavioral, cognitive, or emotional strategies used to ward off the terror and distress caused by reexperiencing and hyperarousal symptoms.

Avoidant symptoms include efforts to avoid thoughts, feelings, activities, places, and people related to the original traumatic event as well as psychogenic amnesia for trauma-related memories.

Numbing symptoms are psychological mechanisms through which PTSD sufferers anesthetize themselves against the intolerable panic, terror, and pain evoked by reexperiencing symptoms. These include psychic numbing, in which the person suppresses all feelings in order to block out the intolerable ones. This can come at a very high price since numbing intolerable, trauma-related feelings requires also anesthetizing loving feelings necessary to sustain an intimate, loving relationship. Other numbing symptoms include diminished interest or participation in significant activities, feeling detached or estranged from others, and believing that one will not experience a normal future (e.g., lifespan, career, or marriage).

Hyperarousal Symptoms

These symptoms are the most apparent manifestations of the excessive physiologic arousal that is part of the PTSD syndrome and include insomnia, irritability, startle reactions, and hypervigilance.

Hypervigilance is the excessive preoccupation with danger and perceived vulnerability mentioned previously. Hyperarousal symptoms make up a hyperreactive psychophysiological state that makes it very difficult for people with PTSD to concentrate or perform other cognitive tasks. For example, PTSD impairs the capacity to focus on intellectual tasks at school, work, or home.

The Duration (E) Criterion

In *DSM–IV*, PTSD may be diagnosed at any time after a traumatic event, except during the first month. The rationale is that a 1-month window must be allowed before diagnosing PTSD in order to permit normal recovery to occur and to avoid pathologizing normal acute posttraumatic distress.

Sometimes the interval between trauma and positive diagnosis may be of many years' duration. This aspect of *DSM–IV* has had a significant impact in compensation claims where the claimant may not have exhibited PTSD symptoms for many years. As reviewed by Bryant and Harvey (2002), delayed onset may represent unrecognized PTSD, subsyndromal PTSD that later escalates to the full syndrome, or a true delay of syndrome onset.

Functional Impairment—the F Criterion

A major change from *DSM–III* to *DSM–IV* (affecting many Axis I diagnoses, in addition to PTSD) was the F Criterion. This is the stipulation that PTSD must cause "clinically significant distress or impairment in social, occupational or other areas of functioning."

Associated Features
Danger to Self and Others

There is evidence of a positive association between the number of previous traumatic events and the likelihood of a suicide attempt. Furthermore, PTSD is often comorbid (see below) with other conditions that are associated with suicidal behavior such as depression, substance use, panic attacks, and severe anxiety (APA, 2000b).

There are no data to suggest that PTSD, per se, is associated with harm to others. Given their preoccupation with threat and danger, however, PTSD patients may sometimes engage in (what they consider) protective behaviors that may be perceived as aggressive actions by onlookers.

Intolerance of Ongoing Stressors

Patients with PTSD often exhibit a reduced capacity to cope with the ordinary and predictable challenges of life. Such stressors include marital, familial, workplace, or social stressors. The persistence of ongoing or secondary stressors are risk factors for the persistence of PTSD (Schnurr, Lunney, & Sengupta, 2004).

Social Support

Social support is a powerful protective factor (Brewin, Andrews, & Valentine, 2000) that includes the capacity of an individual to accept or utilize social support when it is made available (Benight & Bandura, 2004). This may be especially problematic in PTSD where symptoms such as avoidance, alienation, and detachment impair affected individuals from benefiting from available marital, family, and social support.

Risk of Reactivation and Relapse

Given the fact that PTSD patients are extremely sensitive to stimuli or situations associated with the original traumatic event, exposure to such traumatic reminders may have a profound and instantaneous impact on clinical course. Among patients with active PTSD, exposure to such cues may produce a significant exacerbation of their symptoms. Among patients who have achieved clinical remission, such exposure may precipitate a clinical relapse.

As a result, the longitudinal course of PTSD may exhibit different trajectories in different individuals. As noted earlier, the onset of PTSD may occur as early as 1 month after traumatic exposure or be delayed as much as 20 years later. The course may also fluctuate, as in other chronic medical and psychiatric disorders, with a series of remissions interspersed between relapses. Close inspection of such fluctuations often indicates that they can be understood as a result of shifting conditions with respect to ongoing stressors, reexposure to traumatic reminders, and the degree of social support.

Comorbidity

The National Comorbidity Study indicates that 80% of individuals with PTSD will meet criteria for at least one other psychiatric disorder (Kessler et al., 1995). The most common coexisting disorders with PTSD include major depressive disorder (48%), dysthymic disorder (22%), specific phobia (30%), social phobia (28%), panic disorder (7%/13%; men/women), generalized anxiety disorder (16%), alcohol abuse/dependence (28%/52%; women/men), and other drug abuse/dependence (27%/35%; women/men).

One reason for so much comorbidity is the overlap in symptoms that characterize different psychiatric disorders. For example, PTSD shares symptoms of autonomic arousal with panic disorder and GAD, and impaired concentration and insomnia with GAD and depression. It has been suggested previously that extensive comorbidity is an artifact of a diagnostic system that relies entirely on phenomenology.

Cross-Cultural Factors

The PTSD diagnosis has been criticized as a Euro-American construct that has little relevance to posttraumatic syndromes encountered in traditional societies (Summerfield, 2004). For example, two cardinal symptoms of posttraumatic reactions in traditional societies, somatization and dissociation (Kirmayer, 1996), are missing from *DSM–IV* diagnostic criteria for PTSD. Acknowledging that there may be culture-specific idioms of distress that provide a better characterization of chronic posttraumatic distress syndromes found in some ethnocultural contexts (Marsella, Friedman, Gerrity, & Scurfield, 1996), PTSD has been documented throughout the world (Green et al., 2003), including non-Western nations subjected to war or internal conflict (de Jong et al., 2001). A recent comparison between Kenyan survivors of the bombing of the American embassy in Nairobi with American survivors of the bombing of the Federal Building in Oklahoma City indicated similar PTSD prevalence among Africans and Americans exposed to each traumatic event, respectively (North et al., 2005).

Acute Stress Disorder

Most people exposed to a traumatic event will exhibit a transient acute stress reaction that may be briefly incapacitating, at most. It generally consists of *emotional reactions* (e.g., shock, fear, grief, anger, guilt, shame, numbing, etc.); *cognitive reactions* (e.g., confusion, disorientation, difficulty concentrating, self-blame, unwanted memories, etc.); *physical reactions* (tension, fatigue, insomnia, hyperarousal, insomnia, etc.); and *interpersonal reactions* (distrust, irritability, withdrawal, alienation, etc.). A significant minority of people will not recover from this transient reaction and will develop high magnitude and clinically significant distress within the first month following traumatic exposure. This has been defined as acute stress disorder (ASD) by the *DSM–IV*.

The symptoms of PTSD and ASD are similar in terms of reexperiencing, avoidant, and hyperarousal symptoms, except that only one symptom from each cluster is needed for the diagnosis. The PTSD numbing symptoms are subsumed under ASD dissociative symptoms.

The major difference between ASD and PTSD is the greater emphasis placed on symptoms of dissociation. To meet ASD diagnostic criteria, an acutely traumatized individual must exhibit three (out of five) dissociative symptoms, while it is possible to diagnose PTSD with none. ASD dissociative symptoms include reduction in awareness, derealization, depersonalization, psychic numbing, and traumatic amnesia. Empirical justification for including dissociative symptoms as a major diagnostic criterion for ASD is sparse.

Approximately 70%–80% of people with ASD develop PTSD. However, since so many people who develop PTSD never exhibit ASD (Bryant & Harvey, 1998), the utility of this diagnosis has been called into question.

Other Posttraumatic Syndromes
Partial/Subsyndromal PTSD

In recent years, more than 50 publications have reported on the prevalence or morbidity of "partial" or "subsyndromal" PTSD. Findings from either population surveys or clinical samples have identified cohorts of individuals who had been exposed to an extremely stressful event, failed to meet full PTSD criteria, exhibited a number of B, C, and D symptoms, met the F criterion for functional impairment, and exhibited clinically significant symptoms. Generally the partial PTSD cohort has exhibited less symptom severity and functional impairment than the full PTSD group, but more symptom severity than a comparison group that met neither full nor partial PTSD diagnostic criteria. It should be noted that there is some difficulty interpreting this literature since partial/subsyndromal PTSD has been defined differently by different investigators. Furthermore, it may be important to distinguish between individuals who previously met full PTSD criteria and are now in partial remission from those who have never met full diagnostic criteria (see Friedman & Karam, 2008, for references).

Complex PTSD and Disorders of Extreme Stress Not Otherwise Specified (DESNOS)

Many clinicians who have worked with individuals exposed to severe and protracted traumatic exposure (most notably, childhood sexual abuse and torture within the context of political incarceration) maintain that *DSM–IV* PTSD criteria fail to characterize the most significant symptoms among such individuals. They argue that the most significant clinical sequelae include *behavioral difficulties* (such as impulsivity, aggression, sexual acting out, alcohol/drug misuse, and self-destructive actions); *emotional difficulties* (such as affective lability, rage, depression, and panic); *cognitive difficulties* (such as dissociation, amnesia, and pathological changes in personal identity—dissociative identity disorder); *interpersonal difficulties;* and *somatization* (Herman, 1992).

The *DSM–IV* did not include Complex PTSD/DESNOS because results from the *DSM–IV* Field Trials indicated that 92% of individuals with Complex PTSD/DESNOS also met criteria for PTSD. Under the circumstances, it was decided that there was little scientific support for this new diagnosis and that it would be superfluous to include it as a separate nosological category (Kilpatrick, D. G. et al. 1998).

Other Post- (Traumatic/Nontraumatic) Stress Syndromes

It is noteworthy that in medicine the major emphasis is on "stress" per se, rather than "traumatic stress." Indeed, there is a rich literature dating back to the seminal work of Selye (1946), showing how chronic stress might produce medical illness. This is embodied in the concept of "allostatic load" (McEwen, 1998), which has more recently been applied to PTSD (Friedman & McEwen, 2004). Such a theoretical orientation integrates a wealth of scientific evidence showing that prevalence of medical illness is greater among people with PTSD than among those without the disorder (Schnurr & Green, 2004).

Epidemiology

A consistent finding in all research on PTSD is a dose response relationship between the severity of exposure to trauma and the onset of PTSD. Therefore, in the United States, where lifetime trauma exposure is 50%–60%, PTSD prevalence is 7.8%, whereas in Algeria where trauma exposure is 92%, PTSD prevalence is 37.4% (de Jong et al., 2001; Kessler et al., 1995). This dose-response association has held up whether the traumatic experience has been sexual assault, war-zone exposure, a natural disaster, or terrorist attack (Galea et al., 2002; Kessler et al., 1995; Norris et al., 2002a; Norris, Friedman, & Watson, 2002b). It is important to recognize, however, that traumatic events differ in their capacity to precipitate PTSD. For example, in the United

States, the toxicity of interpersonal violence, as in rape, is much higher than that of accidents; whereas 45.9% female rape victims are likely to develop PTSD, only 8.8% female accident survivors will develop the disorder (Kessler et al., 1995). In developing nations, however, natural disasters are much more likely to produce PTSD because of the magnitude of resource loss associated with such exposure (Norris et al., 2002a, 2002b). Furthermore, direct exposure to a life-threatening event is more toxic than "being confronted with" or informed about a traumatic event, as in the A_1 criterion of *DSM–IV*.

Risk Factors

Some people are more vulnerable and others more resistant to developing PTSD after exposure to a traumatic event. Indeed, most people are resilient and do not develop persistent PTSD. Even among female victims of rape, 54.1% will not exhibit full PTSD after 3 months, whereas 91.2% female accident survivors never develop PTSD (Riggs, Rothbaum, & Foa, 1995; Rothbaum, Foa, Riggs, Murdock, & Walsh, 1992). Research on risk factors generally divides them into pretraumatic, peritraumatic, and posttraumatic factors. *Pretraumatic* factors include age, gender, previous trauma history, personal or family psychiatric history, educational level, and the like. Such pretraumatic factors have relatively low power to predict the likelihood of PTSD onset following traumatic exposure (Brewin et al., 2000).

Peritraumatic risk factors concern the nature of the traumatic experience itself as well as one's reaction to it. The dose-response relationship between trauma exposure and PTSD onset, mentioned previously, applies here so that the severity of traumatic exposure predicts the likelihood of PTSD symptoms. Other peritraumatic risk factors include exposure to atrocities, peritraumatic dissociation, panic attacks, and other emotions (Vogt, King, & King, 2007).

The major posttraumatic factor is whether the traumatized person received social support (Brewin et al., 2000). Indeed, social support appears to be the most important risk factor of all, receipt of which can protect trauma-exposed individuals from developing PTSD.

Another posttraumatic risk factor, related more to the persistence rather than the onset of PTSD, is ongoing lifetime stressors. As mentioned previously, recovery from PTSD is less likely when there is a lack of emotional sustenance or social support and recent exposure to adverse life events (Schnurr et al., 2004).

Clinical Issues

It is essential that the clinician conduct diagnostic and therapeutic interviews in a manner that acknowledges the patient's worst fears and that provides an environment of sensitivity, safety, and trust. Clinicians should always be mindful that they are asking the PTSD patient to take a tremendous risk and abandon all the avoidance behaviors, protective strategies, and other psychological strategies that have developed to buffer them from the intolerable memories and feelings associated with the traumatic event. In the case of chronic PTSD, where such protective layers have solidified for years or decades, the clinician must be patient and obtain the trauma history at a pace that the patient can tolerate. It is usually helpful for clinicians to let the patient know that they understand how difficult it must be to revisit emotionally charged traumatic material. It is also helpful for clinicians to instruct the patient to indicate when the interview has become too upsetting. At such times, clinicians should back off immediately and stop discussing traumatic material. By exhibiting clinical behavior that communicates patience, sensitivity, and competence, it is usually possible to work effectively with the most anxious, avoidant, and hypervigilant patient.

References

American Psychiatric Association. (1980). *Diagnostic and statistical manual of mental disorders* (3rd ed.). Washington, DC: Author.

American Psychiatric Association. (1994). *Diagnostic and statistical manual of mental disorders* (4th ed.). Washington, DC: Author.

American Psychiatric Association. (2000a). *Diagnostic and statistical manual of mental disorders* (4th ed. revised). Washington, DC: Author.

American Psychiatric Association. (2000b). Practice guidelines for the treatment of acute stress and posttraumatic stress disorder. *American Journal of Psychiatry, 161,* 1–31.

Benight, C., & Bandura, A. (2004). Social cognitive theory of posttraumatic recovery: The role of perceived self-efficacy. *Behavior Research and Therapy, 42,* 1129–1148.

Brewin, C. R., Andrews, B., & Valentine, J. D. (2000). Meta-analysis of risk factors for posttraumatic stress disorder in trauma-exposed adults. *Journal of Consulting and Clinical Psychology, 68,* 748–766.

Bryant, R. A., & Harvey, A. G. (1998). Relationship between acute stress disorder and posttraumatic stress disorder following mild traumatic brain injury. *American Journal of Psychiatry, 155,* 625–629.

Bryant, R. A., & Harvey, A. G. (2002). Delayed-onset posttraumatic stress disorder: A prospective evaluation. *Australian and New Zealand Journal of Psychiatry, 36,* 205–209.

Charney, D. S. (2004). Psychobiological mechanisms of resilience and vulnerability: Implications for the successful adaptation to extreme stress. *American Journal of Psychiatry, 161,* 195–216.

Davis, M., & Whalen, P. J. (2001). The amygdala: Vigilance and emotion. *Molecular Psychiatry, 1,* 13–34.

De Jong, J.T.V., Komproe, I. H., Van Ommeren, M., El Masri, M., Mesfin, A., Khaled, N., et al. (2001). Lifetime events and posttraumatic stress disorder in 4 postconflict settings. *Journal of the American Medical Association, 286,* 555–562.

Foa, E. B., & Kozak, M. J. (1986). Emotional processing of fear: Exposure to corrective information. *Psychological Bulletin, 99,* 20–35.

Friedman, M. J., & Karam, E. G. (2008). PTSD: Looking toward *DSM–V* and *ICD–11.* In G. Andrews, D. Charney, P. Sirovatka, & D. Regier (Eds.), *Stress-induced fear circuitry disorders: Refining the research agenda for DSM–V* (pp. 3–32). Washington, DC: American Psychiatric Association.

Friedman, M. J., & McEwen, B. S. (2004). PTSD, allostatic load, and medical illness. In P. P. Schnurr & B. L. Green (Eds.), *Trauma and health: Physical health consequences of exposure to extreme stress* (pp. 157–188). Washington, DC: American Psychological Association.

Galea, S., Ahern, J., Resnick, H. S., Kilpatrick, D. G., Bucuvalas, M. J., Gold, J., et al. (2002). Psychological sequelae of the September 11 terrorist attacks in New York City. *New England Journal of Medicine, 346,* 982–987.

Green, B. L., Friedman, M. J., de Jong. J., Solomon, S. D., Keane, T. M., Fairbank, J. A., et al. (Eds.). (2003). *Trauma interventions in war and peace: Prevention, practice, and policy.* Amsterdam: Kluwer Academic/Plenum.

Herman, J. L. (1992). Complex PTSD: A syndrome in survivors of prolonged and repeated trauma. *Journal of Traumatic Stress, 5,* 377–391.

Janoff-Bulman, R. (Ed.). (1992). *Shattered assumptions: Towards a new psychology of trauma.* New York: Free Press.

Keane, T. M., Zimering, R. T., & Caddell, J. M. (1985). A behavioral formulation of posttraumatic stress disorder in Vietnam veterans. *Behavior Therapist, 8,* 9–12.

Kessler, R. C., Sonnega, A., Bromet, E., Hughes, M., & Nelson, C. B. (1995). Posttraumatic stress disorder in the National Comorbidity Survey. *Archives of General Psychiatry, 52,* 1048–1060.

Kilpatrick, D. G., Resick, H. S., Freedy, J. R., Pelcovitz, D., Resick, P. A., Roth, S., et al. (1998). Posttraumatic stress disorder field trial: Evaluation of the PTSD construct—criteria A through E. In T. A. Widiger, A. J. Frances, H. A. Pincus, et al. (Eds.). *DSM–IV sourcebook* (pp. 803–838). Washington, DC: American Psychiatric Association.

Kirmayer, L. J. (1996). Confusion of the senses: Implications of ethnocultural variations in somatoform and dissociative disorders for PTSD. In A. J. Marsella, M. J. Friedman, E. T. Gerrity, & R. M. Scurfield (Eds.), *Ethnocultural aspects of post-traumatic stress disorder: Issues, research, and clinical applications* (pp. 131–163). Washington, DC: American Psychological Association.

Kolb, L. C. (1987). A neuropsychological hypothesis explaining posttraumatic stress disorders. *American Journal of Psychiatry, 144,* 989–995.

Lifton, R. J. (Ed.). (1967). *Death in life: Survivors of Hiroshima.* New York: Random House.

Marsella, A. J., Friedman, M. J., Gerrity, E. T., & Scurfield, R. M. (Eds.). (1996). *Ethnocultural aspects of post-traumatic stress disorder: Issues, research, and clinical applications.* Washington, DC: American Psychological Association.

McEwen, B. S. (1998). Protective and damaging effects of stress mediators. *New England Journal of Medicine, 338,* 171–179.

Norris, F. H., Friedman, M. J., Watson, P. J., Byrne, C. M., Diaz, E., & Kaniasty, K. Z. (2002a). 60,000 disaster victims speak, part I: An empirical review of the empirical literature, 1981–2001. *Psychiatry, 65,* 207–239.

Norris, F. H., Friedman, M. J., & Watson, P. J. (2002b). 60,000 disaster victims speak, part II: Summary and implications of the disaster mental health research. *Psychiatry, 65,* 240–260.

North, C. S., Pfefferbaum, B., Narayanan, P., Thielman, S. B., McCoy, G., Dumont, C. E., et al. (2005). Comparison of post-disaster psychiatric disorders after terrorist bombings in Nairobi and Oklahoma City. *British Journal of Psychiatry, 186,* 487–493.

Riggs, D. S., Rothbaum, B. O., & Foa, E. B. (1995). A prospective examination of symptoms of posttraumatic stress disorder in victims of nonsexual assault. *Journal of Interpersonal Violence, 10,* 201–214.

Rothbaum, B. O., Foa, E. B., Riggs, D. S., Murdock, T. B., & Walsh, W. (1992). A prospective examination of posttraumatic stress disorder in rape victims. *Journal of Traumatic Stress, 5,* 455–475.

Schnurr, P. P., & Green, B. L. (Eds.). (2004). *Trauma and health: Physical health consequences of exposure to extreme stress.* Washington, DC: American Psychological Association.

Schnurr, P. P., Lunney, C. A., & Sengupta, A. (2004). Risk factors for the development versus maintenance of post-traumatic stress disorder. *Journal of Traumatic Stress, 17,* 85–95.

Selye, H. (1946). The general adaptation syndrome and the diseases of adaptation. *Journal of Clinical Endocrinology, 6,* 117–230.

Southwick, S. M., Krystal, J. H., Morgan, A. C., Johnson, D. R., Nagy, L. M., Nicolaou, A. L., et al. (1993). Abnormal noradrenergic function in post-traumatic stress disorder. *Archives of General Psychiatry, 50,* 266–274.

Summerfield, D. A. (2004). Cross-cultural perspectives on the medicalization of human suffering. In G. M. Rosen (Ed.), *Posttraumatic stress disorder: Issues and controversies* (pp. 233–245). Chichester, England: Wiley.

Vogt, D. S., King, D. W., & King, L. A. (2007). Risk pathways for PTSD: Making sense of the literature. In M. J. Friedman, T. M. Keane, & P. A. Resick (Eds.), *PTSD: Science and practice: A comprehensive handbook* (pp. 99–115). New York: Guilford Press.

Approaches to Understanding Anxiety Disorders

Preclinical Approaches to Understanding Anxiety Disorders

Victoria B. Risbrough *and* Mark A. Geyer

Abstract

This chapter reviews rodent tests most commonly used to screen experimental manipulations (e.g., pharmacological, genetic mutation) on murine anxiety-like behavior, and highlight recent strategies for examining basic systems related to anxiety and stress (e.g., glyoxalase 1, corticotropin releasing factor, serotonin, and stathmin). The animal models described in this chapter (e.g., fear-potentiated startle, conditioned fear, and approach/avoidance conflict tests) have been instrumental to examine the physiological underpinnings of state anxiety and fear, develop anxiolytic compounds, and, more recently, to understand genetic and environmental influences on "trait" anxiety.

Keywords: animal model, anxiety, fear, mutation, stress, startle

This chapter will focus on briefly describing the tests most commonly used to screen experimental (e.g., pharmacological, genetic) manipulations on murine anxiety-like behavior, and highlight some of the recent findings of genetic effects on anxiety-like and stress-related behaviors in rodents. The animal models described in this chapter have been instrumental to: (1) examine the physiological underpinnings of state anxiety and fear; (2) develop anxiolytic compounds; and (3) more recently, understand genetic and environmental influences on "trait" anxiety (e.g., Levine, 2005).

Validity of Animal Models of Anxiety

As discussed extensively in Geyer and Markou (2002), assessing animal models typically involves consideration of three types of validity: face, predictive, and construct. Face validity involves the phenomenological similarity between the behavior exhibited by the animal model and the specific symptoms of the human condition (Mosier, 1947). Although face validity is an intuitively appealing cri-

terion and contributes to hypothesis generation, it is not scientifically necessary, is often misleading, and almost invariably involves subjective arbitrary arguments that are not accepted by all investigators in the field. Predictive validity assesses the ability of a model to make correct predictions about the human phenomenon of interest. In psychopharmacology, the term is often used in the narrow sense of making predictions about the therapeutic value of a drug in humans (i.e., pharmacological isomorphism, Matthysse, 1986). Predictive validity, however, can also be demonstrated by evidence that manipulations have similar influences in both the experimental preparation and the modeled phenomenon (Segal & Geyer, 1985). Construct validity of a model is defined as the accuracy with which the test measures what it is intended to measure. The construct need not have anything to do with the presumed etiology of an illness. The process of construct validation of a model is not different in any essential way from the general scientific procedure for developing and testing theories (Cronbach & Meehl, 1955). Because theoretical constructs of a disease are constantly being refined, construct validation can never be the only type of validity met. Nevertheless, the process of construct validation is valuable in the never-ending process of further development and refinement of the model.

Common Rodent Dependent Measures of Anxiety-Like Behavior

This section will help readers unfamiliar with preclinical models of anxiety by providing a brief overview of the most common dependent measures of anxiety-like behavior in rodents and those described in probing systems involved in anxiety. The goal is to highlight the uses of each model and its most common confounds, with specific references given for more detailed and in-depth reviews of each measure.

Avoidance/Locomotor Behavior

The most commonly used animal models of anxiety-like behavior are the elevated plus maze, open field, and light dark box (Cryan & Holmes, 2005). These ethological models measure the conflict between a rodent's innate tendency to avoid novel, open, and/or lit spaces versus the tendency to explore its environment (Montgomery, 1958). All measures are thus based on a ratio of exploration versus avoidance, with avoidance of the brightly lit and open areas of the apparatus being used as an operational measure of anxiety-like behavior. Anxiolytic drugs act in these models by causing the rodent to explore regions or objects that are normally avoided, while anxiogenic drugs reduce exploration even further than control levels (Pellow, Chopin, File, & Briley, 1985). The advantage of these models is that they are sensitive to a wide range of anxiety-modulating compounds, are fairly quick and easy to use (no training is required, they are usually 5–10 minutes and can be automated), and are supported by an extensive pharmacological and empirical literature (e.g., Belzung, 2001). They are also mostly independent of learning and memory, which is a potential confound for fear-conditioning models. The disadvantage of these models is the potential for false positives due to nonspecific effects on general locomotor activity or on novelty seeking. Others have also argued that they may only probe anxiety systems that are sensitive to benzodiazepines, hampering their use to probe non-GABAergic systems (Belzung, 2001; Rodgers, 1997).

Freezing

Another species-specific operational measure of anxiety-like behavior is freezing. Freezing behavior is a very specific posture that the rodent adopts in a threatening environment (e.g., after foot shock, in brightly lit open areas, or in the presence of predator odors) (Blanchard, Yudko, Rodgers, & Blanchard, 1993; Conti, Maciver, Ferkany, & Abreu, 1990). It is characterized by an open stance and a complete cessation of movement, and presumably aids in reducing detection by predators. Freezing is presumed to be a more specific fear behavior than avoidance; however, it can also be confounded by alterations in locomotor activity. Additionally, there have been some arguments that reduction of freezing does not immediately indicate less "anxiety" but could also be due to increases in other competing anxiety behaviors (e.g., attempting to escape). Reductions in freezing may also be more due to a diminution in the ability of the animal to perform the behavior, which some have argued occurs with hippocampal lesions, than to a reduction in "anxiety" per se (Gewirtz, McNish, & Davis, 2000). Like avoidance behaviors, freezing behavior is species-specific, and thus does not have explicit face validity. Measures of degree of freezing in the presence of cues previously conditioned to fear-invoking stimuli (e.g., foot shock, conditioned fear) is one of the most commonly used models of fear and has been instrumental in our understanding of fear circuitry (LeDoux, 2000).

Defensive Startle

The startle response is a cross-species phenomenon that consists of a series of involuntary reflexes elicited by a sudden, intense auditory or tactile stimulus. The startle reflex is argued to be a defensive behavior evolved to protect the body from impact during attack, or perhaps to facilitate flight (Yeomans, Li, Scott, & Frankland, 2002). It is a highly conserved behavior across mammalian species and is well suited to translational studies of pathology across animals and humans (Braff & Geyer, 1990). Responses to tactile (e.g., an airpuff to the throat) or acoustic stimuli are recorded in animals as a whole body "flinch response" (in humans, startle is measured as the strength of the eyeblink response using EMG electrodes at the orbicularis oculi muscles). Cortical and limbic brain regions, many of which are functionally or structurally abnormal in anxiety disorders (as measured by fMRI or PET, e.g., Gilbertson et al., 2002; Hull, 2002; Lorberbaum et al., 2004; Neumeister et al., 2004; Schneider et al., 1999), modulate startle responses (Davis, 1998b; Funayama, Grillon, Davis, & Phelps, 2001; Kumari et al., 2003; Swerdlow, Geyer, & Braff, 2001; Weike et al., 2005). The magnitude of the response is modulated by environmental stimuli. Fear-inducing stimuli increase startle (Brown, Kalish, & Farber, 1951; Davis, Walker, & Lee, 1997), while threat-reducing stimuli or appetitive stimuli (Lang, Bradley, & Cuthbert, 1990) sometimes reduce the startle response. Startle reflex measures have been argued to be valuable translational tools for anxiety research. First, unlike other rodent tests of anxiety that depend on responses to novel stimuli or environments, startle behavior remains relatively stable across repeated testing sessions in mice, rats, healthy humans, and clinically stable psychiatric patients, enabling longitudinal designs to explore the mechanisms underlying recovery from stressor manipulations (Braff, Geyer, & Swerdlow, 2001; Cadenhead, Carasso, Swerdlow, Geyer, & Braff, 1999; Risbrough, Hauger, Pelleymounter, & Geyer, 2003). Assessing behavioral recovery may be a particularly important aspect in developing animal models of posttraumatic stress disorder (Cohen & Zohar, 2004; Rothbaum & Davis, 2003; Shalev et al., 2000). Second, startle plasticity measures are not as confounded by differences in locomotor activity, as are avoidance and freezing (Davis, Cassella, Wrean, & Kehne, 1986). Third, startle behavior paradigms involve fairly rapid tests that involve highly controlled, simple stimuli, increasing their ease of use and their reproducibility in both preclinical and clinical settings. Fourth, one of the translational values of studying the startle response is that the neuroanatomical and neurochemical substrates mediating and modulating startle plasticity are relatively well defined in animals and increasingly so in humans, allowing greater hypothesis generation and interpretability before and after obtaining results (Braff et al., 2001; Geyer, Krebs-Thomson, Braff, & Swerdlow, 2001; Swerdlow et al., 2001).

Startle plasticity, however, is not a selective probe for anxiety systems. For example, a number of drugs that have no effect on anxiety in humans can reduce (Abduljawad, Langley, Bradshaw, & Szabadi, 2001) or increase (Walker & Davis, 2002a) startle reactivity, possibly via sedation or changes in muscle tone of the subject. Hence changes in startle reactivity can rarely be used alone to interpret anxiety or fear states in humans or animals. To increase specificity to anxiety systems, startle is usually assessed in experimental contexts in which startle reactivity is increased via presentation of anxiety- or fear-producing stimuli (i.e., fear-potentiated startle; for preclinical and clinical reviews, see Davis, 1998a and Grillon & Baas, 2003).

Autonomic Responses to Stressors

Physiological measures of fear that have face and predictive validity for similar measures in humans that are linked to anxiety and stress responses are being used in rodents, such as heart rate changes (Tovote et al., 2005), stress-induced changes in body temperature (Zethof, van der Heyden, Tolboom, & Olivier, 1995), and stress-induced effects on neuroendocrine responses such as corticosterone and adrenocorticotropin release. These reliable physiological measures can provide additional confirmation of experimental manipulations on anxiety-related behavior and are sometimes more sensitive probes of anxiety or stress responses than behavioral analyses (Groenink et al., 2003).

Learned Fear

The fear-potentiated startle (FPS) model of conditioned fear (Brown et al., 1951; Davis, 1979) and the conditioned freezing model have been used extensively to study the chemical and anatomical substrates involved in formation of associations between aversive stimuli and environmental cues (Davis, 1998b; LeDoux, 2000; Walker & Davis, 2002b). Fear-potentiated startle and conditioned fear are based on classical conditioning engendered by the pairing of a neutral cue (conditioned stimulus—CS) with a noxious stimulus such as electrical foot shock (unconditioned stimulus—US). After sufficient pairing trials, the presentation of the cue alone elicits a fear- or anxious-like state in the subject (conditioned response) without presentation of the US. In FPS, the conditioned fear response is measured operationally by quantifying the reflex response elicited by startling stimuli, with increased startle response magnitudes being observed in the presence of the cue (CS), relative to the absence of the cue. In conditioned freezing, the operational measure of fear is the amount of freezing in the presence of the cue compared to when the cue is not present. Both conditioned fear and FPS are mediated extensively by the amygdala in rodents, a brain region also known to be active during fear learning in humans (Davis, 1993; Groenink, Joordens, Hijzen, Dirks, & Olivier, 2000; Heldt, Sundin, Willott, & Falls, 2000; LaBar, Gatenby, Gore, LeDoux, & Phelps, 1998; Pare, Quirk, & LeDoux, 2004; Phelps et al., 2001). These models have been used extensively to explore the substrates required for acquisition, expression and extinction[1] of fear behaviors, many of which are hypothesized to be altered in anxiety disorder populations (Grillon & Baas, 2003; Lissek et al., 2005; Rothbaum & Davis, 2003).

Examples of Systems Implicated in Modulating Anxiety-Like Behavior

This section will illustrate two of the more well-studied systems involved in anxiety in both humans and rodents as well as newer peptides that alter cell plasticity and cell viability and have also been implicated in anxiety-like behaviors preclinically.

5-HT1A Receptor

The role of the serotonin (5-HT) 1A receptor in anxiety and fear has been studied extensively using both pharmacological and more recently knockout (KO) mouse techniques (for review, see Gross, Santarelli, Brunner, Zhuang, & Hen, 2000; for review, see Millan, 2003; Toth, 2003). Both receptor activation and loss of function studies support an inhibitory role of the 5-HT_{1A} receptor in anxiety and fear responding. For example, 5-HT_{1A} receptor agonists are effective in reducing anxiety in clinical populations (e.g., Davidson, DuPont, Hedges, & Haskins, 1999; Feighner & Boyer, 1989). Conversely, low levels of 5-HT_{1A} receptor binding are correlated with high anxiety in both control (Tauscher et al., 2001) and panic disorder patients (Neumeister et al., 2004). In animals, 5-HT_{1A} receptor activation via selective agonists has been shown to block innate or unlearned anxiety or fear responses (Millan, 2003; Toth, 2003). Animals with reduced 5-HT_{1A} receptor function due to chronic stress (Daniels, Pietersen, Carstens, Daya, & Stein, 2000) or genetic factors (Overstreet et al., 2003; Stork et al., 1999) also exhibit greater anxiety-like behaviors. Mice with a constitutive loss of function of the 5-HT_{1A} receptor exhibit anxiety-like behavior in conflict tests (e.g., open field and elevated plus maze, Heisler et al., 1998; Parks, Robinson, Sibille, Shenk, & Toth, 1998; Ramboz et al., 1998), increased autonomic responses to novelty (Pattij et al., 2002), and increased freezing after foot shock (Gross et al., 2000). Taken together, these findings support a tonic inhibitory role of the 5-HT_{1A} receptor on unconditioned anxiety.

There is also pharmacological evidence that the 5-HT_{1A} receptor may be involved in conditioned fear behaviors and aversive learning (Bertrand, Lehmann, Lazarus, Jeltsch, & Cassel, 2000; Micheau & van Marrewijk, 1999; Misane, Johansson, & Ogren, 1998; Misane & Ogren, 2000; Stiedl, Misane, Spiess, & Ogren, 2000). Although predominantly expressed as an autoreceptor on the cell bodies of serotonergic neurons, the 5-HT_{1A} receptor also acts as a postsynaptic receptor at regions important for cognitive function such as the neocortex, hippocampus, septum, and amygdaloid complex (for review, see Lanfumey & Hamon, 2000). Physiological studies support a potential role of 5-HT_{1A} receptors in fear learning specifically, as they reduce neuronal discharge rate and inhibit glutamate release in the amygdala, a neuroanatomical substrate for fear learning (Cheng, Wang, & Gean, 1998; Lin et al., 2001a; Stein, Davidowa, & Albrecht, 2000; Walker & Davis, 2002b). In conditioned fear tasks, infusion of selective 5-HT_{1A} agonists into the hippocampus interferes with acquisition and early consolidation of context-dependent fear conditioning (Stiedl et al., 2000), while infusion into the amygdala decreases the expression of cue-dependent fear conditioning (Groenink et al., 2000) and learned avoidance (Liang, 1999; Zangrossi, Viana, & Graeff, 1999).

In humans, a number of studies have revealed inverse correlations between anxiety traits and brain 5-HT_{1A} receptor binding (for review, see Lesch, Zeng, Reif, & Gutknecht, 2003; Neumeister et al., 2004; Tauscher et al., 2001), and associations between affective disorders and polymorphisms in genes that affect serotonergic tone (Frodl et al., 2004; Lemonde et al., 2003; Lesch et al., 2003). Targeted genetic mutation and specific breeding strategies in animals have further supported the role of 5-HT in the development of normal emotional systems (for review, see Gingrich, Ansorge, Merker, Weisstaub, & Zhou, 2003; Overstreet et al., 2003; Toth, 2003). For example, mice with either a deletion in the gene for the 5-HT transporter or the 5-HT_{1A} receptor exhibit increased anxiety-like responses in a number of behavioral models (for review, see Overstreet et al., 2003). The 5-HT_{1A} receptor expression also appears to be critical for development of anxiety behaviors, with reduced forebrain expression during postnatal development resulting in increased anxiety-like behavior (Gross et al., 2002). Although these gene deletion models are probably not perfect reflections of most genetic pathology in affective disorders (i.e., they involve total loss of gene function in both alleles), these models do have strong heuristic value in quantifying the relative importance of these genes in development of normal anxiety and fear systems.

Corticotropin Releasing Factor (CRF)

Over 20 years of animal research has indicated a role for Corticotropin Releasing Factor (CRF, or Corticotropin releasing hormone, CRH), a 41 amino acid peptide, in anxiety responses. In response to stress, CRF is released from the median eminence of the hypothalamus, where it subsequently binds to receptors at the anterior pituitary and increases ACTH release into the bloodstream. This ACTH consequently acts at the adrenal cortex to facilitate release of glucocorticoids such as cortisol. This system, known as the hypothalamic pituitary adrenal axis (HPA), is activated as an important component of the response to stress, and has been shown to be dysregulated in both anxiety and depressive disorders. Corticotropin releasing factor dysregulation may also be implicated in anxiety disorders, although more research in this area is needed (Risbrough & Stein, 2006). Corticotropin releasing factor receptors are required for this important stress response (Bale et al., 2002), which modifies peripheral physiological responses to support "fight or flight" reactions, such as mobilizing energy stores (Pecoraro, Gomez, & Dallman, 2005). Detailed reviews of CRF effects on emotional behavior in animals can be found in Reul and Holsboer, 2002.

Corticotropin releasing factor–containing neurons are not confined to hypothalamic regions; they are also found in a number of neural circuits that mediate information processing, cognition, feeding, and stress responses. For example, in nonhuman primates strong CRF immunoreactive fibers and/or perikarya are observed in the cortex, amygdalar complex, hippocampus, and hindbrain (for review, see Risbrough & Stein, 2006). Corticotropin releasing factor has been shown to modulate diverse neurotransmitter systems, including glutamate, dopamine, serotonin, and norepinephrine (Lavicky & Dunn, 1993; Price & Lucki, 2001; Valentino & Commons, 2005). It acts via at least two known G-protein couple receptors, CRF_1 and CRF_2 (for review, see Dautzenberg & Hauger, 2002 and Eckart et al., 2002). In rodents, both receptors are expressed in relatively discrete nuclei of the neocortex, amygdala, and extended amygdala (bed nucleus stria terminalis and nucleus accumbens), hypothalamus, pituitary, and sensory relay nuclei. However, CRF_1 appears to predominate in cortical and hindbrain regions (Van Pett et al., 2000). In nonhuman primates and humans, there is stronger CRF_2 receptor binding in neocortex and pituitary than found in rodents, suggesting that CRF_2 receptor functions may be more varied in primates as compared to rodents (Kostich, Chen, Sperle, & Largent, 1998; Sanchez, Young, Plotsky, & Insel, 1999). In primates, CRF_1 receptors have been visualized in cortex, limbic regions, and sensory relay nuclei in the brainstem (Kostich, Grzanna, Lu, & Largent, 2004; Sanchez et al., 1999). The consensus

appears to be that the CRF system plays a predominant role in the stress response, shifting behavior toward defensive responding by increasing avoidance and fear-related behaviors with the concomitant suppression of appetitive behaviors such as feeding and reproduction.

The consistent finding that CRF_1 receptor blockade or gene deletion decreases defensive behaviors and attenuates physiological stress responses (e.g., autonomic and neuroendocrine activation) indicates this receptor is a primary mediator of the stress response. In stressed nonhuman primates, administration of the CRF_1 antagonist antalarmin reduced anxiety-like responses and shifted responding toward exploratory and sexual behaviors that are normally suppressed during stress (Habib et al., 2000). The anxiogenic-like effects of CRF_1 receptor activation support its potential as a target for pharmacotherapy for anxiety disorders (Dautzenberg & Hauger, 2002; Reul & Holsboer, 2002; Zorrilla & Koob, 2004). The role of CRF_2 receptors in anxiety is less clear. There is evidence for both anxiolytic- and anxiogenic-like functions after CRF_2 receptor activation or gene deletion (for review, see Hauger, Risbrough, Brauns, & Dautzenberg, 2006). A predominant hypothesis is that CRF_2 receptors facilitate recovery of stress responding and act to inhibit initial CRF_1 induced stress responses (Bale et al., 2000; Coste, Heard, Phillips, & Stenzel-Poore, 2006; Coste, Murray, & Stenzel-Poore, 2001; Kishimoto et al., 2000). Another intriguing hypothesis is that with chronic stress CRF_2 receptors may play a role in facilitating behavioral shifts toward depressive-like behaviors over immediate defensive behaviors normally mediated by CRF_1 activation (but see Bale & Vale, 2003; Hammack et al., 2002; Hammack et al., 2003). Thus the CRF system appears to be active in a number of animal models of anxiety, and there is some evidence that CRF may play similar roles in humans, as CRF genes and CRF system dysregulation have been implicated in some anxiety and depressive disorders (for review, see Risbrough & Stein, 2006). Pharmaceutical companies have been actively creating small molecule CRF_1 antagonists, and initial studies are suggesting that they have efficacy to reduce anxiety, although various toxicology issues with some early compounds have hampered their progress to market (Grigoriadis, 2005; Zobel et al., 2000).

Strategies for Discovery of New Genes and Systems Using Rodents

One successful approach to discovery of novel systems and genes that are specific to anxiety and fear functions has been to pinpoint peptides that have selective expression in brain systems that modulate emotional behavior, such as the cingulate cortex and amygdala.

Cingulate Cortex Specific Genes

A recent study from Carolee Barlow's group at the Salk Institute employed a strategy of determining genes whose expression levels in the brain correlated with anxiety phenotypes in different inbred mouse strains (Hovatta et al., 2005). Hovatta et al. examined gene expression profiles of six inbred mouse strains across a number of anxiety-relevant brain systems, including hypothalamus, pituitary, amygdala, cingulate cortex, periaqueductal grey, and hippocampus. They then determined which genes had expression levels that correlated with the amount of anxiety-like behavior each mouse strain exhibited (as measured by approach-avoidance behaviors, see the previous section, "Avoidance/Locomotor Behavior"). Expression levels of 17 genes correlated either negatively or positively with anxiety-like behavior; and they chose two genes in this group for further examination, glyoxalase 1 and glutathione reductase 1. These genes were expressed significantly more in the amygdala and cingulate cortex of the presumably high anxiety mouse strains compared to the lower anxiety strains. Lentivirus-mediated overexpression of these genes in the cingulate cortex resulted in increased anxiety-like behaviors, while knockdown of the expression of glyoxalase 1 resulted in reduced anxiety-like behavior, supporting the hypothesis that expression of these genes modulates anxiety functions. Both genes code for enzymes that are involved in controlling oxidation in the brain, which has been implicated in trait anxiety in humans and mice (Kromer et al., 2005; Kuloglu, Atmaca, Tezcan, Ustundag, & Bulut, 2002).

Amygdala Specific Genes

The laboratory of Eric Kandel has also recently discovered two genes that modulate performance in learned fear (amygdala dependent) tasks without affecting spatial working memory (nonamygdala dependent). They used representation difference analysis to probe for genes that are expressed selectively in glutamatergic pyramidal cells of the basolateral amygdala and not in hippocampal neurons. The expression profile of genes encoding gastrin related peptide (GRP) and oncoprotein 18/stathmin fit this specific pattern (Shumyatsky et al., 2005, 2002). Basolateral amygdala slices from *Grp* mutant mice or wild-type slices treated with a GRP

antagonist exhibited greater long-term potentiation (LTP, a cellular event associated with memory formation) than control slices. The *Grp* null mutation mice exhibited increased conditioned fear responses 24 but not 4 hours posttraining, and exhibited normal acute stress responses, suggesting that gastrin-related peptide plays a role in long-term consolidation of Pavlovian fear conditioning (Shumyatsky et al., 2002). In contrast, *stathmin* null mutation mice exhibit impaired amygdala LTP, reduced fear conditioning, and less anxiety-like behavior as measured by reduced avoidance of open, brightly lit spaces (Shumyatsky et al., 2005). These data indicate stathmin plays a role in both learned and "innate" fear responses. Both *stathmin* and *Grp* null mutation mice exhibit no differences in spatial working memory or pain sensitivity tasks, suggesting their effects are specific to fear behaviors. Stathmin may produce its effects on learned fear via modulation of microtubule assembly and hence synaptic plasticity (Shumyatsky et al., 2005). In rodent brain, GRP has been suggested to be a co-transmitter for glutamate (Lee et al., 1999). Once released, GRP activates a G-protein coupled receptor leading to intracellular Ca^{2+} release and subsequent activation of the mitogen activated kinase (MAPK) pathway (Sharif, Luo, & Sharif, 1997), which plays an important role in neural plasticity and memory processes. Gastrin-related peptide is a bombesin family peptide that has been implicated in a number of cellular and behavioral functions, including cell growth, feeding, thermoregulation, and smooth muscle contraction (for review, see Ohki-Hamazaki, Iwabuchi, & Maekawa, 2005). Stathmin also plays an important role in mitosis and has been associated with oncogenesis and malignant tumor growth in peripheral cells (e.g., Mistry, Bank, & Atweh, 2005). Thus, although these peptides regulate fear learning specifically as compared to global cognition, their involvement in other important peripheral cellular processes could make them less attractive as targets for pharmacotherapy. The impact of functional mutations to the stathmin gene on anxiety in humans is also unknown, although genes that regulate GRP signaling have been implicated in autism (Ishikawa-Brush et al., 1997).

The extracellular signal-regulated kinase (ERK) pathway (activated by MAPK pathways) is a cellular second messenger system that appears to be required for amygdala-dependent fear acquisition and extinction (Apergis-Schoute, Debiec, Doyere, LeDoux, & Schafe, 2005; Lin et al., 2001b; Lu, Walker, & Davis, 2001; Schafe et al., 2000). These cell signaling pathways produce transcription factors to modulate gene expression and have been shown to play a role in a number of neuronal plasticity events. These pathways have also been shown to be activated by acute stress (Meller et al., 2003; Shen, Tsimberg, Salvadore, & Meller, 2004), and might play a role in acute stress responses (Dautzenberg & Hauger, 2002). Indeed, stress-induced enhancement of fear learning also appears to be via activation of ERK signaling (perhaps via CRF release; Sananbenesi, Fischer, Schrick, Spiess, & Radulovic, 2003). Thus the molecules that regulate ERK signaling provided an exciting new avenue for anxiety and fear research. As these animal models produce a greater understanding of the cellular mechanisms of learned fear and anxiety responses, new gene candidates for incurring both vulnerability and resilience to clinical anxiety will continue to emerge. Whether these candidates will be "drugable" however, is open for debate, although some oncology research indicates that these second messenger peptides can be selectively modulated by pharmacological interventions (Smith, Dumas, Adnane, & Wilhelm, 2006).

Another strategy for discovery of genes that relate to anxiety behavior has been to use quantitative genetics approaches, either via selective breeding for specific traits, or more recently, taking advantage of the high genetic and phenotypic divergence of inbred mouse strains and high throughput gene expression analysis. Fullerton (2006) argues that using murine anxiety-like phenotypes for genetic analysis circumvents some of the problems for such studies in humans, such as heterogeneity of sample, small sample size, and unknown genetic or haplotypic backgrounds of the qualitative trait nucleotides. Sample size in particular may be an important issue that animal studies can better overcome to probe for genes that may have a low effect size at the individual gene level. Just as in humans, however, anxiety-like phenotypic traits in mice are likely heterogeneous in genetic origin and are modulated via multiple interacting systems. Turri, Datta, DeFries, Henderson, & Flint (2001) found that different quantitative trait loci (QTLs) appeared to influence many of the common avoidance behavior tasks in animals, which until recently were considered to probe similar aspects of avoidance behavior. They also found that overlapping genetic influences in these paradigms may influence activity levels more than anxiety per se (Turri et al., 2001). The use of larger batteries of anxiety and fear behaviors has produced QTLs that load across multiple tests; however, the genes

underlying these QTLs are yet to be discovered (Fernandez-Teruel et al., 2002).

Never Forget the Environment

The elegant story that has recently emerged from the laboratory of Michael Meaney best illustrates the complex interaction between "fixed" gene effects and environment. In rats, offspring that had low maternal care exhibited increased neuroendocrine and anxiety-like responding to stress and reduced hippocampal glucocorticoid receptor (GR) expression as adults compared to pups with high levels of maternal care (Weaver et al. 2004). Weaver et al. found that the GR promoter in the high but not low maternal care offspring had more DNA de-methylation, allowing greater access by transcription factors to express GR. Exogenous de-methylation treatment reversed the low GR expression and exaggerated neuroendocrine phenotypes of the low maternal care pups, indicating GR de-methylation via maternal care is critical for these phenotypes. These data suggest that the environment, in this case maternal care, can have stable, lasting changes on gene expression and ultimately "program" stress responding. Weaver et al. speculated that "among mammals, natural selection may have shaped offspring to respond to subtle variations in parental behavior as a forecast of the environmental conditions they will ultimately face once they become independent of the parent" (p. 852). Future studies of how these effects may interact with "vulnerability" genes (e.g., 5-HTT) for anxiety disorders will be truly exciting.

Validity Issues: Conceptual Challenges for Animal Models of Anxiety

It is important to note that the predictive validity of current animal models for clinical anxiolytics (other than benzodiazepines) is under spirited debate, especially when used for phenotyping as opposed to drug screening (Cryan & Holmes, 2005). In individual labs, these tests are not always validated for sensitivity to anxiolytic and anxiogenic manipulations before they are used in phenotyping, which can make interpretation of the phenotyping results more difficult, and cast doubt on conclusions. The use of a battery of anxiety models is also an important component to understanding either genetic or pharmacological effects on anxiety responding, as some tests are not bidirectional (sensitive to both anxiolytic and anxiogenic effects [Risbrough & Stein, 2006]) and many tests appear to probe orthogonal anxiety systems (e.g., Holmes, Yang, & Crawley, 2002). Finally, the majority of the models are used predominantly to test anxiolysis after single acute dosing, which is perhaps no longer the best way to model the clinical reality of chronic dosing (e.g., with serotonin reuptake inhibitors) used to treat anxiety (Borsini, Podhorna, & Marazziti, 2002).

These issues are now being addressed in behavioral pharmacology and genetics, with the creation of more sophisticated models of anxiety responding and the merging of a number of physiological and behavioral measures to produce a more interpretable picture of stress responses in model organisms (Cohen & Zohar, 2004; Stiedl, Meyer, Jahn, Ogren, & Spiess, 2005). Similarly, the use of repeatable anxiety tests in individual subjects, such as the use of startle, provides avenues to test models of chronic stress or anxiety (Adamec, 1997; Rainnie et al., 2004). Additionally, in keeping with the notion that there are different types of anxiety disorders in humans, more ethological measures of anxiety such as social interaction and social defeat may add new dimensions such as social anxiety to preclinical models (Berton et al., 2006; Moy et al., 2004).

Notes

We would like to acknowledge support by NIH grants MH074697 and DA02925 and the Veterans Administration Center of Excellence for Stress and Mental Health.

1. Loss of fear responses to a CS that has been repeatedly presented without the US, thus losing predictive value for the US.

References

Abduljawad, K.A.J., Langley, R. W., Bradshaw, C. M., & Szabadi, E. (2001). Effects of clonidine and diazepam on prepulse inhibition of the acoustic startle response and the N1/P2 auditory evoked potential in man. *Journal of Psychopharmacology, 15,* 237–242.

Adamec, R. (1997). Transmitter systems involved in neural plasticity underlying increased anxiety and defense—implications for understanding anxiety following traumatic stress. *Neuroscience and Biobehavioral Reviews, 21,* 755–765.

Apergis-Schoute, A. M., Debiec, J., Doyere, V., LeDoux, J. E., & Schafe, G. E. (2005). Auditory fear conditioning and long-term potentiation in the lateral amygdala require ERK/MAP kinase signaling in the auditory thalamus: A role for presynaptic plasticity in the fear system. *Journal of Neuroscience., 25,* 5730–5739.

Bale, T. L., Contarino, A., Smith, G. W., Chan, R., Gold, L. H., Sawchenko, P. E., et al. (2000). Mice deficient for corticotropin-releasing hormone receptor-2 display anxiety-like behaviour and are hypersensitive to stress. *Nature Genetics, 24,* 410–414.

Bale, T. L., Picetti, R., Contarino, A., Koob, G. F., Vale, W. W., & Lee, K. F. (2002). Mice deficient for both corticotropin-releasing factor receptor 1 (CRFR1) and CRFR2 have an impaired stress response and display sexually dichotomous anxiety-like behavior. *Journal of Neuroscience, 22,* 193–199.

Bale, T. L., & Vale, W. W. (2003). Increased depression-like behaviors in corticotropin-releasing factor receptor-2-deficient mice: Sexually dichotomous responses. *Journal of Neuroscience, 23,* 5295–5301.

Belzung, C. (2001). Rodent models of anxiety-like behaviors: Are they predictive for compounds acting via non-benzodiazepine mechanisms? *Current Opinion in Investigational Drugs, 2,* 1108–1111.

Berton, O., McClung, C. A., DiLeone, R. J., Krishnan, V., Renthal, W., Russo, S. J., et al. (2006). Essential role of BDNF in the mesolimbic dopamine pathway in social defeat stress. *Science, 311,* 864–868.

Bertrand, F., Lehmann, O., Lazarus, C., Jeltsch, H., & Cassel, J. C. (2000). Intraseptal infusions of 8-OH-DPAT in the rat impairs water-maze performances: Effects on memory or anxiety? *Neuroscience Letters, 279,* 45–48.

Blanchard, R. J., Yudko, E. B., Rodgers, R. J., & Blanchard, D. C. (1993). Defense system psychopharmacology: An ethological approach to the pharmacology of fear and anxiety. *Behavioural Brain Research, 58,* 155–165.

Borsini, F., Podhorna, J., & Marazziti, D. (2002). Do animal models of anxiety predict anxiolytic-like effects of antidepressants? *Psychopharmacology, 163,* 121–141.

Braff, D. L., & Geyer, M. A. (1990). Sensorimotor gating and schizophrenia: Human and animal model studies. *Archives of General Psychiatry, 47,* 181–188.

Braff, D. L., Geyer, M. A., & Swerdlow, N. R. (2001). Human studies of prepulse inhibition of startle: normal subjects, patient groups, and pharmacological studies. *Psychopharmacology, 156,* 234–258.

Brown, J. S., Kalish, H. I., & Farber, I. E. (1951). Conditioned fear as revealed by magnitude of startle response to an auditory stimulus. *Journal of Experimental Psychology, 41,* 317–328.

Cadenhead, K. S., Carasso, B. S., Swerdlow, N. R., Geyer, M. A., & Braff, D. L. (1999). Prepulse inhibition and habituation of the startle response are stable neurobiological measures in a normal male population. *Biological Psychiatry, 45,* 360–364.

Cheng, L. L., Wang, S. J., & Gean, P. W. (1998). Serotonin depresses excitatory synaptic transmission and depolarization-evoked Ca2+ influx in rat basolateral amygdala via 5-HT1A receptors. *European Journal of Neuroscience, 10,* 2163–2172.

Cohen, H., & Zohar, J. (2004). An animal model of posttraumatic stress disorder: The use of cut-off behavioral criteria. *Annals of the New York Academy of Science, 1032,* 167–178.

Conti, L. H., Maciver, C. R., Ferkany, J. W., & Abreu, M. E. (1990). Footshock-induced freezing behavior in rats as a model for assessing anxiolytics. *Psychopharmacology, 102,* 492–497.

Coste, S. C., Heard, A. D., Phillips, T. J., & Stenzel-Poore, M. P. (2006). Corticotropin-releasing factor receptor type 2-deficient mice display impaired coping behaviors during stress. *Genes, Brain, and Behavior, 5,* 131–138.

Coste, S. C., Murray, S. E., & Stenzel-Poore, M. P. (2001). Animal models of CRH excess and CRH receptor deficiency display altered adaptations to stress. *Peptides, 22,* 733–741.

Cronbach, L. J., & Meehl, P. E. (1955). Construct validity in psychological tests. *Psychological Bulletin, 52,* 281–302.

Cryan, J. F., & Holmes, A. (2005). The ascent of mouse: Advances in modelling human depression and anxiety. *Nature Reviews—Drug Discovery, 4,* 775–790.

Daniels, W. M., Pietersen, C. Y., Carstens, M. E., Daya, S., & Stein, D. (2000). Overcrowding induces anxiety and causes loss of serotonin 5HT-1a receptors in rats. *Metabolic Brain Disease, 15,* 287–295.

Dautzenberg, F. M., & Hauger, R. L. (2002). The CRF peptide family and their receptors: Yet more partners discovered. *Trends in Pharmacological Sciences, 23,* 71–77.

Davidson, J. R., DuPont, R. L., Hedges, D., & Haskins, J. T. (1999). Efficacy, safety, and tolerability of venlafaxine extended release and buspirone in outpatients with generalized anxiety disorder. *Journal of Clinical Psychiatry, 60,* 528–535.

Davis, M. (1979). Diazepam and flurazepam: Effects on conditioned fear as measured with the potentiated startle paradigm. *Psychopharmacology, 62,* 1–7.

Davis, M. (1993). Pharmacological analysis of fear-potentiated startle. *Brazilian Journal of Medical and Biological Research, 26,* 235–260.

Davis, M. (1998a). Anatomic and physiologic substrates of emotion in an animal model. *Journal of Clinical Neurophysiology, 15,* 378–387.

Davis, M. (1998b). Are different parts of the extended amygdala involved in fear versus anxiety? *Biological Psychiatry, 44,* 1239–1247.

Davis, M., Cassella, J. V., Wrean, W. H., & Kehne, J. H. (1986). Serotonin receptor subtype agonists: Differential effects on sensorimotor reactivity measured with acoustic startle. *Psychopharmacology Bulletin, 22,* 837–843.

Davis, M., Walker, D. L., & Lee, Y. (1997). Amygdala and bed nucleus of the stria terminalis: Differential roles in fear and anxiety measured with the acoustic startle reflex. *Philosophical Transactions of the Royal Society of London, Series B, Biological Sciences, 352,* 1675–1687.

Eckart, K., Jahn, O., Radulovic, J., Radulovic, M., Blank, T., Stiedl, O., et al. (2002). Pharmacology and biology of corticotropin-releasing factor (CRF) receptors. *Receptors and Channels, 8,* 163–177.

Feighner, J. P., & Boyer, W. F. (1989). Serotonin-1A anxiolytics: An overview. *Psychopathology, 22*(Suppl. 1), 21–26.

Fernandez-Teruel, A., Escorihuela, R. M., Gray, J. A., Aguilar, R., Gil, L., Gimenez-Llort, L., et al. (2002). A quantitative trait locus influencing anxiety in the laboratory rat. *Genome Research, 12,* 618–626.

Frodl, T., Meisenzahl, E. M., Zill, P., Baghai, T., Rujescu, D., Leinsinger, G., et al. (2004). Reduced hippocampal volumes associated with the long variant of the serotonin transporter polymorphism in major depression. *Archives of General Psychiatry, 61,* 177–183.

Fullerton, J. (2006). New approaches to the genetic analysis of neuroticism and anxiety. *Behavior Genetics, 36,* 147–161.

Funayama, E. S., Grillon, C., Davis, M., & Phelps, E. A. (2001). A double dissociation in the affective modulation of startle in humans: Effects of unilateral temporal lobectomy. *Journal of Cognitive Neuroscience, 13,* 721–729.

Gewirtz, J. C., McNish, K. A., & Davis, M. (2000). Is the hippocampus necessary for contextual fear conditioning? *Behavioural Brain Research, 110,* 83–95.

Geyer, M. A., Krebs-Thomson, K., Braff, D. L., & Swerdlow, N. R. (2001). Pharmacological studies of prepulse inhibition models of sensorimotor gating deficits in schizophrenia: A decade in review. *Psychopharmacology, 156,* 117–154.

Geyer, M. A., & Markou, A. (2002). The role of preclinical models in the development of psychotropic drugs. In K. L. Davis, D. S. Charney, J. T. Coyle, & C. Nemeroff (Eds.), *Neuropsychopharmacology: The fifth generation in progress* (pp. 445–455). Philadelphia: Lippincott, Williams & Wilkins.

Gilbertson, M. W., Shenton, M. E., Ciszewski, A., Kasai, K., Lasko, N. B., Orr, S. P., et al. (2002). Smaller hippocampal volume predicts pathologic vulnerability to psychological trauma. *Nature Neuroscience, 5,* 1242–1247.

Gingrich, J. A., Ansorge, M. S., Merker, R., Weisstaub, N., & Zhou, M. (2003). New lessons from knockout mice: The role of serotonin during development and its possible contribution to the origins of neuropsychiatric disorders. *CNS Spectrums, 8,* 572–577.

Grigoriadis, D. E. (2005). The corticotropin-releasing factor receptor: A novel target for the treatment of depression and anxiety-related disorders. *Expert Opinion on Therapeutic Targets, 9,* 651–684.

Grillon, C., & Baas, J. (2003). A review of the modulation of the startle reflex by affective states and its application in psychiatry. *Clinical Neurophysiology, 114,* 1557–1579.

Groenink, L., Joordens, R. J., Hijzen, T. H., Dirks, A., & Olivier, B. (2000). Infusion of flesinoxan into the amygdala blocks the fear-potentiated startle. *Neuroreport, 11,* 2285–2288.

Groenink, L., Pattij, T., De Jongh, R., van der Gugten, J., Oosting, R. S., Dirks, A., et al. (2003). 5-HT1A receptor knockout mice and mice overexpressing corticotropin-releasing hormone in models of anxiety. *European Journal of Pharmacology, 463,* 185–197.

Gross, C., Santarelli, L., Brunner, D., Zhuang, X., & Hen, R. (2000). Altered fear circuits in 5-HT(1A) receptor KO mice. *Biological Psychiatry, 48,* 1157–1163.

Gross, C., Zhuang, X., Stark, K., Ramboz, S., Oosting, R., Kirby, L., et al. (2002). Serotonin1A receptor acts during development to establish normal anxiety-like behaviour in the adult. *Nature, 416,* 396–400.

Habib, K. E., Weld, K. P., Rice, K. C., Pushkas, J., Champoux, M., Listwak, S., et al. (2000). Oral administration of a corticotropin-releasing hormone receptor antagonist significantly attenuates behavioral, neuroendocrine, and autonomic responses to stress in primates. *Proceedings of the National Academy of Sciences of the United States of America, 97,* 6079–6084.

Hammack, S. E., Richey, K. J., Schmid, M. J., LoPresti, M. L., Watkins, L. R., & Maier, S. F. (2002). The role of corticotropin-releasing hormone in the dorsal raphe nucleus in mediating the behavioral consequences of uncontrollable stress. *Journal of Neuroscience, 22,* 1020–1026.

Hammack, S. E., Schmid, M. J., LoPresti, M. L., Der-Avakian, A., Pellymounter, M. A., Foster, A. C., et al. (2003). Corticotropin releasing hormone type 2 receptors in the dorsal raphe nucleus mediate the behavioral consequences of uncontrollable stress. *Journal of Neuroscience, 23,* 1019–1025.

Hauger, R. L., Risbrough, V., Brauns, O., & Dautzenberg, F. M. (2006). Corticotropin releasing factor (CRF) receptor signaling in the central nervous system: New molecular targets. *CNS and Neurological Disorders Drug Targets, 5,* 453–479.

Heisler, L. K., Chu, H. M., Brennan, T. J., Danao, J. A., Bajwa, P., Parsons, L. H., et al. (1998). Elevated anxiety and antidepressant-like responses in serotonin 5-HT1A receptor mutant mice. *Proceedings of the National Academy of Sciences of the United States of America, 95,* 15049–15054.

Heldt, S., Sundin, V., Willott, J. F., & Falls, W. A. (2000). Post-training lesions of the amygdala interfere with fear-potentiated startle to both visual and auditory conditioned stimuli in C57BL/6J mice. *Behavioral Neuroscience, 114,* 749–759.

Holmes, A., Yang, R. J., & Crawley, J. N. (2002). Evaluation of an anxiety-related phenotype in galanin overexpressing transgenic mice. *Journal of Molecular Neuroscience, 18,* 151–165.

Hovatta, I., Tennant, R. S., Helton, R., Marr, R. A., Singer, O., Redwine, J. M., et al. (2005). Glyoxalase 1 and glutathione reductase 1 regulate anxiety in mice. *Nature, 438,* 662–666.

Hull, A. M. (2002). Neuroimaging findings in post-traumatic stress disorder: Systematic review. *British Journal of Psychiatry, 181,* 102–110.

Ishikawa-Brush, Y., Powell, J. F., Bolton, P., Miller, A. P., Francis, F., Willard, H. F., et al. (1997). Autism and multiple exostoses associated with an X;8 translocation occurring within the GRPR gene and 3' to the SDC2 gene. *Human Molecular Genetics, 6,* 1241–1250.

Kishimoto, T., Radulovic, J., Radulovic, M., Lin, C. R., Schrick, C., Hooshmand, F., et al. (2000). Deletion of Crhr2 reveals an anxiolytic role for corticotropin-releasing hormone receptor-2. *Nature Genetics, 24,* 415–419.

Kostich, W. A., Chen, A., Sperle, K., & Largent, B. L. (1998). Molecular identification and analysis of a novel human corticotropin-releasing factor (CRF) receptor: The CRF2gamma receptor. *Molecular Endocrinology, 12,* 1077–1085.

Kostich, W. A., Grzanna, R., Lu, N. Z., & Largent, B. L. (2004). Immunohistochemical visualization of corticotropin-releasing factor type 1 (CRF1) receptors in monkey brain. *Journal of Comparative Neurology, 478,* 111–125.

Kromer, S. A., Kessler, M. S., Milfay, D., Birg, I. N., Bunck, M., Czibere, L., et al. (2005). Identification of glyoxalase-I as a protein marker in a mouse model of extremes in trait anxiety. *Journal of Neuroscience, 25,* 4375–4384.

Kuloglu, M., Atmaca, M., Tezcan, E., Ustundag, B., & Bulut, S. (2002). Antioxidant enzyme and malondialdehyde levels in patients with panic disorder. *Neuropsychobiology, 46,* 186–189.

Kumari, V., Gray, J. A., Geyer, M. A., Ffytche, D., Soni, W., Mitterschiffthaler, M. T., et al. (2003). Neural correlates of tactile prepulse inhibition: A functional MRI study in normal and schizophrenic subjects. *Psychiatry Research: Neuroimaging, 122,* 99–113.

LaBar, K. S., Gatenby, J. C., Gore, J. C., LeDoux, J. E., & Phelps, E. A. (1998). Human amygdala activation during conditioned fear acquisition and extinction: A mixed-trial fMRI study. *Neuron, 20,* 937–945.

Lanfumey, L., & Hamon, M. (2000). Central 5-HT(1A) receptors: Regional distribution and functional characteristics. *Nuclear Medicine and Biology, 27,* 429–435.

Lang, P. J., Bradley, M. M., & Cuthbert, B. N. (1990). Emotion, attention, and the startle reflex. *Psychological Review, 97,* 377–395.

Lavicky, J., & Dunn, A. J. (1993). Corticotropin-releasing factor stimulates catecholamine release in hypothalamus and prefrontal cortex in freely moving rats as assessed by microdialysis. *Journal of Neurochemistry, 60,* 602–612.

LeDoux, J. E. (2000). Emotion circuits in the brain. *Annual Review of Neuroscience, 23,* 155–184.

Lee, K., Dixon, A. K., Gonzalez, I., Stevens, E. B., McNulty, S., Oles, R., et al. (1999). Bombesin-like peptides depolarize rat hippocampal interneurones through interaction with subtype 2 bombesin receptors. *Journal of Physiology, 518(Pt 3),* 791–802.

Lemonde, S., Turecki, G., Bakish, D., Du, L., Hrdina, P. D., Bown, C. D., et al. (2003). Impaired repression at a 5-hydroxytryptamine 1A receptor gene polymorphism associated with major depression and suicide. *Journal of Neuroscience, 23,* 8788–8799.

Lesch, K. P., Zeng, Y., Reif, A., & Gutknecht, L. (2003). Anxiety-related traits in mice with modified genes of the serotonergic pathway. *European Journal of Pharmacology, 480,* 185–204.

Levine, S. (2005). Developmental determinants of sensitivity and resistance to stress. *Psychoneuroendocrinology, 30,* 939–946.

Liang, K. C. (1999). Pre- or post-training injection of buspirone impaired retention in the inhibitory avoidance task: Involvement of amygdala 5-HT1A receptors. *European Journal of Neuroscience, 11,* 1491–1500.

Lin, C. H., Huang, Y. C., Tsai, J. J., & Gean, P. W. (2001a). Modulation of voltage-dependent calcium currents by serotonin in acutely isolated rat amygdala neurons. *Synapse, 41,* 351–359.

Lin, C. H., Yeh, S. H., Lin, C. H., Lu, K. T., Leu, T. H., Chang, W. C., et al. (2001b). A role for the PI-3 kinase signaling pathway in fear conditioning and synaptic plasticity in the amygdala. *Neuron, 31,* 841–851.

Lissek, S., Powers, A. S., McClure, E. B., Phelps, E. A., Woldehawariat, G., Grillon, C., et al. (2005). Classical fear conditioning in the anxiety disorders: A meta-analysis. *Behaviour Research and Therapy, 43,* 1391–1424.

Lorberbaum, J. P., Kose, S., Johnson, M. R., Arana, G. W., Sullivan, L. K., Hamner, M. B., et al. (2004). Neural correlates of speech anticipatory anxiety in generalized social phobia. *Neuroreport, 15,* 2701–2705.

Lu, K. T., Walker, D. L., & Davis, M. (2001). Mitogen-activated protein kinase cascade in the basolateral nucleus of amygdala is involved in extinction of fear-potentiated startle. *Journal of Neuroscience, 21*(RC162), 1–5.

Matthysse, S. (1986). Animal models in psychiatric research. *Progress in Brain Research, 65,* 259–270.

Meller, E., Shen, C., Nikolao, T. A., Jensen, C., Tsimberg, Y., Chen, J., et al. (2003). Region-specific effects of acute and repeated restraint stress on the phosphorylation of mitogen-activated protein kinases. *Brain Research, 979,* 57–64.

Micheau, J., & van Marrewijk, B. (1999). Stimulation of 5-HT1A receptors by systemic or medial septum injection induces anxiogenic-like effects and facilitates acquisition of a spatial discrimination task in mice. *Progress in Neuropsychopharmacology and Biological Psychiatry, 23,* 1113–1133.

Millan, M. J. (2003). The neurobiology and control of anxious states. *Progress in Neurobiology, 70,* 83–244.

Misane, I., Johansson, C., & Ogren, S. O. (1998). Analysis of the 5-HT1A receptor involvement in passive avoidance in the rat. *British Journal of Pharmacology, 125,* 499–509.

Misane, I., & Ogren, S. O. (2000). Multiple 5-HT receptors in passive avoidance: Comparative studies of p-chloroamphetamine and 8-OH-DPAT. *Neuropsychopharmacology, 22,* 168–190.

Mistry, S. J., Bank, A., & Atweh, G. F. (2005). Targeting stathmin in prostate cancer. *Molecular Cancer Therapeutics, 4,* 1821–1829.

Montgomery, K. C. (1958). The relation between fear induced by novel stimulation and exploratory behaviour. *Journal of Comparative and Physiological Psychology, 8,* 254–260.

Mosier, C. I. (1947). A critical examination of the concepts of face validity. *Educational and Psychological Measurement, 7,* 191–205.

Moy, S. S., Nadler, J. J., Perez, A., Barbaro, R. P., Johns, J. M., Magnuson, T. R., et al. (2004). Sociability and preference for social novelty in five inbred strains: An approach to assess autistic-like behavior in mice. *Genes, Brain and Behavior, 3,* 287–302.

Neumeister, A., Bain, E., Nugent, A. C., Carson, R. E., Bonne, O., Luckenbaugh, D. A., et al. (2004). Reduced serotonin type 1A receptor binding in panic disorder. *Journal of Neuroscience, 24,* 589–591.

Ohki-Hamazaki, H., Iwabuchi, M., & Maekawa, F. (2005). Development and function of bombesin-like peptides and their receptors. *International Journal of Developmental Biology, 49,* 293–300.

Overstreet, D. H., Commissaris, R. C., De La Garza, II, R., File, S. E., Knapp, D. J., & Seiden, L. S. (2003). Involvement of 5-HT1A receptors in animal tests of anxiety and depression: Evidence from genetic models. *Stress, 6,* 101–110.

Pare, D., Quirk, G. J., & Ledoux, J. E. (2004). New vistas on amygdala networks in conditioned fear. *Journal of Neurophysiology, 92,* 1–9.

Parks, C. L., Robinson, P. S., Sibille, E., Shenk, T., & Toth, M. (1998). Increased anxiety of mice lacking the serotonin 1A receptor. *Proceedings of the National Academy of Sciences of the United States of America, 95,* 10734–10739.

Pattij, T., Groenink, L., Hijzen, T. H., Oosting, R. S., Maes, R. A., van der Gugten, J., et al. (2002). Autonomic changes associated with enhanced anxiety in 5-HT(1A) receptor knockout mice. *Neuropsychopharmacology, 27,* 380–390.

Pecoraro, N., Gomez, F., & Dallman, M. F. (2005). Glucocorticoids dose-dependently remodel energy stores and amplify incentive relativity effects. *Psychoneuroendocrinology, 30,* 815–825.

Pellow, S., Chopin, P., File, S. E., & Briley, M. (1985). Validation of open:closed arm entries in an elevated plus-maze as a measure of anxiety in the rat. *Journal Neuroscience Methods, 14,* 149–167.

Phelps, E. A., O'Connor, K. J., Gatenby, J. C., Gore, J. C., Grillon, C., & Davis, M. (2001). Activation of the left amygdala to a cognitive representation of fear. *Nature Neuroscience, 4,* 437–441.

Price, M. L., & Lucki, I. (2001). Regulation of serotonin release in the lateral septum and striatum by corticotropin-releasing factor. *Journal of Neuroscience, 21,* 2833–2841.

Rainnie, D. G., Bergeron, R., Sajdyk, T. J., Patil, M., Gehlert, D. R., & Shekhar, A. (2004). Corticotrophin releasing factor-induced synaptic plasticity in the amygdala translates stress into emotional disorders. *Journal of Neuroscience, 24,* 3471–3479.

Ramboz, S., Oosting, R., Amara, D. A., Kung, H. F., Blier, P., Mendelsohn, M., et al. (1998). Serotonin receptor 1A knockout: An animal model of anxiety-related disorder. *Proceedings of the National Academy of Sciences of the United States of America, 95,* 14476–14481.

Reul, J. M., & Holsboer, F. (2002). Corticotropin-releasing factor receptors 1 and 2 in anxiety and depression. *Current Opinion in Pharmacology, 2,* 23–33.

Risbrough, V. B., Hauger, R. L., Pelleymounter, M. A., & Geyer, M. A. (2003). Role of corticotropin releasing factor (CRF) receptors 1 and 2 in CRF-potentiated acoustic startle in mice. *Psychopharmacology, 170,* 178–187.

Risbrough, V. B., & Stein, M. B. (2006). Role of corticotropin releasing factor in anxiety disorders: A translational research perspective. *Hormones and Behavior, 50,* 550–561.

Rodgers, R. J. (1997). Animal models of "anxiety": Where next? *Behavioral Pharmacology, 8,* 477–496; discussion 497–504.

Rothbaum, B. O., & Davis, M. (2003). Applying learning principles to the treatment of post-trauma reactions. *Annals of the New York Academy of Science, 1008,* 112–121.

Sananbenesi, F., Fischer, A., Schrick, C., Spiess, J., & Radulovic, J. (2003). Mitogen-activated protein kinase signaling in the hippocampus and its modulation by corticotropin-releasing factor receptor 2: A possible link between stress and fear memory. *Journal of Neuroscience, 23,* 11436–11443.

Sanchez, M. M., Young, L. J., Plotsky, P. M., & Insel, T. R. (1999). Autoradiographic and in situ hybridization localization of corticotropin-releasing factor 1 and 2 receptors in nonhuman primate brain. *Journal of Comprehensive Neurology, 408,* 365–377.

Schafe, G. E., Atkins, C. M., Swank, M. W., Bauer, E. P., Sweatt, J. D., & LeDoux, J. E. (2000). Activation of ERK/MAP kinase in the amygdala is required for memory consolidation of pavlovian fear conditioning. *Journal of Neuroscience, 20,* 8177–8187.

Schneider, F., Weiss, U., Kessler, C., Muller-Gartner, H. W., Posse, S., Salloum, J. B., et al. (1999). Subcortical correlates of differential classical conditioning of aversive emotional reactions in social phobia. *Biological Psychiatry, 45,* 863–871.

Segal, D. S., & Geyer, M. A. (1985). Animal models of psychopathology. In L. L. Judd & P. M. Groves (Eds.), *Psychobiological foundations of clinical psychiatry* (Chapter 45). Philadelphia: J. B. Lippincott.

Shalev, A. Y., Peri, T., Brandes, D., Freedman, S., Orr, S. P., & Pitman, R. K. (2000). Auditory startle response in trauma survivors with posttraumatic stress disorder: A prospective study. *American Journal of Psychiatry, 157,* 255–261.

Sharif, T. R., Luo, W., & Sharif, M. (1997). Functional expression of bombesin receptor in most adult and pediatric human glioblastoma cell lines: Role in mitogenesis and in stimulating the mitogen-activated protein kinase pathway. *Molecular and Cellular Endocrinology, 130,* 119–130.

Shen, C. P., Tsimberg, Y., Salvadore, C., & Meller, E. (2004). Activation of Erk and JNK MAPK pathways by acute swim stress in rat brain regions. *BMC Neuroscience, 5,* 36.

Shumyatsky, G. P., Malleret, G., Shin, R.-M., Takizawa, S., Tully, K., Tsvetkov, E., et al. (2005). Stathmin, a gene enriched in the amygdala, controls both learned and innate fear. *Cell, 123,* 697–709.

Shumyatsky, G. P., Tsvetkov, E., Malleret, G., Vronskaya, S., Hatton, M., Hampton, L., et al. (2002). Identification of a signaling network in lateral nucleus of amygdala important for inhibiting memory specifically related to learned fear. *Cell, 111,* 905–918.

Smith, R. A., Dumas, J., Adnane, L., & Wilhelm, S. M. (2006). Recent advances in the research and development of RAF kinase inhibitors. *Current Topics in Medicinal Chemistry, 6,* 1071–1089.

Stein, C., Davidowa, H., & Albrecht, D. (2000). 5-HT(1A) receptor-mediated inhibition and 5-HT(2) as well as 5-HT(3) receptor-mediated excitation in different subdivisions of the rat amygdala. *Synapse, 38,* 328–337.

Stiedl, O., Meyer, M., Jahn, O., Ogren, S. O., & Spiess, J. (2005). Corticotropin-releasing factor receptor 1 and central heart rate regulation in mice during expression of conditioned fear. *Journal of Pharmacology and Experimental Therapeutics, 312,* 905–916.

Stiedl, O., Misane, I., Spiess, J., & Ogren, S. O. (2000). Involvement of the 5-HT1A receptors in classical fear conditioning in C57BL/6J mice. *Journal of Neuroscience, 20,* 8515–8527.

Stork, O., Welzl, H., Wotjak, C. T., Hoyer, D., Delling, M., Cremer, H., et al. (1999). Anxiety and increased 5-HT1A receptor response in NCAM null mutant mice. *Journal of Neurobiology, 40,* 343–355.

Swerdlow, N. R., Geyer, M. A., & Braff, D. L. (2001). Neural circuit regulation of prepulse inhibition of startle in the rat: Current knowledge and future challenges. *Psychopharmacology, 156,* 194–215.

Tauscher, J., Bagby, R. M., Javanmard, M., Christensen, B. K., Kasper, S., & Kapur, S. (2001). Inverse relationship between serotonin 5-HT(1A) receptor binding and anxiety: A [(11)C]WAY-100635 PET investigation in healthy volunteers. *American Journal of Psychiatry, 158,* 1326–1328.

Toth, M. (2003). 5-HT1A receptor knockout mouse as a genetic model of anxiety. *European Journal of Pharmacology, 463,* 177–184.

Tovote, P., Meyer, M., Pilz, P. K., Ronnenberg, A., Ogren, S. O., Spiess, J., et al. (2005). Dissociation of temporal dynamics of heart rate and blood pressure responses elicited by conditioned fear but not acoustic startle. *Behavioral Neuroscience, 119,* 55–65.

Turri, M. G., Datta, S. R., DeFries, J., Henderson, N. D., & Flint, J. (2001). QTL analysis identifies multiple behavioral dimensions in ethological tests of anxiety in laboratory mice. *Current Biology, 11,* 725–734.

Valentino, R. J., & Commons, K. G. (2005). Peptides that fine-tune the serotonin system. *Neuropeptides, 39,* 1–8.

Van Pett, K., Viau, V., Bittencourt, J. C., Chan, R. K., Li, H. Y., Arias, C., et al. (2000). Distribution of mRNAs encoding CRF receptors in brain and pituitary of rat and mouse. *Journal of Comprehensive Neurology, 428,* 191–212.

Walker, D. L., & Davis, M. (2002a). Quantifying fear potentiated startle using absolute versus proportional increase scoring methods: Implications for the neurocircuitry of fear and anxiety. *Psychopharmacology, 164,* 318–328.

Walker, D. L., & Davis, M. (2002b). The role of amygdala glutamate receptors in fear learning, fear-potentiated startle, and extinction. *Pharmacology, Biochemistry, and Behavior, 71,* 379–392.

Weaver, I. C., Cervoni, N., Champagne, F. A., D'Alessio, A. C., Sharma, S., Seckl, J. R., et al. (2004). Epigenetic programming by maternal behavior. *Nature Neuroscience, 7,* 847–854.

Weike, A. I., Hamm, A. O., Schupp, H. T., Runge, U., Schroeder, H. W. S., & Kessler, C. (2005). Fear conditioning following unilateral temporal lobectomy: Dissociation of conditioned startle potentiation and autonomic learning. *Journal of Neuroscience, 25,* 11117–11124.

Yeomans, J. S., Li, L., Scott, B. W., & Frankland, P. W. (2002). Tactile, acoustic and vestibular systems sum to elicit the startle reflex. *Neuroscience and Biobehavioral Review, 26,* 1–11.

Zangrossi, H., Jr., Viana, M. B., & Graeff, F. G. (1999). Anxiolytic effect of intra-amygdala injection of midazolam and 8-hydroxy-2-(di-n-propylamino)tetralin in the elevated T-maze. *European Journal of Pharmacology, 369,* 267–270.

Zethof, T.J.J., van der Heyden, J.A.M., Tolboom, J.T.B.M., & Olivier, B. (1995). Stress-induced hyperthermia as a putative anxiety model. *European Journal of Pharmacology, 294,* 125–135.

Zobel, A. W., Nickel, T., Kunzel, H. E., Ackl, N., Sonntag, A., Ising, M., et al. (2000). Effects of the high-affinity corticotropin-releasing hormone receptor 1 antagonist R121919 in major depression: The first 20 patients treated. *Journal of Psychiatric Research, 34,* 171–181.

Zorrilla, E. P., & Koob, G. F. (2004). The therapeutic potential of CRF1 antagonists for anxiety. *Expert Opinion in Investigational Drugs, 13,* 799–828.

Heritability and Genetics of Anxiety Disorders

Joel Gelernter *and* Murray B. Stein

Abstract

This chapter reviews issues related to the inheritance of anxiety disorders and related traits. Studies in genetic epidemiology (twin and family studies) were used to establish first that traits were heritable, then to examine the range of genetic expression of relevant traits. Molecular studies (linkage and association studies) were used to identify chromosomal regions that might harbor risk genes, and to establish relationships of variation in specific candidate genes with specific traits, respectively. Rapid advances in methodology applicable to complex trait genetics (including psychiatric traits) have led to considerable progress in recent years, with the promise of much more to come with the advent of genomewide association methods.

Keywords: anxiety disorders, association, family studies, genetic epidemiology, linkage, molecular genetics, psychiatric genetics, twin studies

Genetic Epidemiology of Anxiety Disorders and Related Traits

Introduction

Many psychiatric illnesses and, more generally, many behavioral phenotypes have genetic components (Bouchard, Lykken, McGue, Segal, & Tellegen, 1990). Genes, and genetic polymorphism, must therefore explain some of the differences in behavior between different individuals. Anxiety disorders, including panic disorder (PD), agoraphobia (AG), social phobia (SocP), specific or simple phobia (SimpP), and obsessive-compulsive disorder (OCD), are genetically influenced. A few specific genes that contribute to the causation of these disorders have been identified; progress in the last 5 years has provided considerable evidence supporting specific chromosomal locations for additional genes.

Anxiety disorders are important causes of morbidity in the United States. Results from the (United States) National Comorbidity Study (NCS), based on criteria from the *Diagnostic and Statistical Manual of Mental Disorders,* 3rd ed., revised (*DSM–III–R;* American Psychiatric Association [APA], 1987), found a lifetime prevalence of *DSM–III–R*–defined PD of 3.5%, and lifetime prevalence of *DSM–III–R* AG without PD of 5.3% (Kessler et al., 1994). Both disorders showed approximately twice the prevalence in females as in males. The NCS Replication (based on *DSM–IV* criteria; APA, 1994) showed consistent results: rates of 3.7% for PD-only, and 0.8% for PD plus AG; lifetime prevalence for isolated panic attacks alone was estimated at 22.7% (Kessler et al., 2006). Comorbidity with other anxiety disorders was, in general, quite high. For example, subjects with PD+AG had rates of 25.8% for SimpP, 66.5% for SocP, and 39.6% for posttraumatic stress disorder (PTSD); rate for comorbidity with any other anxiety disorder was 93.6% (Kessler et al., 2006). There was also a 73.3% rate of comorbidity with mood disorders for this group (i.e., PD+AG), and 37.3% comorbidity with substance use disorders. Thus,

PD is quite common, and it carries a high burden of comorbidity. Also in the NCS, the lifetime prevalence of SimpP was 11.3%, and the prevalence of SocP was 13.3% (Magee, Eaton, Wittchen, McGonagle, & Kessler, 1996). In another study based on the NCS, Sareen, Cox, Clara, & Asmundson (2005) showed that anxiety disorders are also associated with increased comorbidity with physical disorders.

Evidence for Familial Aggregation and Heritability

TWIN STUDIES

Twin studies have provided insight into the heritability of the anxiety disorders, and also into the structure of the genetic risk factors. Findings from twin studies (in females) are consistent, with heritability of PD of about 44% (Kendler et al., 1995), and heritability of AG of about 61% (Kendler, Karkowski, & Prescott, 1999; this estimate derived from a study with correction for assessment reliability). Twin studies have also shown that at least a modest portion of the familial resemblance in social anxiety is heritable (Kendler, Heath, Neale, Kessler, & Eaves, 1992; Kendler et al., 1999; Kendler, Myers, Prescott, & Neale, 2001; Skre, Onstad, Torgersen, Lygren, & Kringlen, 1993; Torgersen, 1983). Kendler et al. (1999) studied heritability for social phobia and phobias in a population-based sample of female twins with two assessments conducted 8 years apart. Heritability of social phobia was estimated as 51%. A similar heritability estimate (48%) was obtained for a measure of social anxiety–related cognitions (i.e., fear of negative evaluation) in twins (Stein, Jang, & Livesley, 2002). Kendler et al. (2001) reported heritability of 24% for social phobia in a set of male twins (without correction for unreliability). These studies support a moderate role for genetic influences on the risk for social phobia (Hettema, Neale, & Kendler, 2001). Heritability data for animal phobia, blood/injury phobia, and situational phobia were also reported by Kendler et al. (1999, 2001). Estimated heritabilities for these three were 47%, 59%, and 46%, respectively. Kendler et al. (2001) considered a sample of male twins; estimated heritabilities were 35%, 28%, and 25%, respectively (uncorrected for measurement unreliability). The estimated female heritabilities, if uncorrected, are similar to the male heritabilities. Twin studies support heritability of about 45%–65% for obsessive-compulsive disorder (OCD) in children and provide limited support for OCD heritability in the range of 27%–47% in adults

(van Grootheest, Cath, Beekman, & Boomsma, 2005).

Twin studies have also been used to investigate the shared genetic contribution to anxiety disorders and disorders that are comorbid with them. Kendler et al. (1995), using a large epidemiologic sample of female monozygotic (MZ) and dizygotic (DZ) twins, demonstrated existence of a genetic factor influencing risk for PD, phobia, and bulimia nervosa. Generalized anxiety disorder and major depression were influenced by a second genetic factor. An individual-specific environmental factor showed moderate loading for PD and phobia. Scherrer et al. (2000) reported that a common genetic factor can contribute to risk for PD and generalized anxiety disorder, based on the Vietnam Era Twin Registry data. Hettema et al. (2001) completed a meta-analysis of the genetic epidemiology literature for anxiety disorders and concluded that the familial aggregation for PD and phobias was explained more by genetic than by nongenetic factors, whereas for generalized anxiety disorder, genetic etiology was less well supported. Hettema, Prescott, Myers, Neale, & Kendler (2005) used structural equation modeling (SEM) to assess common contributions of genetic factors to multiple anxiety diagnosis and found evidence for two genetic factors influencing anxiety disorder risk. One factor was found to influence PD, AG, and generalized anxiety disorder, and another factor was found to influence animal phobia and situational phobia (which can be very difficult to distinguish from AG in some cases). Both of these factors loaded on social phobia. Hettema, Neale, Myers, Prescott, & Kendler (2006) also used SEM in a large twin sample to study the relationship between neuroticism and internalizing disorders (which include major depression and the anxiety disorders). They found that genetic factors shared with neuroticism accounted for between one-third and one-half of the genetic risk across the internalizing disorders, and that a separate neuroticism-independent genetic factor accounted for additional variance in the genetic risk for major depression, generalized anxiety disorder, and panic disorder. This type of knowledge of genetic substructure should assist in the search for susceptibility genes for anxiety disorders.

FAMILY STUDIES

Family studies cannot demonstrate that a disorder is genetically influenced (because of possible environmental confounds), but they provide supporting information and can suggest a range of comorbid disorders that might be influenced by the same genetic factors. Noyes et al. (1986) considered diagnoses in relatives of subjects with AG (alone). In their study, a degree of specificity was supported for PD and AG. The study found that AG was observed more frequently in relatives of subjects with AG than in relatives of subjects with PD (11.6% versus 1.9%), and PD was more common in relatives of subjects with PD than in relatives of subjects with AG (17.3% versus 8.3%). Wittchen, Redd, & Kessler (1998) considered the coaggregation of AG and PD in a German sample. In this sample, lifetime prevalence of *DSM–IV* PD was 1.6% (0.8% with AG and 0.8% without AG); lifetime prevalence of AG was 8.5%. Stein, Chartier, Lizak, & Jang (2001) studied probands with generalized SocP and their first-degree relatives; they demonstrated that relatives of subjects with SocP have increased scores on a range of social anxiety–related measures, and the Tridimensional Personality Questionnaire Harm Avoidance scale (Cloninger, 1987). Pauls, Alsobrook, Goodman, Rasmussen, & Leckman (1995) and Nestadt et al. (2000) applied family study methodology to the index diagnosis of OCD, and demonstrated that relatives of OCD cases have increased prevalence of OCD (10.3% and 11.7%, respectively) compared to controls (1.9% and 2.7%). Relatives of subjects with OCD also have increased prevalence of tic disorders (Grados et al., 2001; Pauls et al., 1995).

Mode of inheritance is important for model-based genetic analysis, which was the only form of linkage analysis widely used in the early days of psychiatric genetics. Early segregation analyses suggested that PD inheritance is consistent with a Mendelian single major locus dominant model (Pauls, Noyes, & Crowe, 1979; Pauls, Crowe, & Noyes, 1979). Hopper, Judd, Derrick, MacAskill, & Burrows (1990), in an analysis of data from a large family study, demonstrated vertical transmission of PD, and also found evidence for a sibship environment component. The data established increased incidence of PD in relatives of PD patients, again consistent with (but not proving) heritability (Crowe, Noyes, Pauls, & Slymen, 1983; Harris, Noyes, Crowe, & Chaudhry, 1983), and supported a possible genetic distinction between PD and GAD. Based on pedigree segregation analysis, Pauls, Bucher, Crowe, & Noyes (1980) suggested that PD may be inherited in a dominant fashion with about 75% penetrance; Crowe et al. (1983) proposed that it is transmitted by a dominant gene. Although single major locus autosomal dominant transmission of PD was consistent with segregation analyses, mode of transmission could not be established unambiguously (Judd, Burrows, & Hay, 1987; Vieland, Goodman, Chapman, & Fyer, 1996). Vieland et al. reported similar support for dominant and recessive models. Some recent data support a parent-of-origin effect (Haghighi, Fyer, Weissman, Knowles, & Hodge, 1999). Overall, the data do not consistently identify a mode of inheritance (Crowe et al., 1983; Pauls et al., 1980; Vieland et al., 1996)—which is most consistent with our current view of PD as a complex genetic trait, influenced by many genes (cf. Gelernter et al., 2001). This now-accepted complex model is also consistent with current knowledge of other complex neurobehavioral traits; they are almost always influenced by numerous genes of small to moderate effect. Nestadt et al. (2000) reported evidence for a major gene affecting OCD risk, based on segregation analysis.

In summary, PD, SocP, AG, SimpP, OCD, and certain anxiety-related traits have all been shown to be genetically influenced. Several studies have shown that it is likely that some genetic factors load on more than one anxiety disorder. Thus, it is rational to search for genes that influence major anxiety disorders and related quantitative traits, individually and jointly.

Molecular Genetics of Anxiety Disorders
Introduction: Issues of Definition of Phenotype

It is not exactly clear yet what the primary manifestation of an inherited predisposition to anxiety would look like. It is possible that it would be a *DSM–IV*–like syndrome, such as PD, but this is certainly not something we can count on. If we knew exactly what traits to look for in defining an individual as "affected," we would have an easier time at uncovering the pathophysiology related to that trait. There has thus been a fair amount of discussion and experimentation around this issue. Perhaps a risk gene predisposes to behavioral inhibition (BI), which would then itself predispose to any of several *DSM–IV* diagnoses. Or, it could be that a risk gene predisposes to the combination of social phobia and PD, only as a comorbid combination. Or there could be a gene that predisposes only to blood injury phobia, in isolation. Investigators in anxiety genetics have taken numerous ideas such as these as the starting points for their studies.

Linkage Studies in PD, AG, SocP, OCD, and Related Traits

Linkage studies can generally be used to implicate chromosomal regions that contain the more important genes that influence a trait. Risch showed that power for detecting linkage depends largely on the risk ratio characterizing a given trait, the recombination fraction, θ, and informativeness of the markers studied (Risch, 1990). For sib-pairs, λ_s is the probability of PD in sibs of affected individuals compared to unrelated population individuals; this is a key figure. Smoller and Tsuang (1998) estimated λ_s for PD as 5–10 (compared to 10 for schizophrenia and bipolar disorder, 2–4 for migraine, and 2–3 for major depression). This places PD in a range where linkage studies should clearly be usable to identify risk loci, and PD is the most-studied of the anxiety disorders via linkage methods.

Linkage studies have implicated numerous chromosomal regions as possibly, or probably, containing genes than influence risk for PD. The first such studies did not take a genomewide approach; Crowe et al. (1987, 1990) tested classical genetic markers (which provide relatively little information for analysis, compared to the molecular markers used today) for linkage in PD families without identifying a significant linkage. Limited candidate gene studies likewise failed to demonstrate significant linkage signals.

Genomewide linkages studies can theoretically provide evidence for linkage for disease-influencing loci wherever they map in the genome, if the marker map is dense enough and the study is otherwise adequately powered. However, adequately powered studies for complex traits like anxiety disorders need to be large and are expensive, and therefore, most published studies have faced power limitations. Knowles et al. (1998) published the first complete genome scan for PD. They described a "first-pass" screen with up to 23 families. Their six highest lod scores were between 1.0 and 2.0, two under a dominant model, on chromosomes 1p and 20p, and four under a recessive model, on chromosomes 7p, 17p, 20q, and X/Y. Smoller et al. (1999) reported a PD genome scan in a single large family, with 103 markers on 10 chromosomes studied; their most significant result showed pointwise (as opposed to genomewide), $p = 0.009$, for a chromosome 1 locus. Crowe et al. (2001) reported the second genome-wide linkage scan for PD, also with 23 families; they reported results of pairwise lod score analyses and multipoint nonparametric lod (NPL) analyses. They identified two lod scores > 2.0, both on chromosome 7, as well as numerous lod scores between 1 and 2. A Bayesian reanalysis of this dataset (Logue, Vieland, Goedken, & Crowe, 2003) revealed greatly increased evidence for a chromosome 7 locus.

Gelernter et al. (2001) published the third such study. These authors described a 10 cM genome-wide linkage scan in a set of 20 American pedigrees (153 subjects), ascertained through probands with panic disorder (PD). For PD, two genomic regions meet criteria for "suggestive" linkage. One of these regions was on chromosome 1 (lod score = 2.04); this region coincided with a region that generated a lod score of 1.1 in a previous genome scan (Crowe et al., 2001). The other, with lod score = 2.01, was located on chromosome 11p near markers at the cholecystokinin B receptor (CCKBR) locus, one of 8 candidate genes examined. For agoraphobia, the most promising potential linkage was on chromosome 3 (pointwise $p = 0.005$). This was accounted for mostly by a single family that by itself generated an NPL score of 10.01 ($p = 0.0039$), and a lod score of 2.10. These results provided initial evidence for a genetic locus on chromosome 3 that contributes to risk for agoraphobia. Overall, the results suggested that PD and AG are complex traits that share some, but not all, of their susceptibility loci. Note that none of the studies described above provided "genomewide-significant" evidence for the map location of a risk locus, that is, evidence still significant after correction for the many statistical tests required for a study of genomewide extent.

The most recent genomewide study for PD is also the largest, and was done by the DeCode group in Iceland (Thorgeirsson et al., 2003). Twenty-five extended pedigrees were included, and 976 short tandem repeat markers were genotyped. They identified the first genomewide-significant linkage signal related to (but not generated entirely by) panic disorder, a lod score of 4.18 on chromosome 9q31. For the analysis that generated this remarkable lod score, they included subjects with other anxiety diagnoses, besides PD. While this locus has not, to our knowledge, been replicated in other anxiety disorders, we observed a linkage peak for habitual cigarette smoking in families ascertained through panic probands, that is, the same family series studied previously for PD, at this same location (Gelernter, Liu, Hesselbrock, Page, Goddard, et al., 2004). One possible explanation is that this locus is related to some anxiety-related phenotype that has not yet been correctly discerned.

Weissman et al. (2000) described a possible PD syndrome, characterized by combinations of PD, kidney or bladder problems, thyroid abnormalities, and several other medical conditions. Their clinical sample included the subjects described in Knowles et al. (1998) plus additional families. When their analysis was restricted to families where the syndrome was present, they identified a chromosomal region with significant linkage on chromosome 13. Further evidence in support of this syndrome, and a chromosome 13 risk locus, was reported by Hamilton et al. (2003). These findings show how careful clinical observation in the identification of a PD subset seemingly led to a more genetically homogenous subgroup among PD families. If a gene can be identified that is related to this syndrome specifically, it is likely to lead to important insights about the pathophysiologic mechanisms that result in PD.

Smoller et al. (1999) reported a "targeted" linkage study for PD and related traits, selecting chromosomal regions for query based on homology with regions that had shown evidence for anxiety-related quantitative trait loci (QTL) in mouse studies. They identified "suggestive" evidence for linkage on (human) chromosomes 10q, 12q13, and 1q. Finally, Cheng et al. (2006) reported a genomewide linkage scan in a large sample of pedigrees selected because they segregated bipolar affective disorder, but which were also informative for other traits, including PD. Cheng et al. identified regions possibly linked to PD, including one at chromosome 7q21.

Gelernter et al. (2003) reported the only genomewide linkage scans for the trait of simple (specific) phobia. This was also the first report of a genetic linkage for a *DSM*-defined anxiety disorder that met genomewide significance criteria, with an observed lod score > 3.3 on chromosome 14. Gelernter, Page, Stein, and Woods (2004) also reported the only genomewide linkage scan for social phobia; this research yielded only "suggestive" linkage evidence, with support for linkage to markers on chromosomes 16, 9, 14, and 18.

Two studies (Hanna et al., 2002; Willour et al., 2004) have provided "suggestive" evidence for linkage of OCD to markers on chromosome 9p. Shugart et al. (2006) conducted a genomewide linkage scan of OCD in a set of 219 families, with "suggestive" evidence for linkage at multiple chromosomal locations. The family collection was based on the work of a large collaborative genetic linkage study of OCD (Samuels et al., 2006). Linkage analysis based on ordinal traits, which is an innovative way to conduct the analysis that accounts for differences in severity of phenotype between subjects, has been applied to the OCD-related trait of hoarding, with the demonstration of statistically significant evidence for linkage to three separate loci (Feng, Leckman, & Zhang, 2004).

One additional finding merits mention; Gratacòs et al. (2001) reported a chromosome 15 interstitial duplication, which they designated DUP25, and reported to be linked and associated to a range of anxiety disorders, together with joint laxity; DUP25 shows non-Mendelian inheritance. The linkage described was observed between the DUP25 *phenotype* and various diagnostic constructs. This result has not been replicated, and in fact, Tabiner et al. (2003) reported that DUP25 was observed neither in anxiety disorder patients, nor in cell lines reported by Gratacòs et al. to contain the variant. However, fixed cell lines sent to members of the Barcelona group were read by them to be DUP25 positive. At this point, it is difficult to provide a good explanation for these disparate observations.

Association Studies in Anxiety Disorders and Related Traits

Numerous candidate gene association studies have been published for anxiety-related traits. Many early negative reports were underpowered. Deckert et al. (1998) suggested possible association between adenosine 2A receptor gene (*ADORA2A*) variants and PD; since then there has been more evidence in support of linkage or association (e.g., Hamilton et al., 2004). Kato, Wang, Zoega, & Crowe (1996) identified a missense mutation in the *CCKBR* gene that was not significantly associated with PD nor linked in a small number of informative pedigrees. Wang, Valdes, Noyes, Zoega, & Crowe (1998) studied a polymorphism in the cholecystokinin promoter (*CCK*-36C/T) and reported possible LD with PD, depending on disease model; their linkage study was uninformative. Kennedy et al. (1999) supported genetic association between *CCKBR* and PD; however, Hamilton et al. (2001) found neither association or linkage of *CCKBR* to PD, using a different polymorphism. Hosing et al. (2004) found a significant association between a *CCKBR* variant and PD in a German sample. Consistent with the notion that genetic variation in the CCK neurotransmitter system may affect risk for PD, Hattori et al. (2001) reported an association between *CCK* alleles and haplotypes and PD in a Japanese population. Gelernter et al. (2001) studied a different *CCK* polymorphism in a European-American PD linkage series and did not find evidence for linkage, but this could be attributable to the difference in the populations studied.

Stein, Schork, & Gelernter (2004) demonstrated that a functional variant at the β_1 adrenergic receptor locus is associated with introversion (low extraversion), a trait that is characteristic of persons with social phobia and enriched in their first-degree relatives (Stein et al., 2001). Another heritable trait characteristic of some anxious youth, identified as high risk on the basis of having a parent with panic disorder, is behavioral inhibition to the unfamiliar (BI) (Kagan, Reznick, & Snidman, 1988; Kagan & Snidman, 1999). A subset of behaviorally inhibited children go on to develop SocP in adulthood, and it has consequently been suggested that BI may be an intermediate phenotype for certain anxiety disorders such as SocP that is more amenable to genetic dissection than are the clinical disorders themselves. In this regard, Smoller and colleagues have found strong evidence of association between the corticotropin releasing hormone (CRH) gene and BI (Smoller et al., 2003; Smoller et al., 2005). It has recently been shown that adults who had been designated in childhood with BI show a heightened amygdala response to novelty as demonstrated with functional magnetic resonance imaging (fMRI) (Schwartz, Wright, Shin, Kagan, & Rauch, 2003). This type of observation raises the possibility that brain responses to emotional stimuli may constitute an even more proximate phenotype (sometimes called an "endophenotype") than temperamental traits such as BI, and that it may be possible to use functional neuroimaging in combination with genetic techniques to uncover susceptibility factors for SocP and related disorders.

The catechol-O-methyltransferase (COMT) gene has been studied in panic disorder, and in a wide range of anxiety-related phenotypes. The best-known COMT variant is a functional single nucleotide polymorphism (SNP) that is responsible for an approximately 4-fold difference in enzyme activity, val158met (rs4680; Lachman et al., 1996). In a sample of 1,234 female nurses, McGrath et al. (2004) found association of val158met genotype with a quantitative trait measuring phobic anxiety, with "val" alleles associated with increased anxiety in a dose-related fashion. For PD, four recent studies support COMT (but not necessarily val158met) as a possible risk locus (Domschke et al., 2004; Hamilton et al., 2002; Woo, Yoon, & Yu, 2002; Woo et al., 2004). Hamilton et al. (2002) reported a haplotypic association with COMT; val158met was not significantly associated. Enoch, Xu, Ferro, Harris, & Goldman (2003) reported an association of the val158met "met" allele with elevated harm avoidance in women. Stein, Fallin, Schork, & Gelernter (2005) investigated three COMT variants, including val158met, in

a college student sample, and found association of two SNPs and the three SNP haplotype with low extraversion, also in women. These authors tested formally for population stratification, and in this case, were able to exclude stratification as the cause of the result. Nackley et al. (2006) demonstrated that synonymous SNPs at the COMT locus identify haplotypes that are associated with differences in protein expression, consistent with these results.

Several other genes have recently been identified in association analyses with anxiety-relevant traits. Hettema, An, et al. (2006) found an association between several SNPs in one of the genes (GAD1) encoding glutamic acid decarboxylase enzymes (which synthesize GABA from glutamate) and an anxiety- and depression-related factor using a case-control design with subjects selected for scoring at the extremes (i.e., high or low) of that factor. Wray et al. (2007) found several SNPs in the gene encoding plexin A2 (PLXNA2) to be associated with measures of anxiety (including anxiety and depression diagnoses, and neuroticism) using an extreme discordant and concordant sib-pair design extracted from a large population-based twin sample. It is likely that many more genes possibly conferring risk for anxiety-related traits and/or disorders will be identified in the near future. The challenge for the field will be to replicate the results, and then to determine the molecular mechanism(s) by which these genes confer risk. Such information will lead to the development of novel therapeutics for anxiety disorders.

We will highlight several of the many relevant candidate gene results for OCD. McDougle, Epperson, Price, & Gelernter (1998) used the transmission-disequilibrium test to demonstrate association of the "L" allele at the well-known serotonin transporter protein gene (SLC6A4) promoter region functional variant 5-HTTLPR. with OCD. This result was recently replicated by Hu et al. (2006), who extended the result to show that the association was accounted for by the "L_A" allele. Also, Dickel et al. (2006) reported association between markers at the SLC1A1 locus, which codes for a glutamate transporter gene, and early-onset OCD; this result is of particular interest because the gene maps to the previously identified chromosome 9p possible linkage region.

Summary and Conclusions

Studies using the techniques of genetic epidemiology have demonstrated that the major anxiety disorders are both familial and genetically influenced.

This demonstration has several implications, the most important of which is that there must be genes that influence these traits. Such genes have been localized by genetic linkage analysis, and identified by genetic association analysis.

However, compared to many other psychiatric disorders that cause significant morbidity in the population, there has been quantitatively less genetics research in anxiety disorders, and there have been fewer efforts to recruit and study the kinds of large clinical samples that are necessary for sufficient power to identify risk loci for genetically complex traits. Such efforts have, historically, been both very expensive and labor-intensive. Recent methodological advances in genetics research may make it easier in future to obtain more risk genes at lower cost—most specifically, by means of whole genome association study (WGAS) methodology. A WGAS uses case-control samples that are then genotyped very densely, with, generally, somewhere in the range of 100,000 to 1,500,000 markers per subject—this is a density that has been made feasible through application of genotyping array methodology. This kind of methodology has recently been responsible for notable successes in gene mapping for complicated and subtle behavioral traits such as memory performance (Papassotiropoulos et al., 2006) and nicotine dependence (Beirut et al., 2007), and has obvious applicability for anxiety disorder genetics as well.

Another recent development in psychiatric genetic is the realization that gene-by-environment (GxE) interaction can be taken into account, and that some of these effects are surprisingly large. GxE interaction refers to the situation in which environmental factors influence risk for a certain trait, but this influence varies depending on genotype. The GxE effects have been demonstrated for depressive symptoms (Caspi et al., 2003; Kaufman et al., 2004) and alcohol use (Covault et al., 2007; Kaufman et al., 2007), among other behavior phenotypes. It seems likely that it will be productive to take GxE effects into consideration for future studies of anxiety disorders as well. In this regard, we have recently reported a GxE effect for childhood maltreatment and the anxiety risk trait, anxiety sensitivity (Stein, Schork, & Gelernter, 2007).

Note

This work was supported in part by the U.S. Department of Veterans Affairs Medical Research Program, the U.S. Department of Veterans Affairs Depression Research Enhancement Award Program (VA CT REAP), and NIH (NIDA) K24 DA10515.

References

American Psychiatric Association. (1987). *Diagnostic and statistical manual of mental disorders* (3rd ed. revised). Washington, DC: Author.

American Psychiatric Association. (1994). *Diagnostic and statistical manual of mental disorders* (4th ed.). Washington, DC: Author.

Bierut, L., Madden, P.A.F., Breslau, N., Johnson, E. O., Hatsukami, D., Pomerleau, O. F., et al. (2007). Novel genes identified in a high-density genome wide association study for nicotine dependence. *Human Molecular Genetics, 16,* 24–35.

Bouchard, T. J., Lykken, D. T., McGue, M., Segal, N. L., & Tellegen, A. (1990). Sources of human psychological differences: The Minnesota Study of Twins Reared Apart. *Science, 250,* 223–228.

Caspi, A., Sugden, K., Moffitt, T. E., Taylor, A., Craig, I. W., Harrington, H., et al. (2003). Influence of life stress on depression: moderation by a polymorphism in the 5-HTT gene. *Science, 301,* 386–389.

Cheng, R., Juo, S. H., Loth, J. E., Nee, J., Iossifov, I., Blumenthaal, R., et al. (2006). Genome-wide linkage scan in a large bipolar disorder sample from the National Institute of Mental Health genetics initiative suggests putative loci for bipolar disorder psychosis, suicide, and panic disorder. *Molecular Psychiatry, 11,* 252–260.

Cloninger, C. R. (1987). A systematic method for clinical description and classification of personality variants. *Archives of General Psychiatry, 44,* 573–578.

Covault, J., Tennen, H., Armeli, S., Conner, T. S., Herman, A. I, Cillessen, A. H., et al. (2007). Interactive effects of the serotonin transporter 5-HTTLPR polymorphism and stressful life events on college student drinking and drug use. *Biological Psychiatry, 61,* 609–616.

Crowe, R., Goedken, R., Samuelson, S., Wilson, R., Nelson, J., & Noyes, R., Jr. (2001). Genomewide survey of panic disorder. *American Journal of Medical Genetics (Neuropsychiatric Genetics), 105,* 105–109.

Crowe, R., Noyes, R., Pauls, D. L., & Slymen, D. (1983). A family study of panic disorder. *Archives of General Psychiatry, 40,* 1065–1069.

Crowe, R. R., Noyes, R., Samuelson, S., Wesner, R., & Wilson, R. (1990). Close linkage between panic disorder and α-haptoglobin excluded in 10 families. *Archives of General Psychiatry, 47,* 377–380.

Crowe, R. R., Noyes, R., Wilson, A. F., Elston, R. C. & Ward, L. J. (1987). A linkage study of panic disorder. *Archives of General Psychiatry, 44,* 933–937.

Deckert, J., Nöthen, M. M., Franke, P., Delmo, C., Fritze, J., Knapp, M., et al. (1998). Systematic mutation screening and association study of the A1 and A2a adenosine receptor genes in panic disorder suggest a contribution of the A2a gene to the development of disease. *Molecular Psychiatry, 3,* 81–85.

Dickel, D., Veenstra-VanderWeele, J., Cox, N. J., Wu, X., Fischer, D. J., van Etten-Lee, M., et al. (2006). Association testing of the positional and functional candidate gene SLC1A1/EAAC1 in early-onset obsessive-compulsive disorder. *Archives of General Psychiatry, 63,* 778–785.

Domschke, K., Freitag, C. M., Kuhlenbaumer, G., Schirmacher, A., Sand, P., Nyhuis, P., et al. (2004). Association of the functional V158M catechol-O-methyl-transferase polymorphism with panic disorder in women. *International Journal of Neuropsychopharmacology, 7,* 183–188.

Enoch, M., Xu, K., Ferro, E., Harris, C. R., & Goldman, D. (2003). Genetic origins of anxiety in women: A role for a functional catechol-O-methyltransferase polymorphism. *Psychiatric Genetics, 13*, 33–41.

Feng, R., Leckman, J. F., & Zhang, H. (2004). Linkage analysis of ordinal traits for pedigree data. *Proceedings of the National Academy of Sciences of the United States of America, 101*, 16739–16744.

Gelernter, J., Bonvicini, K., Page, G., Woods, S. W., Goddard, A. W., Kurger, S., et al. (2001). Linkage genome scan for loci predisposing to panic disorder or agoraphobia. *American Journal of Medical Genetics (Neuropsychiatric Genetics), 105*, 548–557.

Gelernter, J., Liu, X., Hesselbrock, V., Page, G. P., Goddard, A., & Zhang, H. (2004). Results of a genomewide linkage scan: Support for chromosomes 9 and 11 loci increasing risk for cigarette smoking. *American Journal of Medical Genetics (Neuropsychiatric Genetics), 128*, 94–101.

Gelernter, J., Page, G., Bonvicini, K., Woods, S. W., Pauls, D. L., & Kruger, S. (2003). A chromosome 14 risk locus for simple phobia: Results from a genomewide linkage scan. *Molecular Psychiatry, 8*, 71–82.

Gelernter, J., Page, G., Stein, M., & Woods, S. W. (2004). Genome-wide linkage scan for loci predisposing to social phobia: Evidence for a chromosome 16 risk locus. *American Journal of Psychiatry, 161*, 59–66.

Grados, M. A., Riddle, M. A., Samuels, J. F., Liang, K. Y., Hoehn-Saric, R., Bienvenu, O. J., et al. (2001). The familial phenotype of obsessive-compulsive disorder in relation to tic disorders: The Hopkins OCD family study. *Biological Psychiatry, 50*, 559–565.

Gratacòs, M., Nadai, M., Martin-Santos, R., Pujana, M. A., Gago, J., Peral, B., et al. (2001). A polymorphic genomic duplication on human chromosome 15 is a susceptibility factor for panic and phobic disorders. *Cell, 106*, 367–379.

Haghighi, F., Fyer, A., Weissman, M., Knowles, J. A., & Hodge, S. E. (1999). Parent-of-origin effect in panic disorder. *American Journal of Medical Genetics (Neuropsychiatric Genetics), 88*, 131–135.

Hamilton, S., Fyer, A., Durner, M., Heiman, G. A., Baisre de Leon, A., Hodge, S. E., et al. (2003). Further genetic evidence for a panic disorder syndrome mapping to chromosome 13q. *Proceedings of the National Academy of Sciences, 100*, 2550–2555.

Hamilton, S., Slager, S., De Leon, A., Heiman, G. A., Klein, D. F., Hodge, S. E., et al. (2004). Evidence for genetic linkage between a polymorphism in the adenosine 2A receptor and panic disorder. *Neuropsychopharmacology, 29*, 558–565.

Hamilton, S., Slager, S., Heiman, G., Deng, Z., Haghighi, F., Klein, D. F., et al. (2002). Evidence for a susceptibility locus for panic disorder near the catechol-O-methyltransferase gene on chromosome 22. *Biological Psychiatry, 51*, 591–601.

Hamilton, S., Slager, S., Helleby, L., Heiman, G. A., Klein, D. F., Hodge, S. E., et al. (2001). No association or linkage between polymorphisms in the genes encoding cholecystokinin and the cholecystokinin B receptor and panic disorder. *Molecular Psychiatry, 6*, 59–65.

Hanna, G., Veenstra-VanderWeele, J., Cox, N. J., Boehnke, M., Himle, J. A., Curtis, G. C., et al. (2002). Genome-wide linkage analysis of families with obsessive-compulsive disorder ascertained through pediatric probands. *American Journal of Medical Genetics, 114*, 541–552.

Harris, E., Noyes, R., Crowe, R., & Chaudhry, D. R. (1983). Family study of agoraphobia. *Archives of General Psychiatry, 40*, 1061–1064.

Hattori, E., Ebihara, M., Yamada, K., Ohba, H., Shibuya, H., & Yoshikawa, T. (2001). Identification of a compound short tandem repeat stretch in the 5'-upstream region of the cholecystokinin gene, and its association with panic disorder but not with schizophrenia. *Molecular Psychiatry, 6*, 465–470.

Hettema, J., Neale, M., & Kendler, K. (2001). A review and meta-analysis of the genetic epidemiology of anxiety disorders. *American Journal of Psychiatry, 58*, 1568–1578.

Hettema, J. M., An, S. S., Neale, M. C., Bukszar, J., van den Oord, E. J., Kendler, K. S., et al. (2006). Association between glutamic acid decarboxylase genes and anxiety disorders, major depression, and neuroticism. *Molecular Psychiatry, 11*, 752–762.

Hettema, J. M., Neale, M. C, Myers, J. M., Prescott, C. A., & Kendler, K. S. (2006). A population-based twin study of the relationship between neuroticism and internalizing disorders. *American Journal of Psychiatry, 163*, 857–864.

Hettema, J., Prescott, C., Myers, J., Neale, M. C., & Kendler, K. S. (2005). The structure of genetic and environmental risk factors for anxiety disorders in men and women. *Archives of General Psychiatry, 62*, 182–189.

Hopper, J., Judd, F., Derrick, P., MacAskill, G. T., & Burrows, G. D. (1990). A family study of panic disorder: Reanalysis using a regressive logistic model that incorporates a sibship environment. *Genetic Epidemiology, 7*, 151–161.

Hosing, V., Schirmacher, A., Kuhlenbaumer, G., Freitag, C., Sand, P., Schlesiger, C., et al. (2004). Cholecystokinin- and cholecystokinin-B-receptor gene polymorphisms in panic disorder. *Journal of Neural Transmission, 68*(Suppl.), 147–156.

Hu, X.-Z., Lipsky, R. H., Zhu, G., Akhtar, L. A., Taubman, J., Greenberg, B. D., et al. (2006). Serotonin transporter promoter gain-of-function genotypes are linked to obsessive-compulsive disorder. *American Journal of Human Genetics, 78*, 815–826.

Judd, F., Burrows, G., & Hay, D. (1987). Panic disorder: Evidence for genetic vulnerability. *Australian and New Zealand Journal of Psychiatry, 21*, 197–208.

Kagan, J., Reznick, S., & Snidman, N. (1988). Biological bases of childhood shyness. *Science, 240*, 167–171.

Kagan, J., & Snidman, N. (1999). Early childhood predictors of adult anxiety disorders. *Biological Psychiatry, 46*, 1536–1541.

Kato, T., Wang, Z., Zoega, T., & Crowe, R. R. (1996). Missense mutation of the cholecystokinin B receptor gene: Lack of association with panic disorder. *American Journal of Medical Genetics (Neuropsychiatric Genetics), 67*, 401–405.

Kaufman, J., Yang, B.-Z., Douglas-Palumberi, H., Crause-Artus, M., Lipschitz, D., Kristal, J. H., et al. (2007). Genetic and environmental predictors of early alcohol use. *Biological Psychiatry, 61*, 1228–1234.

Kaufman, J., Yang, B.-Z., Douglas-Palumberi, H., Houshyar, S., Lipschitz, D., Krystal, J. H., et al. (2004). Social supports and serotonin transporter gene moderate depression in maltreated children. *Proceedings of the National Academy of Sciences of the United States of America, 101*, 17316–17321.

Kendler, K., Heath, A., Neale, M., Kessler, R. C., & Eaves, L. J. (1992). A population-based twin study of alcoholism in women. *Journal of the American Medical Association, 268*, 1877–1882.

Kendler, K., Karkowski, L., & Prescott, C. (1999). Fears and phobias: Reliability and heritability. *Psychological Medicine, 29*, 539–553.

Kendler, K., Myers, J., Prescott, C., & Neale, M. C. (2001). The genetic epidemiology of irrational fears and phobias in men. *Archives of General Psychiatry, 58,* 257–265.

Kendler, K., Walters, E., Neale, M., Kessler, R. C., Heath, A. C., & Eaves, L. J. (1995). The structure of the genetic and environmental risk factors for six major psychiatric disorders in women: Phobia, generalized anxiety disorder, panic disorder, bulimia, major depression, and alcoholism. *Archives of General Psychiatry, 52,* 374–383.

Kennedy, J. L., Bradwejn, J., Koszycki, D., King, N., Crowe, R., Vincent, J., et al. (1999). Investigation of cholecystokinin system genes in panic disorder. *Molecular Psychiatry, 4,* 284–285.

Kessler, R. C., Chiu, W. T., Jin, R., Ruscio, A. M., Shear, K., & Walters, E. E. (2006). The epidemiology of panic attacks, panic disorder, and agoraphobia in the National Comorbidity Survey Replication. *Archives of General Psychiatry, 63,* 415–424.

Kessler, R. C., McGonagle, K. A., Zhao, S., Nelson, C. B., Hughes, M., Eshleman, S., et al. (1994). Lifetime and 12-month prevalence of *DSM–III–R* psychiatric disorders in the United States. Results from the National Comorbidity Survey. *Archives of General Psychiatry, 51,* 8–19.

Knowles, J. A., Fyer, A. J., Vieland, V. J., Weissman, M. M., Hodge, S. E., Heiman, G. A., et al. (1998). Results of a genome-wide genetic screen for panic disorder. *American Journal of Medical Genetics, 81,* 139–147.

Lachman, H. M., Papolos, D. F., Saito, T., Yu, Y. M., Szumlanski, C. L., & Weinshilboum, R. M. (1996). Human catechol-O-methyltransferase pharmacogenetics: Description of a functional polymorphism and its potential application to neuropsychiatric disorders. *Pharmacogenetics, 6,* 243–250.

Logue, M. W., Vieland, V. J., Goedken, R. J., & Crowe, R. R. (2003). Bayesian analysis of a previously published genome screen for panic disorder reveals new and compelling evidence for linkage to chromosome 7. *American Journal of Medical Genetics (Neuropsychiatric Genetics), 121,* 95–99.

Magee, W., Eaton, W. W., Wittchen, H.-U., McGonagle, K. A., & Kessler, R. C. (1996). Agoraphobia, simple phobia, and social phobia in the National Comorbidity Survey. *Archives of General Psychiatry, 53,* 159–168.

McDougle, C., Epperson, C. N., Price, L. H., & Gelernter, J. (1998). Evidence for linkage disequilibrium between serotonin transporter protein gene (SLC6A4) and obsessive-compulsive disorder. *Molecular Psychiatry, 3,* 270–274.

McGrath, M., Kawachi, I., Ascherio, A., Colditz, G. A., Hunter, D. J., & De Vivo, I. (2004). Association between catechol-O-methyltransferase and phobic anxiety. *American Journal of Psychiatry, 161,* 1703–1705.

Nackley, A., Shabalina, S. A., Tchivileva, I. E., Satterfield, K., Korchynskyi, O., Makarov, S. S., et al. (2006). Human catechol-O-methyltransferase haplotypes modulate protein expression by altering mRNA secondary structure. *Science, 314,* 1930–1933.

Nestadt, G., Samuels, J., Riddle, M., Bienvenu, O. J., III, Liang, K. Y., LaBuda, M., et al. (2000). A family study of obsessive-compulsive disorder. *Archives of General Psychiatry, 57,* 358–363.

Noyes, R., Jr., Crowe, R. R., Harris, E. L., Hamra, B. J., McChesney, C. M., & Chaudhry, D. R. (1986). Relationship between panic disorder and agoraphobia: A family study. *Archives of General Psychiatry, 43,* 227–232.

Papassotiropoulos, A., Stephan, D. A., Huentelman, M. J., Hoerndli, F. J., Craig, D. W., Pearson, J. V., et al. (2006). Common kibra alleles are associated with human memory performance. *Science, 314,* 475–478.

Pauls, D. L., Alsobrook, J. P., II, Goodman, W., Rasmussen, S., & Leckman, J. F. (1995). A family study of obsessive-compulsive disorder. *American Journal of Psychiatry, 152,* 76–84.

Pauls, D. L., Bucher, K. D., Crowe, R. R., & Noyes, R., Jr. (1980). A genetic study of panic disorder pedigrees. *American Journal of Human Genetics, 32,* 639–644.

Pauls, D. L., Crowe, R. R., & Noyes, R., Jr. (1979). Distribution of ancestral secondary cases in anxiety neurosis (panic disorder). *Journal of Affective Disorders, 1,* 387–390.

Pauls, D. L., Noyes, R., Jr., & Crowe, R. R. (1979). The familial prevalence in second-degree relatives of patients with anxiety neurosis (panic disorder). *Journal of Affective Disorders, 1,* 279–285.

Risch, N. (1990). Linkage strategies for genetically complex traits. III. The effect of marker polymorphism on analysis of affected relative pairs. *American Journal of Human Genetics, 46,* 242–253.

Samuels, J. F., Riddle, M. A., Greenberg, B. D., Fyer, A. J., McCracken, J. T., Rauch, S. L., et al. (2006). The OCD collaborative genetics study: Methods and sample description. *American Journal of Medical Genetics (Neuropsychiatric Genetics), 141,* 201–207.

Sareen, J., Cox, B. J., Clara, I., & Asmundson, G. J. (2005). The relationship between anxiety disorders and physical disorders in the U.S. National Comorbidity Survey. *Depression and Anxiety, 21,* 193–202.

Scherrer, J. F., True, W. R., Xian, H., Lyons, M. J., Eisen, S. A., Goldberg, J., et al. (2000). Evidence for genetic influences common and specific to symptoms of generalized anxiety and panic. *Journal of Affective Disorders, 57,* 25–35.

Schwartz, C., Wright, C., Shin, L., Kagan, J., & Rauch, S. L. (2003). Inhibited and uninhibited infants "grown up": Adult amygdalar response to novelty. *Science, 300,* 1952–1953.

Shugart, Y. Y., Samuels, J., Willour, V. L., Grados, M. A., Greenberg, B. D., Knowles, J. A., et al. (2006). Genomewide linkage scan for obsessive-compulsive disorder: Evidence for susceptibility loci on chromosomes 3q, 7p, 1q, 15q, and 6q. *Molecular Psychiatry, 11,* 763–770.

Skre, I., Onstad, S., Torgersen, S., Lygren, S., & Kringlen, E. (1993). A twin study of *DSM–III–R* anxiety disorders. *Acta Psychiatrica Scandinavica, 88,* 85–92.

Smoller, J. W., Acierno, J. S., Jr., Rosenbaum, J. F., Biederman, J., Pollack, M. H., Meminger, S., et al. (1999). Targeted genome screen of panic disorder and anxiety disorder proneness using homology to murine QTL regions. *American Journal of Medical Genetics, 105,* 195–206.

Smoller, J. W., Rosenbaum, J. F., Biederman, J., Kennedy, J., Dai, D., Raclette, S. R., et al. (2003). Association of a genetic marker at the corticotropin-releasing hormone locus with behavioral inhibition. *Biological Psychiatry, 54,* 1376–1381.

Smoller, J. W., & Tsuang, M. T. (1998). Panic and phobic anxiety: Defining phenotypes for genetic studies. *American Journal of Psychiatry, 155,* 1152–1162.

Smoller, J. W., Yamaki, L. H., Fagerness, J. A., Biederman, J., Racette, S., Laird, N. M., et al. (2005). The corticotropin releasing hormone gene and behavioral inhibition in children at risk for panic disorder. *Biological Psychiatry, 57,* 1485–1492.

Stein, M. B., Chartier, M. J., Lizak, M. V., & Jang, K. L. (2001). Familial aggregation of anxiety-related quantitative traits in generalized social phobia: Clues to understanding "disorder" heritability? *American Journal of Medical Genetics, 105,* 79–83.

Stein, M. B., Fallin, M. D., Schork, N. J., & Gelernter, J. (2005). COMT polymorphisms and anxiety-related personality traits. *Neuropsychopharmacology, 30,* 2092–2102.

Stein, M. B., Jang, K. L., & Livesley, W. J. (2002). Heritability of social anxiety-related concerns and personality characteristics: A twin study. *Journal of Nervous and Mental Disease, 190,* 219–224.

Stein, M. B., Schork, N. J., & Gelernter, J. A. (2004). Polymorphism of the beta1-adrenergic receptor is associated with low extraversion. *Biological Psychiatry, 56,* 217–224.

Stein, M. B., Schork, N. J., & Gelernter, J. A. (2008). Gene-by-environment (serotonin transporter and childhood maltreatment) interaction for anxiety sensitivity, an intermediate phenotype for anxiety disorders. *Neuropsychopharmacology 33* (2): 312–319.

Tabiner, M., Youings, S., Dennis, N., Baldwin, D., Buis, C., Mayers, A., et al. (2003). Failure to find DUP25 in patients with anxiety disorders, in control individuals, or in previously reported positive control cell lines. *American Journal of Human Genetics, 72,* 535–538.

Thorgeirsson, T. E., Oskarsson, H., Desnica, N., Kostic, J. P., Stefansson, J. G., Kolbeinsson, H., et al. (2003). Anxiety with panic disorder linked to chromosome 9q in Iceland. *American Journal of Human Genetics, 72,* 1221–1230.

Torgersen, S. (1983). Genetic factors in anxiety disorders. *Archives of General Psychiatry, 40,* 1085–1089.

Van Grootheest, D., Cath, D. C., Beekman, A. T., & Boomsma, D. I. (2005). Twin studies on obsessive-compulsive disorder: A review. *Twin Research and Human Genetics, 5,* 450–458.

Vieland, V. J., Goodman, D. W., Chapman, T., & Fyer, A. J. (1996). New segregation analysis of panic disorder. *American Journal of Medical Genetics, 67,* 147–153.

Wang, Z., Valdes, J., Noyes, R., Zoega, T., & Crowe, R. R. (1998). Possible association of a cholecystokinin promotor polymorphism (CCK-36CT) with panic disorder. *American Journal of Medical Genetics, 81,* 228–234.

Weissman, M. M., Fyer, A. J., Haghighi, F., Heiman, G., Deng, Z., Hen, R., et al. (2000). Potential panic disorder syndrome: Clinical and genetic linkage evidence. *American Journal of Medical Genetics, 96,* 24–35.

Willour, V. L., Shugart, Y. Y., Samuels, J., Grados, M., Cullen, B., Bienvenu, O. J., III, et al. (2004). Replication study supports evidence for linkage to 9p24 in obsessive-compulsive disorder. *American Journal of Human Genetics, 75,* 508–513.

Wittchen, H.-U., Reed, V., & Kessler, R. C. (1998). The relationship of agoraphobia and panic in a community sample of adolescents and young adults. *Archives of General Psychiatry, 55,* 1017–1024.

Woo, J. M., Yoon, K. S., Choi, Y. H., Oh, K. S., Lee, Y. S., & Yu, B. H. (2004). The association between panic disorder and the L/L genotype of catechol-O-methyltransferase. *Journal of Psychiatric Research, 38,* 365–370.

Woo, J. M., Yoon, K. S., & Yu, B. H. (2002). Catechol O-methyltransferase genetic polymorphism in panic disorder. *American Journal of Psychiatry, 159,* 1785–1787.

Wray, N. R., James, M. R., Mah, S. P., Nelson, M., Andrews, G., Sullivan, P. F., et al. (2007). Anxiety and comorbid measures associated with PLXNA2. *Archives of General Psychiatry, 64,* 318–326.

Neuroanatomy and Neuroimaging of Anxiety Disorders

Jennifer C. Britton *and* Scott L. Rauch

Abstract

Neuroimaging methods can be used to examine functional brain differences between healthy individuals and those with anxiety disorders. After the brain regions implicated in the pathophysiology of anxiety disorders (e.g., amygdalo-cortical circuitry) are reviewed, neuroimaging studies of posttraumatic stress disorder (PTSD), social anxiety disorder (SAD), specific phobia (SP), and panic disorder (PD) that report activations in these regions are discussed. Studies of obsessive-compulsive disorder (OCD) implicate a distinct neurocircuitry profile (i.e., cortico-striatal-thalamic circuit) compared to the other anxiety disorders. Few neuroimaging studies of generalized anxiety disorder (GAD) have been conducted. In addition, results from functional connectivity analyses and the effects of treatment on neuroimaging findings are summarized.

Keywords: amygdala, cingulate, fMRI, hippocampus, insula, medial prefrontal cortex, neuroanatomy, neurocircuitry, neuroimaging

The functional brain differences present in anxiety disorders (i.e., posttraumatic stress disorder (PTSD), social anxiety disorder (SAD), specific phobia (SP), panic disorder (PD), and obsessive-compulsive disorder (OCD)) compared to healthy individuals can be examined using neuroimaging methods (for methods review, see Dougherty & Rauch, 2003; Toga & Mazziotta, 1996). Given the similarities in some symptoms across anxiety disorders, a common underlying neural correlate is expected to subserve the shared symptom profile of anxiety. However, anxiety disorders also have unique clinical features, such as distinct triggering mechanisms (e.g., external or internal) that may in turn be mediated by distinct neural substrates. A better understanding of the neural circuitry involved may aid in determining appropriate treatment strategies that target abnormal function. In this chapter, we will: (1) review the features of each anxiety disorder pertinent for our discussion; (2) review the function of brain re-

gions implicated in the pathophysiology of anxiety disorders; and (3) review neuroimaging studies conducted in anxiety disorder populations, including those studies showing effects of treatment.

Anxiety Disorders: Phenomenology and Diagnosis

Although detailed descriptions of the anxiety disorders have been provided elsewhere in this volume (Chapters 3 through 6), it is important to highlight key features of these disorders that will be helpful in understanding the functional neuroimaging data reviewed below.

Most anxiety disorders are characterized by exaggerated and inappropriate fear responses to various stimuli distinctive to the disorder. Individuals with *PTSD* develop a constellation of anxiety symptoms, including heightened arousal, hypervigilance, emotional numbing, and nightmares/flashbacks, in response to reminders of an emotionally traumatic event. In the case of flashbacks, these symptoms can occur spontaneously and are possibly due to heightened sensitivities to the environment. *Phobias* are characterized by exaggerated anxiety responses to feared objects (e.g., social situations in SAD, objects or places in SP) that to most individuals appear nonthreatening. *PD* is characterized by spontaneous and recurring episodes of anxiety, usually accompanied by a series of physical symptoms (e.g., rapid heartbeat, sweating, or nausea). Since the symptoms in PD are often sudden and unexpected, the individual may have a hypersensitivity to external cues in the absence of conscious awareness. A full-scale anxiety response may result as the individual's attention is drawn to internal cues (e.g., shortness of breath or racing heart) because the external trigger is unknown and cognitive strategies to regulate these unexpected responses may be difficult or lagging. In *OCD,* obsessions are recurrent, persistent, and irrational impulses, thoughts, or images that cause marked anxiety or distress; compulsions are ritualistic, repetitive, and purposeful behaviors (e.g., checking) or mental acts (e.g., counting) that an individual performs in response to the obsessions or concomitant increased anxiety.

Functional Neuroanatomy: Key Circuits Implicated

Several neurocircuitry models of anxiety disorders have been developed based on functional neuroanatomy (Figure 1) and clinical phenomenology. For instance, stimulus-driven anxiety detected in PTSD, SAD, SP, and PD may result from abnormalities in bottom-up processing, while cognition-driven anxiety in OCD may result from abnor-

malities in top-down processing. Contemporary models of anxiety disorders hypothesize hyperresponsivity of the amygdala, a structure implicated in fear processing, in response to threat-related stimuli (Figure 2). Decreased thresholds to detect threat, increased threat sensitivity or exaggerated conditioned responses to particular classes of stimuli (e.g., traumatic reminders in PTSD, social situations in SAD, objects in SP, unconscious environmental cues in PD) may account for exaggerated amygdala activation. The amygdala hyperactivity may also be accompanied by deficient top-down regulation (e.g., failure to extinguish fear-conditioned responses) by the medial prefrontal cortex (mPFC), a region that exerts cortical influence over the amygdala. Based on its unique symptomatology, OCD may involve a distinct neurocircuitry, specifically, the cortico-striatal-thalamic circuit (Figure 3). Previous evidence suggests that inappropriate gating of the thalamus by the striatum may yield hyperactivity of the orbitofrontal cortex (OFC) and anterior cingulate cortex (ACC). Although models of anxiety disorders have typically emphasized the amygdalo-cortical and cortio-striatal-thalamic circuitry, other regions may be involved as well and will be reviewed in the upcoming sections.

Pertinent Neurocircuitry

Previous studies of anxiety disorders have concentrated on the amygdalo-cortical circuitry; yet evidence suggests that the amygdala, ACC, mPFC, insula, hippocampus, and posterior cingulate cortex (PCC) all play a role in anxiety disorders. The discussion is organized to highlight the regions most central to various emotional processes: threat assessment,

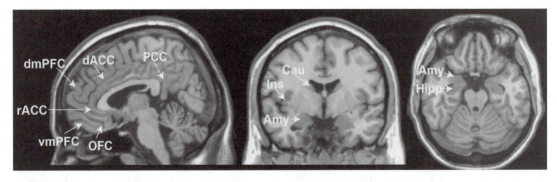

Fig. 1 Neuroanatomical locations. In sagittal view, dorsomedial prefrontal cortex (dmPFC), ventromedial prefrontal cortex (vmPFC[1]), orbitofrontal cortex (OFC), dorsal anterior cingulate cortex (dACC), rostral anterior cingulate cortex (rACC), thalamus (Tha), and posterior cingulate cortex (PCC). In the coronal view, caudate (Cau), insula (Ins), amygdala (Amy). In axial view, amygdala and hippocampus (Hipp).

[1] In the literature, the vmPFC is inconsistently defined and often encompasses the more circumscribed regions of OFC and rostral ACC in addition to more rostral medial regions as shown.

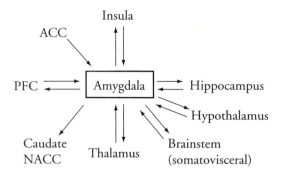

Fig. 2 Amygdalocentric neurocircuitry model of anxiety disorders.

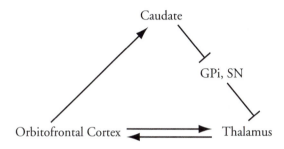

Fig. 3 Cortico-striatal-thalamic circuitry model of obsessive compulsive disorder (OCD). For simplicity, only the indirect basal ganglia pathway from the striatum to the thalamus is shown.

conditioned fear acquisition, and mediation of the fear response (amygdala); attention to emotional stimuli (ACC); emotion regulation (mPFC); interoception and visceral response (insula); and explicit as well as contextual memory (hippocampus and PCC). In doing so, we will provide functional evidence that these regions and their dysregulation may be common across the anxiety disorders. We have opted to discuss OCD and Generalized Anxiety Disorder (GAD) separately, reflecting the unique profiles and foreshadowing the potential recategorization of psychiatric diagnoses (i.e., separating OCD and GAD from the other anxiety disorders).

Amygdala

The amygdala is most notably associated with anxiety disorders because of its role in threat assessment, fear conditioning, and the fear response (for review, see Rauch, Shin, & Wright, 2003). Exaggerated fear responses are noted as key features of PTSD, SAD, SP, and PD. In this section, we review the functional differences in amygdala response to (1) generalized stimuli, and (2) disorder-specific stimuli (e.g., trauma-related stimuli for PTSD, facial

expression and social stress in SAD, phobic-related stimuli in SP, and panic-related stimuli in PD).

PTSD

General—Both PTSD and trauma-exposed non-PTSD control (TENC) subjects exhibit amygdala activation in response to fearful faces compared to happy faces when presented overtly (Shin et al., 2005) or masked (Rauch et al., 2000). In addition, this amygdala activation to fearful faces was greater in PTSD subjects relative to TENC subjects. On the other hand, in one study, while control groups activated the amygdala in response to general negative pictures, PTSD subjects failed to activate the amygdala. In that study, the amygdala response was greater in the TENC and healthy control groups relative to the PTSD subjects (Phan, Britton, Taylor, Fig, & Liberzon, 2006).

PTSD-specific—Since PTSD develops following a traumatic insult, traumatic reminders often trigger states of anxiety and these stimuli tend to activate the amygdala. Functional studies often report amygdala activations in PTSD participants in response to traumatic reminders, including combat sounds relative to white noise (Liberzon et al., 1999), script-driven imagery of the traumatic event relative to a neutral event (Rauch et al., 1996), and combat imagery relative to the combat perception (Shin, Kosslyn, et al., 1997). Liberzon and colleagues were the first to examine activation patterns in PTSD, TENC, and healthy controls and showed a different amygdala response in each group. During script-driven imagery of traumatic/stressful events, amygdala activation was reported in healthy noncombat exposed participants, amygdala deactivation in TENC participants, and no amygdala activity in PTSD participants (Britton, Phan, Taylor, Fig, & Liberzon, 2005). The failure to find amygdala activation in response to script-driven imagery in PTSD patients is consistent with other studies (Bremner, Narayan, et al., 1999; Shin et al., 1999). In addition, the amygdala deactivation in TENC participants is consistent with another study examining combat relative to negative perception (Shin, Kosslyn et al., 1997) and may reflect a compensatory mechanism (i.e., psychological resilience) that the PTSD patients cannot adequately engage.

SAD

Social-specific—In SAD, bilateral amygdala activations have been reported in response to disorder-specific stimuli (e.g., facial stimuli and social stress);

such responses have been observed to correlate with indices of SAD severity and are found to be greater in SAD subjects than in control subjects. Amygdala activations in response to neutral faces during an emotional rating task (Birbaumer et al., 1998), in response to harsh faces (Stein, Goldin, Sareen, Zorrilla, & Brown, 2002; Straube, Kolassa, Glauer, Mentzel, & Miltner, 2004) and in response to neutral faces paired with negative odors have been reported in SAD patients (Schneider et al., 1999). During an emotion identification task, symptom severity was associated with increased amygdala activity in response to harsh relative to happy faces (Phan, Fitzgerald, Nathan, & Tancer, 2006). In healthy adolescents, amygdala activation in response to fearful faces relative to fixation correlated with anxiety pertaining to social stressors as opposed to nonsocial stressors (Killgore & Yurgelun-Todd, 2005), possibly reflecting increased social anxiety in these individuals. When anticipating a public speech, a highly stressful social event, SAD participants exhibited amygdala activation and the amygdala activity correlated with fear ratings (Tillfors et al., 2001). During public speaking, amygdala activation was greater in SAD patients than in healthy controls (Tillfors et al., 2001).

SP

General—Amygdala activation has been reported in response to fear-inducing and disgust-inducing pictures relative to neutral pictures and this activation was greater in SP compared to healthy controls (Schienle, Schafer, Walter, Stark, & Vaitl, 2005). Although some findings support exaggerated amygdala activation to fearful and disgust stimuli, one study did not detect amygdala activation in response to fearful faces (Wright, Martis, McMullin, Shin, & Rauch, 2003). In one study, SP participants deactivated the amygdala in response to general pictures paired with an acoustic startle (Pissiota et al., 2003).

Phobia-specific—Individuals with phobias have an exaggerated fear response to specific objects (e.g., spiders) or situations (e.g., enclosed spaces); amygdala activations have been reported in response to these stimuli. Individuals with SP activated the amygdala (Carlsson et al., 2004) and showed exaggerated amygdala activation compared to healthy controls in response to phobia-relevant pictures relative to neutral pictures (Dilger et al., 2003; Schienle, Schafer, Walter et al., 2005; Straube, Mentzel, & Miltner, 2006). Even though some findings support exaggerated amygdala activity to phobia-relevant stimuli, other studies using phobic-related films or

phobic-related objects did not find amygdala activations in SP, though such studies lacked healthy comparison groups and used imaging methods with more limited temporal resolution (Rauch et al., 1995; Wik et al., 1993).

PD

General—Greater glucose utilization in bilateral amygdala has been reported in PD patients relative to healthy controls (Sakai et al., 2005). In children with anxiety disorders, including PD and generalized anxiety disorder (GAD), amygdala activation in response to fearful faces was detected and this activation both correlated with symptom severity and was greater in anxious children compared to healthy controls (Thomas et al., 2001). In addition, exaggerated amygdala responses to masked faces were found in PD patients relative to healthy controls (Whalen, Pollack, Shin, & Rauch, 2001). However, amygdala activation was not detected when PD subjects were judging the valence of threat relative to neutral words (Maddock, Buonocore, Kile, & Garrett, 2003).

Panic-specific—Patients with PD, relative to OCD patients and healthy controls, showed greater amygdala response to panic-related words in an emotional Stroop task (van den Heuvel et al., 2005).

Anterior Cingulate Cortex

The ACC is divided into rostral (BA 24, 25, 32, 33) and dorsal subterritories (BA 24, 32). Some evidence suggests that the rostral ACC (rACC) processes more emotional task demands and dorsal ACC (dACC) processes more cognitive task demands (e.g., performance monitoring, error detection, allocation of attention, and subjective awareness) (see Bush, Luu, & Posner, 2000). The altered rACC and dACC activity in anxiety disorders may reflect a heightened sensitivity or lowered perceptual thresholds to various stimuli, and/or deficient regulation. Of note, the boundary between rACC and dACC is not well defined and is continually being refined. In addition, the nomenclature of the ACC territories (e.g., using anterior midcingulate [aMCC] versus dACC) is evolving (Vogt, Berger, & Derbyshire, 2003). Evolving demarcations of cingulate cortex subdivisions as well as the emergence of new subterritory names has made reading the literature difficult because clear definitions and consistency are lacking.

PTSD

The rACC (BA 24, 32, 25) response to fearful faces (Shin et al., 2005), script-driven imagery

(Bremner, Narayan, et al., 1999; Britton et al., 2005; Shin et al., 1999), and combat perception (Bremner, Staib, et al., 1999) was lower in PTSD patients compared to control groups, which could be explained by lower activation or greater deactivation. To general stimuli (e.g., fearful faces) (Shin et al., 2005), the rACC activated in both PTSD and TENC groups, but in response to PTSD-relevant stimuli (e.g., script-driven imagery and combat perception), the rACC deactivated in PTSD subjects (Bremner, Narayan, et al., 1999; Bremner, Staib, et al., 1999; Britton et al., 2005; Shin et al., 1999).

As for the dACC, a variety of studies report activations in response to fearful faces (Shin et al., 2005), aversive pictures (Phan, Britton, et al., 2006), PTSD-related pictures (Bremner, Narayan, et al., 1999), and script-driven imagery in the TENC group (Bremner, Staib, et al., 1999; Shin, McNally, et al., 1997; Shin et al., 1999), possibly reflecting increased regulation for general and trauma-related stimuli. Studies report dACC activations in response to aversive pictures (Phan, Britton, et al., 2006), script-driven imagery (Britton et al., 2005; Rauch et al., 1996), and traumatic imagery in the PTSD group (Shin, Kosslyn, et al., 1997), while some studies report dACC deactivations (Shin, Kosslyn, et al., 1997; Shin et al., 2005). As a consequence, TENCs showed greater response to script-driven imagery than the PTSD group (Lanius et al., 2001; Shin et al., 1999; Shin, Orr, et al., 2004). As stated above, the disparity in findings may be attributed, at least in part, to varying definitions of the rACC/dACC boundary.

SAD

A greater dACC response to harsh faces relative to neutral faces has been detected in SAD patients compared to healthy controls, demonstrating an attentional bias to social threat (Phan, Fitzgerald, et al., 2006). However, when anticipating giving a public speech, healthy controls showed greater ACC activation than individuals with SAD (Lorberbaum et al., 2004), possibly reflecting an inability on the part of individuals with SAD to regulate during stressful social events.

SP

In response to general pictures paired with an acoustic startle, dACC deactivations were reported in SP (Pissiota et al., 2003). Dorsal ACC activation has been reported in symptom provocation studies using fear-related objects (Rauch et al., 1995) and phobia-relevant stimuli (Carlsson et al., 2004;

Pissiota et al., 2003; Straube, Mentzel, & Miltner, 2005) and this response was greater in SP (Straube, Glauer, Dilger, Mentzel, & Miltner, 2006), reflecting heightened sensitivities to stimuli.

PD

Panic patients, like healthy controls, show increased dACC responses to threat words (Maddock et al., 2003). Group differences in rACC and dACC response to panic-related words during an emotional Stroop task were detected (van den Heuvel et al., 2005).

Medial Prefrontal Cortex

Given the reciprocal connections and tendency of the mPFC and amygdala to co-activate, the mPFC serves a regulatory role in modulating the amygdala (Ochsner, Bunge, Gross, & Gabrieli, 2002; Ongur & Price, 2000). The addition of cognitive tasks (e.g., rating), which increases mPFC activation, is associated with reduced amygdala activity (Taylor, Phan, Decker, & Liberzon, 2003). Likewise, reappraising or suppressing negative emotion is associated with increased mPFC activation and decreased amygdala activation (Ochsner et al., 2002). Some subregions of the mPFC may have more specialized roles. The more dorsal mPFC (dmPFC, BA 8, 9) may be more involved in cognitive-emotional interactions (Liberzon et al., 2000; Simpson et al., 2000). The ventral mPFC (vmPFC, BA 10, 11, 32) is involved in fear extinction (Phelps, Delgado, Nearing, & LeDoux, 2004) and extinction recall is correlated with medial OFC cortical thickness (Milad et al., 2005). The vmPFC tends to be involved in the integration of affective information, decision making, and "gut feelings" (Bechara, Tranel, & Damasio, 2000). In addition, the vmPFC has been shown to deactivate less when processing "self" in comparison to greater deactivations to "other" (Kelley et al., 2002) and its activity is modulated during the performance of a self-association task (Phan et al., 2004).

Regulatory processes may be dysfunctional across anxiety disorders, implicating the mPFC. For example, a decreased dmPFC response, reflecting deficient regulation, may explain anxiety symptoms. In addition, vmPFC deactivations may reflect deficiencies in fear extinction recall capacities as well as "self" processing that may be especially relevant to SAD.

PTSD

Trauma-exposed non-PTSD controls exhibited dmPFC activation in response to fearful faces and this response was greater than PTSD patients (Shin et al., 2005), suggesting PTSD patients fail to activate regulatory structures adequately. Likewise, in response to aversive relative to neutral pictures, healthy controls activated the dmPFC, but the TENCs and PTSD patients did not activate these structures (Phan, Britton, et al., 2006). Patients with PTSD deactivated the dmPFC in response to combat relative to negative pictures (Shin, Kosslyn, et al., 1997). On the other hand, in one study, the PTSD patients had greater response in this region than the TENCs (Bremner, Narayan, et al., 1999), which may have reflected the increased effort for successful regulation.

Control groups had greater vmPFC/OFC response to fearful faces (Shin et al., 2005), negative pictures (Phan, Britton, et al., 2006) and neutral word recall (Shin, Shin, et al., 2004). This greater response was a result of vmPFC deactivation in response to fearful faces in PTSD patients (Shin et al., 2005) and vmPFC activation in response to aversive pictures in the healthy controls (Phan, Britton, et al., 2006). Patients with PTSD showed less vmPFC activity in response to script-driven imagery (Bremner, Narayan, et al., 1999; Lanius et al., 2001; Shin, Orr, et al., 2004). In another script-driven imagery study, TENCs and healthy controls, unlike PTSD patients, deactivated the vmPFC, possibly suggesting PTSD patients were engaged in more self-relevant processing (Britton et al., 2005). The OFC was activated in response to script-driven imagery in PTSD patients and this OFC response in PTSD patients was greater than the TENC group (Shin et al., 1999), possibly reflecting greater processing of punishment.

SAD

Dorsal mPFC activation in response to angry faces was reported in SAD patients and this response was greater than healthy controls (Stein et al., 2002; Straube, Kolassa, et al., 2004), possibly reflecting the increased need to regulate exaggerated amygdala activity. Giving a public speech resulted in vmPFC deactivations, but SAD patients deactivated to a greater extent than healthy controls (Tillfors et al., 2001). Although the explanation for this phenomenon is unclear, we speculate that the finding is consistent with convergent evidence that vmPFC activity is often inversely correlated with both fear expression and amygdala activation (Milad & Quirk, 2002; Phelps et al., 2004; Shin, Orr, et al., 2004).

SP

Activations in the dmPFC were detected in response to phobic-related stimuli (Straube, Glauer,

et al., 2006). In addition, medial vmPFC/OFC activations were detected during symptom provocation (Rauch et al., 1995) and in response to phobia-related words (Dilger et al., 2003) as well as pictures (Carlsson et al., 2004; Schienle, Schafer, Walter, et al., 2005), while other studies report OFC deactivation in response to phobic-related stimuli (Wik et al., 1993).

PD

A trend toward increased OFC glucose metabolism has been reported in patients relative to healthy controls (Nordahl et al., 1990). Group differences in dmPFC and vmPFC response to panic-related words during an emotional Stroop task were detected (van den Heuvel et al., 2005).

Insula

Given the visceral responses and experience of negative emotion that accompanies states of anxiety and exaggerated fear responses, the field has been increasingly recognizing that the insula, a region involved in somatic/visceral responses as well as interoceptive awareness, may play a role in anxiety disorders. The anxiety sensitivity index (ASI), a measure of the fear of anxiety sensations (e.g., respiratory, cardiovascular, public displays of anxiety, and fear of losing cognitive control), represents a means for exploring related clinical features in anxiety disorders, such as PD (Taylor & Cox, 1998). In fact, a recent editorial hypothesizes that individuals with high anxiety sensitivity perceive an exaggerated differential between observed and predicted body state (i.e., heightened interoceptive prediction signal) (Paulus & Stein, 2006).

PTSD

Both PTSD subjects and TENC groups exhibited insula activations during a PTSD-related counting Stroop, and each group had a greater insula response in different subterritories (Shin et al., 2001). Insula activation has been reported for symptom provocation, but may be specific to the type of trauma insult or symptom profile (e.g., hyperarousal, emotional numbing). Combat-exposed PTSD subjects exhibited insula activation during script-driven imagery (Britton et al., 2005; Rauch et al., 1996), which has been associated with increased flashback intensity (Osuch et al., 2001). However, some reports using script-driven imagery involving sexually abused PTSD subjects did not report insula activation (Bremner, Narayan, et al., 1999; Shin et al., 1999). In these cases, the TENC group exhibited insula activation while recounting the sexual assault or had greater insula responses than did PTSD patients.

SAD

SAD patients exhibited insula activation in response to viewing angry relative to neutral faces and this insula response was statistically greater compared to healthy controls (Straube, Kolassa, et al., 2004). However, other studies have not reported group differences in insula response to harsh versus happy faces (Phan, Fitzgerald, et al., 2006; Stein et al., 2002). On the other hand, SAD patients had greater insula responses than healthy controls when anticipating a public speech (Lorberbaum et al., 2004). Yet, in another study, SAD patients exhibited insula deactivations and lesser responses than healthy controls during public speaking relative to making a private speech (Tillfors et al., 2001).

SP

Individuals with SP exhibited insula activation to fearful pictures (Schienle, Schafer, Walter, et al., 2005) and greater magnitude of insula activation than healthy controls in response to fearful faces (Wright et al., 2003). Insula activation has been detected in response to exposure to feared phobic objects (e.g., real rodents, snakes, and spiders) (Rauch et al., 1995), pictures (Carlsson et al., 2004; Dilger et al., 2003; Schienle, Schafer, Walter, et al., 2005; Straube, Mentzel, et al., 2006) and words (Straube, Mentzel, Glauer, & Miltner, 2004). In most cases, the insula activation was significantly greater than that observed in healthy controls.

Hippocampus

Regions responding to memory retrieval, such as the hippocampus, may be preferentially involved in anxiety disorders (Maren, 2005). In PTSD, diminished recruitment of the hippocampus may serve as a vulnerability factor to developing anxiety symptoms. In studies of SAD and SP, the hippocampus seems to exhibit greater responses than healthy controls. Finally, in PD, a distinct pattern is less clear, but nonetheless, the findings highlight abnormalities in the hippocampus.

PTSD

General stimuli used in the context of explicit learning paradigms show diminished hippocampal recruitment during recall in the PTSD group compared to the TENC group (e.g., word recall) (Shin, Shin, et al., 2004). In response to disorder relevant stimuli, hippocampal deactivations have been reported. In TENCs, this deactivation was observed in response to combat-related pictures and sounds (Bremner, Staib, et al., 1999); whereas, in PTSD patients, this deactivation was observed in response to script-driven imagery (Bremner, Narayan, et al., 1999). In one study, hippocampus/parahippocampus response was correlated with flashback intensity in PTSD (Osuch et al., 2001).

SAD

Patients with SAD exhibited hippocampal/parahippocampal activations to harsh faces and had greater responses than healthy controls (Phan, Fitzgerald, et al., 2006; Stein et al., 2002; Straube, Kolassa, et al., 2004). In addition, SAD patients exhibited a greater response than healthy controls when anticipating delivering a public speech (Lorberbaum et al., 2004).

SP

Studies have reported hippocampal/parahippocampal activation to disgust and phobic-related pictures in SP patients and this response was greater than in healthy controls (Schienle, Schafer, Walter, et al., 2005). However, some studies have reported hippocampal/parahippocampal deactivations to phobia-related films (Wik et al., 1993).

PD

Greater right-to-left asymmetry in parahippocampus activity has been reported across several different studies of PD. For instance, such findings were reported in the context of tasks involving valenced judgment of threat-related compared to neutral words (Maddock et al., 2003), and auditory detection (Nordahl et al., 1990) as well as resting measures of oxygen metabolism and blood flow in patients vulnerable to lactate-induced panic episodes (Reiman et al., 1986). Compared to healthy controls, a PD group exhibited greater hippocampal response to panic-related words during an emotional Stroop task (van den Heuvel et al., 2005).

Posterior Cingulate Cortex

Investigators have recently become more interested in the PCC and its potential involvement in anxiety disorders because of its role in memory processing. Of note, most studies reporting abnormalities in PCC function are in response to disorder-specific stimuli, possibly reflecting the fact that the PCC responds to personal memories.

PTSD

Patients with PTSD exhibited greater PCC activation compared to TENCs in response to fearful faces (Shin et al., 2005). Compared to PTSD subjects, TENCs showed greater PCC response during script-driven imagery (Bremner, Narayan, et al., 1999; Shin et al., 1999). The TENCs exhibited PCC activations in response to trauma-related pictures (Shin, Kosslyn, et al., 1997) and script-driven imagery (Shin, McNally, et al., 1997). In other studies, PCC deactivations were reported in response to trauma-related pictures in the TENC group (Bremner, Staib, et al., 1999; Liberzon et al., 1999), in response to script-driven imagery in PTSD (Liberzon et al., 1999; Rauch et al., 1996), and in response to trauma-related sounds in PTSD, TENCs, and healthy controls (Liberzon et al., 1999). In a functional connectivity analysis using a locus within ACC as the seed voxel, PTSD patients exhibited a greater correlation with PCC activity during script-driven imagery than TENCs, suggesting that the PTSD patients used greater nonverbal memory retrieval (Lanius et al., 2004).

SAD

Healthy controls activated the PCC during a public speech and showed greater responses than SAD patients (Tillfors et al., 2001).

SP

Studies of SP have reported PCC activation to phobic-related words, which was greater than in healthy controls (Straube, Mentzel, et al., 2004). Other studies report PCC deactivation in SP patients in response to phobia-related films and pictures, resulting in significant group differences (Dilger et al., 2003; Wik et al., 1993).

PD

Studies have reported PCC activation to threat-related words in both PD and healthy control groups, but PD patients showed greater activation (Maddock et al., 2003).

Functional Connectivity

Though the amygdala, ACC, mPFC, insula, hippocampus, and PCC are implicated in the pathophysiology of anxiety disorders, few studies have investigated the functional connectivity between these regions in these disorders. This approach may be important in identifying abnormal connections between these regions as well as in appreciating pathophysiology at the network level. Using

script-driven imagery in PTSD patients, functional connectivity analysis using an amygdalar seed voxel determined a general pattern of connectivity of the amygdala. In both PTSD and TENCs, the amygdala activity was correlated with right prefrontal cortex, hippocampus, and visual cortex. Amygdala activation to scripts exhibited a greater correlation with the visual cortex, subcallosal ACC, and dACC in PTSD patients compared with controls. These data suggest differential modulation of autonomic and visual activity (Gilboa, Winocur, Grady, Hevenor, & Moscovitch, 2004).

OCD

Obsessive-compulsive disorder seems to have a neurocircuitry profile that is quite distinct from the other anxiety disorders. In particular, the OFC, ACC, striatum, and thalamus compose the circuit implicated in OCD. A recent movement to decompose the clinical features of OCD into symptom dimensions, via factor analysis, further complicates the landscape in this regard (Mataix-Cols et al., 2004).

At rest, hypermetabolism of the OFC, ACC, and striatum have been repeatedly observed (Baxter, Schwartz, Guze, Bergman, & Szuba, 1990; Saxena, Brody, Schwartz, & Baxter, 1998). The cortico-striatal-thalamic system is also activated in symptom provocation studies (Rauch et al., 1994). Moreover, increased OFC metabolic activity has often been found to correlate with symptom severity (Rauch et al., 1994; Swedo et al., 1992) and effective treatment (whether by medication or cognitive behavioral therapy, CBT) has been shown to reduce hyperactivity in these same regions (Schwartz, Stoessel, Baxter, Martin, & Phelps, 1996). Increased ACC metabolic activity and rCBF in OCD patients may reflect exaggerated attention or failure to filter out extraneous information. Event-related potential (ERP) data suggest that adult OCD patients have increased ACC activity when performing a Stroop task (Hajcak & Simons, 2002). In a continuous monitoring task, ACC activation in adult OCD patients was greater for error-related and conflict monitoring and this activity was correlated with symptom severity (Ursu, Stenger, Shear, Jones, & Carter, 2003). Dorsal ACC activation has been reported when making errors during a response incompatibility task in healthy and OCD adult populations; however, OCD patients exhibited greater rACC activation that correlated with symptom severity (Fitzgerald et al., 2005). Increased metabolic activity and brain activation in the caudate correlated with severity and treatment response (Saxena et al., 2003).

Initial studies using implicit learning tasks, such as the serial reaction time task, have indicated OCD patients and healthy controls perform equally well on this task, but OCD patients exhibit less activation of the striatum and aberrant hippocampal recruitment (Rauch et al., 1997; Rauch et al., 2007; Rauch, Whalen, et al., 2001). Patients with OCD may recruit the medial temporal lobe structures to compensate for deficient striatal function (Deckersbach et al., 2002; Rauch, Whalen, et al., 2001).

In addition to recruiting the cortico-striatal-thalamic system, the amygdala and insula may also play a role in OCD; however, the functions of these two structures behave quite differently than in other anxiety disorders. Even though anxiety disorders, such as PTSD, are typically characterized by exaggerated amygdala activity, this exaggerated response may not be the case for OCD. Recent evidence suggests the amygdala response to happy, neutral, and fearful faces (compared to fixation) is lower in adults with OCD relative to healthy controls (Cannistraro et al., 2004). Despite this amygdala hyporesponsivity across all face conditions, the differential response between face conditions was similar for OCD and healthy control groups. On the other hand, both amygdala and insula activation have been reported during symptom provocation in OCD (Breiter et al., 1996).

Increased obsessive-compulsive behaviors have been associated with increased disgust sensitivity (Schiene et al., 2003; Tolin, Woods, & Abramowitz, 2006), yet OCD patients have deficits in recognizing disgust on facial expressions (Sprengelmeyer et al., 1997). Insula activation has been linked to disgust face perception, possibly reflecting the visceral responses associated with the disgusted feeling experienced (Phillips et al., 1997). Studies in OCD and healthy participants report activations of the insula, caudate, and thalamus in response to disgust pictures depicting decaying bodies and food contamination (Phillips et al., 2000) and OCD patients show greater insula activation (Shapira et al., 2003). This greater insula activation may not be dependent on disorder-specific disgust stimuli (Schiene, Schafer, Stark, Walter, & Vaitl, 2005), but a general greater sensitivity to disgust per se.

Generalized Anxiety Disorder (GAD)

Few neuroimaging studies have been conducted in individuals with GAD; therefore, this disorder will be discussed in brief. Compared to healthy adolescents, individuals with GAD demonstrated a bias away from angry faces and greater ventrolateral prefrontal cortex activation in response to angry-neutral face pairs during an attention task. The ventrolateral prefrontal cortex activation was inversely correlated with anxiety symptoms, suggesting that the response bias may reflect the use of avoidance as a compensatory mechanism for ameliorating heightened anxiety levels (Monk et al., 2006). Contrary to other anxiety disorders, amygdala activation was not detected in this study; however, exaggerated amygdala activation in response to fearful faces was detected in a combined group of PD and GAD children (Thomas et al., 2001). Future studies need to study these groups separately, and extend this line of inquiry to include adults with GAD.

Treatment Studies

Neuroimaging studies can be used to determine the neural effects of treatment interventions, such as medication, CBT, and surgical procedures. Pharmacological treatment of anxiety disorders typically involves the prescription of selective serotonin reuptake inhibitors (SSRIs). The effects are not seen immediately but are typically delayed for 2–4 weeks. Cognitive behavioral therapy typically uses exposure or extinction-based techniques to improve regulation of fear responses to anxiety-provoking triggers (i.e., enhancing top-down cortical modulation of the amygdala) (Rothbaum & Davis, 2003). In cases of extreme treatment resistance, patients can elect surgical interventions (e.g., anterior capsulotomy or anterior cingulotomy). In this section, we will review neuroimaging studies that have used these treatment methods to examine the neural correlates of symptom reduction in each anxiety disorder. Given that the amygdala, ACC, mPFC, insula, hippocampus, and PCC are implicated in the pathophysiology of anxiety disorders, these regions are potential targets for treatment intervention.

PTSD

Patients with civilian trauma–related PTSD receiving eye movement desensitization and reprocessing (EMDR), a behavioral modification therapy, for 3 weekly 90-minute sessions showed reductions in Clinician Administered PTSD Scale (CAPS) scores and Impact of Events (IES) scores; patients also exhibited parallel increases in ACC and frontal lobe rCBF during script-driven imagery (Levin, Lazrove, & van der Kolk, 1999). Patients with PTSD identified through the emergency room as trauma victims participated in CBT (details not specified). Following treatment, PTSD patients showed reduced reexperiencing, avoidance, and hyperarousal symptoms measured by the CAPS. In addition, posttreatment fMRI showed increased PCC activation to forgivability judgments (Farrow et al., 2005).

SAD

SAD patients were treated with 3-hour weekly CBT sessions or citalopram with average dose of 40 ± 9.8 mg/day for 9 weeks. Both treatment interventions showed reductions in social phobia scores and reduced amygdala activity as well as reduced hippocampal activity during public speaking. Amygdala and hippocampal reductions correlated with symptom improvement (Furmark et al., 2002).

SP

SP patients were gradually exposed to spiders, phobic-related stimuli, scheduled in four weekly sessions. Self-reported fear to spider films decreased with treatment. In addition, dorsolateral prefrontal cortical and parahippocampal activity was reduced to normal levels (Paquette et al., 2003).

PD

Following CBT or antidepressant therapy, anxiety and PD severity scores were reduced. The two treatments had somewhat similar profiles of brain changes, mostly right-sided changes. Of note, the CBT group showed increases in left insula activation, but no changes were detected in limbic regions for either group (Prasko et al., 2004).

OCD

In OCD, neuroimaging indices have been identified as predictors of treatment response. Numerous studies have indicated that pretreatment OFC activity is inversely correlated with subsequent response to various SSRIs (Brody et al., 1998; Rauch et al., 2002; Swedo et al., 1992). Conversely, one study found that pretreatment OFC metabolism is positively correlated with subsequent response to CBT (Brody et al., 1998). In addition, pretreatment PCC activity correlated with treatment response to fluvoxamine, an SRI (Rauch et al., 2002). In addition, preoperation glucose metabolism in the PCC correlated with Yale Brown Obsessive Compulsive Scale (YBOCS) improvement in treatment-resistant OCD patients following anterior cingulotomy (Rauch, Dougherty, et al., 2001).

Additionally, brain changes have been associated with successful treatment. Twelve-week fluvoxamine or CBT treatment was associated with reductions in OCD symptoms and reductions in OFC and ACC activity when generating OCD-relevant words relative to neutral words (Nakao et al., 2005). Paroxetine treatment for 12–20 weeks reduced OCD symptoms and was associated with reduced caudate metabolism. Further, the magnitude of metabolism reduction correlated with symptom severity reduction (Hansen, Hasselbalch, Law, & Bolwig, 2002). Deep-brain stimulation of the ventral anterior internal capsule/ventral striatum also showed increased OFC, ACC, striatum, and globus pallidus activity (Rauch et al., 2006).

Although studies have examined the neural correlates of treatment response in anxiety disorders, the field needs to replicate these findings and extend the investigation to determine appropriate treatments for particular individuals.

Summary and Conclusions

In summary, neuroimaging studies enable investigators to examine the functional integrity of various brain regions in anxiety disorders. For most anxiety disorders, amygdalo-cortical circuitry has been central for explaining the failure to regulate exaggerated fear responses; nevertheless, the model needs to be extended and refined with respect to the inclusion of mPFC, ACC, insula, hippocampus, and PCC as relevant cortical/subcortical territories. As reviewed, PTSD, SAD, SP, and PD differentially recruit these structures. However, these disorders also show distinct clinical profiles with respect to triggers, symptomatology, and underlying neural circuitry. In contrast, the cortico-striatal-thalamic system has been central to neurocircuitry models of OCD. However, the amygdala and insula may also be involved, but show different responses compared with the other anxiety disorders. Additional work is needed to better delineate whether neural correlates within these regions can be classified as general phenomena or anxiety disorder–specific. Finally, treatment studies using neuroimaging may pave the way for clinical indications, by virtue of providing predictive information to potentially guide treatment decisions. Replication of imaging findings in the context of longitudinal treatment studies will be necessary before such clinical utility can be realized.

References

Baxter, L. R., Schwartz, J. M., Guze, B. H., Bergman, K., & Szuba, M. P. (1990). Neuroimaging in obsessive-compulsive disorder: Seeking the mediating neuroanatomy. In M. A. Jenike, L. Baer, & W. E. Minichiello (Eds.), *Obsessive-compulsive* disorder: *Theory and management* (2nd ed., pp. 167–188). Chicago: Year Book Medical Publishers.

Bechara, A., Tranel, D., & Damasio, H. (2000). Characterization of the decision-making deficit of patients with ventromedial prefrontal cortex lesions. *Brain, 123*(Pt 11), 2189–2202.

Birbaumer, N., Grodd, W., Diedrich, O., Klose, U., Erb, M., Lotze, M., et al. (1998). fMRI reveals amygdala activation to human faces in social phobics. *Neuroreport, 9,* 1223–1226.

Breiter, H. C., Rauch, S. L., Kwong, K. K., Baker, J. R., Weisskoff, R. M., Kennedy, D. N., et al. (1996). Functional magnetic resonance imaging of symptom provocation in obsessive-compulsive disorder. *Archives of General Psychiatry, 53,* 595–606.

Bremner, J. D., Narayan, M., Staib, L. H., Southwick, S. M., McGlashan, T., & Charney, D. S. (1999). Neural correlates of memories of childhood sexual abuse in women with and without posttraumatic stress disorder. *American Journal of Psychiatry, 156,* 1787–1795.

Bremner, J. D., Staib, L. H., Kaloupek, D., Southwick, S. M., Soufer, R., & Charney, D. S. (1999). Neural correlates of exposure to traumatic pictures and sound in Vietnam combat veterans with and without posttraumatic stress disorder: A positron emission tomography study. *Biological Psychiatry, 45,* 806–816.

Britton, J. C., Phan, K. L., Taylor, S. F., Fig, L. M., & Liberzon, I. (2005). Corticolimbic blood flow in posttraumatic stress disorder during script-driven imagery. *Biological Psychiatry, 57,* 832–840.

Brody, A. L., Saxena, S., Schwartz, J. M., Stoessel, P. W., Maidment, K., Phelps, M. E., et al. (1998). FDG-PET predictors of response to behavioral therapy and pharmacotherapy in obsessive-compulsive disorder. *Psychiatry Research, 84,* 1–6.

Bush, G., Luu, P., & Posner, M. I. (2000). Cognitive and emotional influences in anterior cingulate cortex. *Trends in Cognitive Sciences, 4,* 215–222.

Cannistraro, P. A., Wright, C. I., Wedig, M. M., Martis, B., Shin, L. M., Wilhelm, S., et al. (2004). Amygdala responses to human faces in obsessive-compulsive disorder. *Biological Psychiatry, 56,* 916–920.

Carlsson, K., Petersson, K. M., Lundqvist, D., Karlsson, A., Ingvar, M., & Ohman, A. (2004). Fear and the amygdala: Manipulation of awareness generates differential cerebral responses to phobic and fear-relevant (but nonfeared) stimuli. *Emotion, 4,* 340–353.

Deckersbach, T., Savage, C. R., Curran, T., Bohne, A., Wilhelm, S., Baer, L., et al. (2002). A study of parallel implicit and explicit information processing in patients with obsessive-compulsive disorder. *American Journal of Psychiatry, 159,* 1780–1782.

Dilger, S., Straube, T., Mentzel, H. J., Fitzek, C., Reichenbach, J. R., Hecht, H., et al. (2003). Brain activation to phobia-related pictures in spider phobic humans: An event-related functional magnetic resonance imaging study. *Neuroscience Letters, 348,* 29–32.

Dougherty, D. D., & Rauch, S. L. (2003). Brain imaging in psychiatry. In A. Tasman, T. Kay, & J. A. Lieberman (Eds.), *Psychiatry* (2nd ed., pp. 573–582). London: Wiley.

Farrow, T. F., Hunter, M. D., Wilkinson, I. D., Gouneea, C., Fawbert, D., Smith, R., et al. (2005). Quantifiable change in functional brain response to empathic and forgivability judgments with resolution of posttraumatic stress disorder. *Psychiatry Research, 140,* 45–53.

Fitzgerald, K. D., Welsh, R. C., Gehring, W. J., Abelson, J. L., Himle, J. A., Liberzon, I., et al. (2005). Error-related hyperactivity of the anterior cingulate cortex in obsessive-compulsive disorder. *Biological Psychiatry, 57,* 287–294.

Furmark, T., Tillfors, M., Marteinsdottir, I., Fischer, H., Pissiota, A., Langstrom, B., et al. (2002). Common changes in cerebral blood flow in patients with social phobia treated with citalopram or cognitive-behavioral therapy. *Archives of General Psychiatry, 59,* 425–433.

Gilboa, A., Winocur, G., Grady, C. L., Hevenor, S. J., & Moscovitch, M. (2004). Remembering our past: Functional neuroanatomy of recollection of recent and very remote personal events. *Cerebral Cortex, 14,* 1214–1225.

Hajcak, G., & Simons, R. F. (2002). Error-related brain activity in obsessive-compulsive undergraduates. *Psychiatry Research, 110,* 63–72.

Hansen, E. S., Hasselbalch, S., Law, I., & Bolwig, T. G. (2002). The caudate nucleus in obsessive-compulsive disorder. Reduced metabolism following treatment with paroxetine: A PET study. *International Journal of Neuropsychopharmacology, 5,* 1–10.

Kelley, W. M., Macrae, C. N., Wyland, C. L., Caglar, S., Inati, S., & Heatherton, T. F. (2002). Finding the self? An event-related fMRI study. *Journal of Cognitive Neuroscience, 14,* 785–794.

Killgore, W. D., & Yurgelun-Todd, D. A. (2005). Social anxiety predicts amygdala activation in adolescents viewing fearful faces. *Neuroreport, 16,* 1671–1675.

Lanius, R. A., Williamson, P. C., Densmore, M., Boksman, K., Gupta, M. A., Neufeld, R. W., et al. (2001). Neural correlates of traumatic memories in posttraumatic stress disorder: A functional MRI investigation. *American Journal of Psychiatry, 158,* 1920–1922.

Lanius, R. A., Williamson, P. C., Densmore, M., Boksman, K., Neufeld, R. W., Gati, J. S., et al. (2004). The nature of traumatic memories: A 4-T fMRI functional connectivity analysis. *American Journal of Psychiatry, 161,* 36–44.

Levin, P., Lazrove, S., & van der Kolk, B. (1999). What psychological testing and neuroimaging tell us about the treatment of posttraumatic stress disorder by eye movement desensitization and reprocessing. *Journal of Anxiety Disorders, 13,* 159–172.

Liberzon, I., Taylor, S. F., Amdur, R., Jung, T. D., Chamberlain, K. R., Minoshima, S., et al. (1999). Brain activation in PTSD in response to trauma-related stimuli. *Biological Psychiatry, 45,* 817–826.

Liberzon, I., Taylor, S. F., Fig, L. M., Decker, L. R., Koeppe, R. A., & Minoshima, S. (2000). Limbic activation and psychophysiologic responses to aversive visual stimuli: Interaction with cognitive task. *Neuropsychopharmacology, 23,* 508–516.

Lorberbaum, J. P., Kose, S., Johnson, M. R., Arana, G. W., Sullivan, L. K., Hamner, M. B., et al. (2004). Neural correlates of speech anticipatory anxiety in generalized social phobia. *Neuroreport, 15,* 2701–2705.

Maddock, R. J., Buonocore, M. H., Kile, S. J., & Garrett, A. S. (2003). Brain regions showing increased activation by threat-related words in panic disorder. *Neuroreport, 14,* 325–328.

Maren, S. (2005). Building and burying fear memories in the brain. *Neuroscientist, 11,* 89–99.

Mataix-Cols, D., Wooderson, S., Lawrence, N., Brammer, M. J., Speckens, A., & Phillips, M. L. (2004). Distinct neural correlates of washing, checking, and hoarding symptom dimensions in obsessive-compulsive disorder. *Archives of General Psychiatry, 61,* 564–576.

Milad, M. R., Quinn, B. T., Pitman, R. K., Orr, S. P., Fischl, B., & Rauch, S. L. (2005). Thickness of ventromedial prefrontal cortex in humans is correlated with extinction memory. *Proceedings of the National Academy of Sciences of the United States of America, 102,* 10706–10711.

Milad, M. R., & Quirk, G. J. (2002). Neurons in medial prefrontal cortex signal memory for fear extinction. *Nature, 420* (6911), 70–74.

Monk, C. S., Nelson, E. E., McClure, E. B., Mogg, K., Bradley, B. P., Leibenluft, E., et al. (2006). Ventrolateral prefrontal cortex activation and attentional bias in response to angry faces in adolescents with generalized anxiety disorder. *American Journal of Psychiatry, 163,* 1091–1097.

Nakao, T., Nakagawa, A., Yoshiura, T., Nakatani, E., Nabeyama, M., Yoshizato, C., et al. (2005). Brain activation of patients with obsessive-compulsive disorder during neuropsychological and symptom provocation tasks before and after symptom improvement: A functional magnetic resonance imaging study. *Biological Psychiatry, 57,* 901–910.

Nordahl, T. E., Semple, W. E., Gross, M., Mellman, T. A., Stein, M. B., Goyer, P., et al. (1990). Cerebral glucose metabolic differences in patients with panic disorder. *Neuropsychopharmacology, 3,* 261–272.

Ochsner, K. N., Bunge, S. A., Gross, J. J., & Gabrieli, J. D. (2002). Rethinking feelings: An fMRI study of the cognitive regulation of emotion. *Journal of Cognitive Neuroscience, 14,* 1215–1229.

Ongur, D., & Price, J. L. (2000). The organization of networks within the orbital and medial prefrontal cortex of rats, monkeys and humans. *Cerebral Cortex, 10,* 206–219.

Osuch, E. A., Benson, B., Geraci, M., Podell, D., Herscovitch, P., McCann, U. D., et al. (2001). Regional cerebral blood flow correlated with flashback intensity in patients with posttraumatic stress disorder. *Biological Psychiatry, 50,* 246–253.

Paquette, V., Levesque, J., Mensour, B., Leroux, J. M., Beaudoin, G., Bourgouin, P., et al. (2003). "Change the mind and you change the brain": Effects of cognitive-behavioral therapy on the neural correlates of spider phobia. *Neuroimage, 18,* 401–409.

Paulus, M. P., & Stein, M. B. (2006). An insular view of anxiety. *Biological Psychiatry, 60,* 383–387.

Phan, K. L., Britton, J. C., Taylor, S. F., Fig, L. M., & Liberzon, I. (2006). Corticolimbic blood flow during nontraumatic emotional processing in posttraumatic stress disorder. *Archives of General Psychiatry, 63,* 184–192.

Phan, K. L., Fitzgerald, D. A., Nathan, P. J., & Tancer, M. E. (2006). Association between amygdala hyperactivity to harsh faces and severity of social anxiety in generalized social phobia. *Biological Psychiatry, 59,* 424–429.

Phan, K. L., Taylor, S. F., Welsh, R. C., Ho, S. H., Britton, J. C., & Liberzon, I. (2004). Neural correlates of individual ratings of emotional salience: A trial-related fMRI study. *Neuroimage, 21,* 768–780.

Phelps, E. A., Delgado, M. R., Nearing, K. I., & LeDoux, J. E. (2004). Extinction learning in humans: Role of the amygdala and vmPFC. *Neuron, 43,* 897–905.

Phillips, M. L., Marks, I. M., Senior, C., Lythgoe, D., O'Dwyer, A. M., Meehan, O., et al. (2000). A differential neural response in obsessive-compulsive disorder patients with washing compared with checking symptoms to disgust. *Psychological Medicine, 30,* 1037–1050.

Phillips, M. L., Young, A. W., Senior, C., Brammer, M., Andrew, C., Calder, A. J., et al. (1997). A specific neural substrate for perceiving facial expressions of disgust. *Nature, 389,* 495–498.

Pissiota, A., Frans, O., Michelgard, A., Appel, L., Langstrom, B., Flaten, M. A., et al. (2003). Amygdala and anterior cingulate cortex activation during affective startle modulation: A PET study of fear. *European Journal of Neuroscience, 18,* 1325–1331.

Prasko, J., Horacek, J., Zalesky, R., Kopecek, M., Novak, T., Paskova, B., et al. (2004). The change of regional brain metabolism (18FDG PET) in panic disorder during the treatment with cognitive behavioral therapy or antidepressants. *Neuro Endocrinology Letters, 25,* 340–348.

Rauch, S. L., Dougherty, D. D., Cosgrove, G. R., Cassem, E. H., Alpert, N. M., Price, B. H., et al. (2001). Cerebral metabolic correlates as potential predictors of response to anterior cingulotomy for obsessive-compulsive disorder. *Biological Psychiatry, 50,* 659–667.

Rauch, S. L., Dougherty, D. D., Malone, D., Rezai, A., Friehs, G., Fischman, A. J., et al. (2006). A functional neuroimaging investigation of deep brain stimulation in patients with obsessive-compulsive disorder. *Journal of Neurosurgery, 104,* 558–565.

Rauch, S. L., Jenike, M. A., Alpert, N. M., Baer, L., Breiter, H. C., Savage, C. R., et al. (1994). Regional cerebral blood flow measured during symptom provocation in obsessive-compulsive disorder using oxygen 15-labeled carbon dioxide and positron emission tomography. *Archives of General Psychiatry, 51,* 62–70.

Rauch, S. L., Savage, C. R., Alpert, N. M., Dougherty, D., Kendrick, A., Curran, T., et al. (1997). Probing striatal function in obsessive-compulsive disorder: A PET study of implicit sequence learning. *Journal of Neuropsychiatry Clinical Neuroscience, 9,* 568–573.

Rauch, S. L., Savage, C. R., Alpert, N. M., Miguel, E. C., Baer, L., Breiter, H. C., et al. (1995). A positron emission tomographic study of simple phobic symptom provocation. *Archives of General Psychiatry, 52,* 20–28.

Rauch, S. L., Shin, L. M., Dougherty, D. D., Alpert, N. M., Fischman, A. J., & Jenike, M. A. (2002). Predictors of fluvoxamine response in contamination-related obsessive-compulsive disorder: A PET symptom provocation study. *Neuropsychopharmacology, 27,* 782–791.

Rauch, S. L., Shin, L. M., & Wright, C. I. (2003). Neuroimaging studies of amygdala function in anxiety disorders. *Annals of the New York Academy of Science, 985,* 389–410.

Rauch, S. L., van der Kolk, B. A., Fisler, R. E., Alpert, N. M., Orr, S. P., Savage, C. R., et al. (1996). A symptom provocation study of posttraumatic stress disorder using positron emission tomography and script-driven imagery. *Archives of General Psychiatry, 53,* 380–387.

Rauch, S. L., Wedig, M. M., Wright, C. I., Martis, B., McMullin, K. G., Shin, L. M., et al. (2007). Functional magnetic resonance imaging study of regional brain activation during implicit sequence learning in obsessive-compulsive disorder. *Biological Psychiatry, 61,* 330–336.

Rauch, S. L., Whalen, P. J., Curran, T., Shin, L. M., Coffey, B. J., Savage, C. R., et al. (2001). Probing striato-thalamic function in obsessive-compulsive disorder and Tourette syndrome using neuroimaging methods. *Advances in Neurology, 85,* 207–224.

Rauch, S. L., Whalen, P. J., Shin, L. M., McInerney, S. C., Macklin, M. L., Lasko, N. B., et al. (2000). Exaggerated amygdala response to masked facial stimuli in posttraumatic stress disorder: A functional MRI study. *Biological Psychiatry, 47,* 769–776.

Reiman, E. M., Raichle, M. E., Robins, E., Butler, F. K., Herscovitch, P., Fox, P., et al. (1986). The application of positron emission tomography to the study of panic disorder. *American Journal of Psychiatry, 143,* 469–477.

Rothbaum, B. O., & Davis, M. (2003). Applying learning principles to the treatment of post-trauma reactions. *Annals of the New York Academy of Science, 1008,* 112–121.

Sakai, Y., Kumano, H., Nishikawa, M., Sakano, Y., Kaiya, H., Imabayashi, E., et al. (2005). Cerebral glucose metabolism associated with a fear network in panic disorder. *Neuroreport, 16,* 927–931.

Saxena, S., Brody, A. L., Ho, M. L., Zohrabi, N., Maidment, K. M., & Baxter, L. R., Jr. (2003). Differential brain metabolic predictors of response to paroxetine in obsessive-compulsive disorder versus major depression. *American Journal of Psychiatry, 160,* 522–532.

Saxena, S., Brody, A. L., Schwartz, J. M., & Baxter, L. R. (1998). Neuroimaging and frontal-subcortical circuitry in obsessive-compulsive disorder. *British Journal of Psychiatry—Supplementum, 35,* 26–37.

Schienle, A., Schafer, A., Stark, R., Walter, B., Franz, M., & Vaitl, D. (2003). Disgust sensitivity in psychiatric disorders: A questionnaire study. *Journal of Nervous and Mental Disease, 191,* 831–834.

Schienle, A., Schafer, A., Stark, R., Walter, B., & Vaitl, D. (2005). Neural responses of OCD patients towards disorder-relevant, generally disgust-inducing and fear-inducing pictures. *International Journal of Psychophysiology, 5,* 69–77.

Schienle, A., Schafer, A., Walter, B., Stark, R., & Vaitl, D. (2005). Brain activation of spider phobics towards disorder-relevant, generally disgust- and fear-inducing pictures. *Neuroscience Letters, 388,* 1–6.

Schneider, F., Weiss, U., Kessler, C., Muller-Gartner, H. W., Posse, S., Salloum, J. B., et al. (1999). Subcortical correlates of differential classical conditioning of aversive emotional reactions in social phobia. *Biological Psychiatry, 45,* 863–871.

Schwartz, J. M., Stoessel, P. W., Baxter, L. R., Jr., Martin, K. M., & Phelps, M. E. (1996). Systematic changes in cerebral glucose metabolic rate after successful behavior modification treatment of obsessive-compulsive disorder. *Archives of General Psychiatry, 53,* 109–113.

Shapira, N. A., Liu, Y., He, A. G., Bradley, M. M., Lessig, M. C., James, G. A., et al. (2003). Brain activation by disgust-inducing pictures in obsessive-compulsive disorder. *Biological Psychiatry, 54,* 751–756.

Shin, L. M., Kosslyn, S. M., McNally, R. J., Alpert, N. M., Thompson, W. L., Rauch, S. L., et al. (1997). Visual imagery and perception in posttraumatic stress disorder: A positron emission tomographic investigation. *Archives of General Psychiatry, 54,* 233–241.

Shin, L. M., McNally, R. J., Kosslyn, S. M., Thompson, W. L., Rauch, S. L., Alpert, N. M., et al. (1997). A positron emission tomographic study of symptom provocation in PTSD. *Annals of the New York Academy of Science, 821,* 521–523.

Shin, L. M., McNally, R. J., Kosslyn, S. M., Thompson, W. L., Rauch, S. L., Alpert, N. M., et al. (1999). Regional cerebral blood flow during script-driven imagery in childhood sexual abuse-related PTSD: A PET investigation. *American Journal of Psychiatry, 156,* 575–584.

Shin, L. M., Orr, S. P., Carson, M. A., Rauch, S. L., Macklin, M. L., Lasko, N. B., et al. (2004). Regional cerebral blood flow in the amygdala and medial prefrontal cortex during traumatic imagery in male and female Vietnam veterans with PTSD. *Archives of General Psychiatry, 61,* 168–176.

Shin, L. M., Shin, P. S., Heckers, S., Krangel, T. S., Macklin, M. L., Orr, S. P., et al. (2004). Hippocampal function in posttraumatic stress disorder. *Hippocampus, 14,* 292–300.

Shin, L. M., Whalen, P. J., Pitman, R. K., Bush, G., Macklin, M. L., Lasko, N. B., et al. (2001). An fMRI study of anterior cingulate function in posttraumatic stress disorder. *Biological Psychiatry, 50,* 932–942.

Shin, L. M., Wright, C. I., Cannistraro, P. A., Wedig, M. M., McMullin, K., Martis, B., et al. (2005). A functional magnetic resonance imaging study of amygdala and medial prefrontal cortex responses to overtly presented fearful faces in posttraumatic stress disorder. *Archives of General Psychiatry, 62,* 273–281.

Simpson, J. R., Ongur, D., Akbudak, E., Conturo, T. E., Ollinger, J. M., Snyder, A. Z., et al. (2000). The emotional modulation of cognitive processing: An fMRI study. *Journal of Cognitive Neuroscience, 12*(Suppl. 2), 157–170.

Sprengelmeyer, R., Young, A. W., Pundt, I., Sprengelmeyer, A., Calder, A. J., Berrios, G., et al. (1997). Disgust implicated in obsessive-compulsive disorder. *Proceedings in Biological Science, 264,* 1767–1773.

Stein, M. B., Goldin, P. R., Sareen, J., Zorrilla, L. T., & Brown, G. G. (2002). Increased amygdala activation to angry and contemptuous faces in generalized social phobia. *Archives of General Psychiatry, 59,* 1027–1034.

Straube, T., Glauer, M., Dilger, S., Mentzel, H. J., & Miltner, W. H. (2006). Effects of cognitive-behavioral therapy on brain activation in specific phobia. *Neuroimage, 29,* 125–135.

Straube, T., Kolassa, I. T., Glauer, M., Mentzel, H. J., & Miltner, W. H. (2004). Effect of task conditions on brain responses to threatening faces in social phobics: An event-related functional magnetic resonance imaging study. *Biological Psychiatry, 56,* 921–930.

Straube, T., Mentzel, H. J., Glauer, M., & Miltner, W. H. (2004). Brain activation to phobia-related words in phobic subjects. *Neuroscience Letters, 372,* 204–208.

Straube, T., Mentzel, H. J., & Miltner, W. H. (2005). Common and distinct brain activation to threat and safety signals in social phobia. *Neuropsychobiology, 52,* 163–168.

Straube, T., Mentzel, H. J., & Miltner, W. H. (2006). Neural mechanisms of automatic and direct processing of phobogenic stimuli in specific phobia. *Biological Psychiatry, 59,* 162–170.

Swedo, S. E., Pietrini, P., Leonard, H. L., Schapiro, M. B., Rettew, D. C., Goldberger, E. L., et al. (1992). Cerebral glucose metabolism in childhood-onset obsessive-compulsive disorder: Revisualization during pharmacotherapy. *Archives of General Psychiatry, 49,* 690–694.

Szeszko, P. R., Robinson, D., Alvir, J. M., Bilder, R. M., Lencz, T., Ashtari, M., et al. (1999). Orbital frontal and amygdala volume reductions in obsessive-compulsive disorder. *Archives of General Psychiatry, 56,* 913–919.

Taylor, S., & Cox, B. J. (1998). Anxiety sensitivity: Multiple dimensions and hierarchic structure. *Behaviour Research and Therapy, 36,* 37–51.

Taylor, S. F., Phan, K. L., Decker, L. R., & Liberzon, I. (2003). Subjective rating of emotionally salient stimuli modulates neural activity. *Neuroimage, 18,* 650–659.

Thomas, K. M., Drevets, W. C., Dahl, R. E., Ryan, N. D., Birmaher, B., Eccard, C. H., et al. (2001). Amygdala response to fearful faces in anxious and depressed children. *Archives of General Psychiatry, 58,* 1057–1063.

Tillfors, M., Furmark, T., Marteinsdottir, I., Fischer, H., Pissiota, A., Langstrom, B., et al. (2001). Cerebral blood flow in subjects with social phobia during stressful speaking tasks: A PET study. *American Journal of Psychiatry, 158,* 1220–1226.

Toga, A., & Mazziotta, J. (1996). *Brain mapping: The methods.* San Diego: Academic Press.

Tolin, D. F., Woods, C. M., & Abramowitz, J. S. (2006). Disgust sensitivity and obsessive-compulsive symptoms in a nonclinical sample. *Journal of Behavior Therapy and Experimental Psychiatry, 37,* 30–40.

Ursu, S., Stenger, V. A., Shear, M. K., Jones, M. R., & Carter, C. S. (2003). Overactive action monitoring in obsessive-compulsive disorder: Evidence from functional magnetic resonance imaging. *Psychological Science, 14,* 347–353.

Van den Heuvel, O. A., Veltman, D. J., Groenewegen, H. J., Witter, M. P., Merkelbach, J., Cath, D. C., et al. (2005).

Disorder-specific neuroanatomical correlates of attentional bias in obsessive-compulsive disorder, panic disorder, and hypochondriasis. *Archives of General Psychiatry, 62,* 922–933.

Vogt, B. A., Berger, G. R., & Derbyshire, S.W.G. (2003). Structural and functional dichotomy of human midcingulate cortex. *European Journal of Neuroscience, 18,* 3134–3144.

Wik, G., Fredrikson, M., Ericson, K., Eriksson, L., Stone-Elander, S., & Greitz, T. (1993). A functional cerebral response to frightening visual stimulation. *Psychiatry Research, 50,* 15–24.

Whalen, P. J., Pollack, M. H., Shin, L. M., & Rauch S. L. (2001). [Amygdala response to masked faces in panic disorder]. Unpublished raw data.

Wright, C. I., Martis, B., McMullin, K., Shin, L. M., & Rauch, S. L. (2003). Amygdala and insular responses to emotionally valenced human faces in small animal specific phobia. *Biological Psychiatry, 54,* 1067–1076.

10 Neuroendocrinology of Anxiety Disorders

Samir Khan, Anthony P. King, James L. Abelson *and* Israel Liberzon

Abstract

The hypothalamic-pituitary-adrenal (HPA) axis response to stress is well documented. However, less is established regarding the role of this neuroendocrine system in stress-related psychopathology. The current chapter reviews the scientific literature on HPA functioning in panic disorder, posttraumatic stress disorder (PTSD), social and specific phobia, and generalized anxiety disorder. More specifically, it examines studies that have characterized biological rhythms of HPA axis hormones at basal state, the endocrine response to laboratory and naturalistic challenges, the response to direct pituitary and adrenal stimulation, and the sensitivity of inhibitory feedback mechanisms. While the current literature does not directly support a link between symptoms and HPA dysfunction, several abnormalities have been identified and evidence suggests further study may prove fruitful in understanding the pathophysiology of specific disorders.

Keywords: anxiety disorders, cortisol, HPA, panic, phobia, posttraumatic stress disorder, reactivity, stress

Within moments of a threat, two physiological systems are activated, designed to assist the organism in coping with the impending danger: an autonomic nervous system (ANS) response and a neuroendocrine response. The neuroendocrine response includes activation of the limbic-hypothalamic-pituitary-adrenal (LHPA) axis, which serves to mobilize energy stores, modulate immune responses, and perform other functions designed to respond to the threat and sustain or restore homeostatic balance. Extensive research has provided us with detailed understanding of the basic neurobiology of both systems, with much of that work focusing on how stress, challenge, or threat elicit physiological and neuroendocrine responses, and on the harmful consequences of prolonged or repeated activation of these systems. In early work it was thought that dysregulation within autonomic systems was likely to be more closely tied to anxiety disorders, and that

HPA axis dysregulation was more closely linked to affective disorders. However, advances in basic science have shown that these systems are intimately linked to each other and the clinical research has made it clear that it is quite unlikely that any psychiatric disorder is going to be linked to a single defect in one of these systems.

In the last 15 years there has been increased interest in examining neuroendocrine functioning in abnormal anxiety states, fears, and phobias. More specifically, investigators have examined whether there are changes in the neuroendocrine stress axis that characterize particular anxiety disorders, and whether these changes relate to specific symptoms. While a number of neuroendocrine systems are likely activated in response to stress or perceived threat and may play important mediating roles in symptom development, the overwhelming amount of research has focused on the HPA axis. Though clear, specific, abnormal HPA axis profiles have not yet been identified for anxiety disorders, there is evidence to suggest that further study of this system in patients may well prove fruitful in understanding the pathophysiology of specific disorders. Our goal in this chapter is to provide a review of the scientific literature on neuroendocrine function in anxiety disorders, focusing on the HPA axis, where there is the most information.

The HPA Axis

Description

The HPA axis is the body's principal neuroendocrine stress response system. In response to threat or stress signals from cortico-limbic circuitry, neurons in the paraventricular nucleus (PVN) at the hypothalamus, projecting to the external zone of the median eminence, secrete corticotrophin-releasing hormone (CRH) and arginine vasopressin (AVP). These peptides are then transported by the portal blood system to the anterior portion of the pituitary gland where they synergistically stimulate the release of adrenocorticotropin hormone (ACTH). Stimulation of glucocorticoid release, including cortisol, represents the final step in the chain of HPA activation and occurs upon ACTH stimulation of the adrenal glands.

In normal, basal conditions, HPA activity fluctuates within a circadian rhythm. Both CRH and AVP are released in a pulsatile fashion with a frequency of about one to three secretory episodes per hour. In humans, the amplitude of CRH and AVP pulses are highest early in the morning and gradually decrease throughout the day. This results in the characteristic diurnal pattern observed for cortisol and ACTH (also released in a pulsatile manner) whereby circulating levels are also highest in the morning and lowest in the evening. This normal pattern can be disrupted by changes in systemic conditions (e.g., light or feeding schedules, medications), internal milieu (physical activity, infection, insulin-induced hypoglycemia), or the onset of stress. During acute stress, the amplitude and synchronization of CRH and AVP pulses increase significantly, with consequent increases in ACTH and glucocorticoid release.

Secreted in response to stress, glucocorticoids exert many different effects aimed at redirecting energy stores to cope with the stress or perceived threat, and at providing a negative feedback signal to prevent stressor-activated defense mechanisms from overshooting or overcompensating to the detriment of the organism. More specifically, the effects of glucocorticoids include: (1) elevation of blood glucose levels by stimulating gluconeogenesis in the liver and lipolysis, as well as by inhibiting insulin secretion, (2) suppression of immune and inflammatory activity, and (3) termination of the stress response through inhibition of CRH and ACTH via multiple feedback loops at sites in the pituitary, hypothalamus, and hippocampus. This final step is critical since prolonged or excessive cortisol activation can lead to specific pathophysiology such as adrenal hypertrophy and thymus hypotrophy and has been implicated in the pathogenesis of a number of ailments, including diabetes, asthma, hypertension, affective disorders, and neurodegenerative disease.

Role of CRH in Stress Responses

In addition to being a primary effector of the HPA axis, extra hypothalamic CRH also serves as a neurotransmitter with an important role in stress response and adaptation. CRH and CRH receptor mRNA and protein have major sites of expression in brain regions involved in mediating autonomic arousal, processing emotions, and in modulating stress responses, including the locus cereleleus, PVN, amygdala, hippocampus, and cerebral cortex. In animal models, central or intra-amygdala administration of CRH reliably produces behavioral, neuroendocrine, and physiological effects akin to natural stressors. This includes ANS and HPA activation, as well as stresslike behavioral effects, including inhibition of feeding and sexual behaviors, and increases in defensive burying. The CRH antagonists also produce antianxiety effects in various animal models of stress, although more consistently in behavioral tests involving stimulus-specific fear (e.g., shock, conflict, predator). In tests involving more ambiguous environmental circumstances (e.g., novelty or exploration), CRH antagonists are less consistent in reducing anxiety-like behaviors.

Based in large part on the extensive basic science evidence, CRH1 and CRH2 targeted agents have been proposed as putative pharmacological interventions for the treatment of stress-related disorders. Potent, orally administrable CRH1 antagonists have been developed for human investigation and there are some initial, promising studies examining these compounds in major depressive disorder. However, studies demonstrating clinical efficacy for these compounds in anxiety disorders are ongoing and no clear results are yet available.

Methods of Studying the HPA Axis in Humans

Study of the human HPA axis has been central to the development of modern biological psychiatry, starting with the discovery of excessive HPA activity in major depressive disorder (Carroll et al., 1981). Psychiatric study of the HPA axis in humans requires careful attention as context, anticipation, and perceptual factors can play significant roles, and different strategies are used to investigate specific components. To capture its biological rhythms at basal state, frequent blood, saliva, or urine sampling is commonly done, either prior to a particular challenge or at multiple time points over a predetermined interval (e.g., over 24 h). Acute reactivity can be captured using various laboratory or naturalistic stressors (e.g., problem solving, public speaking) or by direct infusion of a pharmacological probe (e.g., an anxiogenic agent). Assessing the system's central drive is often done by pharmacological stimulation and/or inhibition of components within the chain of HPA activation. For instance, infusion of CRH or ACTH can be used to test the system's responsiveness to direct pituitary or adrenal stimulation. Conversely, the response of the system to changes in central drive can be assessed by reducing circulating cortisol levels using a synthesis inhibitor such as metyrapone. Finally, testing the sensitivity of inhibitory feedback mechanisms is commonly done by administering the glucocorticoid receptor agonist dexamethasone. Dexamethasone stimulates glucocorticoid receptors at the pituitary, facilitating feedback inhibition by combining with the endogenous cortisol to further inhibit ACTH release. If inhibitory feedback mechanisms are hypersensitive, then administering dexamethasone usually produces an exaggerated ACTH suppression, but if they are subsensitive, then elevated circulating ACTH (i.e., an *escape* from suppression) is typically observed.

Investigating the neuroendocrine profile of patients with anxiety or other psychiatric disorders has usually involved looking for abnormalities in these areas: basal state (either prechallenge or in their circadian rhythm), acute reactivity, central drive, and feedback inhibition.

Anxiety Disorders
Panic Disorder

Many of the more typical symptoms of a panic attack appear quite similar to those involved in the classical *fight or flight* response to stress. These include heart palpitations, shortness of breath, sweating, dizziness, hyperventilation, or nausea. More severe symptoms may include sensations of choking or even a fear of dying. Not surprisingly, there has been a fair amount of investigation into potential relationships between the neuroendocrine stress response and panic disorder. However, despite considerable research, a consistent HPA axis profile in panic patients has not yet emerged.

BASAL STATE

Basal state studies have examined CRH, ACTH, and cortisol levels in patients with panic disorder. The few studies examining basal CRH levels in cerebrospinal fluid (CSF) have failed to find a significant difference between panic patients and healthy controls (Fossey et al., 1996; Jolkkonen, Lepola, Bissette, Nemeroff, & Riekkinen, 1993). Studies examining prechallenge or circadian levels of plasma ACTH or cortisol have generally reported either normal or somewhat elevated levels. Roy-Byrne et al., (1986) observed elevated cortisol levels prior to CRH infusion when using a short accommodation period. However, in two other studies, normal cortisol levels were observed when longer preinfusion periods were used (Curtis, Abelson, & Gold, 1997; Holsboer, von Bardeleben, Buller, Heuser, & Steiger, 1987). One explanation is that prolonged accommodation periods may have effectively desensitized patients to contextual effects. Animal and human research has shown that novel stimuli or situations are particularly salient to the HPA axis, and panic patients may show hypersensitivity to an unfamiliar laboratory or experimental setting. The extended baseline period may have served to normalize the cortisol response to these variables prior to the CRH challenge.

A 24 h sampling study found that panic patients had normal daytime, but elevated night-time cortisol levels (Abelson & Curtis, 1996). The night-time elevations were significantly predicted by sampling-related sleep disruption. Interestingly, Bandelow et al. (1997) also reported elevated nocturnal cortisol in patients with panic disorder and observed that nocturnal awakenings might account for this elevation. Other studies examining the circadian rhythm of panic patients have shown inconsistent results. Twenty-four-hour urine cortisol levels appear to be normal in "uncomplicated" patients (i.e., without agoraphobia or other psychiatric diagnoses) (Uhde, Joffe, Jimerson, & Post, 1988). Where elevated levels were observed in 24 h sampling studies, they were accounted for by a comorbid diagnosis of depression, agoraphobia, or both (Kathol, Anton, Noyes, Lopez, & Reich, 1988; Lopez, Kathol, & Noyes, 1990). In contrast to these results, elevated basal ACTH (Goldstein, Halbreich, Asnis, Endicott, & Alvir, 1987) and cortisol (Brambilla et al., 1992) have been observed in "uncomplicated" panic patients, although these results were obtained using a small number of time points, rather than continuous sampling throughout the day. At this point, therefore, there appears to be some evidence for elevated nocturnal cortisol levels in panic patients, perhaps related to sleep disturbances, but characterization of the full circadian profile in panic patients has not yet provided consistent evidence of an abnormality. It may be particularly difficult to capture true "resting" state levels in panic patients as they may be overly reactive to the novel experimental manipulations needed to obtain biological samples from them, and this reactivity might account for at least some of the ACTH and cortisol elevations reported in the basal state literature.

ACUTE REACTIVITY

Given the similarities between panic attacks and many components of the physiological stress response, a particularly intriguing finding is the lack of congruity between panic attacks produced in many laboratory challenge models and HPA activation. In fact, using a wide range of biological panicogens, it has been reliably demonstrated that panic attacks can be induced or stimulated in panic patients without significant cortisol activation (Abelson, Weg, Nesse, & Curtis, 1996; Cameron, Lee, Curtis, & McCann, 1987; Hollander et al., 1989; Levin et al., 1987; Peskind et al., 1998; Seier et al., 1997; Sinha et al., 1999). Furthermore, studies using agents that both provoke panic and stimulate the HPA axis, such as CCK-B agonists, show no correlation between the intensity of panic symptoms and the magnitude of ACTH or cortisol release (Abelson, Liberzon, Young, & Khan, 2005). Spontaneous or naturally occurring panic attacks can also occur without a concomitant cortisol activation (Cameron et al., 1987; Woods, Charney, McPherson, Gradman, & Heninger, 1987), although there is evidence that cortisol levels are higher during real-life panic than they are 24 h later (Bandelow et al., 2000).

In some cases, challenge models have produced abnormal HPA activation, although it is unclear how closely activation was related to the anxious experience. For instance, exaggerated cortisol responses have been observed in response to yohimbine (Gurguis, Mefford, & Uhde, 1991) and fenfluramine (Targum & Marshall, 1989), although in these studies at least half the subjects received the challenge on their first lab visit. A potentially inherent confound, therefore, is the interaction between heightened HPA axis sensitivity to contextual factors, such as a novel or unfamiliar laboratory setting, and

sensitivity to the panicogenic compound. Elevated ACTH and cortisol levels were observed during the first lab visit in a CCK-B challenge model, an effect that was not produced during the second visit (Abelson, Khan, Liberzon, & Young, 2006). Unfortunately, most studies provide limited information on procedures surrounding the challenge paradigm, such as details about accommodation periods, prior exposure to the lab setting, and subject preparation. As a result, in many challenge studies, the effects of specific contextual factors, with known modulatory effects on the HPA axis, cannot be discounted. Future studies specifically designed to examine the role of this potential confound are needed.

CENTRAL DRIVE AND FEEDBACK INHIBITION

As described earlier, the dexamethasone suppression test (DST) is commonly used to assess the sensitivity of inhibitory feedback mechanisms within the HPA axis. For instance, using this test, an escape from ACTH suppression (i.e., nonsuppression) has been reliably observed in patients with major depressive disorder (MDD), suggesting reduced sensitivity of inhibitory feedback mechanisms (Carroll et al., 1981). In patients with panic disorder, however, the data have been less consistent. Most studies have shown either a normal DST response or nonsuppression in a minority of subjects (Curtis, Cameron, & Nesse, 1982; Goldstein et al., 1987; Lieberman et al., 1983; Poland et al., 1985; Sheehan et al., 1983). When abnormalities have been detected using the DST, they appear to be associated with the presence of agoraphobia (Westberg, Modigh, Lisjo, & Eriksson, 1991) or depression (Coryell, Noyes, & Schlechte, 1989). In addition, whereas nonsuppression has predicted the probability of relapse and long-term disability, it was not predictive of anxiety or panic symptom intensity (Coryell & Noyes, 1988).

Schreiber, Lauer, Krumrey, Holsboer, and Krieg (1996) observed higher cortisol levels in panic patients in response to a combined dexamethasone–CRH test. However, the cortisol response in this study showed a degree of gender-dependence, which complicates interpretation, as the panic group was predominantly female and the control group male. More recently, Erhardt et al. (2006) administered dexamethasone to panic patients at 23:00 h on Day 1 and obtained baseline neuroendocrine measures at 15:00 h the following day. Patients were then infused with CRH at 15:02 h. Panic patients showed higher preinfusion ACTH and cortisol levels compared to healthy controls, suggesting abnormal escape (or nonsuppression) from dexamethasone and subsensitivity in inhibitory feedback mechanisms. However, panic patients presented themselves to the laboratory setting for the first time 45 min before infusion, and had an intravenous catheter inserted 30 min later. Therefore, sensitivity to the effects of a first visit to a novel laboratory setting on preinfusion ACTH or cortisol may have contributed to the elevated levels. Interestingly, although there was a positive correlation between anxiety measures and preinfusion cortisol levels, no correlation was reported between changes in anxiety and the ACTH or cortisol response. This might suggest that sensitivity to panic symptoms and HPA axis sensitivity to certain psychosocial/environmental stimuli could be mediated by some similar mechanisms in panic patients, contributing to simultaneous increases in prechallenge hormone levels and greater panic symptom intensity.

Studies directly investigating the central drive of panic patients have utilized CRH infusions and have produced mixed results. The CRH challenge has been shown to produce a blunted (Roy-Byrne et al., 1986), a normal (Brambilla et al., 1992), and an enhanced ACTH response (Schreiber et al., 1996) in panic patients. As alluded to earlier, contextual factors that have not been accounted for may influence or interact with the sensitivity of the HPA axis to CRH, and contribute to the inconsistent results. For instance, the blunted ACTH response observed in the Roy-Byrne et al. (1986) study may result from a shorter accommodation period, which led to elevated prechallenge cortisol level. This in turn may have inhibited ACTH release through stimulation of inhibitory feedback mechanisms. Curtis et al. (1997) did in fact find a normal ACTH response to CRH following a prolonged accommodation period. However, this would not explain all findings. Von Bardeleben and Holsboer (1988) also found a blunted ACTH response to CRH, despite a 6 h accommodation period and normal pre-CRH cortisol levels.

Thus far, in studies examining both central drive and feedback inhibition, the current results are too inconsistent to conclude that abnormalities in either system are present in panic patients. Although some studies suggest elevated cortisol levels in certain contexts, further study is required to replicate these results and to address potential confounds.

Posttraumatic Stress Disorder

Posttraumatic stress disorder (PTSD) develops following exposure to a traumatic event that provokes fear, helplessness, or horror. It is characterized by several types of symptoms, including reexperiencing, avoidance of traumatic reminders, and hyperarousal, and is often associated with maladaptive stress responses. As with panic disorder, it has received considerable attention with regard to investigating potential HPA axis abnormalities.

BASAL STATE

In assessing central hormone levels in PTSD patients, Baker et al. (2005) observed elevated CSF cortisol and CRH levels over a 6 h sampling period, with CRH and cortisol levels being correlated. Elevated CSF CRH levels were also observed in two prior studies (Baker et al., 1999; Bremner et al., 1997). Assessment of 24 h peripheral cortisol in PTSD patients has produced varying results, with studies showing levels to be similar (Baker et al., 1999; Rasmusson et al., 2001), significantly lower (Mason, Giller, Kosten, Ostroff, & Podd, 1986; Yehuda et al., 1995; Yehuda et al., 1990), and significantly higher (Lemieux & Coe, 1995; Maes et al., 1998; Pitman & Orr, 1990) than control subjects. In a large longitudinal epidemiological study, saliva (Young & Breslau, 2004b) and urine (Young & Breslau, 2004a) cortisol measures were obtained in patients with PTSD, patients with trauma exposure but no PTSD, and healthy controls. It was found that PTSD was associated with elevated evening saliva cortisol levels but only in individuals with a comorbid diagnosis of MDD. Patients with PTSD alone showed normal evening saliva and urine cortisol levels.

The clinical relevance of potential group differences, if they exist, still remains unclear. Baker et al. (1999) reported a negative correlation between 24 h urinary cortisol levels and PTSD symptoms in combat veterans in general, but actually failed to find group differences in circulating cortisol between veterans with and without a PTSD diagnosis. Rasmusson et al. (2001) reported an inverse correlation between cortisol levels and time since trauma onset in female subjects but no relationship with PTSD diagnosis. A negative correlation between baseline plasma cortisol levels and avoidance and arousal symptoms has been observed in adolescents with PTSD (Goenjian et al., 1996), and Olff, Guzelcan, de Vries, Assies, and Gersons (2006) did find a negative relationship between cortisol levels and the severity of reexperiencing symptoms, an effect particularly strong in patients with higher symptom severity. Interestingly, Anisman, Griffiths, Matheson, Ravindran, and Merali (2001) also found a relationship between patients with the highest PTSD symptom severity and those with the lowest cortisol levels.

A summary of the results thus far suggests that the presence of abnormalities in circadian cortisol levels in PTSD patients remains unproven, although there are enough positive results to suggest that in certain conditions, abnormalities may exist. There does seem to be some evidence for a link between PTSD and low 24 h cortisol levels in some patients, which contrasts with the hypercortisolemia seen in depression. The degree to which changes in cortisol levels might result from trauma exposure itself, rather than PTSD per se, requires further investigation. As well, whether different circadian levels represent consequences of PTSD or vulnerability factors that are present at the time of trauma and increase the risk of developing PTSD also remains unresolved.

The presence and relevance of differences in circulating cortisol levels in PTSD patients may become more apparent when focused on certain time points. In a study examining 2,490 Vietnam veterans, 8:00 a.m. cortisol levels were significantly lower (by 4%) in PTSD patients compared with healthy controls (Boscarino, 1996). Interestingly, lower awakening cortisol has been associated with current or lifetime PTSD or a past diagnosis of depression in women recently (i.e., 6 months) diagnosed with breast cancer (Luecken, Dausch, Gulla, Hong, & Compas, 2004). As well, a civilian PTSD group showed substantially reduced "cortisol response to awakening" (i.e., in the first 60 min after awakening) compared to control groups (Wessa, Rohleder, Kirschbaum, & Flor, 2006), and PTSD symptoms were found correlated with dampened cortisol response to awakening in active duty police officers (Neylan et al., 2005). However, another recent report found cortisol response to awakening did not predict PTSD symptom severity and was only nonsignificantly lower among firefighters with "high PTSD risk" (Heinrichs et al., 2005). These data add to the evidence for some link between PTSD and reduced levels of circulating cortisol, but the nature of that linkage remains unclear.

ACUTE REACTIVITY

Only a few studies have examined the effects of psychological challenges on neuroendocrine responses in PTSD patients. Liberzon, Abelson, Flagel, Raz, and Young (1999) observed higher autonomic (i.e., skin conductance and heart rate) and catecholamine responses to white noise and combat-related sounds in PTSD patients, but a normal ACTH and cortisol response. In individuals with abuse-related PTSD (i.e., history of childhood physical or sexual abuse), a 20 min cognitive challenge (e.g., arithmetic and problem-solving tasks) also produced normal cortisol response in patients (Bremner et al., 2003). However, Elzinga, Schmahl, Vermetten, van Dyck, and Bremner (2003) exposed women with abuse-related PTSD to personalized trauma scripts and found that PTSD patients showed significantly higher cortisol levels before and during script exposure. Furthermore, there was a highly significant correlation between PTSD symptom severity and cortisol levels during exposure. The higher baseline cortisol levels may indicate sensitivity to certain anticipatory cues. However, the size of the cortisol response and the correlation with symptoms perhaps also indicates a hypersensitivity in PTSD patients to stressors with a greater personal relevance, rather than to challenges that are trauma-related though not trauma-specific, or that are nonspecific cognitive challenges.

Our group recently examined HPA axis responses to trauma-specific (autobiographical trauma script-driven imagery) and nonspecific (IAPS pictures) aversive emotional stimuli in a large ($n = 46$) positron-emission tomography (PET) study of Vietnam combat PTSD patients, Vietnam combat veterans without a history of PTSD symptoms, and noncombat healthy controls. We found evidence of HPA axis (plasma ACTH) responses to trauma recall, but not to other emotional stimuli. Both groups of combat veterans (with or without PTSD) showed significant acute ACTH responses to the trauma scripts, but not to aversive IAPS pictures, suggesting that sensitized HPA axis responses observed in this paradigm were related to trauma-exposure rather than PTSD per se. However, the magnitude of ACTH response was positively correlated with the severity of symptoms in PTSD subjects. In contrast, noncombat-exposed controls did not have ACTH responses to aversive autobiographical scripts or IAPS pictures. While the general and trauma-specific aversive challenges elicited strong subjective emotional responses among all participants, acute ACTH responses were seen only to personalized trauma scripts in combat-exposed groups, supporting the notion that the human HPA axis responds to specific psychological stimuli (in this case, memories of personal threat) rather than to general emotional distress.

CENTRAL DRIVE AND FEEDBACK INHIBITION

Results examining CRH-mediated central drive in PTSD patients have also provided mixed results.

Smith et al. (1989) reported a blunted ACTH response to CRH in patients with combat-related PTSD; however, this was only found in patients with a comorbid diagnosis of MDD. In premenopausal women with PTSD, most of whom had been exposed to physical or sexual abuse, Rasmusson et al. (2001) found a trend toward a higher CRH-induced ACTH response and a significantly higher and delayed cortisol response in patients. However, when examining a group of 11 women and 6 men who developed PTSD following assault or a motor vehicle accident, Kellner, Yassouridis, Hubner, Baker, and Wiedemann (2003) found no significant differences in basal or total CRH-stimulated ACTH or cortisol release between PTSD patients and healthy controls.

Using the DST, results have been somewhat more consistent. Several studies have shown a significant reduction in ACTH following dexamethasone treatment, suggesting sensitized inhibitory feedback mechanisms (Goenjian et al., 1996; Yehuda et al., 1995; Yehuda, Southwick, Krystal, Charney, & Mason, 1993). Those PTSD patients with early childhood abuse also showed hypersuppression of ACTH following dexamethasone treatment (Newport, Heim, Bonsall, Miller, & Nemeroff, 2004). However, despite a consistency of effects, a correlation between DST response and PTSD symptom severity has only been reported in two studies (Yehuda, Golier, Halligan, Meaney, & Bierer, 2004; Yehuda et al., 1995). In PTSD patients receiving metyrapone, which decreases circulating cortisol, Yehuda et al. (1996) found significantly elevated ACTH and 11-deoxycortisol levels compared to controls, suggesting increased pituitary and adrenal activity, respectively. However, at least three subsequent studies have shown either no group difference, or an actual decrease in ACTH response (Kanter et al., 2001; M. Kellner et al., 2004; Neylan et al., 2003). Thus, while feedback mechanisms in PTSD patients may be particularly sensitive to overstimulation by glucocorticoids, understimulation appears to produce inconsistent results.

Social Anxiety

Social anxiety disorder or social phobia involves exaggerated fear or anxiety responses in social situations or other situations involving evaluation. In contrast to panic disorder and PTSD, far fewer studies have characterized neuroendocrine profiles in social anxiety and other anxiety disorders. Thus far, studies have failed to find abnormal circadian or morning cortisol levels (Laufer et al., 2005; Potts, Davidson, Krishnan, Doraiswamy, & Ritchie, 1991; Uhde, Tancer, Gelernter, & Vittone, 1994) or an abnormal DST response (Uhde et al., 1994) in patients with social anxiety disorder.

Examination of HPA axis responsivity to psychological or physiological stressors has produced mixed results. Condren, O'Neill, Ryan, Barrett, and Thakore (2002) observed an elevated cortisol response in social phobics performing cognitive tasks in front of an audience. However, in another study of 19 social phobics performing a public speaking task, while some patients showed an elevated cortisol response, more than half either showed normal or decreased cortisol levels (Furlan, DeMartinis, Schweizer, Rickels, & Lucki, 2001). As well, Martel et al. (1999) found cortisol responses to be similar to control subjects in 27 adolescent girls with social phobia performing a modified version of the Trier Social Stress Test (TSST, a public speaking task involving evaluation). Similarly, in a pharmacological challenge study, Katzman, Koszycki, and Bradwejn (2004) found a normal cortisol response to a laboratory panicogen (a CCK-B agonist) in 12 patients with social phobia.

The absence of a sensitized cortisol response in public speaking tasks is of particular interest since the threat of negative public evaluation is a core concern of individuals with social anxiety. As well, in their meta-analysis of psychological activators of the HPA axis, Dickerson and Kemeny (2004) found that tasks introducing a threat to social esteem or negative social evaluation (such as the TSST) produced the most robust HPA activation, more so than tasks that simply produced subjective distress or fatigue. One explanation for the failure to observe sensitized HPA responses is a potential "ceiling" effect. Since all subjects (healthy and social phobic) show pronounced cortisol increases during evaluative public speaking, discerning a group difference is more difficult. However, in a study of social phobics with and without comorbid depression, Young, Abelson, & Cameron (2004) showed that pure social phobics had a normal ACTH response to the TSST, but those with both social phobia and depression showed an exaggerated response. These data suggest that the failure of social phobia itself to be associated with excessive HPA reactivity to social challenge is not the result of a simple ceiling effect.

Indeed, the relationship between cortisol and subjective anxiety in phobic patients may be quite complex. A recent study by Soravia et al. (2006) found that in social phobics engaged in the TSST, stress-induced cortisol levels actually correlated negatively with fear ratings. In fact, administration of 25 mg of cortisone 1 h prior to a speech task significantly reduced fear levels in social phobics at all stages of the task (anticipation, exposure, and recovery). Thus, rather than provide a "marker" or indicator of subjective fear, cortisol in certain phobic situations may potentially serve a protective role.

Specific Phobia

Specific phobias involve heightened fear or anxiety regarding a specific object or situation (e.g., animals, flight, heights). Perhaps not surprisingly, the few neuroendocrine studies in this area have focused on hormone responses to a specific phobic challenge. Two early studies found that in vivo exposure to a phobic stimuli produced either an anxiety response with no cortisol activation (Curtis, Buxton, Lippman, Nesse, & Wright, 1976) or a cortisol response that did not show a consistent relationship with level of anxiety (Nesse et al., 1985). Fredrikson, Sundin, and Frankenhaeuser (1985) did find greater cortisol release (as well as subjective distress and psychophysiological responses) following exposure to a phobic slide (e.g., of snakes or spiders) as compared to a neutral slide. However, the relationship between cortisol release and anxiety was not particularly strong.

Thus, at this point, the relationship between cortisol and anxiety generated by stimulus-specific phobic exposure remains unclear. Interestingly, in one study cortisol pretreatment actually reduced subjective fear ratings in phobics presented with a slide of their phobic object (e.g., spider) (Soravia et al., 2006). As with the study of HPA axis and panic disorder, it may be of interest to examine the role of psychosocial contextual variables interacting with the stressor in understanding mediators of HPA activation in phobic situations. For instance, a preliminary investigation with eight spider and snake phobics examined the role of perceived control on cortisol response to exposure (Khan, Himle, Liberzon, & Abelson, 2007). Subjects were exposed to their feared object using rapid, systematic exposure, with phobics in one group controlling the pace of exposure and very closely matched phobics in a second group having the object moved closer at time points predetermined by their yoked-comparison subject (thus having no control over pace of exposure). Interestingly, having control had little effect on the actual anxiety response, although perceived control strongly and significantly predicted the size of the cortisol response. This correlation was far more pronounced than that between

cortisol and measures of perceived fear, stressfulness, or danger, which were not significant. Although these data represent a small group of subjects, they do suggest that in understanding the HPA response to phobic stimuli, some attention might be placed on the role of the psychosocial context of exposure, particularly with regard to circumstances that create or enhance a sense of uncertainty or control.

Generalized Anxiety Disorder

Generalized anxiety disorder (GAD) is characterized by excessive anxiety and worry about various life events. A limited number of studies have examined its neuroendocrine profile. Normal CSF CRH levels were found in two studies of GAD patients (Banki, Karmacsi, Bissette, & Nemeroff, 1992; Fossey et al., 1996). As well, Tafet et al. (2001) observed normal morning but elevated evening plasma cortisol levels, which were similar to a comparison group with MDD. Patients with GAD receiving 48 twice-weekly cognitive therapy sessions showed a significant decline in afternoon cortisol levels, but not symptoms, after 24 weeks, whereas levels for untreated subjects stayed the same (Tafet, Feder, Abulafia, & Roffman, 2005). Psychosocial components of therapy (e.g., perceived social support) rather than changes in actual anxiety levels may have influenced cortisol levels. In one of the few challenge studies conducted, Goddard et al. (1999) observed a normal cortisol response in GAD patients to a serotonergic receptor challenge (m-chlorophenylpiperazine or mCPP). Clearly, current evidence is insufficient to establish a clear HPA axis profile for GAD patients.

Summary and Conclusions

The relationship between the HPA axis and anxiety disorders is complex. Extensive basic science data suggest an important mediating role for central CRH in behavioral, physiological, and endocrine stress responses. This has provided some promise that pharmacological interventions involving CRH antagonism might demonstrate therapeutic efficacy in anxiety disorders. Although published studies demonstrating this have not yet emerged, the need for more specific and effective treatments for anxiety disorders remains clear, and CRH antagonists remain under active development and are of considerable interest as potential anxiolytics.

In patients with panic disorder, there is thus far limited evidence suggesting a relationship between panic attacks or panic symptom intensity and the magnitude of ACTH or cortisol release. Interestingly, a number of studies do suggest enhanced sensitivity in panic patients to contextual variables surrounding a panicogenic challenge, such as the novelty of the experience. Using other measures of HPA functioning, the data thus far are too inconsistent to reliably conclude that there are abnormalities in basal state, central drive, and feedback inhibition in panic patients. The few studies suggesting elevated basal cortisol levels would benefit from further replication in experiments directly addressing confounds related to comorbidity and sensitivity to contextual variables. At this point, however, it appears unlikely that peripherally measured HPA axis activity is going to lead us to HPA axis deficits critically involved in the pathophysiology of this disorder. It seems more likely that HPA axis abnormalities in panic are due to dysregulated functioning in extra-hypothalamic circuits that modulate hypothalamic output.

In PTSD patients, there is more consistent evidence to suggest hypersensitive feedback inhibition mechanisms under specific conditions, although the relationship of this sensitivity to PTSD symptom development or intensity is not yet established. Studies examining differences in circadian cortisol levels have been inconsistent, although some studies have suggested a potential relationship between low cortisol levels and trauma exposure and with especially high symptom severity. It seems likely that HPA axis dysregulation might be more closely related to the central pathophysiology of PTSD than is the case for panic disorder. However, it remains unclear whether the dysregulations documented reflect a consequence of trauma exposure, preexisting alterations that constitutes traumatic vulnerability, or a more specific correlate of the disease process. It is also possible that cortisol itself, when secreted in response to a traumatic stressor, plays a protective role and a failure of adequate cortisol release in the face of trauma contributes to central conditions that set the stage for subsequent vulnerability to PTSD.

With regard to more situation-specific anxiety disorders (i.e., social or specific phobias), the limited availability of neuroendocrine data makes definitive conclusions difficult. However, the data thus far do not provide strong evidence of a link between cortisol responses and anxious symptom severity in either patient population. Indeed, there is preliminary evidence indicating that cortisol levels are negatively correlated with anxious systems following phobic exposure, and cortisol treatment prior to a phobic challenge may in fact have therapeutic benefits.

Taken together, some of these results may suggest a different approach to understanding the relationship between changes in anxiety levels and HPA activation. In part due to the extensive basic science literature showing a close association between stress exposure and HPA axis activation it has perhaps been assumed that pathological fears or anxiety might also be associated with abnormal cortisol responses or abnormalities in other components of HPA functioning. However, the relationship between neuroendocrine measures and anxious situations is probably more complex. Animal literature has long suggested that novelty and threat are salient to the HPA axis, particularly in the absence of control, social support, or coping responses. A growing body of data in the human literature now also suggest that experimental contexts that are novel, threatening, or uncontrollable may increase ACTH and cortisol levels in healthy subjects and patients with certain anxiety disorders. It is possible that individuals with anxious symptoms that are, themselves, characterized by a certain lack of control and unpredictability have an HPA axis that is more sensitive to these contextual variables and the system may remain active in the presence of perceived (though not necessarily "real") homeostatic threats. A failure to account for and control many of these contextual variables in clinical studies may be contributing to the high degree of inconsistency in results. Future work should directly test this hypothesis by addressing these potential confounds.

It appears unlikely that the full explanation of any specific anxiety disorder is going to be found within the HPA axis itself, but ongoing study of this system is likely to enhance our understanding of the real etiology and pathophysiology of these important sources of human suffering and dysfunction.

References

Abelson, J. L., & Curtis, G. C. (1996). Hypothalamic-pituitary-adrenal axis activity in panic disorder: 24-hour secretion of corticotropin and cortisol. *Archives of General Psychiatry, 53,* 323–331.

Abelson, J. L., Khan, S., Liberzon, I., & Young, E. A. (2006). HPA axis activity in patients with panic disorder: Review and synthesis of four studies. *Depression and Anxiety, 24,* 66–76.

Abelson, J. L., Liberzon, I., Young, E. A., & Khan, S. (2005). Cognitive modulation of the endocrine stress response to a pharmacological challenge in normal and panic disorder subjects. *Archives of General Psychiatry, 62,* 668–675.

Abelson, J. L., Weg, J. G., Nesse, R. M., & Curtis, G. C. (1996). Neuroendocrine responses to laboratory panic: Cognitive intervention in the doxapram model. *Psychoneuroendocrinology, 21,* 375–390.

Anisman, H., Griffiths, J., Matheson, K., Ravindran, A. V., & Merali, Z. (2001). Posttraumatic stress symptoms and salivary cortisol levels. *American Journal of Psychiatry, 158*, 1509–1511.

Baker, D. G., Ekhator, N. N., Kasckow, J. W., Dashevsky, B., Horn, P. S., Bednarik, L., et al. (2005). Higher levels of basal serial CSF cortisol in combat veterans with posttraumatic stress disorder. *American Journal of Psychiatry, 162,* 992–994.

Baker, D. G., West, S. A., Nicholson, W. E., Ekhator, N. N., Kasckow, J. W., Hill, K. K., et al. (1999). Serial CSF corticotropin-releasing hormone levels and adrenocortical activity in combat veterans with posttraumatic stress disorder. *American Journal of Psychiatry, 156*, 585–588.

Bandelow, B., Sengos, G., Wedekind, D., Huether, G., Pilz, J., Broocks, A., et al. (1997). Urinary excretion of cortisol, norepinephrine, testosterone, and melatonin in panic disorder. *Pharmacopsychiatry, 30,* 113–117.

Bandelow, B., Wedekind, D., Pauls, J., Broocks, A., Hajak, G., & Ruther, E. (2000). Salivary cortisol in panic attacks. *American Journal of Psychiatry, 157,* 454–456.

Banki, C. M., Karmacsi, L., Bissette, G., & Nemeroff, C. B. (1992). Cerebrospinal fluid neuropeptides in mood disorder and dementia. *Journal of Affective Disorders, 25,* 39–45.

Boscarino, J. A. (1996). Posttraumatic stress disorder, exposure to combat, and lower plasma cortisol among Vietnam veterans: Findings and clinical implications. *Journal of Consulting and Clinical Psychology, 64,* 191–201.

Brambilla, F., Bellodi, L., Perna, G., Battaglia, M., Sciuto, G., Diaferia, G., et al. (1992). Psychoimmunoendocrine aspects of panic disorder. *Neuropsychobiology, 26,* 12–22.

Bremner, J. D., Licinio, J., Darnell, A., Krystal, J. H., Owens, M. J., Southwick, S. M., et al. (1997). Elevated CSF corticotropin-releasing factor concentrations in posttraumatic stress disorder. *American Journal of Psychiatry, 154,* 624–629.

Bremner, J. D., Vythilingam, M., Anderson, G., Vermetten, E., McGlashan, T., Heninger, G., et al. (2003). Assessment of the hypothalamic-pituitary-adrenal axis over a 24-hour diurnal period and in response to neuroendocrine challenges in women with and without childhood sexual abuse and posttraumatic stress disorder. *Biological Psychiatry, 54,* 710–718.

Cameron, O. G., Lee, M. A., Curtis, G. C., & McCann, D. S. (1987). Endocrine and physiological changes during "spontaneous" panic attacks. *Psychoneuroendocrinology, 12,* 321–331.

Carroll, B. J., Feinberg, M., Greden, J. F., Tarika, J., Albala, A. A., Haskett, R. F., et al. (1981). A specific laboratory test for the diagnosis of melancholia: Standardization, validation, and clinical utility. *Archives of General Psychiatry, 38,* 15–22.

Condren, R. M., O'Neill, A., Ryan, M. C., Barrett, P., & Thakore, J. H. (2002). HPA axis response to a psychological stressor in generalised social phobia. *Psychoneuroendocrinology, 27,* 693–703.

Coryell, W., & Noyes, R. (1988). HPA axis disturbance and treatment outcome in panic disorder. *Biological Psychiatry, 24,* 762–766.

Coryell, W., Noyes, R., & Schlechte, J. (1989). The significance of HPA axis disturbance in panic disorder. *Biological Psychiatry, 25,* 989–1002.

Curtis, G. C., Abelson, J. L., & Gold, P. W. (1997). ACTH and cortisol responses to CRH: Changes in panic disorder and effects of alprazolam treatment. *Biological Psychiatry, 41,* 76–85.

Curtis, G. C., Buxton, M., Lippman, D., Nesse, R., & Wright, J. (1976). "Flooding *in vivo*" during the circadian phase of minimal cortisol secretion: Anxiety and therapeutic success without adrenal cortical activation. *Biological Psychiatry, 11,* 101–107.

Curtis, G. C., Cameron, O. G., & Nesse, R. M. (1982). The dexamethasone suppression test in panic disorder and agoraphobia. *American Journal of Psychiatry, 139,* 1043–1046.

Dickerson, S. S., & Kemeny, M. E. (2004). Acute stressors and cortisol responses: A theoretical integration and synthesis of laboratory research. *Psychological Bulletin, 130,* 355–391.

Elzinga, B. M., Schmahl, C. G., Vermetten, E., van Dyck, R., & Bremner, J. D. (2003). Higher cortisol levels following exposure to traumatic reminders in abuse-related PTSD. *Neuropsychopharmacology, 28,* 1656–1665.

Erhardt, A., Ising, M., Unschuld, P. G., Kern, N., Lucae, S., Putz, B., et al. (2006). Regulation of the hypothalamic-pituitary-adrenocortical system in patients with panic disorder. *Neuropsychopharmacology, 31,* 2515–2522.

Fossey, M. D., Lydiard, R. B., Ballenger, J. C., Laraia, M. T., Bissette, G., & Nemeroff, C. B. (1996). Cerebrospinal fluid corticotropin-releasing factor concentrations in patients with anxiety disorders and normal comparison subjects. *Biological Psychiatry, 39,* 703–707.

Fredrikson, M., Sundin, O., & Frankenhaeuser, M. (1985). Cortisol excretion during the defense reaction in humans. *Psychosomatic Medicine, 47,* 313–319.

Furlan, P. M., DeMartinis, N., Schweizer, E., Rickels, K., & Lucki, I. (2001). Abnormal salivary cortisol levels in social phobic patients in response to acute psychological but not physical stress. *Biological Psychiatry, 50,* 254–259.

Goddard, A. W., Woods, S. W., Money, R., Pande, A. C., Charney, D. S., Goodman, W. K., et al. (1999). Effects of the CCK(B) antagonist CI-988 on responses to mCPP in generalized anxiety disorder. *Psychiatry Research, 85,* 225–240.

Goenjian, A. K., Yehuda, R., Pynoos, R. S., Steinberg, A. M., Tashjian, M., Yang, R. K., et al. (1996). Basal cortisol, dexamethasone suppression of cortisol, and MHPG in adolescents after the 1988 earthquake in Armenia. *American Journal of Psychiatry, 153,* 929–934.

Goldstein, S., Halbreich, U., Asnis, G., Endicott, J., & Alvir, J. (1987). The hypothalamic-pituitary-adrenal system in panic disorder. *American Journal of Psychiatry, 144,* 1320–1323.

Gurguis, G.N.M., Mefford, I. N., & Uhde, T. W. (1991). Hypothalamic-pituitary-adrenocortical activity in panic disorder: Relationship to plasma catecholamine metabolites. *Biological Psychiatry, 30,* 502–506.

Heinrichs, M., Wagner, D., Schoch, W., Soravia, L. M., Hellhammer, D. H., & Ehlert, U. (2005). Predicting posttraumatic stress symptoms from pretraumatic risk factors: A 2-year prospective follow-up study in firefighters. *American Journal of Psychiatry, 162,* 2276–2286.

Hollander, E., Liebowitz, M. R., Gorman, J. M., Cohen, B., Fyer, A., & Klein, D. F. (1989). Cortisol and sodium lactate-induced panic. *Archives of General Psychiatry, 46,* 135–140.

Holsboer, F., von Bardeleben, U., Buller, R., Heuser, I., & Steiger, A. (1987). Stimulation response to corticotropin-releasing hormone (CRH) in patients with depression, alcoholism and panic disorder. *Hormone and Metabolic Research, 16*(Suppl.), 80–88.

Jolkkonen, J., Lepola, U., Bissette, G., Nemeroff, C., & Riekkinen, P. (1993). CSF corticotropin-releasing factor is not affected in panic disorder. *Biological Psychiatry, 33,* 136–138.

Kanter, E. D., Wilkinson, C. W., Radant, A. D., Petrie, E. C., Dobie, D. J., McFall, M. E., et al. (2001). Glucocorticoid feedback sensitivity and adrenocortical responsiveness in posttraumatic stress disorder. *Biological Psychiatry, 50,* 238–245.

Kathol, R. G., Anton, R., Noyes, R., Lopez, A. L., & Reich, J. H. (1988). Relationship of urinary free cortisol levels in patients with panic disorder to symptoms of depression and agoraphobia. *Psychiatry Research, 24,* 211–221.

Katzman, M. A., Koszycki, D., & Bradwejn, J. (2004). Effects of CCK-tetrapeptide in patients with social phobia and obsessive-compulsive disorder. *Depression and Anxiety, 20,* 51–58.

Kellner, M., Schick, M., Yassouridis, A., Struttmann, T., Wiedemann, K., & Alm, B. (2004). Metyrapone tests in patients with panic disorder. *Biological Psychiatry, 56,* 898–900.

Kellner, M., Yassouridis, A., Hubner, R., Baker, D. G., & Wiedemann, K. (2003). Endocrine and cardiovascular responses to corticotropin-releasing hormone in patients with posttraumatic stress disorder: A role for atrial natriuretic peptide? *Neuropsychobiology, 47,* 102–108.

Khan, S., Himle, J., Liberzon, I., & Abelson, J. L. (2007). *Effect of controlled exposure on cortisol release in specific phobia.* Paper presented at the meeting of the Anxiety Disorders Association of America, St. Louis, MO.

Laufer, N., Maayan, R., Hermesh, H., Marom, S., Gilad, R., Strous, R., et al. (2005). Involvement of GABAA receptor modulating neuroactive steroids in patients with social phobia. *Psychiatry Research, 137,* 131–136.

Lemieux, A. M., & Coe, C. L. (1995). Abuse-related posttraumatic stress disorder: Evidence for chronic neuroendocrine activation in women. *Psychosomatic Medicine, 57,* 105–115.

Levin, A. P., Doran, A. R., Liebowitz, M. R., Fyer, A. J., Gorman, J. M., Klein, D. F., et al. (1987). Pituitary adrenocortical unresponsiveness in lactate induced panic. *Psychiatry Research, 21,* 23–32.

Liberzon, I., Abelson, J. L., Flagel, S. B., Raz, J., & Young, E. A. (1999). Neuroendocrine and psychophysiologic responses in PTSD: A symptom provocation study. *Neuropsychopharmacology, 21,* 40–50.

Lieberman, J. A., Brenner, R., Lesser, M., Coccaro, E., Borenstein, M., & Kane, J. M. (1983). Dexamethasone suppression tests in patients with panic disorder. *American Journal of Psychiatry, 140,* 917–919.

Lopez, A. L., Kathol, R. G., & Noyes, R. (1990). Reduction in urinary free cortisol during benzodiazepine treatment of panic disorder. *Psychoneuroendocrinology, 15,* 23–28.

Luecken, L. J., Dausch, B., Gulla, V., Hong, R., & Compas, B. E. (2004). Alterations in morning cortisol associated with PTSD in women with breast cancer. *Journal of Psychosomatic Research, 56,* 13–15.

Maes, M., Lin, A., Bonaccorso, S., van Hunsel, F., van Gastel, A., Delmeire, L., et al. (1998). Increased 24-hour urinary cortisol excretion in patients with post-traumatic stress disorder and patients with major depression, but not in patients with fibromyalgia. *Acta Psychiatrica Scandinavica, 98,* 328–335.

Martel, F. L., Hayward, C., Lyons, D. M., Sanborn, K., Varady, S., & Schatzberg, A. F. (1999). Salivary cortisol levels in socially phobic adolescent girls. *Depression and Anxiety, 10,* 25–27.

Mason, J. W., Giller, E. L., Kosten, T. R., Ostroff, R. B., & Podd, L. (1986). Urinary free-cortisol levels in posttraumatic stress disorder patients. *Journal of Nervous and Mental Disease, 174,* 145–149.

Nesse, R., Curtis, G., Thyer, B., McCann, D., Huber-Smith, M., & Knopf, R. (1985). Endocrine and cardiovascular responses during phobic anxiety. *Psychosomatic Medicine, 47,* 320–332.

Newport, D. J., Heim, C., Bonsall, R., Miller, A. H., & Nemeroff, C. B. (2004). Pituitary-adrenal responses to standard and low-dose dexamethasone suppression tests in adult survivors of child abuse. *Biological Psychiatry, 55,* 10–20.

Neylan, T. C., Brunet, A., Pole, N., Best, S. R., Metzler, T. J., Yehuda, R., et al. (2005). PTSD symptoms predict waking salivary cortisol levels in police officers. *Psychoneuroendocrinology, 30,* 373–381.

Neylan, T. C., Lenoci, M., Maglione, M. L., Rosenlicht, N. Z., Metzler, T. J., Otte, C., et al. (2003). Delta sleep response to metyrapone in post-traumatic stress disorder. *Neuropsychopharmacology, 28,* 1666–1676.

Olff, M., Guzelcan, Y., de Vries, G. J., Assies, J., & Gersons, B. P. (2006). HPA- and HPT-axis alterations in chronic posttraumatic stress disorder. *Psychoneuroendocrinology, 31,* 1220–1230.

Peskind, E. R., Jensen, C. F., Pascualy, M., Tsuang, D., Cowley, D., Martin, D. C., et al. (1998). Sodium lactate and hypertonic sodium chloride induce equivalent panic incidence, panic symptoms, and hypernatremia in panic disorder. *Biological Psychiatry, 44,* 1007–1016.

Pitman, R. K., & Orr, S. P. (1990). Twenty-four hour urinary cortisol and catecholamine excretion in combat-related posttraumatic stress disorder. *Biological Psychiatry, 27,* 245–247.

Poland, R. E., Rubin, R. T., Lane, L. A., Martin, D. J., Rose, D. E., & Lesser, I. M. (1985). A modified dexamethasone suppression test for endogenous depression. *Psychiatry Research, 15,* 293–299.

Potts, N. L., Davidson, J. R., Krishnan, K. R., Doraiswamy, P. M., & Ritchie, J. C. (1991). Levels of urinary free cortisol in social phobia. *Journal of Clinical Psychiatry, 52*(Suppl.), 41–42.

Rasmusson, A. M., Lipschitz, D. S., Wang, S., Hu, S., Vojvoda, D., Bremner, J. D., et al. (2001). Increased pituitary and adrenal reactivity in premenopausal women with posttraumatic stress disorder. *Biological Psychiatry, 50,* 965–977.

Roy-Byrne, P. P., Uhde, T. W., Post, R. M., Gallucci, W., Chrousos, G. P., & Gold, P. W. (1986). The corticotropin-releasing hormone stimulation test in patients with panic disorder. *American Journal of Psychiatry, 143,* 896–899.

Schreiber, W., Lauer, C. J., Krumrey, K., Holsboer, F., & Krieg, J. C. (1996). Dysregulation of the hypothalamic-pituitary-adrenocortical system in panic disorder. *Neuropsychopharmacology, 15,* 7–15.

Seier, F. E., Kellner, M., Yassouridis, A., Heese, R., Strian, F., & Wiedemann, K. (1997). Autonomic reactivity and hormonal secretion in lactate-induced panic attacks. *American Journal of Physiology, 272,* H2630–H2638.

Sheehan, D. V., Claycomb, J. B., Surman, O. S., Baer, L., Coleman, J., & Gelles, L. (1983). Panic attacks and the dexamethasone suppression test. *American Journal of Psychiatry, 140,* 1063–1064.

Sinha, S. S., Coplan, J. D., Pine, D. S., Martinez, J. A., Klein, D. F., & Gorman, J. M. (1999). Panic induced by carbon dioxide inhalation and lack of hypothalamic-pituitary-adrenal axis activation. *Psychiatry Research, 86,* 93–98.

Smith, M. A., Davidson, J., Ritchie, J. C., Kudler, H., Lipper, S., Chappell, P., et al. (1989). The corticotropin-releasing hormone test in patients with posttraumatic stress disorder. *Biological Psychiatry, 26,* 349–355.

Soravia, L. M., Heinrichs, M., Aerni, A., Maroni, C., Schelling, G., Ehlert, U., Roozendaal, B., de Quervain, D. J. (2006). Glucocorticoids reduce phobic fear in humans. *Proceedings of the National Academy of Sciences, 103*(14), 5585–5590.

Tafet, G. E., Feder, D. J., Abulafia, D. P., & Roffman, S. S. (2005). Regulation of hypothalamic-pituitary-adrenal activity in response to cognitive therapy in patients with generalized anxiety disorder. *Cognitive, Affective, and Behavioral Neuroscience, 5*(1), 37–40.

Tafet, G. E., Idoyaga-Vargas, V. P., Abulafia, D. P., Calandria, J. M., Roffman, S. S., Chiovetta, A., et al. (2001). Correlation between cortisol level and serotonin uptake in patients with chronic stress and depression. *Cognitive, Affective, and Behavioral Neuroscience, 1,* 388–393.

Targum, S. D., & Marshall, L. E. (1989). Fenfluramine provocation of anxiety in patients with panic disorder. *Psychiatry Research, 28,* 295–306.

Uhde, T., Joffe, R. T., Jimerson, D. C., & Post, R. M. (1988). Normal urinary free cortisol and plasma MHPG in panic disorder: Clinical and theoretical implications. *Biological Psychiatry, 23,* 575–585.

Uhde, T. W., Tancer, M. E., Gelernter, C. S., & Vittone, B. J. (1994). Normal urinary free cortisol and postdexamethasone cortisol in social phobia: Comparison to normal volunteers. *Journal of Affective Disorders, 30,* 155–161.

Von Bardeleben, U., & Holsboer, F. (1988). Human corticotropin releasing hormone: Clinical studies in patients with affective disorders, alcoholism, panic disorder and in normal controls. *Progress in Neuropsychopharmacology and Biological Psychiatry, 12*(Suppl.), S165–S187.

Wessa, M., Rohleder, N., Kirschbaum, C., & Flor, H. (2006). Altered cortisol awakening response in posttraumatic stress disorder. *Psychoneuroendocrinology, 31,* 209–215.

Westberg, P., Modigh, K., Lisjo, P., & Eriksson, E. (1991). Higher postdexamethasone serum cortisol levels in agoraphobic than in nonagoraphobic panic disorder patients. *Biological Psychiatry, 30,* 247–256.

Woods, S. W., Charney, D. S., McPherson, C. A., Gradman, A. H., & Heninger, G. R. (1987). Situational panic attacks: Behavioral, physiologic, and biochemical characterization. *Archives of General Psychiatry, 44,* 365–375.

Yehuda, R., Golier, J. A., Halligan, S. L., Meaney, M., & Bierer, L. M. (2004). The ACTH response to dexamethasone in PTSD. *American Journal of Psychiatry, 161,* 1397–1403.

Yehuda, R., Kahana, B., Binder-Brynes, K., Southwick, S. M., Mason, J. W., & Giller, E. L. (1995). Low urinary cortisol excretion in Holocaust survivors with posttraumatic stress disorder. *American Journal of Psychiatry, 152,* 982–986.

Yehuda, R., Levengood, R. A., Schmeidler, J., Wilson, S., Guo, L. S., & Gerber, D. (1996). Increased pituitary activation following metyrapone administration in post-traumatic stress disorder. *Psychoneuroendocrinology, 21,* 1–16.

Yehuda, R., Southwick, S. M., Krystal, J. H., Bremner, D., Charney, D. S., & Mason, J. W. (1993). Enhanced suppression of cortisol following dexamethasone administration in posttraumatic stress disorder. *American Journal of Psychiatry, 150,* 83–86.

Yehuda, R., Southwick, S. M., Nussbaum, G., Wahby, V., Giller, E. L., Jr., & Mason, J. W. (1990). Low urinary cortisol excretion in patients with posttraumatic stress disorder. *Journal of Nervous and Mental Disease, 178,* 366–369.

Young, E. A., Abelson, J. L., & Cameron, O. G. (2004). Effect of comorbid anxiety disorders on the hypothalamic-pituitary-adrenal axis response to a social stressor in major depression. *Biological Psychiatry, 56,* 113–120.

Young, E. A., & Breslau, N. (2004a). Cortisol and catecholamines in posttraumatic stress disorder: an epidemiologic community study. *Archives of General Psychiatry, 61,* 394–401.

Young, E. A., & Breslau, N. (2004b). Saliva cortisol in posttraumatic stress disorder: A community epidemiologic study. *Biological Psychiatry, 56,* 205–209.

Developmental Approaches to Understanding Anxiety Disorders

Richie Poulton, Jessica R. Grisham *and* Gavin Andrews

Abstract

We illustrate the value of a developmental perspective for understanding anxiety disorders by: (1) reviewing evidence for continuity of the anxiety phenotype from childhood to adulthood to show how these findings have implications for nosology, research, and prevention; (2) use posttraumatic stress disorder (PTSD) to reveal how developmental origins can be identified much earlier in life, far removed from traumatic precipitating events; (3) consider the interplay of biological, cognitive, personality, and environmental factors in etiology of panic disorder, with or without agoraphobia; and (4) take an in-depth look at obsessive-compulsive disorder (OCD) to highlight how a developmental approach may be essential for progress to be made in our understanding of this and other anxiety disorders.

Keywords: anxiety disorders, developmental, etiology, longitudinal

In the developed world, mental disorders account for one-eighth of the disability adjusted life years due to disease and rank third in importance after cardiovascular disease and cancer (Mathers, Vos, & Stevenson, 1999). Leaving aside the burden of premature mortality, mental disorders are the leading cause of disability (Murray & Lopez, 1996) and the anxiety disorders account for a quarter of the disability attributed to mental disorders. Even though sufferers seldom generate risks to themselves or to others and so do not come to attention, they are a serious cause of the loss of human potential, mainly through avoidance or failure to perform in educational, vocational, and relationship spheres. In time, comorbidity involves substance use and depression, and the additional impact is considerable (Andrews & Slade, 2002).

To reduce the burden of anxiety disorders, we need to prevent the emergence of disorder, prevent the appearance of comorbidity, and provide effective treatment promptly and efficiently. In short, if

we were serious about averting the burden of anxiety disorders, we should strive to do three things: identify preventable causes or risk factors, educate the workforce to deliver existing treatments with more fidelity, and discover better treatments.

Longitudinal-developmental studies can be particularly helpful in these tasks if they collect risk factor information at time 1 that turns out to be predictive of the disorder at time 2. Such risk factors might then elucidate an aspect of the cause. Such studies are even more valuable if they have information that can be used to rule out alternative explanations for the observed associations between risk exposures and anxiety disorders. Critically, developmental data also provide information about *when* interventions could be better targeted to the vulnerable age group.

But what is the vulnerable age group? Kessler et al. (2005) reported that in the National Comorbidity Survey Replication, the median age of onset of anxiety disorders was 11 years (25th percentile

6 years), which infers that effective prevention should begin in kindergarten, and good treatment should begin in grade school. These data include specific phobia and separation anxiety disorder, both of which have median ages of onset of 7 years. If these disorders are excluded, and neither have been the focus of significant deployment of services, the median age of onset of the other anxiety disorders rises to late teens and the 25th percentile to the early teens, figures that make the task of developing prevention and intervention programs for anxiety disorders more manageable.

Our goal in this chapter is to describe the value of a developmental perspective for understanding anxiety disorders. We do this by: (1) selectively reviewing evidence for continuity of the anxiety phenotype from childhood to adulthood to show how these findings have implications for nosology, research, and prevention; (2) use posttraumatic stress disorder (PTSD) to reveal how developmental origins can be identified much earlier in life, far removed from traumatic precipitating events; (3) consider the interplay of biological, cognitive, personality, and environmental factors in etiology of panic disorder, with or without agoraphobia; and (4) take an in-depth look at obsessive-compulsive disorder (OCD) to highlight how a developmental approach may be essential for progress to be made in our understanding of this and other anxiety disorders.

Continuity of Anxiety Disorders from Childhood to Adulthood

Most adult psychiatric disorders have their roots in early life (e.g., Kim-Cohen et al. 2003; Pine, Cohen, Gurley, Brook, & Ma, 1998). Yet "it is apparent that the amount of lifespan information that is incorporated into the *DSM–IV* is only the tip of the iceberg of what should in fact be known" (Widiger & Clark, 2000, p. 955). Despite researchers developing a range of sophisticated methodologies to enhance the accuracy of retrospective reports, it is generally accepted that biases remain with this type of approach, particularly when respondents are required to estimate the age-of-onset of disorders that may have emerged many years earlier (Kessler et al. 2005; Simon & Von Korff, 1995). Currently, then, prospective follow-back studies remain the best method for obtaining precise information about the developmental histories of anxiety disorders.

Several large prospective-developmental studies have demonstrated linkages between childhood measures of emotional distress and adult anxiety disorders (e.g., Goodwin, Fergusson, & Horwood,

2004; Hofstra, van der Ende, & Verhulst, 2002). For example, in the Christchurch Health and Development Study, Goodwin et al. found that after adjustment for social and family factors during childhood and adolescence, the associations between childhood and adult psychopathology remained significant for social phobia (OR = 3.37 95%CI 1.54–7.39) and specific phobia (OR = 3.89 95%CI 1.89–8.02). Both these studies relied on broad classification schemes in childhood, yet they provide clear evidence of continuity of anxious symptomatology over many years. Indeed stronger associations may have been expected with more narrowly defined syndromes, to the extent that continuity for disorders across development results from specific associations with more narrowly defined syndromes.

In this regard Pine et al. (1998) assessed a community sample (*n* = 776) of young Americans, beginning in 1983 when the sample was aged between 9 and 18 years, and again in 1985 and 1992, using structured interviews that provided *DSM* diagnoses. In simple logistic models, adolescent anxiety disorders were associated with a two to threefold increase in risk for adult anxiety disorders. There was some evidence for homotypic continuity in the course of simple and social phobia but less so for generalized anxiety disorder (GAD) or depression. In analyses adjusted for age, ethnicity, social class, and sex, adolescent simple phobia predicted adult simple phobia only (OR = 3.79 [2.37–6.05]). Adolescent social phobia (OR = 3.29 95%CI 1.52–7.10) as well as overanxious disorder (OR = 2.27 95%CI 1.06–7.10) predicted adult social phobia, indicating considerable homotypic continuity. Interestingly, latent Markov analyses revealed that approximately half of adolescent anxiety disorders were no longer present in adulthood, yet the vast majority of adult anxiety disorders were preceded by some type of disorder during adolescence.

A similar pattern of findings emerged in the Dunedin birth cohort study where psychiatric diagnoses were made according to *DSM* criteria at 11, 13, 15, 18, 21, and 26 years (*n* = 976). Among adult cases interviewed age 26, 50% had received a diagnosis before 15 years of age and 74% before 18 years of age. Among the subset receiving treatment, similar patterns were observed with 60% receiving a diagnosis before 15 years and 78% before age 18. Follow-back analyses of adult anxiety disorder (any of panic disorder, agoraphobia, specific phobia, social phobia, PTSD, GAD, and OCD) showed evidence of homotypic continuity, that is, adults suffering from anxiety disorders had also suffered from anxiety disorders in childhood or adolescence (Kim-Cohen et al., 2003). Adults with anxiety were also at elevated risk of having had juvenile externalizing-spectrum diagnoses of attention-deficit hyperactivity disorder (ADHD) and conduct/oppositional defiant disorder (CD/ODD). However, this follow-back analysis was limited because all seven *DSM* anxiety disorders were treated as a single group, potentially obscuring important differences in continuity patterns between the disorders.

To overcome this limitation, Gregory et al. (2007) used the same follow-back design, in the same sample, to examine continuity between juvenile disorders and *specific* adult anxiety disorders up to age 32 years. Six key findings emerged. First, the age at which study members were first diagnosed with a disorder was similar regardless of the type of anxiety disorder experienced. Second, adults with anxiety disorders experienced their first disorder early in life, that is, there weren't many new-onset cases in adulthood. Third, there was evidence for *strict homotypic continuity* because adults with anxiety disorders (except panic) had experienced significantly more anxiety disorders as juveniles. These juvenile anxiety disorders were also the most common disorders experienced by those with adult anxiety diagnoses. Fourth, there was also evidence for *broad homotypic continuity,* such that adults with most types of anxiety disorder also had a juvenile history of depression. Fifth, there was little evidence for *heterotypic continuity* as adult anxiety diagnoses were not typically associated with a history of externalizing disorders or psychotic symptoms. Sixth, there was some evidence of *specificity:* adults with PTSD had juvenile histories of conduct disorder and/or oppositional defiant disorder. There was also a trend, albeit not significant, for childhood reports of delusional beliefs and hallucinatory to be more frequent among adults with OCD (OR = 2.49) but not other anxiety disorders; and there was some evidence of specificity within phobias, such that adult specific phobias were preceded by juvenile phobias but not other anxiety disorders. These trends appeared despite the high levels of comorbidity between the anxiety disorders in adulthood, and they are consistent with previous research examining these associations.

Implications for Nosology, Research, and Prevention

With regard to nosology, the previous findings (also see Fergusson, Horwood, & Boden, 2006)

suggest that a general approach to the classification of anxiety disorders may be justified. For example, in the most recent study by Gregory et al. (2007), there were similarities in the developmental histories of the different anxiety disorders in terms of age of onset and the types of disorders occurring previously—typically internalizing disorders. Given the high rates of comorbidity among anxiety disorders, this finding is perhaps not surprising. However, other findings, for example, specific phobias in adulthood were associated with juvenile phobias but not other disorders, suggest that some disorders may be best classified independent of other anxiety disorders. More generally, these data support a hierarchical approach to classification, distinguished by a broad class of internalizing disorders, and locating the individual anxiety disorders within it (Watson, 2005).

The findings also emphasize the need for etiological research to begin early in life, and the corollary—that prevention efforts should also begin early in life. The results of the Gregory et al. (2007) study suggest who might be best targeted for prevention efforts—those experiencing depression or anxiety as juveniles (especially phobias that preceded all but one of the adult anxiety disorders). Clinically, knowing that the cognitions and behaviors that characterize most adult anxiety disorders may have emerged much earlier may help the clinician to map (and treat) the developmental origins of these problematic thoughts and behaviors.

If, as these data suggest, adult anxiety disorders have their roots in early life, then focusing on childhood and adolescence will be critical to understanding their etiology and advancing taxonomy. Developmental research on antisocial behavior (e.g., Moffitt & Caspi, 2001) and depression (e.g., Jaffee et al., 2002) has demonstrated the value of distinguishing between persistent (from child to adult) cases from those limited to specific developmental periods. In particular, risk factors often differ according to age of onset and persistence and this distinction may also prove useful for the anxiety disorders. However, it is important to realize that demonstrating continuity is not the same as understanding the processes that give rise to such continuity. A major challenge ahead is to describe *how, when, why,* and *for whom* continuity exists.

Developmental Origins of Anxiety Disorders

It is almost universally accepted that the capacity to experience fear and anxiety is adaptive, enabling as it does rapid and energetic response to imminent danger, or preparation for more distal challenges. However, the nature of maladaptive fear and anxiety remains controversial (Poulton & Menzies, 2002) and, despite many hopeful leads, there is still no consensus about the etiology of any of the anxiety disorders. They could reflect perturbations in core features of individual's responses to imminent danger. Alternatively, anxiety disorders could reflect an intact "core" response to danger that is elicited by inappropriate circumstances or that cannot be terminated appropriately. Moreover, distinct disorders may reflect distinct perturbations. Indeed, the current anxiety disorders in *DSM–IV* are characterized by enormous (developmental) etiological heterogeneity, some of which we review here.

Posttraumatic Stress Disorder

Posttraumatic stress disorder is unique among psychiatric disorders because exposure to a traumatic event is a diagnostic criterion (*DSM–IV*, p. 427), and therefore, it is the quintessential *conditioning* or stress-diathesis disorder. Risk factors for PTSD are of two main types: (1) those that increase risk of trauma exposure, and (2) those that lead to the development of symptoms subsequent to that exposure. Importantly, epidemiologic studies tell us that trauma exposure is not randomly distributed in the population (Breslau, 2002). Indeed, factors driving trauma exposure might be quite different from those that increase psychological vulnerability following trauma. Thus, identification of those factors that contribute to risk at each stage is required. This will help guide different interventions aimed at either preventing exposure in the first instance, or at preventing the development of PTSD once exposure has occurred.

A recent study sought to identify these two sets of risk factors in the first decade of life that were associated with developing PTSD in adulthood (Koenen, Moffitt, Poulton, Martin, & Caspi, 2007). The first set of factors affected both the risk of trauma exposure as well as the risk of developing PTSD once exposed. These risk factors included children's externalizing characteristics (including difficult temperament, antisocial behavior, and hyperactivity), family history of mental-health difficulties (including maternal reports of distress), and family adversities (including loss of a parent). The second set of factors affected risk for PTSD only. These risk factors included low IQ and chronic environmental stressors such as low socioeconomic status. The effect of cumulative childhood risk

was striking: more than half of those scoring in the highest-risk quartile for three developmental factors had PTSD by age 26 compared to only a quarter of those without high risk on any of these factors.

Three key findings emerge from this lifecourse study. First, in contrast to research suggesting that low IQ may be a result of PTSD (De Bellis, 2001), this study, as well as several other prospective studies of military personnel (Kremen et al., 2007; Macklin et al., 1998; Pitman, Orr, Lowenhagen, Macklin, & Altman, 1991), suggests that low IQ may predispose to the development of PTSD. Although the exact mechanism is unclear, it is possible that greater cognitive capacity allows either translation of traumatic events into narratives (Pennebaker, 1999) and/or facilitates extraction of meaning (Janoff-Bulman, 1992). Interestingly, low IQ is a risk factor for other forms of psychopathology (Fergusson, Horwood, & Ridder, 2005), including externalizing disorders, which themselves increase the risk of trauma exposure and subsequent PTSD.

Second, the findings underscore the importance of early environmental conditions for sensitizing individuals to the effects of later stressors. In this regard, animal models have shown that offspring reared under stressful conditions are insecurely attached, emotionally dysregulated (Coplan et al., 1998; Rosenblum & Paully, 1984), and show long-term alterations in functioning of the hypothalamic-pituitary adrenal (HPA) axis (Gorman, Mathew, & Coplan, 2002; Heim & Nemeroff, 2002). Dysregulation of the HPA axis is thought to be involved in the etiology of PTSD, and this might provide a plausible mechanism through which early environmental adversity and the development of PTSD are linked (Yehuda, 2002).

Third, the prospective relation between childhood externalizing problems and risk of PTSD in adulthood is consistent with earlier retrospective reports (e.g. Kulka et al., 1990). Difficult temperament, antisocial behavior, and hyperactivity may all reflect impaired self-regulation, which in turn elevates risk of trauma exposure. Individuals who struggle with self-regulation, broadly defined by the inability "to modulate behavior according to the cognitive, emotional, and social demands of a particular situation" (Calkins & Fox, 2002, p. 479), may be at risk of developing PTSD because they lack the emotional range or "tolerance" required to adequately process the traumatic event. Instead, they may react angrily, and act out, or use avoidance coping strategies that interfere with PTSD recovery in community samples (Koenen, Stellman, Stellman, & Sommer, 2003).

A developmental approach to the epidemiology of PTSD has a lot to recommend it. In terms of research, recent findings show that a developmental perspective is just as valuable for understanding adult PTSD as it is for studies of childhood PTSD. Developmental capacities and conditions of early childhood appear to increase both risk of trauma exposure and the likelihood that symptoms will result, highlighting the importance developmental epidemiology for increasing knowledge about PTSD etiology. From the clinical perspective, therapists may benefit from gathering "developmental" information, particularly that related to chronic adversity, and integrating this into their case formulations. In this regard, psychotherapy that seeks to combine developmental information related to a client's emotional and interpersonal capacities with more traditional trauma-focused treatment is likely to be highly effective in treating adult PTSD (Cloitre, Cohen, & Koenen, 2006). Lastly, prevention efforts should concentrate on factors that increase risk exposure such as antisocial behavior, as well as aiming to minimize exposure to chronic adversity during early development.

Panic Disorder and Phobias

Children's principal fears follow a developmental path. Separation anxiety and specific phobias are first seen in early childhood, social anxiety is first seen in middle childhood, and panic disorder is first seen in early adolescence. Each of these four types of fears parallel the child's increased ability to conceptualize threats and therefore the consequences of the fear. If panic is really the fear that the next panic attack will result in bodily collapse and death, then it is difficult to develop typical panic disorder until a child is old enough to realize the permanence of collapse and death. Ollendick (1998) argues that panic attacks in children are often associated with specific cues rather than being spontaneous and that noncatastrophic interpretations of the symptoms of panic prevail. Thus, any longitudinal study might have to include atypical specific phobias and complaints of somatic symptoms related to anxiety as possible early manifestations of panic disorder in children.

We will use panic disorder with or without agoraphobia and the related condition agoraphobia without panic (both mostly shortened to *panic disorder*) as an exemplar for this approach. In the Kessler et al. study (2005), panic disorder with or without agoraphobia and agoraphobia without panic had a

lifetime prevalence of 7.6%. The median age of onset was 23 years and the 25th percentile was 15 years. This makes data from a developmental perspective of considerable value because there is time to prevent both the disorder and its complications, and time to intervene therapeutically.

Fifteen years ago we thought we knew the cause of panic disorder. However, Taylor (2006), in a clinical review in the *British Medical Journal,* stated that, "The cause of panic disorder is unknown," (p. 952) before going on to mention the importance of genetic factors and oversensitive fear circuitry, the value of the psychological construct of "fear of fear," and the relation between the onset of panic attacks and traumatic events, excessive caffeine, and the misuse of drugs. Katon (2006), in a clinical practice article in the *New England Journal of Medicine,* identified many of the same constructs. In other words, while we do know about risk factors and precipitants, we do not know the precise pathways that lead to the development of the disorder. The situation appears similar for social phobia (e.g., Rapee & Spence, 2004).

While the precise cause of panic disorder may be unknown, two risk factors, even necessary precursors, are of particular interest. The first is a difference in amygdala function, usually measured by functional magnetic resonance imaging (fMRI). The second is a change in vulnerability due to inherited and learned propensity to becoming anxious, fearful, and anticipating the worst. It is usually measured by questionnaires labeled trait anxiety, neuroticism, or more closely related to panic, anxiety sensitivity.

Amygdala, Stress, and Panic

Gorman, Kent, Sullivan, and Coplan (2000) revised their neuroanatomical hypothesis of panic disorder to emphasize "a remarkable similarity between the . . . consequences of response to a conditioned fear stimulus and a panic attack. In animals these responses are mediated by a 'fear network' in the brain that is centered in the amygdala and involves its interaction with the hippocampus and the prefrontal cortex . . . It is speculated that a similar network is involved in panic disorder" (p. 493). Pine et al. (2001) published methods for developmental studies of fear conditioning circuitry using fMRI to examine changes in amygdala activity during noxious conditioning. What is interesting is that, despite very well developed theories based on detailed findings from animal models (Anand & Shekhar, 2003; Pare, Quirk, & Le Doux, 2004), very little direct examination of people with panic disorder against an appropriate control group has appeared.

The results of the animal models were seen as very relevant, and following the 9/11 tragedy, Le Doux and Gorman (2001) exhorted Americans to use their cortex rather than their amygdala to remain calm in the face of the threat. Hariri and Weinberger (2003) report that normal subjects with 5-HTT "short" allele genotype as against the "long" variant had an increased amygdala response to fearful stimuli. None were reported as having a panic attack. Bertolino et al. (2005) found that a "phobic prone group n = 14" selectively, as compared with eating disorder subjects, recruit the amygdala when faced with threatening stimuli. None were described as having panic disorder. To date, brain imaging findings in anxiety disorders in general suggest group differences in amygdala-cortical structure and function. Many of these findings are not reliable or specific, and further research is needed to disentangle the neural substrates of risk. Given the strong position taken by Gorman et al. (2002) or by Pine et al. (2001), one would have expected a comprehensive body of replicated findings to have emerged in respect to panic disorder. It hasn't—yet. Biological markers of sensitivity or vulnerability to panic disorder would be of great value for prognosis and for indicated prevention. At this point, there are no candidate markers.

The Role of Genes and Other Vulnerability Factors

Studies of the contribution of genes to panic disorder are of increasing interest. Hettema, Neale, Myers, Prescott, and Kendler (2006) used multivariate structural equation modeling to explore the relation between neuroticism and the internalizing disorders in 9,000 twins. Genetic factors shared with neuroticism accounted for one-third of the risk of panic disorder and agoraphobia. In addition, the authors could identify a neuroticism independent genetic factor that significantly increased the risk for panic disorder but not for agoraphobia or, for that matter, the other phobias. This is consistent with the view that agoraphobia is not an automatic complication of panic disorders but reflects the pattern of avoidance that occurs in a fear-prone individual with panic disorder. Previous work with the same twins had favored the view that vulnerability to phobias is largely innate, not learned (Kendler, Myers, & Prescott, 2002).

We have already referred to genetic factors that are shared between neuroticism (or trait anxiety or negative emotionality) and panic. Unfortunately,

there is little specificity. This personality trait is associated with all of the internalizing disorders. Anxiety sensitivity posits that there is a trait-like belief in the danger of anxiety symptoms that is normally distributed in the population, and that it is this belief that makes some susceptible to the development of panic disorder. It would therefore appear to be a vulnerability factor specific to panic that could be of value in prospective studies, particularly as there is both a childhood and adult form of the anxiety sensitivity index. There are, however, problems. While Air Force recruits who had high scores did develop more panic attacks during a very stressful basic training, high scores also predicted other anxiety symptoms and depression (Schmidt, Lerew, & Jackson, 1997). This work has been replicated. Hayward, Killen, Kraemer, and Taylor (2000) and Muris, Schmidt, Merckelbach, and Schouten (2001) confirmed the predictive relationship between high scores on the Anxiety Sensitivity Index and the onset of panic. They found that it and trait anxiety both accounted for unique proportions of the variance in anxiety disorder symptoms. Hayward et al. (2000) found it less powerful but more specific than a measure of negative affectivity: "Negative affectivity appears to be a nonspecific risk factor for panic attacks and major depression, whereas anxiety sensitivity appears to be a specific factor that increases the risk for 4-symptom panic attacks in adolescents" (p. 207). Bouton, Mineka, and Barlow (2001) considered that panic disorder develops because exposure to panic attacks causes the conditioning of anxiety to exteroceptive and introceptive cues. As there is a childhood version of the Anxiety Sensitivity Index, it is certainly a candidate marker for those at risk of developing panic disorder.

That it could predict those at risk is interesting, but if it is a vulnerability factor, is this able to be modified? It has been shown to change in people with panic disorder receiving cognitive behavioral treatment. Kenardy, McCafferty, and Rosa (2003) delivered CBT via the Internet to students with high Anxiety Sensitivity Index scores deemed to be at risk of developing anxiety disorders. Compared to the control group, many indicators of vulnerability improved but the change in the Anxiety Sensitivity Index was not significant.

Obsessive-Compulsive Disorder

Significant limitations exist in our understanding of obsessive-compulsive disorder (OCD). Research has not yet been able to identify specific genetic contributions, neuropsychological deficits are highly variable, and biological and psychological models of OCD have not been adequately synthesized to provide a cohesive model of the underlying pathogenic mechanism. A developmental perspective is essential to our understanding of the etiology and course of OCD, including our ability to identify markers of risk and distinguish them from markers of the disease.

Neurobiological Risk Factors and Correlates

Substantial evidence indicates that OCD is associated with distinct patterns of brain dysfunction, particularly altered activity in the orbitofrontal cortex, dorsal anterior cingulate cortex, the basal ganglia (especially the caudate), and hippocampus (Insel, 1992; Rauch et al., 1994, 1997; Saxena, Brody, Schwartz, & Baxter, 1998). Several theories propose that this dysregulation leads thoughts and motivations to persist and become obsessions because the brain fails to reset the state of thinking (Rauch et al., 1994). Obsessions then result in compulsions, actions that are performed over and over again due to the failure of the brain to reset. Neuroanatomical explanations of the development of OCD concentrate on the orbitofrontal frontal cortex and the basal ganglia, especially the striatum. The structural evidence that the frontal lobes and striatum are possible sites of dysfunction in OCD has been discordant. Of the six magnetic resonance studies that have been performed, three MRI studies have found abnormal caudate volumes in OCD (Robinson et al., 1995; Rosenberg & Keshavan, 1998; Scarone et al., 1992). These discrepant findings are probably due to different study methods and the small sample sizes of the studies.

Several findings suggest that OCD is associated with a neurodevelopmental deviation, including the finding that as many of 80% of all cases of OCD have their onset in childhood and adolescence (Pauls et al., 1995), and the comorbidity of OCD with Tourrette syndrome, a neurodevelopmental disorder (American Psychiatric Association, 2004). The presentation of OCD in children is similar to its presentation in adulthood, suggesting that the risk for OCD emerges during early childhood development (Bolton, 1996). A neurodevelopmental model of OCD (Rosenberg & Keshavan, 1998) suggests that a developmentally mediated network dysplasia in ventral prefrontal cortical (VPFC) circuits could manifest clinically by disrupting brain functions that are responsible for purposive behaviors.

To test their model of the development of OCD, Rosenberg and Keshavan (1998) compared psychotropic-naive, pediatric OCD patients to healthy control participants and found that the pediatric OCD patients had significant larger anterior cingulate volumes than control participants. Severity of OCD symptoms, but not illness duration, were positively correlated with VPFC and striatal volumes. Although these findings indicated a developmental rather than an acquired degenerative process, one limitation of the study is that it was cross-sectional rather than prospective. Therefore, the results did not preclude a degenerative process occurring before symptom onset or prior to symptoms reaching a clinical threshold of severity. New prospective developmental studies will be essential for comparing neuroimaging markers with current diagnostic designations in the prediction of outcome. In addition, longitudinal studies before and after treatment are necessary to distinguish illness-related brain changes from medication-induced changes.

Some researchers have suggested that streptococcal infection may be associated with a form of early-onset OCD that involves an abrupt onset of obsessive-compulsive symptoms and co-occurring tics, often abbreviated PANDAS for pediatric autoimmune disorders associated with strep (Guilino et al., 2002; Murphy et al., 2004; Snider & Swedo, 2003). At the present time, however, there is a lack of direct evidence for this hypothesis and additional studies are needed to investigate whether childhood streptococcal infection constitutes a true risk factor for OCD.

Psychological Models of Etiology

There are two major psychological models for the development of OCD, behavioral and cognitive. Behavioral models for OCD are based on learning theory, applied principles of contingent reinforcement and punishment, and the two-stage theory of fear and avoidance. Behavioral theories of OCD posit that a neutral event acquires the capacity to provoke fear because of its pairing with an aversive stimulus. In the second stage of this model, compulsions provide relief from obsessional anxiety or discomfort, which negatively reinforces the compulsions. Thus, the frequency of compulsive actions increases in future situations, which triggers an obsessional concern. Substantial evidence supports a behavioral account of OCD in which obsessions increase discomfort and compulsions reduce it; however, behavioral accounts of the development of OCD are limited.

According to the cognitive theory of OCD, the reaction to negative intrusive experiences in people with OCD depends on underlying beliefs, particularly an exaggerated sense that one is responsible to prevent harm to oneself or others, and that one must act to prevent it (Salkovskis, 1985). Thus, an obsessional patient may interpret the intrusive thought "I will kill my baby" as meaning that there is a risk she will unless she does something to avoid it, such as avoiding being alone with her child, seeking reassurance, or performing some type of ritual. This interpretation results in increased discomfort, anxiety, and depression; greater accessibility of the original thought and related ideas; and neutralizing responses. Neutralization, such as washing, checking, and thought suppression, reduces the level of perceived responsibility in the moment, but increases the probability of intrusive thoughts in the longer term. The increase in intrusive thoughts is due to the greater amount of attention and salience attributed to the thoughts, in that suppressing thought highlights the thinking itself. Research on the nature and measurement of obsessional responsibility, as well as experimental manipulations of responsibility, lend support to this theory (Rheaume, Ladocuceur, Freeston, & Letarte, 1994; Salkovskis, Westbrook, Davis, Jeavons, & Gledhill, 1997; Shafran, 1997).

From a developmental perspective, cognitive-behavioral theories of OCD emphasize a diathesis-stress interaction in which the tendency to think and behave in ways that lead to obsessional problems is cultivated through prior experiences. Yet empirical studies of cognitive-behavioral theories of OCD have largely been correlational, which precludes any firm conclusions that distorted beliefs are the cause of OCD. A longitudinal study demonstrating that premorbid obsessional beliefs predict the onset of OCD would provide empirical support for the cognitive-behavioral account of the disorder.

Psychosocial Risk Factors

Probably related to the dearth of longitudinal studies, there are no known environmental risk factors for OCD. Brown, Campbell, Lehman, Grisham, and Mancill (2001) reported that statistically significant covariation between lifetime PTSD and OCD was attributable to cases in which a principal diagnosis of PTSD was followed by a secondary diagnosis of OCD. This finding indicates the possibility that precipitants or features of PTSD may act as causal factors in OCD. Other studies suggest that OCD may be linked to a history of physical and sexual abuse during childhood (e.g., Lochner et al., 2002). A recent study (Gothelf, Aharonovsky,

Horesh, Carty, & Apter, 2004) found that children with OCD had significantly more total life events and more negative life events in the year before onset than normal controls, and they perceived the life events as having more impact.

All of these studies, however, are reliant on retrospective self-report limiting the conclusions that can be drawn. In one of the few studies of prospective predictors of OCD using the Dunedin sample (Douglass, Moffitt, Dar, McGee, & Silva, 1995), individuals who were assessed as having OCD at age 18 were significantly more depressed and anxious, and had a higher level of substance use than comparison groups at age 15. Additional developmental studies are underway with the Dunedin cohort to evaluate whether substance abuse, traumatic experiences, including childhood physical and sexual abuse, or other psychosocial stressors contribute risk to the future development of OCD.

Heterogeneity of OCD

Research into OCD has been hindered by the heterogeneity of the diagnosis, with specific symptom subtypes associated with genetic, neural, and neuropsychological correlates underlying different symptom dimensions (Alsobrook, Leckman, Goodman, Rasmussen, & Pauls 1999; Mataix-Cols et al., 2004; Rauch et al., 1998). This heterogeneity has the potential to reduce power and obscure findings. From a developmental perspective, subtypes of OCD may follow distinct developmental trajectories, reflected in age of onset and course of symptoms over time. Studies have consistently identified several symptom dimensions that may have different developmental pathways, including (1) obsessions about aggression, harm, sex, religion, and checking compulsions; (2) obsessions about a need for symmetry or exactness, repeating rituals, counting compulsions, and ordering/arranging compulsions; (3) contamination obsessions and cleaning/washing compulsions; and (4) hoarding obsessions and compulsions (Leckman et al., 1997). Emerging data suggest that these stable dimensional phenotypes may be useful in studies of the natural history, genetics, and treatment response of OCD, and are congruent with developmental perspectives (for a review, see Mataix-Cols, Rosario-Campos, & Leckman, 2005). Rettew, Swedo, Leonard, Lenane, & Rapoport (1992) reported that OCD symptoms frequently change over time, often with no clear pattern of progression. It seems that although the pattern or type of symptoms may change over time, the absolute number of symptoms typically remains constant (Piacentini & Bergman, 2000), although this is another area that requires further longitudinal data.

In addition to symptom dimensions, *age at onset* has been used to explore the clinical, neurobiological, and genetic heterogeneity of obsessive-compulsive disorder. There seems to be two OCD subgroups according to age of onset, with different clinical profiles (Hanna, Himle, Curtis, & Gillespie, 2005). Earlier age of onset has been associated with male preponderance, higher rates of comorbid tic disorder, and higher frequency of ticlike compulsions, higher symptom severity ratings, sensory phenomena, and compulsions not preceded by obsessions (Fontenelle, Mendlowicz, Marques, & Versiani, 2003; Geller et al., 1998; Rosario-Campos et al., 2001). Age of onset is also one of the most consistent predictors of poorer pharmacological response and prognosis in OCD (Skoog & Skoog, 1999). It has also been associated with higher rates of attention-deficit hyperactivity disorder (ADHD) and multiple anxiety disorders (Geller et al., 2001). In family studies using adult probands, an early age at onset of OCD symptoms has been strongly associated with a more familial form of OCD (Nestadt et al., 2000; Pauls et al., 1995).

One possible explanation for differences between males and females in age of onset of OCD is androgen levels. Certain studies seem to show that higher androgen levels are associated with worsening symptoms of OCD and these may decrease with antiandrogenic drugs (Eriksson, 2000; Weiss, Baerg, Wiseborc, & Temple, 1995). In cases of adult onset of OCD, most often experienced by females, it is much more likely to be a sudden onset, triggered by a significant life event such as pregnancy, illness, or loss. These cases will more often be episodic rather than chronic. A developmental study evaluating differences between early and late onset OCD, including the effect of gender, would constitute a valuable contribution to our understanding of the disorder.

Natural History and Clinical Course

Older studies on the longitudinal course of OCD suggested that OCD symptoms tend to wax and wane over a chronic, lifelong course (Goodwin, Guze, & Robins, 1969). More recently, Rasmussen and Eisen (1989) reported that continuous or deteriorative course was most prevalent, with less than 2% pursuing an episodic course. Several more recent studies, however, suggest that the outcome of OCD is better than generally assumed, with 43%–75% of patients remaining at least partially improved at follow-up periods of between 2 and 13 years after treatment (Skoog & Skoog, 1999; Steketee, Eisen, Dyck, Warshaw, & Rasmussen, 1999). A study of 22 individuals with OCD by Angst et al. (2004) involving six evaluations over a 20-year period of OCD cases reported favorable long-term outcomes. Although only one-third of the cases had received treatment, after a mean follow-up period of 12.9 years, 86% had no symptoms, 9% had symptoms and moderate distress, and only 5% met *DSM–IV* diagnostic criteria.

Few studies, however, have examined the portion of individuals with subclinical OCD symptoms in childhood who progress to full OCD (Berg et al., 1989; Flament et al., 1988; Valleni-Basil et al., 1994). Attempts to describe the natural history and course of OCD have been limited by the methodological constraints of available studies, including differences in sampling settings, and reliance on retrospective report. It is unclear whether subclinical OCD represents a precursor of clinical disorder, or a level of severity on a continuum that does not necessarily progress to OCD. Valleni-Basil et al. (1994) found the correlates of subclinical OCD were different from those of OCD. Developmental studies of OCD are required to examine the processes underpinning continuity and discontinuity of OCD over time.

New Research

Applying a developmental perspective will be crucial to disentangling the controversial findings on risk factors and etiology of OCD. Existing studies examining etiological hypotheses (both biological and cognitive-behavioral) are largely correlational, thus not affording definitive conclusions about causation. It is important for future research to evaluate possible predictors of OCD without relying exclusively on retrospective self-report. It is unlikely that there is a single etiology of OCD; risk for the disorder is likely shaped by many developmental factors. Identification of the risk factors and course of OCD may foster early intervention and prevention efforts aimed at adolescents who are exhibiting symptoms of the disorder. Information on the origins of OCD may also help improve clinicians' conceptualization and treatment of the disorder.

Future Directions

Advances in our understanding of the developmental aspects of anxiety disorders will likely come from a greater integration between epidemiology and basic neuroscience. Progress in this direction has been slow, partly due to the complexity of both areas. However, the current understanding of anxiety disorders as perturbations in information processing may help speed this process. For example, threat-related information appears to influence measures of attention among both children and adults with anxiety disorders (see Mogg & Bradley, 1998; Pine et al., 2005) and this capacity may result from the ability of threat-related information to engage a specific neural circuit that regulates mammals' responses to threats. Brain imaging studies support the hypothesis that anxiety disorders result from perturbations in this core circuitry (Monk et al., 2006). Moreover, imaging studies also show that such perturbations in circuitry may arise from genetic and environmental influences' capacity to shape brain function and behavior (Pezawas et al., 2005). These recent findings clearly point to the potential benefits of integrating epidemiological, clinical, and genetic perspectives through research in the neurosciences.

We also need to know more about how risk for psychopathology is transmitted from parents to children, and the conditions under which these transgenerational cycles can be broken. Currently we don't fully understand (1) how parents' mental health affects children's development across multiple domains—both positive and negative outcomes; (2) the *how* (or mechanism[s]) of risk transmission; (3) what factors are associated with discontinuities in risk transmission; (4) the impact of mothers' *and* fathers' mental health on their children's development; and (5) the two-way nature of parents' and children's relationships, that is, children have effects on their parents just as parents have effects on their children (Jaffee & Poulton, 2006).

In this regard, Harper (2005) has suggested epigenetic inheritance as a mechanism of interest. Epigenetic processes explain the transmission to children of parental responses to environmental challenges— even when the young don't actually experience these challenges. In other words, genetic inheritance is not altered; gene expression is. Weissman et al. (2005) have also highlighted the importance of three-generation cohort designs by showing how the association between parental depression and child diagnosis of anxiety was moderated by grandparental depression. Clearly, more evidence from intergenerational studies of risk transmission (occurring via secular, social learning, and/or biological mechanisms) will help to deepen our understanding of the developmental aspects of anxiety disorders.

References

Alsobrook, J. P., Leckman, J. F., Goodman, W. K., Rasmussen, S. A., & Pauls, D. L. (1999). Segregation analysis of obsessive-compulsive disorder using symptom-based factor scores. *American Journal of Medical Genetics (Neuropsychiatric Genetics), 88,* 669–675.

American Psychiatric Association. (2004). *Diagnostic and statistical manual of mental disorders* (4th ed.). Washington, DC: Author.

Anand, A., & Shekhar, A. (2003). Brain imaging studies in mood and anxiety disorders. *Annals of the New York Academy of Sciences, 985,* 370–388.

Andrews, G., & Slade, T. (2002). Deconstructing current comorbidity. *British Journal of Psychiatry, 181,* 306–314.

Angst, J., Gamma, A., Endrass, J., Goodwin, R., Ajdacic, V., Eich, D., et al. (2004). Obsessive-compulsive severity spectrum in the community: Prevalence, comorbidity, and course. *European Archives of Psychiatry and Clinical Neuroscience, 254,* 154–164.

Berg, C. L., Rapoport, J. L., Whitaker, A., Davies, M., Leonard, H., Swedo, S. E., et al. (1989). Childhood obsessive compulsive disorder: A two-year prospective follow-up of a community sample. *American Academy of Child and Adolescent Psychiatry, 28,* 528–533.

Bertolino, A., Arciero, G., Rubino, V., Latorre, V., De Candia, M., Mazzola, V., et al. (2005). Variation of human amygdala response during threatening stimuli as a function of 5HT-TLPR genotype and personality style. *Biological Psychiatry, 57,* 1515–1525.

Bolton, D. (1996). Annotation: Developmental issues in obsessive-compulsive disorder. *Journal of Child Psychology and Psychiatry, 37,* 131–137.

Bouton, M. E., Mineka, S., & Barlow, D. H. (2001). A modern learning theory perspective on the etiology of panic disorder. *Psychological Review, 108,* 4–32.

Breslau, N. (2002). Epidemiologic studies of trauma, posttraumatic stress disorder, and other psychiatric disorders. *Canadian Journal of Psychiatry, 47,* 923–929.

Brown, T. A., Campbell, L. A., Lehman, C. L., Grisham, J. R., & Mancill, R. B. (2001). Current and lifetime comorbidity of the *DSM–IV* anxiety and mood disorders in a large clinical sample. *Journal of Abnormal Psychology, 110,* 585–599.

Calkins, S. D., & Fox, N. A. (2002). Self-regulatory processes in early personality development: A multilevel approach to the study of childhood social withdrawal and aggression. *Development and Psychopathology, 14,* 477–498.

Cloitre, M., Cohen, L. R., & Koenen, K. C. (2006). *Treating the trauma of childhood abuse: Psychotherapy for the interrupted life.* New York: Guilford Press.

Coplan, J. D., Trost, R. C., Owens, M. J., Cooper, T. B., Gorman, J. M., Nemeroff, C. B., et al. (1998). Cerebrospinal fluid concentrations of somatostatin and biogenic amines in grown primates reared by mothers exposed to manipulated foraging conditions. *Archives of General Psychiatry, 55,* 473–477.

De Bellis, M. D. (2001). Developmental traumatology: The psychobiological development of maltreated children and its implications for research, treatment, and policy. *Development and Psychopathology, 13,* 539–564.

Douglass, H. M., Moffitt, T. E., Dar, R., McGee, R., & Silva, P. (1995). Obsessive-compulsive disorder in a birth cohort of 18-year-olds: Prevalence and predictors. *Journal of the*

American Academy of Child and Adolescent Psychiatry, 34, 1424–1431.

Eriksson, T. (2000). Antiandrogenic treatment for obsessive-compulsive disorder. *American Journal of Psychiatry, 157*, 483.

Fergusson, D. M., Horwood, L. J., & Boden, J. (2006). Structure of internalising symptoms in early adulthood. *British Journal of Psychiatry, 189*, 540–546.

Fergusson, D. M., Horwood, L. J., & Ridder, E. M. (2005). Show me the child at seven II: Childhood intelligence and later outcomes in adolescence and young adulthood. *Journal of Child Psychology and Psychiatry and Allied Disciplines, 46*, 850–858.

Flament, M. F., Whitaker, A., Rapoport, J. L., Davies, M., Berg, C. Z., Kalikow, K., et al. (1988). Childhood obsessive-compulsive disorder: A prospective study. *Journal of Child Psychology and Psychiatry, 31*, 363–380.

Fontenelle, L. F., Mendlowicz, M. V., Marques, C., & Versiani, M. (2003). Early- and late-onset obsessive-compulsive disorder in adult patients: An exploratory clinical and therapeutic study. *Journal of Psychiatric Research, 37*, 127–133.

Geller, D. A., Biederman, J., Faraone, S., Agranat, A., Cradock, K., Hagermoser, L., et al. (2001). Developmental aspects of obsessive-compulsive disorder: Findings in children, adolescents, and adults. *Journal of Nervous and Mental Disease, 189*, 471–477.

Geller, D. A., Biederman, J., Jones, J., Shapiro, S., Schwartz, S., & Park, K. S. (1998). Obsessive-compulsive disorder in children and adolescents: A review. *Harvard Review of Psychiatry, 5*, 260–273.

Goodwin, D. W., Guze, S. B., & Robins, E. (1969). Follow-up studies in obsessional neurosis. *Archives of General Psychiatry, 20*, 182–187.

Goodwin, R. D., Fergusson, D. M., & Horwood, L. J. (2004). Early anxious/withdrawn behaviours predict later internalising disorders. *Journal of Child Psychology and Psychiatry, 45*, 874–883.

Gorman, J. M., Kent, J. M., Sullivan, G. M., & Coplan, J. D. (2000). Neuroanatomical hypothesis of panic disorder, revised. *American Journal of Psychiatry, 157*, 493–505.

Gorman, J. M., Mathew, S., & Coplan, J. (2002). Neurobiology of early life stress: Nonhuman primate models. *Seminars in Clinical Neuropsychiatry, 7*, 96–103.

Gothelf, D., Aharonovsky, O., Horesh, N., Carty, T., & Apter, A. (2004). Life events and personality factors in children and adolescents with obsessive-compulsive disorder and other anxiety disorders. *Comprehensive Psychiatry, 45*, 192–198.

Gregory, A. M., Caspi, A., Moffitt, T. E., Koenen, K., Eley, T. C., & Poulton, R. (2007). Juvenile mental health histories of adults with anxiety disorders. *American Journal of Psychiatry, 164*, 301–308.

Guilino, L., Gammon, P., Sullivan, K., Franklin, M., Foa, E., Maid, R., et al. (2002). Is parental report of upper respiratory infection at the onset of obsessive-compulsive disorder suggestive of pediatric autoimmune neuropsychiatric disorder associated with streptococcal infection? *Journal of Child and Adolescent Psychopharmacology, 12*, 157–164.

Hanna, G. L., Himle, J. A., Curtis, G. C., & Gillespie, B. W. (2005). A family study of obsessive-compulsive disorder with pediatric probands. *Human Heredity, 60*, 1–9.

Hariri, A. R., & Weinberger, D. R. (2003). Imaging genomics. *British Medical Bulletin, 65*, 259–270.

Harper, L. V. (2005). Epigenetic inheritance and the intergenerational transfer of experience. *Psychological Bulletin, 131*, 340–360.

Hayward, C., Killen, J. D., Kraemer, H. C., & Taylor, C. B. (2000). Predictors of panic attacks in adolescence. *Journal of the American Academy of Child and Adolescent Psychiatry, 39*, 207–214.

Heim, C., & Nemeroff, C. B. (2002). Neurobiology of early life stress: Clinical studies. *Seminar in Clinical Neuropsychiatry, 7*, 147–159.

Hettema, J. M., Neale, M. C., Myers, J. M., Prescott, C. A., & Kendler, K. S. (2006). A population based twin study of the relationship between neuroticism and internalizing disorders. *American Journal of Psychiatry, 163*, 857–864.

Hofstra, M. B., van der Ende, J., & Verhulst, F. C. (2002). Child and adolescent problems predict *DSM–IV* disorders in adulthood: A 14-year follow-up of a Dutch epidemiological sample. *Journal of the American Academy of Child and Adolescent Psychiatry, 41*, 182–189.

Insel, T. R. (1992). Toward a neuroanatomy of obsessive-compulsive disorder. *Archives of General Psychiatry, 49*, 739–744.

Jaffee, S. R., Moffitt, T. E., Caspi, A., Fombonne, E., Poulton, R., & Martin, J. (2002). Differences in early childhood risk factors for juvenile-onset and adult-onset depression. *Archives of General Psychiatry, 59*, 215–222.

Jaffee, S. R., & Poulton, R. (2006). Reciprocal effects of mothers' depression and children's problem behaviors from middle childhood to early adolescence. In A. C. Huston & M. Ripke (Eds.), *Middle childhood contexts of development* (pp. 107–129). New York: Cambridge University Press.

Janoff-Bulman, R. (1992). *Shattered assumptions: Towards a New Psychology of Trauma.* New York: Free Press.

Katon, W. J. (2006). Panic disorder. *New England Journal of Medicine, 354*, 2360–2367.

Kenardy, J., McCafferty, K., & Rosa, V. (2003). Internet delivered indicated prevention for anxiety disorders. *Behavioural and Cognitive Psychotherapy, 31*, 279–289.

Kendler, K. S., Myers, J., & Prescott, C. A. (2002). The etiology of phobias: An evaluation of the stress-diathesis model. *Archives of General Psychiatry, 59*, 242–248.

Kessler, R. C., Berglund, P., Demler, O., Jin, R., Merikangas, K. R., & Walters, E. E. (2005). Lifetime prevalence and age-of-onset distributions of *DSM–IV* disorders in the National Comorbidity Survey Replication. *Archives of General Psychiatry, 62*, 593–602.

Kim-Cohen, J., Caspi, A., Moffitt, T. E., Harrington, H., Milne, B. J., & Poulton, R. (2003). Prior juvenile diagnoses in adults with mental disorder: Developmental follow-back of a prospective-longitudinal cohort. *Archives of General Psychiatry, 60*, 709–717.

Koenen, K., Moffitt, T. E., Poulton, R., Martin, J., & Caspi, A. (2007). Early childhood factors associated with the development of post-traumatic stress disorder: Results from a longitudinal birth cohort. *Psychological Medicine, 37*, 181–192.

Koenen, K. C., Stellman, J. M., Stellman, S. D., & Sommer, J.F.J. (2003). Risk factors for course of PTSD among Vietnam veterans: A 14-year follow-up of American Legionnaires. *Journal of Consulting and Clinical Psychology, 71*, 980–986.

Kremen, W. S., Koenen, K. C., Boake, C., Purcell, S., Eisen, S. A., Franz, C. E., et al. (2007). Pretrauma cognitive ability and risk for posttraumatic stress disorder—a twin study. *Archives of General Psychiatry, 64*, 361–368.

Kulka, R. A., Schlenger, W. E., Fairbank, J. A., Hough, R. L., Jordan, B. K., Marmar, C. R., et al. (1990). *Trauma and the Vietnam war generation: Report of findings from the National Vietnam Veterans Readjustment study*. New York: Bruner/Mazel.

Leckman, J. F., Grice, D. E., Boardman, J., Zhang, H., Vitale, A., Bondi, C., et al. (1997). Symptoms of obsessive-compulsive disorder. *American Journal of Psychiatry, 154*, 911–917.

Le Doux, J. E., & Gorman, J. M. (2001). A call to action: Overcoming anxiety through active coping. *American Journal of Psychiatry, 158*, 1953–1955.

Lochner, C., du Toit, P. L., Zungu-Dirwayi, N., Marais, A., van Kradenburg, J., Curr, B., et al. (2002). Childhood trauma in obsessive-compulsive disorder, trichotillomania, and controls. *Depression and Anxiety, 15*, 66–68.

Macklin, M. L., Metzger, L. J., Litz, B. T., McNally, R. J., Lasko, N. B., Orr, S. P., et al. (1998). Lower precombat intelligence is a risk factor for posttraumatic stress disorder. *Journal of Consulting and Clinical Psychology, 66*, 323–326.

Mataix-Cols, D., Rosario-Campos, M. C., & Leckman, J. F. (2005). A multidimensional model of obsessive-compulsive disorder. *American Journal of Psychiatry, 162*, 228–238.

Mataix-Cols, D., Wooderson, S., Lawrence, N., Brammer, M. J., Speckens, A., & Phillips, M. L. (2004). Distinct neural correlates of washing, checking, and hoarding symptom dimensions in obsessive-compulsive disorder. *Archives of General Psychiatry, 61*, 564–576.

Mathers, C., Vos, T., & Stevenson, C. (1999). *The burden of disease and injury in Australia*. Canberra: Australian Institute of Health and Welfare.

Moffitt, T. E., & Caspi, A. (2001). Childhood predictors differentiate life-course persistent and adolescence-limited antisocial pathways among males and females. *Development and Psychopathology, 13*, 355–375.

Mogg, K., & Bradley, B. P. (1998). A cognitive-motivational analysis of anxiety. *Behaviour Research and Therapy, 36*, 809–848.

Monk, C. S., Nelson, E. E., McClure, E. B., Mogg, K., Bradley, B. P., Leibenluft, E., et al. (2006). Ventrolateral prefrontal cortex activation and attentional bias in response to angry faces in adolescents with generalized anxiety disorder. *American Journal of Psychiatry, 163*, 1091–1097.

Muris, P., Schmidt, H., Merckelbach, H., & Schouten, E. (2001). Anxiety sensitivity in adolescents. *Behaviour Research and Therapy, 29*, 89–100.

Murphy, T. K., Sajid, M., Soto, O., Shapira, N., Edge, P., & Yang, M., et al. (2004). Detecting pediatric autoimmune neuropsychiatric disorders associated with streptococcus in children with obsessive-compulsive disorder and tics. *Biological Psychiatry, 55*, 61–68.

Murray, C. J., & Lopez, A. D. (1996). *The global burden of disease*. Boston: Harvard School of Public Health.

Nestadt, G., Samuels, J., Riddle, M., Bienvenu, O. J., Liang, K. Y., LaBuda, M., et al. (2000). A family study of obsessive-compulsive disorder. *Archives of General Psychiatry, 57*, 358–363.

Ollendick, T. H. (1998). Panic disorder in children and adolescents. *Journal of Clinical Child Psychology, 27*, 234–245.

Pare, D., Quirk, G. J., & Le Doux, J. E. (2004). New vistas on amygdala networks in conditioned fear. *Journal of Neurophysiology, 92*, 1–9.

Pauls, D. L., Alsobrook, J.P.I., Phill, M., Goodman, W., Rasmussen, S., & Leckman, J. F. (1995). A family study of obsessive-compulsive disorder. *American Journal of Psychiatry, 152*, 76–84.

Pennebaker, J. W. (1999). The effects of traumatic disclosure on physical and mental health: The values of writing and talking about upsetting events. *International Journal of Emerging Mental Health, 1*, 9–18.

Pezawas, L., Meyer-Lindenberg, A., Drabant, E. M., Verchinski, B. A., Munoz, K. E., Kolachana, B. S., et al. (2005). 5-HT-TLPR polymorphism impacts human cingulate-amygdala interactions: A genetic susceptibility mechanism for depression. *Nature Neuroscience, 8*, 828–834.

Piacentini, J., & Bergman, R. L. (2000). Obsessive-compulsive disorder in children. *Psychiatric Clinics of North America, 23*, 519–533.

Pine, D. S., Cohen, P., Gurley, D., Brook, J., & Ma, Y. (1998). The risk for early-adulthood anxiety and depressive disorders in adolescents with anxiety and depressive disorders. *Archives of General Psychiatry, 55*, 56–64.

Pine, D. S., Fyer, A., Grun, J., Phelps, E. A., Szeszko, P. R., Koda, V., et. al. (2001). Methods for developmental studies of fear conditioning circuitry. *Biological Psychiatry, 50*, 225–228.

Pine, D. S., Mogg, K., Bradley, B. P., Montgomery, L., Monk, C. S., McClure, E., et al. (2005). Attention bias to threat in maltreated children: Implications for vulnerability to stress-related psychopathology. *American Journal of Psychiatry, 162*, 291–296.

Pitman, R. K., Orr, S. P., Lowenhagen, M. J., Macklin, M. L., & Altman, B. (1991). Pre-Vietnam contents of posttraumatic stress disorder veterans' service medical and personnel records. *Comprehensive Psychiatry, 32*, 416–422.

Poulton, R., & Menzies, R. G. (2002). Non-associative fear acquisition: A review of the evidence from retrospective and longitudinal research. *Behaviour Research and Therapy, 40*, 127–149.

Rapee, R. M., & Spence, S. H. (2004). The etiology of social phobia: Empirical evidence and an initial model. *Clinical Psychology Review, 24*, 737–767.

Rasmussen, S. A., & Eisen, J. L. (1989). Clinical features and phenomenology of obsessive-compulsive disorder. *Psychiatric Annals, 19*, 67–73.

Rauch, S. L., Dougherty, D. D., Shin, L. M., Alpert, N. M., Mazo, P., Leahy, L., et al. (1998). Neural correlates of factor-analyzed OCD symptom dimensions: A PET study. *CNS Spectrums, 3*, 37–43.

Rauch, S. L., Jenike, M. A., Alpert, N. M., Baer, L., Bretter, H.C.R., Savage, C. R., et al. (1994). Regional cerebral blood flow measured during symptom provocation in obsessive-compulsive disorder using oxygen 15-labeled carbon dioxide and positron emission tomography. *Archives of General Psychiatry, 51*, 62–70.

Rauch, S. L., Savage, C. R., Alpert, N. M., Curran, T., Brown, H. D., Manzo, P., et al. (1997). Probing striatal function in obsessive compulsive disorder: A PET study of implicit sequence learning. *Journal of Neuropsychiatry, 9*, 568–573.

Rettew, D. C., Swedo, S. E., Leonard, H. L., Lenane, M. C., & Rapoport, J. L. (1992). Obsessions and compulsions across time in 79 children and adolescents with obsessive-compulsive disorder. *Journal of the American Academy of Child and Adolescent Psychiatry, 31*, 1050–1056.

Rheaume, J., Ladocuceur, R., Freeston, M. H., & Letarte, H. (1994). Inflated responsibility in obsessive-compulsive disorder: Psychometric studies of a semidiographic measure.

Journal of Psychopathology and Behavioral Assessment, 46, 265–276.

Robinson, D., Wu, H., Munne, R. A., Ashtari, M., Alvir, J. M., Lerner, G., et al. (1995). Reduced caudate nucleus volume in obsessive-compulsive disorder. *Archives of General Psychiatry, 52,* 393–398.

Rosario-Campos, M. C., Leckman, J. F., Mercadante, M. T., Shavitt, R. G., Prado, H. S., Sada, P., et al. (2001). Adults with early onset obsessive-compulsive disorder. *American Journal of Psychiatry, 158,* 1899–1903.

Rosenberg, D. R., & Keshavan, M. S. (1998). Toward a neuro-developmental model of obsessive-compulsive disorder. *Biological Psychiatry, 43,* 623–640.

Rosenblum, L. A., & Paully, G. S. (1984). The effects of varying environmental demands on maternal and infant behavior. *Child Development, 55,* 305–314.

Salkovskis, P. M. (1985). Obsessive-compulsive problems: A cognitive-behavioral analysis. *Behavior Research and Therapy, 23,* 571–583.

Salkovskis, P. M., Westbrook, D., Davis, J., Jeavons, A., & Gledhill, A. (1997). Effects of neutralizing on intrusive thought: An experiment investigating the etiology of obsessive-compulsive disorder. *Behaviour Research and Therapy, 35,* 211–219.

Saxena, S., Brody, A. L., Schwartz, J. M., & Baxter, L. R. (1998). Neuroimaging and frontal-subcortical circuitry in obsessive-compulsive disorder. *British Journal of Psychiatry Suppl. 35,* 26–37.

Scarone, S., Colombo, C., Livian, S., Abbruzzese, M., Ronchi, P., Locatelli, M., et al. (1992). Increased right caudate nucleus size in obsessive-compulsive disorder: Detection with magnetic resonance imaging. *Psychiatry Research, 45,* 115–121.

Schmidt, N. B., Lerew, D. R., & Jackson, R. J. (1997). The role of anxiety sensitivity in the pathogenesis of panic. *Journal of Abnormal Psychology, 3,* 355–364.

Shafran, R. (1997). The manipulation of responsibility in obsessive-compulsive disorder. *British Journal of Clinical Psychology, 36,* 397–407.

Simon, G. E., & Von Korff, M. (1995). Recall of psychiatric history in cross-sectional surveys: Implications for epidemiologic research. *Epidemiologic Reviews, 17,* 211–227.

Skoog, G., & Skoog, I. (1999). A 40-year follow-up of patients with obsessive-compulsive disorder. *Archives of General Psychiatry, 56,* 121–127.

Snider, L. A., & Swedo, S. E. (2003). Childhood-onset obsessive-compulsive disorder and tic disorders: A case report and literature review. *Journal of Child and Adolescent Psychopharmacology, 13,* S81–S88.

Steketee, G., Eisen, J., Dyck, I., Warshaw, M., & Rasmussen, S. (1999). Predictors of course in obsessive-compulsive disorder. *Psychiatry Research, 89,* 229–238.

Taylor, C. B. (2006). Panic disorder. *British Medical Journal, 332,* 951–955.

Valleni-Basil, L. A., Garrison, C. Z., Jackson, K. L., Waller, J. L., McKeown, R. E., Addy, C. L., et al. (1994). Frequency of obsessive-compulsive disorder in a community sample of young adolescents. *Journal of American Academy of Child and Adolescent Psychiatry, 33,* 782–791.

Watson, D. (2005). Rethinking the mood and anxiety disorders: A quantitative hierarchical model for *DSM–V. Journal of Abnormal Psychology, 114,* 522–536.

Weiss, B., Baerg, E., Wiseboard, S., & Temple, J. (1995). The influence of gonadal hormones on periodicity of obsessive-compulsive disorder. *Canadian Journal of Psychiatry, 40,* 205–207.

Weissman, M. M., Wickramaratne, P., Nomura, Y., Warner, V., Verdeli, H., Pilowsky, D. J., et al. (2005). Families at high and low risk for depression: A 3-generation study. *Archives of General Psychiatry, 62,* 29–36.

Widiger, T., & Clark, A. L. (2000). Toward *DSM–V* and the classification of psychopathology. *Psychological Bulletin, 126,* 946–963.

Yehuda, R. (2002). Current status of cortisol findings in post-traumatic stress disorder. *Psychiatric Clinics of North America, 25,* 341–368.

chapter 12

Information-Processing Approaches to Understanding Anxiety Disorders

Richard J. McNally *and* Hannah E. Reese

Abstract

Experimental psychopathologists have used cognitive psychology paradigms to elucidate information-processing biases in the anxiety disorders. A vast literature now suggests that patients with anxiety disorders are characterized by an attentional bias for threatening information and a bias toward threatening interpretations of ambiguous information. A memory bias favoring recall of threatening information occurs in panic disorder, but rarely in other anxiety disorders. New treatments involving the experimental modification of cognitive biases are promising.

Keywords: attention, attentional bias, bias, cognitive bias modification, covariation bias, interpretive bias, memory

Traditional approaches to understanding aberrant cognition in people with anxiety disorders rely on the introspection of patients as disclosed during clinical interviews or on questionnaires (Beck, Emery, & Greenberg, 1985). This approach has proven valuable for identifying maladaptive beliefs and appraisals. For example, the tendency to regard fear-related bodily sensations as harbingers of danger, as measured by the Anxiety Sensitivity Index (ASI) (Reiss, Peterson, Gursky, & McNally, 1986), predicts the eruption of unexpected, "spontaneous" panic attacks (Schmidt, Lerew, & Jackson, 1999) and the subsequent emergence of panic disorder and related syndromes (Schmidt, Zvolensky, & Maner, 2006). Likewise, correcting catastrophic misappraisals of bodily sensations is an efficacious means of treating panic disorder (Clark et al., 1999).

Despite their importance (McNally, 2001), introspective methods are seldom capable of disclosing the mechanisms that give rise to the phenomenology of anxiety disorders (MacLeod, 1993).

Accordingly, during the past two decades experimental psychopathologists have used cognitive psychology paradigms to elucidate biases in attention, memory, and interpretation constitutive of anxiety disorders at the information-processing level of analysis (Harvey, Watkins, Mansell, & Shafran, 2004; Williams, Watts, MacLeod, & Mathews, 1988, 1997).

In this field, the term *bias* refers to a systematic difference in the processing of emotionally relevant information between people with anxiety disorders (or those at risk for them) versus healthy control subjects. It does not necessarily imply inaccuracy or distortion of reality (Mathews & MacLeod, 2005). These content-dependent cognitive *biases* differ from cognitive *deficits,* such as general distractibility, that are apparent irrespective of the emotional significance of the information processed. Our purpose is to review highlights of information-processing research in the field of anxiety and the anxiety disorders. The field is now vast, and hence our coverage is perforce synoptic.

Attention

Because the human information-processing system has limited capacity, people can only attend to a subset of stimuli at any point in time. Accordingly, any tendency to attend preferentially to threatening stimuli should result in heightened propensity to experience anxiety. People characterized by high trait anxiety, especially those suffering with anxiety disorders, should therefore exhibit an attentional bias favoring the processing of threat-related stimuli.

To test this hypothesis, researchers have developed the emotional Stroop paradigm (Mathews & MacLeod, 1985). In this paradigm, subjects view words of varying emotional significance and are asked to name the colors of the words while ignoring their meaning. Delays in color-naming ("emotional Stroop interference") occur when the meaning of a word captures the subject's attention despite his or her effort to focus on its color. A bias for threat occurs when subjects take longer to name the colors of threat words than to name the colors of either positive or neutral words.

Patients with anxiety disorders, relative to healthy control subjects, have exhibited greater Stroop interference for threat words than for nonthreat words (for a review, see Williams, Mathews, & MacLeod, 1996). This effect has occurred in specific (spider) phobia (Watts, McKenna, Sharrock, & Trezise, 1986), social phobia (Hope, Rapee, Heimberg, & Dombeck, 1990), posttraumatic stress disorder (PTSD) (McNally, Kaspi, Riemann, & Zeitlin, 1990), panic disorder (Ehlers, Margraf, Davies, & Roth, 1988), generalized anxiety disorder (GAD) (Mathews & MacLeod, 1985), and obsessive-compulsive disorder (OCD) (Foa, Ilai, McCarthy, Shoyer, & Murdock, 1993). There have also been failures to replicate the effect (e.g., PTSD: Freeman & Beck, 2000; panic disorder and OCD: Kampman, Keijsers, Verbraak, Näring, & Hoogduin, 2002).

Most studies, however, suggest that emotionality per se is insufficient to provoke Stroop interference. In one study, panic disorder patients took longer to color-name threat words (e.g., *collapse*) than to color-name positive words (e.g., *cheerful*) even though they rated the latter as more emotional than the former (McNally, Riemann, Louro, Lukach, & Kim, 1992). In another study, positive words signifying the opposite of threat (e.g., *relaxed*) provoked interference in a mixed group of anxious patients (Mathews & Klug, 1993), whereas in other studies of panic disorder (McNally et al., 1994) and OCD (Lavy, van Oppen, & van den Hout, 1994) this

did not occur. Taken together, these findings suggest that positive material seldom produces as much Stroop interference as threatening material except, perhaps, when it is conceptually linked to the patient's main concerns.

Studying college students, Riemann and McNally (1995) selected Stroop stimuli idiographically, based on whether the word was relevant to either a subject's positive current concerns (e.g., a new romantic relationship) or a subject's negative current concerns (e.g., financial worries). Subjects exhibited greater interference for words strongly related to either positive or negative current concerns relative to words only weakly related to these concerns or to control words unrelated to current concerns. This finding raises the possibility that Stroop interference effects arise in anxiety disorder patients because words deeply relevant to their current concerns are seldom relevant for healthy control subjects or to patients with anxiety disorders whose concerns lie elsewhere.

Researchers have investigated whether the emotional Stroop effect is automatic. Tradition holds that an automatic process does not consume cognitive capacity, can operate outside of awareness, and occurs involuntarily (e.g., Shiffrin & Schneider, 1977). These diagnostic criteria for automaticity, however, do not always covary when individuals process threat-relevant material (McNally, 1995). Clearly, the emotional Stroop effect does not constitute automatic processing in the sense of being capacity-free. Indeed, processing the meaning of a threat cue comes at the expense of naming its color, thanks to resources being captured by the meaning of the word. Researchers have asked whether emotional Stroop interference can occur outside of awareness—another sense of the term automatic. Typically researchers present Stroop words very briefly, and then follow each word with a mask (e.g., $#%#*+) comprising characters having the same color as the Stroop word subliminally preceding it. Patients with panic disorder (Lundh, Wikström, Westerlund, & Öst, 1999), GAD (Bradley, Mogg, Millar, & White, 1995; Mogg, Bradley, Williams, & Mathews, 1993), PTSD (Harvey, Bryant, & Rapee, 1996), and spider phobia (van den Hout, Tenney, Huygens, & de Jong, 1997) have exhibited subliminal Stroop interference for threat words. Depressed patients do not exhibit the effect (McNally, Amir, & Lipke, 1996; Mogg & Bradley, 2004).

Despite its seeming obligatory character, the emotional Stroop effect can be overridden when anxious subjects anticipate an imminent, more stressful experience, such as a possible encounter with the feared animal in snake-fearful individuals (Mathews & Sebastian, 1993), viewing a Vietnam combat video in PTSD patients (Constans, McCloskey, Vasterling, Brailey, & Mathews, 2004), or giving a speech in patients with social phobia (Amir et al., 1996). The signature of this strategic override appears to be a speeding up of color-naming across the board, not only for threat words (Williams et al., 1996).

Although delayed color-naming of threat cues may occur because they capture attention, it may also result from threat cues triggering momentary emotional distress that disrupts task performance, or by capacity consumption arising from patients' struggling to attend to color and avoid being distracted by threat (de Ruiter & Brosschot, 1994; Mathews, 1990). Moreover, the effect does not measure attentional shift toward threat cues; indeed, both semantic and color cues occupy the same physical space (Fox, 1993).

Ambiguities about the mechanism of the emotional Stroop prompted MacLeod, Mathews, and Tata (1986) to devise the dot-probe paradigm as a better measure of attentional bias for threat. In this task, subjects perform a neutral response (a button press) to a neutral stimulus (a dot) that replaces either member of a pair of words appearing simultaneously for 500 ms on a computer screen. On some trials, one member of the word pair is threat-relevant (e.g., *cancer*). On occasional trials, a dot appears, replacing either the threat word or the nonthreat word. MacLeod et al. found that subjects with GAD, relative to either depressed or healthy subjects, were faster to respond to probes that replaced threat words and slower to respond to probes that replaced neutral words. This pattern suggests that the attention of GAD patients was drawn to threat words—a tendency that either speeded or slowed probe detection, depending on whether the probe appeared in the location of a threat or neutral cue, respectively.

To increase the sensitivity of the attentional bias task, researchers have modified it in several ways. In one variant, a threat word appears on each trial, and the subject indicates whether the subsequent dot probe replaced either the upper or lower word (Mogg, Bradley, & Williams, 1995). The reaction time (RT) to ascertain probe position is the measure of attentional deployment. In another version, the probe consists of a pair of dots aligned either vertically (:) or horizontally (..), and the subject classifies the probe as either vertical or horizontal as quickly as possible (Mogg & Bradley, 1999).

Another innovation has been the use of facial expressions of emotion as the stimuli preceding the probe. For example, Mogg and Bradley (1999) simultaneously showed subjects two photographs of the same person, one appearing on the left side of the screen and the other appearing on the right. One face displayed anger, and the other joy. An attentional bias for threat occurred when subjects were faster to respond to the probe that replaced the threat face.

In another experiment, compared to healthy control subjects, those with GAD were faster to detect probes that replaced angry facial expressions than those that replaced neutral facial expressions (Bradley, Mogg, White, Groom, & de Bono, 1999). Each emotional face, either angry or happy, was paired with a neutral face of the same person. Interestingly, over the course of the experiment, the GAD patients exhibited a similar attentional bias for happy faces versus neutral ones.

Using a variant of the dot-probe paradigm, Mansell, Clark, Ehlers, and Chen (1999) found that socially anxious subjects exhibited attentional avoidance of faces displaying either positive (joy) or negative (fear, anger, disgust) emotions, but only when subjects were anticipating having to give a speech. In the absence of speech threat, there was no difference in attentional deployment between high and low social anxiety subjects. The authors interpreted these findings as consistent with the hypothesis that social anxiety is associated with reduced processing of external cues. On the other hand, Gilboa-Schechtman, Foa, and Amir (1999) found that patients with generalized social phobia were faster to detect angry than happy faces in a pictorial display relative to nonanxious control subjects. One possibility is that social anxiety is associated with rapid detection of social threat followed quickly by attentional avoidance.

In an influential theoretical formulation, Williams et al. (1988, pp. 166–184) proposed that anxiety is associated with biased attention to threat, including at the preconscious stage of stimulus processing. In response to stimulus input, an affective decision mechanism classifies the input as posing either high threat or no threat. The resource allocation mechanism of those with high versus low trait anxiety theoretically responds differently if high threat is registered. If the affective decision mechanism indicates the presence of high threat, then those with high trait anxiety allocate attention to the threat, whereas those with low trait anxiety shift their attention elsewhere.

But if rapid detection of threat cues is deemed an adaptive feature of the human information-processing system, what, then, distinguishes those with and without an anxiety disorder? Moreover, surely it cannot be adaptive to shift attention away from mortal danger.

Several theorists simultaneously proposed an answer to this question (Mathews & Mackintosh, 1998; Mogg & Bradley, 1998). The key idea here is that individuals varying in trait anxiety differ in terms of when they switch from attentional avoidance to attentional vigilance. Presumably, the threshold for switching from avoidance to vigilance is lower among high trait anxious individuals, including those with anxiety disorders, than among low trait anxious individuals. As Mogg and Bradley (2004) suggested, "biases in the evaluation of threat cues, rather than attentional biases, underlie vulnerability to anxiety" (p. 71). In other words, attentional bias for threat per se is not the fundamental abnormality in anxiety disorders. What distinguishes those with anxiety disorders, or those prone to develop them, is that relatively nonthreatening stimuli are classified as highly threatening, thereby leading to attentional capture by these stimuli. Attentional bias is parasitic on a more fundamental interpretive bias.

Consistent with this view, Wilson and MacLeod (2003) found that both low and high trait anxious subjects exhibit attentional avoidance for faces displaying minimal anger, whereas both groups exhibit attentional vigilance for faces displaying intense anger. Where the groups differ is in their processing of faces displaying moderate anger: high trait anxious subjects, relative to low trait anxious subjects, exhibit attentional vigilance for these faces. Hence, high trait anxious subjects attend to moderate threat as if it signified high threat.

Another issue concerns whether attentional bias reflects rapid capture by threatening stimuli, difficulty disengaging from threat stimuli, or both. Fox and her colleagues found that individuals with elevated trait anxiety experience difficulty disengaging from words associated with threat (Fox, Russo, Bowles, & Dutton, 2001).

Research on attentional bias continues to become increasingly sophisticated. In addition to using reaction-time measures of attentional deployment, researchers have incorporated eye-tracking procedures to study attentional shifts directly. Tracking subjects' eye movements during a dot-probe task, Mogg, Millar, and Bradley (2000) found that GAD subjects without comorbid depression were more likely to direct their gaze at angry than at neutral faces, and they were more likely to shift their gaze more quickly to threat faces than away from them. Neither healthy subjects, nor those with major depression, exhibited these attentional biases for threat.

In other research, psychologists determined that spider phobic subjects, relative to subjects without spider phobia, exhibited attentional capture by spider pictures only when such stimuli were part of a background context they had been told to ignore (Miltner, Krieschel, Hecht, Trippe, & Weiss, 2004). This research team used both reaction time and eye tracking as the basis for its inferences about attentional deployment. As Miltner et al. observed, attentional bias for threat occurs in anxious subjects primarily when they simultaneously confront stimuli of competing valence, a conclusion confirming previous work (MacLeod & Mathews, 1991; Mogg, Mathews, Eysenck, & May, 1991).

Unraveling the complexities of attentional vigilance, avoidance, or both in anxiety is best accomplished by tracking the course of these attentional effects over time (Mogg & Bradley, 2004). There are two ways to do this. In one approach, stimulus duration varies (e.g., 200 ms, 500 ms, 1500 ms). Shorter durations best capture automatic, obligatory attentional capture, whereas longer durations permit strategic avoidance. In the other approach, eye-tracking equipment tracks attentional shifts in real time. Studies of subclinical blood phobics (Mogg, Bradley, Miles, & Dixon, 2004) and subclinical spider phobics (Hermans, Vansteenwegen, & Eelen, 1999; Pflugshaupt et al., 2005; Rinck & Becker, 2006) have documented attentional vigilance for threat cues followed by attentional avoidance. As Pflugshaupt et al. (2005) noted, "As a consequence of initial hypervigilance, phobics are more likely to detect potentially threatening events and thus perceive the world as a dangerous place, while subsequent cognitive avoidance prevents objective evaluation and habituation to such events" (p. 115).

Memory

Most research on memory bias in the anxiety disorders has concerned explicit expressions of memory. Memory is revealed explicitly when task performance requires conscious recollection of previous experiences on free recall, cued recall, or recognition tests. Free recall is usually more sensitive to emotional variables, such as diagnostic status and word valence, than is either cued recall or recognition. A common approach is to have anxious and control subjects encode words of varying emotional valence by having them either rate the self-descriptiveness of each word (McNally, Foa, & Donnell, 1989) or having them generate an image involving themselves and each word (Becker, Roth, Andrich, & Margraf, 1999). Subjects are later asked to remember the items they encountered previously. A memory bias for threat occurs when anxious patients recall more threat words than either neutral or positive words, relative to control subjects. Another variant is to expose subjects to photographs of faces, and have subjects rate them as exhibiting either a critical (threatening) or accepting (nonthreatening) expression prior to testing memory for the faces (Lundh & Öst, 1996).

Researchers have also studied implicit memory bias for threat (Amir & Selvig, 2005). Memory is revealed implicitly when previous experiences facilitate ("prime") performance on a task that does not require deliberate, conscious recollection of these previous experiences (Schacter, 1987). Word-stem completion, perceptual identification, lexical decision, and white noise judgment paradigms are common implicit memory tasks. For the first three tasks, investigators expose subjects to a list of words (e.g., *coffin*). They later have them perform another putatively unrelated task, such as asking them to complete a word stem with the first word that comes to mind (e.g., *cof*), identify words that are briefly flashed on a computer screen, or judge whether briefly flashed letter strings form legitimate words (e.g., *coffin*) or not (e.g., *ceffen*). None of these tasks require conscious recollection of having encountered material previously. But evidence of implicit memory for preexposed material occurs when subjects disproportionately complete word stems with these words (e.g., *coffin*) than with new ones (e.g., *coffee*), identify briefly flashed preexposed words more often than new ones, and make correct lexical decisions more often for preexposed words than for new ones. In a variant of the white noise paradigm (Jacoby, Allan, Collins, & Larwill, 1988), subjects listen and repeat aloud disorder-relevant threat sentences (e.g., "The anxious woman panicked in the supermarket") and neutral sentences (e.g., "The shiny apple sat on the table"). They subsequently hear these old sentences again, intermixed with new threat and neutral sentences. Each sentence is now embedded in white noise of varying volumes, and subjects are asked to rate the volume of the white noise. Evidence of priming occurs when the noise accompanying old sentences seems less loud than that accompanying new sentences. For all of these

paradigms, an implicit memory bias occurs when priming is greater for threatening than for non-threatening material in the anxiety disorder group than in the control group.

Evidence of memory bias for threat is mixed, and it varies as a function of diagnosis and task (Coles & Heimberg, 2002). With few exceptions (e.g., Rapee, 1994), studies have shown that subjects with panic disorder exhibit a free recall bias for negative or threat-relevant words (e.g., Becker, Rinck, & Margraf, 1994; Becker et al., 1999; Cloitre & Liebowitz, 1991; Lim & Kim, 2005; McNally et al., 1989). The bias is sometimes evident on cued recall tests (Cloitre, Shear, Cancienne, & Zeitlin, 1994; Lundh, Czyzykow, & Öst, 1997), but not always (Otto, McNally, Pollack, Chen, & Rosenbaum, 1994), and with few exceptions (Lundh & Öst, 1996), not on recognition tests (Beck, Stanley, Averill, Baldwin, & Deagle, 1992; Ehlers et al., 1988). Vietnam veterans with PTSD likewise are characterized by a free recall bias for negative emotional words (Vrana, Roodman, & Beckham, 1995).

There is very little evidence for explicit memory bias favoring recall of threat-related words in GAD (Bradley, Mogg, & Williams, 1995; Mathews, Mogg, May, & Eysenck, 1989; Mogg, Mathews, & Weinman, 1987; Otto et al., 1994), spider phobia (Watts & Coyle, 1993), or social phobia (Cloitre, Cancienne, Heimberg, Holt, & Liebowitz, 1995; Rapee, McCallum, Melville, Ravenscroft, & Rodney, 1994; Rinck & Becker, 2005; but see Lundh & Öst, 1996).

Although researchers have seldom demonstrated a memory bias favoring threat words among anxiety-disordered patients, work by Friedman, Thayer, and Borkovec (2000) has illuminated why this might be the case. They reported a pronounced free recall bias favoring threat words in GAD patients when these subjects were not constrained by instructions on how to encode the material. As Mathews (2006) has concluded, anxious individuals may very well encode material in terms of its personal emotional threat-value when the task does not require them to encode it in some other manner, and this, in turn, may result in the elusive explicit memory bias for threat appearing.

Conclusions about memory bias, or the lack thereof, must not rest solely on whether anxiety disorder patients are better at recalling threat-related words than words unrelated to threat. For example, Radomsky and Rachman (1999) found that OCD patients with washing rituals, relative to anxious and nonanxious control subjects, had superior memory for objects that had been "contaminated" by the experimenter than for clean objects, thereby underscoring the importance of ecologically relevant stimuli in cognitive research.

Although some studies have suggested an implicit memory bias for threat in word-stem completion (Mathews et al., 1989) and perceptual identification (MacLeod & McLaughlin, 1995) paradigms, others have not (Mathews, Mogg, Kentish, & Eysenck, 1995; McNally & Amir, 1996; Otto et al., 1994). In retrospect, these implicit memory tasks may not have been the best choice to study automatic processing of emotionally relevant information. Priming effects on both tasks are strongly influenced by the perceptual characteristics of the input, not by meaning, emotional or otherwise (e.g., Schacter, 1992). For example, priming effects are attenuated if subjects are preexposed to words appearing in lowercase letters, but then encounter test stimuli appearing in uppercase letters. In other words, the perceptual rather than the conceptual or semantic aspects of the stimuli drive priming effects on these tasks, rendering them of uncertain relevance to the study of emotional meaning and memory.

To study conceptual implicit memory biases for threat in panic disorder, Amir and colleagues adapted the "white noise" paradigm (Amir, McNally, Riemann, & Clements, 1996). Panic patients tended to exhibit greater priming for threat sentences than for neutral ones, whereas control subjects exhibited the opposite pattern. Similar findings occurred in studies of PTSD patients (Amir, McNally, & Wiegartz, 1996) and social phobia patients (Amir, Foa, & Coles, 2000), but not in one concerning patients with OCD (Foa, Amir, Gershuny, Molnar, & Kozak, 1997). Although this task is clearly conceptually more complex than most implicit memory tasks, it is unclear whether it taps conceptual implicit memory. Confidence that it is a conceptual implicit memory task would be bolstered if the effect occurs when, say, a male voice read the sentences at encoding and a female voice read them at test.

Directed Forgetting and Memory Inhibition

Most research on memory bias in the anxiety disorders considers the possibility that information about threat is characterized by heightened accessibility as revealed on either explicit or implicit memory tasks. Researchers have also tested the ability of anxiety-disordered patients to disengage attention from threat cues in an effort to forget them

(McNally, 2005). In one study, researchers administered an item-cuing directed forgetting procedure to three groups of women (McNally, Metzger, Lasko, Clancy, & Pitman, 1998). One group had PTSD related to childhood sexual abuse (CSA). Another group had been exposed to CSA, but had no PTSD, and a third group had never been sexually abused. Each subject viewed a series of words from one of three categories: trauma-relevant, positive, and neutral. Each word appeared for two seconds and was replaced by either an instruction to forget the word or an instruction to remember. Subjects were later asked to recall all words, irrespective of the original instructions. Both control groups exhibited a directed forgetting effect; they recalled words followed by remember instructions more often than those followed by forget instructions, irrespective of the valence of the words. The PTSD group, however, did not exhibit a directed forgetting effect because they experienced difficulty recalling neutral and positive words they were supposed to remember, and experienced difficulty forgetting trauma words they were supposed to forget.

Several other anxiety disorder groups have likewise either exhibited a breakdown in the ability to forget negative material (OCD: Tolin, Hamlin, & Foa, 2002; Wilhelm, McNally, Baer, & Florin, 1996) or no heightened ability to forget threat material (panic disorder: McNally, Otto, Yap, Pollack, & Hornig, 1999; Power, Dalgleish, Claudio, Tata, & Kentish, 2000). Patients with acute stress disorder, however, are characterized by a superior ability to forget trauma-related words (Moulds & Bryant, 2002, 2005).

Memory Functioning in OCD

Patients with OCD, especially those with checking rituals, seem to suffer impairment in their memory for actions. After having just locked the door, turned off the gas, and so forth, they feel compelled to check or repeat these actions again and again to assure themselves that they did, in fact, perform them rather than merely imagined having performed them. Although this phenomenon seems to imply a deficit in reality monitoring—the capacity to distinguish representations resulting from perception ("reality") from those arising from imagination ("fantasy"), researchers have failed to confirm such deficits (Brown, Kosslyn, Breiter, Baer, & Jenike, 1994; Constans, Foa, Franklin, & Mathews, 1995; McNally & Kohlbeck, 1993); instead they have a deficit in their confidence in their memory (McNally & Kohlbeck, 1993), especially under conditions of heightened responsibility (Radomsky, Rachman, & Hammond, 2001).

In an important series of experiments, van den Hout and Kindt (2003) may have identified the basis for memory distrust in OCD. In their analogue research, they had college students either check the knobs on a virtual gas stove ("relevant checking") or check whether virtual light bulbs were turned off ("irrelevant checking"). They found that repeated checking did not diminish the accuracy of memory for the knobs last checked, but it did diminish the subjects' memory vividness, memory detail, and, most important, confidence in the accuracy of their memory. As the authors emphasized, the problem is not why memory distrust persists despite repeated checking. Indeed, repetitive checking itself impairs memory confidence.

Also testing college students, others have likewise demonstrated that repeated checking undermines confidence in one's memory for actions (Coles, Radomsky, & Horng, 2006; Radomsky, Gilchrist, & Dussault, 2006). Radomsky et al. (2006) demonstrated the effect with a genuine, rather than computerized virtual, stove. Coles et al. (2006) found that memory confidence begins to decline after 2 to 10 checks.

Interpretation

People often encounter situations in everyday life whose meaning is far from obvious. Pain in one's chest may signify a heart attack or merely tense muscles. A ringing phone in the middle of the night may bring news of the death of a loved one or it may merely be a wrong number. Any tendency for interpreting ambiguous stimuli as threatening should be associated with increased anxiety. As noted above, interpretive biases have assumed an increasingly prominent role in information-processing theories of anxiety and the anxiety disorders (e.g., Mogg & Bradley, 2004; Richards, 2004).

Pioneering the study of interpretive bias, Butler and Mathews (1983) developed a booklet consisting of ambiguous scenarios and had patients with generalized anxiety, depression, or no disorder write down the first interpretation that came to mind (e.g., "You wake with a start in the middle of the night, thinking you heard a noise, but all is quiet. What do you think woke you up?"). After responding to each scenario, subjects turned the page and ranked three experimenter-provided interpretations in terms of the likelihood of each coming to mind in a similar situation. Only one interpretation was threatening. Butler and Mathews found that both

depressed and anxious patients exhibited a threat bias relative to the control group.

Others have adapted this ambiguous scenario approach, altering the content of the scenarios to capture the concerns of patients with other syndromes. Patients with agoraphobia and panic interpret scenarios involving internal and external ambiguous stimuli as threatening (McNally & Foa, 1987), whereas those with panic disorder exhibit an interpretive bias confined to ambiguous bodily sensations having an abrupt onset rather than ambiguous social or other bodily stimuli (Clark et al., 1997; Westling & Öst, 1995).

These studies suggest that GAD and panic disorder are associated with a bias for interpreting ambiguity as threatening. Because these scenarios might be subject to demand effects, Mathews, Richards, and Eysenck (1989) devised another method for assessing interpretive bias. They presented GAD patients, recovered GAD patients, and healthy control subjects with an audiotaped series of homophones interpretable in either a threatening (e.g., *die*) or nonthreatening (e.g., *dye*) fashion. When asked to write down the words they heard, subjects with GAD produced more threatening spellings than did healthy control subjects, whereas recovered GAD patients did so to an intermediate degree.

This team devised an even more ecologically relevant method for gauging interpretive bias (Eysenck, Mogg, May, Richards, & Mathews, 1991). They had GAD subjects, recovered GAD subjects, and healthy control subjects listen to audiotaped sentences such as "The doctor examined little Emma's growth." They later asked subjects to identify which sentences had the same meaning of those they had heard previously, and the options included disambiguated versions that were either threatening (e.g., "The doctor looked at little Emma's cancer") or neutral (e.g., "The doctor measured little Emma's growth"). The GAD subjects endorsed threatening and neutral versions to an equal extent, whereas the recovered GAD subjects and the healthy control subjects exhibited a "positivity bias" of sorts by endorsing nonthreatening versions more than threatening ones.

But these findings are consistent with an anxiety-linked response bias for endorsing the threat-related option as well as an interpretive bias for threat. That is, anxious subjects might entertain neutral as well as threatening options, but then choose the threat-related one, at least before having been treated for their anxiety disorder. To rule out response bias, MacLeod and Cohen (1993) devised a text comprehension program that distinguishes interpretive bias from response bias. They had college students with either high or low trait anxiety read pairs of sequentially presented sentences on a computer screen. The first sentence of each pair had either a threatening, a nonthreatening, or an ambiguous meaning, whereas the second sentence provided a plausible continuation of the first, and had either a threatening or a nonthreatening meaning. Subjects pushed a button to advance from the first sentence to the second one, and pushed it again to advance from the second sentence to the first one of the next pair. This arrangement enabled MacLeod and Cohen to measure the subjects' reading time. The reading comprehension latency for second sentences that follow ambiguous ones revealed patterns of interpretive bias. That is, comprehension latency for the second sentence is inversely correlated with its plausibility as a continuation of the preceding ambiguous one. Hence, if subjects assume a threatening interpretation of an ambiguous first sentence, then they should be faster to read the second sentence if it constitutes a threatening continuation of the first sentence. The advantage of this paradigm is that subjects merely read sentences and push buttons, thereby minimizing the likelihood of a response bias interpretation of the results. Consistent with their hypothesis, MacLeod and Cohen found that subjects with high trait anxiety were more likely to impose the threatening interpretation on the ambiguous sentences, whereas the low trait anxiety subjects did the opposite.

The study of interpretive bias for threat has become increasingly sophisticated (Richards, 2004). In one paradigm (Amir, Foa, & Coles, 1998), subjects read sentences ending in either a homograph or a nonhomograph that has either a socially threatening or nonthreatening possible meaning, and then decide whether a word appearing either 100 ms or 850 ms later is related to the sentence. For example, subjects might view the sentence "She wrote down the mean" and then decide whether the word "unfriendly" is related to the sentence. Longer decision latencies for words following homographic versus nonhomographic sentences imply that the inappropriate meaning was activated. Amir et al. found that decision latencies in the social phobia group implied activation of the inappropriate meaning for social threat homographic sentences (e.g., "mean" as "cruel" versus "mean" as "average") at 100 ms, but the opposite at 850 ms. This pattern, Amir et al. concluded, implies an automatic activation of threat meaning followed by strategic inhibition of threat in

response to ambiguity—a pattern consistent with a vigilance-avoidance style of threat-related information processing (Mogg, Bradley, Bono, & Painter, 1997). Interestingly, precisely the opposite pattern of results emerged in a study of civilian trauma survivors either with or without PTSD (Amir, Coles, & Foa, 2002). Patients with PTSD, relative to healthy trauma survivors, had difficulty inhibiting threat meanings at the strategic stage of processing, but exhibited enhanced inhibition of threat meanings at the automatic stage of processing.

Most studies on interpretive bias rely on verbal material—scenarios, sentences, and homographs. Amir, Beard, and Bower (2005) developed an ecologically more valid approach to testing for interpretive bias in socially anxious individuals. Amir et al. developed videotaped scenarios, each involving an actor who approached the camera and made either a negative, a positive, or an ambiguous comment (e.g., "That is an interesting shirt you have on"). Subjects were asked to imagine themselves as the recipient of the comment, and to rate the emotional valence of each scenario. Socially anxious students, relative to either high trait anxious students, dysphoric students, or nonanxious ones, rate the ambiguous scenarios are more emotionally negative, thereby confirming their interpretive bias.

Do patients with social phobia impose negative interpretations on ambiguous social stimuli online? Or do they do so retrospectively? To address this issue, Hirsch and Mathews (2000) had subjects read brief social scenarios that included ambiguous passages, and then make speeded lexical decisions about words that implied either a benign or negative interpretation of the passage. Response latencies indicated that nonanxious control subjects made online benign interpretations of ambiguous passages in the text, whereas social phobics did not seem to make any online emotional inferences. That is, social phobics seem to lack a positivity bias that is present in nonanxious control subjects. Others have likewise found that socially anxious individuals seem best characterized by an attenuated positivity bias in the face of ambiguous social cues rather than an outright negative interpretive bias (Constans, Penn, Ihen, & Hope, 1999). In fact, patients with social anxiety disorder appear to experience deficits in acquiring positive interpretations of ambiguous social stimuli (Amir, Beard, & Przeworski, 2005).

Covariation Bias

Covariation bias is the tendency to overestimate the frequency with which two stimuli co-occur.

Researchers have hypothesized that the tendency to overestimate the frequency with which feared stimuli occur with negative consequences may play a role in the development and maintenance of anxiety disorders. This may be one reason why individuals continue to fear certain objects, animals, or situations despite the absence of a correlation between the feared object and a negative outcome in their environment.

Devising an illusory correlation procedure, Tomarken, Mineka, and Cook (1989) pioneered the study of covariation bias. High and low spider- or snake-fearful individuals viewed photographs of their feared animal (snake or spider), mushrooms, and flowers one at a time. Each photograph was followed randomly by one of three outcomes: a mild electric shock, a tone, or nothing. Subjects were instructed to pay attention to the relationship between the photographs and the outcomes. After the experiment, subjects were asked to estimate the frequency with which each type of photograph was paired with each outcome. Although there was no correlation between photograph type and outcome, high-fear subjects significantly overestimated the frequency with which their feared animal and the shock were paired relative to all other stimulus-outcome pairs and relative to the true frequency. Low-fear subjects displayed a similar, but attenuated pattern of estimates. Tomarken et al. interpreted this covariation bias as evidence that fearful individuals processed information during the experiment in a manner that confirmed their fear.

Other researchers, however, suggested that perhaps the tendency to associate feared stimuli with a negative outcome is not the result of biased online processing, but is present in fearful individuals even before the experiment begins (de Jong & Merckelbach, 1990). To test this hypothesis, Davey (1992) asked nonfearful individuals to participate in a threat conditioning paradigm in which they viewed a series of photographs and were told that some of the photographs may be followed by an electric shock. Although no shock was ever delivered, Davey found that individuals who viewed fear-relevant stimuli (snakes and spiders) expected shock to occur significantly more often than those individuals who viewed fear-irrelevant stimuli (kittens and pigeons) providing support for an expectancy bias for phylogenetically fear-relevant stimuli. McNally and Heatherton (1993) asked high and low snake-fearful participants to *imagine* that they were to participate in an illusory correlation paradigm nearly identical to that conducted by Tomarken et al. (1989).

Subjects were then asked to predict the frequency with which each photograph type would be paired with each outcome. The results closely mirrored those of Tomarken et al. (1989); all subjects demonstrated an expectancy bias for fear-relevant stimuli, although it was attenuated in low-fear subjects. This suggests that an expectancy bias for phylogenetically fear-relevant stimuli may be influenced by, but not dependent upon, prior fear. McNally and Heatherton then tested individuals with high or low fear of damaged electrical outlets, and found that both groups exhibited an expectancy bias for damaged electrical outlets and shock regardless of prior fear level, suggesting that expectancy bias is not specific to phylogenetically fear-relevant stimuli. Given that postexperimental covariation biases had occurred for phylogenetically fear-relevant stimuli, but not for ontogenetically fear-relevant ones (Sutton, Mineka, & Tomarken, 1991), McNally and Heatherton suggested that expectancy biases involving phylogenetic threat cues may be characterized by a disconfirmation insensitivity.

Kennedy, Rapee, and Mazurski (1997) sought to clarify some of the early findings in this area by conducting a study in which individuals high and low in fear of both snakes or spiders *and* damaged electrical outlets made both pre- and postexperimental covariation estimates within the same experiment. Following McNally and Heatherton (1993), they had subjects first predict the frequency with which spiders, electrical outlets, and flowers would be paired with a shock, tone, or nothing in an imaginary illusory correlation paradigm. After making these expectancy estimates, subjects then participated in the illusory correlation paradigm they had just imagined and made postexperimental covariation estimates. The authors found that all individuals demonstrated expectancy biases for both the ontogenetically and phylogenetically fear-relevant stimuli and shock regardless of fear level. However, covariation bias was only exhibited by high-fearful individuals for the phylogenetic stimuli. The authors concluded that perhaps both prior fear and fear-relevance of the stimuli influence the degree to which expectancy biases are modified by the illusory correlation paradigm.

In a similar study, Amin and Lovibond (1997) had undergraduates participate in an illusory correlation paradigm in which fear-relevant stimuli (either phylogenetic or ontogenetic), flowers, and mushrooms were followed by a shock, a tone, or nothing. The authors measured online expectancy biases as well as postexperimental biases. Confirming

Kennedy et al.'s findings, an expectancy bias occurred for both classes of stimuli and was not influenced by prior fear level. Only high-fearful subjects exhibited a covariation bias for the phylogenetically fear-relevant stimuli. Taken together, these studies suggest that expectancy biases exist for both phylogenetically and ontogenetically fear-relevant stimuli and are not influenced by prior fear level. In contrast, covariation biases may be influenced by both the prior fear level of the individual and whether the stimuli are phylogenetically or ontogenetically fear-relevant. However, the results by Amin and Lovibond cast some doubt on the hypothesis that covariation biases are merely expectancy biases that have not been modified by situational information during the illusory correlation paradigm. In their measurements of online expectancies, the authors found that the expectancy bias for the phylogenetically fear-relevant stimuli and the shock had disappeared by the end of the experiment, and so the covariation bias cannot simply be a continuation of the expectancy bias. The authors argue that perhaps covariation biases are influenced by biases in memory such that even though subjects have corrected their online estimates by the end of the experiment, they place more weight on their prior expectancies when making their postexperimental estimates.

Researchers have also examined various attributes of the stimuli and outcomes that may influence expectancy and covariation biases. Work by Davey and Dixon (1996) suggests that estimates of the dangerousness of the stimuli, as well as the degree of similarity between the stimuli and the outcomes with regard to valence, arousal, and anxiety may influence the degree to which an expectancy bias occurs. Indeed, a study by Davey and Craigie (1997) found that experimentally increasing an individual's estimates of the dangerousness of one of the experimental stimuli led to significantly greater expectancy and postexperimental covariation estimates for that stimulus and the negative outcome. Tomarken, Sutton, and Mineka (1995) present evidence to suggest that the degree of affective response matching between the stimulus and the outcome is more relevant than the degree of semantic belongingness between the stimulus and outcome in determining covariation bias.

The findings in snake and spider fear have usually been replicated in panic disorder (Pauli, Montoya, & Martz, 1996, 2001; Wiedemann, Pauli, & Dengler, 2001). In contrast, a different pattern of results has emerged for blood-injury injection phobia and social anxiety disorder. Pury and Mineka (1997) found that all individuals regardless of fear level significantly overestimated the frequency with which photographs of surgery and mutilated bodies were paired with shock. Similarly, de Jong, Merckelbach, Bögels, and Kindt (1998) found preexperimental and online expectancy bias, as well as postexperimental covariation biases, for angry faces and shock regardless of subjects' level of prior social anxiety. Thus, prior fear may not moderate covariation bias in these two areas. In both of these cases the authors argue that the blood-related stimuli and the angry faces may be inherently negative, whereas spiders, snakes, and panic-relevant scenes are only negative for those individuals who fear those stimuli. Therefore, there may be an affective match between the blood-related stimuli or angry faces and the shock for all individuals regardless of fear.

Are Biases Correlates or Causes of Anxiety Disorders? Cognitive Bias Modification

Clinical recovery is accompanied by the attenuation or elimination of attentional biases for threat in PTSD (Foa, Feske, Murdock, Kozak, & McCarthy, 1991), spider phobia (Lavy, van den Hout, & Arntz, 1993; Watts et al., 1986), OCD (Foa & McNally, 1986), and GAD (Mathews et al., 1995; Mogg, Bradley, Millar, & White, 1995). Mattia, Heimberg, and Hope (1993) found that patients with social phobia treated successfully with either phenelzine or group cognitive behavior therapy (CBT) no longer exhibited delayed color-naming of social threat words, whereas those remaining symptomatic continued to exhibit the emotional Stroop effect. Interpretive biases for threat likewise diminish or remit in patients with panic disorder (Clark et al., 1997; McNally & Foa, 1987; Westling & Öst, 1995) and GAD following treatment (Eysenck et al., 1991; Mathews, Richards, et al., 1989). There is mixed evidence regarding covariation bias. Treatment has abolished postexperimental covariation bias for spiders and shock in spider phobics in some (de Jong & Merckelbach, 1993; de Jong, Merckelbach, Arntz, & Nijman, 1992), but not all (de Jong & Merckelbach, 1991), studies. Additionally, de Jong, van den Hout, and Merckelbach (1995) found that the degree of residual covariation bias after treatment significantly predicted the degree of return of fear 2 years posttreatment. De Jong, Merckelbach, and Arntz (1995) found that, although treated spider phobics no longer exhibited a preexperimental bias for spiders and shock, both treated and untreated phobics demonstrated an online expectancy bias and a postexperimental covariation bias. The authors suggest that perhaps treatment eliminated the expectancy bias, but the presentation of spider-shock pairings during the experiment may have reinstated the previous bias.

Studies have shown that a subliminal attentional bias for threat predicted emotional distress to a subsequent stressor (MacLeod & Hagan, 1992; van den Hout, Tenney, Huygens, Merckelbach, & Kindt, 1995). Using the homograph interpretive bias paradigm, Amir and Beard (2004) found that students with elevated ASI scores (but no history of panic) exhibited automatic activation of threat meanings relative to those with low ASI scores, a finding consistent with previous research on interpretive bias and anxiety sensitivity in nonpanickers (McNally, Hornig, Hoffman, & Han, 1999). Of course, a third variable might be fostering the prodromal cognitive bias and elevating risk for later disorder or intense distress. Accordingly, the most convincing demonstration that they play a causal role in the emergence of disorder is to manipulate biases and to ascertain their emotional consequences (MacLeod, Campbell, Rutherford, & Wilson, 2004).

MacLeod and colleagues modified the dot-probe task so that the probe either always replaced the threat word for one group of subjects or always replaced the neutral word for another group of subjects (MacLeod, Rutherford, Campbell, Ebsworthy, & Holker, 2002). The subjects were students scoring in the mid-range in terms of trait anxiety. After training was completed, a block of dot-probe trials confirmed that the first group had, indeed, acquired an attentional bias for threat, whereas the second group acquired an attentional avoidance for threat. All subjects then completed a series of difficult anagrams under timed conditions. The negative emotional response to this stressor was attenuated in the group that had undergone attentional avoidance training relative to the group that had undergone attentional bias training. A second experiment replicated the findings of the first, and it also documented that the magnitude of the anxiety response to the stressor was directly related to the extent to which the attentional bias was modified.

Researchers have likewise explored attempts to modify interpretive bias (Yiend & Mackintosh, 2004). The core feature of these procedures is that subjects are exposed to ambiguous material that subjects, in turn, use to perform a subsequent task. For one group of subjects, a threatening interpretation of the ambiguous material fosters successful performance of the later task, whereas for another group of subjects a benign interpretation facilitates

task performance. Interpolated test trials confirm that subjects in each group have acquired either the negative or the benign interpretive bias.

For example, Grey and Mathews (2000) presented subjects with homographs (e.g., *batter*) followed by a word fragment whose solution disambiguated the homograph in either a benign (e.g., p_nc_ke [pancake]) or negative (e.g., ass_ _lt [assault]) manner. Subjects pressed a key as soon as they had guessed the complete word, and then they typed in the first missing letter. Subjects received trials involving either benign or negative solutions before being tested on new items. Confirmation of the acquired interpretive bias was evinced by faster responses for solutions that matched the valence of the solutions presented during training.

Researchers have shown how an interpretive bias established with one procedure generalizes to a very different format (Hertel, Mathews, Peterson, & Kintner, 2003). Hertel et al. trained college students to interpret homographs in either a threat-related or threat-unrelated manner prior to having them generate visual images prompted by single words, some of which were homographs potentially related to threat. Subjects trained to disambiguate stimuli in a threat-related fashion exhibited a heightened tendency to generate negative images in response to homographic prompt words.

Mathews and Mackintosh (2000) devised methods involving more complex textual material. During the training phase, subjects read brief accounts of ambiguous social scenarios, each concluding with a word fragment whose solution disambiguated the preceding text. So, one example read:

> Your partner asks you to go to an anniversary dinner that their company is holding. You have not met any of their work colleagues before. Getting ready to go, you think that the new people you will meet will find you [either b_r_ng or fr_e_dly].

Subjects in the negative condition saw the fragment whose solution imposed a negative interpretation on the passage (*boring*), whereas those in the other condition saw the fragment whose solution imposed a benign interpretation on the passage (*friendly*). After completing the fragment, subjects in each condition answered questions designed to reinforce either a negative or benign interpretive bias (e.g., "Will you be disliked by your new acquaintances?"), compelling the subject to answer either "yes" or "no," depending on the condition.

Following training, subjects then viewed another set of ambiguous scenarios, each followed by a word fragment completion and a comprehension question, but these remained ambiguous and hence did not constrain interpretation. Accordingly, Mathews and Mackintosh were able to assess whether subjects had acquired either a negative or benign interpretive bias by examining how subjects disambiguated these test scenarios. Additionally, they had subjects perform a recognition task by rating each of four sentences with regard to how closely they captured the gist of the preceding text. So, for example, subjects read about "The wedding reception" scenario (Yiend & Mackintosh, 2004):

Your friend asks you to give a speech at her wedding reception. You prepare some remarks and, when the time comes, get to your feet. As you speak, you notice that some people in the audience start to l_ _ gh [i.e., *laugh*]

Subjects then answered the (ambiguous) comprehension question:

Did you stand up to speak? [yes/no]

And then they provided recognition ratings of the following four sentences, two involving a positive interpretation of the scenario, and two involving a negative interpretation. Within each valence, one sentence was a target that constituted a paraphrase of the scenario, whereas the other was a valence-congruent foil. For the previous example, the negative foil, positive foil, negative target, and positive target were as follows:

As you speak, some people in the audience start to yawn.
As you speak, some people in the audience applaud your comments.
As you speak, some people in the audience find your efforts laughable.
As you speak, people in the audience laugh appreciatively.

The results of this research indicate that subjects acquiring a negative interpretive bias provide higher ratings for both negative sentences than for positive ones, and more so for the negative target than for the negative foil. This suggests that subjects are exhibiting a general negative interpretive bias.

Further research indicates that this induced negative interpretive bias persists for at least 24 hours (Yiend, Mackintosh, & Mathews, 2005), but results are mixed regarding whether it heightens subsequent affect in response to a laboratory stressor. In one study, subjects who received negative interpretive bias training did exhibit heightened negative emotional reactivity in response to stressful videos involving television news footage of disasters and emergencies (Wilson, MacLeod, Mathews, & Rutherford, 2006), whereas in another study it did not result in heightened reactivity to a stressful anagram task (Salemink, van den Hout, & Kindt, 2007).

Summary and Conclusions

Work on cognitive biases associated with anxiety and the anxiety disorders began with the assumption that anxiety would affect all aspects of cognitive processing: attention, interpretation, memory, and so forth, and it would operate similarly across the anxiety disorders. The aforementioned synoptic review documents how data-driven theorizing has evolved during the past two decades. Anxiety has much more robust effects on attention and interpretation than it does on explicit memory, with several notable exceptions, and certain abnormalities have emerged that appear unique to certain disorders. For example, work on OCD shows that impaired confidence in one's memory for action appears to be a consequence rather than a cause of repeated checking.

The most important recent developments concern the establishment of the causal status of attentional and interpretive biases for threat. This work, in turn, has inspired the development of new treatments for anxiety disorders based on the direct manipulation of attentional and interpretive biases.

Finally, researchers have begun to explore the neural substrates of processing of emotional material (Mathews, 2006). If this work bears fruit, we will witness a cognitive neuroscience of information-processing bias to supplement the now-established cognitive psychology of this aspect of psychopathology.

References

Amin, J. M., & Lovibond, P. F. (1997). Dissociations between covariation bias and expectancy bias for fear-relevant stimuli. *Cognition and Emotion, 11,* 273–289.

Amir, N., & Beard, C. (2004). Inhibitory difficulties and anxiety sensitivity. *Cognitive Therapy and Research, 28,* 283–292.

Amir, N., Beard, C., & Bower, E. (2005). Interpretation bias and social anxiety. *Cognitive Therapy and Research, 29,* 433–443.

Amir, N., Beard, C., & Przeworski, A. (2005). Resolving ambiguity: The effect of experience on interpretation of ambiguous events in generalized social phobia. *Journal of Abnormal Psychology, 114,* 402–408.

Amir, N., Coles, M. E., & Foa, E. B. (2002). Automatic and strategic activation and inhibition of threat-relevant information in posttraumatic stress disorder. *Cognitive Therapy and Research, 26,* 645–655.

Amir, N., Foa, E. B., & Coles, M. E. (1998). Automatic activation and strategic avoidance of threat-relevant information in social phobia. *Journal of Abnormal Psychology, 107,* 285–290.

Amir, N., Foa, E. B., & Coles, M. E. (2000). Implicit memory bias for threat-relevant information in individuals with generalized social phobia. *Journal of Abnormal Psychology, 109,* 713–720.

Amir, N., McNally, R. J., Riemann, B. C., Burns, J., Lorenz, M., & Mullen, J. T. (1996). Suppression of the emotional Stroop effect by increased anxiety in patients with social phobia. *Behaviour Research and Therapy, 34,* 945–948.

Amir, N., McNally, R. J., Riemann, B. C., & Clements, C. (1996). Implicit memory bias for threat in panic disorder: Application of the "white noise" paradigm. *Behaviour Research and Therapy, 34,* 157–162.

Amir, N., McNally, R. J., & Wiegartz, P. S. (1996). Implicit memory bias for threat in posttraumatic stress disorder. *Cognitive Therapy and Research, 20,* 625–635.

Amir, N., & Selvig, A. (2005). Implicit memory tasks in clinical research. In A. Wenzel & D. C. Rubin (Eds.), *Cognitive methods and their application to clinical research* (pp. 153–171). Washington, DC: American Psychological Association.

Beck, A. T., Emery, G., & Greenberg, R. L. (1985). *Anxiety disorders and phobias.* New York: Basic Books.

Beck, J. G., Stanley, M. A., Averill, P. M., Baldwin, L. E., & Deagle, E. A., III. (1992). Attention and memory for threat in panic disorder. *Behaviour Research and Therapy, 30,* 619–629.

Becker, E., Rinck, M., & Margraf, J. (1994). Memory bias in panic disorder. *Journal of Abnormal Psychology, 103,* 396–399.

Becker, E. S., Roth, W. T., Andrich, M., & Margraf, J. (1999). Explicit memory in anxiety disorders. *Journal of Abnormal Psychology, 108,* 153–163.

Bradley, B. P., Mogg, K., Millar, N., & White, J. (1995). Selective processing of negative information: Effects of clinical anxiety, concurrent depression, and awareness. *Journal of Abnormal Psychology, 104,* 532–536.

Bradley, B. P., Mogg, K., White, J., Groom, C., & de Bono, J. (1999). Attentional bias for emotional faces in generalized anxiety disorder. *British Journal of Clinical Psychology, 38,* 267–278.

Bradley, B. P., Mogg, K., & Williams, R. (1995). Implicit and explicit memory for emotion-congruent information in clinical depression and anxiety. *Behaviour Research and Therapy, 33,* 755–770.

Brown, H. D., Kosslyn, S. M., Breiter, H. C., Baer, L., & Jenike, M. A. (1994). Can patients with obsessive-compulsive disorder discriminate percepts and mental images? A signal detection analysis. *Journal of Abnormal Psychology, 103,* 445–454.

Butler, G., & Mathews, A. (1983). Cognitive processes in anxiety. *Advances in Behaviour Research and Therapy, 19,* 233–243.

Clark, D. M., Salkovskis, P. M., Hackmann, A., Wells, A., Ludgate, J., & Gelder, M. (1999). Brief cognitive therapy for panic disorder: A randomized controlled trial. *Journal of Consulting and Clinical Psychology, 67,* 583–589.

Clark, D. M., Salkovskis, P. M., Öst, L.-G., Breitholz, E., Koehler, K. A., Westling, B. E., et al. (1997). Misinterpretation of body sensations in panic disorder. *Journal of Consulting and Clinical Psychology, 65,* 203–213.

Cloitre, M., Cancienne, J., Heimberg, R. G., Holt, C. S., & Liebowitz, M. (1995). Memory bias does not generalize across anxiety disorders. *Behaviour Research and Therapy, 33,* 305–307.

Cloitre, M., & Liebowitz, M. R. (1991). Memory bias in panic disorder: An investigation of the cognitive avoidance hypothesis. *Cognitive Therapy and Research, 15,* 371–386.

Cloitre, M., Shear, M. K., Cancienne, J., & Zeitlin, S. B. (1994). Implicit and explicit memory for catastrophic associations to bodily sensation words in panic disorder. *Cognitive Therapy and Research, 18,* 225–240.

Coles, M. E., & Heimberg, R. G. (2002). Memory biases in the anxiety disorders: Current status. *Clinical Psychology Review, 22,* 587–627.

Coles, M. E., Radomsky, A. S., & Horng, B. (2006). Exploring the boundaries of memory distrust from repeated checking: Increasing external validity and examining thresholds. *Behaviour Research and Therapy, 44,* 995–1006.

Constans, J. I., Foa, E. B., Franklin, M. E., & Mathews, A. (1995). Memory for actual and imagined events in OC checkers. *Behaviour Research and Therapy, 33,* 665–671.

Constans, J. I., McCloskey, M. S., Vasterling, J. J., Brailey, K., & Mathews, A. (2004). Suppression of attentional bias in PTSD. *Journal of Abnormal Psychology, 113,* 315–323.

Constans, J. I., Penn, D. L., Ihen, G. H., & Hope, D. A. (1999). Interpretive biases for ambiguous stimuli in social anxiety. *Behaviour Research and Therapy, 37,* 643–651.

Davey, G.C.L. (1992). An expectancy model of laboratory preparedness effects. *Journal of Experimental Psychology: General, 121,* 24–40.

Davey, G.C.L., & Craigie, P. (1997). Manipulation of dangerousness judgements to fear-relevant stimuli: Effects on *a priori* UCS expectancy and *a posteriori* covariation assessment. *Behaviour Research and Therapy, 35,* 607–617.

Davey, G.C.L., & Dixon, A. L. (1996). The expectancy bias model of selective associations: The relationship of judgements of CS dangerousness, CS-UCS similarity and prior fear to *a priori* and *a posteriori* covariation estimates. *Behaviour Research and Therapy, 34,* 235–252.

De Jong, P. J., & Merckelbach, H. (1990). Illusory correlation, on-line probability estimates, and electrodermal responding in a (quasi) conditioning paradigm. *Biological Psychology, 31,* 210–212.

De Jong, P. J., & Merckelbach, H. (1991). Covariation bias and electrodermal responding in spider phobics before and after behavioural treatment. *Behaviour Research and Therapy, 29,* 307–314.

De Jong, P. J., & Merckelbach, H. (1993). Covariation bias, classical conditioning, and phobic fear. *Integrative Physiological and Behavioral Science, 28,* 167–170.

De Jong, P. J., Merckelbach, H., & Arntz, A. (1995). Covariation bias in phobic women: The relationship between a priori expectancy, on-line expectancy, autonomic responding, and a posteriori contingency judgement. *Journal of Abnormal Psychology, 104,* 55–62.

De Jong, P. J., Merckelbach, H., Arntz, A., & Nijman, H. (1992). Covariation detection in treated and untreated spider phobics. *Journal of Abnormal Psychology, 101,* 724–727.

De Jong, P. J., Merckelbach, H., Bögels, S., & Kindt, M. (1998). Illusory correlation and social anxiety. *Behaviour Research and Therapy, 36,* 1063–1073.

De Jong, P. J., van den Hout, M., & Merckelbach, H. (1995). Covariation bias and the return of fear. *Behaviour Research and Therapy, 33,* 211–213.

De Ruiter, C., & Brosschot, J. F. (1994). The emotional Stroop interference effect in anxiety: Attentional bias or cognitive avoidance? *Behaviour Research and Therapy, 32,* 315–319.

Ehlers, A., Margraf, J., Davies, S., & Roth, W. T. (1988). Selective processing of threat cues in subjects with panic attacks. *Cognition and Emotion, 2,* 201–219.

Eysenck, M. W., Mogg, K., May, J., Richards, A., & Mathews, A. (1991). Bias in interpretation of ambiguous sentences related to threat in anxiety. *Journal of Abnormal Psychology, 100,* 144–150.

Foa, E. B., Amir, N., Gershuny, B., Molnar, C., & Kozak, M. J. (1997). Implicit and explicit memory in obsessive-compulsive disorder. *Journal of Anxiety Disorders, 11,* 119–129.

Foa, E. B., Feske, U., Murdock, T. B., Kozak, M. J., & McCarthy, P. R. (1991). Processing of threat-related information in rape victims. *Journal of Abnormal Psychology, 100,* 156–162.

Foa, E. B., Ilai, D., McCarthy, P. R., Shoyer, B., & Murdock, T. B. (1993). Information processing in obsessive-compulsive disorder. *Cognitive Therapy and Research, 17,* 173–189.

Foa, E. B., & McNally, R. J. (1986). Sensitivity to feared stimuli in obsessive-compulsives: A dichotic listening analysis. *Cognitive Therapy and Research, 10,* 477–485.

Fox, E. (1993). Attentional bias in anxiety: Selective or not? *Behaviour Research and Therapy, 31,* 487–493.

Fox, E., Russo, R., Bowles, R., & Dutton, K. (2001). Do threatening stimuli draw or hold visual attention in subclinical anxiety? *Journal of Experimental Psychology: General, 130,* 681–700.

Freeman, J. B., & Beck, J. G. (2000). Cognitive interference for trauma cues in sexually abused adolescent girls with posttraumatic stress disorder. *Journal of Clinical Child Psychology, 29,* 245–256.

Friedman, B. H., Thayer, J. F., & Borkovec, T. D. (2000). Explicit memory bias for threat words in generalized anxiety disorder. *Behavior Therapy, 31,* 745–756.

Gilboa-Schechtman, E., Foa, E. B., & Amir, N. (1999). Attentional biases for facial expressions in social phobia: The face-in-the-crowd paradigm. *Cognition and Emotion, 13,* 305–318.

Grey, S., & Mathews, A. (2000). Effects of training on interpretation of emotional ambiguity. *Quarterly Journal of Experimental Psychology, 53A,* 1143–1162.

Harvey, A. G., Bryant, R. A., & Rapee, R. M. (1996). Preconscious processing of threat in posttraumatic stress disorder. *Cognitive Therapy and Research, 20,* 613–623.

Harvey, A., Watkins, E., Mansell, W., & Shafran, R. (2004). *Cognitive behavioural processes across psychological disorders: A transdiagnostic approach to research and treatment.* Oxford, England: Oxford University Press.

Hermans, D., Vansteenwegen, D., & Eelen, P. (1999). Eye movement registration as a continuous index of attention deployment: Data from a group of spider anxious students. *Cognition and Emotion, 13,* 419–434.

Hertel, P. T., Mathews, A., Peterson, S., & Kintner, K. (2003). Transfer of training emotionally biased interpretations. *Applied Cognitive Psychology, 17,* 775–784.

Hirsch, C. R., & Mathews, A. (2000). Impaired positive inferential bias in social phobia. *Journal of Abnormal Psychology, 109,* 705–712.

Hope, D. A., Rapee, R. M., Heimberg, R. G., & Dombeck, M. J. (1990). Representations of the self in social phobia: Vulnerability to social threat. *Cognitive Therapy and Research, 14,* 177–189.

Jacoby, L. L., Allan, L. G., Collins, J. C., & Larwill, L. K. (1988). Memory influences subjective experience: Noise judgments. *Journal of Experimental Psychology: Learning, Memory, and Cognition, 14,* 240–247.

Kampman, M., Keijsers, G.P.J., Verbraak, M.J.P.M., Näring, G., & Hoogduin, C.A.L. (2002). The emotional Stroop: A comparison of panic disorder patients, obsessive-compulsive patients, and normal controls, in two experiments. *Journal of Anxiety Disorders, 16,* 425–441.

Kennedy, S. J., Rapee, R. M., & Mazurski, E. J. (1997). Covariation bias for phylogenetic versus ontogenetic fear-relevant stimuli. *Behaviour Research and Therapy, 35,* 415–422.

Lavy, E., van den Hout, M., & Arntz, A. (1993). Attentional bias and spider phobia: Conceptual and clinical issues. *Behaviour Research and Therapy, 31,* 17–24.

Lavy, E., van Oppen, P., & van den Hout, M. (1994). Selective processing of emotional information in obsessive-compulsive disorder. *Behaviour Research and Therapy, 32,* 243–246.

Lim, S.-L., & Kim, J.-H. (2005). Cognitive processing of emotional information in depression, panic, and somatoform disorder. *Journal of Abnormal Psychology, 114,* 50–61.

Lundh, L.-G., Czyzykow, S., & Öst, L.-G. (1997). Explicit and implicit memory bias in panic disorder with agoraphobia. *Behaviour Research and Therapy, 35,* 1003–1014.

Lundh, L.-G., & Öst, L.-G. (1996). Recognition bias for critical faces in social phobics. *Behaviour Research and Therapy, 34,* 787–794.

Lundh, L.-G., Wikström, J., Westerlund, J., & Öst, L.-G. (1999). Preattentive bias for emotional information in panic disorder with agoraphobia. *Journal of Abnormal Psychology, 108,* 222–232.

MacLeod, C. (1993). Cognition in clinical psychology: Measures, methods or models? *Behaviour Change, 10,* 169–195.

MacLeod, C., Campbell, L., Rutherford, E., & Wilson, E. (2004). The causal status of anxiety-linked attentional and interpretive bias. In J. Yiend (Ed.), *Cognition, emotion and psychopathology: Theoretical, empirical and clinical directions* (pp. 172–189). Cambridge, England: Cambridge University Press.

MacLeod, C., & Cohen, I. L. (1993). Anxiety and the interpretation of ambiguity: A text comprehension study. *Journal of Abnormal Psychology, 102,* 238–247.

MacLeod, C., & Hagan, R. (1992). Individual differences in the selective processing of threatening information, and emotional responses to a stressful life event. *Behaviour Research and Therapy, 30,* 151–161.

MacLeod, C., & Mathews, A. (1991). Biased cognitive operations in anxiety: Accessibility of information or assignment of processing priorities? *Behaviour Research and Therapy, 29,* 599–610.

MacLeod, C., Mathews, A., & Tata, P. (1986). Attentional bias in emotional disorders. *Journal of Abnormal Psychology, 95,* 15–20.

MacLeod, C., & McLaughlin, K. (1995). Implicit and explicit memory bias in anxiety: A conceptual replication. *Behaviour Research and Therapy, 33,* 1–14.

MacLeod, C., Rutherford, E., Campbell, L., Ebsworthy, G., & Holker, L. (2002). Selective attention and emotional vulnerability: Assessing the causal basis of their association through the experimental manipulation of attentional bias. *Journal of Abnormal Psychology, 111,* 107–123.

Mansell, W., Clark, D. M., Ehlers, A., & Chen, Y.-P. (1999). Social anxiety and attention away from emotional faces. *Cognition and Emotion, 13,* 673–690.

Mathews, A. (1990). Why worry? The cognitive function of anxiety. *Behaviour Research and Therapy, 28,* 455–468.

Mathews, A. (2006). Emotional encoding of fear-related information. In B. O. Rothbaum (Ed.), *Pathological anxiety:*

Emotional processing in etiology and treatment (pp. 25–38). New York: Guilford Press.

Mathews, A., & Klug, F. (1993). Emotionality and interference with color-naming in anxiety. *Behaviour Research and Therapy, 31,* 57–62.

Mathews, A., & Mackintosh, B. (1998). A cognitive model of selective processing in anxiety. *Cognitive Therapy and Research, 22,* 539–560.

Mathews, A., & Mackintosh, B. (2000). Induced emotional interpretation bias and anxiety. *Journal of Abnormal Psychology, 109,* 602–615.

Mathews, A., & MacLeod, C. (1985). Selective processing of threat cues in anxiety states. *Behaviour Research and Therapy, 23,* 563–569.

Mathews, A., & MacLeod, C. (2005). Cognitive vulnerability to emotional disorders. *Annual Review of Clinical Psychology, 1,* 167–195.

Mathews, A., Mogg, K., Kentish, J., & Eysenck, M. W. (1995). Effect of psychological treatment on cognitive bias in generalized anxiety disorder. *Behaviour Research and Therapy, 33,* 293–303.

Mathews, A., Mogg, K., May, J., & Eysenck, M. W. (1989). Implicit and explicit memory bias in anxiety. *Journal of Abnormal Psychology, 98,* 236–240.

Mathews, A., Richards, A., & Eysenck, M. W. (1989). Interpretation of homophones related to threat in anxiety states. *Journal of Abnormal Psychology, 98,* 31–34.

Mathews, A., & Sebastian, S. (1993). Suppression of emotional Stroop effects by fear-arousal. *Cognition and Emotion, 7,* 517–530.

Mattia, J. I., Heimberg, R. G., & Hope, D. A. (1993). The revised Stroop color-naming task in social phobics. *Behaviour Research and Therapy, 31,* 305–313.

McNally, R. J. (1995). Automaticity and the anxiety disorders. *Behaviour Research and Therapy, 33,* 747–754.

McNally, R. J. (2001). On the scientific status of cognitive appraisal models of anxiety disorder. *Behaviour Research and Therapy, 39,* 513–521.

McNally, R. J. (2005). Directed forgetting tasks in clinical research. In A. Wenzel & D. C. Rubin (Eds.), *Cognitive methods and their application to clinical research,* (pp. 197–212). Washington, DC: American Psychological Association.

McNally, R. J., & Amir, N. (1996). Perceptual implicit memory for trauma-related information in post-traumatic stress disorder. *Cognition and Emotion, 10,* 551–556.

McNally, R. J., Amir, N., & Lipke, H. J. (1996). Subliminal processing of threat cues in posttraumatic stress disorder? *Journal of Anxiety Disorders, 10,* 115–128.

McNally, R. J., Amir, N., Louro, C. E., Lukach, B. M., Riemann, B. C., & Calamari, J. E. (1994). Cognitive processing of idiographic emotional information in panic disorder. *Behaviour Research and Therapy, 32,* 119–122.

McNally, R. J., & Foa, E. B. (1987). Cognition and agoraphobia: Bias in the interpretation of threat. *Cognitive Therapy and Research, 11,* 567–581.

McNally, R. J., Foa, E. B., & Donnell, C. D. (1989). Memory bias for anxiety information in patients with panic disorder. *Cognition and Emotion, 3,* 27–44.

McNally, R. J., & Heatherton, T. F. (1993). Are covariation biases attributable to *a priori* expectancy biases? *Behaviour Research and Therapy, 31,* 653–658.

McNally, R. J., Hornig, C. D., Hoffman, E. C., & Han, E. M. (1999). Anxiety sensitivity and cognitive biases for threat. *Behavior Therapy, 30,* 51–61.

McNally, R. J., Kaspi, S. P., Riemann, B. C., & Zeitlin, S. B. (1990). Selective processing of threat cues in posttraumatic stress disorder. *Journal of Abnormal Psychology, 99,* 398–402.

McNally, R. J., & Kohlbeck, P. A. (1993). Reality monitoring in obsessive-compulsive disorder. *Behaviour Research and Therapy,* 31, 249–253.

McNally, R. J., Metzger, L. J., Lasko, N. B., Clancy, S. A., & Pitman, R. K. (1998). Directed forgetting of trauma cues in adult survivors of childhood sexual abuse with and without posttraumatic stress disorder. *Journal of Abnormal Psychology, 107,* 596–601.

McNally, R. J., Otto, M. W., Yap, L., Pollack, M. W., & Hornig, C. D. (1999). Is panic disorder linked to cognitive avoidance of threatening information? *Journal of Anxiety Disorders, 13,* 335–348.

McNally, R. J., Riemann, B. C., Louro, C. E., Lukach, B. M., & Kim, E. (1992). Selective processing of emotional information in panic disorder. *Behaviour Research and Therapy, 30,* 143–149.

Miltner, W.H.R., Krieschel, S., Hecht, H., Trippe, R., & Weiss, T. (2004). Eye movements and behavioral responses to threatening and nonthreatening stimuli during visual search in phobic and nonphobic subjects. *Emotion, 4,* 323–339.

Mogg, K., & Bradley, B. P. (1998). A cognitive-motivational analysis of anxiety. *Behaviour Research and Therapy, 36,* 809–848.

Mogg, K., & Bradley, B. P. (1999). Some methodological issues in assessing attentional biases for threatening faces in anxiety: A replication study using a modified version of the probe detection task. *Behaviour Research and Therapy, 37,* 595–604.

Mogg, K., & Bradley, B. P. (2004). A cognitive-motivational perspective on the processing of threat information and anxiety. In J. Yiend (Ed.), *Cognition, emotion and psychopathology: Theoretical, empirical and clinical directions* (pp. 68–85). Cambridge, England: Cambridge University Press.

Mogg, K., Bradley, B. P., Bono, J. D., & Painter, M. (1997). Time course of attentional bias for threat information in non-clinical anxiety. *Behaviour Research and Therapy, 35,* 297–303.

Mogg, K., Bradley, B. P., Miles, F., & Dixon, R. (2004). Time course of attentional bias for threat scenes: Testing the vigilance-avoidance hypothesis. *Cognition and Emotion, 18,* 689–700.

Mogg, K., Bradley, B. P., Millar, N., & White, J. (1995). A follow-up study of cognitive bias in generalized anxiety disorder. *Behaviour Research and Therapy, 33,* 927–935.

Mogg, K., Bradley, B. P., & Williams, R. (1995). Attentional bias in anxiety and depression: The role of awareness. *British Journal of Clinical Psychology, 34,* 17–36.

Mogg, K., Bradley, B. P., Williams, R., & Mathews, A. (1993). Subliminal processing of emotional information in anxiety and depression. *Journal of Abnormal Psychology, 102,* 304–311.

Mogg, K., Mathews, A., Eysenck, M., & May, J. (1991). Biased cognitive operations in anxiety: Artefact, processing priorities or attentional search? *Behaviour Research and Therapy, 29,* 459–467.

Mogg, K., Mathews, A., & Weinman, J. (1987). Memory bias in clinical anxiety. *Journal of Abnormal Psychology, 96,* 94–98.

Mogg, K., Millar, N., & Bradley, B. P. (2000). Biases in eye movements to threatening facial expressions in generalized anxiety disorder and depressive disorder. *Journal of Abnormal Psychology, 109,* 695–704.

Moulds, M. L., & Bryant, R. A. (2002). Directed forgetting in acute stress disorder. *Journal of Abnormal Psychology, 111,* 175–179.

Moulds, M. L., & Bryant, R. A. (2005). An investigation of retrieval inhibition in acute stress disorder. *Journal of Traumatic Stress, 18,* 233–236.

Otto, M. W., McNally, R. J., Pollack, M. H., Chen, E., & Rosenbaum, J. F. (1994). Hemispheric laterality and memory bias for threat in anxiety disorders. *Journal of Abnormal Psychology, 10,* 828–831.

Pauli, P., Montoya, P., & Martz, G. (1996). Covariation bias in panic-prone individuals. *Journal of Abnormal Psychology, 105,* 658–662.

Pauli, P., Montoya, P., & Martz, G. (2001). On-line and *a posteriori* covariation estimates in panic prone individuals: Effects of a high contingency of shocks following fear-irrelevant stimuli. *Cognitive Therapy and Research, 25,* 103–116.

Pflugshaupt, T., Mosimann, U. P., von Wartburg, R., Schmitt, W., Nyffeler, T., & Müri, R. M. (2005). Hypervigilance-avoidance pattern in spider phobia. *Journal of Anxiety Disorders, 19,* 105–116.

Power, M. J., Dalgleish, T., Claudio, V., Tata, P., & Kentish, J. (2000). The directed forgetting of emotional material. *Journal of Affective Disorders, 57,* 147–157.

Pury, C. L., & Mineka, S. (1997). Covariation bias for blood-injury stimuli and aversive outcomes. *Behaviour Research and Therapy, 35,* 35–47.

Radomsky, A. S., Gilchrist, P. T., & Dussault, D. (2006). Repeated checking really does cause memory distrust. *Behaviour Research and Therapy, 44,* 305–316.

Radomsky, A. S., & Rachman, S. (1999). Memory bias in obsessive-compulsive disorder (OCD). *Behaviour Research and Therapy, 37,* 605–618.

Radomsky, A. S., Rachman, S., & Hammond, D. (2001). Memory bias, confidence and responsibility in compulsive checking. *Behaviour Research and Therapy, 39,* 813–822.

Rapee, R. M. (1994). Failure to replicate a memory bias in panic disorder. *Journal of Anxiety Disorders, 8,* 291–300.

Rapee, R. M., McCallum, S. L., Melville, L. F., Ravenscroft, H., & Rodney, J. M. (1994). Memory bias in social phobia. *Behaviour Research and Therapy, 32,* 89–99.

Reiss, S., Peterson, R. A., Gursky, D. M., & McNally, R. J. (1986). Anxiety sensitivity, anxiety frequency and the prediction of fearfulness. *Behaviour Research and Therapy, 24,* 1–8.

Richards, A. (2004). Anxiety and resolution of ambiguity. In J. Yiend (Ed.), *Cognition, emotion and psychopathology: Theoretical, empirical and clinical directions* (pp. 130–148). Cambridge, England: Cambridge University Press.

Riemann, B. C., & McNally, R. J. (1995). Cognitive processing of personally-relevant information. *Cognition and Emotion, 9,* 325–340.

Rinck, M., & Becker, E. S. (2005). A comparison of attentional biases and memory biases in women with social phobia and major depression. *Journal of Abnormal Psychology, 114,* 62–74.

Rinck, M., & Becker, E. S. (2006). Spider fearful individuals attend to threat, then quickly avoid it: Evidence from eye movements. *Journal of Abnormal Psychology, 115,* 231–238.

Salemink, E., van den Hout, M., & Kindt, M. (2007). Trained interpretive bias and anxiety. *Behaviour Research and Therapy, 45,* 329–340.

Schacter, D. L. (1987). Implicit memory: History and current status. *Journal of Experimental Psychology: Learning, Memory, and Cognition, 13,* 501–518.

Schacter, D. L. (1992). Understanding implicit memory: A cognitive neuroscience approach. *American Psychologist, 47,* 559–569.

Schmidt, N. B., Lerew, D. R., & Jackson, R. J. (1999). Prospective evaluation of anxiety sensitivity in the pathogenesis of panic: Replication and extension. *Journal of Abnormal Psychology, 108,* 532–537.

Schmidt, N. B., Zvolensky, M. J., & Maner, J. L. (2006). Anxiety sensitivity: Prospective prediction of panic attacks and Axis I pathology. *Journal of Psychiatric Research, 40,* 691–699.

Shiffrin, R. M., & Schneider, W. (1977). Controlled and automatic human information processing: II. Perceptual learning, automatic attending, and a general theory. *Psychological Review, 84,* 127–190.

Sutton, S. K., Mineka, S. & Tomarken, A. J. (1991, May). *Affective versus semantic determinants of covariation bias between fear-relevant stimuli and aversive outcomes.* Paper presented at the meeting of the Midwestern Psychological Association, Chicago, IL.

Tolin, D. F., Hamlin, C., & Foa, E. B. (2002). Directed forgetting in obsessive-compulsive disorder: Replication and extension. *Behaviour Research and Therapy, 40,* 793–803.

Tomarken, A. J., Mineka, S., & Cook, M. (1989). Fear-relevant selective associations and covariation bias. *Journal of Abnormal Psychology, 98,* 381–394.

Tomarken, A. J., Sutton, S. K., & Mineka, S. (1995). Fear-relevant illusory correlations: What types of associations promote judgemental bias? *Journal of Abnormal Psychology, 104,* 312–326.

Van den Hout, M., & Kindt, M. (2003). Repeated checking causes memory distrust. *Behaviour Research and Therapy, 41,* 301–316.

Van den Hout, M., Tenney, N., Huygens, K., & de Jong, P. (1997). Preconscious processing bias in specific phobia. *Behaviour Research and Therapy, 35,* 29–35.

Van den Hout, M., Tenney, N., Huygens, K., Merckelbach, H., & Kindt, M. (1995). Responding to subliminal threat cues is related to trait anxiety and emotional vulnerability: A successful replication of MacLeod and Hagan (1992). *Behaviour Research and Therapy, 33,* 451–454.

Vrana, S. R., Roodman, A., & Beckham, J. C. (1995). Selective processing of trauma-relevant words in post-traumatic stress disorder. *Journal of Anxiety Disorders, 9,* 515–530.

Watts, F. N., & Coyle, K. (1993). Phobics show poor recall of anxiety words. *British Journal of Medical Psychology, 66,* 373–382.

Watts, F. N., McKenna, F. P., Sharrock, R., & Trezise, L. (1986). Colour naming of phobia-related words. *British Journal of Psychology, 77,* 97–108.

Westling, B. E., & Öst, L.-G. (1995). Cognitive bias in panic disorder patients and changes after cognitive-behavioral treatments. *Behaviour Research and Therapy, 33,* 585–588.

Wiedemann, G., Pauli, P., & Dengler, W. (2001). A priori expectancy bias in patients with panic disorder. *Journal of Anxiety Disorders, 15,* 401–412.

Wilhelm, S., McNally, R. J., Baer, L., & Florin, I. (1996). Directed forgetting in obsessive-compulsive disorder. *Behaviour Research and Therapy, 34,* 633–641.

Williams, J.M.G., Mathews, A., & MacLeod, C. (1996). The emotional Stroop task and psychopathology. *Psychological Bulletin, 120,* 3–24.

Williams, J.M.G., Watts, F. N., MacLeod, C., & Mathews, A. (1988). *Cognitive psychology and emotional disorders.* Chichester, England: Wiley.

Williams, J.M.G., Watts, F. N., MacLeod, C., & Mathews, A. (1997). *Cognitive psychology and emotional disorders* (2nd ed.). Chichester, England: Wiley.

Wilson, E., & MacLeod, C. (2003). Contrasting two accounts of anxiety-linked attentional bias: Selective attention to varying levels of stimulus threat intensity. *Journal of Abnormal Psychology, 112,* 212–218.

Wilson, E., MacLeod, C., Mathews, A., & Rutherford, E. (2006). The causal role of interpretive bias in anxiety reactivity. *Journal of Abnormal Psychology, 115,* 103–111.

Yiend, J., & Mackintosh, B. (2004). The experimental modification of processing biases. In J. Yiend (Ed.), *Cognition, emotion and psychopathology: Theoretical, empirical and clinical directions* (pp. 190–210). Cambridge, England: Cambridge University Press.

Yiend, J., Mackintosh, B., & Mathews, A. (2005). Enduring consequences of experimentally induced biases in interpretation. *Behaviour Research and Therapy, 43,* 779–797.

CHAPTER 13

Understanding Anxiety Disorders from a "Triple Vulnerability" Framework

Liza M. Suárez, Shannon M. Bennett, Clark R. Goldstein *and* David H. Barlow

Abstract

This chapter provides a review of research findings on the nature of anxiety and panic, and a summary and update of Barlow's (1988, 2000, 2002) theory of triple vulnerability in the etiology of anxiety and its disorders. A description of the nature of anxiety is followed by an explication of the emotion of fear, and panic. A model of an integrated set of vulnerabilities is summarized, including a generalized biological (heritable) vulnerability, a generalized psychological vulnerability based on early experiences that contributes to the development of a sense of control over salient events, and a more specific psychological vulnerability associated with learning experiences that serve to focus anxiety on specific objects or situations.

Keywords: animals, anxiety disorders, behavioral genetic, development, temperament, theories of etiology, traits, vulnerability

Anxiety disorders are extremely common, chronic, and crippling. They are the most prevalent class of mental disorders in the population (Barlow, 2002) and are associated with substantial cost to health care systems (Greenberg et al., 1999; Hofmann & Barlow, 1999; Rice & Miller, 1993) and loss of productivity (DuPont et al., 1996). Thus, understanding the causes of anxiety and related disorders is crucial. In this chapter, we review what research findings have uncovered about the nature of anxiety and panic, and summarize and update Barlow's (1988, 2000, 2002) theory of triple vulnerability in the etiology of anxiety and its disorders. We begin with a description of the nature of anxiety, followed by an explication of the related, but separate, emotion of fear, and panic. We consider fear and panic together since evidence supports the idea that a panic attack, whether triggered by a specific object or situation, as in a specific phobia, or experienced as unexpected and uncued (based on the patient's report) as in panic disorder, is the

basic emotion of fear occurring at an inappropriate time.

The Nature of Anxiety and Panic
The Nature of Anxiety

Anxiety is best described as a unique and coherent cognitive-affective structure within our defensive motivational system (Barlow, 1988, 2000, 2002). What distinguishes anxiety from a state of fear in which danger is perceived as actual, present, and impending is a sense of uncontrollability focused on the possibility of future threat, danger, or other potentially negative events. Due to this self-perception of one's inability to predict, control, or obtain desired outcomes in personally salient situations or contexts, anxiety can also be described as a state of helplessness. This negative affective state is associated with a powerful physiological component that has been hypothesized to be a substrate of readiness, which prepares the organism to counteract helplessness. Indeed, research has linked the somatic aspect of anxiety to activation of distinct brain circuits, including the corticotrophin-releasing factor (CRF) system and Gray's behavioral inhibition system (Chorpita & Barlow, 1998; Gray & McNaughton, 1996; Sullivan, Kent, & Coplan, 2000). Lending further support to this hypothesis is the occurrence of characteristic anxious behavior reflecting vigilance, or an expectation of danger in the surrounding environment, and a continuous effort to prepare for danger or other potentially negative events. Chronic anxiety is typified by persistent central nervous system tension and arousal, autonomic inflexibility (Thayer, Friedman, & Borkovec, 1996), and functional brain asymmetry (Heller, Nitschke, Etienne, & Miller, 1997), which seem to reflect the consequences of a state of perpetual readiness to confront danger.

While there is an abundance of situations or stimuli, both external and internal, that may induce anxiety, conscious evaluation is not necessary for this process to occur and individuals often experience anxiety without realizing the specific trigger or cue that elicited the emotion. In their review of studies on the role of conscious awareness in Pavlovian conditioning, Lovibond and Shanks (2002) reported that while most evidence suggests that awareness is necessary but not sufficient for conditioned performance, some studies suggested that conditioning without awareness is possible and worthy of further investigation. Individuals with posttraumatic stress disorder, for example, might respond with anxiety to a reminder of their traumatic experience without directly recalling the association. Analogously, individuals with panic disorder anxiously react to internal somatic sensations and often attribute these sensations to a specific external environment that is subsequently perceived as threatening. Arntz, de Groot, and Kindt (2004) suggest that emotion promotes perceptual memory by better encoding perceptual aspects of the emotional experience, and purport that this finding may be linked to the perceptual memories experienced by individuals with posttraumatic stress disorder.

Anxiety cues can be very broad, as is often the case in generalized social phobia or generalized anxiety disorder, or quite narrow as in specific phobias and sexual dysfunction. Whether conscious or unconscious, broad or narrow, personally specific and salient triggers indicate the need for appropriate and effective performance or reaction, thus inducing the preparatory state of anxiety with its associated tension, arousal, and negative valence. With anxiety comes an attentional shift to a hyperfocus on the

self and a characteristically critical, irrational, or inaccurate evaluation of the self. Attention may also rapidly shift in its focus from the potentially threatening stimulus to the capacity of the individual to deal with the threat, which is typically deemed by the individual to be inadequate. This shift to self-focused attention has been found to further increase arousal and negative affect, creating its own feedback loop (Barlow, 1988, 2002). Increased negative self-focused attention can, in turn, also affect future performance out of awareness, perpetuating the cycle. For example, research examining sexual arousal disorder has shown that efficacy expectancies and subsequent physiological responding to sexual content was lowered by false negative feedback about performance (Bach, Brown, & Barlow, 1999) and by neutral distraction (van Lankveld & van den Hout, 2004), without affecting subjective sexual arousal or negative affect.

As attention narrows to focus on the source of threat or danger, distorted processing of these cues often occurs, either through attentional or interpretive biases, reflecting preexisting hypervalent cognitive schemas. As mentioned earlier, individuals become hypervigilant for cues or stimuli that they associate with the source of their anxiety. This process in humans has been compared to animal models of behavioral inhibition; for example, Gray's (1987; Gray & McNaughton, 1996) *stop, look, and listen* state. In a study comparing children and adolescents with generalized anxiety disorder, posttraumatic stress disorder, and major depressive disorder on a range of cognitive tasks measuring attention, memory, and prospective cognition with both threat- and depression-related material, investigators found that anxious children showed a greater selective attention bias for threat (Dalgleish et al., 2003). Findings revealed that anxious children showed an other-referent bias in prospective risk estimations, and both of these biases were absent in the depressed children. A hyperfocus on anxiety cues and self-evaluation can disrupt concentration and performance in the moment, potentially fulfilling the expectation for inadequate performance. It is important to note that anxiety is seldom pathological, even when intense, until it becomes chronic and consistently interferes with performance, engagement, and/or enjoyment in life.

There are two primary consequences of the process of anxiety described earlier that develop as one attempts to cope with anxiety and its triggers. First, a propensity to avoid entering a state of anxiety is constantly present and this tendency becomes more prominent, noticeable, and interfering as the intensity of the anxiety increases and the cue or context that evoked the anxiety is more relevant and specific. Linear regression analyses have suggested that anxiety sensitivity, or anxiety focused on somatic cues, serves as a precursor to avoidant behavior in adolescents when controlling for gender, trait anxiety, panic attacks, and baseline avoidance (Wilson & Hayward, 2006). For individuals whose anxiety has generalized to many different cues or contexts, avoidance may not be an available coping strategy, leading to the development of equally maladaptive coping strategies such as more subtle avoidance behaviors, engagement in rituals or superstitious behaviors, and attachment to objects or persons who offer a false sense of safety.

The second consequence that can develop is chronic worry driven by anxiety that can be very difficult to control at more severe levels (Borkovec, 1994; Borkovec, Alcaine, & Behar, 2004; Brown, Dowdall, Côté, & Barlow, 1994). This worry process can be best understood as another unsuccessful attempt to cope with the unpleasant affective and physical experience of anxiety. Similar to anxiety, the process of worry in itself is not always maladaptive and interfering; in some cases, it is warranted and even adaptive, until it becomes quite frequent, intense, and uncontrollable. When avoidance and/or worry become chronically interfering, intervention may be warranted to interrupt the self-perpetuating cycle of pathological anxiety.

As a negative affect state, intense anxiety feels uncomfortable and, for some, intolerable. Affect intensity has been found to significantly predict the perceived intensity of panic-relevant physical (e.g., breathlessness, smothering sensations) and cognitive symptoms (e.g., fear of going crazy), but not objective physiological arousal (e.g., heart rate), following a hyperventilation physiological challenge test (Vujanovic et al., 2006). Most likely, this finding reflects the attention narrowing on somatic cues mentioned earlier.

The Nature of Fear and Panic

As noted above, we make a distinction between anxiety and fear that is increasingly supported. Two primary types of empirical evidence support the distinction (Bouton, 2005). Quantitative analyses of outpatient reports of anxiety and mood symptoms have differentiated a state of intense fear and autonomic arousal seemingly associated with panic from a state of apprehension and tense worry that appears to be more consistent with anxiety (Brown, Chorpita, & Barlow, 1998). Further, behavioral

neuroscience research has distinguished anxiety and fear at both behavioral and neural levels. For example, lesions of the amygdala eliminate fear conditioning in rats (e.g., Fanselow, 1994; Kim, Campeau, Falls, & Davis, 1993; Le Doux, 1996) but do not eradicate behavioral measures of anxiety in rats (Treit, Pesold, & Rotzinger, 1993). Moreover, similar lesions of another part of the extended amygdala, the bed nucleus of the stria terminalis (BNST), abolish anxious responding in established animal behavioral measures of anxiety but do not affect fear conditioning (Davis, Walker, & Yee, 1997). Bouton (2005) points out that this pattern suggests a double dissociation between behavioral tasks affected by lesions of the amygdala (fear) and the BNST (anxiety). Finally, as an emergency defensive reaction system, one fear circuit bypasses the cortex for a direct connection from the retina to the emotional brain (the low road), (Le Doux, 1996).

It is important to mention here, and explicate further below, the specific nature and unique heritability of panic. It is well established that panic attacks are fairly common in the general population with approximately between 10%–14% of individuals experiencing unexpected, uncued panic each year (Deacon & Valentiner, 2001; Rapee, Ancis, & Barlow, 1988; Wittchen & Essau, 1991). In the absence of panic disorder these attacks are termed *nonclinical panic*. Typically, panic attacks are less intense and less frequent in nonclinical panickers than in individuals diagnosed with anxiety disorders. Panic attacks are also known to occur during sleep in nonclinical panickers and are found more often in the families of these individuals than in families of individuals who had not experienced panic (Craske, 1999; Norton, Dorward, & Cox, 1986). However, not everyone who experiences a panic attack will develop panic disorder, and generally how one reacts to a panic attack differentiates "nonclinical panickers" from those diagnosed with clinical panic disorder. Panic, by definition (i.e., sudden feelings of marked apprehension and impending doom that are associated with a wide range of distressing physical sensations), mirrors a definition for fear in other contexts. Hence, in order to understand the nature of panic and why panic attacks occur, we must explore the nature of fear and mammalian fear systems, thus differentiating true alarms (appropriate fear in the presence of actual danger) from false alarms (panic) when no objective danger is present within this alarm system.

Understanding the nature of panic became a burgeoning research pursuit in the mid-1980s. A wealth of research has indicated that panic is a complex biopsychosocial process that involves the interaction of an innate, evolutionary alarm system that is crucial for survival with inappropriate and maladaptive learning, resulting in cognitive and affective complications. This alarm system, or the fear system, is activated when people are faced with an impending threat to safety and survival and has been protecting the species since our earliest ancestors were fighting or fleeing from wild animals. Though today an impending attack from a wild animal is a rare occurrence in our society, significant threats that activate our fear system in the same way still exist, such as speeding cars, guns, terrorist attacks, and seeing a child's safety threatened. In the face of such dangers, fear represents a true alarm that activates us physically and cognitively to take action, typically through escaping the threat by running away or occasionally through facing or countering the threat with direct action such as a counterattack. Sometimes the fear system affords us superhuman capabilities, such as exceptional speed, endurance, or strength, which result in actions that might not be possible under alternative circumstances.

These reactions are characteristic of the *fight or flight* response (i.e., Cannon, 1929), which represents action tendencies exhibited by most organisms for the sake of preservation. These two linked responses have extensive evolutionary evidence and significance. A third response, freezing or tonic immobility, is evidenced if the other action tendencies are impossible or unsuccessful (e.g., Fuse, Forsyth, Marx, Gallup, & Weaver, 2007; Gallup, 1974; Heidt, Marx, & Forsyth, 2005). Sometimes these responses of escape, aggression, or immobility can be inappropriate or counterproductive; for example, bolting out of an important meeting, or struggling in deep water when it is more protective to be still and float.

Barlow and colleagues (Barlow, 2000, 2002; Carter & Barlow, 1995; Forsyth & Eifert, 1996) have described the phenomenon of false alarms, or *spontaneous* (uncued and unexpected) panic, which appears internally and externally identical to fear, except for the lack of actual identifiable objective threat or danger. Panic is marked by sudden feelings of dread and imminent doom, as well as a number of uncomfortable and distressing physical sensations such as racing heart, difficulty breathing, sweating, shaking, stomach and muscle tension, and so forth, that mimic the physical experience of fear that occurs when the body is preparing to combat actual danger. Researchers have persistently sought various causes of false alarms, particularly initial false alarms, as well as anxiety and related phenomena, and have

explored the complex interactions between preexisting biological and psychological vulnerabilities and simultaneous events or life stressors (i.e., Barlow, 2000; Bouton, Mineka, & Barlow, 2001). It is to this topic that we now turn.

The Origins of Anxiety and Related Emotional Disorders: Triple Vulnerability

Evidence for an interacting set of three vulnerabilities or diatheses relevant to the development of anxiety, anxiety disorders, and related emotional disorders has emerged in recent years (Barlow, 1988, 2000, 2002). First, genetic contributions to the development of anxiety and negative affect constitute a generalized (heritable) biological vulnerability. Second, evidence also supports a generalized psychological vulnerability to experience anxiety and related negative affective states characterized by a diminished sense of control arising from early developmental experiences. Although the unfortunate co-occurrence of generalized biological and psychological vulnerabilities may be sufficient to produce anxiety and related states, particularly generalized anxiety disorder and depression, a third vulnerability seems necessary to account for the development of at least some specific anxiety disorders. That is, early learning experiences in some instances seem to focus anxiety on certain life circumstances. These circumstances or events, such as social evaluation or the experience of certain somatic sensations, become associated with a heightened sense of threat and danger. It is this specific psychological vulnerability that, when coordinated with generalized biological and psychological vulnerabilities mentioned earlier, seems to contribute to the development of specific anxiety-related disorders, such as social phobia or social anxiety disorder, obsessive-compulsive disorder, panic disorder, specific phobias, and specific psychogenic sexual dysfunction, among others. We review briefly each of these vulnerabilities in turn.

Generalized Biological Vulnerability: Genetic Contributions

Genetic contributions to personality traits or temperaments serve as a biological diathesis for anxiety. Evidence from trait theory, neuroanatomy, genetic studies, and family studies elucidate the role of neurobiology in the etiology and course of anxiety disorders.

TRAITS AND TEMPERAMENTS

The study of trait or temperament models of anxiety with a neurobiological basis has advanced in recent years. Hans Eysenck (1961, 1981) based his trait theory on variations of levels or intensities of cortical arousal. He posited that positive emotions are associated with moderate levels of arousal while unpleasant emotions are associated with under- or overarousal. The construct of *neuroticism* was defined on a continuum with *stability*. These factors were thought to be tied to an underlying biological factor of autonomic nervous system reactivity, which, in turn, feeds back into the limbic system. Emotion, and particularly anxiety, is conceptualized as an interaction between individual traits of cortical arousal and autonomic nervous system reactivity. Gershuny and Sher (1998) found in a sample of 466 young adults that the combination of high neuroticism and low extraversion may play an important and predisposing role in anxiety.

In a related trait theory, Gray (1982; Gray & McNaugton, 1996) described neurobiological correlates to a Behavioral Inhibition System (BIS), Behavioral Approach System (BAS), and flight-flight System (FFS). In Gray's theory, the biological basis for anxiety is the BIS's (over)reaction to novel signals or punishment with exaggerated inhibition. High levels on Gray's BIS roughly relate to high levels of neuroticism and introversion in Eysenck's model. The FFS involves unconditioned escape behavior (i.e., flight) and/or defensive aggression (i.e., fight) in response to unconditioned punishment, such as pain, and unconditioned frustrative nonrewards (Gray, 1991; Gray & McNaughton, 1996). As such, the FFS may represent a biological vulnerability to fear/panic. Gray's BAS system roughly corresponds to high extraversion, stability, and positive affect (Barlow, 2002).

In another trait theory, Kagan (1989, 1994) examined behavioral inhibition in children through their approach and withdrawal behavior. These behavioral profiles were fairly stable. Kagan (1989) defined these profiles as temperaments and found physiological correlates of behavioral inhibition, such as increased salivary cortisol levels and muscle tension, greater pupil dilation, and elevated urinary catecholamine levels. Kagan suggested that temperament is strongly heritable (Robinsion, Kagan, Reznick, & Corley, 1992). Temperamentally inhibited children are at greater risk for developing multiple anxiety disorders (Biederman et al., 1993; Hirshfeld, Rosenbaum & Biederman, 1992). However, only 30% of children who clearly met criteria for behavioral inhibition as young children went on to develop anxiety disorders (Biederman et al., 1990). Moreover, the temperament (as described

in Kagan & Snidman, 1991) appears to be somewhat malleable, which suggests that environmental factors are also important determinants in temperament and anxiety vulnerability. These findings support the notion of a "constraining" biological vulnerability (in contrast with a "determining" role of temperament) in the development of anxiety in adolescence and adulthood.

Finally, in one of the best-known modern conceptualizations of temperaments related to anxiety and depression, Clark and Watson (1991) proposed two genetically based core dimensions of temperament–neuroticism/negative affect, and extraversion/positive affect—as part of their tripartite theory (Clark, 2005; Clark, Watson, & Mineka, 1994; Watson, 2005). These concepts are also closely related to Gray's constructs of behavioral inhibition and behavioral activation, both conceptually and empirically. In 1998 we proposed a revision to this theory and demonstrated that considerable covariance among the *DSM–IV* anxiety and mood disorders could be explained by higher-order dimensions of neuroticism/negative affectivity and extraversion/positive affectivity (Brown, Chorpita, & Barlow, 1998). But these two temperaments related differently to the different *DSM* disorder constructs. Specifically, neuroticism/negative affect accounts for a substantial proportion of the variance in all of the *DSM–IV* disorders with the possible exception of specific phobia, whereas (low) positive affect is more specific to depression and social phobia (Brown et al., 1998; Mineka, Watson, & Clark, 1998). While the above reviewed traits may turn out to be distinct in some way, current evidence in this area from our center and elsewhere (Clark, 2005; Watson, 2005) lump these concepts together in a heritable temperament that we label *neurotocism/behavioral inhibition* (N-BI) and *behavioral activation positive affect* (BA/P) (Brown, 2007; Brown et al., 1998; Campbell-Sills, Liverant, & Brown, 2004).

BEHAVIORAL GENETIC STUDIES

Investigators have also examined genetic contributions, presumably mediated by N-BI to various anxiety (and related) disorders directly. Family studies have examined the prevalence rates among participants with particular anxiety disorders (and controls) and their relatives. For example, lifetime prevalence rates in the first-degree relatives of those with panic disorder with agoraphobia range from 7.9% to 41% while the rate for controls has been found to be 8% or lower (Barlow, 2002). However, family studies cannot rule out the potential confound that commonalities in environment are responsible for the development or acquisition of disorders. Thus, twin studies are of particular interest since it is possible to examine people who share identical genes but at least somewhat different environmental influences. In an early twin study from Norway, Torgersen (1983) compared 32 monozygotic twins and 53 dizygotic same-sex adult twins. At least one member of each pair of the twins had an anxiety disorder. A likely genetic component to panic was found. When all panic-related anxiety disorders (except for generalized anxiety disorder) were lumped together, the concordance rate was 15% for dizygotic twins and 45% in monzygotic twins, a statistically significant difference in this relatively small sample. Of note, however, liberal criteria were used to define inclusion in the Torgersen's "anxiety disorder with panic attack" category (Barlow, 2002). Other twin studies have also suggested a specific genetic contribution to panic disorder (Carey & Gottesman, 1981; Skre, Onstad, Torgersen, Lygren, & Kringlen, 1993).

Specific fears and phobias also seem to evidence a marked genetic contribution based on twin studies. Numerous studies have found that monozygotic twins are more strongly concordant than dizygotic twins for specific fears and phobias (Kendler, Myers, & Prescott, 2002; Kendler, Neale, Kessler, Heath, & Eaves, 1992). However, many of the studies, with the notable exceptions of Kendler et al. (1992, 2002), focused primarily on "normal" fears rather than clinically diagnosable disorders. Moreover, family studies have supported the role of genetic contributions in specific phobias. Fyer et al. (1990) found that 49 first-degree relatives of those with specific phobia were more likely to have a specific phobia than 119 first-degree relatives of those with no history of mental illness (31% versus 11% and a relative risk of 3.3). Interestingly, female relatives were more likely to have a specific phobia than male relatives (48% versus 13%). In a further study, Fyer, Mannuzza, Chapman, Martin, and Klein (1995) compared the relatives of probands suffering from social phobia and panic disorder with agoraphobia, as well as those who had never been mentally ill, with 79 relatives of 15 probands with specific phobia. They found that relatives of the probands seemed to be at greater risk for developing the same phobia as the proband. Family and twin studies generally support that panic disorder and specific phobias share a genetic contribution to their development.

A body of evidence has emerged, particularly over the last 15 years, indicating that this genetic vulnerability for anxiety and related disorders, with the likely exception of phobias, is relatively nonspecific. Behavioral geneticist Kenneth Kendler and colleagues examined a sample of more than 3,700 pairs of twins from Australia and found that approximately 27% of anxiety and depressive symptoms evidenced heritability based on questionnaire responses (Kendler, Heath, Martin, & Eaves, 1987). Interestingly, they found that generalized anxiety disorder and major depressive disorder share a common genetic contribution and that their expression varies based on environmental stressors (Kendler, 2006; Kendler et al., 1992).

More recently, Hettema, Prescott, Myers, Neale, and Kendler (2005) examined the structure of genetic and environmental risk factors for anxiety disorders by employing multivariate structural equation modeling based on more than 5,000 members of the Virginia Adult Twin Study of Psychiatric and Substance Use Disorders. The authors interpreted the best-fitting model as supporting the notion that two additive genetic factors were common across disorders, with one loading most strongly onto generalized anxiety disorder, panic disorder, and agoraphobia (and probably depression), and the other loading primarily onto the two types of specific phobias that were examined (animal and situational phobias such as claustrophobia).

After a review of available research comparing the contributions of behavioral genetic influences, as well as shared and nonshared environmental influences to childhood anxiety, Eley (2001) concluded that genetic influences account for approximately one-third of the variance. Family and genetic studies suggest a genetic "vulnerability" to develop anxiety disorders generally, as opposed to a specific clinical syndrome itself, most likely, mediated by temperament (Kendler et al., 1995), and investigators are now attempting to identify clusters of genes that may be relevant to clarifying this genetic contribution. For example, recent studies of a gene that promotes a corticotropin-releasing hormone (CRH) indicate that activation of this gene influences inhibited temperament and places children at an increased risk for developing panic disorder and possibly phobias (Smoller et al., 2003, 2005), although it is possible that risks for other emotional disorders are enhanced as well. It is likely that genetic influences in the development and maintenance of anxiety are mediated to a substantial degree by this system, as reviewed below.

In a particularly well-designed study, Caspi et al. (2003) examined a group of 847 individuals who had received various assessments since age 3. When these participants were 26 years old, they were assessed for the experience of a major depressive episode over the previous 12 months. Stressful life events were recorded throughout the course of the participants' lives. Overall, 17% of the participants had met criteria for a major depressive episode during the previous year. The most innovative part of the study was that the genetic makeup of the individuals was examined (in particular, a gene that affects the transmission of serotonin, a major neurotransmitter). Caspi et al. studied two alleles (or versions) of this gene—a long and short allele. Since the investigators had been recording stressful life events throughout the participants' lives, they were able to test the relationship between stressful life events and how the variations in the alleles might impact the experience of a major depressive episode. They found that people with the short alleles were much more likely than those with long alleles to develop depression if they had experienced at least four stressful life events. However, allele variation made no difference in the expression of depression in adulthood for those who did not experience stressful life events. This study, epitomizing the new emphasis on gene-environment interactions, demonstrates that neither gene nor environmental factors can fully explain the onset of mental disorders such as anxiety and depression, and that a genetic predisposition is an important but not fully determinative factor in the expression of psychopathology. This study has now been replicated a sufficient number of times to solidify confidence in its findings for depression. Presumably, similar results will be forthcoming for the anxiety disorders (Rutter, Moffitt, & Caspi, 2006). To quote Rutter et al. (2006):

> It should be no surprise, therefore, that the susceptibility genes found so far for mental disorders do not involve a pathogenic effect that knocks out a vital function, but rather represent particular allelic variations of common genes. We are only just at the beginning of the phase of being able to understand just what these genes do, but the likelihood is that they affect particular physiological pathways that make a psychiatric condition more or less likely, but the genes do not cause a mental disorder at all directly. (p. 242)

It is also highly unlikely, as Rutter et al. (2006) suggest, that there is a single gene associated with one specific pathophysiological function that is responsible for anxiety. Instead, evidence suggests that a number of genes (polygenic model) exert weak contributions from several areas on chromosomes that impact a vulnerability to anxiety (Kendler et al., 1995; Kendler, 2006; Plomin, DeFries, McClearn, & Rutter, 1997; Rutter et al., 2006).

Taken as a whole, the evidence supports that some may inherit a tendency to be "nervous" or "emotional." In other words, some people simply seem more predisposed to be biologically reactive to various environmental stressors. This seems most likely to be expressed as a general biological vulnerability to develop anxiety (or depression) when certain psychological vulnerabilities are present. However, there may be separate, yet overlapping, genetic differences between being temperamentally anxious (i.e., frequently being prepared for danger) and having a lower threshold for a flight-or-flight type reaction when danger occurs (as more often occurs in panic and various specific fears and phobias; Barlow, 2002; Hettema et al., 2005). In the next section, additional clarification on the role of psychological and environmental factors is discussed as a prerequisite to developing a more complete theory on the origins of anxiety and related disorders.

Generalized Psychological Vulnerability: A Diminished Sense of Control

At the core of anxiety lies a marked sense of uncontrollability when individuals are faced with certain tasks or challenges that may be in some way threatening (Barlow, 2000, 2002). For these individuals, failures or perceived deficiencies are indications of a chronic inability to cope with unpredictable and uncontrollable negative events, and this sense of uncontrollability is associated with negatively valenced emotional responding. Functional or "normal" individuals, on the other hand, seem to manifest what has been described as an "illusion of control," in which response deficiencies are attributed to passing external causes or to trivial temporary internal states (Barlow, 2002).

In order to fully understand and isolate important variables that contribute to the development of anxiety and related disorders, research with humans has been characterized by retrospective searches of the patient's history and longitudinal studies conducted over the course of decades to examine the factors that place children at risk for the development of certain disorders. However, the ability to produce an emotional disorder in the laboratory is an enormously important step in the area of etiology. Experimentally induced anxiety permits systematic exploration of the factors contributing to the disorder.

THE PRODUCTION OF EXPERIMENTAL NEUROSIS IN ANIMALS

Findings from studies employing laboratory analogues of anxious apprehension suggest that severe anxious apprehension can be produced in the laboratory. For more than 50 years, investigators such as Pavlov, Masserman, Liddell, and Gantt have produced behavior characterized by extreme agitation, restlessness, distractibility, hypersensitivity, increased autonomic responding, muscle tension, and interference with ongoing performance. The phenomenon they produced was commonly termed "experimental neurosis." This phenomenon has been produced in animals by a number of different procedures, including the punishment of appetitive responses, the presentation of insoluble problems, accompanied by the punishment of mistakes, long periods of restraint and monotony, and the introduction of extremely difficult discriminations that are required to obtain food. In an important early review, Mineka and Kihlstrom (1978) suggested that the cause of anxiety in these animals is that "environmental events of vital importance to the organism become unpredictable, uncontrollable, or both" (p. 257). This body of basic experimental work has been reviewed extensively by Barlow (2002). Briefly, evidence suggests that the predictability and controllability of events important to the organism, such as the acquisition of food and escape from pain, are crucial in the development of anxiety and depression (Mineka, Cook, & Miller, 1984; Mineka & Kihlstrom, 1978; Seligman, 1975). Even aversive events of substantial intensity or duration will be better tolerated (with marked individual differences) if they occur predictably, and if the organism at least perceives that some control over these events is possible. Lack of predictability of these "stressful" events seems to lead to chronic anxiety and/or depression (Seligman, 1975; Mineka & Kihlstrom, 1978). More recently, Amat et al. (2005) found that certain areas of the rat brain (in this study, the infralimbic and prelimbic regions of the ventral medial prefrontal cortex) detect whether a stressor is under an organism's control and suggest that the presence of a sense of control may inhibit stress-induced neural activity. (For comprehensive reviews, see Gunnar & Fisher, 2006; Levine, 2005.)

In infant rhesus monkeys, Roma, Champoux, and Suomi (2006) attempted to replicate earlier experiments (Insel, Scanlan, Champoux, & Suomi, 1988; Mineka, Gunnar, & Champoux, 1986) illustrating the causal relationship between controllability of appetitive stimuli and adaptive responses

to novel situations, with an important difference. The authors gathered physiological data (salivary cortisol) to shed light on the impact of controllable versus uncontrollable stress on HPA axis regulation in early development. Results indicated that "master" monkeys (reared in conditions with increased control over food availability through lever pressing) were significantly more active and exhibited reduced cortisol reactivity in response to novel stimuli relative to their "yoked" counterparts (with noncontingent access to food). These findings suggest that environmental control in infancy results in increased competence, which in turn buffers stress reactivity. When taken together, these studies are significant in that they demonstrate the negative influence of experiences with uncontrollability in the early environment. In addition, whereas experimental neurosis paradigms suggest the importance of control over aversive stimuli, this evidence suggests that control over appetitive stimuli may be equally important in the development of mastery and competence in response to stressful situations. This finding underscores the centrality of a sense of control, rather than the particular experiences that are associated with it.

This concept is also illustrated in studies of cortisol reactivity among dominant and subordinate baboons (Sapolsky 1990; Sapolsky, Alberts, & Altmann, 1997; Sapolsky & Ray, 1989). Investigators examined levels of cortisol in these animals as a function of their social rank and discovered that dominant males have lower resting levels of cortisol than subordinate males. However, when some "emergency" occurs, levels of cortisol rise more quickly in the dominant males than in the subordinate males. Cortisol, of course, is the final step in a cascade of hormone secretion that begins with the limbic system in the brain during periods of stress or anxiety. The hippocampus is very responsive to corticosteroids. When stimulated by these hormones during hypothalamic-pituitary-adrenocortical (HPA) axis activity, the hippocampus contributes to a down-regulation of the stress response, thus articulating the close link between the limbic system and various parts of the HPA axis. When produced chronically, cortisol can have damaging effects on a variety of physiological systems, ultimately causing damage to the hippocampus and the immune system (McEwen & Magarinos, 2004). This damage to the hippocampus after a period of chronic stress may then lead to reduced negative feedback sensitivity, to chronic secretion of stress hormones, and ultimately, to physical disease and death. Thus, it seems that

Sapolsky's subordinate baboons are caught in a perpetual state of scanning for danger, probably as a function of perceived lack of control over their condition, resulting in chronic arousal and reduced reactivity (autonomic restriction) to actual stressors.

Studies of the relationship between early experiences and corticotropin-releasing factor (CRF) in macaques also point to important implications about the impact of unpredictability (Coplan, Paunica, & Rosenblum, 2004). Coplan et al. (1996) and Coplan et al. (1998) evaluated the development of anxiety among infant bonnet macaques whose nursing mothers were subjected to three different conditions involving foraging for food, which led to differential interactions with their infants. Findings revealed that infants that were subjected to mothers exposed to a condition of unpredictability in food availability exhibited heightened anxietylike behavior during development, as well as substantially increased behavioral inhibition to a variety of novel and anxiety-producing contexts relative to infants of mothers exposed to high or low, but predictable, food availability (Coplan, Rosenblum, & Gorman, 1995). Of more importance, CRF levels in the cerebrospinal fluid of these monkeys were persistently elevated, and cortisol levels depressed (Coplan et al., 1996). CRF levels were also correlated with heightened cerebrospinal fluid levels of serotonin and dopamine metabolites (Coplan et al., 1998), and these changes persisted into adulthood (Coplan et al., 2004).

Coplan et al. (1998) concluded that increasing adversity during early childhood results in enhanced CRF activity, which in turn causes alteration in other systems underlying the adult expression of stress and anxiety. Behaviors associated with the variable foraging demand condition included inconsistent, erratic, and dismissive behaviors on the part of the mother—behaviors likely to result in diminished maternal attachment. Furthermore, the results seemed due to the unpredictability of this condition, since adult mothers engaged in predictable high foraging demand condition did not exhibit elevated CRF concentrations. Thus Coplan et al. (1998) suppose, as do Nemeroff and his colleagues (Gillespie & Nemeroff, 2007; Heim, Owens, Plotsky, & Nemeroff, 1997) and others (e.g., Gunnar & Fisher, 2006; Ladd et al., 2000; Levine, 2005), that adverse early experience—in combination, of course, with a genetic predisposition—creates a neurobiological diathesis. This diathesis becomes activated in later life by the experience of additional stressful life events or other triggers, completing the diathesis–stress model of the development of anxiety.

In their work with "anxiety" in primates, Sapolsky (Sapolsky, 1990; Sapolsky et al., 1997; Sapolsky & Ray, 1989) and Coplan et al. (1996, 1998, 2004) have characterized a neurobiological process associated with anxiety and stress that develops as a consequence of early experience with uncontrollability. This process involves increased corticotropin-releasing factor (CRF) production combined with diminished sensitivity of the pituitary gland, increased production of stress hormones (cortisol), reduced negative feedback sensitivity with lessened ability to regulate cortisol production, and ultimately, hippocampal degeneration.

Finally, some recent findings from cross-fostering studies in rhesus monkeys have important implications for a discussion of the contribution of parenting styles to a generalized psychological vulnerability to develop anxiety in humans. In these studies with rhesus monkeys, Suomi and colleagues (1999, 2000) experimented with a particularly emotional and stress-reactive group of young monkeys by cross-fostering them to nonreactive mothers. Reactive young animals that were raised by calm mothers for the first 6 months of their lives were able to overcome their biological vulnerability to be reactive. These animals developed normally, demonstrating the kinds of social competence characteristic of nonreactive animals. Furthermore, these changes in their "temperaments" seemed to be permanent, in that they raised their own offspring in a nonreactive and calm manner, much to the benefit of their offspring. On the other hand, infants with the same biological vulnerability raised by emotional and stress-reactive mothers retained their emotionality, perhaps because they developed a synergistic psychological vulnerability. Recent findings indicate the specific early learning experiences actually alter gene expression through some specific mechanisms, such as DNA methylation of specific promoter genes, in a way that produces permanent changes (e.g., Cameron, Champagne, & Parent, 2005; Rutter et al., 2006). These findings, of course, have implications for the prevention of anxiety (and depression), although we are still a long way from understanding how this process might work in humans. A discussion of the effects of parenting styles on the development of anxiety in humans is provided later in the chapter.

Findings from the animal laboratories have important implications for the relationship of experiences with unpredictability and uncontrollability to fear and panic. For example, monkeys evidenced more extreme fear (alarm, panic) when confronted with a potentially life-threatening situation if they had experienced unpredictability or uncontrollability over important life events, even positive events (Mineka et al., 1986; Roma et al., 2006). This evidence indicates that in animals at least, early stress—particularly uncontrollable and/or unpredictable life events—leads to increased HPA axis responding, negative emotionality (chronic anxious apprehension), and alarm reactions. Instillation of a sense of mastery or control during development seems to protect against the likelihood of an anxious response. The development of coping responses that imply a sense of control (whether real or apparent) buffers anxiety as well (Suomi, 1986; Coplan et al., 1996). With this suggestive evidence in mind, it becomes possible to examine findings on the etiology of human anxious apprehension.

THE DEVELOPMENT OF ANXIETY IN HUMANS: LOCUS OF CONTROL AND PARENTING STYLES

Evaluation of the role of control in humans has led to the development of constructs such as "locus of control" and "attributional style." Rotter (1966) suggested that one's "locus of control" could be rated along a dimension of internal to external causality, and developed an instrument to measure perception of control. These ideas sparked the development of psychometrically sound questionnaires to measure these constructs, including the Nowicki-Strickland Locus of Control Scale (Barlow, Chorpita, & Turovsky, 1996) and the Anxiety Control Questionnaire (Brown, White, Forsyth, & Barlow, 2004; Rapee, Craske, Brown, & Barlow, 1996). Findings using these measures suggest that perceived control acts as a diathesis or vulnerability to the experience of negative emotional states (McCauley, Mitchell, Burke, & Moss, 1988; Nunn, 1988; Siegel & Griffin, 1984; Skinner, Chapman, & Baltes, 1988; Weisz & Stipek, 1982; White, Brown, Somers, & Barlow, 2006).

Abramson, Seligman, and Teasdale (1978) reformulated Seligman's theory of learned helplessness, suggesting that the relationship between negative life events and learned helplessness is *moderated* by one's attributional style. That is, the experience of negative events is not sufficient to develop helplessness. Rather, negative life events are most likely to lead to learned helplessness when a person makes internal, global, and stable attributions regarding negative events. Abramson, Metalsky, and Alloy

(1989) modified this theory further and emphasized the role of hopelessness rather than helplessness as more specific to depression. They suggested that for many forms of depression, attributions play a causal role only when they contribute to a sense of hopelessness in which individuals despair of ever attaining any influence over important events in their world. Helplessness, in their view, is more relevant to anxiety.

Nolen-Hoeksema, Girgus, and Seligman (1992) provided important information regarding the development and subsequent effects of cognitive response styles in childhood and early adolescence. In this 5-year longitudinal study, the authors found that in early childhood, negative life events rather than control cognitions or explanatory style were the best predictors of depression. They also found that the presence of depression in early childhood led to a deterioration of explanatory style. Specifically, children who experienced depression at a young age developed an increased tendency to make internal, stable, and global attributions for negative life events, and to make external, unstable, and specific attributions for positive events. This pessimistic explanatory style was found to predict a recurrence of depression in later childhood, with negative life events predicting the specific time at which relapse occurred. In other words, there is a suggestion that cognitive style comes to *moderate* negative life events and depression in older children. The results of this study suggest that adult models of depression (e.g., Abramson et al., 1978) may apply only to older children. The data indicate that by early adolescence, certain cognitive response styles develop. Maladaptive cognitive response styles (which may result from childhood depression, early negative life events, or a combination) serve as a psychological vulnerability or diathesis. Thus, when faced with negative life events, adolescents with such cognitive styles seem to be at a greater risk of developing depression.

There is also evidence to suggest that anxiety is the first consequence of this negative cognitive style traditionally associated with depression. Results from a prospective longitudinal study of anxiety and depression among children (Cole, Peeke, Martin, Truglio, & Seroczynski, 1998) clearly supported the temporal hypothesis that anxiety leads to depression in children and adolescents. In fact, this finding had been repeatedly obtained in prior studies, albeit with less satisfactory methodologies (Hershberg, Carlson, Cantwell, & Strober, 1982; Kovacs, Gatsonis, Paulauskas, & Richards, 1989; Orvaschel, Lewinsohn, & Seeley, 1995).

In a similar vein, Luten, Ralph, and Mineka (1997) reported that a pessimistic attributional style was related more strongly to underlying negative affect than to anxiety or depression specifically. They also suggest that a generalized psychological vulnerability—as represented by a pessimistic attributional style reflecting a sense of uncontrollability—may lead initially to anxiety, followed by depression.

Studies on early environment and the role of parenting styles shed some light on the possible origins of the development of a sense of control in children. Shear (1991) notes that human infants exert control over their environment through their effects on caretakers. When parents are insensitive to their child's expressive, exploratory, and independent behaviors, the child is at risk of developing inhibition and a sense of uncontrollability over his or her world, which may contribute to anxiety.

Parenting styles and family characteristics have been linked to the development of a sense of control (Schneewind, 1995) as well to the development of anxiety and depression (Turner, Beidel, & Costello, 1987). Consistent with attachment theory (Bowlby, 1980; Thompson, 1998), specific parenting dimensions that facilitate or inhibit the development of a sense of control in children have been described as (1) warmth or sensitivity, consistency, and contingency; and (2) encouragement of autonomy and absence of intrusion or of an overcontrolling style (Barlow, 2002). Empirical support for the relation of both dimensions of parenting to the development of a sense of control has been thoroughly reviewed elsewhere (Barlow, 2002; Chorpita, 2001). Both parental dimensions (warmth, consistency, and contingency on the one hand, and encouraging autonomy on the other) appear to provide opportunities for a child to experience control over reinforcing events in early development, through social contingency and mastery of the environment. Over time, such experiences can become part of the child's stored (learned) information and contribute to a generalized sense of control (e.g., Carton & Nowicki, 1994).

Several studies have implicated the same two dimensions of parenting behavior to the development of anxiety and depression. Siqueland, Kendall, and Steinberg (1996), for example, assessed families with and without children who had an anxiety disorder to examine differences in family interactions. Ratings by independent observers during a videotaped interaction task indicated that parents of children with anxiety disorders gave their children less psychological autonomy than did parents of children without an anxiety disorder. In addition, children with anxiety disorders rated their parents as less accepting than did nonanxious children. More recently, Hudson and Rapee (2002) also found that mothers of anxious children were more intrusive in their interactions with their child and sibling relative to mothers of nonanxious children. Taken together, these studies provide evidence that overcontrolling, intrusive parenting styles are associated with anxiety disorders in children, and similar parenting styles have been linked to depression (Ingram & Ritter, 2000; Reiss et al., 1995).

DEVELOPMENTAL CONSIDERATIONS

Having reviewed factors that contribute to a generalized psychological vulnerability or diathesis, we can now consider developmental issues in the activation of this vulnerability (see Barlow et al., 1996; Chorpita & Barlow, 1998). It is generally accepted that negative life events interact with preexisting generalized biological and psychological vulnerabilities to result in emotional disorders. Chorpita, Brown, and Barlow (1998) utilized a cross-sectional design to evaluate this "diathesis–stress" model of the development of anxiety through structural equation modeling. The major hypothesis was that an overcontrolling family environment that fosters diminished personal control should in fact produce a sense of uncontrollability, as reflected in a more external locus of control. This external locus of control should in turn contribute to increased negative affect, and ultimately, to clinical symptoms. Based on evidence from childhood depression studies, the role of attributional style as a mediator in the model was also evaluated.

Compared to a number of alternative models, the model depicting a diminished sense of personal control (external locus of control) functioning as a mediator between a family environment fostering less autonomy and subsequent negative affect and clinical symptoms was the best fit for the data. These findings once again suggest that a family environment characterized by limited opportunity for personal control is associated with later anxiety and negative affect. This relationship is mediated by low perceived control in the children, which appears to be a more robust mediator than attributional style.

In summary, there is evidence supporting a model of the development of anxiety and depression characterized by a generalized psychological vulnerability (or sense of relative uncontrollability) as a mediator between salient events and anxiety or depression early in development. Interestingly, this mediational model in early childhood contrasts with a moderational model that seems to operate for late childhood and adulthood (Chorpita et al., 1998; Chorpita, 2001; Cole & Turner, 1993; Nolen-Hoeksema et al., 1992). An important developmental progression in the formulation of this vulnerability can be derived from these findings. That is, the environment may help to foster a (cognitive) template, with early experience contributing to the formation of a vulnerability (i.e., mediational model). Later in development, this vulnerability may then begin to operate as an amplifier for environmental events (i.e., moderational model). Recent data from the Center for Anxiety and Related Disorders at Boston University support this moderational role in patients with panic disorder. Specifically, anxiety was positively associated with agoraphobia severity, but this relationship was moderated by perceived control in that this association was stronger in patients with low perceived control (White et al., 2006).

In another study, Hedley, Hoffart, and Sexton (2001) evaluated the relationships between perceived control, anxiety sensitivity, and the presence of avoidance and catastrophic thoughts. Support for triple vulnerability theory was based on the finding that beliefs about losing control predicted a fear of bodily sensations, which in turn predicted the presence of avoidance and catastrophic thoughts about physical and social harm. This model fit the data better than (1) a cognitive model, in which it was hypothesized that catastrophic beliefs would lead to both anxiety about body sensations and avoidance, and (2) a behavioral model, in which the anxiety about bodily sensations was thought to lead to catastrophic beliefs and avoidance.

On the other hand, in a recent test of the *moderational* versus *mediational* role of perceived control in the relationship between family functioning and anxiety, Ballash, Pemble, Usui, Buckley, and Woodruff-Borden (2006) found support for only the mediating effects of perceived control using the Anxiety Control Questionnaire in a nonclinical sample of young adults. Results showed that while family communication and general family functioning directly predicted anxiety, affective involvement, behavioral control, and family communication were predictive of a perceived lack of control, which in turn predicted increased anxiety. Limitations of the study included the exclusion of a clinical sample and a limited age range among participants (ages 18–25). Also, in an application of the triple vulnerability model to social anxiety using structural

equation modeling, Hofmann (2005) found that the relationship between catastrophic thinking (the estimated cost of negative events) and social anxiety among patients with social phobia was mediated by the participants' perception of control. A moderational model was not tested.

NEUROENDOCRINE FUNCTION

Earlier, we reviewed the relation between early experiences and HPA axis functioning in animals and the likelihood that HPA axis functioning mediates, to some extent, genetic influences on the development and maintenance of anxiety. Several studies have examined the profound effect of early stressful experiences and neuroendocrine function (typically associated with anxiety and depression) as evidenced by elevated basal cortisol levels in humans. For example, Gunnar, Larson, Hertsgaard, Harris, and Brodersen (1992) demonstrated that 9-month-old infants showed an elevated cortisol response when separated from their mothers, but that this effect was eliminated when an infant was accompanied by a highly responsive caretaker versus a less responsive caretaker.

Granger, Weisz, and Kauneckis (1994) specifically examined the effects of a sense of control, as well as of current behavioral and emotional problems, on cortisol levels in children as a function of a parent–child conflict task. They found that children with higher neuroendocrine activation were more socially withdrawn and socially anxious, had more social problems, and perceived themselves as having less personal control over the outcomes of their lives. They also tended to perceive social outcomes as being less contingent on their actions in general than did low reactors. Although the findings are correlational, they suggest that children with a lower sense of control during parent–child conflict may evidence exaggerated HPA axis reactivity in the face of stressors.

In a recent review of the literature, Gunnar and Fisher (2006) summarized accumulating evidence for the influence of social regulation of cortisol levels in early human development and described possible mechanisms at work in this relationship. Although this brief account oversimplifies their detailed account, the authors noted that in early development, cortisol activity is sensitive to social regulation. With sensitive and responsive caregiving, high cortisol responsivity diminishes, and it becomes more difficult to provoke increases in cortisol. These children, in turn, learn that attachment behaviors and distress reactions will result in helpful responses from caregivers. When exposed to lesser levels of responsive care, cortisol levels increase, particularly among temperamentally vulnerable children (those that are easily angered and frustrated, or anxious and fearful). The authors further suggest that abusive and neglectful care will hurt an individual's ability to respond to threat in a healthy physiological manner and ultimately affect their viability. Furthermore, unlike rodents for whom these influences on the developing brain are only operative for a week or two after birth, in humans, this vulnerability seems to last throughout childhood (Gunnar & Fisher, 2006).

These studies, then, create an important link between the effects of early stressful experiences (particularly those associated with intrusive, controlling parenting styles) and the development of a generalized psychological vulnerability (manifested as diminished control cognitions). This vulnerability in turn directly influences the expression of clinical and neurobiological correlates of anxiety and depression in both humans and animals.

CONCLUSIONS

Earlier in this chapter we reviewed genetic influences on the development and maintenance of anxiety. We discussed important characteristics associated with anxiety, such as increased psychological arousal and tendencies toward temperamental inhibition and or low positive affect. Evidence suggests that a reciprocal relationship exists between an inherited tendency to be "nervous," "emotional," or "inhibited" and important environmental factors (such as exposure to early adverse events and inconsistent or overcontrolling parenting styles), which in turn lead to the development of an overall diminished sense of control.

While genetic factors contribute to the development of temperaments associated with anxious apprehension, the evidence reviewed earlier supports the notion that neurobiological processes underlying anxious apprehension that may emerge from this biological (genetic) diathesis seem to be influenced substantially by early psychological processes, thus contributing to a generalized psychological vulnerability. In this sense, early experiences with controllability and predictability, based in large part (but not exclusively) on interactions with caregivers,

contributes to something of a psychological template, which at some point becomes relatively fixed and diathetic. Stated another way, this psychological dimension of a sense of control is possibly a mediator

between stressful experience and anxiety, and over time this sense becomes a somewhat stable moderator of the expression of anxiety. (Chorpita & Barlow, 1998, p. 16)

This relationship also reflects current thinking on gene–environment intersection (Rutter et al., 2006).

In summary, a synergism of generalized biological (genetic) and generalized psychological (early experience) vulnerabilities contribute to temperaments that are likely to lead to the clinical syndromes of generalized anxiety disorder and the depressive disorders. False alarms (panic attacks) may occur as a function of stressful life events, facilitated by high levels of baseline anxiety, emerging as a function of these synergistic generalized vulnerabilities. But these false alarms are not in themselves implicated in a clinical disorder. For that to occur, an additional layer of more specific psychological vulnerabilities must be considered.

Specific Psychological Vulnerabilities: Learning What Is Dangerous

As noted earlier, the combination of biological vulnerabilities and generalized psychological vulnerabilities by themselves seem insufficient to fully explain the development of all individual anxiety disorders. A specific type of psychological vulnerability is relevant, particularly for anxiety disorders in which anxious apprehension is focused on features perceived as dangerous. Vicarious learning of anxiety can occur with an emphasis on actual objects, situations, and/or internal sensations. For instance, in panic disorder, somatic (or interoceptive) cues are viewed as signals or triggers of impending panic attacks. In specific phobias, these specific psychological vulnerabilities impact what situations and/or objects are feared. In obsessive-compulsive disorder, in which obsessional images, thoughts, or urges become the focus of the sufferer, some evidence suggests that those afflicted with OCD have come to believe that thoughts themselves can cause dangerous actions to occur (also known as thought-action fusion). Moreover, in social phobia, evidence supports the notion that parents and/or other important caregivers communicate the potential danger of social evaluation or performance (Barlow, 2002). For instance, parents of socially anxious children tended to speak of the potentially threatening nature of various social situations and reinforced their children's tendency to avoid these situations (Barrett, Rapee, Dadds, & Ryan, 1996).

Numerous studies have found that vicarious learning and direct experiences as well as straightforward information transmission impact the development and expression of fear and anxiety. The well-known concept of modeling seems important. Ehlers (1993) found that adults with panic disorder and those with infrequent panic attacks as youngsters received more encouragement from caregivers of sick role behavior with the implicit message that noticeable somatic sensations are likely to be dangerous compared to their counterparts without a history of panic attacks. For instance, those with panic attacks or a history of attacks more often heard messages such as, "Take care of yourself, and avoid strenuous activity." Taylor and Rachman (1994) and McNally and Eke (1996) found that preexisting and previously learned sensitivity to specific interoceptive cues differentially predicted the experience of panic attacks to respiratory challenges. Craske, Poulton, Tsao, and Plotkin (2001) found that individuals whose relatives had chronic obstructive pulmonary disease while growing up were more likely than those who did not to have a specific sensitivity to interpreting their own respiratory symptoms as potentially hazardous. Finally, a retrospective study by Muris, Merckelbach, and Meesters (2001) found that the manner in which parents speak to their children about how dangerous it is to experience somatic symptoms impacts children's sensitivity to somatic cues. Specifically, parents' transmission of the idea that somatic symptoms might be dangerous was significantly associated with levels of anxiety sensitivity. Since a number of these studies mentioned have focused on retrospective reports, it is not possible to establish with certainty that these individuals' experience with ill relatives caused the specific psychological vulnerability that triggered an expression of anxiety to interoceptive cues.

There are at least three ways by which a specific psychological vulnerability might develop. One person might develop a disorder after direct involvement in a situation that results in real danger or pain (e.g., a person who, previously unafraid of dogs, is painfully bitten by a dog and subsequently becomes fearful around canines). Experiencing a false alarm in a specific situation can also be a specific vulnerability. For example, a person may develop a fear of public speaking after experiencing a panic attack when giving a speech. Despite a lack of negative feedback, or any indication of poor performance, the person begins to associate public speaking with panic and/or anxiety and becomes fearful in similar situations. Third, vicarious conditioning can also function as a specific vulnerability. Vicarious conditioning involves developing anxiety or panic in response to witnessing or even being told that a situation is dangerous (Barlow, 2002). For instance, a person who watches a movie in which a character appears to vomit after consuming a seemingly contaminated piece of food becomes concerned that he or she will become ill from consuming contaminated food and begins to develop rituals around food (e.g., excessive checking or washing) in an attempt to inoculate himself or herself against thoughts that his or her food is contaminated. Ollendick, Vasey, and King (2001) depict the observational learning and vicarious acquisition of anxious avoidance within an operant conditioning framework. For example, a child might observe the parent model fearful responses to a stimuli (e.g., spiders), and thus respond in a similar way when faced with the same type of situation. Additionally, children may learn to cope with anxiety through avoidance after observing that parental anxiety is reduced by their own avoidant behaviors.

Studies have examined these pathways. Munjack (1984) found that half of those people with a specific phobia of driving who could recall when their phobia began recalled a traumatic event (e.g., a car accident), but the other half had a "false alarm" such as experiencing a panic attack and/or catastrophic thoughts while driving. However, retrospective studies can be imprecise and unreliable (Henry, Moffitt, Caspi, Langley, & Silva, 1994). Due to ethical considerations, it is difficult to design human experiments that examine the role of vicarious learning in the development of anxiety disorders (Craske & Waters, 2005). However, animal research has shown that monkeys can develop a phobia simply by seeing another monkey experience fear (Mineka, Davidson, Cook, & Keir, 1984).

Models of social phobia tend to look somewhat similar to models of panic disorder and specific phobia (Barlow, 2002). Social phobia triggers can result from true alarms (e.g., being laughed at in a social situation by peers) or false alarms (e.g., having a panic attack when initiating a conversation). In addition, social phobia can develop without any kind of alarm. For instance, a person may perceive that he or she has poor social skills. While the person may or may not be accurate in his or her self-evaluation, the key factor is the person's own perception of his or her social skills. A key specific vulnerability in the development of social phobia is the socially phobic person's belief that social evaluation is dangerous (Barlow, 2002). Bruch and Heimberg (1994) and

Rapee and Melville (1997) found that parents of patients with social phobia are significantly more socially fearful and concerned about what others think of them than are parents of patients with panic disorder, and there is evidence to suggest that these views are passed on to their children (Lieb et al., 2000). Specific beliefs about oneself as a social object (e.g., "I'm a boring person") and the use of rigid rules and standards (e.g., "I must be thought of as very smart, and there can be no pauses in my speech") can strengthen the development of social anxiety (Wells & Clark, 1997). The combination of perceiving oneself as inadequate, having unrealistically high social standards, perceiving the cost of a negative social interaction as high, and increased self-focused attention can make social situations particularly scary (Wells & Clark, 1997; Hofmann & Barlow, 2002).

A key specific vulnerability for the development of OCD is the idea that certain thoughts are dangerous and unacceptable (Barlow, 2002). Thought-action fusion, in which thoughts are equated with particular actions, is prevalent in those suffering from OCD. The specific vulnerability involved in generating this thought-action fusion may be the result of childhood incidents in which excessive feelings of responsibility and guilt develop, and unpleasant thoughts are associated with evil intent (Salkovskis, Shafran, Rachman, & Freeston, 1999; Steketee & Barlow, 2002). Several studies have demonstrated that the strength of religious beliefs, regardless of the type of belief, can be associated with thought-action fusion and OCD severity (Rassin & Koster, 2003; Steketee, Quay, & White, 1991). Of course, not everyone with strong religious beliefs develops OCD, but high levels of religiosity may be a specific vulnerability for some people. Additionally, believing that certain thoughts are unacceptable and, consequently, must be suppressed may put one at greater risk of developing OCD (Amir, Cashman, & Foa, 1997; Parkinson & Rachman, 1981; Salkovskis & Campbell, 1994).

The aforementioned examples describe the development of various anxiety disorders with an emphasis on possible specific psychological vulnerabilities. However, it is important to note that the specific symptoms and disorders that develop, if any develop at all, are also impacted by biological and generalized psychological vulnerabilities. If the biological and generalized psychological vulnerabilities are seen as the powder keg and gunpowder, respectively, specific psychological vulnerabilities are the fuses running to the keg. Each fuse is potentially capable of lighting the gunpowder (and, thus, bringing about the expression of a disorder). If one particular fuse had not been lit, it is likely another would have been, perhaps resulting in a different symptom cluster, but resulting in a manifestation of an emotional disorder nonetheless.

Summary and Conclusions

In conclusion, this chapter summarizes the recent literature pertaining to the development of anxiety and related emotional disorders from a triple vulnerability framework. Drawing heavily on emotion theory and on scientific findings from the laboratories of experimental psychology, specifically, cognitive science, neuroscience, developmental psychology, and learning theory, support is presented for the existence of the triple vulnerabilities consisting of generalized biological, generalized psychological, and specific psychological diatheses. Support is, of course, stronger for some aspects of the theory such as the role of early experiences in contributing to a diminished sense of control, which may mediate and later moderate emotional disorders, than it is for the development of specific psychological vulnerabilities, the evidence for which is mostly retrospective self-report. And our understanding of the nature of gene-environment interaction is rapidly changing and advancing, as is our knowledge of epigenetics, or the ability of experience to change gene expression. Prospective risk factor research along with the study of longitudinal structural relations among the hypothetical diatheses using sophisticated data analytic procedures is ongoing in our center and elsewhere. This work will sharpen the hypothetical statements and advance our ideas.

References

Abramson, L. Y., Metalsky, G. I., & Alloy, L. B. (1989). Hopelessness depression: A theory-based subtype of depression. *Psychological Review, 96,* 358–372.

Abramson, L. Y., Seligman, M. E., & Teasdale, J. D. (1978). Learned helplessness in humans: Critique and reformulation. *Journal of Abnormal Psychology, 87,* 49–74.

Amat, J., Baratta, B. V., Paul, E., Bland, S. T., Watkins, L. R., & Maier, S. F. (2005). Medial prefrontal cortex determines how stressor controllability affects behavior and dorsal raphe nucleus. *Nature Neuroscience, 8,* 365–371.

Amir, N., Cashman, L., & Foa, E. B. (1997). Strategies of thought control and obsessive-compulsive disorder. *Behaviour Research and Therapy, 35,* 775–777.

Arntz, A., de Groot, C., & Kindt, M. (2004). Emotional memory is perceptual. *Journal of Behavior Therapy and Experimental Psychiatry, 36,* 19–34.

Bach, A. K., Brown, T. A., & Barlow, D. H. (1999). The effects of false negative feedback on efficacy expectancies and sexual arousal in sexually functional males. *Behavior Therapy, 30,* 79–95.

Ballash, N. G., Pemble, M. K., Usui, W. M., Buckley, A. F., & Woodruff-Borden, J. (2006). Family functioning, perceived control, and anxiety: A mediational model. *Journal of Anxiety Disorders, 20,* 486–497.

Barlow, D. H. (1988). *Anxiety and its disorders: The nature and treatment of anxiety and panic.* New York: Guilford Press.

Barlow, D. H. (2000). Unraveling the mysteries of anxiety and its disorders from the perspective of emotion theory. *American Psychologist, 55,* 1245–1263.

Barlow, D. H. (2002). *Anxiety and its disorders: The nature and treatment of anxiety and panic* (2nd ed.). New York: Guilford Press.

Barlow, D. H., Chorpita, B. F., & Turovsky, J. (1996). Fear, panic, anxiety, and disorders of emotion. In D. A. Hope (Ed.), *Nebraska Symposium on Motivation: Vol. 43. Perspectives on anxiety, panic, and fear: Current theory and research in motivation* (pp. 251–328). Lincoln: University of Nebraska Press.

Barrett, P. M., Rapee, R. M., Dadds, M. M., & Ryan, S. M. (1996). Family enhancement of cognitive style in anxious and aggressive children. *Journal of Abnormal Child Psychology, 24,* 187–203.

Biederman, J., Rosenbaum, J., Hirshfeld, D. R., Faraon, S. V., Bolduc, E. A., Gersten, M., et al. (1990). Psychiatric correlates of behavioral inhibition in young children of parents with and without psychiatric disorders. *Archives of General Psychiatry, 47,* 21–26.

Biederman, J., Rosenblum, J., Bolduc-Murphy, E. A., Faraone, S. V., Chaloff, J., Hirsfeld, D. R., et al. (1993). A three-year follow-up of children with and without behavioral inhibition. *Journal of the American Academy of Child and Adolescent Psychiatry, 32,* 814–821.

Borkovec, T. D. (1994). The nature, functions, and origins of worry. In G.C.L. Davey & F. Tallis (Eds.), *Worrying: Perspectives on theory, assessment, and treatment* (pp. 5–33). New York: Wiley.

Borkovec, T. D., Alcaine, O., & Behar, E. (2004). Avoidance theory of worry and generalized anxiety disorder. In R. G. Heimberg, C. L. Turk, & D. S. Mennin (Eds.), *Generalized anxiety disorder: Advances in research and practice* (pp. 77–108). New York: Guilford Press.

Bouton, M. E. (2005). Behavior systems and the contextual control of anxiety, fear, and panic. In L. Feldman Barrett, P. Niedenthal, & P. Winkielman (Eds.), *Emotion, conscious and unconscious* (pp. 205–227). New York: Guilford Press.

Bouton, M. E., Mineka, S., & Barlow, D. H. (2001). A modern learning-theory prospective on the etiology of panic disorder. *Psychological Review, 108,* 4–32.

Bowlby, J. (1980). *Attachment and loss: Vol. 3. Loss: Sadness and depression.* New York: Basic Books.

Brown, T. A. (2007). Temporal course and structural relationships among dimensions of temperament and DSM–IV anxiety and mood disorder constructs. *Journal of Abnormal Psychology, 116,* 313–328.

Brown, T. A., Chorpita, B. F., & Barlow, D. H. (1998). Structural relationships among dimensions of the *DSM–IV* anxiety and mood disorders and dimensions of negative affect, positive affect, and autonomic arousal. *Journal of Abnormal Psychology, 107,* 179–192.

Brown, T. A., Dowdall, D. J., Côté, G., & Barlow, D. H. (1994). Worry and obsessions: The distinction between generalized anxiety disorder and obsessive-compulsive disorder. In G. Davey & F. Tallis (Eds.), *Worrying: Perspectives on theory, assessment, and treatment* (pp. 229–246). New York: Wiley.

Brown, T. A., White, K. S., Forsyth, J. P., & Barlow, D. H. (2004). The structure of perceived emotional control: Psychometric properties of a revised Anxiety Control Questionnaire. *Behavior Therapy, 35,* 75–99.

Bruch, M. A., & Heimberg, R. G. (1994). Differences in perceptions of parental and personal characteristics between generalized and non-generalized social phobics. *Journal of Anxiety Disorders, 8,* 155–168.

Cameron, N. M., Champagne, F. A., & Parent, C. (2005). The programming of individual differences in defensive responses and reproductive strategies in the rat through variations in maternal care. *Neuroscience and Biobehavioral Reviews, 29,* 843–865.

Campbell-Sills, L., Liverant, G. I., & Brown, T. A. (2004). Psychometric evaluation of the behavioral inhibition/behavioral activation scales in a large sample of outpatients with anxiety and mood disorders. *Psychological Assessment, 16,* 244–254.

Cannon, W. B. (1929). *Bodily changes in pain, hunger, fear and rage* (2nd ed.). New York: Appleton-Century-Crofts.

Carey, G., & Gottesman, I. I. (1981). Twin and family studies of anxiety, phobic, and obsessive disorders. In D. F. Klein & J. G. Rapkin (Eds.), *Anxiety: New research and changing concepts* (pp. 117–136). New York: Raven Press.

Carter, M. M., & Barlow, D. H. (1995). Learned alarms: The origins of panic. In W. O'Donohue & L. Krasner (Eds.), *Theories of behavior therapy: Exploring behavior changes* (pp. 209–228). Washington, DC: American Psychological Association.

Carton, J. S., & Nowicki, S. (1994). Antecedents of individual differences in locus of control of reinforcement: A critical review. *Genetic, Social, and General Psychology Monographs, 120,* 31–81.

Caspi, A., Sugden, K., Moffitt, T. E., Taylor, A., Craig, I. W., Harrington, H., et al. (2003). Influence of life stress on depression: Moderation by a polymorphism in the 5-HTT gene. *Science, 301,* 386–389.

Chorpita, B. F. (2001). Control and the development of negative emotion. In M. W. Vasey & M. R. Dadds (Eds.), *The developmental psychopathology of anxiety* (pp. 112–142). New York: Oxford University Press.

Chorpita, B. F., & Barlow, D. H. (1998). The development of anxiety: The role of control in the early environment. *Psychological Bulletin, 124,* 3–21.

Chorpita, B. F., Brown, T. A., & Barlow, D. H. (1998). Perceived control as a mediator of family environment in etiological models of childhood anxiety. *Behavior Therapy, 29,* 457–476.

Clark, L. A. (2005). Temperament as a unifying basis for personality and psychopathology, *Journal of Abnormal Psychology, 114,* 505–521.

Clark, L. A., & Watson, D. (1991). Tripartite model of anxiety and depression: Psychometric evidence and taxonomic implications. *Journal of Abnormal Psychology, 100,* 316–336.

Clark, L. A., Watson, D., & Mineka, S. (1994). Temperament, personality and the mood and anxiety disorders. *Journal of Abnormal Psychology, 103,* 103–116.

Cole, D. A., Peeke, L. G., Martin, J. M., Truglio, R., & Seroczynski, A. D. (1998). A longitudinal look at the relation between depression and anxiety in children and adolescents. *Journal of Consulting and Clinical Psychology, 66,* 451–460.

Cole, D. A., & Turner, J. E. (1993). Models of cognitive mediation and moderation in child depression. *Journal of Abnormal Psychology, 102*, 271–281.

Coplan, J. D., Andrew, M. W., Rosenblum, L. A., Owens, M. J., Friedman, S., Gorman, J. M., et al. (1996). Persistent elevations of cerebrospinal fulid concentrations of corticotropin-releasing factor in adult nonhuman primates exposed to early life stressors: Implications for the pathophysiology of mood and anxiety disorders. *Proceedings of the National Academy of Science of the United States of America, 93*, 1619–1623.

Coplan, J. D., Paunica, A. D., & Rosenblum, L. A. (2004). Neuropsychobiology of the variable foraging demand paradigm in nonhuman primates. In J. M. Gorman (Ed.), *Fear and anxiety: The benefits of translational research* (pp. 47–64). Washington, DC: American Psychiatric Press.

Coplan, J. D., Rosenblum, L. A., & Gorman, J. M. (1995). Primate models of anxiety: Longitudinal perspectives. *Psychiatric Clinics of North America, 18*, 727–743.

Coplan, J. D., Trost, R. C., Owens, M. J., Cooper, T. B., Gorman, J. M., Nemeroff, C. B., et al. (1998). Cerebrospinal fluid concentrations of somatostatin and biogenic amines in grown primates reared by mothers exposed to manipulated foraging conditions. *Archives of General Psychiatry, 55*, 473–477.

Craske, M. G. (1999). *Anxiety disorders: Psychological approaches to theory and treatment.* Boulder, CO: Westview Press.

Craske, M. G., Poulton, R., Tsao, J., & Plotkin, D.C.P. (2001). Paths to panic disorder/agoraphobia: An exploratory analysis from age 3 to 21 in an unselected birth cohort. *Journal of the American Academy of Child and Adolescent Psychiatry, 40*, 556–563.

Craske, M. G., & Waters, A. M. (2005). Panic disorder, phobias, and generalized anxiety disorder. *Annual Review of Clinical Psychology, 1*, 197–225.

Dalgleish, T., Taghavi, R., Neshat-Doost, H., Moradi, A., Canterbury, R., & Yule, W. (2003). Patterns of processing bias for emotional information across clinical disorders: A comparison of attention, memory, and prospective cognition in children and adolescents with depression, generalized anxiety, and posttraumatic stress disorder. *Journal of Clinical Child and Adolescent Psychology, 32*, 10–21.

Davis, M., Walker, D. L., & Yee, Y. (1997). Roles of the amygdala and bed nucleus of the stria terminalis in fear and anxiety measured with the acoustic startle reflex: Possible relevance to PTSD. *Annals of the New York Academy of Sciences, 821*, 305–331.

Deacon, B. J., & Valentiner, D. P. (2001). Dimensions of anxiety sensitivity and their relationship to nonclinical panic. *Journal of Psychopathology and Behavioral Assessment, 23*, 25–33.

DuPont, R. L., Rice, D. P., Miller, L. S., Shiraki, S. S., Rowland, C. R., & Harwood, H. J. (1996). Economic costs of anxiety disorders. *Anxiety, 2*, 167–172.

Ehlers, A. (1993). Somatic symptoms and panic attacks: A retrospective study of learning experiences. *Behaviour Research and Therapy, 31*, 269–278.

Eley, T. C. (2001). Contributions of behavioral genetics research: Quantifying genetic, shared environmental and nonshared environmental influences. In M. W. Vasey & M. R. Dadds (Eds.), *The developmental psychopathology of anxiety* (pp. 45–59). New York: Oxford University Press.

Eysenck, H. J. (1961). *The handbook of abnormal psychology.* New York: Basic Books.

Eysenck, H. J. (1981). *A model for personality.* New York: Springer-Verlag.

Fanselow, M. S. (1994). Neural organization of the defensive behavior system responsible for fear. *Psychonomic Bulletin and Review, 1*, 429–438.

Forsyth, J. P., & Eifert, G. H. (1996). Systemic alarms in fear conditioning: I. A reappraisal of what is being conditioned. *Behavior Therapy, 27*, 441–462.

Fuse, T., Forsyth, J. P., Marx, B., Gallup, G. G., & Weaver, S. (2007). Factor structure of the Tonic Immobility Scale in female sexual assault survivors: An exploratory and confirmatory factor analysis. *Journal of Anxiety Disorders. 21*, 265–283.

Fyer, A. J., Mannuzza, S., Chapman, F., Martin, L. Y., & Klein, D. F. (1995). Specificity in familial aggregation of phobic disorders. *Archives of General Psychiatry, 52*, 564–573.

Fyer, A. J., Mannuzza, S., Gallops, M. S., Martin, L. Y., Aaronson, C., Gorman, J. G., et al. (1990). Familial transmission of simple phobias and fears: A preliminary report. *Archives of General Psychiatry, 47*, 252–256.

Gallup, G. G., Jr. (1974). Animal hypnosis: Factual status of a fictional concept. *Psychological Bulletin, 81*, 836–853.

Gershuny, B. S., & Sher, K. J. (1998). The relation between personality and anxiety: Findings from a 3-year prospective study. *Journal of Abnormal Psychology, 107*, 252–262.

Gillespie, C. F., & Nemeroff, C. B. (2007). Corticotropin-releasing factor and the psychobiology of early-life stress. *Current Directions in Psychological Science, 16*, 85–89.

Granger, D. A., Weisz, J. R., & Kauneckis, D. (1994). Neuroendocrine reactivity, internalizing behavior problems, and control-related cognitions in clinic-referred children and adolescents. *Journal of Abnormal Psychology, 103*, 267–276.

Gray, J. A. (1982). *The neuropsychology of anxiety.* New York: Oxford University Press.

Gray, J. A. (1987). *The psychology of fear and stress.* New York: Cambridge University Press.

Gray, J. A. (1991). Fear, panic, and anxiety: What's in a name? *Psychological Inquiry, 2*, 72–96.

Gray, J. A., & McNaughton, N. (1996). The neuropsychology of anxiety: A reprise. In D. A. Hope (Ed.), *Nebraska Symposium on Motivation: Vol. 43. Perspectives on anxiety, panic, and fear: Current theory and research in motivation* (pp. 61–134). Lincoln: University of Nebraska Press.

Greenberg, D. B., Sisitsky, T., Kessler, R. C., Finkelstein, S. N., Berndt, E. R., Davidson, J.R.T., et al. (1999). The economic burden of anxiety disorders in the 1990s. *Journal of Clinical Psychiatry, 60*, 427–435.

Gunnar, M. R., & Fisher, P. A. (2006). Bringing basic research on early experience and stress neurobiology to bear on preventive interventions for neglected and maltreated children. *Development and Psychopathology, 18*, 651–677.

Gunnar, M. R., Larson, M. C., Hertsgaard, L., Harris, M. L., & Brodersen, L. (1992). The stressfulness of separation among nine-month-old infants: Effects of social context variables and infant temperament. *Child Development, 63*, 290–303.

Hedley, L. M., Hoffart, A., & Sexton, H. (2001). The change process in a cognitive-behavioral therapy: Testing a cognitive, a behavioral, and an integrated model of panic disorder with agoraphobia. *Psychotherapy Research, 11*, 401–413.

Heidt, J. M., Marx, B. P., & Forsyth, J. P. (2005). Tonic immobility and childhood sexual abuse: A preliminary report evaluating the sequela of rape-induced paralysis. *Behaviour Research and Therapy, 43*, 1157–1171.

Heim, C., Owens, M. J., Plotsky, P. M., & Nemeroff, C. B. (1997). The role of early adverse life events in the etiology of depression and posttraumatic stress disorder: Focus on corticotropin-releasing factor. *Annals of the New York Academy of Sciences, 821,* 194–207.

Heller, W., Nitschke, J. B., Etienne, M. A., & Miller, G. A. (1997). Patterns of regional brain activity differentiate types of anxiety. *Journal of Abnormal Psychology, 106,* 376–385.

Henry, B., Moffitt, T. E., Caspi, A., Langley, J., & Silva, P. (1994). On the "remembrance of things past": A longitudinal evaluation of the retrospective method. *Psychological Assessment, 6,* 92–101.

Hershberg, S. G., Carlson, G. A., Cantwell, D. P., & Strober, M. (1982). Anxiety and depressive disorders in psychiatrically disturbed children. *Journal of Clinical Psychiatry, 43,* 358–361.

Hettema, J. M., Prescott, C. A., Myers, J. M., Neale, M. C., & Kendler, K. S. (2005). The structure of genetic and environmental risk factors for anxiety disorders in men and women. *Archives of General Psychiatry, 62,* 182–189.

Hirshfeld, D. R., Rosenbaum, J. F., & Biederman, J. (1992). Stable behavioral inhibition and its association with anxiety disorder. *Journal of the American Academy of Child & Adolescent Psychiatry, 31,* 103–111.

Hofmann, S. G. (2005). Perception of control over anxiety mediates the relation between catastrophic thinking and social anxiety in social phobia. *Behaviour Research and Therapy, 43,* 885–895.

Hofmann, S. G., & Barlow, D. H. (1999). The costs of anxiety disorders: Implications for psychosocial interventions. In N. E. Miller & K. M. Magruder (Eds.), *Cost-effectiveness of psychotherapy: A guide for practitioners, researchers, and policymakers* (pp. 224–234). New York: Oxford University Press.

Hofmann, S. G., & Barlow, D. H. (2002). Social phobia (social anxiety disorder). In D. H. Barlow (Ed.), *Anxiety and its disorders: The nature and treatment of anxiety and panic* (2nd ed., pp. 454–476). New York: Guilford Press.

Hudson, J. L., & Rapee, R. M. (2002). Parent-child interactions in clinically anxious children and their siblings. *Journal of Clinical Child and Adolescent Psychology, 31,* 548–555.

Ingram, R. E., & Ritter, J. (2000). Vulnerability to depression: Cognitive reactivity and parental bonding in high-risk individuals. *Journal of Abnormal Psychology, 109,* 588–596.

Insel, T. R., Scanlan, J., Champoux, M., & Suomi, S. J. (1988). Rearing paradigm in a nonhuman primate affects response to beta-CCE challenge. *Psychopharmacology, 96,* 81–86.

Kagan, J. (1989). Temperamental contributions to social behavior. *American Psychologist, 44,* 668–674.

Kagan, J. (1994). *Galen's prophecy.* New York: Basic Books.

Kagan, J., & Snidman, N. (1991). Temperamental factors in human development. *American Psychologist, 46,* 856–862.

Kendler, K. S. (2006). Reflections on the relationship between psychiatric genetics and psychiatric nosology. *American Journal of Psychiatry, 163,* 1138–1146.

Kendler, K. S., Heath, A. C., Martin, N. G., & Eaves, L. J. (1987). Symptoms of anxiety and symptoms of depression: Same genes, different environments? *Archives of General Psychiatry, 44,* 451–457.

Kendler, K. S., Myers, J., & Prescott, C. A. (2002). The etiology of phobias: An evaluation of the stress-diathesis model. *Archives of General Psychiatry, 59,* 242–248.

Kendler, K. S., Neale, M. C., Kessler, R. C., Heath, A. C., & Eaves, L. J. (1992). The genetic epidemiology of phobias in women: The interrelationship of agoraphobia, social phobia, situational phobia, and simple phobia. *Archives of General Psychiatry, 49,* 273–281.

Kendler, K. S., Walters, E. E., Neale, M. C., Kessler, R. C., Heath, A. C., & Eaves, L. J. (1995). The structure of genetic and environmental risk factors for six major psychiatric disorders in women: Phobias, generalized anxiety disorder, panic disorder, bulimia, major depression, and alcoholism. *Archives of General Psychiatry, 52,* 374–382.

Kim, M., Campeau, S., Falls, W. A., & Davis, M. (1993). Infusion of the non-NMDA receptor agonist CNQX into the amygdala blocks the expression of fear-potentiated startle. *Behavioral and Neural Biology, 59,* 5–8.

Kovacs, M., Gatsonis, C., Paulauskas, S. L., & Richards, C. (1989). Depressive disorders in childhood: IV. A longitudinal study of comorbidity with and risk for anxiety disorders. *Archives of General Psychiatry, 46,* 776–782.

Ladd, C. O., Huot, R. L., Thrivikraman, K. V., Nemeroff, C. B., Meaney, M. J., & Plotsky, P. M. (2000). Long-term behavioral and neuroendocrine adaptations to adverse early experience. *Progress in Brain Research, 122,* 81–103.

Le Doux, J. E. (1996). *The emotional brain: The mysterious underpinnings of emotional life.* New York: Simon & Schuster.

Levine, S. (2005). Developmental determinants of sensitivity and resistance to stress. *Psychoneuoendocrinology, 30,* 939–946.

Lieb, R., Wittchen, H. U., Höfler, M., Fuetsch, M., Stein, M. B., & Merikangas, K. R. (2000). Parental psychopathology, parenting styles, and the risk of social phobia in offspring. *Archives of General Psychiatry, 57,* 859–866.

Lovibond, P. F., & Shanks, D. R. (2002). The role of awareness in Pavlovian conditioning: Empirical evidence and theoretical implications. *Journal of Experimental Psychology, 28,* 3–26.

Luten, A. G., Ralph, J. A., & Mineka, S. (1997). Pessimistic attributional style: Is it specific to depression versus anxiety versus negative affect? *Behaviour Research and Therapy, 35,* 703–719.

McCauley, E., Mitchell, J. R., Burke, P. M., & Moss, S. J. (1988). Cognitive attributes of depression in children and adolescents. *Journal of Consulting and Clinical Psychology, 56,* 903–908.

McEwen, B. S., & Magarinos, A. M. (2004). Does stress damage the brain? In J. M. Gorman (Ed.), *Fear and anxiety: The benefits of translational research* (pp. 23–45). Washington, DC: American Psychiatric Press.

McNally, R. J., & Eke, M. (1996). Anxiety, sensitivity, suffocation fear, and breath-holding duration as predictors of response to carbon dioxide challenge. *Journal of Abnormal Psychology, 105,* 146–149.

Mineka, S., Cook, M., & Miller, S. (1984). Fear conditioned with escapable and inescapable shock: Effects of a feedback stimulus. *Journal of Experimental Psychology: Animal Behavior Processes, 10,* 307–323.

Mineka, S., Davidson, M., Cook, M., & Keir, R. (1984). Observational conditioning of snake fear in rhesus monkeys. *Journal of Abnormal Psychology, 93,* 355–372.

Mineka, S., Gunnar, M., & Champoux, M. (1986). Control and early socioemotional development: Infant rhesus monkeys reared in controllable versus uncontrollable environments. *Child Development, 57,* 1241–1256.

Mineka, S., & Kihlstrom, J. (1978). Unpredictable and uncontrollable aversive events. *Journal of Abnormal Psychology, 87,* 256–271.

Mineka, S., Watson, D., & Clark, L. A. (1998). Comorbidity of anxiety and unipolar mood disorders. *Annual Review of Psychology, 49,* 377–412.

Munjack, D. J. (1984). The onset of driving phobias. *Journal of Behavior Therapy and Experimental Psychiatry, 15,* 305–308.

Muris, P., Merckelbach, H., & Meesters, C. (2001). Learning experiences and anxiety sensitivity in normal adolescents. *Journal of Psychopathology and Behavioral Assessment, 23,* 279–283.

Nolen-Hoeksema, S., Girgus, J. S., & Seligman, M. E. (1992). Predictors and consequences of childhood depressive symptoms: A 5-year longitudinal study. *Journal of Abnormal Psychology, 101,* 405–422.

Norton, G. R., Dorward, J., & Cox, B. J. (1986). Factors associated with panic attacks in nonclinical subjects. *Behavior Therapy, 17,* 239–252.

Nunn, G. D. (1988). Concurrent validity between the Nowicki-Strickland Locus of Control Scale and the State-Trait Anxiety Inventory for Children. *Educational and Psychological Measurement, 48,* 435–438.

Ollendick, T. H., Vasey, M. W., & King, N. J. (2001). Operant conditioning influences in childhood anxiety. In M. W. Vasey & M. R. Dadds (Eds.), *The developmental psychopathology of anxiety* (pp. 231–252). New York: Oxford University Press.

Orvaschel, H., Lewinsohn, P. M., & Seeley, J. R. (1995). Continuity of psychopathology in a community sample of adolescents. *Journal of the American Academy of Child and Adolescent Psychiatry, 34,* 1525–1535.

Parkinson, L., & Rachman, S. (1981). The nature of intrusive thoughts. *Advances in Behaviour Research and Therapy, 3,* 101–110.

Plomin, R., De Fries, J. C., McClearn, G. E., & Rutter, M. (1997). *Behavioral genetics: A primer* (3rd ed.). New York: Freeman Press.

Rapee, R. M., Ancis, J. R., & Barlow, D. H. (1988). Emotional reactions to physiological sensations: Panic disorder patients and non-clinical subjects. *Behaviour Research and Therapy, 26,* 265–269.

Rapee, R. M., Craske, M. G., Brown, T. A., & Barlow, D. H. (1996). Measurement of perceived control over anxiety-related events. *Behavior Therapy, 27,* 279–293.

Rapee, R. M., & Melville, L. E. (1997). Recall of family factors in social phobia and panic disorder: Comparison of mother and offspring reports. *Depression and Anxiety, 5,* 7–11.

Rassin, E., & Koster, E. (2003). The correlation between thought-action fusion and religiosity in a normal sample. *Behaviour Research and Therapy, 41,* 361–368.

Reiss, D., Hetherington, M., Plomin, R., Howe, G. W., Simmens, S. J., Henderson, S. H., et al. (1995). Genetic questions for environmental studies: Differential parenting and psychopathology in adolescence. *Archives of General Psychiatry, 52,* 925–936.

Rice, D. P., & Miller, L. S. (1993). The economic burden of mental disorders. *Advances in Health Economics and Health Services Research, 14,* 37–53.

Robinson, J. L., Kagan, J., Reznick, J. S., & Corley, R. (1992). The heritability of inhibited and uninhibited behavior: A twin study. *Developmental Psychology, 28,* 1030–1037.

Roma, P. G., Champoux, M., & Suomi, S. J. (2006). Environmental control, social context, and individual differences in behavioral and cortisol responses to novelty in infant rhesus monkeys. *Child Development, 77,* 118–131.

Rotter, J. B. (1966). Generalized expectancies for internal versus external control of reinforcement. *Psychological Monographs: General and Applied, 80,* 1–28.

Rutter, M., Moffitt, T. E., & Caspi, A. (2006). Gene-environment interplay and psychopathology: Multiple varieties but real effects. *Journal of Child Psychology and Psychiatry, 47,* 226–261.

Salkovskis, P. M., & Campbell, P. (1994). Thought suppression induces intrusion in naturally occurring negative intrusive thoughts. *Behaviour Research and Therapy, 32,* 1–8.

Salkovskis, P., Shafran, R., Rachman, S., & Freeston, M. H. (1999). Multiple pathways to inflated responsibility beliefs in obsessional problems: Possible origins and implications for therapy and research. *Behaviour and Therapy Research, 37,* 1055–1072.

Sapolsky, R. M. (1990). Stress in the wild. *Scientific American, 262,* 116–123.

Sapolsky, R. M., Alberts, S. C., & Altmann, J. (1997). Hypercortisolism associated with social subordinance or social isolation among wild baboons. *Archives of General Psychiatry, 54,* 1137–1143.

Sapolsky, R. M., & Ray, J. C. (1989). Styles of dominance and their endocrine correlates among wild olive baboons (Papio anubis). *American Journal of Primatology, 18,* 1–13.

Schneewind, K. A. (Ed.). (1995). *Impact of family processes on control beliefs.* New York: Cambridge University Press.

Seligman, M.E.P. (1975). *Helplessness: On depression, development and death.* San Francisco: Freeman Press.

Shear, M. K. (1991). The concept of uncontrollability. *Psychological Inquiry, 2,* 88–93.

Siegel, L. J., & Griffin, N. J. (1984). Correlates of depressive symptoms in adolescents. *Journal of Youth and Adolescence, 13,* 475–487.

Siqueland, L., Kendall, P. C., & Steinberg, L. (1996). Anxiety in children: Perceived family environments and observed family interaction. *Journal of Clinical Child Psychology, 25,* 225–237.

Skinner, E. A., Chapman, M., & Baltes, P. B. (1988). Control, means-ends, and agency beliefs: A new conceptualization and its measurement during childhood. *Journal of Personality and Social Psychology, 54,* 117–133.

Skre, I., Onstad, S., Torgersen, S., Lygren, S., & Kringlen, E. (1993). A twin study of DSM–III–R anxiety disorders. *Acta Psychiatrica Scaninavica, 88,* 85–92.

Smoller, J. W., Rosenbaum, J. F., Biederman, J., Kennedy, J., Dai, D., Racette, S. R., et al. (2003). Association of a genetic marker at the corticotropin-releasing hormone locus with behavioral inhibition. *Biological Psychiatry, 54,* 1376–1381.

Smoller, J. W., Yamaki, L. H., Fagerness, J. A., Biederman, J., Racette, S., Laird, N. M., et al. (2005). The corticotropin-releasing hormone gene and behavioral inhibition in children at risk for panic disorder. *Biological Psychiatry, 57,* 1485–1492.

Steketee, G., & Barlow, D. H. (2002). Obsessive-compulsive disorder. In D. H. Barlow, *Anxiety and its disorders: The nature and treatment of anxiety and panic* (2nd ed., pp. 516–550). New York: Guilford Press.

Steketee, G., Quay, S., & White, K. (1991). Religion and guilt in OCD patients. *Journal of Anxiety Disorders, 5,* 359–367.

Sullivan, G. M., Kent, J. M., & Coplan, J. D. (2000). The neurobiology of stress and anxiety. In D. I. Mostofsky & D. H. Barlow (Eds.), *The management of stress and anxiety in medical disorders* (pp. 15–35). Needham Heights, MA: Allyn & Bacon.

Suomi, S. J. (1986). Anxiety-like disorders in young nonhuman primates. In R. Gittelman (Ed.), *Anxiety disorders of childhood* (pp. 1–23). New York: Guilford Press.

Suomi, S. J. (Ed.). (1999). *Attachment in rhesus monkeys.* New York: Guilford Press.

Suomi, S. J. (Ed.). (2000). *A biobehavioral perspective on developmental psychopathology: Excessive aggression and serotonergic dysfunction in monkeys.* Dordrecht, Netherlands: Kluwer Academic Publishers.

Taylor, S., & Rachman, S. J. (1994). Klein's suffocation theory of panic. *Archives of General Psychiatry, 51,* 505–506.

Thayer, J. R., Friedman, G. H., & Borkovec, T. D. (1996). Autonomic characteristics of generalized anxiety disorder and worry. *Society of Biological Psychiatry, 39,* 255–266.

Thompson, R. A. (1998). Early sociopersonality development. In W. Damon (Series Ed.) & N. Eisenberg (Vol. Ed.), *Handbook of child psychology: Vol. 3. Social, emotional, and personality development* (5th ed., pp. 25–104). New York: Wiley.

Torgersen, S. (1983). Genetics of neurosis: The effects of sampling variation upon the twin concordance ration. *British Journal of Psychiatry, 142,* 126–132.

Treit, D., Pesold, C., & Rotzinger, S. (1993). Noninteractive effects of diazepam and amygdaloid lesions in two animal models of anxiety. *Behavioral Neuroscience, 107,* 1099–1105.

Turner, S. M., Beidel, D. C., & Costello, A. (1987). Psychopathology in the offspring of anxiety disorders patients. *Journal of Consulting and Clinical Psychology, 55,* 229–235.

Van Lankveld, J.J.D.M., & van den Hout, M. A. (2004). Increasing neutral distraction inhibits genital but not subject sexual arousal of sexually functional and dysfunctional men. *Archives of Sexual Behavior, 33,* 549–558.

Vujanovic, A. A., Zvolensky, M. J., Gibson, L. E., Lynch, T. R., Leen-Feldner, E. W., Feldner, M. T., et al. (2006). Affect intensity: Association with anxious and fearful responding to bodily sensations. *Journal of Anxiety Disorders, 20,* 192–206.

Watson, D. (2005). Rethinking the mood and anxiety disorders: A quantitative hierarchical model for *DSM–V. Journal of Abnormal Psychology, 114,* 522–536.

Weisz, J. R., & Stipek, D. J. (1982). Competence, contingency, and the development of perceived control. *Human Development, 25,* 250–281.

Wells, A., & Clark, D. M. (1997). SAD: A cognitive approach. In G.C.L. Davey (Ed.), *Phobias: A handbook of theory, research, and treatment* (pp. 3–26). New York: Wiley.

White, K. S., Brown, T. A., Somers, T. J., & Barlow, D. H. (2006). Avoidance behavior in panic disorder: The moderating influence of perceived control. *Behaviour Research and Therapy, 44,* 147–157.

Wilson, K. A., & Hayward, C. (2006). Unique contributions of anxiety sensitivity to avoidance: A prospective study in adolescents. *Behaviour Research and Therapy, 44,* 601–609.

Wittchen, H.-U., & Essau, C. A. (1991). The epidemiology of panic attacks, panic disorder, and agoraphobia. In J. R. Walker, G. R. Norton, & C. A. Ross (Eds.), *Panic disorder and agoraphobia* (pp. 103–149). Monterrey, CA: Brooks/Cole.

Familial and Social Environments in the Etiology and Maintenance of Anxiety Disorders

Jennifer L. Hudson *and* Ronald M. Rapee

Abstract

To understand the variables responsible for the development of anxiety disorders, this chapter reviews data on the influence of both the individual's familial and social environments. Considerably more attention is paid in the literature to understanding the familial rather than the nonfamilial (i.e., social) environment. Nevertheless, data are identified that address the influence not only of parents but also of partners, siblings, peers, and culture. Empirical evidence regarding family and social relationships and treatment outcome for individuals with anxiety disorders is reviewed. Finally, the chapter examines evidence regarding the value of involving the family in the treatment of anxiety disorders.

Keywords: anxiety, cultural factors, environment, etiology, family, parent-child attachment, parenting, peers, social relationship, threat information

Although anxiety disorders have a significant heritable component, genetic factors explain only around 40% of the variance in symptoms and disorder (e.g., Andrews, Stewart, Allen, & Henderson, 1990). Hence, factors in the individual's environment are likely to provide additional understanding of why one vulnerable individual may develop an anxiety disorder and another may not. Mounting attention has been given to understanding critical environments associated with increased risk for anxiety disorders (Manassis, Hudson, Webb, & Albano, 2004). Results from studies of adult twins with anxiety disorders have indicated that it is an individual's specific environment (nonshared) that accounts for the most environmental influence, and variables common to family members (shared environment) account for limited interest in understanding adult anxiety disorder (Jardine, Martin, & Henderson, 1984). In contrast, some studies in children have shown significant influences of the shared environment for separation anxiety disorder and fearfulness (e.g., Lichtenstein & Annas, 2000).

To understand the environmental influences impacting on the development and maintenance of anxiety disorders, gene-environment correlations and interactions must also be considered (Eley & Lau, 2005). Individuals with specific genetic vulnerabilities may elicit particular environments. For example, a child with an anxious temperament may elicit certain behaviors from others in his or her social and familial environment (i.e., an evocative gene-environment correlation). Also, individuals at genetic risk who are exposed to a relevant environmental factor may show an increased morbidity compared to those individuals not exposed to the harmful environment (i.e., gene-environment interaction). A child who is genetically vulnerable to anxiety may show an increased probability of developing anxiety when exposed to encouragement of avoidance compared to a genetically vulnerable child who is not exposed, or to a genetically nonvulnerable child who is exposed to the same encouragement of avoidance. Thus, the impact of the environment needs to be understood through its complex relationships with genes. Although knowledge of these relationships with respect to the anxiety disorders is currently limited, they are becoming of increasing interest to behavior geneticists and should lead to increased insight into the etiology of anxiety disorders.

In attempting to understand the variables in the individual's environment that may be responsible for the development of anxiety disorders, both the familial and social environments are considered. Although significantly more attention has been paid in the literature to understanding the familial rather than the nonfamilial (i.e., social) environment, the literature regarding both of these environments will be reviewed. This chapter will also review the empirical evidence regarding the impact of family and social relationships on treatment outcome for individuals with anxiety disorders and the impact treatment may have on the individual's familial and social worlds. Finally, the chapter will examine the evidence regarding the value of involving the family in the treatment of anxiety disorders.

The Role of the Family in Anxiety Disorders
Parenting

Perhaps the most widely studied facet of the individual's environment is parenting behavior. Given the clearly established link between avoidance of threatening stimuli and the maintenance of anxiety disorders (Barlow, 2002), parenting behaviors that serve to accommodate or enhance avoidant strategies are likely to impact on the maintenance of anxiety disorders and perhaps also contribute to the development of anxiety disorders in individuals with an existing anxious vulnerability (Rapee, 2001). In line with this, an accumulating body of research indicates that there is a significant and positive relationship between the anxiety disorders and parenting that is controlling, overprotective, or lacking in autonomy granting (Gar, Hudson, & Rapee, 2005; McLeod, Wood, & Weisz, 2007). The ultimate consequence of overprotective parenting is that the child avoids potentially threatening situations and is prevented from potentially learning the situation is not as dangerous as predicted and he or she is able to exert some control in the situation.

Despite the significant methodological limitations of much of the research examining parenting, support for the link between anxiety and parental overprotection/control has been surprisingly consistent (Rapee, 1997). Although far less reliable, there is some evidence to suggest that parenting high in

negativity and rejection and low in warmth is also associated with anxiety disorders. The bulk of the research into the relationship between parenting styles and anxiety disorders comes from retrospective studies of anxious adults. Despite the inherent bias in such research design, these studies consistently show that anxious adults are more likely to report higher degrees of overprotection/control and rejection/negativity than nonanxious adults (e.g., Rapee & Melville, 1997). In support of retrospective reports, a recent study of adults with social phobia showed that retrospective accounts of overprotective parenting were related to poorer social interactions during a laboratory task (Taylor & Alden, 2006).

Using samples of clinically anxious children, evidence has accumulated for the relationship between certain parenting behaviors and anxiety disorders (Ginsburg, Siqueland, Masia-Warner, & Hedtke, 2004). In this research observational studies have produced more consistent results than studies using child report and self-report of parenting (Hudson & Rapee, 2001; Muris, Meesters, Schouten, & Hoge, 2004). A significant issue arising with parent or child report of parenting is the potential influence of social desirability. Given the stigma associated with being a "bad parent," parents may be reluctant to endorse items that indicate higher levels of control and negativity. In an attempt to avoid this reporting bias, Hudson and Rapee (2001) observed parents while the child completed a difficult cognitive task. Parents were informed that the researchers were interested in the child's cognitive abilities as opposed to their parenting. The task was specifically designed to elicit overinvolved parenting: parents were given the answers to difficult puzzles but told "only help if the child really needs it." In this study, parents of children with anxiety disorders were more involved and more intrusive in the task than parents of nonclinical children. Similarly, a number of observational tasks have also shown that parents of anxious children were more likely to demonstrate overinvolved and controlling behaviors during interactions with their children (e.g., Dumas, LaFreniere, & Serketich, 1995; Hudson & Rapee, 2001; Mills & Rubin, 1998).

The majority of studies examining the relation between parenting behavior and the anxiety disorders are cross-sectional in design, thus limiting their ability to test causality. A recent longitudinal study has indicated an interaction effect between temperament and parenting over time, providing increased understanding of potential causal effects (Rubin, Burgess, & Hastings, 2002). For children whose mothers demonstrated high levels of intrusive, controlling behaviors and critical comments, toddler's inhibition was associated with reticence at 4 years of age. This relationship was not observed in children of mothers who were not intrusive or critical. In a second study by Rubin and colleagues, parents' lack of encouragement at age 2 failed to predict parent reports of their child's shyness at age 4. However, the reverse was true: parents' reports of their child's shyness at age 2 predicted their lack of encouragement of independence of their child at age 4 (Rubin, Nelson, Hastings, & Asendorpf, 1999). In support of an interaction between parenting and child temperament, Arcus (cited in Kagan, Snidman, Arcus, & Reznick, 1994) showed that the degree to which mothers held their infants when the child did not need help predicted the child's fear approximately a year later, but only for high reactive infants. In combination these studies suggest parental overprotection/control on its own may not be sufficient to cause increased anxiety, but point to the importance of a temperament/parenting interaction in the development of anxiety.

Temperamental factors may not only interact with parent behavior, but may also play a role in eliciting overprotective parenting. Hudson, Doyle, and Gar (2008) observed mothers of anxiety disordered children ($n = 62$) and mothers of nonclinical children ($n = 60$) interacting during a speech preparation task with their own child, with a biologically unrelated child from the same group as their child (i.e., anxious or nonanxious), and with a biologically unrelated child from a different group as their child. For mothers' interactions with unrelated children, mothers were observed to be more involved with anxious children in comparison to nonclinical children. This finding suggests that the child's anxious behaviors influence the degree of maternal overinvolvement. The longitudinal study by Rubin and colleagues (1999) discussed above supports the direction of this effect. An anxious child may in fact elicit increased involvement and help from their environment. This increased help, however, will serve to decrease the child's autonomy and increase avoidance of novel anxiety-provoking situations and ultimately maintain the child's vulnerability to anxiety. These suggestions are consistent with the longitudinal findings of Rubin et al. (2002).

Our discussion on parenting behaviors has so far focused on the constructs of overprotection/control and rejection/negativity. As mentioned earlier, these styles of parenting are likely to be important etiologically because they may reduce the child's

opportunity to approach novel situations and to experience confidence and independence (Hudson & Rapee, 2004; Rapee, 2001). Barrett, Rapee, Dadds, and Ryan (1996) conducted a study clearly demonstrating that parents of anxious children are in fact more likely to support avoidant responding to ambiguously threatening situations. In this study children were asked to respond to a series of hypothetical scenarios that were ambiguously threatening, before and after a discussion of the situation with their parents. Barrett et al. found that for clinically anxious children the likelihood of devising an avoidant strategy to deal with the perceived threat increased significantly after the family discussion. This Familial Enhancement of Avoidant Responding (FEAR) effect was not evident in oppositional or nonclinical children. Despite some support of this effect in further studies (Chorpita & Albano, 1996), enhancement of avoidant responding following parent-child discussion has been shown to be influenced by the context of the assessment (e.g., greater FEAR effect after acceptance into a treatment program), increased maternal distress, and the nature of the situation (evident in socially and not physically ambiguous situations: Shortt et al., 2001). Further, Cobham, Dadds, and Spence (1999) found that parent-child discussions did not increase the child's anxiety or avoidance in a real-life anxiety-provoking situation. One interpretation of these findings is that enhancement of avoidance in anxious children may occur in the context of ambiguously threatening situations rather than situations of clear threat. Familial enhancement of avoidant responding in anxious children is clearly sensitive to context and requires further investigation to understand the situations in which it is most likely to occur and influence anxious responding.

Parental anxiety has also been hypothesized to be important in exacerbating the degree of overprotection/overcontrol and lack of warmth. Despite these theoretical links, the empirical research has only provided partial support for this hypothesis. In support of the link between parental anxiety and overprotection/lack of warmth, Whaley, Pinto, and Sigman (1999) found that anxious mothers showed less autonomy granting, less warmth, and greater criticisms during interactions with their children. In contrast, Moore, Whaley, and Sigman (2004) showed that the presence of child anxiety but not maternal anxiety was associated with autonomy granting and lower warmth. Also, Turner, Beidel, Roberson-Nay, and Tervo (2003) found that although anxious parents reported higher levels of distress and apprehension when their children were engaged in play activities that involved some risk (e.g., climbing ropes), they did not actively inhibit or criticize their children from engaging in play compared to nonanxious mothers. These studies, however, were not fully able to assess the comparative impact of maternal and child anxiety due to the absence of or minimal numbers of anxious mothers with nonanxious children. To more comprehensively assess the unique contributions made by maternal and child anxiety, Gar and Hudson (2008) observed anxious and nonanxious mothers with and without anxious children. The study showed that maternal anxiety was related to maternal warmth and criticism but not maternal overinvolvement. This finding indicates that maternal anxiety may not in fact impact on the parent's degree of control but may be associated with increased criticism and negativity.

In summary, the key parenting variables that have been associated with anxiety disorders are parenting that is (1) overprotective/controlling and lacking in autonomy granting, (2) negative and lacking in warmth, and (3) parenting that enhances the child's avoidance of ambiguously threatening situations. The sparse evidence from longitudinal research indicates that these parenting variables are of most importance in the context of a temperamentally vulnerable child. That is, a child who is born with a more inhibited temperament and is raised in an environment that discourages autonomy has an increased risk of developing an anxiety disorder.

Family Environment

In addition to specific parenting behaviors, there are a number of more general facets of the family environment that may be of interest in understanding the development of anxiety disorders. Despite limited evidence for associations between anxiety and family demographic variables (such as maternal age, family composition, and family size), components of the family environment such as cohesion, interparental conflict, stressful and negative family environments have been associated with an increased risk of anxiety. For example, families of individuals with anxiety disorders report environments that are lower in cohesion, expressiveness, and support (Turner et al., 2003; Arbel & Stravynski, 1991). There is also a strong body of literature that shows a causal link between interparental conflict and increased anxiety symptoms (see Hudson, 2005). Children who witness unresolved, aggressive, and hostile interparental conflict are more likely to demonstrate increased rates of internalizing symptoms. The research in this

area suggests that there is an important role for the child's perceptions of self-blame and threat, as well as the child's coping response and emotional security, in determining the child's response to parental conflict.

In support of a causal link between family environment and anxiety symptoms, Grover, Ginsburg, and Ialongo (2004) conducted a longitudinal study following predominantly African American children from 1st to 7th grade. Children with more negative family environments in grade 1 showed higher levels of anxiety in grade 7. Similarly, Spence, Najman, Bor, O'Callaghan, and Williams (2002) showed that poverty, distressed marital relationship, and marital break-up before the child turned 5 were associated with an increased risk of anxiety and depression at 14 years of age. In another longitudinal study, Shaw, Keenan, Vondra, Delliquadri, and Giovannelli (1997) found that disorganized attachment classification, exposure to childrearing disagreements, and parenting hassles in infancy predicted internalizing symptoms in preschool children. On the whole, the research indicates that children exposed to negative family environments are at greater risk of developing anxiety, although at present this research has been minimal and characterized by lack of construct specificity.

There are also a number of other family-related traumas, such as parental death and intrafamilial sexual abuse, that have been shown to place an individual at risk for increased anxiety (Molnar, Buka, & Kessler, 2001; Stein et al., 1996; Tweed, Schoenbach, George, & Blazer, 1989). In a population sample of female twin pairs, Kendler, Neale, Kessler, Heath, and Eaves (1992) showed an association between the death of a parent before the age of 17 and panic disorder and specific phobia. With regard to sexual abuse, Chaffin, Silovsky, and Vaughn (2005) recently demonstrated a temporal link between the onset and ending of sexual abuse and onset of childhood anxiety disorders. The onset of anxiety disorders was associated with the onset of sexual abuse. Decreases in hazard trajectories were observed when sexual abuse ended. The role of trauma in the development of anxiety disorders is covered more comprehensively elsewhere in this volume (see Chapter 19).

Parent-Child Attachment

The absence of a secure attachment has been repeatedly linked to increased anxiety symptoms (see Gar et al., 2005). For example, Warren and colleagues (1997) assessed attachment (using the

"Strange Situation" procedure) as well as infant temperament and maternal anxiety when infants were 1 year old. At 17 years of age, a structured diagnostic interview was administered to assess for psychological disorders. Children with an insecure ambivalent attachment style at age 1 were significantly more likely to be diagnosed with an anxiety disorder at age 17. Infant attachment predicted later anxiety to a greater degree than maternal anxiety and temperament.

Another study examined the potential interaction between temperament, attachment, and the presence of anxiety disorders by assessing attachment in 3- to 4-year-old behaviorally inhibited and behaviorally uninhibited children (Shamir-Essakow, Ungerer, & Rapee, 2005). Despite the presence of a main effect for attachment and inhibition, no interaction between these two variables was evident after controlling for maternal anxiety. This finding suggests that having either an insecure attachment *or* an inhibited temperament places an individual at risk for anxiety. Interestingly, though, children who were behaviorally inhibited and insecurely attached and had a mother who was also anxious had the highest rates of anxiety symptoms.

Parental Modeling and Transmission of Threat Information

Considerable theoretical and popular perspectives have assumed that part of the development of fears and phobias comes from observation and verbal information about potential dangers from external sources (Cook & Mineka, 1989; Muris, Steerneman, Merckelbach, & Meesters, 1996; Ollendick & King, 1991; Rachman, 1977). Following these suggestions, a number of studies have asked people with phobias to introspect about the origins of their fears (Menzies & Clarke, 1993; Öst & Hugdahl, 1983). This research has consistently identified a proportion of individuals (both adults and children) who attribute onset of their fears to observation of traumatic experiences or verbal information from others about potential dangers. Of course, the limitations of this research are obvious. Even if social learning influences are relevant to the development of fears, they are most likely to be complex, idiosyncratic, and extremely subtle. Hence, it is highly unlikely that individuals would have either the insight or the accurate recollection of these processes. Several other strong criticisms of this research have been raised (Menzies & Clarke, 1994).

Along similar lines, some retrospective research has suggested an association between experience of

panic attacks with reports of early observations of parental sick role behaviors and parental encouragement of offspring sick role behaviors (Ehlers, 1993; Stewart et al., 2001). This research has shown that panic attacks were only associated with parental modeling related specifically to symptoms of arousal and not to other nonarousal symptoms, suggesting some specificity in the relationships. While some of the same criticisms as above can be raised in response to this research, the fact that respondents weren't being asked to report on factors that "caused" their panic attacks means that insight becomes less of an issue. However, this different method does not allow causality to be inferred since the associations may be related to an unmeasured third factor (such as shared parent/child genes).

Several retrospective studies have also found that adults with social phobia report recollections of lower levels of sociability and social interactions among their family of origin than do nonanxious controls or people with panic disorder (Bruch & Heimberg, 1994; Rapee & Melville, 1997). As above, the associative nature of this research does not allow causal conclusions to be distinguished from the effects of a common third factor such as shared genetic influence. However, interesting information on this issue can be found from one of the only adoption studies conducted in the anxiety area. In this study, significant relationships were demonstrated between levels of infants' shyness and the sociability of their adoptive mothers (Daniels & Plomin, 1985). Given that the parties share no common genetic material, at least this very major alternate explanation can be ruled out. Thus, it is possible that restricted social interaction early in life allows the child to acquire information about threat posed by social interactions. Alternately, it may be that lack of social interactions does not afford the habituation to social scrutiny that may be found in nonanxious families.

From a more developmental perspective, there is growing evidence that children's fears can be learned at a very young age via observation of fear in their mother. Gerull and Rapee (2002) conducted a study examining avoidance and approach behavior of infants aged 15–20 months following exposure to a rubber snake or spider paired with either fearful or happy facial expressions modeled by their mothers. After 1- and 10-minute delays, the infants were presented with the stimuli again in the context of neutral facial expressions. Children were more likely to avoid the object on follow-up trials when the stimuli had previously been paired with a fearful expression. The results from this study show the capacity of one single facial expression to impact on the child's avoidance of an object for at least a 10-minute period. Outside the laboratory, repeated exposure to fearful expressions is likely to have a far more lasting effect, particularly if the child is temperamentally inclined to avoid novel stimuli. Some interesting data have shown similar patterns with socially relevant information—infants have been shown to react more fearfully to a stranger after watching their mother react negatively in the presence of that person (de Rosnay, Cooper, Tsigaras, & Murray, 2006). Infants of mothers with social phobia have also been shown to display greater increases in fear of a stranger over time than control infants, but only when their mothers displayed overt anxiety to that stranger (Murray, Cooper, de Rosnay, Pearson, & Sack, in press).

In combination, these studies suggest that the modeling of anxious behavior and verbal instruction of threat information can be associated with increased anxiety in the offspring. It is those individuals with anxious parents who are at greater risk of exposure to parental anxious modeling and verbal instruction than individuals without anxious parents. Findings clearly show that the presence of parental anxiety places an individual at increased risk of anxiety symptoms (Spence et al., 2002). Parent anxiety is likely to have an impact on offspring anxiety not only through genetic pathways but through modeling of anxious behavior and transmission of threat information. For example, an anxious parent may be more likely to provide unrealistic estimates of threat to her child and be more likely to encourage avoidant behavior. In support of this, Shortt, Barrett, Dadds, and Fox (2001) showed that maternal distress significantly predicted the child's increased avoidance of ambiguously threatening situations following family discussions. Similarly, Whaley et al. (1999) found that anxious mothers displayed more negative cognitions (i.e., catastrophizing cognitions) during parent-child interactions compared to nonanxious mothers.

Partner and Sibling Relationships

Despite the significant degree of research examining the impact of parental behavior on the anxiety disorders (e.g., overinvolvement), little research has examined the degree to which other relationships within the family context may impact on the development or maintenance of the anxiety disorders. Nevertheless, siblings and spouse who also display such behaviors when interacting with a vulnerable individual (e.g., overinvolvement, lack of warmth, anxious modeling) may also have a significant impact on the development of anxiety disorder (Hudson & Rapee, 2004). Fox, Barrett, and Shortt (2002) observed clinically anxious children interacting with their siblings during a 5-minute discussion task. Compared to nonclinical children, interactions involving clinically anxious children were characterized by more control (by both children) and less warmth. Also, siblings of anxious children reported significantly higher levels of self-reported conflict with their sibling than nonclinical children.

Some research has emerged examining the role of family members (e.g., spouse and siblings) in the accommodation of obsessive-compulsive disorder (OCD) (Barrett, Healy-Farrell, & March, 2004). For example, Calvocoressi et al. (1995) showed that most primary caregivers accommodated the patient's OCD symptoms in some way. For example, the family may change its routine to accommodate the compulsions or assist the individual in his or her rituals. This accommodation was significantly associated with the patient's symptom severity and functioning, and interestingly also associated with the caregiver's own OCD symptoms. Similarly, Amir, Freshman, and Foa (2000) showed that accommodation of the patient's symptoms was associated with increased anxiety and depression symptoms in the family members.

Aside from the limited research in individuals with OCD, this is a largely underexplored area. Future research is needed to explore the potential role of other family members in the development of anxiety disorders to provide a more complete picture of the family's etiological role in anxiety.

Social Relationships and Anxiety Disorders
Social Rejection and Neglect

There is little investigation into the social interactions of anxious children and even less on anxious adults (Alden & Taylor, 2004). The greatest amount of research has focused on the sheer quantity of social interactions. Findings have indicated that anxious individuals engage in fewer social interactions than do nonclinical controls. The bulk of this research has focused specifically on social phobia since social interactions are clearly part of the central focus of the disorder. Less work has examined the social interactions of children or adults with other anxiety disorders, and it is not yet clear whether deficits in social relationships are relatively limited to social anxiety or shared across the anxiety disorders.

Empirical surveys have shown that both children and adults with anxiety disorders generally have fewer friends than controls (Rapee & Melville, 1997; Whisman, Sheldon, & Goering, 2000). For example, in a cross-sectional survey of almost 5,000 participants, lack of close friendships was associated with generalized anxiety disorder, agoraphobia, and social phobia, as well as with major depression (Whisman et al., 2000). Socially anxious students have also been shown to engage in fewer daily social interactions than low anxious students (Dodge, Heimberg, Nyman, & O'Brien, 1987). This difference also extends to intimate relationships: people with social phobia have shown a reduced likelihood of getting married (Lampe, Slade, Issakidis, & Andrews, 2003; Wittchen & Fehm, 2001). Having never been married does not appear to be a feature of anxiety disorders in general and some surveys have indicated that people with social phobia are less likely to be ever married than people with other anxiety disorders (Magee, Eaton, Wittchen, McGonagle, & Kessler, 1996; Sanderson, Di Nardo, Rapee, & Barlow, 1990). Even when they do marry, high socially anxious people are more likely to marry their first partner than are less socially anxious people (Caspi, Elder, & Bem, 1988). In addition, people with anxiety disorders report a poorer quality of relationship with their spouse than do others (McLeod, 1994; Whisman et al., 2000). Similarly, social anxiety in children has been associated with poorer quality and reduced intimacy in their relationships with close friends (La Greca & Moore, 2005; Vernberg, Abwender, Ewell, & Beery, 1992).

A related and somewhat controversial literature has examined social skills in anxious individuals. Once again, the main focus has been on social phobia. In adults evidence has been mixed (Rapee, 1995). Some empirical studies have failed to demonstrate clear differences between individuals with social phobia and controls on broad indicators of performance while other research has shown some differences, although this research has been mixed with respect to the specific deficits demonstrated (Beidel, Turner, & Dancu, 1985; Rapee & Lim, 1992). In comparisons with other anxiety disorders, the little research suggests that people with social phobia perform somewhat worse, although those with other anxiety disorders perform worse than nonanxious controls, possibly due to heightened social anxiety (Baker & Edelmann, 2002; Stopa & Clark, 1993). While the distinction between social skills and social performance has been difficult to clarify, some research has shown that socially anxious adults can perform perfectly adequately on tasks that are structured or provide clear expectations for performance, but perform worse on tasks where expectations are vague (Alden & Wallace, 1995; Thompson & Rapee, 2002). This suggests that by adulthood people with social phobia have the requisite skills but fail to use them under all circumstances. In contrast, the less extensive literature on social skills in anxious children has indicated poorer skills among socially anxious children (Spence, Donovan, & Brechman-Toussaint, 1999).

Naturally, none of these sources of data can shed light on the causal status of reduced social interactions. Considerable data have indicated that anxious behaviors most likely elicit negative reactions and oversight from others; however, it is still possible that these reactions in turn help to maintain the disorder. Several studies have shown that anxious children are less popular than nonanxious children among their peers (Gazelle & Ladd, 2003; La Greca & Lopez, 1998). Similarly, studies have indicated that anxious behaviors in adulthood are viewed less positively by interaction partners. During interactions, socially anxious individuals are rated as less warm, positive, and interested by their interaction partners (Alden & Wallace, 1995). Overall, this means that shy individuals tend to be perceived as less likeable and others are less likely to want further interaction with them than with others (Alden & Wallace, 1995; Papsdorf & Alden, 1998).

There is some evidence that low peer acceptance among socially anxious children is partly mediated by poor social skills (Greco & Morris, 2005). During specific interactions, socially anxious children have been shown to elicit fewer positive reactions from their interaction partner than do nonanxious peers (Spence et al., 1999). Some research has also shown that socially anxious children have difficulty identifying emotional cues in others (Simonian, Beidel, Turner, Berkes, & Long, 2001) and that their own expression and communication of emotion is limited (Melfsen, Osterlow, & Florin, 2000).

Thus, theoretically, it is likely that socially withdrawn and inhibited behavior may lead to reduced social interaction skills, and that these restricted displays lead to peer rejection. However, it is possible that, in turn, peer rejection and lack of peer interactions leads to increased anxiety, especially social anxiety (Rapee & Spence, 2004). In a longitudinal study of young children from kindergarten to grade 4, Gazelle and Ladd (2003) demonstrated that increases in anxious solitude over time were predicted by higher levels of peer exclusion.

Peer Victimization

In many ways, victimization can be viewed as the extreme example of peer rejection described above. But its overt evaluative and aggressive overtones provide it with some unique properties. A number of studies have shown that experiences of teasing and bullying are associated with increases in anxiety as well as depression (Hawker & Boulton, 2000). To date, most of the research into peer victimization and anxiety has focused on social anxiety (Grills & Ollendick, 2002; Storch & Masia-Warner, 2004). Further research is needed to determine whether other forms of anxiety are also associated with victimization; however, there may be theoretical reasons to expect that peer victimization may be associated relatively specifically with more social forms of anxiety. Indeed, at least one study based on retrospective reports from a clinical population has indicated a greater history of victimization during childhood in adults with social phobia than those without this disorder or with other anxiety disorders (McCabe, Antony, Summerfelt, Liss, & Swinson, 2003). Once again, direction of causality is difficult to determine from the mostly cross-sectional research. However, it is very likely that there is a bidirectional relationship whereby higher levels of anxiety and negative affect lead to victimization, which in turn increases levels of anxiety and/or depression. At least one longitudinal study using a large sample has demonstrated that the direction of relationship is at least partly from victimization to symptoms (Bond, Carlin, Thomas, Rubin, & Patton, 2001). In this study adolescents (aged 13 years) who reported being bullied on at least one occasion demonstrated increases in anxiety and depression 12 months later.

Peers and Social Learning

The impact of anxious modeling is not likely specific to the parent-child relationship. An individual's peers and nonfamilial social environment are also likely to provide important models that shape an individual toward or away from anxiety disorders, over and above the impact of parental modeling. The most experimentally sound demonstrations of the modeling effect comes from landmark research by Mineka, Tomarken, and colleagues in Rhesus monkeys (Tomarken, Cook, & Mineka, 1989). In this research, laboratory-reared monkeys that were naïve to the sight of snakes observed wild-reared monkeys acting either fearfully or passively in the presence of either fear-relevant (e.g., snakes) or fear-irrelevant (e.g., flowers) stimuli. Observation of peers acting fearfully in the presence of fear stimuli resulted in marked increases in fearful behaviors in response to fear-relevant, but not to fear-irrelevant, stimuli.

In humans, some simple demonstrations of anxious modeling using nonfamilial models have been observed. For example, Egliston and Rapee (2002) showed that 15- to 20-month-old toddlers showed fearful reactions and avoidance of a toy snake or spider up to 10 minutes after a stranger had reacted negatively to the same object. However, when the infant's mother had previously reacted positively to that same object, fearful reactions were prevented. This study reinforces the important influence of maternal modeling in shaping the impact of other nonfamilial modeling experiences.

Field, Argyris, and Knowles (2001) conducted a study showing that children's fear beliefs about a novel stimulus (i.e., monster) changed when information about the monster was presented verbally by an adult (teacher or stranger). Fear beliefs about the monster did not change when the information was presented via video or was verbally given by a peer. When children were provided with negative information about the monster, children reported increased fear. Similarly, Field (2006) showed that after hearing negative information about a novel animal, children acquired an attentional bias in the left visual field toward that animal. In combination, these studies show that hearing negative information from adults can impact on fear beliefs and attentional biases.

Partner Support of Inhibition

From a theoretical perspective, friendships may play a maintaining role in disorder through the information they impart. Rapee (Hudson & Rapee, 2004; Rapee, 2001) has suggested that anxious children may associate with other anxious children and this may help to maintain or even exacerbate their anxiety through shared goals, attitudes, and support of avoidant behaviors. Later, these functions may be passed on to the spouse. There is currently little empirical support for these suggestions. A few hints in the literature support the hypothesis that friends will be more similar to each other in levels of anxiety or internalizing than they are to other people (Hogue & Steinberg, 1995; Mariano & Harton, 2005). One recent study by Rubin, Wojslawowicz, Rose-Krasnor, Booth-LaForce, and Burgess (2006) examined mutual best friendships in a sample of shy/withdrawn and control children. The study showed that shy/withdrawn children were more likely to have shy/withdrawn and victimized friends than control children.

A recent study has shown that children higher on internalizing symptoms are more likely than others to extensively and negatively discuss their problems (termed *co-rumination* by the author) (Rose, 2002). Of course, it is possible that co-rumination occurs because more distressed children have more problems to discuss. However, co-rumination was shown to mediate the relationship between gender and internalizing, suggesting the possibility that girls score higher on internalizing at least partly because they co-ruminate (Rose, 2002). From another perspective some recent data have indicated that adolescents with more anxiety symptoms are more likely to engage in conservative and risk-avoidant activities with their friends (Rapee, 2004).

Cultural Influences

There is a growing literature on the role of cultural factors in the expression and possibly the development of anxiety. To date, this literature is still sparse, and as with several previously discussed factors, focuses mostly on social anxiety.

There is a common belief that Eastern (more collectivistic) cultures display higher levels of social reticence and anxiety than do Western (more individualistic) cultures. At least some studies have indicated higher scores on measures of social anxiety in populations from Eastern countries, including Japan and Korea, than those from Western countries, including Europe, North America, and Australia (Heinrichs et al., 2006; Kleinknecht, Dinnel, & Kleinknecht, 1997). In seeming contrast to these findings, there is evidence that the clinical diagnosis of social phobia is less common in Eastern than Western countries (Furmark, 2002). To make sense of these seemingly contrary findings, it has been suggested that more collectivistic cultures may have a more positive appraisal of socially withdrawn behaviors, and as a result, these behaviors may not produce the life interference in these countries that they do in more individualistic cultures (Heinrichs et al., 2006; Rapee & Spence, 2004). Rapee and Spence (2004) have argued that one of the principal influences of culture is to affect the diagnostic threshold of a disorder. In other words, cultural norms may influence psychopathology by determining the level at which symptoms are perceived as problematic in the individual's life. Consistent with this suggestion, some studies have shown that parents in some Asian countries are considerably less distressed by their child's internalizing behaviors relative to externalizing behaviors, whereas the reverse is true in Western countries (Weisz, Suwanlert, Chaiyasit, &

Walter, 1987). Further, in Eastern countries childhood shyness predicts later positive functioning in adolescence (Chen, Rubin, Li, & Li, 1999).

In a similar fashion to social phobia, differences between rates of acute stress disorder and posttraumatic stress disorder (PTSD) have also been found across countries. For example, rates of PTSD following traumatic injury in Switzerland (Schnyder, Moergeli, Klaghofer, & Buddeberg, 2001) are markedly lower than rates reported in Australia (Harvey & Bryant, 1998), England (Murray, Ehlers, & Mayou, 2002), or the United States (Blanchard et al., 1996). Similarly, a number of epidemiological surveys of refugee populations have found varied, and rather low, rates of PTSD (Silove, 1999). These findings suggest that the prevalence and/or expression of PTSD may also vary markedly, depending on the cultural context in which it is assessed.

From a slightly different perspective, the form of anxious expression may vary across cultures. Again, the majority of empirical comparison has focused on social reticence. The *DSM* describes a disorder known as *taijin kyofusho* (TK) in Japanese, which refers to a fear of social interactions due to concern about causing distress to another. In contrast, social phobia is characterized by a fear of negative evaluation of the self by another. Once again, comparisons across cultures are difficult; however, some research has suggested that symptoms of TK are reported more frequently in Japanese and Korean samples than in American or Australian (Kleinknecht et al., 1997). Certainly clinical diagnoses of taijin kyofusho are rarely made in Western countries and are restricted to the occasional case study (Clarvit, Schneier, & Liebowitz, 1996; McNally, Cassiday, & Calamari, 1990).

A few other culture-specific forms of anxiety have been reported (Dobkin de Rios, 1981; Guarnaccia, 1993; Russell, 1989; Sachdev, 1990), but empirical evaluation and comparison to Western notions of anxiety have not been systematic. It is likely that the underlying experience and influences on anxiety are a consistent human characteristic. But the surface expression of anxiety, the subjective experience, and the ways in which anxiety interferes with daily functioning, and hence, becomes a disorder are likely to be at least partly influenced by cultural considerations.

Summary of Familial and Social Factors

The etiological pathways toward the anxiety disorders are likely to be complex. The concepts of both multifinality and equifinality are integral in understanding the complexity and intricacy of causal processes (Cicchetti & Rogosch, 1996). That is, there may be multiple pathways to a given disorder (*equifinality*) and a single pathway may have multiple outcomes (*multifinality*). The presence of a parent who is overprotective may contribute to the development of an anxiety disorder in one child but not another. Likewise, the presence of an anxiety disorder does not necessitate the presence of a parent who is overprotective. A number of both familial and social environmental variables have been identified. Clearly, our knowledge of these intricate pathways, while advancing rapidly, is significantly limited. Future research is needed to further enrich our understanding of these processes.

Relationships and Treatment Outcome

Having discussed the current knowledge of the role of familial and social environments in the development of anxiety disorders, our discussion now shifts to examining the impact of familial and social relationships on the treatment of anxiety disorders. First, we will discuss how family and social relationships may be important in treatment outcome for individuals with anxiety disorders, and conversely, how receiving treatment may improve family and social relationships. Finally, we will examine the evidence regarding the value of involving the family in the treatment of anxiety disorders.

Do Relationships Affect Treatment Outcome?

Stemming from seminal work in schizophrenia treatment, the construct of Expressed Emotion (criticism, hostility, and emotional overinvolvement) has been investigated as a predictor of treatment outcome for a range of psychopathology (e.g., depression: Hooley & Gotlib, 2000). Far less attention has been given to examining EE and treatment outcome in the anxiety disorders and much of this limited research has focussed on OCD and panic disorder/agoraphobia. Nevertheless, on the whole, studies seem to show that individuals from families with high levels of perceived criticism and negative family environments show poorer treatment outcome (Leonard et al., 1993; Renshaw, Chambless, & Steketee, 2003). In a sample of more than 100 patients with OCD or panic disorder with agoraphobia, Chambless and Steketee (1999) showed that higher perceived family criticism and hostility predicted poorer treatment outcome. In this study emotional overinvolvement (EOI) was not associated with treatment outcome, however, EOI and hostility predicted treatment dropout.

In contrast to the main body of findings, some mixed results regarding criticism have emerged. One small study of individuals with agoraphobia showed that at 1–2 year follow-up, individuals with a more critical spouse in fact showed greater improvements (Peter & Hand, 1988). Similarly, Chambless and Steketee (1999) showed that nonhostile criticisms (i.e., expressions of dissatisfaction) predicted positive treatment outcome, suggesting that when criticism is not hostile, it may in fact be motivational. These findings await further replication.

A number of studies have also shown that greater family dysfunction at pretreatment is associated with less treatment change (e.g., Steketee, 1993). The majority of support for this relationship again comes from studies with OCD populations (Barrett, Fox, & Farrell, 2005). For example, Piacentini, Gitow, Jaffar, Graae, and Whitaker (1994) showed children with OCD from families demonstrating high levels of conflict and poorer social functioning did worse in behavioral treatment than families with lower conflict and better social functioning. One study examining children with a range of anxiety disorders demonstrated results consistent with the findings in OCD samples (Crawford & Manassis, 2001). In this study, family dysfunction and parenting stress measured at pretreatment were significantly associated with a poorer response to cognitive behavioral therapy (CBT). Psychosocial adversity was also associated with poorer outcome following treatment.

In studies of adults with anxiety disorders, the link between spousal relationships and treatment outcome has been controversial. While some studies have demonstrated a link between the spousal relationship (satisfaction/communication: e.g., Dewey & Hunsley, 1990; Durham, Allan & Hackett, 1997) and outcome, a number of studies have emerged that fail to show a significant association (Steketee & Shapiro, 1995). In support of the association, Craske, Burton, and Barlow (1989) examined couple satisfaction and communication in a small sample of individuals with agoraphobia with or without panic disorder. Individuals who responded favorably to treatment rated more positive partner communication concerning their fears at pre- and mid-treatment compared to individuals who did not respond to treatment. In contrast, a number of studies have failed to find an association between the marital relationship and an individual's success in CBT, particularly at posttreatment. Steketee and Shapiro (1995) concluded that marital satisfaction may be a more robust predictor of long-term outcome as opposed to posttreatment outcome.

Parental psychopathology has also been shown to be a significant predictor of outcome in the treatment of childhood anxiety disorders (e.g., Southam-Gerow, Kendall, & Weersing, 2001). Berman, Weems, Silverman, & Kurtines (2000) showed that parental symptoms of depression, hostility, and paranoia predicted poor outcome in exposure-based cognitive behavioral treatments for children and adolescents. In this study, parental symptoms were a more robust predictor of outcome for younger compared to older children. Similarly, Cobham, Dadds, and Spence (1998) showed that children with anxious parents receiving standard CBT family treatment had a remission rate of 39% at posttest compared to 82% of children without anxious parents. These findings have been recently replicated in a study by Gar and Hudson (2008), showing that anxious children with anxious mothers (diagnosed using a structured diagnostic interview) were significantly less likely to be free of their primary diagnosis at posttreatment compared to anxious children without anxious mothers.

Taken together, these findings provide preliminary evidence that children from families with greater dysfunction, hostility, and parental psychopathology will show a less favorable response to cognitive behavioral treatments. Adults with anxiety disorders are also likely to respond less positively to treatment when they come from hostile, tense, less communicative family/marital environments. On the other hand, adults who live in a positive, supportive, and communicative environment are more likely to show a favorable treatment response.

Does Treatment Affect Relationships?

In addition to research showing that family relationships impact on the success of treatment for individuals with anxiety disorders, there is research, albeit limited, to suggest that treatment for anxiety disorders has positive effects on the individual's family and social interactions (Mendlowicz and Stein, 2000). Following 16 weeks of psychopharmacological treatment (i.e., imipramine), Mavissakalian, Perel, Talbott-Green, and Sloan (1998) found that patients with moderate to severe panic disorder and agoraphobia showed significant changes in quality of life (particularly social functioning). Cognitive behavioral treatments have also produced positive results regarding familial and social relationships in individuals with panic disorder, OCD, and social phobia (Bystritsky et al., 1999; Moritz et al., 2005). Telch, Schmidt, Jaimez, Jacquin, and Harrington (1995) showed that following CBT, individuals

with panic disorder demonstrated significant improvements in quality of life, including family functioning, marital relationships, functioning in the extended family, and social and leisure activities. In individuals with social phobia, Safren and colleagues (1998) and Eng and colleagues (2005) showed significant improvements on quality of life and life satisfaction measures (including social relationships) following CBT. In these studies, however, posttreatment scores remained significantly lower than normative groups, indicating persistent impairment in relationships.

Studies comparing family functioning pre- and posttreatment have produced mixed results. Barrett, Rapee, Dadds, and Ryan (1996) showed that the negative influence of family discussions on avoidant problem solutions was significantly reduced in children receiving cognitive behavioral therapy compared to waitlist children. In contrast, Crawford and Manassis (2001) showed no significant changes in family functioning based on parent and child report following CBT, although mothers and fathers reported significantly less frustration at the end of treatment. Few studies have in fact observed family interactions pre- and posttreatment to assess changes in the quality of relationships.

Despite targeting child anxiety, family CBT has demonstrated flow on effects to parental psychopathology. Crawford and Manassis (2001) showed that mother-rated psychopathology (as measured by the Brief Symptom Index) showed significant reductions following cognitive behavioral family treatment for the child's anxiety. Cobham et al. (1998) also showed significant reductions in maternal self-reported anxiety (based on the State Trait Anxiety Inventory) for mothers who scored high on anxiety at pretreatment following either standard CBT for anxious youth or standard CBT plus a five-session parent anxiety management training.

Involving the Family in Treatment

Given the potential role of the family in the development and maintenance of anxiety disorders and the impact familial variables have on treatment outcome, involving family members in treatment may lead to enhanced outcomes (Manassis, 2005). The majority of empirical evidence evaluating the benefit of involving family members in treatment comes from studies of children with anxiety disorders (e.g., Mendlowitz et al., 1999; Spence, Donovan, & Brechman-Toussaint, 2000) and from adults with panic disorder/agoraphobia and OCD (Barlow, O'Brien, & Last, 1984; Cerny, Barlow,

Craske, & Himadi, 1987; see also Carter, Turovsky, & Barlow, 1984).

Several child studies have compared family CBT to a waitlist condition, showing that family CBT is superior to waitlist (e.g., Shortt, Barrett, & Fox, 2001). The superiority of family CBT to individual CBT is less clear. Providing the most positive evidence for family involvement, Barrett, Dadds, and Rapee (1996) conducted a randomized controlled trial comparing family CBT (CBT + FAM) to individual CBT and waitlist in a sample of 79 children (aged 7–14 years) diagnosed with a primary diagnosis of GAD, social phobia, or SAD. Parents in the family condition were included in each session and were taught skills to more effectively manage their child's anxiety (e.g., contingency management, communication skills, and problem solving). Despite some inconsistency across time points, enhanced effects were demonstrated for the CBT + FAM condition compared to CBT only. At post-treatment and 12-month follow-up, a significantly greater percentage of children no longer met criteria for their primary diagnosis in the CBT + FAM condition compared to the CBT only and waitlist. Further analysis revealed that this effect was specific to younger children (7–10 years) and female children. Despite these initial promising findings, few studies have been able to demonstrate significant differences between family CBT and individual CBT (e.g., Spence et al., 2000).

A significant limitation for many of these studies is inadequate sample size, and hence, limited power to detect differences between two active conditions. In an attempt to overcome power limitations, a recent meta-analysis combined samples from studies comparing family and individual treatment (Deveney, Baillie, Hudson, & Rapee, 2006). The meta-analysis showed enhanced benefits for family CBT compared to child CBT on diagnostic but not symptom measures. The remission rate of principal anxiety diagnoses was significantly greater in the family CBT group (74%) compared to the child-only CBT group (56%). Barmish and Kendall (2005) reported that although treatments including parents have larger effect sizes, there is insufficient evidence due to the limited numbers of studies and significant variability within studies to conclude with confidence that adding parents as co-clients is uniformly superior.

Research examining the impact of including family members in the treatment of adult anxiety disorders is sparse. Some research has been conducted with OCD and panic disorder, providing inconsistent evidence regarding the value of family involvement in treatment (see Byrne, Carr, & Clark, 2004). In treatment for agoraphobia with panic disorder, Barlow and colleagues have shown that involving the spouse in treatment leads to significantly greater improvements in symptoms compared to no spouse involvement (Barlow, O'Brien, & Last, 1984; Cerny, Barlow, Craske, & Himaldi, 1987). In contrast, other studies have shown no enhanced benefits (Cobb, Mathers, Childs-Clarke, & Blowers, 1984). For example, Emmelkamp et al. (1992) demonstrated that behavioral treatment with or without the individual's partner was effective in reducing agoraphobic symptoms. Interestingly, marital quality did not impact on the effectiveness of the spouse-assisted therapy. In the case of OCD, studies have shown spouse- or family-assisted exposure and response prevention has led to significantly greater improvements in OCD symptoms compared to standard exposure and response prevention (Grunes, Neziroglu, & McKay, 2001; Mehta, 1990).

Overall, the majority of evidence supports the value of family involvement in treatment for the anxiety disorders. When family members are involved, behaviors that may have assisted in developing or, more important, maintaining the anxiety can be addressed. Excluding family members may allow maladaptive patterns to go unchanged, possibly increasing the chance of relapse. On the other hand, involving family members may merely hinder the anxious individual from gaining independence and autonomy. Despite the fact that some (but not all) studies show the quality of the spouse/family relationship does not impact on the value of family involvement, one would expect some family members to be better coaches/therapists than others. Perhaps there may be some, yet to be identified, traits that make one family member more appropriate to assist in the therapy process than others. Future research may provide further insights regarding the circumstances under which family involvement in treatment may be particularly beneficial.

References

Alden, L. E., & Taylor, C. T. (2004). Interpersonal processes in social phobia. *Clinical Psychology Review, 24,* 857–882.

Alden, L. E., & Wallace, S. T. (1995). Social phobia and social appraisal in successful and unsuccessful social interactions. *Behaviour Research and Therapy, 33,* 497–506.

Amir, N., Freshman, M., & Foa, E. B. (2000). Family distress and involvement in relatives of obsessive-compulsive disorder patients. *Journal of Anxiety Disorders, 14,* 209–217.

Andrews, G., Stewart, G., Allen, R., & Henderson, A. S. (1990). The genetics of six neurotic disorders: A twin study. *Journal of Affective Disorders, 19,* 23–29.

Arbel, N., & Stravynski, A. (1991). A retrospective study of separation in the development of adult avoidant personality disorder. *Acta Psychiatrica Scandinavica, 83,* 174–178.

Baker, S. R., & Edelmann, R. J. (2002). Is social phobia related to lack of social skills? Duration of skill-related behaviours and ratings of behavioural adequacy. *British Journal of Clinical Psychology, 41,* 243–257.

Barlow, D. H. (2002). *Anxiety and its disorders: The nature and treatment of anxiety and panic* (2nd ed.). New York: Guilford Press.

Barlow, D. H., O'Brien, G. T., & Last, C. G. (1984). Couples treatment of agoraphobia. *Behavior Therapy. 15,* 41–58.

Barmish, A. J., & Kendall, P. C. (2005). Should parents be co-clients in cognitive-behavioral therapy for anxious youth? *Journal of Clinical Child and Adolescent Psychology, 34,* 569–581.

Barrett, P. M., Dadds, M. R., & Rapee, R. M. (1996). Family treatment of childhood anxiety: A controlled trial. *Journal of Consulting and Clinical Psychology, 64,* 333–342.

Barrett, P. M., Fox, T., & Farrell, L. J. (2005). Parent-child interactions with anxious children and with their siblings: An observational study. *Behaviour Change, 22,* 220–235.

Barrett, P. M., Healy-Farrell, L. M., March, J. S. (2004). Cognitive-behavioral family treatment of childhood obsessive-compulsive disorder: A controlled trial. *Journal of the American Academy of Child and Adolescent Psychiatry, 43,* 46–62.

Barrett, P. M., Rapee, R. M., Dadds, M. M., & Ryan, S. M. (1996). Family enhancement of cognitive style in anxious and aggressive children. *Journal of Abnormal Child Psychology, 24,* 187–203.

Beidel, D. C., Turner, S. M., & Dancu, C. V. (1985). Physiological, cognitive and behavioral aspects of social anxiety. *Behaviour Research and Therapy, 23,* 109–117.

Berman, S. L., Weems, C. F., Silverman, W. K., & Kurtines, W. M. (2000). Predictors of outcome in exposure-based cognitive and behavioral treatments for phobic and anxiety disorders in children. *Behavior Therapy, 31,* 713–731.

Blanchard, E. B., Hickling, E. J., Barton, K. A., Taylor, A. E., Loos, W. R., & Jones Alexander, J. (1996). One-year prospective follow-up of motor vehicle accident victims. *Behaviour Research and Therapy, 34,* 775–786.

Bond, L., Carlin, J. B., Thomas, L., Rubin, K., & Patton, G. (2001). Does bullying cause emotional problems? A prospective study of young teenagers. *British Medical Journal, 323,* 480–484.

Bruch, M. A., & Heimberg, R. G. (1994). Differences in perceptions of parental and personal characteristics between generalized and nongeneralized social phobics. *Journal of Anxiety Disorders, 8,* 155–168.

Byrne, M., Carr, A., & Clark, M. (2004). The efficacy of couple-based interventions for panic disorder with agoraphobia. *Journal of Family Therapy, 26,* 105–125.

Bystritsky, A., Saxena, S., Maidment, R. N., Vapnik, T., Tarlow, G., & Rosen, R. (1999). Quality of life changes among patients with obsessive-compulsive disorder in a partial hospitalization program. *Psychiatric Services, 50,* 412–414.

Calvocoressi, L., Lewis, B., Harris, M., Trufan, S. J., Goodman, W. K., McDougle, C. J., et al. (1995). Family accommodation in obsessive-compulsive disorder. *American Journal of Psychiatry, 152,* 441–443.

Carter, M. M., Turovsky, J., & Barlow, D. H. (1984). Interpersonal relationships in panic disorder with agoraphobia: A review of empirical evidence. *Clinical Psychology: Science and Practice, 1,* 25–34.

Caspi, A., Elder, G. H., Jr., & Bem, D. J. (1988). Moving away from the world: Life-course patterns of shy children. *Developmental Psychology, 24,* 824–831.

Cerny, J. A., Barlow, D. H., Craske, M. G., Himadi, W. G. (1987). Couples treatment of agoraphobia: A two-year follow-up. *Behavior Therapy, 18,* 401–415.

Chaffin, M., Silovsky, J. F., & Vaughn, C. (2005). Temporal concordance of anxiety disorders and child sexual abuse: Implications for direct versus artifactual effects of sexual abuse. *Journal of Clinical Child and Adolescent Psychology, 34,* 210–222.

Chambless, D. L., & Steketee, G. (1999). Expressed emotion and behavior therapy outcome: A prospective study with obsessive-compulsive and agoraphobic outpatients. *Journal of Consulting and Clinical Psychology, 67,* 658–665.

Chen, X., Rubin, K. H., Li, B., & Li, D. (1999). Adolescent outcomes of social functioning in Chinese children. *International Journal of Behavioral Development, 23,* 199–223.

Chorpita, B. F., & Albano, A. M. (1996). Cognitive processing in children: Relation to anxiety and family influences. *Journal of Clinical Child Psychology, 25,* 170–176.

Cicchetti, D., & Rogosch, F. A. (1996). Equifinality and multifinality in developmental psychopathology. *Development and Psychopathology, 8,* 597–600.

Clarvit, S. R., Schneier, F. R., & Liebowitz, M. R. (1996). The offensive subtype of taijin-kyofu-sho in New York City: The phenomenology and treatment of a social anxiety disorder. *Journal of Clinical Psychiatry, 57,* 523–527.

Cobb, J. P., Mathers, A. M., Childs-Clarke, A., & Blowers, C. M. (1984). The spouse as co-therapist in the treatment of agoraphobia. *British Journal of Psychiatry, 144,* 282–287.

Cobham, V. E., Dadds, M. R., & Spence, S. H. (1998). The role of parental anxiety in the treatment of childhood anxiety. *Journal of Consulting and Clinical Psychology, 66,* 893–905.

Cobham, V. E., Dadds, M. R., & Spence, S. H. (1999). Anxious children and their parents: What do they expect? *Journal of Clinical Child Psychology, 28,* 220–231.

Cook, M., & Mineka, S. (1989). Observational conditioning of fear to fear-relevant versus fear-irrelevant stimuli in Rhesus monkeys. *Journal of Abnormal Psychology, 98,* 448–459.

Craske, M. G., Burton, T., & Barlow, D. H. (1989). Relationships among measures of communication, marital satisfaction and exposure during couples treatment of agoraphobia. *Behaviour Research and Therapy, 27,* 131–140.

Crawford, A. M., & Manassis, K. (2001). Familial predictors of treatment outcome in childhood anxiety disorders. *Journal of the American Academy of Child and Adolescent Psychiatry, 40,* 1182–1189.

Daniels, D., & Plomin, R. (1985). Origins of individual differences in infant shyness. *Developmental Psychology, 21,* 118–121.

de Rosnay, M., Cooper, P. J., Tsigaras, N., & Murray, L. (2006). Transmission of social anxiety from mother to infant: An experimental study using a social referencing paradigm. *Behaviour Research and Therapy, 44,* 1165–1175.

Deveney, C., Baillie, A. J., Hudson, J. L., & Rapee, R. M. (2006). *Does CBT with the families of anxious children and adolescents lead to a greater reduction in symptoms and diagnoses of anxiety disorders than CBT for the child or adolescent alone?* Manuscript submitted for publication.

Dewey, D., & Hunsley, J. (1990). The effects of marital adjustment and spouse involvement on the behavioral treatment of agoraphobia: A meta-analytic review. *Anxiety Research, 2,* 69–83.

Dobkin de Rios, M. (1981). Saladerra—a culture-bound misfortune syndrome in the Peruvian Amazon. *Culture, Medicine and Psychiatry, 5,* 193–213.

Dodge, C. S., Heimberg, R. G., Nyman, D., & O'Brien, G. T. (1987). Daily heterosocial interactions of high and low socially anxious college students: A diary study. *Behavior Therapy, 18,* 90–96.

Dumas, J. E., LaFreniere, P. J., & Serketich, W. J. (1995). "Balance of power": A transactional analysis of control in mother-child dyads involving socially competent, aggressive, and anxious children. *Journal of Abnormal Psychology, 104,* 104–113.

Durham, R. C., Allan, T., & Hackett, C. A. (1997). On predicting improvement and relapse in generalized anxiety disorder following psychotherapy. *British Journal of Clinical Psychology, 36,* 101–119.

Egliston, K.-A., & Rapee, R. M. (2005). Inhibition of fear acquisition in toddlers following positive modelling by their mothers. *Behaviour Research and Therapy, 45,* 1871–1882.

Ehlers, A. (1993). Somatic symptoms and panic attacks: A retrospective study of learning experiences. *Behaviour Research and Therapy, 31,* 269–278.

Eley, T. C., & Lau, J.Y.F. (2005). Genetics and the family environment. In J. L. Hudson & R. M. Rapee (Eds.), *Psychopathology and the family* (pp. 3–19). Oxford, England: Elsevier.

Emmelkamp, P. M., van Dyck, R., Bitter, M., Heins, R., Onstein, E. J., & Eisen, B. (1992). Spouse-aided therapy with agoraphobics. *British Journal of Psychiatry, 160,* 51–56.

Eng, W., Coles, M. E., Heimberg, R. G., & Safren, S. A. (2005). Domains of life satisfaction in social anxiety disorder: Relation to symptoms and response to cognitive-behavioral therapy. *Journal of Anxiety Disorders, 19,* 143–156.

Field, A. P. (2006). Watch out for the beast: Fear information and attentional bias in children. *Journal of Clinical Child and Adolescent Psychology, 35,* 431–439.

Field, A. P., Argyris, N. G., & Knowles, K. A. (2001). Who's afraid of the big bad wolf: A prospective paradigm to test Rachman's indirect pathways in children. *Behaviour Research and Therapy, 39,* 1259–1276.

Fox, T. L., Barrett, P. M., & Shortt, A. L. (2002). Sibling relationships of anxious children: A preliminary investigation. *Journal of Clinical Child and Adolescent Psychology, 31,* 375–383.

Furmark, T. (2002). Social phobia: Overview of community surveys. *Acta Psychiatrica Scandinavica, 105,* 84–93.

Gar, N. S., & Hudson, J. L. (2008). *The impact of maternal anxiety on child anxiety treatment outcome.* Manuscript submitted for publication.

Gar, N. S., Hudson, J. L., & Rapee, R. M. (2005). Family factors and the development of anxiety disorders. In J. L. Hudson & R. M. Rapee (Eds.), *Psychopathology and the family* (pp. 125–145). Oxford, England: Elsevier.

Gazelle, H., & Ladd, G. W. (2003). Anxious solitude and peer exclusion: A diathesis-stress model of internalizing trajectories in childhood. *Child Development, 74,* 257–278.

Gerull, F. C., & Rapee, R. M. (2002). Mother knows best: Effects of maternal modelling on the acquisition of fear and avoidance behaviour in toddlers. *Behaviour Research and Therapy, 40,* 279–287.

Ginsburg, G. S., Siqueland, L., Masia-Warner, C., & Hedtke, K. A. (2004). Anxiety disorders in children: Family matters. *Cognitive and Behavioral Practice, 11,* 28–43.

Greco, L. A., & Morris, T. L. (2005). Factors influencing the link between social anxiety and peer acceptance: Contributions of social skills and close friendships during middle childhood. *Behavior Therapy, 36,* 197–205.

Grills, A. E., & Ollendick, T. H. (2002). Peer victimization, global self-worth, and anxiety in middle school children. *Journal of Clinical Child and Adolescent Psychology, 31,* 59–68.

Grover, R. L, Ginsburg, G. S, & Ialongo, N. (2004). Childhood predictors of anxiety symptoms: A longitudinal study. *Child Psychiatry and Human Development, 36,* 133–153.

Grunes, M. S., Neziroglu, F., & McKay, D. (2001). Family involvement in the behavioral treatment of obsessive-compulsive disorder: A preliminary investigation. *Behavior Therapy, 32,* 803–820.

Guarnaccia, P. J. (1993). Ataques de nervios in Puerto Rico: Culture-bound syndrome or popular illness? *Medical Anthropology, 15,* 157–170.

Harvey, A. G., & Bryant, R. A. (1998). Relationship of acute stress disorder and posttraumatic stress disorder following motor vehicle accidents. *Journal of Consulting and Clinical Psychology, 66,* 507–512.

Hawker, D.S.J., & Boulton, M. J. (2000). Twenty years' research on peer victimization and psychosocial maladjustment: A meta-analytic review of cross-sectional studies. *Journal of Child Psychology and Psychiatry, 41,* 441–455.

Heinrichs, N., Rapee, R. M., Alden, L. A., Bögels, S. M., Hofmann, S. G., Oh, K. J., & Sakano, Y. (2006). Cultural differences in perceived social norms and social anxiety. *Behaviour Research and Therapy, 44,* 1187–1197.

Hogue, A., & Steinberg, L. (1995). Homophily of internalized distress in adolescent peer groups. *Developmental Psychology, 31,* 897–906.

Hooley, J. M., & Gotlib, I. H. (2000). A diathesis-stress conceptualization of expressed emotion and clinical outcome. *Applied and Preventive Psychology, 9,* 135–151.

Hudson, J. L. (2005). Interparental conflict, violence and psychopathology. In J. L. Hudson & R. M. Rapee (Eds.), *Psychopathology and the family* (pp. 53–69). Oxford, England: Elsevier.

Hudson, J. L., Doyle, A., & Gar, N. S. (2008). *Child and maternal influence on parenting behavior in clinically anxious children.* Manuscript submitted for publication.

Hudson, J. L., & Rapee, R. M. (2001). Parent-child interactions and anxiety disorders: An observational study. *Behaviour Research and Therapy, 39,* 1411–1427.

Hudson, J. L., & Rapee, R. M. (2004). From anxious temperament to disorder: An etiological model. In R. G. Heimberg, C. L. Turk, & D. S. Mennin (Eds.), *Generalized anxiety disorder: Advances in research and practice* (pp. 51–76). New York: Guilford Press.

Jardine, R., Martin, N. G., & Henderson, A. S. (1984). Genetic covariance between neuroticism and the symptoms of anxiety and depression. *Genetics Epidemiology, 1,* 89–107.

Kagan, J., Snidman, N., Arcus, D., & Reznick, J. S. (1994). *Galen's prophecy: Temperament in human nature.* New York: Basic Books.

Kendler, K. S., Neale, M. C., Kessler, R. C., Heath, A. C., & Eaves, L. J. (1992). Childhood parental loss and adult psychopathology in women: A twin study perspective. *Archives of General Psychiatry, 49,* 109–116.

Kleinknecht, R. A., Dinnel, D. L., & Kleinknecht, E. E. (1997). Cultural factors in social anxiety: A comparison of social phobia symptoms and taijin kyofusho. *Journal of Anxiety Disorders, 11,* 157–177.

La Greca, A. M., & Lopez, N. (1998). Social anxiety among adolescents: Linkages with peer relations and friendships. *Journal of Abnormal Child Psychology, 26,* 83–94.

La Greca, A. M., & Moore, H. H. (2005). Adolescent peer relations, friendships, and romantic relationships: Do they predict social anxiety and depression? *Journal of Clinical Child and Adolescent Psychology, 34,* 49–61.

Lampe, L., Slade, T., Issakidis, C., & Andrews, G. (2003). Social phobia in the Australian National Survey of Mental Health and Well-Being (NSMHWB). *Psychological Medicine, 33,* 637–646.

Leonard, H. L., Swedo, S. E., Lenane, M. C., Rettew, D. C., Hamburger, S. D., Bartko, J. J., et al. (1993). A two to seven year follow-up study of 54 obsessive-compulsive children and adolescents. *Archives of General Psychiatry, 50,* 429–439.

Lichtenstein, P., & Annas, P. (2000). Heritability and prevalence of specific fears and phobias in childhood. *Journal of Child Psychology and Psychiatry and Allied Disciplines, 41,* 927–937.

Magee, W. J., Eaton, W. W., Wittchen, H.-U., McGonagle, K. A., & Kessler, R. C. (1996). Agoraphobia, simple phobia, and social phobia in the national comorbidity survey. *Archives of General Psychiatry, 53,* 159–168.

Manassis, K. (2005). Family involvement in psychotherapy: What's the evidence? In J. L. Hudson & R. M. Rapee (Eds.), *Psychopathology and the family* (pp. 283–300). Oxford, England: Elsevier.

Manassis, K., Hudson, J. L., Webb, A., & Albano, A. M. (2004). Beyond behavioral inhibition: Etiological factors in childhood anxiety. *Cognitive and Behavioral Practice, 11,* 3–12.

Mariano, K. A., & Harton, H. C. (2005). Similarities in aggression, inattention/hyperactivity, depression, and anxiety in middle childhood friendships. *Journal of Social and Clinical Psychology, 24,* 471–496.

Mavissakalian, M. R., Perel, J. M., Talbott-Green, M., & Sloan, C. (1998). Gauging the effectiveness of extended imipramine treatment for panic disorder with agoraphobia. *Biological Psychiatry, 43,* 848–854.

McCabe, R. E., Antony, M. M., Summerfelt, L. J., Liss, A., & Swinson, R. P. (2003). Preliminary examination of the relationship between anxiety disorders in adults and self-reported history of teasing or bullying experiences. *Cognitive Behaviour Therapy, 32,* 187–193.

McLeod, J. D. (1994). Anxiety disorders and marital quality. *Journal of Abnormal Psychology, 103,* 767–776.

McLeod, B. D., Wood, J. J., & Weisz, J. R. (2007). Examining the association between parenting and childhood anxiety: A meta-analysis. *Clinical Psychology Review, 27*(2), 155–172.

McNally, R. J., Cassiday, K. L., & Calamari, J. E. (1990). Taijin-kyofu-sho in a black American woman: Behavioral treatment of a "culture-bound" anxiety disorder. *Journal of Anxiety Disorders, 4,* 83–87.

Mehta, M. (1990). A comparative study of family-based and patient-based behavioural management in obsessive-compulsive disorder. *British Journal of Psychiatry, 157,* 133–135.

Melfsen, S., Osterlow, J., & Florin, I. (2000). Deliberate emotional expressions of socially anxious children and their mothers. *Journal of Anxiety Disorders, 14,* 249–261.

Mendlowicz, M. V., & Stein, M. B. (2000). Quality of life in individuals with anxiety disorders. *American Journal of Psychiatry, 157,* 669–682.

Mendlowitz, S. L., Manassis, K., Bradley, S., Scapillato, D., Miezitis, S., & Shaw, B. F. (1999). Cognitive-behavioral group treatments in childhood anxiety disorders: The role of parental involvement. *Journal of the American Academy of Child and Adolescent Psychiatry, 38,* 1223–1229.

Menzies, R. G., & Clarke, J. C. (1993). The etiology of childhood water phobia. *Behaviour Research and Therapy, 31,* 499–501.

Menzies, R. G., & Clarke, J. C. (1994). Retrospective studies of the origins of phobias: A review. *Anxiety, Stress, and Coping, 7,* 305–318.

Mills, R.S.L., & Rubin, K. H. (1998). Are behavioural and psychological control both differentially associated with childhood aggression and social withdrawal? *Canadian Journal of Behavioural Science, 30,* 132–136.

Molnar, B. E., Buka, S. L., & Kessler, R. C. (2001). Child sexual abuse and subsequent psychopathology: Results from the National Comorbidity Survey. *American Journal of Public Health, 91,* 753–760.

Moore, P. S., Whaley, S. E., & Sigman, M. (2004). Interactions between mothers and children: Impacts of maternal and child anxiety. *Journal of Abnormal Psychology, 113,* 471–476.

Moritz, S., Rufer, M., Fricker, S., Karow, A., Morfeld, M., Jelinek, L., et al. (2005). Quality of life in obsessive-compulsive disorder before and after treatment. *Comprehensive Psychiatry, 46,* 453–459.

Muris, P., Meesters, C., Schouten, E., & Hoge, E. (2004). Effects of perceived control on the relationship between perceived parental rearing behaviors and symptoms of anxiety and depression in nonclinical preadolescents. *Journal of Youth and Adolescence, 33,* 51–58.

Muris, P., Steerneman, P., Merckelbach, H., & Meesters, C. (1996). The role of parental fearfulness and modelling in children's fear. *Behaviour Research and Therapy, 34,* 265–268.

Murray, L., Cooper, P. J., de Rosnay, M., Pearson, J., & Sack, C. (in press). Intergenerational transmission of maternal social anxiety: The role of social referencing processes. *Child Development.*

Murray, J., Ehlers, A., & Mayou, R. A. (2002). Dissociation and post-traumatic stress disorder: Two prospective studies of road traffic accident survivors. *British Journal of Psychiatry, 180,* 363–368.

Ollendick, T. H., & King, N. J. (1991). Origins of childhood fears: An evaluation of Rachman's theory of fear acquisition. *Behaviour Research and Therapy, 29,* 117–123.

Öst, L.-G., & Hugdahl, K. (1983). Acquisition of agoraphobia, mode of onset and anxiety response patterns. *Behaviour Research and Therapy, 21,* 623–631.

Papsdorf, M. P., & Alden, L. (1998). Mediators of social rejection in socially anxious individuals. *Journal of Research in Personality, 32,* 351–369.

Peter, H., & Hand, I. (1988). Patterns of patient-spouse interaction in agoraphobics: Assessment by Camberwell Family Interview and impact on outcome of self-exposure treatment. In I. Hand & H.-U. Wittchen (Eds.), *Panic and phobias: 2. Treatments and variables affecting course and outcome* (pp. 240–251). Berlin: Springer-Verlag.

Piacentini, J., Gitow, A., Jaffar, M., Graae, F., & Whitaker, A. (1994). Outpatient behavioural treatment of child and adolescent obsessive compulsive disorder. *Journal of Anxiety Disorders, 8,* 277–289.

Rachman, S. (1977). The conditioning theory of fear acquisition: A critical examination. *Behaviour Research and Therapy, 15,* 375–387.

Rapee, R. M. (1995). Descriptive psychopathology of social phobia. In R. G. Heimberg, M. R. Liebowitz, D. A. Hope, &

F. R. Schneier (Eds.), *Social phobia: Diagnosis, assessment, and treatment* (pp. 41–66). New York: Guilford Press.

Rapee, R. M. (1997). Potential role of childrearing practices in the development of anxiety and depression. *Clinical Psychology Review, 17,* 47–67.

Rapee, R. M. (2001). The development of generalized anxiety. In M. W. Vasey & M. R. Dadds (Eds.), *The developmental psychopathology of anxiety* (pp. 481–503). New York: Oxford University Press.

Rapee, R. M. (2004, July). *A longitudinal study of risk for anxiety in adolescent girls.* Paper presented at the World Congress of Behavioural and Cognitive Therapies, Kobe, Japan.

Rapee, R. M., & Lim, L. (1992). Discrepancy between self and observer ratings of performance in social phobics. *Journal of Abnormal Psychology, 101,* 727–731.

Rapee, R. M., & Melville, L. F. (1997). Recall of family factors in social phobia and panic disorder: Comparison of mother and offspring reports. *Depression and Anxiety, 5,* 7–11.

Rapee, R. M., & Spence, S. H. (2004). The etiology of social phobia: Empirical evidence and an initial model. *Clinical Psychology Review, 24,* 737–767.

Renshaw, K. D., Chambless, D. L., & Steketee, G. (2003). Perceived criticism predicts severity of anxiety symptoms after behavioral treatment in patients with obsessive-compulsive disorder and panic disorder with agoraphobia. *Journal of Clinical Psychology, 59,* 411–421.

Rose, A. J. (2002). Co-rumination in the friendships of girls and boys. *Child Development, 73,* 1830–1843.

Rubin, K. H., Burgess, K. B., & Hastings, P. D. (2002). Stability and social-behavioral consequences of toddlers' inhibited temperament and parenting behaviors. *Child Development, 73,* 483–495.

Rubin, K. H., Nelson, L. J., Hastings, P., & Asendorpf, J. (1999). The transaction between parents' perceptions of their children's shyness and their parenting styles. *International Journal of Behavioral Development, 23,* 937–957.

Rubin, K. H., Wojslawowicz, J. C., Rose-Krasnor, L., Booth-LaForce, C., & Burgess, K. B. (2006). The best friendships of shy/withdrawn children: Prevalence, stability, and relationship quality. *Journal of Abnormal Child Psychology, 34,* 139–153.

Russell, J. G. (1989). Anxiety disorders in Japan: A review of the Japanese literature on shinkeishitsu and taijin-kyofu-sho. *Culture, Medicine, and Psychiatry, 13,* 391–403.

Sachdev, P. S. (1990). Whakama: Culturally determined behaviour in the New Zealand Maori. *Psychological Medicine, 20,* 433–444.

Safren, S. A., Heimberg, R. G., Brown, E. J., & Holle, C. (1998). Quality of life in social phobia. *Depression and Anxiety, 4,* 126–133.

Sanderson, W. C., Di Nardo, P. A., Rapee, R. M., & Barlow, D. H. (1990). Syndrome co-morbidity in patients diagnosed with a *DSM–III–R* anxiety disorder. *Journal of Abnormal Psychology, 99,* 308–312.

Schnyder, U., Moergeli, H., Klaghofer, R., & Buddeberg, C. (2001). Incidence and prediction of posttraumatic stress disorder symptoms in severely injured accident victims. *American Journal of Psychiatry, 158,* 594–599.

Shamir-Essakow, G., Ungerer, J. A., & Rapee, R. M. (2005). Attachment, behavioural inhibition, and anxiety. *Journal of Abnormal Child Psychology, 33,* 131–143.

Shaw, D. S., Keenan, K., Vondra, J. I., Delliquadri, E., & Giovannelli, J. (1997). Antecedents of preschool children's internalizing problems: A longitudinal study of low-income families. *Journal of the American Academy of Child and Adolescent Psychiatry, 36,* 1760–1767.

Shortt, A. L., Barrett, P. M., Dadds, M. R., & Fox, T. L. (2001). The influence of family and experimental context on cognition in anxious children. *Journal of Abnormal Child Psychology, 29,* 585–598.

Shortt, A. L., Barrett, P. M., & Fox, T. L. (2001). Evaluating the FRIENDS Program: A cognitive-behavioral group treatment for anxious children and their parents. *Journal of Clinical Child Psychology, 30,* 525–535.

Silove, D. (1999). The psychosocial effects of torture, mass human rights violations, and refugee trauma: Toward an integrated conceptual framework. *Journal of Nervous and Mental Disease, 187,* 200–207.

Simonian, S. J., Beidel, D. C., Turner, S. M., Berkes, J. L., & Long, J. H. (2001). Recognition of facial affect by children and adolescents diagnosed with social phobia. *Child Psychiatry and Human Development, 32,* 137–145.

Southam-Gerow, M. A., Kendall, P. C., & Weersing, V. R. (2001). Examining outcome variability: Correlates of treatment response in a child and adolescent anxiety clinic. *Journal of Clinical Child Psychology, 30,* 422–436.

Spence, S. H., Donovan, C., & Brechman-Toussaint, M. (1999). Social skills, social outcomes, and cognitive features of childhood social phobia. *Journal of Abnormal Psychology, 108,* 211–221.

Spence, S. H., Donovan, C., & Brechman-Toussaint, M. (2000). The treatment of childhood social phobia: The effectiveness of a social skills training-based, cognitive-behavioural intervention, with and without parental involvement. *Journal of Child Psychology and Psychiatry and Allied Disciplines, 41,* 713–726.

Spence, S. H., Najman, J. M., Bor, W., O'Callaghan, M. J., & Williams, G. M. (2002). Maternal anxiety and depression, poverty and marital relationship factors during early childhood as predictors of anxiety and depressive symptoms in adolescence. *Journal of Child Psychology and Psychiatry, 43,* 457–469.

Stein, M. B., Walker, J. R., Anderson, G., Hazen, A. L., Ross, C. A., Eldridge, G., et al. (1996). Childhood physical and sexual abuse in patients with anxiety disorders and in a community sample. *American Journal of Psychiatry, 153,* 275–277.

Steketee, G. (1993). Social support and treatment outcome of obsessive-compulsive disorder at 9-month follow-up. *Behavioural Psychotherapy, 21,* 81–95.

Steketee, G., & Shapiro, L. J. (1995). Predicting behavioral treatment outcome for agoraphobia and obsessive compulsive disorder. *Clinical Psychology Review, 15,* 317–346.

Stewart, S. H., Taylor, S., Jang, K. L., Cox, B. J., Watt, M. C., Fedoroff, I. C., et al. (2001). Causal modelling of relations among learning history, anxiety sensitivity, and panic attacks. *Behaviour Research and Therapy, 39,* 443–456.

Stopa, L., & Clark, D. M. (1993). Cognitive processes in social phobia. *Behaviour Research and Therapy, 31,* 255–267.

Storch, E. A., & Masia-Warner, C. (2004). The relationship of peer victimization to social anxiety and loneliness in adolescent females. *Journal of Adolescence, 27,* 351–362.

Taylor, C. T., & Alden, L. E. (2006). Parental overprotection and interpersonal behavior in generalized social phobia. *Behavior Therapy, 37,* 14–24.

Telch, M. J., Schmidt, N. B., Jaimez, T. L., Jacquin, K. M., & Harrington, P. J. (1995). Impact of cognitive-behavioral treatment on quality of life in panic disorder patients. *Journal of Consulting and Clinical Psychology, 63,* 823–830.

Thompson, S., & Rapee, R. M. (2002). The effect of situational structure on the social performance of socially anxious and non-anxious participants. *Journal of Behavior Therapy and Experimental Psychiatry, 33,* 91–102.

Tomarken, A. J., Cook, M., & Mineka, S. (1989). Fear-relevant selective associations and covariation bias. *Journal of Abnormal Psychology, 98,* 381–394.

Turner, S. M., Beidel, D. C., Roberson-Nay, R., & Tervo, K. (2003). Parenting behaviors in parents with anxiety disorders. *Behaviour Research and Therapy, 41,* 541–554.

Tweed, J. L., & Schoenbach, V. J., George, L. K., & Blazer, D. G. (1989). The effects of childhood parental death and divorce on six-month history of anxiety disorders. *British Journal of Psychiatry, 154,* 823–828.

Vernberg, E. M., Abwender, D. A., Ewell, K. K., & Beery, S. H. (1992). Social anxiety and peer relationships in early adolescence: A prospective analysis. *Journal of Clinical Child Psychology, 21,* 189–196.

Warren, S. L., Huston, L., Egeland, B., & Sroufe, L. A. (1997). Child and adolescent anxiety disorders and early attachment. *Journal of the American Academy of Child and Adolescent Psychiatry, 36,* 637–644.

Weisz, J. R., Suwanlert, S., Chaiyasit, W., & Walter, B. R. (1987). Over- and undercontrolled referral problems among children and adolescents from Thailand and the United States: The Wat and Wai of cultural differences. *Journal of Consulting and Clinical Psychology, 55,* 719–726.

Whaley, S. E., Pinto, A., & Sigman, M. (1999). Characterizing interactions between anxious mothers and their children. *Journal of Consulting and Clinical Psychology, 67,* 826–836.

Whisman, M. A., Sheldon, C. T., & Goering, P. (2000). Psychiatric disorders and dissatisfaction with social relationships: Does type of relationship matter? *Journal of Abnormal Psychology, 109,* 803–808.

Wittchen, H.-U., & Fehm, L. (2001). Epidemiology, patterns of comorbidity, and associated disabilities of social phobia. *The Psychiatric Clinics of North America, 24,* 617–641.

15 Personality Factors in the Anxiety Disorders

Jina Pagura, Brian J. Cox *and* Murray W. Enns

Abstract

This chapter describes a theoretical framework based on hierarchical models of personality and the anxiety disorders that is able to reflect both the *DSM–IV* organization of anxiety disorders as a distinct internalizing cluster (separate from mood disorders) as well as the diagnostic specificity within the category of anxiety disorders. The literature examining relationships between higher-order personality dimensions, such as Neuroticism and Extraversion, as well as lower-order facets of personality, such as self-criticism, perfectionism, and anxiety sensitivity, and the anxiety disorders is reviewed. Several mechanisms of interaction between personality factors and anxiety disorders are considered, specifically, vulnerability, scar, and pathoplasty models. Based on this literature, specific personality profiles associated with each anxiety disorder are proposed.

Keywords: anxiety, anxiety sensitivity, extraversion, general anxiety disorder, neuroticism, obsessive-compulsive disorder, panic, perfectionism, phobia, posttraumatic stress disorder, self-criticism

The purpose of this chapter is to discuss the relationships between broad and specific personality dimensions and traits and the anxiety disorders. Rather than providing an exhaustive review, we have chosen to focus on studies examining personality factors that fit within a theoretical framework based on hierarchical models of personality and the anxiety disorders. Personality factors related to anxiety disorders in general as well as personality factors relevant to each anxiety disorder will be discussed with reference to mechanisms through which personality affects the anxiety disorders.

The five-factor model (FFM), which describes a hierarchical organization of personality consisting of five broad dimensions or higher-order factors within which specific facets or lower-order factors are nested, is a widely accepted model of personality that has received significant empirical support and validation (Costa & McCrae, 1992). Although a consensus has been reached within the field that personality consists of five basic dimensions,

debate still exists concerning the definition of each particular dimension (Digman, 1990). The FFM conceptualization of Costa and McCrae (1985) defines the five broad domains of personality as Neuroticism, Extraversion, Agreeableness, Conscientiousness, and Openness and describes six specific facets nested within each. Neuroticism, reflecting proneness to distress or negative affectivity, and Extraversion, reflecting positive emotionality, are the dimensions of the FFM most agreed-upon within the field of personality, while consensus on the dimensions of Agreeableness, Conscientiousness, and Openness remains difficult to reach (see McCrae & John, [1992] for a description of these dimensions). Neuroticism is the higher-order domain of personality most broadly relevant to the anxiety disorders. Various personality traits developed separately from the FFM such as anxiety sensitivity, self-criticism, and perfectionism can be thought of as lower-order traits nested within Neuroticism and these traits form an important addition to the hierarchical model of personality. The hierarchical perspective of the FFM serves as the guiding framework of personality for the current discussion. In this regard, we will refer to the names for the dimensions described above throughout this chapter, although a number of different names have been used for these five dimensions by different personality theorists (Digman, 1990).

The hierarchical model of personality is especially relevant to understanding the Integrative Hierarchical Model of Anxiety and Depression (IHM) (Mineka, Watson, & Clark, 1998), which was developed as an extension of the Tripartite Model (Clark & Watson, 1991) in order to incorporate the hierarchical organization of the anxiety disorders (Zinbarg & Barlow, 1996). The original Tripartite Model suggests that negative affect underlies both depression and anxiety, while anxious arousal is specific to anxiety disorders and low positive affect is specific to depression. Neuroticism and Extraversion are the FFM personality traits representative of the temperamental cores of negative affect and positive affect, respectively, and substantial overlap between each affect and the representative personality domain exists (Clark, Watson, & Mineka, 1994; Watson & Clark, 1997). In examining the structure of anxiety disorders, Zinbarg and Barlow (1996) found support for a model in which the broad dimension of Neuroticism is represented across anxiety disorders and differentiates them from the absence of disorder while associations between lower-order factors and specific anxiety disorders suggested the possibility that these factors may be able to reliably differentiate between anxiety disorders.

Incorporating evidence from the Tripartite Model and the hierarchical structure of anxiety disorders, the IHM posits that specific disorders contain both a shared and unique component, with the main extension of the IHM lying in the recognition of the heterogeneity of the anxiety disorders. Although Neuroticism is hypothesized to relate to all anxiety disorders, the IHM recognizes that it is more strongly related to some disorders, specifically those characterized by pervasive distress. Anxious arousal is not proposed as a characteristic of all anxiety disorders, but instead specific factors are posited to differentiate the anxiety disorders. Mineka and colleagues (1998) did not detail the specific personality factors that may be involved in each anxiety disorder and a goal of this discussion is to suggest potential candidate factors or combinations of factors that may serve this purpose. Guided by these theories of personality and anxiety disorders, this chapter takes a hierarchical approach to personality that is able to reflect both the *DSM–IV* organization of anxiety disorders as a distinct internalizing cluster (separate from mood disorders) as well as the diagnostic specificity within the category of anxiety disorders.

Within this hierarchical model of personality and the anxiety disorders, the roles of specific dimensions and traits are varied and a number of mechanisms exist through which these factors could be associated with anxiety. Three potential models of the effects of personality on anxiety disorders are especially relevant to the current discussion (Clark, Watson, & Mineka, 1994). First, numerous models reflecting vulnerability hypotheses have been proposed. These models posit that personality traits act as vulnerability factors for the subsequent development of disorders, thus playing a causal role in the development of the disorder. The ideal test of the vulnerability model would require prospective, longitudinal methodologies. However, studies of this nature are expensive and difficult to conduct. Second, the pathoplasty model posits that personality factors affect the course or expression of the disorder. Instead of directly affecting the development of the disorder, this approach suggests that personality factors result in variations in a given disorder or in the expression of symptoms between individuals. Finally, the scar model asserts that disorders directly affect personality and personality traits change as a consequence of mental disorder.

All three models have been examined in the anxiety disorders, although most studies are cross-sectional and reveal only associations (which are not necessarily causal) between personality factors and the anxiety disorders. These results are difficult to interpret in that it cannot be determined whether these personality factors represent a vulnerability to the given disorder, a temporary consequence of the disorder, or a change in personality due to the disorder. Although not the ideal test of any of the models discussed, these studies still provide important information relevant to the discussion of personality factors in the anxiety disorders. Longitudinal studies that are able to examine the vulnerability model have been conducted and have yielded important evidence that personality can act as a vulnerability factor for anxiety disorders, but these studies are rare compared to other research designs. In addition, relatively little research has been devoted to specifically examining the patho-plasty and scar models. Focusing on the mechanisms through which personality affects anxiety disorders is important for both treatment and research. Further study needs to be devoted to understanding these mechanisms of action and increased understanding will have the potential to improve subsequent interventions.

Research has supported some of the assertions of the Tripartite Model in relation to anxiety disorders, although it is evident from the literature and IHM that additional factors must be considered. Numerous studies have found support for the role of Neuroticism in both mood and anxiety disorders in a variety of samples (Norton, Sexton, Walker, & Norton, 2005; Sexton, Norton, Walker, & Norton, 2003; Trull & Sher, 1994; Watson, Gamez, & Simms, 2005; Weinstock & Whisman, 2006; Zinbarg & Barlow, 1996). Although low Extraversion was initially posited as specific to depression, a number of studies have found low Extraversion to be associated with some anxiety disorders as well (Bienvenu et al., 2001b; Brown, Chorpita, & Barlow, 1998; Trull & Sher, 1994; Watson et al., 2005). Trull and Sher (1994) conducted a study in a large nonclinical sample of young adults examining associations between Axis I disorders and the FFM. Individuals with any anxiety disorder (of agoraphobia, social phobia, posttraumatic stress disorder, and specific phobia) were characterized by significantly higher Neuroticism and Openness, as well as lower Extraversion, Agreeableness, and Conscientiousness scores than those without an anxiety disorder. Further, these authors found that some personality scales showed differential sensitivity for specific disorders. For example, Neuroticism and Extraversion were significantly more sensitive to a diagnosis of social phobia while Agreeableness was less sensitive. Other studies have also found that, although Neuroticism appears to relate to all anxiety disorders, it may be more strongly related to disorders that are characterized by more distress, such as panic disorder and social phobia, and less strongly related to disorders not primarily characterized by distress, such as specific phobia (Bienvenu et al., 2001b; Mineka et al., 1998; Watson et al., 2005; Weinstock & Whisman, 2006). Finally, research suggests that anxious arousal has a less important role in the anxiety disorders than originally proposed. Instead of underlying all anxiety disorders, anxious arousal appears to have a specific role in panic disorder (Brown et al., 1998). These studies examined variations in broad dimensions of personality; however,

as the hierarchical perspective suggests, the lower-order traits may be more useful in distinguishing specific disorders. We now turn to a more detailed examination of personality factors related to specific anxiety disorders.

Panic Disorder

The evolution from the Tripartite Model to the IHM occurred in part as a result of recognition that the anxious arousal component of the Tripartite Model appeared to have a more important role in panic disorder, instead of underlying all anxiety disorders as originally proposed (Brown et al., 1998; Mineka et al., 1998). It appeared that the other anxiety disorders were related to other aspects of anxiety than anxious arousal. An important construct that has the potential to add significantly to the IHM in terms of specific components related to both panic disorder and the other anxiety disorders is anxiety sensitivity (AS).

Anxiety sensitivity refers to a fear of anxiety, specifically a fear of anxiety-related sensations (Reiss & McNally, 1985). Individuals high in AS interpret bodily sensations indicative of anxiety as threatening or dangerous, instead of interpreting them as normal, passing sensations. Although not directly represented in the initial conceptualization of the FFM, AS likely represents a lower-order trait nested within one of the higher-order dimensions of personality. A review of studies examining the role of AS in the structure of personality (Lilienfeld, 1999) suggested that, although preliminary relationships have been demonstrated between AS and a number of personality dimensions, AS might be best conceptualized within the FFM as a lower-order trait nested within Neuroticism. It has been shown to be moderately to highly related to this higher-order dimension and also to possess incremental validity over this dimension, supporting its conceptualization as a lower-order trait nested within Neuroticism (Cox, Borger, Taylor, Fuentes, & Ross, 1999).

An abundance of research also suggests that the construct of AS comprises at least three lower-order facets described as fear of somatic symptoms (physical concerns), fear of cognitive symptoms (mental incapacitation), and fear of publicly observable symptoms (social concerns) (Cox, 1996; Taylor, 1996; Zinbarg, Barlow, & Brown, 1997). As these facets are even more specific than AS, they have the potential to demonstrate further specificity within the IHM.

Although most research examining the role of personality in panic disorder centers on the role of

AS, a number of studies have examined the role of the higher-order dimensions and lower-order facets of the FFM. Neuroticism has been associated with panic disorder in a number of samples (Bienvenu et al., 2004; Weinstock & Whisman, 2006). Further at a lower-order level, some studies have revealed associations between the low positive emotions facet of Extraversion (Bienvenu et al., 2004) as well as the competence facet of Conscientiousness (Bienvenu et al., 2001b).

Much research has been devoted to the study of AS in panic disorder using a number of methodologies. One laboratory method known as the biological challenge paradigm has often been used to investigate the role of AS in panic. This paradigm involves exposing participants to an anxiety-inducing biological manipulation (e.g., hyperventilation) and studying the effects of AS on subsequent panic symptoms and affective responding. In nonclinical samples, AS has been shown to be associated with greater anxiety and panic symptoms following hyperventilation challenge (Donnell & McNally, 1989), caffeine consumption challenge (Telch, Silverman, & Schmidt, 1996), and carbon dioxide inhalation (Harrington, Schmidt, & Telch, 1996; Schmidt & Mallott, 2006). Importantly, these associations have been demonstrated to be independent of a history of panic (Donnell & McNally, 1989; Telch et al., 1996), suggesting that the association between AS and anxiety does not occur only among those who have experienced panic attacks. This suggests that AS may have a causal role in the development of panic attacks, although further longitudinal research is necessary.

A number of prospective studies utilizing questionnaires have also been undertaken in order to examine the role of AS in panic. A 4-year prospective study in which a large sample of high school students were assessed at yearly interviews revealed that individuals who experienced panic attacks had higher levels of AS throughout the study compared to those who did not experience panic, and further, adolescents with stable high or escalating levels of AS were significantly more likely to experience a panic attack than adolescents with stable low levels of AS (Weems, Hayward, Killen, & Taylor, 2002). A 3-year prospective study of college students found AS scores to be associated with the frequency and intensity of panic attacks at follow-up (Maller & Reiss, 1992). Even after adjusting for state and trait anxiety, AS scores were associated with the occurrence of panic attacks at follow-up. Subjects with high AS in this study were five times more likely to

have an anxiety disorder during the follow-up period than those with low AS.

Three 5-week prospective studies of large samples of cadets in the U.S. Air Force followed over the highly stressful period of military basic training have provided strong evidence for AS as a vulnerability factor in the development of anxiety and panic attacks (Schmidt & Lerew, 2002; Schmidt, Lerew, & Jackson, 1997; Schmidt, Lerew, & Jackson, 1999). In all three studies, AS predicted the development of spontaneous panic attacks after controlling for history of panic attacks and trait anxiety. These studies also demonstrated that AS predicts anxiety and depression symptomatology after controlling for the baseline level of anxiety and depression, trait anxiety, functional impairment due to anxiety, and disability.

A recent study examining the ability of AS to predict future anxiety symptoms and panic attacks found that AS was able to predict the development of spontaneous panic attacks among individuals with no history of panic, after controlling for trait anxiety (Schmidt, Zvolensky, & Maner, 2006). Furthermore, AS was found to predict the incidence of both anxiety disorder and Axis I diagnoses among individuals with no history of Axis I diagnoses, after controlling for trait anxiety. In sum, although the available literature shows clear evidence in support of the role of AS in vulnerability to panic symptomatology, studies suggest that AS may function as a general risk factor predisposing individuals to all Axis I psychopathology.

Cross-sectional questionnaire studies have also demonstrated important relationships between AS and panic symptomatology in children, adolescents, college students, and patients with anxiety disorders (Calamari et al., 2001; Lau, Calamari, & Waraczynski, 1996). Further questionnaire studies in college student samples have demonstrated the importance of AS in both spontaneous and cued panic attacks. Significantly higher proportions of individuals in a high AS group compared to medium and low AS groups reported spontaneous panic attacks (Donnell & McNally, 1990) and were classified as at least moderately anticipating future spontaneous panic attacks (Cox, Endler, Norton, & Swinson, 1991). Finally, in a structural equation modeling analysis of university students, AS directly influenced panic frequency (Stewart et al., 2001).

Anxiety sensitivity clearly has an important relationship with panic in nonclinical populations across age, suggesting that AS likely plays an important role in panic disorder. Elevated levels of AS have been found in patients with panic disorder compared to patients with an anxiety disorder other than panic disorder (Taylor, Koch, & Crockett, 1991; Taylor, Koch, & McNally, 1992). The items that differentiated patients with panic disorder and those with other anxiety disorders represented the facets of fear of physical symptoms and fear of cognitive symptoms and were relevant to the "catastrophic misinterpretation of sensations and experiences associated with anxiety" (Taylor et al., 1991, p. 305). These findings suggest the importance of these facets of AS in panic disorder and demonstrate the potential specificity of the facets of AS to differentiate anxiety disorders.

The importance of examining the lower-order facets of AS with respect to panic symptomatology and panic disorder has been further demonstrated both in factor analytic studies and in the development of an expanded measure of AS (Taylor & Cox, 1998). A prospective study with three annual follow-ups conducted in a large sample of students from public schools in California found important effects of the facets of AS (Hayward, Killen, Kraemer, & Taylor, 2000). Negative affectivity and AS were able to predict onset of 4-symptom panic attacks when entered simultaneously after adjusting for past or concurrent depression. When all facets of AS were entered simultaneously after controlling for past or concurrent depression, only the AS facet fear of somatic symptoms predicted onset of 4-symptom panic attacks. Specificity for AS in panic symptomatology was demonstrated, as none of the factors of AS, nor the AS total score, were able to predict depression onset after controlling for the effects of past or concurrent panic attacks. Similarly, Schmidt, Zvolensky, and Maner (2006) found that only the fear of somatic symptoms facet was able to predict spontaneous panic attacks after controlling for trait anxiety among individuals with no history of panic attacks.

Schmidt and colleagues (Schmidt, Lerew, & Joiner, 1998; Schmidt et al., 1999) have also examined the role of AS facets in prospective studies of cadets involved in basic training. Using a covariance analytic strategy wherein baseline and follow-up levels of anxiety and depression are taken into account (rather than using change scores), both of Schmidt and colleagues' studies found the facet of fear of somatic symptoms to relate specifically to anxiety, but not depression or hopelessness. The roles of the other two facets of AS in anxiety appear to be less straightforward. Fear of publicly observable symptoms was significantly related to anxiety in one study (Schmidt et al., 1998), although this

finding was not replicated in the second study (Schmidt et al., 1999). Additionally, although the facet of fear of cognitive symptoms was significantly related to anxiety in both studies, it was also related to depression in one study (Schmidt et al., 1998). The authors suggest that fear of cognitive symptoms is nonspecific and is likely to account for the association between AS and depression.

A recent cross-sectional study examining the role of AS facets in anxiety and depression in a large community sample of women revealed different results (McWilliams, Becker, Margraf, Clara, & Vriends, 2007). After adjusting for Neuroticism, only the fear of cognitive symptoms facet was significantly associated with a diagnosis of panic disorder. In sum, studies using nonclinical samples clearly demonstrate an important role of the AS facet of fear of somatic symptoms in panic and anxiety symptomatology. The role of the other two facets is less clear and requires further study.

Similar findings have also been reported in studies examining facets of AS using clinical samples of patients with anxiety disorders (Brown, Smits, Powers, & Telch, 2003; Zinbarg, Brown, Barlow, & Rapee, 2001). The lack of important associations observed between AS facets fear of cognitive symptoms and fear of publicly observable symptoms and panic symptomatology suggests that neither of these facets play a central role in panic disorder (Zinbarg et al., 2001). The importance of AS and AS facets was, however, clearly demonstrated in a study directly comparing these traits in samples of patients with major depressive disorder and panic disorder (Cox, Enns, Walker, Kjernisted, & Pidlubny, 2001). In a hierarchical logistic regression analysis that adjusted for Neuroticism, Extraversion, and anxious arousal, AS was a significant predictor of panic disorder. Further, in an identical regression that included the lower-order facets of AS as predictors, only the facet of fear of somatic symptoms emerged as a significant predictor of panic disorder. It appears that the lower-order facets of AS may be important in determining specificity of anxiety disorders, in particular, panic disorder, in the IHM.

Few studies have been devoted to testing other models through which personality factors can influence panic disorder, although a few preliminary studies show evidence that the relationship between AS and this disorder might function through pathoplasty or scar mechanisms. In a one-year prospective study, AS was related to panic frequency, Axis I comorbidity, panic attack maintenance, and symptom relapse, suggesting a pathoplastic role of AS (Ehlers,

1995). A rare study dedicated specifically to testing a scar model of AS using a sample of cadets assessed over basic training did find support for the scar model, in that panic attacks led to increased levels of total AS, fear of somatic symptoms and fear of cognitive symptoms at two short-term follow-ups, after controlling for baseline levels (Schmidt, Lerew, & Joiner, 2000). In contrast, a 4-year prospective study of high school students did not find support for the scar model with respect to panic attacks and AS (Weems et al., 2002), suggesting that the scar effect of AS may not be lasting.

Another lower-order factor likely nested within Neuroticism that may show improved specificity in models such as the IHM is perfectionism. This trait refers to a desire to attain perfection evidenced by high personal standards of performance that are associated with overly critical self-evaluation (Frost, Marten, Lahart, & Rosenblate, 1990). Two groups of investigators independently developed multidimensional measures of the construct of perfectionism. Frost and colleagues (1990) hypothesized a construct of perfectionism composed of six dimensions known as concern over mistakes, doubts about actions, personal standards, parental criticism, parental expectations, and organization, and developed a corresponding Multidimensional Perfectionism Scale (F-MPS). Alternatively, Hewitt and Flett (1991) hypothesized a construct composed of three dimensions known as self-oriented perfectionism, other-oriented perfectionism, and socially prescribed perfectionism. Hewitt and Flett's measure of perfectionism is also known as the Multidimensional Perfectionism Scale (H-MPS). Researchers have examined perfectionism in relation to anxiety disorders using both of these conceptualizations, and it appears that perfectionism and its dimensions can offer valuable information to the IHM.

Perfectionism has mostly been studied in relation to social anxiety disorder and obsessive-compulsive disorder (OCD). However, a number of recent studies have examined the role of perfectionism in panic disorder. Two studies showed F-MPS scores to be significantly elevated among patients with panic disorder with or without agoraphobia relative to community controls (Antony, Purdon, Huta, & Swinson, 1998; Frost & Steketee, 1997). Further studies have indicated that perfectionism may be more related to agoraphobia among those with panic disorder rather than panic disorder itself (Iketani et al., 2002b, 2002a). Finally, Frost and Steketee (1997) found patients with panic disorder with agoraphobia to score significantly higher on concern over mistakes than community control participants, although they did not differ significantly from patients with OCD on this dimension. These results suggest that, although perfectionism may not have a significant role in panic disorder compared to other anxiety disorders, it appears to be important in agoraphobia among individuals with panic disorder. It may be that perfectionism has a pathoplastic role in determining the expression of a more severe form of panic disorder, that which includes agoraphobia, and this is an area that merits further research.

Social Anxiety Disorder (Social Phobia)

Another important factor that contributed to the revision of the Tripartite Model was the recognition that low positive affect or Extraversion was not specifically related to depression (Mineka et al., 1998). Using structural equation modeling, Brown and colleagues (1998) found that positive affectivity contributed directly (negatively) to depression as well as to social phobia. This association was of the same magnitude after controlling for negative affect, that is, low positive affect was directly related to both depression and social phobia. Another study found individuals with social phobia to be characterized by higher levels of Neuroticism and lower levels of Extraversion, compared to those without this diagnosis (Trull & Sher, 1994). The relationship between social anxiety and low levels of Extraversion has also been demonstrated in nonclinical samples of college students (Darvill, Johnson, & Danko, 1992; Norton, Cox, Hewitt, & McLoed, 1997) as well as large community samples (Bienvenu et al., 2001b; Bienvenu et al., 2004), wherein social anxiety shows large negative associations with Extraversion. Extraversion also accounted for variance in the prediction of both generalized and nongeneralized social anxiety among college students (Norton et al., 1997) and was the only higher-order personality dimension significantly associated with social phobia after controlling for gender and general distress (Trull & Sher, 1994).

Similar to low Extraversion (Introversion) is the construct of shyness. Shyness appears to be an important personality factor that has the potential to act as a vulnerability factor for the development of social phobia. Although relying solely on cross-sectional methodologies, researchers have demonstrated relationships between the severity of shyness and likelihood of social phobia in a large sample of college students (Chavira, Stein, & Malcarne, 2002) and the general population (Cox, MacPherson, & Enns, 2005).

Another specific personality factor that has been studied in relation to social phobia is self-criticism. This personality trait is characterized by persistent and harsh self-scrutiny and self-evaluation and was originally conceptualized as a vulnerability factor for the development of depression (Blatt, 1974). Within the FFM, self-criticism can be conceptualized as a lower-order trait nested within Neuroticism. Since Neuroticism shows broad associations with many different mental disorders, the examination of lower-order traits such as self-criticism might offer increased specificity and predictive validity. Although there is a broad literature on self-criticism and depression, only recently have researchers begun to consider the potential relationships between self-criticism and the anxiety disorders.

Using a large nationally representative sample of the U.S. population, Cox, Fleet, and Stein (2004) found that self-criticism was significantly elevated in individuals with current social phobia and those with a past history of social phobia compared to those with no psychiatric disorder. Further, self-criticism remained significantly associated with lifetime social phobia after controlling for current emotional distress, Neuroticism, and lifetime histories of mood, anxiety, and substance use disorders. In another study, although self-criticism was elevated in patients with major depression, the highest levels of self-criticism were observed in patients with comorbid social phobia and depression (Cox et al., 2000). Comparing the scores of the social phobia patients to a previously assessed group of panic disorder patients also demonstrated that the social phobia patients had a level of self-criticism almost three times higher than the panic disorder patients, demonstrating the possibility for self-criticism to show specificity among anxiety disorders (Cox et al., 2000). Finally, a cognitive behavioral group therapy study assessed social phobia outpatients before and after treatment and found that self-criticism was associated with social phobia symptom severity prior to treatment, even after controlling for depressed mood (Cox, Walker, Enns, & Karpinski, 2002). Additionally, the change in levels of self-criticism over the course of treatment was significantly associated with improvement in social phobia symptoms.

Perfectionism has also been examined in social phobia through several cross-sectional studies. When compared to controls, patients with social phobia tend to score higher on the F-MPS dimensions of concern over mistakes, doubts about actions, and parental criticism (Juster et al., 1996; Lundh & Öst, 1996; Saboonchi & Lundh, 1997;

Saboonchi, Lundh, & Öst, 1999). Patients with social phobia have also been shown to score higher than controls on socially prescribed perfectionism (Bieling & Alden, 1997), while the presence of social anxiety among undergraduate students has also been associated with this construct (Alden, Bieling, & Wallace, 1994). Important differences in perfectionism have also been elucidated between patients with social phobia and those with other anxiety disorders. Antony and colleagues (1998) found patients with social phobia to score significantly higher on the concern over mistakes, doubts about actions, and parental criticism dimensions of the F-MPS as well as the socially prescribed perfectionism dimension of the H-MPS relative to groups of patients with panic disorder, OCD, and specific phobia. Another study also found that patients with social phobia scored higher than panic disorder patients on concern over mistakes and doubts about actions (Saboonchi et al., 1999). Future longitudinal studies are needed to clarify the role of these dimensions of perfectionism in social phobia, but, nonetheless, specific dimensions of perfectionism appear to be important for the conceptualization of social phobia within the IHM.

Research on AS in relation to social phobia is somewhat limited. Although AS has been found to be elevated in patients social phobia (Taylor et al., 1992), relatively few studies on AS in social phobia have been conducted. In a study where social phobia patients were exposed to a social threat Stroop task and a behavior test where subjects were exposed to a simulation of a personally relevant feared situation, AS was found to be an important predictor of anxious reactions (Orsillo, Lilienfeld, & Heimberg, 1994). Among undergraduate students, AS was found to predict a large portion of variance in circumscribed social anxiety, although it contributed a much smaller amount of variance in generalized social anxiety (Norton et al., 1997). This suggests a potential pathoplastic role of AS in social phobia, that is, AS may be particularly important in nongeneralized (compared to generalized) social phobia whereas self-criticism may be more important in generalized social phobia.

Finally, a recent study in a community sample of German women examined the role of lower-order AS facets in a variety of anxiety disorders (McWilliams et al., 2007). After controlling for Neuroticism, the AS facets of fear of cognitive symptoms and fear of publicly observable symptoms were both significantly associated with a diagnosis of social phobia. Although these studies provide a limited examination of the role of AS, they do suggest an important role of AS in social phobia. Future studies should further examine the role of the lower-order facets of AS, especially the facet of fear of publicly observable symptoms, also known as social concerns, as it appears especially relevant to social phobia.

Posttraumatic Stress Disorder

The diagnosis of posttraumatic stress disorder (PTSD) is unique among the anxiety disorders in that it is the only diagnosis that requires or specifies the influence of an external, precipitating event. However, despite the fact that many individuals experience a traumatic event, only a minority of these individuals develop PTSD (Kessler, Sonnega, Bromet, Hughes, & Nelson, 1995; La Greca & Silverman, 2006). Although the experience of a traumatic event is necessary in the development of PTSD, it is not sufficient, and the potential of personality factors to influence the development of PTSD is significant. The presence of the traumatic event further introduces the possibility for personality factors to act as vulnerability factors for the experience of traumatic events, as well as for the subsequent development of PTSD. Relative to individuals without PTSD, those with this diagnosis have been shown to display higher levels of Neuroticism and lower levels of Extraversion, Agreeableness, and Conscientiousness, with Neuroticism showing the greatest sensitivity for this diagnosis (Trull & Sher, 1994). Although an abundance of research has examined the role of personality factors in PTSD, this diagnosis has often been overlooked in studies specifically examining the hierarchical model of anxiety disorders (Zinbarg & Barlow, 1996).

Vulnerability to Exposure to Traumatic Events

Conscientiousness, Extraversion, and Neuroticism appear to be related to vulnerability to exposure to traumatic events. The role of Conscientiousness is revealed primarily through associations between antisocial behavior and exposure, as antisocial behaviors appear to be best represented in the FFM as low levels of Conscientiousness (Krueger, Caspi, Moffitt, Silva, & McGee, 1996). A history of childhood antisocial acts has been associated with the likelihood of being beaten or mugged among those in the general population (Helzer, Robins, & McEvoy, 1987) and the likelihood of any traumatic exposure among college students (Lauterbach & Vrana, 2001).

Extraversion has also been implicated as an important factor reflecting vulnerability to traumatic exposure. Breslau and colleagues (Breslau, Davis, & Andreski, 1995; Breslau, Davis, Andreski, & Peterson, 1991) found that Extraversion was related to an increased likelihood of trauma exposure both cross-sectionally and prospectively in a large community sample of young adults. Cross-sectionally, this relationship was significant even when controlling for all other risk factors for exposure, and prospectively, the relationship was marginally significant when controlling for past exposure. Traumatized police officers have also been shown to score significantly lower on measures of Introversion, compared to a normative sample (Carlier, Lamberts, & Gersons, 1997).

The role of Conscientiousness and Extraversion in trauma exposure is likely a result of risk-taking behavior, and most authors have argued in favor of this interpretation. However, Lauterbach and Vrana (2001) found that sensation seeking did not have a significant association with exposure after accounting for antisocial behaviors, suggesting that the hostile component of antisocial behavior might be more important in predicting trauma exposure.

Breslau and colleagues (1991, 1995) also found that Neuroticism was related to an increased likelihood of trauma exposure both cross-sectionally when adjusting for all other risk factors for exposure and prospectively when controlling for past trauma exposure. Similarly, burn survivors displayed a higher level of Neuroticism relative to a normative national sample (Fauerbach, Lawrence, Schmidt, Munster, & Costa, 2000).

Vulnerability to Posttraumatic Stress Disorder After Trauma

As discussed previously, the vulnerability model is best tested using longitudinal prospective designs. Although numerous associations have been observed between PTSD and measures of personality, the interpretation of these findings is open to debate. Elevated Neuroticism has been associated with PTSD in large community samples (Breslau et al., 1991; Cox, MacPherson, et al., 2004) and in various more specific samples as well (Bunce, Larsen, & Peterson, 1995; Casella & Motta, 1990; Gamez, Watson, & Doebbeling, 2007; Hyer et al., 1994; Lauterbach & Vrana, 2001; Lewin, Carr, & Webster, 1998; Lonigan, Shannon, Taylor, Finch, & Sallee, 1994; Roca, Spence, & Munster, 1992; Talbert, Braswell, Albrecht, Hyer, & Boudewyns, 1993; Weiss, Marmar, Metzler, & Ronfeldt, 1995).

Additionally, Neuroticism was the only significant predictor of a diagnosis of PTSD after controlling for gender and general distress among a nonclinical sample of adults (Trull & Sher, 1994). In these cross-sectional studies, it is impossible to delineate the role of personality factors, that is, they could be interpreted as predispositions, scars of the disorder, or simply concomitants of current distress and mental illness. As a result, our discussion of personality factors conferring vulnerability to PTSD subsequent to trauma will focus on studies using pretrauma and posttrauma prospective designs, that is, studies that measure personality factors either prior to trauma (pretrauma) or soon after trauma exposure (posttrauma) and follow participants to examine the development of PTSD.

Longitudinal studies have been conducted in samples from a number of populations, although each consisted of individuals exposed to a specific type of trauma, be it combat experience, the death of a child, a devastating fire, or suffering a heart attack or burn injury. A pretrauma prospective study of PTSD has yet to be conducted in a general population sample and it is important to acknowledge that findings from longitudinal studies thus far may not generalize to all traumas. However, consistent results across these studies do lend support to the function of these personality factors in PTSD subsequent to any type of trauma.

Nearly every longitudinal study employing a measure of Neuroticism has yielded findings that this personality dimension is related to the development of PTSD. Pretrauma levels of negative affect were predictive of elevated PTSD symptoms among children exposed to Hurricane Katrina after adjusting for sex, pretrauma PTSD symptoms, number of hurricane-related events, and trait anxiety (Weems et al., 2007). Higher Neuroticism measured pretrauma was found in Australian Vietnam veterans who later developed PTSD compared to those who did not (O'Toole, Marshall, Schureck, & Dobson, 1998). Similarly, predeployment elevations on Neuroticism predicted PTSD symptoms among Dutch peacekeepers (Bramsen, Dirkzwager, & van der Ploeg, 2000), and Neuroticism measured prior to childbirth was able to predict PTSD symptoms among pregnant female volunteers (Engelhard, van den Hout, & Kindt, 2003). Although measured posttrauma, Neuroticism measured prior to hospital discharge has been found to predict severity of PTSD symptoms 3 months later among patients admitted for myocardial infarction (Bennett, Owen, Koutsakis, & Bisson, 2002) and development of

PTSD 4 and 12 months later among burn survivors (Fauerbach et al., 2000). Finally, Neuroticism measured within 2 weeks of a traumatic bushfire was able to predict the development of PTSD symptoms 11 and 29 months later in volunteer firefighters (McFarlane, 1989, 1992). These studies clearly reveal an important role of Neuroticism in the development of PTSD following trauma; however, not all of them are without problems of interpretation. In studies where personality traits are measured in a group of individuals already exposed to a certain trauma (posttrauma), it is not clear whether the personality trait reflects trauma exposure or is in fact an antecedent risk factor for PTSD. The studies that assess personality prior to trauma exposure avoid this limitation.

A number of studies have also provided evidence for roles of Extraversion and Conscientiousness in PTSD, although findings around these broad personality dimensions have not been extensively replicated. The role of elevated Extraversion in PTSD has been observed in studies of war veterans (Dalton, Aubuchon, Tom, Pederson, & McFarland, 1993; Davidson, Kudler, & Smith, 1987; Hyer, Woods, Boudewyns, Bruno, & O'Leary, 1988) and burn survivors (Fauerbach et al., 2000). The role of Conscientiousness has been demonstrated in a study of Australian Vietnam veterans (O'Toole et al., 1998).

Consistent findings of the role of Neuroticism in PTSD are expected; however, increased precision and predictive validity might be achieved by the examination of lower-order personality traits. Relatively few studies have examined the role of lower-order traits nested within Neuroticism and most studies that have are cross-sectional. Nonetheless, these studies have yielded important relationships that with further research may prove important in the development of PTSD.

One lower-order trait of interest is self-criticism (Blatt, 1974). This personality trait has been found to be cross-sectionally associated with a diagnosis of PTSD among trauma-exposed men and women in the general population (Cox, McPherson et al., 2004). Further, self-criticism was able to predict PTSD among men in hierarchical regressions controlling for types of trauma significantly associated with PTSD among men, other risk factors for PTSD, and Neuroticism. Among help-seeking female victims of domestic violence, self-criticism was also able to predict the intensity of PTSD symptoms after adjusting for sociodemographic factors (Sharhabani-Arzy, Amir, & Swisa, 2005). These studies suggest that self-criticism may potentially have important longitudinal associations with PTSD, and these should be investigated in future research.

A second lower-order trait examined in relation to PTSD is AS. This trait has been found to be elevated in patients diagnosed with PTSD (Taylor et al., 1992). Further, AS assessed among pregnant women at 36 weeks gestation was significantly correlated with PTSD symptoms measured 2 weeks postpartum (Keogh, Ayers, & Francis, 2002). This relationship was slightly stronger for the fear of publicly observable symptoms and fear of somatic symptoms facets, although only fear of publicly observable symptoms was able to predict PTSD symptoms after controlling for psychological distress. Another study of women exposed to trauma with and without PTSD found AS scores to be higher among women with PTSD compared to women exposed to trauma who did not develop PTSD (Lang, Kennedy, & Stein, 2002). Further, women with PTSD had significantly higher scores on fear of somatic symptoms and fear of cognitive symptoms than women with trauma exposure but no PTSD. There was no difference between these two groups on fear of publicly observable symptoms. There has been some suggestion that the mental incapacitation facet of AS may be important in PTSD (Cox, Borger, & Enns, 1999; Cox, Taylor, & Enns, 1999) and this study partially supports this assertion. In summary, these studies on AS suggest important avenues of research that could expand knowledge of the vulnerability to PTSD that AS may confer.

Pathoplasty Models in Posttraumatic Stress Disorder

A recent review by Miller (2003) focused on a three-factor model of the etiology and expression of PTSD. Miller proposed a model for the expression of PTSD asserting that Neuroticism represents the primary vulnerability factor for PTSD, while Extraversion and Conscientiousness serve as moderating factors that affect the expression of the disorder. Miller proposed that high levels of Neuroticism in combination with low levels of Extraversion could result in an internalizing expression of PTSD, while high levels of Neuroticism in combination with low levels of Conscientiousness could result in an externalizing form of PTSD. Using large samples of Vietnam veterans, Miller has found support for these subtypes of PTSD (Miller, Greif, & Smith, 2003; Miller, Kaloupek, Dillon, & Keane, 2004). Cluster analyses in both studies revealed a three-cluster solution that yielded a low pathology

cluster, an internalizing cluster, and an externalizing cluster. Individuals in both the internalizing and externalizing clusters were characterized by higher Neuroticism than the low pathology group, but did not differ significantly from each other on this dimension. The internalizing cluster was defined by lower scores on Extraversion compared to the externalizing cluster, and individuals in this cluster showed higher rates of unipolar depressive disorder and panic disorder diagnoses. In contrast, the externalizing cluster was defined by lower scores on Conscientiousness compared to the internalizing cluster, and individuals in this cluster were most likely to have substance-related disorders and antisocial personality disorder diagnoses. Miller and colleagues' (2003, 2004) studies demonstrate the ability of the personality domains of Extraversion and Conscientiousness to exert a pathoplastic effect on PTSD.

Obsessive-Compulsive Disorder

As previously mentioned, controversy over the role of autonomic arousal in anxiety disorders has been an important factor influencing the revision of the Tripartite Model. Although initially posited as an underlying commonality of anxiety disorders, autonomic arousal does not appear to be important in a number of anxiety disorders. Indeed, research suggests that hyperarousal does not appear to be an essential feature of OCD (Hoehn-Saric, McLeod, & Hipsley, 1995). Considerable research has been devoted to determining personality factors important in OCD, and this holds much value in evaluating the hierarchical model of the anxiety disorders.

As expected, OCD patients consistently score higher on measures of Neuroticism compared to control participants (Fullana et al., 2004; Hoehn-Saric et al., 1995; Samuels et al., 2000; Scarrabelotti, Duck, & Dickerson, 1995). Low levels of Extraversion are also commonly found in OCD patients (Fullana et al., 2004; Samuels et al., 2000; Scarrabelotti et al., 1995), although some studies have failed to find a difference (Hoehn-Saric et al., 1995). These differences in Neuroticism and Extraversion appear to persist after controlling for depressive symptoms and state anxiety (Fullana et al., 2004). In contrast to consistent findings of high Neuroticism and low Extraversion, a combination that is seen as conferring vulnerability to obsessive disorders (Eysenck & Eysenck, 1985), less consistent findings have been reported for the other factors of the FFM, although one study demonstrated an association between OCD and high Openness (Bienvenu et al., 2004).

Although they offer increased specificity, few studies have examined the lower-order facets of the FFM. A recent epidemiological study yielded preliminary findings concerning the lower-order facets within the FFM (Samuels et al., 2000). Two facets of Openness, fantasy and feelings, were significantly higher in individuals with lifetime OCD compared to controls. These might reflect an open-mindedness that would predispose individuals to developing new obsessions or prevent them from dismissing obsessions. Individuals with OCD also scored significantly lower than controls on two facets of Conscientiousness, competence and self-discipline. Although preliminary and cross-sectional, these results suggest that specific lower-order facets might be important in vulnerability to OCD.

Perfectionism, a trait that has long been considered in conceptualizations of OCD by theorists of various orientations and noted in clinical reports of OCD (Frost & DiBartolo, 2002), may serve as a specific factor associated with OCD within the IHM. Increased levels of perfectionism have been shown to be associated with more obsessive-compulsive symptoms in both OCD patient samples (Antony et al., 1998; Frost & Steketee, 1997), as well as nonclinical samples (Frost et al., 1990; Gershuny & Sher, 1995). Although mostly utilizing nonclinical, undergraduate samples, factors of both the F-MPS and H-MPS have been shown to be correlated with OCD symptomatology. Symptoms of OCD have been positively associated with self-oriented and socially prescribed perfectionism (Frost & Gross, 1993; Yorulmaz, Karanci, & Tekok-Kilic, 2006) as well as most subscales of the F-MPS, although concern over mistakes and doubts about actions appear to be most closely associated (Frost & Gross, 1993; Rheaume, Freeston, Dugas, Letarte, & Ladouceur, 1995). Additionally, college students with various OCD symptoms have been consistently found to score higher on concern over mistakes and doubts about actions (Frost & Shows, 1993; Frost, Steketee, Cohn, & Griess, 1994; Frost & Gross, 1993). Patients with OCD have also been shown to score significantly higher on concern over mistakes and doubts about actions, compared to community control subjects (Frost & Steketee, 1997). Finally, facets of perfectionism have been shown to distinguish patients with OCD from other patient groups. Comparing F-MPS scores among patients with OCD and panic disorder with agoraphobia, Frost and Steketee (1997) found OCD patients to score significantly higher on doubts about actions than patients with panic disorder with agoraphobia.

Antony and colleagues (1998) also found doubts about actions scores to be significantly elevated among patients with OCD relative to patients with panic disorder, social phobia, and specific phobia, further suggesting the potential specificity of this dimension of perfectionism in OCD. Theorists of various orientations have described the relationship between perfectionism and OCD, the common theme among these being that perfectionistic tendencies (both thoughts and behaviors) are established in order to avoid something unpleasant (see Frost & DiBartolo [2002] for a review). As Frost and DiBartolo note: "Either perfectionism develops in an attempt to avoid uncertainty or in an attempt to establish control, or perfectionism is at the core and produces uncertainty and a desire for control over one's environment. In either case, the major feature is the avoidance of mistakes rather than the achievement of goals" (p. 361).

To our knowledge, no longitudinal studies examining the role of FFM factors or perfectionism in OCD have been conducted. These studies are necessary to demonstrate personality factors as vulnerability factors important for the development of the disorder. Most studies thus far reveal important associations that should be further studied in longitudinal designs. In addition, very few studies have examined other ways in which personality factors can influence OCD. One exception, however, is a recent study by Rector, Richter, and Bagby (2005). These authors examined the ability of the higher-order dimensions and lower-order facets of the FFM to predict severity of OCD symptomatology in hierarchical linear regressions. No facets of Neuroticism, Extraversion, Agreeableness, or Conscientiousness were significantly associated with symptom severity after controlling for depressive symptoms. In contrast, lower scores on the actions facet of Openness were significantly associated with the severity of compulsions, while lower scores on the ideas facet of Openness were significantly associated with the severity of obsessions after controlling for depression. The authors suggest that low scores on actions may be related to the tendency to get caught in a pattern of ritualistic behaviors while low scores on openness may relate to the tendency to interpret thoughts or obsessions as unacceptable and worthy of concern. It appears that, although Neuroticism has nonspecific associations with OCD symptomatology, other factors such as the lower-order facets of actions and ideas can impact the specific expression of the disorder. Further study of vulnerability, pathoplasty, and scar models is warranted.

Generalized Anxiety Disorder

Evidence derived from studies of the hierarchical model of the anxiety disorders has fostered some controversy around the diagnosis of generalized anxiety disorder (GAD). First, studies have shown that features of GAD appear to overlap more with the mood disorders than other anxiety disorders (Brown et al., 1998). Krueger's seminal paper on the structure of mental disorders in the National Comorbidity Survey revealed that GAD fit in an "anxious-misery" cluster of internalizing disorders, along with major depression and dysthymia, in contrast to the other anxiety disorders assessed (social phobia, specific phobia, agoraphobia, and panic disorder), which fit in a "fear" cluster of internalizing disorders (Krueger, 1999). Studies have also revealed that GAD is rarely associated with anxious arousal, but to the contrary, is associated with autonomic suppression and inflexibility (Brown et al., 1998). Further debate exists around the conceptualization of GAD. Researchers have variously suggested that GAD might reflect a pathological personality configuration (Akiskal, 1998; Beck, Stanley, & Zebb, 1996), a vulnerability to developing anxiety and mood disorders (Brown, Barlow, & Liebowitz, 1994), and a basic anxiety disorder, reflecting processes common to all anxiety disorders (Barlow, 1988).

In accordance with these alternate conceptualizations of GAD, numerous studies have revealed strong associations between this disorder and Neuroticism. Compared to controls, patients with GAD scored significantly higher on measures of Neuroticism and Neuroticism was able to differentiate GAD patients from controls after accounting for Extraversion and trait anxiety (Gomez & Francis, 2003). Other authors have also found Neuroticism to be one of the most consistent predictors of chronic anxiety symptoms (De Beurs, Beekman, Deeg, Van Dyck, & Van Tilburg, 2000). In a nationally representative sample of the United States, individuals with GAD scored significantly higher on Neuroticism than those with social phobia, simple phobia, PTSD, and no disorder, and did not differ significantly from those with panic disorder and comorbid disorders after adjusting for gender (Weinstock & Whisman, 2006). A study of a large sample of Gulf War veterans found that GAD was strongly related to negative temperament (Gamez et al., 2007). Taking a different approach, researchers have found that genetic factors influencing GAD overlap substantially with those influencing Neuroticism, further emphasizing the strong relationship between these constructs (Hettema, Prescott, & Kendler,

2004; Kendler, Gardner, Gatz, & Pedersen, 2007). The conceptualization of GAD remains controversial and further research is necessary to determine exactly how this diagnosis fits into psychiatric nosology.

Low levels of Extraversion also appear to have an important role in GAD. Compared to controls, patients with GAD show lower levels of Extraversion (Gomez & Francis, 2003). Further, Extraversion is able to differentiate patients with GAD from controls after accounting for Neuroticism and trait anxiety. This study also demonstrated the potential for Neuroticism and Extraversion to act as pathoplastic factors in GAD. The severity of GAD was significantly positively correlated with Neuroticism and significantly negatively correlated with Extraversion. Neuroticism and Extraversion, entered simultaneously, were significant predictors of GAD severity in logistic regressions. Neuroticism has also been found to be significantly higher among GAD patients whose anxiety symptoms began before age 20 (early-onset) relative to GAD patients whose anxiety began later (Hoehn-Saric, Hazlett, & McLeod, 1993). The early-onset patients also displayed increased depression, obsessional traits, interpersonal sensitivity, and marital difficulties. The role of Neuroticism and Extraversion as pathoplastic factors in GAD warrants further study.

Neuroticism and Extraversion appear to be important in GAD, although studies of the role of personality factors in GAD have been limited to cross-sectional studies examining broad personality dimensions. Further research using longitudinal methodologies and methodologies appropriate for investigating alternative mechanisms of personality factors are necessary to better understand the role of Neuroticism and Extraversion in GAD and the appropriate conceptualization of GAD.

Specific Phobias

Very little research has been devoted to the study of personality factors in specific phobias, consistent with behavioral models of fear acquisition and learning theory conceptualizations of this disorder, wherein specific phobias are conceptualized as conditioned fear responses that can be easily treated with exposure therapy (Lindemann, 1999). Those studies that have been conducted have yielded few consistent results concerning the role of personality factors in specific phobia.

Trull and Sher (1994) found that individuals with specific phobia did not differ from those without specific phobia on any dimension of the FFM.

Additionally, none of the higher-order dimensions were significantly related to a diagnosis of specific phobia in logistic regressions adjusting for gender and general distress. Similarly, specific phobia was not associated with high Neuroticism among participants in the Epidemiological Catchment Follow-up Study (Bienvenu et al., 2001b; Bienvenu et al., 2004), in accordance with studies showing Neuroticism to be weakly related to disorders characterized by behavioral avoidance, such as specific phobia (Watson et al., 2005). In the above-mentioned studies, participants with specific phobia often had significantly higher levels of Neuroticism compared to controls; however, both groups had Neuroticism scores in the average range. In addition, although some studies have reported significant associations between Neuroticism and specific phobia, there appears to be less of an effect of Neuroticism in specific phobia compared to other anxiety disorders (Gamez et al., 2007). Although Neuroticism was higher among those with specific phobia relative to controls in a nationally representative sample of the U.S. population, levels of this personality dimension were significantly higher among patients with GAD and panic disorder relative to those with specific phobia (Weinstock & Whisman, 2006).

Studies have reported associations between specific phobia and several lower-order facets of the FFM. Specific phobia has been associated with low self-discipline, a lower-order facet of Conscientiousness, in two community samples (Bienvenu et al., 2001b; Bienvenu et al., 2004). Additionally, one community sample found two lower-order facets of Agreeableness, trust and compliance, to be associated with specific phobia (Bienvenu et al., 2001b). Although AS and perfectionism are associated with a number of anxiety disorders, studies suggest that AS is not elevated among patients with specific phobia (Taylor et al., 1992), and that no differences in perfectionism on either the F-MPS or H-MPS exist between patients with specific phobia and controls (Antony et al., 1998). One notable exception is a recent study that found the fear of somatic symptoms facet of AS to be associated with specific phobia after adjusting for Neuroticism (McWilliams et al., 2007).

Studies examining the role of personality traits in specific phobia have found few notable relationships. Importantly, the studies discussed that did find significant associations between specific phobia and personality factors did not exclude other diagnoses from the specific phobia group or control for comorbidity in some other way. Elevations of personality traits found in the specific phobia group are

therefore likely related to comorbidity with other disorders. In any case, the personality factors discussed throughout this chapter have the least relevance to specific phobia compared to the other anxiety disorders.

Summary and Conclusions

The literature on personality factors in the anxiety disorders is vast and the findings presented in this chapter are not exhaustive. With the guiding theories of the FFM and the IHM, we have attempted to present a detailed but succinct review of this literature. Studies of the Tripartite Model and IHM thus far have yielded extensive data suggesting that Neuroticism is a shared component of all anxiety disorders, although its importance varies across disorders. Specifically, Neuroticism is strongly related to disorders characterized by chronic and pervasive subjective distress like GAD and PTSD, less strongly related to disorders with more circumscribed patterns of distress like panic disorder, and weakly related to disorders not marked by subjective distress, but characterized by patterns of avoidance like specific phobia.

The unique components associated with each anxiety disorder remain difficult to define, although it is clear that these unique components represent lower-order personality traits nested within Neuroticism rather than the broad dimensions of the FFM. The fact that a number of associations between lower-order personality traits or facets and each anxiety disorder exist suggests that a specific personality profile for each anxiety disorder might emerge in future research. Instead of the unique component of each anxiety disorder being a single trait, it might be a collection of lower-order personality traits. For example, a plausible collection of traits associated with social phobia based on the available data would be high Neuroticism, low Extraversion, and high self-criticism. In line with this hypothesis, a discriminant function analysis of a number of self-report anxiety measures in a sample of patients admitted to an anxiety disorders clinic yielded four lower-order discriminant functions that were able to differentiate among anxiety disorders (Zinbarg & Barlow, 1996). Additionally, different personality factors might be associated with different symptom dimensions within each disorder. These possibilities represent avenues for future research that might contribute to additional revisions and expansions of the IHM.

Studies that have been done point to personality traits and facets that should be considered as potential unique components of different anxiety disorders within the IHM. Anxiety sensitivity and particularly the lower-order AS facet fear of bodily sensations as well as perfectionism and its lower-order dimension of concern over mistakes appear important in panic disorder. Low Extraversion, elevated self-criticism, and the concern over mistakes, doubts about actions, parental criticism, and socially prescribed dimensions of perfectionism appear particularly important in social phobia. Neuroticism appears to be the major factor involved in PTSD, although AS and self-criticism and the pathoplastic factors of Extraversion and Conscientiousness warrant further research. Openness and its lower-order facets as well as the doubts about actions and socially prescribed dimensions of perfectionism hold potential as unique components of OCD. Neuroticism appears to be the major factor involved in GAD, although low Extraversion may have an important role as well. Research ventures should also be devoted to elucidating the best conceptualization of GAD within current psychiatric nosology as this holds important implications for the role of personality factors. Finally, specific phobia is least related to personality factors, although some lower-order factors of Conscientiousness and Agreeableness show associations with this diagnosis.

A recent study was the first to propose and test a preliminary model of personality and anxiety disorders, which the authors refer to as the multilevel trait predictor model of anxiety disorders (MTPM), (Kotov, Watson, Robles, & Schmidt, 2007). Based on the current literature and the IHM, the MTPM proposes the following relationships between personality and anxiety disorders: (1) Neuroticism is a general factor involved in all anxiety disorders; (2) Low Extraversion is a specific factor with a strong link to social phobia and a lesser association with GAD; (3) AS is a specific factor in panic disorder and may also be related to PTSD, social phobia, and GAD; and (4) Negative evaluation sensitivity is a unique factor in social phobia. The authors tested this model by examining continuous measures of panic disorder, social phobia, OCD, and GAD symptoms in a large college student sample and found significant support for the MTPM. All hypothesized associations were confirmed using hierarchical linear regressions, with the exception of the associations between Extraversion and GAD and between AS and social phobia. Additionally, an unexpected association between negative evaluation sensitivity and GAD emerged. Results also indicated that controlling for the traits involved in the MTPM

considerably reduces correlations between different anxiety disorder symptoms and likely accounts for comorbidity between anxiety disorders. The authors note the preliminary status of the model and the need to include all anxiety disorders and elucidate other important traits to be added to the model in future research. Nonetheless, this study represents an important development in the study of the relationship between personality factors and the anxiety disorders and a positive initial step toward a fully elaborated model.

Further research in the field of personality factors in anxiety disorders would benefit from the use of longitudinal, prospective methodologies that have the ability to test the hypothesis that personality traits act as vulnerability factors in the development of anxiety disorders. Multiple interpretations of results exist when studies are of a cross-sectional nature, as are the majority of studies examining personality in the anxiety disorders. Relationships between personality factors and anxiety disorders derived from cross-sectional studies could be interpreted as personality factors leading to anxiety disorders, anxiety disorders affecting personality, or personality changes simply being reflections of current mental illness. Future studies should specifically test these different mechanisms through which personality factors can affect the anxiety disorders. Studies devoted to testing scar models as well as elucidating pathoplastic factors involved in the anxiety disorders would be extremely valuable.

Comorbidity of mental disorders poses a significant problem for treatment of mental disorders as well as psychiatric nosology at a more basic level. It appears that the shared component of anxiety and mood disorders, Neuroticism, has important implications for this problem. Neuroticism has been found to account for a significant proportion of comorbidity within internalizing disorders, suggesting that this personality dimension might be a broad vulnerability factor for comorbid psychiatric disorders in addition to single disorders (Khan, Jacobson, Gardner, Prescott, & Kendler, 2005). Additionally, in a nationally representative sample of the United States, associations between major depressive disorder, panic disorder, and phobic disorders are significantly reduced after Neuroticism and Extraversion are taken into account (Bienvenu et al., 2001a). Comorbidity of mental disorders is related to severity of mental disorders and acknowledging the role of personality dimensions like Neuroticism in this comorbidity has important implications for theories of anxiety disorders as well as treatment.

In sum, personality factors have important effects on the anxiety disorders. Future directions for research on the relationships between personality and anxiety disorders are numerous. Elucidating vulnerability factors for the development of anxiety disorders introduces the potential for primary prevention efforts. Additionally, knowledge of how personality traits can affect the expression of anxiety disorders allows for informed treatment planning. The role of personality traits in the comorbidity of mental disorders has potentially important implications for the treatment of multiple mental disorders within an individual. Interventions targeted to the treatment of lower-order personality factors nested within Neuroticism (e.g., self-criticism, perfectionism), rather than directed treatment of the specific symptoms of each mental disorder, may prove valuable.

References

Akiskal, H. S. (1998). Toward a definition of generalized anxiety disorder as an anxious temperament type. *Acta Psychiatrica Scandinavica, 98*(Supp. 393), 66–73.

Alden, L. E., Bieling, P. J., & Wallace, S. T. (1994). Perfectionism in an interpersonal context: A self-regulation analysis of dysphoria and social anxiety. *Cognitive Therapy and Research, 18*, 297–316.

Antony, M. M., Purdon, C. L., Huta, V., & Swinson, R. P. (1998). Dimensions of perfectionism across the anxiety disorders. *Behaviour Research and Therapy, 36*, 1143–1154.

Barlow, D. H. (1988). *Anxiety and its disorders: The nature and treatment of anxiety and panic.* New York: Guilford Press.

Beck, J. G., Stanley, M. A., & Zebb, B. J. (1996). Characteristics of anxiety disorder in older adults: A descriptive study. *Behaviour Research and Therapy, 34*, 225–234.

Bennett, P., Owen, R. L., Koutsakis, S., & Bisson, J. (2002). Personality, social context, and cognitive predictors of posttraumatic stress disorder in myocardial infarction patients. *Psychology and Health, 17*, 489–500.

Bieling, P. J., & Alden, L. E. (1997). The consequences of perfectionism for patients with social phobia. *British Journal of Clinical Psychology, 36*, 387–395.

Bienvenu, O. J., Brown, C., Samuels, J. F., Liang, K., Costa, P. T., Eaton, M. W., et al. (2001a). Normal personality traits and comorbidity among phobic, panic and major depressive disorders. *Psychiatry Research, 102*, 73–85.

Bienvenu, O. J., Nestadt, G., Samuels, J. F., Costa, P. T., Howard, W. T., & Eaton, M. W. (2001b). Phobic, panic and major depressive disorders and the Five-Factor Model of personality. *Journal of Nervous and Mental Disease, 189*, 154–161.

Bienvenu, O. J., Samuels, J. F., Costa, P. T., Reti, I. M., Eaton, M. W., & Nestadt, G. (2004). Anxiety and depressive disorders and the Five-Factor Model of personality: A higher and lower-order personality trait investigation in a community sample. *Depression and Anxiety, 20*, 92–97.

Blatt, S. J. (1974). Levels of object representation in anaclitic and introjective depression. *The Psychoanalytic Study of the Child, 29*, 107–157.

Bramsen, I., Dirkzwager, A.J.E., & van der Ploeg, H. M. (2000). Predeployment personality traits and exposure to trauma as predictors of posttraumatic stress symptoms: A prospective study of former peacekeepers. *American Journal of Psychiatry, 157*, 1115–1119.

Breslau, N., Davis, G. C., & Andreski, P. (1995). Risk factors for PTSD-related traumatic events: A prospective analysis. *American Journal of Psychiatry, 152*, 529–535.

Breslau, N., Davis, G. C., Andreski, P., & Peterson, E. (1991). Traumatic events and posttraumatic stress disorder in an urban population of young adults. *Archives of General Psychiatry, 48*, 216–222.

Brown, T. A., Barlow, D. H., & Liebowitz, M. R. (1994). The empirical basis of generalized anxiety disorder. *American Journal of Psychiatry, 151*, 1272–1280.

Brown, T. A., Chorpita, B. F., & Barlow, D. H. (1998). Structural relationships among dimensions of the *DSM–IV* anxiety and mood disorders and dimensions of negative affect, positive affect, and autonomic arousal. *Journal of Abnormal Psychology, 107*, 179–192.

Brown, M., Smits, J.A.J., Powers, M. B., & Telch, M. J. (2003). Differential sensitivity of the three ASI factors in predicting panic disorder patients' subjective and behavioral response to hyperventilation challenge. *Anxiety Disorders, 17*, 583–591.

Bunce, S. C., Larsen, R. J., & Peterson, C. (1995). Life after trauma: Personality and daily life experiences of traumatized people. *Journal of Personality, 63*, 165–188.

Calamari, J. E., Hale, L. R., Heffelfinger, S. K., Janeck, A. S., Lau, J. J., Weerts, M. A., et al. (2001). Relations between anxiety sensitivity and panic symptoms in nonreferred children and adolescents. *Journal of Behavior Therapy and Experimental Psychiatry, 32*, 117–136.

Carlier, I.V.E., Lamberts, R. D., & Gersons, B.P.R. (1997). Risk factors for posttraumatic stress symptomatology in police officers: A prospective analysis. *Journal of Nervous and Mental Disease, 185*, 498–506.

Casella, L., & Motta, R. W. (1990). Comparison of characteristics of Vietnam veterans with and without posttraumatic stress disorder. *Psychological Reports, 67*, 595–605.

Chavira, D. A., Stein, M. B., & Malcarne, V. L. (2002). Scrutinizing the relationship between shyness and social phobia. *Anxiety Disorders, 16*, 585–598.

Clark, L., & Watson, D. (1991). Tripartite model of anxiety and depression: Psychometric evidence and taxonomic implications. *Journal of Abnormal Psychology, 100*, 316–336.

Clark, L., Watson, D., & Mineka, S. (1994). Temperament, personality and the mood and anxiety disorders. *Journal of Abnormal Psychology, 103*, 103–116.

Costa, P. T., Jr., & McCrae, R. R. (1985). *The NEO Personality Inventory.* Odessa, FL: Psychological Assessment Resources.

Costa, P. T., & McCrae, R. R. (1992). *Revised NEO Personality Inventory (NEO-PI-R) and NEO Five-Factor Inventory (NEO-FFI) professional manual.* Odessa, FL: Psychological Assessment Resources.

Cox, B. J. (1996). The nature and assessment of catastrophic thoughts in panic disorder. *Behaviour Research and Therapy, 34*, 363–374.

Cox, B. J., Borger, S. C., & Enns, M. W. (1999). Anxiety sensitivity and emotional disorders: Psychometric studies and their theoretical implications. In S. Taylor (Ed.), *Anxiety sensitivity: Theory, research, and treatment of the fear of anxiety* (pp. 115–148). Mahwah, NJ: Erlbaum.

Cox, B. J., Borger, S. C., Taylor, S., Fuentes, K., & Ross, L. M. (1999). Anxiety sensitivity and the five-factor model of personality. *Behaviour Research and Therapy, 37,* 633–641.

Cox, B. J., Endler, N. S., Norton, G. R., & Swinson, R. P. (1991). Anxiety sensitivity and nonclinical panic attacks. *Behaviour Research and Therapy, 29,* 367–369.

Cox, B. J., Enns, M. W., Walker, J. R., Kjernisted, K., & Pidlubny, S. R. (2001). Psychological vulnerabilities in patients with major depression vs. panic disorder. *Behaviour Research and Therapy, 39,* 567–573.

Cox, B. J., Fleet, C., & Stein, M. B. (2004). Self-criticism and social phobia in the U.S. National Comorbidity Survey. *Journal of Affective Disorders, 82,* 227–234.

Cox, B. J., MacPherson, P.S.R., & Enns, M. W. (2005). Psychiatric correlates of childhood shyness in a nationally representative sample. *Behaviour Research and Therapy, 43,* 1019–1027.

Cox, B. J., MacPherson, P.S.R., Enns, M. W., & McWilliams, L. A. (2004). Neuroticism and self-criticism associated with posttraumatic stress disorder in a nationally representative sample. *Behaviour Research and Therapy, 42,* 105–114.

Cox, B. J., Rector, N. A., Bagby, M., Swinson, R. P., Levitt, A. J., & Joffe, R. T. (2000). Is self-criticism unique for depression? A comparison with social phobia. *Journal of Affective Disorders, 57,* 223–228.

Cox, B. J., Taylor, S., & Enns, M. W. (1999). Fear of cognitive dyscontrol in relation to depression symptoms: Comparisons between original and alternative measures of anxiety sensitivity. *Journal of Behavior Therapy and Experimental Psychiatry, 30,* 301–311.

Cox, B. J., Walker, J. R., Enns, M. W., & Karpinski, D. C. (2002). Self-criticism in generalized social phobia and response to cognitive-behavioral treatment. *Behavior Therapy, 33,* 479–491.

Dalton, J. E., Aubuchon, I. N., Tom, A., Pederson, S. L., & McFarland, R. E. (1993). MBTI profiles of Vietnam veterans with post-traumatic stress disorder. *Journal of Psychological Type, 26,* 3–8.

Darvill, T. J., Johnson, R. C., & Danko, G. P. (1992). Personality correlates of public and private self-consciousness. *Personality and Individual Differences, 13,* 383–384.

Davidson, J., Kudler, H., & Smith, R. (1987). Personality in chronic post-traumatic stress disorder: A study of the Eysenck Inventory. *Journal of Anxiety Disorders, 1,* 295–300.

De Beurs, E., Beekman, A.T.F., Deeg, D.J.H., Van Dyck, R., & Van Tilburg, W. (2000). Predictors of change in anxiety symptoms of older persons: Results from the Longitudinal Aging Study Amsterdam. *Psychological Medicine, 30,* 515–527.

Digman, J. M. (1990). Personality structure: Emergence of the five-factor model. *Annual Review of Psychology, 41,* 417–440.

Donnell, C. D., & McNally, R. J. (1989). Anxiety sensitivity and history of panic as predictors of response to hyperventilation. *Behaviour Research and Therapy, 27,* 325–332.

Donnell, C. D., & McNally, R. J. (1990). Anxiety sensitivity and panic attacks in a nonclinical population. *Behaviour Research and Therapy, 28,* 83–85.

Ehlers, A. (1995). A 1-year prospective study of panic attacks: Clinical course and factors associated with maintenance. *Journal of Abnormal Psychology, 104,* 164–172.

Engelhard, I. M., van den Hout, M. A., & Kindt, M. (2003). The relationship between neuroticism, pre-traumatic stress, and post-traumatic stress: A prospective study. *Personality and Individual Differences, 35,* 381–388.

Eysenck, H. J., & Eysenck, M. W. (1985). *Personality and individual differences: A natural science approach.* New York: Plenum Press.

Fauerbach, J. A., Lawrence, J. W., Schmidt, C. W., Jr., Munster, A. M., & Costa, P. T., Jr. (2000). Personality predictors of injury-related posttraumatic stress disorder. *Journal of Nervous and Mental Disease, 188,* 510–517.

Frost, R. O., & DiBartolo, P. M. (2002). Perfectionism, anxiety, and obsessive-compulsive disorder. In G. L. Flett & P. L. Hewitt (Eds.), *Perfectionism: Theory, research and treatment* (pp. 341–371). Washington, DC: American Psychological Association.

Frost, R. O., & Gross, R. C. (1993). The hoarding of possessions. *Behaviour Research and Therapy, 31,* 367–381.

Frost, R. O., Marten, P., Lahart, C., & Rosenblate, R. (1990). The dimensions of perfectionism. *Cognitive Therapy and Research, 14,* 449–468.

Frost, R. O., & Shows, D. L. (1993). The nature and measurement of compulsive indecisiveness. *Behaviour Research and Therapy, 31,* 683–692.

Frost, R. O., & Steketee, G. (1997). Perfectionism in obsessive-compulsive disorder patients. *Behaviour Research and Therapy, 35,* 291–296.

Frost, R. O., Steketee, G., Cohn, L., & Griess, K. (1994). Personality traits in subclinical and non-obsessive-compulsive volunteers and their parents. *Behaviour Research and Therapy, 32,* 47–56.

Fullana, M. A., Mataix-Cols, D., Trujillo, J. L., Caseras, X., Serrano, F., Alonso, P., et al. (2004). Personality characteristics in obsessive-compulsive disorder and individuals with subclinical obsessive-compulsive problems. *British Journal of Clinical Psychology, 43,* 387–398.

Gamez, W., Watson, D., & Doebbeling, B. N. (2007). Abnormal personality and the mood and anxiety disorders: Implications for structural models of anxiety and depression. *Journal of Anxiety Disorders, 21,* 526–539.

Gershuny, B. S., & Sher, K. J. (1995). Compulsive checking and anxiety in a nonclinical sample: Differences in cognition, behavior, personality, and affect. *Journal of Psychopathology and Behavioral Assessment, 17,* 19–38.

Gomez, R., & Francis, L. M. (2003). Generalised anxiety disorder: Relationships with Eysenck's, Gray's and Newman's theories. *Personality and Individual Differences, 34,* 3–17.

Harrington, P. J., Schmidt, N. B., & Telch, M. J. (1996). Prospective evaluations of panic potentiation following 35% CO_2 challenge in nonclinical subjects. *American Journal of Psychiatry, 153,* 823–825.

Hayward, C., Killen, J. D., Kraemer, H. C., & Taylor, C. B. (2000). Predictors of panic attacks in adolescents. *Journal of the American Academy of Child and Adolescent Psychiatry, 39,* 207–214.

Helzer, J. E., Robins, L. N., & McEvoy, L. (1987). Posttraumatic stress disorder in the general population: Findings from the Epidemiological Catchment Area Survey. *New England Journal of Medicine, 317,* 1630–1634.

Hettema, J. M., Prescott, C. A., & Kendler, K. S. (2004). Genetic and environmental sources of covariation between generalized anxiety disorder and neuroticism. *American Journal of Psychiatry, 161,* 1581–1587.

Hewitt, P. L., & Flett, G. L. (1991). Perfectionism in the self and social contexts: Conceptualization, assessment and association with psychopathology. *Journal of Personality and Social Psychology, 60,* 456–470.

Hoehn-Saric, R., Hazlett, R. L., & McLeod, D. R. (1993). Generalized anxiety disorder with early and late onset of anxiety symptoms. *Comprehensive Psychiatry, 34,* 291–298.

Hoehn-Saric, R., McLeod, D. R., & Hipsley, P. (1995). Is hyperarousal essential to obsessive-compulsive disorder? Diminished physiologic flexibility, but not hyperarousal characterizes patients with obsessive-compulsive disorder. *Archives of General Psychiatry, 52,* 688–693.

Hyer, L., Braswell, L., Albrecht, B., Boyd, S., Boudewyns, P., & Talbert, S. (1994). Relationship of NEO-PI to personality styles and severity of trauma in chronic PTSD victims. *Journal of Clinical Psychology, 50,* 699–707.

Hyer, L., Woods, M. G., Boudewyns, P. A., Bruno, R., & O'Leary, W. C. (1988). Concurrent validation of the Millon Clinical Multiaxial Inventory among Vietnam veterans with posttraumatic stress disorder. *Psychological Reports, 63,* 271–278.

Iketani, T., Kiriike, N., Stein, M. B., Nagao, K., Nagata, T., Minamikawa, N., et al. (2002a). Relationship between perfectionism, personality disorders and agoraphobia in patients with panic disorder. *Acta Psychiatrica Scandinavica, 106,* 171–178.

Iketani, T., Kiriike, N., Stein, M. B., Nagao, K., Nagata, T., Minamikawa, N., et al. (2002b). Relationship between perfectionism and agoraphobia in patients with panic disorder. *Cognitive Behaviour Therapy, 31,* 119–128.

Juster, H. R., Heimberg, R. G., Frost, R. O., Holt, C. S., Mattia, J. I., & Faccenda, K. (1996). Social phobia and perfectionism. *Personality and Individual Differences, 21,* 403–410.

Kendler, K. S., Gardner, C. O., Gatz, M., & Pedersen, N. L. (2007). The sources of co-morbidity between major depression and generalized anxiety disorder in a Swedish national twin sample. *Psychological Medicine, 37,* 453–462.

Keogh, E., Ayers, S., & Francis, H. (2002). Does anxiety sensitivity predict post-traumatic stress symptoms following childbirth? A preliminary report. *Cognitive Behaviour Therapy, 31,* 145–155.

Kessler, R. C., Sonnega, A., Bromet, E., Hughes, M., & Nelson, C. B. (1995). Posttraumatic stress disorder in the National Comorbidity Survey. *Archives of General Psychiatry, 52,* 1048–1060.

Khan, A. A., Jacobson, K. C., Gardner, C. O., Prescott, C. A., & Kendler, K. S. (2005). Personality and comorbidity of common psychiatric disorders. *British Journal of Psychiatry, 186,* 190–196.

Kotov, R., Watson, D., Robles, J. P., & Schmidt, N. B. (2007). Personality traits and anxiety symptoms: The multilevel trait predictor model. *Behaviour Research and Therapy, 45,* 1485–1503.

Krueger, R. F. (1999). The structure of common mental disorders. *Archives of General Psychiatry, 56,* 921–926.

Krueger, R. F., Caspi, A., Moffitt, T. E., Silva, P. A., & McGee, R. (1996). Personality traits are differentially linked to mental disorder: A multitrait-multidiagnosis study of an adolescent birth cohort. *Journal of Abnormal Psychology, 105,* 299–312.

La Greca, A. M., & Silverman, W. K. (2006). Children and disasters and terrorism. In P. C. Kendall (Ed.), *Child and adolescent therapy: Cognitive-behavioral procedures* (3rd ed., pp. 356–382). New York: Guilford Press.

Lang, A. J., Kennedy, C. M., & Stein, M. B. (2002). Anxiety sensitivity and PTSD among female victims of intimate partner violence. *Depression and Anxiety, 16,* 77–83.

Lau, J. J., Calamari, J. E., & Waraczynski, M. (1996). Panic attack symptomatology and anxiety sensitivity in adolescents. *Journal of Anxiety Disorders, 10,* 355–364.

Lauterbach, D., & Vrana, S. (2001). The relationship among personality variables, exposure to traumatic events and severity of posttraumatic stress symptoms. *Journal of Traumatic Stress, 14,* 29–45.

Lewin, T. J., Carr, V. J., & Webster, R. A. (1998). Recovery from post-earthquake psychological morbidity: Who suffers and who recovers? *Australian and New Zealand Journal of Psychiatry, 32,* 15–20.

Lilienfeld, S. O. (1999). Anxiety sensitivity and the structure of personality. In S. Taylor (Ed.), *Anxiety sensitivity: Theory, research, and treatment of the fear of anxiety* (pp. 149–180). Mahwah, NJ: Erlbaum.

Lindemann, C. (1999). Phobias. In B. B. Wolman & G. Stricker (Eds.), *Anxiety and related disorders: A handbook* (pp. 161–175). New York: Wiley-Interscience.

Lonigan, C. J., Shannon, M. P., Taylor, C. M., Finch, A. J., & Sallee, F. R. (1994). Risk factors for the development of post-traumatic symptomatology. *Journal of the American Academy of Child and Adolescent Psychiatry, 33,* 94–105.

Lundh, L., & Öst, L. (1996). Stroop interference, self-focus and perfectionism in social phobics. *Personality and Individual Differences, 20,* 725–731.

Maller, R. G., & Reiss, S. (1992). Anxiety sensitivity in 1984 and panic attacks in 1987. *Journal of Anxiety Disorders, 6,* 241–247.

McCrae, R. R., & John, O. P. (1992). An introduction to the Five-Factor Model and its applications. *Journal of Personality, 60,* 175–215.

McFarlane, A. C. (1989). The aetiology of post-traumatic morbidity: Predisposing, precipitation and perpetuating factors. *British Journal of Psychiatry, 154,* 221–228.

McFarlane, A. C. (1992). Avoidance and intrusion in posttraumatic stress disorder. *Journal of Nervous and Mental Disease, 180,* 439–445.

McWilliams, L. A., Becker, E. S., Margraf, J., Clara, I. P., & Vriends, N. (2007). Anxiety disorder specificity of anxiety sensitivity in a community sample of young women. *Personality and Individual Differences, 42,* 345–354.

Miller, M. W. (2003). Personality and the etiology and expression of PTSD: A three-factor model perspective. *Clinical Psychology: Science and Practice, 10,* 373–393.

Miller, M. W., Greif, J. L., & Smith, A. A. (2003). Multidimensional Personality Questionnaire profiles of veterans with traumatic combat exposure: Externalizing and internalizing subtypes. *Psychological Assessment, 15,* 205–215.

Miller, M. W., Kaloupek, D. G., Dillon, A. L., & Keane, T. M. (2004). Externalizing and internalizing subtypes of combat-related PTSD: A replication and extension using the PSY-5 scales. *Journal of Abnormal Psychology, 113,* 636–645.

Mineka, S., Watson, D., & Clark, L. (1998). Comorbidity of anxiety and unipolar mood disorders. *Annual Review of Psychology, 49,* 377–399.

Norton, G. R., Cox, B. J., Hewitt, P. L., & McLoed, L. (1997). Personality factors associated with generalized and non-generalized social anxiety. *Personality and Individual Differences, 22,* 655–660.

Norton, P. J., Sexton, K. A., Walker, J. R., & Norton, G. R. (2005). Hierarchical model of vulnerabilities for anxiety: Replication and extension with a clinical sample. *Cognitive Behaviour Therapy, 34,* 50–63.

Orsillo, S. M., Lilienfeld, S. O., & Heimberg, R. G. (1994). Social phobia and response to challenge procedures: Examining the interaction between anxiety sensitivity and trait anxiety. *Journal of Anxiety Disorders, 8,* 247–258.

O'Toole, B. I., Marshall, R. P., Schureck, R. J., & Dobson, M. (1998). Risk factors for posttraumatic stress disorder in Australian Vietnam veterans. *Australian and New Zealand Journal of Psychiatry, 32,* 21–31.

Rector, N. A., Richter, M. A., & Bagby, R. M. (2005). The impact of personality on symptom expression in obsessive-compulsive disorder. *Journal of Nervous and Mental Disease, 193,* 231–236.

Reiss, S., & McNally, R. J. (1985). Expectancy model of fear. In S. Reiss & R. R. Bootzin (Eds.), *Theoretical issues in behavior therapy* (pp. 107–121). San Diego, CA: Academic Press.

Rheaume, J., Freeston, M. H., Dugas, M. J., Letarte, H., & Ladouceur, R. (1995). Perfectionism, responsibility and obsessive-compulsive symptoms. *Behaviour Research and Therapy, 33,* 785–794.

Roca, R. P., Spence, R. J., & Munster, A. M. (1992). Posttraumatic adaptation and distress among adult burn survivors. *American Journal of Psychiatry, 149,* 1234–1238.

Saboonchi, F., & Lundh, L. (1997). Perfectionism, self-consciousness and anxiety. *Personality and Individual Differences, 22,* 921–928.

Saboonchi, F., Lundh, L., & Öst, L. (1999). Perfectionism and self-consciousness in social phobia and panic disorder with agoraphobia. *Behaviour Research and Therapy, 37,* 799–808.

Samuels, J. F., Nestadt, G., Bienvenu, O. J., Costa, P. T., Jr., Riddle, M. A., Liang, K., et al. (2000). Personality disorders and normal personality dimensions in obsessive-compulsive disorder. *British Journal of Psychiatry, 177,* 457–462.

Scarrabelotti, M. B., Duck, J. M., & Dickerson, M. M. (1995). Individual differences in obsessive-compulsive behaviour: The role of the Eysenckian dimensions and appraisals of responsibility. *Personality and Individual Differences, 18,* 413–421.

Schmidt, N. B., & Lerew, D. R. (2002). Prospective evaluation of perceived control, predictability, and anxiety sensitivity in the pathogenesis of panic. *Journal of Psychopathology and Behavioral Assessment, 24,* 207–214.

Schmidt, N. B., Lerew, D. R., & Jackson, R. J. (1997). The role of anxiety sensitivity in the pathogenesis of panic: Prospective evaluation of spontaneous panic attacks during acute stress. *Journal of Abnormal Psychology, 106,* 355–364.

Schmidt, N. B., Lerew, D. R., & Jackson, R. J. (1999). Prospective evaluation of anxiety sensitivity in the pathogenesis of panic: Replication and extension. *Journal of Abnormal Psychology, 108,* 532–537.

Schmidt, N. B., Lerew, D. R., & Joiner, T. E., Jr. (1998). Anxiety sensitivity and the pathogenesis of anxiety and depression: Evidence for symptom specificity. *Behaviour Research and Therapy, 36,* 165–177.

Schmidt, N. B., Lerew, D. R., & Joiner, T. E., Jr. (2000). Prospective evaluation of the etiology of anxiety sensitivity: Test of a scar model. *Behaviour Research and Therapy, 28,* 1083–1095.

Schmidt, N. B., & Mallott, M. (2006). Evaluating anxiety sensitivity and other fundamental sensitivities predicting anxiety symptoms and fearful responding to biological challenge. *Behaviour Research and Therapy, 44,* 1681–1688.

Schmidt, N. B., Zvolensky, M. J., & Maner, J. K. (2006). Anxiety sensitivity: Prospective prediction of panic attacks and Axis I pathology. *Journal of Psychiatric Research, 40,* 691–699.

Sexton, K. A., Norton, P. J., Walker, J. R., & Norton, G. R. (2003). A hierarchical model of generalized and specific vulnerabilities in anxiety. *Cognitive Behaviour Therapy, 32,* 1–13.

Sharhabani-Arzy, R., Amir, M., & Swisa, A. (2005). Self-criticism, dependency and posttraumatic stress disorder among a female group of help-seeking victims of domestic violence in Israel. *Personality and Individual Differences, 38,* 1231–1240.

Stewart, S. H., Taylor, S., Jang, K. L., Cox, B. J., Watt, M. C., Fedoroff, I. C., et al. (2001). Causal modeling of relations among learning history, anxiety sensitivity, and panic attacks. *Behaviour Research and Therapy, 39,* 443–456.

Talbert, S., Braswell, L. C., Albrecht, J. W., Hyer, L. A., & Boudewyns, P. A. (1993). NEO-PI profiles in PTSD as a function of trauma level. *Journal of Clinical Psychology, 49,* 663–669.

Taylor, S. (1996). Nature and measurement of anxiety sensitivity: Reply to Lilienfeld, Turner and Jacob. *Journal of Anxiety Disorders, 10,* 425–451.

Taylor, S., & Cox, B. J. (1998). Anxiety sensitivity: Multiple dimensions and hierarchic structure. *Behaviour Research and Therapy, 36,* 37–51.

Taylor, S., Koch, W. J., & Crockett, D. J. (1991). Anxiety sensitivity, trait anxiety and the anxiety disorders. *Journal of Anxiety Disorders, 5,* 293–311.

Taylor, S., Koch, W. J., & McNally, R. J. (1992). How does anxiety sensitivity vary across the anxiety disorders? *Journal of Anxiety Disorders, 6,* 249–259.

Telch, M. J., Silverman, A., & Schmidt, N. B. (1996). Effects of anxiety sensitivity and perceived control on emotional responding to caffeine challenge. *Journal of Anxiety Disorders, 10,* 21–35.

Trull, T. J., & Sher, K. J. (1994). Relationship between the five-factor model of personality and Axis I disorders in a nonclinical sample. *Journal of Abnormal Psychology, 103,* 350–360.

Watson, D., & Clark, L. A. (1997). Extraversion and its positive emotional core. In R. Hogan & J. Johnson (Eds.), *Handbook of personality psychology* (pp. 767–791). San Diego, CA: Academic Press.

Watson, D., Gamez, W., & Simms, L. J. (2005). Basic dimensions of temperament and their relation to anxiety and depression: A symptom-based perspective. *Journal of Research in Personality, 39,* 46–66.

Weems, C. F., Hayward, C., Killen, J., & Taylor, C. B. (2002). A longitudinal investigation of anxiety sensitivity in adolescence. *Journal of Abnormal Psychology, 111,* 471–477.

Weems, C. F., Pina, A. A., Costa, N. M., Watts, S. E., Taylor, L. K., & Cannon, M. F. (2007). Predisaster trait anxiety and negative affect predict posttraumatic stress in youths after Hurricane Katrina. *Journal of Consulting and Clinical Psychology, 75,* 154–159.

Weinstock, L. M., & Whisman, M. A. (2006). Neuroticism as a common feature of the depressive and anxiety disorders: A test of the Revised Integrative Hierarchical Model in a national sample. *Journal of Abnormal Psychology, 115,* 68–74.

Weiss, D. S., Marmar, C. R., Metzler, T. J., & Ronfeldt, H. M. (1995). Predicting symptomatic distress in emergency services personnel. *Journal of Consulting and Clinical Psychology, 63,* 361–368.

Yorulmaz, O., Karanci, A. N., & Tekok-Kilic, A. (2006). What are the roles of perfectionism and responsibility in checking and cleaning compulsions? *Anxiety Disorders, 20,* 312–327.

Zinbarg, R. E., & Barlow, D. H. (1996). Structure of anxiety and the anxiety disorders: A hierarchical model. *Journal of Abnormal Psychology, 105,* 181–193.

Zinbarg, R. E., Barlow, D. H., & Brown, T. A. (1997). Hierarchical structure and general factor saturation of the Anxiety Sensitivity Index: Evidence and implications. *Psychological Assessment, 9,* 277–284.

Zinbarg, R. E., Brown, T. A., Barlow, D. H., & Rapee, R. M. (2001). Anxiety sensitivity, panic, and depressed mood: A reanalysis teasing apart the contributions of the two levels in the hierarchical structure of the Anxiety Sensitivity Index. *Journal of Abnormal Psychology, 110,* 372–377.

Psychological Models of Phobic Disorders and Panic

Sheila R. Woody *and* Elizabeth Nosen

Abstract

This chapter provides a brief survey of major elements of psychodynamic, behavioral, and cognitive theories of the etiology and maintenance of panic and phobias. Each approach is described in turn, including relevant findings from psychopathology research. The chapter touches on theories that spring from diverse foundations, including intrapsychic accounts, conditioning theories such as Mowrer's two-factor model accounting for the role of avoidance, and cognitive formulations of social phobia and panic. Other psychological factors in phobic disorders and panic, including anxiety sensitivity, temperament, evolutionary pressures, and culture, are also discussed. The chapter concludes with a discussion of commonalities across these diverse theories on points such as the importance of life events and beliefs about feared stimuli and the consequences of anxiety.

Keywords: behavioral, cognitive, etiological models, fear, panic, phobias, psychodynamic, social anxiety

Many people have strong fears, including fear of death, specific animals or insects, heights, air travel, public speaking, medical procedures, or thunderstorms. Phobias for which people seek treatment usually include those described as types of specific phobia in the *DSM–IV:* phobias of animals, environmental situations (e.g., water) or events (e.g., storms), blood/injury, and specific situations such as enclosed places. Many people suffer with a phobia for decades, seeking treatment only when the phobia's interference with daily functioning escalates (Öst, 1987). An example would be someone with blood/injury phobia who develops a medical problem for which he or she is unable to obtain appropriate treatment due to the phobia. Clients do not often present for treatment with a specific phobia as their only complaint unless they have multiple phobias or phobias that are complicated by panic (Chapman, Fyer, Mannuzza, & Klein, 1993).

Panic attacks are characterized by a sudden wave of fear or alarm, including intense physical sensations of arousal and frightening thoughts about dying, losing control, or going insane. In response to repeated panic attacks, some individuals begin to avoid specific places or situations due to fear of panic (agoraphobia), while others take some safety precautions (such as carrying a mobile phone) without avoidance. The protective effect of a trusted companion objectively reduces distress, catastrophic cognitions, and physiological arousal during biological challenge experiments (Carter, Hollon, Carson, & Shelton, 1995).

Although individuals with social phobia may experience panic attacks related to social situations, the cardinal feature of social phobia is fear of negative evaluation. Persons with social phobia have a strong fear of situations in which they are open to possible scrutiny from others, and the basic fear in these situations is that of being embarrassed or humiliated. In social situations requiring interaction with others, the phobic person often fears being unable to carry on a conversation or leaving an impression of being strange, incompetent, or terrified. Situations that involve potential scrutiny from others, even without direct interaction, can also be problematic, including musical performances, eating or drinking in public, writing in public (e.g., signing a check), using public washrooms, or simply engaging in publicly observable behavior (e.g., bowling). Public speaking is the most commonly feared situation, although most people with social phobia fear and avoid more than one situation (Turner, Beidel, Dancu, & Keys, 1986).

Chapter 3 describes phobias and panic disorder in more detail, including the diagnostic criteria and associated features. The purpose of this chapter is to outline psychological theories about the development and maintenance of these disorders. We will begin with psychodynamic or interpersonal formulations, followed by behavioral models, and we conclude with cognitive models and a discussion of some commonalities across theories. We will describe each approach in turn, including relevant findings from psychopathology research.

Psychodynamic Formulations

Briefly, the classic psychoanalytic formulation of phobias, as described by Goisman (1983), involves an anxiety-provoking impulse, often primitive and socially unacceptable, that is repressed because it is too threatening to be acknowledged. The impulse and its associated anxiety are displaced onto a symbolically or temporally associated object. Generalization may occur, in which similar objects also come to provoke anxiety. The displacement of anxiety onto a symbolic object is considered to be functional because it creates a "threatening" stimulus that can be avoided, unlike intrapsychic conflict. In this account, neurotic anxiety arises purely internally. The formation of a phobic symptom is seen as an attempt to "bind" the anxiety so that it can masquerade as a realistic external fear, and hence be avoided (Compton, 1992). The common element to these accounts of the development of phobias is in the intrapsychic source of anxiety; different writers diverge in their view of the specific impulse being defended against.

The explanatory power of classic psychoanalytic theory is diminished by what appear to be arbitrary interpretations of the specific symptoms of anxiety. For example, Snaith (1968) attributes claustrophobia as well as fear of being alone to a defensive reaction against the temptation to masturbate, and the agoraphobic fear of "going shopping" is taken to indicate a wish to take mother's place beside father.

Other writers target the "discovery of the genital difference" as the precipitating event for childhood phobias (Compton, 1992). These explanations leave no avenue to verify their accuracy, and different writers often disagree on the basis of the same information. Freud's explanation for Little Hans's horse phobia, for example, was based in Oedipal rivalry for his mother, but Lief (1968) argues that the boy's phobia was based on fear of punishment for masturbation.

In contrast to classic psychoanalytic theory, contemporary psychodynamic writers emphasize the personal meaning of the feared stimulus, in closer association with learning and cognitive theories. Salzman's (1968) account takes the psychoanalysts' aggressive or sexual impulse theory and expands it to include any potential threat to the patient's capacity for self-control. The humiliating and threatening consequences of losing control lead to attendant fears of public display of inadequacy and imperfection. The phobia is seen as a "ritual of inaction" (avoidance) designed to exert control over the threat of unmasking of one's inadequacies. Consistent with this idea, the most common feared outcomes endorsed by clients with specific phobia involve the consequences of panic, such as losing control and public humiliation (McNally & Steketee, 1985). Those who argue that the success of treatment for specific phobia is due to restoring a sense of self-efficacy (Williams, Turner, & Peer, 1985) or changing core beliefs about the consequences of experiencing anxiety (Thorpe & Salkovskis, 1995) do not seem to be too far from Salzman's formulation.

From a psychodynamic perspective, symptoms of panic or intense anxiety are indicative of an unconscious conflict, often related to separation versus independence from important others. Shear, Cooper, Klerman, Busch, Shapiro, (1993) postulate that early experiences with frightening and overcontrolling parental behaviors render individuals vulnerable to conflicts between dependence and independence as an adult. Fantasies reflecting anxiety-provoking early life experiences, such as angry separation, critical or unsupportive parents, and relationship entrapment, are hypothesized to engender feelings of resentment and difficulty modulating anger. Shear et al. argue that clients with immature defenses, who tend to maintain a problem focus, are unable to adequately suppress the fear and anxiety associated with this conflict, leaving them feeling unsafe.

Indeed, psychodynamic theorists have noted on the basis of case reviews that adults with panic often report stressful interpersonal problems as a precipitant to the onset of panic (Shear et al., 1993). Among 50 participants with agoraphobia, Kleiner and Marshall (1987) reported that 42 recalled significant marital or relationship conflicts prior to the onset of the phobia. Many other commonly reported stressors at the time of onset were also of an interpersonal nature, including family conflicts, social isolation, or moving to a new home (Kleiner & Marshall, 1987). Agoraphobic individuals also report higher prevalence of parental divorce and maternal separation in their childhood than do controls (Faravelli, 1985). Early childhood physical or sexual abuse is associated with greater risk of subsequent panic (Goodwin, Fergusson, & Horwood, 2005; Safren, Gershuny, Marzol, Otto, & Pollack, 2002) and phobias (Evren, Kural, & Cakmak, 2006; Saunders, Villepointeaux, & Lipovsky, 1992; Stein, Walker, & Anderson, 1996). In particular, retrospective reports of childhood sexual abuse are more common among individuals with panic disorder than among controls or individuals with other types of anxiety disorders (Goodwin et al., 2005; Leskin & Sheikh, 2002; Safren et al., 2002; Stein et al., 1996).

Contemporary interpersonal perspectives on panic and social phobia also point to unacceptable emotions such as anger. Busch, Milrod, and Singer (1999) offer the clinical observation that many clients with panic disorder are unaware of their deep angry feelings and the interpersonal conflict that these feelings engender (in combination with a fear of loss of important relationships). Busch et al. propose panic sometimes serves as an unconscious self-punishment for aggressive transgressions such as individuating from family members. Although panic attacks are highly unpleasant events, Busch et al. suggest that conflicts involving separation and independence have potential to evoke even more intense negative affect, so panic represents the "least unpleasurable" outcome. Evidence suggests that individuals with panic disorder do experience more difficulties identifying and labeling emotions compared to nonanxious individuals; they also show a marked tendency to try to control or "bottle up" feelings of anger, unhappiness, and anxiety (Baker, Holloway, Thomas, Thomas, & Owens, 2004).

Although shame is potentially more important than anger in social phobia (Gabbard, 1992), Miller (1985) argues that unconscious aggressive impulses also underlie the fear of looking foolish. In this view, socially phobic individuals focus on the risk of humiliation rather than their unacceptable hostile impulses, a strategy that preserves personal relationships. Indeed, Erwin, Heimberg, and Schneier (2003) have found that socially phobic individuals exhibit more anger and exert more effort to suppress anger in comparison to nonanxious individuals. Anger suppression is in turn associated with poorer response to cognitive behavioral therapy (CBT) for social phobia (Erwin et al., 2003). Researchers have often neglected psychodynamic and interpersonal models in favor of behavioral or cognitive theories, so many of these ideas are not yet well tested.

Behavioral Models

Conditioning theories of anxiety describe the process by which one learns to be afraid. They propose that fears are acquired through a process of learned association, in which neutral stimuli that are present during a traumatic event subsequently elicit fear on their own. Fear of a neutral stimulus is attributed to a co-occurrence of the stimulus with an aversive incident at some point in the client's history. Examples of inherently aversive incidents include pain, threat of abandonment, spontaneous panic attack, or loss of consciousness. The fear stemming from the aversive incident is presumed to generalize beyond the original fearful stimulus to include the neutral (now conditioned or phobic) stimulus as well. The aversive stimulus can be external or internal to the individual (Bouton, Mineka, & Barlow, 2001; Rescorla, 1988). This new fear is considered to be "conditional" or "conditioned," as the original neutral stimuli provokes fear only through its association with a particular condition (Barlow, 2002).

This process, whereby people (or other animals) become afraid of something once it has been paired with an aversive event, has been demonstrated many times in laboratories. Factors influencing the intensity of the conditioned fear response include the number of times the previously neutral stimulus (i.e., the conditioned stimulus) and the original source of the fear (i.e., the unconditioned stimulus) are paired together temporally, the level of similarity between the two stimuli, and the intensity of fear originally elicited by the unconditioned stimuli (Dickinson & Mackintosh, 1978).

Research has thus shown that classical conditioning *can* initiate phobias, but whether naturally occurring phobias are *typically* due to a conditioning process is more difficult to say. Only a minority of clients with specific phobia actually recall a traumatic onset of their phobia (McNally & Steketee, 1985; Öst & Hugdahl, 1981). On the other hand, the onset of specific phobias, particularly the animal phobias, may occur so early in life that the triggering event is forgotten. Phobias, particularly nonanimal phobias with an onset in adulthood, have been documented to occur following aversive events. For example, 38% of a group of 55 survivors of automobile accidents subsequently developed a driving phobia (Kuch, Cox, Evans, & Shulman, 1994). In addition, a primary basis of choking and dental phobias is a previous frightening experience such as choking on food or having a painful dental visit (Greenberg, Stern, & Weilburg, 1988; Moore, Brodsgaard, & Birn, 1991).

One puzzle associated with early conditioning accounts of phobias was how avoidance could be maintained. Mowrer (1939) furthered conditioning theories by proposing that fears will fail to extinguish when the object of fear is successfully avoided. In this view, agoraphobic (or social) avoidance is negatively reinforced by the reduction in anxiety that occurs when the person escapes or decides to avoid a feared situation. Cessation of anxiety thereby reinforces avoidance, increasing the probability that the individual will avoid similar situations in the future. This two-factor avoidance model is particularly useful for explaining how fears can persist over extremely long periods of time.

Social Anxiety

Conditioning models are not limited to explaining specific phobias. Social phobia may arise from classical conditioning in the same manner. In this model, social anxiety is thought to develop through a history of aversive outcomes to social interactions, such as rejection, humiliation, or shame. Retrospectively recalling their childhoods, adults with social phobia frequently report a history of severe teasing or other direct traumatic conditioning experiences that they relate to the development of their social phobia (McCabe, Antony, Summerfeldt, Liss, & Swinson, 2003; Stemberger, Turner, Deborah, & Calhoun, 1995).

For individuals with poor social skills, operant conditioning principles may promote social avoidance and fear. Some socially anxious individuals unwittingly elicit negative reactions from others through behavioral deficiencies such as nonassertiveness, poor eye contact, low self-disclosure, restricted conversation, trembling, and other signs of visible anxiety. Accordingly, these individuals miss out on positive reinforcement of prosocial behavior. Even further, interaction partners are often put off by such unskilled behavior, which can be interpreted as unfriendliness, prompting rejection of the anxious person. As such, the unskilled person often experiences social interactions as unpleasant and anxiety-provoking, which perpetuates a vicious cycle of social fear, withdrawal, and rejection. In operant conditioning terms, the individual with skills deficits experiences social situations as punishing and avoidance or safety behaviors as negatively reinforced.

Although persons with social phobia generally exhibit ineffective social interaction behaviors (Baker & Edelmann, 2002; Stopa & Clark, 1993), it is unclear whether this arises from a deficient behavioral repertoire or whether intense anxiety simply prevents the competent display of adequate latent skills. Socially phobic children are rated as less socially competent and skilled than their peers, and their interactions with other children are less frequent and of poorer quality (Beidel, Turner, & Morris, 1999; Spence, Donovan, & Brechman-Toussaint, 1999). Some studies suggest that, under the right conditions, individuals with social phobia can perform socially as well as nonanxious persons (Rapee & Lim, 1992; Thompson & Rapee, 2002). Recent research with socially anxious children has found these children present comparably to nonanxious children, but the anxious children believe their skills to be deficient (Cartwright-Hatton, Hodges, & Porter, 2003; Cartwright-Hatton, Tschernitz, & Gomersall, 2005). Thus, socially phobic persons may possess the requisite social skills but fail to use them appropriately.

Panic and Fainting as Unconditioned Stimuli

Spontaneous panic attacks are well known to provoke generalized fear of situations in which the attacks occur, and more than 90% of people with animal phobias report that their primary phobic concern is related to panicking, rather than being harmed by the animal (McNally & Steketee, 1985). Moreover, panic attacks are themselves inherently frightening and represent a powerful unconditioned stimulus. For this reason, the location in which the panic occurred often becomes a conditioned stimulus for provoking future anxiety and hence avoidance. This process helps explain the occurrence of situationally cued panic attacks, a phenomenon common to specific and social phobias, as well as agoraphobia. Conditioning theories have also been employed to account for the uncued or "spontaneous" attacks that occur in panic disorder. In this process, which Goldstein and Chambless (1978) termed *fear of fear,* low levels of anxiety and arousal can also serve as the conditioned stimulus for eliciting higher levels of anxiety and panic. Most people with panic disorder describe clear memories of a specific traumatic panic attack that marked the beginning of the disorder (Öst & Hugdahl, 1983). Mild physiological arousal subsequently comes to serve as a trigger for panic (Margraf, Ehlers, & Roth, 1986).

Blood and injury phobia presents an unusual case because it is associated with an atypical and sometimes dramatic physiological response—a vasovagal response. Öst, Sterner, and Lindahl (1984) provided a fascinating account of a group of blood/injury phobics who were asked to watch a gruesome video of thoracic surgery. Participants were permitted to turn off the video when it became too intense. During the baseline (before they knew the video was coming), a stable physiological pattern was observed. During the few minutes of instructions and exposure to the video, heart rate and blood pressure rose markedly. Blood pressure and heart rate then began to *decrease,* consistently reaching their lowest point about 4 minutes after the participant had turned off the video. Five participants who fainted or came closest to fainting were examined in more detail. Some participants experienced a gradual decline in heart rate and blood pressure for a few minutes and then a dramatic drop, which was often followed by the participant turning off the video. In one individual, heart rate dropped as low as 28 beats per minute. Öst et al. observed frequent periods of asystole (when the heart stops contracting) in almost all participants, varying from 2 to 9 seconds.

Some researchers have investigated biological influences on the vasovagal response to blood/injury stimuli (Accurso et al., 2001; Kendler, Myers, Prescott, & Neale, 2001). Loss of consciousness can also serve as a potent unconditioned stimulus. Kleinknecht and Lenz (1989) found a positive relationship between history of fainting and fear of blood/injury/injection and further reported more avoidance of medical situations among individuals who fainted in response to blood/injury stimuli than among those who feared such situations but did not faint.

Vicarious Conditioning

In addition to direct conditioning, Rachman (1977) pointed to two cultural pathways to acquisition of fear. He proposed that fears can also be acquired vicariously, by watching someone respond fearfully to a stimulus, or through transmission of frightening information about the object or situation. Subsequent experiments suggest that phobias can be acquired vicariously (Mineka, Davidson, Cook, & Keir, 1984; Öst & Hugdahl, 1981). Social anxiety and avoidance may be modeled in families with socially phobic parents (Bruch & Heimberg, 1994). Acquiring fears through information would include hearing frightening warnings from family members about the dangers of the neutral stimulus. This phenomenon is readily observed in those clients with a phobia of flying who have never taken an airplane trip.

Fear of bodily sensations may also be acquired though early learning experiences. Ehlers (1993) found that individuals with panic disorder, as well as infrequent panickers, reported more chronic illnesses in their households while growing up compared with those with other anxiety disorders or controls, a finding replicated by Laraia, Stuart, and Frye (1994). Through such experiences, individuals may learn that physical symptoms are dangerous and a cause for concern. Indeed, people with anxiety disorders (both panic and other types), as well as people with high levels of anxiety sensitivity, report more exposure to uncontrolled parental behaviors (e.g., drunkenness, anger) than do controls (Ehlers, 1993; Watt, Stewart, & Cox, 1998). This exposure may serve as an experiential learning basis for fears of losing control.

Perhaps not surprisingly, given the common symptoms of panic, experience with respiratory illness is a risk factor for both panic and phobias (Bussing, Burket, & Kelleher, 1996; Goodwin, Jacobi, & Thefeld, 2003). Researchers hypothesize that airway restriction associated with asthma and other respiratory illnesses may act as an unconditioned stimulus, sensitizing fear of suffocation and sensitivity to more subtle changes in respiratory function (Carr, 1998). Indeed, fears of suffocation have been associated with both panic and specific phobia (Antony, Brown, & Barlow, 1997; Vernberg, Griez, & Meijer, 1994). Anxiety in asthmatics has also been strongly related to perceptions of airway restriction, independent of changes in actual bronchial airflow (Isenberg, Lehrer, & Hochron, 1992). Personal experience with other chronic illnesses may similarly facilitate fears of bodily sensations.

Beliefs about the danger of somatic symptoms may also be acquired through parental modeling. Parental sick role behaviors, such as staying home from work or going to the hospital, may encourage negative evaluations of physical symptoms. Watt et al. (1998), for example, found that individuals with high anxiety sensitivity not only experienced more anxiety and cold symptoms in their youth, but also reported more parental encouragement of sick role behavior than did low anxiety sensitivity individuals. As might be expected, panickers reported more learning experiences specific to anxiety-related symptoms than did nonpanickers. Panickers also retrospectively report observing more anxiety-related parental sick-role behavior at home (Ehlers, 1993). These findings provide some support for the role of instrumental learning in acquisition of anxiety.

Temperament

Behavioral inhibition is a term that describes a temperament of responding to novel stimuli with reticence, withdrawal, or caution (Kagan, 1999). Other labels that have been used to describe this temperament include shyness, withdrawal, and inhibition (Rapee & Spence, 2004). Behaviorally inhibited children appear to be more likely to develop social phobia in later life (Hayward, Killen, Kraemer, & Taylor, 1998; Neal, Edelmann, & Glachan, 2002), although a substantial proportion of behaviorally inhibited children do not (Biederman et al., 2001; Schwartz, Snidman, & Kagan, 1999).

Some evidence suggests that social reticence is more predictive of subsequent social phobia than is the physical fear component of behavioral inhibition (Neal et al., 2002; van Ameringen, Mancini, & Oakman, 1998), although this pattern leaves open the possibility that behavioral inhibition is simply an early manifestation of the behavioral patterns that characterize socially anxious individuals. Interestingly, children classified as behaviorally inhibited at 21 months of age are more vulnerable to developing various anxiety disorders by the time they are 7 or 8 years old (Hirschfeld et al., 1992).

Learning experiences in childhood and adolescence that promote avoidance in the face of anxiety-evoking situations may shape an avoidant coping style. Ehlers (1993) explored early learning experiences about somatic symptoms, for example. Compared to controls, individuals with anxiety disorders reported more frequent parental instructions to avoid strenuous or social activities. Barrett, Rapee, Dadds, and Ryan (1996) also found that family discussion bolstered anxious children's plans for avoidance.

Cultural Factors

Overall, women often report more intense fears than do men (Fredrikson, Annas, Fischer, & Wik, 1996), and women are more avoidant than are men when confronted with a fear-provoking stimulus such as a snake. Even when men and women are matched for how scared they say they are, once confronted with an actual snake, women are more avoidant, look more anxious, and report feeling more fear (Speltz & Bernstein, 1976; Woody & Chambless, 1989). This difference in fearful behavior is also evident in prevalence rates for phobias; community studies show that women outnumber men with specific phobias 2:1 (Bourdon et al., 1988; Magee, Eaton, Wittchen, McGonagle, & Kessler, 1996).

Why are women overrepresented among phobics? One theory blames sociocultural factors (Chambless, 1987). The traditional masculine sex role involves bravery and prizes assertive, instrumental behavior. Developing boys who display fear may be encouraged to confront their fears; they are almost certainly teased for avoiding or running away. The expectations for girls are different. While fearful behavior may not be actively encouraged, it is certainly tolerated to a greater extent than among boys. Thus, girls may feel less pressure to perform fearlessly, which constitutes a low-demand situation. As discussed above, this circumstance is more likely to be associated with avoidant behavior in the face of fear than a high-demand situation such as the one boys are likely to be facing. If this theory is accurate, social pressure creates a high level of demand for boys and men to behave as though they are not afraid, even when they are. As Chambless (1987) hypothesizes, this active, instrumental behavior may be prophylactic against potential phobias; exposure to feared stimuli may prevent incipient phobias from developing.

Culturally transmitted social goals and expectancies are another form of social learning likely to influence the experience and expression of social anxiety. Cultural context shapes one's sense of self as well as expectations of appropriate and successful social behavior. In a North American context, for example, social pressure encourages self-promotion within culturally prescribed limits and discourages overt submissiveness and reticence. Socially phobic North Americans worry that others will see them as passive or uninteresting, and on average they are more behaviorally reticent than nonanxious persons in socially threatening situations (Alden & Bieling, 1998). Asian social norms, on the other hand, favor less dominant, more avoidant styles of communication (Kim, 1994; Oetzel, 1998a, 1998b). These cultural groups encourage social strategies that are often associated with display of anxiety in a North American context, such as submissiveness or self-effacement (Triandis, 1995). As might be anticipated given these cultural differences, Asians generally endorse higher social anxiety than do Westerners (Norasakkunkit & Kalick, 2002; Okazaki, 2002; Okazaki & Kallivayalil, 2002). Foreign-born East Asians also report higher social anxiety than do those born in the United States (Okazaki, 2000). For reasons that are not yet understood, however, rates of social phobia appear to be lower in Asian countries than in Western countries (Weissman et al., 1996; Wittchen & Fehm, 2001) .

Evolutionary Theories

Seligman (1971) and others have noted that the stimuli featured in common phobias are not random. Phobias of certain stimuli, such as snakes or heights, are relatively prevalent, but other familiar potential sources of danger, such as guns or moving cars, are never (or almost never) reported as phobic objects. Apparently, not every neutral stimulus has equal potential to signal danger even if paired with a frightening event. Preparedness theory proposes that evolutionary pressure has shaped a biological predisposition toward rapidly associating select stimuli with aversive events. An innate predilection to acquire fear of objects or situations that posed threats to ancestral humans (such as heights or snakes) would conceivably be shaped through evolutionary pressure. Modern dangers, such as electrical outlets, would not have had time (in evolutionary terms) to influence survival rates.

Arne Öhman and his colleagues have conducted elegant experiments to test this theory (Mineka & Öhman, 2002). They have found that snakes and spiders more easily elicit conditioned responses than flowers, mushrooms, or electrical outlets (Öhman, Dimberg, & Öst, 1985; Öhman & Mineka, 2001). Prepared stimuli, but not fear-irrelevant stimuli, can become conditioned stimuli even when presented subliminally (Öhman & Soares, 1993). Cook and Mineka (1989, 1990) demonstrated similar phenomena in lab-reared Rhesus monkeys. Although the monkeys had no previous experience with snakes or crocodiles, they more easily acquired fears of these stimuli than of flowers or rabbits. The theory also extends to social stimuli. Research participants detect angry faces in a crowd faster than they detect neutral or negative faces (Juth, Lundqvist, Karlsson, & Öhman, 2005), and angry faces elicit greater skin conductance responses (Merckelbach, van Hout, van den Hout, & Mersch, 1989). Conditioned fears of angry faces are more resistant to extinction than those conditioned to happy or neutral faces (Öhman & Dimberg, 1978).

Cognitive Theories
Misinterpretation of Bodily Sensations

In what has become a classic paper, Clark (1986) proposed a cognitive theory of panic in which he suggested that the basis for panic attacks is a catastrophic misinterpretation of bodily sensations, specifically those sensations typically associated with anxiety (see Figure 1). According to this model, a sensation, such as transient lightheadedness, is perceived as threatening by individuals who are frightened of bodily sensations of arousal (later termed *anxiety sensitivity*). Perceived threats are naturally followed by anxious apprehension, which intensifies the physical sensations of anxiety. For individuals who fear these sensations, catastrophic misinterpretation can follow. For example, lightheadedness may be taken as a sign of a brain aneurysm or stroke. As Figure 1 illustrates, this misinterpretation of the bodily sensation provides further perception of threat, completing the cycle. Catastrophic outcomes typically imagined during a panic attack include dying from an imminent health emergency, going insane, or losing control followed by public humiliation. Such misinterpretations evoke fear, which in turn exacerbates the experience of somatic sensations, resulting in a vicious cycle of rapidly escalating fear.

Anxiety sensitivity is conceptualized as fear of sensations associated with anxiety (Peterson & Reiss, 1987). This trait is believed to engender the misinterpretation of the sensations that initiates the cycle schematized in Figure 1. Schmidt, Lerew, and Jackson (1997) prospectively examined the role of anxiety sensitivity in the development of panic under periods of acute stress. They followed a group of first-year undergraduate cadets through 5 weeks of basic military training. After controlling for history of panic attacks and trait anxiety, anxiety sensitivity at baseline predicted the development of spontaneous panic attacks and subsequent functional impairment and disability due to anxiety.

Other cognitive features of panic and agoraphobia provide support for a cognitive view of these problems. Clients with panic disorder tend to interpret ambiguous bodily sensations as signs of immediate personal danger (Clark et al., 1997). During anxious moments, clients with agoraphobia are more afraid of losing control and being embarrassed than are persons with specific phobia or no anxiety disorder (Belfer & Glass, 1992). Even more telling, these clients express stronger belief in their interpretations of the bodily sensations than is expressed by normal control subjects or other anxiety patients

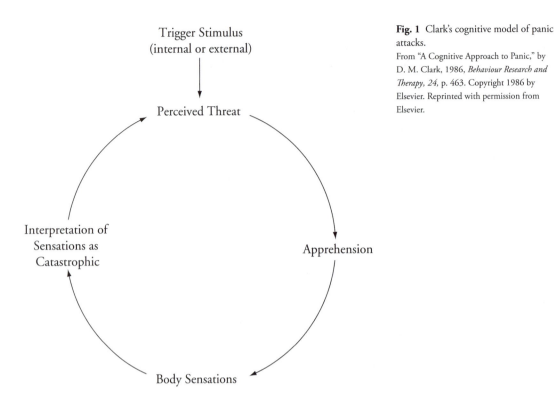

Trigger Stimulus
(internal or external)

↓

Perceived Threat

Apprehension

Body Sensations

Interpretation of
Sensations as
Catastrophic

Fig. 1 Clark's cognitive model of panic attacks.
From "A Cognitive Approach to Panic," by D. M. Clark, 1986, *Behaviour Research and Therapy, 24,* p. 463. Copyright 1986 by Elsevier. Reprinted with permission from Elsevier.

(Clark et al., 1997). Taken together, these findings suggest systematic biases in the way in which clients with panic disorder or agoraphobia process information about physical sensations.

Why do some clients develop agoraphobic avoidance in response to panic attacks, whereas others do not? Growing evidence indicates cognitive variables may be linked to the development of agoraphobia. Agoraphobics tend to expect more panic attacks, focus on the potential negative consequences of an attack (e.g., social humiliation, physical danger), and subsequently feel unable to cope with these events (Clum & Knowles, 1991). Social scrutiny also appears to play a significant role in agoraphobic avoidance. If the first attack occurred in public or caused embarrassment for the client, then avoidance is more likely to follow (Amering et al., 1997). In a behavioral avoidance task, clients with panic disorder were more likely to avoid assigned tasks during a grocery shopping trip if they had been asked to speak to a store clerk or another customer during their shopping experience than if no social interaction was required (Whittal & Goetsch, 1997).

Clark (1993) has further proposed a cognitive explanation for the occurrence of panic during biological challenge experiments, in which a substance (e.g., carbon dioxide [CO_2]–enriched air)

reliably provokes a panic attack among those with panic disorder but less often for those without panic disorder. Clark notes that these procedures induce various physical sensations, which his model argues provoke fear among those with panic. Furthermore, cognitions involving the misinterpretation of bodily sensations occur at the time of challenge-induced panic attacks (Clark, 1993).

In one such study, Sanderson, Rapee, and Barlow (1989) manipulated perception of control during a 20-minute test period. Participants with panic disorder were shown a signal light that would ostensibly indicate times when they would be able to regulate the composition of the gas mixture they were inhaling. Participants understood they would not be able to regulate the gas mixture when the light was not illuminated. In reality, the controls did not affect the gas mixture. All participants inhaled the same 5% CO_2–enriched air, although the light was turned on for half of the participants, creating an illusion of control. Participants in the *Illusion of Control* condition reported fewer catastrophic thoughts compared to those in the *No Control* condition. Similarly, panic-disordered participants with a perception of no control were much more likely to experience a panic attack (80%) than were those with an illusion of control (20%), despite receiving the same amount of CO_2.

The proposal that misinterpretation of bodily sensations contributes to maladaptive anxiety is not limited to panic. An important element of the social phobia model proposed by Rapee and Heimberg (1997) is that internal cues of anxiety color one's mental image of how one appears to others involved in the social situation (see Figure 2). Essentially, clients with social phobia believe they look as terrified and unsure as they feel, which is discrepant from how they believe others expect them to look in a social situation. This discrepancy provokes an assessment of the anticipated consequences of negative evaluation, which results in elevated anxiety that feeds back to the mental representation of the self. Behavioral symptoms of anxiety, if sufficiently severe, can affect social partners. People tend to be less comfortable interacting with someone who has an unsteady voice, trembling hands, or other signs of severe anxiety. In addition, as described earlier, social partners can misperceive reticence as aloofness or indifference, neither of which facilitates social success. Indeed, Stopa and Clark (1993) found

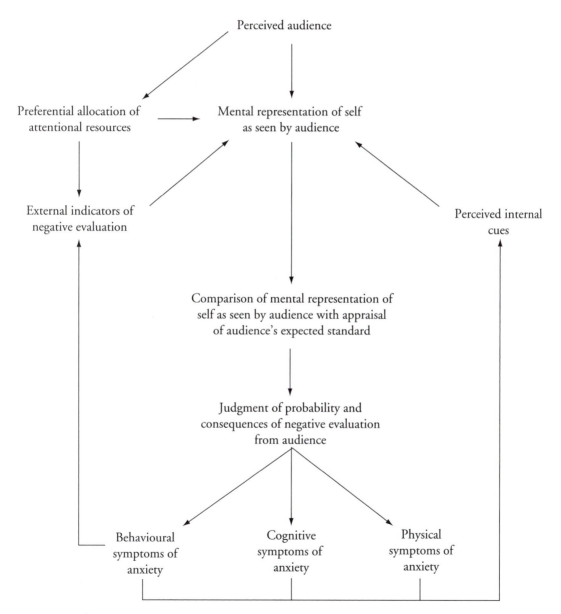

Fig. 2 Rapee and Heimberg model of social phobia.
From "A Cognitive-Behavioral Model of Anxiety in Social Phobia," by R. M. Rapee and R. G. Heimberg, 1997, *Behaviour Research and Therapy, 35,* p. 743. Copyright 1997 by Elsevier. Reprinted with permission from Elsevier.

that observers perceived individuals with social phobia as less outgoing and warm.

Perhaps surprisingly, even clients with specific phobias freely express fear about the consequences of experiencing intense anxiety. In a sample of diverse types of specific phobias, most respondents expressed at least a 40% degree of belief in ideas related to fear of physical consequences of anxiety—similar to those observed in anxiety sensitivity or panic disorder (Thorpe & Salkovskis, 1995). The most common catastrophic physical consequences endorsed by participants in the Thorpe and Salkovskis sample were, "I will make a fool of myself," "I will feel faint," "I will lose control," "I will be unable to escape," and "I will feel trapped." These thoughts were endorsed in the context of being in the same room with the phobic stimulus.

Cognitive Processes

Individuals with social phobia express beliefs that appear to engender anxiety and fear, including beliefs about themselves, beliefs about social standards, and beliefs about the importance of emotional control. In terms of themselves, socially phobic persons anticipate that they are likely to bungle various social situations, behaving in a socially unskilled or unacceptable manner. Related to social standards, social phobics hold unrealistic performance standards (e.g., "I must always have something interesting to say") or overestimate the probability of negative outcomes like loss of status or opportunities (e.g., "If others see me blush, then they will think I am weak"). Rapee and Heimberg (1997) suggest that the socially anxious person believes that other people are inherently critical and likely to evaluate the individual negatively, leading to social rejection and humiliation.

In terms of beliefs about the importance of emotional control, some theorists argue that individuals with social phobia avoid social interactions because they anticipate a lack of control over their emotional responses (Hofmann, 2005). Socially phobic persons believe they lack internal control (Leung & Heimberg, 1996) but that other people can control such events (Cloitre, Heimberg, Liebowitz, & Gitow, 1992). Hofmann (2005) found that perceptions of control over anxiety responses mediated the relationship between social anxiety and estimations of the consequences of negative social interactions (i.e., social cost).

In addition to anxiogenic beliefs, cognitive theories emphasize specific cognitive processes that are hypothesized to maintain such beliefs, including self-focused attention, safety behaviors, and distorted cognitive processing (Clark & Wells, 1995; Rapee & Heimberg, 1997).

Self-focused attention can be a problematic cognitive process for both social phobia and panic disorder. When individuals with social phobia sense a threat of negative evaluation, they will pay close and careful attention to thoughts and internal sensations of anxiety to infer how others may perceive them. As seen in Figure 2, however, self-focused attention increases salience of one's own anxiety response and contributes to a negative mental representation of how one looks to others. Research has confirmed that individuals who are highly socially anxious report higher levels of self-focused attention than less socially anxious individuals (Mellings & Alden, 2000). Further, self-focused attention is believed to impair social performance because it detracts attention from the core task of communicating with others. Self-focused attention increases anxiety in both socially phobic and normal individuals (Bögels & Lamers, 2002; Woody, 1996; Woody & Rodriguez, 2000).

Hypervigilance to bodily sensations is also a feature of panic disorder and is correlated with severity of agoraphobia (Hughes, Budd, & Greenaway, 1999), although the interpretations of sensations differ from panic to social phobia. Whereas the person with social phobia interprets physical events as a possible indicator of outward appearance, the person with panic interprets physical events as possibly indicating illness or malfunction. Conscious attendance to internal cues appears to be a normal adaptive process, as there is wide variability in the general population with regard to how much people attend to their bodily sensations (Schmidt, Lerew, & Trakowski, 1997). The normal process of attending to internal sensations appears to be exaggerated in those with panic disorder (Schmidt et al., 1997), although the extent to which this vigilance causes or is due to the experience of panic attacks is debatable. During anxious moments, clients with agoraphobia are more aware of autonomic signs of arousal than are persons with specific phobia or no anxiety disorder (Belfer & Glass, 1992).

Safety behaviors are designed to reduce the risk of feared events, such as being negatively evaluated, encountering a phobic stimulus, or losing consciousness. Clinical examples include reading a speech rather than speaking extemporaneously (for social phobia), keeping one's feet off the floor while sitting (for spider phobia), and grabbing a physical support in response to momentary lightheadedness (for panic disorder). Cognitive theorists believe such behaviors are problematic because they prevent unambiguous disconfirmation of feared outcomes. Essentially, by engaging in these behaviors, the client can plausibly continue to believe that the feared event would have occurred if the safety behavior had not been performed. If no negative event occurs when a safety behavior has been performed, the individual is likely to attribute the positive outcome to performance of the safety behavior rather than reevaluating the threat-related beliefs that maintain anxiety.

At least with social anxiety, safety behaviors appear to be performed more frequently under circumstances of higher threat. Alden and Bieling (1998), for example, led research participants to believe that they were going to interact with either a critical or accepting partner. Although the partner behaved the same in both conditions, social phobics who anticipated negative evaluation used more safety behaviors during the conversation than did nonanxious controls. Socially anxious individuals did not behave differently from controls in the positive expectation condition, however, indicating that a social skills deficit could not account for the result.

Research also supports the idea that safety behaviors interfere with treatment gains during exposure therapy. Sloan and Telch (2002), for example, assigned claustrophobic individuals to one of three exposure treatments: exposure alone, exposure accompanied by guided threat focus and reappraisal, or exposure accompanied by safety behaviors. Participants in the safety behavior condition were encouraged to use various safety strategies at their discretion during the exposure, including opening a window, standing near an exit door, talking to the experimenter via intercom, and checking that the chamber door was indeed unlocked. They found that individuals encouraged to use safety behaviors during exposure showed less fear reduction between trials and reported significantly more fear at posttreatment than did participants in either of the other two conditions.

Distorted information processing is believed to play a role in maintaining maladaptive fear and has been most extensively studied in the context of social anxiety. Information processing includes attention, memory, interpretation, and other cognitive processes. Individuals with social phobia are hypervigilant for signs of negative evaluation from others. They notice cues of criticism more efficiently than positive social cues (Veljaca & Rapee, 1998),

interpret ambiguous social cues negatively (Amir, Foa, & Coles, 1998; Stopa & Clark, 2000), and discount or fail to notice positive social cues. Empirical studies confirm that social phobics show reduced processing of information when under threat of social evaluation, in the form of attentional bias away from faces (Mansell, Clark, Ehlers, & Chen, 1999), degraded processing of faces (Chen, Ehlers, Clark, & Mansell, 2002), and poorer memory for details of social interactions (Hope, Heimberg, & Klein, 1990; Mellings & Alden, 2000). Postevent processing involves recalling embarrassing moments in a previous social situation and can extend the time of anxious suffering well beyond the duration of the social event itself. Rachman, Grüter-Andrew, and Shafran (2000) found that highly socially anxious individuals engage in longer postevent processing than nonsocially anxious persons, and such processing was associated with subsequent situational avoidance.

Perceptual distortion is a cognitive phenomenon that appears to exacerbate anxiety. Rachman and Cuk (1992) related several interesting clinical anecdotes of patients with anxiety disorders who experience what appear to be distortions in their perception of feared stimuli. In the case of a snake that is perceived to be longer than it actually is or to dart more quickly than it really does, distortions or misperceptions are easy to understand. Some of the patients' perceptions went further, however, with misperceptions of roads and bridges that appeared to tilt dangerously as the patient approached. In a systematic study of perceptual distortion among snake-fearful college students, Taylor and Rachman (1994) found that bias in estimating properties of the stimulus prospectively predicted anxiety during an opportunity to touch a snake. Distortions in the properties of the stimulus also led participants to overpredict the amount of fear they would experience if they were to approach the snake. Taylor and Rachman suggested that global stimulus biases (e.g., estimate of overall dangerousness) were more influential than perceptual errors about specific features of the stimulus (e.g., length, activity level).

The mental representation of the self in a social situation is key to the Rapee and Heimberg cognitive formulation of social phobia (see Figure 2) and represents a likely example of perceptual distortion. This mental representation of the self is formed from many sources, including memory of past events, feedback from others, and current somatic sensations, resulting in a distorted image of how the individual imagines others are seeing him or her in a given moment. In the context of a belief that others expect perfect social performance, such a mental representation induces the individual to begin to consider anticipated social consequences of this substandard performance, generating anxiety that further fuels the negative mental representation as well as robbing attentional resources from the task at hand.

These theories highlight the role of individual's perception of control in the onset and maintenance of emotional disorders. Studies suggest that a lack of perceived control is distressing (Geer, Davison, & Gatchel, 1970; Glass, Reim, & Singer, 1971; Sanderson et al., 1989). Theories of emotional control suggest that individuals who suffer from emotional disorders are vulnerable to experience unexpected bursts of emotion, which causes them to view their emotions and bodily reactions as out of control (Hofmann, 2005). Individuals are believed to avoid situations in which they fear a loss of control.

Conclusions and Future Directions

This chapter has provided a brief survey of major elements of psychodynamic, behavioral, and cognitive theories of the etiology and maintenance of panic and phobias. As discussed, these theories spring from distinct traditions and diverge markedly in many respects. Despite these differences, however, numerous meeting points exist.

Although the details differ across theories, all three major theories of panic and phobias posit some idiographic meaning of the feared stimulus. The meaning in psychodynamic theories is often symbolic, representative of critical intra- or interpersonal conflicts the individual is unable to consciously acknowledge. From a behavioral perspective, the meaning of the stimulus is generally related to learning history; without conscious effort, the individual has come to associate the object or situation with a traumatic outcome with which it was paired in the past. Cognitive theories focus on the feared consequences of entering the situation or engaging with the object; sensations signify impending physical catastrophe in the case of panic disorder, while conversations with strangers signal rejection and humiliation for a person with social phobia.

In each theory, the meaning of a feared stimulus or situation is strongly influenced by previous experiences. An individual's historical experience with adverse events (e.g., interpersonal conflict, illness, spontaneous panic) is clearly important, although the proposed mechanism of action differs.

Psychodynamic theories postulate that early childhood events form the root of interpersonally oriented fears. Looking at it from a different perspective, behavioral theories suggest that exposure to conditioning situations is critical in the formation of phobias. While cognitive theories rarely discuss the origins of maladaptive beliefs about experiencing anxiety, presumably these beliefs are learned in the same way as other values, preferences, and attitudes.

Other similarities between psychodynamic theories on phobias and contemporary cognitive-behavioral ideas include mechanism of generalization. All three theories offer explanations for how fear generalizes from one object to another, essentially growing from a focal fear to a broader problem that involves fear and avoidance of a constellation of objects or situations. Learning theory points to stimulus similarity as the main mechanism for generalization; fear responses are more likely to generalize to related stimuli if they share many characteristics with the original phobic stimulus. For example, going to visit a friend in the hospital is likely to arouse fear for a blood phobic, as hospitals are filled with stimuli likely to have been encountered during injections or blood draws. Visiting the same friend in a college dormitory is unlikely to provoke the fear response, as dormitories share few stimulus characteristics with doctors' offices.

Though stemming from the psychodynamic tradition, Saltzman's (1968) view of generalization is in many ways consistent with those of early behavioral psychopathologists who were his contemporaries. Salzman proposed that generalization can be driven by similarities in the *symbolic* meaning of the stimulus. As an example, he pointed to "feeling trapped," which might underlie fear and avoidance of numerous specific situations, such as elevators, having one's hair cut, or wearing heavy clothing or a seatbelt. A contemporary cognitive-behavioral therapist, hearing this constellation of feared stimuli, would also probably ask about the feared consequences of these situations in an attempt to discover a feared consequence that ties these stimuli together. Researchers are investigating whether generalization occurs because of functional displacement of anxiety, similarities in conditioned stimuli, or cognitive processing biases.

Evidence is also growing to support the notion that beliefs about the consequences of anxiety and associated sensations play a central role in the development of panic and phobias. Across the theories and disorders reviewed, important feared consequences tend to be primarily interpersonal in nature (e.g., embarrassment, rejection) or focused on personal well-being (e.g., death, going crazy). Theorists believe that fear of losing control or being humiliated, for example, are naturally aversive prospects that encourage emotional overcontrol, flawed information processing, and avoidance—all mechanisms theorized to foster future anxiety. Evidence suggests that avoidance may be the most functionally impairing aspect of panic and phobias, and it appears to play a pivotal causal role in escalating fear. Although it is generally agreed that avoidance is detrimental, researchers have not yet determined the specific mechanisms involved.

Although the theoretical formulations overlap in some ways, psychodynamic, behavioral, and cognitive theories certainly suggest disparate intervention strategies. Interventions grounded in cognitive and behavioral theories have been remarkably successful from an empirical perspective, although they require strengthening in relation to several areas (e.g., agoraphobia and social phobia). While little empirical evidence is available on the efficacy of psychodynamic interventions, support is growing for strategies inspired by contemporary aspects of the theory (e.g., interpersonal therapy). These developments are encouraging and provide interesting avenues for future research. At present, little is known about the causal mechanisms underlying effective treatment, and multitheory research can be one avenue for rigorously testing hypotheses about treatment mediators. Examining intersections between major theories, including the important roles of biological vulnerabilities, early experiences, temperament, cultural factors, and cognitive processing, holds promise for expanded understanding of the aetiology, maintenance, and amelioration of panic and phobias.

References

Accurso, V., Winnicki, M., Shamsuzzaman, A. S., Wenzel, A., Johnson, A. K., & Somers, V. K. (2001). Predisposition to vasovagal syncope in subjects with blood/injury phobia. *Circulation, 104,* 903–907.

Alden, L. E., & Bieling, P. (1998). Interpersonal consequences of the pursuit of safety. *Behaviour Research and Therapy, 36,* 53–64.

Amering, M., Katschnig, H., Berger, P., Windhaber, J., Baischer, W., & Dantendorfer, K. (1997). Embarrassment about the first attack predicts agoraphobia in panic disorder patients. *Behaviour Research and Therapy, 35,* 517–521.

Amir, N., Foa, E. B., & Coles, M. E. (1998). Automatic activation and strategic avoidance of threat-relevant information in social phobia. *Journal of Abnormal Psychology, 107,* 285–290.

Antony, M. M., Brown, T. A., & Barlow, D. H. (1997). Response

to hyperventilation and 5.5% CO_2 inhalation of subjects with types of specific phobia, panic disorder, or no mental disorder. *American Journal of Psychiatry, 154,* 1089–1095.

Baker, R., Holloway, J., Thomas, P. W., Thomas, S., & Owens, M. (2004). Emotional processing and panic. *Behaviour Research and Therapy, 42,* 1271–1287.

Baker, S. R., & Edelmann, R. J. (2002). Is social phobia related to lack of social skills? Duration of skill-related behaviours and ratings of behavioural adequacy. *British Journal of Clinical Psychology, 41,* 243–257.

Barlow, D. H. (2002). *Anxiety and its disorders: The nature and treatment of anxiety and panic* (2nd ed.). New York: Guilford Press.

Barrett, P. M., Rapee, R. M., Dadds, M. M., & Ryan, S. M. (1996). Family enhancement of cognitive style in anxious and aggressive children. *Journal of Abnormal Child Psychology, 24,* 187–203.

Beidel, D. C., Turner, S. M., & Morris, T. L. (1999). Psychopathology of childhood social phobia. *Journal of the American Academy of Child and Adolescent Psychiatry, 38,* 643–650.

Belfer, P. L., & Glass, C. R. (1992). Agoraphobic anxiety and fear of fear: Test of a cognitive-attentional model. *Journal of Anxiety Disorders, 6,* 133–146.

Biederman, J., Hirschfeld-Becker, D. R., Rosenbaum, J. F., Hérot, C., Friedman, D., Snidman, N., et al. (2001). Further evidence of association between behavioral inhibition and social anxiety in children. *American Journal of Psychiatry, 158,* 1673–1679.

Bögels, S. M., & Lamers, C.T.J. (2002). The causal role of self-awareness in blushing-anxious, socially-anxious and social phobic individuals. *Behaviour Research and Therapy, 40,* 1367–1384.

Bourdon, K. H., Boyd, J. H., Rae, D. S., Burns, B. J., Thompson, J. W., & Locke, B. Z. (1988). Gender differences in phobias: Results of the ECA Community Survey. *Journal of Anxiety Disorders, 2,* 227–242.

Bouton, M. E., Mineka, S., & Barlow, D. H. (2001). A modern learning theory perspective on the etiology of panic disorder. *Psychological Review, 108,* 4–32.

Bruch, M. A., & Heimberg, R. G. (1994). Differences in perceptions of parental and personal characteristics between generalized and nongeneralized social phobics. *Journal of Anxiety Disorders, 8,* 155–168.

Busch, F. N., Milrod, B. L., & Singer, M. B. (1999). Theory and technique in psychodynamic treatment of panic disorder. *Journal of Psychotherapy Practice and Research, 8,* 234–242.

Bussing, R., Burket, R. C., & Kelleher, E. T. (1996). Prevalence of anxiety disorders in a clinic-based sample of pediatric asthma patients. *Psychosomatics: Journal of Consultation Liaison Psychiatry, 37,* 108–115.

Carr, R. E. (1998). Panic disorder and asthma: Causes, effects and research implications. *Journal of Psychosomatic Research, 44,* 43–52.

Carter, M. M., Hollon, S. D., Carson, R., & Shelton, R. C. (1995). Effects of a safe person on induced distress following a biological challenge in panic disorder with agoraphobia. *Journal of Abnormal Psychology, 104,* 156–163.

Cartwright-Hatton, S., Hodges, L., & Porter, J. (2003). Social anxiety in childhood: The relationship with self and observer rated social skills. *Journal of Child Psychology and Psychiatry, 44,* 737–742.

Cartwright-Hatton, S., Tschernitz, N., & Gomersall, H. (2005). Social anxiety in children: Social skills deficit or cognitive distortion? *Behaviour Research and Therapy, 43,* 131–141.

Chambless, D. L. (1987, September). *Gender and phobia.* Paper presented at the European Association for Behavior Therapy Congress, Amsterdam, the Netherlands.

Chapman, T. F., Fyer, A., Mannuzza, S., & Klein, D. F. (1993). A comparison of treated and untreated simple phobia. *American Journal of Psychiatry, 150,* 816–818.

Chen, Y.-P., Ehlers, A., Clark, D. M., & Mansell, W. (2002). Patients with generalized social phobia direct their attention away from faces. *Behaviour Research and Therapy, 40,* 677–687.

Clark, D. M. (1986). A cognitive approach to panic. *Behaviour Research and Therapy, 24,* 461–470.

Clark, D. M. (1993). Cognitive mediation of panic attacks induced by biological challenge tests. *Advances in Behaviour Research and Therapy, 15,* 75–84.

Clark, D. M., Salkovskis, P. M., Öst, L.-G., Breitholtz, E., Koehler, K. A., Westling, B. E., et al. (1997). Misinterpretation of bodily sensations in panic disorder. *Journal of Consulting and Clinical Psychology, 65,* 203–213.

Clark, D. M., & Wells, A. (1995). A cognitive model of social phobia. In R. G. Heimberg, M. R. Liebowitz, D. A. Hope, & F. R. Schneier (Eds.), *Social phobia: Diagnosis, assessment, and treatment* (pp. 69–93). New York: Guilford Press.

Cloitre, M., Heimberg, R. G., Liebowitz, M. R., & Gitow, A. (1992). Perceptions of control in panic disorder and social phobia. *Cognitive Therapy and Research, 16,* 569–577.

Clum, G. A., & Knowles, S. L. (1991). Why do some people with panic disorders become avoidant? A review. *Clinical Psychology Review, 11,* 295–313.

Compton, A. (1992). The psychoanalytic view of phobias. Part III: Agoraphobia and other phobias of adults. *Psychoanalytic Quarterly, 61,* 400–425.

Cook, M., & Mineka, S. (1989). Observational conditioning of fear to fear-relevant versus fear-irrelevant stimuli in Rhesus monkeys. *Journal of Abnormal Psychology, 98,* 448–459.

Cook, M., & Mineka, S. (1990). Selective associations in the observational conditioning of fear in monkeys. *Journal of Experimental Psychology: Animal Behavior Processes, 16,* 372–389.

Dickinson, A., & Mackintosh, N. J. (1978). Classical conditioning in animals. *Annual Review of Psychology, 29,* 587–612.

Ehlers, A. (1993). Somatic symptoms and panic attacks: A retrospective study of learning experiences. *Behaviour Research and Therapy, 31,* 269–278.

Erwin, B. A., Heimberg, R. G., & Schneier, F. R. (2003). Anger experience and expression in social anxiety disorder: Pretreatment profile and predictors of attrition and response to cognitive-behavioral treatment. *Behavior Therapy, 34,* 331–350.

Evren, C., Kural, S., & Cakmak, D. (2006). Clinical correlates of childhood abuse and neglect in substance dependents. *Addictive Behaviors, 31,* 475–485.

Faravelli, C. (1985). Prevalence of traumatic early life events in 31 agoraphobic patients with panic attacks. *American Journal of Psychiatry, 142,* 1493–1494.

Fredrikson, M., Annas, P., Fischer, H., & Wik, G. (1996). Gender and age differences in the prevalence of specific fears and phobia. *Behaviour Research and Therapy, 34,* 33–39.

Gabbard, G. O. (1992). Psychodynamics of panic disorder and social phobia. *Bulletin of the Menninger Clinic, 56*(2, Suppl. A), A3–A13.

Geer, J. H., Davison, G. C., & Gatchel, R. I. (1970). Reduction of stress in humans through nonveridical perceived control of aversive stimulation. *Journal of Personality and Social Psychology, 16,* 731–738.

Glass, D. C., Reim, B., & Singer, J. E. (1971). Behavioral consequences of adaptation to controllable and uncontrollable noise. *Journal of Experimental Social Psychology, 7,* 244–257.

Goisman, R. M. (1983). Therapeutic approaches to phobia: A comparison. *American Journal of Psychotherapy, 37,* 227–234.

Goldstein, A., & Chambless, D. (1978). A reanalysis of agoraphobia. *Behavior Therapy, 9,* 47–59.

Goodwin, R. D., Fergusson, D. M., & Horwood, L. J. (2005). Childhood abuse and familial violence and the risk of panic attacks and panic disorder in young adulthood. *Psychological Medicine, 35,* 881–890.

Goodwin, R. D., Jacobi, F., & Thefeld, W. (2003). Mental disorders and asthma in the community. *Archives of General Psychiatry, 60,* 1125–1130.

Greenberg, D. B., Stern, T. A., & Weilburg, J. B. (1988). The fear of choking: Three successfully treated cases. *Psychosomatics, 29,* 126–129.

Hayward, C., Killen, J. D., Kraemer, H. C., & Taylor, C. B. (1998). Linking self-reported childhood behavioral inhibition to adolescent social phobia. *Journal of the American Academy of Child and Adolescent Psychiatry, 37,* 1308–1316.

Hirschfeld, D. R., Rosenbaum, J. F., Biederman, J., Bolduc, E. A., Faraone, S. V., Snidman, N., et al. (1992). Stable behavioral inhibition and its association with anxiety disorder. *Journal of the American Academy of Child and Adolescent Psychiatry, 31,* 103–111.

Hofmann, S. G. (2005). Perception of control over anxiety mediates the relation between catastrophic thinking and social anxiety in social phobia. *Behaviour Research and Therapy, 43,* 885–895.

Hope, D. A., Heimberg, R. G., & Klein, J. F. (1990). Social anxiety and the recall of interpersonal information. *Journal of Cognitive Psychotherapy, 4,* 185–195.

Hughes, I., Budd, R., & Greenaway, S. (1999). Coping with anxiety and panic: A factor analytic study. *British Journal of Clinical Psychology, 38,* 295–304.

Isenberg, S., Lehrer, P. M., & Hochron, S. M. (1992). The effects of suggestion on airways of asthmatic subjects breathing room air as a suggested bronchoconstrictor and bronchodilator. *Journal of Psychosomatic Research, 36,* 769–776.

Juth, P., Lundqvist, D., Karlsson, A., & Öhman, A. (2005). Looking for foes and friends: Perceptual and emotional factors when finding a face in the crowd. *Emotion, 5,* 379–395.

Kagan, J. (1999). The concept of behavioral inhibition. In L. A. Schmidt & J. Schulkin (Eds.), *Extreme fear, shyness, and social phobia: Origins, biological mechanisms, and clinical outcomes* (pp. 3–13). New York: Oxford University Press.

Kendler, K. S., Myers, J., Prescott, C. A., & Neale, M. C. (2001). The genetic epidemiology of irrational fears and phobias in men. *Archives of General Psychiatry, 58,* 257–265.

Kim, M.-S. (1994). Cross-cultural comparisons of the perceived importance of conversational constraints. *Human Communication Research, 21,* 128–151.

Kleiner, L., & Marshall, W. L. (1987). The role of interpersonal problems in the development of agoraphobia with panic attacks. *Journal of Anxiety Disorders, 1,* 313–323.

Kleinknecht, R. A., & Lenz, J. (1989). Blood-injury fear, fainting and avoidance of medically-related situations: A family correspondence study. *Behaviour Research and Therapy, 27,* 537–547.

Kuch, K., Cox, B. J., Evans, R. E., & Shulman, I. (1994). Phobias, panic, and pain in 55 survivors of road vehicle accidents. *Journal of Anxiety Disorders, 8,* 181–187.

Laraia, M. T., Stuart, G. W., & Frye, L. H. (1994). Childhood environment of women having panic disorder with agoraphobia. *Journal of Anxiety Disorders, 8,* 1–17.

Leskin, G. A., & Sheikh, J. I. (2002). Lifetime trauma history and panic disorder: Findings from the National Comorbidity Survey. *Journal of Anxiety Disorders, 16,* 599–603.

Leung, A. W., & Heimberg, R. G. (1996). Homework compliance, perceptions of control, and outcome of cognitive-behavioral treatment of social phobia. *Behaviour Research and Therapy, 34,* 423–432.

Lief, H. I. (1968). Generic and specific aspects of phobic behavior. *International Journal of Psychiatry, 6,* 470–473.

Magee, W. J., Eaton, W. W., Wittchen, H.-U., McGonagle, K. A., & Kessler, R. C. (1996). Agoraphobia, simple phobia, and social phobia in the National Comorbidity Survey. *Archives of General Psychiatry, 53,* 159–168.

Mansell, W., Clark, D. M., Ehlers, A., & Chen, Y.-P. (1999). Social anxiety and attention away from emotional faces. *Cognition and Emotion, 13,* 673–690.

Margraf, J., Ehlers, A., & Roth, W. T. (1986). Biological models of panic disorder and agoraphobia: A review. *Behaviour Research and Therapy, 24,* 553–567.

McCabe, R. E., Antony, M. M., Summerfeldt, L. J., Liss, A., & Swinson, R. P. (2003). Preliminary examination of the relationship between anxiety disorders in adults and self-reported history of teasing or bullying experiences. *Cognitive Behaviour Therapy, 32,* 187–193.

McNally, R. J., & Steketee, G. S. (1985). The etiology and maintenance of severe animal phobias. *Behaviour Research and Therapy, 23,* 431–435.

Mellings, T.M.B., & Alden, L. E. (2000). Cognitive processes in social anxiety: The effects of self-focus, rumination and anticipatory processing. *Behaviour Research and Therapy, 38,* 243–257.

Merckelbach, H., van Hout, W., van den Hout, M. A., & Mersch, P.P.A. (1989). Psychophysiological and subjective reactions of social phobics and normals to facial stimuli. *Behaviour Research and Therapy, 27,* 289–294.

Miller, S. (1985). *The shame experience.* Hillsdale, NJ: Erlbaum.

Mineka, S., Davidson, M., Cook, M., & Keir, R. (1984). Observational conditioning of snake fear in Rhesus monkeys. *Journal of Abnormal Psychology, 93,* 355–372.

Mineka, S., & Öhman, A. (2002). Phobias and preparedness: The selective, automatic, and encapsulated nature of fear. *Biological Psychiatry, 52,* 927–937.

Moore, R., Brodsgaard, I., & Birn, H. (1991). Manifestations, acquisition, and diagnostic categories of dental fear in a self-referred population. *Behaviour Research and Therapy, 29,* 51–60.

Mowrer, O. H. (1939). A stimulus-response analysis of anxiety and its role as a reinforcing agent. *Psychological Review, 46,* 553–565.

Neal, J. A., Edelmann, R. J., & Glachan, M. (2002). Behavioural inhibition and symptoms of anxiety and depression: Is there a specific relationship with social phobia? *British Journal of Clinical Psychology, 41,* 361–374.

Norasakkunkit, V., & Kalick, S. M. (2002). Culture, ethnicity, and emotional distress measures: The role of self-construal and self-enhancement. *Journal of Cross-Cultural Psychology, 33,* 56–70.

Oetzel, J. G. (1998a). The effects of self-construals and ethnicity on self-reported conflict styles. *Communication Reports, 11,* 133–144.

Oetzel, J. G. (1998b). Explaining individual communication processes in homogeneous and heterogeneous groups through individualism-collectivism and self-construal. *Human Communication Research, 25,* 202–224.

Öhman, A., & Dimberg, U. (1978). Facial expressions as conditioned stimuli for electrodermal responses: A case of "preparedness"? *Journal of Personality and Social Psychology, 36,* 1251–1258.

Öhman, A., Dimberg, U., & Öst, L.-G. (1985). Animal and social phobias: Biological constraints on the learned fear response. In S. Reiss & R. Bootzin (Eds.), *Theoretical issues in behavior therapy* (pp. 123–175). New York: Academic Press.

Öhman, A., & Mineka, S. (2001). Fears, phobias, and preparedness: Toward an evolved module of fear and fear learning. *Psychological Review, 108,* 483–522.

Öhman, A., & Soares, J. (1993). On the automatic nature of phobic fear: Conditioned electrodermal responses to masked fear-relevant stimuli. *Journal of Abnormal Psychology, 102,* 121–132.

Okazaki, S. (2000). Asian American and White American differences on affective distress symptoms: Do symptom reports differ across reporting methods? *Journal of Cross-Cultural Psychology, 31,* 603–625.

Okazaki, S. (2002). Self-other agreement on affective distress scales in Asian Americans and White Americans. *Journal of Counseling Psychology, 49,* 428–437.

Okazaki, S., & Kallivayalil, D. (2002). Cultural norms and subjective disability as predictors of symptom reports among Asian Americans and White Americans. *Journal of Cross-Cultural Psychology, 33,* 482–491.

Öst, L.-G. (1987). Age of onset in different phobias. *Journal of Abnormal Psychology, 96,* 223–229.

Öst, L.-G., & Hugdahl, K. (1981). Acquisition of phobias and anxiety response patterns in clinical patients. *Behaviour Research and Therapy, 19,* 439–447.

Öst, L.-G., & Hugdahl, K. (1983). Acquisition of agoraphobia, mode of onset and anxiety response patterns. *Behaviour Research and Therapy, 21,* 623–631.

Öst, L.-G., Sterner, U., & Lindahl, I.-L. (1984). Physiological responses in blood phobics. *Behaviour Research and Therapy, 22,* 109–117.

Peterson, R. A., & Reiss, S. (1987). *Anxiety Sensitivity Index manual.* Palos Heights, IL: International Diagnostic Systems.

Rachman, S. (1977). The conditioning theory of fear acquisition: A critical examination. *Behaviour Research and Therapy, 15,* 375–387.

Rachman, S., & Cuk, M. (1992). Fearful distortions. *Behaviour Research and Therapy, 30,* 583–589.

Rachman, S., Grüter-Andrew, J., & Shafran, R. (2000). Post-event processing in social anxiety. *Behaviour Research and Therapy, 38,* 611–617.

Rapee, R. M., & Heimberg, R. G. (1997). A cognitive-behavioral model of anxiety in social phobia. *Behaviour Research and Therapy, 35,* 741–756.

Rapee, R. M., & Lim, L. (1992). Discrepancy between self and observer ratings of performance in social phobics. *Journal of Abnormal Psychology, 101,* 727–731.

Rapee, R. M., & Spence, S. H. (2004). The etiology of social phobia: Empirical evidence and an initial model. *Clinical Psychology Review, 24,* 737–767.

Rescorla, R. A. (1988). Pavlovian conditioning: It's not what you think it is. *American Psychologist, 43,* 151–160.

Safren, S. A., Gershuny, B. S., Marzol, P., Otto, M. W., & Pollack, M. H. (2002). History of childhood abuse in panic disorder, social phobia, and generalized anxiety disorder. *Journal of Nervous and Mental Disease, 190,* 453–456.

Salzman, L. (1968). Obsessions and phobias. *International Journal of Psychiatry, 6,* 451–476.

Sanderson, W. C., Rapee, R. M., & Barlow, D. H. (1989). The influence of an illusion of control on panic attacks induced via inhalation of 5.5% carbon dioxide-enriched air. *Archives of General Psychiatry, 46,* 157–162.

Saunders, B. E., Villepointeaux, L. A., & Lipovsky, J. A. (1992). Child sexual assault as a risk factor for mental disorders among women: A community survey. *Journal of Interpersonal Violence, 7,* 189–204.

Schmidt, N. B., Lerew, D. R., & Jackson, R. J. (1997). The role of anxiety sensitivity in the pathogenesis of panic: Prospective evaluation of spontaneous panic attacks during acute stress. *Journal of Abnormal Psychology, 106,* 355–364.

Schmidt, N. B., Lerew, D. R., & Trakowski, J. H. (1997). Body vigilance in panic disorder: Evaluating attention to bodily perturbations. *Journal of Consulting and Clinical Psychology, 65,* 214–220.

Schwartz, C. E., Snidman, N., & Kagan, J. (1999). Adolescent social anxiety as an outcome of inhibited temperament in childhood. *Journal of the American Academy of Child and Adolescent Psychiatry, 38,* 1008–1015.

Seligman, M.E.P. (1971). Phobias and preparedness. *Behavior Therapy, 2,* 307–320.

Shear, M. K., Cooper, A. M., Klerman, G. L., Busch, F. N., & Shapiro, D. A. (1993). A psychodynamic model of panic disorder. *American Journal of Psychiatry, 150,* 859–866.

Sloan, T., & Telch, M. J. (2002). The effects of safety-seeking behavior and guided threat reappraisal on fear reduction during exposure: An experimental investigation. *Behaviour Research and Therapy, 40,* 235–251.

Snaith, R. P. (1968). A clinical investigation of phobias. *British Journal of Psychiatry, 114,* 673–697.

Speltz, M. L., & Bernstein, D. A. (1976). Sex differences in fearfulness: Verbal report, overt avoidance, and demand characteristics. *Journal of Behavior Therapy and Experimental Psychiatry, 7,* 117–122.

Spence, S. H., Donovan, C., & Brechman-Toussaint, M. (1999). Social skills, social outcomes, and cognitive features of childhood social phobia. *Journal of Abnormal Psychology, 108,* 211–221.

Stein, M. B., Walker, J. R., & Anderson, G. (1996). Childhood physical and sexual abuse in patients with anxiety disorders and in a community sample. *American Journal of Psychiatry, 153,* 275–277.

Stemberger, R. T., Turner, S. M., Deborah, D. C., & Calhoun, K. S. (1995). Social phobia: An analysis of possible developmental factors. *Journal of Abnormal Psychology, 104,* 526–531.

Stopa, L., & Clark, D. M. (1993). Cognitive processes in social phobia. *Behaviour Research and Therapy, 31,* 255–267.

Stopa, L., & Clark, D. M. (2000). Social phobia and interpretation of social events. *Behaviour Research and Therapy, 38,* 273–283.

Taylor, S., & Rachman, S. J. (1994). Stimulus estimation and the overprediction of fear. *British Journal of Clinical Psychology, 33,* 173–181.

Thompson, S., & Rapee, R. M. (2002). The effect of situational structure on the social performance of socially anxious and non-anxious participants. *Journal of Behavior Therapy and Experimental Psychiatry, 33,* 91–102.

Thorpe, S. J., & Salkovskis, P. M. (1995). Phobic beliefs: Do cognitive factors play a role in specific phobias? *Behaviour Research and Therapy, 33,* 805–816.

Triandis, H. C. (1995). *Individualism and collectivism.* Boulder, CO: Westview Press.

Turner, S. M., Beidel, D. C., Dancu, C. V., & Keys, D. J. (1986). Psychopathology of social phobia and comparison to avoidant personality disorder. *Journal of Abnormal Psychology, 95,* 389–394.

Van Ameringen, M., Mancini, C., & Oakman, J. M. (1998). The relationship of behavioral inhibition and shyness to anxiety disorder. *Journal of Nervous and Mental Disease, 186,* 425–431.

Veljaca, K.-A., & Rapee, R. M. (1998). Detection of negative and positive audience behaviours by socially anxious subjects. *Behaviour Research and Therapy, 36,* 311–321.

Vernberg, K., Griez, E., & Meijer, J. (1994). A 35% carbon dioxide challenge in simple phobias. *Acta Psychiatrica Scandinavica, 90,* 420–423.

Watt, M. C., Stewart, S. H., & Cox, B. J. (1998). A retrospective study of the learning history origins of anxiety sensitivity. *Behaviour Research and Therapy, 36,* 505–525.

Weissman, M. M., Bland, R. C., Canino, G. J., Greenwald, S., Lee, C.-K., Newman, S. C., et al. (1996). The cross-national epidemiology of social phobia: A preliminary report. *International Clinical Psychopharmacology, 11,* 9–14.

Whittal, M. L., & Goetsch, V. L. (1997). The impact of panic expectancy and social demand on agoraphobia avoidance. *Behaviour Research and Therapy, 35,* 813–821.

Williams, S. L., Turner, S. M., & Peer, D. F. (1985). Guided mastery and performance desensitization treatments for severe acrophobia. *Journal of Consulting and Clinical Psychology, 53,* 237–247.

Wittchen, H.-U., & Fehm, L. (2001). Epidemiology, patterns of comorbidity, and associated disabilities of social phobia. *Psychiatric Clinics of North America, 24,* 617–641.

Woody, S. R. (1996). Effects of focus of attention on social phobics' anxiety and social performance. *Journal of Abnormal Psychology, 105,* 61–69.

Woody, S. R., & Chambless, D. L. (May 1989). *Social and personality factors predicting sex differences in fearful behavior.* Paper presented at the annual meeting of the Eastern Psychological Association, Boston, MA.

Woody, S. R., & Rodriguez, B. (2000). Social anxiety and self-focused attention in social phobics and normal controls. *Cognitive Therapy and Research, 24,* 473–488.

Psychological Models of Worry and Generalized Anxiety Disorder

Peter L. Fisher *and* Adrian Wells

Abstract

This chapter reviews the four main psychological models and theories of generalized anxiety disorder (GAD). These are cognitive avoidance theory, metacognitive model, intolerance of uncertainty theory, and the emotional dysregulation model. The empirical support for each is critically appraised. Although each theory offers a cognitive behavioral analysis, they differ in their emphasis on the psychological processes involved in the maintenance of pathological worry. As a result they give rise to four distinct treatments. The clinical implications and the treatment efficacy of the four approaches are briefly reviewed. The chapter concludes with a comparative analysis of how well each theory accounts for the cardinal feature of GAD, namely, excessive and uncontrollable worry.

Keywords: anxious apprehension, cognition, emotion, generalized anxiety disorder, generalized anxiety disorder theories, metacognition, models, uncertainty

Generalized anxiety disorder (GAD) has undergone substantial taxonomic development since its inception in the third edition of the *Diagnostic and Statistical Manual of Mental Disorders (DSM–III)* (American Psychiatric Association, 1980) and is now conceptualized primarily as a disorder of worry; indeed the cardinal feature is excessive and uncontrollable worry. This represents a considerable shift in emphasis away from the somatic components of GAD to the cognitive processes thought to be responsible for the pathogenesis and maintenance of this pervasive and debilitating disorder. Over the past two decades this diagnostic change has resulted in the development of a number of empirically supported psychological theories and treatments of GAD and its core component, worry.

In this chapter, we begin with brief overviews of Beck's cognitive theory of anxiety (Beck, Emery, & Greenberg, 1985), and the generic model of anxious apprehension proposed by Barlow

(2000). Next, four specific psychological theories of GAD and worry are presented: (1) the cognitive avoidance theory (Borkovec, Ray, & Stober, 1998), (2) the metacognitive model of GAD (Wells, 1995), (3) the intolerance of uncertainty model (Dugas, Gagnon, Ladouceur, & Freeston, 1998), and (4) the emotion dysregulation model (Mennin, Heimberg, Turk, & Fresco, 2002). Each theory is described, followed by a review of the empirical literature supporting each model/theory. The clinical implications of each approach are then briefly presented, followed by a review of treatment efficacy.

Generic Theories
Beck's Schema Theory
The cognitive or schema theory of emotional disorders developed by Beck (1976) and Beck et al. (1985) has three core elements: schemas, negative automatic thoughts, and systematic biases in thinking styles. A schema or core belief can be thought of

as a filter through which individuals evaluate themselves and interpret the future and events. In anxiety, it is assumed that the basic schema is the belief that "the world is a dangerous place," which guides interpretation of events and subsequently behavior. Outputs of schema activation are termed negative automatic thoughts (NATs), which can reflect different classes of mentation such as verbal thoughts or images. In GAD, NATs center on themes of danger such as, "What if my partner has a car crash?" or "What if I can't cope?" Such thoughts intrude rapidly into consciousness and are viewed by the individual as statements of truth that need to be responded to. The final component of the Beckian model of anxiety disorders involves thinking biases that are typically congruent with the danger-related schemas, and that prevent modification of the core beliefs. For example, in anxiety disorders, it is common for individuals to selectively attend to threat-related information, rather than make a balanced appraisal of all available information.

Barlow's Model of Anxious Apprehension

Barlow (2000) proposed a generic model of GAD that incorporates biological, environmental, and psychological factors. In this model, GAD is conceptualized as "anxious apprehension" and constitutes the "basic" anxiety disorder. It is suggested that individuals have biological and psychological vulnerabilities that when triggered will result in negative affect characterized by a sense of uncontrollability, physiological response, and activation of specific brain circuits (e.g., the behavioral inhibition system). Consequently, the individual becomes self-focused on his or her physiological arousal and is hypervigilant for threat, which produces attempts to cope with the resultant anxiety. The predominant coping strategies proposed in this model are behavioral avoidance and worry in an attempt to problem solve and reduce negative affect.

These two generic theories have been extremely important in the development of a cognitive understanding of both GAD and other anxiety disorders. However, neither theory elucidates the key psychological processes that are specific to GAD and pathological forms of worry.

Specific Models and Theories

Current psychological formulations of GAD emphasize excessive worry that the individual experiences as difficult to control as the core feature of the disorder. These models focus on understanding the nature of worry and the psychological processes by which it continues. Four of the leading theories of worry are described and critically evaluated below.

The Cognitive Avoidance Theory of Worry

This theory is predicated on a behaviorist approach to understanding anxiety and worry. Over the past 20 years, Borkovec and colleagues (cf. Borkovec, Alcaine, & Behar, 2004) have conducted extensive research into the nature of worry and GAD, which has culminated in an empirically validated theory of worry. A crucial piece of phenomenological research paved the way for the development of the cognitive avoidance theory. Worry is predominantly a verbal linguistic activity, with a relatively low level of imagery (Borkovec & Inz, 1990). This led to the hypothesis that worry functions to avoid unpleasant imagery and its associated negative affect. Once an internal threat (e.g., an aversive image) or an external threat is detected, somatic arousal occurs, and the individual is motivated to escape both the distressing imagery and accompanying somatic symptoms. Attention moves away from imaginal activity to conceptual verbal activity (worry), removing the aversive imagery and dampening down the somatic arousal, thereby negatively reinforcing worry. Unfortunately, avoidance of the aversive imagery and affect prevents emotional processing and the anxious meanings are maintained and possibly strengthened. This is consistent with Foa and Kozak's (1986) theory of emotional processing of fear. Within this model, it is argued that fear is represented by three interrelated processes stored in memory, termed a *fear structure*. This incorporates information about the feared stimulus, the response possibilities to the stimulus, and information about the meaning of the stimulus and response. The structure is conceptualized as a program for avoidance or escape from the feared stimulus and in order for the fear structure to be "reprogrammed," the fear structure must be fully activated to permit new information to be encoded, thus creating a new memory. If worry serves an avoidant function, the fear structure is never fully activated. This prevents the encoding of new information, or in behavioral terms, prevents the extinction of fear.

Thus far, the cognitive avoidance model states that worry reduces negative affect and removes aversive imagery. These are relatively immediate avoidant functions; however, worry also serves a longer-term avoidant function, in that people believe that worrying helps to avoid future negative events and helps them to cope in unavoidable difficult circumstances. In reality, the majority of feared events never materialize and people tend to cope better than anticipated. Patients with GAD believe that worry leads to the nonoccurrence of the negative events and enables more effective coping in difficult circumstances. The final avoidant function is that worry may also prevent exposure to more emotionally distressing topics, specifically, previous traumas, adverse childhood experiences, and interpersonal relationships. Specifically, it is suggested that GAD patients are worrying about surface level topics rather than "deeper" concerns.

Empirical Support

There is extensive empirical support for aspects of the cognitive avoidance theory of worry. The theory is predicated on the replicated finding that worry comprises predominately verbal rather than imaginal mentation (e.g., Borkovec & Inz, 1990; Freeston, Dugas, & Ladouceur, 1996). The proposition that worry decreases somatic arousal is also a consistent finding. Tucker and Newman (1981) found people use verbal thought to inhibit emotional arousal in response to distressing stimuli and that verbal thought is associated with less cardiovascular activity than imagery (Vrana, Cuthbert, & Lang, 1986). Worry does appear to reduce the amount of distressing mental imagery and accompanying arousal an individual experiences (see Sibrava & Borkovec, 2006, for a comprehensive review). The critical empirical question concerns how worry leads to lower levels of imagery and autonomic arousal. One answer may lie in the reduced-concreteness theory of worry (Stober, 1998; Stober & Borkovec, 2002). Worry comprises less concrete and more abstract thought, meaning the chain of thoughts contains less imagery, and therefore, less emotional processing takes place. Thinking in an abstract manner will reduce the frequency of imagery, help to avoid autonomic arousal and heightened affective experiences in the short term, but will serve to maintain and even exacerbate the frequency of aversive imagery (e.g., Butler, Wells, & Dewick, 1995).

Borkovec et al. (2004) speculate that individuals with GAD may worry to avoid more emotionally distressing topics. One study indicated that when worriers were instructed to engage in catastrophizing (i.e., a succession of "what if" questions to each thought generated), they generated more steps in the process, with increasing levels of discomfort, whereas nonworriers produced fewer steps and discomfort remained relatively constant across the process (Vasey & Borkovec, 1992). One interpretation of this result is that worriers have a rich associative memory network containing themes of past trauma and thoughts relating to difficult childhood and adult interpersonal encounters. This raises the intriguing possibility that GAD patients are volitionally worrying about topics that have less emotional saliency in order to avoid thinking about more distressing past events or current situations.

Finally, worry is an attempt to avoid future aversive experiences or an attempt to be able to prepare for the worst happening. A great deal of research evidence supports the view that people believe worry is an effective coping strategy. This is a common theme across the theoretical accounts of worry, namely, people with GAD have positive beliefs about the function of worry, relative to people without GAD (e.g., Borkovec & Roemer, 1995; Cartwright-Hatton & Wells, 1997; Freeston, Rheaume, Letarte, Dugas, & Ladouceur, 1994; Tallis, Davey, & Capuzzo, 1994; Wells & Papageorgiou, 1998).

Summary

The avoidance theory of worry argues that worry enables individuals to avoid aversive imagery, anxious arousal, and deeper level concerns that predominately relate to past and present interpersonal issues. Furthermore, worry becomes negatively reinforced through the removal of aversive images, reduction in somatic arousal, and nonoccurrence of anticipated catastrophes. Substantial empirical research exists to support the central tenets of this theory. It provides a good account of the phenomenological aspects of the disorder, and treatment predicated on the theory has been shown to be efficacious (e.g., Borkovec, Newman, Pincus, & Lytle, 2002). Furthermore, it provides a detailed behavioral account of the psychological and physiological processes that serve to maintain excessive worry and GAD. However, it is important for any model of GAD to be able to differentiate between people with high levels of worry and people with GAD. At the present time, it is not clear how the cognitive avoidance theory addresses this issue.

Intriguingly, within the model are clues about the nature of worry that cannot be explained by a behavioral theory. It is assumed that patients with GAD switch from imagery to verbal conceptual activity and that people may be worrying in order to avoid more emotionally distressing topics. If this proposition is considered from an information-processing framework, then it is possible that worry is not an automatic conditioned process, but instead is a volitional maladaptive coping strategy. Following this line of argument, one of the limitations of the cognitive avoidance model may be that it does not pay sufficient attention to people's belief systems, which guide and regulate both thinking and behavior.

Metacognitive Model of GAD

Wells (1995, 1999) developed the metacognitive model of pathological worry and GAD. It is grounded in a wider information-processing theory of self-regulation in psychological disorder (Wells & Matthews, 1994, 1996). The starting point for the model was the observation that GAD and nonpatient worriers appear to differ little in their topological features, specifically content. Wells (1995) proposed that the disabling consequences of worry could be better explained in terms of metacognitive appraisal and control of worry. The model distinguishes between two types of worry: Type 1 worry is worry about external events and internal noncognitive issues (e.g., physical symptoms). Type 2 worry, or meta-worry, in contrast, consists of negative interpretation of worry as uncontrollable and harmful. A central concept is that worry becomes problematic because it is negatively appraised as uncontrollable and harmful; these appraisals are threatening and lead to increased anxiety and extended worry. In addition to this mechanism, a conflict exists in self-regulation in which negative and positive beliefs about worry exert a co-joint effect on the person's ability to regulate worrying.

A period of intense worry is commonly activated by an intrusive thought in the form of a "What if?" question (e.g., "What if I fail my test?"). This activates positive metacognitive beliefs about the need to sustain the worry process in order to anticipate future problems and generate coping options. Thus, Type 1 worrying is sustained and can lead to increased anxiety and negative affect as a range of negative outcomes are generated. However, as the "work of worry" nears its objective, anxiety decreases because the person appraises that he or she has generated ways of coping or that he or she subjectively "feels able to cope." Worrying is not benign, and the model proposes that it may generate problems of its own, such as blocking the processing of images normally required for emotional processing; thus, negative emotional states may be incubated or prolonged by the worry process. Problems are compounded and GAD arises when negative metacognitive beliefs about worry develop and are activated. When this occurs, the person appraises the worrying and the symptoms associated with it as uncontrollable and dangerous. The feared consequences of

worrying include losing one's mind, damaging one's body, or ceasing to function effectively.

As negative beliefs increase anxiety and signal further threat, it becomes increasingly difficult for the individual to reach a suitable stop signal for worrying, and so the need to continue with worrying as a strategy for coping persists. In addition, the (erroneous) belief that worry is uncontrollable leads to incomplete attempts or an absence of attempts to interrupt the worry process once initiated. This lack of disengagement of the process removes opportunities to challenge the erroneous belief that worry is uncontrollable.

Finally, because of the emerging concerns about worry and its consequences, the person with GAD tries to avoid situations that might trigger worrying, but this further restricts opportunities to discover worry is controllable and harmless. Some individuals use unhelpful metacognitive control strategies such as trying not to think about topics that might trigger worrying. However, thought suppression is not consistently effective; a result that can be misinterpreted as evidence of loss of control. In this way, behaviors contribute to a persistence of negative metacognitive beliefs about uncontrollability and the danger of worry.

Empirical Support

There is extensive empirical support for central predictions of the metacognitive model of worry. The model predicts that worrying may interfere with other self-regulatory processes such as emotional processing following threat. Two studies have examined this assertion in analogue samples exposed to stressful film material (Butler, Wells, & Dewick, 1995; Wells and Papageorgiou, 1995). In these studies worrying briefly after exposure to a stressful film led to an increase in the frequency of intrusive images over a subsequent 3-day monitoring period. These data suggest that the process of worrying and the act of using worry as a coping strategy can lead to problems in the regulation of thoughts and emotion.

A central idea in the model is that it is not worry itself (Type 1 worry) that is linked to pathological worry and GAD but negative metacognitions concerning worry. Several studies provide evidence addressing this prediction. Wells and Carter (1999) showed that Type 2 worry was a better predictor of pathological worry than Type 1 worry. A later study (Wells & Carter, 2001) found negative metacognitions characterized patients with *DSM–III–R* GAD and discriminated them from groups of patients with panic disorder or groups with social phobia. Wells (2005) removed the uncontrollability dimension from the meta-worry construct and focused on assessing the danger dimension in testing for its specificity to GAD consistent with a *DSM–IV* diagnosis. Frequency of negative metacognitions concerning danger discriminated GAD participants from those with somatic anxiety or no anxiety.

The contribution of negative metacognitions to pathological worry has also been found cross-culturally in a Lebanese sample (Nassif, 1999, study 1). Nuevo, Montorio, and Borkovec (2004) replicated the study of Wells and Carter (1999) and extended it by examining the relationship between meta-worry and worry severity in an elderly Spanish sample. Meta-worry consistently emerged as a significant predictor of both pathological worry and interference from worry, even when trait anxiety and Type 1 worry was controlled.

While the above studies have tended to focus on Type 2 worry, other studies have sought to test the effects of negative metacognitive beliefs as predicted by the model. Cartwright-Hatton and Wells (1997) found that *DSM–III–R* GAD patients endorsed significantly higher levels of negative beliefs about uncontrollability and danger than groups with other (mixed) anxiety disorders. Wells and Papageorgiou (1998) aimed to rule out possible confounds that might cause a spurious relationship between negative metacognitive beliefs and pathological worry (in nonpatients). They demonstrated that negative meta-beliefs contributed to pathological worry even when positive metacognitive beliefs and obsessive-compulsive symptoms were controlled. Davis and Valentiner (2000) showed that GAD subjects had higher scores than nonworried subjects on two dimensions of negative metacognitions: uncontrollability and danger, and beliefs concerning a need to control thoughts.

Ruscio and Borkovec (2004) examined differences in the experience of worry and in the appraisal of worry among high worriers with and without GAD. This is an important study for the model because it enables an evaluation of whether it is differences in worry or in the appraisal of worry that distinguish high worriers from those with GAD. Their results are consistent with the metacognitive model in demonstrating that worry was similar across both groups but that more substantial differences emerged in two separate negative belief dimensions: uncontrollability and danger.

There is a large body of evidence supporting an association between positive beliefs about worry and either a diagnosis of GAD or the presence of elevated pathological worry. The metacognitive model does not consider positive metacognitions to be specific to GAD, but it does implicate them in the development of pathological worry, and therefore, these relationships are consistent with the model.

The cross-sectional nature of most studies on metacognitive beliefs and meta-worry limits support for the causal effects of metacognition implicated in the model. However, a prospective study by Nassif (1999, study 2) examined longitudinal predictors of pathological worry and GAD. Over a period of 12–15 weeks, meta-worry, but not Type 1 worry measured at time 1, predicted the later development of GAD. Negative metacognitive beliefs concerning uncontrollability and danger at time 1 predicted the presence of GAD at time 2, controlling for GAD status, trait anxiety, and Type 1 worry at time 1.

Summary

The metacognitive model provides an explanation of how worry becomes generalized, excessive, and difficult to control in GAD. It also makes a distinction between GAD and high levels of non-GAD worry in terms of the negative appraisals and negative beliefs held about worrying. It is the first model to give a central role to negative metacognitive beliefs and appraisals. Another novel feature is its consideration of the dynamic disturbances that exist, specifically in the way patients attempt to avoid intrusive thoughts but fail to disengage the worry process due to uncontrollability beliefs or the pressure of positive beliefs about the need to worry. It also explains how some coping strategies or failure to disengage worry lead to a perpetuation of negative metacognitions.

There is a good level of support from a range of sources supporting key aspects of the metacognitive model. But as yet, much of the data are cross-sectional and further evaluations of the causal significance of negative metacognitions are required. The limited amount of data that do exist, however, support a causal effect of worry on negative outcomes involving intrusive thoughts and traumatic reactions following stress. Meta-worry and negative meta-beliefs are also associated with the later development of GAD.

This is a model of the transition to GAD and its maintenance, and the model was not intended to address how erroneous metacognitions develop in the first instance. While this is not a limiting factor for the development of model-based treatment, it does not address questions concerning early detection and prevention of GAD in high-risk groups.

Intolerance of Uncertainty Model of GAD

Dugas et al. (1998) developed the intolerance of uncertainty model of GAD, which has four principal components: intolerance of uncertainty, negative problem orientation, positive beliefs about worry, and cognitive avoidance. At the heart of the model lies the construct of intolerance of uncertainty, considered to be fundamental in the development and maintenance of worry and GAD. One definition of intolerance of uncertainty (IU) is "the tendency to react negatively on an emotional, cognitive and behavioral level to uncertain situations and events" (Dugas, Buhr, & Ladouceur, 2004, pp. 143–144). It is proposed that IU has both direct and indirect links with worry. Specifically, the model proposes that IU directly leads to worry through enhancing cognitive biases, and that positive beliefs about worry, negative problem orientation, and cognitive avoidance indirectly lead to excessive worry. Each feature of the IU model will now be described in more detail.

Intolerance of uncertainty is viewed as a personality trait, derived from a collection of core beliefs about uncertainty. Such beliefs include: "Uncertainty makes life intolerable; uncertainty makes me anxious; and uncertainty stops me from functioning." Collectively, these beliefs or schemas give rise to the view that possible future negative events are unacceptable, regardless of the probability of their occurrence. So within this model, the belief that uncertainty is unacceptable and aversive drives the cognitive, behavioral, and affective components of GAD (Freeston et al., 1994). Clearly, uncertainty is unavoidable, so for people with a low tolerance of uncertainty, everyday situations become extremely difficult to manage and therefore these individuals respond with worry.

Positive beliefs about worry are the second component of this model and are held to be a manifestation of IU. Examples of positive beliefs include: "Worrying is motivating; worry helps to solve problems; it prevents disappointment when negative outcomes occur and worry means I am a caring person" (Freeston et al., 1994). Such beliefs are maintained through both positive and negative reinforcement. Positive reinforcement occurs when worry is followed by a good outcome such as finding a solution to a feared situation. As described in the cognitive avoidance model, worry is negatively reinforced via the nonoccurrence of an imagined catastrophe and reduction in affect.

The third aspect of the IU model concerns a particular aspect of problem solving called *negative problem orientation* (Maydeu-Olivares & D'Zurilla, 1996). Problem orientation can be either positive or negative. Typical beliefs of an individual with a positive problem orientation would be: "All problems can be solved; problems are a challenge to overcome." In contrast, the IU model suggests that GAD patients have a negative problem orientation (Ladouceur, Blais, Freeston, & Dugas, 1998) with a corresponding set of beliefs, which relate to doubts, fears, and pessimism about their ability to solve problems. Therefore, GAD patients do not have deficient problem-solving skills, but rather their attitudes and beliefs about problem solving interfere with the process of active problem solving. Such beliefs prevent the implementation of problem-solving skills, thereby perpetuating the beliefs that problems are impossible to solve as the person is likely to engage in behaviors that would modify this belief.

The final component is cognitive avoidance, which is an attempt to stop or diminish distressing thoughts and images. Patients can use a wide range of avoidance strategies, including thought suppression, thought replacement, mental distraction, and avoidance of triggering stimuli. This component of the IU model is largely drawn from Borkovec's cognitive avoidance theory of worry and has already been described in detail.

Empirical Support

Evidence is rapidly accumulating that supports each of the four core components of the intolerance of uncertainty model and their relationship with worry and GAD (cf. Koerner & Dugas, 2006). A central prediction derived from the model is that people high in intolerance of uncertainty should evidence information-processing biases that are related to both the development and maintenance of worry. In two related studies, Dugas et al. (2005) found evidence of both (1) biased recall of information relating to uncertainty, and (2) a tendency for ambiguous situations to be interpreted as more threatening by a group high in IU, relative to a low IU group. The tendency to make more threatening interpretations remained after controlling for worry, anxiety, and depression.

A number of studies have provided support for the specificity of IU to worry or GAD. In three nonclinical studies, IU was more highly related to worry than to panic or obsessive compulsive symptoms (Dugas, Gosselin, & Ladouceur, 2001), depressive symptoms (Dugas, Schwartz, & Francis, 2004) perfectionism, the need for control, or intolerance of ambiguity (Buhr & Dugas, 2006). Further evidence comes from clinical studies indicating that GAD patients are more intolerant of uncertainty than panic patients (Dugas, Marchand, & Ladouceur, 2005) and a mixed anxiety disorders group (predominately OCD patients) (Ladouceur et al., 1999). In terms of specificity within the model, it appears that IU is a better predictor of worry than the other three features of the IU model.

Positive beliefs about worry have been implicated in the maintenance of GAD in the cognitive avoidance theory, the metacognitive theory, and in the IU model. There is strong support that GAD patients hold positive beliefs about the function of worry (e.g., Cartwright-Hatton & Wells, 1997). Although Koerner and Dugas (2006) speculate that positive beliefs about worry may be a manifestation of IU, further work is required to substantiate this claim.

A demonstrable relationship exists between worry and negative problem orientation (e.g., Davey, Jubb, & Cameron, 1996; Robichaud & Dugas, 2005), but a fundamental question is: How do IU and a negative problem orientation combine to produce high levels of worry and GAD? The argument is that uncertainty is inherent in problem solving and therefore people with a high intolerance of uncertainty are more likely to worry. However, the precise nature of this relationship remains unclear and requires empirical scrutiny.

Summary

There is increasing support for the intolerance of uncertainty model of GAD, and controlled evaluations of the treatment based on the model produced promising results (Dugas et al., 2003; Ladouceur, Dugas, et al., 2000). The intolerance of uncertainty model appears to be firmly based within schema theory. Indeed, it is postulated that intolerance of uncertainty acts as a cognitive filter through which experiences are encoded and evaluated, and therefore, ultimately guide behavior. Although the IU model is a disorder specific model of GAD, placing it within a generic schema framework means it becomes subject to the same limitations as the traditional Beckian model of emotional disorders. In particular, intolerance of uncertainty (like a danger schema) may be the consequence rather than the cause of worry.

Despite the claim that intolerance of uncertainty is most specific to worry and GAD and a good deal of evidence that exists to support this position, a question has been raised as to whether intolerance of uncertainty is specific to GAD or is applicable to a broader range of psychological disorders. For instance, intolerance of uncertainty is viewed as an important construct in OCD (Steketee, Frost, & Cohen, 1998; Tolin, Abramowitz, Brigidi, & Foa, 2003). In a study of the role of IU in analogue GAD and OCD, Holaway, Heimberg, & Coles (2006) found IU was associated as much with OCD as with GAD. Although this is only one study, it appears that intolerance of uncertainty may have a prominent role in both GAD and OCD. Further research is required to clarify whether IU is GAD specific or GAD relevant. No direct comparisons of the role of IU in clinical samples of GAD and OCD have been conducted; such studies need to be undertaken to clarify this issue. Another issue raised by Starcevic and Berle (2006) is a problem with the definition of IU. Specifically, IU appears to be defined differently by other research groups (e.g., Sookman & Pinard, 1995), and also by Dugas and colleagues, with at least three definitions appearing in the literature. This represents a significant problem as different operationalized constructs will clearly result in different associations with psychopathological symptoms and processes. As Starcevic and Berle (2006) point out, a consistent and clear definition of IU may contribute to a better understanding of the relationship that IU has with worry and GAD.

Emotional Dysregulation Model

The emotional dysregulation model of GAD (Mennin et al., 2002; Mennin, Turk, Heimberg, & Carmin, 2004) takes its starting point from the central tenet of the cognitive avoidance theory of worry (Borkovec et al., 2004), namely, that worry facilitates escape from aversive emotional experiences. However, Mennin and colleagues argue that it remains somewhat of a mystery why some people find particular affective states so distressing that they use avoidant strategies such as worry (Mennin, 2004). It follows that in order to develop a greater understanding of GAD, an elucidation of the nature of emotion and emotional regulation is required. Mennin and colleagues use emotion theory (Gross, 1998) to conceptualize GAD. In this theory, emotions have an informational value and often act as guides for subsequent actions. Emotional regulation is concerned with the adaptive function of emotion and how an individual manages, expresses, and responds to emotion. This research group posits that GAD should be conceptualized as a syndrome that comprises four interacting components: (1) heightened intensity of emotions, (2) limited understanding of emotions, (3) negative responses to current emotion, and (4) unhelpful management of emotions. The model suggests that people with GAD are very sensitive to emotions. They also find them problematic to understand, coupled with a fear of aversive emotional states and few emotional regulation skills to manage high levels of affect. In summary, Mennin et al. (2002, 2004) suggest that GAD is characterized by deficits in emotional regulation and excessive reliance on cognitive control strategies such as worry in order to reduce the affective experience.

Empirical Support

Some initial evidence exists that supports the components of this model. In a series of studies (Mennin, Heimberg, Turk, & Fresco, 2005), an analogue GAD sample (undergraduates meeting criteria for GAD on the Generalized Anxiety Disorder Questionnaire—IV [GAD-Q-IV]) (Newman et al., 2002) had greater difficulty in identifying and describing their emotions relative to a control group. In addition, the GAD group rated emotional experiences as significantly more intense. In a mood induction experiment, they had greater difficulty understanding their reactions to the induced mood state. The GAD group also reported greater fear of a range of positive and negative emotions and fear of sadness and anxiety made unique contributions to the detection of GAD.

However, not all studies support the predictions derived from the emotion dysregulation models. Indeed, a study by Novick-Kline, Turk, Mennin, Hoyt, & Gallagher (2005) obtained results that contradicted a central assertion of the model. Contrary to the prediction that individuals with GAD should have lower levels of emotional awareness than controls, the study actually found that individuals with GAD had greater levels of emotional awareness than a control group. Novick-Kline et al. (2005) suggested that the result could be due to methodological issues as levels of emotional awareness were rated by clinicians in this study rather than by self-report as in the previous studies. An alternative explanation suggested by Novick-Kline et al. (2005) is that the emotional awareness component of the model may require modification. Turk, Heimberg, Luterek, Mennin, & Fresco (2005) examined the specificity of the emotional dysregulation model to GAD by comparing analogue GAD and social anxiety groups. Overall, there were few differences in emotional regulation deficits between the two groups. Both the GAD and social anxiety group had

a limited understanding of emotions and no differences existed in terms of negative responses to emotions or in the ability to self-soothe. This study also failed to replicate the previous finding that GAD participants were more expressive of negative emotions relative to a control group. However, the GAD group did report a greater emotional intensity than the social phobia group.

Summary

The emotional dysregulation model of GAD is in the early stages of development and has some preliminary support. A number of significant issues need to be addressed, one of the most important being whether emotional dysregulation is specific to GAD or is a transdiagnostic process inherent to all psychopathology. Evidence exists to illustrate that emotional dysregulation and related constructs are present in a broad range of clinical disorders, including depression, eating disorders, panic disorder, and borderline personality disorder. The emotional dysregulation model attempts to answer the question of why people with GAD find anxiety so distressing and why they use strategies including worry to avoid it. This is a potentially important research question that warrants further investigation.

Clinical Implications

The approaches reviewed here are linked to different types of treatment, offering a specific focus in each case. The two generic theories of anxiety proposed by Beck et al. (1985) and Barlow (2000) do not explicitly target worry, and therefore, cognitive therapy (CT) based on these approaches is not distinguishable from CT for other anxiety disorders. Treatment consists of challenging the content of negative automatic thoughts, training in relaxation, and modifying underlying beliefs about the world being a dangerous place and the self being unable to cope. It is interesting to note that this approach does not make an explicit distinction between negative automatic thoughts and worry, and so it is not clear if the treatment is one that could be considered as targeting worry at all. A pessimistic view is that it may simply remove the negative thoughts that trigger worrying, rather than deal with worry, which could otherwise be construed as a maladaptive coping process.

The other models provide, with varying levels of specificity, treatments that focus on worry and underlying mechanisms. The treatment implied by the avoidance theory should logically consist of imagery exposure (i.e., exposing individuals to their feared images and preventing avoidance, in order to promote extinction). However, a difficulty lies in establishing and identifying the *core* worries of the individual with GAD, which potentially negates the usefulness of worry exposure as a treatment strategy. Instead, the treatment incorporates a range of cognitive and behavioral strategies designed to address the diagnostic components of GAD. Following self-monitoring to increase awareness of the triggers for worrying, clients are taught a range of coping strategies. These include applied relaxation in response to anxiety cues to countercondition the habitual anxiety response and allow corrective information to be encoded within the fear structure. Traditional verbal reattribution strategies are used to modify dysfunctional beliefs about the usefulness of worry as a coping mechanism. Imagery rehearsal is also used to enable the individual to deploy new coping methods (i.e., a relaxation response in response to anxiety-triggering thoughts).

The metacognitive model has a close fit between model and treatment. Here, treatment consists of constructing an idiosyncratic case formulation based on the model. This is followed by helping the patient to see that the core problem in GAD is erroneous beliefs about worry and unhelpful patterns of self-regulation of thinking. Treatment proceeds through a series of stages in which negative beliefs about the uncontrollability of worry are modified first. This is followed by challenging beliefs about the harmful consequences of worry. Finally, positive metacognitive beliefs are challenged as a prerequisite for strengthening alternative ways of dealing with stress and intrusive thoughts.

Treatment based on the intolerance of uncertainty model appears to include a broad range of treatment strategies in a similar way to the treatment predicated on the avoidance theory. The IU treatment begins with an illustration of the process and consequences of worrying. First, patients are given worry awareness training to help in the recognition of the worry process. The intolerance of uncertainty construct is then presented and both verbal and behavioral reattribution methods are used to increase acceptance and tolerance of uncertainty. This construct forms the basis for the subsequent treatment components. Beliefs about the usefulness of worry as a method of coping with uncertainty are challenged and modified. The next treatment phase involves changing the patient's negative problem orientation to a positive orientation, enabling the patient to be more confident in his or her ability to solve problems and to confront rather than avoid uncertain situations. Finally, imaginal exposure to

the individual's *core fears* is used to enable emotional processing to occur.

Treatment Efficacy

Each of the specific treatments based on the cognitive avoidance model, the metacognitive model, and the intolerance of uncertainty model have been evaluated in controlled studies. A controlled evaluation of the efficacy of emotional regulation therapy for GAD has yet to be conducted. A review of the clinical effectiveness of psychological treatments for GAD (Fisher, 2006) based on standardized criteria on the State-Trait Anxiety Inventory (STAI-T) (Spielberger, Gorsuch, Lushene, Vagg, & Jacobs, 1983) and a specific measure of the worry, the Penn State Worry Questionnaire (PSWQ) (Meyer, Miller, Metzger, & Borkovec, 1990), found an aggregated recovery rate of 50% for cognitive behavioral treatments, but this masks possible differences between treatments. Recovery rates for the treatments based on the cognitive avoidance model, the metacognitive model, and the IU model are briefly summarized below. In the two controlled trials conducted by Borkovec and colleagues (Borkovec & Costello, 1993; Borkovec et al., 2002), the recovery rates achieved by CBT (a combined treatment package of applied relaxation and cognitive therapy) at posttreatment were 63% and 57% on the STAI-T and 53% and 44% on the PSWQ. At 1-year follow-up, these recovery rates were maintained with approximately 50% of patients recovered on both the STAI-T and PSWQ.

So far there has been an open trial of metacognitive therapy (MCT) for GAD (Wells & King, 2006) and one small controlled trial comparing MCT with applied relaxation (Wells, Welford, King, Wisely, & Mendel, 2007). In this later trial, MCT achieved a recovery rate of 80% at posttreatment on both the STAI-T and the PSWQ. These treatment gains were largely maintained through to the 12-month follow-up with recovery rates of 70% on the STAI-T and 80% on the PSWQ. The only data available for the clinical significance review for the IU treatment was a controlled trial evaluating the efficacy of that treatment in a small group format against a waitlist control condition (Dugas et al., 2003). The IU treatment produced recovery rates of 48% at posttreatment and 64% at 1-year follow-up on the PSWQ. An earlier study examining the efficacy of the IU treatment in an individual format (Ladouceur, Dugas, et al., 2000) found 62% of participants achieved high end state functioning at posttreatment and 58% at 1-year follow-up with comparable results achieved in the group treatment, although there were higher attrition rates in the group approach.

Summary and Conclusions

The theories reviewed offer a range of cognitive behavioral conceptualizations of pathological worry and GAD, and while they share some features, there are significant differences among them. The cognitive avoidance theory, metacognitive model, and intolerance of uncertainty model each deal explicitly with worrying, which in each case may be construed as a response to other types of internal events (including negative thoughts). Each theory incorporates the notion that worry can prevent emotional processing, leading to an exacerbation of negative affect. Similarly, the cognitive avoidance theory, the intolerance of uncertainty model, and the metacognitive model all highlight the important role that positive beliefs about worry play in the maintenance of the disorder. In addition, each theory would suggest that worry involves thinking about possible future negative situations and the generation of potential outcomes or solutions to those scenarios.

So how do the specific models differ? The avoidance theory places cognitive-emotional avoidance in central stage, while the metacognitive theory gives a central role to negative metacognitions and difficulties in the regulation of worry caused by conflicting positive and negative beliefs about worry. In contrast the IU model focuses on a dispositional construct (schema) leading to the interpretation of uncertainty as being toxic. In comparison, the dysregulation model suggests that GAD patients have a deficit in self-regulation. This is the only model to suggest a deficit (e.g., in emotional identification) rather than just a bias in cognition and behavior. One way to draw out the differences between these theoretical approaches is to examine how each one accounts for the cardinal features of pathological worry. The features to be explained are (1) the excessiveness of worry, (2) the generalized nature of worry, and (3) perceived uncontrollability.

The cognitive avoidance model suggests that worry becomes excessive, generalized, and uncontrollable primarily through reinforcement contingencies. Each time a person experiences a triggering thought or image and accompanying somatic arousal, the person's worry is activated to ameliorate the distress, but unfortunately, this results in a strengthening and widening of stimuli that contain anxious meanings. This creates a richer associative network in memory, thereby increasing the number of situations or stimuli that lead to the conditioned response of worry. Because worry is a conditioned response to an internal stimulus, it is viewed as uncontrollable; in other words, people with GAD no longer have discriminative control over the worry process.

How does the metacognitive model explain the three cardinal features of pathological worry? According to this model, worry becomes excessive and generalized because patients overselect worry as a coping strategy, and then, when negative beliefs about worry are activated, this undermines the coping strategy, leading to greater worry and anxiety. Uncontrollability is a belief, appraisal, and experience that is maintained and strengthened by choice of ineffective self-control strategies. In particular, positive and negative beliefs give rise to conflicting or vacillating motivations to engage in and interrupt the worry process. Attempts to suppress the thoughts that act as triggers for worrying can backfire and increase preoccupation with worry topics. In each case negative appraisals/beliefs about uncontrollability are strengthened or maintained, when in fact, worry can be readily interrupted.

The intolerance of uncertainty model argues that individuals with GAD have an increased sensitivity to a broad array of uncertain situations in life. Because almost every situation carries a degree of uncertainty, it is argued that this explains why worry becomes generalized and excessive. More specifically, people who are intolerant of uncertainty appear to engage in biased information processing, meaning that they interpret ambiguous or uncertain situations as more threatening than people who do not possess an intolerance of uncertainty schema. This interpretative bias is responded to with worry in an attempt to remove uncertainty from real and imagined scenarios, and therefore, people will worry excessively about multiple topics. The other components, namely positive beliefs about worry, negative problem orientation, and cognitive avoidance, serve to maintain this high level of worry. However, there is no explicit account of how intolerance of uncertainty leads to perceived uncontrollability of worry. One possibility is that avoidance and repeated failed attempts to stop worrying lead to the perception that worry is uncontrollable.

In conclusion, the view of psychological processes in GAD is quite different from the perspective of each of the models discussed in this chapter. Each approach is associated with a different emphasis in treatment, with interventions ranging from a general to a relatively tight focus on particular cognitive behavioral factors. Preliminary evidence is encouraging, suggesting that the specific model-based treatments are effective, but they might not be equivalently effective. Controlled comparisons of these interventions and empirical tests of the relative strengths of the theories are now required.

References

American Psychiatric Association. (1980). *Diagnostic and statistical manual of mental disorders* (3rd ed.). Washington, DC: Author.

Barlow, D. H. (2000). Unravelling the mysteries of anxiety and its disorders from the perspective of emotion theory. *American Psychologist, 55*, 1248–1263.

Beck, A. T. (1976). *Cognitive therapy and the emotional disorders.* New York: International Universities Press.

Beck, A. T., Emery, G., & Greenberg, R. (1985). *Anxiety disorders and phobias: A cognitive perspective.* New York: Basic Books.

Borkovec, T. D., Alcaine, O., & Behar, E. (2004). Avoidance theory of worry and generalized anxiety disorder. In R. G. Heimberg, C. L. Turk, & D. S. Mennin (Eds.), *Generalized anxiety disorder: Advances in research and practice* (pp. 77–108). New York: Guilford.

Borkovec, T. D., & Costello, E. (1993). Efficacy of applied relaxation and cognitive-behavioral therapy in the treatment of generalised anxiety disorder. *Journal of Consulting and Clinical Psychology, 61*, 611–619.

Borkovec, T. D., & Inz, J. (1990). The nature of worry in generalized anxiety disorder: A predominance of thought activity. *Behaviour Research and Therapy, 31*, 153–158.

Borkovec, T. D., Newman, M., Pincus, A., & Lytle, R. (2002). A component analysis of cognitive behavioral therapy for generalized anxiety disorder and the role of interpersonal problems. *Journal of Consulting and Clinical Psychology, 70*, 288–298.

Borkovec, T. D., Ray, W. J., & Stober, J. (1998). Worry: A cognitive phenomenon intimately linked to affective, physiological and interpersonal behavioral processes. *Cognitive Therapy and Research, 22*, 561–576.

Borkovec, T. D., & Roemer, L. (1995). Perceived functions of worry among generalized anxiety disorder subjects: Distraction from more emotional topics? *Journal of Behavior Therapy and Experimental Psychiatry, 21*, 9–16.

Buhr, K., & Dugas, M. J. (2006). Investigating the construct validity of intolerance of uncertainty and its unique relationship with worry. *Journal of Anxiety Disorders, 20*, 222–236.

Butler, G., Wells, A., & Dewick, H. (1995). Differential effects of worry and imagery after exposure to a stressful stimulus. *Behavioural and Cognitive Psychotherapy, 23*, 45–56.

Cartwright-Hatton, S., & Wells, A. (1997). Beliefs about worry and intrusions: The Meta-Cognitions Questionnaire and its correlates. *Journal of Anxiety Disorders, 11*, 279–296.

Davey, G.C.L., Jubb, M., & Cameron, C. (1996). Catastrophic worry as a function of changes in problem solving confidence. *Cognitive Therapy and Research, 20*, 333–344.

Davis, R. N., & Valentiner, D. P. (2000). Does meta-cognitive theory enhance our understanding of pathological worry and anxiety? *Personality and Individual Differences, 29*, 513–526.

Dugas, M. J., Buhr, K., & Ladouceur, R. (2004). The role of intolerance of uncertainty in etiology and maintenance. In R. G. Heimberg, C. L. Turk, & D. S. Mennin (Eds.), *Generalized anxiety disorder: Advances in research and practice* (pp. 143–163). New York: Guilford Press.

Dugas, M. J., Gagnon, F., Ladouceur, R., & Freeston, M. H. (1998). Generalized anxiety disorder: A preliminary test of a conceptual model. *Behaviour Research and Therapy, 36*, 215–226.

Dugas, M. J., Gosselin, P., & Ladouceur, R. (2001). Intolerance of uncertainty and worry: Investigating specificity in a non-clinical sample. *Cognitive Therapy and Research, 25*, 551–558.

Dugas, M. J., Hedayati, M., Karavidas, A., Buhr, K., Francis, K., & Phillips, N. (2005). Intolerance of uncertainty and information processing: Evidence of biased recall and interpretations. *Cognitive Therapy and Research, 29*, 57–70.

Dugas, M. J., Ladouceur, R., Leger, E., Freeston, M. H., Langlois, F., Provencher, M., et al. (2003). Group cognitive-behavioural therapy for generalized anxiety disorder: Treatment outcome and long-term follow-up. *Journal of Consulting and Clinical Psychology, 71*, 821–825.

Dugas, M. J., Marchand, A., & Ladouceur, R. (2005). Further validation of a cognitive behavioral model of generalized anxiety disorder: Diagnostic and symptom specificity. *Journal of Anxiety Disorders, 19*, 329–343.

Dugas, M. J., Schwartz, A., & Francis, K. (2004). Intolerance of uncertainty, worry and depression. *Cognitive Therapy and Research, 28*, 835–842.

Fisher, P. L. (2006). The efficacy of psychological treatments for generalized anxiety disorder. In G.C.L. Davey & A. Wells (Eds.), *Worry and its psychological disorders: Theory, assessment and treatment* (pp. 359–377). Chichester, England: Wiley.

Foa, E. B., & Kozak, M. J. (1986). Emotional processing of fear: Exposure to corrective information. *Psychological Bulletin, 99*, 20–35.

Freeston, M. H., Dugas, M. J., & Ladouceur, R. (1996). Thoughts, images, worry, and anxiety. *Cognitive Therapy and Research, 20*, 265–273.

Freeston, M. H., Rheaume, J., Letarte, H., Dugas, M. J., & Ladouceur, R. (1994). Why do people worry? *Personality and Individual Differences, 17*, 791–802.

Gross, J. J. (1998). The emerging field of emotion regulation: An integrative review. *Review of General Psychology, 2*, 271–299.

Holaway, R. M., Heimberg, R. G., & Coles, M. E. (2006). A comparison of intolerance of uncertainty in analogue obsessive-compulsive disorder and generalized anxiety disorder. *Journal of Anxiety Disorders, 20*, 158–174.

Koerner, N., & Dugas, M. J. (2006). A cognitive model of generalized anxiety disorder: The role of intolerance of uncertainty. In G.C.L. Davey & A. Wells (Eds.), *Worry and its psychological disorders: Theory, assessment and treatment* (pp. 201–216). Chichester, England: Wiley.

Ladouceur, R., Blais, F., Freeston, M. H., & Dugas, M. J. (1998). Problem solving and problem orientation in generalized anxiety disorder. *Journal of Anxiety Disorders, 12*, 139–152.

Ladouceur, R., Dugas, M. J., Freeston, M. H., Leger, E., Gagnon, F., & Thibodeau, N. (2000). Efficacy of a cognitive-behavioral treatment for generalized anxiety disorder: Evaluation in a controlled clinical trial. *Journal of Consulting and Clinical Psychology, 68*, 957–964.

Ladouceur, R., Dugas, M. J., Freeston, M. H., Rheaume, J., Blais, F., & Boisvert, J. (1999). Specificity of generalized anxiety disorder symptoms and processes. *Behavior Therapy, 30,* 191–207.

Ladouceur, R., Gosselin, P., & Dugas, M. J. (2000). Experimental manipulation of intolerance of uncertainty: A study of a theoretical model of worry. *Behaviour Research and Therapy, 38,* 933–941.

Maydeu-Olivares, A., & D'Zurilla, T. J. (1996). A factor-analytic study of the Social Problem Solving Inventory: An integration of theory and data. *Cognitive Therapy and Research, 20,* 115–133.

Mennin, D. S. (2004). Emotion regulation therapy for generalized anxiety disorder. *Clinical Psychology and Psychotherapy, 11,* 17–29.

Mennin, D. S., Heimberg, R., Turk, C. L., & Fresco, D. M. (2002). Applying an emotion regulation framework to integrative approaches to generalized anxiety disorder. *Clinical Psychology: Science and Practice, 9,* 85–90.

Mennin, D. S., Heimberg, R. G., Turk, C. L., & Fresco, D. M. (2005). Preliminary evidence for an emotion dysregulation model of generalized anxiety disorder. *Behaviour Research and Therapy, 43,* 1281–1310.

Mennin, D. S., Turk, C. L., Heimberg, R. G., & Carmin, C. N. (2004). Focusing on the regulation of emotion: A new direction for conceptualizing and treating generalized anxiety disorder. In M. A. Reinecke & D. A. Clark (Eds.), *Cognitive therapy over the lifespan: Evidence and practice* (pp. 60–89). New York: Cambridge University Press.

Meyer, T. J., Miller, M. L., Metzger, R. L., & Borkovec, T. D. (1990). Development and validation of the Penn State Worry Questionnaire. *Behaviour Research and Therapy, 28,* 487–495.

Nassif, Y. (1999). *Predictors of pathological worry.* Unpublished master's thesis, University of Manchester, Manchester, England.

Nuevo, R., Montorio, I., & Borkovec, T. D. (2004). A test of the role of meta-worry in the prediction of worry severity in an elderly sample. *Journal of Behavior Therapy and Experimental Psychiatry, 35,* 209–218.

Newman, M. G., Zuellig, A. R., Kachin, K. E., Constantino, M. J., Przeworski, A., Erickson, T., et al. (2002). Preliminary reliability and validity of the Generalized Anxiety Disorder Questionnaire–IV: A revised self-report diagnostic measure of generalized anxiety disorder. *Behavior Therapy, 33,* 215–233.

Novick-Kline, P., Turk, C. L., Mennin, D. S., Hoyt, E. A., & Gallagher, C. L. (2005). Level of emotional awareness as a differentiating variable between individuals with and without generalized anxiety disorder. *Journal of Anxiety Disorders, 19,* 557–572.

Robichaud, M., & Dugas, M. J. (2005). Negative problem orientation (Part II): Construct validity and specificity to worry. *Behaviour Research and Therapy, 43,* 403–412.

Ruscio, A. M., & Borkovec, T. D. (2004). Experience and appraisal of worry among high worriers with and without generalized anxiety disorder. *Behaviour Research and Therapy, 42,* 1469–1482.

Sibrava, N. J., & Borkovec, T. D. (2006). The cognitive avoidance theory of worry. In G.C.L. Davey & A. Wells (Eds.), *Worry and its psychological disorders: Theory, assessment and treatment.* Chichester, England: Wiley.

Sookman, D., & Pinard, G. (1995, July). *The cognitive schemata scale: A multidimensional measure of cognitive schemas in obsessive-compulsive disorder.* Paper presented at the World Congress of Behavioural and Cognitive Therapies, Copenhagen, Denmark.

Spielberger, C. D., Gorsuch, R. L., Lushene, R., Vagg, P. R., & Jacobs, G. A. (1983). *Manual for the State-Trait Anxiety Inventory (Form Y Self-Evaluation Questionnaire).* Palo Alto, CA: Consulting Psychologists Press.

Starcevic, V., & Berle, D. (2006). Cognitive specificity of anxiety disorders: A review of selected key constructs. *Depression and Anxiety, 23,* 51–61.

Steketee, G., Frost, R. O., & Cohen, I. (1998). Beliefs in obsessive-compulsive disorder. *Journal of Anxiety Disorders, 12,* 525–537.

Stober, J. (1998). Worry, problem elaboration and suppression of imagery: The role of concreteness. *Behaviour Research and Therapy, 36,* 751–756.

Stober, J., & Borkovec, T. D. (2002). Reduced concreteness of worry in generalized anxiety disorder: Findings from a therapy study. *Cognitive Therapy and Research, 26,* 89–96.

Tallis, F., Davey, G.C.L., & Capuzzo, N. (1994). The phenomenology of nonpathological worry: A preliminary investigation. In G.C.L. Davey & F. Tallis (Eds.), *Worrying: Perspectives on theory, assessment and treatment* (pp. 61–89). Chichester, England: Wiley.

Tolin, D. F., Abramowitz, J. S., Brigidi, B. D., & Foa, E. B. (2003). Intolerance of uncertainty in obsessive-compulsive disorder. *Journal of Anxiety Disorders, 17,* 233–242.

Tucker, D. M., & Newman, J. P. (1981). Verbal versus imaginal cognitive strategies in the inhibition of emotional arousal. *Cognitive Therapy and Research, 5,* 197–202.

Turk, C. L., Heimberg, R. G., Luterek, J. A., Mennin, D. S., & Fresco, D. M. (2005). Emotion dysregulation in generalized anxiety disorder: A comparison with social anxiety disorder. *Cognitive Therapy and Research, 29,* 89–106.

Vasey, M. W., & Borkovec, T. D. (1992). A catastrophizing assessment of worrisome thoughts. *Cognitive Therapy and Research, 16,* 505–520.

Vrana, S. R., Cuthbert, B. N., & Lang, P. J. (1986). Fear imagery and text processing. *Psychophysiology, 23,* 247–253.

Wells, A. (1995). Meta-cognition and worry: A cognitive model of generalised anxiety disorder. *Behavioural and Cognitive Psychotherapy, 23,* 301–320.

Wells, A. (1997). *Cognitive therapy of anxiety disorders: A practice manual and conceptual guide.* Chichester, England: Wiley.

Wells, A. (1999). A metacognitive model and therapy for generalised anxiety disorder. *Clinical Psychology and Psychotherapy, 6,* 86–96.

Wells, A. (2005). The metacognitive model of GAD: Assessment of meta-worry and relationship with *DSM–IV* generalized anxiety disorder. *Cognitive Therapy and Research, 29,* 107–121.

Wells, A., & Carter, K. (1999). Preliminary tests of a cognitive model of generalized anxiety disorder. *Behaviour Research and Therapy, 37,* 585–594.

Wells, A., & Carter, K. (2001). Further tests of a cognitive model of generalized anxiety disorder: Metacognitions in GAD, panic disorder, social phobia, depression and non-patients. *Behavior Therapy, 32,* 85–102.

Wells, A., & King, P. (2006). Metacognitive therapy for generalized anxiety disorder: An open trial. *Journal of Behavior Therapy and Experimental Psychiatry, 37,* 206–212.

Wells, A., & Matthews, G. (1994). *Attention and emotion: A clinical perspective.* Hove, England: Erlbaum.

Wells, A., & Matthews, G. (1996). Modelling cognition in emotional disorder: The S-REF Model. *Behaviour Research and Therapy, 34,* 881–888.

Wells, A., & Papageorgiou, C. (1995). Worry and the incubation of intrusive images following stress. *Behaviour Research and Therapy, 33,* 579–583.

Wells, A., & Papageorgiou, C. (1998). Relationships between worry, obsessive-compulsive symptoms and meta-cognitive beliefs. *Behaviour Research and Therapy, 36,* 899–913.

Wells, A., Welford, M., King, P., Wisely, J., & Mendel, E. (2007). *A randomized trial of metacognitive therapy versus applied relaxation in the treatment of GAD.* Unpublished manuscript.

Psychological Approaches to Understanding Obsessive-Compulsive Disorder

Christine Purdon

Abstract

In this chapter, cognitive behavioral approaches to understanding the development, persistence, and treatment of OCD are described, with emphasis on the work of Foa, Rachman, and Salkovskis. Developments of these central models by D. A. Clark, Frost, O'Connor, and Purdon are also described. Brief summaries of the empirical evidence supporting those models and of the efficacy of CBT in the treatment of OCD are provided.

Keywords: cognition, cognitive behavioral theories, cognitive behavioral therapy, exposure with response prevention, hoarding, obsessive-compulsive disorder

Psychological approaches to understanding and treating obsessive-compulsive disorder (OCD) have gained prominence in the last two decades, when the benefits of prolonged exposure to obsessional triggers with simultaneous ritual prevention ("exposure with response prevention") were discovered (Foa, Franklin, & Kozak, 1998; Rachman & Hodgson, 1980). Exposure with response prevention (ERP) is based on the conceptualization of obsessions as "noxious" stimuli to which the individual's fear has failed to extinguish. Compulsions are overt and covert (i.e., mental) acts that are performed to reduce the psychophysiological and subjective disturbances caused by the thought. This reduction in distress reinforces performance of the compulsion (Rachman, 1976; Rachman & Hodgson, 1980).

Exposure with response prevention involves active generation of the obsession while the individual refrains from performing the compulsive ritual. This allows the discomfort associated with the obsession to subside naturally in the absence of the compulsive ritual, thereby restoring normal mood state, increasing cognitive control, and making the ritual obsolete (Rachman, 1976; Rachman & Hodgson, 1980). In a

comprehensive analysis of the processes involved in habituation, Foa and Kozak (1986) described fear/anxiety as being represented as a "structure" in memory that consists of information about the feared stimulus situation, responses to the situation, and the meaning of the stimulus and response elements of the structure. In order for this structure to be modified, it must first be completely activated, and then the individual must be exposed to information that is incompatible with it. If the structure is fully activated, the incompatible information can be integrated into the structure, thereby changing its nature.

The fear structure is fully activated only when the individual is exposed to the fear-evoking stimulus. If rituals and avoidance strategies are prevented, fear reduction occurs. That is, the discomfort associated with the stimulus declines in the absence of the escape or avoidance strategies, and the existing stimulus-response elements become dissociated. The lowered level of arousal facilitates integration of corrective information about the meaning of the feared stimuli and responses. A new structure then emerges, in which the stimulus is now represented as fairly benign, which in turn makes the ritual and avoidance behavior obsolete, the hypervigilance to cues of the feared stimulus dissipates, and there is an overall reduction in discomfort. Foa and Kozak (1996) observed high treatment success rates of ERP, with an average immediate response rate of 83% and a long-term follow-up rate of success of about 76%. Similarly, in a meta-analysis of existing treatment studies, Abramowitz (1996) reported that ERP has a very large effect size.

However, when treatment refusal and drop-out rates are taken into consideration, along with the number of treatment nonresponders and the number of individuals who technically "respond" but continue to exhibit debilitating symptoms, the actual treatment success rate could be as low as 50% (Stanley & Turner, 1995). There has been growing acknowledgment that cognitive appraisal plays an important role in the obsessive-compulsive cycle, and that the original model on which ERP is based may not be comprehensive enough to account for all aspects of the disorder, nor all symptom subtypes (e.g., Foa & McNally, 1996; Rachman & Hodgson, 1980; Salkovskis, 1985, 1989). Furthermore, one key predictor of treatment refusal and drop-out is fear of ERP itself (Foa, Steketee, Grayson, & Doppelt, 1983; Maltby & Tolin, 2003; Vogel, Stiles, & Götestam, 2004). Salkovskis (1988, 1996, 1998) argued that the obsession cannot be experienced as "noxious" unless it is appraised negatively. That is, the emotional response to obsessions must be driven by erroneous, negative beliefs about and interpretations of the meaning of the obsession. Thus, it is no surprise that ERP is an unpalatable intervention for many. Treatment refusal and dropout may be decreased substantially if the obsession is "detoxified" in advance through reappraisal of the thought's meaning. As a result of these observations, cognitive-behavioral models of OCD have gained considerable prominence.

Salkovskis's Cognitive Behavioral Model

The starting point of Salkovskis's model is the observation that obsessional thoughts lie on a continuum with normal thoughts that everyone experiences (Salkovskis, 1985, 1989). He then noted that the negative automatic thoughts of individuals with obsessional problems tend to reflect themes of personal responsibility for harm or danger befalling self or others. According to Salkovskis, Richards, and Forrester (1995), the term *responsibility* refers to:

> The belief that one has the power which is pivotal to bring about or prevent subjectively crucial negative

outcomes. These outcomes may be actual, that is, having consequences in the real world, and/or at a moral level. (p. 285)

In accordance with Beck's (1976) schema-based theory, Salkovskis (1985) argued that the negative automatic thoughts evoked by the occurrence of an obsessional thought derive from preexisting dysfunctional schemata, which in the case of OCD constitute beliefs about one's personal responsibility to prevent harm to self or others. Examples of such beliefs include "Having a thought about an action is like performing an action," "Failing to prevent or trying to prevent harm to self or others is the same as having caused the harm in the first place," "Responsibility is not attenuated by other factors (e.g., low probability of occurrence)," "Not neutralizing when an intrusion has occurred is similar or equivalent to seeking or wanting the harm involved in that intrusion to happen," and "One can and should control one's thoughts" (p. 579).

Salkovskis (1998) also suggested that beliefs reflecting the construct of "thought-action fusion" (Shafran, Thordarson, & Rachman, 1996) are important manifestations of responsibility beliefs. Examples of such beliefs are: "Thinking about something makes it happen," and "Having a thought about an immoral action is akin to carrying out that action." Finally, he made the observation that whereas most individuals feel less responsible for acts of omission that result in negative consequences (e.g., failing to straighten out a carpet that someone later trips over) than for acts of commission (e.g., deliberately pulling the carpet out from someone, causing her or him to trip), individuals with OCD lack this bias. Instead, individuals with OCD possess the belief that "*any* influence over a negative outcome equals responsibility for that outcome."

Responsibility beliefs give rise to specific appraisals of the thought that may concern either the thought's content (e.g., "This thought is immoral, therefore, I am immoral for having it") or the thought's occurrence (e.g., "The more I have this thought, the more I'm in danger of losing control and acting on it"). The affective disturbance characteristic of obsessional problems, then, derives not from the obsessional thought itself, but rather from the negative appraisal to which it gives rise, which in turn arises from preexisting beliefs about responsibility. If the thought evokes appraisals involving harm, danger, or loss, without the concomitant sense of responsibility, the resulting affective state will be general anxiety or depression, respectively (Salkovskis,

1985, 1989, 1996, 1998, 2002; Salkovskis et al., 1995).

When the obsession activates concerns that the thought might be acted upon or otherwise come true and that the individual would thus be responsible for potential harm ensuing from the thought, mood disturbance results. The individual then attempts to avert the possibility of being responsible for harm by engaging in some sort of ameliorative action (e.g., seeking reassurance that harm has not occurred, sharing responsibility for the potential harm by telling others about the possibility of harm, conducting overt or covert rituals designed to ward off potential harm, etc). These "neutralizing" activities have three primary consequences. First, they result in a reduction in the mood disturbance, so they are more likely to be repeated in response to future occurrences of the obsession. Second, when the feared event represented in the obsession does not happen (e.g., the house does not burn down) after the performance of the neutralizing act, the event's nonoccurrence is attributed to the neutralizing act. Third, the neutralizing act is highly salient and is closely linked to the thought, so it can become a powerful stimulus for the obsession.

Meanwhile, in an insidious feedback cycle, negative mood states will also "prime" obsessional thoughts as well as negative appraisal of obsessional thoughts, which in turn increase negative mood. Finally, the individual will begin avoiding stimuli that trigger the obsessional thought, thereby sustaining negative beliefs about the thought in the same way that avoidance of a phobic stimulus sustains the individual's fears. Such avoidance behaviors can become pervasive in the same manner as agoraphobic avoidance (Salkovskis, 1985, 1989, 1996, 1998, 2002; Salkovskis et al., 1995). Avoidance can also occur in the form of suppression of the obsession. Individuals with obsessional problems will deem it necessary to pay close attention to their mental processes in order to prevent the occurrence of intrusions or to be aware of and limit the implications for responsibility. As a result, they become engaged in effortful strategies to control their obsessions. Salkovskis (1989) argues that suppression will lead to an ironic increase in the frequency of the obsession.

Rachman's Cognitive Behavioral Model

Rachman conducted much of the pioneering research on behavioral approaches to obsessional problems and cognitive behavioral therapy (CBT) models of OCD owe much to this work. Rachman's (1971, 1997, 1998) formulation of obsessions begins with the observation that the important themes of all moral systems (e.g., aggression, sex, and blasphemy) are reflected in the main themes of obsessions and intrusive thoughts. As such, this type of thought is particularly vulnerable to being experienced as sinful, disgusting, alarming, or threatening. Thus, the content of the obsessional thought is of central importance in the escalation of the disorder. Obsessional problems develop when such appraisals are elaborated, and the individual believes that an intrusive thought reveals something meaningful and heretofore unknown about themselves, that it is a warning sign that a negative event will come true, that the thought will bring about some feared event (e.g., going to hell, being locked up, being rejected by friends and family), or that it is an indication that the individual is in danger of losing control. This *catastrophic misinterpretation* of obsessional thoughts is said to result in the development and persistence of the disorder by many of the same processes involved in the development of panic disorder, which involves a catastrophic misinterpretation of bodily sensations (Rachman, 1997).

The obsession will persist as long as the thought is interpreted as being catastrophic, and it will diminish when the misinterpretations are weakened (Rachman, 1998). Once an intrusive thought is interpreted as having personal significance and possibly portending threat, it will give rise to active resistance to the obsession (i.e., thought suppression), in addition to avoidance (i.e., avoiding knives or avoiding being alone with one's child) and attempts to ameliorate the potential negative outcome (i.e., neutralizing). Such acts relieve the discomfort associated with the thought, and so they are increasingly likely to be repeated, even though that relief would have occurred spontaneously in the absence of the act. Neutralizing acts also serve to preserve the catastrophic misinterpretation of the obsession and the subsequent elaborations of the thought's meaning. Meanwhile, as the individual's conviction that the thought portends danger strengthens, the number of external cues that are relevant to the thought increases (e.g., obsessions involving stabbing a loved one may result in fear and avoidance of all sharp objects, which suddenly all become potential weapons). Thus, the range of threats in the individual's environment increases, which means that the number of triggers for the obsession increases. Meanwhile, the individual may begin to deduce that threat is present simply from the activation of the anxious response ("I'm feeling anxious, therefore, danger must be present"), as well as concerns that when one is anxious, one is more likely to behave in ways that could be harmful.

Rachman (1998) proposed that there are a number of factors that may cause some individuals to misinterpret the personal significance of particular intrusive thoughts. First, vulnerable individuals may possess preexisting beliefs about the significance and dangerousness of certain types of thoughts. For example, a person who believes that "if you think about stabbing a person, it means you have a violent streak" might be more inclined to interpret aggressive intrusive thoughts as highly meaningful and dangerous. People of "tender conscience," or with strong religious convictions, may thus be more prone to finding intrusive thoughts objectionable. Second, internal and external sources of provocation, such as exposure to stress, the occurrence of bodily sensations with the intrusion, the reduction in discomfort associated with ameliorative actions, and failures in thought control can enhance appraisals of significance and even the very occurrence of the intrusive thought itself.

Cognitive biases such as "thought-action fusion" (TAF) also promote misinterpretations of significance. Thought-action fusion includes beliefs that having an unacceptable thought increases the likelihood of the negative event represented in the thought coming true, and that having a morally repugnant thought is the moral equivalent to committing a morally repugnant deed. Rachman argued that the beliefs about responsibility emphasized by Salkovskis derive from the TAF cognitive bias. Individuals with this general cognitive bias, then, are more vulnerable to developing obsessional problems. Closely linked to the TAF bias is the bias that when one is responsible for an outcome, things are more likely to go wrong. This particular bias contributes to anxious feelings and increases threat-sensitivity. Finally, negative mood states like dysphoria can also lead to an escalation and maintenance of obsessions by increasing the accessibility of negative interpretations of the thought as well as the thought itself.

Clark and Purdon: Thought Control and Ego-Dystonicity

Clark and Purdon have offered further elaborations of these models (Clark & Purdon, 1993; Purdon & Clark, 1999). Clark (1989) proposed that all individuals hold certain beliefs or assumptions about thinking and about how to control unwanted thoughts. Individuals may be vulnerable to developing obsessions if such beliefs are rigid,

unrealistic, and dysfunctional. For example, beliefs that perfect control over thoughts is possible and desirable, that failing to control thoughts is a sign of mental weakness and instability, and that failures in thought control potentiate loss of control over any or all other domains of functioning may be particularly relevant to OCD.

If an individual holds such beliefs, her or his stake in thought control will be very high. However, as evidenced by the thought suppression literature, perfect control is rarely, if ever, achieved. Even in studies where suppression was not associated with an actual increase in frequency, perfect suppression is seldom observed (e.g., Purdon, Rowa, & Antony, 2005). Given the individual's beliefs about thoughts, failures in thought control will be experienced as particularly catastrophic, and will result in escalating attempts at thought control and a subsequent decline in mood state. As suggested by the thought suppression literature, this in turn will make thoughts even more difficult to control. At this point, other strategies for ameliorating the distress associated with the thoughts, or, neutralizing strategies, may develop.

Purdon and Clark (1999) observed that one cardinal feature that distinguishes obsessions from other types of negative thoughts is that they are typically experienced as being *ego-dystonic*. Although this term has not been consistently defined, Purdon and Clark suggest that the ego-dystonic quality of an obsession refers to the individual's sense that the thought is inconsistent with specific and important aspects of the self that are especially valued by the person. Purdon and Clark (1999) suggest that ego-dystonicity is a feature of all obsessions and is a key factor in the escalation and persistence of the disorder. For example, an obsession of stabbing or harming a loved one is ego-dystonic in that it is inconsistent with the person's explicit feelings about the loved one, as well as with her or his values and sense of morality. An obsession that one has left an appliance on and caused a fatal accident is ego-dystonic in that it violates the individual's sense of herself or himself as a conscientious, reliable, caring, and cautious person. Finally, an obsession that one has become contaminated is ego-dystonic because it violates that individual's sense of herself or himself as a clean person.

An obsessional thought, then, is inconsistent with one's sense of self and with the kinds of beliefs an individual would expect herself or himself to have. As such, the thought represents a threat to the self-view. The individual is then faced with the task of reconciling the experience of having a thought that is inconsistent with the self-view. Drawing from information-processing theory, Purdon and Clark (1999) suggest that one strategy for resolving the inconsistency would be to accommodate the self-schema to incorporate the experience of the thought (e.g., "I suppose even a person like me can have a thought like this, but of course a person like me would never act on this thought"). This may characterize the response of the majority of individuals to their obsessional thoughts. The alternative strategy would be to assimilate the thought (e.g, "Maybe I am the kind of person who would stab a loved one").

Given that the thought itself is initially the only evidence that the undesirable personality qualities exist, the individual is likely to assume that its absence signifies that the trait in fact is not present. This, in combination with preexisting beliefs about control leads to an enormous stake in controlling the thought. By the same token, failures in thought control will be perceived as catastrophic and the individual is likely to increase attempts to control thoughts. Consistent with Salkovskis (Salkovskis et al., 1995; Salkovksis, 1996, 1998), this urgent need for cognitive control will result in a preoccupation with the stream of consciousness and a heightened vigilance for thought cues, which has the ironic effect of lowering the threshold for detecting cues and intensifies the need to control thoughts.

The individual's conviction that such undesirable personality characteristics may exist will strengthen in the face of failures in thought control, and may eventually cause the individual to behave as if they actually do exist. Once the individual begins to believe that personality traits could be consistent with the thought, he or she is likely to begin using neutralizing strategies to protect the self or others against the harm that he or she may cause. These strategies will terminate exposure to the obsession, will disallow for corrective learning about the thought's meaning, and will make the thought more salient and hence more frequent.

O'Connor and Robillard: Faulty Inference Processes

O'Connor is concerned with treatment of OCD that is characterized by overvalued ideation or poor insight (O'Connor, 2002; O'Connor & Robillard, 1995). He argues that the essential factor in the development and maintenance of OCD is faulty inference processes. In fact, he argues that an obsession *is* an inference about a state of affairs

meaningful to the individual, rather than a discrete thought (O'Connor, 2002). The specific inference processes that perpetuate the faulty belief system in OCD bear little similarity to those driving depression and other anxiety disorders. Rather, people with obsessional problems are unique in that their affective response to the feared stimulus is driven by concerns about what might *possibly* be there, even though their senses say otherwise. In other words, what the obsessional person imagines *could* be there becomes an *actual probability* in her or his mind, resulting in a fear of what is unseen rather than a fear of what is actually seen. Thus, a completely fictional narrative becomes confused with a remote probability. This results from faulty inference processes whereby the obsessional person revises the evidence in the face of the hypothesis, rather than revising the hypothesis in the face of the evidence. For example, a client's hypothesis may be that a table is "dirty" (i.e., covered in dust). Although the table itself looks clean, the client recalls another table that was dirty, but which otherwise resembles the present table, and infers that the present table, too, must be dirty. O'Connor makes the important point that such faulty inference processes are only observed in reference to the obsessional stimuli, and inference processes are very much intact in all other areas of functioning.

According to O'Connor and Robillard (1995) and O'Connor (2002), performance of the compulsive ritual results in simple rehearsal of the imaginary doubt, and no new information about the situation is absorbed. More important, however, because the feared event is wholly imaginary, there is very little objective evidence in the environment that the individual can use to disconfirm the conviction, and existing evidence is discounted on the basis that if the person were to probe more deeply, evidence confirming the conviction would be found (e.g., "If I had a microscope, I'm sure I would find dirt on this table"). This results in repeated attempts to redress the concern (i.e., the neutralizing act), which persists until the individual achieves an adequate sense of certainty that the ritual is no longer necessary (e.g., there is no longer a chance of harm). Of course, there is no objective evidence available to the individual by which to judge whether harm has been averted. What happens instead is that the individual relies on feedback from sources irrelevant to the actual task in hand, such as anxiety reduction, as a cue for termination of rituals.

O'Connor and Robillard (1995) identify four types of faulty inferences, then, that they perceive as significant in the persistence of the disorder. These include inverse inference about reality (i.e., the feared state of affairs exists until proven otherwise), going beyond present reality to a deeper reality (i.e., although the feared state of affairs does not appear to exist at first, it could readily be found to exist given the proper investigative tools, such as a microscope), relying on feedback from a nonpertinent modality (i.e., in the absence of solid objective evidence to disconfirm the conviction, nonrelevant information is used, such as anxiety reduction or the "correct" number of repetitions), and irrelevant associations (e.g., the linking of incidental to genuine connections).

Frost and Colleagues: A Model for Understanding Hoarding

Frost and colleagues have offered a model for understanding hoarding, which may present as a subtype of OCD known to be especially difficult to treat (e.g., Winsberg, Cassic & Koran, 1999). Frost and Gross (1993) examined differences between individuals who hoard and those who do not to find that hoarders are distinguished by greater indecisiveness, greater concern over making mistakes, and a sentimental attachment to possessions. In a preliminary analysis of the development and persistence of hoarding, Frost and colleagues argue that individuals who hoard possessions have perfectionistic tendencies that cause them to view mistakes as catastrophic (Frost, Hartl, Christian, & Williams, 1995). When faced with the decision of whether an object should be saved or discarded, the hoarder is faced with potentially making the wrong decision, which could cause future "harm" (e.g., the item might be needed in future and will not be available at the same price or the information contained in the item may not be retrievable) for which he or she is responsible. In order to avoid the anxiety to which this concern gives rise, the hoarder adopts the highly conservative, cautious strategy of not discarding anything.

At the same time, the individual strives to determine a flawless strategy for organizing the possessions. The enormous difficulty in deciding how to organize items (e.g., should it be organized by color, by size, by purpose, by chronology, etc.?) leads to the equally cautious strategy of having separate stacks for individual items or items that are highly similar, or to complete procrastination of organizing, due to feeling wholly overwhelmed by the prospect of doing it "correctly." In the latter case, most items are stacked together in a pile (or piles) mentally tagged

as "to be organized." In addition, individuals with hoarding problems are characterized by a sentimental attachment to objects such that even trivial items become imbued as being an "extension of the self" or as "safety signals" (i.e., as familiar and friendly objects that provide considerable comfort). The individual then develops a feeling of responsibility for protecting the item from harm (i.e., the individual does not want others to touch, move, or share or use the possession) (Frost et al., 1995). Thus, perfectionistic tendencies interact with a sentimental attachment to possessions and with responsibility beliefs, leading to the individual's appraisal of items as valuable, as extremely difficult to organize, but as potentially dangerous to discard.

Frost and Hartl (1996) further proposed that hoarding develops and persists as a result of the following interrelated factors: (1) information-processing deficits; (2) emotional attachment problems (overly sentimental attachment to objects); (3) behavioral avoidance; and (4) beliefs about the nature of possessions, about responsibility, and about the necessity for perfection. The information-processing deficits identified by Frost and Hartl include difficulties in making decisions, in categorizing and organizing, and in memory.

Reasonable decisions about what is worth keeping and what should be discarded are not made by the hoarder for two reasons. First, the individual has an overly sentimental attachment to objects and an exaggerated sense of responsibility to protect the item from harm. The individual also feels an enormous sense of responsibility to prevent future harm that could come of throwing out something that is later needed, or failing to have on hand something that is needed. Due to perceived memory deficits, the individual believes that he or she may not be able to retrieve information from memory in the future when it is needed, and that the information may be irretrievable from any other source when required. Second, the individual with hoarding problems has significant deficits in organization and classification. This is driven by perfectionistic tendencies that cause the individual to strive for the "perfect" but wholly elusive organizational structure for retaining and classifying items. This is further complicated by the sentimental attachment to objects, which causes the individual to observe and prize the uniqueness of each item. As such, similarities across items are difficult to identify and objects are therefore difficult to group.

In addition to piling everything together to be organized "later," individuals with hoarding problems are reluctant to file items away out of sight out of concern that they will not remember that the item exists and it will be technically lost. New items are acquired regularly both out of a ready ability to develop a sentimental attachment to objects and the fear that unless one takes advantage of the opportunity to acquire potentially useful objects, one might be caught without them in future, thereby being responsible for subsequent harm.

Areas of Convergence and Divergence

Each of the approaches described here assumes that obsessions have their roots in normal thoughts that are experienced by the majority of the population. However, there is considerable variance in the explanation of how such normal thoughts escalate into a clinical problem for a small minority of individuals, and the assertions are quite tentative and nonspecific. Salkovskis's model postulates that any thought will become an obsession if it activates deeply held, preexisting beliefs about responsibility and thereby results in neutralizing acts. Thus, responsibility beliefs and neutralizing are necessary, if not sufficient, factors for the development of obsessional problems. In contrast, Rachman (1997, 1998) argues that thoughts reflecting moral themes are more likely to become obsessions than other types of thoughts, and that personality factors, such as having a "tender conscience," are a vulnerability factor in their development. Beliefs about the thought's dangerousness and beliefs reflecting the TAF bias (from which responsibility beliefs are said to derive) will ensure that the thought becomes the focus of attention and will evoke feelings of anxiety and depression, which, in turn, reduce thought controllability and intensify the perception that the thought is dangerous.

In a somewhat similar vein, Purdon and Clark (1999) argue that thoughts that violate the individual's most valued self-schema are more likely to become obsessional. The interplay between the subsequent stake in controlling such thoughts and interpretations of failures in thought control result in the escalation in frequency and intensity of the normal thoughts into clinical obsessions. Individuals with few self-schema are more likely to experience thoughts as ego-dystonic.

O'Connor's model excepted, the models share a common emphasis in the assertion that it is not the obsession itself that is problematic, but rather the erroneous appraisal that the obsession has relevance for important areas of the individual's functioning. The general goal of therapy recommended by each model would be to have the individual experience the obsession without the negative cognitive, affective, and behavioral response to it. There is also general agreement that efforts directed at "correcting" the potential harm ensuing from the thought play a crucial factor in the persistence of the disorder because they do not permit the individual to learn any new information about the amount of threat represented by the thought. Furthermore, the models discussed here recognize that emotional reasoning plays a role in the persistence of the disorder as well. If the individual has the chance to experience the thought in the absence of an anxious response (i.e., after a period of exposure to the thought while the ritual is prohibited), the thought will likely come to have much less meaning. Thus, in general, the models emphasize ERP as an important component of therapy, in addition to proscribing avoidance of thought triggers and use of other ameliorative strategies that prevent full exposure to the thought and that may enhance the meaning ascribed to the thought (e.g., reassurance seeking, distraction, thought suppression).

It is important to note that none of the models would advocate cognitive restructuring around the probability or likelihood of the feared event alone. It is generally agreed that the individual with OCD knows that the chances of the feared event happening or having happened are remote, yet feels compelled to protect against them nonetheless (different models offer different explanations as to why this is the case). Discussion about the realistic probability of an event is likely to simply serve as a form of reassurance, which, like neutralizing, might result in temporary relief from the distress associated with the thought but which will disallow corrective learning about the dangerousness of experiencing the thought itself. The various models presented here would instead argue that the beliefs that maintain the idea that the thought requires immediate attention are instead what need to be addressed. However, the models diverge in terms of which specific beliefs are deemed to be most important to the development and persistence of the obsessive-compulsive cycle.

In 1995, an international group of researchers studying cognitive appraisal in OCD was formed. The Obsessive-Compulsive Cognitions Working Group (OCCWG) has held a number of formal meetings to identify and assess general types of beliefs and specific types of cognitive appraisal that are relevant to OCD. The OCCWG has identified six categories of beliefs relevant to OCD, which include beliefs reflective of inflated responsibility, tendency to overestimate threat, perfectionism, intolerance of uncertainty, overimportance of thoughts (thought-action fusion), and need to control thoughts (OCCWG, 1997, 2001). Three categories of appraisal were also identified. These include responsibility, overimportance of thoughts (thought-action fusion), and need to control thoughts. The Obsessive Beliefs Questionnaire (OBQ) and the Interpretation of Intrusions Inventory (III) were developed to assess beliefs and appraisal respectively (OCCWG, 1997, 2001).

Empirical Validation of CBT Models

At this time, there has been little empirical investigation of the development of OCD. There is some evidence that obsessions may lie on a continuum with normal intrusive thoughts experienced by most people (e.g., Purdon & Clark, 1994; Rachman & de Silva, 1978). There is also some evidence that obsessions may reflect self-schema. Rowa, Purdon, Summerfeldt, and Antony (2005) asked individuals with OCD to report on the circumstances under which their most and least upsetting obsession developed. Both types of obsession were reported as arising within the context of current life concerns, and the content tended to reflect those concerns (e.g., a harming obsession arising when the individual was applying to train in a helping profession). However, most upsetting obsessions were rated as being more meaningful at the time of their onset and as contradicting valued aspects of self to a greater degree than least upsetting obsessions. The same was found in a nonclinical sample (Rowa & Purdon, 2003). This supports Purdon and Clark's assertions that self-schema play an important role in the development of OCD, although the findings are far from conclusive, given the reliance on retrospective self-report.

There is a large body of work on the relationship between obsessions and compulsions, and the "two-factor" model whereby obsessions give rise to an aversive emotional response that is alleviated by the compulsion is well documented (see Rachman & Hodgson, 1980). There appears to be a strong link between beliefs and appraisal and symptoms of OCD, with studies showing moderate correlations between measures of beliefs and appraisal and measures of symptom severity, even when general distress is partialled out (OCCWG, 2003; Tolin, Woods, & Abramowitz, 2003; Wilson & Chambless, 1999). However, the three scales of the III and the six scales of the OBQ are highly intercorrelated, which

suggests that perhaps these constructs are less distinguishable than would be argued by the cognitive models (OCCWG, 2003).

Rhéaume and Ladouceur (2000) examined change in appraisal of the obsession in relation to changes in the frequency of checking rituals in participants receiving ERP versus ERP plus a formal cognitive restructuring component in a small ($n = 15$) time series analysis. They found that for all those in the ERP group and for one-third those in the CBT group, change on at least one type of appraisal preceded a decrease in checking rituals, although for each participant, decreased checking rituals also preceded change in appraisal at least once. These findings support the link between appraisal and compulsions asserted by cognitive models, and also suggest that changes in appraisal may actually cause change in use of compulsive strategies.

In experimental research in which responsibility is manipulated, decreased perception of responsibility for a negative outcome has been associated with a decrease in urges to check in a sample of compulsive checkers (Lopatka & Rachman, 1995), and high responsibility has been associated with greater checking in a nonclinical sample (Bouchard, Rhéaume, & Ladouceur, 1999). Foa, Amir, Bogert, Molnar, and Prezworski (2001) found that compared to anxious and nonanxious controls, OCD patients with compulsive checking reported greater distress and greater urge to rectify hypothetical scenarios in which there was low to moderate responsibility for harm. This supported the assertion that appraisals of responsibility play a key role in the persistence of OCD.

However, in a follow-up study using the same paradigm, Foa, Sacks, Tolin, Prezworksi, and Amir (2002) also included a group of OCDs without checking compulsions. They found that the OCD noncheckers were similar to the anxious and nonanxious controls in their reported distress over and urge to rectify the situation presented in the various scenarios. This suggests that responsibility appraisal may not be a key factor in all types of OCD, but rather is especially important to OCD characterized by checking. This finding is consistent with other work in which responsibility appears to be important only in particular contexts (e.g., Rachman, Thordarson, Shafran, & Woody, 1995). There is a growing consensus that "mini-models" of OCD that account for specific subtypes may be required. Frost's model of hoarding is an excellent example of this.

The cognitive models also assert that suppression of the obsession is a key factor in the persistence of the disorder. To date, there is no solid evidence that suppression leads to an ironic increase in the frequency of obsessions, at least in the short term (see Purdon, 2004, for a review). However, failures in controlling obsessions may intensify negative appraisal of the obsession, and thought recurrences while suppression is underway appear to be associated with more negative mood state (Purdon et al., 2005). Furthermore, in one study, individuals with OCD were more likely to attribute difficulties with thought control to internal ("weak mind") rather than external ("no one can control all of their thoughts") reasons (Tolin, Abramowitz, Hamlin, Foa, & Synodi, 2002). Finally, Purdon, Rowa, and Antony (2007) found that individuals with OCD spent a significant amount of time per day attempting to suppress obsessions, and that suppression typically interfered with ability to function in a number of areas. Thus, even if suppression does not have an ironic effect on frequency, it may affect other important domains, such as thought appraisal, mood state, and daily functioning.

O'Connor's model asserts that the central problem in OCD is faulty inductive reasoning and probability estimation. Pélissier and O'Connor (2002) examined deductive and inductive reasoning, as well as probability estimations, in a sample of individuals with OCD, anxious controls (individuals with generalized anxiety disorder), and nonanxious controls. All three groups completed a series of written and oral reasoning tasks. No differences in deductive reasoning were observed across groups, as expected. However, the OCD group showed deficits in inductive reasoning and probabilistic reasoning compared to the other two groups. Pélissier and O'Connor interpret their findings to mean that individuals with OCD may produce too many inductive inferences, which causes them to doubt their initial inferences, and obsess about unreal possibilities.

Research on Treatment Efficacy

Several studies have now examined the efficacy of treatment protocols derived from the current cognitive model. For simplicity, protocols that include a formal and substantial ERP component in addition to cognitive restructuring will be referred to as *cognitive behavioral therapy* (CBT) and those that include a formal and substantial cognitive component with no ERP will be referred to as *cognitive therapy* (CT). Ladouceur, Freeston, Gagnon, Thibodeau, and Dumont (1995) examined the efficacy of CBT in a multiple baseline case study of three people with OCD. They found that CBT resulted in a significant reduction in discomfort and an increase in professional or interpersonal functioning for all three and that treatment gains were maintained at 8–11-month follow-up. Freeston et al. (1997) found that CBT resulted in a significant reduction in OCD symptoms posttreatment and at 6-month follow-up, compared to no intervention (waitlist control). Van Oppen et al. (1995) offered the first comparison of ERP to CT, and found CT to be modestly superior, with equal dropout rates. In a small sample of OCD patients, Vogel et al. (2004) found that CBT was equivalent to ERP (with a relaxation control for the cognitive component) in reducing symptoms. The treatment dropout rate was lower in the CBT condition.

In a larger-scale study comparing group treatment with *pure* CT, ERP, or waitlist control, McLean et al. (2001) found that ERP was marginally more effective than CT both posttreatment and at 3-month follow-up, and that both were superior to no intervention. However, there were more dropouts in the ERP condition. They suggested that CT in group format may not be the most ideal means of offering treatment, and that there may be advantages to offering CT individually. Warren and Thomas (2001) had an 84% treatment response using CBT in a routine clinical practice setting, suggesting that the treatment is fairly generalizable to settings at which most people receive their care. Hartl and Frost (1999) found that treatment based on their model of hoarding resulted in improvement in a small sample of individuals in a case study design.

O'Connor, Todorov, Robillard, Borgeat, and Brault (1999) compared CBT alone, selective serotonin reuptake inhibitors (SSRIs) alone, and the combination of SSRIs with CBT to a waitlist control condition. The combined treatment was superior to the individual active treatments, which in turn were more efficacious than no treatment. Van Balkom et al. (1998) examined the efficacy of adding CT or ERP to medication (fluvoxamine) at week 9, compared to the efficacy of each psychotherapy alone and to a waitlist control. All treatment groups were found to be equally effective as compared to the waitlist control. In a large-scale ($n = 122$) double-blind, multisite treatment efficacy study comparing CBT (ERP with no formal cognitive component but an emphasis on discussion of appraisal during exposure), Foa et al. (2005) found that the efficacy of CBT alone was equal to CBT plus an SSRI, and that both were superior to SSRI alone (all interventions were superior to placebo). In a meta-analysis of studies comparing psychotherapy and ERP, CBT, or CT, Eddy, Dutra, Bradley, and Weston (2004) concluded that CBT and ERP were marginally more effective than CT, although all had strong effects. Furthermore, there was a stronger effect size when these treatments were administered individually, rather than in group format.

Finally, O'Connor et al. (2005) compared the efficacy of ERP, CBT, and an inference-based approach (IBA) in a small sample ($n = 54$) of individuals with OCD. The IBA protocol follows directly from O'Connor's model of OCD, in which faulty inferences processes, as opposed to appraisal content, are implicated as the key factor in the persistence of the disorder. In IBA, the primary inference is identified as an obsessional doubt, and treatment focuses on the reasoning patterns that led to the doubt. No exposure or cognitive restructuring is done. All three treatments produced a significant, but equivalent, reduction in OCD symptoms. There appeared to be an advantage in using IBA for patients with higher levels of obsessional conviction, or, overvalued ideation.

In sum, at this point few studies have compared *pure* CT (no formal exposure component) or CBT to ERP. It appears that CBT, CT, and ERP are effective treatments of OCD to about the same degree. However, there is some indication that there may be a therapeutic advantage to retaining an ERP component to treatment, and for administering CT in an individual, rather than group, format. There is very limited evidence that treatment dropout rates may be lower for CT interventions compared to ERP. Given the limited empirical evidence, all conclusions must be made with caution.

Future Directions

Obsessive-compulsive disorder is a heterogenous disorder with at least four clearly identifiable subtypes that include (1) sexual, religious, somatic, and aggressive obsessions, associated with checking rituals; (2) symmetry obsessions, associated with ordering, repeating, and counting compulsions; (3) contamination obsessions associated with cleaning rituals; and (4) hoarding (Leckman, Grice, Boardman, & Zhang, 1997). It may be the case that these different subtypes are best understood in terms of slightly different models. Frost and colleagues have already developed a separate model for understanding hoarding that is far more useful in understanding how to treat the problem than existing models have been. All of the main models reviewed here emphasize the role of thought suppression in the disorder. However, different kinds

of thoughts may give rise to different levels of active resistance. For example, people with symmetry and exactness obsessions may not engage in suppression to anywhere near the extent of someone with harm and aggression obsessions. Appraisal may differ substantially across subtypes, as suggested in the research on responsibility appraisal. Research directed at understanding the distinct epidemiology and phenomenology of OCD subtypes may yield continued advancements in our ability to understand, and therefore treat, OCD.

References

Abramowitz, J. S. (1996). Variants of exposure and response prevention in the treatment of obsessive-compulsive disorder: A meta-analysis. *Behavior Therapy, 27,* 583–600.

Beck, A. T. (1976). *Cognitive therapy and the emotional disorders.* New York: International Universities Press.

Bouchard, C., Rhéaume, J., & Ladouceur, R. (1999). Responsibility and perfectionism in OCD: An experimental study. *Behaviour Research and Therapy, 37,* 239–248.

Clark, D. A. (1989, June). *A schema-control model of negative thoughts.* Paper presented at the World Congress of Cognitive Therapy, Oxford, England.

Clark, D. A., & Purdon, C. (1993). New perspectives for a cognitive theory of obsessions. Invited Essay. *Australian Psychologist, 28,* 161–167.

Eddy, K. T., Dutra, L., Bradley, R., & Weston, D. (2004). A multidimensional meta-analysis of psychotherapy and pharmacotherapy for obsessive-compulsive disorder. *Clinical Psychology Review, 24,* 1011–1030.

Foa, E. B., Amir, N., Bogert, K.V.A., Molnar, C., & Prezworski, A. (2001). Inflated perceptions of responsibility for harm in obsessive-compulsive disorder. *Journal of Anxiety Disorders, 15,* 259–275.

Foa, E. B., Franklin, M. E., & Kozak, M. J. (1998). Psychosocial treatments for obsessive-compulsive disorder. In R. P. Swinson, M. M. Antony, S. Rachman, & M. A. Richter (Eds.), *Obsessive-compulsive disorder: Theory, research and treatment* (pp. 258–276). New York: Guilford Press.

Foa, E. B., & Kozak, M. J. (1986). Emotional processing of fear: Exposure to corrective information. *Psychological Bulletin, 99,* 20–35.

Foa, E. B., & Kozak, M. J. (1996). Psychological treatment for obsessive-compulsive disorder. In M. R. Mavissakalian and R. F. Prien (Eds.), *Long-term treatments of anxiety disorders* (pp. 285–309). Washington, DC: American Psychiatric Association.

Foa, E. B., Liebowitz, M. R., Kozak, M. J., Davies, S., Campeas, R., Franklin, M. E., et al. (2005). Randomized, placebo-controlled trial of exposure and ritual prevention, clomipramine, and their combination in the treatment of obsessive-compulsive disorder. *American Journal of Psychiatry, 162,* 151–161.

Foa, E. B., & McNally, R. J. (1996). Mechanisms of change in exposure therapy. In R. M. Rapee (Ed.), *Current controversies in the anxiety disorders* (pp. 329–343). New York: Guilford Press.

Foa, E. B, Sacks, M. B., Tolin, D. E., Prezworski, A., & Amir, N. (2002). Inflated perception of responsibility for harm in OCD patients with and without checking compulsions:

A replication and extension. *Journal of Anxiety Disorders, 16,* 443–453.

Foa, E. B., Steketee, G., Grayson, J. B., & Doppelt, H. G. (1983). Treatment of obsessive compulsives: When do we fail? In E. B. Foa & P.M.G. Emmelkamp (Eds.), *Failures in behavior therapy.* New York: Wiley.

Freeston, M. H., Ladouceur, R., Gagnon, F., Thibodeau, N., Rhéaume, J., Letarte, H., et al. (1997). Cognitive-behavioral treatment of obsessive thoughts: A controlled study. *Journal of Clinical and Consulting Psychology, 65,* 405–413.

Frost, R. O., & Gross, R. C. (1993). The hoarding of possessions. *Behaviour Research and Therapy, 31,* 367–381.

Frost, R. O., & Hartl, T. L. (1996). A cognitive-behavioral model of compulsive hoarding. *Behaviour Research and Therapy, 34,* 341–350.

Frost, R. O., Hartl, T. L., Christian, R., & Williams, N. (1995). The value of possessions in compulsive hoarding: Patterns of use and attachment. *Behaviour Research and Therapy, 33,* 897–902.

Hartl, T. L., & Frost, R. O. (1999). Cognitive-behavioral treatment of compulsive hoarding: A multiple baseline experimental case study. *Behaviour Research and Therapy, 37,* 451–461.

Ladouceur, R., Freeston, M. H., Gagnon, F., Thibodeau, N., & Dumont, J. (1995). Cognitive behavioral treatment of obsessions. *Behavior Modification, 19,* 247–257.

Leckman, J. F., Grice, D. E., Boardman, J., & Zhang, H. (1997). Symptoms of obsessive-compulsive disorder. *American Journal of Psychiatry, 154,* 911–917.

Lopatka, C., & Rachman, S. (1995). Perceived responsibility and compulsive checking: An experimental analysis. *Behaviour Research and Therapy, 33,* 673–684.

Maltby, N., & Tolin, D. F. (2003). Overview of treatments for OCD and spectrum conditions: Conceptualization, theory and practice. *Brief Treatment and Crisis Intervention, 3,* 127–144.

McLean, P. D., Whittal, M. L., Sochting, I., Koch, W. J., Paterson, R., Thordarson, D. S., et al. (2001). Cognitive versus behavior therapy in the group treatment of obsessive-compulsive disorder. *Journal of Consulting and Clinical Psychology, 69,* 205–214.

Obsessive Compulsive Cognitions Working Group. (1997). Cognitive assessment of obsessive-compulsive disorder. *Behaviour Research and Therapy, 35,* 667–681.

Obsessive Compulsive Cognitions Working Group. (2001). Development and initial validation of the Obsessive Beliefs Questionnaire and the Interpretation of Intrusions Inventory. *Behaviour Research and Therapy, 39,* 987–1006.

Obsessive Compulsive Cognitions Working Group. (2003). Psychometric validation of the Obsessive Beliefs Questionnaire and the Interpretation of Intrusions Inventory: Part I. *Behaviour Research and Therapy, 41,* 863–878.

O'Connor, K. (2002). Intrusions and inferences in obsessive-compulsive disorder. *Behavioural and Cognitive Psychotherapy, 9,* 38–46.

O'Connor, K. P., Aardema, F., Bouthillier, D., Fournier, S., Guay, S., Robillard, S., et al. (2005). Evaluation of an inference-based approach to treating obsessive-compulsive disorder. *Cognitive Behaviour Therapy, 34,* 148–163.

O'Connor, K., & Robillard, S. (1995). Inference processes in obsessive-compulsive disorder: Some clinical observations. *Behaviour Research and Therapy, 33,* 887–896.

O'Connor, K., Todorov, C., Robillard, S., Borgeat, F., & Brault, M. (1999). Cognitive behaviour therapy and medication in

the treatment of obsessive-compulsive disorder: A controlled study. *Canadian Journal of Psychiatry, 44,* 64–71.

Pélissier, M. C., & O'Connor, K. P. (2002). Deductive and inductive reasoning in obsessive-compulsive disorder. *British Journal of Clinical Psychology, 41,* 15–27.

Purdon, C. (2004). Empirical investigations of thought suppression in OCD. *Journal of Behavior Therapy and Experimental Psychiatry, 35,* 121–136.

Purdon, C., & Clark, D. A. (1994). Obsessional intrusive thoughts in nonclinical subjects. Part II: Cognitive appraisal, emotional response and thought control strategies. *Behaviour Research and Therapy, 32,* 403–410.

Purdon, C., & Clark, D. A. (1999). Metacognition and obsessions. *Clinical Psychology and Psychotherapy, 6,* 96–101.

Purdon, C., Rowa, K., & Antony, M. M. (2005). Thought suppression and its effects on thought frequency, appraisal and mood state in individuals with obsessive-compulsive disorder. *Behaviour Research and Therapy, 43,* 93–108.

Purdon, C., Rowa, K., & Antony, M. M. (2007). Diary records of thought suppression attempts by individuals with obsessive-compulsive disorder. *Behavioural and Cognitive Psychotherapy, 35,* 47–59.

Rachman, S. (1971). Obsessional ruminations. *Behaviour Research and Therapy, 9,* 229–235.

Rachman, S. (1976). The modification of obsessions: A new formulation. *Behaviour Research and Therapy, 14,* 437–443.

Rachman, S. (1997). A cognitive theory of obsessions. *Behaviour Research and Therapy, 35,* 793–802.

Rachman, S. (1998). A cognitive theory of obsessions: Elaborations. *Behaviour Research and Therapy, 36,* 385–401.

Rachman, S., & de Silva, P. (1978). Abnormal and normal obsessions. *Behaviour Research and Therapy, 16,* 233–248.

Rachman, S. J., & Hodgson, R. J. (1980). *Obsessions and compulsions.* Englewood Cliffs, NJ: Prentice-Hall.

Rachman, S. J., Thordarson, D. S., Shafran, R., & Woody, S. R. (1995). Perceived responsibility: Structure and significance. *Behaviour Research and Therapy, 33,* 779–784.

Rhéaume, J., & Ladouceur, R. (2000). Cognitive and behavioural treatment of checking behaviour: An examination of individual and cognitive change. *Clinical Psychology and Psychotherapy, 7,* 118–127.

Rowa, K., & Purdon, C. (2003). Why are certain intrusive thoughts more upsetting than others? *Behavioural and Cognitive Psychotherapy, 31,* 1–11.

Rowa, K., Purdon, C., Summerfeldt, L. J., & Antony, M. M. (2005). Why are some obsessions more upsetting than others? *Behaviour Research and Therapy, 43,* 1453–1465.

Salkovskis, P.M. (1985). Obsessional-compulsive problems: A cognitive-behavioural analysis. *Behaviour Research and Therapy, 23,* 571–584.

Salkovskis, P. M. (1988). Intrusive thoughts and obsessional disorders. In D. Glasgow & N. Eisenberg (Eds.), *Current issues in clinical psychology, 4.* London: Gower.

Salkovskis, P. M. (1989). Cognitive-behavioural factors and the persistence of intrusive thoughts in obsessional problems. *Behaviour Research and Therapy, 27,* 677–682.

Salkovskis, P. M. (1996). Cognitive-behavioural approaches to the understanding of obsessive compulsive problems. In R. M. Rapee (Ed.), *Current controversies in the anxiety disorders* (pp. 103–133). New York: Guilford Press.

Salkovskis, P. M. (1998). Psychological approaches to the understanding of obsessional problems. In R. P. Swinson, M. M. Antony, S. Rachman, & M. A. Richter (Eds.),

Obsessive-compulsive disorder: Theory, research and treatment (pp. 33–50). New York: Guilford Press

Salkovskis, P. M. (2002). Understanding and treating obsessive-compulsive disorder. *Behaviour Research and Therapy, 37,* S29–S52.

Salkovskis, P. M., Richards, H. C., & Forrester, E. (1995). The relationship between obsessional problems and intrusive thoughts. *Behavioural and Cognitive Psychotherapy, 23,* 281–299.

Shafran, R., Thordarson, D. S., & Rachman, S. (1996). Thought-action fusion in obsessive-compulsive disorder. *British Journal of Psychology, 36,* 397–408.

Stanley, M. A., & Turner, S. M. (1995). Current status of pharmacological and behavioral treatment of obsessive-compulsive disorder. *Behavior Therapy, 26,* 163–186.

Tolin, D. F., Abramowitz, J. S., Hamlin, C., Foa, E. B., & Synodi, D. S. (2002). Attributions for thought suppression failure in obsessive-compulsive disorder. *Cognitive Therapy and Research, 26,* 505–517.

Tolin, D. F., Woods, C. M., & Abramowitz, J. S. (2003). Relationship between obsessive beliefs and obsessive-compulsive symptoms. *Cognitive Therapy and Research, 27,* 657–669.

Van Balkom, A.J.L., de Haan, E., van Oppen, P., Spinhoven, P., Hoogduin, K., & Dyke, R. (1998). Cognitive and behavioral therapies alone versus in combination with fluvoxamine in the treatment of obsessive-compulsive disorder. *Journal of Nervous and Mental Disease, 186,* 492–499.

Van Oppen, P., de Haan, E., van Balkom, A.J.L.M., Spinhoven, P., Hoogduin, K., & van Dyck, R. (1995). Cognitive therapy and exposure in vivo in the treatment of obsessive-compulsive disorder. *Behaviour Research and Therapy, 4,* 379–390.

Vogel, P., Stiles, T. C., & Götestam, K. G. (2004). Adding cognitive therapy elements to exposure therapy for obsessive-compulsive disorder: A controlled study. *Behavioural and Cognitive Psychotherapy, 32,* 275–290.

Warren, R., & Thomas, J. C. (2001). Cognitive-behavior therapy of obsessive-compulsive disorder in private practice: An effectiveness study. *Journal of Anxiety Disorders, 15,* 277–285.

Wilson, K. A., & Chambless, D. L. (1999). Inflated perceptions of responsibility and obsessive compulsive symptoms. *Behaviour Research and Therapy, 37,* 325–335.

Winsberg, M. E., Cassic, K. S., & Koran, I. M. (1999). Hoarding in obsessive-compulsive disorder: A report of 20 cases. *Journal of Clinical Psychiatry, 60,* 591–597.

Psychological Models of Posttraumatic Stress Disorder and Acute Stress Disorder

Lori A. Zoellner, Afsoon Eftekhari *and* Michele Bedard-Gilligan

Abstract

This chapter first reviews early learning theories of posttraumatic stress disorder (PTSD). This section highlights the role of classical and operant conditioning, as these forms of conditioning are the basis for many of the contemporary theories of PTSD and still shape a preponderance of thought on the nature of the disorder. Yet, as is pointed out, these conditioning models fail to account for some of the complexities seen in PTSD. The next section reviews alternative conceptualizations regarding new learning theory models, information-processing models, and emotional processing models, forming the basis for more contemporary thought. The chapter concludes with a brief discussion of challenges in the conceptualization of trauma exposure and PTSD symptoms.

Keywords: acute stress disorder, classical conditioning, emotion, memory, posttraumatic stress disorder, psychological models, theory, trauma exposure

Under its original formulation, the distinguishing characteristic of posttraumatic stress disorder was not the clusters of symptom criteria, but the traumatic event itself. Unlike the vast majority of *DSM–IV–TR* disorders, the occurrence of an external event is required for a diagnosis of either acute stress disorder (ASD) or posttraumatic stress disorder (PTSD) (American Psychiatric Association [APA], 2000). This exposure to a potentially traumatic event such as combat, a motor vehicle accident, nonsexual and sexual assault, a natural disaster, and so on, serves as the *gatekeeper* for the diagnosis and is assumed to be the root cause of presenting symptoms (Davidson & Foa, 1991). Accordingly, the traumatic event itself dramatically shapes the conceptualization and treatment of the disorder (Rosen, 2005). Throughout the theories discussed in this chapter, a common theme is the role of extreme fear, helplessness, or horror and accompanying stress hormone release at the time of the traumatic event.

Despite this emphasis on event exposure, the initial psychological reactions following a traumatic event are not necessarily pathological; as it is assumed that any event of a given magnitude would result in a constellation of "normal reactions." Rather, the symptoms of PTSD are defined not only by their *existence* but also by their *persistence* over time (APA, 2000). These symptoms include reexperiencing of the traumatic event, avoidance of trauma-related thoughts and reminders, emotional numbing, and chronic hyperarousal. Accordingly, another theme evident in the theories reviewed in this chapter is the emphasis on explaining the persistence of the symptoms rather than their initial presence and on differentiating between those individuals whose reaction is temporary and those whose reaction persists.

In this chapter, we will first review early learning theories of PTSD. In this section, we will highlight the roles of classical and operant conditioning, as these forms of conditioning are the basis for many of the contemporary theories of PTSD and still shape a preponderance of thought on the nature of the disorder. Yet, as will be pointed out, these conditioning models fail to account for some of the complexities seen in PTSD. In the next section, we will review alternative conceptualizations, including new learning theory models, information-processing models, and emotional processing models that form the basis for more contemporary thought. Finally, we will conclude with a brief discussion of challenges in the conceptualization of trauma exposure and PTSD symptoms.

Early Learning Theory Models of PTSD
Classical Conditioning

As discussed earlier, the proximal cause or precipitating event is relatively simple in ASD and PTSD (Barlow, 2002). This proximal cause or precipitating event is exposure to a potentially traumatic event. With this exposure, the most straightforward explanation for the development of subsequent fear and PTSD symptoms is that classical, or Pavlovian, conditioning occurs, where real danger leads to the development of learned danger signals. This classical conditioning process is perhaps one of the best-understood and well-established learning principles. Using an animal-learning paradigm, a shock serves as an unconditioned stimulus (UCS), which elicits an unconditioned response of fear (UCR). This shock is then paired with a neutral stimulus such as a tone, which serves as a conditioned stimulus (CS). After this pairing, the neutral stimulus comes to also elicit fear, a conditioned response (CR), indicating that classical conditioning has taken place. Thus, the animal eventually comes to respond to the previously neutral stimulus in the same manner it did to the original unconditioned stimulus (CS → CR). This same pairing of previously neutral stimuli associated with the traumatic event (e.g., time of day, sights, sounds, people) is thought to underlie the development of persistent fear-based reactions such as reexperiencing of the trauma memory and physiological reactivity upon exposure to nondangerous but trauma-related reminders.

Rachman (1978, 1990) and others (e.g., Mineka, 1985) criticized the application of classical conditioning for its inability to capture the broad range of etiologic factors associated with the development of fear-related disorders. Rachman (1978), in addition to traumatic conditioning, pointed to both vicarious conditioning and informational transmission pathways of fear acquisition. These alternative pathways are consistent with the current definitions of traumatic stressors in the *DSM–IV–TR* (APA, 2000), which allow for both witnessed and confronted events, and findings that suggest that individuals do not have to witness a trauma to develop PTSD (e.g., Sutker, Uddo, Brailey, Vasterling, & Errera, 1994). This said, many conceptualize these other forms of transmission as conditioning as well (e.g., Siddle & Bond, 1988). Another primary criticism is that if a traumatic event is conceptualized as a central etiologic event underlying the development of PTSD, then it should follow that exposure to such an event should almost inevitably result in disorder. Yet, it does not. In fact, although many experience psychological reactions in the immediate aftermath of exposure, with time, only the minority rather than the majority of individuals experience persistent PTSD symptoms (e.g., Kessler, Sonnega, Bromet, Hughes, & Nelson, 1995; Rothbaum, Foa, Riggs, Murdock, & Walsh, 1992).

Dose-dependent response model. To better account for the range of responding following trauma exposure, one intuitively appealing variant of classical conditioning theory is a dose-dependent response or stressor-dose model. The dose-dependent model of PTSD suggests that the severity, duration, and proximity to a traumatic event, or *dose* of trauma exposure, are the most critical factors in who will and who will not develop PTSD. This dose model is embodied in both the past and the current *DSM–IV–TR* (APA, 2000). From a pragmatic standpoint, the dose-dependent model of trauma exposure and subsequent PTSD makes strong intuitive sense: the worse the traumatic event, the more severe the psychological reaction. Also, from a scientific standpoint, this model has a strong empirical basis derived from a solid animal, biological stress tradition (see Bowman & Yehuda, 2003). However, this classical conditioning variant, as well, fails to capture the complexities of who will and will not develop PTSD. Across three meta-analytic studies of predictors of psychopathology (Brewin, Andrews, & Valentine, 2000; Ozer, Best, Lipsey, & Weiss, 2003; Weaver & Clum, 1995), traumatic event characteristics only explained a modest amount of the variance, with other factors emerging as equal if not stronger predictors. Similarly, if a sufficiently strong UCR is required for the development of a CR, physiological arousal at the time of the traumatic event should predict the development of chronic PTSD. Yet, this predictor is unstable and often only captures a modest amount of the variance (e.g., Blanchard, Hickling, Galovski, & Veazey, 2002; Bryant, Harvey, Guthrie, & Moulds, 2000; Shalev et al., 1998). Furthermore, assessment of the *dose* is fraught with difficulty. For example, in the assessment of subjective event intensity, a ceiling effect often occurs with the traumatic event being an individual's most distressing experience, thus rendering quantitative measurement difficult. In addition, it is becoming increasingly clear that current clinical status affects how trauma-exposed individuals remember both objective and subjective characteristics of the traumatic event (e.g., McNally, 2003a; Roemer, Litz, Orsillo, Ehlich, & Friedman, 1998; Southwick, Morgan, Nicolaou, & Charney, 1997; Zoellner, Sacks, & Foa, 2001). Thus, retrospective reports, upon which many of these predictor studies rest, may inadvertently inflate the association between trauma *dosage* and subsequent psychopathology (McNally, 2003a). Accordingly, current models of PTSD must address not only normative outcomes of natural recovery following trauma exposure but also must move beyond simplistic notions of dose-dependent responding.

Two-Factor Theory

To better account for the complexity of responding following trauma exposure, one of the earliest and still most commonly utilized behavioral formulations of PTSD is the application of two-factor theory by Keane, Zimering, and Caddell (1985). Mowrer's two-factor theory (Mowrer, 1939, 1947) implicates both classical and operant conditioning principles in the learning and maintenance of a fear. Specifically, the two factors refer to the acquisition of fear as a motivator, and the acquisition of an arbitrary response through fear-reducing reinforcement. Because of the classical conditioning pairing of the CS and UCS, the animal is motivated to escape the CS; and this escape results in the reduction of the CR, which reinforces this escape response. Thus, fears acquired through classical conditioning are hypothesized to be maintained by the fear-reducing properties of avoidance behavior. Keane and colleagues proposed that through this same process, individuals with PTSD come to fear and avoid a number of stimuli surrounding the traumatic event.

In applying this model specifically to PTSD, Keane and colleagues (1985) suggested that, although this two-factor theory can account for some PTSD symptoms, the complexity of the symptom constellation needs to be further understood through revision of this model and through other high-order conditioning and stimulus generalization principles. Because of lack of robust and stable avoidant responding with the original two-factor conceptualization, Keane and colleagues applied modifications suggested by Stampfl and Levis (1967) that emphasized serial presentation of different CSs prior to the UCS, which results in more powerful avoidant responding. In addition, they also highlighted the process of higher-order conditioning that occurs when a CS is paired with another previously neutral stimulus. For instance, if the tone mentioned in the previous example is paired with a light, the light will become a higher-ordered CS, eventually eliciting fear and anxiety (higher-order CR). Thus, cues that were conditioned during trauma exposure can be paired with new stimuli, and these new stimuli also become able to evoke fear responses. Keane and colleagues also proposed that stimulus generalization helps account for the wide variety of stimuli that evoke the trauma memory and physiological components in individuals with PTSD. This refers to the notion that the more similar a novel, neutral stimulus is to the CS, the stronger the fear response will be to that neutral stimulus. For example, Keane and colleagues (1985) provided the examples of a car backfiring and firecrackers being similar enough to gunfire that they elicit startle responses equivalent to that experienced by gunfire directly. Taken together, these additions to the two-factor model more broadly capture the stable avoidance and widespread responding to trauma-related cues seen in PTSD.

With this two-factor model, just as classical conditioning approaches do not fully capture necessary complexities, the operant conditioning side of two-factor theory also has been called into question. A key problem is whether avoidance maintains fear. Specifically, avoidance behavior can persist even after fear of the conditioned stimulus has diminished (e.g., Siddle & Bond, 1988); and conversely, the experience of distress in a feared situation can also persist even after avoidance has been overcome (Barlow, 2002). Thus, avoidance does not appear necessary for the maintenance of fear. In a broader context, Bolles (1972, 1989) wrote extensively on the failures of reinforcement theory. He argued that reinforcers require a tangible event, such as the removal of something present, for reinforcement to occur and that something not happening does not qualify as a tangible event capable of having reinforcing qualities (see Fanselow, 1997). For a more extensive discussion of these issues and an alternative perspective on avoidance, see species-specific defense reaction theory (Bolles, 1970).

New Learning, Memory, and Emotional Processing Models of PTSD

Although both classical conditioning and operant conditioning principles are clearly implicated in the development of PTSD, problems with these models discussed earlier have spurred the development of more specific and also more comprehensive models. The focus of many PTSD theories now is on individual difference factors of resilience and vulnerability that operate before, during, and after trauma exposure. Specifically, the goal with these models is to identify individual differences that either protect or make an individual vulnerable to experience chronic psychopathology. Yet, the search for these factors is elusive. Most notably, it is often difficult to ascertain whether the feature predicts the disorder, is a consequence of having the disorder, or is a mere correlate of the disorder (McNally, 2003a).

The most formalized attempt to identify vulnerability factors for PTSD was the advent of acute stress disorder (ASD) in the *DSM–IV*. In essence, ASD is a diagnosis aimed at predicting the development of a subsequent disorder, PTSD (Marshall, Spitzer, & Liebowitz, 1999, 2000). Specifically, ASD targets transient but impairing dissociative symptoms often present in the aftermath of trauma and thought to be predictive of worse subsequent psychological functioning (APA, 1994). However, a growing body of knowledge suggests that acute dissociative symptoms are not necessary for the development of chronic PTSD and do not adequately identify all individuals who are at risk for developing chronic PTSD (Barton, Blanchard, & Hickling, 1996; Bryant, 2003; Bryant & Harvey, 1997, 1998; Zoellner, Jaycox, Watlington, & Foa, 2003). Consequently, the importance of ASD as a vulnerability factor and the status of ASD as a disorder itself are questionable.

When identifying resilience and vulnerability factors, in their meta-analytic studies, both Brewin et al. (2000) and Ozer et al. (2003) suggested that preevent factors such as lower intelligence, prior psychopathology, and prior adversity or trauma exposure only accounted for a small amount of the variance in predicting who will and will not develop chronic PTSD. Instead, trauma-related factors such as trauma severity and postevent factors such as lack of social support and life stress accounted for more of the variance. Consistent with these findings, the models presented below all acknowledge preevent factors providing a diathesis for the development of PTSD but instead emphasize factors that relate to the experience of the traumatic event and how

this event is subsequently processed as critical factors in the development of PTSD. These theories fall into three general categories: modifications of earlier learning theories, memory and information-processing theories, and emotional processing theories. At the outset, it should be acknowledged that there is considerable overlap across these categories, the category labels themselves are not sufficiently inclusive, and the theorists themselves may disagree with the placement of these models solely within a single category.

New Learning Theory Models

Modifications to the classical and operant conditioning approaches emphasize a shift in focus from the event itself to the cognitive representation of the event, such as perceptions of predictability and controllability, to better capture the complexities in responding seen in PTSD. This shift in focus is not necessarily incompatible with conditioning theories, as conditioning may modify cognitive processes such as expectancies (Davey, 1992). Three learning-based models, which draw heavily from the empirical animal literature, are presented below.

Uncontrollability and unpredictability in PTSD (Foa, Zinbarg, & Rothbaum, 1992). Foa, Zinbarg, and Rothbaum (1992) propose that behavioral disturbances observed in animals repeatedly exposed to uncontrollable and unpredictable aversive events resemble symptoms seen in chronic PTSD. The idea behind both controllability and predictability is quite simple. Controllability refers to the organism's ability to either prevent or terminate the experience of a US; whereas, predictability refers to the presence or absence of a signal that corresponds to the onset or termination of a US. Foa et al. (1992) specifically hypothesize that, all other factors being equal, the degree to which a traumatic event is uncontrollable and unpredictable is related to the likelihood of the development of PTSD. Just like trauma survivors who experience an uncontrollable, unpredictable traumatic event, animals who undergo extensive exposure to an uncontrollable or unpredictable US display behaviors that are consistent with reexperiencing, avoidance, numbing, and hyperarousal clusters of symptoms seen in humans.

Extending findings from the animal literature, Foa et al. (1992) suggest that for trauma survivors their daily life is marked by a sense of impending doom because survival can neither be predicted or controlled. Symptoms such as psychogenic amnesia, detachment, restricted range of affect, and dissociation may help to cognitively modulate the psychological impact of the trauma in a similar manner as avoidance and escape behaviors in animals. They further suggest that the mechanisms underlying avoidance and numbing might be different, in that avoidance may be a strategic psychological process and numbing may be an automatic process resembling freezing in animals.

Adopting an information-processing perspective, Foa et al. (1992) propose that preexisting memory networks influence an organism's perception of a traumatic event experience in at least two ways. First, they predict an increased likelihood of developing chronic PTSD when a traumatic event strongly violates preexisting beliefs about the predictability and controllability (and all else is held constant), such as when a trauma occurs in a previously safe or pleasant environment. In contrast, in the absence of this violation, repeated exposure to uncontrollable, unpredictable stress is necessary for the formation of expectations that danger can occur at any time and is inescapable. Once the perception of a pervasively threatening world is developed, the organism becomes sensitized to the effects of future uncontrollable, unpredictable stressors. In summary, the bottom line of this model is that not only must a stressor be perceived as a threat to survival but it must also be perceived as uncontrollable or unpredictable.

Contemporary learning theory perspective (Mineka & Zinbarg, 2006). Consistent with Foa et al. (1992), Mineka and Zinbarg (2006) similarly suggest that, from the animal model, the more a traumatic event is perceived to be uncontrollable and unpredictable, the more likely it is to result in PTSD. They similarly propose that organisms differ in how they respond to this stress and that this differing response affects psychological outcomes. Prior to trauma exposure, previous uncontrollable stress helps sensitize an organism to the harmful effects of subsequent exposure to a stressful event and previous control over stressful events helps immunize against these harmful effects of this subsequent exposure. In particular, they suggest that the amount of trauma exposure may be less predictive of later functioning than the organism's psychological state of resistance versus mental defeat (Başoğlu & Mineka, 1992). Importantly, differences in the degree of perceived controllability and predictability experienced by the individual during the event help predict whether such things as prior trauma exposure either sensitize to or buffer against the harmful effects of stress by helping an individual to be more or less psychologically ready.

Following trauma exposure, Mineka and Zinbarg, similar to Foa et al. (1992), suggest that CSs elicit CRs that are analogous to PTSD reexperiencing symptoms, suggesting that the severity of reexperiencing following trauma exposure predicts the development of PTSD. They also highlight the post-event processes of reevaluation and reinstatement of the US as a means of altering or exacerbating the course of PTSD symptoms. For example, they provide a case of post-event reevaluation where a trauma survivor experiences an increase in PTSD symptoms upon learning that his or her attacker was a murderer. Taken together, Mineka and Zinbarg's (2006) contemporary learning theory in the development of PTSD implicates pretrauma vulnerabilities such as prior learning, event-related characteristics (in particular, perceptions of predictability and controllability), response-related characteristics such as the quality and intensity of the association, and postevent factors such as US inflation and reevaluation.

Stress-induced enhancement of fear learning (Rau, DeCola, & Fanselow, 2005). Rau, DeCola, and Fanselow (2005) also sought to provide an updated framework for understanding PTSD within the context of animal learning paradigms. Moving beyond traditional classical conditioning, they propose an animal model potentially analogous to human PTSD. This model utilizes preexposure to a stressor of repeated foot shock that sensitizes conditional fear responding to a single context-shock pairing. Rau and colleagues suggest that this is consistent with PTSD, showing how a mild stressor can trigger a reaction similar to initial trauma exposure and why new fears are easily formed. Interestingly, this sensitization is resistant to both extinction and administration of N-methyl-D-aspartate (NMDA) receptor antagonist, suggesting that alternative means besides extinction and amnesic agents may be necessary in treating behavioral sensitization to stressors similar to the original traumatic event. They suggest that the possible mechanism for this state change is kindling of the neural pathways associated with fear and anxiety. Through repeated reexperiencing of the traumatic event or repeated exposure to mild stressors, the recurring reactivation of the stress response becomes dysregulated, having lower threshold of activation and facilitating sensitized reactions to neutral, but perceived threatening, stimuli.

Summary. All of the above learning-based models seek to address criticisms made of traditional classical conditioning and two-factor theories. These models rely heavily on the animal-based experimental literature for their major suppositions. Accordingly, they generate clear testable hypotheses and serve to advance further translational research within the area of PTSD. One of the major limitations of these models is their ability to clarify the role of cognitive processes and subjectively assessed symptoms (e.g., nightmares, flashbacks, intrusive thoughts). As noted by Foa et al. (1992), if these symptoms are seen as conditioned responses, then animal models have the potential to expand our understanding of these more subjective symptoms. Furthermore, cognitive factors such as perceptions of threat and control may be inferred but cannot be completely understood at the complex level that parallels cognitive processes in humans. Although these animal models may not be able to capture the cognitive complexities associated with posttrauma reactions, they may be able to provide key underlying frameworks and testable hypotheses for solid translational research.

Memory and Information-Processing Theories

Memory and information-processing models of PTSD help fill in some of the gaps left by learning-based theories and highlight the role of the way the trauma memory is initially encoded and subsequently processed as the key mechanism underlying the development of PTSD. Across models, there is an emphasis on the extreme levels of stress at the time of encoding and on the resulting disconnection or lack of integration of the trauma memory with the general autobiographical memory base. In the following section, several main information-processing models will be reviewed, moving from sensitization or overconsolidation models to dual processing models and finally to attribution-based models.

Overconsolidation model (Pitman, 1989). In Pitman's overconsolidation model (1989), a key premise is that extremely stressful traumatic events overstimulate endogenous stress-responsive hormones and neuromodulators, and this overstimulation results in an overconsolidation of traumatic memories. Specifically, Pitman hypothesizes that if cortisol levels are low at the time of a traumatic event due to risk factors such as prior trauma history, there may be a failure to contain the sympathetic nervous system response, resulting in an increase in catecholamines at the time of the trauma. The increased catecholamines at the time of the traumatic event, and shortly thereafter, may interfere with the normal processing of traumatic memories.

This overstimulation results in "superconditioning" (Pitman, 1988), where there is an overconsolidation of the traumatic memory. By overconsolidation, Pitman suggests that the traumatic memory is deeply engraved, which manifests itself as intrusive recollections and conditioned emotional responses. Thus, PTSD may result from an exaggerated response of neuropeptides and catecholamines at the time of the trauma, and these hormones initiate a process in which traumatic memories become overconsolidated or especially well remembered due to high levels of stress.

Dual processing models of PTSD. Two of the best-known memory-based models of PTSD are dual processing models (Brewin, 2001; Brewin, Dalgleish, & Joseph, 1996; van der Kolk, 1987, 1994, 1996; van der Kolk, Burbidge, & Suzuki, 1997), suggesting trauma memories are qualitatively different from memories of other personal events; hence, dual memory processes are at work. These theories posit that trauma memories are separate from the individual's overall memory network, disproportionately characterized by sensory aspects and without a coherent verbal representation.

Drawing on the early theoretical work of Pierre Janet (1907), van der Kolk (1987, 1994, 1996) suggests that trauma memories can be organized entirely on an implicit or perceptual level, absent of a narrative of what happened (van der Kolk & Fisler, 1995). Although ordinary memories are converted into coherent narratives and incorporated into an individual's personal experiences, trauma specifically interferes with declarative memory but does not impact implicit or nondeclarative memory. Specifically, the massive release of stress hormones during and immediately after trauma exposure results in qualitatively unique biochemical pathways in the processing of the trauma memory. Due to this unique processing, trauma memories are imprinted as sensory experiences, are invariable (i.e., not changing over time), and do not become integrated into the individual's personal experiences. This separation then prohibits the traumatic material from interacting with memories for normal events and the normal associative network. Thus, the trauma experience remains cut off from the memory system and exists in a nonelaborated form that lacks meaning and is difficult to access verbally. As van der Kolk (1996) states, "traumatic memories come back as emotional and sensory states with little verbal representation. This failure to process information on a symbolic level, which is essential for proper categorization and integration with other experiences, is at the very core of the pathology of PTSD" (p. 296). Trauma memories are also seen as highly state-dependent in that the extreme emotion during the trauma makes it difficult to recall parts or all of the trauma memory in different emotional states. Accordingly, this state-dependency helps explain dissociative amnesia where an individual can be partially or completely amnesic for the traumatic event.

Similar to van der Kolk's psychobiological theory, Brewin also postulates a dual representation model of PTSD (Brewin, 2001; Brewin et al., 1996; Brewin & Holmes, 2003), proposing two memory systems that account for both integrated, ordinary trauma memories and sensory-based, vivid reliving of the event. Specifically, Brewin and colleagues put forward that personal experiences are processed by two memory systems, verbally accessible memory (VAM) and situationally accessible memory (SAM). The VAM representations are initially consciously processed in working memory prior to transfer into long-term memory. Thus, these representations are coherent, integrated into the individual's larger memory system, and easy to access, recall, and edit consciously and verbally. In contrast, memories represented in SAM receive very little conscious processing but extensive perceptual processing. Information in SAM contains more extensive lower-level perceptual processing of the traumatic event such as external sights and sounds and internal bodily responses that were too brief to receive extensive conscious attention and not recorded in VAM. Accordingly, SAM representations are poorly elaborated and dissociated from other personal experiences in memory. Although SAM representations are difficult to recall verbally, they arise as nondeliberate reexperiencing of the trauma memory such as nightmares, flashbacks, and physiologic reactivity from cues that match those of the trauma. Thus, according to Brewin's theory, PTSD develops when the trauma memories are overrepresented in SAM without conversion to VAM, where they remain poorly inhibited and easily triggered by situational cues and reminders.

Attribution-based models. In contrast to both overconsolidation and dual processing models, attribution models of PTSD focus on the attributions an individual makes about themselves, others, and the world regarding the trauma and related sequelae. Janoff-Bulman (1985, 1992), in one of the first attribution-based models, put forward that PTSD results from shattered assumptions about the self, such as the self is worthy, and the world around

them, such as the world is benevolent and meaningful. The central feature of PTSD, in Janoff-Bulman's model, is a form of "information shock" regarding these assumptions from trauma exposure. This focus on cognitive shifts that occur due to the trauma provides the foundation for other attribution-based models such as Ehlers and Clark's (2000) cognitive processing model of PTSD.

Specifically, Ehlers and Clark (2000) propose that one of the most crucial aspects for the development of PTSD is processing the trauma in a way that leads to a sense of serious current threat. Both appraisals of the trauma and its sequelae and the nature of the trauma memory itself are capable of generating this sense of current threat. One belief in particular, termed *mental defeat,* where an individual perceives a loss of personal autonomy to influence his or her fate, is thought to be particularly influential. This specific belief during trauma exposure is viewed as a risk factor for future negative appraisals about oneself and the world.

Ehlers and Clark further draw attention to how specific information is processed within the autobiographical memory base. Through associations with thematically and temporally related experiences, information is stored in this autobiographical base. Increased elaborative associations facilitate the intentional retrieval of memories through higher-order search strategies and inhibit direct, lower-level retrieval through matching sensory cues. If a trauma memory is poorly elaborated within this autobiographical memory base, it will be more vulnerable to unintentional triggering by matching sensory cues and intentional retrieval will be impaired. Accordingly, PTSD is characterized by a lack of adaptive, conceptual processing and instead characterized by an excess of data-driven processing. Further, unorganized memories seen in persistent PTSD may be in part a result of an inability to establish a self-referential perspective during the trauma, not allowing traumatic memories to be integrated into the autobiographical memory base.

Summary. At the forefront of the application of memory models to the understanding of PTSD comes the assertion that traumatic memories have "special properties" that distinguish them from ordinary memories in the way they are encoded, processed, and retrieved (Shobe & Kihlstrom, 1997). The main underlying assumption is that the high levels of stress experienced during trauma exposure change the way information is encoded and processed. Accordingly, these conditions cannot be replicated in the human laboratory; and thus, the knowledge gleaned from general memory research and theory is often viewed as only partially applicable. While a review of the general memory theory is beyond the scope of this chapter (see Tulving & Craik, 2000), several findings from the general memory literature run contrary to certain underlying assumptions of a few of these models.

As discussed earlier, some of the theorists posit that traumatic stress, via high levels of stress hormones, results in strongly imprinted implicit sensory, motor, and affective representations; but these high levels dramatically interfere with the consolidation of a verbalized, explicit trauma memory. Yet, it is generally believed that high levels of stress hormones both in humans and in animals enhances rather than impairs explicit memory (e.g., McGaugh, 1992). Even within the traumatic stress literature, it is unclear whether explicit traumatic memories seen in PTSD are more fragmented than in those without PTSD or in comparison to other types of events (e.g., Zoellner & Bittinger, 2004). Moreover, the assertion that trauma memories are indelible runs contrary to the broader memory literature suggesting the reconstructive, rather than fixed, nature of memory. Finally, very little evidence exists to suggest that individuals can acquire Pavolvian conditioned responses in the absence of awareness (Lovibond & Shanks, 2002; but see also Manns, Clark, & Squire, 2002). Thus, implicit conditioning in the absence of awareness or declarative knowledge (see McNally, 2003b, for a discussion) as a key underlying mechanism for PTSD may be a relatively untenable construct contrary to the broader memory and conditioning literature. Regardless of the tension about whether trauma memories have special properties that mitigate the importance of general memory theories, the information-processing models above all attempt to capture the memory-related complexities and the key role of the trauma memory in the persistence of trauma-related symptoms. Ehlers and Clark's (2000) model, in particular, is reminiscent of cognitive processes discussed in the new learning theories. Furthermore, these models are intuitively appealing both for the ability to capture the complex clinical presentation seen in PTSD and for their capacity to integrate aspects of cognitive neuroscience into their models.

Emotional Processing Models

Similar to some of the information-processing models described earlier, emotional processing models draw heavily on associative network theories of information processing. Although there are more similarities than differences, the main difference between emotion and information-processing models is the primary focus on key emotions and processing of emotional experiences rather than on the processing of the information per se. Thus, extreme emotions such as being overwhelmed and fearful become the focus in these models. However, as will be seen below, processing of trauma-related information is often viewed as a means toward successful emotional processing of the traumatic experience.

Stress response theory (Horowitz, 1976, 1986). One of the early and most influential theories of PTSD was presented by Horowitz (1976, 1986). Horowitz proposes that individuals initially experience a profound realization that the trauma occurred and then attempt to assimilate this experience with their prior knowledge. The attempted assimilation reflects a fundamental psychological need of the individual to reconcile old and new information. For many individuals, this attempted reconciliation results in an experience of being unable to assimilate the trauma experience and in being psychologically overwhelmed. To cope with this psychological quandary, individuals experience alternating psychological defense reactions of intrusions and denial. Intrusions help gradually work through the assimilation process, and denial helps protect the individual from being too overwhelmed. Intrusions are characterized by reexperiencing and heightened emotions, whereas denial is characterized by avoidance and numbing to minimize the strong reactions brought on during the intrusion phase. Individuals are thought to alternate between these two states in an effort to work through the trauma information, with increased integration resulting in the intensity of states decreasing until resolution occurs. Failure to process or adequately integrate the trauma information leads to the persistence of psychological reactions.

Emotional processing theory (Foa & Kozak, 1986; Foa & Riggs, 1993; Foa & Rothbaum, 1998; Foa, Steketee, & Rothbaum, 1989). Similar to Horowitz, at the heart of emotional processing theory, PTSD reflects impairment in emotional processing of the traumatic experience and special processing efforts are required to successfully process a traumatic experience. Drawing from Lang's bioinformational model (1979, 1985) and Rachman's emotional processing theory (1980), Foa and colleagues highlight the role of pathological fear structures in the development of PTSD. These fear structures include information about the feared stimulus, fear responses, and interpretative information about the meaning of the stimulus and responses. Fear structures become pathological when they contain excessive response elements that are resistant to modification, including when avoidance or physiological reactivity is present or when these structures include unrealistic elements. Subsequent elaboration of emotional processing theory emphasizes the role of unrealistic, pathological cognitions elements, namely, that the world is extremely dangerous and the victim is extremely incompetent (Foa & Rothbaum, 1998). For emotional processing to take place, fear-relevant information must be made available such that the fear memory can be activated; and the information made available must contain elements that are incompatible with some of those that exist so that a new memory can be formed. Specifically, Foa and colleagues argue that recovery following a traumatic event involves the modification of the pathological fear structure and that these modifications are the essence of emotional processing.

Similarly, Litz and colleagues (Litz, 1992; Litz & Gray, 2002; Litz, Orsillo, Kaloupek, & Weathers, 2000) propose a model more specific to understanding emotional numbing, arguing that emotional processing deficits in PTSD are dependent on fear cues in the environment. Individuals with PTSD do not lose their capacity to experience or express a full range of emotions, rather they react primarily with conditioned aversive emotional reactivity and reexperiencing symptoms. Specifically, trauma networks become overgeneralized across a range of thoughts, images, actions, and feelings, and these networks are subsequently more accessible and easily triggered. When the trauma network is activated, other, more adaptive responses are less accessible. Positive responses, in particular, are less accessible when individuals are in a state of stress (e.g., reexperiencing, arousal, exposure to trauma stimuli). However, these positive emotional responses are still accessible to individuals with chronic PTSD in the proper context and with the right cues. Individuals with PTSD become oversensitive to negatively valenced stimuli for negative emotional responses to occur and over time become less sensitive to positively valenced stimuli for positive emotional responses to occur.

Summary. All of the emotional processing models of PTSD underscore the need of the trauma survivor to work through or emotionally process the traumatic experience. Yet, probably one of the most persistent critiques of the emotional processing theories is the question regarding what exactly is emotional processing. That is, there is a gap in the description of the assimilation process, between

providing incompatible information and the shifting of the network. Across models a description of the mechanism underlying changes is not fully elaborated. For example, in emotional processing theory, extinction is discussed (Foa & Kozak, 1986); however, this provides a description of the process rather than the underlying mechanism. Another criticism of these models is the potentially circular nature of the theories. According to Foa and Kozak (1986), the main indicators of emotional processing are within- and between-session habituation. Thus, emotional processing has occurred when a reduction of symptoms has occurred, with the indicators of processing and the end state being identical. Further, Brewin and Holmes (2003) question whether associative network models themselves are too simple and have sufficient flexibility to account for contradictory and complex phenomena of PTSD, arguing instead that the meaning of emotional events are often much more multilayered and highly complex than these models suggest. Yet, these models bring into the forefront crucial emotional aspects of PTSD, namely, the intense fear and other related emotions associated with the disorder. Further, these models provide a solid theoretical account for successful PTSD treatment strategies, particularly exposure-based treatment.

Challenges to Our Current Conceptualizations

Across current learning, information processing, and emotional processing models of PTSD, although there are clear differences and areas of emphasis, all focus on the extreme nature of the traumatic event itself as a central etiologic event and all attempt to explain the complex symptom constellations associated with PTSD. In addition, even though not extensively discussed, these theories recognize pretrauma vulnerabilities that increase the likelihood of chronic psychopathology but simultaneously emphasize the processing of the event itself and subsequent information processing. Undoubtedly, before, during, and after event factors interact with one another in a complex manner, underlying individual differences in resilience and vulnerability.

Nevertheless, the very focus on these commonalities across models is fraught with potential confounds. Just as the traumatic event itself serves as the gatekeeper for the PTSD diagnosis, the potentially expanding definition of what constitutes a traumatic event proposes key challenges to the conceptualization of the disorder (Rosen, 2005). The key issue here is differentiating PTSD from reactions to other, potentially non-traumatic but also life-changing, stressful experiences. These other experiences include such events as loss of a job, divorce, miscarriages, failed in vitro procedures, a cancer diagnosis, and so on. For example, even classic PTSD symptoms such as reexperiencing and emotional numbing fail to differentiate between traumatic and stressful experiences (e.g., Gold, Marx, Soler-Baillo, & Sloan, 2005). Thus, one of the major issues facing the conceptualization of PTSD is differentiating it from reactions to other stressful life events. Another related challenge to the conceptualization of PTSD is differentiating what is general psychopathology and what is truly unique to posttraumatic stress disorder. Notably, many of the symptoms of PTSD such as concentration problems, loss of interest, irritability/anger, and having problems sleeping co-occur with other *DSM–IV* disorders. Clearly, basic diathesis stress models suggest that, given an underlying vulnerability, undergoing a stressful experience will bring out many forms of psychopathology. The question then arises what symptoms make PTSD unique from other disorders and, as discussed above, from reactions to other stressful experiences.

It may be that there is solely a quantitative rather than a qualitative difference in reaction to various types of stressful events, and the general stress literature is much more applicable than currently applied. Alternatively, as some of the theories reviewed in this chapter suggest, the extreme nature of trauma exposure such as the experience of life threat and accompanying stress hormone release may render reactions to these types of events truly qualitatively different from other stressful experiences, such that special theories are needed. Ultimately, the PTSD diagnosis has a unique place within the *DSM–IV* and the conceptualization of mental disorders. No other disorder is so dependent on the experience of an external event, the symptoms themselves are the persistence of normal reactions, and, without the presence of a traumatic event, the symptoms also may not be adequately differentiated from those of other disorders or other stressful experiences. What then is PTSD? As McNally (2003b) suggests, citing constructs delineated by Ian Hacking (1999), PTSD may be best construed as an interactive kind rather than a natural kind. That is, the notion of an interactive kind suggests that the process of classification itself affects PTSD. Thus, the definition of PTSD and the problems associated with defining the construct may ultimately change the conceptualization of the disorder and the disorder itself. Regardless of these potential problems, a comprehensive understanding of psychological reactions following traumatic events requires the synthesis of conditioning, memory, and emotion research–related fields. The understanding of these reactions not only facilitates our understanding of extreme and potentially pathological processes, but also extends our understanding of fundamental processes of conditioning, memory, and emotion.

References

American Psychiatric Association. (1994). *Diagnostic and statistical manual of mental disorders* (4th ed.). Washington, DC: Author.

American Psychiatric Association. (2000). *Diagnostic and statistical manual of mental disorders* (4th ed. text revision). Washington, DC: Author.

Barlow, D. H. (2002). *Anxiety and its disorders: The nature and treatment of anxiety and panic* (2nd ed.). New York: Guilford Press.

Barton, K. A., Blanchard, E., & Hickling, E. J. (1996). Antecedents and consequences of acute stress disorder among motor vehicle accident victims. *Behaviour Research and Therapy, 34*, 805–813.

Başoğlu, M., & Mineka, S. (1992). The role of uncontrollability and unpredictability of stress in the development of post-torture stress symptoms. In M. Başoğlu (Ed.), *Torture and its consequences: Current treatment approaches* (pp. 182–225). Cambridge, England: Cambridge University Press.

Blanchard, E. B., Hickling, E. J., Galovski, T., & Veazey, C. (2002). Emergency room vital signs and PTSD in a treatment seeking sample of motor vehicle accident survivors. *Journal of Traumatic Stress, 15*, 199–204.

Bolles, R. C. (1970). Species-specific defense reactions and avoidance learning. *Psychological Review, 77*, 32–48.

Bolles, R. C. (1972). Reinforcement, expectancy, and learning. *Psychological Review, 79*, 394–409.

Bolles, R. C. (1989). Acquired behaviors: Aversive learning. In R. J. Blanchard, P. F. Brain, D. C. Blanchard, & S. Parmigiani (Eds.), *Ethoexperimental approaches to the study of behavior* (pp. 167–179). NATO ASI Series D, 48. Boston: Kluwer Academic.

Bowman, M. L., & Yehuda, R. (2003). Risk factors and the adversity-stress model. In G. Rosen (Ed.), *Posttraumatic stress disorder: Issues and controversies* (pp. 15–39). New York: Wiley.

Brewin, C. R. (2001). A cognitive neuroscience account of posttraumatic stress disorder and its treatment. *Behaviour Research and Therapy, 39*, 373–393.

Brewin, C. R., Andrews, B., & Valentine, J. D. (2000). Meta-analysis of risk factors for posttraumatic stress disorder in trauma-exposed adults. *Journal of Consulting and Clinical Psychology, 68*, 748–766.

Brewin, C. R., Dalgleish, T., & Joseph, S. (1996). A dual representation theory of post traumatic stress disorder. *Psychological Review, 103*, 670–686.

Brewin, C. R., & Holmes, E. A. (2003). Psychological theories of posttraumatic stress disorder. *Clinical Psychology Review, 23*, 339–376.

Bryant, R. A. (2003). In the aftermath of trauma: Normative reactions and early interventions. In G. Rosen (Ed.), *Posttraumatic stress disorder: Issues and controversies* (pp. 187–212). New York: Wiley.

Bryant, R. A., & Harvey, A. G. (1997). Acute stress disorder: A critical review of diagnostic issues. *Clinical Psychology Review, 17,* 757–773.

Bryant, R. A., & Harvey, A. G. (1998). Relationship between acute stress disorder and posttraumatic stress disorder following mild traumatic brain injury. *American Journal of Psychiatry, 155,* 625–629.

Bryant, R. A., Harvey, A. G., Guthrie, R., & Moulds, M. (2000). A prospective study of acute psychophysiological arousal, acute stress disorder, and posttraumatic stress disorder. *Journal of Abnormal Psychology, 109,* 341–344.

Davey, G.C.L. (1992). Classical conditioning and the acquisition of human fears and phobias: A review and synthesis of the literature. *Advances in Behaviour Research and Therapy, 14,* 29–66.

Davidson, J.R.T., & Foa, E. B. (1991). Diagnostic issues in posttraumatic stress disorder: Considerations for the *DSM–IV*. *Journal of Abnormal Psychology, 100,* 346–355.

Ehlers, A., & Clark, D. M. (2000). A cognitive model of posttraumatic stress disorder. *Behaviour Research and Therapy, 38,* 219–345.

Fanselow, M. S. (1997). Species-specific defense reactions: Retrospect and prospect. In M. E. Bouton & M. S. Fanselow (Eds.), *Learning, motivation, and cognition: The functional behaviorism of Robert C. Bolles* (pp. 321–341). Washington, DC: American Psychological Association.

Foa, E. B., & Kozak, M. J. (1986). Emotional processing of fear: Exposure to corrective information. *Psychological Bulletin, 99,* 20–35.

Foa, E. B., & Riggs, D. S. (1993). Posttraumatic stress disorder in rape victims. In J. Oldham, M. Riba, & A. Tasman (Eds.), *American Psychiatric Press Review of Psychiatry, Vol. 12* (pp. 273–303). Washington, DC: American Psychiatric Press.

Foa, E. B., & Rothbaum, B. O. (1998). *Treating the trauma of rape: Cognitive behavioral therapy for PTSD.* New York: Guilford Press.

Foa, E. B., Steketee, G., & Rothbaum, B. O. (1989). Behavioral/cognitive conceptualization of post-traumatic stress disorder. *Behavior Therapy, 20,* 155–176.

Foa, E. B., Zinbarg, R., & Rothbaum, B. O. (1992). Uncontrollability and unpredictability in post-traumatic stress disorder: An animal model. *Psychological Bulletin, 112,* 218–238.

Gold, S. D., Marx, B. P., Soler-Baillo, J. M., & Sloan, D. M. (2005). Is life stress more traumatic than traumatic stress? *Journal of Anxiety Disorders, 19,* 687–698.

Hacking, I. (1999). *The social construction of what?* Cambridge, MA: Harvard University Press.

Horowitz, M. (1976). *Stress response syndrome.* New York: Jason Aronson.

Horowitz, M. (1986). *Stress response syndrome* (2nd ed.). New York: Jason Aronson.

Janet, P. (1907). *The major symptom of hysteria.* New York: Macmillan.

Janoff-Bulman, R. (1985). The aftermath of victimization: Rebuilding shattered assumptions. In C. R. Figlery (Ed.), *Trauma and its wake: The study and treatment of post-traumatic stress disorder* (pp. 15–35). New York: Bruner/Mazel.

Janoff-Bulman, R. (1992). *Shattered assumptions: Toward a new psychology of trauma.* New York: Free Press.

Keane, T. M., Zimering, R. T., & Caddell, J. M. (1985). A behavioral formulation of posttraumatic stress disorder in Vietnam veterans. *The Behavior Therapist, 8,* 9–12.

Kessler, R., Sonnega, A., Bromet, E., Hughes, M., & Nelson, C. (1995). Posttraumatic stress disorder in the National Comorbidity Survey. *Archives of General Psychiatry, 52,* 1048–1060.

Lang, P. J. (1979). A bio-informational theory of emotional imagery. *Journal of Psychophysiology, 16,* 495–512.

Lang, P. J. (1985). The cognitive psychophysiology of emotion: Fear and anxiety. In J. Master & A. Tuma (Eds.), *Anxiety and the anxiety disorders* (pp. 131–170). Hillsdale, NJ: Erlbaum.

Litz, B. T. (1992). Emotional numbing in combat-related posttraumatic stress disorder: A critical review and reformulation. *Clinical Psychology Review, 12,* 417–432.

Litz, B. T., & Gray, M. J. (2002). Emotional numbing in posttraumatic stress disorder: Current and future research directions. *Australian and New Zealand Journal of Psychiatry, 36,* 198–204.

Litz, B. T., Orsillo, S. M., Kaloupek, D., & Weathers, F. (2000). Emotional processing in posttraumatic stress disorder. *Journal of Abnormal Psychology, 109,* 26–39.

Lovibond, P. H., & Shanks, D. R. (2002). The role of awareness in Pavlovian conditioning: Empirical evidence and theoretical implications. *Journal of Experimental Psychology: Animal Behavior Processes, 28,* 3–26.

Manns, J. R., Clark, R. E., & Squire, L. R. (2002). Standard delay of eyeblink classical conditioning is independent of awareness. *Journal of Experimental Psychology: Animal Behavior Processes, 28,* 32–37.

Marshall, R. D., Spitzer, R., & Liebowitz, M. R. (1999). Review and critique of the new *DSM–IV* diagnosis of acute stress disorder. *American Journal of Psychiatry, 156,* 1677–1685.

Marshall, R. D., Spitzer, R., & Liebowitz, M. R. (2000). New *DSM–IV* diagnosis of acute stress disorder. *American Journal of Psychiatry, 157,* 1890–1891.

McGaugh, J. L. (1992). Affect, neuromodulatory systems, and memory storage. In S.-A. Christianson (Ed.), *The handbook of emotion and memory: Research and theory* (pp. 245–268). Hillsdale, NJ: Erlbaum.

McNally, R. J. (2003a). Conceptual problems with *DSM–IV* criteria for posttraumatic stress disorder. In G. Rosen (Ed.), *Posttraumatic stress disorder: Issues and controversies* (pp. 1–14). New York: Wiley.

McNally, R. J. (2003b). *Remembering trauma.* Cambridge, MA: Belknap Press of Harvard University Press.

Mineka, S. (1985). Animal models of anxiety-based disorders: Their usefulness and limitations. In J. Maser & A. Tuma (Eds.), *Anxiety and the anxiety disorders* (pp. 199–244). Hillsdale, NJ: Erlbaum.

Mineka, S., & Zinbarg, R. (2006). A contemporary learning theory perspective on the etiology of anxiety disorders. *American Psychologist, 61,* 10–26.

Mowrer, O. H. (1939). A stimulus-response analysis of anxiety and its role as a reinforcing agent. *Psychological Review, 46,* 553–564.

Mowrer, O. H. (1947). On the dual nature of learning: A reinterpretation of "conditioning" and "problem solving." *Harvard Educational Review, 17,* 102–148.

Ozer, E. J., Best, S. R., Lipsey, T. L., & Weiss, D. S. (2003). Predictors of posttraumatic stress disorder and symptoms in adults: A meta-analysis. *Psychological Bulletin, 129,* 52–73.

Pitman, R. K. (1988). Post-traumatic stress disorder, conditioning, and network theory. *Psychiatric Annals, 18,* 182–189.

Pitman, R. K. (1989). Post-traumatic stress disorder, hormones, and memory. *Biological Psychiatry, 26,* 221–223.

Rachman, S. (1978). *Fear and courage.* New York: W. H. Freeman.

Rachman, S. (1980). Emotional processing. *Behaviour Research and Therapy, 18,* 51–60.

Rachman, S. (1990). *Fear and courage* (2nd ed.). New York: W. H. Freeman.

Rau, V., DeCola, J. P., & Fanselow, M. S. (2005). Stress-induced enhancement of fear learning: An animal model of posttraumatic stress disorder. *Neuroscience & Biobehavioral Reviews, 29,* 1207–1223.

Roemer, L., Litz, B. T., Orsillo, S. M., Ehlich, P. J., & Friedman, M. J. (1998). Increases in retrospective accounts of war-zone exposure over time: The role of PTSD symptom severity. *Journal of Traumatic Stress, 11,* 597–605.

Rosen, G. M. (2005). Traumatic events, criterion creep, and the creation of posttraumatic stress disorder. *The Scientific Review of Mental Health Practice, 3,* 39–42.

Rothbaum, B. O., Foa, E. B., Riggs, D. S., Murdock, T., & Walsh, W. (1992). A prospective examination of posttraumatic stress disorder in rape victims. *Journal of Traumatic Stress, 5,* 455–475.

Shalev, A. Y., Sahar, T., Freedman, S., Peri, T., Glick, N., Brandes, D., et al. (1998). A prospective study of heart rate responses following trauma and the subsequent development of PTSD. *Archives of General Psychiatry, 55,* 553–559.

Shobe, K. K., & Kihlstrom, J. K. (1997). Is trauma memory special? *Current Directions in Psychological Science, 6,* 70–74.

Siddle, D.A.T., & Bond, N. W. (1988). Avoidance learning, Pavlovian conditioning, and the development of phobias. *Biological Psychology, 27,* 167–183.

Southwick, S. M., Morgan, C. A., Nicolaou, A. L., & Charney, D. S. (1997). Consistency of memory for combat-related traumatic events in veterans of Operation Desert Storm. *American Journal of Psychiatry, 154,* 173–177.

Stampfl, T. G., & Levis, D. J. (1967). Essentials of implosive therapy: A learning-based psychodynamic behavior therapy. *Journal of Abnormal Psychology, 72,* 157–163.

Sutker, P. B., Uddo, M., Brailey, K., Vasterling, J. J., & Errera, P. (1994). Psychopathology in war-zone deployed and non-deployed Operation Desert Storm troops assigned graves registration duties. *Journal of Abnormal Psychology, 103,* 383–390.

Tulving, E., & Craik, F.I.M. (Eds.). (2000). *The Oxford handbook of memory.* Oxford, England: Oxford University Press.

van der Kolk, B. A. (1987). *Psychological trauma.* Washington, DC: American Psychiatric Press.

van der Kolk, B. A. (1994). The body keeps score: Memory and the evolving psychobiology of posttraumatic stress. *Harvard Review of Psychiatry, 1,* 253–265.

van der Kolk, B. A. (1996). The body keeps score: Approaches to the psychobiology of posttraumatic stress disorder. In B. A. van der Kolk, A. C. McFarlane, & L. Weisaeth (Eds.), *Traumatic stress: The effects of overwhelming experience on mind, body, and society* (pp. 214–241). New York: Guilford Press.

van der Kolk, B. A., Burbridge, J., & Suzuki, J. (1997). The psychobiology of traumatic memory. Clinical implications of neuroimaging studies. In R. Yehuda & A. McFarlane (Eds.), *Psychobiology of posttraumatic stress disorder* (pp. 99–113). New York: Annals of the New York Academy of Sciences.

van der Kolk, B. A., & Fisler, R. (1995). Dissociation and the fragmentary nature of traumatic memories: Overview and exploratory study. *Journal of Traumatic Stress, 8,* 505–525.

Weaver, T. L., & Clum, G. A. (1995). Psychological distress associated with interpersonal violence: A meta-analysis. *Clinical Psychology Review, 15,* 115–140.

Zoellner, L. A., & Bittinger, J. (2004). On the uniqueness of trauma memories in PTSD. In G. Rosen (Ed.), *Posttraumatic stress disorder: Issues and controversies.* New York: Wiley.

Zoellner, L. A., Jaycox, L. A., Watlington, C. G., & Foa, E. B. (2003). Are the dissociative criteria in ASD useful? *Journal of Traumatic Stress, 16,* 341–350.

Zoellner, L. A., Sacks, M. B., & Foa, E. B. (2001). Stability of emotions for traumatic memories for acute and chronic PTSD. *Behaviour Research and Therapy, 39,* 671–711.

PART 4

Classification and Assessment

Classification and Boundaries Among Anxiety-Related Problems

Amy E. Lawrence *and* Timothy A. Brown

Abstract

This chapter examines issues related to the classification of anxiety and related disorders. The chapter reviews evidence of the reliability and validity of DSM-IV disorder categories, patterns of comorbidity, models of the relationships between disorders and higher-order personality variables, and evidence of shared genetic vulnerabilities for anxiety disorders. Future research directions, including the movement toward a dimensional classification system, are discussed.

Keywords: anxiety disorders, classification, comorbidity, differential diagnosis, emotional disorders, interview, reliability, validity

Currently, anxiety disorders are classified into 12 categories found in the fourth edition of the *Diagnostic and Statistical Manual of Mental Disorders* (*DSM-IV*) (American Psychiatric Association [APA], 1994). These categories reflect a shift that occurred with the publication of the third edition (APA, 1980) to an atheoretical classification system that offers prototypical descriptions of disorders, but does not specify shared processes underlying clusters of symptoms. The term *neurosis,* which had encompassed all current mood and anxiety diagnoses and implied that hypothetical, unconscious conflicts maintained symptoms, was removed from the nomenclature and replaced with descriptions of the observable features of disorders. The *DSM–IV* currently includes the following disorder categories: panic disorder (PD), panic disorder with agoraphobia (PDA), agoraphobia without a history of panic disorder, social phobia (also called social anxiety disorder), specific phobia, generalized anxiety disorder (GAD), obsessive-compulsive disorder (OCD), posttraumatic stress disorder (PTSD), acute stress

disorder, anxiety disorder due to a general medical condition, substance-induced anxiety disorder, and anxiety disorder not otherwise specified (NOS). Although the proliferation of diagnostic categories over time reflects an expansion in our knowledge of anxiety disorders and facilitates research in classification, some have argued that greater differentiation of disorders has obscured their shared features (e.g., Andrews, 1996). Furthermore, the expansion of diagnostic categories may have resulted in compromised discriminant validity, such that our current nosology may distinguish disorders that are merely variations of broader, underlying syndromes. Specification of these shared features of mood and anxiety symptoms may enhance our understanding of the prevention, etiology, course, and treatment of disorders.

The sections that follow evaluate the current classification system in terms of reliability and validity. In addition, structural analyses that describe the shared features that may account for much of the variance in anxiety and mood disorders are discussed. A research agenda is proposed that would enable a more sophisticated understanding of these shared features and allow refinement of the current classification scheme. Topics addressed include the movement toward a dimensional classification system and explication of personality-psychopathology relationships.

Reliability

Standardized interview protocols are typically used in investigations of the reliability and validity of diagnostic categories. The semistructured interviews most often used in the study of anxiety disorders include the *Structured Clinical Interview for DSM–IV Axis I Disorders* (SCID) (First, Spitzer, Gibbon, & Williams, 1997) and the *Anxiety Disorders Interview Schedule* (ADIS), which has been revised several times in accordance with revisions to the *DSM* and allows detailed inquiry into anxiety and mood disorder symptoms. The most recent iteration, the *Anxiety Disorders Interview Schedule for DSM–IV: Lifetime Version* (ADIS-IV-L) (Di Nardo, Brown, & Barlow, 1994), enables assessment of both current and lifetime anxiety and mood disorders, and includes screening questions for addictive, psychotic, and relevant organic disorders. The ADIS-IV-L also enables dimensional assessment of key and associated features of disorders, regardless of whether a formal diagnosis is under consideration. The assessment of disorder features along continua allows for the determination of the severity of disorders and the presence of subthreshold symptoms (i.e., disorder manifestations that do not meet the interference-distress criterion). Dimensional data can be also more useful than categorical, "presence-absence" ratings in measuring outcomes of clinical trials (e.g., Brown & Barlow, 1995) and as dimensional indicators in studies of latent structure (e.g., Brown, Chorpita, & Barlow, 1998; Waller & Meehl, 1997).

Studies of diagnostic reliability, or the extent to which two or more independent evaluators agree on the presence or absence of a particular diagnosis, have provided evidence that may inform revisions to the *DSM*. In addition to identifying those diagnoses with inadequate discriminant validity, these studies have identified sources of unreliability. The studies most often cited in this chapter relied on "test-retest" methods, in which the patient was interviewed by different independent evaluators (e.g., Brown, Di Nardo, Lehman, & Campbell, 2001; Di Nardo, Moras, Barlow, Rapee, & Brown, 1993). In such studies, the most widely used index of interrater

agreement is the kappa coefficient (κ; Fleiss, Nee, & Landis, 1979), which ranges in value from 0 (chance agreement) to 1.00 (perfect agreement).

Large-scale *DSM–III–R* and *DSM–IV* reliability studies have provided evidence of good to excellent reliability for most mood and anxiety disorder diagnoses (Brown et al., 2001; Di Nardo et al., 1993). In both studies, a random sample of patients was selected from normal clinic flow to receive two independent assessments using the ADIS, with the second interview typically occurring within 2 weeks of the initial assessment. Collapsing across principal and additional diagnoses, reliability coefficients were highest for PDA (κ = .81), OCD (κ = .75), social phobia (κ = .77), and panic disorder (with or without agoraphobia) (κ = .79). Diagnoses exhibiting good reliability included specific phobia (κ = .71), GAD (κ = .65), and any mood disorder (dysthymic disorder or major depressive disorder [MDD]) (κ = .63). With the exception of OCD (which exhibited excellent reliability in *DSM–III–R* studies) and dysthymic disorder (κ = .22; Brown et al., 2001), all diagnostic categories exhibited greater reliability relative to *DSM–III–R* diagnoses (Di Nardo et al., 1993). Notably, interrater reliability for dimensional ratings of disorder features was generally acceptable, with the lowest rates of agreement occurring for single-item ratings (e.g., rating of avoidance of dental or medical procedures [r = .41] in the specific phobia section of the ADIS). For all disorders except for dysthymic disorder (r = .36), the dimensional clinical severity rating (CSR), a 0–8 rating of disorder severity, exhibited favorable reliability.

Sources of diagnostic unreliability varied by disorder, such that disagreements involving social phobia, specific phobia, and OCD typically entailed dispute about whether symptoms met the threshold for a clinical disorder. Overall, however, "difference in patient report" was the largest source of unreliability. Instances in which clinicians disagreed about the diagnosis assigned most often involved disorders with overlapping features (e.g., specific phobia and PD, MDD and dysthymic disorder) (Brown et al., 2001). Frequent disagreements were also observed involving anxiety disorder NOS diagnoses, such that one interviewer judged that clinically significant features of a disorder were present, whereas another judged that not all criteria for a formal *DSM–IV* diagnosis were met. The high rate of disagreements involving threshold issues and NOS diagnoses suggest the limitations of a purely categorical diagnostic system (Brown & Barlow, 2005).

These findings indicate that most current diagnostic categories are associated with good to excellent interrater agreement and that revisions to diagnostic criteria between *DSM–III–R* and *DSM–IV* have resulted in improved reliability for most disorder categories, with PD and GAD exhibiting the most improved reliability (Di Nardo et al., 1993). Generalized anxiety disorder and specific phobias continued to have significant rates of disagreement involving other diagnoses with overlapping features (mood disorders and agoraphobia, respectively). Disagreements involving GAD and mood disorders are noteworthy in light of evidence that these disorders share a common vulnerability.

Validity

Reasonably reliable definitions of anxiety and mood disorders have allowed researchers to address the validity of diagnostic categories, most often through studies of convergent and discriminant validity. As indicated earlier, anxiety disorder categories have increased in recent editions of the *DSM*, resulting in greater differentiation among disorders. Nevertheless, comorbidity studies of *DSM–III–R* criteria indicated that at least 50% of patients with a principal anxiety disorder have one or more additional diagnoses at the time of assessment (e.g., Brown & Barlow, 1992; Sanderson, Di Nardo, Rapee, & Barlow, 1990). In response to these findings, some have argued in favor of a *general neurotic syndrome* that assumes a homogeneous diathesis for a heterogeneous expression of symptoms and collapses the spectrum of anxiety and mood disorders into a single entity (Andrews, 1996; Andrews, Stewart, Morris-Yates, Holt, & Henderson, 1990). Research bearing on this debate is discussed in the remainder of this section. In particular, diagnostic comorbidity, structural relationships between disorder constructs and with higher-order trait dimensions, and relationships between specific disorders are addressed.

Diagnostic Comorbidity

A study of current and lifetime comorbidity of *DSM–IV* anxiety and mood disorders in a large clinical sample has indicated that the current and lifetime prevalence of additional Axis I disorders in principal anxiety and mood disorders is 57% and 81%, respectively (Brown, Campbell, Lehman, Grisham, & Mancill, 2001). Derived from a large sample (*n* = 1,127) of patients diagnosed using the ADIS-IV-L, these findings are based on an outpatient sample subject to exclusion criteria (e.g., no active substance use disorders, no more than one hospitalization in the previous 5 years). Diagnoses associated with the most comorbidity included PTSD, MDD, GAD, and PDA, whereas those with the lowest rates of comorbidity were specific phobia and social phobia. Collapsing across all anxiety disorders, 30% of patients had an additional mood disorder at the time of the evaluation.

This comorbidity study highlights the misleading findings that may be produced by adhering to *DSM–IV* hierarchy rules. Although many hierarchy rules were eliminated in *DSM–IV*, those stating that GAD should not be diagnosed if the symptoms occurred entirely within the context of a mood disorder or PTSD remain. Intended to assist interviewers in choosing among related diagnoses, these rules allow a diagnosis to be excluded if its symptoms are "due to" a disorder occupying a higher position in the hierarchy. When hierarchy rules were adhered to in this study, GAD occurred infrequently as an additional diagnosis. When these rules were ignored, however, GAD was highly comorbid with MDD and dysthymic disorder (67% and 90%, respectively) (Brown, Campbell, et al., 2001). This finding is consistent with other studies indicating that GAD is highly comorbid with other disorders (e.g., Wittchen, Zhao, Kessler, & Eaton, 1994). Clearly, following *DSM–IV* hierarchy rules may impede our ability to determine true rates of comorbidity among anxiety and mood disorders.

Large-scale epidemiological studies have also indicated significant overlap between anxiety and mood disorder diagnoses (Kessler, Chiu, Demler, & Walters, 2005). In addition, these studies have revealed significant comorbidity between certain anxiety and substance use disorders, as well as between anxiety and impulse control disorders. High rates of comorbidity have supported the notion that a shared diathesis underlies many disorders. Structural analyses of disorder features have specified shared vulnerabilities for anxiety and mood disorders.

Structural Relationships Between DSM–IV Disorder Constructs

High rates of comorbidity among anxiety and mood disorders (e.g., Brown, Campbell, et al., 2001), the finding that various diagnoses respond similarly to the same treatments (e.g., Hudson & Pope, 1990), and evidence that comorbid diagnoses often remit after treatment of another anxiety disorder (Brown, Antony, & Barlow, 1995) suggest that these disorders may share a similar pathogenesis.

Unfortunately, many studies addressing the validity of the current classification system have been conducted at the diagnostic level. This approach is limited by its adherence to the diagnostic system under evaluation. Furthermore, the use of categorical *DSM* diagnoses ignores the dimensional nature of many features of anxiety and mood disorders and introduces measurement error by requiring the artificial collapse of variability above and below a diagnostic threshold (MacCallum, Zhang, & Preacher, 2003). Performing a dimensional assessment of disorder features (i.e., assigning ratings to each criterion of a *DSM* diagnosis) allows for the examination of relationships between these features and of the latent structure of disorder constructs. Studies examining the classification of anxiety and mood disorders have also been limited by the assessment of specific disorders in isolation from one another (Watson, Clark, & Harkness, 1994). For example, because the associated features of GAD overlap considerably with symptoms of depression, assessing GAD in isolation may obscure its boundary with mood disorders (Brown, Barlow, & Liebowitz, 1994). Therefore, evaluation of the latent structure of anxiety disorders ideally entails dimensional assessment of both anxiety and mood disorder features.

Although anxiety and depression have traditionally been regarded as conceptually distinct, dimensional measures of these constructs have demonstrated considerable overlap (Brown et al., 1998). Cases of *pure* depression (i.e., patients who present with mood disorders with no current or past anxiety disorder) are relatively rare (e.g., Mineka, Watson, & Clark, 1998). The limited utility of questionnaire measures and clinical ratings in differentiating anxiety and depression have suggested the presence of higher-order factors, or general shared negative affect and absence of positive affect, that might account for the overlap between these two affective states (Clark & Watson, 1991). The tripartite model expanded on the two-factor affective model proposed by Tellegen (1985) by including a third factor, physiological hyperarousal (characterized by such symptoms as shortness of breath, dizziness, and trembling). Clark and Watson (1991) initially proposed that negative affect is a shared feature of anxiety and depression (and includes symptoms such as sleep disturbance and poor concentration), whereas autonomic arousal is specific to anxiety and the absence of positive affect is specific to depression. Numerous studies have lent support to the tripartite structure of anxiety and mood disorders (e.g., Watson et al., 1995). The model was also validated

in children and adolescents (Chorpita, Albano, & Barlow, 1998; Joiner, 1996). Psychophysiological studies have also supported the model, in that the factors hypothesized to be specific to anxiety and depression, autonomic arousal and anhedonia, respectively, show distinct patterns of brain activity (e.g., Bruder et al., 1997).

A large-scale study was conducted to address limitations of previous classification research and to test the validity of the tripartite model (Brown et al., 1998). This study has contributed to the refinement of hierarchical models that specify the relationship between anxiety and mood disorders, and the relationship of these constructs to higher-order vulnerability factors (e.g., Barlow, 2000; Mineka et al., 1998). The study entailed examination of the latent structure of the dimensional features of the mood and anxiety disorders and tripartite model constructs (negative affect, positive affect, and autonomic arousal) and description of the relationships among these variables in a large clinical sample (Brown et al., 1998). Confirmatory factor analysis of dimensional symptom measures (questionnaire scores and clinician ratings) supported the discriminant validity of selected emotional disorders. A five-factor *DSM–IV* disorder model distinguishing mood disorders, PD with and without agoraphobia, social phobia, GAD, and OCD provided the best fit to the data. Notably, a four-factor solution in which GAD and mood disorders were collapsed into a single factor provided a significantly poorer fit, suggesting the distinctiveness of these disorders despite the considerable overlap between their latent factors ($r = .63$). Consistent with the tripartite model, the best-fitting model specified significant paths between the negative affect factor and all five *DSM–IV* disorder factors, though the strongest paths were observed between negative affect and the GAD and mood disorder factors. Decreased positive affect was associated with greater social phobia and depression, though this higher-order factor was not associated with any other anxiety disorder.

Contrary to the predictions of the tripartite model, autonomic arousal was not found to be a discriminating feature for all anxiety disorders, but instead was a lower-order factor primarily related to PD (Brown et al., 1998). In the structural model, the path from GAD to autonomic arousal was negative ($-.22$), indicating that an increase in the GAD factor was associated with a decrease in autonomic arousal. A positive correlation, however, was observed between GAD and autonomic arousal at the zero-order level. This discrepancy suggests a suppressor effect, such that the strong overlap between negative affect and GAD obscured the true relationship between autonomic arousal and GAD. Once the variance associated with negative affect was removed in the structural model, the true relationship between GAD and autonomic arousal was clarified. This finding, as well as nonsignificant paths between autonomic arousal OCD and social phobia, indicate that autonomic arousal may be only weakly related to several anxiety disorders. Overall, the results of this study support the notion that higher-order trait variables, positive affect and negative affect/neuroticism, likely act as shared risk factors for the development of anxiety and mood disorders. Notably, GAD exhibited the greatest degree of overlap with other disorder constructs, as well as a high zero-order correlation with the negative affect latent factor. This finding is consistent with conceptualizations of GAD as the basic emotional disorder, whose features (including chronic worry and negative affect) are evident to some extent in all emotional disorders.

Genetic Vulnerabilities for Anxiety Disorders

Studies examining genetic vulnerabilities for mental disorders have generally supported the notion that a shared vulnerability underlies anxiety disorders. For example, there appears to be a shared genetic diathesis for GAD, panic disorder, agoraphobia and, to a lesser extent, social phobia, with the remaining variance explained by unique and shared environment factors (Hettema, Prescott, Myers, Neale, & Kendler, 2005). Specific phobias load primarily on a second genetic factor, which may indicate that their etiology, particularly that of animal and situational phobias, is distinct from other anxiety disorders. A meta-analysis of genetic epidemiology studies has also indicated that several anxiety disorders (including PD, GAD, phobias, and OCD) aggregate in families and the major source of familial risk is genetic (Hettema, Neale, & Kendler, 2001). The observation of shared genetic variance for mental disorders is not unique to anxiety and mood disorders. Multivariate genetic analyses have indicated that a small number of genetic and environmental risk factors may account for patterns of comorbidity observed among a number of mental and substance use disorders (Kendler, Prescott, Myers, & Neale, 2003).

Genetic studies have been useful in corroborating findings from structural analyses. Consistent with the finding that social phobia and depression share a relationship with positive affect not observed in other emotional disorders, these two disorders appear to share a common genetic diathesis (Eley & Brown, 2008). As previously discussed, latent structural analyses of anxiety and mood disorders have indicated that the higher-order factor of negative affect/neuroticism accounts for much of the variance in emotional disorders and exhibits significant overlap with the GAD factor (Brown et al., 1998). This finding has been supported in a large-scale twin study, which indicated significant covariation between GAD and neuroticism (Hettema, Prescott, & Kendler, 2004).

Findings from studies of the genetic basis for emotional disorders may have significant implications for the classification of anxiety and mood disorders. For example, the observation that neuroticism and GAD share a significant proportion of their genetic vulnerability may point to a revision of GAD's role in diagnostic nosology. GAD has been referred to as the *pure* or fundamental anxiety disorder because its features are observed to some degree in all anxiety disorders (Brown et al., 1994). Hettema et al. (2004) speculate that GAD's overlap with neuroticism may indicate that it is better conceptualized as an anxious personality type rather than an Axis I syndrome.

Extant genetic research has focused on specifying shared genetic vulnerabilities for emotional disorders, though researchers have begun to look more specifically at the genes associated with these disorders. Linkage studies have identified several candidate genes that may confer increased risk for anxiety disorders (e.g., Thorgeirsson et al., 2003), though more studies are necessary to link particular genes with symptoms of emotional disorders.

Relationships Between Specific Disorders

In addition to specifying a framework in which to understand the relationships among all anxiety and mood disorders, comorbidity studies and structural analyses have provided insight into relationships between particular disorders.

Social phobia and depression. A somewhat surprising finding from the aforementioned investigation of the structural relationships among disorders was that decreased positive affect is uniquely associated with social phobia and depression, whereas negative affect is associated with all anxiety and mood disorders (Brown et al., 1998). The social phobia latent factor had a significantly stronger zero-order relationship with positive affect than did the other anxiety disorder factors, suggesting that social phobia and depression share a vulnerability not associated with other emotional disorders (Brown et al., 1998). This finding is consistent with the observation of high comorbidity between social phobia and depression, such that principal diagnoses of MDD and dysthymic disorder had the highest rates of comorbid social phobia (41% and 48%, respectively) (Brown, Campbell, et al., 2001). Social phobia is also associated with more severe comorbid mood disorder symptoms (Kessler, Stang, Wittchen, Stein, & Walters, 1999). Not surprisingly, individuals diagnosed with generalized social phobia, characterized by apprehension and avoidance of most social situations, report higher levels of depression than do individuals with the nongeneralized subtype (Holt, Heimberg, & Hope, 1992; Turner, Beidel, & Townsley, 1992).

GAD and OCD. Although OCD is a highly reliable diagnostic category (κ = .75; Brown et al., 2001), the disorder's phenomenological similarity to GAD has been noted (e.g., Craske, Rapee, Jackel, & Barlow, 1989). Worry and obsessions may appear similar, as might compulsions and reassurance-seeking behavior. In a review of the literature on obsessions and worry, Turner, Beidel, and Stanley (1992) concluded that existing data could not point to whether they were distinct phenomena. They noted that both are present to some degree in clinical and nonclinical populations, appear similar in form and content, are more frequent and less controllable in clinical populations, are both unaccompanied by negative affect, and appear to have a shared vulnerability. The *DSM–IV* offers some guidelines for differentiating obsessions and worry. The definition of OCD, for example, specifies that obsessions are not simply excessive worries about real-life problems. Rather, OCD is characterized by preoccupations that are intrusive and often ego-dystonic, or bizarre and alien to the individual (Rachman, 1973). Furthermore, intrusive thoughts in OCD may elicit a phobic or panic reaction and are typically avoided or resisted, whereas worry thoughts, even if intrusive or repetitive, are typically not resisted (Steketee & Barlow, 2002).

The aforementioned study of the structural relationships among disorder features supports the notion that GAD and OCD have shared features (Brown et al, 1998). In this study, GAD exhibited the highest degree of overlap with other *DSM–IV* diagnosis factors, as well as significant overlap with the nonspecific negative affect factor. The OCD latent factor was most strongly correlated with the GAD factor ($r = .52$), a finding perhaps attributable

to similarity between chronic worry and obsessions, which both may be conceptualized as excessive and/or uncontrollable cognitive processes associated with negative affect.

Despite the similarity between chronic worry and obsessions and the structural relationship between the disorder constructs, a low rate of co-occurrence has been observed between OCD and GAD in some studies (Brown, Campbell, et al., 2001; Brown, Moras, Zinbarg, & Barlow, 1993), whereas others have reported that more than 30% of adults with OCD have a lifetime history of GAD (Andrews et al., 1990; Crino & Andrews, 1996). In a sample consisting of 31 patients with a primary diagnosis of OCD and 46 with a primary diagnosis of GAD, patients with GAD were more likely to describe themselves as worriers and/or as having a tendency to worry about minor matters than were patients with OCD, and patients ultimately diagnosed with OCD were more likely to respond affirmatively to the ADIS screening questions for obsessions and compulsions (Brown et al., 1993). In addition, patients with OCD received significantly higher scores on a self-report measure of obsessions than did patients diagnosed with GAD, though significant correlations between scores on measures of obsessions and compulsions and worry were observed. Other studies have also indicated similarities between compulsions in OCD and worry-driven behaviors in GAD. In one sample, more than half of the patients with GAD reported engaging in some "corrective, preventative, or ritualistic" act in response to their worry (Craske et al., 1989). A measure of thought-action fusion, or the tendency to assume causal relationships between one's own thoughts and the external world (Rachman, 1993), has been used to differentiate obsessions from worry in an undergraduate sample, though this finding has not been replicated in a clinical sample (Coles, Mennin, & Heimberg, 2001). Studies on nonclinical samples have also indicated that individuals are more aware of the triggers of worry than of obsessions and that they consider obsessions less voluntary, though worry content and the presence of worry are more distressing than obsessions (Langlois, Freeston, & Ladouceur, 2000).

Despite the shared variance between worry and obsessions and compulsions, the diagnoses can be reliably distinguished from one another by trained interviewers. In a large-scale reliability study (Brown et al., 2001), diagnostic disagreements involving OCD were relatively uncommon; in the two disagreements involving another disorder, the other disorder involved was anxiety disorder NOS. The low rate of co-occurrence of GAD and OCD and the high diagnostic reliability for OCD observed in these samples may indicate that interviewers observed features of both disorders in patients, but subsumed the features of one under the principal diagnosis. This interpretation is unlikely, however, given the absence of diagnostic disagreements involving principal diagnoses of OCD and GAD. Despite the phenomenological similarity between worry and obsessions, this study indicates that OCD and GAD may be reliably differentiated. Nevertheless, there remains no definitive method by which to distinguish worries from obsessions.

PDA and PTSD. Both PD with and without agoraphobia are characterized by increased autonomic arousal. Lifetime PTSD was the only anxiety or mood disorder in a large-scale comorbidity study associated with an elevated risk of PDA (relative risk [RR] = 1.53) and the presence of PDA conferred a twofold risk for PTSD (RR = 2.06; Brown, Campbell, et al., 2001). PTSD was often temporally primary to the development of PDA, suggesting that it may be conceptualized as a risk factor for the latter disorder. Extensive comorbidity between PTSD and other anxiety disorders was also observed in the National Comorbidity Survey, in which the risk of panic among individuals with PTSD was elevated (RR = 4.11; Kessler, Sonnega, Bromet, Hughes, & Nelson, 1995). The hypothesis that PTSD serves as a risk factor for panic disorder is consistent with the finding that individuals with PD experience lifetime traumatic experiences at higher rates than typically found in individuals meeting criteria for mental illness (Leskin & Sheikh, 2002; Stein et al., 1996). Furthermore, several authors have noted the phenomenologic similarities between PD and PTSD; both disorders are characterized by autonomic arousal, fear-based avoidance of situations, and may entail flashbacks, nightmares, and numbing (Davidson & Foa, 1991; Jones & Barlow, 1990). Panic attacks observed in PTSD may be conceptualized as cued versions of the uncued panic attacks that occur in PD.

Laboratory studies have also indicated similarities between PD and PTSD. Both disorders are presumed to involve an abnormality in noradrenergic pathways (Southwick et al., 1993) and individuals with both disorders exhibit a blunted adrenocorticotropic hormone (ACTH) response after administration of corticotropin-releasing hormone (Smith et al., 1989). The two disorders share both phenomenological and biological similarities, though additional research is necessary to understand the nature of their relationship.

Future Directions in Classification
Movement Toward a Dimensional Classification System

Arguments for a dimensional classification system have emerged based on limitations observed in the current nomenclature. Although the prototypical disorder categories in the *DSM* have arguably stimulated research into psychopathology and advanced our understanding of disorders, researchers have long noted the utility of a dimensional classification system (e.g., Barlow, 1988). Currently, only Axis V of the *DSM–IV*'s multiaxial system requires assessors to rate symptoms on a dimensional scale (APA, 1994). Unfortunately, this Global Assessment of Functioning (GAF) score often exhibits poor reliability (Bates, Lyons, & Shaw, 2002). Nevertheless, there are numerous arguments in favor of adopting at least some dimensional elements in *DSM–V*. The current categorical classification system increases measurement error, obscures important clinical information, implies that abnormality and normality exist on separate continua, and reflects the atheoretical approach to its development.

The limitations of the current classification system have become evident in studies of diagnostic reliability. As previously discussed, for many disorder categories (e.g., social phobia, specific phobia), diagnostic disagreements rarely involved boundary issues with other disorders, but were often due to disagreement about whether a patient's symptoms met the threshold for a formal diagnosis (Brown, Campbell, et al., 2001). Disagreements about threshold are also evident in the high rate of NOS diagnoses observed in this study. In these cases, assessors concurred that a patient's symptoms were sufficiently interfering or distressing to warrant a diagnosis, but disagreed as to whether the symptoms met formal criteria for a *DSM–IV* diagnosis. The high rates of NOS diagnoses may suggest that the *DSM–IV* does not provide adequate coverage for clinically significant symptoms that fail to meet criteria for a formal diagnosis. Unreliability was also observed in use of *DSM–IV* categorical severity specifiers (e.g., ratings of MDD as mild, moderate, or severe), although dimensional ratings of the severity of MDD symptoms were reliable ($r = .74$). A categorical diagnostic system that requires dichotomous decisions about the presence or absence of a disorder may undermine diagnostic reliability by introducing measurement error (MacCallum et al., 2003).

Some have argued that the *DSM–IV* fails to adequately distinguish between normality and abnormality. High and inconsistent prevalence rates for anxiety and mood disorders in epidemiologic studies have led some to argue that "syndromes" observed in the community likely represent transient responses to stimuli rather than true disorders (Regier et al., 1998). Others have argued against the assumption that a distinct boundary between psychopathology and normality exists, and against the utility of making a qualitative distinction between the two (e.g., O'Connor, 2002). Currently, the *DSM* does not provide a mechanism to indicate the severity of disorders (the categorical specifiers for major depressive disorder notwithstanding) or to indicate the presence of subclinical symptom manifestations. Clinicians, therefore, are asked to make a judgment about the presence or absence of clinically significantly symptoms, rather than to rate the severity of observed symptoms along a dimension.

The imposition of categories on phenomena presumed to be dimensional may result in the loss of useful clinical information. As previously discussed, *DSM–IV* hierarchy rules may lead to misleading estimates of comorbidity, particularly in cases in which symptoms of GAD occur within the context of a mood disorder (Brown, Campbell, et al., 2001). There is some evidence, for example, that individuals who experience symptoms of both MDD and GAD experience higher levels of suicidal ideation, poorer social functioning, and higher rates of comorbid anxiety, eating, and somatoform disorders than do individuals who only meet criteria for MDD (Zimmerman & Chelminski, 2003). Adherence to the hierarchy rules may obscure important information about patients' functioning and prognosis.

Other patterns of comorbidity may be artifacts of *DSM–IV* differential diagnosis rules. For example, these rules specify that social or specific fear and avoidance judged to be better accounted for by PDA should be subsumed under that diagnosis. Consequently, comorbidity studies have indicated that the presence of PDA is associated with a decreased relative risk of social phobia and specific phobia (Brown, Campbell, et al., 2001). Rather than reflecting a true lack of association between these disorders (which share several phenotypic features), this finding is a byproduct of diagnostic guidelines. Although these guidelines may serve the purpose of limiting comorbidity, they obscure clinical information that is relevant to the severity of the clinical presentation and treatment planning.

According to the *DSM–IV,* "a categorical approach to classification works best when all the members of a diagnostic class are homogenous, when there are clear boundaries between classes, and when the different classes are mutually exclusive" (APA, 1994, p. xxii). As outlined in the previous discussion of diagnostic comorbidity, there is significant overlap among mood and anxiety disorder categories in the *DSM–IV,* as well as substantial overlap between disorder features (Brown, Campbell, et al., 2001). A categorical classification system, therefore, runs counter to empirical studies indicating that *DSM–IV* diagnostic categories are not discrete entities.

Although numerous researchers have advocated moving toward a dimensional system of classification, few specific proposals have been made. Transforming the current nosology into an entirely dimensional system is clinically impractical (Brown & Barlow, 2005; First, 2005). Therefore, authors of *DSM–V* must determine how dimensional components might be incorporated in the *DSM* without compromising its clinical utility. Brown and Barlow (2005) note that the least drastic overhaul of the current system might entail adding dimensional severity ratings to extant diagnostic categories and disorder features, as in the ADIS-IV-L (Di Nardo et al., 1994). More ambitious proposals that suggest reorganizing the *DSM* around higher-order temperament and personality constructs (e.g., Clark, 2005) may more accurately reflect shared genetic and psychosocial diatheses, but be difficult to implement in clinical and research practice. The incorporation of some higher-order constructs, however, may enhance the *DSM*'s clinical utility by making it relevant for the primary and secondary prevention of mental disorders. Inclusion of these constructs would likely not replace existing disorder categories. Rather, the *DSM* might be organized hierarchically, including both higher-order trait dimensions and lower-order disorder categories.

More research is necessary to develop dimensional models of classification and psychopathology. Unfortunately, much psychopathology research is conducted by using *DSM* disorders as units of analysis. An alternate approach is to examine dimensional indicators of disorder features without consideration of *DSM* diagnostic rules. Disadvantages to this dimensional approach to psychopathology research have also been noted (Brown & Barlow, 2005). For example, dimensional approaches are typically cross-sectional in nature, precluding examination of lifetime data. They also fail to capture the functional relationships among disorder features (e.g., whether situational avoidance is due to a specific phobia, panic disorder, or OCD). Therefore, in some instances, the examination of disorders as binary units of analysis may better serve the purposes of the research.

Currently, there appears to be consensus that the *DSM* must move beyond its atheoretical approach to describing prototypes of disorders, and move toward including some dimensional components. One area in which dimensional measures might be particularly useful is in assessing the degree to which individuals exhibit higher-order features that may function as vulnerabilities for emotional disorders. Although there has been progress in specifying higher-order features underlying anxiety and mood disorders (e.g., Brown et al., 1998), more work is needed to determine how constructs like personality, temperament, and biological vulnerability may be incorporated into a coherent classification system.

Personality-Psychopathology Relationships

Studies that assess the overlap between dimensional features of disorder have enabled specification of the relationships between personality and psychopathology. As previously discussed, high rates of comorbidity suggest the presence of underlying trait vulnerabilities for anxiety and mood disorders, and research has indicated that higher-order factors like negative and positive affect confer risk for the development of certain disorders (Brown et al., 1998). Likewise, an investigation of risk factors for the development of adult externalizing disorders has indicated that a continuum of risk underlies the development of antisocial behavior and substance dependence (Krueger, Markon, Patrick, & Iacono, 2005). A similar conceptualization may be useful in understanding emotional disorders. Krueger et al. (2005) suggest that this externalizing spectrum should be explicitly included in *DSM–V.* Their hierarchical-dimensional externalizing spectrum model provides a coherent model of disorder etiology and requires reconsideration of the putative distinction between Axis I and Axis II (as the externalizing dimension transcends both of these axes).

Several models have been proposed that incorporate higher-order factors beyond negative and positive affect in explaining the etiology of the emotional disorders. Clark, Watson, and Mineka (1994) argued that personality factors are important in our understanding of emotional disorders. Although there is evidence that positive and negative affect confer risk for anxiety and mood disorders, the role

of more specific vulnerabilities (e.g., anxiety sensitivity, thought-action fusion) in the etiology of disorders remains unclear. There is some evidence, for example, to suggest that the trait dimensions of behavioral inhibition and activation may influence the severity and course of depression, with low behavioral activation levels associated with worse outcomes (Kasch, Rottenberg, Arnow, & Gotlib, 2002). Further research is necessary to determine if particular disorders are associated with specific vulnerabilities.

In addition, prospective, longitudinal studies are necessary to elucidate the directionality of relationships between vulnerability dimensions and emotional disorders. Much of the research on personality-psychopathology relationships has been conducted at the cross-sectional level, precluding an understanding of the temporal covariance between vulnerability dimensions and disorders. Longitudinal studies may also address the viability of competing accounts of personality-psychopathology relationships (e.g., do temperament dimensions function as vulnerabilities to psychopathology, or does the experience of emotional disorders result in changes in temperament?). Specification of the relationships between personality dimensions and emotional disorders may have important treatment implications. Further research is needed to examine the impact of treatment on vulnerability dimensions and to determine the influence of these dimensions on the course of disorders.

Several researchers have proposed comprehensive theories that account for personality-psychopathology relationships across anxiety and mood disorders (e.g., Clark, 2005). Although these have yet to be empirically validated, such models may help move the *DSM* toward a theoretical model of disorder etiology, an approach that was abandoned with the publication of *DSM–III.*

Summary and Conclusions

Our extant classification system is an imperfect one. Although the diagnostic categories for anxiety and mood disorders in *DSM–IV* are, for the most part, sufficiently reliable, this purely categorical system is associated with measurement error resulting in disagreements about symptom threshold, a high prevalence of NOS diagnoses, and inaccurate rates of comorbidity resulting from adherence to differential diagnosis and diagnostic hierarchy rules (Brown, Campbell, et al., 2001). There is considerable overlap among the current mood and anxiety disorder categories at both diagnostic and symptom levels, such that worry, social anxiety, neuroticism, and panic attacks are found to some degree in many emotional disorders, as well as in individuals who do not meet criteria for a mental disorder. Although latent structural analyses do not support the notion of a *general neurotic syndrome,* they do indicate that clusters of disorder are linked to higher-order traits that are presumed to be genetically conferred and temporally stable.

Findings from studies of diagnostic reliability and comorbidity, as well as heritability studies, will inform future classification systems. As previously discussed, future editions of the *DSM* will likely incorporate some dimensional elements. Not only will a dimensional system reduce measurement error associated with categorical cutoffs, but it will allow for the measurement of higher-order variables, which may include personality variables or temperament dimensions, that are associated with increased risk of mental disorders. Further research is necessary to determine whether higher-order variables like neuroticism predict vulnerability to emotional disorders better than disorder-specific constructs. Now that some higher-order dimensions have been identified, more longitudinal research is necessary to understand directional relationships between disorder constructs and vulnerability dimensions. In addition, heritability and linkage studies will inform our understanding of families of disorders that share genetic vulnerability. Ultimately, classification research will enable the development of sophisticated models that incorporate higher-order risk factors and disorder-specific vulnerabilities.

The publication of *DSM–III* marked a revolution in the classification of mental disorders. Although an atheoretical, nonempirical approach to classification has enhanced the reliability of diagnostic categories, it has met with numerous criticisms and has perhaps obscured the relationships between syndromes by sacrificing parsimony for increased differentiation of disorders. Future editions of the *DSM* may, in some respects, return to the traditions of *DSM–II* in that they will increasingly focus on the underlying vulnerabilities common to emotional disorders. In the future, however, these shared features will be empirically derived and likely result in a *DSM* that organizes disorders and their risk factors in a comprehensive hierarchical model.

References

American Psychiatric Association. (1980). *Diagnostic and statistical manual of mental disorders* (3rd ed.). Washington, DC: Author.

American Psychiatric Association. (1994). *Diagnostic and statistical manual of mental disorders* (4th ed.). Washington, DC: Author.

Andrews, G. (1996). Comorbidity in neurotic disorders: The similarities are more important than the differences. In R. M. Rapee (Ed.), *Current controversies in the anxiety disorders* (pp. 3–20). New York: Guilford Press.

Andrews, G., Stewart, G., Morris-Yates, A., Holt, P., & Henderson, A. S. (1990). Evidence for a general neurotic syndrome. *British Journal of Psychiatry, 157,* 6–12.

Barlow, D. H. (1988). *Anxiety and its disorders: The nature and treatment of anxiety and panic.* New York: Guilford.

Barlow, D. H. (2000). Unraveling the mysteries of anxiety and its disorders from the perspective of emotion theory. *American Psychologist, 55,* 1247–1263.

Bates, L. W., Lyons, J. A., & Shaw, J. B. (2002). Effect of brief training on application of the global assessment of functioning scale. *Psychological Reports, 91,* 999–1006.

Brown, T. A., Antony, M. M., & Barlow, D. H. (1995). Diagnostic comorbidity in panic disorder: Effect on treatment outcome and course of comorbid diagnoses following treatment. *Journal of Consulting and Clinical Psychology, 63,* 408–418.

Brown, T. A., & Barlow, D. H. (1992). Comorbidity among anxiety disorders: Implications for treatment and *DSM–IV. Journal of Consulting and Clinical Psychology, 60,* 835–844.

Brown, T. A., & Barlow, D. H. (1995). Long-term outcome in cognitive-behavioral treatment of panic disorder: Clinical predictors and alternative strategies for assessment. *Journal of Consulting and Clinical Psychology, 63,* 754–765.

Brown, T. A., & Barlow, D. H. (2005). Dimensional versus categorical classification of mental disorders in the fifth edition of the *Diagnostic and statistical manual of mental disorders and beyond:* Comment on the special section. *Journal of Abnormal Psychology, 114,* 551–556.

Brown, T. A., Barlow, D. H., & Liebowitz, M. R. (1994). The empirical basis of generalized anxiety disorder. *American Journal of Psychiatry, 151,* 1272–1280.

Brown, T. A., Campbell, L. A., Lehman, C. L., Grisham, J. R., & Mancill, R. B. (2001). Current and lifetime comorbidity of the *DSM–IV* anxiety and mood disorders in a large clinical sample. *Journal of Abnormal Psychology, 110,* 49–58.

Brown, T. A., Chorpita, B. F., & Barlow, D. H. (1998). Structural relationships among dimensions of the *DSM–IV* anxiety and mood disorders and dimensions of negative affect, positive affect, and autonomic arousal. *Journal of Abnormal Psychology, 107,* 179–192.

Brown, T. A., Di Nardo, P. A., Lehman, C. L., & Campbell, L. A. (2001). Reliability of *DSM–IV* anxiety and mood disorders: Implications for classification of emotional disorders. *Journal of Abnormal Psychology, 110,* 49–58.

Brown, T. A., Moras, K., Zinbarg, R. E., & Barlow, D. H. (1993). Diagnostic and symptom distinguishability of generalized anxiety disorder and obsessive-compulsive disorder. *Behavior Therapy, 24,* 227–240.

Bruder, G. E., Fong, R., Tenke, C. E., Leite, P., Towey, J. P., Stewart, J. E., et al. (1997). Regional brain asymmetries in major depression with and without an anxiety disorder: A quantitative electroencephalographic study. *Biological Psychiatry,* 939–948.

Chorpita, B. F., Albano, A. M., & Barlow, D. H. (1998). The structure of negative emotions in a clinical sample of children and adolescents. *Journal of Abnormal Psychology, 107,* 74–85.

Clark, L. A. (2005). Temperament as a unifying basis for personality and psychopathology. *Journal of Abnormal Psychology, 114*, 505–521.

Clark, L. A., & Watson, D. (1991). Tripartite model of anxiety and depression: Psychometric evidence and taxometric implications. *Journal of Abnormal Psychology, 100*, 316–336.

Clark, L. A., Watson, D., & Mineka, S. (1994). Temperament, personality, and the mood and anxiety disorders. *Journal of Abnormal Psychology, 103*, 103–116.

Coles, M. E., Mennin, D. S., & Heimberg, R. G. (2001). Distinguishing obsessive features and worries: The role of thought-action fusion. *Behaviour Research and Therapy, 39*, 947–959.

Craske, M. G., Rapee, R. M., Jackel, L., & Barlow, D. H. (1989). Qualitative dimensions of worry in *DSM–III–R* generalized anxiety disorder subjects and nonanxious controls. *Behavior Research and Therapy, 27*, 397–402.

Crino, R. D., & Andrews, D. (1996). Obsessive-compulsive disorder and Axis I comorbidity. *Journal of Anxiety Disorders, 10*, 37–46.

Davidson, J.T.R., & Foa, E. B. (1991). Diagnostic issues in posttraumatic stress disorder: Considerations for *DSM–IV*. *Journal of Abnormal Psychology, 100*, 346–355.

Di Nardo, P. A., Brown, T. A., & Barlow, D. H. (1994). *Anxiety Disorders Interview Schedule for DSM–IV: Lifetime Version (ADIS-IV-L)*. New York: Oxford University Press.

Di Nardo, P. A., Moras, K., Barlow, D. H., Rapee, R. M., & Brown, T. A. (1993). Reliability of *DSM–III–R* disorder categories using the Anxiety Disorders Interview Schedule—Revised (ADIS-R). *Archives of General Psychiatry, 40*, 1070–1074.

Eley, T. C., & Brown, T. A. (2008). *Phenotypic and genetic/environmental structure of anxiety and depressive disorder symptoms in adolescence*. Manuscript submitted for publication.

First, M. B. (2005). Clinical utility: A prerequisite for the adoption of a dimensional approach in *DSM*. *Journal of Abnormal Psychology, 114*, 560–564.

First, M. B., Spitzer, R. L., Gibbon, M., & Williams, J. B. W. (1997). *Structured Clinical Interview for DSM–IV Axis I Disorders (SCID-I): Clinical version*. Washington, DC: American Psychiatric Press.

Fleiss, J. L., Nee, J.C.M., & Landis, J. R. (1979). Large sample variance of kappa in the case of different sets of raters. *Psychological Bulletin, 86*, 974–977.

Hettema, J. M., Neale, M. C., & Kendler, K. S. (2001). A review and meta-analysis of the genetic epidemiology of anxiety disorders. *Archives of General Psychiatry, 158*, 1568–1578.

Hettema, J. M., Prescott, C. A., & Kendler, K. S. (2004). Genetic and environmental sources of covariation between generalized anxiety disorder and neuroticism. *Archives of General Psychiatry, 161*, 1581–1587.

Hettema, J. M., Prescott, C. A., Myers, J. M., Neale, M. C., & Kendler, K. S. (2005). The structure of genetic and environmental risk factors for anxiety disorders in men and women. *Archives of General Psychiatry, 62*, 182–188.

Holt, C. S., Heimberg, R. G., & Hope, D. A. (1992). Avoidant personality disorder and the generalized subtype of social phobia. *Journal of Abnormal Psychology, 101*, 318–325.

Hudson, J. I., & Pope, H. G. (1990). Affective spectrum disorder: Does antidepressant response identify a family of disorders with a common pathophysiology? *American Journal of Psychiatry, 147*, 552–564.

Joiner, T. E., Jr. (1996). A confirmatory factor analytic investigation of the tripartite model of depression and anxiety in college students. *Cognitive Therapy and Research, 20*, 521–539.

Jones, J. C., & Barlow, D. H. (1990). The etiology of posttraumatic stress disorder. *Clinical Psychology Review, 10*, 299–328.

Kasch, K. L., Rottenberg, J., Arnow, B. A., & Gotlib, I. H. (2002). Behavioral activation and inhibition systems in the severity and course of depression. *Journal of Abnormal Psychology, 111*, 589–597.

Kendler, K. S., Prescott, C. A., Myers, J., & Neale, M. C. (2003). The structure of genetic and environmental risk factors for common psychiatric and substance use disorders in men and women. *Archives of General Psychiatry, 60*, 929–937.

Kessler, R. C., Chiu, W. T., Demler, O., & Walters, E. E. (2005). Prevalence, severity, and comorbidity of 12-month *DSM–IV* disorders in the National Comorbidity Survey replication. *Archives of General Psychiatry, 62*, 617–627.

Kessler, R. C., Sonnega, A., Bromet, E., Hughes, M., & Nelson, C. B. (1995). Posttraumatic stress disorder in the National Comorbidity Survey. *Archives of General Psychiatry, 52*, 1048–1060.

Kessler, R. C., Stang, P., Wittchen, H.-U., Stein, M., & Walters, E. E. (1999). Lifetime co-morbidities between social phobia and mood disorders in the U.S. National Comorbidity Survey. *Psychological Medicine, 29*, 555–567.

Krueger, R. F., Markon, K. E., Patrick, C. J., & Iacono, W. G. (2005). Externalizing psychopathology in adulthood: A dimensional-spectrum conceptualization and its implications for *DSM–V*. *Journal of Abnormal Psychology, 114*, 537–550.

Langlois, F., Freeston, M. H., & Ladouceur, R. (2000). Differences and similarities between obsessive intrusive thoughts and worry in a non-clinical population: Study 1. *Behaviour Research and Therapy, 38*, 157–173.

Leskin, G. A., & Sheikh, J. I. (2002). Lifetime trauma history and panic disorder: Findings from the National Comorbidity Survey. *Journal of Anxiety Disorders, 16*, 599–603.

MacCallum, R. C., Zhang, S., & Preacher, K. J. (2003). On the practice of dichotomization of quantitative variables. *Psychological Methods, 7*, 19–40.

Mineka, S., Watson, D., & Clark, L. A. (1998). Comorbidity of anxiety and unipolar mood disorders. *Annual Review of Psychology, 49*, 377–412.

O'Connor, B. P. (2002). The search for dimensional structure differences between normality and abnormality: A statistical review of published data on personality and psychopathology. *Journal of Personality and Social Psychology, 83*, 962–982.

Rachman, S. J. (1973). Some similarities and differences between obsessional ruminations and morbid preoccupations. *Canadian Psychiatric Association Journal, 18*, 71–74.

Rachman, S. J. (1993). Obsessions, responsibility and guilt. *Behaviour Research and Therapy, 31*, 149–154.

Regier, D. A., Kaelber, C. T., Rae, D. S., Farmer, M. E., Knauper, B., Kessler, R. C., et al. (1998). Limitations of diagnostic criteria and assessment instruments for mental disorders. *Archives of General Psychiatry, 55*, 109–115.

Sanderson, W. C., Di Nardo, P. A., Rapee, R. M., & Barlow, D. H. (1990). Syndrome comorbidity in patients diagnosed with a *DSM–III–R* anxiety disorder. *Journal of Abnormal Psychology, 99*, 308–312.

Smith, M. A., Davidson, J., Ritchie, J. C., Kudler, H., Lipper, S., Chappell, P., et al. (1989). The corticotropin-releasing hormone test in patients with posttraumatic stress disorder. *Biological Psychiatry, 26*, 349–355.

Southwick, S. M., Krystal, T. A., Morgan, C. A., Johnson, D., Nagy, L. M., Nicolaou, A., et al. (1993). Abnormal noradrenergic function in posttraumatic stress disorder. *Archives of General Psychiatry, 50,* 266–274.

Stein, M. B., Walker, J. R., Anderson, G., Hazen, A. L., Ross, C. A., Eldridge, G., et al. (1996). Childhood physical and sexual abuse in patients with anxiety disorders in a community sample. *American Journal of Psychiatry, 153,* 275–277.

Steketee, G., & Barlow, D. H. (2002). Obsessive-compulsive disorder. In D. H. Barlow (Ed.), *Anxiety and its disorders: The nature and treatment of anxiety and panic* (pp. 516–550). New York: Guilford Press.

Tellegen, A. (1985). Structures of mood and personality and their relevance to assessing anxiety, with an emphasis on self-report. In A. H. Tuma & J. D. Maser (Eds.), *Anxiety and the anxiety disorders* (pp. 681–706). Hillsdale, NJ: Erlbaum.

Thorgeirsson, T. E., Oskarsson, H., Desnica, N., Kostic, J. P., Stefansson, J. G., Kolbeinsson, H., et al. (2003). Anxiety with panic disorder linked to chromosome 9q in Iceland. *American Journal of Human Genetics, 72,* 1221–1230.

Turner, S. M., Beidel, D. C., & Stanley, M. A. (1992). Are obsessional thoughts and worry different cognitive phenomena? *Clinical Psychology Review, 12,* 257–270.

Turner, S. M., Beidel, D. C., & Townsley, R. M. (1992). Social phobia: A comparison of specific and generalized subtypes and avoidant personality disorder. *Journal of Abnormal Psychology, 101,* 326–332.

Waller, N. G., & Meehl, P. E. (1997). *Multivariate taxometric procedures: Distinguishing types from continua.* Newbury Park, CA: Sage.

Watson, D., Clark, L. A., & Harkness, A. R. (1994). Structures of personality and their relevance to psychopathology. *Journal of Abnormal Psychology, 103,* 18–31.

Watson, D., Weber, K., Assenheimer, J. S., Clark, L. A., Strauss, M. E., & McCormick, R. A. (1995). Testing a tripartite model: I. Evaluating the convergent and discriminant validity of anxiety and depression symptom scales. *Journal of Abnormal Psychology, 104,* 3–14.

Wittchen, H.-U., Zhao, S., Kessler, R. C., & Eaton, W. W. (1994). *DSM–III–R* generalized anxiety disorder in the National Comorbidity Survey. *Archives of General Psychiatry, 51,* 355–364.

Zimmerman, M., & Chelminski, I. (2003). Generalized anxiety disorder in patients with major depression: Is *DSM–IV*'s hierarchy correct? *American Journal of Psychiatry, 160,* 504–512.

Assessment of Anxiety Disorders

Jennifer L. Harrington *and* Martin M. Antony

Abstract

Psychological assessment of anxiety disorders is important in both clinical and research settings. This chapter reviews the various purposes of assessment, discusses issues related to diagnostic assessment, and highlights other areas that are relevant in the evaluation process (e.g., anxiety triggers, avoidance behavior, interference, psychosocial influences, etc.). A variety of assessment methods is discussed, including clinical interviews, behavioral tests, psychophysiological measurement, and behavioral diaries, and the use of multimethod assessment strategies is encouraged. A brief overview of empirically supported assessment measures is also provided.

Keywords: anxiety disorders, assessment, clinical interview, evaluation, inventory, measures, multi-method assessment, psychological assessment, triggers

A thorough assessment is a crucial component in treatment planning and empirical research in the area of anxiety disorders. The purposes of assessment are multifold and have been summarized by Antony (2002; see also Antony & Rowa, 2005; Antony & Swinson, 2000; Ey & Hersen, 2004). They include:

- Establishing the predominant diagnosis and ruling out alternative diagnoses
- Evaluating symptom severity and associated features (e.g., comorbid conditions)
- Case conceptualization and treatment planning
- Selecting participants for inclusion/exclusion in a research study
- Measurement of treatment outcomes
- Program evaluation

Selection of assessment instruments should depend on the purpose of the assessment as well as the context in which the evaluation is to occur. Given the many functions of assessment, practitioners and researchers should carefully consider their primary goals before embarking on the evaluation process. There are a number of different methods that can be used in assessment, each with its own strengths and weaknesses. Logistical issues, such as time constraints and financial resources, will likely play a role in determining which methods are employed, as well as the scope of the assessment. This chapter provides an overview of the assessment process, including available methods, important areas to investigate, and a brief review of empirically validated measures.

Diagnostic Assessment

The first appointment (or several appointments) with a patient usually focus on assessment. Assessments typically begin quite broadly and become more focused as hypotheses about the presenting problem emerge. For example, a patient may complain about feeling anxious in general; however, as information is obtained it may become apparent that the most important concern stems from recurrent unexpected panic attacks. With this information in hand, the diagnostician may choose to employ several additional measures that are more specific to panic-related phenomena (e.g., a self-report measure of anxiety sensitivity, which tends to be elevated in panic disorder). Supplemental measures will serve to validate the diagnosis and facilitate the creation of a comprehensive treatment plan.

Establishing a Diagnosis

Although the diagnostic process can be clear-cut, it is often the case that some careful detective work is needed to determine the nature of the presenting problem. Assessment of anxiety disorders presents a unique challenge to the diagnostician, as these disorders share many common features and are often comorbid with each other and with other psychological disorders. For instance, Rodriguez and colleagues (2004) found that more than 79% of individuals with an anxiety disorder reported symptoms meeting criteria for another Axis I disorder. Furthermore, more than 60% of their sample had more than one anxiety disorder, and more than 40% received a comorbid diagnosis of major depressive disorder. These results were consistent with those of Brown, O'Leary, & Barlow (2001) who also found the co-occurrence of anxiety and mood disorders to be high. Within the anxiety disorders, comorbidity is certainly the rule rather than the exception.

Given the high rates of comorbidity, differential diagnosis becomes an imperative part of psychological evaluation. Treatment decisions often rest on the accuracy of a diagnosis; therefore, clinicians need to exert care when synthesizing information from the assessment. Discriminating between disorders can certainly be a difficult task. For instance, although panic attacks are the hallmark feature of panic disorder, they also occur within the context of other anxiety disorders. For example, it is not uncommon for individuals with social phobia to panic when confronted with a feared performance situation. Similarly, an individual with a specific phobia may experience an acute rise in anxiety after encountering a feared stimulus (e.g., dog, airplane, etc.). In fact, Barlow (2002) noted that 73% of individuals diagnosed with generalized anxiety disorder (GAD) experience occasional panic attacks. A thorough understanding of the phenomenology of the anxiety disorders and diagnostic criteria is necessary to ensure well-informed and accurate diagnoses.

The above discussion highlights the fact that anxiety disorders usually do not occur in isolation, but typically present with at least one other psychological condition. These high rates of comorbidity have a number of important implications. First, comorbidity is associated with higher levels of subjective distress, greater impairment in social and occupational functioning, more severe symptoms, and an increased risk of suicide (Rosenbaum, Pollack, & Pollack, 1996). Second, the clinician is faced with the difficult task of identifying the *predominant* or *principal* disorder—often the one that should be treated first. Antony and Swinson (2000) suggest that selection of the predominant disorder should take into account both the patient's preferences regarding which problem to work on, as well as the clinician's judgment regarding which problem is the most distressing and impairing.

Additional factors to consider when dealing with comorbidity include the likelihood that a particular problem will respond to therapy, and the impact a potential intervention might have on comorbid diagnoses. Indeed, some research indicates that treatment for a particular condition may also decrease comorbid symptoms. For example, studies have consistently shown that treatment designed to target panic disorder also leads to reductions in comorbid problems (Brown, Antony, & Barlow, 1995; Craske et al., 2007; Tsao, Mystkowski, Zucker, & Craske, 2005).

After determining the predominant diagnosis, it is important to evaluate other symptoms that could potentially interfere with a particular therapeutic intervention. More specifically, standard treatment protocols may need to be adjusted given the co-occurrence of other psychological conditions. For instance, individuals with diagnoses of social phobia and panic disorder might experience panic attacks when exposed to feared social situations. Treatment for social anxiety may be compromised if the individual is not willing to engage in exposure exercises for fear of panicking. Consequently, it may be beneficial to offer treatment for both disorders concurrently. Additionally, the presence of a major depressive episode could potentially interfere with treatment, as severe depressive symptoms may limit an individual's ability to fully engage and participate in therapy. Therefore, in some cases it may be advisable to begin with treatment of the depressive disorder. Furthermore, if depression is a concern, clinicians should be vigilant for symptom exacerbation and monitor the course of depression throughout the treatment of the anxiety disorder.

There is some research to suggest that comorbidity can potentially affect treatment efficacy. Several studies have demonstrated that comorbidity has an adverse effect on treatment outcomes. For instance, Steketee, Chambless, and Tran (2001) found an association between comorbid depression and poorer treatment outcome for individuals diagnosed with obsessive-compulsive disorder (OCD) or panic disorder. Conversely, other studies have not found such a relationship (e.g., Joorman, Kosfelder, & Schulte, 2005; McLean, Woody, Taylor, & Koch, 1998). In fact, research has demonstrated that individuals with alcohol dependence benefit from treatment targeting comorbid anxiety symptoms, and this finding held true even for individuals who were more severely addicted to alcohol (Schadé et al., 2007). The effect of comorbidity on treatment outcome has not been a large focus of research attention, and more work is needed before firm conclusions can be drawn. Nonetheless, a thorough assessment should document the existence of comorbid diagnoses. At the very least this will provide qualitative information regarding potential issues that could arise during treatment.

Clinical Interviews

The clinical interview is probably the most commonly used method of assessment in clinical practice, and is typically the first interaction with a patient. This component of the assessment may also be a patient's first experience with a mental health professional. Consequently, many patients approach the first appointment with significant apprehension and unease. In most cases the patient's apprehension will be reduced if the clinician spends the initial portion of the session establishing rapport and developing trust. Once the patient feels more comfortable, he or she will typically be more amenable to discussing personally relevant topics. However, it is important to bear in mind that the assessment itself can be a fear trigger for some patients. People with social phobia often fear interviews in general, and individuals with other anxiety disorders often avoid discussing the situations they fear. For example, people with spider phobias may not be able to say the word *spider*, and people with posttraumatic stress disorder (PTSD) may be unable to discuss their trauma history. Other patients may be embarrassed by their symptoms. For example, individuals with obsessive-compulsive disorder may conceal their repugnant thoughts for fear that they will be perceived as weird or crazy (Newth & Rachman, 2001). Of course, it is important to discuss such information in order to develop an appropriate treatment plan. Providing patients with some general information about the function of assessment and the therapeutic value of discussing fears can often help overcome such barriers (McCabe & Antony, 2002).

In clinical practice, clinicians often rely on unstructured interview formats, despite evidence suggesting that unstructured interviews are considerably less reliable than semistructured interviews (e.g., Miller, 2001; Miller, Dasher, Collins, Griffiths, & Brown, 2001). Fortunately, there has been an increased focus on the development of psychometrically sound assessment tools. A number of structured and semistructured interviews are now available with demonstrated psychometric properties. Indeed, structured and semistructured interviews have become the gold-standard method of assessment in research settings, and are becoming increasingly common in empirically based clinical practices (Summerfeldt & Antony, 2002).

Structured and semistructured interviews are designed with the primary purpose of reducing the sources of variability that contribute to poor diagnostic reliability. Fully structured interviews reduce variability through the inclusion of detailed questions in a standardized format. They are used primarily in epidemiological research, where it is common to use trained lay interviewers, and it is therefore essential that all questions be asked in a standardized manner. By standardizing procedures, structured interviews ensure that assessments are consistent across interviewers and that important diagnostic criteria are not overlooked. Structured interviews provide clinicians with a series of questions regarding specific diagnoses of interest. Typically each section of the interview begins with a general probe, and if the patient responds affirmatively, more detailed questions are asked until a diagnosis has been established, or until it is clear that a diagnostic criterion has *not* been met.

Semistructured interviews are similar to structured interviews, except that they allow the interviewer to follow up responses with additional questions and to provide clarification to the patient. In clinical research settings, as well as some clinical practices, semistructured interviews are commonly used. For a review of issues related to structured and semistructured interviews the interested reader should consult Summerfeldt & Antony (2002).

The Structured Diagnostic Interview for *DSM–IV* (SCID-IV) (First, Spitzer, Gibbon, & Williams,

1996) and the Anxiety Disorders Interview Schedule for *DSM–IV* (ADIS-IV) (Brown, Di Nardo, & Barlow, 1994) are the most widely used semi-structured diagnostic interviews among clinical researchers in the area of anxiety disorders (Antony & Swinson, 2000). The SCID-IV and ADIS-IV are both based on the most recent diagnostic criteria, and they provide a solid foundation by which to assess anxiety disorders as well as other associated conditions (e.g., mood disorders, somatoform disorders, eating disorders, substance use disorders, and psychotic disorders). Space limitations preclude a more complete discussion of these instruments and other structured and semistructured interviews; however, other sources have described these in more detail (e.g., Summerfeldt & Antony, 2002).

It is recommended that clinicians and researchers employ structured and semistructured interviews whenever possible. However, this may not always be feasible given that several hours are often needed for administration. If an unstructured interview is employed, it is advisable to complete the evaluation as systematically as possible. Additionally, the assessment should tap into a number of different domains, which are discussed below.

Domains of Assessment
Development and Course

Information pertaining to a disorder's development can often be beneficial to case conceptualization and treatment planning. Knowing how a disorder began can alert clinicians to thoughts and behaviors that are relevant to symptom maintenance (Antony & Swinson, 2000). For instance, social phobia has been associated with a history of teasing (McCabe, Antony, Summerfeldt, Liss, & Swinson, 2003). Early experiences of this nature may contribute to the development of maladaptive beliefs (e.g., "People will make fun of me") that may need to be targeted during cognitive behavioral treatment. During the assessment process the patient should be asked about the psychosocial environment at the time of symptom onset (e.g., stressors, traumatic events). Additionally, it is often useful to inquire about other developmental factors such as temperament and early parenting. Indeed, understanding the context in which the fear originated is often paramount to the development of an effective treatment plan (Antony & Rowa, 2005).

In addition to obtaining information about symptom onset and development, it is also useful to understand the natural course of the disorder. That is, have symptoms waxed and waned or have

they been relatively stable and consistent over time? If symptoms have been consistent throughout the course of the disorder, it is more likely that any changes seen during treatment can be attributed to the intervention. However, it is not wise to make such assumptions, particularly when a patient's symptoms naturally tend to ebb and flow. In fact, it may be advisable to follow-up and more closely monitor patients who present with symptomatology that varies over time.

Cognitive Components

Cognitive interventions for anxiety disorders focus on changing maladaptive thinking patterns (e.g., beliefs, interpretations, assumptions). Therefore, assessment of cognitions is essential when using these strategies for treating anxiety. Most cognitive behavioral models of emotional disorders emphasize the role of cognitions in symptom maintenance. In fact, cognitive restructuring is a core component of treatment protocols for panic disorder (Craske & Barlow, 2001), GAD (Brown et al., 2001) and social phobia (Turk, Heimberg, & Hope, 2001). Thus, knowledge of a patient's thoughts is very important when devising a treatment plan, and can also inform diagnosis. For instance, an individual may report that he or she is extremely fearful of dogs. Although this statement might initially alert the clinician to the possible existence of a dog phobia, inquiring about underlying thoughts and fears may reveal that the true concern stems from worries about contamination (e.g., dirt, germs), and a possible diagnosis of OCD.

There are several different methods for obtaining information regarding thoughts and beliefs. General questioning during the interview process can often lead to fruitful information. However, it may also be worthwhile to employ monitoring diaries and standard assessment scales.

Anxiety Cues and Triggers

In order to ascertain the nature of the presenting problem, diagnosticians need to determine the antecedents or triggers that provoke an anxiety response. Antecedents can take on a number of different forms. For instance, an individual with contamination concerns may experience anxiety when confronted with stimuli (e.g., doorknobs) that are perceived to be dirty or contaminated. Other individuals may become anxious when in particular situations (e.g., a socially anxious person may have difficulty in dating situations). Furthermore, unusual sensations (e.g., elevated heart rate) can also precipitate anxiety, particularly for those who suffer from panic disorder. General interviewing, as well as monitoring diaries, are helpful for eliciting information of this nature.

Avoidance Behaviors

Avoidance is a common feature of the anxiety disorders. Most individuals who struggle with anxiety describe problems with avoidance behavior and apprehension. Although situational avoidance is perhaps the most obvious form of avoidance, it is important to acknowledge that individuals may also attempt to avoid particular experiences, such as thoughts, images, and physiological symptoms. For instance, individuals with OCD may attempt to suppress their intrusive thoughts (cognitive avoidance). Similarly, individuals with panic disorder may report avoidance of particular substances (e.g., caffeine) or activities (e.g., exercise) that could produce physical sensations reminiscent of panic attacks (interoceptive avoidance).

Determining the pattern and scope of avoidance behavior is important for several reasons. First, it provides useful information regarding an individual's current level of functioning and the interference created by the symptoms. Secondly, exposure-based techniques are an essential feature of most cognitive behavioral interventions; thus, information pertaining to avoidance is useful in developing a comprehensive treatment plan and selecting appropriate exposure exercises. Finally, change in avoidance behaviors can be a useful index of treatment outcome.

Although avoidance behavior can be readily apparent (e.g., the explicit refusal to enter a situation), individuals may also engage in more subtle forms of avoidance or safety behaviors. Broadly speaking, safety behaviors (sometimes referred to as overprotective behaviors) are actions (typically more subtle than complete avoidance or escape from a situation) that an individual uses to alleviate feelings of anxiety or to reduce the likelihood of having a negative outcome occur. Antony and Swinson (2000) suggest several useful probes that can be helpful in identifying such strategies (e.g., "Are there things that you do or items that you carry with you to feel more comfortable when you are in the situation?").

It is also important to inquire about behaviors an individual might engage in *after* contact with a feared situation or stimulus to ameliorate the anxiety. The compulsions that characterize OCD are an example of a behavior that would fall under this category (e.g., excessive hand-washing, repeatedly checking locks, doors, and appliances). However, compulsion-like behaviors are not restricted to OCD. For instance, individuals with GAD might exhibit similar sorts of behaviors (e.g., reassurance seeking, calling loved ones excessively) in response to their worries (Campbell & Brown, 2002).

The ADIS-IV (Brown et al., 1994; Di Nardo, Brown, & Barlow, 1994) is a particularly useful tool for evaluating avoidance and apprehensive behaviors, as it provides a number of checklists of commonly avoided situations for the various anxiety disorders. The clinician inquires about each of these situations to determine the scope and severity of avoidance behavior. Additional information can be obtained through other standardized assessment instruments.

Skills Deficits

Some individuals with anxiety disorders may display skills deficits. This is particularly true for social phobia, as a number of studies have documented that this diagnosis is associated with poorer social performance (e.g., Baker & Edelmann, 2002; Fydrich, Chambless, Perry, Buergener, & Beazley, 1998). Specific phobias may also be associated with skills deficits. For instance, if an individual has avoided certain situations for many years (e.g., swimming, driving) his or her ability to participate in these activities may be compromised. The impact of skills deficits on treatment has not been the focus of much empirical work (Antony & Rowa, 2005); however, there are some data to suggest that the addition of social skills training to cognitive behavioral therapy for social anxiety disorder is beneficial (Herbert et al., 2005).

Physical Sensations and Anxiety Sensitivity

Anxiety sensitivity refers to the belief that anxiety symptoms are dangerous (Reiss, Peterson, Gursky, & McNally, 1986). This construct is thought to contribute to the maintenance of certain phobic disorders and has been shown to be a risk factor for the development of panic disorder (Schmidt, Lerew, & Jackson, 1999). Although anxiety sensitivity is most strongly associated with panic disorder, individuals with other anxiety disorders (e.g., social phobia, PTSD, certain situational phobias) also describe fear over physical symptoms. Therefore, a comprehensive assessment should consider a patient's physiological reaction and his or her beliefs about physical sensations of arousal, especially in the context of exposure to feared stimuli.

As noted earlier, individuals with a diagnosis of panic disorder are typically very fearful of the physical sensations associated with their anxiety (e.g., racing heart, shortness of breath); indeed, knowledge of a patient's response to physical sensations can be beneficial to treatment planning. For instance, interoceptive exposure exercises that target feared sensations have been shown to have a positive impact on treatment outcomes for panic disorder (e.g., Beck, Shipherd, & Zebb, 1997; Griez & van den Hout, 1986).

Fear of physical sensations is not restricted to panic disorder, but rather can occur across the anxiety disorders. For example, individuals with social phobia are often concerned that their physical symptoms (e.g., shaking, blushing, sweating) will be readily apparent to others. Standard cognitive behavioral therapy for social anxiety augmented by interoceptive exposure exercises may be particularly useful for individuals who report these concerns, though this hypothesis remains to be studied. Additionally, certain situational phobias (e.g., claustrophobia) appear to be associated with increased sensitivity to interoceptive cues (Craske & Sipsas, 1992). Individuals with other phobias, such as fears of vomiting and choking, may also be hypervigilant for changes in their physiology.

In addition to the acute episodes of panic, more chronic physical symptoms are also associated with the anxiety disorders. For instance, symptoms such as muscle tension and restlessness are core diagnostic features of GAD. Similarly, to receive a diagnosis of PTSD, an individual must endorse persistent symptoms of increased arousal. Evaluation of physical symptoms, including those related to panic and those related to more generalized arousal and anxiety, is useful for assessing treatment outcome.

Treatment History

It is often useful to ask patients about their previous treatment attempts. Identifying the types of interventions that have worked in the past can be useful for determining what strategies might prove to be beneficial at the present time. However, it is important to recognize that previous interventions may not have been delivered competently, at an effective dosage, or for an adequate duration. Furthermore, determining why a treatment did not work in the past can provide insight into potential problems that may arise during therapy. For instance, if a patient reports a history of treatment noncompliance, it may be necessary to determine the reasons for this so treatment can be adjusted accordingly (e.g., incorporating motivational interviewing, proceeding at a slower pace).

Information regarding past treatment can be obtained through general questioning. Additionally, Steketee and colleagues (1997) have developed an interview measure to determine the frequency and types of treatment (e.g., pharmacotherapy, relaxation training, behavior therapy, cognitive therapy, supportive therapy, and psychodynamic therapy) that a patient has previously received.

Interference

Research has consistently supported the notion that anxiety disorders have a negative impact on an individual's quality of life (Kessler et al., 1994; Rapaport, Clary, Fayyad, & Endicott, 2005). To date, most research on assessment has tended to focus on symptomatology, with much less emphasis on broader areas of functioning (Antony & Rowa, 2005). However, in recent years clinical researchers have become increasingly interested in the impact of anxiety on overall functioning. For instance, in a study examining the impact of psychiatric problems on health-related quality of life, Saarni and colleagues (2007) found that anxiety disorders were associated with significant losses to quality of life—this was particularly true for social phobia and GAD. In fact, the study's data indicated that individuals with GAD experience similar decrements to their health-related quality of life as individuals who are much older and suffering from chronic health problems (e.g., Parkinson's disease, cardiac disease). This finding replicates earlier findings by Antony and colleagues (1998) that individuals with OCD, social phobia, and panic disorder report higher levels of impairment in comparison to individuals with certain chronic medical conditions (e.g., multiple sclerosis). Although these results may reflect a tendency for anxiety patients to exhibit negative reporting biases, at the very least, the results speak to the distress that is associated with these disorders.

To fully determine the functional impact of an anxiety disorder, it is useful to ask questions that address various life areas including relationships, work, leisure activities, social contact, health habits, and any other areas that seem pertinent (Antony & Swinson, 2000). Furthermore, the clinician should inquire about how the patient's current functioning differs from his or her premorbid level of functioning. Improvements in functional impairment and quality of life are important markers of treatment outcome.

Psychosocial Environment

In addition to considering the impact of anxiety disorders on an individual's life, it is important to determine the impact of an individual's anxiety on his or her family (or other important people in the person's life), as well as the extent to which others contribute to the individual's anxiety through accommodation (i.e., helping the individual to avoid or feel safer in feared situations). Examples of accommodation by family members include taking on the grocery shopping for someone with agoraphobia, or washing hands frequently to avoid "contaminating" a loved one who has OCD and fears contamination. Calvocoressi and colleagues (1995) found that accommodation by family members is common in OCD. Furthermore, accommodation is associated with poorer family functioning and appears to be negatively correlated with treatment outcomes (for review, see Steketee & Pruyn, 1998).

Antony and Rowa (2005) discussed how patterns of reinforcement in an individual's environment may perpetuate anxiety symptoms over time. For example, an individual may receive attention and comfort when communicating feelings of anxiety or distress. Similarly, individuals who are excessively clean and organized may receive compliments and accolades for these behaviors. Reinforcement for anxiety-based behaviors may need to be addressed during cognitive behavioral treatment, so it is valuable to assess for these behaviors.

Finally, it is useful to assess for the presence of a support network. Support persons can aid in the treatment process by assisting with exposure exercises (e.g., obtaining materials for exposures, accompanying family members or friends on difficult tasks, modeling nonanxious responses). However, it is important to bear in mind that having an anxiety disorder is often associated with poor social support (e.g., Cramer, Torgersen, & Kringlen, 2005; Kotler, Iancu, Efroni, & Amir, 2001; La Greca & Lopez, 1998), and establishing a support system may be an important treatment goal.

Medical Background

It is important for clinicians to consider the patient's health history and physical status, because anxiety disorders occur frequently in certain medical populations. For instance, asthma is a risk factor for the development of panic disorder (see Carr, 1998, for review), and individuals with anxiety disorders visit their physicians more frequently and report more physical complaints and symptoms than individuals without anxiety disorders (Kroenke, Spitzer, Williams, Monahan, & Lowe, 2007; Katon, Lin, & Kroenke, 2007). A more thorough discussion on comorbidity between the anxiety disorders and physical conditions is available in Chapter 46.

Obtaining medical information is also important to the process of differential diagnosis because certain physical conditions can masquerade as psychological disorders. It is generally recommended that a thorough medical history be taken to determine whether there is any reason to suspect a physical explanation for a patient's symptoms. Medical evaluation is particularly important in the case of panic disorder, as a number of physical conditions can mimic panic symptomatology (e.g., endocrine disorders, hypoglycemia, cardiovascular disease, respiratory disorders, temporal lobe epilepsy, vestibular disorders, and neurological disorders). However, the existence of an underlying medical condition *does not* preclude the diagnosis of an anxiety disorder. For instance, certain physical conditions might predispose individuals to experience panic attacks; however, the anxiety symptoms may continue even after the underlying illness has been treated or resolved (Hoehn-Saric & McLeod, 1988).

Information pertaining to an individual's medical status and history can also be useful for case conceptualization and treatment planning. For instance, the majority of individuals with blood and injection phobias report a history of fainting (Öst, 1992). It is important to take note of this predisposition, as certain therapeutic techniques (i.e., applied tension) are particularly effective for this population (Vögele, Coles, Wardle, & Steptoe, 2003). In addition, a medical assessment can be used to determine the safety and appropriateness of various pharmacological and psychological treatments. For example, individuals who are prone to seizures would likely not be prescribed a tricyclic antidepressant such as imipramine, and conditions such as asthma and cardiac disease would likely exclude patients from certain psychological treatment strategies (e.g., hyperventilation challenges during interoceptive exposure for panic disorder).

Other Assessment Methods
Behavioral Assessment

Behavioral assessment approaches are used to identify target behaviors (excesses or deficits) and the contingencies under which these behaviors occur. Behavioral approaches allow clinicians to directly observe a patient's anxiety response and to identify subtle safety cues of which the patient may not be aware. Furthermore, patients with long-standing anxiety or pronounced avoidance behavior may not be able to articulate their feared cognitions, and completion of behavioral challenges may help to facilitate this process. Finally, behavioral assessment can be used to monitor and evaluate treatment progress and outcome (Chorpita & Taylor, 2001). There are several different types of behavioral assessment, including behavioral approach tests (BATs; also known as behavioral avoidance tests), symptom induction exercises and biological challenges. These different methodologies will be discussed in sequence.

Behavioral approach tests. BATs are the most common method of behavioral assessment. In a BAT, the patient enters a situation that he or she typically avoids or fears. Before and throughout the BAT the patient is asked to provide ratings of his or her fear level. These ratings are typically made using the Subjective Units of Distress Scale (SUDS). This scale ranges from 0 to 100, where 0 = no fear, and 100 = the most fear imaginable. Patients are instructed to remain in the situation as long as possible; however, they are always aware that the task can be discontinued at any point in time.

Because fear and avoidance behavior can be quite discrepant across individuals, behavioral tasks are usually tailored so they are relevant to a particular patient's main concerns. Indeed, one of the major goals of behavioral assessment is to understand the relationship between behavior and environmental factors for the individual in question (Chorpita & Taylor, 2001). Note, however, that standardized BATs have also been employed (e.g., Mavissakalian & Hamman, 1986).

Fear and avoidance hierarchies (FAH) are instrumental for determining which situations to use during BATs. The FAH is a list of specific situations that a patient fears or avoids, ranked in order of difficulty. The list is usually created as part of the assessment process and typically contains 10 to 15 items of varying difficulty. Items from the hierarchy can be selected for the BAT, and they are also used to select practices for exposure therapy.

Antony and Swinson (2000) describe two main types of BAT: progressive and selective. During a *progressive* BAT a patient proceeds to expose himself or herself to increasingly difficult situations involving the feared stimulus or situation. For instance, a BAT for a mouse phobia may begin with the patient standing 10 feet away from a caged animal. Gradually the patient may walk toward the cage, eventually touching the outside of the cage and possibly interacting with the mouse (e.g., petting, holding). The BAT ends when the patient is unable to complete the next step. In a *selective* BAT, patients are asked to enter a specific scenario (e.g., give a presentation, or drive a predetermined route), and his or her responses (e.g., SUDS, cognitions, avoidance behaviors) are measured.

Although BATs have numerous advantages to clinicians and researchers, they are not without shortcomings. For instance, BATs are time-consuming and are thought to be influenced by demand characteristics and limited content validity (McGlynn, Smitherman, & Hammel, 2004). Additionally, BATs are narrow in scope and thus may not be particularly appropriate for individuals with a multitude of feared situations or stimuli (Chorpita & Taylor, 2001).

Biological challenges and symptom induction exercises. Biological challenges and symptom induction exercises are particularly relevant to the study of panic disorder. Both strategies are designed to induce physiological or subjective symptoms of panic, although they utilize different methodologies (Smitherman, 2005). More specifically, biological challenge procedures involve the administration of chemical agents (e.g., carbon dioxide, sodium lactate, caffeine, yohimbine), whereas symptom induction exercises involve specific exercises designed to elicit physiological arousal (e.g., hyperventilation, spinning, running on the spot). Because biological challenges are more invasive, they are less likely to be incorporated into the clinical repertoire. However, research has demonstrated that individuals with panic disorder experience fear after the purposeful induction of symptoms, no matter how these symptoms are produced (for review, see Rapee, 1995). Thus, symptom induction exercises appear to be a convenient and valuable tool for clinical researchers.

Interoceptive assessment provides the clinician with an opportunity to observe a patient's panic symptoms in a controlled setting, which can help to identify important targets for treatment (Forsyth & Karekla, 2001). When completing symptom induction exercises patients are asked to provide several pieces of information, including (1) anticipatory anxiety, (2) anxiety during the task, and (3) the similarity of the sensations to those experienced during an actual panic attack. Typically patients complete a series of activities to produce physical sensations (e.g., Barlow & Craske, 2000, p. 119). Symptom induction exercises appear to be particularly effective for eliciting fear if there is a match between the sensations produced and naturally occurring panic symptoms (Sanderson, Rapee, & Barlow, 1989). Reassessing a patient's response to interoceptive exercises may be a useful measure of treatment outcome.

Psychophysiological Assessment

Although psychophysiological assessment is occasionally used in anxiety disorders research, it is less common in clinical practice, where interviews, self-report scales, and behavioral assessment are most often used. An appeal of psychophysiological measurement is that it is less prone to the biases associated with self-report measures (e.g., malingering, faking, acquiescence) and has therefore been touted as an objective index of symptomatology. However, psychophysiological measures do have a number of methodological problems. First, arousal is influenced by a number of variables other than fear and anxiety; consequently, physiological data can be difficult to interpret. Additionally, there are many ways to assess psychophysiology (e.g., heart rate, galvanic skin response, blood pressure, electromyogram), and these various indices often do not correlate with each other. Nevertheless, Yartz and Hawk (2001) suggest that heart rate can be a useful index to employ when conducting research on anxiety disorders.

Diary Measures

Interviews and questionnaires are retrospective in nature, and thus are subject to reporting biases. Diaries avoid this methodological problem by having the patient record his or her symptoms as they occur or shortly thereafter. Indeed, diary methods are valuable additions to the assessment process, as they help to delineate anxiety cues, associated cognitions, physical sensations, and behavioral responses. Furthermore, self-monitoring can be a useful index of treatment compliance and can be used to monitor treatment outcome. In addition to their clinical utility, diaries may also help patients to better understand their anxiety.

Numerous published self-monitoring forms are available for use in the assessment of anxiety disorders, including Barlow and Craske's (2000) Panic Attack Record, and Brown, O'Leary, and Barlow's (2001) Weekly Record of Anxiety and Depression. Clinicians and researchers often devise their own instruments to evaluate particular phenomena of interest (e.g., exposure practices in social phobia, frequency of intrusive memories in PTSD, triggers for compulsive rituals, etc.). Tompkins (2004) has published a useful guide outlining the use of homework in psychotherapy. This resource has a number of monitoring forms for various problem behaviors (e.g., anxiety, depression, hair-pulling), which may be useful in clinical practice.

Standardized Measures

Standardized instruments are a valuable asset in both research and clinical settings. Most standardized measures are self-report questionnaires. In addition to being cost-effective, self-report questionnaires are easy to administer and provide quick information about baseline levels of symptomatology and change over the course of treatment. Self-report instruments are also particularly well suited for screening; that is, determining whether an individual is likely to meet diagnostic criteria for a particular disorder.

There are hundreds of inventories developed to tap into various facets of the anxiety disorders (e.g., symptom severity, avoidance, cognitions). Researchers and clinicians typically select among the available tools those that best meet their needs and allow them to test hypotheses of interest. Some instruments are strongly tied to diagnostic criteria outlined in the *DSM,* and are therefore useful for the purposes of screening. Other measures tap into more specific features of a disorder that are not necessarily required for a diagnosis (e.g., the strength of particular beliefs); although these are not screening tools, they nevertheless provide valuable information for scientists and practitioners. The measures reviewed in this chapter have all been validated in adult populations, and normative data are available for comparison purposes. Space limitations prevent a comprehensive review of existing measures; however, there are several excellent resource books available that may be of interest to the reader (e.g., Antony & Barlow, 2002; Antony, Orsillo, & Roemer, 2001; Lam, Michalak, & Swinson, 2005).

Measures in this section are organized by diagnostic category, starting with measures for panic disorder and agoraphobia. In addition to the instruments described for each disorder, there are a number of measures that are useful for assessing symptoms across anxiety disorders. For example, the Overall Anxiety Severity and Impairment Scale (OASIS) (Norman, Cissell, Means-Christensen, & Stein, 2006) is a new 5-item scale that measures frequency of anxiety; intensity of anxiety; frequency of avoidance; interference at work, school, or home; and interference in relationships. Preliminary data support the reliability and validity of this very brief measure for assessing the severity of anxiety symptoms, regardless of diagnostic category.

Selected Measures for Panic Disorder and Agoraphobia

Agoraphobia Cognitions Questionnaire (ACQ) (Chambless, Caputo, Bright, & Gallagher, 1984). The ACQ is a self-report questionnaire designed to measure the occurrence and frequency of fearful cognitions associated with panic attacks and anxiety. The ACQ contains 15 items and takes between 5–10 minutes to complete. The ACQ is not a diagnostic measure, but provides some indication of the types of thoughts that may need to be modified during therapy.

Anxiety Sensitivity Index (ASI) (Peterson & Reiss, 1993; Reiss, Peterson, Gursky, & McNally, 1986). The main purpose of the ASI is to assess fear of anxiety-related symptoms. A large body of research has accumulated regarding the relationship between anxiety sensitivity and panic, and the ASI is one of the best-known self-report instruments used in the assessment of panic disorder. The ASI contains 16 items and takes less than 5 minutes to complete. There are several revisions of the ASI available, the newest of which is the 18 item ASI-3 (Taylor et al., 2007).

Mobility Inventory for Agoraphobia (MI) (Chambless, Caputo, Jasin, Gracely, & Williams, 1985). The MI is designed to assess the severity of agoraphobic avoidance behavior and the frequency of panic attacks. The MI is composed of four sections. In the first section patients are asked to rate their avoidance of 26 situations when (1) they are accompanied by another person, and (2) when they are alone. The second section requires patients to identify and circle five items from the first part that are of greatest concern or impairment. The third section contains several questions to assess the frequency of panic attacks (i.e., in the past week, and past 3 weeks) as well as the severity of recent panic attacks. The first section of the MI is used most frequently and has been subject to the most research attention. The MI requires 5–10 minutes for completion.

Panic Disorder Severity Scale (PDSS) (Shear et al., 1997, 2001). The PDSS is a 7-item, clinician-administered scale designed to measure the core dimensions of panic disorder and agoraphobia, including panic attack frequency, distress during panic attacks, severity of anticipatory anxiety, fear and avoidance of agoraphobic situations, fear and avoidance of panic-related sensations, impairment in work functioning, and impairment in social functioning. Preliminary studies suggest that the PDSS is a valid and reliable measure for screening and severity (Shear et al., 1997, 2001), and a self-

report version has recently been developed by the authors.

Selected Measures for Social Anxiety Disorder

Fear of Negative Evaluation Scale (FNE) and Social Avoidance and Distress Scale (SADS). The FNE and SADS are self-report inventories that are intended to be used together (Watson & Friend, 1969). Items on the FNE assess the expectation of negative evaluation and the distress associated with this. The SADS evaluates avoidance of social situations and the degree of distress in social situations. The FNE contains a total of 30 items, and the SADS contains a total of 28 items. Each of the scales takes approximately 15 minutes to complete.

Liebowitz Social Anxiety Scale (LSAS) (Liebowitz, 1987). The LSAS is a popular, clinician-administered scale for social phobia. The scale measures fear and avoidance associated with 24 social and performance situations and has excellent psychometric properties (e.g., Heimberg et al., 1999). A self-report version of the LSAS (LSAS-SR) has also been found to have good psychometric properties (Baker, Heinrichs, Kim, & Hofmann, 2002).

Social Phobia Inventory (SPIN) (Connor et al., 2000). The SPIN is a 17-item, self-report questionnaire designed to measure the core symptoms of social phobia, including fear, avoidance, and physiological arousal. Given its focus on diagnostic criteria for social anxiety, the SPIN can be used as a screening instrument, and research has supported its utility in this context. The SPIN has excellent psychometric properties (Antony, Coons, McCabe, Ashbaugh, & Swinson, 2006), and a briefer version of the SPIN has also been found to be an effective screening instrument (Connor, Kobak, Churchill, Katzelnick, & Davidson, 2001; de Lima Osório, Crippa, Loureiro, 2007).

Social Phobia and Anxiety Inventory (SPAI) (Turner, Beidel, & Dancu, 1996; Turner, Beidel, Dancu, & Stanley, 1989). The SPAI is a self-report measure of social anxiety, which measures somatic, cognitive, and behavioral symptoms of social phobia. There are two subscales: *social* anxiety and *agoraphobia*. The SPAI contains 45 items and requires between 20–30 minutes to complete.

Selected Measures for Obsessive-Compulsive Disorder

Obsessive-Compulsive Inventory (OCI) (Foa, Kozak, Salkovskis, Coles, & Amir, 1998). The OCI is a self-report questionnaire that evaluates the severity of obsessive-compulsive symptoms. Patients provide separate ratings for the frequency and distress associated with various obsessions and compulsions. The OCI consists of 42 items and takes approximately 10–15 minutes to complete. Items from the scale are summed to yield a total score; however, it is also possible to calculate subscale scores (i.e., washing, checking, doubting, ordering, obsessing, hoarding, and neutralizing). A briefer, 18-item version of the OCI, called the OCI-R, has recently been published and validated (Foa et al., 2002; Huppert et al., 2007).

Padua Inventory—Washington State University Revised (PI-WSUR) (Burns, Keortge, Formea, & Sternberger, 1996). The PI-WSUR is a self-report questionnaire designed to assess for obsessions and compulsions. The scale consists of 39 items and requires approximately 10 minutes to complete. A total PI-WSUR score can be obtained by summing all items; additionally, there are a number of subscales (i.e., *contamination obsessions and washing compulsions, dressing/grooming compulsions, checking compulsions, obsessional thoughts of harm to self or others,* and *obsessional impulses to harm self or others*). The PI-WSUR appears to do a particularly good job at discriminating obsessive-compulsive symptoms from general worry, relative to the original *Padua Inventory.*

Yale-Brown Obsessive Compulsive Scale (Y-BOC) (Goodman et al., 1989a, 1989b). The Y-BOCS is a clinician administered semistructured interview that consists of two components. The first component is a checklist that identifies the content of obsessions and compulsions (both current and past). The second component consists of a series of 10 questions to assess the severity of obsessive-compulsive symptoms. In addition to a global severity rating, separate severity scores can be obtained for obsessions and compulsions. In addition to the core severity ratings, there are several additional questions that measure various constructs of interest (e.g., insight, avoidance, indecisiveness, perceived responsibility, slowness), though these are not included in the total score. The Y-BOCS requires approximately 30 minutes for administration; however, clinicians should allot more time if the checklist is completed. A self-report version (Baer, 2000) also appears to have good psychometric properties (Steketee, Frost, & Bogart, 1996).

Selected Measures for Generalized Anxiety Disorder

GAD-7 (Spitzer, Kroenke, Williams, & Löwe, 2006). The GAD-7 is a brief, seven-item scale designed to screen for the presence of GAD. There is good agreement between clinician-administered and self-report versions. A cutoff score of 10 is recommended for distinguishing between those with and without GAD. Spitzer et al. (2006) found that 89% of individuals with GAD had a score of 10 or greater, whereas 82% of individuals without GAD had a score below 10. The GAD-7 appears to have good reliability and validity as a screening tool for GAD as well as for assessing GAD severity.

Generalized Anxiety Disorder Severity Scale (GADSS) (Shear, Belnap, Mazumdar, Houck, & Rollman, 2006). The GADSS is a clinician-administered scale modeled after similar measures, such as the Y-BOCS and PDSS. It assesses target worry content as well as frequency and severity of worry and associated symptoms. A preliminary psychometric investigation found good internal consistency, validity, and sensitivity to change for the GADSS (Shear et al., 2006).

Penn State Worry Questionnaire (PSWQ) (Meyer, Miller, Metzger, & Borkovec, 1990). This popular self-report questionnaire was developed to measure the tendency to worry. It contains 16 items and takes less than 5 minutes to complete. The PSWQ assesses the intensity and excessiveness of worry, rather than worry content. Additionally, the PSWQ appears to be helpful to screen individuals for a possible diagnosis of GAD; this is particularly true for samples that have been referred for excessive worry or anxiety. However, the PSWQ's ability to screen for GAD does not appear to be as strong in unselected samples (Behar, Alcaine, Zuellig, & Borkovec, 2003; Fresco, Mennin, Heimberg, & Turk, 2003).

Worry Domains Questionnaire (WDQ) (Tallis, Eysenck, & Mathews, 1992). The WDQ is a self-report questionnaire that assesses the content of worry. The scale taps into five specific domains of worry, including relationships, lack of confidence, aimless future, work, and finances. The WDQ consists of 25 items and requires approximately 5 minutes to administer. Although the original WDQ was developed to assess worry in nonclinical samples, the scale has been adapted for clinical samples and has been shown to have good psychometric properties as a clinical measure (McCarthy-Larzelere et al., 2001).

Selected Measures for Posttraumatic Stress Disorder

Clinician Administered PTSD Scale (CAPS) (Blake et al., 1990, 1995). The CAPS is a clinician-administered structured interview that is used to diagnose PTSD. The initial portion of the interview consists of a checklist of potentially traumatizing events. Following administration of the checklist the clinician proceeds to ask the patient questions about the incident(s). These questions assess the diagnostic criteria in *DSM–IV*. Administration of the CAPS requires between 45–60 minutes. The CAPS is particularly useful as a diagnostic instrument and to obtain more specific information about the trauma(s); however, it is relatively labor-intensive to administer and as such is not well suited for screening.

Davidson Trauma Scale (DTS) (Davidson et al., 1997). This is a self-report questionnaire that evaluates symptoms of PTSD based on *DSM–IV* criteria. The DTS is not specific to a single type of trauma; thus, it can accommodate a diverse range of experiences (e.g., sexual traumas, crimes, injury). There are three subscales: *intrusions, avoidance/numbing*, and *hyperarousal*. The scale contains 27 items and the time for completion is approximately 10 minutes. Although it is not a diagnostic instrument per se, the DTS appears to be a useful instrument for screening individuals for possible PTSD.

Impact of Event Scale (IES) (Horowitz, Wilner, & Alvarez, 1979; Weiss & Marmar, 1997). The IES is a self-report questionnaire that was designed to assess for intrusions and avoidance behavior that are associated with a past trauma. Prior to answering any questions, the patient identifies a particular stressful situation on which his or her answers are then based. The IES contains 15 items and requires less than 10 minutes to administer. In addition to a total IES score, two subscales (i.e., *intrusions* and *avoidance*) can also be calculated.

After the Initial Assessment
Continued Assessment During and Following Treatment

Assessment should not be limited to the initial consultation with a patient, and in recent years, there has been a greater focus on ongoing assessment, both in research settings and clinical settings. This process may include periodic assessments during treatment, an assessment at the end of treatment, and occasional assessments during follow-up to determine whether gains have been maintained. It may be beneficial to inform patients of the importance of ongoing assessment and to encourage them to periodically assess their own symptoms. Catching exacerbations early may prevent symptoms from worsening and improve the prognosis for recovery (Baker, Patterson, & Barlow, 2002).

Multimethod Assessment

Given the limitations associated with particular types of assessment, it is advisable to incorporate instruments from differing modalities (e.g., self-report, clinician-rated, behavioral, psychophysiological) to capitalize on the various strengths of different methods. Indeed, the use of multiple methods makes it more likely that the diagnostic picture will be representative of the patient and will encompass important domains of the presenting problem (i.e., thoughts, feelings, sensations, behaviors).

Feedback

Following the evaluation it is often useful to provide patients with feedback on their current concerns and the conceptualization of the presenting problem. Feedback serves several purposes. First, it allows the patient to clarify any discrepancies that may exist between his or her understanding of the problem and the clinician's understanding of the problem. Second, it provides the individual with some reassurance that his or her concerns are valid and have been heard. Finally, a discussion about current symptoms can help patients to gain an increased understanding of their difficulties.

Summary and Conclusions

This chapter provides a brief overview of methods used in the assessment of anxiety disorders. Whenever possible, empirically validated assessment tools should be utilized (e.g., semistructured interviews, validated questionnaires). A thorough assessment is important for case conceptualization and treatment planning. Furthermore, assessment is necessary for understanding the phenomenology of a disorder and for developing more effective treatment interventions.

References

Antony, M. M. (2002, August). Determining the empirical status of assessment instruments. In S. O. Lilienfeld (Chair), *Empirically supported assessment instruments: An idea whose time has come?* Symposium presented at the meeting of the American Psychological Association, Chicago, IL.

Antony, M. M., & Barlow, D. H. (Eds.). (2002). *Handbook of assessment and treatment planning for psychological disorders.* New York: Guilford Press.

Antony, M. M., Coons, M. J., McCabe, R. E., Ashbaugh, A. R., & Swinson, R. P. (2006). Psychometric properties of the Social Phobia Inventory: Further evaluation. *Behaviour Research and Therapy, 44,* 1177–1185.

Antony, M. M., Orsillo, S. M., & Roemer, L. (Eds.). (2001). *Practitioner's guide to empirically based measures of anxiety.* New York: Springer.

Antony, M. M., Roth, D., Swinson, R. P., Huta, V., & Devins, G. M. (1998). Illness intrusiveness in individuals with panic disorder, obsessive-compulsive disorder, or social phobia. *Journal of Nervous and Mental Disease, 186,* 311–315.

Antony, M. M., & Rowa, K. (2005). Evidence-based assessment of anxiety disorders in adults. *Psychological Assessment, 17,* 256–266.

Antony, M. M., & Swinson, R. P. (2000). *Phobic disorders and panic in adults: A guide to assessment and treatment.* Washington, DC: American Psychological Association.

Baer, L. (2000). *Getting control: Overcoming your obsessions and compulsions* (rev. ed.). New York: Plume.

Baker, S. L., Heinrichs, N., Kim, H. J., & Hofmann, S. G. (2002). The Liebowitz Social Anxiety Scale as a self-report instrument: A preliminary psychometric analysis. *Behaviour Research and Therapy, 40,* 701–715.

Baker, S. L., Patterson, M. D., & Barlow, D. H. (2002). Panic disorder and agoraphobia. In M. M. Antony & D. H. Barlow (Eds.), *Handbook of assessment and treatment planning for psychological disorders* (pp. 67–112). New York: Guilford Press.

Baker, S. R., & Edelmann, R. J. (2002). Is social phobia related to duration of skill-related behavioural adequacy? *British Journal of Clinical Psychology, 41,* 243–257.

Barlow, D. H. (2002). *Anxiety and its disorders: The nature and treatment of anxiety and panic* (2nd ed.). New York: Guilford Press.

Barlow, D. H., & Craske, M. G. (2000). *Mastery of Your Anxiety and Panic, Third Edition (MAP-3). Client workbook for anxiety and panic.* New York: Oxford University Press.

Beck, J. G., Shipherd, J. C., & Zebb, B. J. (1997). How does interoceptive exposure for panic disorder work? An uncontrolled case study. *Journal of Anxiety Disorders, 11,* 541–556.

Behar, E., Alcaine, O., Zuellig, A. R., & Borkovec, T. D. (2003). Screening for generalized anxiety disorder using the Penn State Worry Questionnaire: A receiver operating characteristic analysis. *Journal of Behavior Therapy and Experimental Psychiatry, 34,* 25–43.

Blake, D. D., Weathers, F. W., Nagy, L. M., Kaloupek, D. G., Gusman, F. D., Charney, D. S., et al. (1995). The development of a clinician-administered PTSD scale. *Journal of Traumatic Stress, 8,* 75–90.

Blake, D. D., Weathers, F. W., Nagy, L. M., Kaloupek, D. G., Lauminzer, G., Charney, D. S., et al. (1990). A clinician rating scale for assessing current lifetime PTSD: The CAPS-1. *The Behavior Therapist, 13,* 187–188.

Brown, T. A., Antony, M. M., & Barlow, D. H. (1995). Diagnostic comorbidity in panic disorder: Effect on treatment outcome and course of comorbid diagnoses following treatment. *Journal of Consulting and Clinical Psychology, 63,* 408–418.

Brown, T. A., Di Nardo, P., & Barlow, D. H. (1994) *Anxiety Disorders Interview Schedule for DSM–IV (Lifetime Version).* New York: Oxford University Press.

Brown, T. A., O'Leary, T. A., & Barlow, D. H. (2001). Generalized anxiety disorder. In D. H. Barlow (Ed.), *Clinical handbook of psychological disorders: A step-by-step treatment manual* (3rd ed., pp. 154–207). New York: Guilford Press.

Burns, G. L., Keortge, S. G., Formea, G. M., & Sternberger, L. G. (1996). Revision of the Padua Inventory of Obsessive Compulsive Disorder Symptoms: Distinctions between worry, obsessions and compulsions. *Behaviour Research and Therapy, 34,* 163–173.

Calvocoressi, L., Lewis, B., Harris, M., Trufan, S. J., Goodman, W. K., McDougle, C. J., et al. (1995). Family accommodation in obsessive-compulsive disorder. *American Journal of Psychiatry, 152,* 441–443.

Campbell, L. A., & Brown, T. A. (2002). Generalized anxiety disorder. In M. M. Antony & D. H. Barlow (Eds.), *Handbook of assessment and treatment planning for psychological disorders* (pp. 147–181). New York: Guilford Press.

Carr, R. E. (1998). Panic disorder and asthma: Causes, effects and research implications. *Journal of Psychosomatic Research, 44,* 43–52.

Chambless, D. L., Caputo, G. C., Bright, P., & Gallagher, R. (1984). Assessment of "fear of fear" in agoraphobics: The Body Sensations Questionnaire and Agoraphobic Cognitions Questionnaire. *Journal of Consulting and Clinical Psychology, 52,* 1090–1097.

Chambless, D. L., Caputo, G. C., Jasin, S. E., Gracely, E. J., & Williams, C. (1985). The Mobility Inventory for Agoraphobia. *Behaviour Research and Therapy, 23,* 35–44.

Chorpita, B. F., & Taylor, A. A. (2001). Behavioral assessment of anxiety disorders. In M. M. Antony, S. M. Orsillo, & L. Roemer (Eds.), *Practitioner's guide to empirically based measures of anxiety* (pp. 19–24). New York: Springer.

Connor, K. M., Davidson, J.R.T., Churchill, L. E., Sherwood, A., Foa, E., & Wesler, R. H. (2000). Psychometric properties of the Social Phobia Inventory (SPIN). *British Journal of Psychiatry, 176,* 379–386.

Connor, K. M., Kobak, K. A., Churchill, L. E., Katzelnick, D., & Davidson, J.R.T. (2001). MINI-SPIN: A brief screening assessment for generalized social anxiety disorder. *Depression and Anxiety, 14,* 137–140.

Cramer, V., Torgersen, S., & Kringlen, E. (2005). Quality of life and anxiety disorders: A population study. *Journal of Nervous and Mental Disease, 193,* 196–202.

Craske, M. G., & Barlow, D. H. (2001). Panic disorder and agoraphobia. In D. H. Barlow (Ed.), *Clinical handbook of psychological disorders* (3rd ed., pp. 1–59). New York: Guilford Press.

Craske, M. G., Farchione, T. J., Allen, L. B., Barrios, V., Stoyanova, M., & Rose, R., (2007). Cognitive behavioral therapy for panic disorder and comorbidity: More of the same or less of more? *Behaviour Research and Therapy, 45,* 1095–1109.

Craske, M. G., & Sipsas, A. (1992). Animal phobias versus claustrophobias: Exteroceptive versus interoceptive cues. *Behaviour Research and Therapy, 30,* 569–581.

Davidson, J.R.T., Book, S. W., Colker, J. T., Tupler, L. A., Roth, S., David, D., et al. (1997). Assessment of a new self-rating scale for posttraumatic stress disorder. *Psychological Medicine, 27,* 153–160.

de Lima Osório, F., Crippa, J. A., & Loureiro, S. R. (2007). A study of the discriminative validity of a screening tool (MINI-SPIN) for social anxiety disorder applied to Brazilian university students. *European Psychiatry, 22,* 239–243.

Di Nardo, P., Brown, T. A., & Barlow, D. H. (1994). *Anxiety Disorders Interview Schedule for DSM–IV.* New York: Oxford University Press.

Ey, S., & Hersen, M. (2004). Pragmatic issues of assessment in clinical practice. In M. Hersen (Ed.), *Psychological assessment in clinical practice: A practical guide* (pp. 3–20). New York: Brunner-Routledge.

First, M. B., Spitzer, R. L., Gibbon, M., & Williams, J. B. W. (1996). *Structured Clinical Interview for DSM–IV Axis I Disorder—Patient Edition (SCID-I/P, Version 2.0).* New York:

Biometrics Research Department, New York State Psychiatric Institute.

Foa, E. B., Huppert, J. D., Leiberg, S., Langner, R., Kichic, R., Hajcak, G., et al. (2002). The Obsessive-Compulsive Inventory: Development and validation of a short version. *Psychological Assessment, 14,* 485–495.

Foa, E. B., Kozak, M. J., Salkovskis, P. M., Coles, M. E., & Amir, N. (1998). The validation of a new obsessive-compulsive disorder scale: The Obsessive Compulsive Inventory. *Psychological Assessment, 10,* 206–214.

Forsyth, J. P., & Karekla, M. (2001). Biological challenge in the assessment of anxiety disorders. In M. M. Antony, S. M. Orsillo, & L. Roemer (Eds.), *Practitioner's guide to empirically based measures of anxiety* (pp. 31–36). New York: Springer.

Fresco, D. M., Mennin, D. S., Heimberg, R. G., & Turk, C. L. (2003). Using the Penn State Worry Questionnaire to identify individuals with generalized anxiety disorder: A receiver operating characteristic analysis. *Journal of Behavior Therapy and Experimental Psychiatry, 34,* 283–291.

Fydrich, T., Chambless, D. L., Perry, K. J., Buergener, F., & Beazley, M. B. (1998). Behavioral assessment of social performance: A rating system for social phobia. *Behaviour Research and Therapy, 36,* 995–1010.

Goodman, W. K., Price, L. H., Rasmussen, S. A., Mazure, C., Delgado, P., Heninger, G. R., et al. (1989a). The Yale-Brown Obsessive Compulsive Scale: II. Validity. *Archives of General Psychiatry, 46,* 1012–1016.

Goodman, W. K., Price, L. H., Rasmussen, S. A., Mazure, C., Fleishmann, R. L., Hill, C. L., et al. (1989b). The Yale-Brown Obsessive Compulsive Scale: I. Development, use and reliability. *Archives of General Psychiatry, 46,* 1006–1011.

Griez, E., & van den Hout, M. (1986). CO_2 inhalation in the treatment of panic attacks. *Behaviour Research and Therapy, 24,* 1145–150.

Heimberg, R. G., Horner, K. J., Juster, H. R., Safren, S. A., Brown, E. J., Schneier, F. R., et al. (1999). Psychometric properties of the Liebowitz Social Anxiety Scale. *Psychological Medicine, 29,* 199–212.

Herbert, J. D., Gaudiano, B. A., Rheingold, A. A., Myers, V., Dalrymple, K., & Nolan, E. M. (2005). Social skills training augments the effectiveness of cognitive behavioral group therapy for social anxiety disorder. *Behavior Therapy, 36,* 125–138.

Hoehn-Saric, R., & McLeod, D. R. (1988). Panic and generalized anxiety disorders. In C. G. Last & M. Hersen (Eds.), *Handbook of anxiety disorders* (pp. 109–126). New York: Pergamon Press.

Horowitz, M., Wilner, N., & Alvarez, W. (1979). Impact of Event Scale: A measure of subjective stress. *Psychosomatic Medicine, 41,* 209–218.

Huppert, J. D., Walther, M. R., Hajcak, G., Yadin, E., Foa, E. B., Simpson, H. B., et al. (2007). The OCI-R: Validation of the subscales in a clinical sample. *Journal of Anxiety Disorders, 21,* 394–406.

Joorman, J., Kosfelder, J., & Schulte, D. (2005). The impact of comorbidity of depression on the course of anxiety treatments. *Cognitive Therapy and Research, 29,* 569–591.

Katon, W. K., Lin, E.H.B., & Kroenke, K. (2007). The association of depression and anxiety with medical symptom burden in patients with chronic medical illness. *General Hospital Psychiatry, 29,* 147–155.

Kessler, R. C., McGonagle, K. A., Zhao, S., Nelson, C. B., Hughes, M., Eshleman, S., et al. (1994). Lifetime and 12-month prevalence of *DSM–III–R* psychiatric disorders in the United States: Results from the National Comorbidity Survey. *Archives of General Psychiatry, 51,* 8–19.

Kotler, M., Iancu, I., Efroni, R., & Amir, M. (2001). Anger, impulsivity, social support, and suicide risk in patients with posttraumatic stress disorder. *Journal of Nervous and Mental Disease, 189,* 162–167.

Kroenke, K., Spitzer, R. L., Williams, J. B., Monahan, P. O., & Lowe, B. (2007). Anxiety disorders in primary care: Prevalence, impairment, comorbidity, and detection. *Annals of Internal Medicine, 146,* 317–325.

La Greca, A. M., & Lopez, N. (1998). Social anxiety among adolescents: Linkages with peer relations and friendships. *Journal of Abnormal Child Psychology, 26,* 83–94.

Lam, R. W., Michalak, E. E., & Swinson, R. P. (2005). *Assessment scales in depression, mania and anxiety.* New York: Taylor & Francis.

Liebowitz, M. R. (1987). Social phobia. *Modern Problems in Pharmacopsychiatry, 22,* 141–173.

Mavissakalian, M., & Hamman, M. S. (1986). Assessment and significance of behavioral avoidance in agoraphobia. *Journal of Psychopathology and Behavioral Assessment, 8,* 317–327.

McCabe, R. E., & Antony, M. M. (2002). Specific and social phobia. In M. M. Antony & D. H. Barlow (Eds.), *Handbook of assessment and treatment planning for psychological disorders* (pp. 113–146). New York: Guilford Press.

McCabe, R. E., Antony, M. M., Summerfeldt, L. J., Liss, A., & Swinson, R. P. (2003). Preliminary examination of the relationship between anxiety disorders in adults and self-reported history of teasing or bullying experiences. *Cognitive Behaviour Therapy, 32,* 187–193.

McCarthy-Larzelere, M., Diefenbach, G. J., Williamson, D. A., Netemeyer, R. G., Bentz, B. G., & Manguno-Mire, G. M. (2001). Psychometric properties and factor structure of the Worry Domains Questionnaire. *Assessment, 8,* 177–191.

McGlynn, F. D., Smitherman, T. A., & Hammel, J. C. (2004). Panic, agoraphobia, and generalized anxiety disorder. In M. Hersen (Ed.), *Psychological assessment in clinical practice: A pragmatic guide* (pp. 35–60). New York: Brunner-Routledge.

McLean, P. D., Woody, S., Taylor, S., & Koch, W. J. (1998). Comorbid panic disorder and major depression: Implications for cognitive-behavioral therapy. *Journal of Consulting and Clinical Psychology, 66,* 240–247.

Meyer, T. J., Miller, M. L., Metzger, R. L., & Borkovec, T. D. (1990). Development and validation of the Penn State Worry Questionnaire. *Behaviour Research and Therapy, 28,* 487–495.

Miller, P. R. (2001). Inpatient diagnostic assessments: 2. Interrater reliability and outcomes of structured vs. unstructured interviews. *Psychiatry Research, 105,* 265–271.

Miller, P. R., Dasher, R., Collins, R., Griffiths, P., & Brown, F. (2001). Inpatient diagnostic assessments: 1. Accuracy of structured vs. unstructured interviews. *Psychiatry Research, 105,* 255–264.

Newth, S., & Rachman, S. (2001). The concealment of obsessions. *Behaviour Research and Therapy, 39,* 457–464.

Norman, S. B., Cissell, S. H., Means-Christensen, A. J., & Stein, M. B. (2006). Development and validation of an Overall Anxiety Severity and Impairment Scale (OASIS). *Depression and Anxiety, 23,* 245–249.

Öst, L. (1992). Blood and injection phobia: Background and cognitive, physiological, and behavioral variables. *Journal of Abnormal Psychology, 101,* 68–74.

Peterson, R. A., & Reiss, S. (1993). *Anxiety Sensitivity Index revised test manual.* Worthington, OH: IDS.

Rapaport, M. H., Clary, C., Fayyad, R., & Endicott, J. (2005). Quality-of-life impairment in depressive and anxiety disorders. *American Journal of Psychiatry, 162,* 1171–1178.

Rapee, R. M. (1995). Psychological factors influencing the affective response to biological challenge procedures in panic disorder. *Journal of Anxiety Disorders, 9,* 59–74.

Reiss, S., Peterson, R. A., Gursky, D. M., & McNally, R. J. (1986). Anxiety sensitivity, anxiety frequency and the prediction of fearfulness. *Behaviour Research and Therapy, 24,* 1–8.

Rodriguez, B. F., Weisberg, R. B., Pagano, M. E., Machan, J. T., Culpepper, L., & Keller, M. B. (2004). Frequency and patterns of psychiatric comorbidity in a sample of primary care patients with anxiety disorders. *Comprehensive Psychiatry, 45,* 129–137.

Rosenbaum, J. F., Pollack, M. H., & Pollack, R. A. (1996). Clinical issues in the long-term treatment of panic disorder. *Journal of Clinical Psychiatry, 57,* 44–48.

Saarni, S. I., Suvisaari, J., Sintonen, H., Pirkola, S., Koskinen, S., Aromaa, A., et al. (2007). Impact of psychiatric disorders on health-related quality of life: General population survey. *British Journal of Psychiatry, 190,* 326–332.

Sanderson, W. C., Rapee, R. M., & Barlow, D. H. (1989). The influence of illusion of control on panic attacks induced by 5.5% carbon dioxide enriched air. *Archives of General Psychiatry, 46,* 157–162.

Schadé, A., Marquenie, L. A., van Balkom, A.J.L.M., Koeter, M.W.J., de Beurs, E., van Dyck, R., et al. (2007). Anxiety disorders: Treatable regardless of the severity of comorbid alcohol dependence. *European Addiction Research, 13,* 109–115.

Schmidt, N. B., Lerew, D. R., & Jackson, R. J. (1999). Prospective evaluation of anxiety sensitivity in the pathogenesis of panic: Replication and extension. *Journal of Abnormal Psychology, 108,* 532–537.

Shear, K., Belnap, B. H., Mazumdar, S., Houck, P., & Rollman, B. L. (2006). Generalized Anxiety Disorder Severity Scale (GADSS): A preliminary validation study. *Depression and Anxiety, 23,* 77–82.

Shear, M. K., Brown, T. A., Barlow, D. H., Money, R., Sholomskas, D. E., Woods, S. W., et al. (1997). Multicenter collaborative Panic Disorder Severity Scale. *American Journal of Psychiatry, 154,* 1571–1575.

Shear, M. K., Rucci, P., Williams, J., Frank, E., Grochocinski, V., Vander Bilt, J., et al. (2001). Reliability and validity of the Panic Disorder Severity Scale: Replication and extension. *Journal of Psychiatric Research, 35,* 293–296.

Smitherman, T. A. (2005). Challenge tests and panic disorder: Implications for clinical assessment. *Professional Psychology: Research and Practice, 36,* 510–516.

Spitzer, R. L., Kroenke, K., Williams, J.B.W., & Löwe, B. (2006). A brief measure for assessing generalized anxiety disorder: The GAD-7. *Archives of Internal Medicine, 166,* 1092–1097.

Steketee, G., Chambless, D. L., & Tran, G. Q. (2001). Effects of Axis I and II comorbidity on behavior therapy outcome for obsessive-compulsive disorder and agoraphobia. *Comprehensive Psychiatry, 42,* 76–86.

Steketee, G., Frost, R., & Bogart, K. (1996). The Yale-Brown Obsessive Compulsive Scale: Interview versus self-report. *Behaviour Research and Therapy, 34,* 675–684.

Steketee, G., Perry, J. C., Goisman, R. M., Warshaw, M. G., Massion, A. O., Peterson, L. G., et al. (1997). The Psychosocial Treatments Interview for Anxiety Disorders: A method for assessing psychotherapeutic procedures in anxiety disorders. *Journal of Psychotherapy Practice and Research, 6,* 194–210.

Steketee, G., & Pruyn, N. A. (1998). Families of individuals with obsessive-compulsive disorder. In R. P. Swinson, M. M. Antony, S. Rachman, & M. A. Richter (Eds.), *Obsessive-compulsive disorder: Theory, research and treatment* (pp. 120–140). New York: Guilford Press.

Summerfeldt, L. J., & Antony, M. M. (2002). Structured and semistructured diagnostic interviews. In M. M. Antony and D. H. Barlow (Eds.), *Handbook of assessment and treatment planning for psychological disorders* (pp. 3–37). New York: Guilford Press.

Tallis, F., Eysenck, M., & Mathews, A. (1992). A questionnaire for the measurement of nonpathological worry. *Personality and Individual Differences, 13,* 161–168.

Taylor, S., Zvolensky, M. J., Cox, B. J., Deacon, B., Heimberg, R. G., Ledley, D. R., et al. (2007). Robust dimensions of anxiety sensitivity: Development and initial validation of the Anxiety Sensitivity Index-3. *Psychological Assessment, 19,* 176–188.

Tompkins, M. A. (2004). *Using homework in psychotherapy: Strategies, guidelines, and forms.* New York: Guilford Press.

Tsao, J.C.I., Mystkowski, J. L., Zucker, B. G., & Craske, M. G. (2005). Impact of cognitive-behavioral therapy for panic disorder on comorbidity: A controlled investigation. *Behaviour Research and Therapy, 43,* 959–970.

Turk, C. L., Heimberg, R. G., & Hope, D. A. (2001). Social anxiety disorder. In D. H. Barlow (Ed.), *Clinical handbook of psychological disorders* (3rd ed., pp. 114–153). New York: Guilford Press.

Turner, S. M., Beidel, D. C., & Dancu, C. V. (1996). *SPAI: Social Phobia and Anxiety Inventory.* North Tonawanda, NY: Multi-Health Systems.

Turner, S. M., Beidel, D. C., Dancu, C. V., & Stanley, M. A. (1989). An empirically derived inventory to measure social fears and anxiety: The Social Phobia and Anxiety Inventory. *Psychological Assessment, 1,* 35–40.

Vögele, C., Coles, J., Wardle, J., & Steptoe, A. (2003). Psychophysiological effects of applied tension on the emotional fainting response to blood and injury. *Behaviour Research and Therapy, 41,* 139–155.

Watson, D., & Friend, R. (1969). Measurement of social-evaluative anxiety. *Journal of Consulting and Clinical Psychology, 33,* 448–457.

Weiss, D. S., & Marmar, C. R. (1997). The Impact of Event Scale—Revised. In J. P. Wilson & T. M. Keane (Eds.), *Assessing psychological trauma and PTSD* (pp. 399–411). New York: Guilford Press.

Yartz, A. R., & Hawk, L. W. (2001). Psychophysiological assessment of anxiety: Tales from the heart. In M. M. Antony, S. M. Orsillo, & L. Roemer (Eds.), *Practitioner's guide to empirically based measures of anxiety* (pp. 25–30). New York: Springer.

PART 5

Treatment of
Anxiety Disorders

Pharmacotherapy for Panic Disorder and Agoraphobia

Mark H. Pollack *and* Naomi M. Simon

Abstract

Panic disorder is a common, often chronic or recurrent, disorder associated with significant distress and dysfunction. Patients with panic disorder experience persistent anxiety about having additional attacks, and worry about the implications or consequences of an attack, and/or change their behavior in response to having panic attacks. In the clinical setting, panic disorder is typically complicated by agoraphobia, that is, anxiety about being in places or situations from which escape might be difficult or embarrassing or in which help may not be available in the event of an attack. Interventions including cognitive behavioral therapy and pharmacotherapy are effective for panic disorder, with this chapter focusing on the medication treatments.

Keywords: agoraphobia, anxiety, cognitive behavioral therapy, panic, pharmacotherapy

Panic disorder is a common, often chronic or recurrent, disorder characterized by the presence of recurrent attacks or paroxysms of extreme anxiety (at least some of which have been unexpected) accompanied by a number of physical symptoms, persistent concerns about having additional attacks, worry about the implications or consequences of an attack (e.g., believing it may be a stroke), and/or changing behavior in response to panic attacks (e.g., visiting an emergency room because of concerns that it reflects a heart attack) (American Psychiatric Association [APA], 1994). For patients presenting in the clinical setting, panic disorder is typically complicated by agoraphobia (i.e., anxiety about being in places or situations from which escape might be difficult or embarrassing, or in which help may not be available in the event of an attack) (APA, 1994).

Panic disorder is relatively common, with a lifetime prevalence of 4.7% in the United States (Kessler et al., 2005). It tends to have a chronic course characterized by persistent symptomatology or frequent relapse and recurrence, and typically onsets by the third decade of life, although individuals may have had a prodromal history of childhood anxiety difficulties (Keller et al., 1994; Pollack et al., 1990; Pollack, Otto, et al., 1996). Panic disorder is associated with a number of negative sequelae in affected individuals, including increased and excessive utilization of general medical services (Katon, 1996; Roy-Byrne et al., 1999); adverse impact on work, family, and social life (Rubin et al., 2000); and increased rates of negative life events, as well as diminished overall quality of life (Cramer, Torgersen, & Kringlen, 2005). Individuals with panic disorder have poor physical and emotional health, increased risk for substance abuse, greater likelihood of suicidal ideation and suicide attempts (Goodwin & Roy-Byrne, 2006), lower educational achievement (Eaton, Kessler, Wittchen, & Magee, 1994), higher likelihood of unemployment and low work productivity (Ettigi, Meyerhoff, Chirban, Jacobs, & Wilson, 1997), impaired social and marital functioning, and financial dependency beyond that attributable to comorbidity with other psychiatric disorders (Markowitz, Weissman, Ouellette, Lish, & Klerman, 1989). Some data suggest that individuals with panic disorder have a magnitude of impairment in quality of life and well-being that is at least the same (Rubin et al., 2000) if not greater (Cramer et al., 2005) than that of patients with depression or serious medical illnesses such as Type II diabetes.

Naturalistic as well as randomized controlled studies of treatment outcomes for panic disorder support its generally chronic nature (Keller et al., 1994; Pollack et al., 1990). Although the majority of patients respond to treatment, symptoms tend to wax and wane over time with periods of improvement and periods of clinical worsening. In follow-up studies of over 20 years, only a minority of treated patients enter sustained remission, with reported remission rates in the range of 10%–35% (Ball, Otto, Pollack, & Rosenbaum, 1994; Eaton et al., 1994; Katschnig & Amering, 1998; Keller & Baker, 1992; Kessler et al., 1994; Pollack & Smoller, 1995; Roy-Byrne & Cowley, 1994; Warshaw, Massion, Shea, Allsworth, & Keller, 1997; Yonkers et al., 1998). The presence of agoraphobia, as well as longer duration of illness, are associated with poorer long term course (Katschnig & Amering, 1998; Warshaw et al., 1997; Yonkers et al., 1998). For instance, in a 1-year follow-up study, patients with uncomplicated panic disorder achieved full remission twice as frequently as those with panic disorder complicated by agoraphobia (Keller et al., 1994). Of interest, though rates of remission of panic disorder are similar in men and women during naturalistic follow-up, rates of recurrence in women were double that of men in a 5-year prospective follow-up study (Yonkers et al., 1998).

Goals of Treatment

The treatment of panic disorder is focused on the elimination of panic attacks, anticipatory anxiety, panic-related situational fears and avoidance behaviors, and, anxiety about and sensitivity to somatic sensations, and functional disabilities (including work, social, and family function); the overarching goal of treatment is to help the patient obtain a good overall quality of life and return to a high level of function (Pollack, 2005). Current conceptualizations of the assessment of treatment response have moved beyond focus on reduction in panic attack frequency (Michelson et al., 1998) and toward the use of broader outcome measures, such as the

Panic Disorder Severity Scale (Shear et al., 2001), which assesses reduction in panic frequency and associated distress, as well as anticipatory anxiety, phobic avoidance of situations and physical sensations, and impairment in work and social function. Finally, treatment of individuals with panic disorder should also aim toward the resolution of comorbid conditions.

Pharmacotherapy of Panic Disorder

The underlying pathophysiology of panic disorder has been attributed to a complex interplay of biologic, psychologic, and environmental factors (Stein, 2005). A recent comprehensive review Roy-Byrne, Craske, & Stein, 2006) discusses current conceptualizations of the etiopathology of panic disorder. Neurobiologic factors that appear to be relevant for the pathophysiology of panic disorder and that may help explain the efficacy of different pharmacologic agents include dysregulation and dysfunction in central neurotransmitter systems such as norepinephrine, serotonin, and gamma aminobutyric acid (GABA) (den Boer & Westenberg, 1988; Gorman, Kent, Sullivan, & Coplan, 2000; Nutt, 1998; Primeau & Fontaine, 1988; Zwanzger & Rupprecht, 2005).

A number of studies support the potential role of norepinephrine in panic disorder. For example, stimulation of the locus coeruleus (LC), a small retropontine nucleus with a high density of norepinephrine-containing neurons, causes panic and increased anxiety (Redmond & Huang, 1979). Further, studies suggest that panic disorder may be associated with abnormalities in central pre- and postsynaptic alpha-2 adrenergic receptors (Charney, Heninger, & Breier, 1984; Nesse, Cameron, Curtis, McCann, & Huber-Smith, 1984). In addition, a number of agents with antipanic efficacy block LC firing, such as the benzodiazepines and antidepressants, including those inhibiting reuptake of norepinephrine such as tricyclics, reboxetine, and venlafaxine (Bakker, van Balkom, & Stein, 2005).

Similarly, there is converging evidence from different lines of inquiry suggesting that abnormalities in central serotonin systems may be associated with panic disorder. For example, one study demonstrated decreased serotonin transport binding in midbrain, temporal lobe, and thalamus in patients with panic compared to normal controls (Maron et al., 2004). Agents with primary effects on serotonergic neurotransmission, including the serotonin selective reuptake inhibitors (SSRIs), serotonin-norepinephrine reuptake inhibitors (SNRIs), and tricyclic antidepressants have also demonstrated efficacy for the treatment of panic disorder (Pollack, Allgulander, et al., 2003).

A variety of studies suggest that abnormalities in the inhibitory neurotransmitter gamma aminobutyric acid (GABA) may also be relevant in the underlying pathophysiology of panic disorder. Benzodiazepines, which are agonists at the benzodiazepine receptor and thus increase GABAergic transmission, are effective for the treatment of panic disorder. Individuals with panic disorder also appear to have decreased benzodiazepine receptor sensitivity (Roy-Byrne, Wingerson, Radant, Greenblatt, & Cowley, 1996). Further, there is a high density of benzodiazepine/GABA receptors in brain regions particularly relevant for fear and anxiety such as the amygdala and hippocampus (Coplan & Lydiard, 1998). Studies using Magnetic Resonance Spectroscopy (MRS) neuroimaging have also documented lower GABA levels in the occipital cortex of patients with panic disorder (Goddard, Mason, et al., 2001). Of interest, the SSRI citalopram has been shown to increase GABA levels in the occipital cortex of normal controls (Bhagwagar et al., 2004); this finding raises the possibility that increased GABAergic neurotransmission may be relevant to the antipanic efficacy of agents previously presumed to exert their primary activity through systems (such as serotonergic) other than the benzodiazepine-GABA receptor complex.

Starting with observations in the 1960s by Klein (Klein & Fink, 1962) that the tricyclic antidepressant imipramine blocks panic attacks, numerous antidepressants from a variety of classes have demonstrated efficacy for treatment of panic disorder. In the decades that followed, benzodiazepines also proved effective antipanic agents. Each medication class has both advantages and disadvantages, and selecting among them involves consideration of several factors, including side-effect profile, cost, history of past response or failure, and patient preference (particularly following review of the relative risks and benefits of each intervention). Further, treatment selection may be guided by the presence of comorbidities and the acuity of the patient's distress. For example, antidepressants are clearly preferable to benzodiazepines for individuals with comorbid depression or substance abuse, whereas the benzodiazepines, which have a more rapid onset of effect, may be particularly useful either as monotherapy or in conjunction with an antidepressant for individuals requiring rapid anxiolysis, or with an inability to tolerate antidepressant initiation (see Table 1).

Antidepressants

Guidelines on the treatment of panic disorder, such as those published by the American Psychiatric Association (APA, 1998), typically recommend antidepressants as first-line pharmacotherapy for the treatment of panic disorder because of their broad spectrum efficacy for common comorbid disorders such as depression, and because antidepressants lack the abuse and dependence liability that complicates benzodiazepine administration. As patients with panic disorder are often very sensitive to medication-related adverse effects, including the potential for exacerbation of anxiety when starting antidepressants, antidepressant pharmacotherapy is typically initiated with lower doses than commonly used for depression, although ultimately effective doses can be similar and may sometimes be higher (Ballenger, Wheadon, Steiner, Bushnell, & Gergel, 1998).

Serotonin Reuptake Inhibitors

Selective serotonin reuptake inhibitors (SSRIs) and serotonin-norepinephrine reuptake inhibitors (SNRIs) are commonly used as first-line pharmacological agents for the treatment of panic disorder, with randomized controlled trials demonstrating the efficacy of the SSRIs citalopram (Lepola et al., 1998; Wade, Lepola, Koponen, Pedersen, & Pedersen, 1997), escitalopram (Stahl, Gergel, & Li, 2003), fluoxetine (Michelson et al., 1998, 1999, 2001), fluvoxamine (Asnis et al., 2001; Bakish et al., 1996; Black, Wesner, Bowers, & Gabel, 1993; de Beurs, van Balkom, Lange, Koele, & van Dyck, 1995; den Boer & Westenberg, 1988; Hoehn-Saric, McLeod, & Hipsley, 1993; Palatnik, Frolov, Fux, & Benjamin, 2001; Sharp, Power, Simpson, Swanson, & Anstee, 1997), paroxetine immediate (Bakker, van Dyck, Spinhoven, & van Balkom, 1999; Ballenger, Wheadon, et al., 1998; Lecrubier, Bakker, Dunbar, & Judge, 1997; Lecrubier & Judge, 1997; Oehrberg et al., 1995; Stein, Seedat, van der Linden, & Zungu-Dirwayi, 2000) and controlled release formulations (Sheehan, Burnham, Iyengar, & Perera, 2005), sertraline (Londborg et al., 1998; Pohl, Wolkow, & Clary, 1998; Pollack, Otto, Worthington, Manfro, & Wolkow, 1998; Sheikh, Londborg, Clary, & Fayyad, 2000), and the immediate (Pollack, Worthington, et al. 1996) and extended release (ER) formulations of the SNRI venlafaxine (Pollack, Mangano, et al., 2007; Pollack, Lepola,

Table 1. Pharmacotherapy of Panic Disorder

Drug	Category of Evidence	Daily Dose Range (mg)	Initial Dose (mg)	Dosing Schedule
SSRIs	A			
Citalopram (Celexa®)		20–60	10–20	qd
Escitalopram (Lexapro®)		10–30	10	qd
Fluoxetine (Prozac®)		10–80	10	qd
Fluvoxamine (Luvox®)		50–300	50	qd
Paroxetine (Paxil®)		10–50	10	qd
Paroxetine CR (Paxil CR®)		12.5–62.5	12.5	qd
Sertraline (Zoloft®)		25–200	25	qd
SNRIs				
Duloxetine (Cymbalta®)	C	30–120	30	qd-bid
Venlafaxine IR	B	75–300	37.5	bid-tid
Venlafaxine Extended-Release (Effexor-XR®)	A	75–225	37.5	qd
TCAs	A			
Clomipramine (Anafranil®)		100–250	12.5–25	qd
Imipramine (Tofranil®)		100–300	10–25	qd
MAOIs				
Phenelzine (Nardil®)	B	60–90	15	bid
Benzodiazepines	A			
Alprazolam (Xanax®)		2–10	0.25–0.5	qid
Clonazepam (Klonopin®)		1–5	0.25	bid
Diazepam (Valium®)		4–50	2.5	bid
Lozarepam (Ativan®)		3–16	1	tid-qid
Other Agents				
Bupropion (Wellbutrin-XR®)	D	100–400	50–100	bid
Buspirone (Buspar®)	E C (augmentation)	15–60	5	bid-tid
Beta Blockers				
Pindolol (Visken®)	B (augmentation)	7.5	2.5	tid
Propranolol (Inderal®)	D C (augmentation)	10–60	10–20	bid
Anticonvulsants				
Carbamazepine (Tegretol®)	E	200–1200	100	tid-qid
Gabapentin (Neurontin®)	D	300–5400	300	bid-tid
Valproate (Depakote®)	C	500–2000	250	bid
Atypical Antipsychotics	C			
Aripiprazole (Abilify®)		2–30	2	qd-bid
Olanzapine (Zyprexa®)		2.5–200	2.5	bid
Quetiapine (Seroquel®)		25–300	25	qd-bid
Risperidone (Risperdal®)		0.5–3	0.5	bid
Ziprasidone (Geodon®)		40–160	40	bid

Levels of Evidence: A = multiple double-blind, placebo controlled studies; B = at least one double-blind randomized control trial; C = case report/series or anecdotal; D = inconsistent results reported; E = negative evidence.

et al., 2007). A more recently introduced SNRI, duloxetine, has also been reported effective for the treatment of panic disorder in case and anecdotal reports, though with no randomized controlled trials published to date (Crippa & Zuardi, 2006). Four of these agents (paroxetine in its immediate and controlled-release formulations, sertraline, fluoxetine, and venlafaxine ER) have Food and Drug Administration (FDA) approval for this indication. Meta-analytic analyses of randomized controlled studies suggest that the magnitude of antidepressant effects compared to placebo is on the order of a medium to large effect size (Bakker, van Balkom, & Spinhoven, 2002; Otto, Tuby, Gould, McLean, & Pollack, 2001); most of the data reflects short-term trials, although several long-term studies demonstrate longer-term efficacy as well (Pollack, Allgulander, et al., 2003).

The SSRIs and SNRIs are generally better-tolerated with less anticholinergic effects and weight gain compared to older classes of agents such as the tricyclic antidepressants (TCAs); they also have a more benign cardiovascular profile and a greater safety margin when taken in overdose relative to the TCAs. Also, SSRIs and SNRIs lack the abuse and dependence liability associated with the benzodiazepines. Further, they have demonstrated efficacy for a wide array of mood and anxiety disorders commonly comorbid with panic disorder, including major depression, social anxiety disorder, generalized anxiety disorder, and posttraumatic stress disorder. However, SSRI and SNRI administration may be associated with a variety of adverse effects, including sexual dysfunction, gastrointestinal disturbance, sleep disturbance, weight gain, dose dependent increases in blood pressure (venlafaxine), urinary retention (duloxetine), and provocation of increased anxiety (particularly at initiation of therapy) that may make their administration problematic for some individuals (Ballenger, Davidson, et al., 1998; Dannon et al., 2004; Modell, Katholi, Modell, & DePalma, 1997). Further, the typical lag in onset of therapeutic efficacy of at least 2–3 weeks can be problematic for acutely distressed individuals. There is no clear evidence of differential efficacy between agents in the SSRI or SNRI classes, although there are potentially relevant differences in side-effect profile (e.g., potential for weight gain, discontinuation-related symptomatology), potential for drug interactions, and recently, availability of generic formulations that may be clinically relevant (Fava, 2006; Fava, Judge, Hoog, Nilsson, & Koke, 2000). Results from one randomized placebo controlled trial suggested greater efficacy on some, though not all, measures for venlafaxine 225 mg/d compared to 40 mg/d of paroxetine, raising the possibility of greater efficacy for the SNRI at higher doses (Pollack, Mangano, et al., 2007); additional data from that study and another one with a similar design demonstrated comparable efficacy for venlafaxine at 75 and 150 mg/d compared to 40 mg/d of paroxetine (Pollack, Mangano, et al., 2007; Pollack, Lepola, et al., 2007).

Tricyclic Antidepressants

Up until they were largely supplanted by the SSRIs and SNRIs, the tricyclic antidepressants (TCAs) were the "gold standard" pharmacotherapy for panic disorder; TCAs were commonly used as first-line agents, with numerous randomized controlled studies of imipramine and clomipramine having demonstrated clear efficacy for this condition and with supportive evidence for other TCAs (Pollack, 2005; Rosenbaum, Pollack, & Fredman, 1998). Although the efficacy of TCAs for panic appears comparable to that of the newer agents (Bakker et al., 1999; den Boer, Westenberg, Kamerbeek, Verhoeven, & Kahn, 1987; Noyes & Perry, 1990), the TCAs have been largely relegated to second-line use due to their greater side-effect burden compared with the newer agents (Bakish et al., 1996), including associated anticholinergic effects, orthostasis, weight gain, delays in cardiac conduction, and potential lethality in overdose. Among patients with panic disorder treated with TCAs the side-effect burden was identified in one study as the primary reason for treatment failure (Cowley, Ha, & Roy-Byrne, 1997). The TCAs also do not appear to have as broad a spectrum of efficacy as the SSRIs, lacking robust efficacy for conditions such as social phobia (Simpson et al., 1998) and for obsessive-compulsive disorder (with the exception of clomipramine), disorders that may present comorbidly with panic disorder.

Monoamine Oxidase Inhibitors

Although widely believed to be effective in clinical practice, the monoamine oxidase inhibitors (MAOIs) have actually not been systematically studied in panic disorder as defined by the current nomenclature, although there is at least one study predating the use of current diagnostic criteria that did likely include a group of panic patients and was consistent with efficacy for the MAOI phenelzine (Sheehan, Ballenger, & Jacobsen, 1980). Although anecdotal reports and clinical lore suggest that MAOIs may be particularly effective for patients with panic disorder refractory to other agents, there is no data that empirically addresses this issue. The MAOIs are typically relegated to third- or fourth-tier use after failure with safer and better-tolerated agents because of the requirement for careful dietary monitoring to avoid tyramine-containing foods, proscriptions against ingestion of sympathomimetic and other agents because of risks of hypertensive reactions, and serotonin syndrome (Lippman & Nash, 1990; Livingston & Livingston, 1996), as well as an aversive side-effect profile, including associated insomnia, weight gain, orthostatic hypotension, and sexual disturbance.

Reversible inhibitors of monoamine oxidase-A (RIMAs), which have a generally more benign side-effect profile and significantly lower risk of hypertensive reactions than the reversible agents such as phenelzine, tranylcypromine, and isocarboxacid, have been studied for the treatment of panic disorder, with reports from randomized controlled trials reporting inconsistent results in terms of efficacy (Bakish, Saxena, Bowen, & D'Souza, 1993; Loerch et al., 1999; Tiller, Bouwer, & Behnke, 1999; van Vliet, den Boer, Westenberg, & Slaap, 1996; van Vliet, Westenberg, & den Boer, 1993). One of the RIMAS examined, brofaromine, never became available for clinical use, and the other, moclobemide, is available in some countries but is not approved for use in the United States. Recently, a transdermal patch for the MAOI selegiline became available in the United States with an indication for treatment of depression. At its lowest dose, use of the selegiline patch does not require the dietary proscriptions of standard MAOIs; however, to date, evaluation of its efficacy for panic disorder has not been reported.

Benzodiazepines

Benzodiazepines remain among the most frequently prescribed medications for the treatment of panic disorder, despite guideline recommendations (APA, 1998) for use of antidepressants as first-line antipanic agents (Bruce et al., 2003; Noyes et al., 1996). While only two high-potency benzodiazepines, alprazolam (immediate and extended-release forms) and clonazepam, have received FDA approval for panic disorder, a number of benzodiazepines of varying potency have demonstrated a similar magnitude of antipanic efficacy in randomized controlled trials, including diazepam (mean dose 43 to 44 mg/d) (Dunner, Ishiki, Avery, Wilson, & Hyde, 1986; Noyes et al., 1996), adinazolam (mean dose 95.5 mg/d) (Davidson et al., 1994), and lorazepam (mean dose 6 to 7.5 mg/d) (Charney & Woods, 1989; Schweizer, Fox, Case, & Rickels, 1988;

Schweizer et al., 1990). The continued common use of benzodiazepines is likely due to their effectiveness for panic disorder, as well as their tolerability, rapid onset of action, and ability to be used on an "as needed" basis for situational anxiety.

Though benzodiazepines are generally well tolerated, their administration may be associated with adverse effects, including sedation, ataxia, and memory impairment (particularly in the elderly and those with prior cognitive impairment) (Stewart, 2005). Though clinicians and patients may be concerned that ongoing administration of benzodiazepines will result in the development of therapeutic tolerance, characterized by loss of therapeutic efficacy or dose escalation, the available evidence suggests that benzodiazepines remain generally effective for panic disorder over time (Nagy, Krystal, Woods, & Charney, 1989; Pollack et al., 1993), and that long-term use is generally not associated with significant dose escalation (Soumerai et al., 2003). However, patients may experience withdrawal symptoms during rapid discontinuation, even after a relatively brief period of regular dosing (Pecknold, Swinson, Kuch, & Lewis, 1988). In one study more than two-thirds of panic disorder patients discontinuing alprazolam experienced a discontinuation syndrome, usually involving increased anxiety and agitation (Rickels, Schweizer, Weiss, & Zavodnick, 1993). Although discontinuation-related adverse effects may be less with longer-acting agents such as clonazepam, they may still occur, and patients with a high level of sensitivity to somatic sensations may find these sensations particularly distressing; a slow taper rate and the addition of cognitive behavioral therapy (Otto et al., 1993) during the discontinuation process each may be helpful in reducing distress associated with benzodiazepine discontinuation. For all patients treated with daily benzodiazepines for more than a very brief period, a taper is recommended to reduce the likelihood of withdrawal symptoms, including in rare cases, seizures. Individuals with a predilection for substance abuse (Kan, Hilberink, & Breteler, 2004) are at risk to abuse benzodiazepines; however, those without this diathesis do not appear to share this risk (Soumerai et al., 2003). Benzodiazepines and alcohol may, however, interact negatively (Gaudreault, Guay, Thivierge, & Verdy, 1991), often rendering the use of these agents in patients with current comorbid alcohol abuse or dependence problematic and further supporting the use of antidepressants as first-line antipanic agents in this comorbid population. Finally, of particular importance given the high rates of comorbid depression associated with panic disorder, benzodiazepines are generally not effective for the treatment of depression and may in fact induce or intensify comorbid depressive symptoms (Greenblatt, Shader, & Abernethy, 1983).

Perhaps in part because of these limitations, monotherapy with benzodiazepines for panic disorder, though still relatively common, has decreased somewhat in recent years, whereas their concomitant prescription with antidepressants has increased (Bruce et al., 2003). Combining benzodiazepine and antidepressants early in treatment offers the potential of accelerating response compared to antidepressants alone, and the possibility of additive or synergistic effects. Studies examining treatment initiation with a combination of an antidepressant and a benzodiazepine compared to an antidepressant alone do suggest earlier onset of therapeutic effect with combination treatment beginning as early as the first week (Goddard, Brouette, et al., 2001; Pollack, Simon, et al., 2003). However, by week 4 or 5 of treatment, the SSRI monotherapy groups achieved comparable efficacy to the combined treatment groups. All groups remained comparably improved from that point forward, regardless of whether patients remained on the combined treatment (Pollack et al., 2003) or tapered off the benzodiazepine (Goddard, Brouette, et al., 2001; Pollack et al., 2003), suggesting that benzodiazepines may be particularly helpful for improving the speed of response when co-initiated with antidepressants but that their ongoing use may not be necessary after the initial weeks of antidepressant pharmacotherapy. In practice, augmentation with a benzodiazepine for individuals remaining symptomatic on antidepressant monotherapy appears effective, although this has not been empirically assessed in systematic study.

Other Agents

Evidence for the potential efficacy of bupropion, a relatively weak reuptake inhibitor of norepinephrine, serotonin, and dopamine for panic disorder is inconsistent, with a small (n = 12) study of the immediate release formulation at relatively high doses demonstrating no benefit (Sheehan, Davidson, Manschreck, & Van Wyck Fleet, 1983), but a more recent open label study of the extended release formulation at standard doses suggesting potential benefit (Simon et al., 2003). Similarly, there is mixed support for the potential efficacy for panic disorder of another noradrenergic agent, the selective reuptake inhibitor reboxetine: a large placebo controlled trial supported the antipanic efficacy of reboxetine (Versiani et al., 2002), while another study comparing the efficacy of reboxetine and paroxetine suggested that the SSRI was more effective than the purely noradrenergic agent, although both agents were efficacious (Bertani et al., 2004).

Buspirone, an azapirone $5HT_{1A}$ partial agonist, indicated for generalized anxiety, appears ineffective for treating panic disorder as monotherapy (Sheehan, Raj, Harnett-Sheehan, Soto, & Knapp, 1993; Sheehan, Raj, Sheehan, & Soto, 1990), but was potentially helpful, based on case reports, as an adjunct to antidepressants and benzodiazepines (Gastfriend & Rosenbaum, 1989) and, in one placebo controlled trial, acutely, though not over the longer term, for cognitive behavioral therapy (CBT) for panic disorder (Bouvard, Mollard, Guerin, & Cottraux, 1997).

Although beta-blockers may reduce the somatic symptoms of arousal associated with panic and anxiety, they are typically used as augmentation for incomplete response to first-line agents and generally not as first-line monotherapy (Munjack et al., 1989). Augmentation with the 5HT-1A partial antagonist and beta-blocker pindolol (2.5 mg tid) for patients with panic disorder remaining symptomatic despite initial treatment with fluoxetine was effective in a small double-blind randomized controlled trial (RCT) (Hirschmann et al., 2000).

A number of small, open label trials or case series have suggested the potential benefit of atypical antipsychotics, including olanzapine (Hollifield, Thompson, Ruiz, & Uhlenhuth, 2005), risperidone (Simon et al, 2006), and aripiprazole (Worthington, Kinrys, Wygant, & Pollack, 2005) as monotherapy or augmentation for the treatment of patients with panic disorder refractory to standard interventions. However, the lack of large RCTs on their efficacy for panic disorder to date, coupled with emerging data demonstrating the association of side effects such as weight gain, hyperlipidemia, and diabetes with some of the atypical agents, do not support the routine first-line use of these agents for panic disorder.

There are limited data supporting a possible secondary role for anticonvulsants for the treatment of panic disorder, and they may be considered for some individuals with panic disorder plus comorbid disorders such as bipolar disorder and substance abuse for which the use of antidepressants and benzodiazepines, respectively, are associated with additional risk. Small studies suggest that some anticonvulsants such as valproic acid (Lum, Fontaine, & Elie, 1990; Woodman & Noyes, 1994), though not others such as carbamazepine (Uhde, Stein, & Post, 1988), have potential benefit for the treatment of panic disorder. A large, double-blind, controlled, multicenter trial of gabapentin did not demonstrate significant benefit compared to placebo for the overall sample of patients with panic disorder, but did show evidence of efficacy for those of at least moderate severity, and the agent appears to be generally well tolerated (Pande et al., 2000). A role for pregabalin, an anticonvulsant with demonstrated utility for generalized anxiety disorder (Rickels et al., 2005), has yet to be demonstrated in panic disorder.

Duration of Treatment

Studies of 6 months to 3 years in duration of the long-term efficacy of pharmacotherapy for panic disorder suggest that ongoing treatment is associated with accruing benefit in terms of reduction of panic attacks, anticipatory anxiety, and agoraphobic avoidance, with persistent maintenance of therapeutic gains, and with reduction in rates of relapse (Lecrubier & Judge, 1997; Lepola et al., 1998; Lydiard, Steiner, Burnham, & Gergel, 1998; Michelson et al., 1999; Rapaport et al., 2001). Guidelines for the treatment of panic disorder, such as those published by the American Psychiatric Association, suggest that patients should continue to receive medication for a minimum of 12 to 18 months after a successful trial of pharmacotherapy, and that discontinuation of treatment should not be attempted until the patient experiences significant improvement or complete remission of symptoms (APA, 1998). Updated practice guidelines for the treatment of panic disorder will be published by the American Psychiatric Association in the near future. Further, while there is a paucity of data examining what to do next for patients who relapse after pharmacotherapy discontinuation, the guidelines and clinical experience suggest that medication should be restarted for patients relapsing following treatment discontinuation and continued for a prolonged period of time. Another set of consensus guidelines (Ballenger et al., 1998) note that full remission of panic disorder may require up to a year of treatment, and suggest that treatment should continue for at least 1 to 2 years, with discontinuation considered only if the patient is in remission and not experiencing significant stressors. These guidelines also suggest that treatment be maintained in patients with a history of severe or recurrent relapses and those individuals currently experiencing persistent symptoms. One study examined the impact of longer-term antidepressant treatment with imipramine on relapse combined patients who were either randomized to placebo discontinuation or openly discontinued after 12–30 months of remission and compared them with those randomized to placebo discontinuation after 6 months of remission; it found that rates of relapse were nearly identical for the two groups (37%) during the follow-up period after discontinuation (Mavissakalian & Perel, 2002). More data are needed to guide recommendations about the optimal length of treatment, and the clinical decision to attempt medication discontinuation should take into account individual patient factors such as the presence of comorbid disorders, prior history of relapse, the initial ease of attainment of treatment response, and the presence of acute psychosocial stressors. However, the achievement of remission prior to treatment discontinuation may be a more critical determinant in preventing relapse than the subsequent duration of maintenance therapy, though this remains to be demonstrated.

Summary and Conclusions

A number of effective pharmacotherapies are available for the treatment of panic disorder with antidepressants, including the SSRIs and SNRIs, and benzodiazepines currently considered as first-line agents. The efficacy of these agents supports ongoing neurobiological research implicating serotonin, norepinephrine, and GABA in panic disorder, as well as abnormalities in amygdala-cortical circuitry. A variety of other medications, though with less evidence supporting their efficacy, may be reasonable alternatives or may have a role as augmentation agents for patients remaining symptomatic or unable to tolerate first-line agents. More research examining the efficacy and safety of newer agents such as atypical antipsychotics and novel anticonvulsants is needed before definitive recommendations can be made about their use in panic disorder; although at this juncture these agents may be considered for some patients. Although the optimal length of pharmacotherapy for panic disorder remains unclear, the goal of treatment should be a full and sustained remission of panic attacks, anticipatory anxiety, agoraphobic fears and avoidance, remission of comorbid mood or anxiety disorders, and a full return to high level of function and quality of life. Further, cognitive behavioral therapy is another first-line intervention that may also have a role in combination with pharmacotherapy or for patients who do not achieve remission with pharmacotherapy alone (Furukawa, Watanabe, & Churchill, 2006). Although it may not be necessary or possible to provide a formal course of cognitive behavioral therapy for all patients receiving pharmacotherapy, integration of cognitive-behavioral principles and encouragement of exposure to phobic situations and sensations, even during relatively brief visits with a clinician, may contribute to a more comprehensive and complete treatment response; research guiding the optimal integration of CBT elements with pharmacotherapy is needed. Additional discussion of the topic of combining medication and CBT for anxiety disorders can be found in Chapter 32. Finally, to improve treatment outcome and overall quality of life and function for individuals with panic disorder, treatment may include therapeutic interventions for relevant psychosocial issues, such as intrapsychic, family, social, and work-related stresses.

References

American Psychiatric Association. (1994). *Diagnostic and statistical manual of mental disorders* (4th ed.). Washington, DC: Author.

American Psychiatric Association. (1998). Practice guideline for the treatment of patients with panic disorder. Work Group on Panic Disorder. *American Journal of Psychiatry, 155*(Suppl. 5), 1–34.

Asnis, G. M., Hameedi, F. A., Goddard, A. W., Potkin, S. G., Black, D., Jameel, M., et al. (2001). Fluvoxamine in the treatment of panic disorder: A multi-center, double-blind, placebo-controlled study in outpatients. *Psychiatry Research, 103*, 1–14.

Bakish, D., Hooper, C. L., Filteau, M. J., Charbonneau, Y., Fraser, G., West, D. L., et al. (1996). A double-blind placebo-controlled trial comparing fluvoxamine and imipramine in the treatment of panic disorder with or without agoraphobia. *Psychopharmacology Bulletin, 32*, 135–141.

Bakish, D., Saxena, B. M., Bowen, R., & D'Souza, J. (1993). Reversible monoamine oxidase-A inhibitors in panic disorder. *Clinical Neuropharmacology, 16*(Suppl. 2), S77–82.

Bakker, A., van Balkom, A. J., & Spinhoven, P. (2002). SSRIs vs. TCAs in the treatment of panic disorder: A meta-analysis. *Acta Psychiatrica Scandinavica, 106*, 163–167.

Bakker, A., van Balkom, A. J., & Stein, D. J. (2005). Evidence-based pharmacotherapy of panic disorder. *International Journal of Neuropsychopharmacology, 8*, 473–482.

Bakker, A., van Dyck, R., Spinhoven, P., & van Balkom, A. J. (1999). Paroxetine, clomipramine, and cognitive therapy in the treatment of panic disorder. *Journal of Clinical Psychiatry, 60*, 831–838.

Ball, S. G., Otto, M. W., Pollack, M. H., & Rosenbaum, J. F. (1994). Predicting prospective episodes of depression in patients with panic disorder: A longitudinal study. *Journal of Consulting and Clinical Psychology, 62*, 359–365.

Ballenger, J. C., Davidson, J. R., Lecrubier, Y., Nutt, D. J., Baldwin, D. S., den Boer, J. A., et al. (1998). Consensus statement on panic disorder from the International Consensus Group on Depression and Anxiety. *Journal of Clinical Psychiatry, 59*(Suppl. 8), 47–54.

Ballenger, J. C., Wheadon, D. E., Steiner, M., Bushnell, W., & Gergel, I. P. (1998). Double-blind, fixed-dose, placebo-controlled study of paroxetine in the treatment of panic disorder. *American Journal of Psychiatry, 155*, 36–42.

Bertani, A., Perna, G., Migliarese, G., Di Pasquale, D., Cucchi, M., Caldirola, D., et al. (2004). Comparison of the treatment with paroxetine and reboxetine in panic disorder: A randomized, single-blind study. *Pharmacopsychiatry, 37*, 206–210.

Bhagwagar, Z., Wylezinska, M., Taylor, M., Jezzard, P., Matthews, P. M., & Cowen, P. J. (2004). Increased brain GABA concentrations following acute administration of a selective serotonin reuptake inhibitor. *American Journal of Psychiatry, 161*, 368–370.

Black, D. W., Wesner, R., Bowers, W., & Gabel, J. (1993). A comparison of fluvoxamine, cognitive therapy, and placebo in the treatment of panic disorder. *Archives of General Psychiatry, 50*, 44–50.

Bouvard, M., Mollard, E., Guerin, J., & Cottraux, J. (1997). Study and course of the psychological profile in 77 patients expressing panic disorder with agoraphobia after cognitive behaviour therapy with or without buspirone. *Psychotherapy and Psychosomatics, 66*, 27–32.

Bruce, S. E., Vasile, R. G., Goisman, R. M., Salzman, C., Spencer, M., Machan, J. T., et al. (2003). Are benzodiazepines still the medication of choice for patients with panic disorder with or without agoraphobia? *American Journal of Psychiatry, 160*, 1432–1438.

Charney, D. S., Heninger, G. R., & Breier, A. (1984). Noradrenergic function in panic anxiety. Effects of yohimbine in healthy subjects and patients with agoraphobia and panic disorder. *Archives of General Psychiatry, 41*, 751–763.

Charney, D. S., & Woods, S. W. (1989). Benzodiazepine treatment of panic disorder: A comparison of alprazolam and lorazepam. *Journal of Clinical Psychiatry, 50*, 418–423.

Coplan, J. D., & Lydiard, R. B. (1998). Brain circuits in panic disorder. *Biological Psychiatry, 44*, 1264–1276.

Cowley, D. S., Ha, E. H., & Roy-Byrne, P. P. (1997). Determinants of pharmacologic treatment failure in panic disorder. *Journal of Clinical Psychiatry, 58*, 555–561; quiz 562–553.

Cramer, V., Torgersen, S., & Kringlen, E. (2005). Quality of life and anxiety disorders: A population study. *Journal of Nervous and Mental Disease, 193*, 196–202.

Crippa, J. A., & Zuardi, A. W. (2006). Duloxetine in the treatment of panic disorder. *International Journal of Neuropsychopharmacology, 9*, 633–634.

Dannon, P. N., Iancu, I., Cohen, A., Lowengrub, K., Grunhaus, L., & Kotler, M. (2004). Three year naturalistic outcome study of panic disorder patients treated with paroxetine. *BMC Psychiatry, 4*, 16.

Davidson, J. R., Beitman, B., Greist, J. H., Maddock, R. J., Lewis, C. P., Sheridan, A. Q., et al. (1994). Adinazolam sustained-release treatment of panic disorder: A double-blind study. *Journal of Clinical Psychopharmacology, 14*, 255–263.

De Beurs, E., van Balkom, A. J., Lange, A., Koele, P., & van Dyck, R. (1995). Treatment of panic disorder with agoraphobia: Comparison of fluvoxamine, placebo, and psychological panic management combined with exposure and of exposure in vivo alone. *American Journal of Psychiatry, 152*, 683–691.

Den Boer, J. A., & Westenberg, H. G. (1988). Effect of a serotonin and noradrenaline uptake inhibitor in panic disorder: A double-blind comparative study with fluvoxamine and maprotiline. *International Clinical Psychopharmacology, 3,* 59–74.

Den Boer, J. A., Westenberg, H. G., Kamerbeek, W. D., Verhoeven, W. M., & Kahn, R. S. (1987). Effect of serotonin uptake inhibitors in anxiety disorders: A double-blind comparison of clomipramine and fluvoxamine. *International Clinical Psychopharmacology, 2,* 21–32.

Dunner, D. L., Ishiki, D., Avery, D. H., Wilson, L. G., & Hyde, T. S. (1986). Effect of alprazolam and diazepam on anxiety and panic attacks in panic disorder: A controlled study. *Journal of Clinical Psychiatry, 47,* 458–460.

Eaton, W. W., Kessler, R. C., Wittchen, H. U., & Magee, W. J. (1994). Panic and panic disorder in the United States. *American Journal of Psychiatry, 151,* 413–420.

Ettigi, P., Meyerhoff, A. S., Chirban, J. T., Jacobs, R. J., & Wilson, R. R. (1997). The quality of life and employment in panic disorder. *Journal of Nervous and Mental Disease, 18,* 368–372.

Fava, M. (2006). Prospective studies of adverse events related to antidepressant discontinuation. *Journal of Clinical Psychiatry, 67*(Suppl. 4), 14–21.

Fava, M., Judge, R., Hoog, S. L., Nilsson, M. E., & Koke, S. C. (2000). Fluoxetine versus sertraline and paroxetine in major depressive disorder: Changes in weight with long-term treatment. *Journal of Clinical Psychiatry, 61,* 863–867.

Furukawa, T. A., Watanabe, N., & Churchill, R. (2006). Psychotherapy plus antidepressant for panic disorder with or without agoraphobia: Systematic review. *British Journal of Psychiatry, 188,* 305–312.

Gastfriend, D. R., & Rosenbaum, J. F. (1989). Adjunctive buspirone in benzodiazepine treatment of four patients with panic disorder. *American Journal of Psychiatry, 146,* 914–916.

Gaudreault, P., Guay, J., Thivierge, R. L., & Verdy, I. (1991). Benzodiazepine poisoning: Clinical and pharmacological considerations and treatment. *Drug Safety, 6,* 247–265.

Goddard, A. W., Brouette, T., Almai, A., Jetty, P., Woods, S. W., & Charney, D. (2001). Early coadministration of clonazepam with sertraline for panic disorder. *Archives of General Psychiatry, 58,* 681–686.

Goddard, A. W., Mason, G. F., Almai, A., Rothman, D. L., Behar, K. L., Petroff, O. A., et al. (2001). Reductions in occipital cortex GABA levels in panic disorder detected with 1h-magnetic resonance spectroscopy. *Archives of General Psychiatry, 58,* 556–561.

Goodwin, R. D., & Roy-Byrne, P. (2006). Panic and suicidal ideation and suicide attempts: Results from the National Comorbidity Survey. *Depression and Anxiety, 23,* 124–132.

Gorman, J. M., Kent, J. M., Sullivan, G. M., & Coplan, J. D. (2000). Neuroanatomical hypothesis of panic disorder, revised. *American Journal of Psychiatry, 157,* 493–505.

Greenblatt, D. J., Shader, R. I., & Abernethy, D. R. (1983). Drug therapy: Current status of benzodiazepines. *New England Journal of Medicine, 309,* 354–358.

Hirschmann, S., Dannon, P. N., Iancu, I., Dolberg, O. T., Zohar, J., & Grunhaus, L. (2000). Pindolol augmentation in patients with treatment-resistant panic disorder: A double-blind, placebo-controlled trial. *Journal of Clinical Psychopharmacology, 20,* 556–559.

Hoehn-Saric, R., McLeod, D. R., & Hipsley, P. A. (1993). Effect of fluvoxamine on panic disorder. *Journal of Clinical Psychopharmacology, 13,* 321–326.

Hollifield, M., Thompson, P. M., Ruiz, J. E., & Uhlenhuth, E. H. (2005). Potential effectiveness and safety of olanzapine in refractory panic disorder. *Depression and Anxiety, 21,* 33–40.

Kan, C. C., Hilberink, S. R., & Breteler, M. H. (2004). Determination of the main risk factors for benzodiazepine dependence using a multivariate and multidimensional approach. *Comprehensive Psychiatry, 45,* 88–94.

Katon, W. (1996). Panic disorder: Relationship to high medical utilization, unexplained physical symptoms, and medical costs. *Journal of Clinical Psychiatry, 57*(Suppl. 10), 11–18; discussion 19–22.

Katschnig, H., & Amering, M. (1998). The long-term course of panic disorder and its predictors. *Journal of Clinical Psychopharmacology, 18*(6 Suppl. 2), 6S–11S.

Keller, M. B., & Baker, L. A. (1992). The clinical course of panic disorder and depression. *Journal of Clinical Psychiatry, 53*(Suppl.), 5–8.

Keller, M. B., Yonkers, K. A., Warshaw, M. G., Pratt, L. A., Gollan, J. K., Massion, A. O., et al. (1994). Remission and relapse in subjects with panic disorder and panic with agoraphobia: A prospective short-interval naturalistic follow-up. *Journal of Nervous and Mental Disease, 182,* 290–296.

Kessler, R. C., Berglund, P., Demler, O., Jin, R., Merikangas, K. R., & Walters, E. E. (2005). Lifetime prevalence and age-of-onset distributions of *DSM–IV* disorders in the National Comorbidity Survey Replication. *Archives of General Psychiatry, 62,* 593–602.

Kessler, R. C., McGonagle, K. A., Zhao, S., Nelson, C. B., Hughes, M., Eshleman, S., et al. (1994). Lifetime and 12-month prevalence of *DSM–III–R* psychiatric disorders in the United States. Results from the National Comorbidity Survey. *Archives of General Psychiatry, 51,* 8–19.

Klein, D. F., & Fink, M. (1962). Psychiatric reaction patterns to imipramine. *American Journal of Psychiatry, 119,* 432–438.

Lecrubier, Y., Bakker, A., Dunbar, G., & Judge, R. (1997). A comparison of paroxetine, clomipramine and placebo in the treatment of panic disorder. Collaborative Paroxetine Panic Study Investigators. *Acta Psychiatrica Scandinavica, 95,* 145–152.

Lecrubier, Y., & Judge, R. (1997). Long-term evaluation of paroxetine, clomipramine and placebo in panic disorder. Collaborative Paroxetine Panic Study Investigators. *Acta Psychiatrica Scandinavica, 95,* 153–160.

Lepola, U. M., Wade, A. G., Leinonen, E. V., Koponen, H. J., Frazer, J., Sjodin, I., et al. (1998). A controlled, prospective, 1-year trial of citalopram in the treatment of panic disorder. *Journal of Clinical Psychiatry, 59,* 528–534.

Lippman, S. B., & Nash, K. (1990). Monoamine oxidase inhibitor update: Potential adverse food and drug interactions. *Drug Safety, 5,* 195–204.

Livingston, M. G., & Livingston, H. M. (1996). Monoamine oxidase inhibitors: An update on drug interactions. *Drug Safety, 14,* 219–227.

Loerch, B., Graf-Morgenstern, M., Hautzinger, M., Schlegel, S., Hain, C., Sandmann, J., et al. (1999). Randomised placebo-controlled trial of moclobemide, cognitive-behavioural therapy and their combination in panic disorder with agoraphobia. *British Journal of Psychiatry, 174,* 205–212.

Londborg, P. D., Wolkow, R., Smith, W. T., DuBoff, E., England, D., Ferguson, J., et al. (1998). Sertraline in the treatment of panic disorder: A multi-site, double-blind, placebo-controlled, fixed-dose investigation. *British Journal of Psychiatry, 173,* 54–60.

Lum, M., Fontaine, R., & Elie, R. (1990). Divalproex sodium's antipanic effect in panic disorder: A placebo-controlled study. *Biological Psychiatry, 27*(Suppl. 1), 164A–165A.

Lydiard, R. B., Steiner, M., Burnham, D., & Gergel, I. (1998). Efficacy studies of paroxetine in panic disorder. *Psychopharmacology Bulletin, 34,* 175–182.

Markowitz, J. S., Weissman, M. M., Ouellette, R., Lish, J. D., & Klerman, G. L. (1989). Quality of life in panic disorder. *Archives of General Psychiatry, 46,* 984–992.

Maron, E., Kuikka, J. T., Shlik, J., Vasar, V., Vanninen, E., & Tiihonen, J. (2004). Reduced brain serotonin transporter binding in patients with panic disorder. *Psychiatry Research 132,* 173–181.

Mavissakalian, M. R., & Perel, J. M. (2002). Duration of imipramine therapy and relapse in panic disorder with agoraphobia. *Journal of Clinical Psychopharmacology, 22,* 294–299.

Michelson, D., Allgulander, C., Dantendorfer, K., Knezevic, A., Maierhofer, D., Micev, V., et al. (2001). Efficacy of usual antidepressant dosing regimens of fluoxetine in panic disorder: Randomised, placebo-controlled trial. *British Journal of Psychiatry, 179,* 514–518.

Michelson, D., Lydiard, R. B., Pollack, M. H., Tamura, R. N., Hoog, S. L., Tepner, R., et al. (1998). Outcome assessment and clinical improvement in panic disorder: Evidence from a randomized controlled trial of fluoxetine and placebo. The Fluoxetine Panic Disorder Study Group. *American Journal of Psychiatry, 155,* 1570–1577.

Michelson, D., Pollack, M., Lydiard, R. B., Tamura, R., Tepner, R., & Tollefson, G. (1999). Continuing treatment of panic disorder after acute response: Randomised, placebo-controlled trial with fluoxetine. The Fluoxetine Panic Disorder Study Group. *British Journal of Psychiatry, 174,* 213–218.

Modell, J. G., Katholi, C. R., Modell, J. D., & DePalma, R. L. (1997). Comparative sexual side effects of bupropion, fluoxetine, paroxetine, and sertraline. *Clinical Pharmacology and Therapeutics, 61,* 476–487.

Munjack, D. J., Crocker, B., Cabe, D., Brown, R., Usigli, R., Zulueta, A., et al. (1989). Alprazolam, propranolol, and placebo in the treatment of panic disorder and agoraphobia with panic attacks. *Journal of Clinical Psychopharmacology, 9,* 22–27.

Nagy, L. M., Krystal, J. H., Woods, S. W., & Charney, D. S. (1989). Clinical and medication outcome after short-term alprazolam and behavioral group treatment in panic disorder: 2.5 year naturalistic follow-up study. *Archives of General Psychiatry, 46,* 993–999.

Nesse, R. M., Cameron, O. G., Curtis, G. C., McCann, D. S., & Huber-Smith, M. J. (1984). Adrenergic function in patients with panic anxiety. *Archives of General Psychiatry, 41,* 771–776.

Noyes, R., Jr., Burrows, G. D., Reich, J. H., Judd, F. K., Garvey, M. J., Norman, T. R., et al. (1996). Diazepam versus alprazolam for the treatment of panic disorder. *Journal of Clinical Psychiatry, 57,* 349–355.

Noyes, R., Jr., & Perry, P. (1990). Maintenance treatment with antidepressants in panic disorder. *Journal of Clinical Psychiatry, 51*(Suppl. A), 24–30.

Nutt, D. J. (1998). Antidepressants in panic disorder: Clinical and preclinical mechanisms. *Journal of Clinical Psychiatry, 59*(Suppl. 8), 24–28; discussion 29.

Oehrberg, S., Christiansen, P. E., Behnke, K., Borup, A. L., Severin, B., Soegaard, J., et al. (1995). Paroxetine in the treatment of panic disorder: A randomised, double-blind, placebo-controlled study. *British Journal of Psychiatry, 167,* 374–379.

Otto, M. W., Pollack, M. H., Sachs, G. S., Reiter, S. R., Meltzer-Brody, S., & Rosenbaum, J. F. (1993). Discontinuation of

benzodiazepine treatment: Efficacy of cognitive-behavioral therapy for patients with panic disorder. *American Journal of Psychiatry, 150,* 1485–1490.

Otto, M. W., Tuby, K. S., Gould, R. A., McLean, R. Y., & Pollack, M. H. (2001). An effect-size analysis of the relative efficacy and tolerability of serotonin selective reuptake inhibitors for panic disorder. *American Journal of Psychiatry, 158,* 1989–1992.

Palatnik, A., Frolov, K., Fux, M., & Benjamin, J. (2001). Double-blind, controlled, crossover trial of inositol versus fluvoxamine for the treatment of panic disorder. *Journal of Clinical Psychopharmacology, 21,* 335–339.

Pande, A. C., Pollack, M. H., Crockatt, J., Greiner, M., Chouinard, G., Lydiard, R. B., et al. (2000). Placebo-controlled study of gabapentin treatment of panic disorder. *Journal of Clinical Psychopharmacology, 20,* 467–471.

Pecknold, J. C., Swinson, R. P., Kuch, K., & Lewis, C. P. (1988). Alprazolam in panic disorder and agoraphobia: Results from a multicenter trial. III. Discontinuation effects. *Archives of General Psychiatry, 45,* 429–436.

Pohl, R. B., Wolkow, R. M., & Clary, C. M. (1998). Sertraline in the treatment of panic disorder: A double-blind multicenter trial. *American Journal of Psychiatry, 155,* 1189–1195.

Pollack, M. H. (2005). The pharmacotherapy of panic disorder. *Journal of Clinical Psychiatry, 66*(Suppl. 4), 23–27.

Pollack, M. H., Allgulander, C., Bandelow, B., Cassano, G. B., Greist, J. H., Hollander, E., et al. (2003). WCA recommendations for the long-term treatment of panic disorder. *CNS Spectrums, 8*(8 Suppl. 1), 17–30.

Pollack, M. H., Lepola, U., Koponen, H., Simon, N. M., Worthington, J. J., Emilien, G., et al. (2007). A double-blind study of the efficacy of venlafaxine extended-release, paroxetine, and placebo in the treatment of panic disorder. *Depression and Anxiety, 24*(1), 1–14.

Pollack, M., Mangano, R., Entsuah, R., Tzanis, E., & Simon, N. M. (2007). A randomized controlled trial of venlafaxine ER and paroxetine in the treatment of outpatients with panic disorder. *Psychopharmacology, 194*(2), 233–242.

Pollack, M. H., Otto, M. W., Rosenbaum, J. F., Sachs, G. S., O'Neil, C., Asher, R., et al. (1990). Longitudinal course of panic disorder: Findings from the Massachusetts General Hospital Naturalistic Study. *Journal of Clinical Psychiatry, 51*(Suppl. A), 12–16.

Pollack, M. H., Otto, M. W., Sabatino, S., Majcher, D., Worthington, J. J., McArdle, E. T., et al. (1996). Relationship of childhood anxiety to adult panic disorder: Correlates and influence on course. *American Journal of Psychiatry, 153,* 376–381.

Pollack, M. H., Otto, M. W., Tesar, G. E., Cohen, L. S., Meltzer-Brody, S., & Rosenbaum, J. F. (1993). Long-term outcome after acute treatment with alprazolam or clonazepam for panic disorder. *Journal of Clinical Psychopharmacology, 13,* 257–263.

Pollack, M. H., Otto, M. W., Worthington, J. J., Manfro, G. G., & Wolkow, R. (1998). Sertraline in the treatment of panic disorder: A flexible-dose multicenter trial. *Archives of General Psychiatry, 55,* 1010–1016.

Pollack, M. H., Simon, N. M., Worthington, J. J., Doyle, A. L., Peters, P., Toshkov, F., et al. (2003). Combined paroxetine and clonazepam treatment strategies compared to paroxetine monotherapy for panic disorder. *Journal of Psychopharmacology, 17,* 276–282.

Pollack, M. H., & Smoller, J. W. (1995). The longitudinal course and outcome of panic disorder. *Psychiatric Clinics of North America, 18,* 785–801.

Pollack, M. H., Worthington, J. J., III, Otto, M. W., Maki, K. M., Smoller, J. W., Manfro, G. G., et al. (1996). Venlafaxine for panic disorder: Results from a double-blind, placebo-controlled study. *Psychopharmacology Bulletin, 32,* 667–670.

Primeau, F., & Fontaine, R. (1988). GABAergic agents and panic disorder. *Biological Psychiatry, 24,* 942–943.

Rapaport, M. H., Wolkow, R., Rubin, A., Hackett, E., Pollack, M., & Ota, K. Y. (2001). Sertraline treatment of panic disorder: Results of a long-term study. *Acta Psychiatrica Scandinavica, 104,* 289–298.

Redmond, D. E., Jr., & Huang, Y. H. (1979). Current concepts: II. New evidence for a locus coeruleus-norepinephrine connection with anxiety. *Life Sciences, 25,* 2149–2162.

Rickels, K., Pollack, M. H., Feltner, D. E., Lydiard, R. B., Zimbroff, D. L., Bielski, R. J., et al. (2005). Pregabalin for treatment of generalized anxiety disorder: A 4-week, multicenter, double-blind, placebo-controlled trial of pregabalin and alprazolam. *Archives of General Psychiatry, 62,* 1022–1030.

Rickels, K., Schweizer, E., Weiss, S., & Zavodnick, S. (1993). Maintenance drug treatment for panic disorder: II. Short- and long-term outcome after drug taper. *Archives of General Psychiatry, 50,* 61–68.

Rosenbaum, J. F., Pollack, M. H., & Fredman, S. J. (1998). The pharmacotherapy of panic disorder. In J. F. Rosenbaum & M. H. Pollack (Eds.), *Panic disorder and its treatment* (pp. 153–180). New York: Marcel Dekker.

Roy-Byrne, P. P., & Cowley, D. S. (1994). Course and outcome in panic disorder: A review of recent follow-up studies. *Anxiety, 1,* 151–160.

Roy-Byrne, P. P., Craske, M. G., & Stein, M. B. (2006). Panic disorder. *Lancet, 368,* 1023–1032.

Roy-Byrne, P. P., Stein, M. B., Russo, J., Mercier, E., Thomas, R., McQuaid, J., et al. (1999). Panic disorder in the primary care setting: Comorbidity, disability, service utilization, and treatment. *Journal of Clinical Psychiatry, 60,* 492–499; quiz 500.

Roy-Byrne, P., Wingerson, D. K., Radant, A., Greenblatt, D. J., & Cowley, D. S. (1996). Reduced benzodiazepine sensitivity in patients with panic disorder: Comparison with patients with obsessive-compulsive disorder and normal subjects. *American Journal of Psychiatry, 153,* 1444–1449.

Rubin, H. C., Rapaport, M. H., Levine, B., Gladsjo, J. K., Rabin, A., Auerbach, M., et al. (2000). Quality of well being in panic disorder: The assessment of psychiatric and general disability. *Journal of Affective Disorders, 57,* 217–221.

Schweizer, E., Fox, I., Case, G., & Rickels, K. (1988). Lorazepam vs. alprazolam in the treatment of panic disorder. *Psychopharmacology Bulletin, 24,* 224–227.

Schweizer, E., Pohl, R., Balon, R., Fox, I., Rickels, K., & Yeragani, V. K. (1990). Lorazepam vs. alprazolam in the treatment of panic disorder. *Pharmacopsychiatry, 23,* 90–93.

Sharp, D. M., Power, K. G., Simpson, R. J., Swanson, V., & Anstee, J. A. (1997). Global measures of outcome in a controlled comparison of pharmacological and psychological treatment of panic disorder and agoraphobia in primary care. *British Journal of General Practice, 47,* 150–155.

Shear, M. K., Rucci, P., Williams, J., Frank, E., Grochocinski, V., Vander Bilt, J., et al. (2001). Reliability and validity of the Panic Disorder Severity Scale: Replication and extension. *Journal of Psychiatric Research, 35,* 293–296.

Sheehan, D. V., Ballenger, J., & Jacobsen, G. (1980). Treatment of endogenous anxiety with phobic, hysterical, and hypochondriacal symptoms. *Archives of General Psychiatry, 37,* 51–59.

Sheehan, D. V., Burnham, D. B., Iyengar, M. K., & Perera, P. (2005). Efficacy and tolerability of controlled-release paroxetine in the treatment of panic disorder. *Journal of Clinical Psychiatry, 66,* 34–40.

Sheehan, D. V., Davidson, J., Manschreck, T., & Van Wyck Fleet, J. (1983). Lack of efficacy of a new antidepressant (bupropion) in the treatment of panic disorder with phobias. *Journal of Clinical Psychopharmacology, 3,* 28–31.

Sheehan, D. V., Raj, A. B., Harnett-Sheehan, K., Soto, S., & Knapp, E. (1993). The relative efficacy of high-dose buspirone and alprazolam in the treatment of panic disorder: A double-blind placebo-controlled study. *Acta Psychiatrica Scandinavica, 88,* 1–11.

Sheehan, D. V., Raj, A. B., Sheehan, K. H., & Soto, S. (1990). Is buspirone effective for panic disorder? *Journal of Clinical Psychopharmacology, 10,* 3–11.

Sheikh, J. I., Londborg, P., Clary, C. M., & Fayyad, R. (2000). The efficacy of sertraline in panic disorder: Combined results from two fixed-dose studies. *International Clinical Psychopharmacology, 15,* 335–342.

Simon, N. M., Emmanuel, N., Ballenger, J., Worthington, J. J., Kinrys, G., Korbly, N. B., et al. (2003). Bupropion sustained release for panic disorder. *Psychopharmacology Bulletin, 37,* 66–72.

Simon, N. M., Hoge, E. A., Fischmann, D., Worthington, J. J., Christian, K. M., Kinrys, G., et al. (2006). An open-label trial of risperidone augmentation for refractory anxiety disorders. *Journal of Clinical Psychiatry, 67,* 381–385.

Simpson, H. B., Schneier, F. R., Campeas, R. B., Marshall, R. D., Fallon, B. A., Davies, S., et al. (1998). Imipramine in the treatment of social phobia. *Journal of Clinical Psychopharmacology, 18,* 132–135.

Soumerai, S. B., Simoni-Wastila, L., Singer, C., Mah, C., Gao, X., Salzman, C., et al. (2003). Lack of relationship between long-term use of benzodiazepines and escalation to high dosages. *Psychiatric Services, 54,* 1006–1011.

Stahl, S. M., Gergel, I., & Li, D. (2003). Escitalopram in the treatment of panic disorder: A randomized, double-blind, placebo-controlled trial. *Journal of Clinical Psychiatry, 64,* 1322–1327.

Stein, D. J. (2005). The neurobiology of panic disorder: Toward an integrated model. *CNS Spectrums, 9*(Suppl. 12), 12–24.

Stein, D. J., Seedat, S., van der Linden, G. J., & Zungu-Dirwayi, N. (2000). Selective serotonin reuptake inhibitors in the treatment of post-traumatic stress disorder: A meta-analysis of randomized controlled trials. *International Clinical Psychopharmacology, 15*(Suppl. 2), S31–39.

Stewart, S. A. (2005). The effects of benzodiazepines on cognition. *Journal of Clinical Psychiatry, 66*(Suppl. 2), 9–13.

Tiller, J. W., Bouwer, C., & Behnke, K. (1999). Moclobemide and fluoxetine for panic disorder. International Panic Disorder Study Group. *European Archives of Psychiatry and Clinical Neuroscience, 249*(Suppl. 1), S7–10.

Uhde, T. W., Stein, M. B., & Post, R. M. (1988). Lack of efficacy of carbamazepine in the treatment of panic disorder. *American Journal of Psychiatry, 145,* 1104–1109.

Van Vliet, I. M., den Boer, J. A., Westenberg, H. G., & Slaap, B. R. (1996). A double-blind comparative study of brofaromine and fluvoxamine in outpatients with panic disorder. *Journal of Clinical Psychopharmacology, 16,* 299–306.

Van Vliet, I. M., Westenberg, H. G., & den Boer, J. A. (1993). MAO inhibitors in panic disorder: Clinical effects of treatment with brofaromine. A double blind placebo controlled study. *Psychopharmacology (Berl), 112,* 483–489.

Versiani, M., Cassano, G., Perugi, G., Benedetti, A., Mastalli, L., Nardi, A., et al. (2002). Reboxetine, a selective norepinephrine reuptake inhibitor, is an effective and well-tolerated treatment for panic disorder. *Journal of Clinical Psychiatry, 63,* 31–37.

Wade, A. G., Lepola, U., Koponen, H. J., Pedersen, V., & Pedersen, T. (1997). The effect of citalopram in panic disorder. *British Journal of Psychiatry, 170,* 549–553.

Warshaw, M. G., Massion, A. O., Shea, M. T., Allsworth, J., & Keller, M. B. (1997). Predictors of remission in patients with panic with and without agoraphobia: Prospective 5-year follow-up data. *Journal of Nervous and Mental Disease, 185,* 517–519.

Woodman, C. L., & Noyes, R., Jr. (1994). Panic disorder: Treatment with valproate. *Journal of Clinical Psychiatry, 55,* 134–136.

Worthington, J. J., III, Kinrys, G., Wygant, L. E., & Pollack, M. H. (2005). Aripiprazole as an augmentor of selective serotonin reuptake inhibitors in depression and anxiety disorder patients. *International Clinical Psychopharmacology, 20,* 9–11.

Yonkers, K. A., Zlotnick, C., Allsworth, J., Warshaw, M., Shea, T., & Keller, M. B. (1998). Is the course of panic disorder the same in women and men? *American Journal of Psychiatry, 155,* 596–602.

Zwanzger, P., & Rupprecht, R. (2005). Selective GABAergic treatment for panic? Investigations in experimental panic induction and panic disorder. *Journal of Psychiatry and Neuroscience, 30,* 167–175.

Psychological Treatment of Panic Disorder and Agoraphobia

Randi E. McCabe *and* Shannon Gifford

Abstract

This chapter provides a review of the research literature on psychological treatment for panic disorder and agoraphobia (PDA). The most extensively studied psychological treatment for PDA is cognitive behavioral therapy (CBT). This chapter summarizes specific CBT strategies and treatment packages, findings from efficacy and effectiveness studies, prevention initiatives, predictors of treatment outcome, and research on long-term outcome. CBT has established efficacy and robust treatment effects that have been demonstrated across a variety of treatment settings and over extended follow-up periods. Further research is needed in the areas of prevention and early intervention, and in the extension of established treatments to underserved or challenging populations.

Keywords: agoraphobia, CBT, cognitive behavioral therapy, effectiveness, efficacy, panic disorder, psychological treatment

The most extensively studied psychological treatment for panic disorder with or without agoraphobia (PDA) is cognitive behavioral therapy (CBT), and the psychological treatment literature on PDA is more advanced than for any other anxiety disorder. As noted by Otto and Deveney (2005), research on CBT for PDA has gone beyond standard efficacy studies on whether CBT works; recent research has included multiarmed combination treatment studies, dismantling studies, effectiveness studies, investigations on cost effectiveness, and prevention research. This chapter provides a review of research on psychological treatment for PDA, including treatment strategies and packages, findings from efficacy and effectiveness studies, prevention initiatives, predictors of treatment outcome, and research on long-term outcome.

Evidence-Based Psychological Treatments for Panic Disorder

Cognitive behavioral therapy is considered a first-line treatment for PDA in practice guidelines published by the American Psychiatric Association (1998) and the Canadian Psychiatric Association (Swinson et al., 2006). The CBT approaches for PDA utilize multiple components that are tailored to meet the treatment needs of the patient. These components include psychoeducation, cognitive restructuring, interoceptive exposure, in vivo exposure, and relaxation-based strategies. The goal of these strategies is to modify an individual's response to panic cues that may be internally based (e.g., a racing heart) or externally based (e.g., sitting in a crowded movie theater) so that a fearful response is replaced by a non-fearful one (for broader discussion, see Allen & Barlow, 2006). Numerous studies demonstrate that these strategies are beneficial for treating the central features of panic disorder, including panic attack frequency, anticipatory anxiety, and agoraphobic avoidance (for review, see Antony & Swinson, 2000; Taylor, 2000).

Treatment Components and Strategies

The psychoeducational component provides information on a number of topics, including the nature of anxiety and fear, understanding panic attacks and the main symptoms of PDA, and the CBT model of the development and maintenance of the disorder (for more detailed description, see Rapee, Craske, & Barlow, 1996). Research has shown that psychoeducation is a beneficial component, leading to reductions in anticipatory anxiety and negative affect (Rees, Richards, & Smith, 1999).

Cognitive restructuring focuses on identifying and modifying misinterpretations of benign physical symptoms (e.g., "When my heart is racing it is a sign of an impending heart attack") as well as panic-related thoughts and beliefs that inflate the perceived cost (i.e., negative consequences) and likelihood of a negative event occurring (e.g., "Panic is dangerous and could kill me," "I need to escape this situation or something terrible will happen"). Cognitive strategies that are more generally focused and do not concentrate on reducing catastrophic misinterpretation of bodily sensations have been shown to be less beneficial in reducing panic symptoms in preliminary research (Salkovskis, Clark, & Hackmann, 1991).

Interoceptive exposure utilizes a range of exercises (e.g., hyperventilation, breathing through a straw, spinning in a chair, and running on the spot) to provoke feared physical sensations (e.g., breathlessness, dizziness, nausea, heart palpitations). The efficacy of interoceptive exposure for reducing PDA symptoms has been supported by studies examining interoceptive exposure as part of a multicomponent treatment approach (Barlow, Gorman, Shear, & Woods, 2000), as well as studies examining the use of interoceptive exposure alone (Craske, Rowe, Lewin, & Noriega-Dimitri, 1997). Evidence demonstrates that interoceptive exposure is a useful intervention for most individuals with PDA. The exercises are effective for inducing anxiety (and panic for some individuals), and anxiety reduction occurs with repeated exposure (Antony, Roth Ledley, Liss, & Swinson, 2006; Schmidt & Trakowski, 2004). Of the standard exercises, the ones that induce the most intense responses include spinning, breathing through a straw, and hyperventilation (Antony et al., 2006; Schmidt & Trakowski, 2004).

Situational or in vivo exposure is an important component of treatment when agoraphobia is present. An exposure hierarchy is used to guide gradual exposure to feared and avoided situations such as riding the bus, crowds, and driving. Exposure is particularly beneficial for targeting agoraphobic avoidance (e.g., Mattick, Andrews, Hadzi-Pavlovic,

& Christensen, 1990). The efficacy of exposure is enhanced when patients are instructed to refrain from engaging in safety behaviors such as carrying a cell phone, medication, or water (Salkovskis, Clark, Hackmann, Wells, & Gelder, 1999). Evidence regarding the benefits of adding panic management strategies (e.g., cognitive therapy, interoceptive exposure) to in vivo exposure for agoraphobia has been mixed, with some studies suggesting an additive effect, and others showing no incremental benefit (Michelson, Marchione, Greenwald, Testa, & Marchione, 1996; Öst, Thulin, & Ramnerö, 2004).

Relaxation-based techniques have also been included in some treatment packages for PDA. Applied relaxation (i.e., progressive muscle relaxation combined with in vivo exposure) is less efficacious than other treatment components and combinations (for review, see Taylor, 2000). The most common relaxation-based technique utilized in PDA treatment is breathing retraining. However, there is some evidence to suggest that breathing retraining does not add to the efficacy of CBT (Schmidt et al., 2000) and may in fact hinder outcome for some individuals by functioning as a safety cue inhibiting corrective learning in response to anxiety and panic symptoms (Antony & Swinson, 2000).

Comprehensive Treatment Approaches

A number of CBT approaches have been developed for PDA, each using some combination of the treatment strategies described earlier. The two best-studied of these approaches are panic control treatment (PCT) (Craske & Barlow, 2007a) developed by David Barlow, Michelle Craske, and colleagues, and cognitive therapy developed by David M. Clark, Paul Salkovskis, and colleagues (Clark et al., 1994, 1999). These approaches share features, though they were developed independently.

Panic Control Treatment

Panic control treatment is the most extensively studied CBT intervention for PDA. Based on a 12- to 15-session manualized treatment protocol (Craske & Barlow, 2007a, 2007b), PCT combines psychoeducation, breathing retraining, cognitive restructuring, interoceptive exposure, and in vivo exposure to the extent that agoraphobic avoidance is a problem (for a review, see Antony & McCabe, 2002). Breathing retraining was added later in the development of PCT, replacing progressive muscle relaxation, which was found to be less beneficial than other PCT components (e.g., Beck, Stanley, Baldwin, Deagle, & Averill, 1994) and potentially interfering with long-term treatment effects (Craske, Brown, & Barlow, 1991). This treatment has been adapted for use in various populations, including treatment of adolescents (e.g., Hoffman & Mattis, 2000) and individuals with schizophrenia (e.g., Hofmann, Bufka, Brady, Du Rand, & Goff, 2000), as well as relapse prevention following benzodiazepine treatment in PDA (Spiegel, Bruce, Gregg, & Nuzzarello, 1994). In addition, PCT has been adapted for use in a primary care setting following a model of collaborative care (Craske et al., 2005). In this context, PCT is combined with medications and delivered by a team consisting of a behavioral health specialist, psychiatrist, and primary care physician. Modifications include fewer sessions, use of telephone booster sessions, and management of comorbidity.

Cognitive Therapy

Clark, Salkovskis, and colleagues (Clark et al., 1994, 1999) developed cognitive therapy for PDA based on Clark's cognitive model of panic (1986, 1988). A range of cognitive and behavioral strategies are used to challenge misinterpretations of bodily sensations as they occur during a panic attack, and to modify catastrophic beliefs underlying these misinterpretations. Behavioral strategies are used to test negative predictions and include situational exposure, elimination of safety behaviors, and induction of feared physical sensations by focusing attention on the body, reading pairs of words linking physical sensations to feared catastrophes, and the use of exercises such as running and hyperventilation.

Other Approaches

A number of approaches have been developed to expand upon and address shortcomings with standard CBT or to approach treatment of the disorder from an alternative theoretical perspective. To date, there are no published randomized controlled trials of the treatment packages reviewed below (with the exception of emotion-focused therapy and panic-focused psychodynamic psychotherapy), although proponents of each have presented promising data from uncontrolled trials.

Sensation-Focused Intensive Therapy (SFIT) (Baker-Morissette, Spiegel, & Heinrichs, 2005). The originators of SFIT note that patients with moderate to severe agoraphobia fare less well in standard CBT than do those with mild or absent situational avoidance, and that patients with residual agoraphobia or fear of physical sensations are at heightened risk of relapse. It is a brief (i.e., 8-day), high-intensity cog-

nitive behavioral treatment package that attempts to completely eliminate agoraphobic avoidance and fear of physical sensations. Following psychoeducation and a "cognitive preparation" phase designed to enhance patient motivation for intensive exposure sessions, patients undergo several days of massed, ungraded exposure to feared stimuli where they are encouraged to tackle their most feared situations immediately. The potency of the exposures is enhanced with symptom-induction exercises. Anything that might distract the patient from the full experience of anxiety (e.g., talking to the therapist, using cognitive restructuring during the exposure) is strongly discouraged. Therapy concludes with a relapse-prevention module.

Acceptance-Enhanced Cognitive Behavioral Therapy for Panic (AE-CBT) (Levitt & Karekla, 2005). Given the significant refusal, dropout, and nonresponder rates associated with CBT outcome trials, Levitt and Karekla (2005) have incorporated ideas from acceptance and commitment therapy (ACT) (Hayes, Strosahl, & Wilson, 1999) into CBT protocols for PDA to further enhance their palatability and short- and long-term efficacy. A central tenet of ACT is that *experiential avoidance,* or the unwillingness to experience painful emotions, thoughts, or bodily sensations, contributes to a variety of emotional problems (Hayes et al., 1999). This treatment adds some components to standard CBT that future research may show to be helpful, such as mindfulness exercises and the explicit inclusion of discussions about the importance of increasing valued activities in the face of potential anxiety. However, core components mirror those of CBT: psychoeducation about panic, interoceptive and situational exposure, and the examination of beliefs about the implications and likely consequences of panic symptoms. Rationales for interventions are framed in terms of accepting emotional experiences and pursuing valued actions. Levitt and Karekla (2005) eliminate cognitive restructuring from their protocol as they view this strategy as an attempt to master and control mental experience. They describe other strategies for gaining perspective on anxious thoughts, however, that seem similar in many respects to cognitive restructuring.

Panic-Focused Psychodynamic Psychotherapy (PFPP) (Milrod et al., 2001). In this manualized, 24-session treatment protocol for PDA, therapists apply psychodynamic principles (e.g., the importance of transference and unconscious thought) and practices (e.g., free association) to the specific problem of panic attacks. The governing idea is that panic attacks are never truly "uncued"; rather, they are seen as the consequences of unconscious conflicts, usually involving themes of separation and independence, rage, or repressed sexual excitement. Therapy involves uncovering the unconscious meanings of panic attacks. In a randomized controlled study (Milrod et al., 2007), PFPP was found to be more effective for reducing panic symptoms than a relaxation-based treatment.

Emotion-Focused Therapy (EFT) (Shear, Houck, Greeno, & Masters, 2001). Shear and colleagues (2001) noted that most people seeking treatment for PDA receive supportive, nonspecific therapy rather than empirically supported interventions specifically targeting PDA symptoms, and that little is known about the efficacy of this therapy. Emotion-focused therapy is a formalized variant of this nonprescriptive, readily available treatment. Shear et al. (2001) conducted a randomized controlled trial of EFT versus CBT, imipramine, and pill placebo for the treatment of panic disorder with no more than mild agoraphobia. Patients found EFT as plausible a treatment as CBT or medication, and patients in this condition had the highest therapy completion rate. However, EFT was not superior to placebo, whereas patients in the CBT and imipramine conditions made significant therapeutic gains, relative to those who received placebo.

Review of Research on CBT for PDA

There is a substantial body of research on CBT for PDA examining various aspects of treatment outcome. This section provides a general overview of the findings from both efficacy and effectiveness studies. Research on the utility of brief CBT interventions is also reviewed.

Efficacy Studies

Numerous randomized controlled trials have established the efficacy of CBT for PDA over placebo, waitlist control, and other active treatments such as applied relaxation (for review, see Taylor, 2000). It has been shown that CBT for PDA is beneficial for reducing associated psychological symptoms and comorbidity, including depression, generalized anxiety disorder, and specific phobia (e.g., Tsao, Mystkowski, Zucker, & Craske, 2002), as well as improving physical health symptom ratings, independent from its impact on anxiety symptoms (Schmidt et al., 2003). In addition, CBT is helpful for patients who have not responded to pharmacotherapy trials (Pollack, Otto, Kaspi, Hammerness, & Rosenbaum, 1994).

The overall effect size for CBT for PDA is large (Butler, Chapman, Forman, & Beck, 2006). For example, in a review of 17 studies published between 1990 and 1998, Westen and Morrison (2001) found a large mean pre- to posttreatment effect size for CBT (Cohen's $d = 1.55$) with 63% of treatment completers and 54% of the intent-to-treat sample classified as improved upon posttreatment. However, it should be noted that, although patients were substantially improved, the average patient continued to have mild symptoms of the disorder at termination.

A more recent meta-analysis of 124 studies conducted by Mitte (2005) found that CBT was superior to no-treatment control and placebo control conditions in the reduction of anxiety and associated depression and improvement in quality of life. Although CBT and behavioral treatment were equally effective in achieving anxiety reduction, CBT was associated with reduced rates of attrition and greater improvement in associated depression symptoms. Self-help treatments were beneficial, although there was variability in the strength of effect sizes across studies. Studies have found that CBT is as efficacious as medication following acute treatment and potentially superior to medication in longer-term follow-up (Barlow, Gorman, Shear, & Woods, 2000; Klosko, Barlow, Tassinari, & Cerny, 1990; Marks et al., 1993; Mitte, 2005).

Combined CBT and Medication. The provision of combined CBT and medication is common in clinical practice. Does a combined treatment provide greater benefit than either treatment alone? Numerous studies using a variety of medications and CBT packages have sought to answer this question. Perhaps the most definitive study addressing this issue is a large-scale multisite clinical trial comparing CBT, imipramine, and their combination conducted by Barlow and colleagues (2000). Following acute treatment, no differences were found among active treatments, all of which were superior to placebo. A slight advantage for combined treatment was suggested following a 6-month maintenance phase where treatments were continued with monthly visits. At 6-month follow up, however, only CBT (and CBT plus placebo) was significantly better than placebo. The effects of medication were reduced following discontinuation. Interestingly, the combined treatment condition was associated with the highest relapse rate at follow-up (48.28%) compared to imipramine (40%), CBT plus placebo (16.67%), and CBT alone (17.86%). A meta-analysis conducted by Mitte (2005) generally supports these findings.

However, other research suggests an advantage for combined treatment, at least in the acute phase. A recent meta-analysis conducted by Furukawa, Watanabe, and Churchill (2006) examined 23 studies (involving 1,709 patients) comparing a combination of psychotherapy and antidepressant pharmacotherapy with either treatment alone for adult patients with PDA. Twenty-two of the 23 studies utilized CBT as the psychotherapy intervention. Combined CBT and medication was superior to either intervention alone following the acute phase of treatment, although combination treatment was associated with a higher dropout rate than CBT alone due to medication-related side effects. At follow-up (6 to 24 months), combined treatment was superior to medication but equivalent to CBT alone. No disadvantage was found for the combined treatment in the long term.

Combined treatment has been recommended for panic when complicated by comorbid conditions (Telch & Lucas, 1994). However, the issue has been raised that medication may interfere with extinction of fear in relation to panic-related triggers and thus impede learning of nonfearful responses (Smits, O'Cleirigh, & Otto, 2006). Moreover, medication may interfere with treatment compliance and increase the risk of dropout due to medication side effects. This is supported by the finding that pharmacotherapy is associated with greater dropout than CBT. For example, in one meta-analytic study, dropout rates were 5.6%, 19.8%, and 22.0% for cognitive behavioral treatments, pharmacological treatments, and combined cognitive behavioral and pharmacological treatment, respectively (Gould, Otto, & Pollack, 1995). Furthermore, withdrawal symptoms may also increase the risk of relapse and interfere with long-term outcome.

Individual Versus Group CBT. There are a number of benefits to delivering CBT in a group format over an individual format. Group CBT is more cost-effective and resource efficient, and less demanding on therapist time. Group CBT has established efficacy (e.g., Dannon, Gon-Usishkin, Gelbert, Lowengrub, & Grunhaus, 2004; Lidren et al., 1994; Telch et al., 1993). Despite the benefits of group treatment, patients display a preference for individual treatment. When given the choice, 95% of patients chose individual over group treatment (Sharp, Power, & Swanson, 2004).

Only a few studies provide a direct comparison of group and individual formats of CBT for PDA. Preliminary results suggest a slight advantage for individual treatment. In one study, both formats were comparable for measures of panic and agoraphobia

at posttreatment and 6-month follow-up but individual treatment was associated with greater alleviation of generalized anxiety and depressive symptoms (Néron, Lacroix, & Chaput, 1995). In another study comparing the two formats in a primary care setting, Sharp and colleagues (2004) found that both formats were superior to waitlist control but did not statistically differ from each other. At posttreatment, a greater proportion of patients in individual treatment achieved clinically significant change (i.e., outcome scores at least two standard deviations below whole-sample pretreatment means) than did those in group treatment. However, this advantage was not evident at 3-month follow-up.

Effectiveness Studies

Effectiveness studies examine treatment outcomes in clinical practice settings under naturalistic conditions (e.g., comorbidity allowed, medication use not controlled) with the purpose of examining the generalizability of findings obtained through randomized controlled trials with strict inclusion and exclusion criteria, conducted in specialized anxiety research settings. The limited generalizability of these efficacy studies to real-world clinical practice was highlighted by Westen and Morrison (2001) who found that the exclusion rate in the efficacy studies they reviewed (which averaged 54%) was correlated positively with the percentage of patients exhibiting improvement, and negatively with the percentage of patients seeking additional treatment. Trials examining treatment outcome for CBT delivered under conditions that more accurately reflect clinical practice therefore represent a particularly important line of research.

The number of effectiveness studies examining CBT for panic disorder outside the research setting has steadily increased over the past 10 years. Overall, findings suggest that CBT is an effective treatment for PDA in community mental health centers and other service-oriented settings. However, not surprisingly, treatment response is not always to the degree that is found in efficacy studies. Some studies have found short- and long-term treatment outcomes comparable to those found in clinical trials (e.g., Stuart, Treat, & Wade, 2000; Wade, Treat, & Stuart, 1998). Other studies suggest more modest effects, possibly due to study criteria and design (e.g., degree of experience of therapists). For example, Addis et al. (2004) found that 42% of patients receiving PCT in a managed care setting achieved clinically significant change compared to 18.8% of patients receiving treatment as usual (TAU). These positive effects were generally maintained over a 2-year follow-up period.

The Collaborative Care for Anxiety and Panic (CCAP) is a three-site primary care study designed to examine clinical and cost-effectiveness of CBT and medication compared to TAU. Patients with PDA were randomized to TAU or pharmacotherapy combined with CBT (i.e., 6 sessions within 3 months; 6 follow-up telephone sessions) provided in a collaborative care model. Combined CBT and pharmacotherapy led to significant improvements in anxiety symptoms and disability compared to TAU (Roy-Byrne, Craske, et al., 2005). In another effectiveness study examining combined CBT and medication versus medication alone in a primary care setting (Craske, Golinelli, et al., 2005), patients who received CBT in addition to medication within the first 3 months of study onset had statistically and clinically significant improvements in anxiety sensitivity, social avoidance, and disability compared to the medication-only group. They were also more improved at 12-month follow-up. An effectiveness study of CBT for PDA in group format found that patients in the CBT condition achieved better outcome on most measures than those in a waitlist control group; however, outcomes were modest in contrast to efficacy study outcomes, and most patients continued to have significant psychological problems following treatment (Rosenberg & Hougaard, 2005).

Brief and Cost-Effective Cognitive Behavioral Interventions

Lack of access to treatment, difficulties with dissemination, limited resources, and treatment costs have driven efforts to develop briefer and more cost-effective interventions such as psychoeducation, Internet-based treatment, and self-help guided by a book or manual (e.g., Antony & McCabe, 2004). From its inception, CBT has been promoted as a relatively brief intervention that trains patients to "become their own therapists." The goal of having patients quickly take control over their treatment has seemed particularly obtainable in the area of PDA, where core treatment elements involve well-specified exercises and extensive psychoeducation. In recent years, many researchers have investigated whether effective treatment for PDA can be provided in less than the standard 10 to 15 hour-long sessions with a therapist.

Research indicates that CBT for PDA can be effectively delivered in an abbreviated number of sessions (e.g., Clark et al., 1999), and with self-help books paired with either limited telephone contact

(e.g., Lidren et al., 1994), several sessions of group-based CBT (e.g., Hecker, Losee, Roberson-Nay, & Maki, 2004), or a limited number of face-to-face "check-in" meetings with therapists (e.g., Hecker, Losee, Fritzler, & Fink, 1996). Internet-based programs show considerable promise (Carlbring et al., 2005), as do interventions making use of palm-held computer technology (Kenardy, Dow, et al., 2003). Based on poor results in trials involving no therapist contact at all (e.g., Febbraro, Clum, Roodman, & Wright, 1999), it seems that many individuals may require some form of contact with a therapist in order to implement the recommended strategies effectively and achieve clinically significant change.

Baillie and Rapee (2004) caution that, although research has generally supported the efficacy of minimal-contact interventions (MCIs) for PDA, some patients may be ill equipped to benefit from these therapies. For example, they point to data suggesting that efficacy and retention rates may drop when samples consist of clinically referred participants, rather than the recruited samples used in most MCI studies. They argue that if treatment effects are less robust for MCIs than for standard protocols, it will be important to learn which patient factors predict response to these limited interventions, and to develop brief, user-friendly screening tools to assess them. At present, there are few data on predictors of treatment outcome in MCIs.

Prevention Research

By the time people obtain treatment for PDA, their symptoms have usually already accrued considerable personal and societal costs. Researchers have begun to ask whether we can take what has been learned about the nature of panic and develop interventions to prevent or arrest the onset of symptoms before they become debilitating. The two factors that have emerged most consistently as signaling elevated risk for PDA are high levels of anxiety sensitivity and the presence of occasional panic attacks. Anxiety sensitivity (AS) is a traitlike individual difference variable representing the extent to which a person fears his or her symptoms of autonomic arousal because of beliefs that such symptoms could have dire physical, mental, or social consequences (Reiss & McNally, 1985). There is considerable evidence that heightened AS is a specific risk factor for development of PDA (see Starcevic & Berle, 2006, for a recent review). In addition, occasional panic attacks have been shown to be associated with increased risk of developing PDA within 1 year (Ehlers, 1995).

Kenardy, McCafferty, and Rosa (2003) conducted an Internet-delivered prevention program intended to reduce AS in college students. Though the program was ineffective in this regard, its cost-effective delivery method (i.e., a self-guided computer-based program) warrants further study. Gardenswartz and Craske (2001) administered a prevention program to individuals without PDA reporting moderate to high AS and at least one uncued panic attack in the preceding year. They found that participants who attended their 5-hour educational workshop were less likely than waitlist controls to develop PDA within the next 6 months (13.6% of the waitlist group developed PDA versus 1.8% of the workshop group). In an earlier study, Swinson, Soulios, Cox, and Kuch (1992) showed that patients presenting to emergency rooms with panic attacks benefited from a single session intervention involving exposure instructions. These individuals compared favorably to participants in a reassurance-only condition on measures of depression, agoraphobic avoidance, and panic frequency administered at 6-month follow-up. This study was not strictly preventive, as 40% of participants already had symptoms meeting criteria for PDA. However, its encouraging findings, in combination with those of Gardenswartz and Craske (2001), point to the likely benefits of further prevention efforts.

Predictors of Treatment Outcome

Although it is clear that CBT is both an efficacious and effective treatment for PDA, it is not beneficial for all patients. In addition to a significant degree of attrition, a portion of treatment completers exhibit a poor response to treatment or experience residual symptoms during follow-up (for review, see McCabe & Antony, 2005). Researchers have tried to identify factors that explain why some individuals derive tremendous benefit from CBT while others see minimal or no gains, in the hopes of identifying areas for further improvement in treatment protocols. Demographic variables such as gender, socioeconomic status, marital status, ethnicity, and age at time of treatment have not been shown to reliably predict dropout or treatment response (see Taylor, 2000, for a review). An array of factors has been examined as predictors of treatment outcome, including the clinical features of PDA, psychiatric comorbidity, medical comorbidity, family interaction patterns, and in-therapy variables such as therapist characteristics and homework completion.

Clinical Features of PDA. Although disorder duration and age of onset have not been shown

to reliably predict treatment outcome, severity of the key clinical features of PDA has been shown to be a strong prognostic factor. The more severe the symptoms at pretreatment (e.g., catastrophic cognitions, self-rated anxiety, anxiety sensitivity, panic frequency, agoraphobic avoidance, and level of functioning), the poorer the treatment outcome (for review, see McCabe & Antony, 2005). However, patients with more severe pretreatment PDA symptoms tend to show the same rate of improvement as patients with less severe symptoms, which means that they may take longer to reach treatment goals and may require a more extended course of treatment (Taylor, 2000).

Individuals with PDA tend to fear that their panic attacks will have catastrophic consequences for their mental health (e.g., "What if I 'snap' and go crazy?"), physical health (e.g., "What if I have a heart attack?"), or social interactions (e.g., "What if I lose control and embarrass myself in public?"). Hicks et al. (2005) found that the presence of pretreatment catastrophic social cognitions (but not fears of mental or physical ill-effects) predicted worse outcome in CBT. They hypothesized that fears of panic attacks causing heart attacks or "mental breakdowns" can be relatively easily allayed when "experts" present contradictory factual information, whereas compelling evidence that one's symptoms have not been noticed or judged by others is more difficult to obtain.

Psychiatric Comorbidity. Detailed, relatively recent reviews of studies examining the impact of comorbid Axis I and II pathology on psychological treatments for PDA are provided by Mennin and Heimberg (2000) and Taylor (2000). Briefly, these reviews indicate that comorbidity in PDA is very common, and that the mere presence of a comorbid disorder does not predict treatment outcome. Looking more closely at the specific nature of comorbid disorders, it appears that the presence of other anxiety disorders such as generalized anxiety disorder or social phobia does not negatively influence treatment response. Of note, however, the impact of posttraumatic stress symptomatology on PDA outcome has been little studied, and clinical observation suggests that these symptoms may well complicate PDA treatment.

Comorbid depression, common in PDA, is an unreliable predictor of outcome. Brown, Antony, and Barlow (1995), for example, found a trend toward poorer outcome immediately posttreatment in patients with major depressive disorder (MDD) or dysthymia, as compared to nondepressed patients, but this difference disappeared by 3-month follow-up. McLean and colleagues (1998) found that co-morbid MDD did not predict the outcome of CBT for PDA, regardless of whether the depression preceded or followed PDA onset. Dimensional measures of depression did show statistically significant associations with global outcome, but the effect sizes were small. Taylor (2000) points out that those with very severe MDD are unlikely to be referred for PDA treatment, and that in these cases it may be necessary to address depressive symptoms prior to offering CBT for PDA.

Individuals with certain other Axis I disorders—that is, those with substance dependence or prominent psychotic or bipolar symptoms—are commonly excluded from treatment trials. For that reason, little is known about how standard protocols should best be modified to benefit these individuals. Alcohol is commonly used to self-medicate against panic symptoms, and there is some evidence that individuals with PDA are at elevated risk for alcoholism (Bibb & Chambless, 1986). When these conditions are comorbid, the presence of one is likely to hamper treatment of the other. Therefore, there is a pressing need to develop integrated treatments for comorbid alcohol dependence and PDA.

Data concerning the impact of personality dysfunction on response to PDA treatment is equivocal. A number of studies suggest that personality pathology negatively impacts treatment outcome and is associated with poorer outcome and slower progress (for review, see Mennin & Heimberg, 2000). Other studies have not found personality variables to be predictive of outcome (e.g., Massion et al., 2002). Steketee, Chambless, and Tran (2001) point out that research in this area is frequently complicated by statistical power issues; in many studies, the impact of specific personality disorders cannot be adequately assessed due to low numbers of participants meeting relevant diagnostic criteria. They responded to this problem by examining the predictive utility of trait clusters (anxious, odd, and dramatic), rather than individual traits or personality disorder diagnoses, and found that each cluster predicted poorer outcome immediately posttreatment. However, this effect disappeared at follow-up. The authors' conclusion that personality difficulties may slow the initial process of engaging in therapy, leading to a lag in gains, is echoed by Berger et al. (2004), who found that the presence of personality disorders predicted a delayed response to PDA treatment. In a recent, large-scale study of individual CBT for anxiety disorders, Weertman, Arntz, Schouten, and Dreessen (2005) found that personality disorders and personality disorder–related beliefs predicted treatment outcome. However, the authors note that the personality variables did not predict treatment dropout, and that the explained variance in treatment outcome (1%–7% of different measures) was smaller than clinical lore might suggest.

Medical Comorbidity. Little research has been done on the impact of comorbid medical illness on treatment outcome in PDA. Roy-Byrne, Stein, and colleagues (2005) took steps to address this gap by examining data from their primary care study on PDA interventions. They rated medical comorbidity by generating a summary illness score for each individual based on self-report information about chronic disease and prescription drug use. The sample was dichotomized into high and low medical comorbidity groups using a median split. Both groups benefited from CBT. Those above the median on medical comorbidity scored higher on pretreatment measures of anxiety sensitivity and agoraphobia, though not on measures of panic attack frequency or anticipatory anxiety. Although this group had greater residual PDA symptomatology at posttreatment than did the low comorbidity group, the authors attributed this difference to their higher baseline anxiety scores. Severity of medical illness was not shown to interact with treatment effectiveness.

We found only one other study assessing the impact of medical comorbidity on CBT for PDA. Schmidt and Telch (1997) found that greater numbers of self-reported chronic health conditions were not associated with more severe PDA symptoms at pretreatment, although self-reported perceived health was. Both the presence of chronic health conditions and perceived ill health predicted a poorer response to treatment, though medical morbidity explained only about 1% of the variance in outcome when perceived health was controlled for. Study methods differed from that of Roy-Byrne, Stein, et al. (2005) in a number of key areas, making it difficult to compare conclusions across studies. Clearly, further research investigating how medical difficulties may slow or impede progress in CBT for PDA is required.

Interpersonal Factors. Renshaw, Chambless, and Steketee (2003) found that patients who reported higher rates of perceived criticism (PC) from an individual sharing their home (most commonly a spouse) responded more poorly to treatment. They argued that it was unlikely this association was due to a process in which higher symptom severity elicited greater criticism from relatives; PC was not associated with concurrent symptom severity, either pre- or posttreatment, and pretreatment PC predicted posttreatment symptom severity when controlling for pretreatment symptom severity. In another study examining the association between family interaction styles and treatment outcome, Chambless and Steketee (1999) found that expressed hostility toward patients predicted treatment dropout and decreased treatment response. Controlling for hostility, critical comments (which frequently involved specific comments on patients' disorder-related behaviors) actually predicted a more positive treatment response on one outcome measure, a behavioral approach test. The authors hypothesized that these "criticisms" may have involved encouraging patients to work through agoraphobic avoidance.

Therapist Variables. Therapist variables have been shown to have little influence on treatment outcome. In a recent multisite study of therapist factors in PDA treatment, for example, Huppert and colleagues (2001) found that years of general therapy experience predicted a small amount of variance in certain PDA-related outcome variables (e.g., anxiety sensitivity) but not in others. No other therapist variables (e.g., age, gender, treatment orientation, specific experiences with CBT) predicted treatment outcome.

Homework Compliance. Research concerning the relationship between CBT homework compliance and treatment outcome for PDA is mixed (for a review, see Schmidt & Woolaway-Bickel, 2000). Schmidt and Woolaway-Bickel (2000) point out that studies assessing homework completion by asking patients to report on the amount of time devoted to these exercises likely miss important information about homework quality. When they assessed the quality of patients' homework (e.g., whether situational exposure tasks evoked appropriate levels of fear; whether exposures were done repeatedly; whether anxiety-provoking cognitions were appropriately identified and evaluated in cognitive work), they found that homework was indeed related to treatment outcome.

Research on Long-Term Outcome

Psychological treatments for PDA are intended to bring about changes in how individuals think about and respond to panic symptoms. Research reviewed earlier demonstrates that these cognitive and behavioral shifts can lessen the frequency and intensity of panic attacks and the functional impairment that accompanies them. But do these changes "stick?" Can we expect that patients who are doing well at the end of therapy will continue to live lives that are not significantly affected by fears of panic?

Studies examining the long-term outcome of CBT for PDA (here arbitrarily defined as outcome after an interval of at least 2 years) are quite encouraging. Results generally show that treatment gains are well maintained over the long term, and some even suggest that patients continue to improve posttherapy. In an early study, Craske, Brown, and Barlow (1991) found that 81% of PDA patients with mild or no agoraphobia who had received exposure-based treatment were panic-free at 2-year follow-up. Brown and Barlow (1995) noted that the percentage of patients achieving more stringent standards of high end-state functioning (e.g., those with no significant agoraphobic avoidance or fear of panic symptoms) after 24 months in that study was notably lower. They pointed out additional reasons for tempered enthusiasm about promising long-term results found in other studies, such as the general lack of information about whether improvement had been stable across the intervening period, or about whether patients had sought additional treatment during those months. In their (1995) study, they found that improvements following CBT for PDA were maintained at 2-year follow-up. There was a trend toward more participants achieving high-functioning status at 24-month than at 3-month follow-up. However, many patients who were classified as *panic free* for the month prior to the final assessment had experienced panic attacks during the preceding months (though the frequency of these was much diminished from pretreatment). A significant number of patients had sought additional treatment.

Fava et al. (2001) followed 200 consecutive patients over a period of up to 12 years who had completed behavioral therapy for PDA at an outpatient clinic. Of the 136 patients who reached panic-free status by the end of treatment, 132 were available for follow-up. Participants were counted as "survivors" if their symptoms did not reach diagnostic criteria for PDA. The authors reported estimated survival rates of 93.1% after 2 years, 82.4% after 5 years, 78.8% after 7 years, and 62.1% after 10 years.

Other studies have since evaluated the long-term effects of CBT in the context of pharmacological treatments. Oei, Llamas, and Evans (1997) found that brief, intensive, group-based CBT had demonstrably lasting positive effects over follow-up intervals ranging from 1.1 to 6.2 (mean 3.3) years. Concurrent medication use did not hurt or enhance outcome. Bruce, Spiegel, and Hegel (1999) investigated the utility of CBT offered during a tapering period of aprazolam, and reported lasting effects 2 to 5 years posttreatment, as measured by panic-free status and absence of further treatment.

In an effectiveness study conducted in a managed care setting, Addis et al. (2006) compared the long-term utility of CBT for PDA versus treatment as usual. Intent-to-treat analyses revealed no differences between groups at 2-year follow-up, but when treatment completers (i.e., those attending at least eight sessions of CBT) were assessed, CBT was significantly more effective than TAU. Twenty-four months after treatment completion, 55% of the participants in the CBT condition had achieved clinically significant change in symptoms, as opposed to 8% in the TAU condition.

Summary and Conclusions

Research reviewed in this chapter clearly demonstrates that psychological treatments—and in particular, those based on cognitive behavioral principles—can effectively alleviate symptoms of PDA. Treatment effects are highly robust; CBT has been shown to be effective across a variety of treatment settings and formats, whether offered alone or in combination with medication, across extended follow-up periods. More research is needed in the areas of prevention and early intervention, and in the extension of established treatments to underserved or challenging populations.

References

Addis, M. E., Hatgis, C., Cardemil, E., Jacob, K., Crasnow, A. D., & Mansfield, A. (2006). Effectiveness of cognitive behavioral therapy for panic disorder versus treatment as usual in a managed care setting: 2-year follow-up. *Journal of Consulting and Clinical Psychology, 74,* 377–385.

Addis, M. E., Hatgis, C., Krasnow, A. D., Jacob, K., Bourne, L., & Mansfield, A. (2004). Effectiveness of cognitive-behavioral treatment for panic disorder versus treatment as usual in a managed care setting. *Journal of Consulting and Clinical Psychology, 72,* 625–635.

Allen, L. B., & Barlow, D. H. (2006). Treatment of panic disorder: Outcomes and basic processes. In B. O. Rothbaum (Ed.), *Pathological anxiety: Emotional processing in etiology and treatment* (pp. 166–180). New York: Guilford Press.

American Psychiatric Association. (1998). Practice guideline for the treatment of patients with panic disorder. *American Journal of Psychiatry, 144*(Suppl. 5), 1–34.

Antony, M. M., & McCabe, R. E. (2002). Empirical basis of panic control treatment. *Scientific Review of Mental Health Practice, 1,* 189–194.

Antony, M. M., & McCabe, R. E. (2004). *10 simple solutions to panic: How to overcome panic attacks, calm physical symptoms and reclaim your life.* Oakland, CA: New Harbinger.

Antony, M. M., Roth Ledley, D., Liss, A., & Swinson, R. P. (2006). Responses to symptom induction exercises in panic disorder. *Behaviour Research and Therapy, 44,* 85–98.

Antony, M. M., & Swinson, R. P. (2000). *Phobic disorders and panic in adults: A guide to assessment and treatment.* Washington, DC: American Psychological Association.

Baillie, A. J., & Rapee, R. M. (2004). Predicting who benefits from psychoeducation and self-help for panic attacks. *Behaviour Research and Therapy, 42,* 513–527.

Baker-Morissette, S., Spiegel, D. A., & Heinrichs, N. (2005). Sensation-focused intensive treatment for panic disorder with moderate to severe agoraphobia. *Cognitive and Behavioral Practice, 12,* 17–29.

Barlow, D. H., Gorman, J. M., Shear, M. K., & Woods, S. W. (2000). Cognitive-behavioral therapy, imipramine, or their combination for panic disorder. *Journal of the American Medical Association, 283,* 2529–2536.

Beck, J. G., Stanley, M. A., Baldwin, L. E., Deagle, E. A., III, & Averill, P. (1994). Comparison of cognitive therapy and relaxation training for panic disorder. *Journal of Consulting and Clinical Psychology, 62,* 818–826.

Berger, P., Sachs, G., Amering, M., Holzinger, A., Bankier, B., & Katschnig, H. (2004). Personality disorder and social anxiety predict delayed response in drug and behavioral treatment of panic disorder. *Journal of Affective Disorders, 80,* 75–78.

Bibb, J. L., & Chambless, D. L. (1986). Alcohol use and abuse among diagnosed agoraphobics. *Behaviour Research and Therapy, 24,* 49–58.

Brown, T. A., Antony, M. M., & Barlow, D. H. (1995). Diagnostic comorbidity in panic disorder: Effects on treatment outcome and course of comorbid diagnoses following treatment. *Journal of Consulting and Clinical Psychology, 63,* 408–418.

Brown, T. A., & Barlow, D. H. (1995). Long-term outcome of cognitive-behavioural therapy of panic disorder: Clinical predictors and alternative strategies for assessment. *Journal of Consulting and Clinical Psychology, 63,* 754–765.

Bruce, T. J., Spiegel, D. A., & Hegel, M. T. (1999). Cognitive-behavioral therapy helps prevent relapse and recurrence of panic disorder following alprazolam discontinuation: A long-term follow-up of the Peoria and Dartmouth studies. *Journal of Consulting and Clinical Psychology, 67,* 151–156.

Butler, A. C., Chapman, J. E., Forman, E. M., & Beck, A. T. (2006). The empirical status of cognitive-behavioral therapy: A review of meta-analyses. *Clinical Psychology Review, 26,* 17–31.

Carlbring, P., Nilsson-Ihrfelt, E., Waara, J., Kollenstam, C., Buhrman, M., Kaldo, V., et al. (2005). Treatment of panic disorder: Live therapy vs. self-help via the internet. *Behaviour Research and Therapy, 43,* 1321–1333.

Chambless, D. L., & Steketee, G. (1999). Expressed emotion and behavior therapy outcome: A prospective study with obsessive-compulsive and agoraphobic outpatients. *Journal of Consulting and Clinical Psychology, 67,* 658–665.

Clark, D. M. (1986). A cognitive approach to panic. *Behaviour Research and Therapy, 24,* 461–470.

Clark, D. M. (1988). A cognitive model of panic attacks. In S. Rachman & J. D. Maser (Eds.), *Panic: Psychological perspectives* (pp. 71–89). Hillsdale, NJ: Erlbaum.

Clark, D. M., Salkovskis, P. M., Hackmann, A., Middleton, H., Anastasiades, P., & Gelder, M. (1994). A comparison of cognitive therapy, applied relaxation and imipramine in the treatment of panic disorder. *British Journal of Psychiatry, 164,* 759–769.

Clark, D. M., Salkovskis, P. M., Hackmann, A., Wells, A., Ludgate, J., & Gelder, M. (1999). Brief cognitive therapy for panic disorder: A randomized controlled trial. *Journal of Consulting and Clinical Psychology, 67,* 583–589.

Craske, M. G., & Barlow, D. H. (2007a). *Mastery of your anxiety and panic (Workbook)* (4th ed.). New York: Oxford University Press.

Craske, M. G., & Barlow, D. H. (2007b). *Mastery of your anxiety and panic (Therapist guide)* (4th ed.). New York: Oxford University Press.

Craske, M. G., Brown, T. A., & Barlow, D. H. (1991). Behavioral treatment of panic disorder: A two-year follow-up. *Behavior Therapy, 22,* 289–304.

Craske, M. G., Golinelli, D., Stein, M. B., Roy-Byrne, P., Bystritsky, A., & Sherbourne, C. (2005). Does the addition of cognitive behavioral therapy improve panic disorder treatment outcome relative to medication alone in the primary-care setting? *Psychological Medicine, 35,* 1645–1654.

Craske, M. G., Rowe, M., Lewin, M., & Noriega-Dimitri, R. (1997). Interoceptive exposure versus breathing retraining within cognitive-behavioural therapy for panic disorder with agoraphobia. *British Journal of Clinical Psychology, 36,* 85–99.

Dannon, P. N., Gon-Usishkin, M., Gelbert, A., Lowengrub, K., & Grunhaus, L. (2004). Cognitive behavioral group therapy in panic disorder patients: The efficacy of CBGT versus drug treatment. *Annals of Clinical Psychiatry, 16,* 41–46.

Ehlers, A. (1995). A 1-year prospective study of panic attacks: Clinical course and factors associated with maintenance. *Journal of Abnormal Psychology, 104,* 164–172.

Fava, G. A., Rafanelli, C., Grandi, S., Conti, S., Ruini, C., Mangelli, L., et al. (2001). Long-term outcome of panic disorder with agoraphobia treated by exposure. *Psychological Medicine, 31,* 891–898.

Febbraro, G.A.R., Clum, G. A., Roodman, A. A., & Wright, J. H. (1999). The limits of bibliotherapy: A study of the differential effectiveness of self-administered interventions in individuals with panic attacks. *Behavior Therapy, 30,* 209–222.

Furukawa, T. A., Watanabe, N., & Churchill, R. (2006). Psychotherapy plus antidepressant for panic disorder with or without agoraphobia: Systematic review. *British Journal of Psychiatry, 188,* 305–312.

Gardenswartz, C., & Craske, M. G. (2001). Prevention of panic disorder. *Behavior Therapy, 32,* 725–737.

Gould, R. A., Otto, M. W., & Pollack, M. H. (1995). A meta-analysis of treatment outcome for panic disorder. *Clinical Psychology Review, 15,* 819–844.

Hayes, S. C., Strosahl, K. D., & Wilson, K. G. (1999). *Acceptance and commitment therapy: An experiential approach to behavior change.* New York: Guilford Press.

Hecker, J. E., Losee, M. C., Fritzler, B. K., & Fink, C. M. (1996). Self-directed versus therapist-directed cognitive behavioral treatment for panic disorder. *Journal of Anxiety Disorders, 10,* 253–265.

Hecker, J. E., Losee, M. C., Roberson-Nay, R., & Maki, K. (2004). Mastery of your anxiety and panic and brief therapist contact in the treatment of panic disorder. *Journal of Anxiety Disorders, 18,* 111–126.

Hicks, T. V., Leitenberg, H., Barlow, D. H., Gorman, J. M., Shear, M. K., & Woods, S. W. (2005). Physical, mental, and social catastrophic cognitions as prognostic factors in cognitive-behavioral and pharmacological treatments for panic disorder. *Journal of Consulting and Clinical Psychology, 73,* 506–514.

Hoffman, E. C., & Mattis, S. G. (2000). A developmental adaptation of Panic Control Treatment for panic disorder in adolescence. *Cognitive and Behavioral Practice, 7,* 253–261.

Hofmann, S. G., Bufka, L. F., Brady, S. M., Du Rand, C., & Goff, D. C. (2000). Cognitive-behavioral treatment of panic in patients with schizophrenia: Preliminary findings. *Journal of Cognitive Psychotherapy, 14,* 381–392.

Huppert, J. D., Bufka, L. F., Barlow, D. H., Gorman, J. M., Shear, M. K., & Woods, S. W. (2001). Therapists, therapist variables, and cognitive-behavioral therapy outcome in a multicenter trial for panic disorder. *Journal of Consulting and Clinical Psychology, 69,* 747–755.

Kenardy, J. A., Dow, M.G.T., Johnston, D. W., Newman, M. G., Thomson, A., Taylor, C., et al. (2003). Comparison of delivery methods of cognitive-behavioral therapy for panic disorder: An international multicenter trial. *Journal of Consulting and Clinical Psychology, 71,* 1068–1075.

Kenardy, J., McCafferty, K., & Rosa, V. (2003). Internet-delivered indicated prevention for anxiety disorders: A randomized controlled trial. *Behavioural and Cognitive Psychotherapy, 31,* 279–289.

Klosko, J. S., Barlow, D. H., Tassinari, R., & Cerny, J. A. (1990). A comparison of alprazolam and behavior therapy in treatment of panic disorder. *Journal of Consulting and Clinical Psychology, 58,* 77–84.

Levitt, J. T., & Karekla, M. (2005). Integrating acceptance and mindfulness with cognitive behavioral treatment for panic disorder. In S. M. Orsillo and L. Roemer (Eds.), *Acceptance and mindfulness-based approaches to anxiety: Conceptualization and treatment* (pp. 165–188). New York: Springer.

Lidren, D. M., Watkins, P., Gould, R. A., Clum, G. A., Asterino, M., & Tulloch, H. L. (1994). A comparison of bibliotherapy and group therapy in the treatment of panic disorder. *Journal of Consulting and Clinical Psychology, 62,* 865–869.

Marks, I. M., Swinson, R. P., Basoglu, M., Kuch, K., Noshirvani, H., O'Sullivan, G., et al. (1993). Alprazolam and exposure alone and combined in panic disorder with agoraphobia: A controlled study in London and Toronto. *British Journal of Psychiatry, 162,* 776–787.

Massion, A. O., Dyck, I. R., Shea, M. T., Phillips, K. A., Warshaw, M. G., & Keller, M. B. (2002). Personality disorders and time to remission in generalized anxiety disorder, social phobia, and panic disorder. *Archives of General Psychiatry, 59,* 434–440.

Mattick, R. P., Andrews, G., Hadzi-Pavlovic, D., & Christensen, H. (1990). Treatment of panic and agoraphobia: An integrative review. *Journal of Nervous and Mental Disease, 178,* 567–576.

McCabe, R. E., & Antony, M. M. (2005). Panic disorder and agoraphobia. In M. M. Antony, D. R. Ledley, & R. Heimberg (Eds.), *Improving outcomes and preventing relapse in cognitive behavioral therapy* (pp. 1–37). New York: Guilford Press.

McLean, P. D., Woody, S., Taylor, S., & Koch, W. J. (1998). Comorbid panic disorder and major depression: Implications for cognitive-behavioral therapy. *Journal of Consulting and Clinical Psychology, 66,* 240–247.

Mennin, D. S., & Heimberg, R. G. (2000). The impact of comorbid mood and personality disorders in the cognitive-behavioral treatment of panic disorder. *Clinical Psychology Review, 20,* 339–357.

Michelson, L. K., Marchione, K. E., Greenwald, M., Testa, S., & Marchione, N. J. (1996). A comparative study of panic disorder with agoraphobia: The relative and combined efficacy of cognitive therapy, relaxation training, and therapist-assisted exposure. *Journal of Anxiety Disorders, 10,* 297–330.

Milrod, B., Busch, F., Leon, A. C., Aronson, A., Roiphe, J., Rudden, M., et al. (2001). A pilot open trial of brief psychodynamic psychotherapy for panic disorder. *Journal of Psychotherapy Practice and Research, 10,* 239–245.

Milrod, B., Leon, A. C., Busch, F., Rudden, M., Schwalberg, M., Clarkin, J., et al. (2007). A randomized controlled clinical trial of psychoanalytic psychotherapy for panic disorder. *American Journal of Psychiatry, 164,* 265–272.

Mitte, K. (2005). A meta-analysis of the efficacy of psycho- and pharmacotherapy in panic disorder with and without agoraphobia. *Journal of Affective Disorders, 88,* 27–45.

Néron, S., Lacroix, D., & Chaput, Y. (1995). Group vs. individual cognitive behaviour therapy in panic disorder: An open clinical trial with a six month follow up. *Canadian Journal of Behavioural Science, 27,* 379–392.

Oei, T.P.S., Llamas, M., & Evans, L. (1997). Does concurrent drug intake affect the long-term outcome of group-cognitive behaviour therapy in panic disorder with or without agoraphobia? *Behaviour Research and Therapy, 35,* 851–857.

Öst, L., Thulin, U., & Ramnerö, J. (2004). Cognitive behavior therapy vs. exposure in vivo in the treatment of panic disorder with agoraphobia. *Behaviour Research and Therapy, 42,* 1105–1127.

Otto, M. W., & Deveney, C. (2005). Cognitive-behavioral therapy and the treatment of panic disorder: Efficacy and strategies. *Journal of Clinical Psychiatry, 66,* 28–32.

Pollack, M. H., Otto, M. W., Kaspi, S. P., Hammerness, P. G., & Rosenbaum, J. F. (1994). Cognitive behavior therapy for treatment-refractory panic disorder. *Journal of Clinical Psychiatry, 55,* 200–205.

Rapee, R. M., Craske, M., & Barlow, D. H. (1996). Psychoeducation. In C. G. Lindemann (Ed.), *Handbook of the treatment of the anxiety disorders* (2nd ed., pp. 311–322). Lanham, MD: Jason Aronson.

Rees, C. S., Richards, J. C., & Smith, L. M. (1999). The efficacy of information-giving in cognitive-behavioural treatment for panic disorder. *Behaviour Change, 16,* 175–181.

Reiss, S., & McNally, R. J. (1985). The expectancy model of fear. In S. Reiss & R. R. Bootzin (Eds.), *Theoretical issues in behavior therapy* (pp. 107–121). New York: Academic Press.

Renshaw, K. D., Chambless, D. L., & Steketee, G. (2003). Perceived criticism predicts severity of anxiety symptoms after behavioral treatment in patients with obsessive-compulsive disorder and panic disorder with agoraphobia. *Journal of Clinical Psychology, 59,* 411–421.

Rosenberg, N. K., & Hougaard, E. (2005). Cognitive-behavioural group treatment of panic disorder and agoraphobia in a psychiatric setting: A naturalistic study of effectiveness. *Nordic Journal of Psychiatry, 59,* 198–204.

Roy-Byrne, P., Craske, M. G., Stein, M. B., Sullivan, G., Bystritsky, A., Katon, W., et al. (2005). A randomized effectiveness trial of cognitive-behavioral therapy and medication for primary care panic disorder. *Archives of General Psychiatry, 62,* 290–298.

Roy-Byrne, P., Stein, M. B., Russo, J., Craske, M., Katon, W., Sullivan, G., et al. (2005). Medical illness and response to treatment in primary care panic disorder. *General Hospital Psychiatry, 27,* 237–243.

Salkovskis, P. M., Clark, D. M., & Hackmann, A. (1991). Treatment of panic attacks using cognitive therapy without exposure or breathing retraining. *Behaviour Research and Therapy, 29,* 161–166.

Salkovskis, P. M., Clark, D. M., Hackmann, A., Wells, A., & Gelder, M. (1999). An experimental investigation of the role of safety behaviours in the maintenance of panic disor-der with agoraphobia. *Behaviour Research and Therapy, 37,* 559–574.

Schmidt, N. B., McCreary, B. T., Trakowski, J., Santiago, H., Woolaway-Bickel, K., & Ialongo, N. (2003). Effects of cognitive-behavioral treatment on physical health status in patients with panic disorder. *Behavior Therapy, 34,* 49–63.

Schmidt, N. B., Telch, M. J. (1997). Nonpsychiatric medical comorbidity, health perceptions, and treatment outcome in patients with panic disorder. *Health Psychology, 16,* 114–122.

Schmidt, N. B., & Trakowski, J. (2004). Interoceptive assessment and exposure in panic disorder: A descriptive study. *Cognitive and Behavioral Practice, 11,* 81–92.

Schmidt, N. B., & Woolaway-Bickel, K. (2000). The effects of treatment compliance on outcome in cognitive-behavioral therapy for panic disorder: Quality versus quantity. *Journal of Consulting and Clinical Psychology, 68,* 13–18.

Schmidt, N. B., Woolaway-Bickel, K., Trakowski, J., Santiago, H., Storey, J., Koselka, M., et al. (2000). Dismantling cognitive-behavioral treatment for panic disorder: Questioning the utility of breathing retraining. *Journal of Consulting and Clinical Psychology, 68,* 417–424.

Sharp, D. M., Power, K. G., & Swanson, V. (2004). A comparison of the efficacy and acceptability of group versus individual cognitive behaviour therapy in the treatment of panic disorder and agoraphobia in primary care. *Clinical Psychology and Psychotherapy, 11,* 73–82.

Shear, M. K., Houck, P. M., Greeno, C., & Masters, S. (2001). Emotion-focused psychotherapy for patients with panic disorder. *American Journal of Psychiatry, 158,* 1993–1998.

Smits, J.A.J., O'Cleirigh, C. M., & Otto, M. W. (2006). Combining cognitive-behavioral therapy and pharmacotherapy for the treatment of panic disorder. *Journal of Cognitive Psychotherapy, 20,* 75–84.

Spiegel, D. A., Bruce, T. J., Gregg, S. F., & Nuzzarello, A. (1994). Does cognitive behavior therapy assist slow-taper alprazolam discontinuation in panic disorder? *American Journal of Psychiatry, 151,* 876–881.

Starcevic, V., & Berle, D. (2006). Cognitive specificity of anxiety disorders: A review of selected key constructs. *Depression and Anxiety, 23,* 51–61.

Steketee, G., Chambless, D. L., & Tran, G. Q. (2001). Effects of Axis I and II comorbidity on behavior therapy outcome for obsessive-compulsive disorder and agoraphobia. *Comprehensive Psychiatry, 42,* 76–86.

Stuart, G. L., Treat, T. A., & Wade, W. A. (2000). Effectiveness of an empirically based treatment for panic disorder delivered in a service clinic setting: 1-year follow-up. *Journal of Consulting and Clinical Psychology, 68,* 506–512.

Swinson, R. P., Antony, M. M., Bleau, P., Chokka, P., Craven, M., Fallu, A., et al. (2006). Clinical practice guidelines: Management of anxiety disorders. *Canadian Journal of Psychiatry, 51*(Suppl. 2), 1S–92S.

Swinson, R. P., Soulios, C., Cox, B. J., & Kuch, K. (1992). Brief treatment of emergency room patients with panic attacks. *American Journal of Psychiatry, 49,* 944–946.

Taylor, S. (2000). *Understanding and treating panic disorder: Cognitive-behavioural approaches.* Chichester, England: Wiley.

Telch, M., & Lucas, R. (1994). Combined pharmacological and psychological treatment of panic disorder: Current status and future directions. In B. E. Wolfe & J. D. Maser (Eds.), *Treatment of panic disorder: A consensus development conference* (pp. 177–197). Washington, DC: American Psychiatric Press.

Telch, M. J., Lucas, J. A., Schmidt, N. B., Hanna, H. H., Jaimez, T. L., & Lucas, R. A. (1993). Group cognitive-behavioral treatment of panic disorder. *Behaviour Research and Therapy, 31,* 279–287.

Tsao, J.C.I., Mystkowski, J. L., Zucker, B., & Craske, M. G. (2002). Effects of cognitive-behavioral therapy for panic disorder on comorbid conditions: Replication and extension. *Behavior Therapy, 33,* 493–509.

Wade, W. A., Treat, T. A., & Stuart, G. L. (1998). Transporting an empirically supported treatment for panic disorder to a service clinic setting: A benchmarking strategy. *Journal of Consulting and Clinical Psychology, 66,* 231–239.

Weertman, A., Arntz, A., Schouten, E., & Dreessen, L. (2005). Influences of beliefs and personality disorders on treatment outcome in anxiety patients. *Journal of Consulting and Clinical Psychology, 73,* 936–944.

Westen, D., & Morrison, K. (2001). A multidimensional meta-analysis of treatments for depression, panic, and generalized anxiety disorder: An empirical examination of the status of empirically supported therapies. *Journal of Consulting and Clinical Psychology, 69,* 875–899.

Pharmacotherapy for Social Anxiety Disorder and Specific Phobia

Michael Van Ameringen, Catherine Mancini *and* Beth Patterson

Abstract

This chapter examines how, over the past two decades, there has been a rapid emergence of pharmacological treatment options for patients with generalized social anxiety disorder (GSAD). Results of treatment and neuroimaging studies suggest the involvement of serotonin, gamma-amino-butyric acid (GABA)/glutamate, and dopamine in GSAD. The literature clearly supports the use of SSRIs and the SNRI venlafaxine ER as first-line pharmacological agents in the treatment of GSAD; however, there is a paucity of data for patients who obtain a partial or nonresponse to first-line treatments as well as strategies to move GSAD individuals from response to remission. Exposure-based treatments are considered to be the gold standard treatment for specific phobias. There is a small literature on the use of pharmacological agents in specific phobias that does not support their use as the primary treatment modality.

Keywords: anxiety, anxiety treatment, pharmacotherapy, social anxiety, social phobia, treatment resistance

This chapter examines results from pharmacological treatment studies in social anxiety disorder (SAD), including combination, augmentation, and comparison (with psychological treatments) studies. Treatment resistance, predictors of treatment response, and relapse prevention will also be discussed. In addition, the pharmacological treatments for specific phobia will be reviewed.

Pharmacotherapy in Social Anxiety Disorder

Selective serotonin reuptake inhibitors (SSRIs) are recognized as the first-line treatment for generalized social anxiety disorder (GSAD) based on their efficacy, safety, tolerability, and effectiveness in treating conditions commonly comorbid with GSAD. The relatively low side-effect profile associated with these agents, as well as consistent evidence of efficacy across treatment studies, have led to their widespread clinical use (Van Ameringen, Mancini, Pipe, & Bennett, 2004b). The efficacy of other agents such as the serotonin noradrenalin reuptake inhibitor (SNRI) venlafaxine, benzodiazepines, monoamine oxidase inhibitors (MAOIs), reversible inhibitors of monoamine oxidase (RIMAs), anticonvulsants, and other agents have also been demonstrated in the treatment of GSAD.

Selective Serotonin Reuptake Inhibitors
FLUVOXAMINE

Fluvoxamine was the first SSRI to show efficacy in controlled studies of social phobia. In a 12-week double-blind placebo-controlled study of fluvoxamine in 30 social phobics, 46% of the patients in the fluvoxamine group were considered responders (a 50% reduction in the Liebowitz Social Anxiety Scale [LSAS] [Liebowitz, 1987] score at 12 weeks), versus 7% of patients taking placebo (van Vliet, den

Boer, & Westenberg, 1994). In a larger controlled study, Stein and colleagues (Stein, Fyer, Davidson, Pollack, & Wiita, 1999) compared fluvoxamine (mean dose of 202 mg/day) to placebo in 92 patients with generalized social phobia. At week 12, using "last observation carried forward analysis" (LOCF), 43% of the patients in the fluvoxamine group were classified as responders according to the Clinical Global Impression–Improvement Scale (CGI-I), (U.S. Department of Health, 1976) compared to only 23% of placebo patients.

More recently, fluvoxamine-controlled release (CR) was examined in comparison to placebo in 279 generalized social phobics (Davidson et al., 2004a). The fluvoxamine CR group (mean daily dose 174 mg/day) displayed clinically and statistically significant reductions in social phobia symptoms compared to placebo based on the primary outcome measure (LSAS). Responders, defined as a CGI-I ≤ 2, were significantly greater in the fluvoxamine CR group (33.9%) as compared to placebo (16.7%) ($p < .001$). Fluvoxamine CR also showed significantly superior efficacy on secondary outcome measures, including the Sheehan Disability Scale (SDS) (Sheehan, 1983) and CGI–Severity (CGI-S) (U.S. Department of Health, 1976).

SERTRALINE

Using a flexible-dose, crossover design, 12 patients meeting *DSM–III–R* (American Psychiatric Association [APA], 1994) criteria for social phobia were randomized to either sertraline or placebo for 10 weeks (Katzelnick et al., 1995). Overall, 50% of the sertraline group (versus 9% in the placebo group) were labeled responders based on the Liebowitz Panic and Social Phobic Disorders Rating Form (Liebowitz et al., 1988). The mean change in the LSAS score from baseline in the sertraline phase was 22, while only a 5.5-point change was reported in the placebo phase ($p < 0.05$).

In a large 20-week, multicenter study conducted in Canada, Van Ameringen et al. (2001) compared sertraline (up to 200 mg/day) to placebo in 204 patients with social phobia using a double-blind, flexible dose design. At week 20, 53% of the sertraline group versus 29% of the placebo group were considered responders according to the CGI-I. The mean reduction on the Brief Social Phobia Scale (BSPS) (Davidson et al., 1997) for the sertraline group was 34.3% compared to 18.6% for placebo ($p < 0.01$).

The efficacy of flexible dose sertraline in 415 individuals with severe generalized SAD (GSAD) was examined in a 12-week double-blind treatment study (Liebowitz et al., 2003). Using LOCF analysis, patients who received sertraline (mean max. dose of 159 mg/day) experienced a clinically significant mean reduction in LSAS score (primary outcome measure) by week 12 of treatment (–31.0), compared to a –21.7 reduction in the placebo group ($p = .001$). A significantly greater proportion of patients in the sertraline group achieved responder status as defined by CGI-I < 2, compared to those taking placebo in both the week 12 completer analysis (55.6% versus 29%; $p < .001$), and intent to treat (ITT)-LOCF analysis (46.8% versus 25.5%; $p < .001$).

PAROXETINE

Paroxetine has been the most-studied SSRI in SAD, with more than five controlled trials of treatment efficacy. Stein and colleagues (1998) compared paroxetine to placebo in a 12-week controlled trial of 187 patients with social phobia. Fifty-five percent of the paroxetine group versus 23% of the placebo group were considered to be responders with a CGI-I ≤ 2 (*or* 3.88, 95% CI, 2.81–5.36). In the paroxetine group, a statistically significant reduction in mean LSAS was reported: 39% versus a 17.4% drop in the placebo group (95% CI, 8.7%–34.7%).

In a 12-week multicentered double-blind, parallel-group, placebo-controlled trial, conducted by Baldwin and colleagues (Baldwin, Bobes, Stein, Scharwachter, & Faure, 1999), 290 patients with social anxiety disorder were randomized to paroxetine (20–50 mg/day; $n = 139$) or placebo ($n = 151$). A clinically significant improvement was found in the paroxetine group as compared to placebo on primary efficacy measures of mean change in LSAS from baseline to endpoint, and in the proportion of responders having a CGI-I < 2. Several subsequent randomized controlled trials (RCTs) with paroxetine (Allgulander, 1999; Liebowitz et al., 2002) and paroxetine controlled-release (paroxetine CR) (Lepola, Bergtholdt, St. Lambert, Davy, & Ruggiero, 2004) have yielded additional confirmatory evidence of efficacy.

FLUOXETINE

In the first placebo-controlled study of fluoxetine in social phobia ($n = 60$), the dose of fluoxetine and placebo was fixed at 20 mg/day for the first 8 weeks of double-blind treatment (Kobak, Greist, Jefferson, & Katzelnick, 2002). The final 6 weeks involved a flexible dose of fluoxetine, up to a maximum of 60 mg/day. There were no significant differences apparent between fluoxetine and placebo on the amount of LSAS change from baseline (primary outcome measure), although a significant change in LSAS was found at week 14 to baseline. The change in fluoxetine treatment response was similar to that reported with other SSRIs; however, the placebo response was greater. These results are important, as this is the first controlled study of an SSRI in social phobia to show lack of efficacy.

ESCITALOPRAM

A statistically superior therapeutic effect was found for escitalopram compared with placebo in a 12-week double-blind comparison of flexible dose escitalopram (10–20 mg/day) and placebo (n = 358). This was based on total LSAS score (p = .005) with a significantly greater rate of response (54% for escitalopram versus 39% with placebo; p < 0.01; LOCF analysis) (Kasper, Stein, Loft, & Nil, 2005). Although a significant improvement was demonstrated, escitalopram only showed a significant separation from placebo at week 12, which is later than found in most studies of SSRIs in GSAD (Kasper et al., 2005).

Overall, there is overwhelming evidence for the efficacy of the SSRIs in GSAD. As well as having established efficacy, they are well tolerated and have the additional benefit of treating comorbid conditions commonly seen with GSAD (Van Ameringen, Mancini, Pipe, & Bennett, 2004b).

SNRIs: Venlafaxine

The SNRI venlafaxine has been shown to be an effective alternative to SSRI agents. In a 12-week double-blind, placebo controlled, parallel group multisite study 272 patients with *DSM–IV* (APA, 1994) social phobia were randomized to either venlafaxine extended release (ER) (flexible doses, 75 to 225 mg/day) or placebo following a 1-week placebo run-in (Rickels, Mangano, & Khan, 2004). At week 12 (LOCF), patients in the venlafaxine-ER group had a significantly lower LSAS total score (primary efficacy measure) than placebo (57.7 versus 66.0, p ≤ .01). As well, significantly more patients were considered responders by CGI-I ≤ 2 at week 12: 50% of venlafaxine ER patients versus 34% in the placebo group (p < .01; LOCF). These results have been supported by a 12-week flexible-dose, randomized controlled trial of venlafaxine ER in 271 patients (Liebowitz, Mangano, Bradwejn, & Asnis, 2005) and a 28-week, double-blind, multicenter design (n = 386) study was completed, in which patients were randomized into three treatment groups: venlafaxine at a fixed low dose (75 mg/day), venlafaxine ER at a flexible high dose (150–225 mg/day), and placebo (Stein, Pollack, Bystritsky, Kelsey, & Mangano, 2005). In this latter study, no significant differences were found between low fixed-dose venlafaxine ER and the higher flexible dose.

Nefazodone

Nefazodone is a serotonergic antidepressant similar to an SSRI, but it also blocks postsynaptic 5-HT$_{2A}$ receptors (DeVane, Grothe, & Smith, 2002). In the only RCT, where 105 patients were randomized to 14-weeks of nefazodone or placebo, nefazodone was found to be no better than placebo (Van Ameringen, et al., 2007).

Tricyclic Antidepressants

It has been the clinical lore that tricyclic antidepressants (with the exception, possibly, of potent serotonin reuptake inhibiting tricyclics such as clomipramine) are not efficacious in social phobia. This has been supported by an 8-week, placebo-controlled study of imipramine in the treatment of 41 patients with social phobia in which the efficacy of imipramine was found to be no better than placebo (Emmanuel, Johnson, & Villarreal, 1998).

Monoamine Oxidase Inhibitors

Evidence for the efficacy of the MAOIs dates back to the 1970s (Liebowitz, Gorman, Fyer, & Klein, 1985), with phenelzine being the first drug to demonstrate efficacy in placebo-controlled trials of social phobia (Gelernter et al., 1991; Heimberg et al., 1998; Liebowitz et al., 1992, 1999). Two landmark studies greatly contributed to the emergence of the MAOIs as the gold standard drug treatment for social phobia. Gelernter and colleagues (1991) found phenelzine to be superior to alprazolam, placebo, and group cognitive behavioral treatment (CBT) (detailed in "Comparative Efficacy in Social Anxiety Treatment"). Liebowitz and colleagues (1992) conducted a controlled trial comparing phenelzine, atenolol, and placebo in 74 individuals with social phobia. After 8 weeks of treatment, phenelzine (in a mean daily dose of 75.7 mg/day) was more effective than atenolol (p = .02) or placebo (p = .009) for relieving social phobic symptoms. Although MAOIs demonstrated robust efficacy in GSAD, due to dietary restrictions, and risk of serious adverse events associated with the use of these agents, including the risk of hypertensive crisis, these medications are now reserved for those nonresponsive to other drug treatments.

Reversible Inhibitors of Monoamine Oxidase Type A

Favorable results for RIMAs have been found in open-label studies examining these agents in social anxiety disorder (Bisserbe & Lepine, 1994; Versiani, Egidio, Figueira, Mendlowicz, & Marques, 1997); however, randomized controlled trials have not been consistent. Brofaromine was shown to be effective in 3 placebo-controlled trials (Fahlen, Nilsson, Borg, Humble, & Pauli, 1995; Lott et al., 1997; van Vliet, den Boer, & Westenberg, 1992). This agent was withdrawn from the world market in 1994 for reasons unrelated to its safety or efficacy. Moclobemide was found to be no different in efficacy than placebo in 3 studies (43–45), but did show superiority to placebo in a long-term study (Stein, Cameron, Amrein, & Montgomery, 2002). When the RIMAs were first released, there were great hopes that they would become a user-friendly MAOI; however, results from randomized controlled trials have been disappointing (Noyes et al., 1997; Schneier et al., 1998). Given these inconsistent results and low effect sizes, these agents do not appear to be very potent as treatments for GSAD and should be reserved for use when trials of other agents have been unsuccessful.

Benzodiazepines

Benzodiazepines are thought to reduce anxiety by enhancing inhibitory GABA neurotransmission. Positive randomized controlled trials of clonazepam (Davidson et al., 1993), alprazolam (Gelernter et al., 1991), and bromazepam (Versiani, Egidio, et al., 1997) have also been reported in SAD.

Davidson and colleagues (1993) compared clonazepam to placebo in 75 social phobics. At endpoint, 78% of the clonazepam group and 20% of the placebo group were rated as improved by CGI-I ≤ 2 ($p = .0001$).

Drawbacks to these agents include possible rebound anxiety, the ineffectiveness of benzodiazepines in the treatment of common comorbid conditions often found with SAD such as depression, as well as the potential for dependence in those patients with comorbid substance abuse (also a common comorbid disorder with SAD). Benzodiazepines should not be considered first-line therapy for this disorder, but should be reserved for use where adjunctive therapy may be needed or in cases where rapid onset of action is required.

Anticonvulsants

Anticonvulsants, or antiepileptics, are thought to modulate the glutamate–gamma-amino-butyric acid (GABA) neurotransmitter systems. Abnormalities in both GABA and glutamate have been associated with various anxiety disorders and evidence support-

ing the use of anticonvulsants in the treatment of social anxiety disorder is rapidly emerging in both open label and in randomized placebo-controlled trials (Van Ameringen, Mancini, Pipe, & Bennett, 2004a). Topiramate (Van Ameringen, Mancini, Pipe, Oakman, & Bennett, 2004), tiagabine (Papp & Ninan, 2004), levetiracetam (Simon et al., 2004), and valproic acid (Kinrys et al., 2003) have all shown improvements in individuals with SAD in open-label trials, although the findings of valproic acid are less robust (Nardi, Mendlowicz, & Versiani, 1997).

Gabapentin

In a 14-week, double-blind, controlled study ($n = 69$), gabapentin (900 to 3,600 mg/day) was compared with placebo in the treatment of social phobia (Pande et al., 1999). In the ITT analysis, 32% of those taking gabapentin versus 14% taking placebo were found to be responders with a 50% reduction in LSAS scores, as well as 38% of the gabapentin group versus 17% of the placebo group being responders according to the CGI-I ≤ 2 ($p = .05$).

Pregabalin

In one controlled study of social phobia, 135 patients were randomized to pregabalin 150 mg/day or 600 mg/day or placebo for 11 weeks (Pande et al., 2004). The primary efficacy measure of the LSAS (total score) was significantly decreased in the pregabalin 600 mg/day group as compared to placebo (mean change from baseline: –28.6 versus –18.4; $p = .03$), but pregabalin 150 mg/day showed no difference in LSAS total score reductions as compared to placebo. Response by CGI-I ≤ 2 was 42.6% in the 600 mg/day group versus 21.7% in the placebo group ($p = 0.03$).

Levetiracetam

Zhang and colleagues (Zhang, Connor, & Davidson, 2005) recently published results of a 7-week randomized, double-blind, placebo-controlled study of levetiracetam (500–3,000 mg/day). In 18 subjects with social anxiety disorder, no significant difference was found between levetiracetam and placebo on the primary BSPS, nor on secondary measures including the LSAS (ITT). Response rate by CGI-I ≤ 2 was 22% for levetiracetam versus 14.3% for placebo.

These trials of anticonvulsants as monotherapy in social anxiety disorder suggest that anticonvulsants could be interesting agents for the growing number of patients who are unable to tolerate SSRIs or who are nonresponsive to first-line treatments.

Atypical Antipsychotics

Atypical antipsychotic agents have been shown in both animal models (Moore, Rees, Sanger, & Tye, 1994) and clinical trials (Klieser et al., 1999; Tollefson, Sanger, Beasley, & Tran, 1998) to have anxiolytic effects and evidence is emerging for their potential use in SAD. Quetiapine monotherapy has been recently examined in an open-label trial in GSAD (Schutters, van Megen, & Westenberg, 2005) with very positive results. In an 8-week, randomized, double-blind, placebo-controlled study in a small sample of 12 patients with GSAD, flexible dose olanzapine (mean dose 9 mg/day) resulted in significantly greater improvement on the primary outcome measures of the BSPS ($p = .02$) and the SPIN ($p = .01$) (ITT) but not on the LSAS (Barnett, Kramer, Casat, Connor, & Davidson, 2002). The ITT response rate by CGI-I $\leq$ 2 was 60% for olanzapine versus 0% for placebo ($p = .17$).

Atypical antipsychotic agents have been generally well tolerated in all the short-term reports thus far, with relatively low dropouts due to adverse events. In other areas of psychiatry, long-term use of these drugs has been associated with significant adverse events over time such as weight gain, diabetes, and high cholesterol (Newcomer, 2004). These agents show promise as either adjunctive agents or in treatment resistance, although at this time, the strength of the data does not support their use as a first-line treatment strategy.

Other Agents

Evidence from open-label trials of selegiline (L-Deprenyl) (Simpson et al., 1998) and reboxetine (Atmaca, Tezcan, & Kuloglu, 2003) has indicated potential efficacy of these alternative agents in the treatment of GSAD. Buproprion SR, an agent with noradrenergic and dopaminergic actions, has demonstrated efficacy in one open-label trial (Emmanuel et al., 2000) but not in others (Emmanuel, Lydiard, & Ballenger, 1991; Sheehan, 1983).

In a 10-week, randomized, placebo-controlled study of 66 women with SP, mirtazepine (30 mg/day) was superior to placebo on the primary self-report outcome measures of the SPIN ($p < .001$) and LSAS ($p < .001$) (69).

The 5-HT$_3$ antagonist ondansetron has been examined in 2 randomized controlled trials; one with slightly positive (Bell & DeVaugh-Geiss, 1994) and one with negative results (Grunes, Yayura-Tobias, & Neziroglu, 1996).

St. John's wort, or *Hypericum perforatum,* is an alternative agent that has been used in the treatment of depression as well as anxiety disorders. Its efficacy was evaluated in a 12-week randomized double-blind, placebo-controlled trial in SAD ($n = 40$), where no significant differences were found on the primary efficacy measure, the mean change from baseline on the LSAS, for St. John's wort as compared to placebo (11.4 versus 13.2, $p = .27$, effect size = $-.09$) (Kobak, Taylor, Warner, & Futterer, 2005).

D-cycloserine (DCS) has recently been shown to be an effective additive intervention to exposure therapy in SAD (Hofmann et al., 2006) in a randomized placebo-controlled trial of 27 patients. The DCS or placebo was administered 1 hour prior to each of 5 exposure sessions. A significant change from baseline in the Social Phobia and Anxiety Inventory (SPAI), the primary outcome measure, was reported ($p = .006$) as well as on the LSAS self-report scale ($p = .02$) (Turner, Beidel, Dancu, & Stanley, 1998).

Comparative Efficacy in Social Anxiety Treatment

Federoff and Taylor (2001) conducted a meta-analysis examining 11 forms of treatment for social phobia. On self-report measures, the largest effect sizes were found for benzodiazepines (2.095, 95% CI 1.40–2.79) and SSRIs (1.697, 95% CI 0.88–2.52) and these conditions did not significantly differ from each other. Observer-rated measures were computed for 8 of the 11 conditions, and exposure emerged with the largest effect size (3.468, 95% CI -3.36–10.30), followed by benzodiazepines (3.150, 95% CI 1.13–5.17) and SSRIs (1.540, 95% CI 1.10–1.98). However, no differences in efficacy were found between treatment conditions. The authors concluded that pharmacotherapies, especially benzodiazepines and SSRIs, seem to be the most efficacious treatments for GSAD.

In another meta-analysis, Blanco and colleagues (2003) compared the efficacy of medications evaluated in placebo-controlled studies of social phobia. They found that the medications with the largest effect sizes were phenelzine (1.02), followed by clonazepam (.97), gabapentin (.78), brofaromine (.66), and finally, SSRIs (.65); however, no statistically significant differences were observed between drug classes. The authors also examined the heterogeneity of the effect sizes and found more stable effect size estimates within the SSRIs and concluded that these agents be used as first-line treatments for SAD.

In a recent meta-analysis conducted by Stein and colleagues (Stein, Isper, & van Balkom, 2005) for the Cochrane Collaboration, the authors concluded that pharmacotherapy was effective in reducing social phobia symptom clusters as well as comorbid depressive symptoms and associated disability, both in the short and long term. This effect was most evident in the SSRIs, where consistent evidence was found in support of their treatment efficacy and tolerability as compared to RIMAs and MAOIs.

A Number Needed to Treat (NNT) analysis of placebo-controlled trials of flexible dose trials of SSRIs and venlafaxine showed a NNT for paroxetine of 3.1, sertraline 4.5, fluoxetine 6.2, escitalopram 6.7, venlafaxine ER 7.1, fluvoxamine 8.7, and for all SSRIs and SNRIs 4.9 (Van Ameringen, Mancini, Patterson, & Bennett, 2005).

Drug versus Drug Comparisons

The dose equivalent head-to-head antidepressant studies have not suggested a difference in efficacy thus far. The findings of these investigations are summarized in Table 1.

Drug and CBT Comparisons

Only a few studies comparing CBT or cognitive behavioral group therapy CBGT to drug show drug to be more efficacious than CBT. Generally, both treatment conditions have been found to be effective compared to placebo, and with only slight differences in efficacy between the two. However, there is some preliminary evidence (based on very small sample sizes) that CBT may be a more enduring treatment with lower relapse rates upon discontinuation. Table 2 summarizes these treatment studies.

Combination Therapy in Treatment of Social Anxiety

The combination of psychological and pharmacological therapies in SAD has been examined in a few clinical studies (Rodebaugh, Holaway, & Heimberg, 2004). Some findings suggest that combining pharmacotherapy with some form of CBT may enhance treatment benefits for patients with SAD (Muller, Koen, Seedat, & Stein, 2005; Rodebaugh et al. 2004), but others do not (Blomhoff et al., 2001; Clark & Agras, 1991; Davidson et al., 2004a, 2004b; Falloon, Lloyd, & Harpin, 1981).

In clinical practice, clinicians have touted the benefits of combination treatment in GSAD that are not supported by the current literature. Methodological issues in the previous combination studies may have accounted for our current negative findings. Generally, clinicians start with one modality

Table 1. Drug Versus Drug Comparisons

Study	N	Duration	Treatment	Outcome
Verisani et al. (1992)	78	16	Moclobemide (MOC) Phenelzine (PHEN) Placebo (PBO)	MOC > PBO PHEN > PBO PHEN > MOC
Liebowitz et al. (1992)	74	8	PHEN Atentolol (ATEN)	PHEN > PBO
Atmaca et al. (2002)	71	8	MOC Citalopram (CIT)	MOC = CIT
Lader (2004)	899	24	Escitalopram (ECIT) Paroxetine (PAR) PBO	ECIT > PBO PAR > PBO ECIT 20 mg > PAR 20 mg
Allgulander et al. (2004)	434	12	Venlafaxine ER (VEN) PAR PBO	VEN = PAR > PBO
Furmark et al. (2005)	36	6	NKI Antagonist (GR205171) CIT PBO	GR205177 > PBO CIT > PBO

Table 2. Drug and CBT Comparison Studies

Study	N	Duration (weeks)	Drug #1	Drug #2	Placebo (PBO)	Psych Intervention	Outcome
Gelertner et al. (1991)	65	12	Phenelzine (PHEN) + Self Exposure (SE)	Alprazolam (ALP) + SE	Yes	Cognitive Behavioral Group Therapy (CBGT)	PHEN = ALP = CBGT All treatments > PBO
Turner et al. (1994)	72	12	PHEN	Atenolol (ATEN)	Yes	CBGT	PHEN > PBO PHEN > ATEN PHEN > CBGT
Heimberg et al. (1998)	133	12	PHEN		Yes	CBGT Educational Support (ES)	CBGT > PBO CBGT > ES PHEN > All other conditions
Otto et al. (2000)	45	12	Clonazepam (CPAM)		Yes	CBGT	CBGT = CPAM
Oosterbann et al. (2001)	82	15	Moclobemide (MOC)		Yes	Cognitive Therapy (CT)	CT > MOC CT = PBO MOC = PBO
Clark et al. (2003)	60	16	Fluoxetine (FLX) + SE		Yes	CT	CT > FLX CT > PBO
Davidson et al. (2004b)	295	14	FLX		Yes	CBGT CBGT + FLX CBGT + PBO	FLX > PBO CBGT > PBO

of treatment allowing for some treatment effect, prior to adding the second modality. This method of combining treatments has not yet been studied in controlled trials, which may lead to superior efficacy for combination treatment.

Treatment Resistance in Social Anxiety Disorder

Evidence is slowly emerging for the clinical management of treatment-resistant GSAD. In most investigations described throughout this chapter, the primary outcome was treatment *response,* typically defined as a CGI-I ≤ 2 (i.e., "very much" or "much improved") or a 50% drop LSAS.

Remission, on the other hand, refers to a complete resolution of symptoms across three domains of improvement: symptom severity, functionality, and well-being or overall improvement (Ballenger et al., 1998). When assessing remission, the Consensus Statement on Social Anxiety Disorder (Ballenger et al., 1998) has suggested the use of a combination of measures, including the LSAS to measure symptom severity, the SDS for functionality, and the CGI-I and CGI-S scales to measure overall improvement. Unfortunately, few, if any clinical trials have used this combination of measures to define remission, or even response. In a study by Mennin and colleagues (2002), results indicated that an LSAS cutoff score of 30 correctly identified more than 93% of those with social phobia with only 6% of those without the disorder being misclassified as socially phobic.

To date, five open trials (Aarre, 2003; Altamura, Pioli, Vitto, & Mannu, 1999; Kelsey, 1995; Simon, Korbly, Worthington, Kinrys, & Pollack, 2002; Van Ameringen, Mancini, & Wilson, 1996) and one double-blind, placebo-controlled, crossover study (Stein, Sareen, Hami, & Chao, 2001) have examined pharmacological agents in treatment-resistant social phobia.

In open-trials conducted by Altamura and colleagues (1999) and Aarre (2003) the effectiveness of switching to venlafaxine or phenelzine, respectively, in patients resistant to traditional social phobia treatment was examined. Both investigations indicated significant reduction in social phobia symptoms with the switch in agents.

Augmentation strategies for nonresponsive patients with SAD often involve the addition of a supplementary drug, usually from a different class. Treatment with SSRI has been augmented by the addition of benzodiazepines, anticonvulsants, as well as other agents (Muller et al., 2005), with positive open-label evidence for risperidone (Simon et al., 2006), aripiprazole (Worthington, Kinrys, Wygant, & Pollack, 2005), tiagabine (Kinrys et al., 2004; Rosenthal, 2003), and buspirone (Van Ameringen et al., 1996).

In a double-blind, placebo-controlled, crossover study, pindolol augmentation (5 mg tid) did not show any significant advantage over placebo in reducing social phobia symptoms in 14 social phobic patients who did not achieve a full response to paroxetine (Stein et al., 2001).

A randomized study of 28 patients with GSAD compared open-label paroxetine (20–40 mg/day) with double-blind placebo or clonazepam (1 to 2 mg/day) for 10 weeks (Seedat & Stein, 2004). At endpoint, only a trend favoring paroxetine/clonazepam treatment was observed, as this group experienced response rates (based on CGI-I ≤ 2) of 79%, versus only 43% in placebo. Low dropout rates due to adverse events indicate that this combination was a well-tolerated treatment option for nonresponsive SAD patients.

At this time there are no controlled data to guide clinicians in the choice of next-step treatments when a patient does not respond, or has a partial response to a standard, first-line treatment.

Predictors of Treatment Response

In examining a variety of medication types and treatment modalities across studies, there appear to be no consistent predictors of treatment response in social phobia. Given the wide variety of efficacious treatments in social phobia, identification of predictors of treatment response would be of great value to clinicians.

Investigations of gene polymorphisms have provided an exciting new direction into studies of predictors of response to pharmacological agents. Stein, Seedat, and Gelernter (2006) recently reported on a study of polymorphism in the serotonin transporter gene promoter 5HTTLPR and SSRI response in GSAD, in which DNA samples were taken from a series of 32 GSAD patients participating in a 12-week SSRI trial and examined and compared to standardized outcome data. Sixty-six percent of the sample were responders to the SSRI. A trend toward a linear association between 5HT-TLPR genotype and likelihood of response to SSRI was found, using both diallelic and triallelic classification. A reduction in LSAS and BSPS scores were significantly ($p < 0.02$) associated with the 5HT-TLPR genotype using both modalities of classification as well. The authors concluded that variation in this functional polymorphism, which is known to influence serotonin reuptake is associated with response to SSRI in individuals with GSAD (Stein et al., 2006).

Summary: Pharmacotherapy of GSAD

Since the emergence of social phobia, or GSAD, into the diagnostic nomenclature, we have seen an exponential expansion in our knowledge regarding effective treatment of this disorder from both pharmacological and psychological perspectives. The literature clearly supports the use of SSRIs and the SNRI venlafaxine ER as first-line pharmacological agents in the treatment of GSAD. Nevertheless, there remains a paucity of data in a number of areas, which indicate a need for further randomized, controlled investigations. For example, treatment resistance is an area where the body of knowledge is increasing, but requires further enhancement. There appears to be a large number of patients who obtain a partial or nonresponse to first-line treatment, and more studies looking at next-step treatments for these patients would be an important measure to guide clinicians more effectively. Potential agents that may be helpful in treatment resistance include anticonvulsants, antipsychotics, benzodiazepines, and MAOIs, but data are currently lacking about their utility in the context of treatment resistance.

The lack of superiority seen in randomized controlled trials of combination treatments such as drug and CBT over either treatment alone has been disappointing, although the new findings on the enhancement of exposure treatments with D-cycloserine (DCS) appear very promising. With the growing number of drug classes that have demonstrated efficacy in GSAD, as well as the demonstrated efficacy of CBT, we need to develop predictors of treatment response that allow matching patient variables to a specific treatment intervention. However, these advances may not successfully occur until genetic or other biological markers are identified that code for subgroups of SAD individuals and we have a better understanding of the interaction between genetic and environmental factors resulting in GSAD.

Pharmacological Treatment of Specific Phobias

Exposure-based treatments are considered to be the gold standard treatment for specific phobias (Antony & Barlow, 2002). There is a dearth of information regarding the pharmacological treatment of specific phobias, however, and even fewer randomized controlled trials. What data exist are lim-

ited by small sample sizes. Nevertheless, there are positive case reports for fluoxetine in flying phobia (Abene & Hamilton, 1998), and fluvoxamine in the treatment of storm phobia (Balon, 1999). Early studies examined benzodiazepines as additive agents to exposure and did not indicate efficacy (Antony & Barlow, 2002) for these agents in specific phobias. Small, randomized, double-blind placebo controlled trials provide tentative evidence in support of paroxetine (Benjamin, Ben-Zion, Karbofsky, & Dannon, 2000) and escitalopram (Connor, Varia, Zhang, & Davidson, 2006), but larger studies are needed before these medications can be recommended for this purpose.

A study of 28 subjects with *DSM–IV* acrophobia (Ressler, et al., 2004) randomly assigned subjects to receive doses of D-cycloserine (DCS) (50 mg or 500 mg) or placebo, prior to virtual reality exposure (VRE) to a glass elevator. Exposure therapy plus DCS resulted in significantly larger reductions of symptoms (1 week posttreatment: $p < .001$; 3 months posttreatment: $p < .05$), independent of dosage. Subjects in DCS condition reported greater improvement in general measures of real-world acrophobia symptoms ($p < .02$), acrophobia anxiety (AAQ: $p < .01$), attitudes toward heights (ATHI: $p < .04$; CGI-I: $p < .01$), and number of self-exposures to real-world heights ($p < .01$). The DCS-enhanced extinction was not found to be state-dependent, and the authors concluded that two sessions of VRE therapy in combination with DCS is sufficient for extinction of fear in the virtual environment for as long as 3 months.

In summary, there is little evidence to support the use of pharmacological agents as the primary treatment modality in specific phobias. It is likely that exposure-based treatment may remain the first-line treatment intervention. Perhaps the role of pharmacotherapy in specific phobia may be to reduce general levels of anxiety, thereby enabling treatment refractory patients to benefit from exposure treatment. However, more controlled studies with larger sample sizes, encompassing a variety of specific phobias are required. Results from the study of adjunctive DCS treatment to exposure therapy are exciting and innovative, suggesting that pharmacotherapeutic interventions may be able to enhance the efficacy of exposure therapy. Future research initiatives may examine the role of pretreatment with an SSRI prior to a course of exposure therapy, which may have a similar effect as adjunctive DCS, as well as the use of other agents such as DCS that can enhance learning.

References

Aarre, T. F. (2003). Phenelzine efficacy in refractory social anxiety disorder: a case series. *Nordic Journal of Psychiatry, 57*(4), 313–315.

Abene, M. V., Hamilton, J. D. (1998). Resolution of fear of flying with fluoxetine treatment. *Journal of Anxiety Disorders, 12,* 599–603.

Allgulander, C. (1999). Paroxetine in social anxiety disorder: a randomized placebo-controlled study. *Acta Psychiatr Scand, 100*(3), 193–198.

Altamura, A. C., Pioli, R., Vitto, M., & Mannu, P. (1999). Venlafaxine in social phobia: A study in selective serotonin reuptake inhibitor non-responders. *Int Clin Psychopharmacol, 14*(4), 239–245

American Psychiatric Association. (1994). *Diagnostic and statistical manual of mental disorders* (4th ed.). Washington, DC: Author.

Antony, M. M., & Barlow, D. H. (2002). Specific phobias. In D. Barlow (Ed.), *Anxiety and its disorders: The nature and treatment of anxiety and panic* (2nd ed., pp. 380–417). New York: Guilford Press.

Atmaca, M., Kuloglu, M., Tezcan, E., & Unal, A. (2002). Efficacy of citalopram and moclobemide in patients with social phobia: some preliminary findings. *Human Psychopharmacology, 17,* 401–405.

Atmaca, M., Tezcan, E., & Kuloglu, M. (2003). An open clinical trial of reboxetine in the treatment of social phobia. *Journal of Clinical Psychopharmacology, 23,* 417–419.

Baldwin, D., Bobes, J., Stein, D. J., Scharwachter, I., & Faure, M. (1999). Paroxetine in social phobia/social anxiety disorder: Randomised, double-blind, placebo-controlled study. Paroxetine Study Group. *British Journal of Psychiatry, 175,* 120–126.

Ballenger, J. C., Davidson, J. R., Lecrubier, Y., Nutt, D. J., Bobes, J., Beidel, D. C., et al. (1998). Consensus statement on social anxiety disorder from the International Consensus Group on Depression and Anxiety. *Journal of Clinical Psychiatry, 59*(Suppl. 17), 54–60.

Balon, R. (1999). Fluvoxamine for phobia of storms. *Acta Psychiatrica Scandinavica, 100,* 244–245.

Barnett, S. D., Kramer, M. L., Casat, C. D., Connor, K. M., & Davidson, J.R.T. (2002). Efficacy of olanzapine in social anxiety disorder: A pilot study. *Journal of Psychopharmacology, 16,* 365–368.

Bell, J., DeVaugh-Geiss, J. (1994, December). *Multicenter trial of a 5-HT3 antagonist, ondansetron, in social phobia.* Poster session presented at the annual meeting of the American College of Neuropsychopharmacology, San Juan, Puerto Rico.

Benjamin, J., Ben-Zion, I. Z., Karbofsky, E., & Dannon, P. (2000). Double-blind placebo-controlled pilot study of paroxetine for specific phobia. *Psychopharmacology, 149,* 194–196.

Bisserbe, J. C., & Lepine, J. P. (1994). Moclobemide in social phobia: A pilot open study. GRP Group. Groupe de Recherche en Psychopharmacologie. *Clinical Neuropharmacology, 17*(Suppl. 1), S88–S94.

Blanco, C., Schneier, F. R., Schmidt, A., Blanco-Jerez, C. R., Marshall, R. D., Sanchez-Lacay, A., et al. (2003). Pharmacological treatment of social anxiety disorder: A meta-analysis. *Depression and Anxiety, 18,* 29–40.

Blomhoff, S., Haug, T. T., Hellstrom, K., Holme, I., Humble, M., Madsbu, H. P., et al. (2001). Randomised controlled general practice trial of sertraline, exposure therapy and combined treatment in generalised social phobia. *British Journal of Psychiatry, 179,* 23–30.

Clark, D. B., & Agras, W. S. (1991). The assessment and treatment of performance anxiety in musicians. *American Journal of Psychiatry, 148,* 598–605.

Clark, D. M., Ehlers, A., McManus, F., Hackmann, A., Fennell, M., Campbell, H., et al. (2003). Cognitive therapy versus fluoxetine in generalized social phobia: A randomized placebo-controlled trial. *Journal of Consulting & Clinical Psychology, 71,* 1058–1067.

Connor, K. M., Varia, I., Zhang, W., & Davidson, J.R.T (2006, May). *Escitalopram for specific phobia: A placebo-controlled pilot study.* Paper presented at the 159th annual meeting of the American Psychiatric Association, Toronto, Ontario, Canada.

Davidson, J., Yaryura-Tobias, J., DuPont, R., Stallings, L., Barbato, L. M., van der Hoop, R. G., et al. (2004a). Fluvoxamine-controlled release formulation for the treatment of generalized social anxiety disorder. *Journal of Clinical Psychopharmacology, 24,* 118–125.

Davidson, J. R., Foa, E. B., Huppert, J. D., Keefe, F. J., Franklin, M. E., Compton, J. S., et al. (2004b). Fluoxetine, comprehensive cognitive behavioral therapy, and placebo in generalized social phobia. *Archives of General Psychiatry, 61,* 1005–1013.

Davidson, J. R., Miner, C. M., Veaugh-Geiss, J., Tupler, L. A., Colket, J. T., & Potts, N. L. (1997). The Brief Social Phobia Scale: A psychometric evaluation. *Psychological Medicine, 27,* 161–166.

Davidson, J. R., Potts, N., Richichi, E., Krishnan, R., Ford, S. M., Smith, R., et al. (1993). Treatment of social phobia with clonazepam and placebo. *Journal of Clinical Psychopharmacology, 13,* 423–428.

DeVane, C. L., Grothe, D. R., & Smith, S. L. (2002). Pharmacology of antidepressants: Focus on nefazodone. *Journal of Clinical Psychiatry, 63*(Suppl. 1), 10–17.

Emmanuel, N. P., Brawman-Mintzer, O., Morton, W. A., Book, S. W., Johnson, M. R., Lorberbaum, J. P., et al. (2000). Bupropion-SR in treatment of social phobia. *Depression and Anxiety, 12,* 111–113.

Emmanuel, N. P., Johnson, M. R., & Villarreal, G. (1998). Imipramine in the treatment of social phobia: A double blind study. Poster. In *Programs and Abstracts of the 36th Annual Meeting of the American College of Neuropsychopharmacology.* [Poster presented at the American College of Neuropsychopharmacology meeting.]

Emmanuel, N. P., Lydiard, R. B., & Ballenger, J. C. (1991). Treatment of social phobia with bupropion. *Journal of Clinical Psychopharmacology, 11,* 276–277.

Fahlen, T., Nilsson, H. L., Borg, K., Humble, M., & Pauli, U. (1995). Social phobia: The clinical efficacy and tolerability of the monoamine oxidase-A and serotonin uptake inhibitor brofaromine. A double-blind placebo-controlled study. *Acta Psychiatrica Scandavica, 92,* 351–358.

Falloon, I. R., Lloyd, G. G., & Harpin, R. E. (1981). The treatment of social phobia: Real-life rehearsal with nonprofessional therapists. *Journal of Nervous and Mental Disease, 169,* 180–184.

Fedoroff, I. C., & Taylor, S. (2001). Psychological and pharmacological treatments of social phobia: A meta-analysis. *Journal of Clinical Psychopharmacology, 21,* 311–324.

Furmark, T., Appel, L., Michelgard, A., Wahlstedt, K., Ahs, F., Zancan, S., et al. (2005). Cerebral blood flow changes after treatment of social phobia with the neurokinin-1 antagonist GR205171, citalopram, or placebo. *Biological Psychiatry, 58,* 132–142.

Gelernter, C. S., Uhde, T. W., Cimbolic, P., Arnkoff, D. B., Vittone, B. J., Tancer, M. E., et al. (1991). Cognitive-behavioral and pharmacological treatments of social phobia. A controlled study. *Archives of General Psychiatry, 48,* 938–945.

Grunes, M. S., Yayura-Tobias, J. A., & Neziroglu, F. A. (1996, May 1–5). Society of Biological Psychiatry 51st annual convention and scientific program, New York. Abstracts. *Biological Psychiatry, 39,* 467–677.

Heimberg, R. G., Liebowitz, M. R., Hope, D. A., Schneier, F. R., Holt, C. S., Welkowitz, L. A., et al. (1998). Cognitive behavioral group therapy vs. phenelzine therapy for social phobia: 12-week outcome. *Archives of General Psychiatry, 55,* 1133–1141.

Hofmann, S. G., Meuret, A. E., Smits, J.A.J., Simon, N. M., Pollack, M. H., Eisenmenger, K., et al. (2006). Augmentation of exposure therapy with D-cycloserine for social anxiety disorder. *Archives of General Psychiatry, 63,* 298–304.

Kasper, S., Stein, D. J., Loft, H., & Nil, R. (2005) Escitalopram in the treatment of social anxiety disorder. *British Journal of Psychiatry, 186,* 222–226.

Katzelnick, D. J., Kobak, K. A., Greist, J. H., Jefferson, J. W., Mantle, J. M., & Serlin, R. C. (1995). Sertraline for social phobia: A double-blind, placebo-controlled crossover study. *American Journal of Psychiatry, 152,* 1368–1371.

Kelsey, J. E. (1995). Venlafaxine in social phobia. *Psychopharmacology Bulleti*n, 31, 767–771.

Kinrys, G., Pollack, M. H., Simon, N. M., Worthington, J. J., Nardi, A. E., & Versiani, M. (2003). Valproic acid for the treatment of social anxiety disorder. *International Clinical Psychopharmacology, 18,* 169–172.

Kinrys, G., Soldani, F., Hsu, D., Pardo, T., Melo, M., & Worthington, J. (2004, May). *Adjunctive tiagabine for treatment of refractory social anxiety disorder.* Poster session presented at the 157th Annual meeting of the American Psychiatric Association, New York.

Klieser, E., Schulte, T., Wurthmann, C., Czekalla, J., Maestele, A., Russ, H., et al. (1999, August). *Open-label study of olanzapine in generalized anxiety disorder (GAD).* Poster session presented at XI World Congress of Psychiatry, Hamburg, Germany.

Kobak, K. A., Greist, J. H., Jefferson, J. W., & Katzelnick, D. J. (2002). Fluoxetine in social phobia: a double-blind, placebo-controlled pilot study. *Journal of Clinical Psychopharmacology, 22,* 257–262.

Kobak, K. A., Taylor, L. V., Warner, G., & Futterer, R. (2005). St. John's wort versus placebo in social phobia: Results from a placebo-controlled pilot study. *Journal of Clinical Psychopharmacology, 25,* 51–58.

Lader, M., Stender, K., Burger, V., & Nil, R. (2004). Efficacy and tolerability of escitalopram in 12- and 24-week treatment of social anxiety disorder: Randomised, double-blind, placebo-controlled, fixed-dose study. *Depression and Anxiety, 19,* 241–248.

Lepola, U., Bergtholdt, B., St Lambert, J., Davy, K. L., & Ruggiero, L. (2004). Controlled-release paroxetine in the treatment of patients with social anxiety disorder. *Journal of Clinical Psychiatry, 65,* 222–229.

Liebowitz, M. R. (1987). Social phobia. *Modern Problems of Pharmacopsychiatry, 22,* 141–173.

Liebowitz, M. R., DeMartinis, N. A., Weihs, K., Londborg, P. D., Smith, W. T., Chung, H., et al. (2003). Efficacy of sertra-line in severe generalized social anxiety disorder: results of a double-blind, placebo-controlled study. *Journal of Clinical Psychiatry, 64,* 785–792.

Liebowitz, M. R., Gorman, J. M., Fyer, A. J., Campeas, R., Levin, A. P., Sandberg, D., et al. (1988). Pharmacotherapy of social phobia: an interim report of a placebo-controlled comparison of phenelzine and atenolol. *Journal of Clinical Psychiatry, 49,* 252–257.

Liebowitz, M. R., Gorman, J. M., Fyer, A. J., & Klein, D. F. (1985). Social phobia: Review of a neglected anxiety disorder. *Archives of General Psychiatry, 42,* 729–736.

Liebowitz, M. R., Heimberg, R. G., Schneier, F. R., Hope, D. A., Davies, S., Holt, C. S., et al. (1999). Cognitive-behavioral group therapy versus phenelzine in social phobia: Long-term outcome. *Depression and Anxiety, 10,* 89–98.

Liebowitz, M. R., Mangano, R. M., Bradwejn, J., & Asnis, G. (2005). A randomized controlled trial of venlafaxine extended release in generalized social anxiety disorder. *Journal of Clinical Psychiatry, 66,* 238–247.

Liebowitz, M. R., Schneier, F., Campeas, R., Hollander, E., Hatterer, J., Fyer, A., et al. (1992). Phenelzine vs. atenolol in social phobia: A placebo-controlled comparison. *Archives of General Psychiatry, 49,* 290–300.

Liebowitz, M. R., Stein, M. B., Tancer, M., Carpenter, D., Oakes, R., & Pitts, C. D. (2002). A randomized, double-blind, fixed-dose comparison of paroxetine and placebo in the treatment of generalized social anxiety disorder. *Journal of Clinical Psychiatry, 63,* 66–74.

Lott, M., Greist, J. H., Jefferson, J. W., Kobak, K. A., Katzelnick, D. J., Katz, R. J., et al. (1997). Brofaromine for social phobia: A multicenter, placebo-controlled, double-blind study. *Journal of Clinical Psychopharmacology, 17,* 255–260.

Mennin, D. S., Fresco, D. M., Heimberg, R. G., Schneier, F. R., Davies, S. O., & Liebowitz, M. R. (2002). Screening for social anxiety disorder in the clinical setting: using the Liebowitz Social Anxiety Scale. *Journal of Anxiety Disorders, 16,* 661–673.

Moore, N. A., Rees, G., Sanger, G., & Tye, N. C. (1994). Effects of olanzapine and other antipsychotic agents on responding maintained by a conflict schedule. *Behavioural Pharmacology, 5,* 196–202.

Muller, J. E., Koen, L., Seedat, S., & Stein, D. J. (2005). Social anxiety disorder: Current treatment recommendations. *CNS Drugs, 19,* 377–391.

Nardi, A. E., Mendlowicz, M., & Versiani, F. M. (1997). Valproic acid in social phobia: An open trial. *Biological Psychiatry, 42,* 118 S.

Newcomer, J. W. (2004). Abnormalities of glucose metabolism associated with atypical antipsychotic drugs. *Journal of Clinical Psychiatry, 65*(Suppl. 18), 36–46.

Noyes, R., Jr., Moroz, G., Davidson, J. R., Liebowitz, M. R., Davidson, A., Siegel, J., et al. (1997). Moclobemide in social phobia: A controlled dose-response trial. *Journal of Clinical Psychopharmacology, 17,* 247–254.

Oosterbaan, D. B., van Balkom, A.J.L.M., Spinhoven, P., van Oppen, P., & van Dyck, R. (2001). Cognitive therapy versus moclobemide in social phobia: A controlled study. *Clinical Psychology and Psychotherapy, 8,* 263–273.

Otto, M. W., Pollack, M. H., Gould, R. A., Worthington, J. J., III, McArdle, E. T., & Rosenbaum, J. F. (2000). A comparison of the efficacy of clonazepam and cognitive-behavioral group therapy for the treatment of social phobia. *Journal of Anxiety Disorders, 14,* 345–358.

Pande, A. C., Davidson, J. R., Jefferson, J. W., Janney, C. A., Katzelnick, D. J., Weisler, R. H., et al. (1999). Treatment of social phobia with gabapentin: A placebo-controlled study. *Journal of Clinical Psychopharmacology, 19,* 341–348.

Pande, A. C., Feltner, D. E., Jefferson, J. W., Davidson, J. R., Pollack, M., Stein, M. B., et al. (2004). Efficacy of the novel anxiolytic pregabalin in social anxiety disorder: A placebo-controlled, multicenter study. *Journal of Clinical Psychopharmacology, 24,* 141–149.

Papp, L. A., & Ninan, P. T. (2004, May). *Tiagabine for the treatment of social anxiety disorder.* Poster session presented at 157th Annual meeting of the American Psychiatric Association, New York.

Ressler, K. J., Rothbaum, B. O., Tannenbaum, L., Anderson, P., Graap, K., Zimand, E., et al. (2004). Cognitive enhancers as adjuncts to psychotherapy. *Archives of General Psychiatry, 61,* 1136–1144.

Rickels, K., Mangano, R., & Khan, A. (2004). A double-blind, placebo-controlled study of a flexible dose of venlafaxine ER in adult outpatients with generalized social anxiety disorder. *Journal of Clinical Psychopharmacology, 24,* 488–496.

Rodebaugh, T. L., Holaway, R. M., & Heimberg, R. G. (2004). The treatment of social anxiety disorder. *Clinical Psychology Review, 24,* 883–908.

Rosenthal, M. (2003). Tiagabine for the treatment of generalized anxiety disorder: A randomized, open-label, clinical trial with paroxetine as a positive control. *Journal of Clinical Psychiatry, 64,* 1245–1249.

Schneier, F. R., Goetz, D., Campeas, R., Fallon, B., Marshall, R., & Liebowitz, M. R. (1998). Placebo-controlled trial of moclobemide in social phobia. *British Journal of Psychiatry, 172,* 70–77.

Schutters, S. I., van Megen, H. J., & Westenberg, H. G. (2005). Efficacy of quetiapine in generalized social anxiety disorder: Results from an open-label study. *Journal of Clinical Psychiatry, 66,* 540–542.

Seedat, S., & Stein, M. B. (2004). Double-blind, placebo-controlled assessment of combined clonazepam with paroxetine compared with paroxetine monotherapy for generalized social anxiety disorder. *Journal of Clinical Psychiatry, 65,* 244–248.

Sheehan, D. V. (1983). *The anxiety disease.* New York: Scribner.

Simon, N. M., Hoge, E. A., Fischmann, D., Worthington, J. J., Christian K. M., & Kinrys, G. (2006). An open label trial of risperidone augmentation for refractory anxiety disorders. *Journal of Clinical Psychiatry, 67,* 381–385.

Simon, N. M., Korbly, N. B., Worthington, J. J., Kinrys, G., & Pollack, M. H. (2002). Citalopram for social anxiety disorder: An open-label pilot study in refractory and nonrefractory patients. *CNS Spectrums, 7,* 655–657.

Simon, N. M., Worthington, J. J., Doyle, A. C., Hoge, E. A., Kinrys, G., Fischmann, D., et al. (2004). Levetricetam for the treatment of social anxiety disorder. *Journal of Clinical Psychiatry, 65,* 1219–1222

Simpson, H. B., Schneier, F. R., Marshall, R. D., Campeas, R. B., Vermes, D., Silvestre, J., et al. (1998). Low dose selegiline (L-Deprenyl) in social phobia. *Depression and Anxiety, 7,* 126–129.

Stein, D. J., Cameron, A., Amrein, R., & Montgomery, S. A. (2002). Moclobemide is effective and well tolerated in the long-term pharmacotherapy of social anxiety disorder with or without comorbid anxiety disorder. *International Clinical Psychopharmacology, 17,* 161–170.

Stein, D. J., Isper, J. C., & van Balkom, A. J. (2005). Pharmacotherapy for social anxiety disorder [Review]. *The Cochrane Collaboration, Cochrane Library,* 1–48.

Stein, M. B., Fyer, A. J., Davidson, J. R., Pollack, M. H., & Wiita, B. (1999). Fluvoxamine treatment of social phobia (social anxiety disorder): A double-blind, placebo-controlled study. *American Journal of Psychiatry, 156,* 756–760.

Stein, M. B., Liebowitz, M. R., Lydiard, R. B., Pitts, C. D., Bushnell, W., & Gergel, I. (1998). Paroxetine treatment of generalized social phobia (social anxiety disorder): A randomized controlled trial. *Journal of the American Medical Association, 280,* 708–713.

Stein, M. B., Pollack, M. H., Bystritsky, A., Kelsey, J. E., & Mangano, R. M. (2005). Efficacy of low and higher dose extended-release venlafaxine in generalized social anxiety disorder: A 6-month randomized controlled trial. *Psychopharmacology (Berl), 177,* 280–288.

Stein, M. B., Sareen, J., Hami, S., & Chao, J. (2001). Pindolol potentiation of paroxetine for generalized social phobia: A double-blind, placebo-controlled, crossover study. *American Journal of Psychiatry, 158,* 1725–1727.

Stein, M. B., Seedat, S., & Gelernter, J. (2006). Serotonin transporter gene polymorphism predicts SSRI response in generalized social anxiety disorder. *Psychopharmacology, 187,* 68–72.

Tollefson, G. D., Sanger, T. M., Beasley, C. M., & Tran, P. V. (1998). A double-blind, controlled comparison of the novel antipsychotic olanzapine versus haloperidol or placebo on anxious and depressive symptoms accompanying schizophrenia. *Biological Psychiatry, 43,* 803–810.

Turner, S. M., Beidel, D. C., Dancu, C. V., & Stanley, M. A. (1998) An empirically derived inventory to measure social fears and anxiety: The Social Phobia and Anxiety Inventory. *Psychological Assessment, 1,* 35–40.

Turner, S. M., Beidel, D. C., & Jacob, R. G. (1994). Social phobia: A comparison of behavior therapy and atenolol. *Journal of Consulting and Clinical Psychology, 62,* 350–358.

United States Department of Health, Employee Assistance and Wellness Program. (1976). *ECDEU assessment manual for psychopharmacoloy.* Rockville, MD: National Institute of Mental Health.

Van Ameringen, M., Mancini, C., Oakman, J., Walker, J., Kjernisted, K., Chokka, P., et al. (2007). Nefazodone in the treatment for generalized social phobia: A randomized, placebo controlled trial. *Journal of Clinical Psychiatry, 68*(2), 288–295.

Van Ameringen, M., Mancini, C., Patterson, B., & Bennett, M. (2005). An evaluation of paroxetine in generalised social anxiety disorder. *Expert Opinion on Pharmacotherapy, 6,* 819–830.

Van Ameringen, M., Mancini, C., Pipe, B., & Bennett, M. (2004a). Antiepileptic drugs in the treatment of anxiety disorders: Role in therapy. *Drugs, 64,* 2199–2220.

Van Ameringen, M., Mancini, C., Pipe, B., & Bennett, M. (2004b). Optimizing treatment in social phobia: A review of treatment resistance. *CNS Spectrums, 9,* 753–762.

Van Ameringen, M., Mancini, C., Pipe, B., Oakman, J., & Bennett, M. (2004). An open trial of topiramate in the treatment of generalized social phobia. *Journal of Clinical Psychiatry, 65,* 1674–1678.

Van Ameringen, M., Mancini, C., & Wilson, C. (1996). Buspirone augmentation of selective serotonin reuptake inhibitors (SSRIs) in social phobia. *Journal of Affective Disorders, 39,* 115–121.

Van Ameringen, M. A., Lane, R. M., Walker, J. R., Bowen, R. C., Chokka, P. R., Goldner, E. M., et al. (2001). Sertraline treatment of generalized social phobia: A 20-week, double-blind, placebo-controlled study. *American Journal of Psychiatry, 158,* 275–281.

Van Vliet, I. M., den Boer, J. A., & Westenberg, H. G. (1992). Psychopharmacological treatment of social phobia: Clinical and biochemical effects of brofaromine, a selective MAO-A inhibitor. *European Neuropsychopharmacology, 2,* 21–29.

Van Vliet, I. M., den Boer, J. A., & Westenberg, H. G. (1994). Psychopharmacological treatment of social phobia: A double blind placebo controlled study with fluvoxamine. *Psychopharmacology (Berl), 115,* 128–134.

Versiani, M., Egidio, N., Figueira, I., Mendlowicz, M., & Marques, C. (1997). Double-blind placebo controlled trial with bromazepam in social phobia. *Jornal Brasileiro de Psiquiatria Marco, 46,* 167–171.

Versiani, M., Nardi, A. E., Mundim, F. D., Alves, A. B., Liebowitz, M. R., & Amrein, R. (1992). Pharmacotherapy of social phobia: A controlled study with moclobemide and phenelzine. *British Journal of Psychiatry, 161,* 353–360.

Worthington, J. J., III, Kinrys, G., Wygant, L. E., & Pollack, M. H. (2005). Aripiprazole as an augmentor of selective serotonin reuptake inhibitors in depression and anxiety disorder patients. *International Clinical Psychopharmacology, 20,* 9–11.

Zhang, W., Connor, K. M., & Davidson, J. R. (2005). Levetiracetam in social phobia: A placebo controlled pilot study. *Journal of Psychopharmacology, 19,* 551–553.

Psychological Treatment of Social Anxiety Disorder and Specific Phobia

Leanne Magee, Brigette A. Erwin *and* Richard G. Heimberg

Abstract

Social anxiety disorder and specific phobia are distinct disorders with distinct courses of illness, etiology, and prevalence rates. This chapter provides an overview of the treatment of social anxiety disorder and specific phobia, empirical support for their efficacy, and factors influencing outcome. For social anxiety disorder, cognitive behavioral therapy appears to be the best-established approach to treatment, and although social skills training as well as psychodynamic, interpersonal, and acceptance and commitment therapies may be beneficial, they require additional investigation. In the treatment of specific phobias, exposure emerges as the treatment of choice. There remains a significant lack of understanding regarding which treatments or combinations of treatments work best and whether individual differences or other variables lead to better treatment outcome.

Keywords: anxiety, cognitive behavioral therapy, psychodynamic therapy, social anxiety disorder, social phobia, social skills training, specific phobia, relaxation strategies

In the last few decades, knowledge about social anxiety disorder and specific phobia has increased considerably. Social anxiety disorder and specific phobia are distinct disorders with distinct courses of illness, etiology, and prevalence rates. Increased knowledge of social anxiety disorder and specific phobia has been associated with significant advances in research into the treatment of these disorders and increased awareness that they respond to different treatment strategies. This chapter provides an overview of the treatment of social anxiety disorder and specific phobia, empirical support for their efficacy, and factors influencing outcome.

Social Anxiety Disorder
Cognitive Behavioral Therapies

Cognitive behavioral therapy (CBT) for social anxiety disorder is a time-limited, present-focused approach with the goal of identifying and modifying distorted beliefs and supporting more adaptive

behaviors in social and performance situations (Heimberg, 2002). Cognitive behavioral treatments, specifically those that employ exposure alone or combined with cognitive restructuring, social skills training, and relaxation training, have received the most attention of any psychotherapeutic approaches in the empirical literature.

Cognitive behavioral models of social anxiety disorder suggest that anxiety is maintained largely by dysfunctional beliefs and biased information-processing strategies (e.g., D. M. Clark & Wells, 1995; Rapee & Heimberg, 1997). These models emphasize the interaction between socially anxious individuals' dysfunctional belief systems and their tendencies toward behavioral and experiential avoidance. As such, cognitive behavioral interventions address both individuals' belief systems as well as their patterns of overt and subtle avoidance. Exposure-based cognitive behavioral treatments have been categorized by the International Consensus

Group on Depression and Anxiety as having good evidence for their efficacy (Ballenger et al., 1998). Comprehensive reviews of CBT for social anxiety disorder have been conducted by Rodebaugh, Holaway, and Heimberg (2004) and Turk, Coles, and Heimberg (2002).

EXPOSURE TREATMENTS

Exposure treatments are designed to reduce anxiety by asking clients to imagine (imaginal exposure) or directly confront (in vivo exposure) anxiety-evoking stimuli in such a way that they remain psychologically engaged. Classical behavioral models suggest that exposure leads to long-term anxiety reduction by promoting the naturally occurring conditioning processes of extinction and habituation, which in turn increase access to positively reinforcing stimuli and decrease behavioral avoidance. In vivo exposure can be directed toward actual or simulated situations in treatment sessions or toward real-life situations during between-session homework assignments. In preparation for exposure, clients are asked to identify and rank order anxiety-provoking situations. Exposure requires clients to progressively confront more anxiety-provoking situations, beginning with ones that elicit a moderate amount of anxiety. Before exposure to the next most anxiety-evoking situation is initiated, exposure to each situation is repeated a sufficient number of times so that it no longer elicits a distressing amount of anxiety. This process is repeated until the anxiety associated with each situation is significantly reduced.

It appears likely that the mechanism underlying exposure involves the acquisition of new learning that does not replace the original anxiety response but rather results in the assimilation of both the original anxiety response and new information derived from exposure experiences (Bouton, 2002). Exposure is maximally effective when clients engage fully with the exposure situation such that emotional and physiological arousal is fully experienced (Foa & Kozak, 1986). Clients often attempt to dilute the intensity of exposures behaviorally (e.g., by engaging in safety behaviors, that is, behaviors that the client erroneously believes are necessary for him or her to successfully "survive" the situation) (Wells et al., 1995) and cognitively (e.g., by removing attention from the feared situation through distraction or by attending to negative and distorted cognition) (Foa & Kozak, 1986). To maximize the effectiveness of exposure interventions, all relevant safety behaviors should be identified in advance and prevented (Wells et al., 1995) and clients should be instructed to maintain attention on the situation (Wells & Papageorgiou, 1998).

Imaginal exposure for social anxiety disorder has not been examined sufficiently. In vivo exposure techniques have demonstrated short- and long-term efficacy in both self-directed and therapist-directed formats (see Rodebaugh et al., 2004, for a review). As a sole treatment for social anxiety disorder, exposure has resulted in greater anxiety reduction than progressive muscle relaxation (Al-Kubaisy et al., 1992; Alström, Nordlund, Persson, Hårding, & Ljungqvist, 1984), pill placebo (Turner, Beidel, & Jacob, 1994), and delayed treatment (Newman, Hofmann, Trabert, Roth, & Taylor, 1994). Methodological problems suggest the need for replication.

Exposure is rarely administered in the absence of other techniques; rather, it is usually combined with other techniques such as cognitive restructuring (Juster & Heimberg, 1995), since the core feature of social anxiety disorder, fear of negative evaluation, is a cognitive construct (Butler, 1985; Turk, Fresco, & Heimberg, 1999). Successful and comprehensive treatment of social anxiety disorder should include attention to information-processing biases and dysfunctional beliefs, which may or may not be best accomplished through a combination of exposure therapy and cognitive restructuring techniques.

EXPOSURE PLUS COGNITIVE RESTRUCTURING TREATMENTS

Cognitive restructuring is designed to help clients challenge maladaptive beliefs about themselves and the world they live in such that they can view the world in a more realistic way. This group of interventions is based on the notion that one's thoughts about a situation, rather than the situation itself, generate anxiety (e.g., A. T. Beck & Emery, 1985). Recent cognitive behavioral models (e.g., D. M. Clark & Wells, 1995; Rapee & Heimberg, 1997) assert that inaccurate beliefs about the potential dangers posed by social situations, negative predictions about the outcomes of such situations, and biased processing of information that occurs in relation to social interactions contribute to the development and maintenance of social anxiety disorder.

Heimberg's cognitive behavioral group therapy (CBGT) (Heimberg & Becker, 2002) is a widely studied and empirically supported cognitive behavioral treatment protocol for social anxiety disorder. Small groups of approximately six clients led by two therapists provide opportunities for exposure to social interactions. In the initial psychoeducation phase of treatment, the therapists accurately inform clients about the cognitive, physiological, and behavioral components of social anxiety and increase the clients' awareness and understanding of their disorder. Next, clients are instructed in cognitive restructuring, which first involves teaching clients to identify negative and irrational thoughts that occur in the context of social and performance situations (e.g., "I won't have anything to say" or "He won't like me"). Therapists and clients work to evaluate and dispute these thoughts by identifying thinking errors (e.g., the tendency to act as though one knows what another person is thinking; the tendency to predict negative outcomes without evidence) (J. S. Beck, 1995) and developing rational alternatives. Cognitive restructuring techniques are maximally effective when used before, during, and after exposure exercises. In this context, exposure is utilized both as a means of habituation and of challenging clients' irrational thoughts and beliefs (Rodebaugh et al., 2004). For homework, clients practice cognitive restructuring in preparation for and after engaging in exposures to anxiety-evoking situations between sessions. This therapy employs both systematic therapist-directed in-session exposures and homework assignments for in vivo exposure and self-administered cognitive restructuring to address each client's individual fears. The format for individual CBT for social anxiety disorder is similar to that of CBGT. For detailed reviews of the use of cognitive restructuring in the treatment of social anxiety disorder, please see Heimberg and Becker (2002) and Hope, Heimberg, Juster, and Turk (2000).

Empirical findings support the efficacy of combining cognitive and exposure techniques in comparison to waitlist control conditions (Butler, Cullington, Munby, Amies, & Gelder, 1984; Hope, Heimberg, & Bruch, 1995), educational supportive control conditions (Heimberg, Dodge, Hope, Kennedy, Zollo, et al., 1990; Heimberg, Holt, Schneier, Spitzer, & Liebowitz, 1993; Heimberg et al., 1998), and pill placebo (Heimberg et al., 1998). Empirical studies have been equivocal regarding the relative efficacy of exposure alone versus exposure plus cognitive restructuring, with some studies demonstrating equivalent outcomes and others finding the combination to be superior and to provide additional gains during the follow-up period (Rodebaugh et al., 2004). There has been a modest tendency for clients treated with exposure alone to show some loss

of gains after discontinuation of treatment, suggesting that additional treatment components may be necessary to maximize durability of improvements. Cognitive techniques may enhance the efficacy of exposure as they appear to reduce the amount of exposure necessary to achieve typically similar positive outcomes (Turk et al. 2002).

SOCIAL SKILLS TRAINING

Social skills training (SST) is based on the assumption that social anxiety is related to a lack of social skill, which provokes negative reactions from others and leads to poor interpersonal outcomes and distress. These programs typically provide education for clients about appropriate social behavior, often in the form of instruction and modeling of target social skills (e.g., eye contact, voice volume, or posture). Clients then rehearse each social skill until it is performed adequately, receiving praise from the therapist for successively better approximations of the desired behavior. Newly acquired social skills are then practiced in real-life situations. Although some studies have demonstrated an inverse relationship between anxiety and the quality of social performance (Halford & Foddy, 1982; Stopa & Clark, 1993), others have found no evidence of impaired social performance among socially anxious persons (Glasgow & Arkowitz, 1975; Rapee & Lim, 1992). Moreover, it is unclear whether any social impairment is due to a lack of social skills or to anxiety-driven behavioral inhibition or underestimation of competence in social situations (Rapee & Lim, 1992; Stopa & Clark, 1993).

Research into the effectiveness of SST is the least advanced and methodologically sophisticated in this literature. No study has demonstrated that SST alone is more effective than a control condition. In the only controlled study of SST, 15 weeks of treatment did not result in significant improvements in social anxiety, social skills, or overall clinical adjustment when compared to a waitlist control group (Marzillier, Lambert, & Kellet, 1976). However, it is unclear how representative the clients treated by Marzillier and colleagues are of the larger population of persons with social anxiety disorder, as this study was conducted before social anxiety disorder became an officially recognized diagnostic category (American Psychiatric Association, 1980). In an uncontrolled study, Turner, Beidel, Cooley-Quille, Woody, and Messer (1994) reported that social effectiveness therapy, which combines SST with education and exposure, was effective in the treatment of clients with generalized social anxiety disorder and that these gains were maintained 2 years after the end of treatment (Turner, Beidel, & Cooley-Quille, 1995). Several other uncontrolled studies found that SST was associated with reductions in self-reported anxiety, depression, and difficulty in social situations (e.g., Falloon, Lloyd, & Harpin, 1981; Stravynski, Marks, & Yule, 1982; Trower, Yardley, Bryant, & Shaw, 1978; Wlazlo, Schroeder-Hartwig, Hand, Kaiser, & Münchau, 1990). However, reductions in social anxiety following SST may not be attributable to remediation of social skills deficiencies. Because SST necessarily involves exposure to anxiety-provoking situations and to corrective cognitive feedback, it appears impossible to separate the effects of such training from those of in vivo exposure (Heimberg, 2002; Turk et al., 2002). Though there is insufficient evidence to recommend SST as a stand-alone intervention, recent research suggests that adding SST to CBGT may add to the treatment's efficacy. A standard CBGT intervention for generalized social anxiety disorder was compared to one that integrated an SST into CBGT. Both treatment groups demonstrated meaningful improvements following the intervention, but the combination group demonstrated significantly greater treatment gains (Herbert et al., 2005).

RELAXATION STRATEGIES

Relaxation training is intended to help clients reduce physiological arousal during or in anticipation of anxiety-provoking situations. Progressive muscle relaxation (Bernstein, Borkovec, & Hazlett-Stevens, 2000) is used to manage the physiological arousal that often accompanies anxiety. Individuals are instructed to focus their attention on different muscle groups as they first tense and then relax the muscles. Progressive muscle relaxation alone has been shown to have minimal effects on social anxiety symptoms (Al-Kubaisy et al., 1992; Alström et al., 1984) and has been used as a control condition in studies comparing cognitive restructuring and exposure treatments for social anxiety disorder (e.g., Al-Kubaisy et al., 1992).

Applied relaxation, which combines gradual exposure to feared situations with progressive muscle relaxation, may be effective in the treatment of social anxiety disorder. Individuals are instructed to recognize physiological symptoms associated with anxiety. Progressive muscle relaxation is then applied to nonanxiety-provoking situations and through graduated exposure to anxiety-provoking situations at the first sign of physiological arousal (Öst, 1987). Applied relaxation has demonstrated

superior efficacy to a waitlist control condition (Jerremalm, Jansson, & Öst, 1986) and is as effective as social skills training (Öst, Jerremalm, & Johansson, 1981). However, applied relaxation may be less effective than self-instructional training (a cognitive intervention) (Jerremalm et al., 1986). A recent randomized controlled trial by D. M. Clark et al. (2006) assigned individuals with social anxiety disorder to cognitive therapy (see D. M. Clark, 2001; D. M. Clark et al., 2003), exposure plus applied relaxation, or a waitlist control. Both active treatment groups demonstrated significantly greater improvement on all outcome measures than the waitlist control group. However, superior efficacy was demonstrated for cognitive therapy, which led to significantly greater improvement on measures of social anxiety than exposure plus applied relaxation and the classification of many more clients as having demonstrated clinically significant gains (76% versus 38%, respectively) (D. M. Clark et al., 2006). No study has compared applied relaxation with exposure alone to determine whether the inclusion of relaxation enhances treatment efficacy.

Meta-Analytic Findings

Five major meta-analyses have examined the components of cognitive behavioral treatments of social anxiety disorder, including exposure alone, cognitive restructuring alone, exposure plus cognitive restructuring, social skills training, and applied relaxation. Effect sizes for all cognitive behavioral interventions have been superior to those of delayed treatment conditions (Chambless & Hope, 1996; Fedoroff & Taylor, 2001; Feske & Chambless, 1995; Gould, Buckminster, Pollack, Otto, & Yap, 1997; Taylor, 1996).

Taylor (1996) found that cognitive restructuring, social skills training, exposure alone, and exposure plus cognitive restructuring were superior to waitlist controls in reducing self-reported symptoms of social anxiety. Significant increases in effect sizes after follow-up periods averaging 3 months in duration suggest that further improvements were made after the end of treatment. There were no significant differences between CBT variants. However, only exposure combined with cognitive restructuring resulted in effect sizes greater than placebo treatment.

A more recent meta-analysis (Fedoroff & Taylor, 2001) found similar results when comparing exposure alone, cognitive restructuring alone, exposure plus cognitive restructuring, social skills training, and applied relaxation. All treatments demonstrated moderate efficacy at posttreatment. However, follow-up assessments revealed maintenance of gains rather than further improvement, and there were no significant differences between the five cognitive behavioral therapies using either self-report or clinician-administered outcome measures.

Though the meta-analyses have not found significant differences in the effect sizes of various cognitive behavioral therapies, there are suggestions that certain variants may be superior to others. Three meta-analyses found that the effect sizes for cognitive restructuring without exposure and social skills training were nonsignificantly smaller than those for exposure plus cognitive restructuring (Fedoroff & Taylor, 2001; Gould et al., 1997; Taylor, 1996). In addition, applied relaxation demonstrated nonsignificantly smaller effects when compared to exposure plus cognitive restructuring (Fedoroff & Taylor, 2001), similar to the findings of the more recent study of D. M. Clark et al. (2006). The failure of these differences to achieve significance may be attributable to lack of power due to the small number of available comparisons. Further examination is necessary before definitive statements about the relative effects of different cognitive behavioral therapies can be made (Rodebaugh et al., 2004).

All five meta-analyses examined the relative efficacy of exposure alone and exposure plus cognitive restructuring, and none found compelling evidence to suggest a meaningful difference between the two. Feske and Chambless (1995) determined that exposure alone and exposure with cognitive restructuring yielded equivalent effect sizes at posttreatment and follow-up based on self-report outcome measures, with no differences in attrition rates. Gould et al. (1997) reported that cognitive behavioral therapies with an exposure component administered either in isolation or in combination with cognitive restructuring resulted in large effects. Taken together, results from these meta-analyses speak to the importance of including an exposure component in CBT for social anxiety disorder (Zaider & Heimberg, 2003). However, as noted earlier, they also suggest that the inclusion of cognitive techniques may reduce the amount of exposure necessary to produce similar outcomes (Turk et al., 2002).

Pharmacological Interventions: Comparison to and Combination With CBT

Pharmacological treatments for social anxiety have demonstrated equivalent (Gould et al., 1997) to superior (Fedoroff & Taylor, 2001) posttreatment effect sizes compared to CBT. Gould et al. (1997) examined effect sizes for 24 controlled trials of CBT or medication treatments. Both were superior to control conditions (controlled effect sizes of .62 and .74, respectively), but they did not differ significantly on treatment response and demonstrated nearly equivalent attrition rates at posttreatment and follow-up.

In contrast, Fedoroff and Taylor (2001) demonstrated that some medication treatments were more efficacious than cognitive behavioral therapies. Specifically, selective serotonin reuptake inhibitors (SSRIs) and benzodiazepines had the largest effect sizes, performing better than control conditions but similarly to each other. Benzodiazapines performed better than monoamine oxidase inhibitors (MAOIs) and CBT, but neither MAOIs or SSRIs were significantly better than CBT. However, because most pharmacotherapy studies lacked follow-up data, Fedoroff and Taylor (2001) were unable to investigate the relative maintenance of treatment gains beyond posttreatment assessment for pharmacotherapies and CBT. Though some forms of pharmacotherapy may be somewhat more effective than CBT in the short term (Fedoroff & Taylor, 2001), assertions that CBT is associated with more durable effects than those produced by medications need additional support from studies with longer follow-up periods (Rodebaugh et al., 2004).

Heimberg and colleagues (1998) compared CBGT to the MAOI phenelzine, pill placebo, and a credible psychological placebo. After 12 weeks of treatment, CBGT and phenelzine were associated with equivalent response rates (75% and 77% of treatment completers, respectively) and rates of attrition, both of which were superior to the pill placebo and attention-placebo conditions. Phenelzine produced more immediate gains and demonstrated greater effects on some measures, with 52% of the participants in the medication group classified as treatment responders at 6 weeks compared to only 28% of individuals receiving group CBT. However, after a 6-month maintenance phase and a 6-month follow-up phase, phenelzine was associated with a greater rate of relapse (50%) than CBGT (17%) (Liebowitz et al., 1999). Although phenelzine resulted in more immediate treatment gains, coping skills learned during group CBT may have aided clients in maintaining gains and preventing relapse (Liebowitz et al., 1999). Similarly, individuals with generalized social anxiety disorder who received CBT based on the model suggested by D. M. Clark and Wells (1995) exhibited superior treatment response at posttreatment and 1-year follow-up compared to individuals who received fluoxetine plus instructions for self-directed exposure or pill placebo plus instructions for self-directed exposure. There were no differences between fluoxetine and pill placebo in this study (D. M. Clark et al., 2003), although fluoxetine was superior to placebo in a study by Davidson et al. (2004).

Other studies comparing the efficacy of cognitive behavioral treatments and pharmacological agents are difficult to interpret due to methodological limitations. Several studies compared CBT to medications that did not surpass placebo in previous research (D. B. Clark & Agras, 1991; Turner, Beidel, & Jacob, 1994), limiting our ability to generalize their findings to medications that have demonstrated efficacy. In some studies, the pharmacotherapy condition also contained instructions for self-directed exposure (D. M. Clark et al., 2003; Gerlernter et al., 1991; Otto et al., 2000), making it difficult to separate the effects of medication and psychological interventions. However, in the study by D. M. Clark et al. (2003), CBT was more efficacious than the combination of fluoxetine and instructions for self-directed exposure.

Based on research indicating the efficacy of cognitive behavioral and pharmacological treatments for social anxiety disorder, interest in combining the two approaches has grown. While some studies have combined CBT with medications that have not performed better than placebo (D. B. Clark & Agras, 1991; Falloon et al., 1981), other studies have provided more appropriate comparisons. Two large-scale multisite studies have more recently examined the combination of CBT with pharmacological agents. Heimberg, Liebowitz, and colleagues (1998) conducted a comparison of CBGT, phenelzine, their combination, and pill placebo. Preliminary data indicate that phenelzine plus CBGT is more likely to be superior to pill placebo than either treatment alone (Heimberg, 2002). A similar study was conducted by Davidson and colleagues (2004) using fluoxetine. They found fluoxetine, group CBT, and their combination all to be superior to placebo, but found no advantage of combining fluoxetine and CBT. Blomhoff and colleagues (2001) compared the efficacy of the SSRI sertraline and pill placebo alone and in combination with physician-directed exposure or general medical care, which included nondirective encouragement. All active treatments were superior to placebo and nondirective encouragement after 12 weeks, but there was no difference between sertraline and exposure. Only sertraline alone or in combination with exposure surpassed placebo at 24 weeks. Though exposure appeared to add somewhat to sertraline, demonstrated by the earlier onset of treatment response in this condition, overall there was no significant difference between sertraline with and without exposure. However, 1-year follow-up suggested that only the patients who received exposure alone continued to improve, whereas patients who received sertraline with or without exposure demonstrated deterioration on a limited set of measures (Haug et al., 2003).

Recent research indicates that D-cycloserine, an antibiotic approved for the treatment of tuberculosis, may enhance the efficacy of exposure trials in animals and humans by augmenting learning and consolidating memory (Myers & Davis, 2002; Schwartz, Hashtroudi, Herting, Schwartz, & Deutsch, 1996). When administered prior to or soon after exposure trials in animals, D-cycloserine appears to facilitate the process of extinction of conditioned fear (Ledgerwood, Richardson, & Cranney, 2003; Walker, Ressler, Lu, & Davis, 2002). For example, a study of fear-potentiated startle response to a light and shock pairing showed that rats administered D-cycloserine prior to extinction trials demonstrated enhanced extinction of the learned fear response (Walker et al., 2002).

In a pilot study of 27 participants with social anxiety disorder, Hofmann et al. (2006) found that those who received D-cycloserine 1 hour prior to exposure reported significantly less social anxiety than those who received placebo prior to exposure. Results suggest that D-cycloserine may enhance an already effective treatment for social anxiety disorder and facilitate extinction, but additional and larger studies are needed to confirm these early findings.

Taken together, results of these studies suggest that, although medication treatments confer an earlier benefit, their use in isolation is associated with a high rate of relapse, which may be reduced by combining them with cognitive behavioral therapies (Rodebaugh et al., 2004). However, combination of treatments does not guarantee increased benefit unless the treatments potentiate each other or act on different aspects of the disorder. In addition, though adding one treatment to another may enhance treatment effects (e.g., medication reduces anxiety such that it is easier to establish a therapeutic alliance), it is possible that one treatment may detract from the effect of the other (e.g., a client who responds well to medication may have little motivation to participate in psychotherapy). It is essential that the interaction of psychotherapy and medication treatments be systematically and rigorously examined (Zaider & Heimberg, 2004).

Other Approaches

Although cognitive behavioral treatments for social anxiety disorder are the most extensively studied, there are a number of psychotherapeutic interventions used widely in clinical practice that have not been investigated rigorously. Case studies and open trials suggest that alternative treatment approaches, such as psychodynamic interventions, interpersonal therapy, and acceptance and commitment therapy, look promising. Rigorous research is needed to ascertain their efficacy in comparison with CBT.

PSYCHODYNAMIC THERAPY

Gabbard (1992) suggested that social anxiety disorder is associated with specific unconscious desires and emotional experiences. He hypothesizes that individuals with social anxiety disorder experience shame regarding an unconscious desire to be the center of attention; guilt regarding an unconscious desire to eliminate social competition; doubt regarding their ability to eliminate social competition; separation anxiety regarding an unconscious desire for autonomy; and loss of a caregiver's love that is a perceived result of autonomy. Gabbard (2005) has further hypothesized that some clients have internalized representations of significant others who are critical, shaming, or abandoning. Expectations of criticism, shame, and rejection are then projected onto others and lead to a desire to avoid potentially threatening social situations.

In psychodynamic therapy, fears are examined in the context of relationship history. Stated fears, expectations of others, and assumptions about others are explored, along with associated emotional experiences such as guilt and shame. Careful identification and exploration of transference to critical, overprotective, shaming, rejecting, or anxious caretakers may be particularly productive (e.g., Barber, Morse, Krakauer, Chittams, & Crits-Christoph, 1997). The goal of psychodynamic therapy for social anxiety disorder is the internalization of more benign and accepting others, which is thought to be associated with reduced symptomatology. Although case studies and conceptualizations of the development and maintenance of social anxiety disorder within a psychodynamic framework have been put forth (e.g., Zerbe, 1997), no controlled studies of psychodynamic treatments for social anxiety disorder have been conducted.

INTERPERSONAL PSYCHOTHERAPY

Interpersonal psychotherapy (IPT) is a time-limited treatment based on the assumption that psychiatric disorders are developed and maintained within a psychosocial and interpersonal context. It was originally developed as a manualized, short-term treatment for depression. Research has found IPT to be efficacious for major depression (Elkin et al., 1989), dysthymic disorder (Markowitz, 1994), and bulimia nervosa (Wilfley et al., 1993), all of which have interpersonal components. The obvious interpersonal nature of social anxiety disorder makes the application of IPT to this disorder appealing.

The goal of IPT for social anxiety disorder is for the client to understand the connection between social anxiety symptoms and current interpersonal problems. This insight is thought to be associated with improvement of social anxiety. There has been one uncontrolled investigation of IPT for social anxiety disorder (Lipsitz, Markowitz, Cherry, & Fyer, 1999). The modified version of IPT employed in this open trial utilized techniques such as exploration and clarification of thoughts and feelings; encouragement of emotional expression; analysis of communication and decision-making styles; and role-play exercises. After 14 weeks of treatment, 7 of 9 (78%) clients were classified as treatment responders by independent evaluators, a rate comparable to those reported in randomized controlled trials of other more empirically supported treatment modalities. Such findings warrant replication in controlled trials with adequate power.

ACCEPTANCE AND COMMITMENT THERAPY

Acceptance and commitment therapy (ACT) is a relatively new treatment modality. It is suggested that ACT works through different processes than traditional CBT. Research is rapidly accumulating and preliminary studies suggest that ACT offers a promising alternative to existing treatment techniques for a wide range of psychological disorders (Hayes, Luoma, Bond, Masuda, & Lillis, 2006). Within an ACT framework, it is suggested that psychopathology is related to psychological inflexibility and avoidance of internal and external experiences. Clients learn that inflexible attempts to control, reduce, or avoid anxiety actually exacerbate anxiety. Acceptance and commitment therapy encourages clients to choose valued life directions in various domains, such as family, career, and spirituality, and to act in ways that are consistent with such values. Finally, ACT encourages commitment to action toward one's values. Committed action can be practiced through behavioral exposures, homework assignments, skills training, and goal setting such as that done in traditional CBT. In practice, ACT employs work within session and as homework assignments to work toward short- and long-term behavior change goals that are consistent with one's values. The processes central to ACT are conceptualized as overlapping and interrelated, and as setting the stage for living a meaningful life that is consistent with one's values (Hayes et al., 2006). Though symptom reduction is not an explicit goal of ACT, symptoms are expected to abate as clients work toward living a fuller and more meaningful life (Eifert & Forsyth, 2005).

Little work has yet been conducted applying ACT to the treatment of social anxiety disorder. However, in a preliminary study, Block and Wulfert (2000) compared three sessions of ACT to three sessions of CBT for the treatment of public speaking anxiety. Participants in the ACT group demonstrated reduced subjective anxiety and greater willingness to speak in front of a group than those in the CBT group.

Factors Influencing Treatment Outcome

Currently, it is unclear whether certain features of social anxiety disorder are associated with preferential response to individual treatment, as much of the research has examined response to cognitive behavioral group therapy. Investigations examining the relationship between clinical characteristics and treatment outcome have produced mixed results. Despite inconsistent findings, there is some information regarding the role that some features may play in the prediction of treatment outcome, including subtype of the disorder, comorbidity with other disorders or emotional states, expectancy for treatment outcome, and compliance with treatment.

SUBTYPES OF SOCIAL ANXIETY DISORDER

There are two subtypes of social anxiety disorder determined by the pervasiveness of one's social fears. Clients are classified as having generalized social anxiety disorder if their fears extend to most social situations and nongeneralized social anxiety disorder if they do not (Heimberg, Holt, Schneier, Spitzer, & Liebowitz, 1993). Studies of CBGT have shown that individuals with generalized social anxiety disorder do not respond as well to treatment as those with the nongeneralized subtype. For example, clients with generalized social anxiety disorder demonstrated more impairment at the beginning of treatment and, despite similar rates of improvement, ended treatment with greater levels of impairment than individuals with nongeneralized social anxiety disorder (Brown, Heimberg, & Juster, 1995). However, generalized social anxiety disorder is a more

severe form of the disorder, and pretreatment severity has also been associated with poorer treatment outcomes (Otto et al., 2000).

COMORBIDITY WITH OTHER MENTAL DISORDERS

Social anxiety disorder commonly co-occurs with other disorders, such as anxiety disorders, depression, and substance abuse and dependence (Kessler et al., 1994; Schneier, Johnson, Hornig, Liebowitz, & Weissman, 1992). Studies have demonstrated similar response to CBT when comparing clients with uncomplicated social anxiety disorder to those with comorbid anxiety disorders (Erwin, Heimberg, Juster, & Mindlin, 2002; Turner, Beidel, Wolff, Spaulding, & Jacob, 1996). However, comorbid mood disorders, such as major depression, can influence response to group CBT. Individuals with comorbid mood disorders showed greater severity of social anxiety symptoms before and after treatment but improved at a comparable rate (Erwin et al., 2002). Another study of group CBGT found pretreatment depression to be the most salient predictor of outcome at posttreatment and 6-month follow-up, with more depressed individuals being less likely to improve and remain improved on measures of anxious apprehension, self-rated anxiety, and self-rated skill in social interactions (Chambless, Tran, & Glass, 1997).

Alcohol abuse and dependence are often comorbid with social anxiety disorder. Approximately 48% of individuals with lifetime social anxiety disorder meet criteria for a lifetime diagnosis of an alcohol use disorder (Grant et al., 2005). Social anxiety disorder is associated with higher rates of alcohol use disorders than most other anxiety disorders (Kessler et al., 1997; Kessler, Chiu, Demler, Merikangas, & Walters, 2005). There is a small amount of research on the effects of social anxiety disorder on the treatment of alcoholic clients. For instance, post hoc analyses of Project MATCH data (Project MATCH Research Group, 1993) indicated that female alcoholics with social anxiety disorder responded more favorably to CBT than traditional 12-step facilitation, whereas the reverse pattern was true of alcoholics without social anxiety disorder (Thevos, Roberts, Thomas, & Randall, 2000). Although they responded better to CBT than 12-step facilitation, they responded less favorably than female alcoholics without social anxiety disorder regardless of treatment condition. Little research has examined the effect of alcoholism on the outcome of treatment for social anxiety disorder.

Compared with uncomplicated social anxiety disorder, social anxiety disorder complicated by Axis II personality disorders (e.g., avoidant, obsessive-compulsive, dependent, and histrionic personality disorders) is consistently associated with greater symptom severity and impairment before and after treatment, but not consistently associated with poorer treatment response (Turner et al., 1996). Avoidant personality disorder most frequently co-occurs with social anxiety disorder, particularly the generalized subtype. The impact of a comorbid diagnosis of avoidant personality disorder on treatment response for social anxiety disorder has received the greatest amount of empirical attention (Brown et al., 1995; Schneier, Spitzer, Gibbon, Fyer, & Liebowitz, 1991), although the effects are inconsistent and small. Two studies suggest that comorbid avoidant personality disorder is associated with poorer treatment response (Chambless et al., 1997; Feske et al., 1996). Several other studies of clients with primary social anxiety disorder found no difference in treatment response between those with and without comorbid avoidant personality disorder (Brown et al., 1995; Hofmann, Newman, Becker, Taylor, & Roth, 1995; van Velzen, Emmelkamp, & Scholing, 1997), a finding that is most robust when the study sample is limited to clients with generalized social anxiety disorder. These findings suggest that, although the presence of avoidant personality disorder at pretreatment is associated with lower posttreatment functioning, such an outcome is likely related to pretreatment severity (Turk et al., 2002).

Though some evidence indicates that individuals with social anxiety disorder may be more likely to experience difficulties with anger than those without an anxiety disorder (Fitzgibbons, Franklin, Watlington, & Foa, 1997; Meier, Hope, Weilage, Etling, & Laguna, 1995), only one study has looked at the role that anger plays in response to CBT for social anxiety disorder (Erwin, Heimberg, Schneier, & Liebowitz, 2003). Higher levels of trait anger were significantly related to premature termination. Among treatment completers, pretreatment elevations in state anger, trait anger, and the tendency to suppress the expression of anger were associated with poorer treatment outcomes. These individuals demonstrated greater posttreatment social anxiety, fear of negative evaluation, and depressive symptoms even after controlling for pretreatment severity of social anxiety. Studies are needed to determine whether anger affects treatment response by increasing attributions for one's anxiety to others' behaviors rather than one's own, which may undermine motivation

for self-change (Rodebaugh et al., 2004). It is also important to investigate whether intervening with problematic anger and anger suppression contributes to the client's openness to treatment (Holaway & Heimberg, 2004).

EXPECTANCIES

Treatment expectancies appear to be associated with outcome, even when pretreatment severity is controlled (Chambless et al., 1997; Safren, Heimberg, & Juster, 1997). Lower outcome expectancies were associated with greater severity of social anxiety, longer duration of symptoms, classification as generalized subtype of social anxiety disorder, and comorbid depression (Safren et al., 1997), all of which are related to poorer treatment response outcome (e.g., Chambless et al., 1997; Turner et al., 1996). Higher outcome expectancies were associated with greater improvement in anxious apprehension, self-rated anxiety, and conversational skill. This finding remained robust after controlling for depression (Chambless et al., 1997). The relationship between outcome expectancies and treatment response may not be causal—for instance, it is possible that clients with low expectancies are accurately predicting their response to treatment (Chambless et al., 1997). Nonetheless, modification of expectancies at the outset of treatment may play an important role in shaping eventual outcome (Safren et al., 1997).

HOMEWORK COMPLIANCE

The completion of between-session homework assignments, such as exposures to anxiety-provoking situations and cognitive restructuring practice, is an integral part of CBT for social anxiety disorder. Studies examining the relationship between homework compliance and treatment outcome have found mixed results. Some studies have shown that adherence to homework assignments is related to better posttreatment outcomes (Leung & Heimberg, 1996). Although other investigations reported that homework compliance was not related to better posttreatment outcomes (Edelman & Chambless, 1995; Woody & Adessky, 2002), 6-month follow-up assessments revealed that homework compliant individuals reported fewer avoidant behaviors, less fear of negative evaluation, and less anxiety when giving a speech compared with less compliant clients (Edelman & Chambless, 1995). These findings suggest that effects of homework compliance not evident at posttreatment may surface once active treatment has ended. Additional research is needed to understand these findings and to more clearly determine the impact of homework compliance on treatment outcome.

Cognitive Change

In a study comparing group CBT, exposure group therapy, and waitlist control conditions, changes in estimated social cost, or negative cognitive appraisal, mediated pretreatment to posttreatment changes in both active treatment groups (Hofmann, 2004). Furthermore, only the group receiving cognitive techniques in addition to exposure continued to show improvement from posttreatment to the 6-month follow-up assessment. Continued benefit was associated with an overall reduction in estimated social cost from pre- to posttreatment assessments, suggesting that the cognitive behavioral intervention is associated with greater treatment gains that are mediated through changes in estimated social cost (Hofmann, 2004).

Specific Phobias
Cognitive Behavioral Interventions

Cognitive behavioral interventions for specific phobias have been the most thoroughly researched, and there is much evidence that they demonstrate greater efficacy in treating specific phobia than other approaches.

EXPOSURE TREATMENTS

In vivo exposure is by far the most studied and effective treatment for specific phobia, and it should be considered the first-line treatment. To date, research has shown that prolonged and repeated in vivo exposure is the most effective intervention for specific phobias (Chambless, 1990; Marks, 1987). Much of the literature has focused on the identification of elements of exposure that lead to the fastest and most effective treatment for specific phobia.

Modeling in the form of observing another client receive treatment prior to the client's own in vivo exposure has been shown to enhance the effects of in vivo exposure and increase the speed with which positive outcomes are attained (Gotestam & Berntzen, 1997). Therapist-directed in vivo exposure is generally more effective than self-directed manual-based exposure (Öst, Salkovskis, & Hellström, 1991), with treatment gains enduring at 1-year (e.g., Öst, Salkovskis, & Hellström, 1991) and 8-year follow-ups (Gotestam & Berntzen, 1997). Addition of self-directed in vivo exposure homework to therapist-directed in vivo exposure treatment may increase the likelihood, speed, and durability of treatment gains.

Several investigations have attempted to determine the minimum number of sessions necessary to produce treatment gains. Multiple exposure sessions are generally considered more effective than a single exposure session and may produce greater treatment effects immediately following treatment (Hellström, Fellenius, & Öst, 1996). However, some studies report positive outcomes for single-session in vivo exposure treatments at posttreatment and 1-year follow-up with adults (Öst, 1996) and youth (Öst, Svensson, Hellström, & Lindwall, 2001). Maintenance programs may improve treatment gains and durability of one-session treatments (Hellström et al., 1996). A related question is the spacing of exposure sessions. Chambless (1990) compared the effects of 10 daily and 10 weekly in vivo exposure sessions for specific phobia and found no differences at posttreatment or 6-month follow-up on outcome or attrition.

VIRTUAL REALITY EXPOSURE TREATMENTS

Immersive computer-generated virtual reality (VR) exposure is an alternative to in vivo exposure for specific phobias and is useful when in vivo exposure situations are difficult to arrange. This exposure involves the three-dimensional simulation of feared situations with which the client can interact in real time. Various display and sensory input technologies, as well as the use of real objects (e.g., toy spiders), help integrate the client into this virtual environment. The sense of presence distinguishes VR interventions from standard imaginal exposures.

The application of virtual reality technology to exposure-based treatment for specific phobias is a relatively recent development. Nonetheless, the body of research is growing and supports the efficacy of VR exposure for specific phobia. Case studies have found VR exposure to be efficacious either alone (Carlin, Hoffman, & Weghorst, 1997; North, North, & Coble, 1997) or in combination with anxiety management training for specific phobia (Rothbaum, Hodges, Watson, Kessler, & Opdyke, 1996). Controlled studies are also beginning to garner support for VR exposure. Despite a small sample size ($n = 17$), the first randomized controlled trial comparing VR exposure with a waiting-list control condition for acrophobia (fear of heights) demonstrated positive effects (Rothbaum et al., 1995). More recently, Rothbaum, Hodges, Smith, Lee, and Price (2000) compared anxiety management training plus VR exposure, anxiety management training plus in vivo exposure, and a waiting-list control condition for fear of flying. Both VR exposure and in vivo exposure resulted in equivalent gains, which were maintained at 6-month follow up ($n = 45$) and 12-month follow up ($n = 24$) (Rothbaum, Hodges, Anderson, Price, & Smith, 2002). Maltby, Kirsch, Mayers, and Allen (2002) compared VR exposure with an attention group therapy control condition for fear of flying and found that VR exposure produced superior treatment gains compared to the control group on measures of flight anxiety and rates of clinically significant change. However, these gains were not maintained at 6-month follow-up. In a study of fear of heights, D-cycloserine in combination with virtual reality exposure was associated with greater treatment efficacy than virtual reality exposure with placebo (Ressler et al., 2004).

APPLIED RELAXATION AND APPLIED TENSION TREATMENTS

Applied relaxation for the treatment of specific phobia targets physiological arousal through systematic tension and relaxation of various muscle groups in the context of gradual exposure to anxiety-provoking stimuli. There are few studies investigating applied relaxation for specific phobia, though Öst, Johansson, and Jerremalm (1982) found that applied relaxation was as effective as in vivo exposure and superior to delayed treatment for claustrophobia.

Applied tension was designed specifically to treat the parasympathetic arousal (i.e., dilation of blood vessels, drop in blood pressure, slowed heart rate, constricted airways) that is unique to blood-injection-injury phobia. Applied tension requires clients to tense muscles in the presence of phobic stimuli in order to elevate blood pressure and thus contains an exposure component. In an uncontrolled study, individuals with phobias for blood, wounds, and injuries responded equally well to applied tension, applied relaxation, and their combination at posttreatment and 6-month follow-up, although applied tension was effective in half the number of sessions (Öst, Sterner, & Fellenius, 1989). A greater percentage of individuals treated with applied tension achieved clinically significant gains at posttreatment and 1-year follow-up compared with individuals treated with in vivo exposure alone (Öst, Fellenius, & Sterner, 1991). Dismantling studies have attempted to parse the effects of muscle tension from those of the exposure component of applied tension (Hellström et al., 1996). Persons treated with applied tension and tension only evidenced similar gains at posttreatment and 1-year follow-up, and these gains were superior to those produced by in vivo exposure. Moreover, the effects of applied tension and tension only may be achieved in one session (Hellström et al., 1996).

COGNITIVE RESTRUCTURING TREATMENTS

The cognitive model of specific phobia posits that irrational thoughts are responsible for the development of the phobia, maintain avoidance behavior, and contribute to physiological symptoms. Cognitive restructuring helps clients to monitor and change these irrational beliefs so that they are better able to confront feared stimuli. A number of studies have provided evidence suggesting that persons with specific phobia have phobia-specific irrational beliefs (e.g., Thorpe & Salkovskis, 1995). When combined with exposure to feared stimuli, cognitive restructuring may be useful. However, there are few studies of cognitive treatments for specific phobia.

Other Treatments

Uncontrolled and controlled studies of eye movement desensitization and reprocessing (EMDR) (Shapiro, 1995) for specific phobias have demonstrated some improvement in phobic symptoms, though empirical support is still scarce. Case studies of blood and injection phobias (Kleinknecht, 1993), snake and insect phobias (Young, 1994), spider phobia (Muris & Merckelbach, 1995), and dental phobias (De Jongh et al., 1995) have demonstrated some efficacy for EMDR. Controlled trials of EMDR among spider-phobic adults have provided mixed support at best. When compared to an assessment only condition, EMDR had no effect on fear of spiders (Bates, McGlynn, Montgomery, & Mattke, 1996). Muris and Merckelbach (1997) randomly assigned 24 spider-phobic adults to 1 hour of either EMDR, imaginal exposure, or a no-treatment control group, all of which were followed by in vivo exposure. EMDR was no better than imaginal exposure, and only after combining it with in vivo exposure were further and significant differences found. However, findings from controlled and uncontrolled investigations of EMDR for specific phobia are troubled by lack of adherence to standardized EMDR treatment protocols (De Jongh, Ten Broeke, & Renssen, 1999), and thus more rigorous research is needed before EMDR can be considered a credible intervention for specific phobias.

There are few controlled investigations of psychodynamic psychotherapy for specific phobia. Any effect of psychodynamic techniques (e.g., psychodynamic interpretation, exploration of the specific phobia as a defense against other unrecognized fears, psychoeducation, hypnosis) is likely attributable to facilitation of self-directed exposure (Gabbard 2005; Schneier, Erwin, Heimberg, Marshall, & Mellman, 2007). Supportive psychodynamic psychotherapy for specific phobia was found to be as effective as in vivo exposure after 26 weeks of treatment (Klein, Zitrin, & Woerner, 1983). However, Klein et al. attributed improvement in supportive psychotherapy to the initiation of self-directed exposure and were therefore unable to justify the use of supportive psychotherapy over behavior therapy.

Predictors of Treatment Outcome

A number of studies suggest that tailoring treatment to individual response patterns will improve outcome. There is some evidence to suggest that physiologically reactivity in response to feared stimuli may respond best to applied relaxation (Öst et al., 1982); behavioral avoidance of feared stimuli may respond best to in vivo exposure; cognitive symptoms may respond best to cognitive interventions (Norton & Johnson, 1983). However, an empirical investigation found no stable predictors of short- or long-term outcome for specific phobia (Hellstrøm & Öst, 1996).

Summary and Conclusions

Recent empirical evidence suggests we have efficacious psychotherapy treatments for social anxiety disorder and specific phobias. For the treatment of social anxiety disorder, CBT appears to be the best-established approach to treatment, and though social skills training as well as psychodynamic, interpersonal, and acceptance and commitment therapies may be beneficial, they require additional investigation. In the treatment of specific phobias, exposure emerges as the treatment of choice. There still remains a significant lack of understanding regarding which treatments or combinations of treatments work best and whether individual differences or other variables lead to better treatment outcome. Inevitably, some clients do not respond optimally to even the most successful treatment approaches. Continued investigation of the influence of particular variables on treatment outcome (e.g., homework compliance, comorbidity, expectations for improvement, cognitive change, etc.) will inform the refinement and combination of existing treatments.

References

Al-Kubaisy, T., Marks, I. M., Logsdail, S., Marks, M. P., Lovell, K., Sungur, M., et al. (1992). Role of exposure homework in phobia reduction: A controlled study. *Behavior Therapy, 23,* 599–621.

Alström, J. E., Nordlund, C. L., Persson, G., Hårding, M., & Ljungqvist, C. (1984). Effects of four treatment methods on social phobia patients not suitable for insight-oriented psychotherapy. *Acta Psychiatrica Scandinavica, 70,* 97–110.

American Psychiatric Association. (1980). *Diagnostic and statistical manual of mental disorders* (3rd ed.). Washington, DC: Author.

Ballenger, J. C., Davidson, J. T., Lecrubier, Y., Nutt, D., Bobes, J., Beidel, D., et al. (1998). Consensus statement on social anxiety disorder from the International Consensus Group on Depression and Anxiety. *Journal of Clinical Psychiatry, 59*(Suppl.), 54–60.

Barber, J. P., Morse, J. Q., Krakauer, I. D., Chittams, J., & Crits-Christoph, K. (1997). Change in obsessive-compulsive and avoidant personality disorders following time-limited supportive-expressive therapy. *Psychotherapy, 34,* 133–143.

Bates, L. W., McGlynn, F., Montgomery, R. W., & Mattke, T. (1996). Effects of eye-movement desensitization versus no treatment on repeated measures of fear of spiders. *Journal of Anxiety Disorders, 10,* 555–569.

Beck, A. T., & Emery G. (1985). *Anxiety disorders and phobias: A cognitive perspective.* New York: Basic Books.

Beck, J. S. (1995). *Cognitive therapy: Basics and beyond.* New York: Guilford Press.

Bernstein, D. A., Borkovec, T. D., & Hazlett-Stevens, H. (2000). *New directions in progressive relaxation training: A guidebook for helping professionals.* Westport, CT: Praeger Press.

Block, J. A., & Wulfert, E. (2000). Acceptance or change: Treating socially anxious college students with ACT or CBGT. *The Behavior Analyst Today, 1,* 3–10.

Blomhoff, S., Haug, T. T., Hellstrøm, K., Holme, I., Humble, M., Madsbu, H. P., et al. (2001). Randomized controlled general practice trial of setraline, exposure therapy, and combined treatment in generalized social phobia. *British Journal of Psychiatry, 179,* 23–30.

Bouton, M. E. (2002). Context, ambiguity, and unlearning: Sources of relapse after behavioral extinction. *Biological Psychiatry, 52,* 976–986.

Brown, E. J., Heimberg, R. G., & Juster, H. R. (1995). Social phobia subtype and avoidant personality disorder: Effect on severity of social phobia, impairment, and outcome of cognitive-behavioral treatment. *Behavior Therapy, 26,* 467–486.

Butler, G. (1985). Exposure as a treatment for social phobia: Some instructive difficulties. *Behaviour Research and Therapy, 23,* 651–657.

Butler, G., Cullington, A., Munby, M., Amies, P., & Gelder, M. (1984). Exposure and anxiety management in the treatment of social phobia. *Journal of Consulting and Clinical Psychology, 52,* 642–650.

Carlin, A. S., Hoffman, H. G., & Weghorst, S. (1997). Virtual reality and tactile augmentation in the treatment of spider phobia: A case report. *Behaviour Research and Therapy, 35,* 153–158.

Chambless, D. L. (1990). Spacing of exposure sessions in treatment of agoraphobia and simple phobia. *Behavior Therapy, 21,* 217–219.

Chambless, D. L., & Hope, D. A. (1996). Cognitive approaches to the psychopathology and treatment of social phobia. In P. M. Salkovskis (Ed.), *Frontiers of cognitive therapy* (pp. 345–382). New York: Guilford Press.

Chambless, D. L., Tran, G. Q., & Glass, C. R. (1997). Predictors of response to cognitive-behavioral group therapy for social phobia. *Journal of Anxiety Disorders, 11,* 221–240.

Clark, D. B., & Agras, W. S. (1991). The assessment and treatment of performance anxiety in musicians. *American Journal of Psychiatry, 148,* 598–605.

Clark, D. M. (2001). A cognitive perspective on social phobia. In W. R. Crozier & L. E. Alden (Eds.), *International handbook of social anxiety* (pp. 405–430). Chichester, England: Wiley.

Clark, D. M., Ehlers, A., Hackman, A., McManus, F., Fennell, M., Grey, N., et al. (2006). Cognitive therapy versus exposure plus applied relaxation in social phobia: A randomized controlled trial. *Journal of Consulting and Clinical Psychology, 74,* 568–578.

Clark, D. M., Ehlers, A., McManus, F., Hackmann, A., Fennell, M., Campbell, H., et al. (2003). Cognitive therapy vs. fluoxetine in generalized social phobia: A randomized placebo controlled trial. *Journal of Consulting and Clinical Psychology, 71,* 1058–1067.

Clark, D. M., & Wells, A. (1995). A cognitive model of social phobia. In R. G. Heimberg, M. R. Liebowitz, D. A. Hope, & F. R. Schneier (Eds.), *Social phobia: Diagnosis, assessment, and treatment* (pp. 69–93). New York: Guilford Press.

Davidson, J. R., Foa, E. B., Huppert, J. D., Keefe, F. J., Franklin, M. E., Compton, J. S., et al. (2004). Fluoxetine, comprehensive cognitive behavioral therapy, and placebo in generalized social phobia. *Archives of General Psychiatry, 61,* 1005–1013.

De Jongh, A., Muris, P., Ter Horst, G., Van Zuuren, F. J., Schoenmakers, N., & Makkes, P. (1995). One-session cognitive treatment of dental phobia: Preparing dental phobics for treatment by restructuring negative cognitions. *Behaviour Research and Therapy, 33,* 947–954.

De Jongh, A., Ten Broeke, E., & Renssen, M. R. (1999). Treatment of specific phobias with eye movement desensitization and reprocessing (EMDR): Protocol, empirical status, and conceptual issues. *Journal of Anxiety Disorders, 13,* 69–85.

Edelman, R. E., & Chambless, D. L. (1995). Adherence during session and homework in cognitive-behavioral group treatment of social phobia. *Behaviour Research and Therapy, 33,* 537–577.

Eifert, G. H., & Forsyth, J. P. (2005). *Acceptance and commitment therapy for anxiety disorders: A practitioner's treatment guide to using mindfulness, acceptance, and values-based behavior change strategies.* Oakland, CA: New Harbinger Publications.

Elkin, I., Shea, M. T., Watkins, J. T., Imber, S. D., Sotsky, S. M., Collins, J. F., et al. (1989). National Institute of Mental Health Treatment of Depression Collaborative Research Program: General effectiveness of treatments. *Archives of General Psychiatry, 46,* 971–982.

Erwin, B. A., Heimberg, R. G., Juster, H., & Mindlin, M. (2002). Comorbid anxiety and mood disorders among persons with social anxiety disorder. *Behaviour Research and Therapy, 40,* 19–35.

Erwin, B. A., Heimberg, R. G., Schneier, F. R., & Liebowitz, M. R. (2003). Anger experience and expression in social anxiety disorder: Pretreatment profile and predictors of attrition and response to cognitive-behavioral treatment. *Behavior Therapy, 34,* 331–350.

Falloon, I.R.H., Lloyd, G. G., & Harpin, R. E. (1981). The treatment of social phobia: Real-life rehearsal with nonprofessional therapists. *Journal of Nervous and Mental Disorders, 169,* 180–184.

Fedoroff, I. C., & Taylor, S. (2001). Psychological and pharmacological treatments for social anxiety disorder: A meta-analysis. *Journal of Clinical Psychopharmacology, 21,* 311–324.

Feske, U., & Chambless, D. L. (1995). Cognitive behavioral versus exposure only treatment for social phobia: A meta-analysis. *Behavior Therapy, 26,* 695–720.

Feske, U., Perry, K. J., Chambless, D. L., Renneberg, B., & Goldstein, A. (1996). Avoidant personality disorder as a predictor for treatment outcome among generalized social phobics. *Journal of Personality Disorders, 10,* 174–184.

Fitzgibbons, L., Franklin, M. E., Watlington, C., & Foa, E. B. (1997, November). *Assessment of anger in generalized social phobia.* Poster session presented at the annual convention of the Association for Advancement of Behavior Therapy, Miami, FL.

Foa, E. B., & Kozak, M. J. (1986). Emotional processing of fear: Exposure to corrective information. *Psychological Bulletin, 99,* 20–35.

Gabbard, G. O. (1992). Psychodynamics of panic disorder and social phobia. *Bulletin of the Menninger Clinic, 56*(Suppl. A), A3–13.

Gabbard, G. O. (2005). *Anxiety disorders in psychodynamic psychiatry in clinical practice.* Washington, DC: American Psychiatric Press.

Gerlenter, C. S., Uhde, T. W., Cimbolic, P., Arnkoff, D. B., Vittone, B. J., Tancer, M. E., et al. (1991). Cognitive-behavioral and pharmacological treatments of social phobia: A controlled study. *Archives of General Psychiatry, 48,* 938–945.

Glasgow, R. E., & Arkowitz, H. (1975). The behavioral assessment of male and female social competence in dyadic heterosexual interactions. *Behaviour Research and Therapy, 6,* 488–498.

Gotestam, K. G., & Berntzen, D. (1997). Use of the modeling effect in one-session exposure. *Scandinavian Journal of Behavior Therapy, 26,* 97–101.

Gould, R. A., Buckminster, S., Pollack, M. H., Otto, M., & Yap, L. (1997). Cognitive behavioral and pharmacological treatment for social phobia: A meta-analysis. *Clinical Psychology: Science and Practice, 4,* 291–306.

Grant, B. F., Hasin, D. S., Blanco, C., Stinson, F. S., Chou, S. P., Goldstein, R. B., et al. (2005). The epidemiology of social anxiety disorder in the United States: Results from the National Epidemiologic Survey on Alcohol and Related Conditions. *Journal of Clinical Psychiatry, 66,* 1351–1361.

Halford, K., & Foddy, M. (1982). Cognitive and social skills correlates of social anxiety. *British Journal of Clinical Psychology, 21,* 17–28.

Haug, T. T., Blomhoff, S., Hellstrøm, K., Holme, I., Humble, M., Madsbu, H. P., et al. (2003). Exposure therapy and sertraline in social phobia: 1-year follow-up of a randomized controlled trial. *British Journal of Psychiatry, 182,* 312–318.

Hayes, S. C., Luoma, J. B., Bond, F. W., Masuda, A., & Lillis, J. (2006). Acceptance and Commitment Therapy: Model, processes, and outcomes. *Behaviour Research and Therapy, 44,* 1–25.

Heimberg, R. G. (2002). Cognitive behavioral therapy for social anxiety disorder: Current status and future directions. *Biological Psychiatry, 51,* 101–108.

Heimberg, R. G., & Becker, R. E. (2002). *Cognitive-behavioral group therapy for social phobia: Basic mechanisms and clinical applications.* New York: Guilford Press.

Heimberg, R. G., Dodge, C. S., Hope, D. A., Kennedy, C. R., Zollo, L., & Becker, R. E. (1990). Cognitive-behavioral group treatment of social phobia: Comparison to a credible placebo control. *Cognitive Therapy and Research, 14,* 1–23.

Heimberg, R. G., Holt, C. S., Schneier, F. R., Spitzer, R. L., & Liebowitz, M. R. (1993). The issue of subtypes in the diagnosis of social phobia. *Journal of Anxiety Disorders, 7,* 249–269.

Heimberg, R. G., Liebowitz, M. R., Hope, D. A., Schneier, F. R., Holt, C. S., Welkowitz, L., et al. (1998). Cognitive-behavioral group therapy versus phenelzine in social phobia: 12 week outcome. *Archives of General Psychiatry, 55,* 1133–1141.

Heimberg, R. G., Salzman, D. G., Holt, C. S., & Blendell, K. A. (1993). Cognitive-behavioral group treatment for social phobia: Effectiveness at five-year follow-up. *Cognitive Therapy and Research, 17,* 325–339.

Hellström, K., Fellenius, J., & Öst, L. G. (1996). One versus five sessions of applied tension in the treatment of blood phobia. *Behaviour Research and Therapy, 34,* 101–112.

Hellström, K., & Öst, L. G. (1996). Prediction of outcome in the treatment of specific phobia: A cross-validation study. *Behaviour Research and Therapy, 34,* 403–411.

Herbert, J. D., Gaudiano, B. A., Rheingold, A. A., Myers, V. H., Dalrymple, K., & Nolan, E. M. (2005). Social skills training augments the effectiveness of cognitive behavioral group therapy for social anxiety disorder. *Behavior Therapy, 36,* 125–138.

Hofmann, S. G. (2004). Cognitive mediation of treatment change in social phobia. *Journal of Consulting and Clinical Psychology, 72,* 392–399.

Hofmann, S. G., Meuret, A. E., Smits, J.A.J., Simon, N. M., Pollack, M. H., Eisenmenger, K., et al. (2006). Augmentation of exposure therapy with D-cycloserine for social anxiety disorder. *Archives of General Psychiatry, 63,* 298–304.

Hofmann, S. G., Newman, M. G., Becker, E., Taylor, C. B., & Roth, W. T. (1995). Social phobia with and without avoidant personality disorder: Preliminary behavior therapy outcome findings. *Journal of Anxiety Disorders, 9,* 427–438.

Holaway, R. M., & Heimberg, R. G. (2004). Cognitive-behavioral therapy for social anxiety disorder: A treatment review. In B. Bandelow & D. J. Stein (Eds.), *Social anxiety disorder—more than shyness: Psychopathology, pathogenesis, and management* (pp. 235–250). New York: Marcel Dekker.

Hope, D. A., Heimberg, R. G., & Bruch, M. A. (1995). Dismantling cognitive-behavioral group therapy for social phobia. *Behaviour Research and Therapy, 33,* 637–650.

Hope, D. A., Heimberg, R. G., Juster, H. R., & Turk, C. L. (2000). *Managing social anxiety: A cognitive-behavioral therapy approach.* New York: Oxford University Press.

Jerremalm, A., Jansson, L., & Öst, L. G. (1986). Cognitive and physiological reactivity and the effects of different behavioral methods in the treatment of social phobia. *Behaviour Research and Therapy, 24,* 171–180.

Juster, H. R., & Heimberg, R. G. (1995). Social phobia: Longitudinal course and long-term outcome of cognitive-behavioral treatment. *Psychiatric Clinics of North America, 18,* 821–842.

Kessler, R. C., Chiu, W. T., Demler, O., Merikangas, K., & Walters, E. E. (2005). Prevalence, severity, and comorbidity of 12-month *DSM–IV* disorders in the National Comorbidity Survey Replication. *Archives of General Psychiatry, 62,* 617–627.

Kessler, R. C., Crum, R. M., Warner, L. A., Nelson, C. B., Schulenberg, J., & Anthony, J. C. (1997). Lifetime co-occurrence of *DSM–III–R* alcohol abuse and dependence with other psychiatric disorders in the National Comorbidity Survey. *Archives of General Psychiatry, 54,* 313–321.

Kessler, R. C., McGonagle, K. A., Zhao, S., Nelson, C. B., Hughes, M., Eshleman, S., et al. (1994). Lifetime and 12-month prevalence of *DSM–III–R* psychiatric disorders in the United States: Results from the National Comorbidity Survey. *Archives of General Psychiatry, 51,* 8–19.

Klein, D. F., Zitrin, C. M., & Woerner, M. G. (1983). Treatment of phobias, 2: Behavior therapy and supportive psychotherapy: Are there any specific ingredients? *Archives of General Psychiatry, 40,* 139–145.

Kleinknecht, R. A. (1993). Rapid treatment of blood and injection phobias with eye movement desensitization. *Journal of Behavior Therapy and Experimental Psychiatry, 24,* 211–217.

Ledgerwood, L., Richardson, R., & Cranney, J. (2003). D-cycloserine facilitates extinction of conditioned fear as assessed by freezing in rats. *Behavioral Neuroscience, 117,* 341–349.

Leung, A. W., & Heimberg, R. G. (1996). Homework compliance, perceptions of control, and outcome of cognitive-behavioral treatment for social phobia. *Behaviour Research and Therapy, 34,* 423–432.

Liebowitz, M. R., Heimberg, R. G., Schneier, F. R., Hope, D. A., Davies, S., Holt, C. S., et al. (1999). Cognitive-behavioral group therapy versus phenelzine in social phobia: Long-term outcome. *Depression and Anxiety, 10,* 89–98.

Lipsitz, J. D., Markowitz, J. C., Cherry, S., & Fyer, A. (1999). Open trial of interpersonal psychotherapy for the treatment of social phobia. *American Journal of Psychiatry, 156,* 1814–1816.

Maltby, N., Kirsch, I., Mayers, M., & Allen, G. J. (2002). Virtual reality exposure therapy for the treatment of fear of flying: A controlled investigation. *Journal of Consulting and Clinical Psychology, 70,* 1112–1118.

Markowitz, J. C. (1994). Psychotherapy of dysthymia. *American Journal of Psychiatry, 151,* 1114–1121.

Marks, I. M. (1987). *Fears, phobias, and rituals: Panic, anxiety, and their disorders.* London: Oxford University Press.

Marzillier, J. S., Lambert, C., & Kellet, J. (1976). A controlled evaluation of systematic desensitization and social skills training for socially inadequate psychiatric patients. *Behaviour Research and Therapy, 14,* 225–238.

Meier, V. J., Hope, D. A., Weilage, M., Etling, D., & Laguna, L. (1995, November). *Anger and social phobia: Its expression and relation to treatment outcome.* Poster session presented at the annual convention of the Association for Advancement of Behavior Therapy, Washington, DC.

Muris, P., & Merckelbach, H. (1995). Treating spider phobia with eye movement desensitization and reprocessing: Two case reports. *Journal of Anxiety Disorders, 9,* 439–449.

Muris, P., & Merckelbach, H. (1997) Treating spider phobics with eye-movement desensitization and reprocessing: A controlled study. *Behavioural and Cognitive Psychotherapy, 25,* 39–50.

Myers, K. M., & Davis, M. (2002). Behavioral and neural analysis of extinction: A review. *Neuron, 36,* 567–584.

Newman, M. G., Hofmann, S. G., Trabert, W., Roth, W. T., & Taylor, S. (1994). Does behavioral treatment of social phobia lead to cognitive changes? *Behavior Therapy, 25,* 503–517.

North, M. M., North, S. M., & Coble, J. R. (1997). Virtual reality therapy for fear of flying. *American Journal of Psychiatry, 154,* 130.

Norton, G. R., & Johnson, W. E. (1983). A comparison of two relaxation procedures for reducing cognitive and somatic anxiety. *Journal of Behavior Therapy and Experimental Psychiatry, 14,* 209–214.

Öst, L. G. (1987). Applied relaxation: Description of a coping technique and review of controlled studies. *Behaviour Research and Therapy, 25,* 397–409.

Öst, L. G. (1996). One-session group treatment of spider phobia. *Behaviour Research and Therapy, 34,* 707–715.

Öst, L. G., Fellenius, J., & Sterner, U. (1991). Applied tension, exposure in vivo, and tension-only in the treatment of blood phobia. *Behaviour Research and Therapy, 29,* 561–574.

Öst, L. G., Jerremalm, A., & Johansson, J. (1981). Individual response patterns and the effects of different behavioral methods in the treatment of social phobia. *Behaviour Research and Therapy, 19,* 1–16.

Öst, L. G., Johansson, J., & Jerremalm, A. (1982). Individual response patterns and the effects of different behavioral methods in the treatment of claustrophobia. *Behavior Research and Therapy, 20,* 445–460.

Öst, L. G., Salkovskis, P., & Hellström, K. (1991). One-session therapist-directed exposure vs. self-exposure in the treatment of spider phobia. *Behavior Therapy, 22,* 407–422.

Öst, L. G., Sterner, U., & Fellenius, J. (1989). Applied tension, applied relaxation, and the combination in the treatment of blood phobia. *Behaviour Research and Therapy, 27,* 109–121.

Öst, L. G., Svensson, L., Hellström, K., & Lindwall, R. (2001). One-session treatment of specific phobias in youth: A randomized clinical trial. *Journal of Consulting and Clinical Psychology, 69,* 814–824.

Otto, M. W., Pollack, M. H., Gould, R. A., Worthington, J. J., McArdle, E. T., Rosenbaum, J. F., et al. (2000). A comparison of the efficacy of clonazepam and cognitive-behavioral group therapy for the treatment of social phobia. *Journal of Anxiety Disorders, 14,* 345–358.

Project MATCH Research Group. (1993). Project MATCH: Rationale and methods for a multisite clinical trial matching patients to alcoholism treatment. *Alcoholism: Clinical and Experimental Research, 17,* 1130–1145.

Rapee, R. M., & Heimberg, R. G. (1997). A cognitive-behavioral model of anxiety in social phobia. *Behaviour Research and Therapy, 35,* 741–756.

Rapee, R. M., & Lim, L. (1992). Discrepancy between self- and observer ratings of performance in social phobics. *Journal of Abnormal Psychology, 101,* 728–731.

Ressler, K. J., Rothbaum, B. O., Tannenbaum, L., Anderson, P., Graap, K., Zimand, E., et al. (2004). Cognitive enhancers as adjuncts to psychotherapy: Use of D-cycloserine in phobic individuals to facilitate extinction of fear. *Archives of General Psychiatry, 61,* 1136–1144.

Rodebaugh, T. L., Holaway, R. M., & Heimberg, R. G. (2004). The treatment of social anxiety disorder. *Clinical Psychology Review, 24,* 883–908.

Rothbaum, B. O., Hodges, L., Anderson, P. L., Price, L., & Smith, S. (2002). Twelve-month follow-up of virtual reality and standard exposure therapies for the fear of flying. *Journal of Consulting and Clinical Psychology, 70,* 428–432.

Rothbaum, B. O., Hodges, L. F., Kooper, R., Opdyke, D., Williford, J., & North, M. M. (1995). Effectiveness of computer-generated (virtual reality) graded exposure in the treatment of acrophobia. *American Journal of Psychiatry, 152,* 626–628.

Rothbaum, B. O., Hodges, L., Smith, S., Lee, J. H., & Price, L. (2000). A controlled study of virtual reality exposure therapy for the fear of flying. *Journal of Consulting and Clinical Psychology, 68,* 1020–1026.

Rothbaum, B. O., Hodges, L., Watson, B. A., Kessler, G. D., & Opdyke, D. (1996). Virtual reality exposure therapy in the treatment of fear of flying: A case report. *Behaviour Research and Therapy, 34,* 477–481.

Safren, S. A., Heimberg, R. G., & Juster, H. R. (1997). Clients' expectancies and their relationship to pretreatment symptomatology and outcome of cognitive-behavioral group treatment for social phobia. *Journal of Consulting and Clinical Psychology, 65,* 694–698.

Schneier, F. R., Erwin, B. A., Heimberg, R. G., Marshall, R. D., & Mellman, S. (2007). Social anxiety disorder and specific phobias. In G. O. Gabbard (Ed.), *Treatment of psychiatric disorders* 4th ed. pp. 495–506). Washington, DC: American Psychiatric Press.

Schneier, F. R., Johnson, J., Hornig, C. D., Liebowitz, M. R., & Weissman, M. M. (1992). Social phobia: Comorbidity and morbidity in an epidemiologic sample. *Archives of General Psychiatry, 49,* 282–288.

Schneier, F. R., Spitzer, R. L., Gibbon, M., Fyer, A. J., & Liebowitz, M. R. (1991). The relationship of social phobia subtypes and avoidant personality disorder. *Comprehensive Psychiatry, 31,* 496–502.

Schwartz, B. L., Hashtroudi, S., Herting, R. L., Schwartz, P., & Deutsch, S. I. (1996). D-cycloserine enhances implicit memory in Alzheimer patients. *Neurology, 46,* 420–424.

Shapiro, F. (1995). *Eye movement desensitization and reprocessing: Basic principles, protocols, and procedures.* New York: Guilford Press.

Stopa, L., & Clark, D. M. (1993). Cognitive processes in social phobia. *Behaviour Research and Therapy, 31,* 255–267.

Stravynski, A., Marks, I., & Yule, W. (1982). Social skills problems in neurotic outpatients: Social skills training with and without cognitive modification. *Archives of General Psychiatry, 39,* 1378–1385.

Taylor, S. (1996). Meta-analysis of cognitive-behavioral treatments for social phobia. *Journal of Behavior Therapy and Experimental Psychiatry, 27,* 1–9.

Thevos, A. K., Roberts, J. S., Thomas, S. E., & Randall, C. L. (2000). Cognitive behavioral therapy delays relapse in female socially phobic alcoholics. *Addictive Behaviors, 25,* 333–345.

Thorpe, S. J., & Salkovskis, P. M. (1995). Phobia beliefs: Do cognitive factors play a role in specific phobias? *Behavior Research and Therapy, 33,* 805–816.

Trower, P., Yardley, K., Bryant, B., & Shaw, P. (1978). The treatment of social failure: A comparison of anxiety-reduction and skills acquisition procedures on two social problems. *Behavior Modification, 2,* 41–60.

Turk, C. L., Coles, M., & Heimberg, R. G. (2002). Psychotherapy for social phobia. In D. J. Stein & E. Hollander (Eds.), *Textbook of anxiety disorders* (pp. 323–339). Washington, DC: American Psychiatric Press.

Turk, C. L., Fresco, D. M., & Heimberg, R. G. (1999). Cognitive behavior therapy. In M. Hersen & A. S. Bellack (Eds.), *Handbook of comparative interventions for adult disorders* (2nd ed., pp. 287–316). New York: Wiley.

Turner, S. M., Beidel, D. C., & Cooley-Quille, M. R. (1995). Two-year follow-up of social phobics treated with social effectiveness therapy. *Behaviour Research and Therapy, 33,* 553–555.

Turner, S. M., Beidel, D. C., Cooley-Quille, M. R., Woody, S. R., & Messer, S. C. (1994). A multi-component behavioral treatment for social phobia: Social Effectiveness Therapy. *Behaviour Research and Therapy, 32,* 381–390.

Turner, S. M., Beidel, D. C., & Jacob, R. G. (1994). Social phobia: A comparison of behavior therapy and atenolol. *Journal of Consulting and Clinical Psychology, 62,* 350–358.

Turner, S. M., Beidel, D. C., Wolff, P. L., Spaulding, S., & Jacob, R. G. (1996). Clinical features affecting treatment outcome of social phobia. *Behaviour Research and Therapy, 34,* 795–804.

Van Velzen, C.J.M., Emmelkamp, P.M.G., & Scholing, A. (1997). The impact of personality disorders on behavioral treatment outcome for social phobia. *Behaviour Research and Therapy, 35,* 889–900.

Walker, D. L., Ressler, K. J., Lu, K. T., & Davis, M. (2002). Facilitation of conditioned fear extinction by systemic administration or intra-amygdala infusions of D-cycloserine as assessed with fear-potentiated startle in rats. *Journal of Neuroscience, 22,* 2343–2351.

Wells, A., Clark, D. M., Salkovskis, P., Ludgate, J., Hackmann, A., & Gelder, M. (1995). Social phobia: The role of in-situation safety behaviors in maintaining anxiety and negative beliefs. *Behavior Therapy, 26,* 153–161.

Wells, A., & Papageorgiou, C. (1998). Social phobia: Effects of external attention in anxiety, negative beliefs, and perspective taking. *Behavior Therapy, 29,* 357–370.

Wilfley, D. E., Agras, W. S., Telch, C. F., Rossiter, E. M., Schneider, J. A., Cole, A. G., et al. (1993). Group cognitive behavioural therapy and group interpersonal therapy for the nonpurging bulimic individual. *Journal of Consulting and Clinical Psychology, 61,* 296–305.

Wlazlo, Z., Schroeder-Hartwig, K., Hand, I., Kaiser, G., & Münchau, N. (1990). Exposure in vivo vs. social skills training for social phobia: Long-term outcome and differential effects. *Behaviour Research and Therapy, 28,* 181–193.

Woody, S. R., & Adessky, R. S. (2002). Therapeutic alliance, group cohesion, and homework compliance during cognitive-behavioral group treatment of social phobia. *Behavior Therapy, 35,* 5–27.

Young, W. (1994). EMDR treatment of phobic symptoms in multiple personality. *Dissociation, 7,* 129–133.

Zaider, T. I., & Heimberg, R. G. (2003). Non-pharmacologic treatments for social anxiety disorder. *Acta Psychiatrica Scandinavica, 108*(Suppl. 417), 1–13.

Zaider, T. I., & Heimberg, R. G. (2004). The relationship between psychotherapy and pharmacotherapy for social anxiety disorder. In B. Bandelow & D. J. Stein (Eds.), *Social anxiety disorder—more than shyness: Psychopathology, pathogenesis, and management* (pp. 299–314). New York: Marcel Dekker.

Zerbe, K. J. (1997). Uncharted waters: Psychodynamic considerations in the diagnosis and treatment of social phobia. In W. W. Menninger (Ed.), *Fear of humiliation: Integrated treatment of social phobia and comorbid conditions* (pp. 1–19). Northvale, NJ: Jason Aronson.

Pharmacotherapy for Generalized Anxiety Disorder

Sanjay J. Mathew *and* Ellen J. Hoffman

Abstract

In this chapter, we review the evidence from double-blind, randomized, placebo-controlled trials for the pharmacotherapy of generalized anxiety disorder (GAD). Selective serotonin reuptake inhibitors are considered first-line medications in the treatment of GAD. There is also evidence for the use of serotonin-norepinephrine reuptake inhibitors. While benzodiazepines have the advantage of rapid onset of action, they lack antidepressant effects and may result in dependence. While there is evidence for the efficacy of the tricyclics and monoamine oxidase inhibitors in anxiety and depressive disorders, their use is limited by their less favorable side-effect profile. Other medication classes that are utilized in GAD include 5-HT1A agonists and anticonvulsants, and recent studies have investigated atypical antipsychotics as adjunctive medications in GAD.

Keywords: anticonvulsant, antidepressant, anxiety, benzodiazepine, experimental therapeutics, pharmacotherapy, serotonin reuptake inhibitor

Pharmacological treatments for generalized anxiety disorder (GAD) have evolved over the last three decades in parallel with the field's evolving conceptualization of this disorder (see Chapter 4). While the pharmacotherapy literature reviewed herein primarily examines studies utilizing *DSM–III–R* or *DSM–IV* criteria, future renditions of *DSM* may classify GAD with the chronic depressive disorders, reflecting these disorders' epidemiological comorbidity and possible shared biology (Sullivan et al., 2005; Mathew & Steinbugler, in press).

Medications for GAD in the United States, with the exception of buspirone, were originally introduced for related anxiety and mood disorders (see Table 1), and were not developed based on an understanding of pathophysiology. As significantly high lifetime comorbidities are observed between GAD and major depression (>60%), antidepressants with anxiolytic properties have been logically used as the first-line medications for GAD

over the past decade (Gorman, 2003), and three of these medications are approved by the U.S. Food and Drug Administration (FDA) (Table 1). There is now evidence from a number of randomized, placebo-controlled, double-blind clinical trials for the use of selective serotonin reuptake inhibitors (SSRIs), including paroxetine, sertraline, and escitalopram, in the treatment of GAD, as well as multiple studies supporting the efficacy of the serotonin norepinephrine reuptake inhibitor (SNRI) venlafaxine XR (Baldwin & Polkinghorn, 2005). While older antidepressants such as the tricyclics (TCAs) and monoamine oxidase inhibitors (MAOIs) have been shown to be effective for many anxiety and depressive disorders, their use is limited by their generally poorer tolerability. Besides the SSRIs and SNRIs, other classes of drugs commonly utilized in GAD include 5-HT1A agonists, benzodiazepines, anticonvulsants, and most recently, atypical antipsychotics.

Table 1. U.S. Food and Drug Administration Approved Medications for Generalized Anxiety Disorder

Medication	Year of Approval	Drug Class	Manufacturer	Daily Dose Range	Other Indications	Key Reference
Diazepam[a] (Valium)	1963 (initial)	Benzodiazepine	Roche[c]	2 mg–10 mg	Anxiety Disorders; short-term relief of anxiety sx	Rickels et al. (1993)
Lorazepam[a] (Ativan)	1971 (initial)	Benzodiazepine	Biovail[c]	1 mg–10 mg	Anxiety Disorders; short-term relief of anxiety sx or anxiety assoc. w/depressive sx	Fontaine et al. (1986)
Alprazolam (Xanax)	1981	Benzodiazepine	Pfizer[c]	0.75 mg–4 mg	PD; Anxiety assoc. w/ depression	Hoehn-Saric et al. (1988)
Busiprone (BuSpar)[b]	1986	Azapirone	Bristol-Myers Squibb[c]	15 mg–60 mg	Anxiety Disorders; short-term relief of anxiety sx	Jacobson et al. (1985)
Venlafaxine XR (Effexor XR)	2000	SNRI	Wyeth	37.5 mg–225 mg	MDD, SAD, PD	Allgulander et al. (2001)
Paroxetine (Paxil)	2001	SSRI	GlaxoSmithKline[c]	10 mg–50 mg	MDD, PD, SAD, OCD, PTSD	Pollack et al. (2001)
Escitalopram (Lexapro)	2003	SSRI	Forest Laboratories	10 mg–20 mg	MDD	Davidson et al. (2004)

Note. SSRI = Selective Serotonin Reuptake Inhibitor; SNRI = Serotonin-Norepinephrine Reuptake Inhibitor; MDD = Major Depressive Disorder; PD = Panic Disorder; SAD = Social Anxiety Disorder; OCD = Obsessive-Compulsive Disorder; PTSD = Posttraumatic Stress Disorder.

[a]Approval preceded FDA designations for specific anxiety disorders; approved for Anxiety Disorders.

[b]Approval preceded FDA designations for specific anxiety disorders; approved for Anxiety Disorders, but clinical trials supporting approval included many patients whose diagnosis would roughly correspond to *DSM–III* Generalized Anxiety Disorder.

[c]Generic available.

This chapter will review the double-blind randomized, placebo-controlled (RCT) pharmacological studies in GAD, and then discuss more recent medication approaches for this chronic, often disabling, and common psychiatric condition. Recommendations for future psychopharmacological targets will be offered.

Antidepressants
Selective Serotonin Reuptake Inhibitors

The efficacy of several SSRIs in the treatment of GAD has been demonstrated in multiple randomized, double-blind studies (see Table 2). In both fixed- and flexible-dose short-term studies of GAD, paroxetine was found to result in significantly greater response and remission rates versus placebo (Pollack et al., 2001; Rickels et al., 2003). Rickels et al. (2003) demonstrated that 62% of patients receiving paroxetine 20 mg/day and 68% of those receiving 40 mg/day were responders (defined as those patients with a Clinical Global Impression-Improvement [CGI-I] rating of 1 or 2) by study endpoint, which was significantly more than the placebo response of 46%. Similarly, a response rate of 62% for paroxetine 20–50 mg/day versus 47% for placebo was found by Pollack et al. (2001). In these two 8-week studies, paroxetine resulted in remission (defined as Hamilton Anxiety Rating Scale [HAM-A] ≤ 7) in approximately one-third of patients (Pollack et al., 2001; Rickels et al., 2003).

In addition, two 3-month flexibly dosed studies of sertraline 50–150 mg/day found that it is significantly more effective than placebo in treating symptoms of GAD (Allgulander et al., 2004; Dahl et al., 2005). Allgulander et al. (2004) identified response and remission rates (63% and 31%, respectively) for sertraline that were similar to paroxetine, while Dahl et al. (2005) showed that 55% of patients receiving sertraline had at least a 50% decrease in their HAM-A scores by study end, which was significantly greater than the percentage of responders given placebo (32%). Escitalopram 10–20 mg/day was found to have similar efficacy in the treatment of GAD in an 8-week, flexibly dosed trial with significant rates of response (58%) and remission (36%) (Davidson, Bose, Korotzer, & Zheng, 2004).

Two long-term studies assessed the risk of relapse in GAD following treatment with paroxetine (Stocchi et al., 2003) and escitalopram (Allgulander, Florea, & Trap Huusom, 2005), and found that significantly more patients who were switched to placebo relapsed during a 6-month period. It was found that 11% of patients who continued on

paroxetine and 19% of those who continued on escitalopram relapsed versus 40% and 56%, respectively, of patients given placebo in the two studies (Allgulander et al., 2005; Stocchi et al., 2003). Similarly, in a study by Davidson, Bose, & Wang (2005), patients who completed three 8-week, double-blind, placebo-controlled trials of escitalopram were allowed to enter a 6-month open-label phase, in which the response rate in the Last Observation Carried Forward (LOCF) analysis was 76% and continuing improvement in HAM-A scores was noted by study endpoint. With respect to evidence for other SSRIs, Baldwin and Polkinghorn (2005) note that there are no published RCTs of citalopram, fluoxetine, and fluvoxamine for GAD.

Ball, Kuhn, Wall, Shekhar, and Goddard (2005) conducted the first head-to-head study of SSRIs in GAD, finding that paroxetine and sertraline had similar efficacy in terms of response and remission rates after 8 weeks. The authors also observed that the two SSRIs had a greater effect on the psychic versus the somatic symptom subscale of the HAM-A (Ball et al., 2005), a distinction that has been described in other SSRI studies (Pollack et al., 2001; Rickels et al., 2003). Of note, patients in this study were allowed to have other Axis I anxiety and depressive disorders only if GAD was the primary disorder; patients with HAM-D scores > 20 were excluded (Ball et al., 2005). Another head-to-head study by Bielski, Bose, & Chang (2005) showed that both paroxetine and escitalopram were similar in reducing HAM-A scores and improving quality of life, though more patients withdrew from the paroxetine group due to adverse effects. An important limitation of the SSRI comparator studies noted above was the absence of placebo controls.

SSRIs in Special Populations in GAD

In a population of older adults (>60 years) with different anxiety disorder diagnoses, including GAD, Lenze et al. (2005) showed that citalopram 10–30 mg/day was effective in reducing anxiety symptoms in a small, 8-week RCT, while Schuurmans et al. (2006) showed that sertraline (titrated from 25 mg/day to 100–150 mg/day) as well as cognitive behavioral therapy led to an improvement in anxiety symptoms. In a pooled analysis of five RCTs in geriatric patients, Katz, Reynolds, Alexopoulos, & Hackett (2002) showed that venlafaxine ER was effective in treating late-life GAD.

In children and adolescents with anxiety disorders, including GAD, separation anxiety, and social phobia, small RCTs have shown that fluvoxamine

(RUPP Anxiety Study Group, 2001) and fluoxetine (Birmaher et al., 2003) are significantly more effective than placebo after 8- and 12-weeks, respectively, in treating anxiety in these disorders. Open-label extensions of RCTs in pediatric populations indicated that continuation of fluoxetine treatment led to improvement of CGI-I and CGI-S scores after 1 year in one study (Clark et al., 2005), while another study found that a majority of the patients who responded to fluvoxamine in the RCT and received open-label continuation treatment for 24 weeks remained in remission. It was found that 71% (10 of 14) of fluvoxamine nonresponders who switched to fluoxetine and 56% (27 of 48) of placebo nonresponders who were started on fluvoxamine showed some improvement in anxiety symptoms during the open-label extension, though there was no comparison made to patients who did not take medication during this time (RUPP Anxiety Study Group, 2002). Finally, in a small RCT (*n* = 22), Rynn, Siqueland, & Rickels (2001) found that sertraline (50 mg/day during weeks 2–9) was effective after 9 weeks in reducing HAM-A and CGI severity and improvement scores in children and adolescents (average age 11–12) with GAD.

Serotonin-Norepinephrine Reuptake Inhibitors: Venlafaxine XR and Duloxetine

There is evidence from multiple short- and long-term RCTs to support the use of venlafaxine XR in the treatment of GAD (see Table 2). In both flexible- and fixed-dose studies, venlafaxine XR resulted in significantly greater response rates versus placebo after 8 weeks (Nimatoudis et al., 2004) and after 24–28 weeks (Allgulander, Hackett, & Salinas, 2001; Gellenberg, Lydiard, Aguiar, Haskins, & Salinas, 2000).

Long-term studies by Allgulander et al. (2001) and Gelenberg et al. (2000) have demonstrated efficacy for venlafaxine XR over placebo. After 24 weeks, venlafaxine XR (37.5, 75, or 150 mg/day) was superior to placebo in reducing HAM-A and CGI-I scores (Allgulander et al., 2001). A flexible-dose, 6-month study found that venlafaxine XR 75–225 mg/day resulted in ≥ 69% response rate (defined here as ≥ 40% reduction in HAM-A scores or CGI-I = 1 or 2) (Gellenberg et al., 2000).

More recent studies have suggested that duloxetine, a SNRI FDA-approved in the United States for major depressive disorder and diabetic peripheral neuropathic pain, may have a role in reducing symptoms of generalized anxiety. For example, Dunner, Goldstein, Mallinckrodt, Lu, and Detke

(2003) examined pooled data from 4 multicenter RCTs of duloxetine in the treatment of patients with major depressive disorder and found that duloxetine decreased anxiety symptoms in depressed patients according to either HAM-A or HAM-D anxiety/somatization subfactor scores. In addition, several trials have investigated the utility of duloxetine in patients with clinically predominant diagnoses of GAD (Allgulander et al., 2006; Koponen et al., 2006; Pollack et al., 2006a; Rynn et al., 2006), and based on these data, the drug's manufacturer filed a supplemental new drug application in May 2006 for the GAD indication, and subsequently received FDA approval in February 2007.

Tricyclic Antidepressants

Tricyclic antidepressants (TCAs) have a long history of use in anxiety and related conditions, and are effective treatments for GAD, although few studies have investigated TCAs in *DSM–IV* defined GAD. Rickels, Downing, Schweizer, and Hassman (1993) conducted an 8-week double-blind, placebo-controlled trial comparing imipramine, diazepam, and trazodone in the treatment of patients with *DSM–III* GAD, in which diazepam resulted in the greatest improvement during the first 2 weeks, after which imipramine was significantly more effective in reducing total HAM-A scores (reviewed in Baldwin & Polkinghorn, 2005); all 3 treatment groups were found to be effective in reducing anxiety symptoms by study end (reviewed in Lydiard & Monnier, 2004). The overall poorer tolerability of the TCAs compared to the SSRIs and SNRI have limited their use in primary care settings and in psychiatric practices (Baldwin & Polkinghorn, 2005; Gorman, 2003).

Anticonvulsants

Recent RCTs have investigated pregabalin, an anticonvulsant FDA-approved for neuropathic pain and adjunct treatment for partial seizures, in the short-term treatment of GAD. Pande et al. (2003) demonstrated significant reductions in HAM-A in both pregabalin groups (150 or 600 mg/day) and in a lorazepam-treated group versus placebo after 4 weeks. Pohl, Feltner, Fieve, and Pande (2005) found that pregabalin resulted in significant response rates after 6 weeks for all doses tested (fixed, divided doses of 200, 400, or 450 mg/day); HAM-A responders = 53%–56% for all pregabalin groups versus 34% for placebo; CGI-I response = 55%–59% versus 34%. In another 4-week, fixed-dose, placebo-controlled

Table 2. Randomized Placebo-Controlled Pharmacotherapy Trials of Antidepressants in Generalized Anxiety Disorder

Medication(s) studied, mg/day	Study	Type, Weeks	n	HAM-A Pre	HAM-A Post	% HAM-A Response[b]	CGI-I Scores or Response %	Remission Rates % (HAM-A ≤ 7 or CGI-S = 1)	Other Outcome Measures	Comment
					Selective Serotonin Reuptake Inhibitors					
Paroxetine 10–40 Serrtraline 25–100	Ball et al. (2005)	Flexible, 8	25 28	20.8 21.4	NA	% reduction in HAM-A scores: 57.3 55.9	NA	40 46	No difference in reductions on IU-GAMS and BAI scores, or improvement of Q-LES-Q between 2 groups.	No placebo; greater reduction in HAM-A psychic vs. somatic subscales in both groups (though equal reductions in psychic and somatic symptoms on IU-GAMS).
Paroxetine 20–50 Escitalopram 10–20	Bielski et al. (2005)	Flexible, 24	61 60	23.4 23.7	10.1 8.4	NA	2.1 1.8	NA	Both drugs led to improvement in quality of life.	No placebo; escitalopram was better tolerated than paroxetine.
Paroxetine 20 Paroxetine 40 Placebo	Rickels et al. (2003)	Fixed, 8	189 197 180	24.1 23.8 24.4	11.6[a] 11.6[a] 15.1	NA	61.7%[a] 68%[a] 45.6%	30[a] 36[a] 20	Significantly greater improvement in SDS in paroxetine groups.	Dropout rate was 11% in both paroxetine groups.
Paroxetine 20–50 Placebo	Stocchi et al. (2003)	Flexible for 8 weeks, then fixed, 32	274 287	NA	In relapse phase: −1.9[a] +4.8	NA	NA	73.0[a] 34.4	Placebo group was almost 5 times more likely to relapse than paroxetine group.	8-week single-blind paroxetine phase followed by 24-week double-blind phase where subjects either continued on paroxetine or switched to placebo to investigate relapse; data for double-blind phase shown.

Paroxetine 20–50 Placebo	Pollack et al. (2001)	Flexible, 8	161 163	24.2 24.1	~12 ~14	NA	62.1%[a] 47.2%	36.0[a] 22.7	Significantly greater improvement in SDS and reduction in HAD scores in paroxetine group.	Mean dose paroxetine 26.8 mg; significant improvement in HAM-A anxious mood item in paroxetine group from week 1.
Sertraline 50–100 Placebo	Dahl et al. (2005)	Flexible, 12	184 189	24.6 25.0	12.9[a] 17	55[a] 32	1.9[a] 2.7	NA	Significantly greater improvement on Q-LES-Q in sertraline group.	Similar levels of reduction in symptom severity in both psychic and somatic HAM-A factors in sertraline group by end of study, though lower effect size noted for somatic factor.
Sertraline 50–150 Placebo	Allgulander et al. (2004)	Flexible, 12	182 188	24.6 25.0	10.88[a] 14.9	NA	63%[a] 37%	31[a] 18	Significantly greater efficacy on HAD and improvement in quality of life in sertraline group.	Anxiolytic response to sertraline seen by week 4.
Sertraline 25 (1st week), then 50 Placebo	Rynn et al. (2001)	Fixed, 9	11 11	20.6 23.3	7.8[a] 21.0	NA	2.1[a] 3.5	NA	Significant differences in some additional anxiety disorder rating scales for children in sertraline group.	Significant reduction in both psychic and somatic symptoms of anxiety in sertraline group; no difference in side effects reported between 2 groups.
Escitalopram 10 (1st 4 weeks), then 10–20 Placebo	Davidson et al. (2004)	Flexible, 8	158 157	23.6 23.2	12.3[a] 15.8	NA	58%[a] 38%	36[a] 16	Quality of life significantly better in escitalopram group.	Significantly greater mean changes in HAM-A in escitalopram group starting at week 1.

Table 2. (*Continued*)

Medication(s) studied, mg/day	Study	Type, Weeks	n	HAM-A Pre	HAM-A Post	% HAM-A Response[b]	CGI-I Scores or Response %	Remission Rates % (HAM-A ≤ 7 or CGI-S = 1)	Other Outcome Measures	Comment
					Selective Serotonin Reuptake Inhibitors					
Escitalopram 20	Allgulander et al. (2005)	Fixed, at least 24, to a maximum of 74	187	NA	In relapse phase; change after 24 weeks: −0.83[a] +0.39	NA	NA	NA	The risk of relapse was 4.04 times higher in placebo vs. escitalopram groups.	12-week open label escitalopram treatment; responders were either continued on escitalopram or given placebo for at least 24 weeks unless patient relapsed or was withdrawn; data for double-blind phase shown.
Placebo			188							
					Serotonin-Norepinephrine Reuptake Inhibitor (Venlafaxine XR)					
Venlafaxine XR 75–150	Nimatoudis et al. (2004)	Flexible, 8	24	27.1	7.9[a]	92[a]	1.8[a]	62.5[a]	Covi anxiety scale changes were not statistically significant.	Patients with less than 30% decrease in HAM-A at end of week 2 doubled dose of venlafaxine; decrease in HAM-A scores for venlafaxine group became significant at day 29.
Placebo			22	28.5	17.7	27	0.6	9.1		
Venlafaxine XR 75	Hackett et al. (2003)	Fixed, 8	185	27.9	13.9	59	81%	NA	HAD anxiety sub-scale reduction in venlafaxine XR groups in secondary analysis.	No significant improvement was observed in any group in primary analysis,
Venlafaxine XR 150			169	27.9	15.1	54	75%			
Diazepam 15			89	28.4	13.6	56	78%			
Placebo			97	27.6	15.9	45	65%			

Study	Design, duration (wk)	Treatment	Analysis	N	HAM-A baseline	HAM-A endpoint	CGI	Response rate	Remission rate	Efficacy results	Comments
Allgulander et al. (2001)	Fixed, 24	Venlafaxine ER 37.5	Primary	138	26.6	12.8[a]	2.3[a]	NA	NA	Significant decrease in BSA total score in all venlafaxine ER groups, and HAD in venlafaxine ER 75 and 150 mg groups.	A dose-response relationship was observed for venlafaxine ER with 150 mg dose having highest responder rates; higher doses also showed earlier onset of action.
		Venlafaxine ER 75	Primary	130	26.3	11.8[a]	1.9[a]	NA	NA		but was noted in venlafaxine XR group *in a secondary analysis* that omitted study centers where there was no difference between diazepam and placebo.
		Venlafaxine ER 150	Primary	137	26.3	10.1[a]	1.9[a]	NA	NA		
		Placebo	Primary	130	26.7	15.5	2.6	NA	NA		
		Venlafaxine ER 37.5	2nd analysis	69	28.0	15.3[a]	NA	60[a]	85%[a]		
		Venlafaxine ER 75	2nd analysis	61	28.0	16.0[a]	NA	59[a]	74%[a]		
		Venlafaxine ER 150	2nd analysis	N/A	N/A	N/A	NA	N/A	N/A		
		Placebo	2nd analysis	35	28.0	20.9	NA	32	43%		
Gellenberg et al. (2000)	Flexible, 28	Venlafaxine XR 75–225		115	25.0	11.6[a]	NA	≥69%[a]	NA	Significantly lower CGI-I, CGI-S, and HAD scores in venlafaxine XR group.	Significant reductions in anxiety scores noted in venlafaxine XR group vs. placebo and maintained during 6 months of study.
		Placebo		123	25.0	16.3	NA	42–46% (defined here as = 40% reduction in HAM-A)	NA		
Rickels et al. (2000)	Fixed, 8	Venlafaxine XR 75		86	24.7	13.5	2.33	NA	NA	Significantly lower HAD scores in all venlafaxine XR groups at week 8.	All 3 venlafaxine doses showed some efficacy, but most positive results were with 225 mg.
		Venlafaxine XR 150		81	24.5	12.1	2.30	NA	NA		
		Venlafaxine XR 225		86	23.6	12.1[a]	2.22[a]	NA	NA		
		Placebo		96	24.1	14.6	2.61	NA	NA		

Table 2. (*Continued*)

Medication(s) studied, mg/day	Study	Type, Weeks	n	HAM-A Pre	HAM-A Post	% HAM-A Response[b]	CGI-I Scores or Response %	Remission Rates % (HAM-A ≤ 7 or CGI-S = 1)	Other Outcome Measures	Comment
Serotonin-Norepinephrine Reuptake Inhibitor (Venlafaxine XR)										
Venlafaxine XR 75	Davidson et al. (1999)	Fixed, 8	87	23.7	13.0	49	62%[a]	NA	Venlafaxine XR was significantly more effective on HAD than placebo (except at weeks 1 [both doses] and 2 [150 mg]) and buspirone (except at week 1).	At week 8, adjusted mean HAM-A psychic anxiety, anxious mood and tension scores were significantly lower in venlafaxine XR group vs. placebo.
Venlafaxine XR 150			87	23.0	13.8	49	49%			
Buspirone 30 (in three divided doses)			93	23.8	14.1	45	55%[a]			
Placebo			98	23.7	15.6	36	39%			

Note. NA = information not available; N/A = not applicable; HAM-A = Hamilton Anxiety Rating Scale; CGI-I = Clinical Global Impression Improvement Scale; CGI-S = Clinical Global Impression Severity Scale; Pre = pretreatment; Post = posttreatment; LOCF = last observation carried forward; IU-GAMS = Indiana University Generalized Anxiety Measurement Scale; BAI = Beck Anxiety Inventory; Q-LES-Q = Quality of Life Enjoyment and Satisfaction Questionnaire; SDS = Sheehan Disability Scale; HAD = Hospital Anxiety and Depression Scale; BSA = Brief Scale for Anxiety; XR or ER = extended-release; MMRM = mixed models repeated-measures. LOCF data given unless otherwise noted. Mean age in most studies was 40 years and % female subjects was 50%–70% except in Rynn et al. (2001), in which average age was 11 years and % female subjects was 19% in sertraline group and 8% in placebo group.

[a]Statistically superior to placebo.

[b]% HAM-A response is either % reduction in HAM-A scores or % HAM-A responders (patients with a 50% decrease in baseline HAM-A score), as defined by the particular study, and is indicated in the table.

trial, Rickels et al. (2005) observed significant decreases in HAM-A scores in all pregabalin groups (fixed, divided doses of 300, 450, or 600 mg/day) as well as in an alprazolam comparator group (1.5 mg/day), but only pregabalin 300 mg/day and 600 mg/day groups had a significant percentage of HAM-A and CGI-I responders compared to placebo on LOCF analysis; the percentage of CGI-I responders was also significant in the alprazolam group. The authors concluded that pregabalin 300 mg/day was of comparable or superior efficacy to the higher doses of pregabalin and alprazolam (Rickels et al., 2005). A major finding from this study was that pregabalin showed comparable efficacy to the benzodiazepine from week 1 onward. Feltner et al. (2003) found that pregabalin 600 mg/day (200 mg tid) and lorazepam (6 mg/day, divided tid), but not pregabalin 150 mg/day (50 mg tid), resulted in significant reductions in HAM-A scores compared to placebo, though there were no significant differences in CGI-I and HAM-A response or remission rates for any of the treatment groups in this study. Montgomery, Tobias, Zornberg, Kasper, and Pande (2006) found that pregabalin 400 mg/day was superior to placebo on all primary and secondary measures in a 6-week RCT of outpatients (in primary care and psychiatric settings) with GAD; a 600 mg/day dose was superior to placebo on some, but not all measures. In September 2004 pregabalin received a nonapprovable letter from the FDA for the GAD indication, but it received EU approval in March 2006.

Recent studies have also intensively investigated the anticonvulsant tiagabine for GAD. A small randomized, open-label trial of tiagabine (4–16 mg/day) versus paroxetine (20–60 mg/day) demonstrated that both medications significantly reduced anxiety symptoms from baseline on HAM-A after 10 weeks, though this study did not include a placebo arm (Rosenthal, 2003). Pollack et al. (2005) found no significant difference in response rates between tiagabine 4–16 mg/day (divided doses) and placebo in an 8-week, flexible-dose study, though reduction of anxiety symptoms was noted in the tiagabine group in the secondary statistical analyses (observed case and mixed models repeated-measures [MMRM] analyses).

Benzodiazepines and Azapirones

A number of RCTs have demonstrated that benzodiazepines are efficacious in the short-term, acute treatment of GAD, and have the advantage of rapid onset of action (reviewed in Baldwin & Polkinghorn, 2005; Gorman, 2003). Rickels et al. (1993) and Rocca, Fonzo, Scotta, Zanalda, and Ravizza (1997) showed the rapid onset of action of benzodiazepines for GAD in their studies. However, benzodiazepines lack antidepressant effects and may result in dependence (reviewed in Baldwin & Polkinghorn, 2005; Gorman, 2003). In addition, the use of benzodiazepines for the long-term treatment of GAD is problematic, as very few patients achieve and sustain remission with benzodiazepine monotherapy.

Because of their overall tolerability, lack of addictive potential, and minimal sexual dysfunction or blood pressure effects, serotonin 1A (5-HT$_{1A}$) partial and full agonists have been extensively investigated in GAD since FDA approval was granted for the azapirone buspirone in 1986. A meta-analysis of 8 clinical trials of buspirone in GAD revealed efficacy comparable to benzodiazepines, and superior benefit to placebo in patients with comorbid depressive symptoms (Gammans et al., 1992). In a direct comparison study of buspirone and venlafaxine XR in GAD patients, both agents were numerically superior to placebo in reducing total scores on the Hamilton Anxiety Scale (HAM-A) scale, but this did not reach statistical significance for either group after 8 weeks; venlafaxine XR was statistically superior to buspirone on the Hospital Anxiety and Depression Scale (Davidson, DuPont, Hedges, & Haskins, 1999).

Several other members of the azapirone chemical class, the majority of 5-HT$_{1A}$ partial or full agonists, include gepirone, zalospirone, and ipsapirone, none of which are FDA approved for GAD. In a double-blind, placebo-controlled study of 198 patients with GAD comparing gepirone and diazepam, Rickels, Schweizer, DeMartinis, Mandos, and Mercer (1997) showed a delayed anxiolytic effect (week 6 of the study) of gepirone compared to diazepam and placebo. A greater number of patients also dropped out from the gepirone group secondary to side effects (nausea, dizziness), which the authors attributed to the drug's narrow therapeutic window. An important limitation to the broad appeal of the azapirones is evidence of decreased efficacy in patients with past benzodiazepine use (DeMartinis, Rynn, Rickels, & Mandos, 2000).

Atypical Antipsychotics

Due to their broad neurochemical effects on postsynaptic 5-HT2 receptors and modulation of 5-HT1A, atypical antipsychotics may have efficacy as anxiolytic medications. A recent small 6-week, double-blind RCT studied olanzapine (mean dose = 8.7 mg/day) augmentation of fluoxetine (20 mg/day) in patients with GAD who did not respond to fluoxetine after 6 weeks (Pollack et al., 2006b). The authors found that olanzapine augmentation resulted in a significant 50% reduction in HAM-A and CGI-S scores (<3), and while remission rates increased in the olanzapine group, this was not statistically significant in this small sample (n = 21) (Pollack et al., 2006b). Olanzapine resulted in sedation and significant weight gain of 11 pounds on average in the treatment group (Pollack et al., 2006b). Another small (n = 39) 4-week, double-blind, placebo-controlled study investigated low-dose risperidone (0.5–1.5 mg/day) as an adjunctive treatment in GAD (Brawman-Mintzer, Knapp, & Nietert, 2005). In this study, patients who did not respond (HAM-A ≥ 18, CGI-S of moderate or greater) to at least 4 weeks of treatment with another medication, either an SSRI, SNRI, benzodiazepine, or other anxiolytic or antidepressant, were randomized to receive either risperidone or placebo for 5 weeks, while continuing the other medication. Patients in the risperidone group had statistically significant reductions in HAM-A total and psychic anxiety scores versus the placebo group, but CGI-I response rates were not significant (Brawman-Mintzer et al., 2005). Improvements were noted on other rating scales, including CGI-S, HAM-A somatic anxiety, and HADS, in the risperidone group versus placebo, but were not significant by study end. Risperidone was noted to be well tolerated overall, though side effects included somnolence, dizziness, and blurred vision (Brawman-Mintzer et al., 2005).

To date, there are no RCTs of quetiapine, ziprasadone, and aripiprazole as monotherapy or adjunctive treatment in GAD.

Experimental Therapeutics in GAD

Glutamate, an excitatory amino acid neurotransmitter extensively localized in neural circuits implicated in anxiety and mood disorders, has received increasing attention as a pharmacological target in anxiety disorders (Mathew, 2005). Several pharmacological approaches that modulate glutamate neurotransmission and serve a neuroprotective, or plasticity enhancing, function have been used in GAD. Riluzole, a glutamate-release inhibitor FDA-approved for amyotrophic lateral sclerosis, was observed in a small open-label pilot study to decrease social anxiety symptoms in patients with GAD, as well as decrease anxiety sensitivity (Mathew, 2005; Mathew et al., 2005). Open-label proof of concept studies of this agent have been conducted in treatment resistant depression (Zarate et al., 2004) and

in bipolar depression (Zarate et al., 2005). Novel classes of glutamatergic drugs, such as AMPA receptor potentiators and metabotropic glutamate receptor (mGluR) agonists, have also been studied in preclinical and clinical studies. The mGluR family, particularly allosteric potentiators and agonists of mGluR2/3, decrease presynaptic glutamate release and induce postsynaptic hyperpolarization, and were developed to provide rapid anxiolysis with minimal abuse liability and tolerance development (see Swanson et al., 2005, for a comprehensive review). In GAD, reductions in anxiety were observed with the mGlu2/3 agonist LY354740 in a large, multicenter placebo and lorazepam-controlled study (data on file, Eli Lilly and Co.), but safety concerns with this particular compound have prompted investigation of alternative mGlu agents.

A potential new area of therapeutics for GAD capitalizes on the relationship between stress-related anxiety and oxidative stress (Hovatta et al., 2005), and involves modulation of glutamate via oxidative stress reduction. N-acetylcysteine (NAC) is an amino acid derivative that is widely used to treat acetaminophen overdose, and regulates glutamate homeostasis by controlling extracellular, extrasynaptic glutamate levels. It supports cellular resynthesis of glutathione, and is one of the major antioxidant systems in eukaryotic cells (Matuszczak et al., 2005). In tissue culture, NAC protects glial cells from glutamate-mediated toxicity and promotes glial clearance of glutamate. Clinically, NAC has been also shown to delay muscle fatigue during exercise (Matuszczak et al., 2005). Inasmuch as oxidative stress is associated with anxietylike behaviors in mice (Hovatta et al., 2005), NAC might be a promising treatment for GAD, which is marked by prominent fatigue and anticipatory anxiety.

Other novel therapeutic approaches in GAD under investigation in phase III studies involve compounds with more selective targeting of the 5-HT1A receptor, such as PRX-00023 (Mathew, Oshana, & Donohue, 2006) and MN-305 (MediciNova). Triple reuptake inhibitors—medications that block reuptake of serotonin, norepinephrine, and dopamine—are currently being investigated in major depressive disorder, and if promising in MDD, will undoubtedly be studied in GAD. These agents are purported to have advantages in speed of onset, efficacy, and tolerability. Finally, agomelatine (Novartis AG), which is undergoing phase III studies for MDD, targets the melatonin receptor system and postsynaptic 5-HT2C receptor. This drug might be a potentially attractive candidate for

GAD, given that circadian dysregulation and sleep difficulties are common complaints.

Summary and Conclusions

Challenges to the development of rational pharmacotherapy for GAD include the following: (1) unclear phenotype, with morphing diagnostic criteria and extensive mood and anxiety disorder comorbidity; (2) high placebo response rates, resulting in many failed trials; and most critically (3) ill-defined biological substrates and brain circuitry, with limited understanding of pathophysiology. While 5-HT1A agonists have been utilized for more than 20 years in GAD, no brain imaging studies in GAD patients have demonstrated discrete 5-HT1A abnormalities. Recent brain imaging studies in both adolescent (Monk et al., 2006) and adult GAD (Mathew et al., 2004) have identified specific right-sided prefrontal cortical abnormalities, but implications for treatment are unknown.

The SSRIs and SNRIs will continue to be the mainstay of pharmacotherapy for GAD for the immediate future, given their efficacy and overall better tolerability than older antidepressants. Over the next decade, further refinements of these monoaminergic-based drugs, including triple reuptake inhibitors, and more selective 5-HT1A agonists, will likely be introduced for GAD. Innovations in the development of ionotropic and metabotropic glutamatergic drugs, as well as anxiety applications for newer anticonvulsants such as pregabalin, may turn out to be valuable alternatives to the benzodiazepines for the induction of rapid anxiolysis. Given the chronicity and low spontaneous remission rates of GAD, the identification of well-tolerated chronic treatments is especially critical.

References

Allgulander, C., Dahl, A. A., Austin, C., Morris, P.L.P., Sogaard, J. A., Fayyad, R., et al. (2004). Efficacy of sertraline in a 12-week trial for generalized anxiety disorder. *American Journal of Psychiatry, 161,* 1642–1649.

Allgulander, C., Florea, I., & Trap Huusom, A. K. (2005). Prevention of relapse in generalized anxiety disorder by escitalopram treatment. *International Journal of Neuropsychopharmacology, 9,* 1–11.

Allgulander, C., Hackett, D., & Salinas, E. (2001). Venlafaxine extended release (ER) in the treatment of generalised anxiety disorder: Twenty-four-week placebo-controlled dose-ranging study. *British Journal of Psychiatry, 179,* 15–22.

Allgulander, C., Koponen, H., Erickson, J., Pritchett, Y., Detke, M., Ball, S., et al. (2006, March). *Duloxetine is an effective treatment for improving painful physical symptoms and functioning associated with generalized anxiety disorder.* Poster session presented at Anxiety Disorders Association of America, Miami, FL.

Baldwin, D. S., & Polkinghorn, C. (2005). Evidence-based pharmacotherapy of generalized anxiety disorder. *International Journal of Neuropsychopharmacology, 8,* 293–302.

Ball, S. G., Kuhn, A., Wall, D., Shekhar, A., & Goddard, A. W. (2005). Selective serotonin reuptake inhibitor treatment for generalized anxiety disorder: A double-blind, prospective comparison between paroxetine and sertraline. *Journal of Clinical Psychiatry, 66,* 94–99.

Bielski, R. J., Bose, A., & Chang, C. C. (2005). A double-blind comparison of escitalopram and paroxetine in the long-term treatment of generalized anxiety disorder. *Annals of Clinical Psychiatry, 17,* 65–69.

Birmaher, B., Axelson, D., Monk, K., Kalas, C., Clark, D. B., Ehmann, M., et al. (2003). Fluoxetine for the treatment of childhood anxiety disorders. *Journal of the American Academy of Child and Adolescent Psychiatry, 42,* 415–423.

Brawman-Mintzer, O., Knapp, R. G., & Nietert, P. J. (2005). Adjunctive risperidone in generalized anxiety disorder: A double-blind, placebo-controlled study. *Journal of Clinical Psychiatry, 66,* 1321–1325.

Clark, D. B., Birmaher, B., Axelson, D., Monk, K., Kalas, C., Ehmann, M., et al. (2005). Fluoxetine for the treatment of childhood anxiety disorders: Open-label, long-term extension to a controlled trial. *Journal of the American Academy of Child and Adolescent Psychiatry, 44,* 1263–1270.

Dahl, A. A., Ravindran, A., Allgulander, C., Kutcher, S. P., Austin, C., & Burt, T. (2005). Sertraline in generalized anxiety disorder: Efficacy in treating the psychic and somatic anxiety factors. *Acta Psychiatrica Scandinavica, 111,* 429–435.

Davidson, J.R.T., Bose, A., Korotzer, A., & Zheng, H. (2004). Escitalopram in the treatment of generalized anxiety disorder: Double-blind, placebo controlled, flexible-dose study. *Depression and Anxiety, 19,* 234–240.

Davidson, J.R.T., Bose, A., & Wang, Q. (2005). Safety and efficacy of escitalopram in the long term treatment of generalized anxiety disorder. *Journal of Clinical Psychiatry, 66,* 1441–1446.

Davidson, J.R.T., DuPont, R. L., Hedges, D., & Haskins, J. T. (1999). Efficacy, safety, and tolerability of venlafaxine extended release and buspirone in outpatients with generalized anxiety disorder. *Journal of Clinical Psychiatry, 60,* 528–535.

DeMartinis, N., Rynn, M., Rickels, K., & Mandos, L. (2000). Prior benzodiazepine use and buspirone response in the treatment of generalized anxiety disorder. *Journal of Clinical Psychiatry, 62,* 657–658.

Dunner, D. L., Goldstein, D. J., Mallinckrodt, C., Lu, Y., & Detke, M. J. (2003). Duloxetine in treatment of anxiety symptoms associated with depression. *Depression and Anxiety, 18,* 53–61.

Feltner, D. E., Crockatt, J. G., Dubovsky, S. J., Cohn, C. K., Shrivastava, R. K., Targum, S. D., et al. (2003). A randomized, double-blind, placebo-controlled, fixed-dose, multicenter study of pregabalin in patients with generalized anxiety disorder. *Journal of Clinical Psychopharmacology, 223,* 240–249.

Fontaine, R., Mercier, P., Beaudry, P., Annable, L., & Chouinard, G. (1986). Bromazepam and lorazepam in generalized anxiety: A placebo-controlled study with measurement of drug plasma concentration. *Acta Psychiatrica Scandinavica, 74,* 451–458.

Gammans, R. E., Stringfellow, J. C., Hvizdos, A. J., Seidehamel, R. J., Cohn, J. B., Wilcox, C. S., et al. (1992). Use of buspirone in patients with generalized anxiety disorder and coexisting depressive symptoms: A meta-analysis of eight, randomized, controlled studies. *Neuropsychobiology, 25,* 193–201.

Gelenberg, A. J., Lydiard, R. B., Rudolph, R. L., Aguiar, L., Haskins, J. T., & Salinas, E. (2000). Efficacy of venlafaxine extended-release capsules in nondepressed outpatients with generalized anxiety disorder: A 6-month randomized controlled trial. *Journal of the American Medical Association, 283,* 3082–3088.

Gorman, J. M. (2003). Treating generalized anxiety disorder. *Journal of Clinical Psychiatry, 64*(Suppl. 2), 24–29.

Hackett, D., Haudiquet, V., & Salinas, E. (2003). A method for controlling for a high placebo response rate in a comparison of venlafaxine XR and diazepam in the short-term treatment of patients with generalised anxiety disorder. *European Psychiatry, 18,* 182–187.

Hoehn-Saric, R., McLeod, D. R., & Zimmerli, W. D. (1988). Differential effects of alprazolam and imipramine in generalized anxiety disorder: Somatic versus psychic symptoms. *Journal of Clinical Psychiatry, 49,* 293–301.

Hovatta, I., Tennant, R. S., Helton, R., Marr, R. A., Singer, O., Redwine, J. M., et al. (2005). Glyoxalase 1 and glutathione reductase 1 regulate anxiety in mice. *Nature, 438,* 662–666.

Jacobson, A. F., Dominguez, R. A., Goldstein, B. J., & Steinbook, R. M. (1985). Comparison of buspirone and diazepam in generalized anxiety disorder. *Pharmacotherapy, 5,* 290–296.

Katz, I. R., Reynolds, C. F., III, Alexopoulos, G. S., & Hackett, D. (2002). Venlafaxine ER as a treatment for generalized anxiety disorder in older adults: Pooled analysis of five randomized placebo-controlled clinical trials. *Journal of the American Geriatric Society, 50,* 18–25.

Koponen, H., Allgulander, C., Pritchett, Y., Erickson, J., Detke, M., Ball, S., et al. (2006, March). *A fixed-dose study of the efficacy and safety of duloxetine for the treatment of generalized anxiety disorder.* Poster session presented at Anxiety Disorders Association of America annual meeting, Miami, FL.

Lenze, E. J., Mulsant, B. H., Shear, M. K., Dew, M. A., Miller, M. D., Pollock, B. G., et al. (2005). Efficacy and tolerability of citalopram in the treatment of late-life anxiety disorders: Results from an 8-week randomized, placebo-controlled trial. *American Journal of Psychiatry, 162,* 146–150.

Lydiard, R. B., & Monnier, J. (2004). Pharmacological treatment. In R. C. Heimberg, C. L. Turk, & D. S. Mennin (Eds.), *Generalized anxiety disorder: Advances in research and practice* (pp. 351–379). New York: Guilford Press.

Mathew, S. J. (2005). Exploring glutamate function in mood and anxiety disorders: Rationale and future directions. *CNS Spectrums, 10,* 806–807.

Mathew, S. J., Amiel, J. A., Coplan, J. D., Fitterling, H., Sackeim, H. A., & Gorman, J. M. (2005). Riluzole in generalized anxiety disorder. *American Journal of Psychiatry, 162,* 2379–2381.

Mathew, S. J., Mao, X., Coplan, J. D., Smith, E.L.P., Sackeim, H. A., Gorman, J. M., et al. (2004). Dorsolateral prefrontal cortical pathology in generalized anxiety disorder: A proton magnetic resonance spectroscopic imaging study. *American Journal of Psychiatry, 161,* 1119–1121.

Mathew, S. J., Oshana, S., & Donohue, S. (2006, June). *Preliminary evidence of short-term efficacy of a novel non-azapirone selective 5-HT1A agonist in generalized anxiety disorder.* Paper presented at the meeting of the New Clinical Drug Evaluation Unit, National Institute of Mental Health, Boca Raton, FL.

Mathew, S. J., & Steinbugler, M. (in press). Neurochemistry of generalized anxiety disorder. In G. Kinrys & P. F. Renshaw

(Eds.), *Understanding anxiety: Its neurobiological basis and treatment.* New York: Informa Healthcare.

Matuszczak, Y., Farid, M., Jones, J., Lansdowne, S., Smith, M. A., Taylor, A. A., et al. (2005). Effects of N-acetylcysteine on glutathione oxidation and fatigue during handgrip exercise. *Muscle and Nerve, 32,* 633–638.

Monk, C. S., Nelson, E. E., McClure, E. B., Mogg, K., Bradley, B. P., Leibenluft, E., et al. (2006). Ventrolateral prefrontal cortex activation and attentional bias in response to angry faces in adolescents with generalized anxiety disorder. *American Journal of Psychiatry, 163,* 1091–1097.

Montgomery, S. A., Tobias, K., Zornberg, G. L., Kasper, S., & Pande, A. C. (2006). Efficacy and safety of pregabalin in the treatment of generalized anxiety disorder: A 6-week, multicenter, randomized, double-blind placebo-controlled comparison of pregabalin and venlafaxine. *Journal of Clinical Psychiatry, 67,* 771–782.

Nimatoudis, I., Zissis, N. P., Kogeorgos, J., Theodoropoulou, S., Vidalis, A., & Kaprinis, G. (2004). Remission rates with venlafaxine extended release in Greek outpatients with generalized anxiety disorder: A double-blind, randomized, placebo controlled study. *International Clinical Psychopharmacoogy, 19,* 331–336.

Pande, A. C., Crockatt, J. G., Feltner, D. E., Janney, C. A., Smith, W. T., Weisler, R., et al. (2003). Pregabalin in generalized anxiety disorder: A placebo-controlled trial. *American Journal of Psychiatry, 160,* 533–540.

Pohl, R. B., Feltner, D. E., Fieve, R. R., & Pande, A. C. (2005). Efficacy of pregabalin in the treatment of generalized anxiety disorder. *Journal of Clinical Psychopharmacology, 25,* 151–158.

Pollack, M., Raskin, J., Swindle, R., Ball, S., Erickson, J., Nunez, M., et al. (2006a, March). *A flexible-dose, progressive-titration, placebo-controlled trial of duloxetine for improving patient-reported functional outcomes in adults with generalized anxiety disorder.* Poster session presented at Anxiety Disorders Association of America annual meeting, Miami, FL.

Pollack, M. H., Simon, N. M., Zalta, A. K., Worthington, J. J., Hoge, E. A., Mick, E., et al. (2006b). Olanzapine augmentation of fluoxetine for refractory generalized anxiety disorder: A placebo controlled study. *Biological Psychiatry, 59,* 211–215.

Pollack, M. H., Roy-Byrne, P. P., Van Ameringen, M., Snyder, H., Brown, C., Ondrasik, J., et al. (2005). The Selective GABA reuptake inhibitor tiagabine for the treatment of generalized anxiety disorder: Results of a placebo-controlled study. *Journal of Clinical Psychiatry, 66,* 1401–1408.

Pollack, M. H., Zaninelli, R., Goddard, A., McCafferty, J., Bellew, K. M., Burnham, D. B., et al. (2001). Paroxetine in the treatment of generalized anxiety disorder: Results of a placebo-controlled, flexible-dosage trial. *Journal of Clinical Psychiatry, 62,* 350–357.

Rickels, K., Downing, R., Schweizer, E., & Hassman, H. (1993). Antidepressants for the treatment of generalized anxiety disorder: A placebo-controlled comparison of imipramine, trazodone, and diazepam. *Archives of General Psychiatry, 50,* 884–895.

Rickels, K., Pollack, M. H., Feltner, D. E., Lydiard, R. B., Zimbroff, D. L., Bielski, R. J., et al. (2005). Pregabalin for treatment of generalized anxiety disorder: A 4-week, multicenter, double-blind, placebo-controlled trial of pregabalin and alprazolam. *Archives of General Psychiatry, 62,* 1022–1030.

Rickels, K., Pollack, M. H., Sheehan, D. V., & Haskins, J. T. (2000). Efficacy of extended-release venlafaxine in nondepressed outpatients with generalized anxiety disorder. *American Journal of Psychiatry, 157,* 968–974.

Rickels, K., Schweizer, E., DeMartinis, N., Mandos, L., & Mercer, C. (1997). Gepirone and diazepam in generalized anxiety disorder: A placebo-controlled trial. *Journal of Clinical Psychopharmacology, 17,* 272–277.

Rickels, K., Zaninelli, R., McCafferty, J., Bellew, K., Iyengar, M., & Sheehan, D. (2003). Paroxetine treatment of generalized anxiety disorder: A double-blind, placebo-controlled study. *American Journal of Psychiatry, 160,* 749–756.

Rocca, P., Fonzo, V., Scotta, M., Zanalda, E., & Ravizza, L. (1997). Paroxetine efficacy in the treatment of generalized anxiety disorder. *Acta Psychiatrica Scandinavica, 95,* 444–450.

Rosenthal, M. (2003). Tiagabine for the treatment of generalized anxiety disorder: A randomized, open-label clinical trial with paroxetine as a positive control. *Journal of Clinical Psychiatry, 64,* 1245–1249.

RUPP Anxiety Study Group. (2001). Fluvoxamine for the treatment of anxiety disorders in children and adolescents. *New England Journal of Medicine, 344,* 1279–1285.

RUPP Anxiety Study Group. (2002). Treatment of pediatric anxiety disorders: An open-label extension of the research units on pediatric psychopharmacology anxiety study. *Journal of Child and Adolescent Psychopharmacology, 12,* 175–188.

Rynn, M., Russell, J., Erickson, J., Detke, M., Ball, S., Dinkel, J., et al. (2006, March). *Efficacy and safety of duloxetine in the treatment of generalized anxiety disorder: A flexible-dose, progressive-titration, placebo-controlled trial.* Poster session presented at Anxiety Disorders Association of America annual meeting, Miami, FL.

Rynn, M. A., Siqueland, L., & Rickels, K. (2001). Placebo-controlled trial of sertraline in the treatment of children with generalized anxiety disorder. *American Journal of Psychiatry, 158,* 2008–2014.

Schuurmans, J., Comijs, H., Emmelkamp, P.M.G., Gundy, C.M.M., Wijnen, I., van den Hout, M., et al. (2006). A randomized, controlled trial of the effectiveness of cognitive-behavioral therapy and sertraline versus a waitlist control group for anxiety disorders in older adults. *American Journal of Geriatric Psychiatry, 14,* 255–263.

Stocchi, F., Nordera, G., Jokinen, R. H., Lepola, U. M., Hewett, K., Bryson, H., & Iyengar, M., for the Paroxetine Generalized Anxiety Disorder Study Team. (2003). Efficacy and tolerability of paroxetine for the long-term treatment of generalized anxiety disorder. *Journal of Clinical Psychiatry, 64,* 250–258.

Sullivan, G. M., Oquendo, M. A., Simpson, N., Van Heertum, R. L., Mann, J. J., & Parsey, R. V. (2005). Brain serotonin 1A receptor binding in major depression is related to psychic and somatic anxiety. *Biological Psychiatry, 58,* 947–954.

Swanson, C. J., Bures, M., Johnson, M. P., Linden, A. M., Monn, J. A., & Schoepp, D. D. (2005). Metabotropic glutamate receptors as novel targets for anxiety and stress disorders. *Nature Reviews—Drug Discovery, 4,* 131–144.

Zarate, C., Payne, J. L., Quiroz, J., Sporn, J., Denicoff, K. K., Luckenbaugh, D., et al. (2004). An open label trial of riluzole in patients with treatment resistant major depression. *American Journal of Psychiatry, 161,* 171–174.

Zarate, C. A., Quiroz, J. A., Singh, J. B., Denicoff, K. D., De Jesus, G., Luckenbaugh, D. A., et al. (2005). An open-label trial of the glutamate-modulating agent riluzole in combination with lithium for the treatment of bipolar depression. *Biological Psychiatry, 57,* 430–432.

Psychological Treatment of Generalized Anxiety Disorder

Melisa Robichaud *and* Michel J. Dugas

Abstract

This chapter reviews the leading psychological treatments being conducted for generalized anxiety disorder (GAD). First, a detailed review is provided about early therapeutic interventions, which largely comprised various cognitive behavioral therapy (CBT) strategies designed to address the generalized experience of anxiety in GAD. In addition, the chapter discusses the difficulties that GAD as a disorder has posed in terms of treatment, such as shifting diagnostic criteria. Finally, both current psychological treatments and future directions are presented, placed within the framework of the theoretical models of excessive worry from which they were derived.

Keywords: anxiety, cognitive behavioral therapy, generalized anxiety disorder, psychological treatment, worry

Of all the anxiety disorders, generalized anxiety disorder (GAD) has proven to be one of the most difficult to treat. Yet GAD is a relatively common disorder, with a 12-month prevalence rate between 2% and 4%, and a lifetime incidence ranging from 4% to 7% among the general population (Blazer, Hughes, George, Schwartz, & Boyer, 1991; Hunt, Issakidis, & Andrews, 2002; Wittchen, Zhao, Kessler, & Eaton, 1994). Moreover, it appears that GAD is the most common anxiety disorder, and the second most frequently occurring mental health disorder, in primary care facilities (Barrett, Oxman, & Gerber, 1988; Wittchen et al., 2002), as well as being associated with significant disability (e.g., Stein & Heimberg, 2004) and cost (Greenberg et al., 1999). As such, there is a need for a highly efficacious treatment for GAD. However, the question of how to appropriately treat GAD remains a subject of debate, and it is only in recent years that independent research teams have begun to develop GAD-specific theoretical models designed to better understand the development and maintenance of the disorder (see Chapter 17 for a discussion of current theoretical models of GAD). From these conceptualizations of GAD, corresponding treatment protocols have been elaborated, all of which are empirically driven and designed to specifically address GAD symptoms and processes.

In this chapter, we provide an overview of the various psychological treatments for GAD by reviewing the earlier, more general treatment interventions, as well as more recent disorder-specific protocols. In addition, we present the challenges GAD has posed in the development of effective treatment, and the results of efficacy research on the various protocols to date. Finally, some new research directions, and their implications for treatment, will be discussed.

Description of Psychological Treatments for GAD
Early Treatment Interventions

A variety of interventions have been used for the treatment of GAD since its first appearance in the *DSM–III* (American Psychiatric Association [APA], 1980). Although there remains no standard treatment for GAD, most treatment packages have included various components of cognitive behavioral therapy (CBT). The most common CBT interventions used for the treatment of GAD have included imagery rehearsal strategies, applied relaxation, stimulus control, and cognitive therapy. We will now review some of these therapeutic components included in many early GAD treatment packages.

IMAGERY REHEARSAL

This component largely involves the application of relaxation techniques to the imaginal presentation of anxiety cues, and is therefore designed to address general anxious arousal. In contrast to imaginal exposure, where patients generate an anxiety-provoking image to allow for gradual extinction of the fear response, imagery rehearsal involves the imaginal practice of coping skills in response to the induction of anxiety. Different variations of this particular strategy have been developed, including anxiety management training (AMT) (Suinn & Richardson, 1971) and self-control desensitization (Goldfried, 1971). In AMT, for example, patients are taught to exert voluntary control over their anxiety by learning relaxation, and then practicing these skills in session through a process of guided rehearsal. Specifically, patients are encouraged to visualize anxiety-inducing scenes, experience the anxiety, and then use their relaxation skills to return to a relaxed state. Once they are proficient in reducing their anxiety in session, patients are instructed to practice these techniques in real-life situations.

APPLIED RELAXATION

Although a variety of relaxation strategies have been used in the treatment of GAD, including progressive muscle relaxation and diaphragmatic breathing, applied relaxation (Öst, 1987) has received the most research attention. As with AMT, applied relaxation was not specifically designed for the treatment of GAD (it was in fact developed to treat phobias), but the technique was seen as ideal for GAD, given its applicability to nonsituational, general anxiety. Applied relaxation involves the gradual skill acquisition of increasingly shorter, and more portable, relaxation strategies. The goal is to ultimately use a 20- to 30-second relaxation technique whenever symptoms of anxiety arise in daily life. Patients are first instructed to monitor their anxiety throughout the day, in order to become proficient at recognizing early signs of incipient anxiety. They are then taught a series of progressively shorter relaxation techniques, beginning with progressive muscle relaxation (the tense and release of major muscle groups), and eventually moving through to rapid relaxation (relaxing in 20–30 seconds) and application training (using rapid relaxation in real-life anxious situations).

STIMULUS CONTROL

This therapeutic intervention involves training GAD patients to postpone their worries when they occur, focus on present-moment experience at that time, and schedule a specific time later in the day when they will worry (see Borkovec, Wilkinson, Folensbee, & Lerman, 1983). The rationale for this strategy is that worry can be triggered by a wide range of environmental circumstances representing a vague fear of future negative outcome possibilities, and is therefore under poor stimulus control. As such, by scheduling a specific time to worry, patients are establishing increased control over its occurrence. Of the three common behavioral techniques described herein, stimulus control is the only treatment strategy that was expressly designed for GAD, based on a specific theory of worry (i.e., poor stimulus control).

COGNITIVE THERAPY

Although there is variability in the way cognitive therapy is used in the treatment of GAD, most protocols have incorporated the work of Beck and Emery (1985), which outlines the following steps: (1) enhancing self-awareness by having patients monitor their thoughts; (2) correcting faulty thinking patterns by encouraging patients to question the evidence for their thoughts; and (3) generating alternative interpretations that take into account a more realistic appraisal of a given situation. Although these steps are not specific to any particular disorder, in terms of GAD, challenging probability estimations and decatastrophizing are the most commonly used cognitive interventions (e.g., Zinbarg, Craske, & Barlow, 2006). Patients are encouraged to reassess the likelihood of a particular feared event (from high probability to low probability), and to develop the worst-case scenario for specific worries in order to evaluate whether a feared event is truly *catastrophic* and whether patients have the ability to cope with the event should it occur.

Rationale for Generalist Treatments

It is evident from the above description of early psychological treatments for GAD that the interventions largely reflect the treatment of "general anxious arousal" rather than the disorder of GAD itself. That is, the therapeutic strategies used were primarily designed to address the pervasive experience of anxiety, rather than the specific processes that might have led to its development and maintenance (with the possible exception of stimulus control). As will be elaborated upon later, the efficacy of these interventions was not optimal, particularly in comparison to the success of CBT for other anxiety disorders (e.g., Clark, 1996). The use of general CBT strategies in the treatment of a specific anxiety disorder such as GAD appears to be the product of several factors, which will now be briefly discussed.

SHIFTING DIAGNOSTIC CRITERIA

Generalized anxiety disorder is unique among the anxiety disorders, as it has only been a diagnosable disorder in the last 25 years, and it has undergone several transformations through successive editions of the *DSM*. When GAD was first introduced into the *DSM–III* (APA, 1980), it was essentially viewed as a residual disorder that could only be diagnosed in the *absence* of other anxiety disorders. In addition, its symptoms were quite vague; a diagnosis of GAD required "persistent anxiety" for at least 1 month and a host of somatic symptoms. The primary feature of GAD later shifted from persistent anxiety to excessive or unrealistic worry with the publication of the *DSM–III–R* (APA, 1987). Although this incarnation of the disorder more closely approximated the current conceptualization of GAD, multiple somatic symptoms were still required for a diagnosis, and the criteria of "unrealistic worry" maintained a qualitative difference between clinical and nonclinical worry. It was not until the advent of the *DSM–IV* (APA, 1994) that the diagnostic criteria for GAD became streamlined, and began to adequately reflect the clinical reality of excessive and uncontrollable worry about daily life events.

The byproduct of these changes to the conceptualization of GAD was that a treatment focus was particularly difficult to establish. For example, a shift from "persistent anxiety" to "excessive worry" as the hallmark of GAD was essentially a change from an emotional/physiological focus to a more cognitive one. It is therefore not surprising that CBT for GAD has incorporated a variety of therapeutic components that might globally be expected to only partially reduce the evolving, and largely abstract, symptomatology of the disorder.

WORRY AS A VAGUE PRIMARY SYMPTOM

A second difficulty with the treatment of GAD lies in its fundamental feature: excessive worry about daily life events. Unlike other anxiety disorders, where there is typically a circumscribed stimulus or trigger to the experience of anxiety (e.g., panic attacks in panic disorder), there is none for GAD. In fact, many GAD patients will report worrying about "everything." Specific CBT interventions such as in-vivo or imaginal exposure to feared situations do not therefore lend themselves as easily to the treatment of GAD. Not only would a myriad of feared situations be required for exposure given the varied nature of GAD worry, but the worries themselves can involve a vague fear about potential future negative events that is incompatible with exposure. As a result, the focus of treatment becomes one of attempting to manage anxious arousal whenever and wherever it arises, rather than addressing the specific fear structure that underlies it.

LACK OF GAD-SPECIFIC RESEARCH

A final noteworthy challenge to the effective treatment of GAD is the lack of research on the disorder itself, and the specific processes that might be related to its development. In reviews of popular research databases, GAD was found to be among the three most infrequently studied anxiety disorders from 1981 to 1992 (Cox, Wessel, Norton, Swinson, & Direnfeld, 1995; Norton, Cox, Asmundson, & Maser, 1995). In an extension of this research to include publications up to 1997, similar findings also emerged (Dugas, 2000). Moreover, an analysis of the content of research inquiry uncovered that the great majority of articles focused on descriptive (e.g., epidemiology, clinical features) and treatment issues (e.g., treatment outcome, psychotherapy, pharmacology). Research devoted to processes involved in GAD, such as etiology and the specific characteristics of the disorder, comprised between 9% and 11% of articles. The preponderance of treatment studies over investigations into the form and function of GAD can be construed as adding to our general knowledge of the disorder, but not the nature of the disorder itself. In addition, it necessarily assumes a lack of disorder-specific treatment protocols, given the small amount of research into processes explicitly linked to GAD.

Disorder-Specific Evidence-Based Treatments for GAD

In contrast to the generalist approaches, several research teams have been developing GAD-specific theoretical formulations in an attempt to understand the factors that contribute to the genesis of the disorder. It is hypothesized that treatment protocols derived from a disorder-specific formulation will more efficaciously target the processes that underlie a given condition, hence providing superior treatment outcomes. In the following section, we will review several of the current therapeutic protocols that have been developed in this fashion. Given that the theoretical models that underlie many of these treatments have already been expanded upon in Chapter 17, this section will primarily be limited to an elaboration of the treatment strategies.

CBT TARGETING AVOIDANCE

The earliest seminal work on GAD and the role of worry was conducted by Thomas Borkovec in the 1980s. Using basic and applied research, Borkovec and colleagues formulated an avoidance theory of worry, wherein worry is viewed as an attempt to avoid potential threats in the future, as well as aversive emotional experiences (see Borkovec, Alcaine, & Behar, 2004). A treatment package was later developed, and although it incorporated many of the CBT strategies elaborated upon earlier, the majority of the therapeutic components were amended in accordance with the avoidance theory of worry. Specifically, the treatment protocol was devised with an emphasis on "present-moment" experience, rather than the future orientation typical of GAD patients. As such, Borkovec's CBT protocol targeting avoidance will be briefly reviewed here.

Four main treatment components are included in the protocol: (1) awareness and self-monitoring; (2) relaxation; (3) cognitive therapy; and (4) imagery rehearsal of coping strategies (see Borkovec, 2006, for review). In terms of the first component, the purpose of this intervention is to assist patients in becoming more proficient at recognizing both their anxiety triggers and their dysfunctional reactions to these triggers. However, the focus in Borkovec's treatment is also to increase patient awareness of present-moment experience by consistently drawing attention to the fact that anxiety is typically triggered by past or future-oriented thoughts, which would not occur if the individual were focused instead on the present moment. A similar temporal orientation is also drawn into the instruction of relaxation. Patients are encouraged to use relaxation when feeling anxious, yet also in everyday situations, in order to become more familiar with a state of tranquility and calm in the present moment. One of the substantive changes to the cognitive therapy component is the inclusion of *expectancy-free living* as a desired goal. That is, rather than continually attempting to correct faulty expectations about future events, an eventual goal of treatment is to help patients refrain from forming any expectations about a given

situation. Borkovec asserts that given the selective attention and disconfirmatory bias that valenced expectations can engender, being expectancy-free will allow for a more accurate appraisal of a given situation, as well as further encourage the notion of living in the present moment. The final treatment component of imagery rehearsal, described earlier in the chapter, was not specifically altered to address "present-moment" experience.

CBT TARGETING INTOLERANCE OF UNCERTAINTY

Dugas and colleagues developed a protocol based on an empirically driven cognitive model of GAD that posits a primary role for intolerance of uncertainty (IU) in the development and maintenance of the disorder (see Dugas & Robichaud, 2007, for a detailed description of the model and protocol). Specifically, it is asserted that individuals with GAD are highly intolerant of any uncertainty in their lives, which subsequently leads them to worry in an attempt to think about, and plan for, any possible eventuality (i.e., "What if X happens? Well, then I could . . ."). However, given that life is necessarily fraught with uncertainty (i.e., no one can know for certain what will happen in the future), individuals with GAD are repeatedly triggered to worry throughout the day, leading to excessive and uncontrollable worry about an ever-changing series of daily events. The primary target in treatment is therefore to assist patients in becoming more tolerant of the uncertainties in life in order to reduce worries to a more manageable level.

The protocol developed by Dugas and colleagues includes four primary treatment modules: (1) uncertainty recognition and behavioral exposure; (2) reevaluation of the usefulness of worry; (3) problem-solving training; and (4) imaginal exposure. Each treatment strategy was designed to address IU either directly or indirectly, and was incorporated into the protocol based on both clinical and nonclinical research substantiating the role of each corresponding component of the cognitive model of GAD (see Koerner & Dugas, 2006, for review). In the first step of treatment, patients are introduced to the concept of IU, the futility of seeking certainty in life, and the time-consuming consequence of this process, as IU engenders a series of coping behaviors that ultimately serve to maintain worry in the long-term. These IU-driven behaviors involve either approaching a given situation in order to eliminate all the uncertain elements (e.g., excessive reassurance) or avoiding an uncertain situation altogether due to its inherent aversiveness (e.g., procrastination). The goal in this first treatment module is to learn to act "as if" one is tolerant of uncertainty, by conducting behavioral experiments where the patient deliberately drops these coping behaviors and tolerates the uncertainty. In the second treatment module, patients are encouraged to acknowledge, and ultimately challenge, the positive beliefs they hold about the usefulness of worry. Positive beliefs about worries tend to fall into five categories, reflecting the beliefs that worrying (1) helps to find solutions to problems; (2) serves a motivating function that ensures that things will get done; (3) can protect from negative emotions; (4) can, in and of itself, prevent negative outcomes; and (5) represents a positive personality trait (Francis & Dugas, 2004). Helping patients to evaluate whether their worries are in fact beneficial is viewed as essential in order to address any ambivalence in treatment.

The remaining treatment modules are designed to provide patients with alternative, more functional, methods of dealing with their concerns, other than through worry. Early on in treatment patients are taught to distinguish between worries that deal with current problems and worries about hypothetical situations, as each worry type is addressed with a specific treatment intervention. For worries about actual current problems, a problem-solving approach is used. Patients are first taught how to improve their problem orientation, that is, to change their negative beliefs about problems and their own problem-solving ability. This is accomplished in several ways, including helping patients to view the relative threat and opportunity of problems on a dimensional, rather than a categorical, level. Patients are encouraged to find the opportunity, or challenge, within a given problematic situation in order to make problem solving less aversive. In addition, the steps to effective problem solving are introduced and practiced both in and out of session. Problem solving is presented as a more action-oriented approach to difficulties, in contrast to worry, which largely involves thinking about problems rather than solving them. The final module of treatment addresses worries about hypothetical situations. Given that one has no control over future events, and that a particular feared outcome might never actually occur, problem solving would be an inappropriate strategy for this type of worry. Instead, patients are taught to process their core fears through imaginal exposure. Research has shown that worry primarily takes the form of verbal-linguistic thoughts rather than mental images, which ultimately decreases physiological arousal and prevents emotional processing (see Sibrava & Borkovec, 2006). As such, patients are instructed to write an exposure script for a frequent worry topic in as much visual and sensory detail as possible, and to conduct daily imaginal exposures to the script until distress levels surrounding the topic are reduced, and the fear has been processed.

It is noteworthy that the protocol does not include interventions that directly address the somatic symptoms associated with GAD. Rather, it is expected that anxiety levels will drop as a result of greater tolerance for uncertainty and reduced worry. Moreover, cognitive techniques such as probability estimation are deliberately not employed. Since intolerance of uncertainty is viewed as the primary force behind GAD worry, patients are expected to react with worry and anxiety to *any* uncertain situation, even when a negative outcome is extremely unlikely. As such, working with patients to help them see that most feared events are highly unlikely would not be particularly beneficial. If patients' intolerance of uncertainty is not addressed, so long as there is any possibility that a feared event could occur, then they would be expected to perseverate in their worries.

METACOGNITIVE THERAPY

Adrian Wells developed a disorder-specific treatment protocol based on a cognitive model of GAD that gives primacy to an individual's beliefs about worry (Wells, 2006a, 2006b). Wells's metacognitive therapy (MCT) is based on the theory that GAD worry develops as a function of both the positive and negative beliefs about worry that patients hold. Briefly, individuals begin worrying due to their positive beliefs about the utility of worry, and stop when a resolution to the particular worry is achieved. As such, the presence of positive beliefs about worry is not necessarily pathological, although it is viewed as potentially inhibiting more adaptive coping behaviors. However, GAD worry is characterized by the addition of negative beliefs about worry (i.e., worry is dangerous and uncontrollable), which subsequently leads to meta-worry (worrying about the act of worry), making it difficult to achieve a resolution to the worry cycle, and thus leading to chronic and excessive worry. The goal of MCT is therefore to modify patients' *beliefs about worry,* rather than address the worries themselves (i.e., worry about daily life events).

The protocol for MCT comprises the following five major components: (1) case formulation; (2) socialization to treatment; (3) modifying negative beliefs about the uncontrollability of worry; (4) modifying beliefs about the danger of worry; and (5) modifying positive beliefs about worry. Given that patients will have their own particular beliefs about the costs and benefits of worry, the first stage of treatment involves the development of an idiographic case formulation, in order to place a patient's specific worry pattern into a pictorial model. The model includes an individual's specific beliefs, Type I (worries about daily life events) and Type II (meta-worry) worries, and the resultant emotional (e.g., anxiety), behavioral (e.g., reassurance-seeking), and cognitive (e.g., thought suppression) consequences thereof. The second module, socialization to treatment, involves presenting the idiographic model to patients, orienting them toward the treatment target of beliefs about worry, and underscoring the ineffectiveness of current coping behaviors. The remainder of treatment is subsequently directed toward modifying beliefs, chiefly through the use of cognitive challenges and selected behavioral experiments. In terms of modifying beliefs about the uncontrollability of worry, examples of strategies include reviewing the evidence for and against the beliefs, engaging in worry postponement to highlight how worry can in fact be controlled, and deliberately worrying to see whether it becomes uncontrollable. Danger metacognitions are similarly addressed with cognitive challenges and behavioral experiments, as well as psychoeducation about the anxiety response. Throughout MCT, patients are repeatedly asked to rate the strength of their negative metacognitions, with experiments being repeated and refined until a belief rating of zero is endorsed. In the final major step of treatment, positive beliefs about worry are modified using several specific cognitive strategies. For example, using a mismatch strategy, patients are instructed to document the disparity between feared and actual outcomes in order to underscore the fact that worry might not be particularly useful or accurate. In addition, patients conduct worry modulation experiments, wherein they alternate days of increasing or reducing worry in order to record whether positive outcomes actually occur with greater frequency on high worry days.

As with CBT targeting IU, MCT does not include any therapeutic interventions designed to reduce somatic symptoms, since anxious arousal is viewed as a consequence of higher-order processes (in this case, negative metacognitions about worry). It is therefore expected that reductions in anxiety will occur once negative and positive worry appraisals are modified. Moreover, MCT does not incor-

porate cognitive challenging strategies designed to address distortions in the content of daily worry (Type I worry) itself, as is typically seen in many earlier CBT protocols. Rather, the contention in the metacognitive model is that the development and maintenance of GAD occurs as a result of Type II meta-worry, and it is at this process level that treatment should be directed in order to obtain an optimal therapeutic outcome (Wells, 1999).

INTEGRATIVE PSYCHOTHERAPIES

In recent years, several researchers have begun developing integrative psychotherapies for the treatment of GAD that include both existing treatment strategies and novel interventions derived from basic and clinical research. Many of these integrative treatments have incorporated therapeutic components typically used in theoretical orientations other than CBT, such as psychodynamic and interpersonal approaches. The overarching logic of these integrational protocols is that current CBT packages for GAD have to date shown only modest treatment effects, and that additional therapeutic components might significantly improve outcomes. The following is therefore a brief review of two of the major integrative psychotherapies that have been elaborated upon in recent years.

Interpersonal/Emotional Processing. Borkovec and colleagues developed an integrative treatment that involves the addition of interpersonal/psychodynamic strategies for improving problematic relationship patterns and facilitating emotional deepening to the existing CBT protocol (Newman, Castonguay, Borkovec, & Molnar, 2004). The rationale for the integration of an interpersonal/emotional processing (I/EP) component is based on several disparate research findings related to interpersonal issues and emotional processing in GAD. In terms of the former, the authors note that patients with GAD often have comorbid social anxiety disorder, frequently worry about interpersonal problems, and score higher than clinical norms on inventories of interpersonal problems. In relation to emotional processing, research on the avoidance theory of worry suggests that GAD patients worry in order to avoid experiencing negative emotions. As such, the inclusion of an I/EP component to treatment was deemed appropriate, given the apparent role of both processes, and would likely enhance the treatment efficacy of CBT alone.

Borrowing from Safran and Segal's (1990) work on interpersonal process in therapy, I/EP integrative psychotherapy involves helping patients to expose themselves to feared emotions, feared critical feedback in interpersonal situations, and fears of being vulnerable, spontaneous, and open with others. These treatment goals are addressed in the second part of 2-hour therapy sessions, wherein the first hour is devoted to standard CBT interventions and the second hour to I/EP. In order to address problematic relationships, the emphasis is placed on exploring current and past relationships and teaching patients alternative ways to handle social interactions, including the provision of social skills training. Clinicians are also encouraged to make use of the patient-therapist relationship to become aware of patients' maladaptive interpersonal behaviors, which is consistent with a psychodynamic orientation of monitoring any transference or countertransference issues. Emotional deepening is addressed through a variety of experiential strategies, where patients are encouraged to express and deepen any unprocessed emotions. One example of an experiential intervention is the "empty chair" exercise, where patients are instructed to express their feelings regarding an unresolved issue by imagining that the other person is sitting in a chair facing them.

Acceptance and Mindfulness. Another integrative approach to the treatment of GAD involves the inclusion of therapeutic strategies derived from acceptance and commitment therapy (ACT) (Hayes, Strosahl, & Wilson, 1999) and dialectical behavior therapy (DBT) (Linehan, 1993). Orsillo and colleagues (2003) developed an integrational protocol based on a rationale that is similar to the underlying logic of I/EP integrative psychotherapy. Specifically, they noted that given the experiential avoidance and restricted range of autonomic responses characteristic of GAD, a protocol that incorporated the acceptance and experience of emotion would be appropriate. The treatment employs ACT interventions by encouraging patients to make choices that are consistent with valued life directions, which often entails experiencing largely avoided emotions and internal experiences. Moreover, mindfulness, the therapeutic stance of observing one's internal and external state in the present moment without judgment, is also incorporated into the protocol, and is taken from the mindfulness strategies used in DBT for borderline personality disorder. This integrational protocol also draws from Borkovec's CBT model targeting avoidance with the presentation of a model of anxiety and worry, as well as somatic management training (e.g., diaphragmatic breathing).

Review of GAD Treatment Efficacy
Efficacy of Generalist Treatment Interventions

Since the first appearance of GAD in the *DSM*, many treatment outcome studies have been conducted in an attempt to find the most efficacious protocol for the disorder's treatment. Most of the earlier investigations compared the efficacy of behavior therapy (BT), cognitive therapy (CT), and CBT to either a control condition or another active treatment in order to extract the most beneficial treatment components. What has constituted BT, CT, and CBT has varied across studies; however, BT typically comprises some form of relaxation or anxiety-management training, while CT makes use of the various cognitive challenging interventions developed by Beck and Emery (1985), and CBT involves a combination thereof. In terms of the efficacy of the different treatments, a meta-analytic review of 13 outcome studies found that CBT was significantly superior to: (1) no treatment in all studies; (2) nonspecific or alternate treatments in 82% and 78% of the comparisons at posttreatment and follow-up, respectively; and (3) BT or CT in 20% and 43% of the comparisons at posttreatment and follow-up, respectively. Moreover, CBT resulted in the largest effect sizes overall in terms of improvement on measures of anxiety and depression at posttreatment and at follow-up (Borkovec & Ruscio, 2001). The authors concluded that CBT for GAD provides a significant therapeutic benefit in both the short- and long-term, and that it is occasionally superior to its component elements (i.e., BT and CT).

Although these results are promising, and ultimately led to CBT being deemed a valid empirical intervention for the treatment of GAD (Chambless et al., 1998), a different pattern of findings has emerged when treatment outcome is evaluated using an index of clinically significant change. Using the criterion of high end-state functioning, which was defined by either a posttreatment score that fell within one standard deviation of normative samples or a score that exceeded a face-valid level of meaningful change for measures without norms, Borkovec and Costello (1993) found that CBT led to meaningful change in 26.3% of participants at posttreatment and 57.9% at 1-year follow-up. These findings were replicated in later investigations, with CBT consistently resulting in clinically significant change in approximately half of patients (Borkovec, Newman, Pincus, & Lytle, 2002; Fisher & Durham, 1999). Considering that indices of meaningful change are notably higher for CBT in other anxiety disorders, for example, clinically significant improvement from CBT for panic disorder is between 80%–85% (Clark, 1996), the salutary effects of psychotherapy for GAD can be improved upon. Moreover, these results highlight how the recent investigations into disorder-specific models of GAD and their corresponding treatment packages are necessary in order to ultimately achieve superior overall treatment effects.

Efficacy of Disorder-Specific Treatment Protocols for GAD

Many of the disorder-specific treatments elaborated upon herein were only recently developed, and as a result few clinical outcome studies have as yet been published, although several clinical trials are currently underway. The following section will therefore briefly review the available outcome data, as well as some of the preliminary uncontrolled results uncovered so far.

COMPLETED OUTCOME RESEARCH

Borkovec's CBT targeting avoidance package has undergone several controlled investigations, and has been compared to nondirective treatment, BT, and CT. In addition, research has been conducted to determine whether lengthening treatment time would enhance therapeutic outcome (Borkovec & Costello, 1993; Borkovec et al., 2002). In general, CBT was superior to nondirective treatment, and at least as efficacious as BT and CT. However, as noted previously, high end-state functioning was only achieved for approximately half of GAD patients, and this result was unchanged even when treatment was lengthened. As such, although this treatment protocol leads to significant improvement of GAD symptoms, it has not yet achieved an ideal level of efficacy.

The CBT protocol targeting IU developed by Dugas and colleagues has also undergone several clinical investigations. In terms of the efficacy of the treatment when compared to waitlist control, statistically significant between-group differences (with superior outcomes in the treatment group) were found on all symptom measures at posttreatment, in both individual and group formats (Dugas, Ladouceur, Léger, Freeston et al., 2003; Ladouceur et al., 2000). Moreover, 65% and 60% of GAD patients met treatment responder status, and 62% and 65% attained high end-state functioning, in individual and group treatment, respectively. These gains were largely maintained over time, with 58% of patients retaining high end-state functioning 1 year following individual treatment, and 66% continuing to report high end-state functioning 1 year after group

treatment. Finally, in terms of GAD diagnostic criteria, the majority of participants (77%) no longer met *DSM–IV* diagnostic criteria for GAD following individual treatment. A similar pattern emerged for group treatment, with the percentages of participants no longer meeting criteria increasing over time (60% at posttreatment, 83% at 1-year follow-up, and 95% at 2-year follow-up). Currently, a randomized clinical trial comparing this treatment protocol to applied relaxation is underway. At present, results suggest that CBT targeting IU is superior to applied relaxation, and this has emerged in terms of GAD diagnostic remission rates (70% versus 55%) and effect sizes for change in overall severity of GAD ($d' = 2.4$ versus $d' = 1.4$; Dugas et al., 2004).

PRELIMINARY RESULTS

Metacognitive Therapy. The MCT protocol developed by Wells is currently being evaluated in a controlled clinical trial; however, results from an initial open trial have already yielded promising results (Wells & King, 2006). Specifically, among 10 patients meeting *DSM–IV* GAD criteria who received three to twelve MCT sessions, significant reductions were reported on measures of anxiety, worry, and depressed mood, with large effect sizes ranging from 1.2 to 2.9. Further, a high number of patients met criteria for clinically meaningful change, both at posttreatment (87.5%) and at 1-year follow-up (75%), and the initial data from a randomized trial comparing MCT to applied relaxation have yielded similar results, with MCT producing 80% recovery rates on measures of trait anxiety and worry. These findings, although highly promising, are still currently tentative, as only 10 GAD patients were included in the analyses to date (see Fisher, 2006).

Integrative Psychotherapies. Borkovec's and colleagues I/EP integrational psychotherapy is currently being subjected to clinical investigation to determine whether the addition of an I/EP component to the CBT protocol targeting avoidance would improve treatment efficacy. Participants receive either CBT plus I/EP or CBT with the addition of a supportive listening component, thereby allowing for the assessment of any possible therapeutic benefit to I/EP, over and above the addition of increased therapy time. Data from this investigation are still currently being gathered; however, tentative results suggest that the addition of I/EP to existing CBT packages does improve treatment outcome. Using the results of 18 participants who met *DSM–IV* diagnostic criteria for GAD and received 15 2-hour sessions of CBT plus

I/EP, Newman et al. (2004) uncovered therapeutic change on several measures. Within-group effect sizes were favorable when compared to those of a prior study evaluating a comprehensive CBT protocol (Borkovec et al., 2002) both at posttreatment ($d' = 2.9$ for CBT + I/EP versus $d' = 2.2$ for CBT) and at 1-year follow-up ($d' = 2.7$ versus $d' = 1.9$). Although these results are quite promising, the tentative nature of the findings should be underscored, as the additive therapeutic benefit of I/EP strategies to the treatment of GAD, when compared to a treatment time and therapeutic contact controlled group, has yet to be determined.

The integrational protocol developed by Orsillo et al. (2003) has also yielded positive preliminary findings in a case series and an open trial. Four participants meeting *DSM–IV* GAD diagnostic criteria received 10 2-hour group sessions of an integrative psychotherapy utilizing acceptance-based and mindfulness techniques. At posttreatment, participants were found to display significant reductions on measures of worry, anxiety, and depression compared to pretreatment. In addition, 75% of the sample met criteria for treatment response and 50% reached high end-state functioning at posttreatment. The authors reported that all four participants made significant positive life changes despite the fact that only half achieved clinically meaningful change. In a subsequent open trial including 16 patients with GAD (Roemer & Orsillo, 2007), 75% of patients were classified as responders (62.5% met criteria for high end-state functioning) at posttreatment, and 50% were classified as responders at 3-month follow-up (with 50% meeting criteria for high end-state functioning, based on a conservative estimate). Patients reported significant reductions in clinician-rated and self-reported GAD symptoms, as well as reductions in associated symptoms (e.g., depression, tendency to avoid internal experiences). Further controlled studies are needed to determine the effectiveness of this treatment, relative to more established treatments.

Future Directions

Although new and exciting psychological interventions have been developed for the treatment of GAD, it still remains a disorder for which the theoretical understanding and resultant treatment lag behind those seen in other anxiety disorders. Many of the current GAD-specific protocols are highly promising; however, as is evident from the influx of integrational interventions, GAD researchers are still striving to refine and improve upon existing treatments in order to raise the efficacy of GAD

treatment to an acceptable level. The following section will therefore briefly review some new areas of inquiry that might hold promise for the enhanced treatment of GAD.

MOTIVATIONAL INTERVIEWING

An intriguing potential addition to existing CBT interventions for GAD is motivational interviewing (MI). Based on Prochaska and DiClemente's (1984) stages of change model, MI is an intervention designed to address treatment ambivalence and resistance by reflecting these feelings back and validating them, rather than confronting patients (Moyers & Rollnick, 2002). Recently, MI strategies have been incorporated into CBT for various anxiety disorders to determine whether the inclusion of MI would reduce resistance and increase homework compliance and engagement in treatment (Westra, 2004). As noted by the author, this adjunctive therapeutic component might be particularly beneficial for the treatment of GAD for several reasons. First, the theoretical formulations underlying both CBT targeting IU and MCT posit that GAD patients hold positive beliefs about the function of worry (Koerner & Dugas, 2006; Wells, 2006b). If patients believe that their worries are somehow beneficial to them, resistance to the therapeutic goal of reducing worry would be expected. Second, in our own research team's clinical trials, the only common therapy factor that significantly predicted outcome was patient motivation (see Dugas, Ladouceur, Léger, Langlois, et al., 2003). If poor treatment motivation and ambivalence about change do in fact play a role in current GAD recovery rates, then MI might be a beneficial addition to existing protocols, although further research will need to be conducted with samples of GAD patients before any conclusions can be drawn.

WRITTEN EMOTIONAL DISCLOSURE

Another exciting area of research into potential treatment strategies for GAD relates to written emotional disclosure. Originally developed by Pennebaker (1997) as an intervention that could lead to improvements in physical health, written emotional disclosure involves asking individuals to write about stressful or traumatic events. The intervention was subsequently used with PTSD patients, and results suggested that it had a positive impact on psychological health, as the severity of PTSD symptoms were significantly reduced following three written emotional disclosure sessions (Sloan, Marx, & Epstein, 2005). Recently, the specific applicability of this therapeutic strategy to worry has become a subject of research. Borkovec, Roemer, and Kinyon (1995) have conceptualized emotional disclosure as an opposing process to worry, since one leads to the resolution of negative emotional experience and the other perpetuates emotional disturbance, despite the fact that they both involve verbal-linguistic mental activity. In fact, they propose that similar to the traumatic coping strategy of cognitively shifting to a "lower level of analysis" (e.g., focusing on daily chores), worry is an example of low-level thinking, given its focus on minor matters and daily events. As such, written emotional disclosure might be particularly beneficial to the treatment of GAD. Our own research team has begun testing a written emotional disclosure paradigm adapted for worry, using non-clinical high worriers, and preliminary results have shown a reduction in worry, GAD somatic symptoms, and depression among participants writing about a feared outcome (Goldman, Dugas, Sexton, & Gervais, 2007). Additional research will need to be conducted with GAD patients, however, to determine whether the procedure might ultimately enhance current treatment outcomes.

Summary and Conclusions

In recent years there has been a great deal of progress in our understanding and treatment of the complex disorder of GAD. New treatment interventions based on specific models of the disorder have emerged, and early results suggest that the overall effectiveness of psychotherapy for GAD is progressively being enhanced. Moreover, new research directions are currently being investigated with the goal of further ameliorating these existing treatments. Despite this, the study of GAD can still be considered a burgeoning field, as our understanding of the disorder pales in comparison to the detailed analysis of processes underlying other anxiety disorders. Moreover, there is to date no ideal or universally accepted psychotherapy for GAD, as recovery rates for the disorder have remained moderate. However, given the promise that GAD researchers have shown in their innovative conceptualization and treatment of the disorder, it is realistic to believe that the recent strides in our ability to deal with GAD will continue to increase over time.

References

American Psychiatric Association. (1980). *Diagnostic and statistical manual of mental disorders* (3rd ed.). Washington, DC: Author.

American Psychiatric Association. (1987). *Diagnostic and statistical manual of mental disorders* (3rd ed. rev.). Washington, DC: Author.

American Psychiatric Association. (1994). *Diagnostic and statistical manual of mental disorders* (4th ed.). Washington, DC: Author.

Barrett, J., Oxman, T. E., & Gerber, P. D. (1988). The prevalence of psychiatric disorders in primary care practice. *Archives of General Psychiatry, 45,* 1100–1106.

Beck, A. T., & Emery, G. (1985). *Anxiety disorders and phobias: A cognitive perspective.* New York: Basic Books.

Blazer, D. G., Hughes, D., George, L. K., Schwartz, M., & Boyer, R. (1991). Generalized anxiety disorder. In L. N. Robins & D. A. Regier (Eds.), *Psychiatric disorders in America: The Epidemiologic Catchment Area Study* (pp. 180–203). New York: Free Press.

Borkovec, T. D. (2006). Applied relaxation and cognitive therapy for pathological worry and generalized anxiety disorder. In G.C.L. Davey & A. Wells (Eds.), *Worry and its psychological disorders: Theory, assessment and treatment* (pp. 273–287). Chichester, England: Wiley.

Borkovec, T. D., Alcaine, O. M., & Behar, E. (2004). Avoidance theory of worry and generalized anxiety disorder. In R. G. Heimberg, C. L. Turk, & D. S. Mennin (Eds.), *Generalized anxiety disorder: Advances in treatment and practice* (pp. 77–108). New York: Guilford Press.

Borkovec, T. D., & Costello, E. (1993). Efficacy of applied relaxation and cognitive-behavioral therapy in the treatment of generalized anxiety disorder. *Journal of Consulting and Clinical Psychology, 61,* 611–619.

Borkovec, T. D., Newman, M. G., Pincus, A. L., & Lytle, R. (2002). A component analysis of cognitive-behavioral therapy for generalized anxiety disorder and the role of interpersonal problems. *Journal of Consulting and Clinical Psychology, 70,* 288–298.

Borkovec, T. D., Roemer, L., & Kinyon, J. (1995). Disclosure and worry: Opposite sides of the emotional processing coin. In J. W. Pennebaker (Ed.), *Emotion, disclosure, and health* (pp. 47–70). Washington, DC: American Psychological Association.

Borkovec, T. D., & Ruscio, A. M. (2001). Psychotherapy for generalized anxiety disorder. *Journal of Clinical Psychiatry, 62,* 37–42.

Borkovec, T. D., Wilkinson, L., Folensbee, R., & Lerman, C. (1983). Stimulus control applications to the treatment of worry. *Behaviour Research and Therapy, 21,* 247–251.

Chambless, D. L., Baker, M. J., Baucom, D. H., Beutler, L. E., Calhoun, K. S., Crits-Christoph, P., et al. (1998). Update on empirically validated therapies: II. *The Clinical Psychologist, 51,* 3–15.

Clark, M. M. (1996). Panic disorder: From theory to therapy. In P. M. Salkovskis (Ed.), *Frontiers of cognitive therapy* (pp. 318–344). New York: Guilford Press.

Cox, B. J., Wessel, I., Norton, G. R., Swinson, R. P., & Direnfeld, D. M. (1995). Publication trends in anxiety disorders research: 1990–1992. *Journal of Anxiety Disorders, 9,* 531–538.

Dugas, M. J. (2000). Generalized anxiety disorder publications: So where do we stand? *Journal of Anxiety Disorders, 14,* 31–40.

Dugas, M. J., Ladouceur, R., Léger, E., Freeston, M. H., Langlois, F., Provencher, M. D., et al. (2003). Group cognitive-behavioral therapy for generalized anxiety disorder: Treatment outcome and long-term follow-up. *Journal of Consulting and Clinical Psychology, 71,* 821–825.

Dugas, M. J., Ladouceur, R., Léger, E., Langlois, F., Provencher, M. D., Boisvert, J.-M., et al. (2003, November). *Group CBT for generalized anxiety disorder: Does change in tolerance for uncertainty predict symptom change beyond non-specific therapy factors?* Poster session presented at the annual convention of the Association for Advancement of Behavior Therapy, Boston, MA.

Dugas, M. J., & Robichaud, M. (2007). *The cognitive-behavioral treatment of generalized anxiety disorder: From science to practice.* New York: Routledge.

Dugas, M. J., Savard, P., Gaudet, A., Turcotte, J., Brillon, P., Leblanc, R., et al. (2004, November). Cognitive-behavioral therapy *versus* applied relaxation for generalized anxiety disorder: Differential outcomes and processes. In H. Hazlett-Stevens (Chair), *New advances in the treatment of chronic worry and generalized anxiety disorder.* Symposium conducted at the annual convention of the Association for Advancement of Behavior Therapy, New Orleans, LA.

Fisher, P. L. (2006). The efficacy of psychological treatments for generalised anxiety disorder? In G.C.L. Davey & A. Wells (Eds.), *Worry and its psychological disorders: Theory, assessment, and treatment* (pp. 359–377). Chichester, England: Wiley.

Fisher, P. L., & Durham, R. C. (1999). Recovery rates in generalized anxiety disorder following psychological therapy: An analysis of clinically significant change in the STAI-T across outcome studies since 1990. *Psychological Medicine, 29,* 1425–1434.

Francis, K., & Dugas, M. J. (2004). Assessing positive beliefs about worry: Validation of a structured interview. *Personality and Individual Differences, 37,* 405–415.

Goldfried, M. R. (1971). Systematic desensitization as training in self-control. *Journal of Consulting and Clinical Psychology, 37,* 228–234.

Goldman, N., Dugas, M. J., Sexton, K. A., & Gervais, N. J. (2007). The impact of written exposure on worry: A preliminary investigation. *Behavior Modification, 31,* 512–538.

Greenberg, P. E., Sisitsky, T., Kessler, R. C., Finkelstein, S. N., Berndt, E. R., Davidson, J.R.T., et al. (1999). The economic burden of anxiety disorders in the 1990s. *Journal of Clinical Psychiatry, 60,* 427–435.

Hayes, S. C., Strosahl, K. D., & Wilson, K. G. (1999). *Acceptance and commitment therapy: An experiential approach to behavior change.* New York: Guilford Press.

Hunt, C., Issakidis, C., & Andrews, G. (2002). DSM–IV generalized anxiety disorder in the Australian National Survey of Mental Health and Well-Being. *Psychological Medicine, 2002,* 649–659.

Koerner, N., & Dugas, M. J. (2006). A cognitive model of generalized anxiety disorder: The role of intolerance of uncertainty. In G.C.L. Davey & A. Wells (Eds.), *Worry and its psychological disorders: Theory, assessment and treatment* (pp. 201–216). Chichester, England: Wiley.

Ladouceur, R., Dugas, M. J., Freeston, M. H., Léger, E., Gagnon, F., & Thibodeau, N. (2000). Efficacy of a cognitive-behavioral treatment for generalized anxiety disorder: Evaluation in a controlled clinical trial. *Journal of Consulting and Clinical Psychology, 68,* 957–964.

Linehan, M. M. (1993). *Skills training manual for cognitive behavioral treatment of borderline personality disorder.* New York: Guilford Press.

Moyers, T. B., & Rollnick, S. (2002). A motivational interviewing perspective on resistance in psychotherapy. *Journal of Clinical Psychology, 58,* 185–194.

Newman, M. G., Castonguay, L. G., Borkovec, T. D., & Molnar, C. (2004). Integrative psychotherapy. In R. G. Heimberg, C. L. Turk, & D. S. Mennin (Eds.), *Generalized anxiety disorder: Advances in research and practice* (pp. 320–350). New York: Guilford Press.

Norton, G. R., Cox, B. J., Asmundson, G.J.G., & Maser, J. D. (1995). The growth of research on anxiety disorders during the 1980s. *Journal of Anxiety Disorders, 9,* 75–85.

Orsillo, S. M., Roemer, L., & Barlow, D. H. (2003). Integrating acceptance and mindfulness into existing cognitive-behavioral treatment for GAD: A case study. *Cognitive and Behavioral Practice, 10,* 222–230.

Öst, L. G. (1987). Applied relaxation: Description of a coping technique and review of controlled studies. *Behaviour Research and Therapy, 25,* 397–409.

Pennebaker, J. W. (1997). Writing about emotional experiences as a therapeutic process. *Psychological Science, 8,* 162–166.

Prochaska, J. O., & DiClemente, C. C. (1984). *The transtheoretical approach: Crossing traditional boundaries of therapy.* Homewood, IL: Dow Jones/Irwin.

Roemer, L., & Orsillo, S. M. (2007). An open trial of an acceptance-based behavior therapy for generalized anxiety disorder. *Behavior Therapy, 38,* 72–85.

Safran, J. D., & Segal, Z. V. (1990). *Interpersonal process in cognitive therapy.* New York: Basic Books.

Sibrava, N. J., & Borkovec, T. D. (2006). The cognitive avoidance theory of worry. In G.C.L. Davey & A. Wells (Eds.), *Worry and its psychological disorders: Theory, assessment, and treatment* (pp. 239–256). Chichester, England: Wiley.

Sloan, D. M., Marx, B. P., & Epstein, E. M. (2005). Further examination of the exposure model underlying the efficacy of written emotional disclosure. *Journal of Consulting and Clinical Psychology, 73,* 549–554.

Stein, M. B., & Heimberg, R. G. (2004). Well-being and life satisfaction in generalized anxiety disorder: Comparison to major depressive disorder in a community sample. *Journal of Affective Disorders, 79,* 161–166.

Suinn, R. M., & Richardson, F. (1971). Anxiety management training: A non-specific behavior therapy program for anxiety control. *Behavior Therapy, 2,* 498–510.

Wells, A. (1999). A metacognitive model and therapy for generalized anxiety disorder. *Clinical Psychology and Psychotherapy, 6,* 86–95.

Wells, A. (2006a). Metacognitive therapy for worry and generalised anxiety disorder. In G.C.L. Davey & A. Wells (Eds.), *Worry and its psychological disorders: Theory, assessment, and treatment* (pp. 259–272). Chichester, England: Wiley.

Wells, A. (2006b). The metacognitive model of worry and generalised anxiety disorder. In G.C.L. Davey & A. Wells (Eds.), *Worry and its psychological disorders: Theory, assessment, and treatment* (pp. 179–199). Chichester, England: Wiley.

Wells, A., & King, P. (2006). Metacognitive therapy for generalized anxiety disorder: An open trial. *Journal of Behavior Therapy and Experimental Psychiatry, 37,* 206–212.

Westra, H. A. (2004). Managing resistance in cognitive behavioural therapy: The application of motivational interviewing in mixed anxiety and depression. *Cognitive Behaviour Therapy, 33,* 161–175.

Wittchen, H.-U., Kessler, R. C., Beesdo, K., Krause, P., Höfler, M., & Hoyer, J. (2002). Generalized anxiety and depression in primary care: Prevalence, recognition, and management. *Journal of Clinical Psychiatry, 63,* 24–34.

Wittchen, H.-U., Zhao, Z., Kessler, R. C., & Eaton, W. W. (1994). DSM–III–R generalized anxiety disorder in the National Comorbidity Survey. *Archives of General Psychiatry, 51,* 355–364.

Zinbarg, R. E., Craske, M. G., & Barlow, D. H. (2006). *Mastery of your anxiety and worry (Therapist guide)* (2nd ed.). New York: Oxford University Press.

Biological Treatment for Obsessive-Compulsive Disorder

S. Evelyn Stewart, Eric Jenike *and* Michael A. Jenike

Abstract

This chapter examines how obsessive-compulsive disorder (OCD) may be effectively treated using biologic approaches. Early recognition and intervention with combined cognitive behavioral and medication therapy limit its subsequent morbidity. Selective serotonin reuptake inhibitors (SSRIs) and clomipramine are central in acute and maintenance pharmacotherapy of OCD, often requiring high dosage. Augmenting agents include low-dose typical and atypical antipsychotic agents, among others. As OCD appears to be a chronic waxing and waning illness, effective medications should be continued for at least 1 to 2 years. Relapse rates tend to be high following medication discontinuation, although a history of cognitive behavioral therapy limits this risk. In severe treatment-refractory cases, surgical and somatic therapies such as deep brain stimulation have been used.

Keywords: deep brain stimulation, medication, obsessive-compulsive disorder, pharmacology, somatic, surgery, treatment

Obsessive-compulsive disorder (OCD) tends to be underdiagnosed and undertreated. As a contributory factor, OCD-affected individuals may be secretive about their illness. Furthermore, many health care providers are not familiar with OCD or are not trained in providing treatment. This is unfortunate, since early diagnosis and treatment can help to avoid OCD-related suffering and lessen the risks of related problems, such as depression and marital or employment difficulties (The Expert Consensus Panel for Obsessive-Compulsive Disorder, 1997). Treatment approaches that help OCD patients include cognitive behavioral therapy (CBT) and medications (Jenike, Baer, & Minichiello, 1998). This chapter covers the medical treatment of OCD by reviewing empirical evidence, which guides subsequent discussion of practical clinical approaches.

To provide a background for OCD treatment, the putative role of neurotransmitters in its patho-physiology will be discussed. Subsequently, the pharmacologic literature will be reviewed with a focus on randomized controlled trials and less studied medications, followed by a description of somatic, nonpharmacologic approaches and long-term outcome. This research review is followed by a practical overview of the pharmacologic treatment of OCD, including when and how to initiate treatment, when to change, augment, or discontinue medication, and treatment in the context of comorbidities and special populations. Resources available for consumers, families, and clinicians are also identified.

Role of Neurotransmitters in OCD

The role of neurotransmitters and neurochemicals in the context of OCD circuitry is not yet fully understood. These are postulated to include serotonin, glutamate, opiates, and selected neuropeptides, among others. However, given the clinical heterogeneity of OCD, it is likely that distinct transmitters or a combination of etiologic agents may be involved in individual OCD subtypes or cases. The *serotonin hypothesis,* suggesting a hypersensitivity of postsynaptic serotonin receptors (Marazziti, 2001) reflects OCD's responsiveness to serotonin reuptake inhibitors (Fineberg, 1996), worsening with serotonin agonists (Hollander et al., 1988), and the association between OCD severity and medication responsiveness with cerebrospinal fluid levels of 5-hydroxyindolacetic acid (Insel, Mueller, Alterman, Linnoila, & Murphy, 1985; Thoren, Asberg, Cronholm, Jornestedt, & Traskman, 1980). Dopamine has been strongly linked to disorders presenting with obsessive-compulsive behavior, such as Tourette's disorder and cocaine use (Marazziti, 2001; McDougle et al., 1990). More recently, lines of study implicate: (1) glutamatergic neurotransmission (Chakrabarty, Bhattacharyya, Christopher, & Khanna, 2005) with increased CSF levels, the SAPAP3 knockout mouse as a putative animal model of OCD (Welch et al., 2007), association with glutamatergic genes (Arnold, Sicard, Burroughs, Richter, & Kennedy, 2006; Dickel et al., 2006; Stewart et al., 2007), and response to glutamatergic modulating agents in OCD (Coric et al., 2005; Lafleur et al., 2006); (2) the neuropeptides oxytocin and vasopressin (Leckman et al., 1994); and (3) opioid peptides (Marazziti, 2001; Shapira et al., 1997).

Review of Pharmacologic Literature

Serotonin reuptake inhibitors (SRIs), which include selective serotonin reuptake inhibitors (SSRIs) and the tricyclic antidepressant clomipramine, are central in acute and maintenance pharmacotherapy of OCD. Clomipramine, the first medication discovered to be effective for OCD, was FDA approved in 1989 and is the only tricyclic antidepressant with significant serotonergic properties (Thoren et al., 1980). The SSRIs were subsequently determined to be effective and successful placebo-controlled OCD trials have been published for all six of the currently marketed SSRIs (Jenike, 2004; Stein et al., 2007). Although SRIs are classified as antidepressants, they also have demonstrated efficacy for OCD treatment in nondepressed patients.

Monotherapy Randomized Controlled Trials

A multitude of OCD controlled trials have been conducted to date. In these trials, *response* is typically defined as a ≥25% or ≥35% decrease in Y-BOCS score or a CGI-I score of much to very

much improved. Studies in the past decade had higher placebo response rates than those previously reported (mean 15%) (Ackerman & Greenland, 2002). Approximately 40% to 60% of patients respond to SRIs with a 20% to 40% reduction of OCD symptoms (Jenike et al., 1998; Pigott & Seay, 1999).

There is some indication from OCD meta-analyses, but not direct comparative trials, that clomipramine may be more effective than SSRIs (Abramowitz, 1997; Ackerman & Greenland, 2002; Eddy, Dutra, Bradley, & Westen, 2004; Geller et al., 2003; Jenike, Baer, & Greist, 1990; Jenike, 2004; Koran, McElroy, Davidson, Rasmussen, Hollander, 1996; Zohar & Judge, 1996). However, given their preferable side effect profile (i.e., less sedation, weight gain, and cardiac effects than clomipramine), SSRIs remain the first line of medical treatment. No significant effect size differences have been found in meta-analyses of adult (Ackerman & Greenland, 2002) or child (Geller et al., 2003) OCD populations. Venlafaxine extended release (XR), a dual serotonin and norepinephrine reuptake inhibitor (SNRI), does not have a specific FDA indication for OCD and has not been studied in placebo controlled trials, but has appeared effective in most open-label case series. Monoamine oxidase inhibitors (MAOIs) continue to be used in some severe OCD cases, although their efficacy has not been proven in controlled trials (Jenike, Baer, Minichiello, Rauch, & Buttolph, 1997) and the associated adverse effects and food restrictions limit their use (McCabe, 1986; Sweet et al., 1995). Improvement in OCD cases has been reported with trazodone in case series and reports (Hermesh, Aizenberg, & Munitz, 1990) but was not shown to be superior to placebo in a randomized controlled trial (Pigott et al., 1992b). Bupropion (Vulink, Denys, & Westenberg, 2005), tricyclic antidepressants other than clomipramine (Foa, Kozak, Steketee, McCarthy, 1992), and antipsychotic monotherapy do not appear to be effective treatments for OCD.

SRI Augmentation and Alternatives

Numerous agents have been studied in combination with SRIs, either when there is no response or a partial response to these medications (Jenike, 1993; Jenike et al., 1998; McDougle & Goodman, 1997; Rauch & Jenike, 1994). These augmentation or alternative agents are summarized in Table 1. The most impressive data on augmentation document benefits of adding low-dose typical (McDougle et al., 1994) or atypical (Denys et al., 2004)

Table 1. Augmentation/Refractory Sample Trials in OCD

First Author	Year	Baseline Medication (mg/d)	Augmenting Agent (mg/d)	Comparison Agent (mg/d)	Sample (N)	Augmentation Effective
SRI-Augmentation						
Grady	1993	Fluoxetine (80)	Buspar (60)	PBO (db)	13	No
McDougle	1990	Fluvoxamine (291) +/− Lithium (1038)	Typical antipsychotic	Fluvoxamine (291) +/− Lithium (1038)	20	Yes
Pallanti	1999	Citalopram (40)	Clomipramine (150)	Citalopram (40)	16	Yes
Hewlett	1992	Clomipramine (250), Clonazepam (10)	Clonidine (1)	Diphenhydramine (250)	28	No
Pigott	1991	Clomipramine	Triiodothyronine/	Lithium (0.54 mEq/l)	16	No
McDougle	1994	Fluvoxamine (300)	Haloperidol (10)	PBO	34	Yes
SRI-Refractory Cases						
Pigott	1992a	Clomipramine (182)	Buspirone (57)	PBO (db)	14	No
McDougle	1993	Fluvoxamine (300)	Buspirone (60)	PBO	33	No
McDougle	1994	SRI with comorbid tic d/o	Haloperidol (10)	PBO	34	Yes
Mundo	1998	Fluvoxamine	Pindolol	PBO	15	No
McDougle	2000	SRI	Risperidone (2.2)	PBO	70	Yes
Dannon	2000	SRI	Pindolol (7.5)	PBO	14	Yes
Atmaca	2002	SRI	Quetiapine (50–200)	PBO (sb)	27	Yes
Hollander	2003b	SRI	Risperidone (0.5–3)	PBO	16	Yes
Bystritsky	2004	SRI	Olanzapine (11.2)	PBO	26	Yes
Denys	2004	SRI	Quetiapine (300)	PBO	40	Yes
Shapira	2004	Fluvoxamine (40)	Olanzapine (6.1)	PBO	42	Yes
Erzegovesi	2005	Fluvoxamine (300)	Risperidone (0.5)	PBO	45	Yes
Carey	2005	SRI	Quetiapine (169)	PBO	41	Yes
Fineberg	2005	SRI	Quetiapine (50–200)	PBO	21	No

Note. SRI = serotonin-reuptake inhibitor; rct = randomized controlled trial; db = double-blind; sb = single-blind; PBO = placebo; n/a = not available; Y-BOCS = Yale-Brown Obsessive-Compulsive Rating Scale used in all studies.

antipsychotic agents to an SRI, though the durability of this approach is unclear (Fineberg, Sivakumaran, Roberts, & Gale, 2005). Double-blind placebo-controlled studies of other atypical antipsychotic agents such as ziprasidone and aripiprazole have yet to be completed.

In a single placebo-controlled study, clonazepam had significant antiobsessional efficacy with an SRI (Hewlett, Vinogradov, & Agras, 1992). Despite positive case reports of lithium as an augmenting agent, two controlled trials had negative results (McDougle, Price, Goodman, Charney, & Heninger, 1991). Encouraging results from uncontrolled trials of buspirone augmentation were followed by marginal success in controlled trials (McDougle et al., 1993; Pigott et al., 1992a). Numerous other agents have been tried in combination with SRIs, including clonidine (Hewlett et al., 1992), pindolol (Dannon et al., 2000; Mundo, Guglielmo, & Bellodi, 1998), tryptophan (Yaryura-Tobias, 1981; Yaryura-Tobias & Bhagavan, 1977), tramadol (Shapira et al., 1997), morphine (Koran et al., 2005), nicotine (Lundberg, Carlsson, Norfeldt, & Carlsson, 2004), and inositol (Fux, Benjamin, & Belmaker, 1999). One promising augmenting agent in an open-label study is the glutamate antagonist, riluzole (Coric et al., 2005). Further study of this and related glutamatergic agents such as memantine is warranted.

In terms of alternatives to SSRIs, venlafaxine placebo-controlled studies are lacking, although several open-label studies have reported positive findings. In these studies, SNRIs appeared as effective as SSRIs. It has also been suggested that venlafaxine might be preferred in certain types of treatment-resistant OCD or with particular comorbid conditions (Dell'Osso, Nestadt, Allen, & Hollander, 2006). Results of controlled monotherapy studies for potential alternatives to SRI's provide inconsistent support for clonazepam (Hollander, Kaplan, & Stahl, 2003b), buspirone (Grady et al., 1993; Pato et al., 1991), inositol (Levine, 1997), mirtazapine (Koran et al., 2005), d-amphetamine (Insel, Hamilton, Guttmacher, Murphy, 1983), methylphenidate (Joffe, Swinson, & Levitt, 1991), and St. John's wort (Kobak et al., 2005). Although a few patients reportedly respond to these medications, given the uncontrolled nature of these observations, no conclusions about their usefulness can be drawn at present.

A more recently studied augmenting agent in OCD and other anxiety disorders is d-cycloserine, given prior to CBT sessions (Otto, Basden, Leyro, McHugh, & Hofmann, 2006). This reportedly improves the speed of extinction learning in OCD (Wilhelm et al., 2008), with a trend towards lower CBT drop-out rates (Kushner et al., 2007).

Surgical/Somatic Approaches

When standard medication and CBT approaches have been unsuccessful in severe debilitating OCD cases, surgical and somatic therapies are occasionally used in treatment.

Transcranial Magnetic Stimulation (TMS)

With TMS, pulses of magnetic energy are intermittently administered to surface regions of the brain through the skull. This modality has been tested in several OCD treatment studies. In two trials using a sham TMS condition, there was significant improvement (Greenberg et al., 1997; Sachdev et al., 2001). In a third smaller controlled trial, no improvement over sham was seen (Alonso et al., 2001). In an open-label trial (Mantovani et al., 2006), there was a mean 60% clinical improvement. These studies had inconsistent study designs, limiting overall conclusions regarding TMS efficacy. However, given that this technique is noninvasive and well tolerated, further study is warranted.

Electroconvulsive Therapy (ECT)

Electroconvulsive therapy was reportedly effective for treatment-resistant OCD in a case series (Maletzky, McFarland, & Burt, 1994) and several case reports (Casey & Davis, 1994; Lavin & Halligan, 1996; Mellman & Gorman, 1984; Strassnig, Riedel, & Muller, 2004; Thomas & Kellner, 2003). This suggests only weak evidence given comorbid depression among subjects and the methodologies used. Thus, ECT has not been adequately proven as an effective modality in OCD.

Deep Brain Stimulation (DBS)

This therapy involves surgical placement of implanted electrodes that may be turned on and off to stimulate or inhibit activity in surrounding brain tissue. This was effective for OCD in case reports (Anderson & Ahmed, 2003; Aouizerate et al., 2004; Fontaine et al., 2004) and two double-blind controlled studies (Abelson et al., 2005; Nuttin, Cosyns, Demeulemeester, Gybels, & Meyerson, 1999; Nuttin, Gabriels, van Kuyck, & Cosyns, 2003) in which quadripolar electrodes were bilaterally implanted in the anterior limbs of the internal capsules. Significant improvements were noted in the first week to 1 month in these studies. Side effects included nausea, diarrhea, and tingling. Thus, DBT, which is reversible and generally well tolerated, is a promising somatic treatment in refractory OCD.

Neurosurgery

Several neurosurgical approaches have been performed for severe, treatment-refractory OCD. Their irreversibility, in addition to potential cognitive/personality change, seizure, weight gain, incontinence and mania are associated risks (Cosgrove & Rauch, 1995). In a study of 44 cingulotomies (Baer et al., 1995; Dougherty et al., 2002; Jenike et al., 1991), 32% had improved at 32-month follow-up. In two bilateral anterior cingulotomy studies, 6/14 (Kim et al., 2003) and 4/15 (Richter et al., 2004) subjects were responders at 1 year. In a bilateral anterior capsulotomy study ($n = 15$), the mean severity decrease was 53% at 1 year (Oliver et al., 2003). In a study of limbic leucotomy at least 4/12 were responders (Montoya et al., 2002), paralleling results of another case study (Hay et al., 1993). Neurosurgery has not been proven in unblinded studies. The availability of less-invasive procedures renders neurosurgery a less-attractive alternative treatment, as it has not been studied compared to sham procedures. However, it may be a viable option for some individuals with very severe and refractory OCD.

Long-Term Outcome
Natural History and Clinical Course

Determining the optimal length of medication treatment requires an understanding of the long-term course and natural history of OCD. However, numerous inconsistencies in long-term outcome studies limit comparison or confirmation of findings. Some studies used retrospective recall approaches, whereas others differed in subject ascertainment and inclusion criteria. In general, OCD has a gradual onset (although acute onset occurs in some cases). The long-term course of OCD has been studied in child, adult, clinical and population samples. In retrospective studies published before the availability of effective OCD medications, with a minimum 10-year follow-up period, improvement rates ranged between 32% and 74% (Skoog & Skoog, 1999). In a landmark study of 144 adult OCD inpatients with a mean 47-year follow-up period, 50% reported a chronic course (≥5 years of continuous symptoms), 25% an intermittent course (≥2 episodes with symptom-free periods), and 12% an episodic course (one episode lasting <5 years) (Skoog & Skoog, 1999).

In other samples, a chronic (Perugi et al., 2002) or waxing and waning course (Rasmussen & Eisen,

1988) was present in at least 70% of cases. In the single long-term outcome study on a nonclinical OCD community sample, only 14% of 22 adult-onset subjects met *DSM–IV* criteria or had symptoms and moderate distress related to OCD at 13-year follow-up (Angst et al., 2004).

In a meta-analysis by Stewart et al. (2004), 22 long-term outcome studies for childhood OCD ($n = 521$ subjects) with follow-up periods ranging between 1–15.6 years were analyzed. Pooled mean persistence rates were 41% for *full* OCD and 19% for *subthreshold* OCD at follow-up. Hence, for many individuals presenting in clinical settings, OCD appears to be a chronic illness with a waxing and waning course. However, with proper treatment, most individuals experience at least mild to moderate improvement.

Discontinuation Studies

Relapse rates tend to be high following SRI discontinuation, in apparent contrast to CBT discontinuation. In one study, almost 90% of patients who received drug therapy without CBT had a relapse after double-blind discontinuation of medical therapy (Pato, Zohar-Kadouch, Zohar, & Murphy, 1988). Among patients who had a response to medication, the mean time to relapse during the use of a substitute placebo was 63 days (Steiner, Bushnell, & Gergel, 1995).

There have been four double-blind SRI discontinuation studies to date in OCD. These are difficult to compare due to contrasting designs and relapse definitions. Relapse rates ranged from 89% for clomipramine responders after 7 weeks (Pato et al., 1988), to 59% for paroxetine responders after 24 weeks (Hollander et al., 2003a), to 32% for fluoxetine responders after 52 weeks (Romano, Goodman, Tamura, & Gonzales, 2001) to 24% for sertraline responders after 28 weeks (Koran, Hackett, Rubin, Wolkow, & Robinson, 2002). Relapse rates significantly differed between placebo and medication continuation groups in two of these studies (Hollander et al., 2003a; Koran et al., 2002), and comparisons were not available in a third (Pato et al., 1988). In an unblinded discontinuation study, reported relapse rates were even higher (Ravizza, Barzega, Bellino, Bogetto, & Maina, 1996).

A multisite study comparing relapse rates between medication and CBT modalities found that CBT responders (with or without clomipramine) had significantly lower relapse rates (12%) and longer time to relapse than responders to clomipramine alone (45%). These rates were measured following

12 weeks of treatment (Foa et al., 2005) and again 12 weeks after discontinuation of treatment (Simpson et al., 2004). This pattern held up when applying several definitions of relapse (Simpson, Franklin, Cheng, Foa, & Liebowitz, 2005). However, context effects may partially underlie relapse rates in OCD combination discontinuation studies as CBT involves state-dependent learning that is not well applied in the new medication-free context (without reinstatement of CBT) (Michael Otto, personal communication, McLean Grand Rounds, February 22, 2008).

Overview of Pharmacologic Treatment
Initial Management Approaches

This section will summarize a practical management approach based upon research evidence. Prior to establishing a treatment plan, a complete diagnostic assessment should be conducted, confirming the OCD diagnosis and assessing functional impact, motivation for treatment, comorbidities, past treatment trials, and family accommodation. A baseline measure of OCD symptoms and severity should be established with an instrument such as the Yale-Brown Obsessive-Compulsive Scale and checklist (Y-BOCS). If the predominant OCD symptom is hoarding, this indicates a lower likelihood of benefit from medication or medication and CBT (Mataix-Cols, Rauch, Manzo, Jenike, & Baer, 1999; Saxena et al., 2002). Insight should be assessed with an instrument such as the Brown Assessment of Beliefs Scale (Eisen et al., 1998), since poor insight has been inconsistently associated with poorer SRI (Eisen et al., 2001) and CBT (Tolin, Maltby, Diefenbach, Hannan, & Worhunsky, 2004) response.

Updated practice guidelines for the treatment of OCD have recently been published by the American Psychiatric Association. The OCD Guidelines published in 1997 recommended first-line use of CBT. For those with severe illness, the use of SSRI medications prior to a trial of CBT was advised. Further, it was suggested that two or three trials of SSRIs should precede a trial of clomipramine (The Expert Consensus Panel for Obsessive-Compulsive Disorder, 1997). Similar OCD practice parameters were published in 1998 for children and adolescents affected by OCD (American Academy of Child and Adolescent Psychiatry, 1998). In summary, current empirical evidence points to both CBT and SSRIs as safe and effective first-line treatments for OCD.

The decision whether to initiate an SSRI alone, CBT alone, or a combination of both depends upon individual patient variables. For those patients preferring medication alone, or those without access to a CBT-trained clinician and/or with poor motivation or insight, an initial trial with an SSRI alone may be suitable. Presence of comorbid depression, psychosis, or other anxiety disorders that may interfere with CBT may indicate that medication should be included in the initial management approach. The selection of a specific SSRI is open to clinical judgment, as head-to-head trials and meta-analyses have not found significant differences in efficacy between these medications. Thus, serial trials are required to determine which agent helps the most while causing the fewest side effects (Jenike et al., 1998). In making this selection, a family history of positive response or adverse reaction to a specific SSRI, potential interactions with other medications and side effect profiles should be considered.

To determine effectiveness of a medication, a 10- to 12-week trial at the highest tolerated specific dose within the advised dose range is required. For treatment of OCD, doses are typically higher than those required for depression (Jenike et al., 1998). Typical OCD medications, their dosages, interaction profiles, and side effects are summarized in Table 2. Before initiating a medication trial, it is often necessary to conduct laboratory investigations such as blood work and an electrocardiogram, depending on the specific agent. A reduction of symptoms is a more common outcome of this trial than remission. If the patient remains significantly impaired by OCD, or is requesting further medication trials, and if benefits are deemed to outweigh risks, then additional medication trials should be considered. Between each step in the treatment plan (see Figure 1), adherence/compliance and adverse effects should be assessed.

Second-Line Management Approaches

Second-line medication strategies include SRI augmentation or replacement. Effective SRI augmenting agents as determined by controlled trials include typical and atypical antipsychotics, clonazepam, buspirone, and lithium (see Table 2). Atypical agents should be attempted prior to typical antipsychotics given the lower risk for tardive dyskinesia, an irreversible adverse effect. Distinct adverse effect profiles exist for certain medications within classes (i.e., ziprasidone and potential QT prolongation) and classwide adverse effects (e.g., weight gain and diabetes for the atypical antipsychotics) are also important for consideration.

Table 2. OCD Medications, Dosages, and Side Effects

Drug Generic Name	Drug Trade Name	Starting Dose (mg/d)	Upper Range Target Dose (mg/d)	Adverse Effects
FIRST-LINE AGENTS				
SSRIs				
Citalopram	Celexa	20	60	**Common:** insomnia, anxiety, GI upset, sexual, dizziness, sedation
Escitalopram	Lexapro	10	40	**Rare:** rash, headache
Fluoxetine	Prozac	20	80	
Fluvoxamine	Luvox	50	300	
Paroxetine	Paxil	20	60	
Sertraline	Zoloft	50	200	
TRICYCLICS				
Clompiramine	Anafranil	25	250	**Common:** anticholinergic s/e, dizziness, sexual, weight gain, tremor **Rare:** EKG changes, seizures
ADJUNCTIVE/SECOND-LINE AGENTS				
Buspirone	Buspar	10 (divided bid)	10–45 (divided bid)	**Common:** dizziness, headache, nausea **Rare:** sedation, rash
SNRIs				
Venlafaxine	Effexor XR	75	225–300	**Common:** GI upset, sexual dysfunction, sweating, insomnia, tremor, hypertension **Rare:** vasodilation, yawning
BENZODIAZEPINES				
Clonazepam	Klonopin	0.25–0.5 (od or divided bid)	0.5–3 (od or divided bid)	**Common:** sedation, tolerance **Rare:** impaired cognition, disinhibition, Ataxia
Lorazepam	Ativan	0.5 (divided bid-tid)	0.5–4 (divided bid-tid)	
ATYPICAL ANTIPSYCHOTICS				
Risperidone	Risperdal	1 (od or divided bid)	0.5–6	**Common:** weight gain, dizziness, sedation, constipation, sexual
Olanzapine	Zyprexa	5	5–20 (od or divided bid)	**Rare:** hyperglycemia, elevated prolactin, extrapyramidal symptoms
Quetiapine	Seroquel	50 (divided bid)	500 (divided bid)	
Aripiprazole	Abilify	10	10–30	
Ziprasidone	Geodon	40 (divided bid)	40–160 (divided bid)	
TYPICAL ANTIPSYCHOTICS				
Haloperidol	Haldol	0.5	0.5–10	**Common:** sedation, extrapyramidal symptoms, sexual, anticholinergic s/e, **Rare:** EKG changes, tardive dyskinesia, neuroleptic malignant syndrome
Pimozide	Orap	1	1–3	
MAOIs				
Phenelzine	Nardil	45 (divided tid)	90 (divided tid)	**Common:** insomnia, dizziness, headache, sedation, tremor, anticholinergic s/e, weight gain, postural hypotension, sexual **Rare:** hypertensive crisis
Tranylcypromine	Parnate	20 (divided bid)	60 (divided bid)	

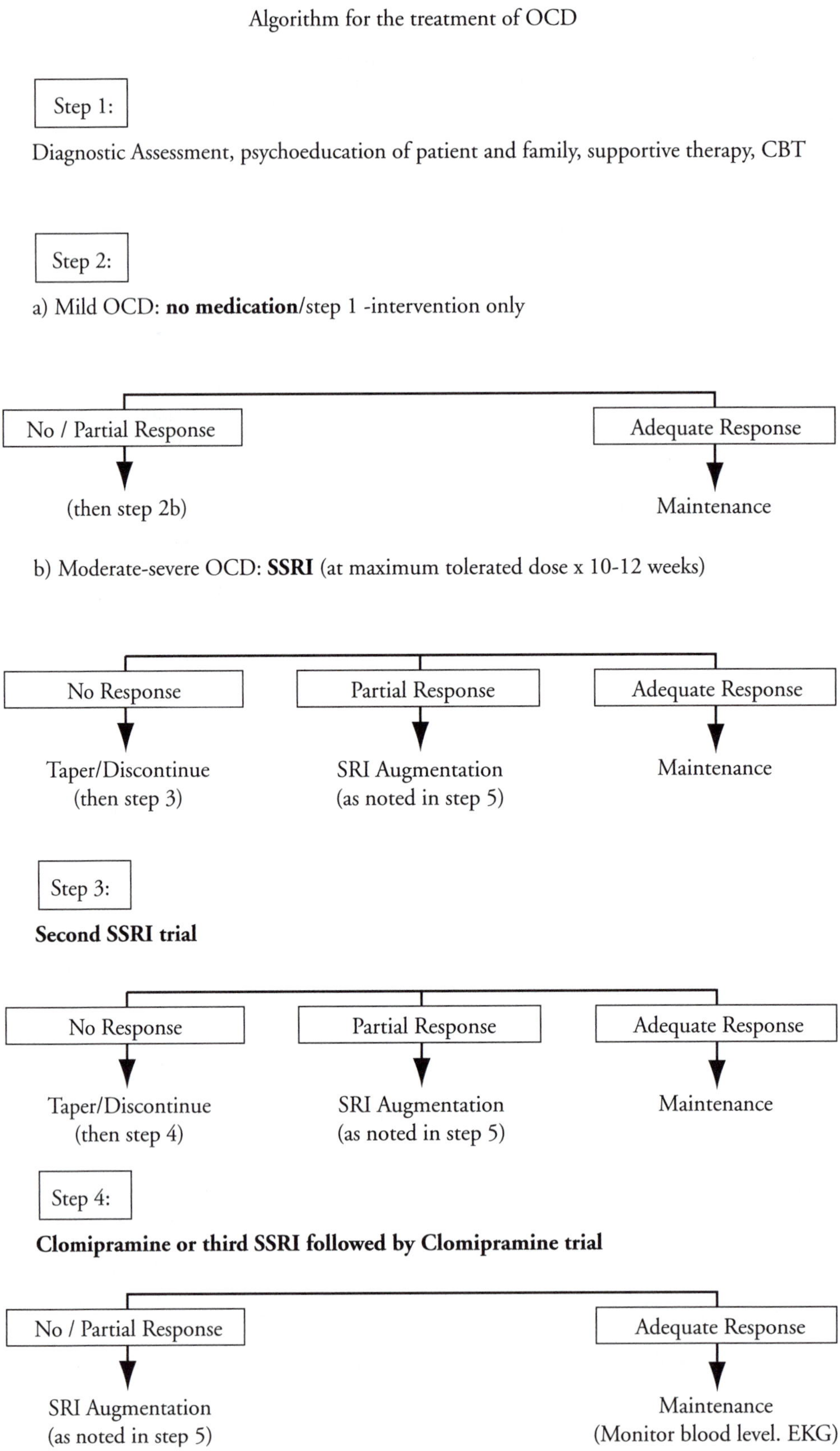

Algorithm for the treatment of OCD

Step 1:

Diagnostic Assessment, psychoeducation of patient and family, supportive therapy, CBT

Step 2:

a) Mild OCD: **no medication**/step 1 -intervention only

No / Partial Response	Adequate Response
↓	↓
(then step 2b)	Maintenance

b) Moderate-severe OCD: **SSRI** (at maximum tolerated dose x 10-12 weeks)

No Response	Partial Response	Adequate Response
↓	↓	↓
Taper/Discontinue (then step 3)	SRI Augmentation (as noted in step 5)	Maintenance

Step 3:

Second SSRI trial

No Response	Partial Response	Adequate Response
↓	↓	↓
Taper/Discontinue (then step 4)	SRI Augmentation (as noted in step 5)	Maintenance

Step 4:

Clomipramine or third SSRI followed by Clomipramine trial

No / Partial Response	Adequate Response
↓	↓
SRI Augmentation (as noted in step 5)	Maintenance (Monitor blood level. EKG)

Fig. 1 Management flowchart.

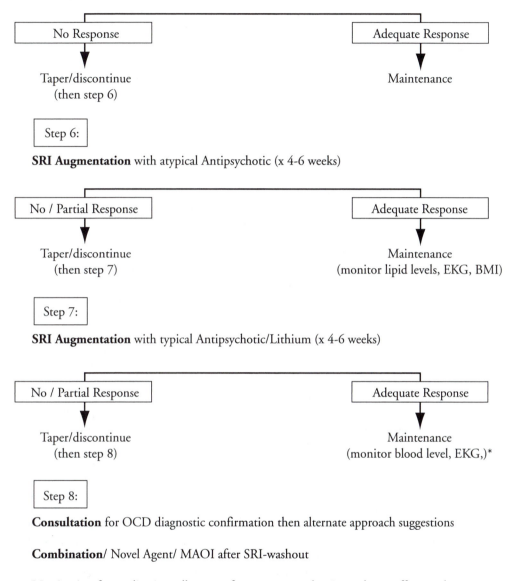

Step 5:

SRI Augmentation/Replacement with Clonazepam/Buspirone (x 4-6 weeks)

No Response	Adequate Response
Taper/discontinue (then step 6)	Maintenance

Step 6:

SRI Augmentation with atypical Antipsychotic (x 4-6 weeks)

No / Partial Response	Adequate Response
Taper/discontinue (then step 7)	Maintenance (monitor lipid levels, EKG, BMI)

Step 7:

SRI Augmentation with typical Antipsychotic/Lithium (x 4-6 weeks)

No / Partial Response	Adequate Response
Taper/discontinue (then step 8)	Maintenance (monitor blood level, EKG,)*

Step 8:

Consultation for OCD diagnostic confirmation then alternate approach suggestions

Combination/ Novel Agent/ MAOI after SRI-washout

Monitoring for medication adherence, for common and serious adverse effects and for interaction with other medication &/ or illness is required throughout.

Fig. 1 *continued.*

Clonazepam and buspirone are used as SRI augmenting agents and occasionally as SRI replacement agents in OCD treatment. There is some evidence that monoamine oxidase inhibitors (MAOIs) may be effective as SRI replacements. However, a prior washout period of at least 2 to 4 weeks for most SRIs, and of 6 to 8 weeks for fluoxetine, is mandatory to avoid serotonin syndrome. Furthermore, while taking MAOIs, patients must not eat tyramine-containing foods and must avoid other interacting medications, or a life-threatening hypertensive crisis may occur. These constraints may limit or preclude the use of MAOIs for some patients.

When to Discontinue Treatment

There is no clear evidence indicating the optimal trial length after treatment response is obtained. In general, once an effective medication and dose are identified, they should be continued for at least 1 to 2 years. Continuation of pharmacotherapy at a lower maintenance dose has also been proposed, but optimal doses remain uncertain. If medications are decreased, very slow tapering every 2 months is optimal. Unfortunately, the relapse rate following medication discontinuation tends to be high. For those having received previous CBT, however, relapse rates may be lower (Foa et al., 2005). CBT reinstatement booster sessions throughout tapering and discontinuation may be advisable because CBT involves state-dependent learning that may benefit from being re-taught in the new medication-free state.

Treatment with Comorbid Illnesses

For individuals with OCD comorbidities, all disorders should be treated and monitored for exacerbation or improvement following medication changes, and the possibility of drug-drug interactions must be considered. For those with comorbid tics, addition of an antipsychotic medication to an SRI may be beneficial (Eapen & Robertson, 2000; McDougle et al., 1994). In the context of depression, medication use should be prioritized as the presence of this comorbidity is associated with poor CBT response (Keeley, Storch, Merlo, & Geffken, 2008).

Other treatment options for comorbid depression include interpersonal or short-term psychodynamic therapy, increasing the SRI dose, addition of bupropion, or in severe cases, electroconvulsive therapy. In the challenging context of comorbid bipolar disorder and OCD, efforts should be made to stabilize mood prior to initiation of an SRI (American Psychiatric Association [APA], 2002). Careful monitoring will be required for potential manic/hypomanic switching when medically treating the OCD. Those with comorbid panic disorder should be started on SRIs at low doses with slow upward titration (APA, 1998) with potential short-term addition of benzodiazepines. For comorbid social phobia, SRIs provide effective treatment, as do venlafaxine extended release (Liebowitz, Mangano, Bradwejn, Asnis, & SAD Study Group, 2005), clonazepam (Davidson et al., 1993) and CBT (Hambrick, Weeks, Harb, & Heimberg, 2003).

In schizophrenia, OCD symptoms may be precipitated or exacerbated by second-generation antipsychotics (Lykouras, Alevizos, Michalopoulou, & Rabavilas, 2003), which occasionally resolve within a few weeks. When schizophrenia and OCD present independently, both must be treated with initial stabilization of psychosis. If clozapine is used, low doses and slow dose titration are recommended to avoid OCD symptom exacerbation (Poyurovsky, Weizman, & Weizman, 2004). For management of OCD symptoms, addition of SRIs (Poyurovsky et al., 2004), switching to another atypical antipsychotic, and addition of CBT should be considered.

Personality disorders are common in OCD (Torres et al., 2006) and may impact treatment outcome (Fricke et al., 2006). Addition of psychodynamic therapy may assist with treatment resistance and transference/countertransference issues (Gabbard, 2005). Comorbid alcohol or substance abuse may impair treatment response and compliance, and may also cause interactions with medications. Treatment guidelines for these disorders have been established (APA, in press).

Treatment in Special Populations

Other individual factors that may impact on the OCD treatment plan should also be considered, including extremes of age as well as pregnancy and medical conditions.

In children and adolescents OCD is also responsive to SRI medications and CBT. Close monitoring is advised due to recent controversy implicating a potential increase in suicidal thinking with antidepressants in this age group, especially in the initial weeks. Of note, SSRIs may be necessary for treating OCD in this age group and should not be unduly avoided (ACNP Task Force et al., 2006).

For pregnant patients, OCD symptoms have been reported to change, by either worsening or improving (Labad et al., 2005; Williams & Koran, 1997). A risk-benefit analysis and psychoeducation should be emphasized in these cases, as fetal well-being is influenced not only by potential medication exposure but also by the mother's health and well-being. Current research does not indicate elevated fetal mortality (Wisner et al., 2000), major malformations (Einarson & Einarson, 2005; Kulin et al., 1998; Simon, Cunningham, & Davis, 2002; Wisner et al., 2000), or developmental deficits at 2–6 years (Nulman et al., 2002; Simon et al., 2002) with prenatal exposure to SSRIs or tricyclics. Although all SSRIs pass into breast milk, related adverse effect rates are reportedly low (Newport, Fisher, Graybeal, & Stowe, 2004; Weissman et al., 2004). There is debate as to whether SSRIs increase risk for premature delivery, low birth weight (Nordeng & Spigset,

2005), or a transitory "neonatal behavioral syndrome" (Moses-Kolko et al., 2005). Further details on perinatal risks of medication exposure are available elsewhere (Newport et al., 2004).

For medically ill patients with OCD, potential drug-drug interactions, ability to metabolize medications, and adverse effects should be considered. Medications to avoid or use with caution include clomipramine in patients with cardiac or seizure disorder and atypical antipsychotics in those with diabetes mellitus (Lehman et al., 2004). Symptoms of OCD may also present or worsen in conditions such as Syndenham's chorea, Parkinson's disease, Huntington's disease, traumatic brain injury trauma, stroke, and encephalitis (Isaacs, Philbeck, Barr, Devinsky, & Alper, 2004; Koran, 1999; Weiss & Jenike, 2000). In these cases, the medical condition should initially be stabilized and treated prior to reassessment and initiation of OCD medications.

Summary and Conclusions

Obsessive-compulsive disorder (OCD) tends to be underdiagnosed and undertreated. However, early diagnosis and treatment can help to avoid OCD-related suffering and lessen the risk of related problems. Standard effective treatment approaches for OCD include medications and/or CBT (Jenike et al., 1998). This chapter covered the medical treatment of OCD by reviewing empirical evidence and discussing practical clinical strategies for various OCD populations.

Consumer/Patient and Clinician Resources

OC Foundation
112 Water Street, Suite 501 Boston, MA 02119
Tel: (617) 973–5801; Fax: (617) 973–5805; www.ocfoundation.org

Scrupulous Anonymous (for those with religious/morality-focused OCD)
http://mission.liguori.org/newsletters/scrupanon.htm

San Francisco Bay Area Resource & Internet Guide for Extreme Hoarding Behavior
http://www.hoarders.org

The American Academy of Child and Adolescent Psychiatry
3615 Wisconsin Ave., NW; Washington, DC 20016–3007
Tel: 202–966–7300;
http://www.aacap.org/;http://www.aacap.org/publications/factsfam/index.htm

Anxiety Disorders Association of America
Tel: 301-231-9350; http://www.adaa.org
Information on the Use of Medication During Pregnancy and Breast Feeding

California Teratogen Information Service and Clinical Research
Tel: 1-800-532-3749 (CA only) or
610-543-2131
www.otispregnancy.org/ctis.html

MGH Women's Mental Health Program
www.womensmentalhealth.com

Resources for General Information on Mental Disorders and Medications:
National Institute of Mental Health (NIMH)
Public Information and Communications Branch
6001 Executive Boulevard, Room 8184, MSC 9663; Bethesda, MD 20892-9663
Tel: 1-866-615-6464; Fax: 301-443-4279

National Alliance on Mental Illness
Tel: 1-800-950-6264; or 703-524-7600
http://www.nami.org

National Mental Health Association
1021 Prince St.; Alexandria, VA 22314-2971
Tel: 1-800-969-6642 or 703-684-7722
Fax: 703-684-5968; www.nmha.org

References

ACNP Task Force, Mann, J. J., Emslie, G., Baldessarini, R. J., Beardslee, W., Fawcett, J. A., et al. (2006). ACNP Task Force report on SSRIs and suicidal behavior in youth. *Neuropsychopharmacology, 31*(3), 473–492.

Abelson, J. L., Curtis, G. C., Sagher, O., Albucher, R. C., Harrigan, M., Taylor, S. F., et al. (2005). Deep brain stimulation for refractory obsessive-compulsive disorder. *Biological Psychiatry, 57*(5), 510–516.

Abramowitz, J. S. (1997). Effectiveness of psychological and pharmacological treatments for obsessive-compulsive disorder: a quantitative review. *Journal of Consulting and Clinical Psychology, 65*(1), 44–52.

Ackerman, D. L., & Greenland, S. (2002). Multivariate meta-analysis of controlled drug studies for obsessive-compulsive disorder. *Journal of Clinical Psychopharmacology, 22,* 309–317.

Alonso, P., Pujol, J., Cardoner, N., Benlloch, L., Deus, J., Menchon, J. M., et al. (2001). Right prefrontal repetitive transcranial magnetic stimulation in obsessive-compulsive disorder: A double-blind, placebo-controlled study. *American Journal of Psychiatry, 158,* 1143–1145.

American Academy of Child and Adolescent Psychiatry. (1998). Practice parameters for the assessment and treatment of children and adolescents with obsessive-compulsive disorder. *Journal of the American Academy of Child and Adolescent Psychiatry, 37,* 27S–45S.

American Psychiatric Association. (1998). Practice guideline for the treatment of patients with panic disorder. Work Group on Panic Disorder. *American Journal of Psychiatry, 155,* 1–34.

American Psychiatric Association. (2002). Practice guideline for the treatment of patients with bipolar disorder (revision). *American Journal of Psychiatry, 159,* 1–50.

American Psychiatric Association. (in press). Practice guideline for the treatment of patients with substance use disorders (2nd ed.). *American Journal of Psychiatry.*

Anderson, D., & Ahmed, A. (2003). Treatment of patients with intractable obsessive-compulsive disorder with anterior capsular stimulation: Case report. *Journal of Neurosurgery, 98,* 1104–1108.

Angst, J., Gamma, A., Endrass, J., Goodwin, R., Ajdacic, V., Eich, D., et al. (2004). Obsessive-compulsive severity spectrum in the community: Prevalence, comorbidity, and course. *European Archives of Psychiatry and Clinical Neuroscience, 254,* 156–164.

Aouizerate, B., Cuny, E., Martin-Guehl, C., Guehl, D., Amieva, H., Benazzouz, A., et al. (2004). Deep brain stimulation of the ventral caudate nucleus in the treatment of obsessive-compulsive disorder and major depression: Case report. *Journal of Neurosurgery, 101,* 682–686.

Arnold, P. D., Sicard, T., Burroughs, E., Richter, M. A., & Kennedy, J. L. (2006). Glutamate transporter gene SLC1A1 associated with obsessive-compulsive disorder. *Archives of General Psychiatry, 63*(7), 769–776.

Atmaca, M., Kuloglu, M., Tezcan, E., & Gecici, O. (2002). Quetiapine augmentation in patients with treatment resistant obsessive-compulsive disorder: A single-blind, placebo-controlled study. *International Clinical Psychopharmacology, 17,* 115–119.

Baer, L., Rauch, S. L., Ballantine, H. T., Jr., Martuza, R., Cosgrove, R., Cassem, E., et al. (1995). Cingulotomy for intractable obsessive-compulsive disorder: Prospective long-term follow-up of 18 patients. *Archives of General Psychiatry, 52,* 384–392.

Bystritsky, A., Ackerman, D. L., Rosen, R. M., Vapnik, T., Gorbis, E., Maidment, K. M., et al. (2004). Augmentation of serotonin reuptake inhibitors in refractory obsessive-compulsive disorder using adjunctive olanzapine: A placebo-controlled trial. *Journal of Clinical Psychiatry, 65,* 565–568.

Carey, P. D., Vythilingum, B., Seedat, S., Muller, J. E., Van Ameringen, M., & Stein, D. J. (2005). Quetiapine augmentation of STIs in treatment refractory obsessive-compulsive disorder: A double-blind, randomised, placebo-controlled study. *BMC Psychiatry, 5,* 5.

Casey, D. A., & Davis, M. H. (1994). Obsessive-compulsive disorder responsive to electroconvulsive therapy in an elderly woman. *Southern Medical Journal, 87,* 862–864.

Chakrabarty, K., Bhattacharyya, S., Christopher, R., & Khanna, S. (2005). Glutamatergic dysfunction in OCD. *Neuropsychopharmacology, 30*(9), 1735–1740.

Coric, V., Taskiran, S., Pittenger, C., Wasylink, S., Mathalon, D. H., Valentine, G., et al. (2005). Riluzole augmentation in treatment-resistant obsessive-compulsive disorder: An open-label trial. *Biological Psychiatry, 58,* 424–428.

Cosgrove, G. R., & Rauch, S. L. (1995). Psychosurgery. *Neurosurgery Clinics of North America, 6,* 167–176.

Dannon, P. N., Sasson, Y., Hirschmann, S., Iancu, I., Grunhaus, L. J., & Zohar, J. (2000). Pindolol augmentation in treatment-resistant obsessive compulsive disorder: A double-blind placebo controlled trial. *European Neuropsychopharmacology, 10,* 165–169.

Davidson, J. R., Potts, N., Richichi, E., Krishnan, R., Ford, S. M., Smith, R., et al. (1993). Treatment of social phobia with clonazepam and placebo. *Journal of Clinical Psychopharmacology, 13,* 423–428.

Dell'Osso, B., Nestadt, G., Allen, A., & Hollander, E. (2006). Serotonin-norepinephrine reuptake inhibitors in the treatment of obsessive-compulsive disorder: A critical review. *Journal of Clinical Psychiatry, 67*(4), 600–610.

Denys, D., de Geus, F., van Megen, H. J., & Westenberg, H. G. (2004). A double-blind randomized, placebo-controlled trial of quetiapine addition in patients with obsessive-compulsive disorder refractory to serotonin reuptake inhibitors. *Journal of Clinical Psychiatry, 65,* 1040–1048.

Dickel DE, Veenstra-VanderWeele J, Cox NJ, Wu X, Fischer DJ, Van Etten-Lee M, Himle JA, Leventhal BL, Cook EH Jr, Hanna GL. (2006). Association testing of the positional and functional candidate gene Slc1a1/Eaac1 in early onset obsessive-compulsive disorder. *Archives of General Psychiatry, 63*(7), 717–720.

Dougherty, D. D., Baer, L., Cosgrove, G. R., Cassem, E. H., Price, B. H., Nierenberg, A. A., et al. (2002). Prospective long-term follow-up of 44 patients who received cingulotomy for treatment-refractory obsessive-compulsive disorder. *American Journal of Psychiatry, 159,* 269–275.

Eapen, V., & Robertson, M. M. (2000). Comorbid obsessive-compulsive disorder and Tourette syndrome: Therapeutic interventions. *CNS Drugs, 13,* 173–183.

Eddy, K. T., Dutra, L., Bradley, R., & Westen, D. (2004). A multidimensional meta-analysis of psychotherapy and pharmacotherapy for obsessive-compulsive disorder. *Clinical Psychology Review, 24*(8), 1011–1030.

Einarson, T. R., & Einarson, A. (2005). Newer antidepressants in pregnancy and rates of major malformations: A meta-analysis of prospective comparative studies. *Pharmacoepidemiol Drug Safety, 14,* 823–827.

Eisen, J. L., Rasmussen, S. A., Phillips, K. A., Price, L. H., Davidson, J., Lydiard, R. B., et al. (2001). Insight and treatment outcome in obsessive-compulsive disorder. *Comprehensive Psychiatry, 42*(6), 494–497.

Eisen, J. L., Phillips, K. A., Baer, L., Beer, D. A., Atala, K. D., & Rasmussen, S. A. (1998). The Brown Assessment of Beliefs Scale: Reliability and validity. *American Journal of Psychiatry, 155,* 102–108.

Erzegovesi, S., Guglielmo, E., Siliprandi, F., & Bellodi, L. (2005). Low-dose risperidone augmentation of fluoxamine treatment in obsessive-compulsive disorder: A double-blind, placebo-controlled study. *European Neuropsychopharmacology, 15,* 69–74.

The Expert Consensus Panel for Obsessive-Compulsive Disorder. (1997). Treatment of obsessive-compulsive disorder. *Journal of Clinical Psychiatry, 58*(Suppl. 4), 2–72.

Fineberg, N. (1996). Refining treatment approaches in obsessive-compulsive disorder. *International Clinical Psychopharmacology, 11*(Suppl. 5), 13–22.

Fineberg, N. A., Sivakumaran, T., Roberts, A., & Gale, T. (2005). Adding quetiapine to SRI in treatment-resistant obsessive-compulsive disorder: A randomized controlled treatment study. *International Clinical Psychopharmacology, 20,* 223–226.

Foa, E. B., Kozak, M. J., Steketee, G. S., & McCarthy, P. R. (1992). Treatment of depressive and obsessive-compulsive symptoms in OCD by imipramine and behaviour therapy. *The British Journal of Clinical Psychology, 31*(Pt 3), 279–292.

Foa, E. B., Liebowitz, M. R., Kozak, M. J., Davies, S., Campeas, R., Franklin, M. E., et al. (2005). Randomized, placebo-controlled trial of exposure and ritual prevention, clomipramine, and their combination in the treatment of obsessive-compulsive disorder. *American Journal of Psychiatry, 162*, 151–161.

Fontaine, D., Mattei, V., Borg, M., von Langsdorff, D., Magnie, M. N., Chanalet, S., et al. (2004). Effect of subthalamic nucleus stimulation on obsessive-compulsive disorder in a patient with Parkinson disease: Case report. *Journal of Neurosurgery, 100*, 1084–1086.

Fricke, S., Moritz, S., Andresen, B., Jacobsen, D., Kloss, M., Rufer, M., et al. (2006). Do personality disorders predict negative treatment outcome in obsessive-compulsive disorders? A prospective 6-month follow-up study. *European Psychiatry: The Journal of the Association of European Psychiatrists, 21*(5), 319–324.

Fux, M., Benjamin, J., & Belmaker, R. H. (1999). Inositol versus placebo augmentation of serotonin reuptake inhibitors in the treatment of obsessive-compulsive disorder: A double-blind cross-over study. *International Journal of Neuropsychopharmacology, 2*, 193–195.

Gabbard, G. O. (2005). *Psychodynamic psychiatry in clinical practice.* Washington, DC: American Psychiatric Press.

Geller, D. A., Biederman, J., Stewart, S. E., Mullin, B., Martin, A., Spencer, T., et al. (2003). Which SSRI? A meta-analysis of pharmacotherapy trials in pediatric obsessive-compulsive disorder. *American Journal of Psychiatry, 160*, 1919–1928.

Grady, T. A., Pigott, T. A., L'Heureux, F., Hill, J. L., Bernstein, S. E., & Murphy, D. L. (1993). Double-blind study of adjuvant buspirone for fluoxetine-treated patients with obsessive-compulsive disorder. *American Journal of Psychiatry, 150*, 819–821.

Greenberg, B. D., George, M. S., Martin, J. D., Benjamin, J., Schlaepfer, T. E., Altemus, M., et al. (1997). Effect of prefrontal repetitive transcranial magnetic stimulation in obsessive-compulsive disorder: A preliminary study. *American Journal of Psychiatry, 154*, 867–869.

Hambrick, J. P., Weeks, J. W., Harb, G. C., & Heimberg, R. G. (2003). Cognitive-behavioral therapy for social anxiety disorder: supporting evidence and future directions. *CNS Spectrums, 8*(5), 373–381.

Hay, P., Sachdev, P., Cumming, S., Smith, J. S., Lee, T., Kitchener, P., et al. (1993). Treatment of obsessive-compulsive disorder by psychosurgery. *Acta Psychiatrica Scandinavica, 87*, 197–207.

Hermesh, H., Aizenberg, D., & Munitz, H. (1990). Trazodone treatment in clomipramine-resistant obsessive-compulsive disorder. *Clinical Neuropharmacology, 13*, 322–328.

Hewlett, W. A., Vinogradov, S., & Agras, W. S. (1992). Clomipramine, clonazepam, and clonidine treatment of obsessive-compulsive disorder. *Journal of Clinical Psychopharmacology, 12*, 420–430.

Hollander, E., Allen, A., Steiner, M., Wheadon, D. E., Oakes, R., & Burnham, D. B. (2003a). Acute and long-term treatment and prevention of relapse of obsessive-compulsive disorder with paroxetine. *Journal of Clinical Psychiatry, 64*, 1113–1121.

Hollander, E., Fay, M., Cohen, B., Campeas, R., Gorman, J. M., & Liebowitz, M. R. (1988). Serotonergic and noradrenergic sensitivity in obsessive-compulsive disorder: Behavioral findings. *American Journal of Psychiatry, 145*(8), 1015–1017.

Hollander, E., Kaplan, A., & Stahl, S. M. (2003b). A double-blind, placebo-controlled trial of clonazepam in obsessive-compulsive disorder. *World Journal of Biological Psychiatry, 4*, 30–34.

Insel, T. R., Hamilton, J. A., Guttmacher, L. B., & Murphy, D. L. (1983). D-amphetamine in obsessive-compulsive disorder. *Psychopharmacology (Berl), 80*(3), 231–235.

Insel, T. R., Mueller, E. A., Alterman, I., Linnoila, M., & Murphy, D. L. (1985). Obsessive-compulsive disorder and serotonin: is there a connection? *Biological Psychiatry, 20*(11), 1174–1188.

Isaacs, K. L., Philbeck, J. W., Barr, W. B., Devinsky, O., & Alper, K. (2004). Obsessive-compulsive symptoms in patients with temporal lobe epilepsy. *Epilepsy and Behavior, 5*, 569–574.

Jenike, M. A. (1993). Augmentation strategies for treatment-resistant obsessive-compulsive disorder. *Harvard Review of Psychiatry, 1*, 17–26.

Jenike, M. A. (2004). Clinical practice: Obsessive-compulsive disorder. *New England Journal of Medicine, 350*, 259–265.

Jenike, M. A., Baer, L., Ballantine, T., Martuza, R. L., Tynes, S., Giriunas, I., et al. (1991). Cingulotomy for refractory obsessive-compulsive disorder: A long-term follow-up of 33 patients. *Archives of General Psychiatry, 48*, 548–555.

Jenike, M. A., Baer, L., & Greist, J. H. (1990). Clomipramine versus fluoxetine in obsessive-compulsive disorder: a retrospective comparison of side effects and efficacy. *Journal of Clinical Psychopharmacology, 10*(2), 122–124.

Jenike, M. A., Baer, L., & Minichiello, W. E. (1998). *Obsessive-compulsive disorders: Practical management* (3rd ed.). St. Louis, MO: Mosby.

Jenike, M. A., Baer, L., Minichiello, W. E., Rauch, S. L., & Buttolph, M. L. (1997). Placebo-controlled trial of fluoxetine and phenelzine for obsessive-compulsive disorder. *American Journal of Psychiatry, 154*(9), 1261–1264.

Joffe, R. T., Swinson, R. P., & Levitt, A. J. (1991). Acute psychostimulant challenge in primary obsessive-compulsive disorder. *Journal of Clinical Psychopharmacology, 11*, 237–241.

Keeley, M. L., Storch, E. A., Merlo, L. J., & Geffken, G. R. (2008). Clinical predictors of response to cognitive-behavioral therapy for obsessive-compulsive disorder. *Clinical Psychology Reviews, 28*, 118–130.

Kim, C. H., Chang, J. W., Koo, M. S., Kim, J. W., Suh, H. S., Park, I. H., et al. (2003). Anterior cingulotomy for refractory obsessive-compulsive disorder. *Acta Psychiatrica Scandinavica, 107*, 283–290.

Kobak, K. A., Taylor, L. V., Bystritsky, A., Kohlenberg, C. J., Greist, J. H., Tucker, P., et al. (2005). St John's wort versus placebo in obsessive-compulsive disorder: Results from a double-blind study. *International Clinical Psychopharmacology, 20*, 299–304.

Koran, L. M. (1999). *Obsessive-compulsive and related disorders in adults: A comprehensive clinical guide.* Cambridge, England: Cambridge University Press.

Koran, L. M., Gamel, N. N., Choung, H. W., Smith, E. H., & Aboujaoude, E. N. (2005). Mirtazapine for obsessive-compulsive disorder: an open trial followed by double-blind discontinuation. *Journal of Clinical Psychiatry, 66*(4), 515–520.

Koran, L. M., Hackett, E., Rubin, A., Wolkow, R., & Robinson, D. (2002). Efficacy of sertraline in the long-term treatment of obsessive-compulsive disorder. *American Journal of Psychiatry, 159*, 88–95.

Koran, L. M., McElroy, S. L., Davidson, J. R., Rasmussen, S. A., Hollander, E., & Jenike, M. A. (1996). Fluvoxamine versus clomipramine for obsessive-compulsive disorder: A double-blind comparison. *Journal of Clinical Psychopharmacology, 16*(2), 121–129.

Kulin, N. A., Pastuszak, A., Sage, S. R., Schick-Boschetto, B., Spivey, G., Feldkamp, M., et al. (1998). Pregnancy outcome following maternal use of the new selective serotonin reuptake inhibitors: A prospective controlled multicenter study. *Journal of the American Medical Association, 279,* 609–610.

Kushner, M. G., Kim, S. W., Donahue, C., Thuras, P., Adson, D., Kotlyar, M., et al. (2007). D-cycloserine augmented exposure therapy for obsessive-compulsive disorder. *Biological Psychiatry, 62,* 835–838.

Labad, J., Menchon, J. M., Alonso, P., Segalas, C., Jimenez, S., & Vallejo, J. (2005). Female reproductive cycle and obsessive-compulsive disorder. *Journal of Clinical Psychiatry, 66,* 428–435; quiz 546.

Lafleur, D. L., Pittenger, C., Kelmendi, B., Gardner, T., Wasylink, S., Malison, R. T., et al. (2006). N-acetylcysteine augmentation in serotonin reuptake inhibitor refractory obsessive-compulsive disorder. *Psychopharmacology (Berl), 184,* 254–256.

Lavin, M. R., & Halligan, P. (1996). ECT for comorbid obsessive-compulsive disorder and schizophrenia. *American Journal of Psychiatry, 153,* 1652–1653.

Leckman, J. F., Goodman, W. K., North, W. G., Chappell, P. B., Price, L. H., Pauls, D. L., et al. (1994). Elevated levels of CSF oxytocin in obsessive compulsive disorder: Comparison with Tourette's syndrome and healthy controls. *Archives of General Psychiatry, 51,* 782–792.

Lehman, A. F., Lieberman, J. A., Dixon, L. B., McGlashan, T. H., Miller, A. L., Perkins, D. O., et al. (2004). Practice guideline for the treatment of patients with schizophrenia (2nd ed.). *American Journal of Psychiatry, 161,* 1–56.

Levine, J. (1997). Controlled trials of inositol in psychiatry. *European Neuropsychopharmacology, 7,* 147–155.

Liebowitz, M. R., Mangano, R. M., Bradwejn, J., Asnis, G., & SAD Study Group. (2005). A randomized controlled trial of venlafaxine extended release in generalized social anxiety disorder. *Journal of Clinical Psychiatry, 66(2),* 238–247.

Lundberg, S., Carlsson, A., Norfeldt, P., & Carlsson, M. L. (2004). Nicotine treatment of obsessive-compulsive disorder. *Progress in Neuro-psychopharmacology & Biological Psychiatry, 28(7),* 1195–1199.

Lykouras, L., Alevizos, B., Michalopoulou, P., & Rabavilas, A. (2003). Obsessive-compulsive symptoms induced by atypical antipsychotics: A review of the reported cases. *Progress in Neuro-psychopharmacology & Biological Psychiatry, 27(3),* 333–346.

Maletzky, B., McFarland, B., & Burt, A. (1994). Refractory obsessive compulsive disorder and ECT. *Convulsive Therapy, 10,* 34–42.

Mantovani, A., Lisanby, S. H., Pieraccini, F., Ulivelli, M., Castrogiovanni, P., & Rossi, S. (2006). Repetitive transcranial magnetic stimulation (rTMS) in the treatment of obsessive-compulsive disorder (OCD) and Tourette's syndrome (TS). *International Journal of Neuropsychopharmacology, 9,* 95–100.

Marazziti, D. (2001). Integrated pathophysiology. In N. Fineberg, D. Marazziti, & D. Stein (Eds.), *Obsessive-compulsive disorder: A practical guide* (pp. 89–102). London: Martin Dunitz.

Mataix-Cols, D., Rauch, S. L., Manzo, P. A., Jenike, M. A., & Baer, L. (1999). Use of factor-analyzed symptom dimensions to predict outcome with serotonin reuptake inhibitors and placebo in the treatment of obsessive-compulsive disorder. *American Journal of Psychiatry, 156(9),* 1409–1416.

McCabe, B. J. (1986). Dietary tyramine and other pressor amines in MAOI regimens: A review. *Journal of the American Dietetic Association, 86,* 1059–1064.

McDougle, C. J., Epperson, C. N., Pelton, G. H., Wasylink, S., & Price, L. H. (2000). A double-blind, placebo-controlled study of risperidone addition in serotonin reuptake inhibitor-refractory obsessive-compulsive disorder. *Archives of General Psychiatry, 57,* 794–801.

McDougle, C. J., & Goodman, W. K. (1997). Combination pharmacological treatment strategies. In E. Hollander & D. J. Stein (Eds.), *Obsessive-compulsive disorders: Diagnosis, etiology, treatment* (pp. 203–225). New York: Marcel Dekker.

McDougle, C. J., Goodman, W. K., Leckman, J. F., Holzer, J. C., Barr, L. C., McCance-Katz, E., et al. (1993). Limited therapeutic effect of addition of buspirone in fluvoxamine-refractory obsessive-compulsive disorder. *American Journal of Psychiatry, 150,* 647–649.

McDougle, C. J., Goodman, W. K., Leckman, J. F., Lee, N. C., Heninger, G. R., & Price, L. H. (1994). Haloperidol addition in fluvoxamine-refractory obsessive compulsive disorder: A double blind placebo-controlled study in patients with and without tics. *Archives of General Psychiatry, 51,* 302–308.

McDougle, C. J., Goodman, W. K., Price, L. H., Delgado, P. L., Krystal, J. H., Charney, D. S., et al. (1990). Neuroleptic addition in fluvoxamine-refractory obsessive-compulsive disorder. *American Journal of Psychiatry, 147,* 652–654.

McDougle, C. J., Price, L. H., Goodman, W. K., Charney, D. S., & Heninger, G. R. (1991). A controlled trial of lithium augmentation in fluvoxamine-refractory obsessive-compulsive disorder: Lack of efficacy. *Journal of Clinical Psychopharmacology, 11(3),* 175–184.

Mellman, L. A., & Gorman, J. M. (1984). Successful treatment of obsessive-compulsive disorder with ECT. *American Journal of Psychiatry, 141,* 596–597.

Montoya, A., Weiss, A. P., Price, B. H., Cassem, E. H., Dougherty, D. D., Nierenberg, A. A., et al. (2002). Magnetic resonance imaging-guided stereotactic limbic leukotomy for treatment of intractable psychiatric disease. *Neurosurgery, 50,* 1043–1049; discussion 1049–1052.

Moses-Kolko, E. L., Bogen, D., Perel, J., Bregar, A., Uhl, K., Levin, B., et al. (2005). Neonatal signs after late in utero exposure to serotonin reuptake inhibitors: Literature review and implications for clinical applications. *Journal of the American Medical Association, 293,* 2372–2383.

Mundo, E., Guglielmo, E., & Bellodi, L. (1998). Effect of adjuvant pindolol on the antiobsessional response to fluvoxamine: A double-blind, placebo-controlled study. *International Clinical Psychopharmacology, 13,* 219–224.

Newport, D. J., Fisher, A., Graybeal, S., & Stowe, Z. N. (2004). Psychopharmacology during pregnancy and lactation. In A. F. Schatzberg & C. B. Nemeroff (Eds.), *American Psychiatric Association textbook of psychopharmacology* (pp. 1109–1149). Washington, DC: American Psychiatric Press.

Nordeng, H., & Spigset, O. (2005). Treatment with selective serotonin reuptake inhibitors in the third trimester of pregnancy: Effects on the infant. *Drug Safety, 28,* 565–581.

Nulman, I., Rovet, J., Stewart, D. E., Wolpin, J., Pace-Asciak, P., Shuhaiber, S., et al. (2002). Child development following exposure to tricyclic antidepressants or fluoxetine throughout fetal life: A prospective, controlled study. *American Journal of Psychiatry, 159,* 1889–1895.

Nuttin, B., Cosyns, P., Demeulemeester, H., Gybels, J., & Meyerson, B. (1999). Electrical stimulation in anterior limbs of internal capsules in patients with obsessive-compulsive disorder. *Lancet, 354*(9189), 1526.

Nuttin, B. J., Gabriels, L., van Kuyck, K., & Cosyns, P. (2003). Electrical stimulation of the anterior limbs of the internal capsules in patients with severe obsessive-compulsive disorder: anecdotal reports. *Neurosurgery Clinics of North America, 14*(2), 267–274.

Oliver, B., Gascon, J., Aparicio, A., Ayats, E., Rodriguez, R., Maestro De Leon, J. L., et al. (2003). Bilateral anterior capsulotomy for refractory obsessive-compulsive disorders. *Stereotactic and Functional Neurosurgery, 81,* 90–95.

Otto, M. W., Basden, S. L., Leyro, T. M., McHugh, R. K., & Hofmann, S. G. (2006). Clinical perspectives on the combination of D-cycloserine and cognitive-behavioral therapy for the treatment of anxiety disorders. *CNS Spectrums, 12,* 51–56.

Pallanti, S., Quercioli, L., Paiva, R. S., & Koran, L. M. (1999). Citalopram for treatment-resistant obsessive-compulsive disorder. *European Psychiatry, 14,* 101–106.

Pato, M. T., Pigott, T. A., Hill, J. L., Grover, G. N., Bernstein, S., & Murphy, D. L. (1991). Controlled comparison of buspirone and clomipramine in obsessive-compulsive disorder. *American Journal of Psychiatry, 148,* 127–129.

Pato, M. T., Zohar-Kadouch, R., Zohar, J., & Murphy, D. L. (1988). Return of symptoms after discontinuation of clomipramine in patients with obsessive-compulsive disorder. *American Journal of Psychiatry, 145,* 1521–1525.

Perugi, G., Toni, C., Frare, F., Travierso, M. C., Hantouche, E., & Akiskal, H. S. (2002). Obsessive-compulsive-bipolar comorbidity: A systematic exploration of clinical features and treatment outcome. *Journal of Clinical Psychiatry, 63,* 1129–1134.

Pigott, T. A., L'Heureux, F., Hill, J. L., Bihari, K., Bernstein, S. E., & Murphy, D. L. (1992a). A double-blind study of adjuvant buspirone hydrochloride in clomipramine-treated patients with obsessive-compulsive disorder. *Journal of Clinical Psychopharmacology, 12,* 11–18.

Pigott, T. A., L'Heureux, F., Rubenstein, C. S., Bernstein, S. E., Hill, J. L., & Murphy, D. L. (1992b). A double-blind, placebo controlled study of trazodone in patients with obsessive-compulsive disorder. *Journal of Clinical Psychopharmacology, 12,* 156–162.

Pigott, T. A., Pato, M. T., L'Heureux, F., Hill, J. L., Grover, G. N., Bernstein, S. E., et al. (1991). A controlled comparison of adjuvant lithium carbonate or thyroid hormone in clomipramine-treated patients with obsessive-compulsive disorder. *Journal of Clinical Psychopharmacology, 11,* 242–248.

Pigott, T. A., & Seay, S. M. (1999). A review of the efficacy of selective serotonin reuptake inhibitors in obsessive-compulsive disorder. *Journal of Clinical Psychiatry, 60,* 101–106.

Poyurovsky, M., Weizman, A., & Weizman, R. (2004). Obsessive-compulsive disorder in schizophrenia: clinical characteristics and treatment. *CNS Drugs, 18*(14), 989–1010.

Rasmussen, S. A., & Eisen, J. L. (1988). Clinical and epidemiologic findings of significance to neuropharmacologic trials in OCD. *Psychopharmacology Bulletin 24,* 466–470.

Rauch, S. L., & Jenike, M. A. (1994). Management of treatment resistant obsessive-compulsive disorder: Concepts and strategies. In Berend, O., E. Hollander, & J. Zohar (Eds), *Current insights in obsessive-compulsive disorder* (pp. 227–244). Chichester, England: John Wiley.

Ravizza, L., Barzega, G., Bellino, S., Bogetto, F., & Maina, G. (1996). Drug treatment of obsessive-compulsive disorder (OCD): Long-term trial with clomipramine and selective serotonin reuptake inhibitors (SSRIs). *Psychopharmacology Bulletin, 32,* 167–173.

Richter, E. O., Davis, K. D., Hamani, C., Hutchison, W. D., Dostrovsky, J. O., & Lozano, A. M. (2004). Cingulotomy for psychiatric disease: Microelectrode guidance, a callosal reference system for documenting lesion location, and clinical results. *Neurosurgery, 54,* 622–628; discussion 628–630.

Romano, S., Goodman, W., Tamura, R., & Gonzales, J. (2001). Long-term treatment of obsessive-compulsive disorder after an acute response: A comparison of fluoxetine versus placebo. *Journal of Clinical Psychopharmacology, 21,* 46–52.

Sachdev, P. S., McBride, R., Loo, C. K., Mitchell, P. B., Malhi, G. S., & Croker, V. M. (2001). Right versus left prefrontal transcranial magnetic stimulation for obsessive-compulsive disorder: A preliminary investigation. *Journal of Clinical Psychiatry, 62,* 981–984.

Saxena, S., Maidment, K. M., Vapnik, T., Golden, G., Rishwain, T., Rosen, R. M., et al. (2002). Obsessive-compulsive hoarding: symptom severity and response to multimodal treatment. *Journal of Clinical Psychiatry, 63*(1), 21–27.

Shapira, N. A., Keck, P. E., Jr., Goldsmith, T. D., McConville, B. J., Eis, M., & McElroy, S. L. (1997). Open-label pilot study of tramadol hydrochloride in treatment-refractory obsessive-compulsive disorder. *Depression and Anxiety, 6,* 170–173.

Shapira, N. A., Ward, H. E., Mandoki, M., Murphy, T. K., Yang, M. C., Blier, P., et al. (2004). A double-blind, placebo-controlled trial of olanzapine addition in fluoxetine-refractory obsessive-compulsive disorder. *Biological Psychiatry, 55,* 553–555.

Simon, G. E., Cunningham, M. L., & Davis, R. L. (2002). Outcomes of prenatal antidepressant exposure. *American Journal of Psychiatry, 159,* 2055–2061.

Simpson, H. B., Franklin, M. E., Cheng, J., Foa, E. B., & Liebowitz, M. R. (2005). Standard criteria for relapse are needed in obsessive-compulsive disorder. *Depression and Anxiety, 21,* 1–8.

Simpson, H. B., Liebowitz, M. R., Foa, E. B., Kozak, M. J., Schmidt, A. B., Rowan, V., et al. (2004). Post-treatment effects of exposure therapy and clomipramine in obsessive-compulsive disorder. *Depression and Anxiety, 19,* 225–233.

Skoog, G., & Skoog, I. (1999). A 40-year follow-up of patients with obsessive-compulsive disorder [see comments]. *Archives of General Psychiatry, 56,* 121–127.

Stein, D. J., Andersen, E. W., Tonnoir, B., & Fineberg, N. (2007). Escitalopram in obsessive-compulsive disorder: a randomized, placebo-controlled, paroxetine-referenced, fixed-dose, 24-week study. *Current Medical Research Opinions 23,* 701–711.

Steiner, M., Bushnell, M. S., & Gergel, I. P. (1995). *Long-term treatment and prevention of relapse of OCD with paroxetine.* 148th Annual Meeting of the American Psychological Association, New York.

Stewart SE, Fagerness JA, Platko J, Smoller JW, Scharf JM, Illmann C, Jenike E, Chabane N, Leboyer M, Delorme R, Jenike MA, Pauls DL. (2007). Association of the SLC1A1 Glutamate Transporter Gene and Obsessive-Compulsive Disorder. *American Journal of Medical Genetics Part B (Neuropsychiatric Genetics) 144B:* 1027–1033.

Stewart, S. E., Geller, D. A., Jenike, M., Pauls, D., Shaw, D., Mullin, B., et al. (2004). Long-term outcome of pediatric obsessive-compulsive disorder: A meta-analysis and qualitative review of the literature. *Acta Psychiatrica Scandinavica, 110,* 4–13.

Strassnig, M., Riedel, M., & Muller, N. (2004). Electroconvulsive therapy in a patient with Tourette's syndrome and co-morbid obsessive compulsive disorder. *World Journal of Biological Psychiatry, 5,* 164–166.

Sweet, R. A., Brown, E. J., Heimberg, R. G., Ciafre, L., Scanga, D. M., Cornelius, J. R., et al. (1995). Monoamine oxidase inhibitor dietary restrictions: What are we asking patients to give up? *Journal of Clinical Psychiatry, 56,* 196–201.

Thomas, S. G., & Kellner, C. H. (2003). Remission of major depression and obsessive-compulsive disorder after a single unilateral ECT. *Journal of ECT, 19,* 50–51.

Thoren, P., Asberg, M., Cronholm, B., Jornestedt, L., & Traskman, L. (1980). Clomipramine treatment of obsessive-compulsive disorder: I. A controlled clinical trial. *Archives of General Psychiatry, 37,* 1281–1285.

Tolin, D. F., Maltby, N., Diefenbach, G. J., Hannan, S. E., & Worhunsky, P. (2004). Cognitive-behavioral therapy for medication nonresponders with obsessive-compulsive disorder: a wait-list-controlled open trial. *Journal of Clinical Psychiatry, 65,* 922–923.

Torres, A. R., Moran, P., Bebbington, P., Brugha, T., Bhugra, D., Coid, J. W., et al. (2006). Obsessive-compulsive disorder and personality disorder: evidence from the British National Survey of Psychiatric Morbidity 2000. *Social Psychiatry and Psychiatric Epidemiology, 41,* 862–867.

Vulink, N. C., Denys, D., & Westenberg, H. G. (2005). Bupropion for patients with obsessive-compulsive disorder: An open-label, fixed-dose study. *Journal of Clinical Psychiatry, 66,* 228–230.

Weiss, A. P., & Jenike, M. A. (2000). Late-onset obsessive-compulsive disorder: A case series. *Journal of Neuropsychiatry and Clinical Neuroscience, 12,* 265–268.

Weissman, A. M., Levy, B. T., Hartz, A. J., Bentler, S., Donohue, M., Ellingrod, V. L., et al. (2004). Pooled analysis of antidepressant levels in lactating mothers, breast milk, and nursing infants. *American Journal of Psychiatry, 161,* 1066–1078.

Welch, J. M., Lu, J., Rodriguiz, R. M., Trotta, N. C., Peca, J., Ding, J. D., et al. (2007). Cortico-striatal synaptic defects and OCD-like behaviors in Sapap3-mutant mice. *Nature, 448,* 871–872.

Wilhelm, S., Buhlmann, U., Tolin, D. F., Meunier, S. A., Pearlson, G. D., Reese, H. E., et al. (2008). Augmentation of behavior therapy with d-cycloserine for obsessive-compulsive disorder. *American Journal of Psychiatry, 165,* 335–341.

Williams, K. E., & Koran, L. M. (1997). Obsessive-compulsive disorder in pregnancy: The puerperium, and the premenstruum. *Journal of Clinical Psychiatry, 58,* 330–334; quiz 335–336.

Wisner, K. L., Zarin, D. A., Holmboe, E. S., Appelbaum, P. S., Gelenberg, A. J., Leonard, H. L., et al. (2000). Risk-benefit decision making for treatment of depression during pregnancy. *American Journal of Psychiatry, 157,* 1933–1940.

Yaryura-Tobias, J. A. (1981). Clinical observations on L-tryptophan in the treatment of obsessive-compulsive disorders. *Biological Psychiatry, 16,* 622–625.

Yaryura-Tobias, J. A., & Bhagavan, H. N. (1977). L-tryptophan in obsessive-compulsive disorders. *American Journal of Psychiatry, 134,* 1298–1299.

Zohar, J., & Judge, R. (1996). Paroxetine versus clomipramine in the treatment of obsessive-compulsive disorder: OCD Paroxetine Study Investigators. *The British Journal of Psychiatry, 169*(4), 468–474.

29 Psychological Treatment of Obsessive-Compulsive Disorder

Jonathan S. Abramowitz, Autumn E. Braddock *and* Elizabeth L. Moore

Abstract

The psychological treatment of obsessive-compulsive disorder (OCD) is one of the great success stories within the field of mental health. Within the span of about 20 years, the prognosis for individuals with OCD changed from poor to very good as a result of the development of cognitive–behavioral techniques. This chapter describes the procedures of exposure, response prevention, and cognitive therapy; their hypothesized mechanisms of action; and the results from treatment outcome research attesting to their efficacy and effectiveness. The chapter also addresses the efficacy of combining exposure therapy techniques with medications in the treatment of OCD.

Keywords: cognitive behavioral therapy, exposure therapy, obsessive-compulsive disorder, psychological treatment

As its name suggests, obsessive-compulsive disorder (OCD) is characterized by obsessions and compulsions (*DSM–IV–TR*) (American Psychiatric Association, 2000). Obsessions are defined as recurrent, unwanted, and often seemingly bizarre thoughts, impulses, or doubts that evoke affective distress (e.g., recurring senseless thoughts that one has offended God by mistake). Compulsions are defined as repetitive behavioral or mental rituals performed in response to obsessions or according to particular rules (e.g., excessive praying and confession).

Research indicates that obsessional fears tend to concern issues related to doubts about personal safety or the safety of others, with compulsive rituals aimed at reducing such doubts. In a large study on the various presentations of OCD, Abramowitz, Franklin, Schwartz, and Furr (2003) found that certain types of obsessions and compulsions co-occur within patients, including (1) obsessions regarding contamination with decontamination rituals (e.g., excessive washing and cleaning); (2) obsessions

regarding responsibility for harm or catastrophe and reassurance-seeking rituals (e.g., compulsive checking); and (3) unwanted, repugnant aggressive/violent, sexual, or blasphemous obsessional thoughts with covert compulsions or "neutralizing strategies" (e.g., mental rituals, praying, repeating routine actions, and thought suppression). Also, some patients have excessive concerns about lucky/unlucky numbers, orderliness, and/or symmetry. Although most OCD sufferers recognize that their symptoms are senseless and excessive, approximately 4% strongly believe that their rituals serve to prevent the occurrence of disastrous consequences (i.e., they have "poor insight") (Foa & Kozak, 1995). Clinical observations suggest that the degree of insight can vary over time and across symptom categories.

The lifetime prevalence rate of OCD in adults is estimated at about 2%–3% (Karno, Golding, Sorenson, & Burnam, 1988). Although symptoms typically wax and wane as a function of general life stress, a chronic and deteriorating course is the norm if adequate treatment is not sought. In many cases, fears, avoidance, and rituals impair various areas of functioning, including job or academic performance, socializing, and leisure activities. Additionally, many individuals with OCD experience other Axis I disorders such as mood and anxiety problems (Crino & Andrews, 1996). When the prevalence and course of OCD are considered along with its associated personal costs, one quickly recognizes the importance of effective treatment for this condition. Hence, this chapter reviews the theoretical underpinnings of effective psychological treatments for OCD and describes the implementation of such treatment procedures. A comprehensive review of the data supporting the efficacy and effectiveness of such treatments is also provided.

Behavior Therapy
Theoretical Basis

Prior to the 1970s, OCD was considered unresponsive to treatment, a label that speaks to the effectiveness (or ineffectiveness) of the dominant treatment strategies used for OCD at that time: psychodynamic and psychoanalytic psychotherapy. By the last quarter of the 20th century, however, the prognostic picture for OCD began to improve dramatically due in large part to the work of Victor Meyer and other behaviorally oriented clinicians and researchers who applied learning theory to the experimental study and treatment of OCD. Briefly, we review some of this early work as it is germane to understanding the development of contemporary behavioral therapy techniques for OCD.

Behavioral models of OCD derive largely from Mowrer's (Mowrer, 1960) two-stage theory of the acquisition and maintenance of fear and avoidance behavior. The first stage involves a classical conditioning process in which neutral stimuli such as objects, thoughts, and images become conditioned stimuli associated with fear and discomfort by being paired with another, unconditioned stimulus that by its nature provokes fear. Although most individuals with OCD do not report traumatic conditioning histories (e.g., Mineka & Zinbarg, 1996), such conditioning might occur through social learning and verbal transmission of threat-related information (Mineka & Zinbarg, 2006). In the second stage of the model, escape and avoidance responses are developed to reduce the conditioned fear response and are maintained by their immediate success (i.e., negative reinforcement). Dollard and Miller (1950) suggested that compulsive rituals develop as active avoidance strategies because obsessional stimuli are

ubiquitous and difficult to avoid. Because rituals serve to reduce fear, they are negatively reinforced and thus become habitual. Escape, avoidance, and rituals maintain conditioned fear responses by preventing the natural extinction of such fears.

Although it remains unclear whether obsessional fear is acquired via classical conditioning, there is strong empirical evidence that (1) obsessions trigger fear and anxiety, and (2) compulsive rituals reduce obsessional anxiety. In a series of elegant experiments on the phenomenology of OCD (primarily washing and checking presentations), Rachman and his colleagues (Rachman & Hodgson, 1980) found that exposure to obsessional cues triggered subjective distress and provoked urges to perform compulsive rituals. For patients permitted to perform such rituals, subjective distress and compulsive urges were immediately reduced. A gradual "spontaneous decay" of compulsive urges was noted when patients were not permitted to execute their rituals. Repeated prevention of rituals resulted in the eventual extinction of subjective distress in response to previously fear-evoking situations and stimuli.

Noting the therapeutic implications of the aforementioned theory and research that were complemented by early animal studies on avoidance learning (see Houts, 2005, for a review), Meyer (1966) persuaded patients hospitalized with OCD to deliberately confront situations and stimuli they usually avoided (e.g., floors, bathrooms) for the purpose of deliberately inducing obsessional fears and urges to ritualize. The patients were simultaneously instructed to refrain from performing compulsive rituals (e.g., washing, checking) to demonstrate the natural reduction in distress that would follow, thus rendering rituals redundant. Ten of Meyer's 15 patients responded extremely well to this exposure and response prevention (ERP) treatment, which extinguished obsessional fear and avoidance, and helped them resist ritualistic urges. The remainder of these patients evidenced partial improvement. Follow-up studies conducted several years later found that only two of those who were successfully treated had relapsed (Meyer, Levy, & Schnurer, 1974).

What began with Mowrer's empirically informed clinical experiment developed into a well-validated treatment for OCD. Contemporary ERP entails (1) systematic prolonged and repeated (therapist-guided and self-directed) exposure to situations that provoke obsessional fear along with (2) abstinence from compulsive behaviors. This might occur in the form of repeated actual confrontation with feared low-risk situations (i.e., in vivo exposure), or in the form of imaginal confrontation with the obsessional thought or feared consequences of exposure (i.e., imaginal exposure). For example, an individual who avoids places of worship because of obsessional sexual thoughts that occur when he or she is attending services would practice going to the house of worship (situational exposure) and purposely thinking sexual thoughts (imaginal exposure).

Refraining from compulsive rituals, or response prevention, is a vital component of behavioral treatment because the performance of such rituals to reduce obsessional anxiety would prematurely discontinue exposure and prevent the patient from learning that (1) the obsessional situation is not truly dangerous, and (2) anxiety subsides on its own even if the ritual is not performed (i.e., habituation). Thus, successful ERP requires that the patient remain in the exposure situation until the obsessional distress decreases spontaneously, without attempting to reduce the distress by withdrawing from the situation or by performing compulsive rituals or neutralizing strategies.

Description of ERP

Exposure and response prevention can be delivered in a number of ways. One highly successful format involves a thorough functional assessment and treatment plan, followed by 16 twice-weekly exposure sessions lasting 90–120 minutes each, spaced over about 8 weeks (Abramowitz, Foa, & Franklin, 2003). Generally, the therapist oversees the patient's exposure tasks during the treatment sessions and then assigns self-exposure practice to be completed by the patient between visits. Depending on the patient's symptom presentation and the practicality of confronting actual feared situations, treatment sessions might involve varying amounts of actual and imaginal exposure practice. Field trips to places that afford realistic exposure practice are also commonly used.

Consistent with this framework, our ERP program (Abramowitz, 2006) typically begins with a consultation to discuss the appropriateness of treatment and the rationale for using the ERP techniques. The initial therapy sessions involve assessment and case conceptualization. The therapist collects information about the following four parameters of the patient's OCD symptoms: (1) obsessional thoughts, ideas, impulses; (2) external stimuli that trigger obsessions; (3) rituals and avoidance behavior; and (4) the anticipated harmful consequences of confronting feared situations without performing rituals. Before beginning any exposure, the therapist socializes the patient to a psychological model of OCD that is based on the principles of learning and emotion (Salkovskis, 1996). The rationale for how ERP is expected to be helpful in reducing OCD is reiterated, including how anxiety will be provoked and allowed to decline naturally (i.e., without rituals) in the presence of the obsessional thought or its trigger. Information gathered during the assessment sessions is then used to plan, collaboratively with the patient, the specific exposure exercises that will be pursued. Next, the patient is acquainted with response prevention procedures. Importantly, the term *response prevention* does not imply that the therapist actively prevents the patient from performing rituals. Instead, the therapist educates patients about the rationale for response prevention and strongly encourages them to decide to resist urges to perform rituals. Self-monitoring of rituals is often used in support of this goal.

Exposure exercises themselves typically begin with moderately distressing situations, stimuli, and images, and escalate up to the most distressing situations. Beginning with less anxiety-evoking exposure tasks increases the likelihood that the patient will learn to manage his or her distress and complete each exposure exercise successfully. Moreover, having success with initial exposures increases confidence in the treatment and helps motivate the patient to persevere during later, more difficult, exercises. At the end of each treatment session, the therapist instructs the patient to continue exposure for several hours and in varied contexts without the therapist. Exposure to the most anxiety-evoking situations is not left to the end of the treatment, but rather, is practiced about mid-way through the schedule of exposure sessions. This tactic allows the patient ample opportunity to repeat exposure to the most difficult situations in different contexts for the purposes of generalization of the treatment effects. During the later treatment sessions, the therapist emphases the importance of the patient's continuing to apply the ERP procedures learned during treatment.

Mechanisms of Action

From a behavioral perspective, ERP is thought to work because it provides an opportunity for the extinction of conditioned fear responses. Specifically, repeated and uninterrupted exposure to feared stimuli produces a natural decrease in conditioned fear. Response prevention blocks the performance of rituals that would foil the extinction process. From a cognitive perspective, ERP is thought to work because these procedures present the patient with information that disconfirms faulty estimates of threat (Foa & Kozak, 1986). For example, when a patient confronts feared situations and refrains from rituals, he or she discovers that (1) obsessional fear declines naturally, and (2) the feared disastrous consequences are unlikely to materialize. This evidence is incorporated into the patient's belief system. Finally, ERP helps patients gain self-efficacy by mastering their fears without having to rely on avoidance or safety behaviors. The importance of this sense of mastery is an oft-overlooked effect of ERP.

Cognitive Therapy
Theoretical Basis

Cognitive perspectives on OCD derive from observations that thoughts are important elements of the pathology of OCD, and the assumption that obsessions and compulsions can be reduced by modifying problematic cognitive processes (Shafran, 2005). Among the most promising cognitive models are those based on Beck's (1976) cognitive specificity hypothesis, which proposes that different types of psychopathology arise from different types of dysfunctional beliefs. As they pertain to OCD, such cognitive models (Salkovskis, 1996) start with the established finding that unwanted intrusive thoughts, images, impulses, and doubts are normal experiences reported by most people (Rachman & de Silva, 1978). Such intrusions reflect the individual's current concerns and are triggered by internal or external reminders of those concerns. For example, the sight of a fire truck might trigger a doubt regarding whether one left the oven on, which could lead to a house fire. Cognitive theorists such as Rachman (1997, 1998), Salkovskis (1996), and others (e.g., Frost & Steketee, 2002) suggest that when such intrusions are appraised as highly significant in some way (e.g., as posing a threat for which the individual is personally responsible), the intrusion escalates into an obsession.

Consider, for example, the intrusive doubt about a house fire mentioned above. Most people experiencing such a thought would regard it as meaningless "mental noise." Such an intrusion, however, might become a clinical obsession if the person appraises it as having serious consequences for which he or she is personally responsible; such as, "Since I'm thinking of this, it must have really happened." Such appraisals evoke anxiety and fear, and motivate the person to try to reduce this affective distress and prevent any harmful events associated with the intrusion (e.g., by returning home and checking the oven).

From the cognitive perspective, compulsive rituals are construed efforts to remove intrusions, distress, and prevent feared consequences. In addition to being negatively reinforced by the reduction in distress that they engender, as espoused by the behavioral model, rituals are thought to contribute to the maintenance of obsessional fear by preventing the person from learning that his or her appraisals are unrealistic (e.g., the person fails to learn that unwanted thoughts about danger are not actually indicative of danger). Rituals also influence the frequency of intrusions by serving as reminders, and thereby triggering their reoccurrence. For example, compulsive hand-washing can remind the person that he or she may have become contaminated. Attempts at distracting oneself from unwanted intrusions paradoxically increase the frequency of intrusions, possibly because the distractors become reminders, or retrieval cues, of the intrusions.

The therapeutic implication of cognitive models of OCD is that unwanted intrusive thoughts are normal experiences, and it is their misinterpretation that causes OCD symptoms. Cognitive therapy therefore aims to obviate obsessions and compulsions by helping the patient reinterpret the unwanted intrusions as nonthreatening. From this perspective, successful treatment must incorporate procedures that (1) help patients correct their dysfunctional beliefs about, and misinterpretations of, otherwise normal intrusive thoughts, and (2) eliminate barriers to the correction of these mistaken cognitions. Specific techniques used in cognitive therapy are discussed below.

Implementation of Cognitive Therapy Procedures

Cognitive therapy typically begins with an explanation of the cognitive model of emotion and its application to OCD. Patients are taught that emotional distress arises not from situations or intrusive thoughts themselves, but rather from how the individual gives meaning to such stimuli (Beck, 1976). Patients learn that their intrusive thoughts—no matter how vulgar, violent, immoral, or otherwise unacceptable—are not harmful or significant per se. Rather, obsessional problems arise when the patient misperceives and misinterprets these stimuli as highly significant. Such misinterpretations cause distress and lead to exaggerated responses such as avoidance, rituals, and other forms of neutralization in an effort to reduce obsessional distress. Additionally, patients learn about the ways in which neutralizing responses reinforce obsessions and prevent the correction of mistaken beliefs about the otherwise normal intrusive thoughts.

A number of techniques have been developed to help patients correct erroneous beliefs about intrusive thoughts (for reviews, see Clark, 2004, and Fama & Wilhelm, 2005). Each of these procedures involves rational discussion of maladaptive assumptions, often using metaphors and Socratic questioning. The therapist guides the patient to (1) identify mistaken, illogical beliefs, (2) challenge faulty ideas by evaluating the relevant evidence, and (3) develop more helpful and logical beliefs, assumptions, interpretations, and responses. The selection of which specific cognitive technique to use is driven by the particular patient's beliefs underlying his or her obsessional fears. In this way, cognitive therapy is highly tailored to the individual patient.

An exemplary cognitive technique for modifying beliefs about the importance of and need to control intrusive thoughts is to give the patient a list of intrusive thoughts reported by non-OCD individuals to demonstrate such intrusions are universal and not harmful. *Behavioral experiments* specifically targeting mistaken beliefs are effective cognitive techniques, as well. These involve the patient entering situations that exemplify mistaken beliefs and gathering evidence to test out the logic of such beliefs. For example, a patient who believes that her intrusive thoughts about the death of a family member will somehow bring about such a tragedy (i.e., thought-action fusion) would be encouraged to deliberately think about and wish for relatives to die. Later, the patient would determine whether thinking these thoughts caused the feared consequences. To ensure that mistaken beliefs are the only explanation for the nonoccurrence of the feared outcome, they should be out of the patient's control and the base rate should be uncommon but not entirely rare (e.g., deaths do occur, but they are not likely at any given time).

Review of the Treatment Outcome Literature
Efficacy of ERP

Over the past 30 to 40 years, numerous treatment studies have been accumulated to indicate that ERP is extremely effective in reducing OCD symptoms. Foa and Kozak (1996) found that across 16 studies of ERP, 83% of the patients were responders (defined as achieving at least 30% improvement) at posttreatment, whereas 76% were at follow-up an average of 29 months later. A meta-analysis of 24 ERP studies totaling over 800 patients conducted from 1975 through 1995 found posttreatment mean effect sizes of 1.16 on self-report measures and 1.41 on clinician-rated, interview measures (Abramowitz, 1996). Follow-up effect sizes were similarly large: 1.10 and 1.57 for self-report and interview scales, respectively. These findings suggest that most OCD patients who undergo treatment with ERP achieve substantial short- and long-term benefit.

Interpreting OCD treatment outcome results is simplified by the fact that most studies use a common outcome measure: the 10-item Yale-Brown Obsessive Compulsive Scale (Y-BOCS) (Goodman et al., 1989a, 1989b). This enables comparisons across investigations and helps readers derive clinically useful data from study results. The Y-BOCS yields a total score ranging from 0 (no symptoms) to 40 (extremely severe). Scores of 0–7 indicate subclinical symptoms, 8–15 indicate mild OCD, 16–25 represent moderate symptomatology, 26–30 represent severe symptoms, and 31–40 indicate extreme symptoms. Because the Y-BOCS possesses adequate psychometric properties, we focus on outcome results for this measure in the review that follows.

Mean Y-BOCS scores from the four existing randomized controlled trials (RCTs) evaluated the efficacy of ERP in comparison with both credible control treatments (e.g., relaxation, anxiety management training, pill placebo) and waitlist (see Table 1). Overall, the findings from these rigorously conducted trials, which were carried out at various international sites, indicate that ERP produces large and clinically meaningful effects on OCD symptoms. Moreover, ERP's superiority over credible pill and psychotherapy placebo treatments indicates that improvement is due to the specific treatment procedures (i.e., exposure and response prevention), over and above nonspecific or common factors of psychotherapy such as attention and time passage.

Effectiveness Studies of ERP

Whereas the studies described above demonstrate the *efficacy* of ERP, their results do not necessarily generalize to typical service delivery settings (e.g., Persons & Silberschatz, 1998); as a result, ERP is grossly underutilized in everyday practice since many clinicians believe that study results are not applicable to their clientele. Indeed, patient samples in RCTs are not always representative of most treatment-referred OCD patients. The RCTs typically exclude individuals with certain comorbid conditions in order to achieve more homogenous

Table 1. Effects of Exposure and Response Prevention (ERP) in Randomized Controlled Trials

		Mean Y-BOCS Total Score					
		ERP Group			Control Group		
Study	Control Condition	n	Pre	Post	n	Pre	Post
Fals-Stewart et al. (1993)	Relaxation	31	20.2	12.1	32	19.9	18.1
Lindsay et al. (1997)	Anxiety management	9	28.7 (4.6)	11.0 (3.8)	9	24.4 (7.0)	25.9 (5.8)
Van Balkom et al. (1998)	Waiting list	19	25.0 (7.9)	17.1 (8.4)	18	26.8 (6.4)	26.4 (6.8)
Foa et al. (2005)	Pill placebo	29	24.6 (4.8)	11.0 (7.9)	26	25.0 (4.0)	22.2 (6.4)

Note. Y-BOCS = Yale-Brown Obsessive Compulsive Scale.

diagnostic samples; yet among people with OCD, comorbidity with mood and anxiety disorders is the norm. Other differences between RCTs and routine clinical practice include therapist training and supervision, use of manuals (i.e., fixed number of sessions), and random assignment. An issue for research is, therefore, to examine whether treatments found efficacious in highly controlled studies work as well with typical OCD patients as encountered in routine practice.

Effectiveness studies, which represent an approach to bridging the research-practice gap described above, are investigations in which empirically supported treatments are evaluated in clinical service contexts with highly representative patients and treatment providers. Four effectiveness studies have examined the effects of ERP among nonresearch outpatient samples. In the earliest study, Kirk (1983) reported on 36 OCD patients treated by nonresearch-oriented behavior therapists in England. Treatment, which involved variations of ERP and was neither manualized nor time-limited, resulted in more than 75% of patients experiencing at least moderate improvement. The majority of patients (81%) sought no further treatment for OCD over a 5-year follow-up period. Because no standardized outcome measures were used to assess outcome as the study was conducted before the Y-BOCS was developed, the clinical effects of the treatment are difficult to determine.

More recently, Franklin, Abramowitz, Kozak, Levitt, and Foa (2000) treated 110 patients with intensive ERP (15 daily sessions over 3 weeks) on a fee-for-service basis. Over half of their sample had psychiatric or medical comorbidities, many patients

reported histories of treatment failure, and many had challenging presentations of OCD such as hoarding, scrupulosity, and severe obsessions with mental rituals. Nevertheless, patients evidenced considerable improvement: mean Y-BOCS scores improved from 26.8 to 11.8 (60% reduction in OCD symptoms). Moreover, only 10 patients dropped out of treatment prematurely.

Although the Franklin et al. (2000) study demonstrated that representative OCD patients respond well to ERP, the study took place in an anxiety disorders specialty unit where many therapists were highly experienced with ERP, and/or received regular supervision from ERP experts. In addition, the intensive treatment regimen was highly demanding and unlikely to be used in most outpatient settings. To address these issues, Warren and Thomas (2001) reported on 26 individuals with OCD treated in a private practice psychotherapy clinic with ERP and formal cognitive techniques. Treatment sessions were held weekly for 1 hour and the total number of therapy hours across patients varied (mean = 16.4 hrs). Thirty-two percent of the patients in this study had comorbid conditions and 50% had previously received treatment for their OCD. Results were highly consistent with Franklin et al.'s (2000) study: Y-BOCS scores improved from 23.0 to 11.6 (48% reduction in OCD symptoms). Moreover, Warren and Thomas (2001) demonstrated that the beneficial effects of cognitive behavioral therapy (CBT) extend to private practice settings in which treatment sessions occur on a once-weekly basis.

In a multicultural naturalistic study, Friedman and colleagues (2003) presented treatment outcome results for a community sample of African American, Caribbean American, and White OCD patients. Therapy involved an average of 20 twice-weekly ERP sessions and was informed by an ERP manual, although therapists did not have to adhere rigidly to the protocol. Whereas treatment was effective in reducing OCD and depressive symptoms, many patients reported significant residual symptoms after therapy: mean Y-BOCS scores for African American patients were 23.5 (pretreatment) and 17.2 (posttreatment; 27% reduction), and for Whites were 26.03 (pretreatment) and 17.65 (posttreatment; 23% reduction). There were no between-group differences in treatment outcome.

When the results of ERP effectiveness studies are benchmarked to the results of RCTs, it appears that OCD patients with substantial comorbidity and histories of treatment failure who received therapy in nonresearch contexts generally fare comparably to the highly selected patient samples treated under controlled conditions in RCTs. This suggests that the substantial effects of ERP for OCD are transportable from research to clinical contexts.

Comparisons Between ERP and Cognitive Therapy

Six studies have directly compared variations of ERP to different forms of CT. In two early trials, Emmelkamp and colleagues compared rational emotive therapy (RET) to ERP (Emmelkamp & Beens, 1991; Emmelkamp & Hoekstra, 1988). RET (Ellis, 1962) included identifying irrational beliefs (e.g., "not washing my hands would be 100% awful"), challenging the basis of these beliefs, and replacing them with rational beliefs that do not lead to anxiety. Exposure in the ERP conditions was self-controlled; meaning patients completed all exposure practice on their own as homework assignments. In the two studies, both RET and self-controlled ERP produced similarly disappointing results. Limitations of these studies included their small sample sizes, lack of adequate assessment (Y-BOCS), and absence of therapist-supervised exposure in ERP. Therefore, definitive conclusions regarding the relative efficacy of ERP and CT on the basis of these studies are not warranted.

Four additional studies that reported outcome using the Y-BOCS compared contemporary CT programs with variations of ERP. The results of these studies are presented in Table 2. Van Oppen et al. (1995) randomly assigned patients to either 16 sessions of CT or 16 sessions of self-controlled ERP. Both treatments led to an improvement in

OCD symptoms with CT being more effective than ERP. Importantly, the brief and infrequent therapist contact (weekly 45-minute sessions), along with reliance upon patients to manage all exposure practices on their own, likely accounted for the relatively modest effects of ERP in this study. Moreover, CT involved behavioral experiments that resembled exposure, which blurred the distinction between the two study treatments. Only after behavioral experiments were introduced at the sixth session did symptom reduction in the CT group approach that of ERP. Thus, it appears that the exposure component of behavioral experiments was key to the efficacy of CT. Consistent with this assertion, van Balkom et al. (1998) found no significant differences between self-controlled ERP and CT with behavioral experiments.

Cottraux et al.'s (2001) study appears to be the most even-handed comparison between CT and ERP. Both treatments involved 20 hours of therapist contact over 16 weeks. The CT included psychoeducation, modification of unrealistic interpretations of intrusive thoughts, and behavioral experiments to test unrealistic assumptions both in session and for homework; ERP involved therapist-supervised and homework-based exposure, as well as complete response prevention. Although the two programs produced comparable immediate outcomes, at 1-year follow-up, patients treated with ERP evidenced further improvement (follow-up mean Y-BOCS = 11.1), whereas those who received CT had not (follow-up mean Y-BOCS = 15.0).

In McLean et al.'s (2001) trial, patients received 12 weekly 2.5 hour group sessions (6 to 8 participants per group) of either CT or ERP, the latter involving in-session and homework-based exposures. Both treatments were more effective than a waitlist control condition, and ERP was associated with greater improvement than CT at both posttreatment (40% and 27% Y-BOCS reductions, respectively) and follow-up (21% and 41% Y-BOCS reductions).

In conclusion, the interpretation of early results from comparison studies as indicating equivalent efficacy of CT and ERP is questionable since both treatments yielded minimal improvements in most studies. The ERP outcome was likely hindered because of the use of suboptimal treatment procedures (e.g., lack of therapist-supervised exposure). At the same time, CT programs appear to have been enhanced by behavioral experiments that likely have similar effects as supervised exposure. Using meta-analytic methods, we found that the

Table 2. Direct Comparisons Between Exposure and Response Prevention (ERP) and Contemporary Cognitive Therapy

		Y-BOCS Total Score					
		Cognitive Therapy Group			ERP Group		
Study	Comments	*n*	Pre	Post	*n*	Pre	Post
Van Oppen et al. (1995)	No therapist-supervised ERP	28	24.1 (5.5)	13.3 (8.5)	29	31.4 (5.0)	17.9 (9.0)
Van Balkom et al. (1998)	Patients overlapped with van Oppen et al. (1995)	25	25.3 (6.6)	13.5 (9.7)	22	25.0 (7.9)	17.1 (8.4)
Cottraux et al. (2001)	Both treatments included exposurelike procedures	30	28.6 (5.1)	16.1 (8.2)	30	28.5 (4.9)	16.4 (7.8)
McLean et al. (2001)	All treatment in groups	31	21.9 (5.8)	16.1 (6.7)	32	21.8 (4.6)	13.2 (7.2)

Note. Y-BOCS = Yale-Brown Obsessive Compulsive Scale.

efficacy of CT for OCD is enhanced by the addition of behavioral experiments (Abramowitz, Franklin, & Foa, 2002). In later studies that incorporated in-session exposure within ERP protocols, the treatment based on behavioral theory appears to be superior to the cognitively oriented treatment.

Adding Cognitive Therapy to ERP

To examine whether adding elements of CT would potentiate the effects of ERP, Vogel and colleagues (2004) randomly assigned 35 OCD patients to receive either ERP plus CT or ERP plus a relaxation (REL; used as a placebo procedure to control for the effects of adding additional techniques to ERP). Treatment involved 12 twice-weekly 2-hour sessions including 90 minutes of therapist-supervised exposure and 30 minutes for either CT or relaxation. Patients were required not to ritualize for 2 hours following exposure. At posttreatment, both groups evidenced substantial improvement in Y-BOCS scores, and there was a nonsignificant trend toward superiority of ERP+REL. At follow-up, however, this trend disappeared. The authors also noted a significantly greater treatment retention rate among the ERP+CT group. Thus, CT might be helpful in promoting perseverance with somewhat challenging ERP programs.

Freeston et al. (1997) examined the effects of combining ERP and CT for OCD patients with severe obsessional thoughts but no overt compulsive rituals (i.e., they had mental rituals only). This therapy entailed (1) education about the universality of intrusive thoughts, (2) ERP consisting of in-session and homework imaginal exposure to intrusive thoughts using audio loop tapes, (3) refraining from neutralizing behaviors, and (4) CT targeting dysfunctional interpretations of the obsessional thoughts. Compared to waitlist, the active treatment produced substantial improvement. Among all patients (*n* = 28) Y-BOCS scores improved from 23.9 to 9.8 after an average of 25.7 sessions over 19.2 weeks. Moreover, patients retained their gains at 6-month follow-up (mean Y-BOCS at follow-up was 10.8). This study demonstrated that ERP and CT could be successfully combined to treat patients with primarily obsessions with mental rituals, a presentation of OCD traditionally considered unresponsive to treatment.

In summary, just as exposure in the form of behavioral experiments augments the effects of CT (Abramowitz et al., 2002), cognitive techniques likely play a critical role in ERP. Regrettably, most descriptions of ERP fail to fully describe the informal cognitive procedures that likely contribute to its efficacy. For example, discussions about overestimates of danger and the costs of avoidance and ritualistic behavior are often required to persuade patients to engage in ERP. The research described above, however, suggests that discussions about mistaken cognitions should *accompany*, rather than *replace*, therapist-supervised exposure. Thus, we use cognitive interventions to "tenderize" catastrophic beliefs (e.g., "I will get deathly ill from using a public bathroom"), thereby making it easier for patients to confront feared situations during ERP.

Comparisons Between ERP and Medication

Given the success of both cognitive behavioral and pharmacological (discussed in chapter 28 of this volume) treatments for OCD, researchers have examined the relative efficacy of these two approaches (e.g., Cottraux et al., 1990; Foa et al., 2005; Marks et al., 1988; Marks, Stern, Mawson, Cobb, & McDonald, 1980). The most straightforwardly designed comparison study, completed by Foa et al. (2005), included 122 patients randomly assigned to (1) intensive ERP, (2) clomipramine (CMI), (3) the combination of ERP and CMI, or (4) pill placebo. The ERP included both in-session (i.e., therapist-supervised) and homework-based exposure. Immediately following treatment, all active therapies produced significant improvement relative to placebo. Moreover, ERP was superior to CMI. Mean pretreatment Y-BOCS scores were 24.6 for the ERP group and 26.3 for the CMI group. At posttreatment, the ERP group had a mean of 11.0, and the CMI group, a mean of 18.2. This corresponds to a 55% reduction for ERP and 32% reduction for CMI. Limitations of this study include that ERP was intensive (15 daily sessions over 3 weeks), provided by expert therapists, and that patients with comorbid conditions (e.g., depression, anxiety disorders) were excluded from the trial. Thus this sample of patients, and the psychotherapy they received, was not highly representative of typical clinical practice.

Augmenting ERP With Medication

In our clinic, nearly 80% of patients seeking psychological treatment have already begun a trial of one or more medications with demonstrated efficacy for OCD. Yet, relatively few studies have examined whether combining these two approaches affords advantages over either treatment as a monotherapy. Indeed, combining ERP and medication could produce a synergistic effect in which combined therapy is superior to either psychological or pharmacological treatment alone (e.g., adding one treatment could facilitate response to the other). Equally likely is that medication and ERP add little to each other (e.g., if either treatment was sufficiently robust that the other had little to contribute). A third possibility is that one treatment detracts from the efficacy of the other (e.g., if patients attribute their improvement to one form of treatment and subsequently do not adhere to the other).

Direct comparison studies generally indicate that combining ERP and medication is more effective than using medication alone for OCD, but not superior to ERP alone (Cottraux et al., 1990; Foa et al., 2005; Franklin, Abramowitz, Bux, Zoellner, & Feeny, 2002; Hohagen et al., 1998; Marks et al., 1980, 1988; O'Connor, Todorov, Robillard, Borgeat, & Brault, 1999; van Balkom et al., 1998). This raises the question of whether adding ERP offers an additional benefit when an adequate medication trial provides an unsatisfactory outcome. This issue has been addressed in four studies to date. Simpson, Gorfinkle, and Liebowitz (1999) offered twice-weekly ERP (17 sessions) to six individuals who had shown only minimal improvement after an adequate SSRI trial. After completing ERP, scores on the Y-BOCS were substantially further reduced (pre-ERP mean = 23.8, post-ERP mean = 12.2), indicating that ERP augments SSRIs in medication-resistant patients. Similar results were reported by Kampman, Keijsers, Hoogduin, and Verbank (2002) who conducted ERP with 14 nonresponders (less than 25% symptom reduction) to fluoxetine. Among the nine patients who completed the study, mean Y-BOCS scores declined from 28.1 before fluoxetine, to 25.7 after 12 weeks on fluoxetine (before ERP commenced), and 15.0 after 12 sessions of CBT.

In a second study, Abramowitz and Zoellner (2002) examined whether the findings reported above extended to OCD patients with primarily obsessions and mental rituals. They found that following 15 sessions of twice-weekly ERP, the 6 study patients improved substantially (mean Y-BOCS scores declined from 23.3 to 8.7) compared to the minimal gains they had made during the 12 weeks before ERP.

Tolin et al. (2004) selected 20 individuals with OCD who had a high rate of comorbid psychological diagnoses and who had not responded adequately to multiple adequate medication trials. After a 1-month waitlist period, these patients received 15 sessions of ERP. Results indicated a statistically significant drop in OCD symptoms following psychological treatment, although posttreatment Y-BOCS scores remained somewhat high. Still, patients who completed the study maintained their gains as far out as 6 months after the end of treatment ollow-up mean Y-BOCS score = 18.7).

Finally, Tenneij et al. (2005) in the Netherlands randomly assigned 96 OCD patients who had evidenced at least a 25% improvement on medication to another 6 months of either ERP or additional drug treatment. Patients who received the addition of ERP showed a significantly greater improvement in Y-BOCS scores than did those who continued with pharmacotherapy alone. Six months following the random allocation to groups, those receiving the addition of ERP had a mean Y-BOCS score of 11.76, while those continuing on medication had a mean score of 17.56. Taken together, these four studies indicate that exposure-based CBT is an appropriate strategy to use for OCD patients who have residual symptoms despite an adequate medication trial. The clinical implications of this research are substantial since medication, which is the most widely available and the most widely used treatment for OCD, produces only limited symptom reduction on average (e.g., 20% to 40%; Rauch & Jenike, 1998).

Predictors of Treatment Outcome

While improvement is the norm for individuals with OCD who receive ERP, about 25%–30% of patients drop out of this therapy prematurely, and among those who remain in treatment, about 20% show little response. This amounts to close to 50% of OCD patients who do not show satisfactory improvement with ERP; an important statistic to consider alongside the impressive data for this treatment's effectiveness. In this section, we review research on predictors of ERP outcome.

Variations in How the Treatment Is Delivered

Three findings have emerged from meta-analytic studies addressing the relationship between treatment outcome and the manner in which ERP is delivered (Abramowitz, 1996, 1997). First, greater short- and long-term improvement in OCD symptoms is associated with more hours of in-session, therapist-supervised exposure practice. Programs in which exposure is carried out exclusively for homework (i.e., without therapist supervision) consistently produce inferior effects to programs in which exposure is conducted in the session with therapist assistance. Indeed, it seems that the therapist's supervision is needed to ensure that the patient fully and systematically confronts exposure stimuli in a way that will produce long-term fear reduction. Second, combining in vivo and imaginal exposure is superior to in vivo exposure alone in reducing anxiety symptoms. This finding is consistent with the

idea that fear in OCD is evoked by mental stimuli (intrusive doubts, images, and ideas) as much as it is evoked by external cues, necessitating exposure to such internal stimuli. Third, ERP programs in which patients refrain *completely* from ritualizing during the treatment period produce superior immediate and long-term effects compared to those that involved only partial response prevention. This highlights the importance of consistency in treatment: patients must reliably have experiences in which obsessional anxiety declines in the absence of compulsive rituals.

To examine whether the robust effects obtained with intensive (daily) ERP are compromised by reducing the session frequency, Abramowitz, Foa, and Franklin (2003) compared 15 sessions of ERP delivered over 3 weeks (5 sessions per week) to twice-weekly sessions over 8 weeks. Whereas intensive therapy was minimally superior to the twice-weekly regimen immediately following treatment (posttreatment Y-BOCS scores were 10.4 [intensive] and 12.7 [twice-weekly]), this difference disappeared at 3-month follow-up (Y-BOCS = 13.13 [intensive] and 14.25 [twice-weekly]). Results of this study suggest that a twice-weekly therapy schedule provides clinicians with a more pragmatic, yet equally effective, alternative to the highly demanding and often impractical intensive protocol.

Poor Insight

Individuals with OCD vary with respect to how strongly they believe that their obsessional fears are realistic and that their compulsive rituals actually serve to prevent disastrous consequences (Foa & Kozak, 1995); a small percentage of patients have poor insight into the senselessness of their symptoms. In a small study with 11 patients, Foa, Abramowitz, Franklin, and Kozak (1999) examined whether the degree of such insight influences ERP outcome, finding that relative to patients who recognize their OCD symptoms are senseless, those with poor insight evidenced attenuated response to ERP. To explain this finding, the authors speculated that patients with poor insight have difficulty consolidating information that is inconsistent with their obsessional fears. Moreover, because of their extreme fear, these patients might not adhere to ERP instructions as closely as do patients with good insight. Although additional studies with larger samples are necessary, insight is likely an important prognostic indicator of response to ERP.

Severe Depression

Research findings consistently indicate that from 25% to 50% of OCD patients also suffer from depressive disorders (Abramowitz, 2004). Using a large sample of 87 patients, Abramowitz and colleagues (e.g., Abramowitz, Franklin, Street, Kozak, & Foa, 2000) examined the effects of comorbid depressive symptoms on the outcome of ERP. Patients were divided into groups on the basis of pretreatment scores on the *Beck Depression Inventory* (BDI) (Beck, Ward, Medelsohn, Mock, & Erlbaugh, 1961): nondepressed, mildly, moderately, and severely depressed. Comparisons across groups indicated attenuated outcome only for the most severely depressed group of patients. The authors suggested that because of their high emotional reactivity, severely depressed individuals fail to undergo a reduction in anxiety/distress that occurs following extended exposure to feared stimuli. Thus, they do not learn that to feel comfortable in the presence of feared stimuli. Motivational difficulties, which often accompany depression, may also account for poor treatment outcome.

Expressed Emotion

Researchers have defined expressed emotion (EE) as responses such as emotional overinvolvement, hostility, and perceived criticism toward a family member with OCD (or any problem). To determine whether these sorts of responses serve as predictors of outcome with ERP, Chambless and Steketee (1999) administered measures of EE to 60 OCD patients and their families prior to the commencement of the patients' treatment. The most consistent predictor of negative treatment outcome was hostility: when relatives were hostile to the identified patient, the odds of premature termination were about six times greater than when relatives were not hostile. Hostility was associated with a poorer response in patients who completed treatment, as well. Once hostility was statistically controlled, however, criticism had a positive effect. This indicates that treatment response can be enhanced if relatives are taught to express constructive dissatisfaction with patients' *symptoms,* but not in a personally rejecting manner.

Personality Disorders

The presence of certain personality traits and personality disorders (PDs) has been shown to hinder response to CBT and to medication for OCD in one study (Steketee, Chambless, & Tran, 2001). Obsessive-compulsive PD and histrionic PD traits, for example, might interfere with developing rapport and adherence to ERP instructions. If, however, a good therapeutic relationship can be developed, ERP can be successful despite these traits. Clinicians should also consider that some patients with dramatic traits gain reinforcement for their OCD symptoms. In such circumstances, psychological treatment approaches are unlikely to succeed because patients do not perceive themselves as gaining rewards for their efforts to reduce obsessions and rituals. Individuals with personality traits in the odd cluster (e.g., schizotypal PD) present a challenge for clinicians because such patients have a reduced ability to profit from corrective information obtained during exposure or cognitive interventions.

Summary and Conclusions

Few psychological disorders result in as much distress and functional impairment as does OCD (Barlow, 2002). Although the specific etiologic factors involved in the *development* of obsessions and compulsions remain elusive, research has led to a very clear understanding of the processes that *maintain* these symptoms. The ERP and CT therapy techniques derived from this understanding have received consistent empirical support, leading to a good prognosis for most individuals with OCD. By far, the most studied psychological intervention for OCD is ERP, which often produces substantial immediate and durable reductions in OCD symptoms. Evidence from effectiveness studies suggests that ERP is transportable to nonresearch settings, and therefore, should be a first-line treatment modality for OCD patients in general clinical settings. Moreover, ERP appears to be quite helpful in further alleviating obsessions and compulsions when these symptoms do not respond satisfactorily to pharmacotherapy. These encouraging results withstanding, full remission with psychological treatment is not typical (Abramowitz, 1998); response is in fact highly variable. We are beginning to uncover factors that reliably predict poor response to ERP, including lack of insight into the senselessness of obsessional fears, severe depression, and family hostility.

As we stand at the dawn of a new century, it is encouraging to look back at how far we have come with respect to the psychological treatment of OCD. We can also look forward with hope that researchers will address a number of critical issues that require further study. For example, treatment programs that incorporate the education of family members about OCD, its treatment, and how to effectively assist with a loved one's therapy, would be useful given the high prevalence of relational problems in families of OCD patients. Motivation to begin treatment, especially given the nature of ERP, is also a problem. Thus, readiness programs in which patients read case histories or discuss treatment with former patients might decrease refusal rates and increase treatment compliance. From the clinician's perspective, engineering and executing successful exposure-based therapy can often be a challenge. Indeed, the greatest barrier to successful treatment of OCD is that relatively few clinicians receive the kind of training needed to become proficient in these procedures. Therefore, research and development of programs for teaching service providers how to implement psychological treatments for OCD will have a major impact on improving access to these effective interventions.

References

Abramowitz, J. S. (1996). Variants of exposure and response prevention in the treatment of obsessive-compulsive disorder: A meta-analysis. *Behavior Therapy, 27,* 583–600.

Abramowitz, J. S. (1997). Effectiveness of psychological and pharmacological treatments for obsessive-compulsive disorder: A quantitative review. *Journal of Consulting and Clinical Psychology, 65,* 44–52.

Abramowitz, J. S. (1998). Does cognitive-behavioral therapy cure obsessive-compulsive disorder? A meta-analytic evaluation of clinical significance. *Behavior Therapy, 29,* 339–355.

Abramowitz, J. S. (2004). Treatment of obsessive-compulsive disorder in patients who have comorbid major depression. *Journal of Clinical Psychology: In Session, 60,* 1133–1141.

Abramowitz, J. S. (2006). *Understanding and treating obsessive-compulsive disorder.* Mahwah, NJ: Erlbaum.

Abramowitz, J. S., Foa, E. B., & Franklin, M. E. (2003). Exposure and ritual prevention for obsessive-compulsive disorder: Effects of intensive versus twice-weekly sessions. *Journal of Consulting and Clinical Psychology, 71,* 394–398.

Abramowitz, J. S., Franklin, M. E., & Foa, E. B. (2002). Empirical status of cognitive-behavioral therapy for obsessive-compulsive disorder: A meta-analytic review. *Romanian Journal of Cognitive and Behavioral Psychotherapies, 2,* 89–104.

Abramowitz, J. S., Franklin, M. E., Schwartz, S. A., & Furr, J. M. (2003). Symptom presentation and outcome of cognitive-behavioral therapy for obsessive-compulsive disorder. *Journal of Consulting and Clinical Psychology, 71,* 1049–1057.

Abramowitz, J., Franklin, M., Street, G., Kozak, M., & Foa, E. (2000). Effects of comorbid depression on response to treatment for obsessive-compulsive disorder. *Behavior Therapy, 31,* 517–528.

Abramowitz, J. S., & Zoellner, L. A. (2002). Cognitive-behavior therapy as an adjunct to medication for obsessive-compulsive disorder with mental rituals: A pilot study. *Romanian Journal of Cognitive and Behavioral Psychotherapies, 2,* 11–22.

American Psychiatric Association. (2000). *Diagnostic and statistical manual of mental disorders* (4th ed., text revision). Washington, DC: Author.

Barlow, D. H. (2002). *Anxiety and its disorders: The nature and treatment of anxiety and panic.* New York: Guilford Press.

Beck, A. T. (1976). *Cognitive therapy of the emotional disorders.* New York: International Universities Press.

Beck, A. T., Ward, C. H., Medelsohn, M., Mock, J., & Erlbaugh, J. (1961). An inventory for measuring depression. *Archives of General Psychiatry, 4,* 561–571.

Chambless, D. L., & Steketee, G. (1999). Expressed emotion and behavior therapy outcome: A prospective study with obsessive-compulsive and agoraphobic outpatients. *Journal of Consulting and Clinical Psychology, 67,* 658–665.

Clark, D. A. (2004). *Cognitive-behavioral therapy for OCD.* New York: Guilford Press.

Cottraux, J., Mollard, E., Bouvard, M., Marks, I., Sluys, M., Nury, A. M., et al. (1990). A controlled study of fluvoxamine and exposure in obsessive compulsive disorder. *International Journal of Clinical Psychopharmacology, 5,* 17–30.

Cottraux, J., Note, I., Yao, S. N., Lafont, S., Note, B., Mollard, E., et al. (2001). A randomized controlled trial of cognitive therapy versus intensive behavior therapy in obsessive compulsive disorder. *Psychotherapy and Psychosomatics, 70,* 288–297.

Crino, R. D., & Andrews, G. (1996). Obsessive-compulsive disorder and Axis I comorbidity. *Journal of Anxiety Disorders, 10,* 37–46.

Dollard, J., & Miller, N. E. (1950). *Personality and psychotherapy: An analysis in terms of learning, thinking, and culture.* New York: McGraw-Hill.

Ellis, A. (1962). *Reason and emotion in psychotherapy.* Secaucus, NJ: Citadel.

Emmelkamp, P.M.G., & Beens, H. (1991). Cognitive therapy with obsessive-compulsive disorder: A comparative evaluation. *Behaviour Research and Therapy, 29,* 293–300.

Emmelkamp, P.M.G., & Hoekstra, R. J. (1988). Cognitive therapy vs. exposure in vivo in the treatment of obsessive-compulsives. *Cognitive Therapy and Research, 12,* 103–114.

Fals-Stewart, W., Marks, A. P., & Schafer, J. (1993). A comparison of behavioral group therapy and individual behavior therapy in treating obsessive-compulsive disorder. *Journal of Nervous and Mental Disease, 181,* 189–193.

Fama, J., & Wilhelm, S. (2005). Formal cognitive therapy: A new treatment for OCD. In J. S. Abramowitz & A. C. Houts (Eds.), *Concepts and controversies in obsessive-compulsive disorder* (pp. 263–281). New York: Springer.

Foa, E. B., Abramowitz, J. S., Franklin, M. E., & Kozak, M. J. (1999). Feared consequences, fixity of belief, and treatment outcome in patients with obsessive-compulsive disorder. *Behavior Therapy, 30,* 717–724.

Foa, E. B., & Kozak, M. J. (1986). Emotional processing of fear: Exposure to corrective information. *Psychological Bulletin, 99,* 20–35.

Foa, E. B., & Kozak, M. J. (1995). DSM–IV field trial: Obsessive-compulsive disorder. *American Journal of Psychiatry, 152,* 90–96.

Foa, E. B., & Kozak, M. J. (1996). Psychological treatment for obsessive-compulsive disorder. In M. R. Mavissakalian & R. F. Prien (Eds.), *Long-term treatments of anxiety disorders* (pp. 285–309). Washington, DC: American Psychiatric Press.

Foa, E. B., Liebowitz, M. R., Kozak, M. J., Davies, S., Campeas, R., Franklin, M. E., et al. (2005). Randomized, placebo-controlled trial of exposure and ritual prevention, clomipramine, and their combination in the treatment of obsessive-compulsive disorder. *American Journal of Psychiatry, 162,* 151–161.

Franklin, M. E., Abramowitz, J. S., Bux, D. A., Jr., Zoellner, L. A., & Feeny, N. C. (2002). Cognitive-behavioral therapy with and without medication in the treatment of obsessive-compulsive disorder. *Professional Psychology: Research and Practice, 33,* 162–168.

Franklin, M. E., Abramowitz, J. S., Foa, E. B., Kozak, M. J., & Levitt, J. T. (2000). Effectiveness of exposure and ritual prevention for obsessive-compulsive disorder: Randomized compared with nonrandomized samples. *Journal of Consulting and Clinical Psychology, 68,* 594–602.

Freeston, M. H., Ladouceur, R., Gagnon, F., Thibodeau, N., Rheaume, J., Letarte, H., et al. (1997). Cognitive-behavioral treatment of obsessive thoughts: A controlled study. *Journal of Consulting and Clinical Psychology, 65,* 405–413.

Friedman, S., Smith, L. C., Halpern, B., Levine, C., Paradis, C., Viswanathan, R., et al. (2003). Obsessive-compulsive disorder in a multi-ethnic urban outpatient clinic: Initial presentation and treatment outcome with exposure and ritual prevention. *Behavior Therapy, 34,* 397–410.

Frost, R. O., & Steketee, S. (2002). *Cognitive approaches to obsessions and compulsions: Theory, assessment, and treatment.* Oxford, England: Elsevier.

Goodman, W. K., Price, L. H., Rasmussen, S. A., Mazure, C., Delgado, P., Heninger, G. R., et al. (1989a). The Yale-Brown Obsessive Compulsive Scale: Validity. *Archives of General Psychiatry, 46,* 1012–1016.

Goodman, W. K., Price, L. H., Rasmussen, S. A., Mazure, C., Fleischmann, R. L., Hill, C. L., et al. (1989b). The Yale-Brown Obsessive Compulsive Scale: Development, use, and reliability. *Archives of General Psychiatry, 46,* 1006–1011.

Hohagen, F., Winkelmann, G., Rasche-Rauchle, H., Hand, I., Konig, A., Munchau, N., et al. (1998). Combination of behaviour therapy with fluvoxamine in comparison with behaviour therapy and placebo. *British Journal of Psychiatry, 173,* 71–78.

Houts, A. C. (2005). Behavioral and animal models of OCD. In J. S. Abramowitz & A. C. Houts (Eds.), *Concepts and controversies in obsessive-compulsive disorder* (pp. 73–86). New York: Springer.

Kampman, M., Keijsers, G.P.J., Hoogduin, C.A.L., & Verbank, M.J.P.M. (2002). Addition of cognitive-behavior therapy for obsessive-compulsive disorder patients non-responding to fluoxetine. *Acta Psychiatrica Scandinavica, 106,* 314–319.

Karno, M., Golding, J., Sorenson, S., & Burnam, A. (1988). The epidemiology of obsessive-compulsive disorder in five U.S. communities. *Archives of General Psychiatry, 45,* 1094–1099.

Kirk, J. W. (1983). Behavioural treatment of obsessional compulsive patients in routine clinical practice. *Behaviour Research and Therapy, 21,* 57–62.

Lindsay, M., Crino, R., & Andrews, G. (1997). Controlled trial of exposure and response prevention in obsessive-compulsive disorder. *British Journal of Psychiatry, 171,* 135–139.

Marks, I. M., Lelliott, P. T., Başoğlu, M., Noshirvani, H., Monteiro, W., Cohen, D., et al. (1988). Clomipramine, self-exposure and therapist-aided exposure for obsessive-compulsive rituals. *British Journal of Psychiatry, 152,* 522–534.

Marks, I. M., Stern, R. S., Mawson, D., Cobb, J., & McDonald, R. (1980). Clomipramine, self-exposure, and therapist-aided exposure for obsessive-compulsive rituals. *British Journal of Psychiatry, 152,* 522–534.

McLean, P. D., Whittal, M. L., Thordarson, D. S., Taylor, S., Söchting, I., Koch, W. J., et al. (2001). Cognitive versus behavior therapy in the group treatment of obsessive-compulsive disorder. *Journal of Consulting and Clinical Psychology, 69,* 205–214.

Meyer, V. (1966). Modification of expectations in cases with obsessional rituals. *Behaviour Research and Therapy, 4,* 273–280.

Meyer, V., Levy, R., & Schnurer, A. (1974). The behavioral treatment of obsessive-compulsive disorders. In H. R. Beech (Ed.), *Obsessional states* (pp. 233–258). London: Methuen.

Mineka, S., & Zinbarg, R. (1996). Conditioning and ethological models of anxiety disorders. In D. A. Hope (Ed.), *Nebraska Symposium on Motivation: Vol. 43. Perspectives on anxiety, panic, and fear: Current theory and research on motivation.* (pp. 135–210). Lincoln: University of Nebraska Press.

Mineka, S., & Zinbarg, R. (2006). A contemporary learning theory perspective on the etiology of anxiety disorders: It's not what you thought it was. *American Psychologist, 61,* 10–26.

Mowrer, O. (1960). *Learning theory and behavior.* New York: Wiley.

O'Connor, K., Todorov, C., Robillard, S., Borgeat, F., & Brault, M. (1999). Cognitive-behaviour therapy and medication in the treatment of obsessive-compulsive disorder: A controlled study. *Canadian Journal of Psychiatry, 44,* 64–71.

Persons, J. B., & Silberschatz, G. (1998). Are results of randomized controlled trials useful to psychotherapists? *Journal of Consulting and Clinical Psychology, 66,* 126–135.

Rachman, S. (1997). A cognitive theory of obsessions. *Behaviour Research and Therapy, 35,* 793–802.

Rachman, S. (1998). A cognitive theory of obsessions: Elaborations. *Behaviour Research and Therapy, 36,* 385–401.

Rachman, S., & de Silva, P. (1978). Abnormal and normal obsessions. *Behaviour Research and Therapy, 16,* 233–248.

Rachman, S. J., & Hodgson, R. J. (1980). *Obsessions and compulsions.* Englewood Cliffs, NJ: Prentice-Hall.

Rauch, S., & Jenike, M. (1998). Pharmacological treatment of obsessive-compulsive disorder. In P. E. Nathan & J. M. Gorman (Eds.), *A guide to treatments that work* (pp. 358–376). New York: Oxford University Press.

Salkovskis, P. (1996). Cognitive-behavioral approaches to the understanding of obsessional problems. In R. Rapee (Ed.), *Current controversies in the anxiety disorders* (pp. 103–133). New York: Guilford Press.

Shafran, R. (2005). Cognitive-behavioral models of OCD. In J. S. Abramowitz & A. C. Houts (Eds.), *Concepts and controversies in obsessive-compulsive disorder* (pp. 229–252). New York: Springer.

Simpson, H. B., Gorfinkle, K. S., & Liebowitz, M. R. (1999). Cognitive-behavioral therapy as an adjunct to serotonin reuptake inhibitors in obsessive-compulsive disorder: An open trial. *Journal of Clinical Psychiatry, 60,* 584–590.

Steketee, G., Chambless, D. L., & Tran, G. Q. (2001). Effects of Axis I and II comorbidity on behavior therapy outcome for obsessive-compulsive disorder and agoraphobia. *Comprehensive Psychiatry, 42,* 76–86.

Tenneij, N., van Megen, H., Denys, D., & Westenberg, H. (2005). Behavior therapy augments response of patients with obsessive-compulsive disorder responding to drug treatment. *Journal of Clinical Psychiatry, 66,* 1169–1175.

Tolin, D. F., Maltby, N., Diefenbach, G., Hannan, S., & Worhunsky, P. (2004). Cognitive-behavioral therapy for medication nonresponders with obsessive-compulsive disorder: A wait-list controlled open trial. *Journal of Clinical Psychiatry, 65,* 922–931.

Van Balkom, A.J.L.M., de Haan, E., van Oppen, P., Spinhoven, P., Hoogduin, K.A.L., & van Dyck, R. (1998). Cognitive and behavioral therapies alone versus in combination with fluvoxamine in the treatment of obsessive-compulsive disorder. *Journal of Nervous and Mental Disorders, 186,* 492–499.

Van Oppen, P., de Haan, E., van Balkom, A.J.L.M., Spinhoven, P., Hoogduin, K., & van Dyck, R. (1995). Cognitive therapy and exposure *in vivo* in the treatment of obsessive compulsive disorder. *Behaviour Research and Therapy, 33,* 379–390.

Vogel, P. A., Stiles, T. C., & Gotestam, K. G. (2004). Adding cognitive therapy elements to exposure therapy for obsessive compulsive disorder: A controlled study. *Behavioural and Cognitive Psychotherapy, 32,* 275–290.

Warren, R., & Thomas, J. C. (2001). Cognitive-behavior therapy of obsessive-compulsive disorder in private practice: An effectiveness study. *Journal of Anxiety Disorders, 15,* 277–285.

Pharmacotherapy for Posttraumatic Stress Disorder and Other Trauma-Related Disorders

Mary F. Dent *and* J. Douglas Bremner

Abstract

Posttraumatic stress disorder (PTSD) can cause serious chronic psychological impairments in a significant number of persons who have been exposed to an extreme traumatic event. Finding effective, well-tolerated pharmacological treatments for this disorder is an ongoing research effort. This chapter reviews recent thinking that PTSD results from dysfunctions in the neural systems mediating fear learning and memory. These systems are modulated by dopamine, GABA, norepinephrine, and serotonin. Drugs that have been investigated to alleviate PTSD symptoms affect these neuromodulators and include all classes of antidepressants, mood stabilizers, and antipsychotics. To date, the SSRI antidepressants, particularly paroxetine, have shown the best evidence for alleviating most PTSD symptoms in most people. Drugs that promote extinction of fear learning are currently being investigated.

Keywords: acute stress, anticonvulsants, antidepressants, antipsychotics, mood stabilizers, neurobiology, pharmacotherapy, posttraumatic stress disorder

Posttraumatic stress disorder (PTSD) is a serious and complex mental disorder, which expresses itself through symptom clusters that include reexperiencing aspects of the initial trauma through intrusive trauma-related thought content, flashbacks, and nightmares; emotional numbing along with social avoidance and withdrawal; and hypervigilance with concentration impairments and sleep disturbance. Increased irritability, anger, and aggressiveness, as well as major depression and substance abuse, are also commonly seen. This disorder became officially recognized as a psychopathological entity with the recognition of the long-term difficulties experienced by war veterans, primarily related to the Vietnam conflict. The prolonged maladjustment problems often seen in soldiers returning from that campaign together with a new appreciation for the general role of trauma as a threat to psychological well-being brought sufficient attention to the syndrome that it

was included in the *DSM–III* in 1980 (reviewed in Lasiuk & Hegadoren, 2006; McNally, 2003).

Many high-profile recent events have brought heightened attention to and concern about this issue. Tsunamis, hurricanes, earthquakes, and other natural disasters along with political events such as the war in Iraq and terrorist bombings create the seed conditions for a dramatic increase in those affected by this disorder in both the military and civilian communities. A recent study suggests that about 17% of soldiers returning from Iraq will experience serious psychological disorders (given that historic levels of violence in that region remain unchanged), with PTSD being the primary outcome (Hoge et al., 2004). Also, personally devastating events such as shootings, car accidents, rapes, and so on continue to negatively affect people's psychological well-being on an everyday basis. The personal and social cost of this disorder, the high number of potential new cases of PTSD, plus its widespread distribution throughout the population highlights the need for widely available, easily used, and effective treatments for acute stress and PTSD.

Posttraumatic stress disorder can be conceptualized, in essence, as a dysfunction of fear learning and memory (Bryant et al., 2005; Elzinga & Bremner, 2002; van Praag, 2004; Williams et al., 2006). It is characterized by anxiety-related behaviors and experiences that first arose as justifiable fear in response to a real threat to self or others; however, these fear responses continue for many years or decades after the initial danger has passed, and under conditions where further harm is highly unlikely. Thus, the fear learning fails to extinguish, plus the context in which the original learning occurred is lost or overgeneralized (Rothbaum & Davis, 2003). In addition, victims may show some degree of amnesia for the time period around the initial trauma, and may show chronic short-term memory impairments.

Understanding these memory dysfunctions may be important for interventions in PTSD. The sequence of events that lead to the development of PTSD are experience of an initial trauma, an intermediate period lasting from a few months to several years, where a variable number of symptoms are experienced, followed by long-term expression of PTSD symptoms. Traditionally, pharmacotherapy approaches have focused on treating the various expressions of anxiety that are the end point of the development of chronic PTSD. This often results in a lifelong regimen of medication. However, a deeper understanding of the neurobiological sequelae that place one at risk for PTSD soon after trauma has occurred has opened up possibilities for intervention much sooner in the PTSD development process. Intervention may be possible during the acute stress response, with the goal of forestalling the future development of dysfunctional fear memories. This approach is receiving increased recent attention, and some drug treatments have shown promise (Morgan, Krystal, & Southwick, 2003). Other research in memory may shed light on the processes involved in the *incubation* period, prior to the development of chronic symptoms. Recent investigations into memory have demonstrated that emotional memories are subject to a consolidation/reconsolidation process (McGaugh, 2004); during reconsolidation phases, memories are labile and subject to alteration, including either strengthening or extinction. This phase, wherein long-term memories are "under construction," may be the process that is occurring during the period after trauma exposure but

before the eruption of full-blown PTSD. Interventions designed to facilitate extinction during this reconsolidation phase could potentially head off the eventual development of chronic PTSD symptoms (Rothbaum & Davis, 2003). Some very encouraging progress has been made in developing treatment approaches based on this understanding (M. Davis, K. M. Myers, J. P. Chhatwal, & K. J. Ressler, 2006).

With these observations in mind, it makes great sense that investigations into the neurobiology of PTSD have focused on the neural systems for fear learning, memory, and stress responses. Since PTSD is the product of the psychological and physiological responses to a traumatic event, exploring how a pharmacotherapy for PTSD might work requires an understanding of the psychological and physiological components of the fear-learning and stress response systems. Our understanding of these interrelated systems has yielded our current knowledge of how known treatments for PTSD might be working and also suggests new avenues for the development of future interventions.

Neurobiology of PTSD: An Overview

How do we come to appreciate that certain stimuli represent a source of threat to us, and should therefore be feared? Primates have very few, if any, instinctive fears; our repertoire of responses to aversive stimuli must be acquired from observation of others' experiences or from our own experiences. This kind of learning usually takes the form of classical conditioning, where a given set of environmental stimuli are linked up or associated with an aversive internal state (i.e., pain perception). Neural circuits that receive both types of stimuli then strengthen in activation to the previously neutral environmental stimuli. This process is the neural underpinning of associative learning, which results in a rat freezing or startling to a tone (CS+) or a person having exaggerated fear responses to stimuli that co-occurred with his or her original trauma. The system that does this learning function in the brain is for the most part subcortical and highly conserved across mammalian species. A well-developed line of research has solidly demonstrated that it is the basolateral nucleus of the amygdala (BLA) that combines sensory stimuli with internal signals produced by an aversive event. The BLA then projects to the central nucleus of the amygdala (CeA), which organizes a range of somatic and psychological responses to the threat including, presumably, the experience of the emotion of fear itself (thoroughly reviewed in M. Davis, 2000; Fanselow & Poulos, 2005; LeDoux, 1996; Phelps &

LeDoux, 2005). Although direct evidence would be hard to obtain, a wealth of research findings predict that at the time of the experience of the initial trauma, the future victim of PTSD would have a highly activated amygdala.

The amygdala is highly interconnected with the hippocampus; the hippocampus has the important functions of encoding information about the context in which the fear learning occurred, mediating the transfer of memories into longer-term storage, and providing a source of inhibition on stress hormone release. The amygdala and hippocampus indirectly project to the paraventricular nucleus of the hypothalamus, which then initiates the hormonal aspect of the stress response (Herman et al., 2003). All of these structures have reciprocal connections with the major neuromodulatory cell body areas, including those for dopamine (DA), acetylcholine (ACh), serotonin (5-HT), and norepinephrine (NE). The drugs that are commonly used to treat PTSD exert their effects by altering the function of one or more of these neuromodulators, which then alters the limbic mediation of the experience and expression of fear and anxiety responses.

Approaches to Pharmacotherapy: Acute Stress

PTSD gradually evolves out of the responses to a specific, known event that is highly distressing. This state of affairs suggests the possibility that if the right kind of intervention is presented at the right time, perhaps the future development of PTSD could be prevented. Several recent reviews have discussed the issues to be considered for this kind of intervention to be successful (J. R. Davidson, 2006; Elsesser, Sartory, & Tackenberg, 2005; Morgan et al., 2003; Shalev, 2002). The sum of the evidence indicates that most people exhibit signs of distress in the aftermath of trauma, including hyperarousal, anxiety, reexperiencing, dissociation, numbing, agitation, and so on. For most of these victims, psychological, social, and physiological coping mechanisms will lead to a successful recovery from the trauma (Rothbaum & Davis, 2003; Shalev, 2002). A minority of trauma survivors go on to develop psychopathologies, including depression and anxiety as well as PTSD (Shalev, Freedman, et al., 1998; Yehuda, McFarlane, & Shalev, 1998). Therefore, an important concept to emerge from this line of investigation is the notion that some of the initial responses to trauma are constructive and should not be interfered with (Rothbaum & Davis, 2003). For example, it might be expected that benzodiazepine administration soon after the trauma would help to reduce hyperreactivity and promote coping responses; however, the few studies that have been done on this topic are quite variable. Beneficial effects (Mellman, Byers, & Augenstein, 1998), no effects (Braun, Greenberg, Dasberg, & Lerer, 1990), and deleterious effects (Gelpin, Bonne, Peri, Brandes, & Shalev, 1996) have all been reported. It appears that benzodiazepine-induced sedation is not conducive to mounting a coping response to the traumatic stressor (McCleery & Harvey, 2004). A more promising approach has been to use drugs that interfere with NE transmission, as it is NE that initiates the sympathetic system–mediated arousal response to immediate threat, and may also participate in the encoding of memories for such events (Hurlemann et al., 2005; Murchison et al., 2004). The β2 blocker propranolol (Famularo, Kinscherff, & Fenton, 1988; Pitman et al., 2002; Vaiva et al., 2003), when administered soon after the occurrence of trauma, was associated with a reduction in indicators of anxiety and PTSD measured 2–3 months after the trauma event. The α1 antagonist prazosin and the α2 receptor antagonist clonidine have been found to alleviate nightmares and emotional reactivity in PTSD subjects (Kinzie & Leung, 1989; Raskind et al., 2002; Taylor et al., 2006); these medications may also be efficacious for acute stress interventions.

One of the hypotheses that has been proposed to account for neurobiological processes that may be occurring during the period between trauma exposure but before the expression of full PTSD symptoms has been the mechanism of amygdalar kindling (Kalynchuk, Pinel, & Meaney, 2006; Kellett & Kokkinidis, 2004). Following this model, the use of anticonvulsants during the period soon after trauma exposure may also be efficacious (Pitman & Delahanty, 2005). Continued investigations of ways to constructively ameliorate the initial effects of trauma, and possibly circumvent the descent into PTSD (and its persistence), are clearly needed.

Approaches to Pharmacotherapy for PTSD

Some of the earliest appraisals of effective pharmacotherapy for PTSD focused on methods to reduce the hyperarousal seen in PTSD, with the expectation that other symptoms would be ameliorated as well. Drugs in use at the time to treat panic disorder and depression were explored for efficacy in PTSD, including the MAOI and tricyclic antidepressants, the benzodiazepines, and the NE antagonists, clonidine and propranolol; these drugs were judged to be possibly useful but not completely satisfactory (Friedman, 1988). By the middle of the next decade, with the development of the serotonin-selective reuptake inhibitors (SSRIs), antidepressant drugs were drawing increased interest and investigation, though few double-blind clinical trials had been completed at that point (Shalev, Bonne, & Eth, 1996). Concurrently, mood stabilizers, such as lithium, valproate, and carbamazepine were explored for efficacy in PTSD, consequent to observations that the retarded onset of PTSD symptoms greatly resembled the effects of amygdalar kindling, and might best be treated with these antikindling medications (Shalev et al., 1996). This rationale continues to be explored, as discussed below. Within the next 5 years, the weight of expert opinion had settled on the SSRIs as "the best first choice" for PTSD pharmacotherapy (Foa, Davidson, & Frances, 1999). This state of consensus has remained essentially unchanged since then (Ballenger et al., 2000; Balon, 2004; Cooper, Carty, & Creamer, 2005; Cyr & Farrar, 2000; Hageman, Andersen, & Jorgensen, 2001; Pearlstein, 2000). However, this is not to say that the SSRIs are completely satisfactory in all respects. The SSRIs are commended for being well tolerated and having a general efficacy in alleviating most of the symptoms of most victims of PTSD, but problems remain, and the motivation is there to find a wider range of pharmacotherapy solutions. As yet, relatively few well-designed controlled studies have been done with any of the novel potential medications for PTSD. Gender, type of trauma (civilian versus war-related), severity of PTSD phenomena, and the presence of comorbidities have been identified as relevant factors influencing drug efficacy. Age is a variable that has been largely ignored in the pharmacotherapy literature for PTSD. A very few studies have looked at potential treatments for children and adolescents, but no studies currently on hand have looked at drug treatments for the elderly. Since brain maturation/degeneration and hepatic capacity change over the course of development, age is potentially a very important variable in determining drug effects. And, of course, the issues of dosage, length of treatment, validity of assessment instruments, sample representativeness, random assignment with placebo controls, and including an adequate sample size are relevant to evaluating this line of research, as is true for all research using clinical drug trials.

Antidepressants. The antidepressant medications, particularly various SSRIs, have drawn the most research attention to date (L. L. Davis, English,

Ambrose, & Petty, 2001). The first antidepressants to be explored for PTSD efficacy were the MAOIs and tricylics, such as phenelzine, amitriptyline, clomipramine, and imipramine. As a group, these studies tended to use small sample sizes, often without placebo controls, and were highly variable in dosages, measurement scales, and duration of drug treatment (reviewed in J. Davidson et al., 1990). There were common problems with drug intolerance due to side effects. Improvements in PTSD-specific symptoms were usually seen, however, which encouraged the continued search for more effective pharmacotherapy medications among the newer antidepressants, the serotonin-selective reuptake inhibitors (SSRIs) such as fluoxetine, sertraline, and paroxetine.

Exploratory studies (J. Davidson, Roth, & Newman, 1991; McDougle, Southwick, Charney, & St. James, 1991; Nagy, Morgan, Southwick, & Charney, 1993) showed modest but significant improvement with fluoxetine treatment, though it was clear that dosing, duration of treatment, and numerous other factors affecting treatment outcome required further investigation. It was encouraging, however, that fluoxetine was associated with alleviation of the PTSD-specific symptoms, most notably the avoidance/numbing aspect, along with improving depression scale scores. Subsequent random controlled trial studies have provided some support for the efficacy of fluoxetine and a greater understanding of factors that influence treatment success. Source of trauma, time since trauma, and length of drug treatment were raised as issues in a study by van der Kolk and colleagues (1994), when they found that, with 5 weeks of fluoxetine, a civilian sample primarily composed of sexual trauma survivors showed a better treatment response than a sample of military veterans with PTSD of 10 or more years duration. A subsequent study by Hertzberg and colleagues (Hertzberg, Feldman, Beckham, Kudler, & Davidson, 2000) failed to establish efficacy for fluoxetine in a sample of only military veterans after 12 weeks of treatment, while a sample of civilians showed substantial improvement with the same duration of treatment (Connor, Sutherland, Tupler, Malik, & Davidson, 1999). A study by Martenyi and colleagues (Martenyi, Brown, Zhang, Prakash, & Koke, 2002) employed subjects who more recently experienced combat. This group showed substantial improvement in PTSD symptoms after 12 weeks of treatment, suggesting that the older veterans in the Hertzberg and van der Kolk studies were a distinct subject group, possibly having more severe PTSD, or more resistance to treatment due to advanced age or chronicity of PTSD. Another suggestion to emerge from the Martenyi study was that higher doses of fluoxetine may be needed to ameliorate PTSD symptoms than those used to treat depression. Prolonged periods of treatment may also be desirable for fluoxetine to avert relapse of PTSD symptoms (J. R. Davidson et al., 2005; Martenyi, Brown, Zhang, Koke, & Prakash, 2002; Martenyi & Soldatenkova, 2006); however, evidence indicates that fluoxetine is well tolerated and safe for this group (Barnett et al., 2002).

Other SSRI antidepressants have been investigated for efficacy with PTSD. Based on its good treatment record for depression and panic disorder, sertraline was a prime candidate for application to PTSD. The initial controlled trial was very promising; sertraline was particularly effective in reducing PTSD-specific impairments in a civilian sample, had a quick onset of action (improvements were noted within 2 weeks of treatment), and was considered safe and well tolerated (K. Brady et al., 2000). Further randomized clinical trials corroborated this evidence for sertraline as an efficacious drug ameliorating PTSD symptoms (J. R. Davidson, Rothbaum, van der Kolk, Sikes, & Farfel, 2001). Longer-term treatment with sertraline was conducive to continued improvement and prevention of relapse (J. Davidson et al., 2001; Londborg et al., 2001). It was especially noteworthy that efficacy was demonstrated for sertraline with a sample of combat veterans, since fluoxetine was not as successful for treating this population (Zohar et al., 2002). Additional studies have demonstrated a particular reduction in anger soon after sertraline doses are initiated (J. Davidson, Landerman, & Clary, 2004), and an improvement in the comorbid conditions of depression and anxiety (K. T. Brady & Clary, 2003) and excess alcohol consumption (K. T. Brady et al., 2005).

Although fluoxetine showed some efficacy in treating PTSD symptoms, and sertraline more so, both of these medications left room for improvement in sufficiently alleviating all three PTSD symptom clusters. Paroxetine was seen as potentially promising due to its history of success in treating other anxiety disorders as well as depression. Controlled trials from two different groups were, in fact, very encouraging (Marshall, Beebe, Oldham, & Zaninelli, 2001; Tucker et al., 2001). Significant improvement in social and occupational quality of life measures were accompanied by significant reductions on all three PTSD symptom clusters by the end of 12 weeks of treatment in these civilian samples. One analysis indicated that long-term treatment with paroxetine continued to improve PTSD and other anxiety disorder symptoms to the point where the patient could be said to be in remission (Ballenger, 2004).

Sertraline and paroxetine showed convincing evidence for alleviating PTSD symptoms; however, each study contained subjects who failed to respond to the chosen drug. Therefore, as is usually the case with psychopharmacology, other drugs continued to be explored for efficacy. Fluvoxamine has received some research attention but only with small-scale studies without placebo controls. Both a civilian sample (Tucker et al., 2000) and a sample of veterans (Escalona, Canive, Calais, & Davidson, 2002) showed improvement in PTSD symptoms and depression with fluvoxamine; especially noted were improvements in quality of sleep and physiological indexes of arousal (Tucker et al., 2000). However, both studies reported higher dropout rates tied to complaints of side effects when compared to studies using sertraline or fluoxetine.

Preliminary investigations have also been done for the SSRIs citalopram and escitalopram. Escitalopram was efficacious at reducing avoidance/numbing and hyperarousal symptoms in an open-label trial with a sample of military veterans (Robert, Hamner, Ulmer, Lorberbaum, & Durkalski, 2006), while citalopram improved all symptom clusters in a short-term trial of a similar sample group (English, Jewell, Jewell, Ambrose, & Davis, 2006). It appears that randomized controlled trials (RCT) of these drugs are warranted.

Mirtazapine is a tetracyclic antidepressant with the ability to enhance both 5-HT and NE systems. Three small-scale studies showed evidence of modest to strong improvement in PTSD symptoms in both civilian and military veteran populations (Bahk et al., 2002; Chung et al., 2004; J. R. Davidson et al., 2003; Kim, Pae, Chae, Jun, & Bahk, 2005). The drug was reported to be well tolerated in all three studies, and large-scale randomized controlled trials were felt to be justified by the authors of these studies.

Drugs that promote both NE and 5-HT are beneficial in treating some depression, and may be efficacious for PTSD as well. Nefazodone is a reuptake inhibitor for both 5-HT and NE that is an alternative for treating SSRI nonresponders. A number of studies have provided evidence that this drug is effective in treating PTSD symptoms as well (Garfield, Fichtner, Leveroni, & Mahableshwarkar, 2001), being especially helpful in regulating sleep disturbances and nightmares (J.R.T. Davidson, Weisler, Malik, & Connor, 1998; Gillin et al., 2001; Hertzberg, Feldman, Beckham, Moore, & Davidson, 1998, 2002; Mellman, David, & Barza, 1999; Neylan et al., 2003); however, this drug is associated with some risk of liver failure, which led the manufacturer to pull it from the U.S. market in 2004. Trazodone likewise has effects on 5-HT and NE reuptake but also blocks the 5-HT2 receptor. This drug has antidepressant and sedating qualities and has also shown some efficacy for ameliorating PTSD symptoms, especially sleep dysfunctions (Hertzberg, Feldman, Beckham, & Davidson, 1996; Warner, Dorn, & Peabody, 2001). Venlafaxine is considered a SNRI (5-HT-NE reuptake inhibitor) and has also shown efficacy for reducing scores on CAPS avoidance and hyperarousal scales in a 12-week RCT (J. Davidson, Rothbaum et al., 2006), performing somewhat better at higher doses than sertraline in this sample. Venlafaxine continued to be effective through a 6-month continuation trial, although full remission of PTSD symptoms was not seen (J. Davidson, Baldwin et al., 2006). Although it is at first blush counterintuitive that NE functional agonists should ameliorate PTSD symptoms, since heightened NE activity has been noted in unmedicated PTSD patients (Bremner, Krystal, Southwick, & Charney, 1996), the NE reuptake inhibitor reboxetine was at least as effective as fluvoxamine in ameliorating PTSD symptoms in a small sample of civilian PTSD subjects (Spivak et al., 2006). Also, the NE functional antagonist guanfacine was not found to be helpful in one study (Neylan et al., 2006).

The primary mechanism of action of the antidepressants has been regarded as being the promotion of serotonergic functionality through a number of different receptor-based mechanisms. However, recently a new mechanism of action of the antidepressants has been revealed: these drugs also act to promote neurogenesis in the hippocampus (Huang & Herbert, 2006; Manji et al., 2003; Namestkova, Simonova, & Sykova, 2005; Warner-Schmidt & Duman, 2006). Evidence indicates that the new cells become integrated and functional in memory processes. This recovery of hippocampal tissue is substantial enough to be visualized in the human brain (Vermetten, Vythilingam, Southwick, Charney, & Bremner, 2003). These findings—which await more widespread replication—give some indication that the antidepressant drugs not only ameliorate the symptoms of PTSD, but may also help in the structural recovery of hippocampal tissue that may have been lesioned by exposure to stressors.

Anticonvulsants-Mood Stabilizers. Anticonvulsant drugs have also received investigative interest based on the rationale that the relatively quiescent period between the time of trauma exposure and the occurrence of PTSD symptoms may reflect the operation of a kindling mechanism in the amygdala (Kalynchuk et al., 2006; Kellett & Kokkinidis, 2004) with effects similar to the physical and psychological effects of temporal lobe epilepsy. The anticonvulsant medications are thought to promote gamma-aminobutyric acid (GABA) function; GABA is the predominant inhibitory transmitter in the brain and has traditionally been considered an important element in dysfunctions of fear and anxiety (Nemeroff, 2003). However, not all GABAergic drugs are desirable for treating chronic conditions such as PTSD. The benzodiazepines have been shown to ameliorate some symptoms of PTSD (Shalev, Bloch, Peri, & Bonne, 1998), but run a high risk of tolerance, abuse, and toxic interactions with alcohol. Therefore, drugs having more indirect effects on GABA function, such as the anticonvulsants and mood stabilizers, are more desirable for long-term treatment.

In preliminary uncontrolled studies, carbamazepine and valproate did significantly alleviate PTSD symptoms, especially in the areas of hyperreactivity, sleep disturbance, and intrusive thoughts in small groups of combat veterans (Fesler, 1991; Lipper et al., 1986). Subsequent studies have recognized the efficacy of sertraline and paroxetine as first-line medications, but recognize the need to find other drugs for treatment-resistant patients or as adjunctive therapy for specific problem areas. Lamotrigine is a newer mood stabilizer that is more easily tolerated than the older anticonvulsants; this drug showed evidence for improving the reexperiencing and avoidance clusters in a small sample composed of both civilian and veteran subjects (Hertzberg et al., 1999). Likewise, the GABA agonists levetiracetam, tiagabine, and topiramate have shown some efficacy, with minimal side effects, in small, exploratory investigations (Berlant & van Kammen, 2002; Connor, Davidson, Weisler, Zhang, & Abraham, 2006; Kinrys, Wygant, Pardo, & Melo, 2006). Topiramate (Berlant & van Kammen, 2002) was noted to be especially effective in reducing the reexperiencing cluster, including flashbacks and nightmares, and should be considered for patients with particular difficulties in that area. However, outcomes were more modest for this drug in a RCT of a civilian sample (Tucker et al., 2007) . Also in line with these findings, a large (*n* = 232 subjects) RCT of tiagabine failed to demonstrate its superiority over placebo in the treatment of patients with PTSD (Davidson, Brady, Mellman, Stein, & Pollack, 2007). Phenytoin is also in the anticonvulsant class, but drew attention for efficacy in PTSD because its purported mechanism of action is as a glutamate antagonist. Theoretically, much of the impairment seen in PTSD victims arises from glutamate-mediated hippocampal damage. A glutamate blocker could feasibly act more directly to remedy the symptoms of PTSD in the structures where they are generated. This theoretical approach was supported by findings of significant improvement in all three PTSD clusters in a small mixed sample treated for 3 months with phenytoin (Bremner et al., 2004).

Antipsychotics. A recurring finding through a number of the studies summarized here has been that the most severe cases of PTSD did not respond to the treatment being offered. At their most extreme expression, the reexperiencing cluster symptoms may take the form of hallucinations and delusions that would be characterized as psychotic. In addition, some PTSD victims have outbursts of anger and aggressiveness that are not very amenable to treatments such as SSRIs. Some researchers have reported the use of antipsychotic medications to address the issues of these more severe cases. This alternative is more attractive now that a number of atypical antipsychotics are available. These drugs generally show fewer side effects, particularly the motor impairments, found with the older antipsychotics. Also, the atypical antipsychotics have effects on 5-HT as well as dopamine systems, and increasing 5-HT functionality is a common route to alleviating PTSD symptoms. Although the first open-label study using olanzapine was disappointing (Butterfield et al., 2001), case reports appeared promising (Jakovljevic, Sagud, & Mihaljevic-Peles, 2003). A second study with a more severely impaired group of military veterans showed very positive results for improvement in PTSD symptoms, especially in the reexperiencing cluster, with few side effects and after only 3 weeks of treatment (Pivac, Kozaric-Kovacic, & Muck-Seler, 2004).

Fluphenazine also alleviated PTSD symptoms but was not tolerated as well (Pivac et al., 2004). Likewise, risperidone was found to be an effective adjunctive medication for alleviating psychotic symptoms, particularly reexperiencing and hyperarousal, in one open-label study (Kozaric-Kovacic, Pivac, Muck-Seler, & Rothbaum, 2005) and four randomized controlled studies (Bartzokis, Lu, Turner, Mintz, & Saunders, 2005; Hamner et al., 2003;

Padala et al., 2006; Reich, Winternitz, Hennen, Watts, & Stanculescu, 2004); risperidone may also be appropriate for patients having special difficulties with irritability and heightened aggressiveness (Monnelly, Ciraulo, Knapp, & Keane, 2003). Quetiapine may also be useful as an adjunctive treatment for sleep disorders (Robert et al., 2005) or as an adjunctive therapy for the spectrum of symptoms in those with an unsatisfactory response to other therapies (Ahearn, Mussey, Johnson, Krohn, & Krahn, 2006; Hamner et al., 2003; Sokolski, Denson, Lee, & Reist, 2003). Likewise, current evidence supports the use of olanzapine, and possibly aripiprazole, as potentially helpful adjunctive therapies for PTSD (Lambert, 2006; Stein, Kline, & Matloff, 2002). Finally, there is evidence of the successful use of clozapine in controlling psychotic symptoms in traumatized adolescents (Kant, Chalansani, Chengappa, & Dieringer, 2004; Wheatley, Plant, Reader, Brown, & Cahill, 2004); however, the use of this drug requires consistent monitoring for agranulocytosis, making clozapine a less desirable choice than other atypical antipsychotics.

Future Directions

Some of the more interesting possibilities for interventions with PTSD have come out of our increased understanding of the brain mediation of the processes of learning and memory. In particular, studies on the neural mechanisms and the neurochemistry of extinction of fear learning have begun to show potential for moving into clinical applications.

Extinction is a process of active inhibition of the pathway encoding the conditioned stimulus-unconditioned stimulus (CS-US) association; it occurs after repeated exposure to the CS in the absence of the US. The inhibition is accomplished via GABAergic mechanisms in the basolateral amygdala (Chhatwal, Myers, Ressler, & Davis, 2005). Compelling evidence is accumulating to show that endogenous cannabinoids are required for the GABAergic mechanism of extinction to function. The primary site of action in the brain for the endocannabinoids is the CB1 receptor (Devane, Dysarz, Johnson, Melvin, & Howlett, 1988; Wilson & Nicoll, 2002), which is expressed at high levels in the basolateral amygdala (Chhatwal et al., 2005). In CB1 knockout mice, there is a near-absence of extinction to a fear-conditioned stimulus, and a CB1 antagonist prevents extinction in intact animals (Marsciano et al., 2002). The compound AM404 promotes the neural activity of the endocannabinoids by inhibiting the breakdown of these molecules and also promotes the course of extinction (Chhatwal, Davis, Maguschak, & Ressler, 2004). If compounds can be developed that are safe for humans and could be taken during exposure therapy, such as reexposure to trauma-associated stimuli with virtual reality, this approach carries the potential of actually "curing" PTSD. This method has already been tried with good results using another extinction promoter, the glutamate partial agonist D-cycloserine, with various anxiety disorders, including PTSD (Heresco-Levy et al., 2002; Hofmann et al., 2006; Ressler et al., 2004). These issues are discussed in more detail in a recent review by Michael Davis and colleagues (M. Davis et al., 2006).

Another line of research indicates that promotion of cannabinoid functionality actually increases the rate of neurogenesis in the hippocampus, as do the SSRI antidepressants, as reviewed above. Rats who show hippocampal neurogenesis after administration of a synthetic cannabinoid also showed reduced anxiety as assessed with a novelty-suppressed feeding paradigm, and reduced depressiveness as assessed with the forced-swim test (Jiang et al., 2005). Findings such as these are opening up new frontiers for the treatment of psychopathologies such as PTSD. We may soon have at our disposal the means to stop PTSD completely in its course, and thereby alleviate a great deal of needless suffering.

References

Ahearn, E. P., Mussey, M., Johnson, C., Krohn, A., & Krahn, D. (2006). Quetiapine as an adjunctive treatment for post-traumatic stress disorder: An 8-week open-label study. *International Clinical Psychopharmacology, 21,* 29–33.

Bahk, W.-M., Pae, C.-U., Tsoh, J., Chae, J.-H., Jun, T.-Y., Kim, C.-L., et al. (2002). Effects of mirtazapine in patients with post-traumatic stress disorder in Korea: A pilot study. *Human Psychopharmacology, 17,* 341–344.

Ballenger, J. C. (2004). Remission rates in patients with anxiety disorders treated with paroxetine. *Journal of Clinical Psychiatry, 65,* 1696–1707.

Ballenger, J. C., Davidson, J.R.T., Lecrubier, Y., Nutt, D. J., Foa, E. B., Kessler, R. C., et al. (2000). Consensus statement of posttraumatic stress disorder from the international consensus group on depression and anxiety. *Journal of Clinical Psychiatry, 61*(Suppl. 5), 60–66.

Balon, R. (2004). Developments in treatment of anxiety disorders: Psychotherapy, pharmacotherapy, and psychosurgery. *Depression and Anxiety, 19,* 63–76.

Barnett, S. D., Tharwani, H. M., Hertzberg, M. A., Sutherland, S. M., Connor, K. M., & Davidson, J. R. (2002). Tolerability of fluoxetine in posttraumatic stress disorder. *Progress in Neuro-Psychopharmacology and Biological Psychiatry, 26,* 363–367.

Bartzokis, G., Lu, P. H., Turner, J., Mintz, J., & Saunders, C. S. (2005). Adjunctive risperidone in the treatment of chronic combat-related posttraumatic stress disorder. *Biological Psychiatry, 57,* 474–479.

Berlant, J., & van Kammen, D. P. (2002). Open-label topiramate as primary or adjunctive therapy in chronic civilian posttraumatic stress disorder: A preliminary report. *Journal of Clinical Psychiatry, 63,* 15–20.

Brady, K., Pearlstein, T., Asnis, G. M., Baker, D., Rothbaum, B., Sikes, C. R., et al. (2000). Efficacy and safety of sertraline treatment of posttraumatic stress disorder. *Journal of the American Medical Association, 283,* 1837–1844.

Brady, K. T., & Clary, C. M. (2003). Affective and anxiety comorbidity in post-traumatic stress disorder treatment trials of sertraline. *Comprehensive Psychiatry, 44,* 360–369.

Brady, K. T., Sonne, S., Anton, R. F., Randall, C. L., Back, S. E., & Simpson, K. (2005). Sertraline in the treatment of co-occurring alcohol dependence and posttraumatic stress disorder. *Alcoholism: Clinical and Experimental Research, 29,* 395–401.

Braun, P., Greenberg, D., Dasberg, H., & Lerer, B. (1990). Core symptoms of posttraumatic stress disorder unimproved by alprazolam treatment. *Journal of Clinical Psychiatry, 51,* 236–238.

Bremner, J. D., Krystal, J. H., Southwick, S. M., & Charney, D. S. (1996). Noradrenergic mechanisms in stress and anxiety: II. Clinical studies. *Synapse, 23,* 39–51.

Bremner, J. D., Mletzko, T., Welter, S., Siddiq, S., Reed, L., Williams, C., et al. (2004). Treatment of posttraumatic stress disorder with phenytoin: An open-label pilot study. *Journal of Clinical Psychiatry, 65,* 1559–1564.

Bryant, R. A., Felmingham, K. L., Kemp, A. H., Barton, M., Peduto, A. S., Rennie, C., et al. (2005). Neural networks of information processing in posttraumatic stress disorder: A functional magnetic resonance imaging study. *Biological Psychiatry, 58,* 111–118.

Butterfield, M. I., Becker, M. E., Connor, K. M., Sutherland, S., Churchill, L. E., & Davidson, J.R.T. (2001). Olanzapine in the treatment of post-traumatic stress disorder: A pilot study. *International Clinical Psychopharmacology, 16,* 197–203.

Chhatwal, J. P., Davis, M., Maguschak, K. A., & Ressler, K. J. (2004). Enhancing cannabinoid neurotransmission augments the extinction of conditioned fear. *Neuropsychopharmacology, 30,* 516–524.

Chhatwal, J. P., Myers, K. M., Ressler, K. J., & Davis, M. (2005). Regulation of gephyrin and $GABA_A$ receptor binding within the amygdala after fear acquistion and extinction. *Journal of Neuroscience, 25,* 502–506.

Chung, M. Y., Min, K. H., Jun, Y. J., Kim, S. S., Kim, W. C., & Jun, E. M. (2004). Efficacy and tolerability of mirtazapine and sertraline in Korean veterans with posttraumatic stress disorder: A randomized open label trial. *Human Psychopharmacology, 19,* 489–494.

Connor, K. M., Davidson, J. R., Weisler, R. H., Zhang, W., & Abraham, K. (2006). Tiagabine for posttraumatic stress disorder: Effects of open-label and double-blind discontinuation treatment. *Psychopharmacology, 184,* 21–25.

Connor, K. M., Sutherland, S. M., Tupler, L. A., Malik, M. L., & Davidson, J.R.T. (1999). Fluoxetine in post-traumatic stress disorder. *British Journal of Psychiatry, 175,* 17–23.

Cooper, J., Carty, J., & Creamer, M. (2005). Pharmacotherapy for posttraumatic stress disorder: Empirical review and clinical recommendations. *Australian and New Zealand Journal of Psychiatry, 39,* 674–682.

Cyr, M., & Farrar, M. K. (2000). Treatment for posttraumatic stress disorder. *Annals of Pharmacotherapy, 34,* 366–376.

Davidson, J., Baldwin, D., Stein, D. J., Kuper, E., Benattia, I., Ahmed, S., et al. (2006). Treatment of posttraumatic stress disorder with venlafaxine extended release: A 6-month randomized controlled trial. *Archives of General Psychiatry, 63,* 1158–1165.

Davidson, J., Kudler, H., Smith, R., Mahorney, S. L., Lipper, S., Hammett, E., et al. (1990). Treatment of posttraumatic stress disorder with amitriptyline and placebo. *Archives of General Psychiatry, 47,* 259–266.

Davidson, J., Landerman, L. R., & Clary, C. M. (2004). Improvement of anger at one week predicts the effects of sertraline and placebo in PTSD. *Journal of Psychiatric Research, 38,* 497–502.

Davidson, J., Pearlstein, T., Londborg, P., Brady, K. T., Rothbaum, B., Bell, J., et al. (2001). Efficacy of sertraline in preventing relapse of posttraumatic stress disorder: Results of a 28-week double-blind, placebo-controlled study [see comment]. *American Journal of Psychiatry, 158,* 1974–1981.

Davidson, J., Roth, S., & Newman, E. (1991). Fluoxetine in post-traumatic stress disorder. *Journal of Traumatic Stress, 4,* 419–423.

Davidson, J., Rothbaum, B. O., Tucker, P., Asnis, G., Benattia, I., & Musgnung, J. J. (2006). Venlafaxine extended release in posttraumatic stress disorder: A sertraline- and placebo-controlled study. *Journal of Clinical Psychopharmacology, 26,* 259–267. [Erratum appears in *Journal of Clinical Psychopharmacology,* October 2006, *26,* 473. Note: dosage error in text.]

Davidson, J. R. (2006). Pharmacologic treatment of acute and chronic stress following trauma: 2006. *Journal of Clinical Psychiatry, 67*(Suppl. 2), 34–39.

Davidson, J. R., Brady, K., Mellman, T. A., Stein, M. B., & Pollack, M. H. (2007). The efficacy and tolerability of tiagabine in adult patients with post-traumatic stress disorder. *Journal of Clinical Psychopharmacology, 27,* 85–88.

Davidson, J. R., Connor, K. M., Hertzberg, M. A., Weisler, R. H., Wilson, W. H., & Payne, V. M. (2005). Maintenance therapy with fluoxetine in posttraumatic stress disorder: A placebo-controlled discontinuation study. *Journal of Clinical Psychopharmacology, 25,* 166–169.

Davidson, J. R., Rothbaum, B. O., van der Kolk, B. A., Sikes, C. R., & Farfel, G. M. (2001). Multicenter, double-blind comparison of sertraline and placebo in the treatment of posttraumatic stress disorder. *Archives of General Psychiatry, 58,* 485–492.

Davidson, J. R., Weisler, R. H., Butterfield, M. I., Casat, C. D., Connor, K. M., Barnett, S., et al. (2003). Mirtazapine vs. placebo in posttraumatic stress disorder: A pilot trial. *Biological Psychiatry, 53,* 188–191.

Davidson, J.R.T., Weisler, R. H., Malik, M. L., & Connor, K. M. (1998). Treatment of posttraumatic stress disorder with nefazodone. *International Clinical Psychopharmacology, 13,* 111–113.

Davis, L. L., English, B. A., Ambrose, S. M., & Petty, F. (2001). Pharmacotherapy for post-traumatic stress disorder: A comprehensive review. *Expert Opinion in Pharmacotherapy, 2,* 1583–1595.

Davis, M. (2000). The role of the amygdala in conditioned and unconditioned fear and anxiety. In J. P. Aggleton (Ed.), *The amygdala: A functional analysis* (pp. 213–288). Oxford, England: Oxford University Press.

Davis, M., Myers, K. M., Chhatwal, J. P., & Ressler, K. J. (2006). Pharmacological treatments that facilitate extinction of fear: Relevance to psychotherapy. *NeuroRx: The Journal of the American Society for Experimental NeuroTherapeutics, 3,* 82–96.

Devane, W. A., Dysarz, F.A.I., Johnson, M. R., Melvin, L. S., & Howlett, A. C. (1988). Determination and characterization of a cannabinoid receptor in rat brain. *Molecular Pharmacology, 34,* 605–613.

Elsesser, K., Sartory, G., & Tackenberg, A. (2005). Initial symptoms and reactions to trauma-related stimuli and the development of posttraumatic stress disorder. *Depression and Anxiety, 21,* 61–70.

Elzinga, B. M., & Bremner, J. D. (2002). Are the neural substrates of memory the final common pathway in posttraumatic stress disorder (PTSD)? *Journal of Affective Disorders, 70,* 1–17.

English, B. A., Jewell, M., Jewell, G., Ambrose, S., & Davis, L. L. (2006). Treatment of chronic posttraumatic stress disorder in combat veterans with citalopram: An open trial. *Journal of Clinical Psychopharmacology, 26,* 84–88.

Escalona, R., Canive, J. M., Calais, L. A., & Davidson, J. R. (2002). Fluvoxamine treatment in veterans with combat-related post-traumatic stress disorder. *Depression and Anxiety, 15,* 29–33.

Famularo, R., Kinscherff, R., & Fenton, T. (1988). Propranolol treatment for childhood posttraumatic stress disorder, acute type: A pilot study. *American Journal of Diseases of Children, 142,* 1244–1247.

Fanselow, M. S., & Poulos, A. M. (2005). The neuroscience of mammalian associative learning. *Annual Review of Psychology, 56,* 207–234.

Fesler, F. A. (1991). Valproate in combat-related posttraumatic stress disorder. *Journal of Clinical Psychiatry, 52,* 361–364.

Foa, E. B., Davidson, J.R.T., & Frances, A. (1999). Expert Consensus Guideline Series: Treatment of posttraumatic stress disorder. *Journal of Clinical Psychiatry, 60*(Suppl. 16), 69–76.

Friedman, M. J. (1988). Toward rational pharmacotherapy for posttraumatic stress disorder: An interim report. *American Journal of Psychiatry, 145,* 281–284.

Garfield, D. A., Fichtner, C. G., Leveroni, C., & Mahableshwarkar, A. (2001). Open trial of nefazodone for combat veterans with posttraumatic stress disorder. *Journal of Traumatic Stress, 14,* 453–460.

Gelpin, E., Bonne, O., Peri, T., Brandes, D., & Shalev, A. Y. (1996). Treatment of recent trauma survivors with benzodiazepines: A prospective study. *Journal of Clinical Psychiatry, 57,* 390–394.

Gillin, J. C., Smith-Vaniz, A., Schnierow, B., Rapaport, M. H., Kelsoe, J., Raimo, E., et al. (2001). An open-label, 12-week clinical and sleep EEG study of nefazodone in chronic combat-related posttraumatic stress disorder. *Journal of Clinical Psychiatry, 62,* 789–796.

Hageman, I., Andersen, H. S., & Jorgensen, M. B. (2001). Post-traumatic stress disorder: A review of psychobiology and pharmacotherapy. *Acta Psychiatrica Scandinavica, 104,* 411–422.

Hamner, M. B., Faldowski, R. A., Ulmer, H. G., Frueh, B. C., Huber, M. G., & Arana, G. W. (2003). Adjunctive risperidone treatment in post-traumatic stress disorder: A preliminary controlled trial of effects on comorbid psychotic symptoms. *International Clinical Psychopharmacology, 18,* 1–8.

Heresco-Levy, U., Kremer, I., Javitt, D. C., Goichman, R., Reshef, A., Blanaru, M., et al. (2002). Pilot-controlled trial of D-cycloserine for the treatment of post-traumatic stress disorder. *International Journal of Neuropsychopharmacology, 5,* 301–307.

Herman, J. P., Figueiredo, H., Mueller, N. K., Ulrich-Lai, Y., Ostrander, M. M., Choi, D. C., et al. (2003). Central mechanisms of stress integration: Hierarchical circuitry controlling hypothalamo-pituitary-adrenocortical responsiveness. *Frontiers in Neuroendocrinology, 24,* 151–180.

Hertzberg, M. A., Butterfield, M. I., Feldman, M. E., Beckham, J. C., Sutherland, S. M., Connor, K. M., et al. (1999). A preliminary study of lamotrigine for the treatment of posttraumatic stress disorder. *Biological Psychiatry, 45,* 1226–1229.

Hertzberg, M. A., Feldman, M. E., Beckham, J. C., & Davidson, J. R. (1996). Trial of trazodone for posttraumatic stress disorder using a multiple baseline group design. *Journal of Clinical Psychopharmacology, 16,* 294–298.

Hertzberg, M. A., Feldman, M. E., Beckham, J. C., Kudler, H. S., & Davidson, J. R. (2000). Lack of efficacy for fluoxetine in PTSD: A placebo controlled trial in combat veterans. *Annals of Clinical Psychiatry, 12,* 101–105.

Hertzberg, M. A., Feldman, M. E., Beckham, J. C., Moore, S. D., & Davidson, J. R. (1998). Open trial of nefazodone for combat-related posttraumatic stress disorder. *Journal of Clinical Psychiatry, 59,* 460–464.

Hertzberg, M. A., Feldman, M. E., Beckham, J. C., Moore, S. D., & Davidson, J. R. (2002). Three- to four-year follow-up to an open trial of nefazodone for combat-related posttraumatic stress disorder. *Annals of Clinical Psychiatry, 14,* 215–221.

Hofmann, S. G., Meuret, A. E., Smits, J. A., Simon, N. M., Pollack, M. H., Eisenmenger, K., et al. (2006). Augmentation of exposure therapy with D-cycloserine for social anxiety disorder. *Archives of General Psychiatry, 63,* 298–304.

Hoge, C. W., Castro, C. A., Messer, S. C., McGurk, D., Cotting, D. I., & Koffman, R. L. (2004). Combat duty in Iraq and Afghanistan, mental health problems, and barriers to care. *New England Journal of Medicine, 351,* 13–22.

Huang, G.-J., & Herbert, J. (2006). Stimulation of neurogenesis in the hippocampus of the adult rat by fluoxetine requires rhythmic change in corticosterone. *Biological Psychiatry, 59,* 619–624.

Hurlemann, R., Hawellek, B., Matusch, A., Kolsch, H., Wollersen, H., Madea, B., et al. (2005). Noradrenergic modulation of emotion-induced forgetting and remembering. *Journal of Neuroscience, 25,* 6343–6349.

Jakovljevic, M., Sagud, M., & Mihaljevic-Peles, A. (2003). Olanzapine in the treatment-resistant, combat-related PTSD—a series of case reports. *Acta Psychiatrica Scandinavica, 107,* 394–396; discussion 396.

Jiang, W., Zhang, Y., Xiao, L., Cleemput, J. V., Ji, S.-P., Bai, G., et al. (2005). Cannabinoids promote embryonic and adult hippocampus neurogenesis and produce anxiolytic- and antidepressant-like effects. *Journal of Clinical Investigation, 115,* 3104–3116.

Kalynchuk, L. E., Pinel, J. P., & Meaney, M. J. (2006). Serotonin receptor binding and mRNA expression in the hippocampus of fearful amygdala-kindled rats. *Neuroscience Letters, 396,* 38–43.

Kant, R., Chalansani, R., Chengappa, K. N., & Dieringer, M. F. (2004). The off-label use of clozapine in adolescents with bipolar disorder, intermittent explosive disorder, or posttraumatic stress disorder. *Journal of Child and Adolescent Psychopharmacology, 14,* 57–63.

Kellett, J., & Kokkinidis, L. (2004). Extinction deficit and fear reinstatement after electrical stimulation of the amygdala:

Implications for kindling-associated fear and anxiety. *Neuroscience, 127,* 277–287.

Kim, W., Pae, C. U., Chae, J. H., Jun, T. Y., & Bahk, W. M. (2005). The effectiveness of mirtazapine in the treatment of post-traumatic stress disorder: A 24-week continuation therapy. *Psychiatry and Clinical Neurosciences, 59,* 743–747.

Kinrys, G., Wygant, L. E., Pardo, T. B., & Melo, M. (2006). Levetiracetam for treatment-refractory posttraumatic stress disorder. *Journal of Clinical Psychiatry, 67,* 211–214.

Kinzie, J. D., & Leung, P. (1989). Clonidine in Cambodian patients with posttraumatic stress disorder. *Journal of Nervous and Mental Disease, 177,* 546–550.

Kozaric-Kovacic, D., Pivac, N., Muck-Seler, D., & Rothbaum, B. O. (2005). Risperidone in psychotic combat-related posttraumatic stress disorder: An open trial. *Journal of Clinical Psychiatry, 66,* 922–927.

Lambert, M. T. (2006). Aripiprazole in the management of posttraumatic stress disorder symptoms in returning global war on terrorism veterans. *International Clinical Psychopharmacology, 21,* 185–187.

Lasiuk, G. C., & Hegadoren, K. M. (2006). Posttraumatic stress disorder part I: Historical development of the concept. *Perspectives in Psychiatric Care, 42,* 13–20.

LeDoux, J. (1996). *The emotional brain.* New York: Simon and Schuster.

Lipper, S., Davidson, J.R.T., Grady, T. A., Edinger, J. D., Hammett, E. B., Mahorney, S. L., et al. (1986). Preliminary study of carbamazepine in post-traumatic stress disorder. *Psychosomatics, 27,* 849–854.

Londborg, P. D., Hegel, M. T., Goldstein, S., Goldstein, D., Himmelhoch, J. M., Maddock, R., et al. (2001). Sertraline treatment of posttraumatic stress disorder: Results of 24 weeks of open-label continuation treatment. *Journal of Clinical Psychiatry, 62,* 325–331.

Manji, H. K., Quiroz, J. A., Sporn, J., Payne, J. L., Denicoff, K., Gray, N. A., et al. (2003). Enhancing neuronal plasticity and cellular resilience to develop novel, improved therapeutics for difficult-to-treat depression. *Biological Psychiatry, 53,* 707–742.

Marsciano, G., Wotjak, C. T., Azad, S. C., Bisogno, T., Rammes, G., Cascio, M. G., et al. (2002). The endogenous cannabinoid system controls extinction of aversive memories. *Nature, 418,* 530–534.

Marshall, R. D., Beebe, K. L., Oldham, M., & Zaninelli, R. (2001). Efficacy and safety of paroxetine treatment for chronic PTSD: A fixed-dose, placebo-controlled study. *American Journal of Psychiatry, 158,* 1982–1988.

Martenyi, F., Brown, E. B., Zhang, H., Koke, S. C., & Prakash, A. (2002). Fluoxetine v. placebo in prevention of relapse in post-traumatic stress disorder [see comment]. *British Journal of Psychiatry, 181,* 315–320.

Martenyi, F., Brown, E. B., Zhang, H., Prakash, A., & Koke, S. C. (2002). Fluoxetine versus placebo in posttraumatic stress disorder. *Journal of Clinical Psychiatry, 63,* 199–206.

Martenyi, F., & Soldatenkova, V. (2006). Fluoxetine in the acute treatment and relapse prevention of combat-related posttraumatic stress disorder: Analysis of the veteran group of a placebo-controlled, randomized clinical trial. *European Neuropsychopharmacology, 16,* 340–349.

McCleery, J. M., & Harvey, A. G. (2004). Integration of psychological and biological approaches to trauma memory: Implications for pharmacological prevention of PTSD. *Journal of Traumatic Stress, 17,* 485–496.

McDougle, C. J., Southwick, S. M., Charney, D. S., & St. James, R. L. (1991). An open trial of fluoxetine in the treatment of posttraumatic stress disorder [letter]. *Journal of Clinical Psychiatry, 11,* 325–327.

McGaugh, J. L. (2004). The amygdala modulates the consolidation of memories of emotionally arousing experiences. *Annual Review of Neuroscience, 27,* 1–28.

McNally, R. J. (2003). Progress and controversy in the study of posttraumatic stress disorder. *Annual Reviews in Psychology, 54,* 229–252.

Mellman, T. A., Byers, P. M., & Augenstein, J. S. (1998). Pilot evaluation of hypnotic medication during acute traumatic stress response. *Journal of Traumatic Stress, 11,* 563–569.

Mellman, T. A., David, D., & Barza, L. (1999). Nefazodone treatment and dream reports in chronic PTSD. *Depression and Anxiety, 9,* 146–148.

Monnelly, E. P., Ciraulo, D. A., Knapp, C., & Keane, T. (2003). Low-dose risperidone as adjunctive therapy for irritable aggression in posttraumatic stress disorder. *Journal of Clinical Psychopharmacology, 23,* 193–196.

Morgan, C. A., Krystal, J. H., & Southwick, S. M. (2003). Toward early pharmacological posttraumatic stress intervention. *Biological Psychiatry, 53,* 834–843.

Murchison, C. F., Zhang, X. Y., Zhang, W. P., Ouyang, M., Lee, A., & Thomas, S. A. (2004). A distinct role for norepinephrine in memory retrieval [see comment]. *Cell, 117,* 131–143.

Nagy, L. M., Morgan, C. A., Southwick, S. M., & Charney, D. S. (1993). Open prospective trial of fluoxetine for posttraumatic stress disorder. *Journal of Clinical Psychopharmacology, 13,* 107–113.

Namestkova, K., Simonova, Z., & Sykova, E. (2005). Decreased proliferation in the adult rat hippocampus after exposure to the Morris water maze and its reversal by fluoxetine. *Behavioural Brain Research, 163,* 26–32.

Nemeroff, C. B. (2003). The role of GABA in the pathophysiology and treatment of anxiety disorders. *Psychopharmacology Bulletin, 37,* 133–146.

Neylan, T. C., Lenoci, M., Maglione, M. L., Rosenlicht, N. Z., Leykin, Y., Metzler, T. J., et al. (2003). The effect of nefazodone on subjective and objective sleep quality in posttraumatic stress disorder. *Journal of Clinical Psychiatry, 64,* 445–450.

Neylan, T. C., Lenoci, M., Samuelson, K. W., Metzler, T. J., Henn-Haase, C., Hierholzer, R. W., et al. (2006). No improvement of posttraumatic stress disorder symptoms with guanfacine treatment. *American Journal of Psychiatry, 163,* 2186–2188.

Padala, P. R., Madison, J., Monnahan, M., Marcil, W., Price, P., Ramaswamy, S., et al. (2006). Risperidone monotherapy for post-traumatic stress disorder related to sexual assault and domestic abuse in women. *International Clinical Psychopharmacology, 21,* 275–280.

Pearlstein, T. (2000). Antidepressant treatment of posttraumatic stress disorder. *Journal of Clinical Psychiatry, 61*(Suppl. 7), 40–43.

Phelps, E. A., & LeDoux, J. E. (2005). Contributions of the amygdala to emotion processing: From animal models to human behavior. *Neuron, 48,* 175–187.

Pitman, R. K., & Delahanty, D. L. (2005). Conceptually driven pharmacological approaches to acute trauma. *CNS Spectrums, 10,* 99–106.

Pitman, R. K., Sanders, K. M., Zusman, R. M., Healy, A. R., Cheema, F., Lasko, N. B., et al. (2002). Pilot study of secondary prevention of posttraumatic stress disorder with propranolol [see comment]. *Biological Psychiatry, 51,* 189–192.

Pivac, N., Kozaric-Kovacic, D., & Muck-Seler, D. (2004). Olanzapine versus fluphenazine in an open trial in patients with psychotic combat-related post-traumatic stress disorder. *Psychopharmacology, 175,* 451–456.

Raskind, M. A., Thompson, C., Petrie, E. C., Dobie, D. J., Rein, R. J., Hoff, D. J., et al. (2002). Prazosin reduces nightmares in combat veterans with posttraumatic stress disorder. *Journal of Clinical Psychiatry, 63,* 565–568.

Reich, D. B., Winternitz, S., Hennen, J., Watts, T., & Stanculescu, C. (2004). A preliminary study of risperidone in the treatment of posttraumatic stress disorder related to childhood abuse in women. *Journal of Clinical Psychiatry, 65,* 1601–1606.

Ressler, K. J., Rothbaum, B. O., Tannenbaum, L., Anderson, P., Graap, K., Zimand, E., et al. (2004). Cognitive enhancers as adjuncts to psychotherapy: Use of D-Cycloserine in phobic individuals to facilitate extinction of fear. *Archives of General Psychiatry, 61,* 1136–1144.

Robert, S., Hamner, M. B., Kose, S., Ulmer, H. G., Deitsch, S. E., & Lorberbaum, J. P. (2005). Quetiapine improves sleep disturbances in combat veterans with PTSD: Sleep data from a prospective, open-label study. *Journal of Clinical Psychopharmacology, 25,* 387–388.

Robert, S., Hamner, M. B., Ulmer, H. G., Lorberbaum, J. P., & Durkalski, V. L. (2006). Open-label trial of escitalopram in the treatment of posttraumatic stress disorder. *Journal of Clinical Psychiatry, 67,* 1522–1526.

Rothbaum, B. O., & Davis, M. (2003). Applying learning principles to the treatment of post-trauma reactions. *Annals of the New York Academy of Sciences, 1008,* 112–121.

Shalev, A. Y. (2002). Acute stress reactions in adults. *Biological Psychiatry, 51,* 532–543.

Shalev, A. Y., Bloch, M., Peri, T., & Bonne, O. (1998). Alprazolam reduces response to loud tones in panic disorder but not in posttraumatic stress disorder. *Biological Psychiatry, 44,* 64–68.

Shalev, A. Y., Bonne, O., & Eth, S. (1996). Treatment of posttraumatic stress disorder: A review. *Psychosomatic Medicine, 58,* 165–182.

Shalev, A. Y., Freedman, S., Peri, T., Brandes, D., Sahar, T., Orr, S. P., et al. (1998). Prospective study of posttraumatic stress disorder and depression following trauma. *American Journal of Psychiatry, 155,* 630–637.

Sokolski, K. N., Denson, T. F., Lee, R. T., & Reist, C. (2003). Quetiapine for treatment of refractory symptoms of combat-related post-traumatic stress disorder. *Military Medicine, 168,* 486–489.

Spivak, B., Strous, R. D., Shaked, G., Shabash, E., Kotler, M., & Weizman, A. (2006). Reboxetine versus fluvoxamine in the treatment of motor vehicle accident-related posttraumatic stress disorder: A double-blind, fixed-dosage, controlled trial. *Journal of Clinical Psychopharmacology, 26,* 152–156.

Stein, M. B., Kline, N. A., & Matloff, J. L. (2002). Adjunctive olanzapine for SSRI-resistant combat-related PTSD: A double-blind, placebo-controlled study [see comment]. *American Journal of Psychiatry, 159,* 1777–1779.

Taylor, F. B., Lowe, K., Thompson, C., McFall, M. M., Peskind, E. R., Kanter, E. D., et al. (2006). Daytime prazosin reduces psychological distress to trauma specific cues in civilian trauma posttraumatic stress disorder. *Biological Psychiatry, 59,* 577–581.

Tucker, P., Smith, K. L., Marx, B., Jones, D., Miranda, R., & Lensgraf, J. (2000). Fluvoxamine reduces physiologic reactivity to trauma scripts in posttraumatic stress disorder. *Journal of Clinical Psychopharmacology, 20,* 367–372.

Tucker, P., Trautman, R. P., Wyatt, D. B., Thompson, J., Wu, S. C., Capece, J. A., et al. (2007). Efficacy and safety of topiramate monotherapy in civilian posttraumatic stress disorder: A randomized, double-blind, placebo-controlled study. *Journal of Clinical Psychiatry, 68,* 201–206.

Tucker, P., Zaninelli, R., Yehuda, R., Ruggiero, L., Dillingham, K., & Pitts, C. D. (2001). Paroxetine in the treatment of chronic posttraumatic stress disorder: Results of a placebo-controlled, flexible-dosage trial. *Journal of Clinical Psychiatry, 62,* 860–868.

Vaiva, G., Ducrocq, F., Jezequel, K., Averland, B., Lestavel, P., Brunet, A., et al. (2003). Immediate treatment with propranolol decreases posttraumatic stress disorder two months after trauma. [see comment]. *Biological Psychiatry, 54,* 947–949. [Erratum appears in *Biological Psychiatry,* December 15, 2003, *54,* 1471].

Van der Kolk, B. A., Dreyfuss, D., Michaels, M., Shera, D., Berkowitz, R., Fisler, R., et al. (1994). Fluoxetine in posttraumatic stress disorder. *Journal of Clinical Psychiatry, 55,* 517–522.

Van Praag, H. M. (2004). The cognitive paradox in posttraumatic stress disorder: A hypothesis. *Progress in Neuro-Psychopharmacology and Biological Psychiatry, 28,* 923–935.

Vermetten, E., Vythilingam, M., Southwick, S. M., Charney, D. S., & Bremner, J. D. (2003). Long-term treatment with paroxetine increases verbal declarative memory and hippocampal volume in posttraumatic stress disorder. *Biological Psychiatry, 54,* 693–702.

Warner, M. D., Dorn, M. R., & Peabody, C. A. (2001). Survey on the usefulness of trazodone in patients with PTSD with insomnia or nightmares. *Pharmacopsychiatry, 34,* 128–131.

Warner-Schmidt, J. L., & Duman, R. S. (2006). Hippocampal neurogenesis: Opposing effects of stress and antidepressant treatment. *Hippocampus, 16,* 239–249.

Wheatley, M., Plant, J., Reader, H., Brown, G., & Cahill, C. (2004). Clozapine treatment of adolescents with posttraumatic stress disorder and psychotic symptoms. *Journal of Clinical Psychopharmacology, 24,* 167–173.

Williams, L. M., Kemp, A. H., Felmingham, K., Barton, M., Olivieri, G., Peduto, A., et al. (2006). Trauma modulates amygdala and medial prefrontal responses to consciously attended fear. *Neuroimage, 29,* 347–357.

Wilson, R. I., & Nicoll, R. A. (2002). Endocannabinoid signaling in the brain. *Science, 296,* 678–682.

Yehuda, R., McFarlane, A. C., & Shalev, A. Y. (1998). Predicting the development of posttraumatic stress disorder from the acute response to a traumatic event. *Biological Psychiatry, 44,* 1305–1313.

Zohar, J., Amital, D., Miodownik, C., Kotler, M., Bleich, A., Lane, R. M., et al. (2002). Double-blind placebo-controlled pilot study of sertraline in military veterans with posttraumatic stress disorder. *Journal of Clinical Psychiatry, 22,* 190–195.

Psychological Treatment of Posttraumatic Stress Disorder and Acute Stress Disorder

David S. Riggs *and* Edna B. Foa

Abstract

A number of programs have been developed to treat posttraumatic stress disorder (PTSD) and acute stress disorder (ASD). Few of these programs have substantial empirical support for their efficacy. Most programs with established efficacy are based on techniques of cognitive behavioral therapy (CBT), including exposure therapy, cognitive therapy, and anxiety management training or, in the case of Eye Movement Desensitization and Reprocessing, incorporate techniques similar to those used in CBT approaches. This chapter describes the major treatment approaches that have been empirically evaluated and reviews the treatment outcome literature for these programs. It concludes that there is substantial evidence for the efficacy of CBT approaches, particularly those that incorporate exposure to the traumatic memory. However, the literature provides little guidance to select among the available treatments as those studies that directly compare two or more treatments show largely equivalent outcomes.

Keywords: acute stress disorder, posttraumatic stress disorder, therapy, trauma, treatment

Traumatic events can trigger a variety of psychological difficulties, including depression, specific phobias, and posttraumatic stress disorder (PTSD). The choice of treatment, then, depends on the specific difficulties experienced by the trauma survivor. In this chapter we will focus on treatments that aim at reducing symptoms of the two disorders specifically tied to traumatic events: posttraumatic stress disorder (PTSD) and acute stress disorder (ASD) (American Psychiatric Association [APA], 1994). Also, rather than trying to review all of the treatments that have been used or suggested for these disorders, we will focus on treatments that have received empirical support for their efficacy. Most of these treatments are based on techniques of cognitive behavioral therapy (CBT), including exposure therapy, anxiety management training, and cognitive therapy (see Foa, Keane, & Friedman, 2000). Though these treatments share many characteristics, there are differences in the specific procedures and

emphasis. Some programs emphasize the use of exposure to trauma-related memories and cues, others focus on training trauma survivors to manage and cope with distressing feelings, and still others stress the role of cognitive restructuring techniques to produce change in cognitions related to the trauma.

Description of Psychological Treatments of Chronic PTSD

A variety of treatment programs have been utilized for posttrauma reactions, particularly since the introduction of PTSD (for a comprehensive review, see Foa et al., 2000). However, the bulk of the research into the efficacy of psychosocial treatments has focused on CBT programs (see Foa & Meadows, 1997; Foa & Rothbaum, 1998; Foa, Rothbaum, & Furr, 2003). Several treatments based on CBT principles have been found to reduce PTSD symptoms in randomized controlled trials using waitlist or minimal attention control groups. The most rigorously studied programs can be broadly grouped into five categories: (1) exposure therapy, (2) anxiety management skills training, (3) cognitive therapy, (4) programs that combine elements of these interventions, and (5) programs that include nonconventional exposure techniques, in particular, eye movement desensitization and reprocessing (EMDR) (Shapiro, 2001).

Exposure Therapy

The fact that PTSD shares certain characteristics with other anxiety disorders led several authors to examine the utility of exposure therapy in reducing PTSD symptoms. Initially, the theoretical basis for exposure therapy to treat PTSD focused on the habituation or extinction of fear reactions. More recently, researchers have conceptualized exposure therapy as producing cognitive changes as well as reducing emotional distress (Foa & Rothbaum, 1998). The core element of exposure therapy programs for PTSD is the repeated intentional recalling of traumatic memories, often referred to as imaginal exposure. Most programs also integrate in vivo exposure to environmental cues (e.g., situations, objects) that elicit trauma-related distress or the traumatic memory. Specific strategies and instructions for implementing imaginal and in vivo exposure can also vary across programs. In addition to the core exposure elements, programs may include other techniques such as relaxation (Keane, Fairbank, Caddell, & Zimering, 1989) or controlled breathing (Foa et al., 1999, 2005), and education about trauma and posttrauma reactions (Foa et al., 1999, 2005).

Anxiety Management Therapies

Some treatments for PTSD teach techniques to control anxiety symptoms or manage ongoing stress associated with the trauma. These approaches used in isolation have not been the focus of as much empirical evaluation as treatments described here, but several studies have used such techniques as comparison treatments for exposure and cognitive therapies (e.g., Foa, Rothbaum, Riggs, & Murdock, 1991; Foa et al., 1999). In addition, many treatment programs for PTSD incorporate the teaching of some anxiety management techniques.

Veronen and Kilpatrick (1983) adapted stress inoculation training (SIT) Meichenbaum, 1974), to treat rape survivors, and several studies have included an evaluation of SIT to treat PTSD (Foa et al., 1991, 1999). Stress inoculation training for PTSD includes a number of different techniques, including education about trauma-related symptoms, breathing and relaxation training to reduce physiological arousal, cognitive restructuring, guided self-talk, assertiveness training, role-playing, covert modeling, and thought-stopping. Some SIT programs include an exposure component (e.g., Veronen & Kilpatrick, 1983), whereas others explicitly preclude structured exposure instructions (e.g., Foa et al., 1991, 1999). Also, programs vary in the number of sessions and the specific anxiety management techniques used.

Cognitive Therapies

Several different cognitive treatments have been developed to treat PTSD. Although specific details of these approaches differ across programs, there are certain characteristics that are consistent. All these treatments aim to help the survivor identify trauma-related cognitive errors that contribute to difficulties in the survivor's life. The programs differ on exactly how the dysfunctional thoughts are identified with some monitoring present-day situations (e.g., Blanchard et al., 2003; Foa et al., 2005) and others focused more directly on the traumatic memory (e.g., Ehlers, Clark, Hackmann, McManus, & Fennell, 2005; Resick, Nishith, Weaver, Astin, & Feuer, 2002). Regardless of how the cognitions are identified, these programs focus on thoughts that reflect exaggerated or inaccurate beliefs about the trauma, oneself, or the world. Once identified, various techniques are used to encourage change in these cognitions that will render them more adaptive. One technique that is common to many cognitive therapies for PTSD is the use of Socratic questioning to challenge the faulty cognitions and replace them with alternative realistic and functional cognitions (e.g., Ehlers et al., 2005; Foa et al., 2005; Resick et al., 2002). Most cognitive therapies incorporate an exposure component, but the methods for doing this differ across programs with three primary techniques (writing about the trauma, imaginal reliving of the trauma, and in vivo exposure) being used alone or in combination. Programs also differ with respect to structural factors such as the length and number of sessions.

Eye Movement Desensitization and Reprocessing

Eye movement desensitization and reprocessing (Shapiro, 1989, 2001) is a treatment that includes aspects of CBT approaches, though the treatment was not initially developed within the CBT tradition. During EMDR sessions, patients generate a mental image of the trauma along with associated negative thoughts and feelings. While focusing on these images and thoughts, the patient is asked to move his or her eyes rapidly back and forth by following the movement of the therapist's finger or other stimulus (e.g., a moving light). Alternatively, the survivor might engage in other bilaterally alternating stimuli such as auditory tones alternating in each ear, or finger tapping. Intermittently, during the treatment session, the client is asked to evaluate the qualities of the images and thoughts as well as the level of the distress they evoke. In later sessions, the client is encouraged to make alternative cognitive appraisals of the trauma or his or her behavior during it, and while focusing on these alternative cognitions, to repeat the rapid eye movements. Originally, Shapiro (1991) suggested that the rapid eye movements were necessary for quick processing of the trauma. However, research has not supported this assertion (for review, see Lohr, Tolin, & Lilienfeld, 1998).

The Efficacy of CBT Treatments for Chronic PTSD

The treatments described above have generally been found effective in treating PTSD after a relatively few sessions (typically 9 to 16 sessions conducted over 5 to 16 weeks). Importantly, these treatments have lasting benefits with a number of studies showing that treatment gains persist over periods as long as 2 years (e.g., Blanchard et al., 2003; Cloitre, Koenen, Cohen, & Han, 2002; Ehlers et al., 2005; Foa et al., 1999, 2005; Resick et al., 2002; Tarrier, et al., 1999; Taylor et al., 2003). Furthermore, CBT for chronic PTSD has been shown to be effective in survivors of a wide variety of traumas. Early studies focused on women who had been sexually or physically assaulted (e.g., Echeburua, Corral, Zubizarreta, & Sarasua, 1997; Foa et al., 1991) and male combat veterans (e.g., Cooper & Clum, 1989; Keane et al., 1989). Subsequent studies have replicated the findings with these populations (Foa et al., 1999, 2005; Glynn et al., 1999; Resick et al., 2002; Rothbaum, Astin, & Marsteller, 2005), as well as with survivors of physical and sexual abuse in childhood (Cloitre et al., 2002; Foa et al., 2005) and motor vehicle accidents (Blanchard et al., 2003; Fecteau & Nicki, 1999). Additional studies have found CBT to be effective in treating PTSD among refugees (Otto et al., 2003; Paunovic & Öst, 2001) and in samples that include survivors of different types of traumas (Bryant, Moulds, Guthrie, Dang, & Nixon, 2003; Marks, Lovell, Noshirvani, Livanou,

& Thrasher, 1998; Power et al., 2002; Tarrier, Pilgrim, et al., 1999; Taylor et al., 2003). Thus, there is strong support for the use of CBT interventions with a variety of traumatized populations.

Exposure Therapy

The efficacy of exposure therapy has been examined in numerous studies. Variations include programs that incorporate both imaginal and in vivo exposure (e.g., Foa et al., 1999, 2005; Resick et al., 2002; Rothbaum et al., 2005), programs utilizing only one form of exposure (e.g., Bryant, Moulds, Guthrie, Dang, & Nixon, 2003; Tarrier et al., 1999), programs that implement imaginal and in vivo exposure concurrently (Foa et al., 1999, 2005; Rothbaum et al., 2005), and others that implement them sequentially (e.g., Marks et al., 1998; Taylor et al., 2003). Additionally, many programs combine exposure therapy with other approaches such as cognitive restructuring, anxiety management, or affect regulation techniques (e.g., Blanchard et al., 2003; Cloitre et al., 2002). Despite these variations, the results of these studies provide consistent support for the efficacy of exposure therapy in treating PTSD.

Prolonged Exposure (PE) therapy, developed by Foa and colleagues (Foa et al., 1991, 1999, 2005), is a program that emphasizes the role of imaginal and in vivo exposure in treating chronic PTSD. Several studies have demonstrated PE to be effective in reducing PTSD compared to waitlist (Foa et al., 1991, 1999, 2005; Resick et al., 2002) or supportive counseling (Foa et al., 1991; Schnurr et al., 2007). Furthermore, all of the studies demonstrated that treatment gains are maintained over time (3–9 months). Studies have also compared PE to other active treatments and found the effects of PE to be comparable to SIT (Foa et al., 1991, 1999), cognitive processing therapy (CPT) (Resick et al., 2002), and EMDR (Rothbaum et al., 2005) in reducing symptoms of PTSD. All of the studies examining the efficacy of PE indicate that it reduces symptoms of depression and anxiety as well as the targeted PTSD symptoms.

A number of studies have examined the potential benefit of combining PE with other treatment techniques, including SIT and cognitive restructuring. In general, these studies have found no advantage of adding treatment techniques to the basic PE protocol. For example, Foa et al. (1999) examined the efficacy of PE combined with SIT and found no greater improvement among survivors treated with the combined treatment over either treatment delivered alone. In a follow-up study, Foa and her colleagues found no advantage for adding formal cognitive therapy to the PE regimen (Foa et al., 2005). Paunovic and Öst (2001) also compared treatment with PE to PE combined with cognitive restructuring and found no added benefit with the combined treatment.

Marks et al. (1998) utilized a protocol that included many of the same techniques as PE, but exposure exercises were conducted sequentially with imaginal exposure exercises conducted in the first five sessions and in vivo exercises during the final five sessions. This treatment was superior to relaxation training and equally effective as cognitive restructuring in reducing PTSD symptoms. As with studies of PE, combining exposure and cognitive restructuring techniques did not produce any added reduction in symptoms compared to either treatment alone. Taylor et al. (2003) used an eight-session version of the Marks et al. (1998) exposure therapy protocol (four sessions of imaginal exposure, followed by four sessions of in vivo exposure) in a study that compared this treatment to EMDR and relaxation training. All groups were improved at the end of treatment, with the exposure group significantly more improved than the relaxation group and (on some measures) the EMDR group. The group treated with EMDR was not significantly different from relaxation. Power et al. (2002) compared Marks et al.'s (1998) combined treatment (imaginal and in vivo exposure plus cognitive restructuring) to EMDR and waitlist. Both active treatments produced a greater reduction in PTSD symptoms than did the waitlist. In this case, though, the two active treatments did not differ.

Other treatment programs that incorporate extensive exposure have also been found to be effective in treating PTSD. For example, a brief treatment that combined education, breathing retraining, imaginal and in vivo exposure, and cognitive restructuring was effective in reducing PTSD symptoms compared to a waitlist (Fecteau & Nicki, 1999). Similarly, Echeburua et al. (1997) reported that a treatment combining gradual exposure and cognitive restructuring reduced PTSD symptoms significantly more than relaxation, though both groups improved. Cloitre et al. (2002) treated women who had been sexually abused as children with imaginal exposure after they had completed training in emotion regulation and relationship skills. Compared to a waitlist, this sequential treatment was effective in reducing PTSD symptoms as well as improving affect regulation and interpersonal functioning.

Interestingly, emotional regulation training did not reduce PTSD symptoms whereas imaginal exposure reduced PTSD symptoms and at the same time increased emotional regulation. Blanchard et al. (2003) found that a CBT program that combined memory exposure (writing and repeatedly reading a trauma-narrative), in vivo exposure, relaxation, and behavioral activation was more effective in reducing PTSD than supportive psychotherapy and a waitlist. In a study comparing imaginal exposure alone, the combination of imaginal exposure and cognitive restructuring, and supportive counseling, both exposure groups improved more than the supportive counseling group (Bryant, Moulds, Guthrie, Dang, & Nixon, 2003). The group that received the combined treatment also showed a greater reduction in reexperiencing and trauma-related cognitions than did the group that received imaginal exposure only.

Cognitive Therapies

Several different cognitive therapy programs have been found to reduce PTSD symptoms. Although these protocols also incorporate some exposure exercises, the focus of treatment is not on exposure and the rationale for including these exercises is often quite different from that provided in exposure therapies. As a result, these cognitive programs tend to use less frequent and shorter exposure exercises than do exposure treatments.

Several studies have examined the efficacy of CPT (Resick & Schnicke, 1992) for treating PTSD symptoms. In addition to the cognitive techniques that are the focus of CPT, patients engage in limited exposure via writing narratives of their traumatic experience and reading the narrative aloud during sessions. Resick et al. (2002) compared CPT to PE and to a waitlist condition, and found that CPT was more effective than waitlist and equally effective to PE in reducing PTSD symptoms depression and anxiety. As with PE, the gains made with CPT appear to be maintained at a 9-month follow-up assessment. The group treated with CPT expressed lower feelings of guilt than did those treated with PE on two out of four measures of guilt. Two additional studies have examined the efficacy of CPT compared to a waitlist condition. One study found that CPT was effective in reducing PTSD and anxiety symptoms in a mixed group of military veterans (Monson et al., 2006). Notably, when clusters of PTSD symptoms were examined, the CPT group improved more than the waitlist group on measures of reexperiencing and emotional numbing, but not on hyperarousal and behavioral avoidance. A third study used a modified version of CPT to address the needs of adult survivors of childhood sexual abuse (Chard, 2005). The protocol used in this study included 17 group and 10 individual sessions and incorporated sessions examining developmental aspects of the trauma, assertiveness, communication skills, sexual intimacy, and social support. Compared to a minimal attention waitlist condition, this modified CPT program produced significant reductions in PTSD symptoms, depression, and dissociation.

Another cognitive therapy approach to treating PTSD focuses specifically on modifying cognitions related to feelings of guilt (Kubany, Hill, & Owens, 2003; Kubany et al., 2004). This program also includes a limited exposure component and training in assertiveness, problem solving, and anger management skills. Compared to a waitlist, this therapy program significantly reduced symptoms of PTSD, depression, guilt, and low self-esteem in female victims of domestic violence.

Ehlers and her colleagues have examined the efficacy of a cognitive therapy for PTSD that is somewhat different from those of Resick and Kubany (Ehlers et al., 2003, 2005). Instead of encouraging change in specific cognitive themes that are theoretically linked to the traumatic experience, the Ehlers treatment aims to (1) modify extremely negative appraisals of the trauma and its aftereffects, (2) change the nature of the survivor's memory for the event, and (3) reduce maladaptive behavioral and cognitive strategies used to provide short-term distress reduction (Ehlers et al., 2005). The Ehlers et al. treatment protocol also includes a number of exposure techniques such as writing about the event, imaginal reliving, and revisiting the site of the trauma. In both of the studies conducted by Ehlers and her colleagues, this cognitive intervention was found to be superior to waitlist in reducing PTSD, depression, and anxiety (Ehlers et al., 2003, 2005). In one study, the cognitive therapy protocol was also more effective than a self-help program based on cognitive-behavioral principles (Ehlers et al., 2003).

Also supportive of the efficacy of cognitive therapy for PTSD are the results of the Marks et al. (1998) study that included a cognitive restructuring (CR) only condition. The results of this study indicated that the CR treatment was more effective than waitlist in reducing PTSD and depression symptoms. Many of the combined treatments discussed in the exposure therapy section also included a substantial cognitive therapy component (Foa et al., 2005; Marks et al., 1998; Paunovic & Öst,

2001). In general, these combined treatments appear as effective as exposure therapy alone.

Eye Movement Desensitization and Reprocessing

Eye movement desensitization and reprocessing has been the topic of extensive empirical study due, at least in part, to the controversial nature of the treatment and the initial claims about it efficacy (it was initially described as a single-session cure for PTSD). It is more effective than waitlist control conditions in reducing PTSD symptoms, but treatment generally takes 8–16 sessions, much like other effective PTSD treatments. For example, a study comparing two sessions of EMDR to no treatment found that neither group improved significantly (Jensen, 1994). In comparison, results from another study that included nine EMDR sessions demonstrate significantly more improvement with EMDR than in a waitlist condition (Rothbaum et al., 2005). There are also indications that EMDR is more effective than standard psychiatric care for reducing PTSD symptoms (Marcus, Marquis, & Sakai, 1997).

Several recent studies compared EMDR to CBT programs with somewhat mixed results. Lee, Gavriel, Drummond, Richards, and Greenwald (2002) compared seven sessions of EMDR to seven sessions of treatment modeled on the PE-SIT protocol developed by Foa and her colleagues (Foa et al., 1999). Both treatments produced significant reductions in PTSD that were comparable at the posttreatment assessment. However, when 3-month follow-up data were analyzed, the EMDR group showed significantly more reduction in PTSD symptoms than did the PE-SIT group. This difference appeared largely due to differences in intrusion symptoms (Lee et al., 2002). Power et al. (2002) found no statistically significant advantage for EMDR, but did report effect sizes favoring EMDR over a combined exposure and cognitive restructuring treatment.

In contrast to the above studies, several studies have found EMDR to underperform compared to CBT programs. In one study, EMDR was compared to a treatment program that combined exposure, cognitive restructuring, and SIT (Devilly & Spence, 1999). At posttreatment and 3-month follow-up assessments, the CBT program produced greater improvements than did EMDR; these differences were most pronounced at the follow-up assessment because of a partial return of symptoms in the EMDR group. Taylor et al. (2003) reported that exposure therapy, but not EMDR, produced significantly better outcome than the control, relaxation training. In perhaps the best-controlled study comparing EMDR and exposure therapy, Rothbaum et al. (2005) compared EMDR to PE and a waitlist. Both active treatments produced significantly greater improvement in PTSD symptoms than the waitlist group, but PTSD symptom reduction in the two active treatments did not differ at posttreatment or follow-up.

Anxiety Management Therapies

Only a few studies have systematically examined the efficacy of anxiety management programs for treating PTSD. However, as noted above, several of the combined treatments that have been examined include a substantial anxiety management (e.g., Blanchard et al., 2003) or emotion regulation (e.g., Cloitre et al., 2002) component. The only program specifically targeting anxiety management skills training alone that has been included in well-controlled studies is SIT. In two studies conducted by Foa and colleagues (Foa et al., 1991, 1999), SIT was compared to other treatments for PTSD and to a waitlist. In both of these studies, SIT was more effective than waitlist immediately after treatment and at follow-up, suggesting that, like other CBT treatments, gains from SIT are maintained over time (Foa et al., 1991, 1999). In both studies, symptom reductions following SIT were comparable to those following PE. However, effect sizes obtained from Foa et al. (1999) suggest somewhat greater gains with PE than with SIT. As noted above, combining PE and SIT treatments did not produce greater treatment gains than either treatment alone (Foa et al., 1999).

Summary of Treatments for Chronic PTSD

Clearly, there are several effective CBT treatment programs for chronic PTSD. Studies examining exposure, cognitive, and skills training programs have found them to be significantly more effective than waitlist or minimal attention control groups. The effect sizes associated with these treatments are typically very large. Importantly, though these treatments are relatively brief (8–16 sessions), the gains persist over time. In addition, these treatment programs targeting PTSD also reduce other symptoms that often co-occur with PTSD such as depression and anxiety. Studies have also shown that CBT treatments for PTSD reduce guilt and shame (Kubany et al., 2003; Resick et al., 2002) and anger (e.g., Cahill, Rauch, Hembree, & Foa, 2003), as

well as increasing self-esteem (Kubany et al., 2003). In the study by Cloitre et al. (2002) that combined training in emotion regulation skills and imaginal exposure, patients reported significant decreases in alexithymia and dissociation relative to waitlist.

The empirical literature offers little guidance for how to choose among the various effective treatment programs. Studies that have directly compared two or more of the available treatment programs have generally found few or no significant differences among active treatments (Foa et al., 1991, 1999; Marks et al., 1998; Power et al., 2002; Resick et al., 2002; Rothbaum et al., 2005; Tarrier et al., 1999). The few studies that did find statistically significant differences between active treatments do not provide consistent differences, so it is not possible to identify a *best* treatment. Because most studies included relatively small samples, the lack of statistically significant differences may reflect a lack of power to detect real differences among the treatments. In a recent study that included large enough samples to ensure sufficient power, PE was superior to present center therapy (Schnurr et al., 2007).

Attempts to improve treatment outcome by combining efficacious CBT protocols have not been particularly fruitful. Foa and her colleagues conducted studies to examine the potential benefits of adding anxiety management (Foa et al., 1999) or cognitive restructuring (Foa et al., 2005) techniques to the PE protocol that includes both imaginal and in vivo exposure exercises. In both these studies, the combined treatment did not produce greater improvement than PE alone. Similar results have been reported by other research groups that have attempted to augment the PE gains with cognitive restructuring techniques (e.g., Marks et al., 1998; Paunovic & Öst, 2001). In only one study did results emerge to suggest that a combined treatment might outperform a single mode treatment. In this study, Bryant and colleagues found that treatment that combined imaginal exposure and cognitive restructuring produced superior results to treatment with imaginal exposure alone (Bryant, Moulds, Guthrie, Dang, & Nixon, 2003). Unfortunately, the study did not include a group treated with imaginal and in vivo exposure. Foa and Cahill (in press) analyzed the gains made with various treatment programs for PTSD and concluded that adding an exposure component to cognitive therapy improved outcome, whereas the addition of cognitive therapy to programs that include both imaginal and in vivo exposure did not enhance to efficacy of the exposure therapy alone.

Treatments for Acute Stress Disorder

In the fourth edition of the *Diagnostic and Statistical Manual for Mental Disorders (DSM–IV)* (APA, 1994), acute stress disorder was included as a distinct disorder. Acute stress disorder shares many characteristics with PTSD, including exposure to a trauma that initiates a number of different symptoms. Like PTSD, ASD includes symptoms of re-experiencing, avoidance, and arousal; in addition to these, dissociative symptoms are also present either during or after the trauma. The primary distinction between the two disorders is the duration for which the symptoms are present. In ASD, the symptoms must occur within the first 4 weeks after the trauma and cannot persist for more than 4 weeks. In comparison, PTSD becomes diagnosable only if the symptoms persist for more than 1 month.

It has been suggested the presence of ASD may be a risk factor for developing chronic PTSD; however, prospective studies do not fully support this hypothesis (Bryant, 2006). Although many people who are diagnosed with ASD during the month after a trauma do develop chronic PTSD, some do not. Conversely, many people who develop chronic PTSD did not have ASD during that first month. Likely, this is because a good number of people develop PTSD without the prominent dissociative symptoms that are included in the ASD diagnosis (Bryant, 2006).

Evaluating early interventions for trauma survivors is complicated for many reasons. First, the vast majority of trauma survivors will recover without treatment over the course of the first few months after the trauma (Foa & Riggs, 1994). Therefore, an effective treatment for ASD must produce more gains than what occurs naturally. Second, recent trauma survivors may not view the difficulties that they are experiencing as problems in need of therapy, but rather as normal reactions to the recent trauma. This can make it difficult to obtain sufficiently large samples to test early intervention programs. Finally, the self-limiting nature of the ASD diagnosis (the disorder cannot be diagnosed more than 4 weeks after the trauma), and the finding that many trauma survivors who develop PTSD do not manifest ASD, can complicate attempts to identify samples or to measure outcome. Some interventions targeting trauma survivors who manifest difficulties shortly after the traumatic event are not necessarily designed to *treat* ASD. Rather, they might be best conceptualized as secondary prevention programs designed to reduce the likelihood that a trauma survivor will develop chronic PTSD. Despite these difficulties, several well-controlled studies of early interventions have been conducted.

Overall, there has been much less research on early interventions for trauma survivors than on treatments for chronic PTSD. Most of the studies that have examined early interventions have utilized brief (4–5 sessions) CBT programs administered 2–4 weeks after the traumatic event. Results of these studies suggest that intervention programs that incorporate many of the techniques used to treat chronic PTSD (education, exposure, cognitive restructuring, anxiety management) can also promote recovery, and prevent chronic PTSD, when administered shortly after the event.

Bryant and colleagues have conducted a series of studies examining the efficacy of early CBT interventions with trauma survivors who met criteria for ASD (Bryant, Harvey, Sackville, Dang, & Basten, 1998; Bryant, Moulds, Guthrie, & Nixon, 2003, 2005; Bryant, Sackville, Dang, Moulds, & Guthrie, 1999). The basic treatment examined in these studies includes several CBT techniques such as education about posttrauma reactions, anxiety management, cognitive restructuring, and imaginal and in vivo exposure. Some of the studies used variations on these core components to determine the relative contribution of specific components of the program. In the first study Bryant et al. (1998) compared five sessions of CBT to five sessions of supportive counseling (SC), which included education about trauma and training in problem-solving skills. Treatments were initiated 2–4 weeks after the trauma and continued for 4 weeks. The results of this study suggested that the CBT program reduced acute symptoms and prevented chronic PTSD. Specifically, 6 months posttreatment only 17% of patients in the CBT group met criteria for a PTSD diagnosis compared to 67% of those in the SC condition. In a second study, Bryant and colleagues (Bryant et al., 1999) compared the full CBT protocol with a CBT treatment that included exposure and cognitive restructuring but no anxiety management skills training. The two CBT treatments appeared equally effective at reducing PTSD in this sample, with 20% of each of the CBT groups having PTSD 6 months after treatment compared to 67% of the people in a supportive counseling treatment. Data collected from a subset of the patients treated in these two studies who were reassessed 4 years after treatment suggest that the gains made with early treatment persist over time (Bryant, Moulds, & Nixon, 2003).

Additional studies further demonstrated the efficacy of this CBT program for trauma survivors diagnosed with ASD (Bryant et al., 2005; Bryant, Moulds, Guthrie, & Nixon, 2003). In one study (Bryant et al., 2005), the researchers examined the possible benefit of adding hypnosis to the CBT protocol. As in the earlier studies, patients who completed the CBT treatment were less likely than those in the SC condition to have PTSD at a 6-month follow-up assessment (21% versus 59%). Similarly, the group treated with CBT and hypnosis showed less PTSD (20%) than the SC group. Outcomes for the two CBT groups were largely similar, though the group that was also treated with hypnosis showed somewhat more reduction on a measure of reexperiencing symptoms than did the CBT alone group. Bryant and colleagues (Bryant, Moulds, Guthrie, & Nixon, 2003) extended their findings with a study that examined the efficacy of brief CBT with patients who had ASD and a mild traumatic brain injury (i.e., lost consciousness during the trauma). Again, the CBT program was more effective than SC, with only 8% of those treated with CBT and 58% of those treated with SC having PTSD at 6 months after treatment.

Additional studies have found similar early CBT interventions to be effective at promoting recovery in survivors who do not necessarily meet criteria for ASD. Indeed, the first study that examined early CBT intervention was conducted before ASD was introduced into the *DSM–IV* (Foa, Hearst-Ikeda, & Perry, 1995). Female assault victims with symptoms severe enough to be diagnosed with PTSD (except for duration) at the time they entered the study (about 2 weeks postassault) were treated with a brief (4-session) CBT program that included exposure, education, relaxation training, and cognitive restructuring. Foa and colleagues compared these patients to a matched group (no random assignment) of survivors who completed repeated assessments. This program reduced the rate of PTSD (10%) at posttreatment compared to the assessment control group (70%). However, at 6 months the groups did not differ on the proportion that had PTSD (11% and 22% for the treated and untreated groups, respectively) due to continued recovery in the untreated group. In a subsequent study by Foa and colleagues, recently assaulted women who met criteria for PTSD were randomly assigned to one of three groups: CBT, supportive counseling (SC), or assessment only (Foa, Zoellner, & Feeney, 2003). It was found that PTSD symptom severity decreased in all three conditions with the CBT group endorsing less severe symptoms than the SC group. The

assessment only condition was no different than either of the other two groups. As in the earlier Foa et al. (1995) study, the groups did not differ at follow-up. Thus, the brief CBT treatment accelerated recovery but in the long run natural recovery eliminated the superiority of the CBT treatment.

In sum, the results of studies examining early interventions for trauma survivors suggest that CBT techniques similar to those used to treat chronic PTSD may also be useful in accelerating recovery or preventing chronic PTSD from developing.

Dissemination of Effective Treatments for PTSD and Other Trauma Reactions

Despite the availability of empirically supported treatments for PTSD and more acute trauma reactions, these programs are not widely used in clinical practice. Based on our experience and the few available data (Becker, Zayfert, & Anderson, 2004), it seems practitioners are slow to adopt the treatments despite their efficacy. This is not unique to PTSD treatments as the translation of other empirically supported and manualized treatments has also been slow (Barlow, Levitt, & Bufka, 1999), but there may be unique concerns about using manualized treatments to treat PTSD (Cook, Schnurr, & Foa, 2004).

There are many issues that can impede clinicians from choosing to use manualized treatments in general and treatments for PTSD in particular. Based on the results of a survey of practicing psychologists, Addis and Krasnow (2000) identified two major factors that impact the decision to use a treatment manual: (1) concern that the use will impair the therapeutic process, and (2) a lack of conviction that the use of the manualized treatment will lead to more positive outcomes. Cook et al. (2004) categorized concerns about adopting manualized treatments for PTSD into six types of concerns: (1) the treatment will interfere with the therapeutic relationship, (2) the treatment will not address all of the client's needs, (3) the treatment will unduly constrain or limit the therapist, (4) the treatment will not work, (5) the treatment will restrict clinical innovation, and (6) learning and adopting the treatment is not feasible. In addition, for some clinicians there are systemic or organizational barriers that can limit the use of manualized and empirically supported treatments (Cook et al., 2004).

These issues may apply to all of the empirically supported treatments described earlier, but an examination of the authors' experience in disseminating PE therapy may provide useful insight into ways of overcoming some of these barriers. Because exposure to trauma memories is included, in one form or another, in many of the treatment programs that have been established as effective for PTSD, our experience with PE may be instructive as other treatments are disseminated.

In a survey of practicing psychologists the reason offered by most of the sample (60%) for not using exposure therapy to treat PTSD was a lack of training in the techniques (Becker et al., 2004). A substantial minority of the respondents also indicated that they did not use exposure therapy because of a preference for individualized versus manualized treatments (25%) and worries that someone treated with exposure could decompensate (22%). Interestingly, these same three issues were of most concern to practitioners who had at least some training in exposure therapy but were not using it currently: lack of training 40%, possible decompensation 35%, discomfort with manualized treatment 31%. These same issues are likely to be raised with any manualized treatment for PTSD, but we are not aware of similar surveys focused on treatments other than exposure. These issues and concerns can be addressed by providing training. Indeed, we have found that after only a few successful cases, many of the concerns voiced by providers decrease dramatically.

We have undertaken a number of different efforts to disseminate PE to various audiences of providers. Some minor differences exist in the specific activities used to train in the use of PE based on the setting in which the training occurs and the reason for conducting the training, but several common components are included. At the highest level, training includes intensive education in the techniques used in PE through multiday workshops and ongoing case supervision/consultation as providers begin to use the protocol to treat trauma survivors. Ongoing case consultation is provided by clinicians who have used the protocol and are familiar with the techniques.

The availability of ongoing consultation after the initial training provides an opportunity for new PE clinicians to obtain feedback and support as they begin to use PE with patients. It also reflects the recognition that simply training a person in the techniques of a treatment program is not sufficient to ensure its use (Becker et al., 2004). The extent to which ongoing support and consultation is necessary varies widely from one clinician to another. In our experience, providers who are experienced

with CBT and those who use exposure with other anxiety disorders may require less consultation to become comfortable with the specific exposure protocol. Other clinicians, particularly those with other theoretical orientations, may require more supervision to ensure that they are applying the techniques correctly and to allow them more time to become comfortable with the protocol.

Throughout the dissemination process, we try to alleviate some of the common concerns that serve as barriers to the use of manualized treatments. To this end, we discuss the ability of clinicians to apply the treatment flexibly. That is, although the protocol incorporates very specific techniques, there are many opportunities for the clinician to adapt treatment to best fit the needs of specific clients (Foa, Hembree, & Rothbaum, 2007). We also describe and discuss the available data that support the safety of PE in treating PTSD (see Riggs, Cahill, & Foa, 2006 for a more complete description). Similarly, we share many case examples from our own experience treating PTSD to illustrate how the treatment can be applied with a variety of trauma survivors. In particular, because clinicians are often concerned that the complicated cases that often present for treatment are excluded from research studies, we emphasize the use of PE with cases that include multiple problems in addition to the PTSD. Also, we build opportunities into the training workshop for trainees to role-play skills. By incorporating information that addresses common concerns into the training and by including opportunities for the providers to practice the skills, we aim to encourage practitioners to overcome any reticence to use the protocol.

Our experience with these dissemination efforts has been quite gratifying. Results from several studies that have utilized this basic approach suggest that the treatment can be successfully disseminated to clinicians with varying levels of training and with different clinical orientations (Foa et al., 2005; Schnurr et al., 2007). Anecdotally, we have found that providers who have a few successful cases with supportive consultation from someone experienced with the treatment will begin to use the treatment more widely. Importantly, we have used a variety of supervision/consultation models, including face-to-face supervision with experts, expert consultation combined with a local supervisor with less PE experience, and expert consultation combined with monitoring of videotaped therapy sessions. All of these approaches appear to be effective for fostering the effective use of the treatment protocol, but it should be noted that providing ongoing consultation does require a great deal of time and resources.

Summary and Conclusions

Research has established a number of treatment programs based on CBT principles that are effective for treating chronic PTSD in a relatively short period of time. These include exposure therapy, cognitive therapy, anxiety management training, and EMDR. Further, there is growing evidence that similar treatments can be effective at accelerating recovery and preventing chronic PTSD when delivered shortly after a trauma. Despite the promise of these treatments, there is substantial room for improvement. Some patients retain residual symptoms despite completion of treatment and others do not complete treatment. More problematic is the fact that many people do not have access to these effective interventions due to the shortage of professionals who have been trained to deliver these treatments and a lack of information about where trauma survivors can find well-trained clinicians. Clearly, there is a need to develop and support more dissemination and training programs to increase access to these treatments.

References

Addis, M. E., & Krasnow, A. D. (2000). A national survey of practicing psychologists' attitudes toward psychotherapy treatment manuals. *Journal of Consulting and Clinical Psychology, 68*, 331–339.

American Psychiatric Association. (1994). *Diagnostic and statistical manual of mental disorders* (4th ed.). Washington, DC: Author.

Barlow, D. H., Levitt, J. T., & Bufka, L. F. (1999). The dissemination of empirically supported treatments: A view to the future. *Behaviour Research and Therapy, 37*, S147–S162.

Becker, C. B., Zayfert, C., & Anderson, E. (2004). A survey of psychologists' attitudes towards and utilization of exposure therapy for PTSD. *Behaviour Research and Therapy, 42*, 277–292.

Blanchard, E. B., Hickling, E. J., Devineni, T., Veazey, C. H., Galovski, T. E., Mundy, E., et al. (2003). A controlled evaluation of cognitive behavioral therapy for posttraumatic stress in motor vehicle accident survivors. *Behaviour Research and Therapy, 41*, 79–96.

Bryant, R. A. (2006). Cognitive-behavioral therapy for acute stress disorder. In A. M. Follette & J. I. Ruzek (Eds.), *Cognitive-behavioral therapies for trauma* (2nd ed., pp. 201–227). New York: Guilford Press.

Bryant, R. A., Harvey, A. G., Sackville, T., Dang, S. T., & Basten, C. (1998). Treatment of acute stress disorder: A comparison between cognitive-behavioral therapy and supportive counseling. *Journal of Consulting and Clinical Psychology, 66*, 862–866.

Bryant, R. A., Moulds, M. L., Guthrie, R. M., Dang, S. T., & Nixon, R.D.V. (2003). Imaginal exposure alone and imaginal exposure with cognitive restructuring in treatment of posttraumatic stress disorder. *Journal of Consulting and Clinical Psychology, 71*, 706–712.

Bryant, R. A., Moulds, M., Guthrie, R., & Nixon, R. D. V. (2003). Treating acute stress disorder following mild traumatic brain injury. *American Journal of Psychiatry, 160*, 585–587.

Bryant, R. A., Moulds, M., Guthrie, R., & Nixon, R. D. V. (2005). The additive benefit of hypnotherapy and cognitive behavior therapy in treating acute stress disorder. *Journal of Consulting and Clinical Psychology, 73*, 334–340.

Bryant, R. A., Moulds, M. L., & Nixon, R.D.V. (2003). Cognitive behaviour therapy of acute stress disorder: A four-year follow-up. *Behaviour Research and Therapy, 41*, 489–494.

Bryant, R. A., Sackville, T., Dang, S. T., Moulds, M., & Guthrie, R. (1999). Treating acute stress disorder: An evaluation of cognitive behavior therapy and supportive counseling techniques. *American Journal of Psychiatry, 156*, 1780–1786.

Cahill, S. P., Rauch, S. A., Hembree, E. A., & Foa, E. B. (2003). Effect of cognitive-behavioral treatments for PTSD on anger. *Journal of Cognitive Psychotherapy, 17*, 113–131.

Chard, K. M. (2005). An evaluation of cognitive processing therapy for the treatment of posttraumatic stress disorder related to childhood sexual abuse. *Journal of Consulting and Clinical Psychology, 73*, 965–971.

Cloitre, M., Koenen, K. C., Cohen, L. R., & Han, H. (2002). Skills training in affective and interpersonal regulation followed by exposure: A phase-based treatment for PTSD related to childhood abuse. *Journal of Consulting and Clinical Psychology, 70*, 1067–1074.

Cook, J. M., Schnurr, P. P., & Foa, E. B. (2004). Bridging the gap between posttraumatic stress disorder research and clinical practice: The example of exposure therapy. *Psychotherapy: Theory, Research, Practice Training, 41*, 374–387.

Cooper, N. A., & Clum, G. A. (1989). Imaginal flooding as a supplementary treatment for PTSD in combat veterans: A controlled study. *Behavior Therapy, 20*, 381–391.

Devilly, G. J., & Spence, S. H. (1999). The relative efficacy and treatment distress of EMDR and a cognitive-behavior trauma treatment protocol in the amelioration of posttraumatic stress disorder. *Journal of Anxiety Disorders, 13*, 131–157.

Echeburua, E., Corral, P. D., Zubizarreta, I., & Sarasua, B. (1997). Psychological treatment of chronic posttraumatic stress disorder in victims of sexual aggression. *Behavior Modification, 21*, 433–456.

Ehlers, A., Clark, D. M., Hackmann, A. H., McManus, F., & Fennell, M. (2005). Cognitive therapy for post-traumatic stress disorder: Development and evaluation. *Behaviour Research and Therapy, 43*, 413–431.

Ehlers, A., Clark, D. M., Hackmann, A., McManus, F., Fennell, M., Herbert, C., et al. (2003). A randomized controlled trial of cognitive therapy, self-help booklet, and repeated assessment as early interventions for PTSD. *Archives of General Psychiatry, 60*, 1024–1032.

Fecteau, G., & Nicki, R. (1999). Cognitive behavioural treatment of post traumatic stress disorder after motor vehicle accident. *Behavioural and Cognitive Psychotherapy, 27*, 201–214.

Foa, E. B., & Cahill, S. P. (in press). Psychosocial treatments for PTSD: An overview. In Y. Neria, R. Gross, R. Marshall, & E. Susser (Eds.), *9/11: Public health in the wake of terrorist attacks*. Cambridge, England: Cambridge University Press.

Foa, E. B., Dancu, C. V., Hembree, E. A., Jaycox, L. H., Meadows, E. A., & Street, G. (1999). The efficacy of exposure therapy, stress inoculation training and their combination in ameliorating PTSD for female victims of assault. *Journal of Consulting and Clinical Psychology, 67,* 194–200.

Foa, E. B., Hearst-Ikeda, D., & Perry, K. J. (1995). Evaluation of a brief cognitive-behavior program for the prevention of chronic PTSD in recent assault victims. *Journal of Consulting and Clinical Psychology, 63,* 948–955.

Foa, E. B., Hembree, E. A., Cahill, S. P., Rauch, S. A., Riggs, D. S., Feeney, N. C., et al. (2005). Randomized trial of prolonged exposure for PTSD with and without cognitive restructuring: Outcome at academic and community clinics. *Journal of Consulting and Clinical Psychology, 73,* 953–964.

Foa, E. B., Hembree, E. A., & Rothbaum, B. O. (2007). *Prolonged exposure therapy for PTSD: Emotional processing of traumatic experiences (therapist guide).* New York: Oxford University Press.

Foa, E. B., Keane, T. M., & Friedman M. J. (2000). *Effective treatments for PTSD: Practice guidelines from the International Society for Traumatic Stress Studies.* New York: Guilford Press.

Foa, E. B., & Meadows, E. A. (1997). Psychosocial treatments for post-traumatic stress disorder: A critical review. *Annual Review of Psychology, 48,* 449–480.

Foa, E. B., & Riggs, D. S. (1994). Incidence of posttraumatic stress disorder in female victims of interpersonal violence. *StressPoints: The newsletter of the International Society for the Study of Traumatic Stress.*

Foa, E. B., & Rothbaum, B. O. (1998). *Treating the trauma of rape: Cognitive-behavioral therapy for PTSD.* New York: Guilford Press.

Foa, E. B., Rothbaum, B. O., & Furr, J. M. (2003). Augmenting exposure therapy with other CBT procedures. *Psychiatric Annals, 33,* 47–53.

Foa, E. B., Rothbaum, B. O., Riggs, D. S., & Murdock, T. B. (1991). Treatment of posttraumatic stress disorder in rape victims: A comparison between cognitive-behavioral procedures and counseling. *Journal of Consulting and Clinical Psychology, 59,* 715–723.

Foa, E. B., Zoellner, L. A., & Feeny, N. C. (2003). An evaluation of three brief programs for facilitating recovery after assault. *Journal of Traumatic Stress, 19,* 29–43.

Glynn, S. M., Eth, S., Randolph, E. T., Foy, D. W., Urbaitis, M., Boxer, L., et al. (1999). A test of behavioral family therapy to augment exposure for combat-related posttraumatic stress disorder. *Journal of Consulting and Clinical Psychology, 67,* 243–251.

Jensen, J. A. (1994). An investigation of Eye Movement Desensitization and Reprocessing (EMD/R) as a treatment for posttraumatic stress disorder (PTSD) symptoms of Vietnam combat veterans. *Behavior Therapy, 25,* 311–325.

Keane, T. M., Fairbank, J. A., Caddell, J. M., & Zimering, R. T. (1989). Implosive (flooding) therapy reduces symptoms of PTSD in Vietnam combat veterans. *Behavior Therapy, 20,* 245–260.

Kubany, E. S., Hill, E. E., & Owens, J. A. (2003). Cognitive trauma therapy for battered women with PTSD: Preliminary findings. *Journal of Traumatic Stress, 16,* 81–91.

Kubany, E. S., Hill, E. E., Owens, J. A., Iannce-Spencer, C., McCaig, M. A., Tremayne, K. J., et al. (2004). Cognitive trauma therapy for battered women with PTSD (CTT-BW). *Journal of Consulting and Clinical Psychology, 72,* 3–18.

Lee, C., Gavriel, H., Drummond, P., Richards, J., & Greenwald, R. (2002). Treatment of PTSD: Stress inoculation training with prolonged exposure compared to EMDR. *Journal of Clinical Psychology, 58,* 1071–1089.

Lohr, J. M., Tolin, D. F., & Lilienfeld, S. O. (1998). Efficacy of Eye Movement Desensitization and Reprocessing: Implications for behavior therapy. *Behavior Therapy, 29,* 123–156.

Marcus, S., Marquis, P., & Sakai, C. (1997). Controlled study of treatment of PTSD using EMDR in an HMO setting. *Psychotherapy, 34,* 307–315.

Marks, I., Lovell, K., Noshirvani, H., Livanou, M., & Thrasher, S. (1998). Treatment of posttraumatic stress disorder by exposure and/or cognitive restructuring. *Archives of General Psychiatry, 55,* 317–325.

Meichenbaum, D. (1974). *Cognitive behavior modification.* Morristown, NJ: General Learning Press.

Monson, C. M., Schnurr, P. P., Resick, P. A., Friedman, M. J., Young-Xu, Y., & Stevens, S. P. (2006). Cognitive processing therapy for veterans with military-related posttraumatic stress disorder. *Journal of Consulting and Clinical Psychology, 74,* 898–907.

Otto, M. W., Hinton, D., Korbly, N. B., Chea, A., Ba, P., Gershuny, B. S., et al. (2003). Treatment of pharmacotherapy-refractory posttraumatic stress disorder among Cambodian refugees: A pilot study of combination treatment with cognitive-behavior therapy vs. sertraline alone. *Behaviour Research & Therapy, 41,* 1271–1276.

Paunovic, N., & Öst, L.-G. (2001). Cognitive-behavior therapy vs. exposure therapy in the treatment of PTSD in refugees. *Behaviour Research and Therapy, 39,* 1183–1197.

Power, K., McGoldrick, T., Brown, K., Buchanan, R., Sharp, D., Swanson, V., et al. (2002). A controlled comparison of eye movement desensitization and reprocessing versus exposure plus cognitive restructuring versus waiting list in the treatment of post-traumatic stress disorder. *Clinical Psychology and Psychotherapy, 9,* 299–318.

Resick, P. A., Nishith, P., Weaver, T. A., Astin, M. C., & Feuer, C. A. (2002). A comparison of cognitive processing therapy with prolonged exposure and a waiting condition for the treatment of posttraumatic stress disorder in female rape victims. *Journal of Consulting and Clinical Psychology, 70,* 867–879.

Resick, P. A., & Schnicke, M. K. (1992). Cognitive processing therapy for sexual assault victims. *Journal of Consulting and Clinical Psychology, 60,* 748–756.

Riggs, D. S., Cahill, S. P., & Foa, E. B. (2006). Exposure treatment of posttraumatic stress disorder. In V. Follette & J. Ruzek (Eds.), *Cognitive-behavioral therapies for trauma* (2nd ed., pp. 65–95). New York: Guilford Press.

Rothbaum, B. O., Astin, M. C., & Marsteller, F. (2005). Prolonged exposure versus eye movement desensitization and reprocessing (EMDR) for PTDS rape victims. *Journal of Traumatic Stress, 18,* 607–616.

Schnurr, P. P., Friedman, M. J., Engel, C. C., Foa, E. B., Shea, M. T., Chow, B. K., et al. (2007). Cognitive behavioral therapy for posttraumatic stress disorder in women: A randomized controlled trial. *Journal of the American Medical Association, 297,* 820–830.

Shapiro, F. (1989). Efficacy of eye movement desensitization procedure in the treatment of traumatic memories. *Journal of Traumatic Stress, 2,* 199–223.

Shapiro, F. (1991). Eye movement desensitization and reprocessing procedure: From EMD to EMDR: A new treatment model for anxiety and related trauma. *The Behavior Therapist, 14,* 133–135.

Shapiro, F. (2001). *Eye movement desensitization and reprocessing: Basic principles, protocols, and procedures* (2nd ed.). New York: Guilford Press.

Tarrier, N., Pilgrim, H., Sommerfield, C., Faragher, B., Reynolds, M., Graham, E., & et al. (1999). A randomized trial of cognitive therapy and imaginal exposure in the treatment of chronic posttraumatic stress disorder. *Journal of Consulting and Clinical Psychology, 67,* 13–18.

Taylor, S., Thordarson, D. S., Maxfield, L., Fedoroff, I. C., Lovell, K., & Ogrodniczuk, J. (2003). Comparative efficacy, speed, and adverse effects of three PTSD treatments: Exposure therapy, EMDR, and relaxation training. *Journal of Consulting and Clinical Psychology, 71,* 330–338.

Veronen, L. J., & Kilpatrick, D. G. (1983). Stress management for rape victims. In D. Meichenbaum & M. E. Jaremko (Eds.), *Stress reduction and prevention* (pp. 341–374). New York: Plenum Press.

Combining Pharmacological and Cognitive Behavioral Therapy in the Treatment of Anxiety Disorders

Michael W. Otto, Evelyn Behar, Jasper A. J. Smits *and* Stefan G. Hofmann

Abstract

This chapter is designed to provide an integrated perspective on the issues and efficacy associated with the application of combined cognitive behavioral therapy (CBT) and pharmacotherapy for the anxiety disorders. Important practice characteristics, including the availability, cost, effort, and tolerability of each treatment, are discussed along with a review of efficacy findings. The ongoing hope that combination treatment (CBT plus antidepressants or benzodiazepines) will provide an especially efficacious or cost-effective treatment has not been realized. The chapter closes with consideration of some of the novel and promising combination treatment strategies (e.g., isolated use of D-cycloserine) that, instead of relying on direct treatment of affective disorders, target pharmacotherapy toward the promotion of more optimal learning in CBT.

Keywords: cognitive behavioral therapy, combination treatment, efficacy, nonresponse, pharmacotherapy, treatment tolerability

With few exceptions, the empirical literature indicates that both cognitive behavioral and pharmacological treatments for anxiety disorders are effective in helping patients reduce their anxiety and anxiety-related disability and increase quality of life. In the case of pharmacotherapy, depending on the anxiety disorder under treatment, patients can benefit from taking any of several classes of pharmacological agents, including selective serotonin reuptake inhibitors (SSRIs), monoamine oxidase inhibitors (MAO-Is), tricyclic antidepressants, and benzodiazepines (Abramowitz, 1997; Gould, Buckminster, Pollack, Otto, & Yap, 1997; Lydiard, Brawman-Mintzer, & Ballenger, 1996; Pollack, 2005; van Etten & Taylor, 1998). Patients can also benefit from cognitive behavioral therapy (CBT), with evidence of consistent efficacy across the anxiety disorders (Deacon & Abramowitz, 2004; Otto, Smits, & Reese, 2004).

Given the efficacy of both CBT and pharmacotherapy, there has long been the hope that these two modalities of treatment can be combined for an especially powerful approach to treating anxiety disorders. This proposition rests on the assumption that the separate actions of pharmacotherapy and CBT are going to be additive, and that the magnitude of the additive benefit is worth the additional effort and costs of engagement in each treatment. In this chapter we review some of the assumptions, mechanisms, and data concerning combined pharmacologic and cognitive behavioral treatment of the anxiety disorders, with attention to whether combined treatment should be considered a default approach for patients with anxiety disorders. We offer a cautionary account of the benefits actually achieved by combination treatment, and underscore the importance of considering the way pharmacotherapy may alter the therapeutic learning achieved with CBT. Furthermore, we discuss recent advances in the field that provide alternatives to the simple combination of two modalities of treatment that are each aimed at anxiolysis, and instead focus on pharmacologic strategies that may more directly enhance the therapeutic learning from exposure-based CBT.

We start our accounting of the nature and efficacy of combined treatment strategies by considering some of the practice characteristics and assumptions about the benefits of combining CBT and pharmacotherapy.

Mechanisms and Efficacy of Each Modality of Treatment

Converging evidence from comparative treatment trials (e.g., Barlow, Gorman, Shear, & Woods, 2000; Davidson et al., 2004; Foa et al., 2005; Heimberg et al., 1998) and meta-analytic studies (Gould et al., 1997; Furukawa, Watanabe, & Churchill, 2006; Heimberg et al., 1998; Kobak, Greist, Jefferson, Katzelnick, & Henk, 1998; Mitte, 2005a, 2005b; Otto et al., 2004) indicates only subtle differences in efficacy between CBT and pharmacotherapy for the acute treatment of many of the anxiety disorders. Depending on the disorder under study, either CBT or pharmacotherapy may show relatively more acute benefit. For example, CBT, particularly intensive CBT, may enjoy subtle advantages over pharmacotherapy for panic disorder and obsessive-compulsive disorder (OCD), whereas medication may have acute advantages over CBT for social anxiety disorder.

Aside from these general similarities in outcome, the two treatment modalities differ significantly in practice characteristics. The hypothesized mechanism of action in pharmacotherapy for anxiety disorders is the modulation of affect via specific biochemical pathways when anxiety is elicited by disorder-specific cues, such as interoceptive cues for panic disorder patients or social scrutiny for social anxiety disorder (e.g., Otto, Safren, Nicolaou, & Pollack, 2003). Treatment benefit is readily seen in the context of acute treatment (e.g., 12 weeks) and is often maintained with ongoing pharmacotherapy. However, when medications are discontinued relapse is common (e.g., Mavissakalian & Perel, 1992; Noyes, Garvey, Cook, & Suelzer, 1991; Stein, Versiani, Hair, & Kumar, 2002; Walker et al., 2000). As such, treatment with pharmacotherapy is a long-term proposition if treatment gains are to be maintained; however, there is some evidence that the subgroup of patients who are able to achieve remission on medications may be most likely to be able to discontinue medication treatment without relapse (Mavissakalian & Perel, 1999).

In contrast to pharmacotherapy, CBT is a learning-based approach targeted to helping patients eliminate the core fears and associated avoidance and anticipatory anxiety that characterizes individual anxiety disorders. Although anxiety management skills such as muscle relaxation and breathing retraining can provide benefit, CBT currently emphasizes helping patients relearn a sense of safety with, rather than simply coping with, feared situations and events (Otto et al., 2004). This systematic relearning utilizes informational, cognitive, and exposure strategies. For example, exposure therapy for patients with social anxiety disorder might include attending social engagements or creating embarrassing situations in which they must engage until anxiety dissipates.

Brief CBT utilizing these treatment elements has been shown to be efficacious in acute treatment trials, providing beneficial outcomes well within the 12-week time frames typical of pharmacotherapy trials (Deacon & Abramowitz, 2004; Otto et al., 2004), and for some disorders, offering benefit following the initial session (Penava, Otto, Maki, & Pollack, 1998). Moreover, the therapeutic learning during acute treatment offers long-term maintenance of gains after termination of formal treatment (for meta-analytic reviews, see Christensen, Hadzi-Pavlovic, Andrews, & Mattick, 1987; Gould, Buckminster, et al., 1997; Gould, Otto, & Pollack, 1995; Gould, Otto, Pollack, & Yap, 1997; Otto, Penava, Pollack, & Smoller, 1996). This longer-term benefit comes at the cost of more intensive learning during the acute treatment phase, where patients have to take an active role in learning to respond differently to the situations, events, and sensations that elicit anxiety.

It is this effort that has provided one rationale for combined treatment: using pharmacotherapy as a strategy to decrease anxiety and promote the tolerance of exposure efforts. But is this an accurate expectation?

The Tolerability of Treatment: Individual and Combined

The greater intensity of sessions and the challenges associated with exposure-based treatment do not translate into poorer tolerability of treatment, as assessed by rates of treatment discontinuation. Indeed, review of dropout rates, as evaluated in meta-analytic reviews of acute pharmacotherapy and CBT trials, indicate that CBT is equal to or more tolerable than pharmacologic alternatives across the anxiety disorders (see Table 1). Accordingly, the belief that concomitant pharmacotherapy may aid the retention of patients in CBT by reducing anxiety severity is challenged by these data.

In addition, there is evidence suggesting that patients who have difficulty adhering to exposure-based treatment also have difficulty complying with pharmacotherapy (Fava et al., 1997). Further, meta-analytic reviews of the panic disorder literature indicate that the dropout rate for combination treatment (22%) is more similar to that for treatment with SSRIs (19.9%) than that for CBT (5.6%). Recent large-scale studies of social anxiety disorder (Davidson et al., 2004) and OCD (Foa et al., 2005) provide similar trends toward a higher dropout rate in combination treatment than CBT, but this trend was not evident in a multicenter trial of panic disorder (Barlow et al., 2000). Given these mixed data, a conservative conclusion is that combination treatment offers no reliable advantages to CBT in terms of the acute retention of patients.

The Availability of Treatment: Individual and Combined

The differential availability of care also raises issues about the feasibility of combined treatment strategies.

Proposals for routine use of combination treatment presume that both pharmacologically and cognitive behaviorally astute clinicians are available for care provision and, if available, both resources should be used. However, the availability in most communities of state-of-the-art CBT differs from that for pharmacotherapy. Given the combined forces of psychiatric specialists and primary care physicians, there is adequate opportunity for patients to seek pharmacotherapy, relative to the more restricted availability of CBT. Indeed, the dissemination of CBT to standard clinical practice has proceeded slowly. Studies of anxiety patients in primary and specialty care indicate that only one-tenth to one-third of patients with anxiety disorders received programs of CBT (Goisman, Warshaw, & Keller, 1999; Stein et al., 2004). This has occurred despite evidence that it is possible to successfully disseminate CBT to community settings (Addis et al., 2004; Stuart, Treat, & Wade, 2000; Wade, Treat, & Stuart, 1998).

If CBT is the limiting resource for combination treatment, two questions should be addressed. First, if full programs of state-of-the art CBT are

Table 1. Dropout Rates in Controlled Trials as Represented by Mean Percentages From Meta-Analytic Reviews

Disorder	Dropout %
Panic Disorder (Gould et al., 1995; Otto et al., 2001)	
CBT	5.6
Benzodiazepines	13.1
Non-SSRI Antidepressants	25.4
SSRIs	19.9
Combined CBT and Medication	22.0
Generalized Anxiety Disorder (Gould et al., 1997b)	
CBT	10.6
Benzodiazepines	13.1
Antidepressants	33.5
Social Anxiety Disorder (Gould et al., 1997a)	
CBT	10.7
Benzodiazepines	12.0
Antidepressants	10.3
Obsessive-Compulsive Disorder (Kobak et al., 1998)	
CBT	16.7
Antidepressants	20.5
Posttraumatic Stress Disorder (Otto et al., 1996)	
CBT	19.0
Pharmacotherapy	38.0

Adapted from "Cognitive-Behavioral Therapy for the Treatment of Anxiety Disorders," by M. W. Otto, J.A.J. Smits, & H. E. Reese, 2004, *Journal of Clinical Psychiatry, 65*(Suppl. 5), p. 39. Copyright 2004 by Physicians Postgraduate Press, Inc .

available, should pharmacotherapy be added to this regimen? Second, if full programs of CBT are not available, should elements of CBT be added to pharmacotherapy?

The second question is addressed readily by research showing that instruction in stepwise exposure offers benefits similar to therapist-guided exposure for some anxiety disorders (Park et al., 2001), and that the addition of *elements* of CBT, particularly instruction in stepwise exposure, has been shown to enhance pharmacologic treatment in both specialty care and primary care settings (Craske et al., 2005; Marks et al., 1988; Mavissakalian & Michelson, 1986; Telch, Agras, Taylor, Roth, & Gallen, 1985). Indeed, the so-called prescription of exposure assignments conjoint with medications has been recommended as standard practice in pharmacotherapy for social anxiety disorder (Sutherland & Davidson, 1995). Accordingly, one strategy for combination treatment is to consider elements of CBT as an "add on" to pharmacotherapy, helping ensure that patients have a framework for reentering and persisting in avoided situations. This approach has the advantage of extending the benefit of pharmacotherapy without substantially increasing costs when a CBT specialist is not available for a full program of treatment. However, it has the limitation of failing to use the more comprehensive programs of CBT that have shown particular acceptability, tolerability, efficacy, and cost-efficacy on their own (Deacon & Abramowitz, 2005; Heuzenroeder et al., 2004; Otto, Pollack, & Maki, 2000).

The issue of adding pharmacotherapy to full packages of CBT requires greater consideration of whether core fears associated with anxiety disorders can be treated adequately when these fears are being attenuated by medication. A number of accounts of the fear reductions from exposure stress the importance of evocation of anxiety during exposure (for review, see Powers, Smits, Leyro, & Otto, 2006). For example, in their emotional processing theory, Foa and Kozak (1986) stress the importance of adequate activation of fear-related memories so that new (safety) information can be incorporated in these memories. Adequate activation depends in part on whether the exposure procedures are a realistic representation of the feared event or situation, including the elicitation of fear itself during exposure. This theoretical account is consistent with findings showing that attenuation of the perceived threat of the exposure situation also attenuates the efficacy of exposure. For example, the availability of escape strategies (Powers, Smits, & Telch, 2004) or strategies such as distraction from the feared stimulus (e.g., Kamphuis & Telch, 2000; Rodriguez & Craske, 1993) or "playing it safe" in the presence of the stimulus (Sloan & Telch, 2002) can each reduce the efficacy of exposure.

A complementary account of these findings focuses attention on the role of context in determining what was learned from exposure. As clinicians know well, context is an important consideration for understanding the fear and avoidance of patients. For example, a drive on a highway might be a comfortable or terrifying experience for a phobic individual depending on whether the patient feels rested, had a calm or tense morning, or has a cell phone or friend present in the car. Likewise, the context of an exposure assignment can help determine what is learned from the exposure.

Research on the extinction of fear indicates that extinction from exposure does not represent the elimination of fear associations, but rather that it represents the learning of an *alternative* meaning of the fear cue. Following extinction training, memories of the original fear learning compete with memories of the extinction learning, and the dominant memory is determined in part by context (for a review, see Bouton, 2002). Contexts may include the physical environment, the time of day, and the presence of important others. More important for issues of combination treatment, contexts also include internal states, which can result in state-dependent (context dependent) learning effects. For example, animal research indicates that internal state (e.g., anxiety reduction from an anxiolytic) is a sufficiently powerful context cue such that new learning of safety (i.e., extinction) may be achieved solely in that context (Bouton, Kenney, & Rosengard, 1990). In an experimental demonstration of a similar context effect in humans, Mystkowski et al. (2003) investigated the effects of shifts in internal context by having participants ingest either caffeine or placebo during a single session of exposure-based treatment for a spider phobia. Both groups demonstrated benefit from the single session of exposure. However, when participants reconfronted the spider 1 week later, participants who had a shift in internal context (i.e., treated while taking caffeine, but tested while taking placebo; or the reverse) had a greater return of fear relative to participants who underwent a consistent internal context (i.e., treated and tested while taking caffeine, or treated and tested while taking placebo).

These studies raise questions regarding whether exposure-based treatments will have the same acute or enduring effects on patients taking medications as those who are medication free at the time of exposure. From the perspective of Foa and Kozak's (1986) emotional processing theory, affect modulation from pharmacotherapy may downgrade the therapeutic learning offered by exposure, and hence, may attenuate the additive effects of the two modalities of treatment. From the perspective of context learning, pharmacotherapy that is discernable by either its affect modulation or side effects may create unique conditions where therapeutic learning is strongest in that context, and may be attenuated once the internal context is changed, that is, upon medication discontinuation (see Otto, Smits, & Reese, 2004; Powers et al., 2006). Accordingly, there are good reasons to expect that the combination of pharmacotherapy with state-of-the-art CBT may fail to show strong additive effects and may engender liabilities upon medication discontinuation.

Efficacy Studies: Individual Versus Combined Treatments

Early indications that combined treatment effects may be weaker than expected (for reviews, see Foa, Franklin, & Moser, 2002; Otto et al., 2004) have been further validated by recent large-scale trials. For example, in the treatment of OCD a number of trials indicated that combination treatment did not achieve superior effects over CBT in isolation (e.g., Cottraux et al., 1990 [6-month follow-up]; Franklin, Abramowitz, Bux, Zoellner, & Feeny, 2002; Hohagen et al., 1998; van Balkom et al., 1998). Reflecting some advantage of intensive CBT over pharmacotherapy, Franklin et al. (2002) did, however, report superiority of combination treatment relative to clomipramine in isolation (posttreatment and follow-up), underscoring the importance of exposure in enhancing medication effects. This finding was further confirmed in the recent multicenter investigation of exposure-based CBT (exposure plus response prevention), clomipramine, and their combination for the treatment of OCD (Foa et al., 2005). All active treatments were superior to placebo at week 12, and further, both the CBT and combination treatment were superior to clomipramine alone. Finally, there was no evidence for differential efficacy between CBT and combination treatment; response rates for CBT were 62% for the intent-to-treat sample and 86% for treatment completers as compared to 70% and 79%, respectively, for combination treatment. Clomipramine response

rates were 42% and 48%, and placebo response rates were 8% and 10% for the intent-to-treat and completer samples, respectively.

In the treatment of social anxiety disorder, there is similar evidence that CBT and combined treatment offer near equal outcomes. In a recent large trial, Davidson and associates (2004) randomized patients with generalized social anxiety disorder to CBT alone, fluoxetine alone, the combination of these treatments, or placebo. Again, all active treatments were superior to placebo on primary outcomes, but investigators found less than a 3% improvement in response rates with the addition of fluoxetine to CBT. Patients treated with CBT plus fluoxetine demonstrated an intent-to-treat response rate of 54% relative to intent-to-treat response rates of 52% for CBT alone, 51% for fluoxetine alone, and 32% for the pill placebo condition. This result offers an interesting point of comparison to a large (n = 387) effectiveness study conducted in a primary care setting. In this study, Blomhoff et al. (2001) trained primary care physicians to provide exposure instructions in the context of brief (15 to 20 minute) sessions. In this trial, a trend (p = .059) for superiority of combined exposure plus sertraline was evident relative to brief exposure alone. However, this difference was not evident at a 1-year follow-up assessment; across the follow-up interval, the exposure alone group achieved additional gains whereas the combination group experienced maintenance or a slight deterioration in outcome scores (Haug et al., 2003). This result is consistent with previous reports favoring the longer-term effects of CBT relative to pharmacotherapy for social anxiety disorder (Liebowitz et al., 1999). It is also consistent with concerns about the role of pharmacotherapy in attenuating gains made in CBT across follow-up periods when medication is discontinued (Otto et al., 2004). These issues are made particularly clear for the treatment of panic disorder.

Studies of panic disorder have yielded a complex picture regarding the value of combination treatment (Furukawa et al., 2006). Research by de Beurs, van Balkom, Lange, Koele, and van Dyke (1995) found superiority of combination CBT plus fluvoxamine relative to exposure-based CBT plus placebo. An additive effect for combination treatment was also found by Barlow et al. (2000) in their large multicenter trial of panic disorder with no or mild agoraphobia. Across a period of maintenance treatment, the combination of imipramine plus CBT emerged as more efficacious than CBT alone on some measures; however, upon discontinuation of imipramine treatment, there was substantial loss of efficacy in the combination treatment condition so that monotherapy with CBT tended toward greater response rates than combination treatment. Similar effects are also evident in a multicenter trial of combination treatment for panic disorder utilizing the benzodiazepine alprazolam. Marks et al. (1993) randomized 154 panic disorder patients to 8 weeks of either alprazolam plus exposure, alprazolam plus relaxation, exposure plus placebo, or placebo plus relaxation. Although combination treatment was associated with marginally greater effects during the acute phase, these gains were lost during medication taper and follow-up, leaving exposure as the strongest treatment by the end of the follow-up period.

This loss of CBT efficacy when it is offered as part of acute combination treatment strategy followed by medication discontinuation is consistent with predictions from accounts of internal context effects; when the internal context was changed upon medication discontinuation, therapeutic learning was attenuated. Patients in the CBT alone condition underwent no context change, and hence, tended to maintain their treatment gains at a stronger level.

Also consistent with context accounts are findings that the beneficial effects of combined treatment can be maintained if CBT is ongoing or reinstated during the period of medication discontinuation—thereby ensuring that CBT is offered both in the medication and postmedication contexts. For example, CBT delivered during benzodiazepine taper has been shown to be effective in reducing panic symptoms and has been associated with longer maintenance of treatment gains during follow-up periods (Hegel, Ravaris, & Ahles, 1994; Otto et al., 1993; Spiegel, Bruce, Gregg, & Nuzzarello, 1994). There is similar evidence suggesting that CBT delivered during antidepressant medication taper also leads to beneficial effects (Schmidt, Wollaway-Bickel, Trakowski Santiago, & Vasey, 2002; Whittal, Otto, & Hong, 2001). For example, Schmidt et al. (2002) found that panic disorder patients who were enrolled in group CBT evidenced improvements in functioning and high levels of end-state functioning, regardless of whether they had been assigned to continue or discontinue SSRI treatment. In terms of context effects, it may be that CBT provides opportunities for safety learning in medication-free contexts, thereby ensuring longer-term maintenance of the safety learning.

In summary, the empirical evidence for the simultaneous application of combined treatment is consistent with cautions based on understandings of the nature and mechanism of exposure-based CBT. The simultaneous initiation of pharmacotherapy with state-of-the-art CBT is associated with none or relatively few treatment benefits depending on the anxiety disorder under study, and may come at the cost of poorer maintenance of treatment gains over the long term. In contrast, the evidence is more positive for the utility of adding exposure interventions at the outset of pharmacotherapy, particularly for the treatment of panic disorder and OCD. Below we consider the difference between combining these modalities at treatment initiation and the additive value seen by crossing over nonresponders to the alternative treatment strategy.

Judicious Use of Combination Treatments

Based on consideration of the availability, tolerability, and efficacy of combined treatment strategies for the anxiety disorders, we believe the available evidence supports the following conclusions. Elements of CBT, particularly instruction in stepwise exposure, offer fairly reliable benefit when combined with the initiation of pharmacotherapy. To the extent that these treatment elements can be provided as part of the care of the pharmacotherapy team, and do not require resources from clinicians who otherwise could be offering full packages of CBT, then routine application of this strategy appears indicated. In contrast, when state-of-the-art CBT is available, this intervention can be offered alone and achieve results that rival combination treatment in many cases and offer the potential for greater durability of treatment and lower cost (e.g., Heuzenroeder et al., 2004; Otto, Pollack, & Sabatino, 1996). As such, clinicians should be cautious about recommending routine combination treatment when full packages of CBT can be provided.

Nonetheless, combination treatment should be considered when nonresponse is encountered in one or the other treatment modalities. For example, a number of small studies indicate that patients who did not respond to pharmacotherapy for panic disorder (Otto, Pollack, Penava, & Zucker, 1999; Pollack, Otto, Kaspi, Hammerness, & Rosenbaum, 1994) and for posttraumatic stress disorder (PTSD) (Otto et al., 2003) benefited from subsequent CBT. There is also evidence suggesting that patients who fail to respond to CBT for panic disorder can achieve beneficial results from subsequent pharmacotherapy (Kampman, Keijsers, Hoogduin, & Hendriks, 2002). Accordingly, combination treatment should be considered a next-step strategy for patients refractory to other approaches.

Novel Combination
Treatment—D-cycloserine

Rather than combining two empirically supported monotherapies, each aimed at anxiolysis, novel combination treatment approaches arising from translational research have instead focused on the use of pharmacotherapy to promote therapeutic learning from CBT. Most prominent among these approaches is the use of the N-Methyl-D-Aspartate (NMDA) partial agonist, D-cycloserine. This strategy is the result of basic research on the neural circuits underlying fear acquisition and extinction (e.g., Davis, Falls, & Gewirtz, 2000; Davis & Myers, 2002). Specifically, animal studies suggest that fear learning and extinction are both blocked by antagonists at the glutamatergic NMDA receptor. Moreover, D-cycloserine (DCS), a partial NMDA agonist, appears to augment learning in animal trials (for review, see Davis, 2002; Richardson, Ledgerwood, & Cranney, 2004). That is, the process of extinction of conditioned fear is facilitated by DCS given in individual doses prior to or soon after extinction (exposure) trials in animals, and may even aid the generalization of extinction to related cues (Ledgerwood, Richardson, & Cranney, 2005).

Thus far, three published studies have examined the ability of DCS to enhance the effects of exposure in the treatment of anxiety disorders. In a groundbreaking study, Ressler et al. (2004) randomly assigned acrophobic patients ($n = 28$) to one of three treatment conditions: (1) virtual-reality exposure therapy plus DCS 500 mg; (2) VRE plus DCS 50 mg, or (3) virtual-reality exposure plus a pill placebo. Pills were administered in a double-blind fashion 1 hour prior to each of two weekly virtual-reality exposure sessions. Results indicated that by the second exposure session, patients who had received DCS reported significantly greater reductions in acrophobia symptoms and skin conductance levels during virtual exposures, as well as greater improvement on general acrophobia symptoms as applied to real-world situations relative to those treated with placebo. Furthermore, this differential benefit was maintained at 3 months following treatment termination.

In an independent replication and extension of this finding, Hofmann et al. (2006) examined the efficacy of adjunctive DCS in a placebo-controlled trial of CBT for social anxiety disorder. The use of patients with social anxiety disorder represents the application of adjunctive DCS to a disorder known for its marked disability and distress that has been the target of more traditional combination treatment strategies (e.g., Da-

vidson et al., 2004). Furthermore, it examined DCS as applied to a longer course of treatment: a total of five sessions of exposure-based CBT, with DCS or placebo administration 1 hour before the final four of these sessions. A total of 27 participants were randomized in a double-blind fashion to receive treatment, and results indicated that patients in the DCS group reported significantly more gains from exposure treatment than those who had received adjunctive placebo plus exposure. These benefits were seen both at posttreatment and at the 1-month follow-up assessment, and reflected between group effect sizes for the advantage of adjunctive DCS versus placebo in the range from medium ($d = 0.72$) to large ($d = 1.43$), according to Cohen's standards.

Furthermore, in a third investigation, Kushner and associates (2007) studied the relative efficacy provided by DCS versus placebo augmentation of exposure-based treatment for obsessive-compulsive disorder (OCD). Unlike previous studies, up to 10 sessions of CBT combined with study pills were provided on an intensive (twice-per-week) schedule. Use of frequent dosing of DCS brings with it the risk of rapid tolerance. For example, investigations of isolated versus chronic dosing (i.e., 20 minutes prior to testing versus daily for 15 days prior) of DCS in animal paradigms has revealed limitations for chronic dosing (Parnas, Weber, & Richardson, 2005; Quartermain, Mower, Rafferty, Herting, & Lanthorn, 1994). As suggested by Ressler et al. (2004), DCS may need to be taken on an isolated rather than a chronic dosing schedule in order for it to have its intended effect on NMDA receptor activity. Hence, the particular design used in the Kushner et al. (2007) trial may have sapped some of the strength of the DCS effects due to the frequent use of DCS. Consistent with this concern, better outcomes for patients receiving DCS were found early in the trial. However, with additional exposure sessions, patients receiving placebo closed the gap between the two treatment groups.

The use of adjunctive DCS to enhance therapeutic learning from exposure is fully congruent with concerns against affect modulation and context effects in combination treatments (for review, see Otto et al., 2007). The DCS is taken only prior to sessions, and hence, exposure practice following each week of therapy is during a drug-free state. Moreover, even during acute administration, DCS is not an anxiolytic and in the 50 mg dose range appears to be virtually free of side effects (e.g., D'Souza et al., 2000; Heresco-Levy et al., 2002; Hofmann et al., 2006; van Berckel et al., 1998). Accordingly,

DCS emerges, at this early stage, as a particularly promising candidate for enhancing CBT.

Ongoing work is seeking to document the efficacy of adjunctive DCS across the anxiety disorders, with trials of panic disorder, OCD, and PTSD now underway. One aspect of DCS treatment that is not known is the number of times it can be used successfully within a treatment episode. To date, the use of DCS on four weekly occasions in the Hofmann et al. (2006) protocol represents the most frequent isolated-dose use of DCS with unambiguously positive results (cf., Kushner et al., 2007). Further research will need to be conducted to determine whether use beyond this amount provides any additional benefit.

Combination Treatment— Frontal Activation

Translational research also provides support for administration of yohimbine hydrochloride (an α_2-receptor antagonist) as an alternative strategy for enhancing extinction learning (Cain, Blouin, & Barad, 2004). Cain et al. (2004) found that fear extinction in mice was accelerated (from 30 trials to 5 trials) following injection of yohimbine hydrochloride (5 mg/kg). Additionally, the mice treated with yohimbine hydrochloride were protected from the negative effects of spacing extinction trials (20-minute intertrial intervals) in comparison to mice treated with placebo.

The theorized mechanism whereby yohimbine hydrochloride's effects emerge is stimulation of the medial prefrontal cortex (mPFC), signaling safety both during and following extinction trials. Specifically, yohimbine hydrochloride stimulates c-Fos expression in the mPFC, making it capable of accelerating fear reduction and enhancing subsequent recall of safety learning. Indeed, the animal literature indicates that mPFC is implicated strongly in extinction learning (Morgan, Romanski, & LeDoux, 1993; Quirk, Russo, Barron, & Lebron, 2000). For example, mPFC activity in healthy rats increases (thereby signaling safety) during testing on the day following extinction learning (Milad & Quirk, 2002), and stimulation of the mPFC in rats enhances extinction learning (Herry & Garcia, 2002; Milad & Quirk, 2002). Likewise, removal of the mPFC in rats precludes the continuation of successful extinction from one day to the next (Morgan et al., 1993; Quirk et al., 2000). The effects of yohimbine hydrochloride administered during exposure in humans have not yet been investigated. However, clinical studies are ongoing, examining its potential enhancing effects on exposure-based interventions for anxiety syndromes.

Another strategy for enhancing frontal functioning relies not on pharmacotherapy but upon region-specific tasks to activate frontal structures. In the affective disorders, early work by Siegle, Ghinassi, and Thase (in press) is noteworthy for using tasks to target frontal areas thought to be involved in depression and depressive rumination. In initial studies, depressed outpatients were asked to complete select cognitive tasks over a 2-week period as an adjunct to the psychotherapy and pharmacotherapy they were receiving for depression. The tasks included Wells's (2000) Attentional Control Training task, designed to improve selective attention during rumination and that hypothetically targets prefrontal functioning (Siegel et al., in press), and the Paced Auditory Serial Attention Task (Gronwall, 1977), which results in activation of the prefrontal cortex during an emotionally distressing and stressful activity. Relative to a group undergoing psychotherapy and pharmacotherapy without the adjunctive cognitive training, the cognitive training patients displayed significantly greater improvements with respect to both their depressive symptoms (as measured by the BDI-II) and degree of rumination (as measured by the RSQ). Furthermore, patients receiving the cognitive control training evidenced improvements in brain mechanisms that were targeted by the cognitive training. Specifically, fMRI results indicated that from pre- to posttreatment, these patients displayed improvements in amygdala functioning and dorsolateral prefrontal cortex functioning.

These results from the depression literature offer promising possibilities in the treatment of anxiety patients. Similar to depressed patients, individuals suffering from anxiety symptoms report high levels of rumination, particularly those individuals for whom ruminative thought processes are an integral part of their diagnosis (e.g., generalized anxiety disorder, obsessive-compulsive disorder). Furthermore, deficits in prefrontal executive functioning have been implicated in certain anxiety disorders (e.g., OCD; for a review, see Otto, 1992). Given that rumination and prefrontal functioning are problematic in the anxiety disorders, patients may benefit from cognitive control training as a novel approach to alleviating anxiety symptoms, given this approach's specific aim of increasing functioning in brain areas that are implicated in these processes.

Summary and Conclusions

Clinical studies have shown that the desired additive benefit between pharmacotherapy and CBT is rarely realized. This is particularly true for the addition of anxiolytic or antidepressant medication to state-of-the-art CBT. Combination treatment appears to have few advantages over monotherapy with CBT, particularly when longer-term management of treatment gains is considered. Nonetheless, when state-of-the art CBT is not available, additional treatment benefits are more reliably achieved by adding elements of CBT, particularly exposure interventions, to pharmacotherapy. In addition, recent advances in translational research have fostered a number of novel approaches to combination treatment strategies. In particular, preliminary findings for the role of D-cycloserine in combination with exposure-based CBT encourages further study of pharmacologic strategies for enhancing therapeutic learning rather than modulating affect.

References

Abramowitz, J. S. (1997). Effectiveness of psychological and pharmacological treatments for obsessive-compulsive disorder: A quantitative review. *Journal of Consulting and Clinical Psychology, 65,* 44–52.

Addis, M. E., Hatgis, C., Krasnow, A. D., Jacob, K., Bourne, L., & Mansfield, A. (2004). Effectiveness of cognitive-behavioral treatment for panic disorder versus treatment as usual in a managed care setting. *Journal of Consulting and Clinical Psychology, 72,* 625–635.

Barlow, D. H., Gorman, J. M., Shear, M. K., & Woods, S. W. (2000). Cognitive-behavioral therapy, imipramine, or their combination for panic disorder: A randomized controlled trial. *Journal of the American Medical Association, 283,* 2529–2536.

Blomhoff, S., Haug, T. T., Hellström, K., Holme, I., Humble, M., Madsbu, H. P., et al. (2001). Randomised controlled general practice trial of sertraline, exposure therapy and combined treatment in generalized social phobia. *British Journal of Psychiatry, 179,* 23–30.

Bouton, M. E. (2002). Context, ambiguity, and unlearning: Sources of relapse after behavioral extinction. *Biological Psychiatry, 52,* 976–986.

Bouton, M. E., Kenney, F. A., & Rosengard, C. (1990). State dependent fear extinction with two benzodiazepine tranquilizers. *Behavioral Neuroscience, 104,* 44–55.

Cain, C. K., Blouin, A. M., & Barad, M. (2004). Adrenergic transmission facilitates extinction of conditional fear in mice. *Learning and Memory, 11,* 179–187.

Christensen, H., Hadzi-Pavlovic, D. Andrews, G., & Mattick, R. (1987). Behavior therapy and tricyclic medication in the treatment of obsessive-compulsive disorder: A quantitative review. *Journal of Consulting and Clinical Psychology, 55,* 701–711.

Cottraux, J., Mollard, E., Bouvard, M., Marks, I., Sluys, M., Nury, A. M., et al. (1990). A controlled study of fluvoxamine and exposure in obsessive-compulsive disorder. *International Clinical Psychopharmacology, 5,* 17–30.

Craske, M. G., Golinelli, D., Stein, M. B., Roy-Byrne, P., Bystritsky, A., & Sherbourne, C. (2005). Does the addition of cognitive behavioral therapy improve panic disorder treatment outcome relative to medication alone in the primary-care setting? *Psychological Medicine, 35,* 1645–1654.

Davidson, J.R.T., Foa, E. B., Huppert, J. D., Keefe, F. J., Franklin, M. E., Compton, J. S., et al. (2004). Fluoxetine, comprehensive cognitive behavioral therapy, and placebo in generalized social phobia. *Archives of General Psychiatry, 61,* 1005–1013.

Davis, M. (2002). Role of NMDA receptors and MAP kinase in the amygdala in extinction of fear: Clinical implications for exposure therapy. *European Journal of Neuroscience, 16,* 395–398.

Davis, M., Falls, W. A., & Gewirtz, J. (2000). Neural systems involved in fear inhibition: Extinction and conditioned inhibition. In M. Myslobodsky & I. Weiner (Eds.), *Contemporary issues in modeling psychopathology* (pp. 113–142). Boston: Kluwer Academic.

Davis, M., & Myers, K. M. (2002). The role of glutamate and gamma-aminobutyric acid in fear extinction: Clinical implications for exposure therapy. *Biological Psychiatry, 52,* 998–1007.

Deacon, B. J., & Abramowitz, J. S. (2004). Cognitive and behavioral treatments for anxiety disorders: A review of meta-analytic findings. *Journal of Clinical Psychology, 60,* 429–441.

Deacon, B. J., & Abramowitz, J. S. (2005). Patients' perceptions of pharmacological and cognitive-behavioral treatments for anxiety disorders. *Behavior Therapy, 36,* 139–145.

De Beurs, E., van Balkom, A. J., Lange, A., Koele, P., & van Dyke, R. (1995). Treatment of panic disorder with agoraphobia: Comparison of fluvoxamine, placebo, and psychological panic management combined with exposure and of exposure in vivo alone. *American Journal of Psychiatry, 152,* 683–691.

D'Souza, D. C., Gil, R., Cassello, K., Morrissey, K., Abi-Saab, D., White, J., et al. (2000). IV glycine and oral D-cycloserine effects on plasma and CSF amino acids in healthy humans. *Biological Psychiatry, 47,* 450–462.

Fava, G. A., Savron, G., Zielezny, M., Grandi, S., Rafanelli, C., & Conti, S. (1997). Overcoming resistance to exposure in panic disorder with agoraphobia. *Acta Psychiatrica Scandinavica, 95,* 306–312.

Foa, E. B., Franklin, M. E., & Moser, J. (2002). Context in the clinic: How well do cognitive-behavioral therapies and medications work in combination? *Biological Psychiatry, 10,* 987–997.

Foa, E. B., & Kozak, M. J. (1986). Emotional processing of fear: Exposure to corrective information. *Psychological Bulletin, 99,* 20–35.

Foa, E. B., Liebowitz, M. R., Kozak, M. J., Davies, S., Campeas, R., Franklin, M. E., et al. (2005). Randomized, placebo-controlled trial of exposure and ritual prevention, clomipramine, and their combination in the treatment of obsessive-compulsive disorder. *American Journal of Psychiatry, 162,* 151–161.

Franklin, M. E., Abramowitz, J. S., Bux, D. A., Zoellner, L. A., & Feeny N. C. (2002). Cognitive-behavioral therapy with and without medication in the treatment of obsessive-compulsive disorder. *Professional Psychology: Research and Practice, 33,* 162–168.

Furukawa, T. A., Watanabe, N., & Churchill, R. (2006). Psychotherapy plus antidepressant for panic disorder with or without agoraphobia. *British Journal of Psychiatry, 188,* 305–312.

Goisman, R. M., Warshaw, M. G., & Keller, M. B. (1999). Psychosocial treatment prescriptions for generalized anxiety disorder, panic disorder, and social phobia, 1991–1996. *American Journal of Psychiatry, 156,* 1819–1821.

Gould, R. A., Buckminster, S., Pollack, M. H., Otto, M. W., & Yap, L. (1997a). Cognitive-behavioral and pharmacological treatment for social phobia: A meta-analysis. *Clinical Psychology: Science and Practice, 4,* 291–306.

Gould, R. A., Otto, M. W., & Pollack, M. H. (1995). A meta-analysis of treatment outcome for panic disorder. *Clinical Psychology Review, 15,* 819–844.

Gould, R. A., Otto, M. W., Pollack, M. P., & Yap, L. (1997b). Cognitive-behavioral and pharmacological treatment of generalized anxiety disorder: A preliminary meta-analysis. *Behavior Therapy, 28,* 285–305.

Gronwall, D. M. (1977). Paced auditory serial-addition task: A measure of recovery from concussion. *Perceptual & Motor Skills, 44,* 367–373.

Haug, T. T., Blomhoff, S., Hellström, K., Holme, I., Humble, M., Madsbu, H. P., et al. (2003). Exposure therapy and sertraline in social phobia: 1-year follow-up of a randomised controlled trial. *British Journal of Psychiatry, 182,* 312–318.

Hegel, M. T., Ravaris, C. L., & Ahles, T. A. (1994). Combined cognitive-behavioral and time-limited alprazolam treatment of panic disorder. *Behavior Therapy, 25,* 183–195.

Heimberg, R. G., Liebowitz, M. R., Hope, D. A., Schneier, F. R., Holt, C. S., Welkowitz, L. A., et al. (1998). Cognitive behavioral group therapy vs. phenelzine therapy for social phobia: 12-week outcome. *Archives of General Psychiatry, 55,* 1133–1141.

Heresco-Levy, U., Kremer, I., Javitt, D. C., Goichman, R., Reshef, A., Blanaru, M., et al. (2002). Pilot-controlled trial of D-cycloserine for the treatment of post-traumatic stress disorder. *International Journal of Neuropsychopharmacology, 5,* 301–307.

Herry, C., & Garcia, R. (2002). Prefrontal cortex long-term potentiation, but not long-term depression, is associated with the maintenance of extinction of learned fear in mice. *Journal of Neuroscience, 22,* 577–583.

Heuzenroeder, L., Donnelly, M., Haby, M. M., Mihalopoulos, C., Rossell, R., Carter, R., et al. (2004). Cost-effectiveness of psychological and pharmacological interventions for generalized anxiety disorder and panic disorder. *Australian and New Zealand Journal of Psychiatry, 38,* 602–612.

Hofmann, S. G., Meuret, A. E., Smits, J.A.J., Simon, N. M., Pollack, M. H., Eisenmenger, K., et al. (2006). Augmentation of exposure therapy with D-cycloserine for social anxiety disorder. *Archives of General Psychiatry, 63,* 298–304.

Hohagen, F., Winkelmann, G., Räsche-Rauschle, H., Hand, I., König, A., Münchau, N., et al. (1998). Combination of behaviour therapy with fluvoxamine in comparison with behaviour therapy and placebo: Results of a multicentre study. *British Journal of Psychiatry, 35*(Suppl.), 71–78.

Kamphuis, J. H., & Telch, M. J. (2000). Effect of distraction and guided threat reappraisal on fear reduction during exposure-based treatments for specific fears. *Behaviour Research and Therapy, 38,* 1163–1181.

Kampman, M., Keijsers, G. P., Hoogduin, C. A., & Hendriks, G. J. (2002). A randomized, double-blind, placebo-controlled study of the effects of adjunctive paroxetine in panic disorder patients unsuccessfully treated with cognitive-behavioral therapy alone. *Journal of Clinical Psychiatry, 63,* 772–777.

Kobak, K. A., Greist, J. H., Jefferson, J. W., Katzelnick, D. J., & Henk, H. J. (1998). Behavioral versus pharmacological treatments of obsessive compulsive disorder: A meta-analysis. *Psychopharmacology, 136,* 205–216.

Kushner, M. G., Kim, S. W., Donahue, C., Thuras, P., Adson, D., Kotlyar, M., et al. (2007). *Biological Psychiatry, 62,* 835–838.

Ledgerwood, L., Richardson, R., & Cranney, J. (2005). D-cycloserine facilitates extinction of learned fear: Effects of reacquisition and generalized extinction. *Biological Psychiatry, 57,* 841–847.

Liebowitz, M. R., Heimberg, R. G., Schneier, F., Hope, D. A., Davies, S., Holt, C. S., et al. (1999). Cognitive-behavioral group therapy versus phenelzine in social phobia: Long term outcome. *Depression and Anxiety, 10,* 89–98.

Lydiard, R. B., Brawman-Mintzer, O., & Ballenger, J. C. (1996). Recent developments in the psychopharmacology of anxiety disorders. *Journal of Consulting and Clinical Psychology, 64,* 660–668.

Marks, I. M., Lelliott, P., Basoglu, M., Noshirvani, H., Monteiro, W., Cohen, D., et al. (1988). Clomipramine, self-exposure and therapist-aided exposure for obsessive-compulsive rituals. *British Journal of Psychiatry, 152,* 522–534.

Marks, I. M., Swinson, R. P., Basaglu, M., Kuch, K., Nasirvani, H., O'Sullivan, G., et al. (1993). Alprazolam and exposure alone and combined in panic disorder with agoraphobia: A controlled study in London and Toronto. *British Journal of Psychiatry, 162,* 776–787.

Mavissakalian, M., & Michelson, L. (1986). Agraophobia: Relative and combined effectiveness of therapist-assisted in vivo exposure and imipramine. *Journal of Clinical Psychiatry, 47,* 117–122.

Mavissakalian, M., & Perel, J. M. (1992). Clinical experience in maintenance and discontinuation of imipramine therapy in panic disorder with agoraphobia. *Archives of General Psychiatry, 49,* 318–323.

Mavissakalian, M., & Perel, J. M. (1999). Long term maintenance and discontinuation of imipramine therapy in panic disorder with agoraphobia. *Archives of General Psychiatry, 56,* 821–827.

Milad, M. R., & Quirk, G. J. (2002). Neurons in medial prefrontal cortex signal memory for fear extinction. *Nature, 420,* 70–74.

Mitte, K. (2005a). Meta-analysis of cognitive-behavioral treatments for generalized anxiety disorder: A comparison with pharmacotherapy. *Psychological Bulletin, 131,* 185–195.

Mitte, K. (2005b). A meta-analysis of the efficacy of psycho- and pharmacotherapy in panic disorder with and without agoraphobia. *Journal of Affective Disorders, 88,* 27–45.

Morgan, M. A., Romanski, L. M., & LeDoux, J. E. (1993). Extinction of emotional learning: Contribution of medial prefrontal cortex. *Neuroscience Letters, 163,* 109–113.

Mystkowski, J. L., Mineka, S., Vernon, L. L., & Zinbarg, R. E. (2003). Changes in caffeine states enhance return of fear in spider phobia. *Journal of Consulting and Clinical Psychology, 71,* 243–250.

Noyes, R., Garvey, M. J., Cook, B., & Suelzer, M. (1991). Controlled discontinuation of benzodiazepine treatment for patients with panic disorder. *American Journal of Psychiatry, 148,* 517–523.

Otto, M. W. (1992). Normal and abnormal information processing: A neuropsychological perspective on obsessive compulsive disorder. *Psychiatric Clinics of North America, 15,* 825–847.

Otto, M. W., Basden, S., Leyro, T. M., McHugh, R. K., & Hofmann, S. G. (2007). Clinical perspectives on the combination of D-cycloserine and CBT for the treatment of anxiety disorders. *CNS Spectrums, 12,* 51–61.

Otto, M. W., Hinton, D., Korbly, N. B., Chea, A., Phalnarith, B., Gershuny, B. S., et al. (2003). Treatment of pharmacotherapy-refractory posttraumatic stress disorder among Cambodian refugees: A pilot study of combination treatment with cognitive-behavior therapy vs. sertraline alone. *Behaviour Research and Therapy, 41,* 1271–1276.

Otto, M. W., Penava, S. J., Pollock, R. A., & Smoller, J. W. (1996). Cognitive-behavioral and pharmacologic perspectives on the treatment of post-traumatic stress disorder. In M. H. Pollack, M. W. Otto, & J. F. Rosenbaum (Eds.), *Challenges in clinical practice: Pharmacologic and psychosocial strategies* (pp. 219–260). New York: Guilford Press.

Otto, M. W., Pollack, M. H., & Maki, K. M. (2000). Empirically-supported treatment for panic disorder: Costs, benefits, and stepped care. *Journal of Consulting and Clinical Psychology, 68,* 556–563.

Otto, M. W., Pollack, M. H., Penava, S. J., & Zucker, B. G. (1999). Cognitive-behavior therapy for patients failing to respond to pharmacotherapy for panic disorder: A clinical case series. *Behaviour Research and Therapy, 37,* 763–770.

Otto, M. W., Pollack, M. H., & Sabatino, S. A. (1996). Maintenance of remission following cognitive-behavior therapy for panic disorder: Possible deleterious effects of concurrent medication treatment. *Behavior Therapy, 27,* 473–482.

Otto, M. W., Pollack, M. H., Sachs, G. S., Reiter, S. R., Meltzer-Brody, S., & Rosenbaum, J. F. (1993). Discontinuation of benzodiazepine treatment: Efficacy of cognitive-behavior therapy for patients with panic disorder. *American Journal of Psychiatry, 150,* 1485–1490.

Otto, M. W., Safren, S. A., Nicolaou, D. C., & Pollack, M. H. (2003). Considering mechanisms of action in the treatment of social anxiety disorder. In M. H. Pollack, N. M. Simon, and M. W. Otto (Eds.), *Social phobia: Presentation, course, and treatment.* New York: Castle Connolly Graduate Medical Publishing.

Otto, M. W., Smits, J.A.J., & Reese, H. E. (2004). Cognitive-behavioral therapy for the treatment of anxiety disorders. *Journal of Clinical Psychiatry, 65*(Suppl. 5), 34–41.

Otto, M. W., Tuby, K. S., Gould, R. A., McLean, R. Y., Pollack, M. H. (2001). An effect-size analysis of the relative efficacy and tolerability of serotonin selective reuptake inhibitors for panic disorder. *American Journal of Psychiatry, 158*(12), 1989–1992.

Park, J. M., Mataix-Cols, D., Marks, I. M., Ngamthipwatthana, T., Marks, M., Araya, R., et al. (2001). Two-year follow-up after a randomised controlled trial of self- and clinician-accompanied exposure for phobia/panic disorders. *British Journal of Psychiatry, 178,* 543–548.

Parnas, A. S., Weber, M., & Richardson, R. (2005). Effects of multiple exposures to D-cycloserine on extinction of conditioned fear in rats. *Neurobiology of Learning and Memory, 83,* 224–231.

Penava, S. J., Otto, M. W., Maki, K. M., & Pollack, M. H. (1998). Rate of improvement during cognitive-behavioral group treatment for panic disorder. *Behaviour Research and Therapy, 36,* 665–673.

Pollack, M. H. (2005). The pharmacotherapy of panic disorder. *Journal of Clinical Psychiatry, 66*(Suppl. 4), 23–27.

Pollack, M. H., Otto, M. W., Kaspi, S. P., Hammerness, P. G., & Rosenbaum, J. F. (1994). Cognitive-behavior therapy for treatment-refractory panic disorder. *Journal of Clinical Psychiatry, 55,* 200–205.

Powers, M. B., Smits, J.A.J., Leyro, T. M., & Otto, M. (2006). Translational research perspectives on maximizing the effectiveness of exposure therapy. In D.C.S. Richard and D. Lauterbach (Eds.), *Comprehensive handbook of the exposure therapies* (pp. 109–126). Burlington, MA: Academic Press.

Powers, M. B., Smits, J. A., & Telch, M. J. (2004). Disentangling the effects of safety-behavior utilization and safety-behavior availability during exposure-based treatment: A placebo-controlled trial. *Journal of Consulting and Clinical Psychology, 72,* 448–454.

Quartermain, D., Mower, J., Rafferty, M. F., Herting, R. L., & Lanthorn, T. H. (1994). Acute but not chronic activation of the NMDA-coupled glycine receptor with D-cycloserine facilitates learning and retention. *European Journal of Pharmacology, 157,* 7–12.

Quirk, G. J., Russo, G. K., Barron, J. L., & Lebron, K. (2000). The role of ventromedial prefrontal cortex in the recovery of extinguished fear. *Journal of Neuroscience, 20,* 6225–6231.

Ressler, K. J., Rothbaum, B. O., Tannenbaum, L., Anderson, P., Graap, K., Zimand, E., et al. (2004). Cognitive enhancers as adjuncts to psychotherapy: Use of D-cycloserine in phobics to facilitate extinction of fear. *Archives of General Psychiatry, 61,* 1136–1144.

Richardson, R., Ledgerwood, L., & Cranney, J. (2004). Facilitation of fear extinction by D-cycloserine: theoretical and clinical implications. *Learning and Memory, 11,* 510–516.

Rodriguez, B. I., & Craske, M. G. (1993). The effects of distraction during exposure to phobic stimuli. *Behaviour Research and Therapy, 31,* 549–558.

Schmidt, N. B., Wollaway-Bickel, K., Trakowski, J. H., Santiago, H. T., & Vasey, M. (2002). Antidepressant discontinuation in the context of cognitive behavioral treatment for panic disorder. *Behaviour Research and Therapy, 40,* 67–73.

Siegle, G. J., Ghinassi, F., & Thase, M. E. (in press). Neurobehavioral therapies in the 21st century: Summary of an emerging field and an extended example of cognitive control training for depression. *Cognitive Therapy and Research.*

Sloan, T., & Telch, M. J. (2002). The effects of safety-seeking behavior and guided threat reappraisal on fear reduction during exposure: An experimental investigation. *Behaviour Research and Therapy, 40,* 235–251.

Spiegel, D. A., Bruce, T. J., Gregg, S. F., & Nuzzarello, A. (1994). Does cognitive behavior therapy assist slow-taper alprazolam discontinuation in panic disorder? *American Journal of Psychiatry, 151,* 876–881.

Stein, D. J., Versiani, M., Hair, T., & Kumar, R. (2002). Efficacy of paroxetine for relapse prevention in social anxiety disorder: A 24-week study. *Archives of General Psychiatry, 59,* 1111–1118.

Stein, M. B., Sherbourne, C. D., Craske, M. G., Means-Christensen, A., Bystritsky, A., Katon, W., et al. (2004). Quality of care for primary care patients with anxiety disorders. *American Journal of Psychiatry, 161,* 2230–2237.

Stuart, G. L., Treat, T. A., & Wade, W. A. (2000). Effectiveness of an empirically based treatment for panic disorder delivered in a service clinic setting: 1-year follow-up. *Journal of Consulting and Clinical Psychology, 68,* 506–512.

Sutherland, S. M., & Davidson, J.R.T. (1995). β-Blockers and benzodiazepines in pharmacotherapy. In M. B. Stein (Ed.), *Social phobia: Clinical and research perspectives* (pp. 323–326). Washington, DC: American Psychiatric Press.

Telch, M. J., Agras, W. S., Taylor, C. B., Roth, W. T., & Gallen, C. (1985). Combined pharmacological and behavioral treatment for agoraphobia. *Behaviour Research and Therapy, 23,* 325–335.

Van Balkom, A. J., de Haan, E., van Oppen, P., Spinhoven, P., Hoogduin, K. A., & van Dyck, R. (1998). Cognitive and behavioral therapies alone and in combination with fluvoxamine in the treatment of obsessive-compulsive disorder. *Journal of Nervous and Mental Disease, 186,* 492–499.

Van Berckel, B. N., Lipsch, C., Gispen-de Wied, C., Wynne, H. J., Blankenstein, M. A., van Ree, J. M., et al. (1998). The partial NMDA agonist D-cycloserine stimulates LH secretion in healthy volunteers. *Psychopharmacology (Berl), 138,* 190–197.

Van Etten, M. L., & Taylor, S. (1998). Comparative efficacy of treatments for post-traumatic stress disorder: A meta-analysis. *Clinical Psychology and Psychotherapy, 5,* 126–144.

Wade, W. A., Treat, T. A., & Stuart, G. L. (1998). Transporting an empirically supported treatment for panic disorder to a service clinic setting: A benchmarking strategy. *Journal of Consulting and Clinical Psychology, 66,* 231–239.

Walker, J. R., Van Ameringen, M. A., Swinson, R., Bowen, R. C., Chokka, P. R., Goldner, E., et al. (2000). Prevention of relapse in generalized social phobia: Results of a 24-week study in responders to 20 weeks of sertraline treatment. *Journal of Clinical Psychopharmacology, 20,* 636–644.

Wells, A. (2000). *Emotional disorders and metacognition: Innovative cognitive therapy.* New York: Wiley.

Whittal, M. L., Otto, M. W., & Hong, J. J. (2001). Cognitive-behavior therapy for discontinuation of SSRI treatment of panic disorder: A case series. *Behaviour Research and Therapy, 39,* 939–945.

Integrated Psychological Treatment of Multiple Anxiety Disorders

Peter J. Norton

Abstract

Transdiagnostic, or nondiagnosis-specific, conceptualizations of anxiety disorder have been gaining in popularity recently. Drawing from multiple lines of evidence, including genetics, comorbidity, and treatment response, the evidence suggests greater overlap than difference among the anxiety diagnoses. As such, multiple groups have begun to investigate the efficacy and utility of transdiagnostic cognitive behavioral treatments for anxiety designed for use with diagnostically heterogeneous groups. The current chapter reviews the theoretical basis underlying these treatments, describes the content of the treatments, and summarizes the emerging efficacy evidence.

Keywords: cognitive behavioral therapy, mixed-diagnosis, pathology, transdiagnostic, unified treatment

Since the release of *DSM–III* (American Psychiatric Association [APA], 1980) and its subsequent editions (APA, 1987, 1994), there has been substantial reclassification and dissection of anxiety disorders from early neurosis-based conceptualizations. *DSM–I* and *II* (APA, 1952, 1965) presented 3 anxiety (neurosis) classifications, which grew to 9 anxiety disorders in *DSM–III* and *III–R,* and 12 in *DSM–IV.* Furthermore, several anxiety disorder diagnoses can be further divided with specifiers and subtypes, such as the specific phobia types or the generalized specification for social anxiety disorder, such that (disregarding distinctions within substance-induced anxiety disorder or anxiety disorder due to a general medical condition) *DSM–IV* currently allows for 25 distinct Axis I diagnoses primarily related to anxiety.

This increasing specificity in anxiety disorder diagnoses has spawned extensive research, and our understanding of the nature and treatment of anxiety disorders has grown considerably. While invaluable knowledge has evolved from research asking, "How do these disorders differ?" one casualty of diagnostic specificity has been research asking, "How are these disorders similar?" Recent years, however, have seen increased discussion of how to best classify anxiety and related disorders. While the structure delineated in *DSM* remains the most widely accepted, many have suggested a move toward alternative models of anxiety, including dimensional models (e.g., Brown, 2002; Goldberg, 1996), models emphasizing a single common anxiety pathology (e.g., Norton, 2006; Norton & Hope, 2005), and models suggesting a common pathology across all affective disorders (e.g., Barlow, Allen, & Choate, 2004). Proponents of each of these models have provided compelling arguments and data to support the validity of the models. Although more thorough discussions are presented elsewhere (e.g., Barlow, Allen & Choate, 2004; Norton, 2006), a brief review of the theoretical model surrounding unified treatment approaches is presented below.

Core Pathology Conceptualization of Anxiety Disorders

Much of the theoretical underpinnings of unified treatment models is based around the constructs of neuroticism (e.g., Eysenck, 1957), trait anxiety (Gray, 1982; Spielberger, 1985), and negative affectivity (Clark & Watson, 1991), models sufficiently similar and overlapping that they likely reflect the same construct (Barlow, 2002; Zinbarg & Barlow 1996). For the purposes of this chapter, the term *Negative Affectivity* (NA) will be used, which has been described generally as "a stable, heritable trait tendency to experience a broad range of negative feelings such as worry, anxiety, self-criticisms, and a negative self-view" (Keogh & Reidy, 2000, p. 108). Clark, Steer, and Beck (1994) further define NA as a temperamental sensitivity to negative stimuli resulting in feelings of fear, anxiety, depression, guilt, and self-dissatisfaction. Craske (1999) and Barlow (1988, 2002) tie this construct of generalized vulnerability to Beck and Emery's (1985) models of danger schemata, and suggest that the vulnerability "is associated with a perceived inability to predict, control, or obtain desired results" (Barlow, 1988, p. 248). Indeed, Barlow (2002) argues that the sensitivity to negative stimuli arises due to perceptions of uncontrollability or unpredictability. Seen as a common underlying factor contributing to both anxiety and mood disorders, NA may explain the high rates of comorbidity and similarity between mood and anxiety disorders (Clark et al., 1994).

Genetic Data Supporting a Core Pathology Conceptualization

A considerable body of evidence suggests a hereditable component in clinical anxiety. Twin studies utilizing multivariate genetic analyses have provided strong support for the idea that genetic transmission does not involve specific anxiety disorders, but rather a common nonspecific diathesis toward anxiety and other NA-related disorders. Jardin, Martin, and Henderson (1984) examined measures of neuroticism and checklists of anxiety and depressive symptoms from nearly 4,000 twin pairs. Their analyses suggested a strong genetic influence on anxiety and depressive symptoms, but nearly all of this genetic influence was shared with the genetic influence on neuroticism. Kendler, Heath, Martin, and Eaves (1987) expanded upon this model and found evidence suggesting that genetic factors did not specifically influence either symptoms of depression or anxiety, but rather, a genetic factor of general distress influences both anxiety and depres-

sion. In short, Kendler et al. (1987) concluded that genetics provide a general predisposition for affective disorders, but environmental factors are largely responsible for determining the specific disorder manifestation. Subsequent studies by Kendler, Neale, Kessler, Heath, and Eaves (1992) and Andrews et al. (Andrews, 1991; Andrews, Stewart, Allen, & Henderson, 1990; Andrews, Stewart, Morris-Yates, Holt, & Henderson, 1990) generally agree that at least a portion of what contributes to the development of anxiety disorders is a general predisposition to experience negative affect.

Comorbidity as Evidence for a Core Pathology

If there exists a single NA vulnerability factor for the development of an anxiety disorder, it would be expected that individuals with this vulnerability would be prone to developing anxiety-related difficulties. That is, vulnerable individuals may experience multiple learning experiences. Should this be the case, it would be anticipated that many vulnerable individuals would present with multiple fears. Under the *DSM* model, this would be expressed as comorbidity. As expected, very high rates of within-anxiety disorder and anxiety/mood disorder comorbidity do exist. Among a clinical sample, Andrews, Stewart, et al. (1990) reported that patients' symptoms met *DSM* criteria for an average of 2.1 depressive and anxiety disorders. Indeed, treatment data (Brown & Barlow, 1992; Sanderson, Di Nardo, Rapee, & Barlow, 1990) also suggest 50%–60% of individuals with an anxiety disorder have a comorbid anxiety or mood disorder diagnosis.

Treatment Effects Supporting a Core Pathology Conceptualization

Treatment Effects on Primary Symptoms. Given the hypothesis that anxiety disorders share the same core pathology, it should follow that treatments acting upon the core pathology should be effective regardless of the specific feared stimuli. According to Barlow and Lehman (1996) and Craske (1999), encouraging efficacy data have been obtained across the range of cognitive behavioral treatment protocols for anxiety-related disorders. Many effective pharmacological treatment options exist as well, including tricyclic and heterocyclic antidepressants, serotonin reuptake inhibitors, monoamine oxidase inhibitors, azapirones, beta-adrenergic blockers, and benzodiazepines (Craske, 1999; Taylor, 1998). Several recent meta-analyses of cognitive behavioral treatment (CBT) outcome studies support the effectiveness of such treatments across the anxiety disorders and, generally, the superior efficacy of CBT approaches over non-CBT psychosocial treatments (e.g., Abramowitz, 1997; Fedoroff & S. Taylor, 2001; Gould, Otto, & Pollack, 1995; Gould, Otto, Pollack, & Yap, 1997; Norton & Price, 2007; van Etten & Taylor, 1998). Overall, these meta-analyses support the efficacy of CBT for anxiety disorders, and treatment effects are relatively similar across diagnoses (Norton & Price, 2007). Indeed, similar treatment effects are not unexpected, as each treatment typically incorporates similar therapeutic techniques: education and self-monitoring, cognitive restructuring, and exposure.

While many similarities exist within the standard manualized treatment protocols, the specific features of the components do differ to varying degrees. Most notably, arousal control techniques differ in not only their presence or absence, but also in the emphasis of specific techniques (e.g., progressive muscular relaxation, breathing retraining, etc.). Differences also exist among the other common components (i.e., psychoeducation, self-monitoring, cognitive restructuring, and exposure). These differences, however, are in *content,* not *function.* For example, the format for exposure depends on the nature of a client's fears, but the rationale for exposure, overcoming fears by facing them, does not vary.

Treatment Effects on Comorbid Conditions. In addition to the fact that functionally or chemically similar treatments are effective across diagnoses, Borkovec, Abel, and Newman (1995) and Brown, Antony, and Barlow (1995) have reported that following treatment for a principal anxiety diagnosis, untargeted comorbid anxiety diagnoses often abate. Borkovec et al. (1995) noted that following treatment for generalized anxiety disorder (GAD), the incidence of comorbid anxiety disorders decreased significantly. Furthermore, the decline in nontargeted comorbid diagnoses varied by outcome, such that those demonstrating superior improvement for GAD showed a greater decline in comorbid diagnoses. Brown et al. (1995) reported that following treatment for panic disorder, rates of comorbidity declined from 51% to 17% at posttreatment. Similar effects on secondary anxiety and depression were described by Blanchard and colleagues (2003) following treatment for motor-vehicle accident posttraumatic stress disorder (PTSD). Norton, Hayes, and Hope (2004) reported that, following a transdiagnostic anxiety treatment, levels of depressiveness decreased significantly compared to no change for controls.

Further, all but one client with a depressive diagnosis showed improvement to subclinical depressive severity following treatment.

Summary of Support for the Core Pathology Conceptualization

Several distinct lines of investigation have been offered in support of the hypothesis that the *DSM–IV* anxiety disorders may represent a single core pathology that may be elicited by different stimuli and manifested in distinct ways. First, considerable research indicates that negative affectivity, a temperamental personality trait characterized by sensitivity to negative emotions due to a low sense of control, underlies the manifestations of clinical anxiety. Second, observed rates of comorbidity within the *DSM–IV* anxiety disorders greatly exceed that which would be predicted if anxiety disorders were independent disorders. One explanation for the high comorbidity is that the comorbid disorders are not independent disorders, but rather multiple manifestations of the same pathology. It is also possible that the high rates of comorbidity could be the result of other mechanisms, such as a common risk factor for two or more independent disorders. However, this alternative explanation appears less tenable in light of the third line of evidence, treatment outcome data. Highly similar CBT and pharmacological treatments are efficacious across the anxiety disorders, suggesting that these treatments are impacting on a core pathology underlying each of these diagnostic groups. This evidence is strengthened by findings that nontargeted comorbid anxiety diagnoses frequently remit after treatment for a principal anxiety diagnosis. While there may be some utility in considering each of the anxiety disorders as distinct entities, the evidence here suggests greater similarity than difference.

Dissemination and Accessibility

While much of the impetus for developing transdiagnostic anxiety treatments was tied to the NA models and aforementioned data, practical concerns such as dissemination and treatment accessibility were also a driving force. Anxiety disorders are among the most responsive disorders to CBT and pharmacological treatment. Indeed, numerous meta-analyses support their efficacy across the anxiety disorders (Abramowitz, 1997; Fedoroff & Taylor, 2001; Gould et al., 1995, 1997; Norton & Price, 2007; van Etten & Taylor, 1998). Despite the availability of efficacious treatments, most individuals with an anxiety disorder never receive appropriate treatment (Young, Klap, Sherbourne, & Wells, 2001). As suggested by Norton and Hope (2005), "the problem lies not with our treatments, but with their delivery" (p. 80).

Two of the largest barriers to treatment delivery are poor dissemination of efficacious treatments to providers, and limited accessibility to efficacious treatment for clients. Regarding the former, the impact of training expenses and time demands on clinicians may play a key role underlying poor dissemination (Addis, Wade, & Hatgis, 1999). Given the high financial and time costs of purchasing and studying treatment materials, attending training seminars, and receiving supervision in the delivery of treatments for one, much less six or more, anxiety diagnoses, this dissemination barrier is not surprising.

The latter barrier to efficacious treatment delivery—accessibility—is a function not only of the poor dissemination described above, but also to resource demands on practitioners who are trained in efficacious treatments. For example, an evidence-based treatment provider can only treat a limited number of clients in any given time period. A common approach to make evidence-based treatments more widely available is through group treatments. Indeed, two treatment groups per day of six clients each would impact as many or more clients than an entire workday of individual treatment sessions. Group treatments may also address other barriers to treatment, such as cost-effectiveness. Cost-effectiveness, if passed along to the clients, directly augments the accessibility of treatment, particularly to lower-income individuals and third-party payers. As noted by the Surgeon General (Office of the Surgeon General, 1999), cost of treatment is a frequently cited reason for not seeking treatment.

Despite the utility of group treatments, they are frequently not practical in settings with a smaller population base or greater therapist saturation. Indeed, it is often difficult to obtain sufficient numbers of patients with the same diagnosis, who present to clinic within a similar time frame, and who have similar availabilities for scheduling treatment. For example, consider a therapist at an anxiety disorder specialty clinic who wishes to recruit six clients for a diagnosis-specific treatment group. Assuming all intakes have an anxiety disorder, based on National Comorbidity Survey prevalence estimates, it would require on average 21 intakes before one would expect to have recruited 6 individuals with a primary diagnosis of specific phobia to form the group. It would require 25 intakes for a six-person social phobia group, 31 intakes for a panic/agoraphobia group, 50 intakes for a PTSD group, 53 intakes for a GAD group, and 199 intakes for an obsessive-compulsive disorder (OCD) group. In contrast, if a clinician wanted to recruit six clients with any anxiety diagnosis for a transdiagnostic group treatment, only six intakes would be required.

Transdiagnostic Treatment Protocols

Given the theoretical evidence and practical advantages, it is not surprising that several independent research groups have begun to develop specific treatment protocols for mixed-diagnosis anxiety groups. Although none have been publicly released, early publications and presentations provide a general overview of the format, content, and emphasis of these treatments. These treatments are described below, and preliminary outcome data for these treatments are presented in the following section. The length and detail of the protocol descriptions vary considerably; this is a function of the amount of available information and does not reflect any statement of the utility or quality of the treatment.

Norton and Hope Protocol. The Norton and Hope (2005) protocol utilizes 12 weekly group sessions, each lasting 2 hours. Groups sizes are typically capped at six to eight clients and two therapists. With the exception of the first session, sessions are active, with skills and treatment components being practiced within the session. Practice of treatment skills outside of session (i.e., "homework") is strongly encouraged, and homework noncompliance is addressed in session as a barrier to recovery.

The initial session and part of the second session are primarily educational, designed to provide an understanding of anxiety and anxiety disorders, thoroughly describe the components of treatment and their purpose, and facilitate group cohesion. During the first session, the concept of a fear-avoidance hierarchy is discussed, and each client develops a hierarchy with assistance from the therapists. Cognitive restructuring is introduced in the second session with a thorough discussion of the importance of thoughts or appraisals. Clients are asked to monitor automatic thoughts during the week as homework. During the third session, thought monitoring homework is reviewed, the concept of thinking errors is discussed, and clients are encouraged to identify any in their monitored thoughts. The process of asking and answering disputing questions is then covered and practiced with the monitored thoughts, initially with therapist assistance. Finally, rational responses are developed based on the thought challenging.

Sessions 4 through 9 are dedicated to in-session graduated exposure and response prevention. At the start of each session, exposure exercises are introduced, negotiated, and planned. Where possible, exposures are devised where multiple group members will draw benefit from participating, such as having two clients with social-evaluative concerns engage in a "political debate." All exposures are preceded by cognitive restructuring of likely automatic thoughts. In previous groups, 50% to 75% of the group clients engage in an exposure each session. Those not engaging in an in-session exposure will be assigned self-exposure homework, and will engage in an in-session exposure during the following session.

In Sessions 10 and 11, the focus returns to cognitive restructuring but the emphasis is shifted from presenting fear to more global experiences of negative affect. These sessions are designed to promote rationally examining thoughts in general, as opposed to only those related to specific fears, in an effort to reduce general susceptibility to negative affect and potentially minimize the future development of similar or new fears. The final session is devoted to termination issues and developing relapse prevention action plans.

Barlow et al. Protocol. Barlow and colleagues (Barlow, Allen, & Choate, 2003, 2004; Allen, Ehrenreich, & Barlow, 2005) are currently refining a similar transdiagnostic treatment protocol. In contrast to the Norton and Hope treatment, however, Barlow and colleagues developed their protocol to be applicable across the spectrum of Negative Affect Syndrome disorders, which includes anxiety and depression, and possibly eating, dissociative, substance use, and somatoform disorders. Early descriptions of their treatment, which covers 10 weekly sessions, emphasized four major therapeutic areas: education (Sessions 1 and 2), reappraisal of emotional cognitions (Sessions 3 and 4), prevention of emotional avoidance (Sessions 5 and 6), and exposure to/approach of emotion-eliciting stimuli (Sessions 7 to 9) (Barlow et al., 2003). The final session covers relapse prevention and termination.

According to Allen et al. (2005) the protocol is currently undergoing revision and modification based on preliminary efficacy data and client feedback. In more recent descriptions (Allen et al., 2005) descriptions of *exposure* are substituted by the concept of *modifying action tendencies*. This concept, which encompasses therapeutic exposure, emphasizes altering the maladaptive behavioral and cognitive tendencies when confronted by negative emotion and the removal of any strategies that are used to decrease the experienced affect.

Larkin et al. Protocol. Larkin, Waller, and Combs-Lane (2003) reported developing an 8-week transdiagnostic group treatment for individuals with any principal anxiety disorder diagnosis except PTSD and OCD. Weekly sessions, which last 90 minutes, focus on teaching and practicing skills, including diaphragmatic breathing retraining, guided imagery, and progressive muscle relaxation (Sessions 2 and 3), cognitive restructuring (Sessions 4 and 5), anxiety hierarchy development and exposure therapy (Sessions 6 and 7), and relapse prevention (Session 8). Unlike many of the other transdiagnostic programs, exposure is not as heavily incorporated into the sessions, as hierarchy development and exposure are only directly introduced and practiced in session during the sixth and seventh sessions. This places a greater onus on the clients to guide and motivate their own exposure without support or guidance from the therapists. Conversely, the Larkin et al. Protocol emphasizes relaxation training skills, which some other protocols have omitted.

Schmidt Protocol. Schmidt (2003; Smith & Schmidt, 2005) describes a 10-session cognitive behavioral group treatment program, entitled False Safety-behavior Elimination Therapy (F-SET), that is designed for individuals with primary diagnoses of panic disorder, social anxiety disorder, and GAD. Similar to the other treatment protocols described here, the emphasis of the treatment is on exposure and response (false safety behaviors) prevention, with additional incorporation of education and cognitive restructuring. Specific session-by-session details of the order, timing, and intensity of the various treatment components, however, have not been reported. Similar to the Barlow et al. (2003, 2004) program, F-SET involves the careful identification and gradual elimination of any overt or covert safety behaviors, including mental behaviors that serve to maintain the strength of the fears. In addition to developing the transdiagnostic protocol, Schmidt also designed the treatment model to be very simple and easy to learn, thereby facilitating dissemination to front-line providers.

Erickson et al. Protocol. Erickson, Janeck, and Tallman (2007) adapted an early transdiagnostic anxiety treatment (see Erickson, 2003), but adopted a somewhat different treatment approach to the aforementioned treatment programs. Similar to other transdiagnostic treatments, weekly sessions are 2 hours in length and are led by two co-therapists. Group sizes are larger, however, ranging from 8 to 12 clients in any one group. Their treatment focuses on building a hierarchy of feared situations and developing specific weekly behavioral goals for approaching the feared situations. In this regard, the Erickson et al. Protocol very heavily emphasizes graduated self-directed exposure. During subsequent sessions, general and diagnosis-specific exposure approaches (e.g., interoceptive, imaginal) are described and practiced by the entire group, and clients are strongly encouraged to repeatedly practice those exposure exercises that elicited anxiety for them. This "try everything and pick the best" approach differs considerably from the more prescriptive "this is what you should do" approach adopted in the other treatments. This approach likely has some advantages and some disadvantages. In terms of disadvantages, most notable are the lack of parsimony and the expense of therapy time practicing exercises that may not be useful for a sizable number of the clients. Additionally, some exposure exercises are not introduced until late in the treatment, which may limit the amount of in-session practice with a therapist's guidance. On the other hand, the practice of multiple exposures may identify previously unknown fear triggers, such as interoceptive hyperventilation exercises identifying a sensitivity to paroxysmal sensations, due to the belief that others notice her breathing, in a social phobic with no panic history.

During the sixth, seventh, and ninth sessions, automatic thoughts are introduced and cognitive restructuring is practiced in session and for homework. In the 11th session, cognitive restructuring continues, but deeper schema-level exploration and challenging is emphasized. In all instances, a typical progression of automatic thought identification, labeling thinking errors, reviewing evidence, and generating alternative hypotheses is followed. Finally, passive and progressive relaxation training and diaphragmatic breathing are presented and practiced in the fourth, fifth, and eighth sessions, respectively. Relapse prevention and progress maintenance are the focus of the final session, where clients create a new set of 11-week behavioral goals.

The Erickson et al. Protocol, as noted above, requires considerable self-direction on the part of the clients. Numerous therapeutic skills and techniques are presented to the entire group and clients are encouraged to identify and utilize those skills or techniques that are most valuable in reaching their treatment goals. While therapists do recommend certain exercises for specific clients based on their presenting complaints, much of the onus for selecting homework exercises is placed on the clients. This approach certainly maximizes the clients' perceptions of empowerment and ownership of the treatment plan, although it runs the risk that some clients will opt to practice less difficult or anxiety-producing techniques, such as repeatedly practicing relaxation over anxiety-producing in vivo exposures.

Lumpkin et al. Protocol. Lumpkin, Silverman, Weems, Markham, and Kurtines (2002) adapted a group treatment protocol for anxious youths (Silverman & Kurtines, 1996) for use with diagnostically mixed anxiety groups, including GAD, specific phobia, separation anxiety disorder, social phobia, and OCD. Groups meet weekly for 12 weeks, and sessions last 50 minutes followed by a 20-minute conjoint period with therapists, clients, and their parents. Initial sessions emphasize contingency management strategies and treatment socialization wherein parents are trained in contingency management skills and principles, followed by controlled application of the principles to facilitate exposure. As treatment progresses, children are trained in thought challenging and self-talk strategies that are used to facilitate self-directed exposure to fears. Simultaneously, parental use of contingency management to facilitate exposure is slowly withdrawn to transfer control to the children. Finally, these self-control skills are applied during graduated exposure conducted in session and as contracted homework.

Preliminary Outcome Data

Given the relatively recent development of transdiagnostic anxiety treatments, it is not surprising that there are only a few outcome trials supporting their efficacy. Still, the collective results of detailed case reviews (Allen et al., 2005; Barlow et al., 2003), uncontrolled pre–post outcome trials (Erickson, 2003; Larkin et al., 2003), small-n experimental studies (Lumpkin et al, 2002), and randomized controlled trials (Norton & Hope, 2005; Norton, Hayes, & Hope, 2004; Erickson et al., 2007; Schmidt, 2003; Smith & Schmidt, 2005) generally converge in support of the efficacy of such treatments.

Case Reports. Barlow et al. (2003) reported preliminary evidence from two initial groups, describing effect sizes similar to those typically seen in diagnosis-specific treatments. One participant, who was diagnosed with comorbid GAD and major depressive disorder, did not respond well to treatment. Following revision to the protocol, Allen et al. (2005) delivered the treatment to six clients of varied anxiety and depressive diagnoses, on an individual basis.

Five of the six clients showed decreases in the severity of their primary diagnoses to subclinical levels. Data from self-report questionnaires generally supported these findings. Currently, as noted by Allen et al. (2005) this group is adapting their protocol for adolescents and children, although efficacy data are not available.

Uncontrolled Trials. Recently, Erickson (2003) reported the results of an uncontrolled trial of a separate transdiagnostic CBT program for anxiety. His results suggested significant decreases in self-reported anxiety and depression among the 70 clients completing the 11-week treatment. Further 6-month follow-up data from 16 participants suggested maintenance of treatment gains. No analyses of outcome by diagnosis were conducted due to power limitations. Larkin et al. (2003) also presented preliminary data from an outcome trial and reported similar results. Participants had principal diagnoses of GAD, social phobia, and panic disorder and/or agoraphobia. Of 46 participants enrolled in the study, 25 treatment completers showed generally consistent reductions on self-report measures of anxiety, clinician-rated global assessment of functioning, and self-monitored anxiety and depression.

Quasi-Experimental Trials. Lumpkin et al. (2002) reported similar treatment effects following a 12-week transdiagnostic treatment with anxious youths. Multiple baseline results suggested notable reductions on measures of anxiety occurring during treatment, but no change during the baseline periods. As well, treatment gains were maintained at 6 and 12 months. Again, however, no analyses by diagnosis were conducted due to the limited sample size.

Randomized Controlled Trials. In the only reported outcome trial of the Schmidt protocol (Schmidt, 2003; Smith & Schmidt, 2005), compared to controls, participants receiving treatment showed considerable improvement. Treatment effects for panic disorder and social anxiety disorder were larger than those for GAD, although clients with GAD still showed good response.

Erickson et al. (2007) evaluated the efficacy of their treatment protocol in a large multisite randomized controlled trial by comparison to a waitlist control condition. Initial reports offer mixed conclusions. Compared to controls, participants receiving treatment evidenced a significantly larger decrease in Beck Anxiety Inventory scores from pre- to posttreatment. Conversely, change on diagnosis-specific outcome measures did not differ between conditions. Further, the data suggest that this was not due to low statistical power when analyzing diagnostic subgroups.

Norton and Hope (2005) conducted a trial of their treatment and found that, compared to clients in a waitlist control condition, clients receiving treatment improved significantly. Roughly 67% of those receiving treatment, as compared to none of the waitlist controls, showed a reduction in diagnostic severity to subclinical levels, and significant improvement was also noted on some, albeit not all, indices of anxiety. Unfortunately, the limited sample size of this study ($n = 23$) precluded analyses of outcome by diagnosis. In a reanalysis of the treatment data, Norton, Hayes, and Hope (2004) also noted significant decreases in depressive symptoms and the diagnostic severity of depressive disorders among those receiving treatment, despite depression not being targeted in treatment, whereas no change in depression was noted for waitlist controls.

Summary and Conclusions

A concern that has been raised regarding transdiagnostic treatments is that by tailoring different exercises (e.g., interoceptive, imaginal, or role-played exposure) to different clients, the transdiagnostic group treatment becomes more similar to six disorder-specific individual treatments occurring simultaneously in the same room. Although this may be the appearance, as we would likely use interoceptive techniques with panickers, imaginal techniques with GAD clients, and in vivo techniques with social phobics, it is not actually the case. The approach in these protocols is to emphasize the *rationale* and *process* of graduated exposure, not the manualization of specific exposure exercises. Such an approach is consistent with an individual case formulation (see Persons & Tompkins, 1997) of the feared stimuli, not diagnosis.

Therefore, the techniques in transdiagnostic treatment are adapted for each client to maximally target his or her specific fears. This is similar to what is done in most diagnosis-specific group treatments, such as those for OCD where different clients may be engaging in different in vivo or imaginal exposures simultaneously. Indeed, most group treatment protocols do not prescribe identical application of treatment components to all group members. Rather, most recognize that the general therapeutic elements must be individually tailored to the individual clients in the group. For example, with regard to group treatment of social anxiety disorder, Heimberg (1991) reported, "it has been our experience that patients with very different specific fears may still relate well to each other's concerns. Thus, patients with different fears [e.g., public speaking versus dating fears] may be mixed in the same group with several benefits" (p. 23; clarification added). Supporting Heimberg's (1991) observation, data from behavioral and cognitive group treatments for OCD suggest that the degree of homogeneity or heterogeneity among OCD subtypes (e.g., contamination/washing, hoarding, etc.) within treatment groups does not influence outcome (Norton & Whittal, 2004). In fact, during the initial trial of the Norton and Hope (2005) Protocol, the heterogeneity contributed to a positive group process as clients realized that the discrepancy between appraisals and reality they saw in others could also be applied to their own fears (e.g., "My fears may be as unrealistic as your fears seem to me"). Thus, differences in the specific features of anxiety disorders do not preclude the development of a transdiagnostic protocol for anxiety, and indeed may make these treatments more flexible as they do not use diagnosis as a proxy for an individual functional analysis.

Many questions remain unanswered. First, few data exist to suggest whether all anxiety disorder diagnoses are amenable to transdiagnostic treatment, and whether they are equally amenable. This clearly stands as an important next step in the research endeavor, although power issues for comparing diagnoses would require a very large outcome study. As noted earlier, even the developers of some of the transdiagnostic treatments are hesitant to include individuals with OCD and PTSD. This stands in contrast to the Barlow et al. (2003, 2004) treatment, which is inclusive of clients with a range of negative affect–related disorders such as depression. Second, no trials have compared the efficacy of a transdiagnostic treatment to the efficacy of diagnosis-specific group treatments, although treatment effect sizes appear comparable to those reported in meta-analyses.

The issue of comparable efficacy to diagnosis-specific treatments is one of frequent opinion but little evidence; however, several possibilities exist. First, equal efficacy could be shown, which would leave the choice of treatment model to each practitioner's preference. This may be the most likely scenario. Second, it may be found that transdiagnostic treatments are efficacious, but not as efficacious as disorder-specific treatments. This appears to be the most commonly held belief. If this is indeed the case, it might suggest a hierarchical treatment model wherein all clients presenting to a clinic or hospital are routed through a transdiagnostic treatment initially, and those with limited or no response

are escalated to more intensive and efficacious disorder-specific treatments. Finally, it is plausible that transdiagnostic treatments may be shown to be more efficacious than diagnosis-specific treatments. Although this may be unlikely, it is possible that being less constrained by diagnosis affords the clinician greater flexibility in devising a treatment plan around a client's individual case formulation as opposed to diagnostic categories.

In summary, this chapter provided a basic overview of the theoretical and practical considerations that have led to, and underlie, the development of cognitive behavioral group treatments designed for diagnostically heterogeneous groups. Several treatment models that are currently under development were outlined, with all advocating exposure (or exposurelike principles) as the central feature of the treatment. Early outcome data are generally supportive of the efficacy of these treatments, and should help guide the continued development and refinement of transdiagnostic treatments for anxiety.

References

Abramowitz, J. S. (1997). Effectiveness of psychological and pharmacological treatments for obsessive-compulsive disorder: A quantitative review. *Journal of Consulting and Clinical Psychology, 65,* 44–52.

Addis, M. E., Wade, W. A., & Hatgis, C. (1999). Barriers to dissemination of evidence-based practices: Addressing practitioners' concerns about manual-based psychotherapies. *Clinical Psychology: Science and Practice, 6,* 430–441.

Allen, L. B., Ehrenreich, J. T., & Barlow, D. H. (2005). A unified treatment for emotional disorders: Applications with adults and adolescents. *Japanese Journal of Behavior Therapy, 31,* 3–31.

American Psychiatric Association. (1952). *Diagnostic and statistical manual of mental disorders.* Washington, DC: Author.

American Psychiatric Association. (1965). *Diagnostic and statistical manual of mental disorders* (2nd ed.). Washington, DC: Author.

American Psychiatric Association. (1980). *Diagnostic and statistical manual for mental disorders* (3rd ed.). Washington, DC: Author.

American Psychiatric Association. (1987). *Diagnostic and statistical manual for mental disorders* (3rd ed. revised). Washington, DC: Author.

American Psychiatric Association. (1994). *Diagnostic and statistical manual for mental disorders* (4th ed.). Washington, DC: Author.

Andrews, G. (1991). Anxiety, personality, and anxiety disorders. *International Review of Psychiatry, 3,* 293–302.

Andrews, G., Stewart, G. W., Allen, R., & Henderson, A. S. (1990). The genetics of six neurotic disorders: A twin study. *Journal of Affective Disorders, 19,* 23–29.

Andrews, G., Stewart, G. W., Morris-Yates, A., Holt, P. E., & Henderson, A. S. (1990). Evidence for a general neurotic syndrome. *British Journal of Psychiatry, 157,* 6–12.

Barlow, D. H. (1988). *Anxiety and its disorders: The nature and treatment of anxiety and panic.* New York: Guilford Press.

Barlow, D. H. (2002). *Anxiety and its disorders: The nature and treatment of anxiety and panic* (2nd ed.). New York: Guilford Press.

Barlow, D. H., Allen, L. B., & Choate, M. L. (2003, November). A unified treatment protocol for the emotional disorders. In P. J. Norton (Chair), *Integrative treatment approaches across anxiety and related disorders.* Symposium conducted at the annual meeting of the Anxiety Disorders Association of America, Toronto, ON, Canada.

Barlow, D. H., Allen, L. B., & Choate, M. L. (2004). Toward a unified treatment for emotional disorders. *Behavior Therapy, 35,* 205–230.

Barlow, D. H. & Lehman, C. L. (1996). Advances in the psychosocial treatment of anxiety disorders: Implications for national health care. *Archives of General Psychiatry, 53,* 727–735.

Beck, A. T., & Emery, G. (1985). *Anxiety disorders and phobias: A cognitive perspective.* New York: Basic Books.

Blanchard, E. B., Hickling, E. J., Devineni, T., Veazey, C. H., Galovski, T. E., Mundy, E., et al. (2003). A controlled evaluation of cognitive behavioral therapy for posttraumatic stress in motor vehicle accident survivors. *Behaviour Research and Therapy, 41,* 79–96.

Borkovec, T. D., Abel, J. A., & Newman, H. (1995). Effects of psychotherapy on comorbid conditions in generalized anxiety disorder. *Journal of Consulting and Clinical Psychology, 63,* 479–483.

Brown, T. A. (2002). Classification of anxiety disorders. In D. J. Stein & E. Hollander (Eds.), *The textbook of anxiety disorders* (pp. 13–28). Washington, DC: American Psychiatric Press.

Brown, T. A., Antony, M. M., & Barlow, D. H. (1995). Diagnostic comorbidity in panic disorder: Effect on treatment outcome and course of comorbid diagnoses following treatment. *Journal of Consulting and Clinical Psychology, 63,* 408–418.

Brown, T. A., & Barlow, D. H. (1992). Comorbidity among anxiety disorders: Implications for treatment and *DSM–IV. Journal of Consulting and Clinical Psychology, 60,* 835–844.

Clark, D. A., Steer, R. A., & Beck, A. T. (1994). Common and specific dimensions of self-reported anxiety and depression: Implications for the cognitive and tripartite models. *Journal of Abnormal Psychology, 103,* 645–654.

Clark, L. A., & Watson, D. (1991). Tripartite model of anxiety and depression: Psychometric evidence and taxonomic implications. *Journal of Abnormal Psychology, 100,* 316–336.

Craske, M. G. (1999). *Anxiety disorders: Psychological approaches to theory and treatment.* Boulder, CO: Westview Press.

Erickson, D. H. (2003). Group cognitive behavioural therapy for heterogeneous anxiety disorders. *Cognitive Behaviour Therapy, 32,* 179–186.

Erickson, D. H., Janeck, A., & Tallman, K. (2007). Group cognitive-behavioral group for patients with various anxiety disorders. *Psychiatric Services, 58,* 1205–1211.

Eysenck, H. J. (1957). *The dynamics of anxiety and hysteria: An experimental application of modern learning theory to psychiatry.* London: Routledge & Kegan Paul.

Fedoroff, I. C., & Taylor, S. (2001). Psychological and pharmacological treatments of social phobia: A meta-analysis. *Journal of Clinical Psychopharmacology, 21,* 311–324.

Goldberg, D. P. (1996). A dimensional model for common mental disorders. *British Journal of Psychiatry, 168,* 44–49.

Gould, R. A., Otto, M. W., & Pollack, M. H. (1995). A meta-analysis of treatment outcome for panic disorder. *Clinical Psychology Review, 15,* 819–844.

Gould, R. A., Otto, M. W., Pollack, M. H., & Yap, L. (1997). Cognitive behavioral and pharmacological treatment of generalized anxiety disorder: A preliminary meta-analysis. *Behavior Therapy, 28,* 285–305.

Gray, J. A. (1982). *The neurobiology of anxiety.* New York: Oxford University Press.

Heimberg, R. G. (1991). *A manual for conducting cognitive-behavioral group therapy for social phobia* (2nd ed.). Unpublished manuscript available from the author.

Jardin, R., Martin, N. G., & Henderson, A. S. (1984). Genetic covariation between neuroticism, and the symptoms of anxiety and depression. *Genetics Epidemiology, 1,* 89–107.

Kendler, K. S., Heath, A. C., Martin, N. G., & Eaves, L. J. (1987). Symptoms of anxiety and symptoms of depression. *Archives of General Psychiatry, 44,* 451–457.

Kendler, K. S., Neale, M. C., Kessler, R. C., Heath, A. C., & Eaves, L. J. (1992). Major depression and generalized anxiety disorder: Same genes, (partly) different environments? *Archives of General Psychiatry, 49,* 716–722.

Keogh, E., & Reidy, J. (2000). Exploring the factor structure of the Mood and Anxiety Symptom Questionnaire (MASQ). *Journal of Personality Assessment, 74,* 106–125.

Larkin, K. T., Waller, S., & Combs-Lane, A. (2003, March). Anxiety management group therapy for multiple anxiety disorder diagnoses. In P. J. Norton (Chair), *Integrative treatment approaches across anxiety and related disorders.* Symposium conducted at the annual meeting of the Anxiety Disorders Association of America, Toronto, ON, Canada.

Lumpkin, P. W., Silverman, W. K., Weems, C. F., Markham, M. R., & Kurtines, W. M. (2002). Treating a heterogeneous set of anxiety disorders in youth with group cognitive behavioral therapy: A partially nonconcurrent multiple-baseline evaluation. *Behavior Therapy, 33,* 163–177.

Norton, P. J. (2006). Toward a clinically-oriented model of anxiety disorders. *Cognitive Behaviour Therapy, 35,* 88–105.

Norton, P. J., Hayes, S. A., & Hope, D. A. (2004). Effects of a transdiagnostic group treatment for anxiety on secondary depressive disorders. *Depression and Anxiety, 20,* 198–202.

Norton, P. J., & Hope, D. A. (2005). Preliminary evaluation of a broad-spectrum cognitive-behavioral group therapy for anxiety. *Journal of Behavior Therapy and Experimental Psychiatry, 36,* 79–97.

Norton, P. J. & Price, E. P. (2007). A meta-analytic review of cognitive-behavioral treatment outcome across the anxiety disorders. *Journal of Nervous and Mental Disease, 195,* 521–531.

Norton, P. J., & Whittal, M. L. (2004). Symptom heterogeneity and clinical outcome in group treatment for obsessive-compulsive disorder. *Depression and Anxiety, 20,* 195–197.

Office of the Surgeon General. (1999). *Mental health: A report of the Surgeon General.* Rockville, MD: U.S. Department of Health and Human Services.

Persons, J. B., & Tompkins, M. A. (1997). Cognitive-behavioral case formulation. In T. D. Eels (Ed.), *Handbook of psychotherapy case formulation* (pp. 314–339). New York: Guilford Press.

Sanderson, W. C., Di Nardo, P. A., Rapee, R. M., & Barlow, D. H. (1990). Syndrome comorbidity in patients diagnosed with a *DSM–III–R* anxiety disorder. *Journal of Abnormal Psychology, 99,* 308–312.

Schmidt, N. B. (2003, November). Unified CBT for anxiety: Preliminary findings from False Safety Behavior Elimination

Therapy (F-SET). In D. F. Tolin (Chair), *Increasing the cost-effectiveness and user-friendliness of cognitive behavior therapy for anxiety disorders*. Symposium conducted at the 37th annual convention of the Association for Advancement of Behavior Therapy, Boston, MA.

Smith, J. D., & Schmidt, N. B. (2005, March). Unified CBT for anxiety: Preliminary findings from False Safety Behavior Elimination Therapy (F-SET). In P. J. Norton (Chair), *Transdiagnostic issues across anxiety and mood disorders*. Symposium conducted at the annual meeting of the Anxiety Disorders Association of America, Seattle, WA.

Silverman, W. K., & Kurtines, W. M. (1996). *Anxiety and phobic disorders: A pragmatic approach*. New York: Plenum Press.

Spielberger, C. D. (1985). Anxiety, cognition and affect: A state-trait perspective. In A. H. Tuma & J. D. Maser (Eds.), *Anxiety and the anxiety disorders* (pp. 171–182). Hillsdale, NJ: Erlbaum.

Taylor, C. B. (1998). Treatment of anxiety disorders. In A. F. Schatzberg & C. B. Nemeroff (Eds.), *Textbook of psychopharmacology* (2nd ed., pp. 775–789). Washington, DC: American Psychiatric Press.

Van Etten, M. L., & Taylor, S. (1998). Comparative efficacy of treatments for post-traumatic stress disorder: A meta-analysis. *Clinical Psychology and Psychotherapy, 5*, 126–144.

Young, A. S., Klap, R., Sherbourne, C. D., & Wells, K. B. (2001). The quality of care for depressive and anxiety disorders in the United States. *Archives of General Psychiatry, 58*, 55–61.

Zinbarg, R. E., & Barlow, D. H. (1996). Structure of anxiety and the anxiety disorders: A hierarchical model. *Journal of Abnormal Psychology, 105*, 181–193.

Complementary and Alternative Approaches to Treating Anxiety Disorders

Kathryn M. Connor *and* Sandeep Vaishnavi

Abstract

Studies suggest that between 20%–50% of adults in industrialized nations use some form of complementary and/or alternative medicine (CAM) to either prevent or treat health problems, with higher rates of CAM use observed in nonindustrialized nations. Frequently used approaches include biologically based treatments, manipulative and body-based practices, and mind-body interventions. This chapter summarizes findings from systematic investigations of CAM in treating anxiety disorders and other anxiety states.

Keywords: alternative medicine, anxiety disorders, botanical CAM, complementary medicine, dietary supplement

Studies over the last decade suggest that between 20%–50% of adults in industrialized nations use some form of complementary and/or alternative medicine (CAM) to either prevent or treat health problems (Astin, Maries, Pelletier, Hansen, & Haskell, 1998; Eisenberg et al., 1998). Frequently used approaches include biologically based treatments, manipulative and body-based practices, and mind-body interventions, as well as other CAM approaches listed in Table 1. A more detailed overview of these categories can be found on the Web site for the National Center for Complementary and Alternative Medicine (NCCAM) at http://nccam.nih.gov/health/.

A 2002 survey of U.S. adults revealed that 62% of respondents used CAM in the last year for health reasons. Consistent with earlier surveys in Western societies, the most common conditions prompting use are recurring pain, colds, anxiety and depression, gastrointestinal discomfort, and insomnia (Astin, 1998; Barnes, Powell-Griner, McFann, & Nahin, 2004; Eisenberg et al, 1998). The principal reason for use is the belief that CAM would improve health when used in combination with conventional medical treatment (Barnes et al., 2004).

Among psychiatric outpatients and other adults with self-defined anxiety and/or depression, rates of CAM use can exceed 50% (Kessler et al., 2001; Knaudt, Connor, Weisler, Churchill, & Davidson, 1999). These treatments are often used in conjunction with care provided by conventional (allopathic) health care providers, but not necessarily with the provider's knowledge (Astin et al., 1998; Knaudt et al., 1999). Systematic evaluation of the effects of CAM for diagnosed mental disorders has been very limited. St. Johns' wort (*Hypericum perforatum*), an herbal product widely used for its mood-elevating properties, is arguably the most extensively investigated CAM therapy. However, evidence to support its use remains inconsistent and confusing (Linde, Mulrow, Berner, & Effer, 2005). By comparison, very few randomized controlled trials (RCTs) have been performed in patients with anxiety disorders meeting criteria from the current *Diagnostic and Statistical Manual of Mental Disorders (DSM)* (American Psychiatric Association, 2000) or

International Classification of Diseases (ICD) (World Health Organization, 1993). Most published works have focused on other clinical populations (e.g., cancer, pre- and postoperative patients, wound-healing, chronic neurologic disorders) and situational anxiety in healthy controls. In this chapter, the authors summarize findings from systematic investigations of CAM in treating anxiety disorders and other anxiety states.

Biologically Based Practices

Biologically based practices are part of an ancient healing tradition dating back to prehistoric times. For example, medicinal herbs were found among the personal effects of the mummified Ice Man discovered in Italy in 1991. Practices included under this rubric are noted in Table 1. Among U.S. adults, the most widely used dietary supplements are botanical products, with two products purported to have psychotropic effects among the top 10 products used in 2002: ginkgo biloba (21%) for cognitive enhancement and St. John's wort (12%) for depression (Barnes et al., 2004).

Botanicals

Kava (*Piper methysticum*) has been used for centuries in South Pacific cultures as a tranquilizing agent and has been adopted in Western Europe for the treatment of anxiety and nervous tension. Findings

Table 1. Commonly Used Complementary and Alternative Medicine Therapies

Biologically based practices: botanicals, animal-derived extracts, vitamins, minerals, fatty acids, amino acids, proteins, prebiotics and probiotics, whole diets, and functional foods

Manipulative and body-based practices: chiropractic and osteopathic manipulation, massage therapies, reflexology

Mind-body intervention strategies: relaxation, hypnosis, visual imagery, meditation, yoga, biofeedback, tai chi, qi gong

Energy medicine: deals with two type of energy fields: (1) veritable (involves use of specific, measurable wavelengths and frequencies to treat patients), and (2) putative (fields that have defied reproducible measurement to date; also called biofields)

Whole medical systems: traditional Chinese medicine, Ayurvedic medicine, naturopathy, homeopathy

from preclinical models suggest anxiolytic effects may be mediated through several neurotransmitter systems (e.g., GABA, serotonin, norepinephrine, and dopamine) (Baum, Hill, & Rommelspacher, 1998; Jossofie, Schmiz, & Hiemke, 1994; Seitz, Schule, & Gleitz, 1997). A 2005 Cochrane Database review found that, compared with placebo, kava was an effective symptomatic short-term treatment (1–24 weeks) for anxiety, with the caveats that (1) the effect was small, (2) there were only a few studies with small sample sizes, and (3) rigorous trials with large samples are needed to further clarify efficacy and safety issues (Pittler & Ernst, 2002). Further examination of the individual studies reveals samples of patients with a broad diagnostic representation, ranging from generalized anxiety disorder (GAD; *DSM-IV*) to nonpsychotic anxiety (*DSM–III–R*) to a variety of situationally bound anxiety states. Findings from subsequent reports have been inconsistent; a meta-analysis of 6 randomized controlled trials (RCTs) using the same kava product in adults with nonpsychotic anxiety suggested an effect for kava (Witte, Loew, & Gaus, 2005), while results from a pooled analysis of 3 RCTs using the same product in adults with *DSM–IV* GAD failed to find any significant clinical effects for kava (Connor, Payne, & Davidson, 2006). While it is possible that kava may be of benefit in milder stress reactions, one must carefully examine the risk-benefit ratio of treating with kava. Given the concerns raised in recent years regarding potential hepatotoxicity with the product (Stikel et al., 2003), at the present time, it is hard to justify kava's use in clinical psychiatry.

Valerian (*Valeriana officinalis*) has been traditionally used as a hypnotic for mild to moderate subjective complaints of insomnia. Valerian contains a number of constituents that have demonstrated central nervous system (CNS) activity, and proposed mechanisms include activity at melatonin, serotonin, and central adenosine receptors, as well as through the inhibitory neurotransmitter GABA (Abourashed, Koetter, & Brattshrom, 2004; Schellenberg, Sauer, Abourashed, Koetter, & Brattsrom, 2004). Systematic data supporting possible anxiolytic effects are scant. In one RCT of 36 patients with *DSM–III–R* GAD treated with valerian extract (81.3 mg/day), diazepam (6.5 mg/day), or placebo for 4 weeks, no differences were noted between any of the treatments on the primary anxiety outcome measures (Andreatini, Sartori, Seabra, & Leite, 2002). The anxiolytic effect of three single doses of valerian in combination with lemon balm (*Mellisa officinalis*) was assessed in a placebo-controlled crossover study in 24 healthy adults subjected to stress in a laboratory setting. Mixed anxiolytic effects were observed, with greater effect at the lowest dose (600 mg), but reduced cognitive performance at all doses (Kennedy, Little, Haskell, & Scholey, 2006).

Other Supplements

Little research exists on the anxiolytic effects of vitamins, minerals, and other dietary supplements. Gotu kola (*Centella asiatica*) has been associated with significant reduction in acoustic startle response in healthy adults, but the effect in patients with clinically significant anxiety is unknown (Bradwejn, Zhou, Koszycki, & Jakov, 2000). One RCT assessed the effect of a multivitamin combination containing calcium, magnesium, and zinc, on psychological well-being in 80 healthy adult males (Carroll, Ring, Suter, & Willemsen, 2000). After 1 month of treatment, the multivitamin combination was superior to placebo in reducing anxiety and perceived stress, suggesting a possible stress-modulating effect for the supplement. While this treatment demonstrated an effect in healthy adults without clinically significant anxiety, the effect in patients with clinically significant anxiety is unknown. Omega-3 fatty acids are popular nutritional supplements that may also have a role in treating anxiety, as suggested by positive findings from open-label studies in test anxiety (Yehuda, Robinovitz, & Mostofsky, 2005) and *DSM–IV* anxiety disorders (Connor, Zhang, Watkins, Payne, & Davidson, 2005). However, larger, well-designed RCTs are needed to further understand the possible role for omega-3 fatty acids in treating anxiety.

Manipulative and Body-Based Practices

Manipulative and body-based practices focus primarily on structures and systems of the body, including bones, joints, soft tissues, and the circulatory and lymphatic systems. Some of these practices are integral components of ancient, traditional medical systems (e.g., traditional Chinese medicine, ayurveda), while others were developed within the last 150 years (chiropractic and osteopathic manipulation). While quite different in many respects, these practices share the following principles: the human body is self-regulating and has the ability to heal itself; and the parts of the human body are interdependent. It is notable that these modalities are among the most common CAM approaches used by mainstream physicians in the United States (Astin et al., 1998).

Chiropractic

Chiropractic focuses on the relationship between the body's structure (particularly the spine) and function. Practitioners use hands-on therapy (called manipulation or adjustment), which often involves rapid movements and is in contrast to some other body-based treatments. The conceptual basis of chiropractic care is that misalignments of the spine interfere with "nerve flow" and lead to disease.

Chiropractic is growing in popularity among suffers of chronic back pain, who tend to perceive the therapy as a valuable component of their health care. Despite this public endorsement, conclusions from systematic assessments provide guarded optimism in chiropractic's role in treating acute lower back pain, neck pain, and muscle tension headaches (Kaptchuk & Eisenberg, 1998). It is notable that these pain syndromes are common in anxiety patients and, while chiropractic has not been studied in an RCT of patients with anxiety disorders, improvement in pain may lead to an indirect reduction in anxiety. One RCT has examined the effect of chiropractic on blood pressure and anxiety, finding reduction in blood pressure, but no difference from placebo on its effect on anxiety (Yates, Lampling, Abram, & Wright, 1988).

Massage

The anxiolytic effects of massage have been investigated in a variety of clinical populations, including women in labor, women with premenstrual dysphoric disorder, patients with subacute lower back pain, poststroke, and prior to surgery. Administered either in a single session or multiple sessions over days or weeks, in comparison to placebo, the benefits were generally noted immediately after treatment (Agarwal et al., 2005; Chang, Wang, & Chen, 2002; Mok & Woo, 2004), although in two trials the differences were noted at follow-up (Preyde, 2000) or at various time points in the study (Hernandez-Reif et al., 2000). Factors that likely contribute to these inconsistencies include the differences in study samples, massage therapy techniques, duration of treatment (single versus multiple treatments), and other study design features.

Massage may also be used in combination with aromatherapy. A meta-analysis of this treatment combination in different populations revealed an effect size comparable to psychotherapy in reducing trait anxiety (Moyer, Rounds, & Hannum, 2004). In a systematic review of lung cancer patients receiving combined massage and aromatherapy, reduction in anxiety was the most consistent clinical finding

(Fellowes, Barnes, & Wilkinson, 2004). While its effect in anxiety disorders is unknown, massage with or without aromatherapy may be of particular benefit for reducing anxiety in patients at risk for poor medication tolerability and/or drug-drug interactions, or in whom conventional therapies have provided limited relief.

Mind-Body Intervention Strategies

Mind-body medicine has been defined as "interventions that use a variety of techniques designed to facilitate the mind's capacity to affect bodily function and symptoms" (Astin, Sharpiro, Eisenberg, & Forys, 2003), and largely focuses on strategies and interventions to promote health. Fundamental precepts include the respect for and enhancement of an individual's capacity for self-knowledge and self-care. Illness is viewed as an opportunity for growth and transformation, with health care providers serving as guides or catalysts in this process. As with other CAM modalities, many of these approaches are components of ancient healing traditions. Yet today, mind-body interventions constitute a large portion of CAM use, with more than 30% of U.S. adults reporting use of relaxation techniques and imagery, biofeedback, and hypnosis in 2002 (Wolsko, Eisenberg, Davis, & Phillips, 2004).

Research in recent decades has empirically demonstrated the physiologic relationship between stress and neuroendocrine responses in animals, with the attribution of the phrase *fight or flight* to describe sympathetic nervous system activation to perceived stress (Cannon, 1932). In humans, mind-body interventions attempt to modify this stress response by reducing sympathetic activation and increasing parasympathetic tone. Examples of treatments in this field include relaxation, hypnosis, meditation, biofeedback, music, aromatherapy, yoga, tai chi, and qi gong. While several of these areas will be discussed below, additional information on meditation-based treatments can be found in Chapter 36.

Hypnosis

Hypnosis is an altered state of consciousness where a hypnotherapist can increase the patient's attention and make the patient more responsive to suggestions. Advocates compare the trancelike state of awareness in hypnosis to the experience of being so intensely focused on a task that one becomes unaware of things in the surrounding environment. Hypnosis may involve the therapist inducing a relaxed state by talking in a way that creates a sense of relaxation and security. The therapist may also help create visual imagery or, alternatively, teach techniques of self-hypnosis.

The putative mechanism of action for the hypnotic effect is unknown, but it may involve activation of medial prefrontal cortex and left dorsolateral prefrontal cortex, thus affecting information processing (Linden, 2006). There is mixed evidence for efficacy of hypnosis in anxiety. An RCT in patients with acute stress disorder demonstrated that hypnosis in conjunction with cognitive behavioral therapy (CBT) is more effective than either CBT or supportive counseling alone (Bryant, Moulds, Guthrie, & Nixon, 2005). However, a systematic review of a form of hypnosis (autogenic training) for stress and anxiety was inconclusive due to the poor methodological quality of the trials (Ernst & Kanji, 2000).

Biofeedback

Biofeedback techniques help patients to control involuntary body responses (e.g., blood pressure, muscle tension, heart rate, or even neural activity) (DeCharms et al., 2005). Treatment sessions involve measuring the patient's physiological responses, with the therapist providing feedback via auditory and visual cues. Over time, the patient associates the physiological response with the symptom, and applies various techniques to reduce these responses (Manuck, 1976). The mechanism of action is not entirely known, although it is hypothesized that so-called autonomic functions (that were thought to be entirely automatic) are under conscious control to some extent. It is noteworthy that some patients with stress-responsive conditions (i.e., hypertension, diabetes) who apply biofeedback skills may experience improvement in their conditions and require lower doses of medication.

With regard to effects on anxiety, findings from one RCT in patients with GAD showed that after 8 sessions, biofeedback significantly reduced state anxiety and physiologic symptoms, with maintenance of effect 6 weeks after treatment (Rice, Blanchard, & Purcell, 1993). A similar finding occurred with alcohol-dependent patients with high anxiety (Clark & Hirschman, 1990).

Music

The therapeutic effects of music have been demonstrated not only through subjective reports of relaxation, but also through observed entrainment of motor and sensory functions that have facilitated recovery in patients with neurologic dysfunction (e.g., cerebral palsy, stroke, traumatic brain injury). While the putative mechanism of action is unknown, evidence suggests that music affects the release of norepinephrine and corticotropin releasing hormone (CRH) (Watkins, 1997).

Evidence supporting the effectiveness of music therapy to treat anxiety is inconclusive. A meta-analysis found music reduces anxiety in hospital patients undergoing normal care, but not in preoperative patients (Evans, 2002). However, a systematic review of the effect of music therapy on anxiety experienced by patients in short-term waiting periods, such as day surgery, was inconclusive (Cooke, Chaboyer, & Hiratos, 2005).

Aromatherapy

Aromatherapy utilizes the application of aromatic oils for therapeutic benefit and is often combined with massage. While the mechanism of action is unknown, there is some evidence to suggest effects on neurotransmitters and perhaps even neuroprotective effects (Perry & Perry, 2006).

In terms of an effect on anxiety, results are mixed. Following a systematic review, Cooke and Ernst (2000) concluded that aromatherapy has mild, transient anxiolytic effects. Three subsequent controlled trials found that aromatherapy was not effective in reducing anxiety in patients with advanced cancer after 4 weeks (Soden, Vincent, Crasken, Lucas, & Ashley, 2004), or in patients receiving radiation therapy (Graham, Browne, Cox, & Graham, 2003), or prior to therapeutic abortion (Wiebe, 2000). However, in a trial of 40 healthy adults, aromatherapy with lavender (considered a relaxing scent) compared to rosemary (considered a stimulating scent) was associated with reduction in anxiety and related EEG changes (Diego et al., 1998). In addition, in patients undergoing magnetic resonance imaging (MRI) testing for a diagnostic cancer workup, aromatherapy was associated with reduced anxiety (Redd, Manne, Peters, Jacobsen, & Schmidt, 1994).

Yoga

Yoga is an ancient practice from India that literally means *to yoke,* the concept being that yoga helps yoke or bind together one's physical, mental, and spiritual dimensions. Yoga incorporates various specific postures to increase the flow of life energy (or *prana* in Sanskrit).

In a systematic review of studies of yoga for anxiety, each of the 8 studies meeting selection criteria (8 controlled trials; 6 were randomized and 2 were not) showed a positive result in favor of yoga. The most methodologically rigorous study provided a positive result as well; of note, a meta-analysis could not be performed because of study heterogeneity, mainly because of the varied conditions studied (Kirkwood, Rampes, Tuffrey, Richardson, & Pilkington, 2005). A subsequent Cochrane Database review was inconclusive; it selected two studies for inclusion, one in which transcendental meditation (TM) reduced anxiety symptoms and electromyography scores comparable with electromyography-biofeedback and relaxation therapy, while the other showed that Kundalini Yoga (KY) did not differentiate from relaxation/mindfulness meditation in lowering anxiety (Krisanaprakornkit, Krisanaprakornkit, Piyavhatkul, & Laopaiboon, 2006). Likely the most rigorous RCT on yoga in the literature compared KY with a relaxation response and mindfulness meditation arm in obsessive-compulsive disorder (OCD) patients and found a significant treatment difference in favor of KY, with a large effect size of 1.10 (Shannahoff-Khalsa et al., 1999).

Less rigorous trials have shown a mixed picture. In other trials examining the effects of a variety of yoga techniques and in which anxiety was not the primary outcome, results have tended to be negative, including in patients with multiple sclerosis (Iyengar yoga; Oken et al., 2004), cancer (Tibetan yoga (TY); Cohen, Warneke, Fouladi, Rodriguez, & Chaoul-Reich, 2004), and irritable bowel syndrome (Taneja et al., 2004). Another RCT did find a reduction in anxiety for mildly depressed patients compared to a waitlist control (Woolery, Myers, Sternlieb, & Zeltzer, 2004). In a sample of healthy young adults, one RCT showed decrease in anxiety and increase in parasympathetic activity (Ray et al., 2001). Similarly, yoga has been shown to decrease basal anxiety and anticipatory anxiety in medical students prior to exams (Malathi & Damodaran, 1999).

Energy Medicine

Energy medicine employs the use of veritable and putative energy fields, veritable fields being mechanical or electromagnetic forces that can be measured, and putative fields being fields that have not yet been measurable. The latter is based on the concept that humans have a subtle form of energy known as *qi* in traditional Chinese medicine, *ki* in Japan, and *prana* in Ayurveda.

Energy medicine proponents believe that illness results from disturbances of these subtle energies. Therapeutic approaches in this category include reiki, qi gong, therapeutic touch, and magnetic therapy. The common aspect of all these approaches is that the practitioners believe that by moving their hands over the patient's body, they can reorient the patient's energies. Although there is not currently established physical proof for these subtle energies, a superconducting quantum interference device (SQUID) has been claimed to measure large frequency-pulsing biomagnetic fields emanating from the hands of Therapeutic Touch practitioners during therapy (Zimmerman, 1990).

A systematic review shows some support for therapeutic touch in anxiety/pain (Spence & Olson, 1997). Another review found no generalizable findings (Wardell & Weymouth, 2004). Several RCTs have shown evidence for efficacy; one study showed a trend toward significant reduction of anxiety with therapeutic touch in high anxiety patients (Olson & Sneed, 1995); another showed therapeutic touch and relaxation were significantly beneficial among psychiatric patients with anxiety (Gagne & Toye, 1994); another showed a significant effect of therapeutic touch in reducing anxiety of institutionalized elderly patients (Simington & Laing, 1993); while another study in burn patients showed a significant reduction in anxiety (Turner, Clark, Gauthier, & Williams, 1998). Similarly, therapeutic touch has been shown to reduce anxiety in healthy volunteers (Lafreniere et al., 1999). Magnetic therapy is also considered part of energy medicine; however, no systematic reviews, meta-analyses, or RCTs in anxiety or anxiety disorders have been published to date.

Whole Medical Systems

Whole medical systems include homeopathy, traditional Chinese medicine (TCM), ayurvedic medicine, and chiropractic medicine. These are systems of medicine that are distinguishable from modern Western (*allopathic*) medicine. They often have their own systems of theory and practice and have evolved separately from Western medicine.

Homeopathy

Homeopathy was developed in Germany and has been practiced in the United States since the early 19th century. One of the key concepts of homeopathy is that patients can heal themselves by invoking their own "vital force." Practitioners believe that when this vital energy is imbalanced, disease occurs. Homeopathic treatment involves giving very small doses of substances that at larger doses can cause the symptoms that are being treated in order to invoke the patient's own healing powers. Dilution, homeopathy posits, actually makes the treatment more

effective by extracting the vital essence of the substance. Homeopathy also posits that treatment must be individualized to the particular patient's emotional and physical state and constitutional type, so that different patients with the same symptoms may necessarily receive different treatments.

No systematic reviews/meta-analyses with homeopathy and anxiety were available. An RCT with GAD patients showed no difference from placebo (Bonne, Shemer, Gorali, Katz, & Shalev, 2003). An animal study showed effects on anxiety in mice with a particular homeopathic preparation (Dhawan, Kumar, & Sharma, 2002).

Traditional Chinese Medicine

Traditional Chinese Medicine (TCM) is a system of healing that dates back more than 2,000 years. The view of TCM is that the body has a balance of two forces, *yin* (the slow or passive principle) and *yang* (the fast or active principle). Health, it is believed, is achieved by balancing yin and yang. Imbalance leads to disease by blockage of vital energy (*qi*) along pathways known as meridians. Herbs, acupuncture, and massage are used to unblock *qi*.

There were no systematic reviews/meta-analyses available on acupuncture or acupressure with anxiety disorders. Several RCTs have found auricular acupuncture to be effective in reducing anxiety in prehospital transport settings (Kober et al., 2003), in preoperative anxiety in surgical outpatients (Wang, Peloquin, & Kain, 2001), and in healthy anxious adults (Wang & Kain, 2001).

Ayurveda

Ayurveda (or "the science of life") is a system of healing from ancient India that places emphasis on balancing mind, body, and spirit. Ayurvedic treatments include diet, massage, use of herbs and metals, exercise, meditation, and yoga. Meditation is covered elsewhere in this chapter and yoga has been discussed earlier. Two ayurvedic herbs have activity to suggest potential anxiolytic effects: *Sesbania grandiflora,* traditionally used to treat so-called epileptic fits; and *Withania somnifera,* used to promote physical and mental health and to defend against disease and adverse environmental influences. In mice, treatment with the leaves of *S. garndiflora* was associated with increased brain levels of GABA and serotonin and with greater time in the open arm of the elevated plus maze, indicating anxiolytic activity (Kasture, Deshmukh, & Chopde, 2002). The roots of *W. somnifera* contain bioactive glycowithanolides (WSG) which, in rats, have shown anxiolytic activity comparable to lorazepam in several models for anxiety as well as in reduction of brain levels of tribulin, an endocoid marker of clinical anxiety, following administration of an anxiogenic agent (pentylenetetrazole) (Bhattacharya, Bhattacharya, Sairam, & Ghosal, 2000). However, while evidence from animal models suggests anxiolytic activity for these herbs, these effects have not been investigated in humans.

Summary and Conclusions

Complementary and alternative medicine practices have immense popularity, although upon critical investigation, many of these practices often do not stand up to scientific scrutiny. Botanical products in particular have to be taken with caution as they do not undergo the same regulatory scrutiny as medications. Drug products undergo rigorous investigation and regulatory review for evidence of efficacy and safety prior to being approved for use in the market. Manufacturers are also required to follow good manufacturing practices (GMP) and any claims of benefit must be submitted to regulatory authorities for review and approval. Different regulatory requirements, however, are applied to dietary supplements, including botanical products. For example, in the United States, supplements are regulated as food products by the Food and Drug Administration (FDA), under the guidance of the Dietary Supplement Health and Education Act (DSHEA) of 1994, and are subject to the same GMP standards of foods, but not of drugs. Manufacturers of supplements are responsible for ensuring the safety of their products and are not subject to premarket approval or a specific postmarketing surveillance period by the FDA. Under DSHEA, manufacturers may make claims of benefit based on the published literature, and the Federal Trade Commission is then responsible for monitoring manufactured products for truth in advertising. This regulatory framework is under review in the United States and, in examining the safety of supplements in 2002, the Institute of Medicine issued a report recommending a framework for the cost-effective and science-based evaluation of supplements by the FDA (Institute of Medicine of the National Academies, 2004).

Given these differences, there are a number of issues to consider when interpreting data from studies of supplements, and for botanical products in particular. Medicinal herbs are complex mixtures of a variety of potentially pharmacologically active compounds, with potentially multiple actions. Herbs are also available in a variety of forms (e.g., fresh, dried, extracts), using different plant parts (e.g., roots, leaves, flowers), and routes of administration (e.g., pills, ointments, oils, suppositories, inhaled smoke, infused beverages). The content of active constituents in a given botanical product varies depending on a number of variables, including the plant part used, growing conditions, procedures used for collection, storage, processing, and stability over time. Thus, there are high levels of interbatch and interproduct variability. Traditionally, these treatments have been used in the restoration of health, whereas drugs are generally designed to affect a specific ailment or disease. Therefore, one could question if the current gold-standard RCT model is appropriate to assess the efficacy of these treatments. Lastly, readers need to consider issues of study methodology when interpreting study results, including but not limited to the following: diagnostic heterogeneity of samples; small sample sizes; variability in products, doses, route of administration, and duration of treatment; adequacy of placebo controls, blinding, and comparators; and use of validated outcome measures.

Despite the lack of scientific evidence to support efficacy and safety in combining CAM with conventional medical treatment, more than half of U.S. adults use CAM for this purpose, believing that this combination will improve their health (Barnes et al., 2004). We know that botanical products are commonly used in this manner and that patients are often reluctant to disclose this use to their health care providers. Therefore, it is the responsibility of health care providers to inquire about use of dietary supplements in all patients at each visit. While very little is known about supplement-medicine and supplement-supplement interactions, several serious interactions have been reported, such as those between St. John's wort and immunosuppressants or antiretrovirals (Izzo, 2004).

In conclusion, systematic research on CAM modalities in anxiety disorders is very limited and has yielded results that are often inconclusive. Given the popularity of CAM worldwide, further research is needed to increase our understanding of the safety and efficacy of these approaches. In addition, it is imperative that health care providers be mindful of patients' use of these therapies and discuss the use of supplements and other CAM treatments with their patients.

References

Abourashed, E. A., Koetter, U., & Brattshrom, A. (2004). In vitro binding experiments with a valerian, hops, and their fixed combination extract (Ze91019) to selected central nervous system receptors. *Phytomedicine, 11,* 633–638.

Agarwal, A., Ranjan, R., Dhiraaj, S., Lakra, A., Kumar, M., & Singh, U. (2005). Acupressure for prevention of pre-operative anxiety: A prospective, randomised, placebo controlled study. *Anaesthesia, 60,* 978–981.

American Psychiatric Association. (2000). *Diagnostic and statistical manual of mental disorders* (4th ed. text revision). Washington, DC: Author.

Andreatini, R., Sartori, V. A., Seabra, M. L., & Leite, J. R. (2002). Effect of valepotriates (valerian extract) in generalized anxiety disorder: A randomized placebo-controlled pilot study. *Phytotherapy Research, 16,* 650–654.

Astin, J. (1998). Why patients use alternative medicine: Results of a national survey. *Journal of the American Medical Association, 279,* 1548–1553.

Astin, J. A., Maries, A., Pelletier, K. R., Hansen, E., & Haskell, W. L. (1998). A review of the incorporation of complementary and alternative medicine by mainstream physicians. *Archives of Internal Medicine, 158,* 2303–2310.

Astin, J. A., Shapiro, S. L., Eisenberg, D. M., & Forys, K. L. (2003). Mind-body medicine: State of the science, implications for practice. *Journal of the American Board of Family Practice, 16,* 131–147.

Barnes, P., Powell-Griner, E., McFann, K., & Nahin, R. (2004, May 27). Complementary and alternative medicine use among adults: United States, 2002. *CDC Advance Data Report #343.*

Baum, S. S., Hill, R., & Rommelspacher, H. (1998). Effect of kava extract and individual kavapyrones on neurotransmitter levels in nucleus acumbens of rats. *Progress in Neuropsychopharmacology and Biological Psychiatry, 22,* 1105–1120.

Bhattacharya, S. K., Bhattacharya, A., Sairam, K., & Ghosal, S. (2000). Anxiolytic-antidepressant activity of Withania somnifera glycowithanolides: An experimental study. *Phytomedicine, 7,* 463–469.

Bonne, O., Shemer, Y., Gorali, Y., Katz, M., & Shalev, A. Y. (2003). A randomized, double-blind, placebo-controlled study of classical homeopathy in generalized anxiety disorder. *Journal of Clinical Psychiatry, 64,* 282–287.

Bradwejn, J., Zhou, Y., Koszycki, D., & Jakov, S. (2000). A double-blind, placebo-controlled study on the effects of gotu kola (Centella asiatica) on acoustic startle response in healthy subjects. *Journal of Clinical Psychopharmacology, 20,* 680–684.

Bryant, R. A., Moulds, M. L., Guthrie, R. M., & Nixon, R.D.V. (2005). The additive benefit of hypnosis and cognitive-behavioral therapy in treating acute stress disorder. *Journal of Consulting and Clinical Psychology, 73,* 334–340.

Cannon, W. B. (1932). *The wisdom of the body.* New York: Norton.

Carroll, D., Ring, C., Suter, M., & Willemsen, G. (2000). The effects of an oral multivitamin combination with calcium, magnesium, and zinc on psychological well-being in healthy young adult male volunteers: A double-blind placebo-controlled trial. *Psychopharmacology, 150,* 220–225.

Chang, M. Y., Wang, S. Y., & Chen, C. H. (2002). Effects of massage on pain and anxiety during labour: A randomized controlled trail in Taiwan. *Journal of Advances in Nursing, 38,* 68–73.

Clark, M. E., & Hirschman, R. (1990). Effects of paced respiration on anxiety reduction in a clinical population. *Biofeedback and Self Regulation, 15,* 273–284.

Cohen, L., Warneke, C., Fouladi, R. T., Rodriguez, M. A., & Chaoul-Reich, A. (2004). Psychological adjustment and sleep quality in a randomized trial of the effects of a Tibetan yoga intervention in patients with lymphoma. *Cancer, 100,* 2253–2260.

Connor, K. M., Payne, V., & Davidson J.R.T. (2006). Kava in generalized anxiety disorder: Three placebo-controlled trials. *International Clinical Psychopharmacology, 21,* 249–253.

Connor, K. M., Zhang, W., Watkins, L., Payne, V., & Davidson, J.R.T. (2005). A pilot study of the effect of omega-3 fatty acids on heart rate variability in anxiety disorders. *Neuropsychopharmacology, 30*(Suppl. 30), S104.

Cooke, B., & Ernst, E. (2000). Aromatherapy: A systematic review. *British Journal of General Practice, 50,* 493–496.

Cooke, M., Chaboyer, W., & Hiratos, M. A. (2005). Music and its effect on anxiety in short waiting periods: A critical appraisal. *Journal of Clinical Nursing, 14,* 145–155.

DeCharms, C. R., Maeda, F., Glover, G. H., Ludlow, D., Pauly, J. M., Soneji, D., et al. (2005). Control over brain activation and pain learned by using real-time functional MRI. *Proceedings of the National Academy of Sciences, 102,* 18626–18631.

Dhawan, K., Kumar, S., & Sharma, A. (2002). Comparative anxiolytic activity profile of various preparations of Passiflora incarnate Linneaus: A comment on medicinal plants' standardization. *Journal of Alternative and Complementary Medicine, 8,* 282–291.

Diego, M. A., Jones, N. A., Field, T., Hernandez-Reif, M., Schanberg, S., Kuhn, C., et al. (1998). Aromatherapy positively effects mood, EEG patterns of alertness and math computations. *International Journal of Neuroscience, 3,* 217–224.

Eisenberg, D. M., David, R. B., Ettner, S. L., Appel, S., Wilkey, S., Van Rompay, M., et al. (1998). Trends in alternative medicine use in the United States, 1990–1997: Results of a follow-up national survey. *Journal of the American Medical Association, 280,* 1569–1575.

Ernst, E., & Kanji, N. (2000). Autogenic training for stress and anxiety: A systematic review. *Complementary Therapies in Medicine, 8,* 106–110.

Evans, D. (2002). The effectiveness of music as an intervention for hospital patients: A systematic review. *Evidence Based Nursing, 37,* 8–18.

Fellowes, D., Barnes, K., & Wilkinson, S. (2004). Aromatherapy and massage for symptom relief in patients with cancer. *Cochrane Database of Systematic Reviews, 2,* CD002287.

Gagne, D., & Toye, R. C. (1994). The effects of therapeutic touch and relaxation therapy in reducing anxiety. *Archives of Psychiatric Nursing, 8,* 184–189.

Graham, P. H., Browne, L., Cox, H., & Graham, J. (2003). Inhalation aromatherapy during radiotherapy: Results of a placebo-controlled double-blind randomized trial. *Journal of Clinical Oncology, 21,* 2372–2376.

Hernandez-Reif, M., Martinez, A., Field, T., Quintero, O., Hart, S., & Burman, I. (2000). Premenstrual symptoms are relieved by massage therapy. *Journal of Psychosomatic Obstetrics and Gynaecology, 21,* 9–15.

Institute of Medicine of the National Academies. (2004). *Dietary supplements: A framework for evaluating safety.* Retrieved October 20, 2006, from www.iom.edu/CMS/3788/4605/19578.aspx

Izzo, A. A. (2004). Drug interactions with St. John's wort (*Hypericum perforatum*): Review of the clinical evidence. *International Journal of Clinical Pharmacology and Therapeutics, 42,* 139–148.

Jossofie, A., Schmiz, A., & Hiemke, C. (1994). Kavapyrone enriched extract from Piper methysticum as a modulator of the GABA binding site in different regions of rat brain. *Psychopharmacology, 116*, 469–474.

Kaptchuk, T. J., & Eisenberg, D. M. (1998). Chiropractic: Origins, controversies, and contributions. *Archives of Internal Medicine, 158*, 2215–2224.

Kasture, V. S., Deshmukh, V. K., & Chopde, C. T. (2002). Anxiolytic and anticonvulsive activity of Sesbania grandiflora leaves in experimental animals. *Phytotherapy Research, 16*, 455–460.

Kennedy, D. O., Little, W., Haskell, C. F., & Scholey, A. B. (2006). Anxiolytic effects of a combination of Melissa officinalis and Valeriana officinalis during laboratory induced stress. *Phytotherapy Research, 20*, 96–102.

Kessler, R. C., Soukup, J., Davis, R. B., Foster, D. F., Wilkey, S. A., Van Rompay, M. I., et al. (2001). The use of complementary and alternative therapies to treat anxiety and depression in the United States. *American Journal of Psychiatry, 158*, 289–294.

Kirkwood, G., Rampes, H., Tuffrey, V., Richardson, J., & Pilkington, K. (2005). Yoga for anxiety: A systematic review of the research evidence. *British Journal of Sports Medicine, 39*, 884–889.

Knaudt, P. R., Connor, K. M., Weisler, R. H., Churchill, L. E., & Davidson, J.R.T. (1999). Alternative therapy use by psychiatric outpatients. *Journal of Nervous and Mental Disease, 187*, 692–695.

Kober, A., Scheck, T., Schubert, B., Strasser, H., Gustorff, B., Bertalanffy, P., et al. (2003). Auricular acupressure as a treatment for anxiety in prehospital transport settings. *Anesthesiology, 98*, 1328–1332.

Krisanaprakornkit, T., Krisanaprakornkit, W., Piyavhatkul, N., & Laopaiboon, M. (2006). Meditation therapy for anxiety disorders. *Cochrane Database of Systematic Reviews*, CD004998.

Lafreniere, K. D., Mutus, B., Cameron, S., Tannous, M., Giannotti, M., Abu-Zahra, H., et al. (1999). Effects of therapeutic touch on biochemical and mood indicators in women. *Journal of Alternative and Complementary Medicine, 5*, 367–370.

Linde, K., Mulrow, C. D., Berner, M., & Egger, M. (2005). St. John's wort for depression: A meta-analysis of randomized controlled trials. *Cochrane Database of Systematic Reviews*, CD000448.

Linden, D.E.J. (2006). How psychotherapy changes the brain—the contribution of functional neuroimaging, *Molecular Psychiatry, 11*, 528–538.

Malathi, A., & Damodaran, A. (1999). Stress due to exams in medical students: Role of yoga. *Indian Journal of Physiology and Pharmacology, 43*, 218–224.

Manuck, S. B. (1976). The voluntary control of heart rate under differential somatic restraint. *Biofeedback and Self-Regulation, 1*, 273–284.

Mok, E., & Woo, C. P. (2004). The effects of slow-stroke back massage on anxiety and shoulder pain in elderly stroke patients. *Complementary Therapies in Nursing and Midwifery, 10*, 209–216.

Moyer, C. A., Rounds, J., & Hannum, J. W. (2004). A meta-analysis of massage therapy research. *Psychological Bulletin, 130*, 3–18.

Oken, B. S., Kishiyama, S., Zajdel, D., Bourdette, D., Carlsen, J., Haas, M., et al. (2004). Randomized controlled trial of yoga and exercise in multiple sclerosis. *Neurology, 62*, 2058–2064.

Olson, M., & Sneed, N. (1995). Anxiety and therapeutic touch. *Issues in Mental Health Nursing, 16*, 97–108.

Perry, N., & Perry, E. (2006). Aromatherapy in the management of psychiatric disorders. *CNS Drugs, 20*, 257–280.

Pittler, M. H., & Ernst, E. (2002). Kava extract for treating anxiety. *Cochrane Database of Systematic Reviews, 2*, CD003383.

Preyde, M. (2000). Effectiveness of massage therapy for subacute low-back pain: A randomized controlled trial. *Canadian Medical Association Journal, 162*, 1815–1820.

Ray, U. S., Mukhopadhyaya, S., Purkayastha, S. S., Asnani, V., Tomer, O. S., Prashad, R., et al. (2001). Effect of yogic exercises on physical and mental health of young fellowship course trainees. *Indian Journal of Physiology and Pharmacology, 45*, 37–53.

Redd, W. H., Manne, S. L., Peters, B., Jacobsen, P. B., & Schmidt, H. (1994). Fragrance administration to reduce anxiety during MR imaging. *Journal of Magnetic Resonance Imaging, 4*, 623–626.

Rice, K. M., Blanchard, E. B., & Purcell, M. (1993). Biofeedback treatments of generalized anxiety disorder: Preliminary results. *Biofeedback and Self Regulation, 18*, 93–105.

Schellenberg, R., Sauer, S., Abourashed, E. A., Koetter, U., & Brattsrom, A. (2004). The fixed combination of valerian and hops (Ze91019) acts via a central adenosine mechanism. *Planta Medica, 70*, 594–597.

Seitz, U., Schule, A., & Gleitz, J. (1997). [^{3}H]-momoamine uptake inhibitor properties of kava pyrones. *Planta Medica, 63*, 548–549.

Shannahoff-Khalsa, D. S., Ray, L. E., Levine, S., Gallen, C. C., Schwartz, B. J., & Sidorowich, J. J. (1999). Randomized controlled trial of yogic meditation techniques for patients with obsessive-compulsive disorder. *CNS Spectrums, 4*, 34–46.

Simington, J. A., & Laing, G. P. (1993). Effects of therapeutic touch on anxiety in the institutionalized elderly. *Clinical Nursing Research, 2*, 438–450.

Soden, K., Vincent, K., Crasken, S., Lucas, C., & Ashley, S. (2004). A randomized controlled trial of aromatherapy massage in a hospice setting. *Palliative Medicine, 18*, 87–92.

Spence, J. E., & Olson, M. A. (1997). Quantitative research on therapeutic touch: An integrative review of the literature 1985–1995. *Scandinavian Journal of Caring Sciences, 11*, 183–190.

Stikel, F., Baumuller, H. M., Seitz, K., Vasilakis, D., Setiz, G., Seitz, H. K., et al. (2003). Hepatitis induced by kava (Piper methysticum rhizome). *Journal of Hepatology, 39*, 62–67.

Taneja, I., Deepak, K. K., Poojary, G., Acharya, I. N., Pandey, R. M., & Sharma, M. P. (2004). Yogic versus conventional treatment in diarrhea-predominant irritable bowel syndrome: A randomized controlled study. *Applied Psychophysiology and Biofeedback, 29*, 19–33.

Turner, J. G., Clark, A. J., Gauthier, D. K., & Williams, M. (1998). The effect of therapeutic touch on pain and anxiety in burn patients. *Journal of Advanced Nursing, 28*, 10–20.

Wang, S. M., & Kain, Z. N. (2001). Auricular acupuncture: A potential treatment for anxiety. *Anesthesia and Analgesia, 92*, 548–553.

Wang, S. M., Peloquin, C., & Kain, Z. N. (2001). The use of auricular acupuncture to reduce preoperative anxiety. *Anesthesia and Analgesia, 93*, 1178–1180.

Wardell, D. W., & Weymouth, K. F. (2004). Review of studies of healing touch. *Journal of Nursing Scholarship, 36*, 147–154.

Watkins, G. R. (1997). Music therapy: Proposed physiological mechanisms and clinical implications. *Clinical Nurse Specialist, 11,* 43–50.

Wiebe, E. (2000). A randomized trial of aromatherapy to reduce anxiety before abortion. *Effective Clinical Practice, 3,* 166–169.

Witte, S., Loew, D., & Gaus, W. (2005). Meta-analysis of the efficacy of the acetonic kava-kava extract WS° 1490 in patients with non-psychotic anxiety disorders. *Phytotherapy Research, 19,* 183–188.

Wolsko, P. M., Eisenberg, D. M., Davis, R. B., & Phillips, R. S. (2004). Use of mind-body medical therapies. *Journal of General Internal Medicine, 19,* 43–50.

Woolery, A., Myers, H., Sternlieb, B., & Zeltzer, L. (2004). A yoga intervention for young adults with elevated symptoms of depression. *Alternative Therapies in Health and Medicine, 10,* 60–63.

World Health Organization. (1993). *International classification of diseases* (10th ed.). Geneva: Author.

Yates, R. G., Lampling, D. L., Abram, N. L, & Wright, C. (1988). Effects of chiropractic treatment on blood pressure and anxiety: A randomized controlled trial. *Journal of Manipulative and Physiologic Therapeutics, 11,* 484–488.

Yehuda, S., Robinovitz, S., & Mostofsky, D. I. (2005). Mixture of essential fatty acids lowers test anxiety. *Nutritional Neuroscience, 8,* 265–267.

Zimmerman, J. (1990). Laying-on-of-hands healing and therapeutic touch: A testable theory. *BEMI Currents Journal of the Bioelectromagnetics Institute, 2,* 8–17.

Exposure-Based Treatments for Anxiety Disorders: Theory and Process

David A. Moscovitch, Martin M. Antony *and* Richard P. Swinson

Abstract

The essential role of exposure in facilitating fear reduction during cognitive behavioral therapy (CBT) for the anxiety disorders is well established. Yet, the precise mechanisms underlying its efficacy have been debated for decades. How and why does fear reduction occur? This question, which is the central focus of the present chapter, is examined in depth via a thorough review of the empirical literature. Clinical applications and implications are discussed in the context of up-to-date experimental research within the broad field of psychological science. Pressing, unanswered research questions are raised, and future research directions are suggested.

Keywords: cognitive behavioral therapy (CBT), emotional processing, exposure, fear extinction, neurobiology, safety learning

Exposure—the repeated and systematic confrontation of feared stimuli—is considered to be an essential ingredient underlying efficacious psychological treatments for most anxiety disorders. Although the central role of exposure in facilitating fear reduction in cognitive behavioral therapy (CBT) has been well established, much about exposure still remains under investigation. For example, what precisely is the purpose of exposure? What are the "feared stimuli" that should be targeted? What is the evidence supporting the theories that guide our understanding of how and why exposure works? What factors moderate and mediate the relationship between exposure and reduction of fear? And, why do a substantial number of individuals with anxiety disorders experience a relapse or return of fear following apparently successful exposure-based CBT?

The purpose of the present chapter is to attempt to answer these and other questions on exposure-based treatments for anxiety disorders via a critical review of the empirical literature. The chapter begins by tracing the history of exposure and briefly describing its current use and efficacy in CBT. Next, mechanisms of exposure are discussed with the goal of understanding how and why fear reduction occurs. This investigation of exposure mechanisms provides the backdrop for a discussion on the importance of the preexposure assessment and the ways in which exposure should be tailored to address idiosyncratic fears across the anxiety disorders. Subsequently, factors related to the process and administration of exposure exercises that have been shown to moderate fear reduction and impact the efficacy of exposure-based treatments are discussed. Finally, the chapter concludes by providing ideas for future directions in research and clinical practice.

Historical Underpinnings of Exposure

Exposure originated from the practice of systematic desensitization, a therapeutic technique popularized by Wolpe (1958, 1961) for the treatment of pathological fear and anxiety. Systematic desensitization rose to prominence during the 1950s and 1960s, during an era in which the field of psychology in North America was dominated by behaviorism. Clinicians who wished to help modify their patients' maladaptive feelings and behaviors began turning to learning theory and the principles of conditioning for direction. Guided by Jacobson's (1938) relaxation techniques, Wolpe and his followers discovered that they could substantially reduce anxiety symptoms in neurotic patients by systematically and repeatedly exposing them imaginally to progressively greater anxiety-provoking descriptions of feared stimuli (prearranged hierarchically) while patients engaged in effortful muscle relaxation. Occasionally, patients were also encouraged to confront anxiety-provoking stimuli in vivo following a prolonged administration of desensitization (e.g., Lazarus, 1963). This paved the way for later researchers (e.g., Agras, Leitenberg, & Barlow, 1968) to discard systematic desensitization and simply treat anxious patients with in vivo exposure by encouraging them to purposely venture away from safe places and directly confront feared cues and situations, an approach that was found to be at least as effective as desensitization plus relaxation (e.g., Emmelkamp & Wessels, 1975). Today, almost five decades after Wolpe's pioneering work, considerable empirical evidence exists from numerous controlled clinical trials demonstrating that exposure-based cognitive behavioral therapies are efficacious first-line psychological interventions for the anxiety disorders (e.g., Barlow, 2002; Barlow, Moscovitch, & Micco, 2004).

Mechanisms of Exposure

Fear reduction is the hallmark of successful exposure, but how and why does fear reduction occur? What are the mechanisms underlying the efficacy of exposure-based treatments for anxiety and why do some individuals either experience relapse after seemingly successful treatment, or fail to benefit from exposure therapy altogether? The essential question here concerns *mediators* of change, which are the variables or processes by which therapeutic change occurs and which account for the relationship between intervention and outcome.

Early Theories

One of the first significant attempts to explain the psychological mechanisms underlying fear acquisition and exposure therapy was based on Mowrer's (1939, 1960) two-stage model. Briefly, Mowrer argued that fears are acquired via classical conditioning

and maintained by the rewarding effects of fear reduction that occurs during escape or avoidance of the aversive stimulus. In simple terms, conditioned fear causes avoidance behavior, which in turn, serves to reinforce the fear. Thus, according to the two-stage theory, exposure directly reduces avoidance behaviors, which subsequently leads to the extinction of learned fear. Although this theory has been extremely influential in shaping our understanding of the relationship between fear and avoidance, as well as the importance of targeting avoidance behaviors in treatment, the two-stage model has been criticized on a number of grounds, which are summarized succinctly by Rachman (1976). Perhaps the most compelling of these critiques is the observation that desynchrony between the three components of fear responding (subjective self-report, physiological arousal, and avoidance behavior) tends to be the rule rather than the exception (e.g., patients often behave courageously despite fear, or alternatively, continue to avoid situations despite low levels of fear). This observation undermined the proposed direct causal link between fear and avoidance and paved the way for new theories to explain the mechanisms underlying exposure.

Early behavior therapists (e.g., Lazarus, 1963; Wolpe, 1958) proposed *reciprocal inhibition* as the mechanism responsible for the therapeutic effects of desensitization, arguing that repeated exposure to fear-evoking stimuli in conjunction with the use of an anxiety-incompatible response in the presence of such stimuli (i.e., relaxation) would ultimately lead to the elimination (or diminution) of learned fear. However, subsequent studies (for reviews, see Kazdin & Wilson, 1978; Yates, 1975) suggested that desensitization works regardless of whether it is paired with relaxation training, thereby negating the explanation of reciprocal inhibition as a possible mechanism of fear reduction.

Habituation

Habituation is frequently cited in the CBT literature as a mechanism of exposure. Habituation refers to a decrement in response as a result of repeated stimulation. In the context of exposure therapy for anxiety disorders, habituation has typically been defined in terms of psychophysiological fear responding (e.g., heart rate, skin conductance), but has also been described in relation to self-reported experiences of fear (e.g., subjective units of distress or SUDS). As outlined by Thompson and Spencer (1966) and reviewed recently by Tryon (2005), the phenomenon of habituation encompasses a number of well-defined characteristics, all of which must be observed in order to conclude that habituation has occurred. However, the pattern of change in fear responding during exposure does not always follow this definition, thus prompting many to criticize this phenomenon as an explanation for the mechanisms that underlie exposure. For example, the principles of habituation require that prolonged exposure will naturally lead to decrements in fear over time, but clinical observation indicates clearly that some patients do not experience or report such decrements, even during lengthy exposures. In addition, habituation implies that a habituated response is always reinstated after exposure to the feared stimulus following an interval or delay, a pattern of responding that would be synonymous with relapse rates of 100% in individuals undergoing exposure therapy, a number that far overestimates actual rates. Moreover, habituation implies that the dishabituated response is transient and likely to quickly rehabituate with restimulation, a pattern of results that is not always achieved even with booster sessions of exposure therapy following the return of fear in individuals with anxiety disorders. Additionally, habituation does not presume that new learning occurs (e.g., Rachman, 1989), but it is now well established that fear reduction involves a process of new learning, as we review in detail below.

Furthermore, anxiety-disordered patients who experience a return of fear typically show increases in self-reported fear without corresponding elevations in psychophysiological responding (e.g., Barlow, 1988), a pattern of results that is impossible to reconcile with habituation theory. Indeed, there is still no convincing evidence that decreased physiological responding is a valid or reliable indicator of anxiety reduction. The literature contains numerous examples of anxiety-disordered patients who experience decreases in physiological responding during exposure but continue to report significant levels of subjective fear, as well as accounts of "courageous" patients (e.g., Rachman, 1978) who experience significant reductions in subjective and behavioral manifestations of anxiety during treatment despite continued high autonomic reactivity (Barlow, 1988). Studies also suggest that, like anxious patients, nonanxious controls experience a gradual decrease in physiological arousal during exposure, even though, for them, exposure stimuli do not arouse any subjective experience of fear (Holdon & Barlow, 1986). Finally, studies on the *return of fear*—the reappearance of fear that has undergone extinction during exposure—have shown that this phenomenon occurs independently of the amount or speed of within-session fear reduction (e.g., Rachman, 1989).

Thus, there are many compelling reasons to discard habituation as an explanation for how exposure leads to fear reduction. Unfortunately, however, habituation enjoys much popularity in the exposure therapy literature because it has, in our view, become a colloquial term synonymous with *fear reduction*. Yet, as discussed above, habituation is a well-defined phenomenon that refers to a specific process that differs from simple fear reduction, which makes its colloquial use inappropriate and confusing. For the sake of clarity, we recommend describing decrements in fear responding during exposure with the term *fear reduction* rather than habituation, and to specifically reference the way in which such decrements are measured (i.e., psychophysiology, self-report, or behavior). We endeavor to do so throughout the remainder of this chapter.

Extinction

Converging research from both animal laboratories and studies on human conditioning suggests that fear reduction during exposure is most parsimoniously understood as a process that is governed by the behavioral principles of *extinction learning*. From a learning theory perspective, Pavlovian extinction is defined as a decrease in responding that occurs when a conditioned stimulus (CS) is presented repeatedly in the absence of the unconditioned stimulus (US). As applied to anxiety disorders, an underlying premise of this view is that pathological fear is a classically conditioned response triggered by a relatively benign CS that has acquired aversive properties through its learned association with a feared US. In practical terms, the CS is the feared stimulus (e.g., an airplane, for an individual with a specific phobia of flying) and the US is the feared consequence (e.g., death by crashing). Thus, individuals with anxiety disorders have been conditioned—though not necessarily through direct traumatic experience (e.g., Mineka & Zinbarg, 2006)—to expect the CS to set the stage for "something bad" to happen and that the ensuing consequences will be "dangerous."

In exposure-based treatments, patients repeatedly and systematically confront feared stimuli under conditions designed to promote extinction of learned fear. Contrary to previous belief, recent evidence (e.g., Rescorla, 2001) has established that the process of behavioral extinction does not involve "unlearning" a previously learned association (e.g., airplane—danger), but rather entails a new, active learning process in which individuals come to attribute novel significance to the CS (airplane—relative safety). Otto and colleagues (e.g., Otto, Smits, & Reese, 2005) have termed this process *safety learning*. During safety learning, the memory of the original meaning is not abolished; rather, separate mental representations of the original and novel meanings of the fear cue (danger versus safety) come to exist in tandem and in competition.

A major implication of this paradigm is that for individuals with anxiety disorders who have undergone exposure therapy and later confront a once-feared stimulus in any particular situation, the current meaning of that stimulus is ambiguous and ultimately depends upon which of the two interpretations is "selected." As Bouton and his colleagues have elegantly shown (for a review, see Bouton, Woods, Moody, Sunsay, & García-Gutiérrez, 2006), which of the two meanings is selected depends heavily upon context. A crucial variable in the selection process appears to be the match or mismatch between the context in which extinction learning occurred and the context in which the fear cue is later confronted. Although *fear acquisition* seems to occur in a relatively context-free manner with wide generalizability, *extinction learning* appears to be particularly context-dependent and discriminatory. This implies, with critical importance for exposure therapy, that if fear of a particular stimulus is extinguished in one context, fear is likely to reemerge if the stimulus is subsequently encountered in a different context (e.g., Bouton, 2004). By this account, *return of fear* reflects the persistence of original conditioning events in memory that are reactivated by contexts other than those associated with successful exposure treatment.

Studies with rats have consistently demonstrated robust context effects leading to a return of fear following extinction. Such effects have been observed for a remarkably wide range of contexts, including both external situations (e.g., rooms, place, environment, background stimuli) and internal states (drugs, hormones, moods, deprivation, recent events, expectancies, and passage of time) (Bouton, 2000, 2002). Numerous controlled studies with human clinical samples indicate that, similar to rats, individuals with anxiety disorders treated with exposure are likely to experience powerful context-dependent learning. In these studies, phobic patients who had been treated with exposure demonstrated return of fear in contexts that contained salient cues that did not match those

associated with extinction, both for distinctive visual cues such as physical setting and characteristics of people in the proximity (e.g., Mineka, Mystkowski, Hladek, & Rodriguez, 1999; Mystkowski, Craske, & Echiverri, 2002; Vansteenwegen et al., 2005), as well as for internal states manipulated by the presence or absence of psychoactive substances (e.g., caffeine versus placebo; Mystkowski, Mineka, Vernon, & Zinbarg, 2003). It should be emphasized that context effects in these studies have been observed for self-reported fear (Mineka et al., 1999; Mystkowski et al., 2002), behavioral indicators of fear (e.g., approach behavior; Mystkowski et al., 2003), and electrodermal response (Vansteenwegen et al., 2005), but have never simultaneously been observed across response types in a concordant fashion within any one study.

Thus, the context-specific nature of safety learning implies that the extinction of learned fear during exposure therapy does not generalize easily to new situations that were not encountered during treatment. Rather, evidence suggests that for safety learning to "stick," retrieval contexts must contain salient internal or external stimuli that match those of the context(s) that predominated during the extinction trials. From a psychotherapeutic standpoint, what follows from this premise is that designing and implementing effective exposures during therapy such that safety learning is accomplished, consolidated, retained, and capable of being retrieved across a broad range of situations requires considerable thought, active effort, and creative collaboration on the part of therapist and patient. Before we discuss these practical and very important clinical considerations, we first take a deeper look at the possible mechanisms underlying extinction learning.

Possible Mechanisms of Extinction Learning

As the preceding discussion highlights, current evidence points to *new learning through the process of behavioral extinction* as the mechanism that best accounts for the relationship between exposure and fear reduction among individuals with anxiety disorders. Indeed, exposure seems to represent the forum that optimally facilitates emotional change through new learning. But precisely what causes extinction learning? In other words, what psychological and biological processes occur or are required to occur during exposure that enable patients to acquire this new association between previously feared cues and a sense of relative safety?

Emotional Processing

Foa and Kozak's (1986) emotional processing theory—later revised by Foa and McNally (1996)—is arguably the most comprehensive and influential account of the processes that govern the encoding of emotional information during exposure. Drawing upon earlier work by Rachman (1980), emotional processing theory builds upon Lang's (1977, 1979) bioinformational framework in which fear is represented as a networked memory structure containing three kinds of information: (1) information about the feared stimulus, situation, or object; (2) information about verbal, autonomic, and behavioral escape/avoidance responses evoked by fear; and (3) critical, idiosyncratic information about the *meaning* of the feared stimulus and fear responses for that individual (e.g., information about threat and/or danger in relation to stimulus and response).

Foa and Kozak (1986) proposed that altering an emotional memory requires *both:* (1) activation of the fear memory, which—in their view—is measured by initial increases in subjective and physiological fear responses during exposure to the feared stimulus; and (2) the encoding of new information that is incompatible with information stored in the existing fear network. In their view, the best indicator of such encoding is what they term *habituation,*[1] defined as within- and across-session reduction in subjective and physiological fear responding following repeated and prolonged exposure to the feared stimulus. Foa and Kozak theorized that four conditions are necessary for such activation and encoding to occur: (1) the content elements of the exposure situation or stimulus must match those contained in the fear structure; (2) the medium through which exposure is conducted (e.g., in vivo versus imaginal) must enable an effective depiction of the fear structure; (3) the duration of each exposure must be sufficient to enable a significant decrease in physiological indicators of fear (e.g., heart rate, skin conductance); and (4) the exposure environment and instructions must permit patients to attend sufficiently to the process of encoding new information.

What, according to emotional processing theory, do anxious individuals learn during exposure that facilitates fear reduction? First, when physiological fear decreases during short-term exposure, new interoceptive information is encoded, signaling the absence of arousal in the presence of the feared stimulus—information that is inconsistent with that contained within the original fear structure. Second, when individuals confront feared stimuli, they encode new information about the *meaning* of such stimuli. Specifically, exposure leads to the inhibition of associations between feared stimuli and propositions about expected threat. Threat propositions include both overestimated probabilities about the likelihood that confronting feared stimuli will produce harmful consequences, as well as catastrophic attributions about the negative valence or so-called badness of such consequences. With respect to overestimated probabilities, patients are likely to have encoded two kinds of information, both of which may require modification: (1) that their anxiety response in the presence of the feared stimulus is likely to persist indefinitely or spiral out of control unless they avoid or escape; and (2) that the fear stimulus itself or their anxiety response to it are likely to cause some kind of identifiable psychological or physical harm. Thus, during within-session short-term fear reduction, the patient "integrates the information that the feared situation constitutes no real danger from without, as well as information that anxiety reactions are of finite intensity and duration" (Foa & Kozak, 1996, p. 28). Repeated exposures over time enable patients to achieve long-term fear reduction as they integrate new information that feared long-term consequences of exposure are also unlikely to occur. In addition, during exposure, patients learn not only that the actual probability of feared consequences occurring is much lower than originally believed, but occasionally also that the consequences themselves are not as aversive as they expected (e.g., an individual with social phobia may indeed blush during exposure but learn that others do not react as negatively as anticipated). This change in valence is accomplished experientially during exposure via contact with information that is incompatible with the original feared beliefs.

Expectancy Violation

Thus, according to emotional processing theory, *fear reduction during exposure requires the learning and integration of new information that is incompatible with existing representations of threat that are coded in memory,* an explanation that is entirely consistent with the extinction learning paradigm discussed earlier. Indeed, current learning theory conceptualizations of the mechanisms underlying extinction learning point to the central role of *expectancy violation.* In Bouton's (2004) words, "each CS presentation arouses a sort of expectation of the US that is disconfirmed on each extinction trial" (p. 491). Thus, for patients with anxiety disorders, the nonoccurrence of feared consequences during exposure violates expectancies, thereby enabling extinction learning to occur. This explanation, which is supported by human laboratory studies of fear acquisition and extinction (for a review, see Vansteenwegen, Dirikx, Hermans, Vervliet, & Eelen, 2006), embodies the notion popularized by Barlow (e.g., Barlow, 1988; Barlow, Allen, & Choate, 2004) that the purpose of exposure and one of the essential components of any psychological treatment for emotional disorders is to facilitate action tendencies (or behaviors) that are opposite those of the dysregulated emotion. Arguably, engaging in *opposite action tendencies* constitutes a powerful learning experience for patients, which violates underlying expectancies about feared stimuli and feared consequences. For example, the agoraphobic patient who behaves opposite his desire to avoid public transportation by choosing to ride on a bus despite extremely high levels of anxiety and fear, learns—contrary to expectation—that his anxiety and fear do not spiral out of control (i.e., *emotional tolerance*) and that feared consequences associated with panicking on the bus (e.g., "I will have a heart attack") are unlikely to occur. Presumably, he also learns a sense of mastery or control over the situation ("I can choose to engage in this behavior despite my anxiety."). This perspective is also consistent with therapeutic models that emphasize *behavioral activation* as a fundamental process underlying reduction of negative emotions (e.g., Jacobson, Martell, & Dimidjian, 2001), as well as cognitive therapy models that highlight the importance of *behavioral experiments* and *hypothesis testing* in facilitating cognitive and emotional change (e.g., Beck, Rush, Shaw, & Emery, 1979; Bennett-Levy et al., 2004).

Neurobiological Mechanisms

What are the corresponding neurobiological mechanisms of extinction learning? Tryon's Parallel Distributed Processing Connectionist Neural Network (PDP-CNN) model (e.g., Tryon, 2005) depicts the processing and learning of new information that occurs during exposure therapy as a cascade of synaptic activation that spreads across different levels of a networked neural system. At its most basic level, this model implies that new learning modifies connection weights between the synapses within the network. According to Tryon, successful cascade changes in the network underlie simultaneous changes in dysregulated cognitions, emotions, and behaviors that constitute the pathological fear response.

Although Tryon's specific model still lacks concrete empirical support, converging evidence from

the field of cognitive neuroscience over the past few decades does support the notion that specific, identifiable brain circuits mediate changes in fear responding that occur as a result of extinction learning. Research has implicated the medial prefrontal cortex and amygdala, and the connections between them, as the primary neural system underlying fear extinction (e.g., Sotres-Bayon, Bush, & Ledoux, 2004). As reviewed by Sotres-Bayon et al. (2004), numerous laboratory studies on both rats and humans indicate that during the process of extinction, the medial prefrontal cortex plays a crucial role in regulating the amygdala-mediated expression of conditioned fear by inhibiting the retrieval of previously learned fear associations. Glutamatergic N-methyl-D-aspartate (NMDA) receptors throughout the brain mediate the process of associative learning, and activation of these receptors within the amygdala appears to be essential for extinction learning in particular. It has been shown that extinction of fear memories can either be blocked or enhanced by administration of NMDA receptor antagonists or agonists, respectively, which act on receptor sites within the amygdala. Sotres-Bayon and colleagues (2004) propose that the context-dependent effects of extinction learning and retrieval may reflect the involvement of the hippocampus in this process. Specifically, hippocampal projections to the medial prefrontal cortex may serve as contextual constraints that set the stage for retrieval of conditioned fear memories.

One of the most significant recent developments in the field of anxiety disorders has been the experimental use of the pharmacological agent D-cycloserine (DCS), a partial NMDA agonist, to augment exposure therapy and facilitate the process of extinction learning. Two double-blind, placebo-controlled trials have now been published demonstrating the superior efficacy of DCS plus brief exposure therapy in comparison to placebo plus brief exposure therapy for patients with specific phobia of heights (Ressler et al., 2004) and social phobia (Hofmann et al., 2006). In these trials, DCS was administered acutely and intermittently prior to exposure sessions with minimal adverse side effects. In their paper, Ressler and collaborators (2004) underscore the point that the augmenting effects of DCS appeared to occur *between* rather than within sessions, suggesting that "the NMDA-dependent phase of extinction training occurs during the post-extinction consolidation period" (p. 1142), a finding that has potentially critical implications for cognitive models that emphasize the central role of information processing biases in the maintenance of anxiety disorders (e.g., Clark, 1986; Clark & Wells, 1995; Ehlers & Clark, 2000). According to such models (e.g., Clark & Wells, 1995), anxiety disorders persist for years—often despite repeated exposure to information that should conceivably disconfirm erroneous beliefs regarding the likelihood and/or cost of the occurrence of feared consequences—because patients engage in inadequate or biased processing of new, incoming information. If these information processing biases interfere with extinction learning, and if DCS enhances extinction learning by facilitating consolidation—a process during which the labile new memory trace undergoes stabilization and is incorporated into long-term memory (e.g., Dudai, 2004)—it would be interesting and important to investigate whether and how the effects of DCS impact (or are impacted by) such information processing biases.

Some Final Thoughts on Mechanisms of Exposure

If, as described above, *new associative learning* mediates the relationship between exposure and fear reduction, it should technically be possible to design studies that establish an unambiguous causal chain linking the three variables in the hypothesized temporal sequence (e.g., Kraemer, Wilson, Fairburn, & Agras, 2002). In other words, such studies should demonstrate that exposure precedes and causes new learning and that new learning precedes and causes fear reduction. Unfortunately, designing such studies presents innumerable methodological challenges. For example, how does one measure the construct of "new learning" in real time (i.e., "online" or while it is occurring)? Even if one determines how to measure learning in real time, how does one do so without relying on participants' self-report, which—if measured online—is likely to interfere with the process of learning itself? Moreover, how is it possible to determine the epoch during which new learning should be measured? Indeed, new learning also involves the process of memory consolidation, which is vital to the ultimate integration of new information into long-term memory and which is likely to persist long after the termination of an exposure (e.g., Dudai, 2004). Thus, it is evident that both new learning and fear reduction occur during exposure, but without clear experimental evidence that establishes a causal, temporally sequenced link between the variables, we are left to wonder: Is it more accurate to state that new learning causes fear reduction or that fear reduction

causes new learning? Future research must determine whether one or both possibilities are factual statements. Furthermore, some writers (e.g., Brewin, 2006) now propose that the integral change process underlying efficacious CBT does not involve the direct modification of fear representations per se; rather, what changes during treatment is the relative salience or accessibility of existing positive versus negative mental representations. According to this view, CBT works by facilitating the accessibility of previously inhibited positive mental representations in response to such cues, which, prior to treatment, automatically activated negative mental representations and concomitant emotional experiences. This intriguing theory requires empirical support.

Maximizing Exposure Outcomes: Moderating Variables

Although much has been written about the benefits and apparent simplicity of "facing one's fears," it is crucial to remember that the extinction of learned fear during exposure is a tenuous, fragile process that requires careful attention to a myriad of variables that may work to moderate (by enhancing or interfering with) the encoding, consolidation, and retrieval of new learning. In this section, we discuss several possible moderating variables and how they may impact exposure process and outcomes.

The Importance of Precise Assessment and Conceptualization of the Anxiety Disorders

What happens when patients report during CBT that a particular exposure is completely ineffective? In these instances, a patient may confront the so-called feared stimulus but experience absolutely no activation or decrease in fear or anxiety, or alternatively, may experience no changes in catastrophic attributions. In our view, one of the most common causes of such failure is inadequate prior conceptualization of the crucial elements of the patient's disorder.

Designing an effective exposure during treatment for any anxiety disorder should begin with a meticulous assessment of the idiosyncratic nature of the patient's fear. Specifically, therapist and patient should work collaboratively to understand the patient's: (1) feared stimuli (what are the precise objects or foci of the patient's fear?); (2) feared consequences (what is the patient afraid will happen if the feared stimuli are confronted?); (3) fear-related avoidance, escape, and safety behaviors (what does the patient typically do to try to prevent his or her feared consequences from occurring?); and finally,

(4) fear triggers and contexts (what cues, contexts, and situations are associated for the patient with his or her feared stimuli and, therefore, likely to trigger feelings of anxiety and use of avoidance behaviors?).

We will use social phobia as an example to illustrate the above framework (for a more detailed review of this framework and its application to social phobia, please see Moscovitch, in press). What is the feared stimulus for individuals with social phobia? Some have argued that patients with social phobia fear embarrassment or criticism and negative evaluation from others. Although they typically do fear such outcomes, we contend that embarrassment or criticism and negative evaluation are the feared consequences rather than the feared stimuli per se. The object of fear, or feared stimulus, in social phobia can be conceptualized as *specific characteristics of self* that one believes are deficient and likely to be criticized if revealed or exposed for public scrutiny. To understand this crucial difference between feared stimuli and feared consequences in social phobia, it may be helpful to consider an analogy to panic disorder: just as in panic disorder, going crazy or dying are the feared consequences of heightened physical sensations and panic, in social phobia, negative evaluation is the "catastrophic" consequence that individuals with social phobia believe will transpire if they reveal to potentially critical others particular aspects of themselves about which they are ashamed.

Although all patients with social phobia share the fear that they will publicly expose "deficient" aspects of themselves to critical others, there is considerable heterogeneity between patients with social phobia in terms of the specific self-attributes they perceive as being deficient. As reviewed by Moscovitch (in press), clinical observation and converging research evidence suggest that perceived self-deficiencies in social phobia can be divided into four general dimensions: (1) perceived flaws in social skills and behaviors (e.g., "I will do something stupid"; "I will have nothing to say"; etc.); (2) perceived flaws in physical appearance (e.g., "I am dressed inappropriately"; "I am ugly"; etc.); (3) perceived flaws in concealing potentially visible signs of anxiety (e.g., "I will sweat"; "My hands will shake"; etc.); and (4) perceived characterological (i.e., personality-related) flaws (e.g., "I am boring"; "I am stupid"; etc.). These are not mutually exclusive categories, as individuals with social phobia, particularly those with the generalized subtype, often report concerns across all four dimensions. However, some individuals with social phobia, particularly those with the nongeneralized or discrete subtypes, may report concerns that are confined to only one or two dimensions.

Once we understand patient's specific feared stimuli and consequences, it is relatively straightforward to predict and assess that patient's avoidance and safety behaviors as well as the contexts and situations that tend to trigger his or her fear. Indeed, in the anxiety disorders, *avoidance behaviors and situational fear triggers are always functionally related to and flow logically from feared stimuli and feared consequences.* Thus, a patient with social phobia who fears that he is dull or boring is likely to be particularly afraid of social situations in which he may have to reveal personal information about himself to others (e.g., one-on-one conversations, dating situations, cocktail parties, etc.). He is likely to avoid such situations or, when confronted with them, to employ safety behaviors such as asking an excessive number of questions of the other person to deflect attention away from himself, or mentally censoring or over-rehearsing what he is going to say before he says it. On the other hand, a patient with social phobia who fears exhibiting physical symptoms of anxiety that may be visible to others, such as blushing or sweating, will likely fear and avoid performance situations (e.g., public speaking, job interviews) or social encounters in which she could become the center of attention (e.g., having dinner with colleagues). This individual might use a different set of safety behaviors, such as wearing clothing that hides perceived "problem areas" (e.g., turtlenecks if the individual is negatively focused on blushing around her neck; or suit jackets if the individual is focused on sweating through her shirt, etc.), carrying items to help cover up or fix perceived problem areas (e.g., "cover up" make-up, hats, scarves, handkerchiefs, etc.,), taking medications (e.g., benzodiazepines) to prevent anxious arousal that leads to visible physical symptoms, and frequently leaving social situations to visibly inspect herself in the mirror.

This framework can be applied by the therapist not only to social phobia, but also to the entire spectrum of anxiety disorders. Once the assessment is complete and precise information has been collected about the patient's feared stimuli, consequences, situational fear triggers, and avoidance/safety behaviors, designing and setting up an effective exposure is straightforward. Collecting this information will enable therapist and patient to collaboratively implement exposures that will allow the patient to confront feared stimuli, perform clear and unambiguous tests of feared consequences, and eliminate avoidance and safety behaviors that interfere with the acquisition of new, corrective learning.

Maximizing Attention to Exposure-Based Learning and Eliminating Safety Behaviors

Successful exposure outcomes require individuals to learn new information that violates expectancies about the feared stimulus, and to integrate such information into existing memory structures. Thus, it is not surprising that research has found exposure outcomes to be enhanced by variables that maximize patient attention to exposure-based learning. Individuals with anxiety disorders tend to engage in negatively biased cognitive processes that interfere with the learning and consolidation of new information and maintain anxious states (e.g., Clark, 1986; Clark & Wells, 1995; Ehlers & Clark, 2000). For example, when faced with social threat, individuals with social phobia shift their attention inward and engage in a process of detailed self-monitoring (e.g., Spurr & Stopa, 2002), during which they neglect the processing of incoming external information and instead focus on spontaneous, recurrent, and excessively negative self-images, which they believe to be accurate (Hackmann, Clark, & McManus, 2000; Hackmann, Surawy, & Clark, 1998). Hirsch and Matthews (2000) reported that, in contrast to nonanxious control participants who tended to construe ambiguous social situations as positive when asked to examine them as they unfolded ("online"), patients with social phobia failed to demonstrate either positive or negative online inferences, suggesting that they might have a tendency to miss important online positive cues and, as a result, may lack the positive inferential online bias that characterizes the cognitive processes of nonanxious controls. Following social encounters, individuals with social phobia tend to engage in negatively biased postevent processing in which they focus on perceived instances of social failure while discounting any indicators of social success that may help disconfirm their pervasive negative beliefs (e.g., Clark & Wells, 1995; Rachman, Grüter-Andrew, & Shafran, 2000).

In an attempt to counteract these information processing biases and maximize the benefits of exposure for their anxiety disordered patients, Wells and Papageorgiou (1998) specifically instructed individuals with social phobia during exposure to focus their attention externally, survey the environment objectively, and notice salient social cues in their environment, such as other people's reactions to them. They found that this simple manipulation led to significant reductions in both social anxiety and negative beliefs. Although researchers have yet to examine directly the mechanisms that may account for these effects, Wells and Papageorgiou (1998) suggested that an external attentional focus may promote these changes by weakening patients' single-minded concentration on interoceptive cues of anxiety, thereby disrupting the ruminative cycle of self-focused attention that facilitates the maintenance of safety behaviors and discourages patients from generating and considering alternative beliefs (e.g., Salkovskis, 1991).

Indeed, preliminary studies suggest that many patients with anxiety disorders can successfully drop their safety behaviors when instructed to do so during exposure (e.g., Wells et al., 1995). In social phobia, dropping safety behaviors leads to reductions in subjective levels of anxiety and perception of social threat, which facilitates exposure outcomes during treatment (Garcia-Palacios & Botella, 2003; Morgan & Raffle, 1999; Wells et al., 1995). Such findings have spurred investigators to pilot test computer-based dot-probe attention training paradigms to treat anxiety disorders, which have shown promising initial results despite the complete absence of traditional therapeutic interventions (Mohlman, 2004). The purpose of such training paradigms is simply to facilitate corrective focus of attention away from feared stimuli and toward other prominent environmental cues.

Thus, during exposure, patients with anxiety disorders are likely to focus their attention on cues in the environment that are consistent with and reinforce elements of their pathological fear structure. Moreover, they will employ subtle avoidance and safety behaviors that will prevent them from fully engaging in the exposure and confronting potentially corrective information in the exposure environment that is inconsistent with existing fear memories. Therefore, it is imperative for therapists to explicitly direct their patients' attention during exposure to the cues that are inconsistent with such memories, so that patients can encode and integrate new safety learning. Some investigators have observed that even subtle cognitive maneuvers, such as distraction, may prevent fear reduction and new learning during or between exposures (Kamphuis & Telch, 2000; Rodriguez & Craske, 1993; Telch et al., 2004), although other studies on distraction have shown that it does not have a detrimental effect on exposure outcomes (e.g., Johnstone & Page, 2004; Oliver & Page, 2003). In addition, recent findings by Telch and colleagues in a cleverly designed study with claustrophobic patients indicated that therapists should design exposures such that patients discard not only the use of safety behaviors, but also their availability (Powers, Smits, & Telch, 2004). Their study demonstrated that for participants who perceived that safety aids were available for use during exposure (to facilitate escape or avoidance of feared stimuli), fear reduction was significantly disrupted—even if such safety aids were never actually used—in comparison to participants who believed that escape or avoidance was not an option.

Context-Specificity

As reviewed in the preceding sections, research from both animal and human studies suggests that extinction learning is remarkably context-specific. It appears that what individuals learn during extinction is the association of CS-no US *within a particular context,* such that safety learning becomes conditional upon the context in which it occurred. With this in mind, Bouton (2000, 2002) and others (e.g., Powers, Smits, Leyro, & Otto, 2007) have recommended certain specific, practical steps that therapists can implement during exposure to ensure that its effects will be more durable and generalizable to multiple contexts. First, numerous exposures should be conducted across multiple contexts during therapy, so that patients can encode and integrate into memory multiple context-specific traces of new learned associations of safety, thereby creating multiple cues for later retrieval of such learning. In addition to maximizing the number of exposure contexts, varying the properties of the exposure stimulus may further increase the durability and generalizability of safety learning (e.g., for an individual with a specific phobia of dogs, exposing him or her to multiple dogs across multiple settings rather than just one dog across multiple settings).

Moreover, it is important for clinicians to be mindful of the patient's internal context during exposure. Research has shown that what medicated rats learn during extinction trials may not transfer well to nonmedicated states due to shifts in internal context (Bouton, Kenney, & Rosengard, 1990). Similarly, patients who undergo exposure therapy while taking psychotropic medications may learn to associate safety cues with the "feel" of being on those medications, thus making them vulnerable to relapse when medications are later discontinued and they confront feared stimuli in the presence of an internal context that is different from the one that predominated during therapy (e.g., Bouton, 2002;

Otto, 2002). As pointed out by Otto, Smits, and Reese (2005), this conceptualization is supported by data from multicenter trials of combined CBT-and-medication treatments for panic disorder with agoraphobia (Barlow, Gorman, Shear, & Woods, 2000; Marks et al., 1993), in which patients who received CBT alone exhibited enhanced long-term outcomes relative to those who received combined treatment with medication discontinuation after the acute phase of therapy. Thus, some investigators (e.g., Otto et al., 2005) recommend that for patients receiving simultaneous CBT-medication treatment, CBT should be extended beyond the period of medication discontinuation. When CBT is conducted without medications, patients will learn to associate extinction learning with an internal emotional context of heightened anxiety. Moreover, ensuring that extinction trials include occasional aversive emotional outcomes (e.g., anxious arousal or panic attacks) may further inoculate patients against relapse.

We also recommend that clinicians collect information during therapy on contexts in which patients might be particularly vulnerable to relapse after therapy, and then specifically instruct patients to conduct exposure practices in those contexts or in the presence of contextual cues that remind them of those contexts. Furthermore, clinicians should experiment with embedding retrieval cues into exposure practices that patients associate with "safety learning" and then train patients to actively recall those cues when confronted later with relapse contexts, thereby providing an aid to help bridge the extinction context with potential relapse contexts (Bouton, 2002). Finally, clinicians should make sure to include a relapse prevention component in therapy in which they prepare patients for inevitable future increases in symptoms due to context-specific return of fear. During this process, patients should list predictable situations or contexts that may predispose them to relapse and outline an active plan that they will follow to extinguish symptom increases via exposure practice.

Exposure Frequency and Duration

How long should an individual exposure session last and how frequently should exposures occur during therapy? Research investigating the optimal duration and spacing of exposure sessions has attained mixed results, although methodological and measurement variability have hampered comparisons across studies. An early study investigating this issue in systematic desensitization therapy for patients with specific phobia of animals found a slight advantage for distributed over massed exposure sessions (Ramsay, Barends, Brueker, & Kruseman, 1966). In a second study, Foa, Jameson, Turner, and Payne (1980) compared outcomes in agoraphobic patients who were randomly assigned to receive either 10 daily (massed) or 10 weekly (spaced) sessions of in-vivo exposure. They reported that both conditions were effective in reducing subjective levels of fear and anxiety, but massed exposure was more effective in reducing agoraphobic avoidance. Other studies have found no differences in outcomes between the two types of exposure schedules (e.g., Chambless, 1990).

In an attempt to address these inconsistent findings, Craske and colleagues have suggested that it is important to investigate the benefits of spacing time *between* exposure sessions (to enable between-session consolidation of learning) while still ensuring that patients receive sufficient time in the presence of feared stimuli *within* exposure sessions (to maximize within-session extinction learning). To this end, Rowe and Craske (1998) and Tsao and Craske (2000) conducted controlled studies in which a massed (single day) exposure schedule was compared to an expanding-spaced exposure schedule (in which the amount of time between sessions increased as treatment progressed, with a massed schedule initially and a more distributed or spaced schedule in the later stages of therapy). Participants in these studies had specific phobia of spiders (Rowe & Craske, 1998) and public speaking anxiety (Tsao & Craske, 2000). Tsao and Craske (2000) also included a uniform-spaced exposure therapy schedule as a control condition. Outcomes were assessed at pretreatment, within each session, posttreatment, and 1-month follow-up. The most consistent finding from both studies was that participants who received a massed exposure schedule experienced significantly *more* return of fear at follow-up compared to the other conditions. In the Rowe and Craske (1998) study, these results were obtained despite findings showing that participants who received massed exposure experienced greater levels of subjective fear reduction across sessions and lower subjective fear, heart rate, and perceived danger at the postassessment, and that participants who received expanding-spaced exposure demonstrated significant increases in heart rate across exposure sessions.

Massed continuous within-session exposures may be important in the initial stages of treatment because they maximize extinction learning by allowing patients to strongly disconfirm negative outcome expectancies, while later distributed exposures allow for the consolidation of such learning (Craske & Mystkowski, 2006). Drawing upon data in the animal literature indicating that extinction is induced most effectively if rats confront a feared stimulus (i.e., the CS) during each exposure trial for a period of time that exceeds the duration of the CS during fear acquisition, Craske and Mystkowski (2006) predict that optimal treatment outcomes will be achieved with exposures that each last as long as it takes patients to learn that confronting feared stimuli does not lead to the occurrence of feared consequences. If this line of reasoning is correct, it would be essential for clinicians to ask their patients explicitly prior to exposure at what point during exposure such expectancies would be disconfirmed, and then to ensure that exposures last at least that long. This notion, which is intriguing, awaits further study.

Fear Activation and Reduction During Exposure

As described earlier, emotional processing theory postulates that successful exposure outcomes are facilitated when (1) the fear structure is activated with stimuli that match those represented in memory; and (2) when physiological arousal is attenuated in the presence of feared stimuli through repeated and prolonged exposure without escape or avoidance. Although most CBT practitioners support the notion that fear activation and attenuation during exposure is necessary for successful outcomes, what story do the data support?

In an early study by Foa, Blau, Prout, and Latimer (1977), rat-phobic participants were assigned to one of three prolonged imaginal exposure conditions that differed according to the level of harshness of scene presentation. Results indicated that participants responded comparably to all three conditions, and showed no differences in both self-reported anxiety and willingness to later approach a live rat. The authors concluded that inducing horror is not necessary for efficacious exposure during flooding, but that prolonged confrontation with the feared stimulus is essential. It is important to note, however, that this study did not directly address the question of fear activation and there may have been a ceiling effect such that all participants—even those in the more pleasant imaginal conditions—were sufficiently aroused during exposure to achieve successful outcomes.

Studies that have directly measured the relationship between fear activation and exposure outcomes have reported mixed findings, with some showing that fear activation during exposure predicts more favorable treatment responses in patients with posttraumatic stress disorder (PTSD) (Foa, Riggs, Massie, & Yarczower, 1995) and obsessive-compulsive disorder (OCD) (Kozak, Foa, & Steketee, 1988), and others demonstrating that greater fear activation during the initial stages of exposure predicts poorer posttreatment outcomes (i.e., less subjective fear reduction) for patients with PTSD (van Minnen & Hagenaars, 2002) and specific phobia of enclosed spaces (Kamphuis & Telch, 2000; Telch et al., 2004; Telch, Valentiner, Ilai, Petruzzi, & Hehmsoth, 2000). These equivocal findings may indicate that while it is crucial to activate underlying fear structures during exposure in order to facilitate new learning associated with disconfirmation of outcome expectancies, very high levels of arousal may disrupt exposure outcomes. Indeed, this notion is consistent with Foa and McNally's (1996) revised emotional processing account, in which they argue that optimal treatment outcomes require *moderate* levels of within-session arousal. This conceptualization is also consistent with converging evidence across therapy orientations that the in-session activation of specific, relevant emotions is important for therapeutic change, provided that emotional engagement is effectively combined with cognitive processing that facilitates conscious reflection and the construction of new meaning (Whelton, 2004). Indeed, too much fear activation may impair the encoding of new information during exposure.

If it is important for exposures to elicit at least moderate levels of anxiety, is it also important for patients to stay in exposure situations until their anxiety decreases? Interestingly, research indicates that treatment outcomes are positively associated with levels of *between-session* but *not* within-session fear reduction (e.g., Kozak et al., 1988; van Minnen & Hagenaars, 2002). There is no evidence to suggest that reductions in self-reported or autonomic arousal during exposure are important for successful treatment. Contrary to common belief, Craske and Mystkowski (2006) propose that conditions that promote *sustained excitation* during exposure may be as effective as conditions that promote reductions in autonomic arousal (e.g., Lang & Craske, 2000), provided—of course—that the exposure lasts long enough to permit new, relevant learning to occur (see also Craske, Kircanski, Zelikowsky, Mystkowski, Chowdhury, et al., 2008). Relatively long exposures that do not facilitate decreased physiological arousal may still be sufficient for patients

to learn both that the feared stimulus is not actually dangerous and that their anxiety, although high, will not spiral out of control. Presumably, such learning is then consolidated and integrated into memory between exposure sessions.

As noted above, Telch and colleagues have shown that variables that interfere with this consolidation process are likely to impair treatment outcomes while factors that facilitate this process are likely to enhance outcomes. For example, Telch et al. (2004) reported that patients who were assigned to exposure conditions that promoted distraction demonstrated slower between-session fear reduction, which led to poorer overall outcomes. Kamphuis and Telch (2000) demonstrated that between-session fear reduction was facilitated by exposure manipulations that guided patients to challenge their negative appraisals of feared stimuli while explicitly focusing their attention on relevant threats during exposure. This condition was also associated with significantly enhanced treatment outcomes.

Other Possible Moderators

A number of other factors that may moderate the efficacy of exposure have been investigated and described in detail in the literature, including (1) the importance of maximizing predictability and patients' perception of control during exposure; (2) the relative efficacy of various exposure modalities (e.g., imaginal exposure, in-vivo exposure, interoceptive exposure, and the use of technologies such as virtual reality to enhance exposure); (3) the impact of vicarious exposure (i.e., therapist modeling) on fear reduction; and (4) the importance and cost-effectiveness of interventions that promote self-directed exposure via homework assignments, self-help books, and the new wave of computer and Internet-based therapies. Unfortunately, space constraints prevent us from undertaking a detailed review of these topics here. We recommend that the interested reader consult a recent overview by Antony and Swinson (2000).

Summary and Future Directions

For many clinical psychologists, the laboratory and the clinic are intricately intertwined. Current research informs clinical practice, while insights gained during therapy instigate the generation of innovative ideas that are tested in controlled studies. In our current era of evidence-based treatment, the dual agenda of both understanding the science and perfecting the practice of exposure-based CBT has risen to new prominence.

Although exposure therapy was known to be an efficacious treatment for anxiety disorders long before we understood why, ongoing research on the processes that mediate and moderate fear reduction has only recently begun to illuminate the mechanisms of exposure. Evidence now indicates that fear reduction during exposure occurs when patients successfully learn and consolidate new, context-dependent information that is incompatible with both existing memory-bound representations of threat and patients' own expectancies of feared consequences. Underlying such learning is an intricate NMDA-mediated neurobiological network involving the prefrontal cortex, amygdala, and hippocampus.

Despite our accumulation of this knowledge, successful exposure outcomes are often elusive, even for experienced and well-informed clinicians. As we've seen, the process of maximizing safety learning relies on a myriad of interconnected variables that are, themselves, moderated by individual differences ranging from the idiosyncratic nature of patients' fears, safety behaviors, and information processing biases, to the internal and external contexts, duration, frequency, and fear-eliciting properties of exposure practices. Clearly, this is a process fraught with many potential pitfalls and one that requires a skillful therapeutic integration of both scientific principles and clinical artistry.

As we have attempted to highlight throughout this chapter, many questions remain to be answered regarding the theory and process of exposure. Future studies will now also be required to clarify the relationship and boundaries between exposure and the so-called "third wave" of behavioral interventions, which emphasize the importance of acceptance-based strategies in the treatment of anxiety disorders (e.g., Acceptance and Commitment Therapy; Hayes, Luoma, Bond, Masuda, & Lillis, 2006). The recent emergence of acceptance- and mindfulness-based therapies as viable, empirically supported interventions for anxiety and its disorders has led many to conceptualize them as conceptually distinct alternatives to traditional exposure-based CBT. In our view, however, experiential acceptance has always been an important component of exposure, in which patients are encouraged to confront and tolerate aversive stimuli without fighting their anxiety, distracting themselves, or avoiding. Perhaps one of the major differences between the two approaches concerns the relative emphasis on the *process* of managing internal experience (e.g., thoughts, feelings, and behaviors). While acceptance-based interventions tend to focus explicitly on one's relationship with one's internal experience and promote acceptance of such experience as a desirable outcome in itself, CBT has traditionally focused on the content of internal experience (e.g., specific thoughts, feelings, and behaviors), even though the process of accepting internal experience has also been emphasized, albeit largely implicitly and not as a desired outcome in itself. Future studies will, no doubt, help elucidate whether a more explicit focus on acceptance enhances CBT outcomes for patients with anxiety disorders, as well as shed light on the numerous additional questions that we have raised on the theory and process of exposure.

Notes

This project was undertaken, in part, thanks to funding from the Canada Research Chairs Program, awarded to the first author.

1. Note that proponents of emotional processing theory (Foa & Kozak, 1986; Foa & McNally, 1996), as well as others, employ the term *habituation* as being synonymous with *fear reduction*, which in our view is a confusing misnomer, as discussed above. Thus, throughout this chapter, we use the term *fear reduction* rather than *habituation* to describe decreases in subjective or physiological fear responses.

References

Agras, W. S., Leitenberg, H., & Barlow D. H. (1968). Social reinforcement in the modification of agoraphobia. *Archives of General Psychiatry, 19,* 423–427.

Antony, M. M., & Swinson, R. P. (2000). *Phobic disorders and panic in adults: A guide to assessment and treatment.* Washington, DC: American Psychological Association.

Barlow, D. H. (1988). *Anxiety and its disorders: The nature and treatment of anxiety and panic.* New York: Guilford Press.

Barlow, D. H. (2002). *Anxiety and its disorders: The nature and treatment of anxiety and panic* (2nd ed.). New York: Guilford Press.

Barlow, D. H., Allen, L. B., & Choate, M. L. (2004). Toward a unified treatment for emotional disorders. *Behavior Therapy, 35,* 205–230.

Barlow, D. H., Gorman, J. M., Shear, M. K., & Woods, S. W. (2000). Cognitive-behavioral therapy, imipramine, or their combination for panic disorder: A randomized control trial. *Journal of the American Medical Association, 283,* 2529–2536.

Barlow, D. H., Moscovitch, D. A., & Micco, J. A. (2004). Psychotherapeutic interventions for phobias. In H. S. Akiskal, A. Okasha, J. J. Lopez-Ibor, & M. Maj (Eds.), *World Psychiatric Association volume on phobias for evidence and experience in psychiatry* (pp. 179–215). Hoboken, NJ: Wiley.

Beck, A. T., Rush, A. J., Shaw, B. F., & Emery, G. (1979). *Cognitive therapy of depression.* New York: Guilford Press.

Bennett-Levy, J., Butler, G., Fennell, M., Hackman, A., Mueller, M., & Westbrook, D. (Eds.). (2004). *Oxford guide to behavioural experiments in cognitive therapy.* New York: Oxford University Press.

Bouton, M. E. (2000). A learning theory perspective on lapse, relapse, and the maintenance of behavior change. *Health Psychology, 19*(1, Suppl.), 57–63.

Bouton, M. E. (2002). Context, ambiguity, and unlearning: Sources of relapse after behavioral extinction. *Biological Psychiatry, 52,* 976–986.

Bouton, M. E. (2004). Context and behavioral processes in extinction. *Learning and Memory, 11,* 485–494.

Bouton, M. E., Kenney, F. A., & Rosengard, C. (1990). State-dependent fear extinction with two benzodiazepine tranquilizers. *Behavioral Neuroscience, 104,* 44–55.

Bouton, M. E., Woods, A. M., Moody, E. W., Sunsay, C., & García-Gutiérrez, A. (2006). Counteracting the context-dependence of extinction: Relapse and some tests of possible methods of relapse prevention. In M. G. Craske, D. Hermans, & D. Vansteenwegen (Eds.), *Fear and learning: From basic processes to clinical implications* (pp. 175–196). Washington, DC: American Psychological Association.

Brewin, C. R. (2006). Understanding cognitive behaviour therapy: A retrieval competition account. *Behaviour Research and Therapy, 44,* 765–784.

Chambless, D. L. (1990). Spacing of exposure sessions in treatment of agoraphobia and simple phobia. *Behavior Therapy, 21,* 217–229.

Clark, D. M. (1986). A cognitive approach to panic. *Behaviour Research and Therapy, 24,* 461–470.

Clark, D. M., & Wells, A. (1995). A cognitive model of social phobia. In R. G. Heimberg, M. R. Liebowitz, D. A. Hope, & F. R. Schneier (Eds.), *Social phobia: Diagnosis, assessment, and treatment* (pp. 69–93). New York: Guilford Press.

Craske, M. G., Kircanski, K., Zelikowsky, M., Mystkowski, J. L., Chowdhury, N., & Baker, A. (2008). Optimizing inhibitory learning during exposure therapy. *Behaviour Research and Therapy, 46,* 5–27.

Craske, M. G., & Mystkowski, J. L. (2006). Exposure therapy and extinction: Clinical studies. In M. G. Craske, D. Hermans, & D. Vansteenwegen (Eds.), *Fear and learning: From basic processes to clinical implications* (pp. 217–233). Washington, DC: American Psychological Association.

Dudai, Y. (2004). The neurobiology of consolidations, or, how stable is the engram? *Annual Review of Psychology, 55,* 51–86.

Ehlers, A., & Clark, D. M. (2000). A cognitive model of post-traumatic stress disorder. *Behaviour Research and Therapy, 38,* 319–345.

Emmelkamp, P.M.G., & Wessels, H. (1975). Flooding in imagination vs. flooding in vivo: A comparison with agoraphobics. *Behaviour Research and Therapy, 13,* 7–15.

Foa, E. B., Blau, J. S., Prout, M., & Latimer, P. (1977). Is horror a necessary component of flooding (implosion)? *Behaviour Research and Therapy, 15,* 397–402.

Foa, E. B., Jameson, J. S., Turner, R. M., & Payne, L. L. (1980). Massed vs. spaced exposure sessions in the treatment of agoraphobia. *Behaviour Research and Therapy, 18,* 333–338.

Foa, E. B., & Kozak, M. J. (1986). Emotional processing of fear: Exposure to corrective information. *Psychological Bulletin, 99,* 20–35.

Foa, E. B., & McNally, R. J. (1996). Mechanisms of change in exposure therapy. In R. Rapee (Ed.), *Current controversies in the anxiety disorders* (pp. 329–343). New York: Guilford Press.

Foa, E. B., Riggs, D. S., Massie, E. D., & Yarczower, M. (1995). The impact of fear activation and anger on the efficacy of exposure treatment for posttraumatic stress disorder. *Behavior Therapy, 26,* 487–499.

Garcia-Palacios, A., & Botella, C. (2003). The effects of dropping in-situation safety behaviors in the treatment of social phobia. *Behavioral Interventions, 18,* 23–33.

Hackmann, A., Clark, D. M., & McManus, F. (2000). Recurrent images and early memories in social phobia. *Behaviour Research and Therapy, 38,* 601–610.

Hackmann, A., Surawy, C., & Clark, D. M. (1998). Seeing yourself through others' eyes: A study of spontaneously occurring images in social phobia. *Behavioural and Cognitive Psychotherapy, 26,* 3–12.

Hayes, S. C., Luoma, J. B., Bond, F. W., Masuda, A., & Lillis, J. (2006). Acceptance and commitment therapy: Model, processes and outcomes. *Behaviour Research and Therapy, 44,* 1–25.

Hirsch, C. R., & Matthews, A. (2000). Impaired positive inferential bias in social phobia. *Journal of Abnormal Psychology, 109,* 705–712.

Hofmann, S. G., Meuret, A. E., Smits, J.A.J., Simon, N. M., Pollack, M. H., Eisenmenger, K., et al. (2006). Augmentation of exposure therapy with D-Cycloserine for social anxiety disorder. *Archives of General Psychiatry, 63,* 298–304.

Jacobson, E. (1938). *Progressive relaxation.* Chicago: University of Chicago Press.

Jacobson, N. S., Martell, C. R., & Dimidjian, S. (2001). Behavioral activation treatment for depression: Returning to contextual roots. *Clinical Psychology: Science and Practice, 8,* 255–270.

Johnstone, K. A., & Page, A. C. (2004). Attention to phobic stimuli during exposure: The effect of distraction on anxiety reduction, self-efficacy and perceived control. *Behaviour Research and Therapy, 42,* 249–275.

Kamphuis, J. H., & Telch, M. J. (2000). Effects of distraction and guided threat reappraisal on fear reduction during exposure-based treatments for specific fears. *Behaviour Research and Therapy, 38,* 1163–1181.

Kazdin, A. E., & Wilson, G. T. (1978). *Evaluation of behavior therapy: Issues, evidence, and research strategies.* Cambridge, MA: Ballinger.

Kozak, M. J., Foa, E. B., & Steketee, G. (1988). Process and outcome of exposure treatment with obsessive-compulsives: Psychophysiological indicators of emotional processing. *Behavior Therapy, 19,* 157–169.

Kraemer, H. C., Wilson, G. T., Fairburn, C. G., & Agras, W. S. (2002). Mediators and moderators of treatment effects in randomized clinical trials. *Archives of General Psychiatry, 59,* 877–884.

Lang, A. J., & Craske, M. G. (2000). Manipulations of exposure-based therapy to reduce return of fear: A replication. *Behaviour Research and Therapy, 38,* 1–12.

Lang, P. J. (1977). Imagery in therapy: An information processing analysis of fear. *Behavior Therapy, 8,* 862–886.

Lang, P. J. (1979). A bio-informational theory of emotional imagery. *Psychophysiology, 16,* 495–512.

Lazarus, A. A. (1963). The results of behaviour therapy in 126 cases of severe neurosis. *Behaviour Research and Therapy, 1,* 69–79.

Marks, I. M., Swinson, R. P., Başoğlu, M., Kuch, K., Noshirvani, H., O'Sullivan, G., et al. (1993). Alprazolam and exposure alone and combined in panic disorder with agoraphobia: A controlled study in London and Toronto. *British Journal of Psychiatry, 162,* 776–787.

Mineka, S., Mystkowski, J. L., Hladek, D., & Rodriguez, B. I. (1999). The effects of changing contexts on return of fear following exposure therapy for spider fear. *Journal of Consulting and Clinical Psychology, 67,* 599–604.

Mineka, S., & Zinbarg, R. (2006). A contemporary learning theory perspective on the etiology of anxiety disorders: It's not what you thought it was. *American Psychologist, 61,* 10–26.

Mohlman, J. (2004). Attention training as an intervention for anxiety: Review and rationale. *The Behavior Therapist, 27,* 37–41.

Morgan, H., & Raffle, C. (1999). Does reducing safety behaviors improve treatment response in patients with social phobia? *Australian and New Zealand Journal of Psychiatry, 33,* 503–510.

Moscovitch, D. A. (in press). What is the core fear in social phobia?: A new model to facilitate individualized case conceptualization and treatment. *Cognitive and Behavioral Practice.*

Mowrer, O. H. (1939). A stimulus-response analysis of anxiety and its role as a reinforcing agent. *Psychological Review, 46,* 553–565.

Mowrer, O. H. (1960). *Learning theory and the symbolic processes.* New York: Wiley.

Mystkowski, J. L., Craske, M. G., & Echiverri, A. M. (2002). Treatment context and return of fear in spider phobia. *Behavior Therapy, 33,* 399–416.

Mystkowski, J. L., Mineka, S., Vernon, L. L., & Zinbarg, R. E. (2003). Changes in caffeine states enhance return of fear in spider phobia. *Journal of Consulting and Clinical Psychology, 71,* 243–250.

Oliver, N. S., & Page, A. C. (2003). Fear reduction during in vivo exposure to blood-injection stimuli: Distraction vs. attentional focus. *British Journal of Clinical Psychology, 42,* 13–25.

Otto, M. W. (2002). Learning and "unlearning" fears: Preparedness, neural pathways, and patients. *Biological Psychiatry, 52,* 917–920.

Otto, M. W., Smits, J.A.J., & Reese, H. E. (2005). Combined psychotherapy and pharmacotherapy for mood and anxiety disorders in adults: Review and analysis. *Clinical Psychology: Science and Practice, 12,* 72–86.

Powers, M. B., Smits, J.A.J., Leyro, T. M., & Otto, M. W. (2007). Translational research perspectives on maximizing the effectiveness of exposure therapy. In D.C.S. Richard & D. L. Lauterbach (Eds.), *Handbook of exposure therapies* (pp. 109–126). Burlington, MA: Academic Press.

Powers, M. B., Smits, J. A., & Telch, M. J. (2004). Disentangling the effects of safety-behavior utilization and safety-behavior availability during exposure-based treatment: A placebo-controlled trial. *Journal of Consulting and Clinical Psychology, 72,* 448–454.

Rachman, S. (1976). The passing of the two-stage theory of fear and avoidance: Fresh possibilities. *Behaviour Research and Therapy,* 125–131.

Rachman, S. (1978). *Fear and courage.* San Francisco: Freeman.

Rachman, S. (1980). Emotional processing. *Behaviour Research and Therapy, 14,* 349–355.

Rachman, S. (1989). The return of fear: Review and prospect. *Clinical Psychology Review, 9,* 147–168.

Rachman, S., Grüter-Andrew, J., & Shafran, R. (2000). Post-event processing in social anxiety. *Behaviour Research and Therapy, 38,* 611–617.

Ramsay, R. W., Barends, J., Brueker, J., & Kruseman, A. (1966). Massed versus spaced desensitization of fear. *Behaviour Research and Therapy, 4,* 205–207.

Rescorla, R. A. (2001). Experimental extinction. In R. R. Mowrer & S. B. Klein (Eds.), *Handbook of contemporary learning theories* (pp. 119–154). Mahwah, NJ: Erlbaum.

Ressler, K. J., Rothbaum, B. O., Tannenbaum, L., Anderson, P., Graap, K., Zimand, E., et al. (2004). Cognitive enhancers as adjuncts to psychotherapy. *Archives of General Psychiatry, 61,* 1136–1144.

Rodriguez, B. I., & Craske, M. G. (1993). The effects of distraction during exposure to phobic stimuli. *Behaviour Research and Therapy, 31,* 549–558.

Rowe, M. K., & Craske, M. G. (1998). Effect of an expanding-spaced vs. massed exposure schedule on fear reduction and return of fear. *Behaviour Research and Therapy, 36,* 701–717.

Salkovskis, P. M. (1991). The importance of behaviour in the maintenance of anxiety and panic: A cognitive account. *Behavioural Psychotherapy, 19,* 6–19.

Sotres-Bayon, F., Bush, D.E.A., & Ledoux, J. E. (2004). Emotional perseveration: An update on prefrontal-amygdala interactions in fear extinction. *Learning and Memory, 11,* 525–535.

Spurr, J. M., & Stopa, L. (2002). Self-focused attention in social phobia and social anxiety. *Clinical Psychology Review, 22,* 947–975.

Telch, M. J., Valentiner, D. P., Ilai, D., Petruzzi, D., & Hehmsoth, M. (2000). The facilitative effects of heart-rate feedback in the emotional processing of claustrophobic fear. *Behaviour Research and Therapy, 38,* 373–387.

Telch, M. J., Valentiner, D. P., Ilai, D., Young, P. R., Powers, M. B., & Smits, J.A.J. (2004). Fear activation and distraction during the emotional processing of claustrophobic fear. *Journal of Behavior Therapy and Experimental Psychiatry, 35,* 219–232.

Thompson, R. F., & Spencer, W. A. (1966). Habituation: A model phenomenon for the study of neuronal substrates of behavior. *Psychological Bulletin, 73,* 16–43.

Tryon, W. W. (2005). Possible mechanisms for why desensitization and exposure therapy work. *Clinical Psychology Review, 25,* 67–95.

Tsao, J.C.I., & Craske, M. G. (2000). Timing of treatment and return of fear: Effects of massed-, uniform-, and expanding-spaced exposure schedules. *Behavior Therapy, 31,* 479–497.

Van Minnen, A., & Hagenaars, M. (2002). Fear activation and habituation patterns as early process predictors of response to prolonged exposure treatment in PTSD. *Journal of Traumatic Stress, 15,* 359–367.

Vansteenwegen, D., Dirikx, T., Hermans, D., Vervliet, B., & Eelen, P. (2006). Renewal and reinstatement of fear: Evidence from human conditioning research. In M. G. Craske, D. Hermans, & D. Vansteenwegen (Eds.), *Fear and learning: From basic processes to clinical implications* (pp. 175–196). Washington, DC: American Psychological Association.

Vansteenwegen, D., Hermans, D., Vervliet, B., Francken, G., Beckers, T., Baeyens, F., et al. (2005). Return of fear in a human differential conditioning paradigm caused by a return to the original acquisition context. *Behaviour Research and Therapy, 43,* 323–336.

Wells, A., Clark, D. M., Salkovskis, P., Ludgate, J., Hackmann, A., & Gelder, M. (1995). Social phobia: The role of in-situation safety behaviors in maintaining anxiety and negative beliefs. *Behavior Therapy, 26,* 153–161.

Wells, A., & Papageorgiou, C. (1998). Social phobia: Effects of external attention on anxiety, negative beliefs, and perspective taking. *Behavior Therapy, 29,* 357–370.

Whelton, W. J. (2004). Emotional processes in psychotherapy: Evidence across therapeutic modalities. *Clinical Psychology and Psychotherapy, 11,* 58–71.

Wolpe, J. (1958). *Psychotherapy by reciprocal inhibition.* Stanford, CA: Stanford University Press.

Wolpe, J. (1961). The systematic desensitization treatment of neuroses. *Journal of Nervous and Mental Disease, 132,* 189–203.

Yates, A. J. (1975). *Theory and practice in behavior therapy.* New York: Wiley.

Mindfulness and Acceptance-Based Treatments for Anxiety Disorders

Lizabeth Roemer, Shannon M. Erisman *and* Susan M. Orsillo

Abstract

This chapter provides an overview of mindfulness and acceptance-based approaches to treating anxiety and anxiety disorders. A description of these therapeutic approaches is provided, followed by a conceptual/empirically based rationale for applying these approaches to psychotherapy for anxiety. Emphasized are the potential role of (1) cultivating expanded, present-moment focus rather than narrowed, future focus; (2) targeting avoidance of and reactivity to internal experiences; (3) facilitating emotional skills and regulation; and (4) promoting mindful, intended action and approach behavior in the successful treatment of anxiety disorders. This is followed by a review of open trial and randomized controlled trials, as well as experimental and case studies, of mindfulness- and acceptance-based treatments for anxiety disorders. Directions for future research conclude the chapter.

Keywords: acceptance, anxiety, anxiety disorders, mindfulness, psychotherapy, treatment

Although mindfulness and acceptance-based approaches to addressing or treating psychological difficulties have a long history (e.g., Buddhist traditions of mindfulness practice to reducing suffering, see Olendzki [2005], for an overview; Rogers's [1961] emphasis on acceptance in psychotherapy), recently, theoretical interest in the role of these constructs in psychological health has been renewed and empirically based approaches to their integration in psychotherapy have flourished (e.g., Baer, 2006; Hayes, Follette, & Linehan, 2004). A full review of the approaches within this domain is beyond the scope of this chapter; instead we provide a brief review of those treatments that integrate mindfulness and acceptance into behavioral or cognitive approaches to treating anxiety and related disorders. Readers should see Orsillo and Roemer (2005) for a book-length presentation of this area.

Description of Acceptance and Mindfulness-Based Approaches

Kabat-Zinn (1994) defines mindfulness as "paying attention, in a particular way: on purpose, in the present moment, nonjudgmentally" (p. 4). Bishop et al. (2004) recently proposed a two-component definition: self-regulation of attention toward immediate experience, with that attention characterized by openness, curiosity, and acceptance. Thus, mindfulness includes both awareness of the present moment and a particular quality of that awareness: compassionate, nonreactive, and nonjudging. Several therapeutic approaches (described in more detail below) have incorporated a wide range of exercises, ranging from formal meditation to mindfully washing the dishes, aimed at cultivating this kind of awareness, under the assumption that this will promote psychological well-being (e.g., Segal, Williams, & Teasdale, 2002).

Mindfulness derives from forms of Buddhist meditation that emphasize nonjudgmental awareness of whatever occurs in the present moment, without attaching to any internal or external content. Although we acknowledge that taking mindfulness out of the context of Buddhist practice and into the domain of psychotherapy involves altering potentially important contextual factors and elements (Walsh & Shapiro, 2006), here we focus primarily on the way that mindfulness has been used by psychologists and other health professionals.

A central element of what we have called acceptance-based behavioral treatments (Orsillo, Roemer, & Holowka, 2005) is accepting or allowing one's internal experiences as opposed to judging, reacting to, or trying to eliminate them. Hayes, Strosahl, and Wilson (1999) highlight the ways that nonacceptance of, or efforts to avoid, one's internal experience (i.e., experiential avoidance) can in fact paradoxically increase distress and impair functioning. Linehan (1993a) emphasizes the importance of balancing acceptance- and change-oriented approaches in treatment. The emphasis in these and other acceptance-based treatment approaches is not on resigning oneself to distress, but rather on recognizing that distressing thoughts, feelings, and sensations are an inevitable part of human experience and therefore reducing futile and often maladaptive efforts to eliminate these experiences. This stance allows distress to rise and fall naturally, and reduces secondary reactions to one's distress that can increase its intensity and duration. Effort can then be more effectively applied to living one's life more fully and approaching previously avoided contexts of value to the individual (Wilson & Murrell, 2004).

Clearly, mindfulness and acceptance are closely related constructs. Mindfulness practice involves bringing an acceptance stance to one's experience (Bishop et al., 2004) and mindfulness practice can be seen as a way of developing acceptance toward one's experience. Both acceptance and mindfulness are thought to involve seeing one's thoughts and feelings as just thoughts and feelings, rather than as a reflection of one's true self or the permanent state of one's life (e.g., decentering, Segal et al., 2002; defusion, Hayes et al., 1999; disidentification, Walsh & Shapiro, 2006). Although a number of distinct acceptance- and mindfulness-based approaches have been developed, considerable overlap exists, prompting Hayes (2004) to propose a third wave of behavior therapy, characterized by approaches that emphasize changing the context surrounding one's internal experiences rather than their content.

Although an extensive review of each specific approach is beyond the scope of this chapter (see Hayes, Follette, & Linehan, 2004, and Baer, 2006, for book-length reviews of a range of acceptance- and mindfulness-based interventions), we briefly review the most researched, broadly applied treatments before discussing the theoretical and empirical basis for applying acceptance- and mindfulness-based treatments to anxiety disorders and the empirical support for these applications.

Acceptance and commitment therapy (ACT) (Hayes et al., 1999) evolved from a comprehensive behavioral account of human language that specifies the ways that humans come to respond to their thoughts as if they were actual events (e.g., the thought "I might be rejected" elicits the same response as an actual rejection), resulting in fear of and efforts to avoid these internal experiences that paradoxically increase distress and also impair functioning. This therapy uses metaphors and experiential exercises to help clients (1) recognize the limits of experiential control efforts, (2) defuse from their internal experiences so that they experience their thoughts and feelings as transient events, and (3) increase their willingness to engage in personally meaningful and valued behaviors. Randomized controlled trials provide preliminary evidence of the efficacy of this approach for psychotic symptoms, smoking cessation, polysubstance abuse, and workplace stress (see Hayes, Masuda, Bissett, Luoma, & Guerrero, 2004, for a review) as well as anxiety, as reviewed below.

Mindfulness-based stress reduction (MBSR) is a health promotion program developed by Jon Kabat-Zinn for individuals with a broad range of medical or psychological presentations. In this 8-week program, which is led like a class, participants are introduced to formal meditation practice, yoga, and other mindfulness exercises. Although this intervention is explicitly not a psychotherapeutic approach (and providers are not necessarily mental health professionals), MBSR has been associated with significant symptom reduction in individuals with anxiety disorders and binge eating disorder (see Baer, 2003, for a review) and was associated with a medium effect on mental health outcomes in a meta-analysis of controlled studies (Grossman, Niemann, Schmidt, & Walach, 2004). It has also been adapted by Segal and colleagues (2002) into mindfulness-based cognitive therapy (MBCT), a program that has been shown to significantly reduce the risk of relapse among individuals who have recovered from depression with a history of at least three prior depressive episodes (see Baer, 2003, for a review).

Dialectical behavior therapy (DBT) (Linehan, 1993a, 1993b), which incorporates individual therapy, group skills training, telephone consultations, and therapist consultation groups, was initially developed to comprehensively treat individuals with borderline personality disorder (BPD), and has more recently expanded to address other presenting problems. Skills groups include a mindfulness skills module, as well as application of mindfulness skills to distress tolerance, emotion regulation, and interpersonal effectiveness. To target the emotion dysregulation thought to underlie borderline personality disorder and other disorders, an emphasis is placed on validating emotional experiences, recognizing that emotional responses are natural and can be beneficial, while also skillfully using and managing one's emotions rather than being overly influenced by them (e.g., choosing actions rather than allowing them to be solely emotionally driven). Randomized controlled trials have demonstrated the efficacy of DBT in treating BPD, with and without comorbid substance abuse, as well as eating disorders (see Hayes, Masuda, et al., 2004, for a review).

Potential Mechanisms of Change

Acceptance and mindfulness-based approaches may enhance treatment of anxiety disorders for a variety of reasons, some disorder-specific and some general. Below we highlight some of the potential mechanisms that apply across the anxiety disorders; see Orsillo and Roemer (2005) for a more extensive review of both general and disorder-specific approaches.

Cultivating Expanded, Present Focus Rather Than Narrowed, Future Focus

A large body of information-processing research (see Chapter 12 for a review) suggests that anxiety is characterized by a preattentive bias toward threat and a focus on potential future threat, rather than present moment experience, resulting in narrowed attention. This has prompted some researchers to propose attentional training as a potential treatment for anxiety disorders (e.g., Wells, 1990), which is characterized by a more focused target of attention than mindfulness. Mindfulness practice is proposed to enhance attentional abilities, including cultivation of an expanded attentional focus.[1] In addition, the emphasis on bringing one's attention to the present moment may reduce the future focus associated with anticipatory anxiety and worry (Borkovec,

2002). This expanded, present-moment focus may also set the stage for more effective efforts at behavioral change due to enhanced ability to detect early cues and make choices regarding alternative actions. The extensive, repeated practice associated with mindfulness interventions may help to counter the rigid, narrowed attentional focus that characterizes individuals with anxiety disorders.

Targeting Avoidance of and Reactivity to Internal Experiences

Fear and avoidance are central characteristics of the range of anxiety disorders, although the focal nature and targets of these responses vary (e.g., social situations for social anxiety disorder, internal and external trauma cues for posttraumatic stress disorder [PTSD], physiological sensations for panic disorder), prompting exposure-based treatments to become treatments of choice for the majority of individuals with these disorders (see Chapter 35). Research on fear of fear (Goldstein & Chambless, 1978) and interoceptive conditioning (Bouton, Mineka, & Barlow, 2001) has highlighted the way that individuals can develop distress responses to their own internal sensations and fearful responses, thus prompting heightened fear and anxiety. Relatedly, research on anxiety sensitivity (Taylor, Koch, & McNally, 1992) has demonstrated that beliefs regarding the harmfulness of anxiety may underlie panic disorder in particular, but also other anxiety disorders. Thus, emotional or cognitive reactions to one's experience of fear and anxiety may play an important role in the development and maintenance of anxiety disorders.

Recent research and theory has identified the clinical relevance of reactivity to and avoidance of a wider range of internal experiences. Fear of emotions (including anger, depression, and positive emotions) is associated with symptoms of generalized anxiety disorder (GAD) (Mennin, Heimberg, Turk, & Fresco, 2005; Roemer, Salters, Raffa, & Orsillo, 2005), social anxiety disorder (SAD) (Turk, Heimberg, Luterek, Mennin, & Fresco, 2005), and fear of panic sensations in the laboratory (Williams, Chambless, & Ahrens, 1997). Efforts to avoid distressing thoughts may have paradoxical effects, contributing to the development and maintenance of anxiety disorders, although some inconsistent findings have been reported (see Purdon, 1999, for a review). Finally, studies have revealed associations between experiential or emotional avoidance and a range of anxious symptoms (see Hayes, Luoma, Bond, Masuda, & Lillis, 2006; Salters-Pedneault,

Tull, & Roemer, 2004, for reviews). Many of these studies have been correlational and used analogue populations; more research is needed to determine the causal or maintaining role and clinical relevance of these processes. However, in a recent study, clients with anxiety and mood disorders rated their emotional responses to a distressing film clip as less acceptable than a nondistressed control group, and reported more efforts to suppress these emotional responses (Campbell-Sills, Barlow, Brown, & Hofmann, 2006a). Further, lower acceptability ratings predicted heightened suppression efforts, which in turn predicted reduced emotional recovery, supporting the model proposed above. Interventions that promote acceptance and mindfulness may effectively target this detrimental experiential reactivity and avoidance.

Facilitation of Emotional Skills and Regulation

The reactivity to emotional experiences and avoidant, ineffective management of emotions that seem to characterize individuals with anxiety disorders can be seen as one aspect of broader deficits in emotional skills and regulation. Mennin (2005) has recently proposed that individuals with anxiety disorders may exhibit a range of difficulties with their emotional responding and its regulation, including poor understanding of their emotions, increased reactivity to their emotions (as described above), and deficits in their ability to manage their emotions (including excessive use of avoidant strategies). Barlow, Allen, and Choate (2004) have similarly noted that individuals with anxiety disorders may exhibit emotional avoidance and a relative inability to modify action tendencies associated with emotional responses that leads to problematic behavioral responses (such as avoidance). Mennin (2005) and Barlow et al. (2004) review the body of research that supports these models (e.g., panic disorder, SAD, and GAD have all been associated with poor clarity of emotional responses, and habitual engagement in emotional action tendencies (i.e., avoidance) characterizes all of the anxiety disorders).

Although interventions such as those proposed by Mennin (2005) and Barlow and colleagues (2004) may more explicitly target these difficulties, mindfulness and acceptance-based approaches may also facilitate effective regulation of emotion in several ways. Enhanced, nonjudgmental awareness of emotional responses is likely to enhance clarity and understanding of emotional responses, as well as reduce emotional reactivity, as described above.

Also, mindfulness practice may decrease automaticity, which would allow clients to notice emotional action tendencies without habitually engaging in them. Further, seeing one's emotions as transient and not fused to one's sense of self can reduce the tendency to avoid (or act on) these emotional responses. Hayes and Feldman (2004) note that mindfulness practice can reduce both overengagement with, and avoidance of, emotional responses, thus facilitating "healthy" engagement with one's emotions, which is characterized by, among other things, awareness and attention to emotions, present-moment focus, and a nonjudgmental stance. Correlational studies have supported the proposed relationship between self-reports of acceptance, mindfulness, and enhanced emotion regulation (e.g., Baer, Smith, Hopkins, Krietemeyer, & Toney, 2006). Further, an experimental study found that acceptance (versus suppression) instructions were associated with enhanced recovery from a distressing stimulus among clients with emotional disorders (Campbell-Sills, Barlow, Brown, & Hofmann, 2006b), suggesting that these processes may affect regulation of emotion.[2]

Promotion of Mindful, Intended Action and Approach Behavior

Anxiety disorders are characterized by both overt behavioral avoidance and more subtle constriction and nonengagement in valued actions (Orsillo, Roemer, Block, & Tull, 2004) as evidenced by the demonstrated reductions in quality of life associated with these clinical disorders (see Orsillo et al., 2005, for a review). Exposure-based treatments, in which clients repeatedly engage in habitually avoided behaviors, gradually broadening restricted behavioral repertoires, have demonstrated efficacy across the anxiety disorders (see Chapter 35). Efficacy of exposure-based treatment requires functional exposure to feared stimuli (Foa & Kozak, 1986), suggesting that present-moment, expanded attentional focus may facilitate its efficacy. (Jacobson, Martell, and Dimidjian [2001] similarly suggest mindfulness may enhance behavioral activation; a client's increased contact with his children will only be naturally reinforced if he is attending to his children while he is with them.) Acceptance-based approaches, such as ACT, which emphasize identifying what is important to the individual, may also provide an important motivational basis for exposures by more explicitly connecting them to the parts of the client's life that have become restricted. This, along with the increased internal awareness associated with mindfulness practice, may facilitate selection of exposure tasks that are broadly meaningful, rather than solely based on sources of fear and anxiety.

The valued action component of ACT, along with the concept of mindful, intended action (e.g., Chodron, 2001) from Buddhist writings, suggest the incorporation of a broad emphasis on behavior in which individuals are encouraged to choose their actions, rather than simply reacting to situations in habitual ways (concepts that are consistent with traditional behavioral approaches to behavior change and Barlow and colleagues' [2004] emphasis on the importance of modification of emotion action tendencies). Cultivation of increased awareness of internal and external contexts, coupled with practice in not reacting to these stimuli, is expected to promote intended, rather than habitual, actions that are consistent with what is important to the individual.

Existing Research

A comprehensive review of correlational research in this area is beyond the scope of this chapter; however, there is a growing body of evidence that mindfulness and acceptance are negatively associated with reports of anxious symptoms (see Hayes et al., 2006; Salters-Pedneault et al., 2004, for reviews). We review below the existing data from analogue studies, case studies, open trials, and randomized controlled trials. We then go on to describe research that is currently in progress, along with other directions for future research.

Experimental/Analogue Research

Several studies have explored the effects of brief acceptance interventions in the laboratory on anxiety or related outcomes. Individuals high in anxiety sensitivity reported lower levels of avoidance, subjective fear, and catastrophic cognitions in response to carbon dioxide (CO_2) exposure following acceptance versus control or no instructions (Eifert & Heffner, 2003), while individuals with panic disorder similarly reported less subjective anxiety, as well as greater willingness to participate in a similar task, in response to CO_2 exposure after acceptance versus suppression instructions or a neutral narrative (Levitt, Brown, Orsillo, & Barlow, 2004). Individuals diagnosed with anxiety or mood disorders showed better cardiac recovery following a distressing film clip in an acceptance than in a suppression condition, although the opposite pattern emerged for reports of negative affect (Campbell-Sills et al.,

2006b). The absence of a no instruction condition in the latter study precludes determination of whether suppression interfered with cardiac recovery or acceptance enhanced it; however, both conclusions support the potential efficacy of acceptance-based interventions in promoting recovery, particularly given that clients with emotional disorders may habitually suppress their emotional responses (Campbell-Sills et al., 2006a). Similarly, Feldner, Zvolensky, Stickle, Bonn-Miller, and Leen-Feldner (2006) found that suppression instructions (compared to observation instructions) led to increased heart rate during the recovery period following CO_2 exposure, although subjective anxiety was not affected by the manipulation. Two studies have also revealed an association between trait levels of experiential avoidance and anxious responding to a biological challenge: Feldner, Zvolensky, Eifert, and Spira (2003) found that individuals with high trait levels of experiential avoidance, compared to those with low trait levels of experiential avoidance, reported heightened subjective anxiety when instructed to suppress their responses during a CO_2 exposure, while Karekla, Forsyth, and Kelly (2004) found that individuals with high levels of experiential avoidance reported heightened subjective responses to CO_2 exposure in the absence of any instructions. Overall, these studies suggest that acceptance may ameliorate anxious responding and/or suppression/experiential avoidance may exacerbate it, with subjective distress affected in the short term and physiological recovery affected over time, indicating that acceptance-based interventions may be efficacious in treating anxiety.

Case Studies

Several case study reports of the use of mindfulness or acceptance-based approaches for individuals with diagnosed anxiety disorders have been published recently. López (2000) treated a 28-year-old man with a 5-year history of panic disorder with agoraphobia with 12 sessions of ACT (in Spanish), resulting in substantial decreases in self-report measures of anxiety and behavioral avoidance. Findings are limited by the absence of formal diagnostic or follow-up assessment, although the report of a "mutual friend" over the course of a 3-year follow-up suggested maintenance of treatment gains. Batten and Hayes (2005) treated a young woman with comorbid PTSD, due to childhood sexual abuse, and substance abuse with 96 sessions of ACT, resulting in sobriety and reported depressive and psychological symptoms below clinical levels at posttreatment as well as at 12-month follow-up, without any additional psychotherapy during this time period. However, the absence of specific assessments of posttraumatic symptomatology precludes unequivocal conclusions regarding the effect of this intervention on PTSD. Orsillo, Roemer, and Barlow (2003) treated four clients with GAD and other comorbid disorders with a pilot group intervention that integrated traditional cognitive behavioral treatment for GAD with mindfulness and acceptance-based strategies (drawing heavily from ACT).[3] Clients demonstrated statistically significant reductions in self-reported worry, depressive and anxious symptoms, as well as in experiential avoidance, posttreatment; however, only two of four clients reached responder and high end state functioning status, suggesting a need for further treatment development. Finally, Singh, Wahler, Winton, and Adkins (2004) treated a 25-year-old woman diagnosed with chronic obsessive-compulsive disorder (OCD), with an extensive history of unsuccessful pharmacological and psychosocial treatments, along with five hospitalizations in the previous year, with a 16-week mindfulness-based intervention that consisted of meditation and mindfulness instruction and a strong emphasis on Buddhist principles of Right Mindfulness and Right Action (all behaviors engaged in mindfully). The client discontinued her medication following treatment and reported substantial decreases in self-reported distress and depression, as well as clinician-rated OCD symptoms at both post- and 2-year follow-up, along with no additional treatment or hospitalizations.

Single Case Designs

An eight-session adaptation of ACT was evaluated using a nonconcurrent multiple baseline across participants design in four individuals diagnosed with OCD (Twohig, Hayes, & Masuda, 2006). Reductions in frequency of compulsive behavior were noted following the implementation of the intervention in all four cases and notable reductions in self-reported OCD, anxious, and depressive symptoms that improved or maintained at 3-month follow-up were observed, along with reductions in reported experiential avoidance and the need to react to obsessions. In a similar study investigating an adaptation of ACT for the treatment of skin picking (Twohig, Hayes, & Masuda, 2006), four of five clients reported reductions in skin picking from pre- to posttreatment, but only one of the five participants maintained these gains at the 3-month follow-up assessment, suggesting a need for future treatment development.

Open Trial and Randomized Controlled Trials

Methodological details from the four published open trial investigations and two randomized controlled trials of acceptance- and mindfulness-based treatments for anxiety are presented in Tables 1 and 2. Evidence suggests that MBSR may effectively target panic and GAD, although an absence of posttreatment diagnostic assessment limits conclusions that can be drawn (Kabat-Zinn et al. 1992). A treatment designed to directly target the self-focused attention that is characteristic of individuals with social phobia shows promising results (Bogels, Sijbers, & Voncken, 2006). This treatment first teaches expanded attention and then teaches clients to focus specifically on the demands of a task, rather than themselves, in order to enhance task performance and reduce anxiety. An ACT treatment that integrates exposure also shows initial promise in the treatment of the generalized subtype of social anxiety disorder (Dalrymple & Herbert, 2007). Another promising intervention is an integrated acceptance-based behavioral therapy for GAD that combines psychoeducation about the function of emotions and problems with emotional control, acceptance- and mindfulness-based strategies, and value-driven action (Roemer & Orsillo, 2007). In the treatment of trichotillomania, ACT shows promise when it is combined with habit reversal training (Woods, Wetterneck, & Flessner, 2006), and ACT alone generally yields comparable results to systematic desensitization in the treatment of math anxiety among students (Zettle, 2003).

Taken together, the existing studies suggest the potential of mindfulness- and acceptance-based treatments for the treatment of anxiety disorders (particularly GAD, OCD, and SAD), although considerably more research is needed to determine if effects are clinically significant, robust, and comparable to or better than those for existing treatments. In particular, given the emphasis on broader functioning in these approaches, whether they have enhanced effects on measures of functioning and quality of life should be more fully explored. Also, although preliminary evidence suggests that these approaches target hypothesized mechanisms of change, more research is needed to determine whether defusion, reduced experiential avoidance, and enhanced acceptance/mindfulness are the active ingredients in these treatments.

Research in Progress

Many other mindfulness- and acceptance-based approaches to treating anxiety disorders are in

Table 1. Summary of Findings From Open-Trial Investigations of Mindfulness- and Acceptance-Based Treatments of Anxiety and Related Disorders

Citation	Sample	Treatment	Posttreatment	Follow-Up	Limitations/Further Details
Kabat-Zinn et al. (1992); Miller, Fletcher, & Kabat-Zinn (1995)	4 Panic 10 Panic w/ agoraphobia 8 GAD completed treatment 2 GAD individuals dropped out of treatment	8 session MBSR	–sig. decrease in self-report, monitoring, and clinician measures of anxiety and depression –20 of 22 participants showed "marked reduction" in Beck and Hamilton depression and anxiety scores –sig. decrease in panic attack frequency	–significant reductions maintained at 3-mo. follow-up –sig. decrease in panic attack frequency among panickers at 3-mo. f/u –effects maintained at 3-year follow-up	–no measure of clinical significance –no post- or f/u diagnostic assessments –some number of participants unavailable for 3 mo. f/u, 4 unavailable for 3-year f/u –11 participants taking psychotropic medication at 3-mo. f/u –9 participants received psychosocial or psychopharmacological treatment during 3-year follow-up period –no separate report of effects by diagnostic group –no control group
Bogels et al. (2006)	9 individuals diagnosed with social phobia completed treatment 1 drop-out	9 session combined mindfulness/task concentration (5 session MBCT)	–sig. decrease (large effect size) in self-report of soc. phobia –7 out of 9 no longer met diagnostic criteria –4 of 9 below clinical cut-off on self-report measure	–maintained significant decrease (large effect size) at 2-month follow-up –5 of 9 below clinical cut-off on self-report measure	–efficacy could be due to inclusion of task concentration training, which has been shown to be efficacious for social phobia, although only a few sessions were devoted to it in this treatment –no diagnostic assessment at follow-up –1 client did not complete post- or f/u –no control group
Roemer & Orsillo (2007)	16 individuals diagnosed with GAD completed treatment 3 dropouts	16-session acceptance-based behavior therapy includes psychoeducation and monitoring, mindfulness/ acceptance-based strategies, and behavioral change in valued domains	–sig. decrease (large effect size) in clinician-assessed severity of GAD, reports of anxious and depressive symptoms, experiential avoidance, and fear of emotions –sig. increase (large effect size) in reports of quality of life –62.5% met criteria for high end state functioning	–maintained significant decrease in all outcomes from post- (with large effect sizes) at 3-month follow-up –maintained significant increase in reported quality of life –58.3% met criteria for high end state functioning	–4 clients unavailable for follow-up assessment –includes standard behavioral elements such as monitoring, psychoeducation and behavioral strategies; need to determine if mindfulness/ acceptance and valued action elements enhance efficacy –although gains were significant at follow-up, nonsignificant declines suggest need for more attention to relapse prevention (which has since been added to the treatment). –no control group

| Dalrymple & Herbert (2007) | 17 individuals diagnosed with social anxiety disorder, generalized subtype 2 dropouts | 10 session ACT with exposure (includes role-play, in vivo exposure, and social skills training) | –sig. decrease (large effect size) in self-report of social anxiety symptoms, self- and other-report of anxiety in behavioral task, and self-report of experiential avoidance
–sig. increase (large effect size) in reports of quality of life and clinician rating of global improvement | –maintained or improved sig. decrease in all outcomes from post- (with large effect sizes) at 3-mo. follow-up
–maintained sig. increase in quality of life | –5 clients unavailable for follow-up assessment
–no post- or follow-up diagnostic assessments
–no measure of clinical significance
–includes standard behavioral elements such as exposure, role-play and social skills training; need to determine if ACT elements enhance efficacy
–no control group |

Table 2. Summary of Findings From Randomized Controlled Trials of Mindfulness- and Acceptance-Based Treatments for Anxiety and Related Disorders

Citation	Sample	Treatment	Comparison	Posttreatment	Follow-Up	Limitations/Further Details
Zettle (2003)	24 participants with self-reported math anxiety were treated 13 participants dropped out of treatment	ACT	Systematic desensitization (SD)	–sig. decreases in self-reported math and test anxiety in both groups –sig. decreases in trait anxiety in the SD group, not the ACT group –6 participants "recovered and improved" in math anxiety in the ACT group, 8 participants in the SD group –sig. decreases in self-reported experiential avoidance in both groups	–maintained decreases in all three measures in both groups –6 participants "recovered and improved" in math anxiety in the ACT group, 7 participants in the SD group –maintained decreases in experiential avoidance	–nonclinical participants –no evidence for incremental efficacy of ACT –no measures of broader functioning
Woods et al. (2006)	25 individuals who met criteria for trichotillomania were treated 2 clients dropped out of treatment	10 session ACT plus Habit Reversal Training	waitlist	–sig. greater decreases in treatment group in self-report, monitoring, and clinician ratings of hair-pulling and self-report of anxiety, depression, and experiential avoidance –66% of those in the treatment group were "clinically improved" by self-report	–no significant increase in monitoring and clinician ratings of hair pulling, depression, anxiety, or experiential avoidance from post- to follow-up –significant increase in self-report assessment of hair pulling from post- to follow-up	–no post- or follow-up diagnostic assessments –not clear if results are due to Habit Reversal Training, an intervention with demonstrated efficacy for trichotillomania, although only a few sessions were devoted to it in this study –no measures of broader functioning

development or currently being researched. Eifert and Forsyth (2005) have developed a unified protocol applying ACT to the anxiety disorders; no data are currently available for its efficacy, but a randomized controlled trial comparing it to cognitive behavior therapy is currently underway (Forsyth, personal communication, 2006). Karekla has developed an acceptance-enhanced CBT for panic disorder, which showed comparable effects on symptoms and quality of life as panic control treatment in a small, unpublished randomized controlled trial (reported in Levitt & Karekla, 2005). Patel (2006) has developed a mindfulness-based treatment for OCD in which she adapted MBSR for individual therapy and added some elements of MBCT and ACT to enhance decentering/defusion; her application of this treatment to a young man with OCD who had failed to respond to previous trials of SSRIs (and refused exposure with response prevention) resulted in clinically significant reductions in OCD symptoms and improvements in quality of life that were maintained at 3-month follow-up. Semple, Reid, and Miller (2005) have adapted MBCT for children with anxiety problems; evidence suggests this approach is acceptable to children, although data are not yet available on the impact of the treatment on symptoms of anxiety. Finally, several authors have described approaches that have yet to be tested: Germer (2005) has outlined methods for applying mindfulness to the treatment of anxiety disorders, Orsillo and Batten (2005) describe an adaptation of ACT for PTSD; Gratz, Tull, and Wagner (2005) have explored the potential utility of adapting DBT mindfulness skills to the treatment of anxiety disorders; and Greco, Blackledge, Coyne, and Ehrenreich (2005) describe the application of ACT to children with anxiety disorders.

Mindfulness- and acceptance-based approaches hold promise in the treatment of anxiety disorders because they directly target the reactivity to and avoidance of internal experiences, attentional biases, and restrictions in functioning and quality of life that characterize these disorders. Efficacy research is still in its early stages, with more well-controlled randomized trials needed to determine incremental efficacy, as well as mechanisms of change. In addition, research determining predictors of treatment, the optimal modes of delivering these interventions (e.g., whether and how much formal practice is necessary), and optimal methods for training therapists in these approaches is needed. Further, because most studies have included predominantly White middle-class participants, research is needed to determine the efficacy of these approaches with clients from diverse backgrounds.

Notes

1. Correlational findings support this claim: experienced mindfulness meditators demonstrated enhanced performance in a sustained attention task and performed significantly better than concentration meditators when the stimulus was unexpected, suggesting that mindfulness practice enhances distributed, rather than focused, attention (Valentine & Sweet, 1999). However, experimental studies are needed to confirm that these findings are due to mindfulness practice, rather than a third variable that characterizes individuals who choose to practice mindfulness meditation.

2. Often confusion arises regarding the apparent contradiction between "accepting" emotional responses and regulating them. As Craske and Hazlett-Stevens (2002) have noted, accepting one's emotional responses might effectively reduce distress (because this stance will reduce the amplification of distress that results from nonacceptance). In our clinical work, we make a distinction between attaching to an outcome of distress reduction (e.g., "I need to reduce my anxiety so that I can give this talk.") versus engaging in actions that might reduce arousal or distress, but not requiring them to do so (e.g., "I am going to focus on my breath here and see if I can bring my anxiety down a little bit. Whether or not that has an effect, I am going to give this talk and do my best to convey this information that is important to me.")

3. The treatment has since been revised and is now administered individually, with a more developed mindfulness component (see Roemer, Salters-Pedneault, & Orsillo, 2006; Roemer & Orsillo, 2007).

References

Baer, R. A. (2003). Mindfulness training as a clinical intervention: A conceptual and empirical review. *Clinical Psychology: Science and Practice, 10,* 125–143.

Baer, R. A. (Ed.). (2006). *Mindfulness-based treatment approaches: Clinician's guide to evidence base and applications.* New York: Elsevier.

Baer, R. A., Smith, G. T., Hopkins, J., Krietemeyer, J., & Toney, L. (2006). Using self-report assessment methods to explore facets of mindfulness. *Assessment, 13,* 27–35.

Barlow, D. H., Allen, L. B., & Choate, M. L. (2004). Toward a unified treatment for emotional disorders. *Behavior Therapy, 35,* 205–230.

Batten, S. V., & Hayes, S. C. (2005). Acceptance and Commitment Therapy in the treatment of comorbid substance abuse and post-traumatic stress disorder: A case study. *Clinical Case Studies, 4,* 246–262.

Bishop, S. R., Lau, M., Shapiro, S., Carlson, L., Anderson, N. D., Carmody, J., et al. (2004). Mindfulness: A proposed operational definition. *Clinical Psychology: Science and Practice, 11,* 230–241.

Bogels, S. M., Sijbers, G.F.V.M., & Voncken, M. (2006). Mindfulness and task concentration training for social phobia: A pilot study. *Journal of Cognitive Psychotherapy: An International Quarterly, 20,* 33–44.

Borkovec, T. D. (2002). Life in the future versus life in the present. *Clinical Psychology: Science and Practice, 9,* 76–80.

Bouton, M. E., Mineka, S., & Barlow, D. H. (2001). A modern learning theory perspective on the etiology of panic disorder. *Psychological Review, 108,* 4–32.

Campbell-Sills, L., Barlow, D. H., Brown, T. A., & Hofmann, S. (2006a). Acceptability and suppression of negative emotion in anxiety and mood disorders. *Emotion, 6,* 587–595.

Campbell-Sills, L., Barlow, D. H., Brown, T. A., & Hofmann, S. (2006b). Effects of suppression and acceptance on emotional responses of individuals with anxiety and mood disorders. *Behaviour Research and Therapy, 44,* 1251–1263.

Chodron, P. (2001). *The places that scare you: A guide to fearlessness in difficult times.* Boston: Shambhala.

Craske, M. G., & Hazlett-Stevens, H. (2002). Facilitating symptom reduction and behavior change in GAD: The issue of control. *Clinical Psychology: Science and Practice, 9,* 69–75.

Dalrymple, K. L., & Herbert, J. D. (2007). Acceptance and Commitment Therapy for generalized social anxiety disorder: A pilot study. *Behavior Modification, 31,* 543–568.

Eifert, G. H., & Forsyth, J. P. (2005). *Acceptance and commitment therapy for anxiety disorders: A practitioner's treatment guide to using mindfulness, acceptance, and values-based behavior change strategies.* Oakland, CA: New Harbinger.

Eifert, G. H., & Heffner, M. (2003). The effects of acceptance versus control contexts on avoidance of panic-related symptoms. *Journal of Behavior Therapy and Experimental Psychiatry, 34,* 293–312.

Feldner, M. T., Zvolensky, M. J., Eifer, G. H., & Spira, A. (2003). Emotional avoidance: An experimental test of individual differences and response suppression using biological challenge. *Behaviour Research and Therapy, 41,* 403–411.

Feldner, M. T., Zvolensky, M. J., Sickle, T. R., Bonn-Miller, M. O., & Leen-Feldner, E. (2006). Anxiety sensitivity-physical concerns as a moderator of the emotional consequences of emotional suppression during biological challenge: An experimental test using growth curve analysis. *Behaviour Research and Therapy, 44,* 249–272.

Foa, E. B., & Kozak, M. J. (1986). Emotional processing of fear: Exposure to corrective information. *Psychological Bulletin, 99,* 20–35.

Germer, C. K. (2005). Anxiety disorders: Befriending fear. In C. K. Germer, R. D. Siegel, & P. R. Fulton (Eds.), *Mindfulness and psychotherapy* (pp. 152–172). New York: Guilford Press.

Goldstein, A. J., & Chambless, D. L. (1978). A reanalysis of agoraphobia. *Behavior Therapy, 9,* 47–59.

Gratz, K. L., Tull, M. T., & Wagner, A. W. (2005). Applying DBT mindfulness skills to the treatment of clients with anxiety disorders. In S. M. Orsillo & L. Roemer (Eds.), *Acceptance and mindfulness-based approaches to anxiety: Conceptualization and treatment* (pp. 147–161). New York: Springer.

Greco, L. A., Blackledge, J. T., Coyne, L. W., & Ehrenreich, J. (2005). Integrating acceptance and mindfulness into treatments for child and adolescent anxiety disorders: Acceptance and Commitment Therapy as an example. In S. M. Orsillo & L. Roemer (Eds.), *Acceptance and mindfulness-based approaches to anxiety: Conceptualization and treatment* (pp. 301–322). New York: Springer.

Grossman, P., Neimann, L., Schmidt, S., & Walach, H. (2004). Mindfulness-based stress reduction and health benefits: A meta-analysis. *Journal of Psychosomatic Research, 57,* 35–43.

Hayes, A. M., & Feldman, G. (2004). Clarifying the construct of mindfulness in the context of emotion regulation and process of change in therapy. *Clinical Psychology: Science and Practice, 11,* 255–264.

Hayes, S. C. (2004). Acceptance and Commitment Therapy, Relational Frame Theory, and the third wave of behavioral and cognitive therapies. *Behavior Therapy, 35,* 639–665.

Hayes, S. C., Follette, V. M., & Linehan, M. M. (2004). *Mindfulness and acceptance: Expanding the cognitive-behavioral tradition.* New York: Guilford Press.

Hayes, S. C., Luoma, J. B., Bond, F. W., Masuda, A., & Lillis, J. (2006). Acceptance and Commitment Therapy: Model, processes and outcomes. *Behaviour Research and Therapy, 44,* 1–25.

Hayes, S. C., Masuda, A., Bissett, R., Luoma, J., & Guerrero, L. F. (2004). DBT, FAP, and ACT: How empirically oriented are the new behavior therapy technologies? *Behavior Therapy, 35,* 35–54.

Hayes, S. C., Strosahl, K. D., & Wilson, K. G. (1999). *Acceptance and commitment therapy: An experiential approach to behavior change.* New York: Guilford Press.

Jacobson, N. S., Martell, C. R., & Dimidjian, S. (2001). Behavioral activation treatment for depression: Returning to contextual roots. *Clinical Psychology: Science and Practice, 8,* 255–270.

Kabat-Zinn, J. (1994). *Wherever you go, there you are.* New York: Hyperion.

Kabat-Zinn, J., Massion, A. O., Kristeller, J., Peterson, L. G., Fletcher, K. E., Pbert, L., et al. (1992). Effectiveness of a Mindfulness-Based Stress Reduction program in the treatment of anxiety disorders. *American Journal of Psychiatry, 149,* 936–943.

Karekla, M., Forsyth, J. P., & Kelly, M. M. (2004). Emotional avoidance and panicogenic responding to a biological challenge procedure. *Behavior Therapy, 35,* 725–746.

Levitt, J. T., Brown, T. A., Orsillo, S. M, & Barlow, D. H. (2004). The effects of acceptance versus suppression of emotion on subjective and psychophysiological response to carbon dioxide challenge in patients with panic disorder. *Behavior Therapy, 35,* 747–766.

Levitt, J. T., & Karekla, M. (2005). Integrating acceptance and mindfulness with cognitive behavior therapy for panic disorder. In S. M. Orsillo & L. Roemer (Eds.), *Acceptance and mindfulness-based approaches to anxiety: Conceptualization and treatment* (pp. 165–188). New York: Springer.

Linehan, M. M. (1993a). *Cognitive-behavioral treatment of borderline personality disorder.* New York: Guilford Press.

Linehan, M. (1993b). *Skills training manual for cognitive behavioral treatment of borderline personality disorder.* New York: Guilford Press.

López, F.J.C. (2000). Acceptance and Commitment Therapy (ACT) in panic disorder with agoraphobia: A case study. *Psychology in Spain, 4,* 120–128.

Mennin, D. S. (2005). Emotion and the acceptance-based approaches to the anxiety disorders. In S. M. Orsillo & L. Roemer (Eds.), *Acceptance and mindfulness-based approaches to anxiety: Conceptualization and treatment* (pp. 37–68). New York: Springer.

Mennin, D. S., Heimberg, R. G., Turk, C. L., & Fresco, D. M. (2005). Preliminary evidence for an emotion dysregulation model of generalized anxiety disorder. *Behaviour Research and Therapy, 43,* 1281–1310.

Miller, J. J., Fletcher, K., & Kabat-Zinn, J. (1995). Three-year follow-up and clinical implications of a mindfulness meditation-based stress reduction intervention in the treatment of anxiety disorders. *General Hospital Psychiatry, 17,* 192–200.

Olendzki, A. (2005). The roots of mindfulness. In C. K. Germer, R. D. Siegel, & P. R. Fulton (Eds.), *Mindfulness and psychotherapy* (pp. 241–261). New York: Guilford Press.

Orsillo, S. M., & Batten, S. V. (2005). Acceptance and Commitment Therapy in the treatment of posttraumatic stress disorder. *Behavior Modification, 29,* 95–129.

Orsillo, S. M., & Roemer, L. (Eds.). (2005). *Acceptance and mindfulness-based approaches to anxiety: Conceptualization and treatment.* New York: Springer.

Orsillo, S. M., Roemer, L., & Barlow, D. H. (2003). Integrating acceptance and mindfulness into existing cognitive-behavioral treatment for GAD: A case study. *Cognitive and Behavioral Practice, 10,* 223–230.

Orsillo, S. M., Roemer, L., Block, J., & Tull, M. T. (2004). Acceptance, mindfulness, and cognitive behavioral therapy: Comparisons, contrasts and application to anxiety. In S. C. Hayes, V. M. Follette, & M. M. Linehan (Eds.), *Mindfulness and acceptance: Expanding the cognitive-behavioral tradition.* New York: Guilford Press.

Orsillo, S. M., Roemer, L., & Holowka, D. W. (2005). Acceptance-based behavioral therapies for anxiety: Using acceptance and mindfulness to enhance traditional cognitive-behavioral approaches. In S. M. Orsillo & L. Roemer (Eds.), *Acceptance and mindfulness-based approaches to anxiety: Conceptualization and treatment* (pp. 3–35). New York: Springer.

Patel, S. R. (2006, March). *Mindfulness-based treatment for OCD: A case report.* Paper presented at the 5th annual Mindfulness Based Stress Reduction International Conference, Worcester, MA.

Purdon, C. (1999). Thought suppression and psychopathology. *Behaviour Research and Therapy, 37,* 1029–1054.

Roemer, L., & Orsillo, S. M. (2007). An open trial of an acceptance-based behavior therapy for generalized anxiety disorder. *Behavior Therapy, 38,* 72–85.

Roemer, L., Salters, K., Raffa, S., & Orsillo, S. M. (2005). Fear and avoidance of internal experiences in GAD: Preliminary tests of a conceptual model. *Cognitive Therapy and Research, 29,* 71–88.

Roemer, L., Salters-Pedneault, K., & Orsillo, S. M. (2006). Incorporating mindfulness and acceptance-based strategies in the treatment of generalized anxiety disorder. In R. Baer (Ed.), *Mindfulness-based treatment approaches: Clinician's guide to evidence base and applications* (pp. 52–74). New York: Academic Press.

Rogers, C. R. (1961). *On becoming a person: A therapist's view of psychotherapy.* Boston: Houghton Mifflin.

Salters-Pedneault, K., Tull, M. T., & Roemer, L. (2004). The role of avoidance of emotional material in the anxiety disorders. *Applied and Preventive Psychology, 11,* 95–114.

Segal, Z. V., Williams, J.M.G., & Teasdale, J. D. (2002). *Mindfulness-based cognitive therapy for depression: A new approach to preventing relapse.* New York: Guilford Press.

Semple, R. J., Reid, E.F.G., & Miller, L. (2005). Treating anxiety with mindfulness: An open trial of mindfulness training for anxious children. *Journal of Cognitive Psychotherapy: An International Quarterly, 19,* 279–392.

Singh, N. N., Wahler, R. G., Winton, A. S., & Adkins, A. D. (2004). A mindfulness-based treatment of obsessive-compulsive disorder. *Clinical Case Studies, 3,* 275–287.

Taylor, S., Koch, W. J., & McNally, R. J. (1992). How does anxiety sensitivity vary across the anxiety disorders? *Journal of Anxiety Disorders, 6,* 249–259.

Turk, C. L., Heimberg, R. G., Luterek, J. A., Mennin, D. S., & Fresco, D. M. (2005). Emotion dysregulation in generalized anxiety disorder: A comparison with social anxiety disorder. *Cognitive Therapy and Research, 29,* 89–106.

Twohig, M. P., Hayes, S. C., & Masuda, A. (2006). A preliminary investigation of acceptance and commitment therapy as a treatment for chronic skin picking. *Behaviour Research and Therapy, 44,* 1513–1522.

Twohig, M. P., Hayes, S. C., & Masuda, A. (2006). Increasing willingness to experience obsessions: Acceptance and Commitment Therapy as a treatment for obsessive-compulsive disorder. *Behavior Therapy, 37,* 3–13.

Valentine, E. R., & Sweet, P. G. (1999). Meditation and attention: A comparison of the effects of concentrative and mindfulness meditation on sustained attention. *Mental Health, Religion, and Culture, 2,* 59–70.

Walsh, R., & Shapiro, S. L. (2006). The meeting of meditative disciplines and Western psychology: A mutually enriching dialogue. *American Psychologist, 61,* 227–239.

Wells, A. (1990). Panic disorder in association with relaxation induced anxiety: An attentional training approach to treatment. *Behavior Therapy, 21,* 273–280.

Williams, K. E., Chambless, D. L., & Ahrens, A. (1997). Are emotions frightening? An extension of the fear of fear construct. *Behaviour Research and Therapy, 35,* 239–248.

Wilson, K. G., & Murrell, A. R. (2004). Values work in acceptance and commitment therapy: Setting a course for behavioral treatment. In S. C. Hayes, V. M. Follette, & M. M. Linehan (Eds.), *Mindfulness and acceptance: Expanding the cognitive-behavioral tradition* (pp. 120–151). New York: Guilford Press.

Woods, D. W., Wetterneck, C. T., & Flessner, C. A. (2006). A controlled evaluation of acceptance and commitment therapy plus habit reversal for trichotillomania. *Behaviour Research and Therapy, 44,* 639–656.

Zettle, R. D. (2003). Acceptance and Commitment Therapy (ACT) vs. Systematic Desensitization in treatment of mathematics anxiety. *The Psychological Record, 53,* 197–215.

Self-Help Treatments for Anxiety Disorders

John R. Walker, Norah Vincent *and* Patricia Furer

Abstract

This chapter considers the effectiveness of self-administered treatments for anxiety—media-based approaches such as manuals, self-help books, audiotapes, computer programs, and Internet sites that allow individuals to help themselves with minimal therapist contact. Systematic and meta-analytic reviews of traditional self-administered treatments or bibliotherapy suggest that in research settings these interventions produce encouraging medium-effect sizes that are smaller than therapist-guided interventions. Web-based treatment, provided through the Internet, has the potential for very wide reach. Some degree of therapist contact during self-administered treatments is related to larger effect sizes, suggesting that therapist monitoring may increase engagement in treatment. Research is needed on approaches to recruitment, screening, increasing engagement, and evaluating the cost of programs.

Keywords: anxiety, bibliotherapy, minimum therapist contact, self-administered treatment, self-help, Web-based treatment

For the purposes of this chapter, self-help treatments are defined as media-based approaches such as manuals, self-help books, audiotapes, computer programs, and Internet sites that allow individuals to help themselves with minimal assistance from a health service provider (Williams, 2003). We will not address the use of self-help groups because there is much less research available in this area (den Boer, Wiersma, & van den Bosch, 2004), even though this is a growing source of assistance for a wide range of health problems (Eisenberg et al., 1998). Instead, we will consider the naturalistic use of self-help treatments, evidence of their effectiveness, and ethical concerns.

A key factor in the interest in self-help approaches is the high level of need in the community. The majority of people with anxiety and depressive disorders do not receive care (Wang, Lane, et al., 2005) and there are long delays before people seek

and receive care (Wang, Berglund, et al., 2005). Among those who do receive care, the care is often inadequate (Wang, Lane, et al., 2005). In a large epidemiological study of the mental health of Canadians age 15 years and over ($n = 36,816$), 8.7% of respondents indicated that they had seen a professional of some kind about their emotions, mental health, or use of alcohol or drugs in the previous 12 months (Sareen, Cox, Afifi, Clara, & Yu, 2005). A further 3% reported that in the previous 12 months there was a time when they needed help for these concerns but did not receive it. Among this group with perceived need for help but no help-seeking, the three types of care most commonly desired were "therapy or counselling" (50%), "help for personal relationships" (22%), and "information on mental illness or treatment" (20%). Only 8% of this subgroup indicated that they wanted medication treatment. The three most common reasons for not seeking care were "preferred to manage [emotional problems] by self" (35%), "did not get around to it" (19%), and "did not know how to get help" (16%). The large proportions among those with a perceived need for care who prefer to manage the problem by themselves, desire information, or do not know how to get help suggest that there are many people who may be receptive to self-help approaches.

Self-help interventions are considered because they may increase the availability and accessibility of help (allowing interventions to be used at convenient times and at home), reduce costs to consumers and the health care system, increase sense of privacy relative to the use of traditional services (where stigma is an issue for many consumers), and increase the consumer's control over (of) the intervention (Griffiths, Lindenmeyer, Powell, Lowe, & Thorogood, 2006; Proudfoot, 2004).

Naturalistic Use of Self-Help Treatments

Controlled studies of self-help treatments typically recruit participants through media advertising or notices in health care settings. Participants are evaluated for the presence of the problem under investigation, symptom severity, and suitability for participation in the study. Newman, Erickson, Przeworski, and Dzus (2003) point out that there is a great deal of variability among controlled trials in the amount of therapist contact. They suggest four categories to describe therapist contact:

1. *self-administered therapy* (therapist contact for assessment at most)

2. *predominantly self-help* (therapist contact beyond assessment is for providing the initial therapeutic rationale and/or for periodic check-ins)

3. *minimal-contact therapy* (active involvement of a therapist in directing the intervention but to a lesser degree than traditional therapy)

4. *predominantly therapist-administered treatments* (regular contact with a therapist for a typical number of sessions with self-help materials used to augment standard therapy)

In the naturalistic use of self-help treatments, there is a similar range of therapist involvement from situations in which the consumer uses material with no therapist contact to situations in which the therapist uses self-help materials to augment therapy sessions. The most widely available and evaluated form of self-help treatment involves the use of traditional text materials. Most bookstores have a large section devoted to self-improvement and self-help approaches for a wide range of problems. There

is no contact with a therapist and consumers evaluate for themselves whether there is a good match between the program and their needs.

Many professionals recommend self-help books as part of their practice. Norcross (2000) provides data from surveys mailed to members of the American Psychological Association Clinical and Counselling Divisions. Self-help books were recommended by 85% of psychologists to an average of 34% of their clients. Clinicians rated many of the resources that are available positively and very few indicated that they felt self-help materials had a harmful effect on their clients. The potential positive impact of the use of high-quality self-help materials is illustrated in a study involving the treatment of panic disorder. Clark et al. (1999) found that they could reduce therapist time from over 12 hours to 6.5 hours with the use of self-study modules with no loss in treatment effectiveness.

In recent years, formats have been developed that take advantage of new technologies. Table 1 describes some of the advantages and challenges associated with the commonly available formats. The most widely available new technology at this point is the Internet (Proudfoot, 2004). An increasing proportion of households throughout the developed and developing world have access to this technology and the Internet is widely used as a source of health information. For example, Sirovatka (2002) reports that 7 million hits are registered every month on the National Institute of Mental Health (NIMH) homepage.

A colorful description of the wide availability of self-help resources is provided by Norcross (2000): "The self-help market resembles a Persian bazaar with proliferating choices and no clear answers: should you nurture others or nurture your "inner child"; seek success or simplicity; just say no or just do it; confront your fears or honor them. Sorely needed is research on the utility and quality of self-help materials" (p. 373).

Reviews of the Effectiveness of Self-Help Treatments
Systematic Review

Newman et al. (2003) describe the results of a systematic review of self-help interventions for anxiety disorders, focusing particularly on the degree of therapist involvement. In examining study methodology, they noted that it was often difficult to make comparisons among studies because they were not clear in specifying the amount of therapist involvement, the cost of the intervention, and the degree to which participants implemented various

Table 1. Advantages and Challenges of Different Approaches to Disseminating Self-Help Interventions

Format	Advantages	Challenges
Limited-production text materials	• Material may be focused on local concerns and resources • No computer resources required	• Time-consuming to produce and keep up-to-date • Limited distribution • Cost of materials • Space required for inventory
Commercially available books	• Existing distribution system through bookstores and Internet • Current availability of a wide range of materials	• Challenge to become familiar with materials on a wide range of topics • Quality of materials and reading level varies • More difficult to tailor the program to the needs of the client
Computer-based programs (e.g., CD)	• Easier to control copying of materials • Modest cost to client • Programs may be interactive and branching to respond to the needs and interests of different clients • May include some audio and video material	• Computer and printer access is required • Younger people are more familiar with this format, older people are often less familiar • Challenging to find an economic model to recover the cost of production and dissemination • High initial development costs • Limited availability of programs
Internet-based programs	• Very widely distributed (internationally) • Content may be modified or expanded easily • Modest or no cost to client • Programs may be interactive and branching to respond to the needs and interests of different clients • May include some audio and video material • Development tools are available in many health and educational settings • Some good examples are currently available	• Computer, printer, and Internet access is required • Younger people are more familiar with this format, older people are often less familiar • Challenging to find an economic model to recover the cost of production and dissemination • Variable quality in publicly available material • High initial development costs

components of the intervention. The programs used diverse materials and it was difficult to determine the quality of the materials. Few studies evaluated the therapeutic alliance, an important factor in the effectiveness of psychological interventions.

The review suggested a number of conclusions related to the degree of therapist involvement in the treatment. For many of the anxiety disorders, there were not enough studies of self-help interventions to draw firm conclusions. The findings indicate that *self-administered therapy* for specific phobia led to more improvement than no treatment and placebo control groups and outcomes were not significantly different from interventions with greater therapist contact. Therapy was more likely to be effective when participants found the self-help tool to be credible and when they were highly motivated for treatment. Self-administered treatment provided in the research clinic setting was generally more effective than the same intervention applied at home, suggesting that some degree of accountability and monitoring had a positive effect on outcome.

Considering *predominantly self-help* interventions, they found that for panic disorder, specific phobia, and mixed anxiety samples, approaches that emphasized in-vivo exposure were superior to no treatment and equivalent to interventions that involved greater therapist contact. For *minimal-contact therapy,* outcome was similar to more intensive treatments for specific phobia, panic disorder (without severe agoraphobia), mixed anxiety samples, and social phobia.

Meta-Analytic Reviews

There are a number of meta-analytic reviews that focus on the effectiveness of self-help treatments. Early meta-analytic studies suggested that self-help approaches may be particularly helpful with anxiety problems (Gould & Clum, 1993; Marrs, 1995) in comparison to habit problems such as smoking, excessive drinking, and weight problems. Other reviews suggested that self-help approaches might rival therapist-directed interventions in terms of magnitude of effect (den Boer et al., 2004; Gould & Clum, 1993; Marrs, 1995; Scogin, Bynum, Stephens, & Calhoon, 1990). Hirai and Clum (2006) report a meta-analysis summarizing 33 randomized controlled trials of self-help treatments for anxiety problems. Most of these studies used traditional text materials. The largest number of studies focused on panic disorder (8), social anxiety disorder (7), and specific phobia (4) while there were few studies of generalized anxiety disorder (GAD), posttraumatic stress disorder (PTSD), test anxiety, and mixed anxiety. They found that the dropout rate in these studies of 12% during the intervention and 9% by the follow-up assessment was similar to the rate in control groups and therapist-directed interventions. The mean effect size for the self-help interventions (calculated using Cohen's d) was .68 compared to waiting list controls and .50 compared to placebo controls. The effect size compared to therapist-directed interventions (−.42) indicated that the therapist-directed interventions produced larger changes in anxiety. The follow-up data available were typically for short periods (1 to 4 months) but suggested reasonable maintenance of gains. Therapist contact during the intervention was related to larger effect size, although the amount and type of therapist contact was not related, suggesting that minimal therapist contact may be enough to increase the effectiveness of self-help treatments. There were some differences in effect size related to diagnosis, suggesting that self-administered treatments were particularly effective with panic disorder.

The authors concluded that there is good support for the effectiveness of self-administered treatments. These treatments generally produce a medium effect size, which is smaller than the effect size of therapist-directed treatment for most problems. This material is also well suited for use in stepped care approaches.

Recent Studies of Self-Help Treatments
Traditional Text Material

In a particularly informative study, Febbraro, Clum, Roodman, and Wright (1999) compared two forms of bibliotherapy with no therapist contact (bibliotherapy alone or bibliotherapy with daily self-monitoring and self-administered feedback) to two control procedures (waiting list or daily self-monitoring and self-administered feedback). All four groups showed similar improvement over time with no additional effect of bibliotherapy. In comparing these results to previous findings, the authors suggested that a key factor may have been the lack of therapist contact for the initial assessment (done by mail in this study) and during the course of the study. Previous studies with positive findings had involved some degree of therapist contact during the assessment and/or intervention. In a follow-up phase to this study, the authors found that participants who entered a 6-month relapse prevention phase with a relapse prevention manual and monthly therapist telephone contacts (up to 15 minutes) had a better outcome on panic measures than participants with no relapse prevention contacts (Wright, Clum, Roodman, & Febbraro, 2000).

A research team from the University of Manchester in England recently evaluated the use of a self-help cognitive behavioral therapy (CBT) program for patients referred from primary care with anxiety or depression. Patients expressed satisfaction with the materials but the degree of improvement with the self-help program was no greater than for treatment as usual when it was used independently after assessment (Fletcher, Lovell, Bower, Campbell, & Dickens, 2005) or with additional meetings with a therapist (Mead et al., 2005).

In a study of the treatment of PTSD following motor vehicle accidents, Ehlers et al. (2003) compared three interventions: a self-help treatment booklet using CBT principles (with a 40-minute introduction by a therapist), repeated clinician assessments, and individual CBT (average of 12 sessions). Individual treatment was much more effective than the other two conditions. The use of the booklet did not produce results superior to the repeated assessment condition.

In one of the few studies focused on children's anxiety, Rapee, Abbott, and Lyneham (2006) compared bibliotherapy to group intervention to a waiting list control condition to teach CBT principles to parents of anxious children. Pre-, post-, and follow-up assessments took place in person but there was no therapist contact in the bibliotherapy condition (or the waiting list condition) during the treatment phase. The dropout rate was twice as high in the bibliotherapy condition (32%) as in the group (16%) and waiting list conditions (14%). There was more improvement in the bibliotherapy condition than in the waiting list condition but less than in the group intervention condition. In the intent-to-treat analysis, the proportion no longer meeting the criteria for any anxiety disorder was approximately 6% in the waiting list condition, 18% in the bibliotherapy condition, and 49% in the group intervention condition. Lyneham and Rapee (2006) evaluated the use of the same bibliotherapy program for parents of anxious children in rural communities with differing forms of therapist support, including scheduled telephone calls, scheduled e-mail contacts and replies, and client-initiated telephone calls (if help was required). Initial and subsequent assessments were completed by using a telephone interview and a questionnaire package returned by mail. Following treatment, the percentage of children no longer meeting criteria for an anxiety disorder was 79% in the scheduled telephone contact condition, 33% in the e-mail condition, 31% in the client-initiated telephone contact condition, and 0% in the waiting list condition. Those in the scheduled telephone contact condition completed an average of 8.3 of the 9 planned telephone contacts with an average duration of 25 minutes. In contrast, only about 30% of those in the client-initiated telephone call condition initiated contacts, with most of these only making one call. At 12-month follow-up these gains were maintained or extended. This study illustrates the dramatic differences in the results of self-help intervention based on the amount of therapeutic contact and the method of contact.

Audio Materials

A few self-help programs such as the Attacking Anxiety program available through the Midwest Center for Stress and Anxiety in Ohio are marketed directly to consumers through infomercials and widely advertised public meetings. A naturalistic study of this program, which relies on audiotapes and text material, by independent assessors suggested that 35% of respondents achieved clinically

significant improvement, a further 23% achieved reliable change, and only 1 of 176 reported negative change (Finch, Lambert, & Brown, 2000). The authors noted that this assessment was based on the one-third of program participants who returned evaluation questionnaires.

Internet Programs

Due to the advantages of Internet-based programs (see Table 1), this approach has supplanted most earlier programs developed for use with desktop computers. Most studies of Web-based programs involve participants who are screened and then referred to the program. Participants may use a password to have access to the program and may be required to complete modules sequentially. In some cases, they are required to complete assessments and even demonstrate some level of knowledge before moving on to the next module. In openly available programs, in contrast, participants find the program on the Internet, they may complete some self-assessment materials, and then they may use the program freely. Participants may attempt some or all of the modules, print or save some of the material, and may return to the site multiple times.

Limited Access Internet Programs

One of the pioneering programs in this area is the *FearFighter* program, first developed as a computer-based program and later modified for use on the Internet. While the program is currently being employed in a number of primary care settings in the United Kingdom, the only large-scale evaluation was carried out in a specialty mental health clinic (Marks, Kenwright, McDonough, Whittaker, & Mataix-Cols, 2004). Individuals with agoraphobia, social phobia, or specific phobia were assigned to the computer-guided self-exposure program (FearFighter, $n = 37$), clinician-guided self-exposure ($n = 39$), and a computer- and audiotape-guided relaxation program ($n = 17$). The relaxation program had a significantly lower dropout rate (6%) than FearFighter (43%) and the clinician-guided programs (24%), which did not differ significantly from each other. Considering only treatment completers, the two self-exposure conditions had comparable improvement and satisfaction at posttreatment assessment, while the relaxation condition showed little clinical improvement in phobic avoidance. Including both completers and dropouts, average therapist contact time was 76 minutes in the computer-guided relaxation program, 76 minutes in the FearFighter program, and 283 minutes in the clinician-guided program. Schneider, Mataix-Cols, Marks, and Bechofen (2005) evaluated two different programs for treatment of panic and phobic anxiety (agoraphobia with or without panic disorder, social phobia, or specific phobia) provided on the Internet after participants were screened by telephone for the study. The FearFighter program, which emphasizes exposure to feared situations, was compared to the Managing Anxiety program, which emphasizes relaxation and cognitive change with no encouragement or discouragement of exposure. The two programs produced equivalent results at the end of a 10-week treatment period, but by the time of the 1-month follow-up, the exposure program produced greater improvement on 5 of 10 measures. Total telephone contact time during the treatment phase was 115 minutes for the FearFighter program and 87 minutes for the Managing Anxiety program. While this study did not have a control condition, the magnitude of change was similar to that found with active treatments and was considerably larger than the changes measured in control groups in previous studies.

Carlbring, Ekselius, and Andersson (2003) describe a study of two Internet interventions for panic disorder. In this *minimal-contact therapy* approach, participants received a 6-module CBT program or a 9-module applied relaxation program. Therapist contact consisted of an in-person diagnostic interview and e-mail contact. The amount of therapist time for contact during the treatment was reduced from an earlier stage of development of the program by using a library of standard e-mail answers to questions from participants. Within group effect size (d) was 0.71 for applied relaxation and 0.42 for CBT. This study had weaker results for the CBT program than a previous study by this group, possibly because of more impersonal e-mail contact, slower response time to e-mail contacts (7 days versus 1 day), and no deadlines for completing modules. Carlbring et al. (2005) extended this study by comparing a 10-session Internet CBT program to 10 sessions of individual therapy for panic disorder. To increase social interaction, the participants were required to post at least one message in an online discussion group about a predetermined topic in every module. A supportive atmosphere developed as participants were able to read and comment on messages. In addition to submitting homework, which was used to determine whether the participants could go on to the next session (feedback was given within 36 hours), participants were free to submit as many messages as they wanted to the therapist. The

mean time spent on administration and responding to the e-mails was 2.5 hours for each participant. The within-group effect size (d) for the Internet treatment (0.80) was very close to that for the individual CBT condition (0.93). Carlbring, Furmark, Steczko, Ekselius, and Andersson (2006) describe an open trial of Web-based treatment of social anxiety disorder using similar methodology. Therapist contact, an average of 3 hours for each participant, was provided by e-mail and an online discussion group was provided as well. The intervention had a within group effect size of 0.88 at posttreatment and improved at a 6-month follow-up to 1.31.

Klein, Richards, and Austin (2006) compared therapist-assisted self-help using either a manual or an Internet program for panic disorder. Both groups showed considerable improvement in comparison to an information-only control group. The Internet intervention was more effective than the CBT manual in reducing clinician-rated agoraphobia and number of general practitioner (GP) visits at postassessment. Both groups received a considerable amount of therapist assistance, via telephone for the manual group (with a once weekly call for a total of 4 hours) and via e-mail for the Internet group (response within 24 hours for an average of 5.5 hours). Satisfaction and treatment credibility were equally high for both groups. Participants tended to complete the treatment in fewer days in the Internet program than in the manual program (45 versus 63 days). The authors suggested that the differences between the two conditions may have been due in part to the faster response provided by e-mail as compared to scheduled weekly telephone contacts.

Lange et al. (2003) describe an interesting approach to the treatment of traumatic stress in clients recruited through the media and a Web site. Screening and assessments were carried out on an Internet site. The treatment involved 10 45-minute writing assignments over 5 weeks. The assignments covered three general themes: "self confrontation" (or exposure), cognitive reappraisal, and "sharing and farewell" (to encourage a symbolic letting go of the event). Assignments were submitted through the Web site and written feedback was provided via the Web site within 24 hours by trained graduate students. Completers in the active treatment showed an impressive proportion with clinically significant improvement (45%–50%) compared to the waiting-list control group (8%). The attrition rate was high with 437 participants being screened positive for participation but only 184 returning the consent form by mail and being randomized to either the treatment or waiting-list control conditions. Of the 122 assigned to the treatment condition, 24 dropped out during the self-confrontation phase (20%), 11 during the cognitive restructuring phase (9%), 9 during the social sharing phase (7%), and 9 did not complete the postassessment (7%). Of the 62 assigned to the control condition, 30 did not complete the postassessment (48%). A proportion of those who dropped out were successfully contacted with a questionnaire about reasons for dropping out. Common reasons for dropping out were difficulties with the computer and network (40%), a preference to see a therapist in person (30%), and discomfort about writing about personal events (30%). No information was provided about the amount of therapists' time involved in this program.

Hirai and Clum (2005) describe a small Internet-based intervention for persons with traumatic event related distress. Participants were recruited from college programs and the community and were screened by mail. An 8-week self-help program produced significant reductions in symptoms compared to a waiting-list control group. There was no direct or e-mail contact with therapists except for reminders to complete assessments and encouragement to complete the program within the fixed time period. The dropout rate was 25%. On a measure of anxiety, 54% in the Internet group and 7% in the control group showed clinically significant improvement. This study suggests that an Internet program may be helpful for individuals who have experienced traumatic events and are experiencing significant distress.

Open Access Internet Programs

There are a number of self-help programs that are widely available on the Internet. Two programs focusing on anxiety are www.Paniccenter.net for panic and www.anxieties.com with brief self-help resources for a range of anxiety disorders. One of the most well developed Web-based programs is www.MySelfHelp.com with modules for depression, grief, insomnia, eating disorders, compulsive shopping, guilt, self-esteem, helping loved ones, and stress management (Bedrosian, 2004). The program is designed as a tool to complement work with a health service provider, although it may also be used as a freestanding service. Providers are encouraged to refer patients to the Web site and in turn participants are encouraged to share summary information about their participation in the program with the health care provider. The program has been the

focus of extensive input by mental health specialists but has no published evaluations.

Farvolden, Denisoff, Selby, Bagby, and Rudy (2005) describe the pattern of usage and outcome data available from www.Paniccenter.net. Over a 17-month period there were 484,695 visits and 1,148,097 page views from 99,695 users of the site. Persons who wanted to use the self-help program aspect of the site were required to register and 1,161 users did so. Of these, 1,059 chose to download the self-help manual. The program was organized into 12 sessions. There was very high attrition from the structured program and only 12 registered users completed all of the 12 sessions. The authors note that some of the users may have worked with the downloaded program and others may have used the program in a nonlinear manner. Considering the larger group of participants who participated in the first part of the program, there was a significant reduction in frequency of panic attacks between Sessions 2 and 3.

Christensen, Griffiths, Korten, Brittliffe, and Groves (2004) evaluated a CBT Web site focused on prevention of depression (called MoodGYM). They compared spontaneous users and persons referred as part of a clinical trial. This study provides a helpful comparison with the study by Farvolden et al. (2005). During the 29-month period covered by the study, 19,607 visitors registered on the site. Of these, 62% completed at least one set of assessment scales but only 16% completed at least 2 of the 5 modules. This compared to 86% of trial participants who completed one set of assessments and 67% who completed 2. There was more attrition by module 4, completed by 1.4% of spontaneous users and 38% of trial users. Spontaneous and trial users reported similar initial levels of depression, well above community norms, and for both groups there were equivalent decreases in depression scores with an increasing number of treatment modules completed. The major difference between the groups was the very high rate of attrition among spontaneous users.

Ethical Concerns About Self-Administered Treatments

Gerald Rosen has expressed concerns for many years about the proliferation of self-help books and excessive claims about their effectiveness in the absence of research evaluating the programs. Recent reviews by Rosen and his colleagues suggest that the dissemination of self-help programs has increased tremendously over the years without a corresponding increase in the proportion that have been evaluated

(Rosen, 1993; Rosen, Glasgow, & Moore, 2003). Rosen provides examples of situations in which treatment manuals have a reasonable level of effectiveness when used with therapist supervision but are not used successfully by most people in unsupervised use. Small changes in procedures may have major effects on program effectiveness. Rosen et al. (2003) suggest a very useful framework for evaluating self-help programs. There is also concern that unsuccessful use of self-help materials may have a negative effect (Rosen, Glasgow, & Moore, 2003). The issue of negative effects of self-help programs has been addressed by a small number of researchers. Scogin et al. (1996) reviewed five studies of treatment of depression using a widely available self-help book and found that there was no evidence that more people experienced a worsening of the problem with depression than in therapist-administered treatments. The number of participants experiencing deterioration was low, especially in comparison to the number experiencing improvement.

Summary and Conclusions

Self-help treatments continue to be widely accepted and used by the public, and self-help resources are often used by clinicians in the field. There are exciting new developments of self-help treatments provided through the Internet. At the same time, systematic reviews and individual studies suggest that there continues to be limited scientific support for the effectiveness of self-help programs when they are used completely independently. The degree of change produced by these programs when they are effective is modest. On the other hand, there is strong evidence that increasing the amount of contact with a therapist increases the effectiveness of self-help programs and produces results that may be similar to programs requiring considerably more therapist time. Given the promise of self-help treatments for increasing the availability and accessibility of services and reducing costs, it is clear that more work on the development of effective programs is warranted. Some of the important factors to evaluate in future research include methods of recruiting participants, approaches to screening and facilitating entry to the program, engagement in the program, contact during the program to encourage participation, follow-up after the program, and cost of the program relative to alternatives.

Richardson and Richards (2006) suggest that it may be possible to improve the effectiveness of programs by paying more attention in the development of self-help materials to common factors that have been studied in psychotherapy. They argue that it may be possible to write materials in ways that increase engagement and the therapeutic alliance, communicate empathy and warmth, provide responsiveness and flexibility, and deal with problems that develop in the course of therapy. The addition of online discussion groups such as the one described by Carlbring et al. (2005) may increase engagement in treatment. Clearly, more study of the process of self-help treatment and involvement in different aspects of treatment may provide information that will assist in improving treatments.

References

Bedrosian, R. C. (2004, November). *One-stop shopping: Designing a family of interactive self-help programs for co-morbid problems.* Paper presented at the meeting of the Association for the Advancement of Behavior Therapy, New Orleans, LA.

Carlbring, P., Ekselius, L., & Andersson, G. (2003). Treatment of panic disorders via the Internet: A randomized trail of CBT vs. applied relaxation. *Journal of Behavior Therapy and Experimental Psychiatry, 34,* 129–140.

Carlbring, P., Furmark, T., Steczkó, J., Ekselius, L., & Andersson, G. (2006). An open study of Internet-based bibliotherapy with minimal therapist contact via email for social phobia. *Clinical Psychologist, 10,* 30–38.

Carlbring, P., Nilsson-Ihrfelt, E., Waara, E., Kollenstam, C., Buhrman, M., Kaldo, V., et al. (2005). Treatment of panic disorders: Live therapy vs. self-help via the Internet. *Behaviour Research and Therapy, 43,* 1321–1333.

Christensen, H., Griffiths, K. M., Korten, A. E., Brittliffe, K., & Groves, C. (2004). A comparison of changes in anxiety and depression symptoms of spontaneous users and trial participants of a cognitive behavior therapy website. *Journal of Medical Internet Research, December 22, 6*(4), e46.

Clark, D. M., Salkovskis, P. M., Hackmann, A., Wells, A., Ludgate, J., & Gelder, M. (1999). Brief cognitive therapy for panic disorder: A randomized controlled trial. *Journal of Consulting and Clinical Psychology, 67,* 583–589.

Den Boer, P.C.M.A., Wiersnia, D., & van den Bosch, R. J. (2004). Why is self-help neglected in the treatment of emotional disorders? A meta-analysis. *Psychological Medicine, 34,* 959–971.

Ehlers, A., Clark, D. M., Hackmann, A., McManus, F., Fennell, M., Herbert, C., et al. (2003). A randomized controlled trial of cognitive therapy, a self-help booklet, and repeated assessments as early interventions for posttraumatic stress disorder. *Archives of General Psychiatry, 60,* 1024–1032.

Eisenberg, D. M., Davis, R. B., Ettner, S. L., Appel, S., Wilkey, S., Van Rompay, M., et al. (1998). Trends in alternative medicine use in the United States, 1990–1997: Results of a follow-up national survey. *Journal of the American Medical Association, 11,* 1569–1575.

Farvolden, P., Denisoff, E., Selby, P., Bagby, R. M., & Rudy, L. (2005). Usage and longitudinal effectiveness of a Web-based self-help cognitive behavioral therapy program for panic disorder. *Journal of Medical Internet Research, 26, 7*(1), e7.

Febbraro, G.A.R., Clum, G. A., Roodman, A. A., & Wright, J. H. (1999). The limits of bibliotherapy: A study of the differential effectiveness of self-administered interventions in individuals with panic attacks. *Behavior Therapy, 30,* 209–222.

Finch, A. E., Lambert, M. J., & Brown, G. (2000). Attacking anxiety: A naturalistic study of a multimedia self-help program. *Journal of Clinical Psychology, 56,* 11–21.

Fletcher, J., Lovell, K., Bower, P., Campbell, M., & Dickens, D. (2005). Process and outcome of a non-guided self-help manual for anxiety and depression in primary care: A pilot study. *Behavioural and Cognitive Psychotherapy, 33,* 319–331.

Gould, R. A., & Clum, G. A. (1993). A meta-analysis of self-help treatment approaches. *Clinical Psychology Review, 13,* 169–186.

Griffiths, F., Lindenmeyer, A., Powell, J., Lowe, P., & Thorogood, M. (2006). Why are health care interventions delivered over the Internet? A systematic review of the published literature. *Journal of Medical Internet Research, 8*(2), e10. Retrieved May 6, 2006, from http://www.jmir.org/2006/2/e10/

Hirai, M., & Clum, G. A. (2006). A meta-analytic study of self-help interventions for anxiety problems. *Behavior Therapy, 37,* 99–111.

Hirai, M., & Clum, G. A. (2005). An Internet-based self-change program for traumatic event related fear, distress, and maladaptive coping. *Journal of Traumatic Stress, 18,* 631–636.

Kleina, B., Richards, J. C., & Austin, D. W. (2006). Efficacy of Internet therapy for panic disorder. *Journal of Behavior Therapy and Experimental Psychiatry, 37,* 213–238.

Lange, A., Rietdijk, D., Hudcovicova, M., van den Ven, J. P., Schrieken, B., & Emmelkamp, P.M.G. (2003). Interapy: A controlled randomized trial of the standardized treatment of posttraumatic stress through the Internet. *Journal of Consulting and Clinical Psychology, 71,* 901–909.

Lyneham, H. J., & Rapee, R. M. (2006). Evaluation of therapist-support parent implemented CBT for anxiety in rural children. *Behaviour Research and Therapy, 44,* 1287–1300.

Marks, I. M., Kenwright, M., McDonough, M., Whittaker, M., & Mataix-Cols, D. (2004). Saving clinicians' time by delegating routine aspects of therapy to a computer: A randomized controlled trial in phobia/panic disorder. *Psychological Medicine, 34,* 9–17.

Marrs, R. W. (1995). A meta-analysis of bibliotherapy studies. *American Journal of Community Psychology, 23,* 843–870.

Mead, N., MacDonald, W., Bower, P., Lovell, K., Richards, D., Roberts, C., et al. (2005). The clinical effectiveness of guided self-help versus waiting-list control in the management of anxiety and depression: A randomized controlled trial. *Psychological Medicine, 35,* 1633–1643.

Newman, M. G., Erickson, T., Przeworski, A., & Dzus, E. (2003). Self-help and minimal contact therapies for anxiety disorder: Is human contact necessary for therapeutic efficacy? *Journal of Clinical Psychology, 59,* 251–274.

Norcross, J. C. (2000). Here comes the self-help revolution in mental health. *Psychotherapy: Theory, Research, Practice, Training, 37,* 370–377.

Proudfoot, J. G. (2004). Computer-based treatment for anxiety and depression: Is it feasible? Is it effective? *Neuroscience and Biobehavioral Reviews, 28,* 353–363.

Rapee, R. M., Abbott, M. J., & Lyneham, H. (2006). Bibliotherapy for children with anxiety disorders using written materials for parents: A randomized controlled trial. *Journal of Consulting and Clinical Psychology, 74,* 436–444.

Richardson, R., & Richards, D. A. (2006). Self-help: Towards the next generation. *Behavioural and Cognitive Psychotherapy, 34,* 13–23.

Rosen, G. M. (1993). Self-help or hype? Comments on psychology's failure to advance self-care. *Professional Psychology: Research and Practice, 24,* 340–345.

Rosen, G. M., Glasgow, R. E., & Moore, T. E. (2003). Self-help therapy: The science and business of giving psychology away. In S. O. Lilienfeld & S. J. Lynn (Eds.), *Science and pseudoscience in clinical psychology* (pp. 399–424). New York: Guilford Press.

Sareen, J., Cox., B. J., Afifi, T. O., Clara, I., & Yu, B. N. (2005). Perceived need for mental health treatment in a nationally representative Canadian sample. *Canadian Journal of Psychiatry, 50,* 643–651.

Schneider, A. J., Mataix-Cols, D., Marks, I. M., & Bachofen, M. (2005). Internet-guided self-help with or without exposure therapy for phobic and panic disorders. *Psychotherapy and Psychosomatics, 74,*154–164.

Scogin, F., Bynum, J., Stephens, G., & Calhoon, S. (1990). Efficacy of self-administered treatment programs: Meta-analytic review. *Professional Psychology: Research and Practice, 21,* 42–47.

Scogin, F., Floyd, M., Jamison, C., Ackerson, J., Landreville, P., & Bissonette, L. (1996). Negative outcomes: What is the evidence on self-administered treatments? *Journal of Consulting and Clinical Psychology, 64,* 1086–1089.

Sirovatka, P. (2002). Hyman leaves NIMH stronger, richer. *Psychiatric Research Reports, 18,* 1–2.

Wang, P. S., Berglund, P., Olfson, M., Pincus, H. A., Wells, K. B., & Kessler, R. C. (2005). Failure and delay in initial treatment contact after first onset of mental disorders in the National Comorbidity Survey Replication. *Archives of General Psychiatry, 62,* 603–613.

Wang, P. S., Lane, M., Olfson, M., Pincus, H. A., Wells, K. B., & Kessler, R. C. (2005). Twelve-month use of mental health services in the United States: Results from the National Comorbidity Survey Replication. *Archives of General Psychiatry, 62,* 629–640.

Williams, C. (2003). New technologies in self-help: Another effective way to get better. *European Eating Disorders Review, 11,* 170–182.

Wright, J., Clum, G., Roodman, A., & Febbraro, G. (2000). A bibliotherapy approach to relapse prevention in individuals with panic attacks. *Journal of Anxiety Disorders, 14,* 483–499.

Prevention of Child and Youth Anxiety and Anxiety Disorders

Paula Barrett *and* Lara Farrell

Abstract

Anxiety is one of the most common mental health problems affecting children and youth today. Prevention approaches offer an alternative and adjunct to treatment, and have become a priority for governments, offering a cost-effective and efficient means of providing services to children and youth prior to the onset of psychopathology. This chapter presents a review of current prevention strategies for anxiety disorders and examines the role of risk and protective factors in the development of anxiety. Current evidence-based prevention strategies are discussed at an indicated, selective, and universal level of prevention. Cognitive behavioral approaches to anxiety prevention are discussed based on a model of risk and resilience. Future directions for prevention practice and research are highlighted.

Keywords: anxiety, child, cognitive behavioral treatment, prevention, protective factors, risk factors, youth

Randomized controlled trials (RCTs) of cognitive behavioral treatment (CBT) for child and youth anxiety have consistently shown evidence of significant symptom reduction (Barrett, Dadds, & Rapee, 1996; Kendall, 1994; Kendall et al., 1997), leading to the current recognition of this intervention modality as being *probably efficacious* (e.g., Albano & Kendall, 2002; Ollendick & King, 1998). Kendall (1994) published the first RCT of CBT for anxiety disorders in children more than 10 years ago, examining the efficacy of the now widely used CBT program *Coping Cat,* with results indicating the program being effective for 64% of the children who participated. The efficacy of CBT for child anxiety disorders has been extended since Kendall's first trial (1994) with a number of published replication studies (i.e., Howard & Kendall, 1996; Kendall, Flannery-Schroeder, Panichelli-Mindel, Southam-Gerow, & Henin & Warman, 1997), long-term follow-up studies (i.e., Kendall, Safford,

Flannery-Schroeder, & Webb, 2004; Kendall & Southam-Gerow, 1996), and further controlled evaluations of CBT by a number of independent research groups (i.e., Barrett, Dadds, & Rapee, 1996; Cobham, Dadds, & Spence, 1998; Silverman et al., 1999). Cognitive behavioral treatment has been demonstrated as an effective intervention in both individual (Barrett et al., 1996; Kendall, 1994; Kendall et al., 1997; King et al., 1998) and group formats (Flannery-Schroeder et al., 2000; Mendlowitz et al., 1999; Shortt, Barrett, & Fox, 2001; Silverman et al., 1999). While results of the RCTs conducted to date provide promise for this treatment, there still remains considerable room for improvement in reducing anxiety disorders during childhood and youth.

Despite the demonstrated effectiveness of CBT in comparison to waitlist control conditions in reducing anxiety symptomatology, there remain a significant number of children and youth within

RCTs who do not remit from their anxiety disorders. Cartwright-Hatton and colleagues (Cartwright-Hatton, Roberts, Chitsabesan, Fothergill, & Harrington, 2004) published a systematic review of CBT for child and youth anxiety, combining the results from 10 published studies that compared CBT to a monitoring condition or a nonactive control group. In this review, the authors examined relative effect sizes of each study, focusing predominantly on the remission rates as their outcome variable. Results demonstrated that overall, when CBT is compared to a no-treatment control condition, CBT offers a significant positive treatment effect. However, when examining remission rates, the overall combined remission rates following CBT across studies was only 56.5% at posttreatment, and 63.75% at follow-up. This finding indicates that more than one-third of anxious children and youth who receive an evidence-based CBT intervention in a controlled trial continue to maintain anxiety diagnoses following completion of treatment and into the years that follow.

And what of the 10%–20% of children and youth with anxiety disorders in the general population (Costello & Angold, 1995; Kashani & Orvachel, 1988; McGee et al., 1990), who do not participate in RCTs? Research indicates that the majority of children and youth with clinical anxiety disorders will not receive treatment in the community (i.e., Tuma, 1989; Verhulst & van der Ende, 1997; Wittchen et al., 1999), and of those who do, many will not receive evidence-based interventions (Knitzer, 1985). One study estimated that about 75% of children with emotional and behavioral disorders in the United States do not receive specialty mental health services (Ringel & Sturm, 2001). In Australia, research suggests that as few as 5% of children and youth with mental health disorders come into contact with a mental health service (Stanley, 2002). The obvious discrepancy between the proportions of children with a mental health disorder in the community versus the proportion who receive specialized mental health services has been a matter of concern for policymakers, clinicians, and researchers alike. Given that anxiety disorders are extremely prevalent during childhood and youth, are associated with the development of other psychiatric illnesses if not treated (Last, Perrin, Hersen, & Kazdin, 1996), and are known to severely compromise a child's functioning through social isolation, interpersonal difficulties, impaired social competence, and school adjustment (Klein & Last, 1989; Messer & Beidel, 1994), there remains

a considerable need to improve intervention delivery and outcomes. One potentially very effective approach to facilitate the early identification of children and youth with anxiety disorders in the community, and to efficiently increase intervention delivery to children and youth, is to offer *preventative* interventions.

The prevention of anxiety and anxiety disorders in children and youth has received notable attention in the field in comparison to other childhood mental health problems, with a modest evidence base emerging and an obvious ongoing commitment from researchers and practitioners alike. In terms of some general, contemporary guidelines for prevention programming and practice, Nation and colleagues (2003) have recently conducted an analysis of the diverse prevention focused research, and identified six core principles for prevention programming and research to guide future research and practice. These six principles for coordinated prevention approaches include (1) use of a research-based risk and protective factor framework that involves families, peers, schools, and communities as partners to target multiple outcomes; (2) should be long-term, age-specific, and culturally appropriate; (3) fosters development of individuals who are healthy and fully engaged through teaching them to apply social-emotional skills and ethical values in daily life; (4) aims to establish policies, institutional practices, and environmental supports that nurture optimal development; (5) selects, trains, and supports interpersonally skilled staff to implement programming effectively; and (6) incorporates and adapts evidence-based programming to meet local community needs through strategic planning and ongoing evaluation, and continues improvement (Nation et al., 2003).

This chapter provides a review of current prevention strategies and outcomes for anxiety disorders, and seeks to examine the current status of this field of research in terms of the above core principles for prevention programming and research. Specifically, this chapter will examine the role of risk and protective factors and describe CBT approaches to prevention based on a model of risk and resilience. Further, this chapter examines the current evidence-base for prevention strategies, examining outcomes at multiple levels of intervention—from indicated, to selective, and universal studies of prevention. Finally, a discussion of the current state of the field in both prevention research and practice will be offered, with directions for future prevention research and practice highlighted.

Prevention Strategies

The most widely accepted model for defining prevention strategies at present is that described by Mrazek and Haggerty (1994), which includes three levels of prevention based upon guidelines for selecting participants. This model of prevention includes *indicated, selective,* and *universal* prevention approaches (Mrazek & Haggerty, 1994). *Indicated* prevention approaches are those applied to individuals or groups who are found to already report mild symptomatology, identifying them as being at increased risk for future development of mental health disorders. Indicated interventions require screening or interviewing children for emotional disturbance to accurately identify those individuals reporting existing symptoms of emotional distress. *Selective* prevention programs are applied to select individuals or subgroups of individuals who present with a significantly higher than average risk of developing a mental health disorder, based on our understanding of associated risk factors for that disorder. Selective interventions do not require screening of children, but rather rely on some other form of participant selection—often parent, teacher, or school nomination of perceived increased risk. *Universal* interventions are those applied to whole populations, regardless of the risk status of individuals, therefore, they eliminate the need to screen or accurately identify an at-risk subgroup of children and/or youth. In some instances, universal interventions are designed to enhance general well-being, whereas others are targeted at preventing a specific disorder(s) such as anxiety disorders.

There are a number of both advantages and disadvantages associated with each of these three levels of prevention. The determining characteristics of a chosen prevention approach for a particular group or subgroup is likely to be driven by the goal of the overriding intervention, and the associated context-specific circumstances, such as the sampling population available for recruiting participants, as well as the financial and human resources available for running the intervention. We believe an ideal situation is when all three levels of prevention are working in synergy—that is, indicated and/or selective interventions are available for those at increased risk, as well as universal approaches being delivered to all children and youth focused on increasing resilience and protective factors regardless of one's risk or life circumstances. In designing and delivering prevention programs and research, it is useful to weigh the pros and cons of each level of intervention to aid in finding the optimal approach to producing effective, yet parsimonious outcomes for all stakeholders involved—particularly the children, youth, and families who will participate.

Indicated and *selective* prevention approaches share many similar advantages, as well as shortcomings. The most obvious advantage of these approaches is that these programs target the most disadvantaged or in-need individuals, therefore, providing the strongest rationale for attracting funding, producing larger effect sizes than universal approaches in terms of statistical significance of outcomes, and having the most robust outcomes at a clinical significance level in terms of reducing suffering. When compared to universal approaches, these programs are generally more time-, cost-, and labor-efficient, and the benefit/cost ratio is more easily calculated, therefore, being more attractive to funding bodies and stakeholders (Donovan & Spence, 2000). Given that indicated and selective interventions target children with increased risk, or with elevated symptoms, it has been argued that participants involved in these programs may demonstrate increased motivation and compliance with the program due to their increased needs.

In terms of shortcomings, indicated and selective programs share a similar fundamental disadvantage in terms of the recruitment of samples. For selective programs, defining suitable "risk" criteria and developing the associated methods for reliably selecting individuals at risk are problematic. While selective interventions targeting children exposed to traumatic life events may prove to be generally straightforward in terms of selecting and recruiting participants, the identification of children and youth at increased risk due to other psychosocial factors is likely to prove more difficult (Donovan & Spence, 2000). Likewise, the selection of reliable and valid measures of risk is essential in delivering indicated interventions. Identifying measures that are sensitive to detecting elevated symptomatology and then deciding upon the appropriate cut-offs to define risk reliably present methodological and clinical quandaries for researchers. To date there no gold standards of measurement in assessing and defining level of risk for anxiety disorders within indicated approaches. Timing of selective and indicated interventions further present challenges to researchers and clinicians alike—when is the optimal time in a child's development to screen or identify potential risk for emotional disturbance? When will an intervention provide the most effective outcomes and prevent escalation of symptoms across a child's development? And how long are prevention outcomes likely to protect a child or youth from developing further emotional problems? All of these questions raise important issues when considering the potential benefits of a selective and/or indicated approach to prevention. Furthermore, given that the nature of these interventions is to "select" or "identify" individuals at increased risk, delivering these programs within the school environment presents a risk in itself—that is, risk of stigmatization for the children or youth who have been identified as requiring additional help within the school. Often for these children, they are called out of class, or they are required to participate in the intervention during their lunch times or after school. It is important that schools delivering indicated and selective interventions employ strategies to protect the confidentiality of students who are involved in such programs, and to also ensure that students are not disadvantaged through their participation in these programs, for example, by missing out on other essential curriculum and learning opportunities.

Universal prevention approaches also have advantages, as well as disadvantages when considering issues associated with both the implementation and evaluation of such programs. Given that universal approaches target entire populations, these interventions have the potential to be of enormous benefit in terms of reducing the prevalence of childhood anxiety disorders. Furthermore, since all children are targeted, regardless of risk level, those who do need assistance to overcome emotional or behavioral problems, but who may never come to the attention of a mental health professional, are nonetheless engaged in a positive program of change within the school environment without the burden of potential stigmatization associated with individualized or targeted programs. Moreover, as comorbidity for childhood anxiety disorders is high, and risk and protective factors frequently overlap among different emotional and behavioral disorders, a single universal preventive intervention has the potential to impact upon multiple problems (Greenberg, Domitrovich, & Bumbarger, 2001). Universal prevention interventions conducted in the school context have further advantages such as reducing the need to screen and recruit participants (all children participate in the classroom program such that there is no requirement to identify and select participants). Universal approaches to prevention have the potential for reaching a broad range of children and adolescents with varying levels of risk for psychopathology, without stigmatization associated with identifying individuals or subgroups.

This approach to prevention focuses on acquiring skills to cope, enhancing peer support, and reducing psychosocial difficulties within the classroom or peer-group—thus promoting learning and healthy emotional development in all children (Evans, 1999; Kubiszyn, 1998).

While the value of promoting emotional competence and positive mental health within schools for all children, regardless of risk, cannot be overlooked, there are some difficulties associated with universal prevention research. First, dealing with large samples of children and youth mean universal prevention research is extremely costly—program evaluation requires screening all children before and after an intervention, and optimally at long-term follow-up to ascertain preventative outcomes. A second potential difficulty for universal prevention research in schools is the burden of research on the school system. Utilizing schools for prevention research potentially presents abundant data opportunities; however, the process of engaging schools and conducting longitudinal research is a complex procedure that requires *ongoing* support and commitment from all involved, including educational authorities, school principals, teaching and administrative staff, as well as parents and students. The benefits of a school-based intervention must be highly valued by all stakeholders if long-term follow-up is to be successful and program implementation sustainable over time. A final questionable disadvantage of a universal approach to prevention is the potentially low dose effect that a universal strategy may offer, and whether classroom-based program delivery by the classroom teacher offers sufficient program duration and intensity to alter the developmental pathways of children already at substantial risk for anxiety. Based on research outcomes to date, it seems that the dose of intervention at a universal level may in fact be sufficient, with evidence suggesting all children, particularly those at *elevated* risk, do receive sufficient exposure to skills in a universal intervention to provide short-term positive impacts on anxiety reduction and prevention (e.g., Barrett & Turner, 2001; Lock & Barrett, 2003; Lowry-Webster, Barrett, & Dadds, 2001). Despite the inherent obstacles in delivering universal prevention programs and conducting universal prevention research, this population-based approach to mental health promotion and prevention offers potentially very promising outcomes for the emotional development of children and youth, and provides an optimistic vision for reducing the increasing prevalence of anxiety and its disorders in

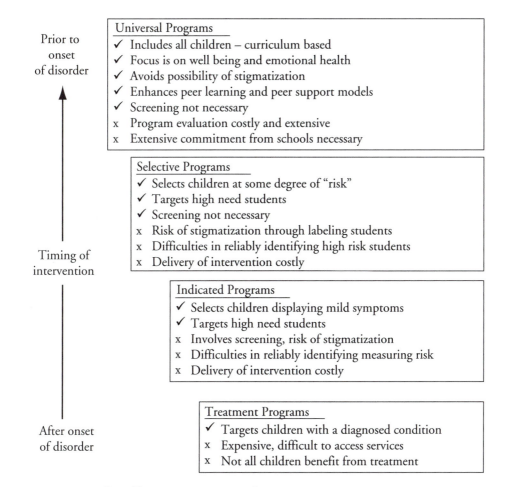

Prior to
onset
of disorder

Universal Programs
✓ Includes all children – curriculum based
✓ Focus is on well being and emotional health
✓ Avoids possibility of stigmatization
✓ Enhances peer learning and peer support models
✓ Screening not necessary
x Program evaluation costly and extensive
x Extensive commitment from schools necessary

Selective Programs
✓ Selects children at some degree of "risk"
✓ Targets high need students
✓ Screening not necessary
x Risk of stigmatization through labeling students
x Difficulties in reliably identifying high risk students
x Delivery of intervention costly

Timing of
intervention

Indicated Programs
✓ Selects children displaying mild symptoms
✓ Targets high need students
x Involves screening, risk of stigmatization
x Difficulties in reliably identifying measuring risk
x Delivery of intervention costly

Treatment Programs
✓ Targets children with a diagnosed condition
x Expensive, difficult to access services
x Not all children benefit from treatment

After onset
of disorder

Fig. 1 The intervention continuum: From treatment to prevention strategies.

childhood and youth. Figure 1 describes the intervention continuum for anxiety and anxiety disorders in children and youth.

Role of Risk and Protective Factors

Nation and colleagues' (2003) six core principles for prevention research and practice highlight first and foremost the need for a research-based risk and protective factor framework that involves families, peers, schools, and communities in targeting specific prevention outcomes. The development of childhood anxiety disorders involves a very complex interplay between risk and protective factors, at a biological, psychological, environmental, and familial level. Empirical evidence to date investigating the etiology of anxiety disorders in childhood has identified a number of potential risk factors; however, research into protective factors is by comparison deficient. While research clearly indicates increased risk for anxiety disorders in offspring of anxious parents; a sizable percent of these children do not become

clinically anxious. Why is it that some children do not develop emotional disturbances, even though they have been exposed to a number of risk factors? The role of protective factors is crucial in explaining why some children and youth are less susceptible to risk. An understanding of specific protective factors associated with increasing resilience against anxiety and anxiety disorders in childhood is an understudied area requiring further investigation. The current research-based framework for the prevention of child anxiety disorders is therefore based primarily on reducing risk, based on our current knowledge of risk factors. In many cases, however, risk factors associated with an increased vulnerability for anxiety may not be acquiescent to change—therefore a model of prevention must lean more toward building strengths and protective factors that intuitively counteract risk and vulnerability. Familial (including genetic), social, psychological, and environmental risk factors for anxiety disorders are covered in chapters 8 and 14 in this book.

Even though there is evidence that the risk factors for anxiety disorders, as reviewed elsewhere in this textbook, are associated with increased vulnerability for anxiety disorders, these risk factors alone are not sufficient in accurately predicting which children/youth will experience clinical anxiety in the face of adversity, and which will not. Certain factors that protect against the development of childhood internalizing disorders in the context of risk factors have been identified. While empirical research for the role of protective factors associated with childhood anxiety is limited, there has been some research to support the protective role of coping strategies and social support in buffering children against emotional distress and anxiety. Coping strategies have been categorized in the literature as either problem-focused, avoidant, or emotion-focused (Billings & Moos, 1981; Carver, Scheier, & Weintraub, 1989). Adaptive coping style is believed to serve a protective function for mental health and well-being in general (Muris et al., 2001). In the case of anxiety disorders, the ability to use problem-focused coping strategies, characterized by approach and engagement, has been suggested to exert a protective influence (e.g., Herman-Stahl & Petersen, 1996; Lengua et al., 1999; Muris et al., 2001; Plancherel & Bolognini, 1995; Windle & Windle, 1996), while emotion-focused coping has been associated with higher levels of emotional and behavioral problems in adolescence (Compas et al., 1988), and avoidant coping has been associated with elevated levels of anxiety and depression (Ebata & Moos, 1991). While research is only preliminary, there is evidence to suggest that problem-focused coping strategies may serve to protect a child or adolescence against the experience of clinical anxiety. Additionally, positive and available social support has been demonstrated to reduce the likelihood of negative psychological outcomes following exposure to traumatic or stressful life events (Cowen, Pedro-Carroll, & Alpert-Gillis, 1990; Jose et al., 1998; Spaccarelli & Fuchs, 1997; White et al., 1998). In one study examining the effects of parental divorce on primary school-aged children, participants with a higher self-rating of perceived overall social support manifested fewer postdivorce difficulties, anxiety, and worry (Cowen et al., 1990). It seems likely that the quality and availability of social support accessible to children and youth may predict one's ability to cope in difficult life circumstances, therefore, increasing one's resilience against anxiety and emotional disturbance.

Based on this brief review of protective factors associated with the development of childhood anxiety, it is clear that our knowledge of existing protective factors is substantially lacking in comparison to our knowledge of risk factors. This discrepancy in the research literature is problematic in developing theoretically and empirically driven models to prevention, particularly models of universal prevention that focus on increasing general well-being and emotional resilience in children and youth. Nevertheless, current interventions for anxiety disorders in children and youth are based on the above-mentioned risk and protective factors, and focus on a cognitive behavioral model that aims at reducing risk factors while enhancing protective factors associated with the development and maintenance of anxiety and anxiety disorders. The cognitive behavioral model of intervention for child and youth anxiety addresses *cognitive, physiological,* and *learning* processes. Interventions typically target *cognitive* processes through teaching children positive thinking strategies and encouraging flexibility in thinking through challenging negative thoughts. *Physiological* processes are addressed through teaching children first, awareness of their internal, physiological body clues when feeling nervous or afraid, and then through providing skills to enable children to self-regulate emotional distress and physiological arousal using relaxation strategies. Finally, *learning* processes are addressed in an anxiety intervention through the acquisition of new skills that help children cope with and manage anxiety and anxiety-provoking situations. These learning and behavioral skills include teaching children and youth problem-focused coping strategies that support a child approaching fears and challenges rather than avoiding situations, and encourage children seeking proactive outcomes to challenging life circumstance. Figure 2 illustrates the cognitive behavioral model of intervention for anxiety and anxiety disorders, describing cognitive, physiological, and learning (behavioral) strategies aimed at reducing risk for anxiety and increasing protective factors associated with emotional resilience.

The accumulating evidence-base for prevention interventions aimed at targeting and reducing anxiety and anxiety disorders has grown rapidly over the past 10 to 12 years. A number of trials have been conducted at each level of prevention, with results suggesting favorable outcomes in terms of both symptoms reduction and reduction of risk for anxiety and anxiety disorders. This review summarizes the field of prevention research to date.

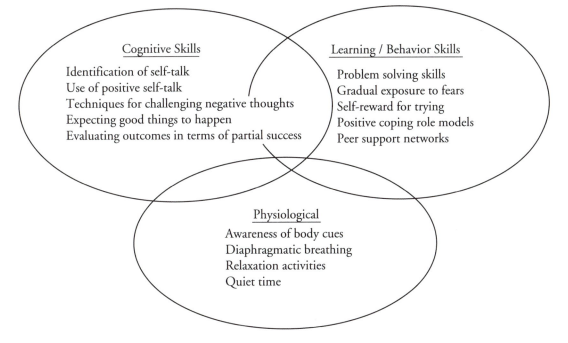

Fig. 2 The cognitive behavioral model of intervention for child and youth anxiety.

Prevention Outcomes for Child and Youth Anxiety Disorders

Indicated Interventions. Three studies have been identified in the literature, which have evaluated school-based *indicated* prevention of anxiety for children and adolescents. The first study, conducted by Kiselica, Baker, Thomas, and Reedy (1994), investigated the effectiveness of a preventive stress inoculation program for adolescents, consisting of a blend of progressive muscle relaxation, cognitive restructuring, and assertiveness training. The program involved eight sessions and was delivered to Grade 9 students ($n = 48$) who reported elevated anxiety scores on self-report measures. Students were compared with a control group on measures of anxiety, stress, and academic performance. Compared with controls, the students who received the indicated intervention demonstrated significantly greater improvements on self-report measures of trait anxiety and stress-related symptoms at posttest and at 4-week follow-up assessment. There were no significant differences between the two groups in academic achievement at either posttest or follow-up. This study provided initial support for a school-based psychosocial intervention in reducing anxiety in youth.

Dadds, Spence, Holland, Barrett, and Laurens (1997) examined the effectiveness of a 10-session school-based group CBT intervention for prevent-ing anxiety symptoms in 7- to 14-year-olds, in comparison to a monitoring only control group. Participants were selected on the basis of subclinical or mild clinical levels of anxiety determined by child self-report, teacher nominations, and parental interviews. In addition to weekly child sessions, parents were invited to attend three parent education sessions. The program delivered was the *Coping Koala* (Barrett, Dadds, & Rapee, 1996), an Australian modification of Kendall's (1994) *Coping Cat* program. The *Coping Koala* program includes group-based delivery of CBT anxiety-management strategies, in combination with parent support and training.

Results demonstrated positive outcomes for all children involved in the study, with both intervention and control children reporting decreased anxiety at postintervention. A significant preventive effect on rate of diagnosis, as well as child and family adjustment, was evident at the 6- and 24-month follow-up time-points for the intervention participants only (Dadds, Spence, Laurens, Mullins, & Barrett, 1999). Of the participants who had subclinical levels of anxiety (but not disorder) at pretreatment, 54% of these control participants progressed to a diagnosable disorder at the 6-month follow-up, compared with only 16% in the intervention group. This study provides preliminary evidence for a prevention effect of anxiety disorders, through delivering a school-based CBT intervention during late childhood.

Bernstein, Layne, Egan, and Tennison (2005) have recently replicated this study, examining the effectiveness of group-based CBT for anxiety, in comparison to group-based CBT plus parent training, and a no-treatment, monitoring only control group. This study involved students 7 through to 11 years of age (*n* = 61) who reported elevated levels of anxiety based on self-report, parent and child diagnostic interviews, and teacher nomination. Children who scored above the clinical cut-off on the anxiety self-report measure and/or who were nominated by their teachers as being anxious were interviewed (along with their parents in a separate interview) for an anxiety diagnosis. Inclusion criteria for this study required participants to have a diagnosis of separation anxiety disorder, generalized anxiety disorder, and/or specific phobia or "features" (one or more diagnostic criteria, but not all) of at least one of these disorders.

The intervention delivered in this study of indicated intervention was the *FRIENDS* program (Barrett et al., 2000a), a published adaptation of the *Coping Koala* program (Barrett, Dadds, & Rapee, 1996). The *FRIENDS* program (Barrett, 2004, 2005) is an empirically validated (Barrett et al., 1996, 2001; Shortt et al., 2001) CBT program for children and adolescents who experience anxiety. The *FRIENDS* program includes two developmentally tailored workbooks for use with either children or youth and can be run in both group and individual settings. *FRIENDS* includes a family-skills component (2 parent sessions) that involves parents in each stage of skill acquisition and provides parent training in anxiety management. The program consists of 10 weekly sessions and two booster sessions 1 and 3 months following the completion of the program. The program teaches children skills associated with affective education and empathy development, emotional regulation, developing positive self-talk, problem-solving skills, building social support networks, coping role models, approaching fears through fear hierarchies, self-reward, and strategies for dealing with conflict. Bernstein and colleagues (2005) evaluated the standard *FRIENDS* group program, in comparison to *FRIENDS* plus an intensive weekly parent support component, and a no-treatment monitoring only control.

The results of this study demonstrated that group-based CBT (with and without parent training), delivered within the school environment, is significantly more effective than no-treatment in reducing anxiety symptoms and diagnosis based on child report, parent report, and diagnostic interviews (Bernstein et al., 2005). This study found significant pre- to postintervention effects between CBT conditions and the no-treatment control group, which improves on outcomes found in the Dadds et al. (1997) study that did not demonstrate significant group differences until 6-month and 24-month follow-up (Dadds et al., 1997). In terms of differences between group CBT and group CBT plus parent training, findings from this study are mixed. On parent report of child anxiety and clinician-rated severity, there were significant differences between group CBT plus parent training and the no-treatment control group, but no difference was found for group CBT alone compared to the no-treatment control. Contrary to these findings, there was evidence that group CBT alone was superior to group CBT plus parent training based on diagnostic status, whereby only group CBT alone was significantly different from the no-treatment control group. The results of this study provide some evidence that group CBT programs delivered within the school environment, alone or in combination with parent training, can effectively reduce anxiety symptoms for some children. Longitudinal follow-up of subjects in this study is warranted to inform about the longer-term preventative outcomes for nonclinical children who participated in this study.

Selective Interventions. A number of preliminary investigations have been conducted in the literature to examine the effectiveness of school-based *selective* interventions, across a range of risk groups, to reduce or prevent anxiety symptoms and disorder. Rapee and Jacobs (2002) piloted the efficacy of a selective prevention (delivered exclusively to parents) of anxiety in preschool-aged (3.5 years to 4.5 years) children who exhibited behavioral inhibition. Children in this study were selected on the basis of parent-rated behavioral inhibition. Parents participated in a six-session group program, which trained them in anxiety-management strategies, understanding of parental modeling and overinvolvement, modeling positive behavior, promoting independence in children, and instruction on how to develop and assist children with exposure hierarchies to address their child's fears. While no immediate postintervention results were reported, findings at 12-month follow-up indicated that the program was superior to the no-treatment comparison group for reducing behavioral inhibition and rate of anxiety disorder diagnosis in children. These preliminary results offer encouraging data to suggest that children as young as 3 and 4 years of age may benefit from interventions targeting anxiety and fostering emotional resilience.

In an extension to this study, Rapee, Kennedy, Ingram, Edwards, and Sweeney (2005) conducted a controlled evaluation of this selective CBT intervention, aimed at preventing anxiety disorders in young children. Children were selected for inclusion in this study if they exhibited a high number of withdrawn/inhibited behaviors, based on maternal report and laboratory observation, and were randomly allocated to either a 6-session parent education group program (n = 73), or a no-treatment monitoring condition (n = 73). Results of this study demonstrated that children of parents in the education program experienced significantly fewer anxiety diagnoses at 12-month follow-up compared to the monitoring group. This study suggests that early intervention, targeted at children at increased risk for anxiety, may reduce or prevent the occurrence of anxiety disorders later in childhood. Longer-term follow-up would shed important light on the actual impact of the intervention in years to come.

In further studies of selective prevention, Barrett and colleagues (Barrett, Moore, & Sonderegger, 2000; Barrett, Sonderegger, & Sonderegger, 2001; Barrett, Sonderegger, & Xenos, 2003) have examined the effects of delivering school-based CBT interventions to diverse cultural groups of children. Cultural change and migration have been found to significantly increase risk for the development of anxiety in childhood and adolescence (Barrett & Turner, 2000). To address this risk factor, a number of studies have evaluated the effectiveness of the *FRIENDS* program (Barrett et al., 2000a) in reducing the psychological distress experienced by migrant children and adolescents of former Yugoslavian, Chinese, and mixed-ethnic backgrounds. Following involvement in this 10-session school-based CBT group intervention, participants reported improvements on measures of self-esteem, internalizing symptoms, and future outlook (Barrett et al., 2000, 2001, 2003), with gains maintained up to 6-month follow-up (Barrett et al., 2003).

Cooley, Boyd, & Grados (2004) conducted a pilot trial of the *FRIENDS* program (Barrett et al., 2000a) with a group of inner-city African American children (n = 10; aged 10 to 11 years) exposed to high levels of community violence and reporting moderate levels of anxiety. The program was implemented biweekly during class time, with postintervention results indicating significantly reduced self-reported anxiety, including significant decreases in contextually relevant anxiety (e.g., safety concerns). Additionally, participants reported a high level of program acceptability and subjectively rated a moderate degree of impact on their behavior at school. This research team has subsequently commenced a larger efficacy trial, with results likely to become available in the near future.

Universal Interventions. To date, the published research evaluating universal prevention outcomes for child and youth anxiety and anxiety disorders has been exclusively conducted by Barrett and colleagues (Barrett, Farrell, Ollendick, & Dadds, 2006; Barrett & Turner, 2000; Lock & Barrett, 2003; Lowry-Webster, Barrett, & Dadds, 2001; Lowry-Webster, Barrett, & Lock, 2003). This current universal prevention research evaluates the well-established anxiety intervention program, *FRIENDS* (Barrett et al., 2000a, 2000b, 2004, 2005), which is now widely used throughout clinics and schools both in Australia and abroad as a treatment, indicated/selective prevention program, and as universal prevention approach in schools. A number of international research groups are currently conducting replication studies of universal prevention using *FRIENDS,* as well as conducting evaluations of similar cognitive behavioral programs aimed at reducing anxiety. The publication of these independent research trials will add substantially to the current status of evidence-base for universal prevention of anxiety and anxiety disorders in children and youth. This review summarizes Barrett and colleagues research evaluations to date, of universal approaches to prevention.

Barrett and Turner (2001) conducted the first preliminary trial of *FRIENDS* as a universal intervention for the prevention of internalizing symptoms in grade 6 children (aged 9–10 years). This study evaluated a "train-the-trainer" model of intervention, whereby children were assigned to one of three conditions: (1) psychologist-led intervention (n = 188), (2) teacher-led intervention (n = 263), and (3) standard curriculum, monitoring only condition (n = 137). Barrett and Turner (2001) trained classroom teachers and psychologists to implement the *FRIENDS* program as part of the standard classroom curriculum. Parents in both the psychologist-led and the teacher-led intervention were invited to attend four parent evenings. Children were screened for symptoms of anxiety using self-report questionnaires. Evaluation of children's self-report measures at postintervention indicated positive intervention effects, with participants reporting significant reductions in anxiety symptoms across psychologist- and teacher-led interventions in comparison to the monitoring only condition. This study provided preliminary evidence for the effectiveness of the *FRIENDS* program, delivered by either trained teachers or psychologists at a school-based population level, integrated within the standard school curriculum.

Following this initial study, Lowry-Webster, Barrett, and Dadds (2001) examined the effectiveness of *FRIENDS* as a universal strategy, in comparison to a monitoring only condition. In total, 594 students, aged 10–13 years, were allocated to either an intervention or control condition on the basis of classroom group. Children were screened using self-report measures of anxiety and depression symptomatology. At postassessment, children from both the intervention and control conditions reported significant reductions in anxiety symptoms, although these decreases were significantly greater in the intervention group compared to the monitoring condition. A significant reduction in self-reported symptoms of depression was also found for the intervention group only. Further analysis of change in risk status for those children within the high-risk category (scoring above clinical cut-off on measures of anxiety) showed positive findings. Of the children in the intervention group identified at high risk at preintervention, 75.3% were no longer at risk at postintervention, compared to 54.8% of high-risk children in the monitoring group. This finding highlights both the general improvement over time in anxiety symptoms for all children in upper primary school, a finding that has been reported by a number of others (i.e., Dadds et al., 1999; Last et al., 1996), as well as the increased reduction in risk for children who received a universal intervention (20% more of high-risk students report reduction of risk).

Lowry-Webster et al. (2003) continued the above investigation by monitoring these children over the following year to assess outcomes at 12-month follow-up. Results indicated that prevention effects were maintained up to 12-month follow-up for children who received the *FRIENDS* program. The children in the intervention group reported lower scores on anxiety self-report measures than children in the control condition, and the high-risk anxiety children from the intervention condition reported reductions in both anxiety and depression scores. Diagnostic interview data demonstrated that 85% of high-risk children in the intervention group were diagnosis free at 12-month follow-up, compared to only 31.2% of high-risk children in the control group. This follow-up study demonstrated both

statistically and clinically significant reductions in anxiety symptoms and disorders from pretest to 12-month follow-up following the *FRIENDS* universal program when delivered by classroom teachers within the standard school curriculum.

Lock and Barrett (2003), in a separate study aimed at replicating the findings of Lowry-Webster et al. (2001), presented the results of a longitudinal school-based study of universal prevention using the *FRIENDS* program across two distinct age groups. This study involved a group of 733 children enrolled in Grade 6 (*n* = 336; aged 9 and 10 years) and Grade 9 (*n* = 401; aged 14 to 16 years) from seven socioeconomically diverse schools in the metropolitan area of Brisbane, Australia. Schools were randomly assigned to either the intervention condition or a monitoring control condition (standard curriculum), and all students completed self-report measures of anxiety (SCAS: Spence, 1998; RCMAS: Reynolds & Richmond, 1978), depression (CDI: Kovacs, 1981), and coping (Brodzinsky, Elias, Steiger, Simon, Gill, & Clarke-Hitt, 1992). Students identified as "high-risk" based on elevated scores on an anxiety measure were interviewed using a structured diagnostic interview. As with previous research (e.g., Dadds et al., 1997, 1999; Lowry-Webster et al., 2001, 2003), this study found general reductions in anxiety across time regardless of intervention condition; however, reductions were significantly greater for students in the intervention condition compared to the monitoring condition at both posttest and 12-month follow-up.

In terms of age differences, this study found that children in Grade 6 reported significantly higher levels of anxiety prior to the intervention and at postintervention, yet evidenced greater reductions in anxiety at 12-month follow-up, as well as lower levels of depression across time compared to Grade 9 children. This finding suggests that the optimal time for preventing anxiety may be in late childhood (9–10 years of age) versus early adolescence. Lock and Barrett (2003) further examined gender differences and found that females were more likely than males to be at-risk of an anxiety disorder at preintervention and tended to report higher levels of anxiety than boys over time. Moreover, Grade 6 females appeared to be most responsive to the intervention, as they reported greater reductions in anxiety compared to females in Grade 9, and males across grades. Lock and Barrett (2003) also examined the effects of the intervention on depressive symptoms. Results indicated that there were significant reductions in depression; however, this effect was only apparent at 12-month follow-up, suggesting a delayed prevention effect for depression. This finding of a delayed effect is consistent with the finding from the Queensland Early Intervention project (Dadds et al., 1997) and is also consistent with Jaycox and colleagues' prevention trial for depression (see Jaycox et al., 1994).

Most recently, Barrett et al. (2006) evaluated the long-term effectiveness of the *FRIENDS* program in reducing anxiety and depression, by reporting long-term (12-, 24-, and 36-month) follow-up data for Lock and Barrett's (2003) original sample of children across Grade 6 and Grade 9. Results of this study indicated that intervention-related reductions in anxiety reported in Lock and Barrett (2003) were maintained for students in Grade 6, with the intervention group reporting significantly lower ratings of anxiety at long-term follow-up. There were no significant group differences for students in Grade 9 at any of the follow-up assessment points. This finding strengthens Lock and Barrett's (2003) suggestion that intervening with universal prevention in Grade 6 may be an optimal time for reducing risk for anxiety and depression. This study reported a significant time by intervention group by gender effect on anxiety, with females in the intervention group reporting significantly lower anxiety than females in the monitoring condition at 12-month and 24-month follow-up, but not at 36-month follow-up. Results also supported a longitudinal prevention effect with significantly fewer high-risk students at 36-month follow-up in the intervention condition than in the control condition. This long-term follow-up study provides evidence for the durability of prevention effects for children who receive a prevention intervention in Grade 6, with outcomes evident up to 3 years following a brief cognitive behavioral intervention, delivered by classroom teachers, within the school curriculum. For girls, however, who reported the highest scores of anxiety at preintervention, and who reported the largest reductions in anxiety up to 12-month follow-up (Lock & Barrett, 2003), it seems that prevention effects may only be durable up to 24-month follow-up. These studies of universal prevention provide promising outcomes for reducing risk for anxiety disorders in children and youth through school-based delivery of evidence-based prevention programs.

Prevention Research and Practice: Current Status and Visions for the Future

A shift in intervention focus, from treatment to prevention, may reduce the overwhelming burden of demand on community treatment providers, and is a seemingly optimistic approach to reducing risk for anxiety symptoms and disorder in children and youth. Based on the research conducted to date, it seems that utilizing schools for proving mental health promotion and prevention offers an encouraging alternative to a community health care system that is failing to reduce the prevalence of emotional disturbance in children and youth.

A review of the prevention research conducted to date presents some promising data that early intervention can make a substantial impact on reducing anxiety symptoms and disorders. Studies of *indicated* prevention have demonstrated that by identifying those children who are already experiencing symptoms and disorders of anxiety, programs can be effectively delivered by psychologists within the school community, which significantly reduce stress, anxiety symptoms, and anxiety diagnoses (Bernstein et al., 2005; Dadds et al., 1997; Kiselica et al., 1994) in both the short-term (i.e., Bernstein et al., 2005), as well as at longer-term follow-up (i.e., Dadds et al., 1997). *Selective* prevention studies, which select children and youth based on some predefined risk factor for anxiety disorders (i.e., children with increased behavioral inhibition, immigrant children, children exposed to violence), have also shown some positive preliminary outcomes. Delivering CBT interventions at school, aimed at increasing resilience and managing anxiety and stress, for children at potential risk for anxiety disorders appears to be effective in reducing stress and anxiety, as well as increasing self-esteem, positive outlook, and positive behaviors within the school context (i.e., Barrett et al., 2000, 2001; Rapee & Jacobs, 2002).

Research examining the effectiveness of *universal* prevention strategies within schools provides possibly the most exciting development in anxiety prevention research, with findings demonstrating reduction in anxiety symptoms for all children, including a preventative effect for high-risk children. Studies conducted to date have provided evidence that teachers can be successfully trained to deliver manualized CBT interventions, with outcomes similar to those found when programs are delivered by psychologists (Barrett & Turner, 2000; Lowry-Webster et al., 2001), within the classroom setting, as part of the standard school educational curriculum. Data from a number of studies that have examined the efficacy of the *FRIENDS* program (Barrett et al., 2000a, 2000b; Barrett, 2004, 2005), have demonstrated significant reductions in anxiety immediately following the intervention (Barrett &

Turner, 2000; Lock & Barrett, 2003; Lowry-Webster et al., 2001), as well as at longer-term follow-up (Barrett et al., 2006; Lock & Barrett, 2003; Lowry-Webster et al., 2003). Additional benefits of universal prevention for anxiety are that many students also experience significant reductions in depression symptoms (Lock & Barrett, 2003; Lowry-Webster et al., 2001), an important finding given the high overlap of anxiety and depression in clinical samples.

Research suggests that timing of universal interventions for reducing anxiety may be critical, with programs likely to achieve greatest change during primary school years, prior to the often stressful transition into high school and prior to the mean age of onset of anxiety diagnoses, which tends to be in middle to late childhood. It also seems important that universal prevention approaches are not seen as a one-off program, but rather are incorporated into schools at multiple levels, beginning as early as preschool and continuing throughout primary and high school. It is likely that prevention outcomes will be more durable, beyond 2 to 3 years, and programs more sustainable in schools, if they become part of the core ongoing learning objectives and curriculum of schools. Universal prevention programs are an attractive approach to intervention for schools and communities, in that all children have the opportunity to benefit from learning positive coping life skills, thereby increasing emotional resilience in all children regardless of risk and fostering positive peer learning and support networks within the school environment. Universal prevention provides possibly the best opportunity to target all children, including those who may be at increased risk for emotional disturbance, without the expense and burden of screening, labeling, and targeting select children for participation in intervention groups outside of the classroom curriculum. These evidence-based programs offer schools a curriculum for teaching social-emotional competence and resilience, while reducing the overall risk for anxiety and depression in students.

In considering the current status of prevention research for child and youth anxiety and anxiety disorders, we can measure the research to date and outcomes of an evidence-based program such as *FRIENDS,* against Nation and colleagues' (2003) six principles for coordinated prevention approaches. What prevention research in child anxiety has achieved to date is (1) the use of a research-based risk and protective factor framework that involves families, peers, and schools in targeting outcomes; (2) evaluation of long-term prevention outcomes (i.e., Barrett et al., 2006), age-specific outcomes (i.e., Lock & Barrett, 2003), and culturally appropriate outcomes (i.e., Barrett et al., 2001, 2003); (3) evaluation of universal approaches that aim to foster the development of individuals who are healthy and fully engaged, through teaching social-emotional skills (i.e., Barrett & Turner, 2000; Barrett et al., 2006; Lock & Barrett, 2003; Lowry-Webster, Barrett, & Dadds, 2001; Lowry-Webster, Barrett, & Lock, 2003); and (4) the evaluation of a train the trainer model of intervention, which supports the principle of selecting, training, and supporting interpersonally skilled staff to implement prevention programs effectively within the school context. What prevention research for child anxiety needs to examine in the future, to meet the current recommended standards suggested by Nation and colleagues (2003), is to establish and evaluate different models of prevention dissemination and practice, which are based on sustainable, community-driven policies and institutional practices, which may serve to meet the needs of schools, as well as improve prevention outcomes. For example, research evaluating multilevel programming, including universal, indicated/selective, and links to treatment services in the community, working in parallel, supported by school policy and procedures, is necessary to inform on comprehensive yet sustainable approaches to prevention in schools. Research addressing school-based prevention practice, such as the cost-benefit ratio, staff training and ongoing professional development, and schools being equipped to measure outcomes, is also imperative to move beyond evidence-based research into community-based practice.

While the current state of the literature provides initial evidence in support of prevention approaches for child and youth anxiety, much research is still needed in terms of (1) establishing efficacy of CBT for anxiety prevention through replication studies by independent research teams; (2) evaluating different models of delivery aimed at improving outcomes and durability of outcomes, for example, through multilevel programming (universal plus indicated/selective), as well as multilayered programming that incorporates ongoing booster sessions or delivery of programs at multiple times across schooling for children and youth; and (3) evaluation of different school-based models of dissemination, aimed at meeting institutional needs and achieving sustainable programs and outcomes for families, schools, and communities. The future challenge that presents itself for policy makers, educational authorities, researchers, and schools alike is in bridging the gap between evidence-based research and actual prevention practice.

References

Albano, A. M., & Kendall, P. C. (2002). Cognitive behavioral therapy for children and adolescents with anxiety disorders: Clinical research advances. *International Review of Psychiatry, 14,* 129–134.

Barrett, P. M. (2004a). *Friends for Life! Program. Group Leader's Workbook for Children* (4th ed.). Brisbane, Australia: Australian Academy Press.

Barrett, P. M. (2004b). *Friends for Life! for Children. Participant Workbook and Leader's Manual.* Brisbane, Australia: Australian Academic Press.

Barrett, P. M. (2005a). *Friends for Life! Program. Group Leader's Workbook for Youth* (4th ed.). Brisbane, Australia: Australian Academy Press.

Barrett, P. M. (2005b). *Friends for Life! for Youth. Participant Workbook and Leader's Manual.* Brisbane, Australia: Australian Academic Press.

Barrett, P. M., Dadds, M. R., & Rapee, R. (1996). Family treatment of childhood anxiety: A controlled trial. *Journal of Consulting and Clinical Psychology, 64,* 333–342.

Barrett, P. M., Duffy, A., Dadds, M., & Rapee, R. (2001). Cognitive behavioral treatment of anxiety disorders in children: Long-term (6 year) follow-up. *Journal of Consulting and Clinical Psychology, 69,* 135–141.

Barrett, P. M., Farrell, L. J., Ollendick, T. H., & Dadds, M. (2006). Long-term outcomes of an Australian universal prevention trial of anxiety and depression symptoms in children and youth: An evaluation of the FRIENDS Program. *Journal of Clinical Child and Adolescent Psychology, 35,* 403–411.

Barrett, P. M., Lowry, H., & Turner, C. (2000a). *Friends Program. Group Leader's Workbook for Children.* Brisbane, Australia: Australian Academy Press.

Barrett, P. M., Lowry, H., & Turner, C. (2000b). *Friends Program. Group Leader's Workbook for Youth.* Brisbane, Australia: Australian Academy Press.

Barrett, P. M., Moore, A. F., & Sonderegger, R. (2000). The FRIENDS program for young former-Yugoslavian refugees in Australia: A pilot study. *Behavior Change, 17,* 124–133.

Barrett, P. M., Sonderegger, R., & Sonderegger, N. L. (2001). Evaluation of an anxiety-prevention and positive-coping program (FRIENDS) for children and adolescents of non-English-speaking background. *Behavior Change, 18,* 78–91.

Barrett, P. M., Sonderegger, R., & Xenos, S. (2003). Using FRIENDS to combat anxiety and adjustment problems among young migrants to Australia: A national trial. *Clinical Child Psychology and Psychiatry, 8,* 241–260.

Barrett, P. M., & Turner, C. M. (2000). Childhood anxiety in ethnic families: Current status and future directions. *Behavior Change, 17,* 113–123.

Barrett, P. M., & Turner, C. M. (2001). Prevention of anxiety symptoms in primary school children: Preliminary results from a universal school-based trial. *British Journal of Clinical Psychology, 40,* 399–410.

Bernstein, G. A., Layne, A. E., Egan, E. A., & Tennison, D. M. (2005). School-based interventions for anxious children. *Journal of the American Academy of Child and Adolescent Psychiatry, 32,* 814–821.

Billings, A. G., & Moos, R. H. (1981). The role of coping responses and social resources in attenuating the impact of stressful life events. *Journal of Behavioral Medicine, 4,* 139–157.

Brodzinsky, D. M., Elias, M. J., Steiger, C., Simon, J., Gill, M., & Clarke-Hitt, J. (1992). Coping scale for children and youth: Scale development and validation. *Journal of Applied Developmental Psychology, 13,* 195–214.

Cartwright-Hatton, S., Roberts, C., Chitsabesan, P., Fothergill, C., & Harrington, R. (2004). Systematic review of the efficacy of cognitive behavior therapies for childhood and adolescent anxiety disorders. *British Journal of Clinical Psychology, 43,* 421–436.

Carver, C. S., Scheier, M. F., & Weintraub, J. K. (1989). Assessing coping strategies: A theoretically based approach. *Journal of Personality and Social Psychology, 56,* 267–283.

Cobham, V. E., Dadds, M. R., & Spence, S. H. (1998). The role of parental anxiety in the treatment of childhood anxiety. *Journal of Consulting and Clinical Psychology, 66,* 893–905.

Compas, B. E., Malcarne, V. L., & Fondascaro, K. M. (1988). Coping with stressful events in older children and young adolescents. *Journal of Consulting and Clinical Psychology, 56,* 405–411.

Cooley, M. R., Boyd, R. C., & Grados, J. J. (2004). Feasibility of an anxiety preventive intervention for community violence exposed African-American children. *Journal of Primary Prevention, 25,* 105–123.

Costello, E. J., & Angold, A. A. (1995). Epidemiology. In J. S. March (Ed.), *Anxiety disorders in children and adolescents* (pp. 109–124). New York: Guilford Press.

Cowen, E. L., Pedro-Carroll, J. L., & Alpert-Gillis, L. J. (1990). Relationships between support and adjustment among children of divorce. *Journal of Child Psychology and Psychiatry and Allied Disciplines, 31,* 727–734.

Dadds, M. R., Spence, S. H., Holland, D., Barrett, P. M., & Laurens, K. (1997). Prevention and early intervention for anxiety disorders: A controlled trial. *Journal of Consulting and Clinical Psychology, 65,* 627–635.

Dadds, M. R., Spence, S. H., Laurens, K., Mullins, M., & Barrett, P. M. (1999). Early intervention and prevention of anxiety disorders in children: Results at 2-year follow-up. *Journal of Consulting and Clinical Psychology, 67,* 145–150.

Donovan, C. L., & Spence, S. H. (2000). Prevention of childhood anxiety disorders. *Clinical Psychology Review, 20,* 509–531.

Ebata, A. T., & Moos, R. H. (1991). Coping and adjustment in distressed and healthy adolescents. *Journal of Applied Developmental Psychology, 12,* 33–54.

Evans, S. W. (1999). Mental health services in schools: Utilization, effectiveness and consent. *Clinical Psychology Review, 19,* 165–178.

Flannery-Schroeder, E. C., & Kendall, P. C. (2000). Group and individual cognitive behavioral treatments for youth with anxiety disorders: A randomised clinical trial. *Cognitive Therapy and Research, 24,* 251–278.

Greenberg, M. A., Domitrovich, C., & Bumbarger, B. (2001). The prevention of mental disorders in school-aged children: Current state of the field. *Prevention and Treatment, 4.* Retrieved from http://journals.apa.org/prevention/volume4/pre004001a.html

Herman-Stahl, M., & Petersen, A. C. (1996). The protective role of coping and social resources for depressive symptoms among young adolescents. *Journal of Youth and Adolescence, 25,* 733–753.

Howard, B. L., & Kendall, P. C. (1996). Cognitive-behavioral family therapy for anxiety-disordered children: A multiple baseline evaluation. *Cognitive Therapy and Research, 20*, 423–443.

Jaycox, L. H., Reivich, K. J., Gilham, J., & Seligman, M. (1994). Preventing depressive symptoms in children and adolescents. *Behavior Research and Therapy, 32*, 801–816.

Kashani, J. H., & Orvaschel, H. (1990). A community study of anxiety in children and adolescents. *American Journal of Psychiatry, 147*, 313–318.

Kendall, P. C. (1994). Treating anxiety disorders in youth: Results of a randomised clinical trial. *Journal of Consulting and Clinical Psychology, 62*, 100–101.

Kendall, P. C., Flannery-Schroeder, E., Panichelli-Mindel, S. M., Southam-Gerow, M., Henin, A., & Warman, M. (1997). Therapy for youth with anxiety disorders: A second randomized clinical trial. *Journal of Consulting and Clinical Psychology, 65*, 366–380.

Kendall, P. C., Safford, S., Flannery-Schroeder, E., & Webb, A. (2004). Child anxiety treatment: Outcomes in adolescence and impact on substance use and depression at 7.4-year follow-up. *Journal of Consulting and Clinical Psychology, 72*, 276–287.

Kendall, P. C., & Southam-Gerow, M. A. (1996). Long-term follow-up of a cognitive-behavioral therapy for anxiety disordered youth. *Journal of Consulting and Clinical Psychology, 64*, 724–730.

King, N. J., Hamilton, D. I., & Ollendick, T. H. (1988). *Children's phobias: A behavioral perspective*. Chichester, England: Wiley.

Kiselica, M. S., Baker, S. B., Thomas, R. N., & Reedy, S. R. (1994). Effects of stress inoculation training on anxiety, stress, and academic performance among adolescents. *Journal of Counseling Psychology, 41*, 335–342.

Klein, R. G., & Last, C. G. (1989). *Anxiety disorders in children*. Thousand Oaks, CA: Sage.

Knitzer, J. (Guest Ed.). (1985). Mental health services to children (Special issue). *Journal of Clinical Child Psychology, 14*, 178–251.

Kovacs, M. (1981). Rating scales to assess depression in school-age children. *Acta Paedopsychiatrica, 46*, 305–315.

Kubiszyn, T. (1998). *Educational testing and measurement: Classroom application and practice*. New York: Wiley.

Last, C. G., Perrin, S., Hersen, M., & Kazdin, A. E. (1996). A prospective study of childhood anxiety disorders. *Journal of the American Academy of Child and Adolescent Psychiatry, 35*, 1502–1510.

Lengua, L. J. Sandler, I. N., West, S. G., Wolchik, S. A., & Curran, P. J. (1999). Emotionality and self-regulation, threat appraisal, and coping in children of divorce. *Development and Psychopathology, 11*, 15–37.

Lock, S., & Barrett, P. M. (2003). A longitudinal study of developmental differences in universal preventive intervention for child anxiety. *Behavior Change, 20*, 183–199.

Lowry-Webster, H. M., Barrett, P. M., & Dadds, M. R. (2001). A universal prevention trial of anxiety and depressive symptomatology in childhood: Preliminary data fom an Australian study. *Behavior Change, 18*, 36–50.

Lowry-Webster, H. M., Barrett, P. M., & Lock, S. (2003). A universal prevention trial of anxiety symptomatology during childhood: Results at 1-year follow-up. *Behavior Change, 20*, 25–43.

McGee, R., Feehan, M., Partridge, F., Silva, P. A., & Kelly, J.A.B. (1990). DSM–III disorders in a large sample of adolescents. *Journal of American Academy of Child and Adolescent Psychiatry, 29*, 611–619.

Mendlowitz, S. L., Manassis, K., Bradley, S., Scapillato, D., Miezitis, & Shaw, B. F. (1999). Cognitive-behavioral group treatments in child anxiety disorders: The role of parental involvement. *Journal of American Academy of Child and Adolescent Psychiatry, 38*, 1223–1229.

Messer, S. C., & Beidel, D. C. (1994). Psychosocial correlates of childhood anxiety disorders. *Journal of the American Academy of Child and Adolescent Psychiatry, 33*, 975–983.

Mrazek, P. J., & Haggerty, R. J. (1994). *Reducing risk for mental disorders: Frontiers for preventive intervention research*. Washington, DC: National Academy Press.

Muris, P., Merckelbach, H., & Meesters, C. (2001). Learning experiences and anxiety sensitivity in normal adolescents. *Journal of Psychopathology and Behavioral Assessment, 23*, 279–283.

Nation, M., Crusto, C., Wandersman, A., Kumpfer, K. L., Seyboldt, D., Morrisey-Kane, E., et al. (2003). What works in prevention: Principles of effective prevention programs. *American Psychologist, 58*, 449–456.

Ollendick, T. H., & King, N. J. (1994). Diagnosis, assessment and treatment of internalising problem in children: The role of longitudinal data. *Journal of Consulting and Clinical Psychology, 62*, 918–927.

Plancherel, B., & Bolognini, M. (1995). Coping and mental health in early adolescence. *Journal of Adolescence, 18*, 459–474.

Rapee, R. M., & Jacobs, D. (2002). The reduction of temperamental risk for anxiety in withdrawn preschoolers: A pilot study. *Journal of Behavioral and Cognitive Psychotherapy, 6*, 271–280.

Rapee, R. M., Kennedy, S., Ingram, M., Edwards, S., & Sweeney, L. (2005). Prevention and early intervention of anxiety disorders in inhibited preschool children. *Journal of Consulting and Clinical Psychology, 73*, 488–497.

Reynolds, C. R., & Richmond, B. O. (1978). What I think and feel: A revised measure of children's manifest anxiety. *Journal of Abnormal Child Psychology, 6*, 271–280.

Ringel, J., & Sturm, R. (2001). National estimates of mental health utilization and expenditure for children in 1998. *Journal of Behavioral Health Services & Research, 28*, 319–332.

Rosenbaum, J. F., Biederman, J., Gerten, M., Hirshfeld, D. R., Meminger, S. R., Herman, J. B., et al. (1988). Behavioral inhibition in children of parents with panic disorder and agoraphobia: A controlled study. *Archives of General Psychiatry, 45*, 463–470.

Shortt, A., Barrett, P. M., & Fox, T. (2001). Evaluating the FRIENDS program: A cognitive-behavioral group treatment of childhood anxiety disorders. *Journal of Clinical Child Psychology, 30*, 525–535.

Shortt, A. L, Barrett, P. M., Dadds, M. R., & Fox, T. L. (2001). The influence of family and experimental context on cognition in anxious children. *Journal of Abnormal Child Psychology, 29*, 585–598.

Silverman, W. K., Kurtines, W. M., Ginsburg, G. S., Weems, C. F., Lumpkin, P. W., & Carmichael, D. H. (1999). Treating anxiety disorders in children with group cognitive-behavioral therapy: A randomised clinical trial. *Journal of Consulting and Clinical Psychology, 67*, 995–1003.

Spaccarelli, S., & Fuchs, C. (1997). Variability in symptom expression among sexually abused girls: Developing multivariate models. *Journal of Clinical Child Psychology, 26*, 24–35.

Spence, S. H. (1998). A measure of anxiety symptoms among children. *Behavior Research and Therapy, 36*, 545–566.

Stanley, F. (2002). *Year Book Australia: Health centenary article—child health since federation*. Canberra, ACT: Australian Bureau of Statistics.

Tuma, J. M. (1989). Mental health services for children: The state of the art. *American Psychologist, 44,* 188–198.

Verhulst, F., & van der Ende, J. (1997). Factors associated with child mental health service use in the community. *Journal of the American Academy of Child and Adolescent Psychiatry, 36,* 901–909.

Windle, M., & Windle, R. C. (1996). Coping strategies, drinking motives, and stressful life events among middle adolescents: Associations with emotional and behavioral problems and with academic functioning. *Journal of Abnormal Psychology, 105,* 551–560.

Wittchen, H.-U., Stein, M. B., & Kessler, R. C. (1999). Social fears and social phobia in a community sample of adolescents and young adults: Prevalence, risk factors and comorbidity. *Psychological Medicine, 29,* 309–323.

Managing Anxiety in Primary Care

Denise A. Chavira, Murray B. Stein *and* Peter Roy-Byrne

Abstract

This chapter discusses how anxiety disorders are common in primary care and are associated with considerable impact. Despite their prevalence and impact, anxiety disorders frequently go undetected and untreated. Furthermore, quality of care for patients with anxiety disorders is often suboptimal. During the past decade, increased efforts have been made to improve care for patients with anxiety disorders. Brief and empirically validated screening instruments have begun to facilitate detection. Treatment outcome data support the utility of integrated anxiety intervention models that often include collaboration with primary care providers, case management, evidence-based psychotherapy, and/or pharmacotherapy. Although barriers to care still exist, sustained efforts to address these barriers and implement evidence-based interventions in primary care will further improve access and quality of care for patients with anxiety disorders.

Keywords: anxiety, assessment, barriers, primary care, treatment

Prevalence

Epidemiological studies suggest that anxiety disorders are the most common psychiatric disorder, with lifetime prevalence rates ranging from 8%–29% (Kessler et al., 2005). Furthermore, in the primary care setting, the prevalence of anxiety is much higher than in the general population. Lifetime rates in this setting typically range from 30%–40% (Allgulander & Nilsoon, 2003; Nisenson, Pepper, Schwenk, & Coyne, 1998), and the 1-month prevalence of any anxiety disorder is 14.6% (Nisenon et al., 1998). Disorder specific rates are 3%–10% for generalized anxiety disorder, 3%–11% for panic disorder, and 2.6% for social phobia (Nisenson et al., 1998; Roy-Byrne et al., 1999; Shear & Schulberg, 1995; Weiller, Bisserbe, Maier, & Lecrubier, 1998). Rates of posttraumatic stress disorder (PTSD) are also high, with estimates in the range of 12%–44% (Bruce et al., 2002; Escalona, Achilles, Waitzkin, & Yager, 2004), particularly in women who have experienced a sexual assault. In general, more women than men have anxiety disorders and rates are higher among younger than older patients (Kroenke, Spitzer, & Williams, 1994). Importantly, many patients with mood and anxiety disorders will receive their only health care from their general medical providers, and ethnic minorities in particular are more apt to present to medical settings for treatment of mental health problems (Olfson et al., 2000; Vega, Kolody, Auguilar-Gaxiola, & Catalano, 1999).

While the quality of care for anxiety disorders in primary care is improving, it remains suboptimal (Stein et al., 2004; Young, Klap, Sherbourne, & Wells, 2001). Recognition of anxiety disorders is low, ranging between 24%–44% (Lang & Stein, 2002), and when anxiety disorders are identified, providers are less likely to provide adequate quality treatment (Young et al., 2001). Service utilization rates are similarly low. In a recent study of primary care patients with a diagnosis of panic disorder, generalized anxiety disorder, social phobia, or PTSD, approximately 33% had received counseling from their provider in the prior 3 months, fewer than 10% had received counseling from a mental health professional who used empirically supported strategies (e.g., cognitive behavioral therapy), and 40% had received appropriate antianxiety medication in the previous 3 months, although only 25% had received appropriate dosing across a sufficient period of time (Stein et al., 2004). In a longitudinal study of primary care patients, 68% of patients identified as anxious had not received any mental health treatment when they were reassessed 7 years later (Colman, Brod, Potter, Buesching, & Rowland, 2004). High prevalence rates accompanied by poor overall recognition and utilization underscore the presence of a substantial unmet need for services in this population.

Detection

Somatization of anxiety symptoms contributes to the challenges of making accurate diagnoses and more indirectly, to increased medical expenditures (DuPont, Rice, & Miller, 1996). Anxiety symptoms can at times present as vague somatic complaints or as a serious medical condition. Symptoms such as chest pain, insomnia, dizziness, headaches, shortness of breath, nausea, palpitations, and numbness may mimic medical illnesses such as cardiac (e.g., ischemic heart disease and arrhythmias), thyroid disorders, or pulmonary problems. In fact, in the presence of acute physical complaints or chronic illness, it becomes more difficult for providers to recognize psychiatric illnesses (Culpepper, 2003; Furedi, Rozsa, Zambori, & Szadoczky, 2003). Many medical conditions can be ruled out by history and physical examination, and in some cases, additional laboratory tests (e.g., blood tests to detect thyroid disorders) may be necessary (Stein et al., 2005). Furthermore, diagnostic accuracy can be facilitated by considering the course of anxiety. For example, given the chronic unremitting course of anxiety, it is less common to see an individual present with sudden anxiety after age 35, in the absence of a significant stressor. In such cases, medical conditions may be more likely (Culpepper, 2003).

Comorbidity
Medical Comorbidity

Although somatic complaints may obscure the detection of anxiety, actual medical comorbidity is common among patients with anxiety disorders (Sareen et al., 2006). Patients with depression or anxiety report an average of 2 to 3 concurrent chronic medical illnesses (Young et al., 2001). Among 134 patients with chronic obstructive pulmonary disease (COPD), 65% screened positive for both depression and anxiety, 10% screened positive for anxiety only, and 5% for depression only (Kunik et al., 2005). Of those, only 31% were receiving treatment for anxiety or depression. Only a small portion of patients with a medical illness comorbid with depression or anxiety will receive appropriate treatment for a psychiatric problem; without treatment, anxiety can worsen the medical condition and sometimes exacerbate the psychiatric problems (Rogers, White, & Warshaw, 1994; Spitzer, Kroenke, Linzer, et al., 1995; Spitzer, Kroenke, & Williams, 1999). Importantly, in one treatment study, patients with panic disorder responded equally well to an anxiety management program regardless of their level of comorbid medical illness (Roy-Byrne, Stein, Russo, et al., 2005). However, patients with medical illness often start off with more severe psychiatric symptoms and may require more intensive treatment to achieve full remission (Roy-Byrne, Stein, Russo, et al., 2005).

Psychiatric Comorbidity

More than 50% of anxious patients in the community suffer from an additional comorbid mood or anxiety disorder (Kessler, Stang, Wittchen, Stein, & Walters, 1999; Roy-Byrne, Stang, et al., 2000) and in primary care, a single anxiety disorder, uncomplicated by comorbidity, is rare. For example, between 27% and 50% of panic disorder patients also have social anxiety disorder, and 36% to 42% percent have generalized anxiety disorder (Olfson et al., 1997; Rodriguez et al., 2004; Roy-Byrne et al., 1999). Among individuals with a current anxiety disorder, 33% to 76% have multiple anxiety disorders (Rodriguez et al., 2004; Spitzer, Kroenke, et al., 1999), 33% to 85% have a depressive disorder (Nisenson et al., 1998; Olfson et al., 1997; Roy-Byrne et al., 1999), and average rates of substance use comorbidity are approximately 15% (Grant et al., 2004; Rodriguez et al., 2004).

In general, comorbidity is associated with greater chronicity, slower recovery (Dew, Reynolds, & Houck, 1997; Hegel et al., 2005), increased rates of psychiatric hospitalizations (Kessler et al., 1998), suicidality (Bartels Coakley, & Oxman, 2002; Roy-Byrne, Stang, et al., 2000) and greater psychosocial disability (Brown, Schulberg, & Shear, 1996; Hirschfeld, 2001; Kessler et al., 1998; Olfson et al.,

1997). Patients with anxiety and comorbid depression often experience more impairment in quality of life than those with either disorder alone (Culpepper, 2003), and a new onset of anxiety puts a patient at a higher risk of developing major depression in the next year (Kessler et al., 1998). Fortunately, among patients with anxiety disorders, having a co-occurring depressive disorder increases the likelihood that the patient will receive counseling and psychotropic medications in the general medical sector (Meredith, Sherbourne, Jackson, Camp, & Wells, 1997; Stein et al., 2004; Weisberg, Dyck, Culpepper, & Keller, 2007), though treatment of comorbid conditions often needs to be more complex and sustained to be effective.

Costs and Functional Impact

The impact of anxiety disorders is a problem of substantial public health significance. The total costs of anxiety disorders is between 42.3 billion and 63.1 billion, which can be attributed to morbidity, mortality, lost productivity, and other indirect costs (Dupont, Rice, & Miller, 1996; Greenberg, Sisitsky, & Kessler, 1999). The annual costs of anxiety are more than the costs for schizophrenia or all affective disorders combined (Rice & Miller, 1998). The proportion of mental illness expenditures devoted to anxiety disorders is 30%, and anxiety accounts for 53% of pharmacotherapy expenditures for mental illnesses (Arikian & Gorman, 2001; Dupont et al., 1996). Difficulties with detection likely contribute to costs associated with outpatient medical utilization, and perhaps indirect costs associated with delaying appropriate treatment (Dupont et al., 1996). Patients with anxiety disorders are high utilizers of medical services, including primary, specialty, and emergency services, even after controlling for initial utilization status (Ford, Trestman, Steinberg, Tennen, & Allen, 2004). Further, patients with anxiety disorders appear to be persistent high utilizers when assessed across a 2-year span, a pattern that was not present for patients with depressive or addictive disorders (Ford, Trestman, Tennen, & Allen, 2005).

Screening

While much research has been conducted on screening programs for depression, unique challenges exist for patients with anxiety disorders. First, multiple anxiety disorders exist, making it difficult for one screening tool to accurately capture all anxiety disorders. Second, the use of multiple screening tools to detect individual disorders is likely a time-consuming, and complicated, task, particularly in primary care settings, where time is limited and screening programs must be simple to implement.

Various screening strategies have been suggested. However, at present there are no data to suggest which program may be the most efficient, cost-effective, or acceptable. For example, the use of a broad-based measure of psychological distress followed by a more lengthy assessment to screen for anxiety diagnoses is one possible option. Also, disorder-specific measures can be used as an initial step, and brief screening instruments to assess multiple anxiety disorders are emerging.

Broad-Based Measures—Clinician-Administered Interviews

The PRIME-MD is a well validated measure (Spitzer et al., 1994) that covers a broad range of psychiatric disorders. It is a two-step system that includes a 26-item self-report questionnaire to screen for five groups of disorders (depressive, anxiety, alcohol, somatoform, and eating disorders) and is followed by a structured interview that typically takes 8.4 minutes and is completed by the physician. Although the Prime-MD has acceptable psychometric properties for mood disorders, panic disorder, and generalized anxiety disorder, it is less useful for other psychological disorders and requires training to be accurately administered.

The Mini International Neuropsychiatric Interview (MINI) (Sheehan et al., 1998) is another structured interview that assesses a broad range of mental disorders. Its psychometric properties are well established (Sheehan et al., 1998), and it can be effective in recognizing anxiety and depression in primary care. The MINI takes 20–30 minutes to administer and requires training in order to properly use. The MINI also has a 17-item preliminary questionnaire that shows promise as a screener given its brevity, relative to the MINI (Ballenger, Davidson, Lecrubier, & Nutt, 2001).

Broad-Based Measures—Self-Report

The Patient Health Questionnaire (PHQ) (Spitzer, Kroenke, Williams, et al., 1999) is entirely self-administered, though the clinician needs to review the completed questionnaire and apply diagnostic algorithms. The PHQ consists of 26 items covering the following broad-based groups of disorders: somatoform, mood, anxiety, eating, and alcohol. The PHQ subscales (e.g., PHQ-9 for depression) can be used to assess disorder specific problems and also yields indices of severity and impairment. The PHQ has psychometric properties comparable to the original

PRIME MD and the MINI, but requires much less time to administer. Overall, it is a well-established, time-efficient measure capable of generating both categorical (i.e., diagnoses) and quantitative (i.e., severity/impairment levels) information.

The *Brief Symptom Inventory-18 (BSI-18)* was derived from the parent, SCL-90-R (Derogatis, 1994) and developed as a quick screen for psychological distress (Derogatis, 2000). It contains 3 subscales, somatization, depression, and anxiety, as well as an overall index, the global severity index (GSI). Cronbach's alphas range from 0.74 to 0.89 and test retest estimates range from 0.68 to 0.90. It has been used with medical populations and shown high levels of sensitivity and specificity in screening for psychological distress (Carlson & Bultz, 2003). The BSI-18 provides a dimensional score that does not correspond to *Diagnostic and Statistical Manual (DSM)* categories. It has the advantage of being well validated, but as a screen in the primary care setting, it still may be somewhat lengthy.

Assessing Multiple Anxiety Disorders

In order to address concerns about brevity and simplicity of use, attempts have been made to create screening measures that consist of single items that correspond to specific anxiety disorders. One such measure is the Anxiety and Depression Detector (ADD) (Means-Christensen, Sherbourne, Roy-Byrne, Craske, & Stein, 2005). The ADD was developed in a primary care setting to screen for panic disorder, PTSD, social phobia, generalized anxiety disorder, and depression in a primary care setting. When items are used in an aggregate (i.e., yes to any of the items) to predict the presence of any diagnosis, the sensitivity values were 0.92 to 0.96 and specificity values were 0.57 to 0.82. When individual items are used, however, values for the social phobia and PTSD items are not adequate and require further examination. At this point, the ADD may be a very time-efficient and user-friendly screen to assist providers in detecting the possible presence of any anxiety disorder.

Assessing Specific Anxiety Disorders

Broad-based measures can be followed up with disorder-specific measures (e.g., a measure for social anxiety, a measure for panic disorder, etc.), or disorder-specific measures can be used as an initial step if providers are fairly certain about the nature of the problem. The psychometric properties for many of these measures are well established (see Antony & Barlow, 2002; Antony, Orsillo, & Roemer, 2001; Antony & Rowa, 2005); however, the training

required, length, and specificity of these measures may render them difficult to administer in primary care. Recently, abbreviated versions of some of these measures have also been developed, including two- and six-item versions of the PTSD Checklist (Lang & Stein, 2005), and a three-item version of the Social Phobia Inventory (SPIN) (Connor, Kobak, Churchill, Katzelnick, & Davidson, 2001). A newly emerging self-report scale to screen for GAD and assess its severity is the GAD-7, which consists of seven items and has good reliability and validity (Spitzer, Kroenke, Williams, & Lowe, 2006).

Treatment Options

Data support pharmacotherapy, psychotherapy (e.g., cognitive behavioral therapy), or some combination thereof, as efficacious treatment options. Determining which intervention often becomes an issue of individual choice, negotiated between the provider and the patient. Possible factors to consider when negotiating this decision include severity of anxiety and possible comorbid depression, previous response to medication and psychotherapy, family history of anxiety and mood disorders, and patient beliefs about medication and psychotherapy.

Pharmacotherapy

First-line pharmacotherapy for anxiety disorders is usually antidepressant therapy, in particular, the selective serotonin reuptake inhibitors (SSRIs) (e.g., paroxetine) or serotonin norepinephrine reuptake inhibitors (SNRIs) (e.g., venlafaxine). Treatment response rates for anxiety disorders are in the range of 50%–70% (Stein, 2005). Current Food and Drug Administration (FDA) indications for various pharmacological interventions are presented in Table 1. In general, doses are usually the same as for the treatment of depression, though it is often advisable to start with lower initial doses, and to titrate upward somewhat more slowly toward therapeutic dosages. The serotonergic agents are particularly desirable as a first-line treatment, because they are simple to use (i.e., do not have complex dosing regimens requiring multiple provider visits), have a low drug interaction, have favorable side-effect profiles, and have large enough therapeutic windows to reduce the risk of overdose (Hirschfeld, 2001). They are also associated with less abuse liability and potential for dependence. Common adverse events include sleep problems, drowsiness, lightheadedness, nausea, diarrhea, and sexual dysfunction (Hirschfeld, 2001). The typical duration of a therapeutic trial is 8–12 weeks, during which time

Table 1. Antidepressant Medications Currently Indicated by the U.S. Food and Drug Administration for Treating Anxiety Disorders

Anxiety Disorder	FDA-Approved Medications
Generalized Anxiety Disorder	• Paroxetine (Paxil) • Venlafaxine ER (Effexor XR) • Escitalopram (Lexapro)
Social Phobia	• Paroxetine (Paxil) and Paroxetine Controlled-Release (Paxil CR) • Sertraline (Zoloft) • Venlafaxine ER (Effexor XR)
Panic Disorder	• Paroxetine (Paxil) and Paroxetine Controlled-Release (Paxil CR) • Sertraline (Zoloft) • Venlafaxine ER (Effexor XR) • Fluoxetine (Prozac)
Posttraumatic Stress Disorder	• Paroxetine (Paxil) • Sertraline (Zoloft)
Obsessive-Compulsive Disorder	• Paroxetine (Paxil) • Sertraline (Zoloft) • Fluoxetine (Prozac) • Fluvoxamine (Luvox) • Clomipramine (Anafranil)

an optimal balance between efficacy and potential adverse effect is sought (Stein, 2005).

TRICYCLIC AND HETEROCYCLIC ANTIDEPRESSANTS

Until the mid-1980s, tricyclic (imipramine, desipramine, etc.) and heterocyclic compounds (e.g., doxepin) were widely used for treating panic disorder with or without agoraphobia, and to a lesser extent, generalized anxiety disorder (GAD). Although effective for these conditions, many patients experience an anticholinergic effect (jitteriness) when using these medications, which can be particularly aversive for anxious patients. Given the presence of anticholingergic and adverse cardiac effects, they are not frequently used for patients with anxiety disorders. An exception is obsessive-compulsive disorder (OCD), where clomipramine (Anafranil) is still widely used as a monotherapy or as an adjunct to SSRIs. In addition, these agents may be quite useful for patients nonresponsive to SSRIs and SNRIs, and are easier to use, despite their side effects, than monoamine oxidase inhibitors (see below).

MONOAMINE OXIDASE INHIBITORS (MAOIs)

The MAOIs (e.g., phenelzine [Nardil] and tranylcypromine [Parnate]) have been shown to be effective in treating panic disorder with or without agoraphobia, and the generalized type of social anxiety disorder (Blanco et al., 2003). Their utility in the treatment of other anxiety disorders is less clear. In a primary care setting, MAOIs are less frequently used because of their side-effect profile, which includes postural hypotension, insomnia, weight gain, and the need for a special (very low tyramine) diet to reduce the risk of a hypertensive crisis. Most often, these medications are reserved for nonresponders to other treatments and are managed by specialty mental health professionals.

OTHER AGENTS

Nefazodone (Serzone), mirtazapine (Remeron), and bupropion (usually prescribed as Wellbutrin SR or XR) are other, newer antidepressants. None of these agents have been well studied for anxiety disorders in large randomized controlled trials, though they may be somewhat useful for depression with comorbid anxious symptoms (Stein, 2005). Buspirone (BuSpar) is indicated for the treatment of chronic anxiety (Gammans et al., 1992); however, its usefulness is probably limited to the treatment of GAD. In placebo-controlled trials, buspirone has not demonstrated efficacy for social anxiety disorder or panic disorder (Sheehan, Raj, Harnett-Sheehan,

Soto, & Knapp, 1993; van Vliet, den Boer, Westenberg, & Ho Pian, 1997).

BENZODIAZEPINES

Benzodiazepines (e.g., alprazolam [Xanax] and clonazepam [Klonopin, Rivotril]) are another pharmacological option for anxiety disorders that are effective, fast-acting, and can be used on an as-needed or *prn* basis for very situational anxiety (Thom, Sartory, & Johren, 2000). An additional advantage of benzodiazepines is that they are not associated with some of the activating effects found in the antidepressants. The drawbacks of benzodiazepine therapy include greater relapse after discontinuation (Gelernter et al., 1991; Thom et al., 2000), possible sedation, cognitive and psychomotor impairment, and interaction effects with alcohol. There is also a potential for physiologic dependence with long-term use and increased potential for abuse, particularly in predisposed individuals (Bandelow, Zohar, & Hollander, 2002; Rickels, Schweizer, Case, & Greenblatt, 1990). While a general guideline is to consider antidepressant therapy first, in some instances, benzodiazepines may be a suitable alternative, particularly if the patient does not have substance abuse problems or a prior history of substance abuse, there is no evidence of concomitant depression, if there are medical illnesses that suggest a contraindication for using antidepressants, in the presence of a bipolar II disorder, and in cases where the patient requires immediate relief of symptoms to be functional.

BETA-ADRENERGIC RECEPTOR ANTAGONISTS

Beta-adrenergic receptor antagonists can also be useful on an as-needed basis, but their use is limited almost exclusively to the management of performance anxiety (Stein, 2005). Beta blockers sometimes used for this purpose include propanolol (Inderal) and atenolol (Tenormin). These medications reduce tachycardia (racing heart) and tremor (shaking), symptoms that often contribute to a cycle of anxiety in patients who have a heightened awareness of their somatic symptoms. Taken on an as-needed basis, beta blockers are usually well tolerated with few side effects (e.g., feelings of dizziness, lightheaded, or fatigue). But they are contraindicated in the presence of certain medical conditions (e.g., asthma) and drug-drug interactions must also be considered.

General Considerations

Pharmacotherapy should not be provided without any instruction. Education about the illness,

recommendations for combating problem behaviors, and advice about how to maximize the response to medication are all useful components of pharmacotherapy. Furthermore, various beliefs about medication may be present (e.g., "Taking medications means I'm crazy"; "I'll become addicted") and should be discussed in order to enhance compliance.

Psychosocial Interventions

Cognitive behavioral therapy (CBT) is an empirically supported psychosocial intervention whose efficacy has been demonstrated in various randomized clinical trials (Deacon & Abramowitz, 2004). Response rates for CBT are also in the range of 50%–70%. Cognitive behavioral therapy targets a problem by addressing an individual's thoughts, behaviors, and feelings. The underlying principle of CBT is that thoughts, actions, and feelings are intertwined and collectively contribute to mood states such as anxiety and depression. In CBT, patients are taught to use a Socratic method of questioning (data gathering and hypothesis testing) to challenge their anxious thinking. They are also taught how to gradually confront situations that they may be avoiding or enduring with great distress. Relaxation strategies (e.g., diaphragmatic breathing, progressive muscle relaxation, visual imagery) may be used to address the more somatic features of anxiety, particularly in the case of generalized anxiety and worry. The CBT therapist assumes a collaborative stance, where the patient and therapist are part of a team, and through trial and error, work to develop effective ways of coping with anxiety symptoms.

CBT is usually short term, lasting anywhere from 3–12 months, and in some studies the sole or adjunctive use of CBT (combined with pharmacotherapy) has been shown to reduce rates of relapse (Heimberg et al., 1998; Marks et al., 1993). It can be prescribed initially, followed by adjunctive pharmacotherapy in the presence of limited or partial response, or CBT can be used to ease medication discontinuation. Data-driven guidelines for sequencing medication and psychosocial interventions like CBT are not yet available.

Integrated Models of Care

Although an efficacious treatment approach, many individuals do not receive CBT, primarily due to problems with availability, access, lack of awareness of treatment options, and insurance coverage. In order to address these issues, various models have been developed for treating anxiety disorders in the primary care setting (Rollman et al., 2005; Roy-Byrne et al., 2005). Many of these models have emerged from the depression literature, where there has been a proliferation of studies examining the effectiveness of collaborative care models for treating depressive disorders in primary care (Katon et al., 1995; Simon, VonKorff, Rutter, & Wagner, 2000). Collaborative care models use a disease management approach in which evidence-based care is delivered by a multidisciplinary team, often including medical providers, psychiatrists, nurse care managers, and/or behavioral health specialists.

In one of the earliest effectiveness studies for anxiety disorders, Roy-Byrne and colleagues (Roy-Byrne, Katon, Cowley, & Russo, 2001) examined a psychiatrist consultation model to assist primary care providers with managing pharmacotherapy for patients with panic disorder. In this study, patients who were randomized to a psychiatrist collaborative care (CC) model received (1) educational tapes and brochures about anxiety, (2) pharmacotherapy with an SSRI, (3) psychiatrist consultation including two in-person visits and follow-up telephone calls, and (4) the primary care provider received notes after every visit. At posttreatment, patients in the CC condition showed greater improvement on various outcome measures, including panic severity, anxiety sensitivity, and overall satisfaction with care. Furthermore, more than twice as many patients reached normal levels on a measure of anxiety sensitivity when compared to treatment as usual (TAU) patients. Data also support that this intervention was cost-effective and could be of high potential value to health care systems (Katon, Roy-Byrne, Russo, & Cowley, 2002).

The Collaborative Care for Anxiety and Panic Study (CCAP) (Roy-Byrne et al., 2005) included a CBT intervention; however, in this study, the original intervention was reduced from 12–16 sessions to 6 sessions in order to be feasible in primary care. In this study, patients were given the option of receiving pharmacotherapy, cognitive behavioral therapy (CBT), or both. Patients randomized to collaborative care (CC) were offered a demonstration video, an educational workbook, six in-person CBT sessions delivered by a behavioral health specialist, six follow-up phone contacts, and algorithm study–based pharmacotherapy by the study psychiatrist. Throughout the intervention, the behavioral health specialist was in frequent contact with the primary care provider, often serving as a liaison between the psychiatrist and the provider. At the end of treatment, patients in the CC condition

had lower symptom severity and higher functioning, which was sustained for 12 months, compared to participants randomized to treatment as usual. Furthermore, 29% of patients randomized to both CBT and pharmacotherapy achieved full remission of their panic disorder compared to the usual care group (16%, $p < .05$). Given similar rates of quality pharmacotherapy found in the CC and TAU groups (Roy-Byrne et al., 2005), and data supporting the efficacy of CBT in panic disorder as well as a dose response relationship, where more CBT sessions were related to better outcomes, it is likely that the outcomes of this intervention were largely driven by the CBT component of this study (Craske, Golinelli, et al., 2005).

Using a somewhat different design, Rollman and colleagues (Rollman et al., 2005) tested a collaborative care telephone intervention to assist primary care providers in the treatment of panic disorder and GAD. In this protocol, case managers were used in primary care settings that were linked by a common electronic medical record system. Patients who screened positive for panic disorder and/or GAD were contacted by telephone and asked which of the following choices they preferred: (1) a self-study workbook about anxiety management, (2) an algorithm-based trial of pharmacotherapy, (3) referral to specialty mental health, (4) a combination of the interventions above, or (5) none of the above. Providers were informed of patient diagnoses and treatment choices and were given recommendations for treatment through the electronic medical record system. Throughout the intervention, the care manager was responsible for telephoning the patient to review lesson plans and to encourage treatment adherence. Patients randomized to the intervention group had greater reductions in anxiety symptoms and depression at the end of the 12-month trial. Significant improvements in quality of life, number of days worked per week, and reductions of absenteeism were also found compared to the usual care group (Rollman et al., 2005). According to the authors, this intervention may be particularly useful for large health care systems and for individuals who lack access to mental health services (e.g., rural populations).

Findings from these studies have been very promising and provide support for anxiety models of care that can be effective in the primary care setting. However, additional research needs to demonstrate that such interventions are generalizable, feasible, cost-effective, and disseminable. In particular, models of treatment to address all anxiety disorders, rather than one or two specific anxiety disorders, would be particularly useful in primary care. Similarly, models that are effective across ethnically and socioeconomically diverse populations warrant further investigation.

Barriers to Care

A discussion of treatment options warrants a review of barriers to care. Barriers at the individual (e.g., beliefs, demographic characteristics), provider (e.g., time constraints), and system levels (e.g., insurance coverage) often affect an individual's ability to access, utilize, adhere to, and accept services. To date, only a few studies have examined the presence of barriers among patients with anxiety disorders. In the Collaborative Care for Anxiety in Primary Care project (CCAP; Roy-Byrne et al., 2005), patients with panic attacks did not favor one treatment modality over the other; approximately 64% were willing to consider medication and 67% were willing to consider psychosocial therapy options (Hazlett-Stevens et al., 2002). Using a standardized assessment (rather than one item about "willingness" to accept treatment) that examined patient beliefs about medication and psychosocial interventions, Wagner and colleagues (Wagner et al., 2005) found that having a diagnosis did not influence beliefs about medication or psychotherapy, nor was the presence of a specific anxiety disorder related to beliefs about either type of treatment. In both of these studies, however, ethnic minorities reported less favorable attitudes toward both medication and therapy. Data from the CCAP study also suggested that only 38% of patients with panic disorder reported unmet need for emotional or mental health problems, even though they were impaired, and the majority of participants had not received any kind of treatment in the past 3 months (Craske, Edlund, et al., 2005). The authors emphasize that a potential barrier for many panic patients may be a perception that their anxiety symptoms do not require treatment. Other commonly reported barriers were being unable to find out where to go for help (43%), cost (40%), having a health plan that would not pay for treatment (35%), and not being able to get an appointment soon enough (35%) (Craske, Edlund, et al., 2005). In another study of primary care patients with anxiety disorders, the most commonly endorsed reason for not receiving pharmacotherapy was "the primary care provider did not recommend it," followed by "didn't believe in taking medication for emotional problems." For psychotherapy, the most commonly endorsed reason was "didn't

believe in psychotherapy for emotional problems," followed by "didn't think he/she had a problem" (Weisberg et al., 2007). Qualitative data from a subsample of economically disadvantaged patients with panic disorder (from the CCAP study) also underscore the importance of logistical barriers (e.g., lack of resources, travel, time) on treatment adherence however, these findings further reveal that decision making regarding adherence (or how much to adhere) is a complex process influenced not only by logistical barriers but also by the patient's beliefs about what will be effective in their individual case as well as their ongoing assessment of their own well-being (Mukherjee et al., 2006).

Additional barriers that may impact recognition and appropriate treatment for patients with anxiety disorders are varied. As mentioned previously, many patients may present their psychiatric symptoms as somatic symptoms (Furedi et al., 2003). Next, the average health care visit is 7–10 minutes, making it difficult for providers to have enough time to detect anxiety disorders. Providers as well as patients may have perceptions that anxiety disorders are not serious problems despite evidence about associated impairment. They may also not perceive interventions outside of pharmacotherapy to be feasible or useful. In a qualitative study where providers were first asked to attend five educational seminars about CBT, barriers such as lack of time, practice distractions and interruptions, and the perception that some patients were not good candidates for CBT were noted as possible barriers to the delivery of CBT (Wiebe & Greiver, 2005). Importantly, barriers may also exist at the system level such as the implementation of screening practices for anxiety disorders, effective collaboration with mental health providers, and better reimbursement policies for evaluation and treatment.

Conclusions

The prominence of anxiety disorders in primary care is substantial and the magnitude of the mental health care burden created by anxiety disorders is concerning. Despite their prevalence, anxiety disorders frequently go undetected and untreated. Providers are in a challenging position as gatekeepers who have the responsibility of identifying and referring individuals with psychiatric disorders, or more often, treating such individuals themselves. The use of brief and valid screening instruments may facilitate this process, but efforts to improve identification raise issues regarding quality of care, accessibility of services, and other barriers to care among this population. Research aimed at improving identification and detection must be accompanied by efforts to develop interventions that are empirically validated, accessible, and effective across settings. Studies currently in progress will inform efforts to successfully develop and implement such models of care.

References

Allgulander, C., & Nilsson, B. (2003). A nationwide study in primary health care: One out of four patients suffers from anxiety and depression. *Lakartidnengen, 100,* 832–838.

Antony, M. M., & Barlow, D. H. (Eds.). (2002). *Handbook of assessment and treatment planning for psychological disorders.* New York: Guilford Press.

Antony, M. M., Orsillo, S. M., & Roemer, L. (Eds.). (2001). *Practitioner's guide to empirically-based measures of anxiety.* New York: Springer.

Antony, M. M., & Rowa, K. (2005). Evidence-based assessment of anxiety disorders in adults. *Psychological Assessment, 17,* 256–266.

Arikian, S., & Gorman, J. (2001). A review of the diagnosis, pharmacologic treatment, and economic aspects of anxiety disorders. *Primary Care Companion Journal of Clinical Psychiatry, 3,* 110–117.

Ballenger, J. C., Davidson, J.R.T., Lecrubier, Y., & Nutt, D. J. (2001). A proposed algorithm for improved recognition and treatment of depression/anxiety spectrum in primary care. *Primary Care Companion Journal of Clinical Psychiatry, 3,* 44–52.

Bandelow, B., Zohar, J., & Hollander, E. (2002). World Federation of Societies of Biological Psychiatry guidelines for the pharmacological treatment of anxiety, obsessive-compulsive and posttraumatic stress disorders. *World Journal of Biological Psychiatry, 3,* 171–199.

Bartels, S. J., Coakley, E., & Oxman, T. E. (2002). Suicidal and death ideation in older primary-care patients with depression, anxiety, and at-risk alcohol use. *American Journal of Psychiatry, 10,* 417–427.

Blanco, C., Schneier, F., Schmidt, A., Blanco-Jerez, C., Marshall, R., Sanchez-Lacay, A., et al. (2003). Pharmacological treatment of social anxiety disorder: A meta-analysis. *Depression and Anxiety, 18,* 29–40.

Brown, C., Schulberg, H., & Shear, M. (1996). Phenomenology and severity of depression and comorbid lifetime anxiety disorders in primary medical care practice. *Anxiety, 2,* 210–218.

Bruce, S., Weisberg, R., Dolan, R., Machan, J., Kessler, R., Manchester, G., et al. (2001). Trauma and posttraumatic stress disorder in primary care patients. *Primary Care Companion Journal of Clinical Psychiatry, 3,* 211–217.

Carlson, L., & Bultz, B. (2003). Cancer distress screening: Needs, models and methods. *Journal of Psychosomatic Research, 55,* 403–409.

Colman, S., Brod, M., Potter, L., Buesching, D., & Rowland, C. (2004). Cross-sectional 7-year follow-up of anxiety in primary care patients. *Depression and Anxiety, 19,* 105–111.

Connor, K., Kobak, K., Churchill, L., Katzelnick, D., & Davidson, J. (2001). Mini-SPIN: A brief screening assessment for generalized social anxiety disorder. *Depression and Anxiety, 14,* 137–140.

Craske, M. G., Edlund, M., Sullivan, G., Roy-Byrne, P., Sherbourne, C., Bystritsky, A., et al. (2005). Perceived unmet need for mental health treatment and barriers to care among patients with panic disorder. *Psychiatric Services, 56,* 988–994.

Craske, M. G., Golinelli, D., Stein, M. B., Roy-Byrne, P., Bystritsky, A., & Sherbourne, C. (2005). Does the addition of cognitive behavioral therapy improve disorder treatment outcome relative to medication alone in the primary-care setting? *Psychological Medicine, 35,* 1–10.

Culpepper, L. (2003). Use of algorithms to treat anxiety in primary care. *Journal of Clinical Psychiatry, 64,* 30–33.

Deacon, B., & Abramowitz, J. (2004). Cognitive and behavioral treatments for anxiety disorders: A review of meta-analytic findings. *Journal of Clinical Psychology, 60,* 429–441.

Derogatis, L. (1994). *Symptom Checklist-90-R (SCL-90-R) administration, scoring, and procedures manual* (3rd ed.). Minneapolis: National Computer Systems.

Derogatis, L. (2000). *BSI-18: Administration, scoring and procedures manual.* Minneapolis: National Computer Systems.

Dew, M. A., Reynolds, C. F., & Houck, P. R. (1997). Temporal profiles of the course of depression during treatment: Predictors of pathways toward recovery in the elderly. *Archives of General Psychiatry, 54,* 1016–1024.

DuPont, R., Rice, D., & Miller, L. (1996). Economic costs of anxiety disorders. *Anxiety, 2,* 167–172.

Escalona, R., Achilles, G., Waitzkin, H., & Yager, J. (2004). PTSD and somatization in women treated at a VA primary care clinic. *Psychosomatics, 45,* 291–296.

Ford, J., Trestman, R., Steinberg, K., Tennen, H., & Allen, S. (2004). Prospective association of anxiety, depressive, and addictive disorders with high utilization of primary, specialty and emergency medical care. *Social Science and Medicine, 58,* 2145–2148.

Ford, J. D., Trestman, R. L., Tennen, H., & Allen, S. (2005). Relationship of anxiety, depression and alcohol use disorders to persistent high utilization and potentially problematic under-utilization of primary medical care. *Social Science and Medicine, 61,* 1618–1625.

Furedi, J., Rozsa, S., Zambori, J., & Szadoczky, E. (2003). The role of symptoms in the recognition of mental health disorders in primary care. *Psychosomatics, 44,* 402–406.

Gammans, R., Stringfellow, J., Hvizdos, A., Seidehamel, R., Cohn, J., Wilcox, C., et al. (1992). Use of buspirone in patients with generalized anxiety disorder and coexisting depressive symptoms: A meta-analysis of eight randomized controlled studies. *Neuropsychobiology, 25,* 193–201.

Gelernter, C., Uhde, T., Cimbolic, P., Arnkoff, D., Vittone, B., Tancer, M., et al. (1991). Cognitive-behavioral and pharmacological treatments of social phobia: A controlled study. *Archives of General Psychiatry, 48,* 938–945.

Grant, B., Stinson, F., Dawson, D., Chou, S., Dufour, M., Comptom, W., et al. (2004). Prevalence and co-occurrence of substance use disorders and independent mood and anxiety disorders: Results from the national Epidemiologic Survey on Alcohol and Related Conditions. *Archives of General Psychiatry, 61,* 807–816.

Greenberg, P., Sisitsky, T., & Kessler, R. (1999). The economic burden of anxiety disorders in the 1990s. *Journal of Clinical Psychiatry, 60,* 427–435.

Hazlett-Stevens, H., Craske, M., Roy-Byrne, P., Sherbourne, C., Stein, M., & Bystritsky, A. (2002). Predictors of willingness to consider medication and psychosocial treatment for panic disorder in primary care patients. *General Hospital Psychiatry, 24,* 316–321.

Hegel, M. T., Unutzer, J., Tang, L., Arean, P. A., Katon, W., Williams, J. W., et al. (2005). Impact of comorbid panic and posttraumatic stress disorder on outcomes of collaborative care for late-life depression in primary care. *American Journal of Geriatric Psychiatry, 13,* 48–58.

Heimberg, R., Liebowitz, M., Hope, D., Schneier, F., Holt, C., Welkowitz, L., et al. (1998). Cognitive behavioral group therapy vs. phenelzine therapy for social phobia. *Archives of General Psychiatry, 55,* 1133–1141.

Katon, W., Von Korff, M., & Lin, E. (1995). Collaborative management to achieve treatment guidelines: Impact on depression in primary care. *Journal of the American Medical Association, 273,* 1026–1031.

Katon, W. J., Roy-Byrne, P., Russo, J., & Cowley, D. (2002). Cost-effectiveness and cost offset of a collaborative care intervention for primary care patients with panic disorder. *Archives of General Psychiatry, 59,* 1098–1104.

Kessler, R., Berglund, P., Demler, O., Jin, R., Merikangas, K., & Walters, E. (2005). Lifetime prevalence and age-of-onset distributions of *DSM–IV* disorders in the National Comorbidity Survey Replication. *Archives of General Psychiatry, 62,* 593–602.

Kessler, R., DuPont, R., Berglund, P., & Wittchen, H.-U. (1999). Impairment in pure and comorbid generalized anxiety disorder and major depression at 12 months in two national surveys. *American Journal of Psychiatry, 156,* 1915–1923.

Kessler, R., Stang, P., Wittchen, H., Ustun, T., Roy-Byrne, P., & Walters, E. (1998). Lifetime panic-depression comorbidity in the National Comorbidity Survey. *Archives of General Psychiatry, 55,* 801–808.

Kroenke, K., Spitzer, R. L., & Williams, J.B.W. (1994). Physical symptoms in primary care: Predictors of psychiatric disorders and functional impairment. *Archives of Family Medicine, 3,* 774–779.

Kunik, M., Roundy, K., Veazy, C., Souchek, J., Richardson, P., Wray, N., et al. (2005). Surprisingly high prevalence of anxiety and depression in chronic breathing disorders. *CHEST, 127,* 1205–1211.

Lang, A., & Stein, M. (2002). Screening for anxiety in primary care: Why bother? *General Hospital Psychiatry, 24,* 365–366.

Lang, A., & Stein, M. (2006). An abbreviated PTSD checklist for use as a screening instrument in primary care. *Behaviour Research and Therapy, 43,* 585–594.

Marks, I. M., Swinson, R. P., Başoğlu, M., Kuch, K., Noshirvani, H., O'Sullivan, G., et al. (1993). Alprazolam and exposure alone and combined in panic disorder with agoraphobia: A controlled study in London and Toronto. *British Journal of Psychiatry, 162,* 776–787.

Means-Christensen, A., Sherbourne, C., Roy-Byrne, P. P., Craske, M. G., & Stein, M. B. (2005). Using five questions to screen for five common mental disorders in primary care. *General Hospital Psychiatry, 28,* 108–118.

Meredith, L., Sherbourne, C., Jackson, C., Camp, P., & Wells, K. (1997). Treatment typically provided for comorbid anxiety disorder. *Archives of Family Medicine, 6,* 231–237.

Mukherjee, S., Sullivan, G., Perry, D., Verdugo, B., Means-Christensen, A., Schraufnagel, T., et al. (2006). Adherence to treatment among economically disadvantaged patients with panic disorder. *Psychiatric Services, 57,* 1745–1750.

Nisenson, L. G., Pepper, C. M., Schwenk, T. L., & Coyne, J. C. (1998). The nature and prevalence of anxiety disorders in primary care. *General Hospital Psychiatry, 20,* 21–28.

Olfson, M., Shea, S., Feder, A., Fuentes, M., Nomura, Y., Gameroff, M., et al. (2000). Prevalence of anxiety, depression, and substance use disorders in an urban general medicine practice. *Annals of Family Medicine, 9,* 876–883.

Rice, D., & Miller, L. (1998). Health economics and cost implications of anxiety and other mental disorders in the United States. *British Journal of Psychiatry, 173,* 4–9.

Rickels, K., Schweizer, E., Case, W., & Greeenblatt, D. (1990). Long-term therapeutic use of benzodiazepines. *Archives of General Psychiatry, 47,* 899–907.

Rodriguez, B., Weisberg, R., Pagano, M., Machan, J., Culpepper, L., & Keller, M. (2004). Frequency and patterns of psychiatric comorbidity in a sample of primary care patients with anxiety disorders. *Comprehensive Psychiatry, 45,* 129–137.

Rogers, M., White, K., & Warshaw, M. (1994). Prevalence of medical illness in patients with anxiety disorders. *International Journal of Psychiatry in Medicine, 24,* 83–96.

Rollman, B. L., Herbeck Belnap, B., Mazumdar, S., Zhu, F., Kroenke, K., Schulberg, H. C., et al. (2005). Symptomatic severity of Prime-MD diagnosed episodes of panic and generalized anxiety disorders in primary care. *Journal of General Internal Medicine, 20,* 623–628.

Roy-Byrne, P., Craske, M., Stein, M., Sullivan, G., Bystritsky, A., Katon, W., et al. (2005). A randomized effectiveness trial of cognitive-behavioral therapy and medication for primary care panic disorder. *Archives of General Psychiatry, 62,* 290–298.

Roy-Byrne, P. P., Katon, W., Cowley, D. S., & Russo, J. (2001). A randomized effectiveness trial of collaborative care for patients with panic disorder in primary care. *Archives of General Psychiatry, 58,* 869–876.

Roy-Byrne, P., Stang, P., Wittchen, H., Ustun, B., Walters, E., & Kessler, R. (2000). Lifetime panic-depression comorbidity in the National Comorbidity Survey: Association with symptoms, impairment, course and help-seeking. *British Journal of Psychiatry, 176,* 229–235.

Roy-Byrne, P., Stein, M. B., Russo, J., Craske, M., Katon, W., Sullivan, G., et al. (2005). Medical illness and response to treatment in primary care panic disorder. *General Hospital Psychiatry, 27,* 237–243.

Roy-Byrne, P., Stein, M. B., Russo, J., Mercier, E., Thomas, R., & McQuaid, J. (1999). Panic disorder in the primary care setting: Comorbidity, disability, service utilization, and treatment. *Journal of Clinical Psychiatry, 60,* 492–499.

Sareen, J., Jacobi, F., Cox, B. J., Balik, S. L., Clara, I., Stein, M. B. (2006). Disability and poor quality of life associated with comorbid anxiety disorders and physical conditions. *Archives of Internal Medicine, 166,* 2109–2116.

Shear, M. K., & Schulberg, H. C. (1995). Anxiety disorders in primary care. *Bulletin of the Menninger Clinic, 59,* A73–A85.

Sheehan, D., Lecrubier, Y., Sheehan, K., Amorim, P., Janavs, J., & Weiller, E. (1998). The Mini-International Neuropsychiatric Interview (M.I.N.I): The developmental and validation of a structured diagnostic psychiatric interview for *DSM–IV* and *ICD–10. Journal of Clinical Psychiatry, 59,* 22–33.

Sheehan, D., Raj, A., Harnett Sheehan, K., Soto, S., & Knapp, E. (1993). The relative efficacy of high-dose buspirone and alprazolam in the treatment of panic disorder: A double blind placebo controlled study. *Acta Psychiatrica Scandinavica, 88,* 1–11.

Simon, G., Von Korff, M., Rutter, C., & Wagner, E. (2000). Randomized trial of monitoring, feedback, and management of care by telephone to improve treatment of depression in primary care. *British Medical Journal, 320,* 550–554.

Spitzer, R., Kroenke, K., Linzer, M., Hahn, S., Williams, J., DeGruy, F., et al. (1995). Health related quality of life in primary care patients with mental disorders: Results from the PRIME-MD 1000 study. *Journal of the American Medical Association, 274,* 1511–1517.

Spitzer, R. L., Kroenke, K., Williams, J., & Lowe, B. (2006). A brief measure for assessing generalized anxiety disorder: The GAD-7. *Archives of Internal Medicine, 166,* 1092–1097.

Spitzer, R. L., Kroenke, K., Williams, J., & PHQPCS Group. (1999). Validation and utility of a self-report version of PRIME-MD: The PHQ primary care study. *Journal of the American Medical Association, 282,* 1737–1744.

Spitzer, R. L., Williams, J.B.W., Kroenke, K., Linzer, M., DeGruy, F., Hahn, S., et al. (1994). The utility of a new procedure for diagnosing mental disorders in primary care: The PRIME-MD 1000 study. *Journal of the American Medical Association, 272,* 1749–1756.

Stein, M. (2005). Anxiety disorders: Somatic teatment. In H. Kaplan & B. Saddock (Eds.), *Comprehensive textbook of psychiatry* (pp. 1780–1788). Baltimore: Williams and Wilkins.

Stein, M. B., Sherbourne, C. D., Craske, M. G., Means-Christensen, A., Bystritsky, A., Katon, W., et al. (2004). Quality of care for primary care patients with anxiety disorders. *American Journal of Psychiatry, 161,* 2230–2237.

Thom, A., Sartory, G., & Johren, P. (2000). Comparison between one-session psychological treatment and benzodiazepines in dental phobia. *Journal of Consulting and Clinical Psychology, 68,* 378–387.

Van Vliet, M., den Boer, J., Westenberg, H., & Ho Pian, K. (1997). Clinical effects of buspirone in social phobia: A double blind, placebo controlled study. *Journal of Clinical Psychiatry, 58,* 164–168.

Vega, W., Kolody, B., Auguilar-Gaxiola, S., & Catalano, R. (1999). Gaps in service utilization by Mexican Americans with mental health problems. *American Journal of Psychiatry, 156,* 928–934.

Wagner, A., Bystritsky, A., Russo, J., Craske, M., Sherbourne, C., Stein, M., et al. (2005). Beliefs about psychotropic medication and psychotherapy among primary care patients with anxiety disorders. *Depression and Anxiety, 21,* 99–105.

Weiller, E., Bisserbe, J., Maier, W., & Lecrubier, Y. (1998). Prevalence and recognition of anxiety syndromes in five European primary care settings. *British Journal of Psychiatry, 34*(Suppl.), 18–23.

Weisberg, R. B., Dyck, I., Culpepper, L., & Keller, M. B. (2007). Psychiatric treatment in primary care patients with anxiety disorders: A comparison of care received from primary care providers and psychiatrists. *American Journal of Psychiatry, 164,* 276–282.

Wiebe, E., & Greiver, M. (2005). Using cognitive behavioural therapy in practice: Qualitative study of family physicians experiences. *Canadian Family Physician, 51,* 992–993.

Young, A. S., Klap, R., Sherbourne, C. D., & Wells, K. B. (2001). The quality of care for depressive and anxiety disorders in the United States. *Archives of General Psychiatry, 58,* 55–61.

PART 6

Other Anxiety-Based Conditions

Hypochondriasis and Health Anxiety

Steven Taylor *and* Gordon J. G. Asmundson

Abstract

This chapter reviews the nature, assessment, and treatment of excessive health anxiety, the most severe form of which is hypochondriasis. Etiologic research suggests that genetic factors play a modest role, and that learning experiences regarding health, disease, and medical treatment play an important role. These experiences appear to give rise to maladaptive beliefs that, in turn, lead to behaviors such as persistent reassurance-seeking and other forms of checking, which can perpetuate health anxiety. Research indicates that cognitive behavioral therapies are among the most effective interventions. The elements of these treatments are reviewed, and important future directions for improving treatment outcome are discussed.

Keywords: cognitive behavioral therapy, health anxiety, hypochondriasis, reassurance-seeking, sick role

Diagnostic and Descriptive Features

We live in a world filled with health threats. Recent, widely publicized examples include the threats of various epidemics—avian influenza, severe acute respiratory syndrome (SARS), bovine spongiform encephalopathy (mad cow disease), and West Nile virus—as well as medications that were previously assumed to be safe but are now reported to be potentially dangerous—some medications used for arthritis (e.g., COX-2 inhibitors such as Vioxx), diet supplements (e.g., those containing ephedrine such as Ephedra), and some antidepressant medications (e.g., selective serotonin reuptake inhibitors administered to children or pregnant women). Most people do not become unduly alarmed about such news, but some do. More generally, most health-related concerns, if they arise, are realistic and well founded; others are disproportionate to the actual degree of threat to the individual. In this chapter we will discuss the nature and treatment of

full-blown hypochondriasis and subclinical forms of the disorder (i.e., various forms of partial or abridged hypochondriasis) where health anxiety is the primary problem and not a secondary feature of another disorder (e.g., panic disorder, generalized anxiety disorder, or major depression).

Although hypochondriasis is currently conceptualized as a somatoform disorder (American Psychiatric Association [APA], 2000), anxiety is a prominent feature. In fact, it has been argued that hypochondriasis should be reclassified as an anxiety disorder (e.g., Mayou et al., 2005). Hypochondriasis is defined by a preoccupation with fears of having, or the idea that one has, a serious disease, based on a misinterpretation of one or more bodily sensations or changes (APA, 2000). Fear persists even though the person receives ample reassurance from physicians that there is no evidence of serious disease, and despite the fact that frightening bodily changes or sensations believed to be symptomatic of disease rarely become progressively worse (as might happen in the case of a genuinely serious disease process). People with hypochondriasis usually resist the idea that they are suffering from a mental disorder. To be diagnosed with hypochondriasis, one has to have these symptoms for at least 6 months. Shorter periods of health anxiety have been called abridged or transient hypochondriasis (e.g., Barsky et al., 1993). In other cases of abridged hypochondriasis, patients may experience mild health anxiety (insufficiently severe or debilitating to meet criteria for hypochondriasis), but this anxiety may persist for years (e.g., Fink et al., 2004).

People with hypochondriasis may perpetually adopt a sick role, living as invalids and avoiding all effortful activities. They typically complain persistently about their health, discussing their concerns at great length with anyone who will listen. This can lead to strained relationships with their family, friends, and physicians. Frustration and anger on the part of physician and patient are not uncommon. Doctor shopping—visiting many different physicians in the hope of finding help—is often the result. This puts people with hypochondriasis at risk of unnecessary or repeated medical and surgical treatments, some of which can produce troubling side effects or treatment complications (e.g., scarring, pain). Thus, hypochondriasis can be worsened by iatrogenic (physician-induced) factors.

Full hypochondriasis has a lifetime prevalence of 1%–5% (APA, 2000), and the abridged version may be even more common. Hypochondriasis can arise at any age, although it most commonly develops in early adulthood (APA, 2000). It is equally common in women and men (Creed & Barsky, 2004) and typically arises when the person is under stress, seriously ill, or recovering from a serious illness, or has suffered the loss of a family member (Barsky & Klerman, 1983). The course of hypochondriasis is often chronic, persisting for years in more than 50% of cases, and it frequently co-occurs with mood disorders, anxiety disorders, and somatization disorder (APA, 2000).

Cultural factors, such as socially transmitted values and expectations, can influence how a person interprets bodily changes and sensations, and whether treatment-seeking is initiated. There appear to be cross-cultural differences in which bodily changes and sensations are feared the most. For example, people in the United Kingdom tend to have excessive concerns about gastrointestinal sensations, whereas those in Germany are more vigilant for cardiopulmonary sensations. There also

tends to be elevated rates of medically unexplained symptoms in China and Latin America compared to other countries (e.g., Gureje, 2004); however, these cross-national differences generally do not follow clear cultural lines, suggesting that factors other than culture may be involved (Gureje, 2004).

Etiology

Many theories of hypochondriasis and health anxiety have been proposed over the years. However, the most well-developed, empirically supported model is the cognitive-behavioral approach, which has led to effective treatment (Salkovskis et al., 2003; Taylor & Asmundson, 2004). The main features of the model are shown in Figure 1. The key concept in this model is that excessive health anxiety (as in hypochondriasis) arises from dysfunctional beliefs about sickness, health, and health care, including beliefs that lead the person to misinterpret the significance and dangerousness of benign bodily changes and sensations. Benign bodily changes and sensations arise from any number of sources, including benign bodily perturbations, minor diseases, and autonomic arousal associated with anxiety or other emotional states. The human body is noisy; bodily sensations are daily or weekly occurrences even for healthy people (Pennebaker, 1982). Many of these sensations are mild or transient and are not associated with disease. However, the dangerousness of these sensations tends to overestimated by people with excessive health anxiety. Examples of dysfunctional beliefs associated with excessive health anxiety are shown in Table 1.

Consistent with the model in Figure 1, the research generally suggests that health-anxious people, compared to nonanxious controls:

• Are more likely to report experiencing a lot of bodily sensations, but are no better at detecting their occurrence (e.g., heartbeats or pain; Barsky et al., 1995; Lautenbacher et al., 1998).
• Are more likely to interpret bodily sensations as indicators of poor health or serious disease (e.g., Haenen et al., 1998; Rief et al., 1998).
• Are more likely to believe that good health is associated with few or no bodily sensations (Barsky et al., 1993).
• Are more likely to believe that they are weak and unable to tolerate stress (Rief et al., 1998).
• Show a greater tendency to overestimate the likelihood of contracting diseases and overestimate the dangerousness of diseases (Ditto et al., 1988; Easterling & Leventhal, 1989).

Table 1. Dysfunctional Beliefs That Are Empirically Associated With Excessive Health Anxiety

Theme	Examples
Meaning of bodily changes and sensations	• I'm healthy only when I don't have any bodily sensations. • Bodily complaints are always a sign of disease. • Red blotches are signs of skin cancer. • Joint pain means that my bones are degenerating. • Real symptoms aren't caused by anxiety.
Meaning and consequences of diseases	• If I get sick I'll be in great pain and suffering. • People will avoid or reject me if I get really ill. • Serious diseases are everywhere. • People don't recover from serious diseases.
View of self as weak, vulnerable, or inadequate	• My circulatory system is very sensitive. • I need to avoid exertion because I'm physically frail. • Illness is a sign of failure and inadequacy. • If I'm ill people will abandon me.
Physicians and medical tests	• It is possible to be absolutely certain about my health. • Doctors should be able to explain all bodily complaints. • Doctors can't be trusted because they often make mistakes. • If a doctor refers me for further medical tests, then he or she must believe that there's something seriously wrong with me. • Medical evaluations are unreliable if you don't have symptoms at the time of the test. • Medical evaluations are unreliable if you don't give your doctor a complete and detailed description of your symptoms. • If the doctor simply listens to you and says, "Your health is fine," then the assessment can't be trusted; a reliable evaluation requires a detailed interview and lab tests.
Adaptiveness of worry and bodily vigilance	• Worrying about my health will keep me safe. • I need to frequently check my body in order to catch the first signs of illness. • I need to carefully watch my health, otherwise something terrible will happen.
Death, the afterlife, and superstitious beliefs	• I'll be trapped and alone forever when I'm dead. • Death means I'll be eternally aware of what I've lost. • God makes bad people die early. • If I tell myself I'm healthy then I'll be tempting fate.

From *Treating Health Anxiety: Cognitive-Behavioral Approaches*, by S. Taylor and G.J.G. Asmundson, 2004, New York: Guilford Press, p. 32. Copyright 2004 by Guilford Press. Reprinted with permission of Guilford Press.

• Are more likely to regard themselves as being at greater risk for developing various diseases, but do not view themselves as being at greater risk for being victims of an accident or criminal assault (Barsky et al., 2001; Haenen et al., 2000).

• Are more likely to selectively attend to, dwell on, and recall health-related information (e.g., Brown et al., 1999; Owens et al., 2004; Pauli & Alpers, 2002). When attention is focused on one's body, the intensity of perceived sensations increases. This is particularly likely to occur when the person is in unstimulating environments, such as while working at a tedious job or sitting in a dull hospital ward (Pennebaker, 1982).

Our recent study of monozygotic and dizygotic twins indicates that genetic factors play a modest role in health anxiety, accounting for 10% to 37% of variance in scores on measures of health anxiety (Taylor et al., 2006). The most important determinants are

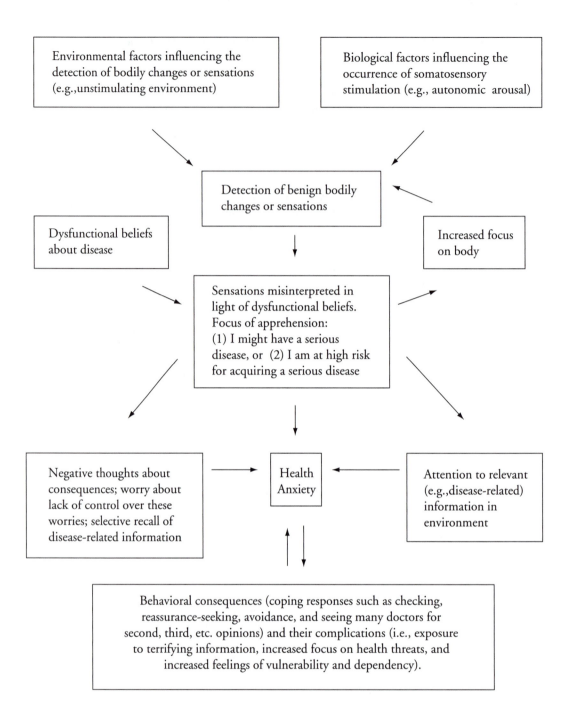

Fig. 1 Factors involved in precipitating and perpetuating episodes of excessive health anxiety.

Adapted from *Treating Health Anxiety: Cognitive-Behavioral Approaches,* by S. Taylor and G.J.G. Asmundson, 2004, New York: Guilford Press, p. 52. Copyright 2004 by Guilford Press. Reprinted with permission of Guilford Press.

environmental in nature. The relevant genes have yet to be identified, but may include the genes implicated in the modulation of emotion, such as the serotonin transporter gene. Important environmental factors include early learning experiences (e.g., episodes of actual illness, receiving treats or other reinforcements only when sick, observing how significant others cope

with illness) that lead one to formulate dysfunctional beliefs about how dangerous bodily changes and sensations are and that one's body is weak (e.g., Robbins & Kirmayer, 1996; Whitehead et al., 1994). Once formed, these beliefs can be activated by exposure to disease-related information (e.g., bodily changes or sensations, media information), which appears to give rise to worries and horrific images of disease (Easterling & Leventhal, 1989; Wells & Hackmann, 1993).

Why do dysfunctional beliefs often persist in people with elevated health anxiety? There are several reasons. First, these individuals typically experience many health-related "false alarms," where their frightening bodily sensations turn out to be innocuous. These experiences sometimes disconfirm beliefs that one's health is at risk. However, often the opposite occurs. That is, the experience is interpreted in a manner that is consistent with the belief. For example, the person may reason that just because a bodily sensation turned out to be benign today does not preclude the possibility that at some point in the future the same sensation could be due to a serious disease ("I was lucky this time. Next time it could be serious."). Second, they tend to implement maladaptive coping behaviors in a misguided attempt to allay their fears.

Among the most important of the maladaptive coping behaviors are persistent reassurance seeking (from physicians, friends, or significant others), and other forms of repetitive checking (e.g., bodily checking). Such behaviors appear to persist because they are associated with short-term reduction in anxiety (Lucock et al., 1998). In the longer term, they can perpetuate health anxiety. For example, repeatedly seeking and receiving reassurance can:

• Prolong the person's preoccupation with illness by extending the amount of time they spend discussing their health, and by exposing them to alarming information about rare but lethal medical conditions.

• Infantilize the person. By repeatedly turning to others for help, people with elevated health anxiety can "train" significant others to repeatedly inquire about their health and offer assurance. This fosters helplessness and reinforces the view that the person is weak and vulnerable.

• Lead to iatrogenic effects, including repeated or unnecessary medical tests and physician-patient miscommunication that can perpetuate health anxiety (see Taylor & Asmundson, 2004, for details).

• Tell the person what they don't have (e.g., "You don't have a heart problem") but fail to give them an adequate explanation for their concerns (e.g., "You are having normal, stress-related skipped heartbeats, which you notice because you are constantly focusing on your heart").

• Fail to provide the person with complete certainty about the absence of disease (i.e., medical tests are rarely, if ever, 100% accurate). Thus, there is always room for doubt about the accuracy of the findings (e.g., "The doctor said that the tests didn't reveal anything wrong with me, but maybe they missed something"). People who are unable or unwilling to tolerate the uncertainty inherent in medical diagnoses often persist in seeking medical reassurance in the hope that obtaining enough diagnostic tests and medical opinions will eventually provide 100% certainty of health. Of course, the greater the number of medical tests, the greater the odds of obtaining a false positive result that, in turn, provides direct but medically inaccurate evidence for their dysfunctional beliefs.

Assessment for Treatment Planning
Assessment Rationale and Targets

The first two steps in assessment for treatment planning involve ruling out general medical conditions that might account for the patient's presenting problems, and ruling in a *DSM–IV–TR* diagnosis of hypochondriasis. Both steps are important in order to determine the best treatment for the patient. In other words, to determine whether an empirically supported treatment for excessive health anxiety, such as cognitive-behavioral treatment for hypochondriasis, is indicated.

By the time that people with severe health anxiety are referred to a mental health professional, they have often had numerous medical evaluations, usually at their insistence, with the results failing to find a general medical condition that could account for their concerns. The shifting nature of the patient's health concerns (e.g., different disease concerns each week, often in response to whatever health threat is currently being discussed in the media) is a further clue that the problem is likely one of health anxiety rather than a general medical condition. Some doctors try to placate the patient by providing medically unnecessary tests. Such forms of "assessment" are not helpful, and may perpetuate health anxiety, because repeated testing can have iatrogenic effects (e.g., scarring and pain due to repeated exploratory surgeries), and can reinforce the patient's mistaken belief that she or he has a serious disease (e.g., "I must have something seriously wrong with me because the doctor has agreed to conduct more tests").

In some cases a general medical condition may be diagnosed in addition to hypochondriasis. In these cases, a diagnosis of hypochondriasis is made when the general medical condition does not fully account for the person's concerns about disease or for their bodily changes or sensations (APA, 2000). Because disease-related fears and beliefs are common in other psychiatric conditions—especially panic disorder, generalized anxiety disorder, obsessive-compulsive disorder, mood disorders, and somatic type delusional disorder—these also need to be ruled out before arriving at a diagnosis of hypochondriasis.

A thorough psychological assessment should include consideration of current *DSM–IV–TR* Axes I and II diagnoses (to assess for comorbid disorders). It should also include an evaluation of the following:

• Personal history, in order to identify the learning experiences that may have contributed to the development of hypochondriasis.

• Current living circumstances, in order to identify stressors, which may contribute to tension or anxiety-related bodily sensations that are misinterpreted as indications of disease, and to assess the patient's relationship with her or his significant others. For example, do family and friends provide excessive reassurance or take on many of the patient's responsibilities?

• Specific features of hypochondriasis, including troubling bodily changes (e.g., rashes, blemishes) or sensations (e.g., pains), disease fears, dysfunctional beliefs and strength of conviction (e.g., beliefs such as "Healthy people never experience bodily sensations"), and avoidance or "safety" behaviors (e.g., remaining in close proximity of hospitals "just in case" of illness).

• Reasons for seeking treatment, in order to identify and address such issues that can interfere with treatment adherence. For example, some patients present for treatment because they have been pressured to do so by their doctor or family members and not because they believe it will help.

Assessment Methods

There are several particular classes of assessment methods that are useful for treatment planning. These include hospital medical records (in order to chart the course of the patient's problems), clinician-administered structured clinical interviews, self-report questionnaires, and prospective monitoring forms. Regarding the structured interviews, the Structured Clinical Interview for *DSM–IV* (First et al., 1996) provides a comprehensive assessment of the more common disorders, along with an assessment of hypochondriasis. For clinicians desiring

a more detailed assessment of hypochondriasis, the Health Anxiety Interview (Taylor & Asmundson, 2004) provides a comprehensive evaluation of the nature and history of the patient's health concerns.

There are numerous self-report measures of hypochondriasis and related constructs. The most widely used of these are reproduced in the appendices of Taylor and Asmundson (2004). The questionnaires differ in several ways, including breadth of assessment, time required for administration and scoring, availability of norms, and the amount of research on their reliability and validity. The choice of scale depends partly on the purpose of the assessment. If the clinician requires a quick assessment of health anxiety, then the Whiteley Index (Pilowsky, 1967) is a particularly good choice because, unlike other brief measures, norms and screening cut-off scores are available. The Whiteley Index is also short enough for periodic readministration throughout treatment to monitor progress. If a more detailed assessment of the various facets of health anxiety is desired, then the Illness Attitude Scales (Kellner, 1986) is a good choice, particularly because it is easy to score, there are a good deal of data on its reliability and validity, and norms are available. Factor analytic research (e.g., Hadjistavropoulos et al., 1999) suggests that it consists of four scales: (1) fear of illness, disease, pain, and death; (2) symptom interference with lifestyle; (3) treatment experience (including reassurance seeking and the effects of receiving reassurance); and (4) disease conviction (i.e., belief that one is ill, despite contrary evidence).

A promising new measure is the Multidimensional Inventory of Hypochondriacal Traits (Longley et al., 2005). This contains four scales: (1) disease conviction, (2) worry about health, (3) reassurance-seeking to allay illness fears, and (4) somatic absorption with bodily sensations. While it covers much the same content as the Illness Attitude Scales and has comparably good psychometric properties, it has not been as widely used. Consequently, there is less information on norms and cut-off scores for identifying clinically severe health anxiety.

Prospective monitoring methods are useful in treatment planning, and can be used throughout therapy in order to monitor the course of treatment. Prospective monitoring involves the use of a daily diary or checklist (e.g., see Appendix 8 of Taylor & Asmundson, 2004). Patients can be asked to complete the diary each day for 1 or 2 weeks prior to treatment and on regular intervals (e.g., every 4 weeks) throughout treatment. This provides a wealth of information regarding the patient's specific health concerns and health behaviors on an episode-by-episode basis.

Description of Treatments
Historical Overview

Based on disappointing results of early, largely psychodynamic treatments, the prognosis of hypochondriasis was once considered to be quite poor, and treatments were thought to be of limited value (e.g., Ladee, 1966). During the 1960s and 1970s, however, there were important, promising developments in behavioral treatments for hypochondriasis (e.g., Leonhard, 1961), which were refined in the 1980s and 1990s into empirically supported cognitive-behavioral interventions. These treatments were based on the assumption that hypochondriasis may arise from mechanisms thought to be involved in other forms of anxiety (especially dysfunctional beliefs and maladaptive coping, as illustrated in Figure 1) and, consequently, that established treatments for other forms of anxiety might be profitably used in the treatment of hypochondriasis. During the 1980s and 1990s, there were also some promising developments in pharmacotherapies for hypochondriasis. These treatments were based on the observation that hypochondriasis is characterized by prominent anxiety and often accompanied by depression. Therefore, medications with anxiolytic and antidepressant properties might be beneficial in treating hypochondriasis. A further rationale for the use of antidepressant medication was the hypothesis that hypochondriasis is actually a masked form of depression (Lesse, 1967); although this hypothesis has now been refuted (Taylor & Asmundson, 2004). In the following paragraphs we describe in more detail the cognitive-behavioral and pharmacological treatments.

General Features of Treatment

Treatment for hypochondriasis, whether psychosocial or pharmacologic, is conducted in the context of good medical management. Primary care physicians play an important role in encouraging patients to try a course of cognitive-behavioral treatment or pharmacotherapy. Patients referred for such treatment are typically those that have failed to respond to simpler interventions, such as physician assurance that their health is fine. To avoid unnecessary medical evaluations, the patient, mental health practitioner, and the patient's primary care physician can generate a tailored list of guidelines for when a physician should be consulted. Specific guidelines for seeking medical care will depend on the nature of

the patient's physical health. For elderly or infirm patients, it may be medically necessary for frequent (e.g., monthly) medical check-ups.

All treatments include nonspecific treatment factors (e.g., therapist warmth and empathy) along with some form of psychoeducation. Nonspecific treatment factors are likely to be very important. People with elevated health anxiety often complain about the lack of understanding from others, including their health care providers. An open and accepting attitude by the therapist may enhance the patient's sense of being understood (Kellner, 1986). A typical course of cognitive-behavioral treatment or pharmacotherapy lasts 12–16 weeks in treatment studies, and typically longer in routine clinical practice, depending on the nature and severity of the patient's problems. Booster sessions are offered, as needed.

Cognitive Behavioral Therapy (CBT) and Related Treatments

There are several interventions that are similar to one another: psychoeducation, explanatory therapy, cognitive therapy, exposure and response prevention, CBT, and behavioral stress management. Table 2 summarizes the components of these interventions and illustrates their similarities and differences. The treatments shown in the table differ in that some packages contain more components than others, and only explanatory therapy uses reassurance as an intervention. The other treatment packages explicitly avoid giving reassurance, because of the concern that reassurance perpetuates health anxiety. Behavioral exercises in CBT are, in many ways, similar to those used in exposure and response prevention. The main difference is that a broader range of behavioral exercises are used in CBT. These exercises are often framed as behavioral experiments that test health-related beliefs. In the following sections we describe each treatment package.

Psychoeducation. This involves the provision of information about the nature of one's concerns and their treatment. The advantage of psychoeducation is that it is simple to administer and can be delivered in groups. Specific content depends on the type of treatment that the patient receives. If treatment is based on a cognitive-behavioral model, for example, then psychoeducation will involve an explanation of the model (consisting of simplified versions of Table 1 and Figure 1, adaptive to the specific characteristics of the patient) and examples of treatment strategies.

Bouman (2002) provides an excellent example of a cognitive-behavioral psychoeducation program

Table 2. Pharmacological and Psychosocial Treatments for Hypochondriasis

	Psycho-education	Explanatory therapy	Cognitive therapy	Exposure and response prevention	Cognitive behavior therapy	Behavioral stress management	Paroxetine	Fluoxetine	Fluvoxamine	Nefazodone
Medical Management										
Medical evaluation	+	+	+	+	+	+	+	+	+	+
Liaison between the physician providing medical management and mental health practitioner	+	+	+	+	+	+	+	+	+	+
Psychosocial treatment component										
Thorough psychiatric evaluation	+	+	+	+	+	+	+	+	+	+
Nonspecific treatment factors (e.g., therapist attention, warmth, and empathy)	+	+	+	+	+	+	+	+	+	+
Psychoeducation about the causes of bodily sensations and health anxiety	+	+	+	+	+	+	+	+	+	+
Monitoring of bodily sensations, emotions, and thoughts	–	–	+	–	+	+	–	–	–	–

Intervention									
Extensive use of cognitive restructuring exercises	–	–	–	+	+	+	–	–	–	–
Systematic exposure exercises	+	–	–	–	+/–	+	–	–	–	–
Relaxation training	–	–	–	–	–	+	–	–	–	–
Assertiveness training	–	–	–	–	–	+	–	–	–	–
Stimulus control exercises for reducing worry	–	–	–	–	–	+	–	–	–	–
Time management training	–	–	–	–	–	+	–	–	–	–
Provision of repeated assurance that patient does not have a serious disease	–	+	–	–	–	–	–	–	–	–
Treatment dropout (%)	22	16	11	14	10	4	18	15	21	18
Pre-post effect size (the larger the number, the larger the reduction in hypochondriasis)	1.05	0.91	0.83	1.00	2.05	1.59	1.34	1.92	NA	1.07

Note. + Intervention used; +/– sometimes used; – not used; NA = not available.
Adapted from "Current Directions in the Treatment of Hypochondriasis," by S. Taylor, G.J.G. Asmundson, and M. J. Coons, 2005, *Journal of Cognitive Psychotherapy, 19*, p. 81. Copyright 2005 by Guilford Press. Used by permission of Springer Publishing Company, Inc., New York 10036.

titled "Coping With Illness Anxiety." This program is community-based and is composed of short lectures, demonstrations, video illustrations, focused group discussions, and brief exercises. Homework assignments are brief and optional (e.g., monitoring and challenging thoughts, identifying avoidance behaviors, monitoring daily hassles). The session contents of Bouman's program are as follows:

- *Session 1.* Overview of the program.
- *Session 2.* Role of thoughts in producing health anxiety, and how to challenge them.
- *Session 3.* Information on the role of selective attention in health anxiety.
- *Session 4.* Education on the role of checking, reassurance-seeking, avoidance, and other maladaptive behaviors in perpetuating health anxiety.
- *Session 5.* Information on the role of stress in producing bodily sensations.
- *Session 6.* Exercises in which participants devise interventions to overcome their health anxiety (e.g., cognitive restructuring exercises) based on their individualized cognitive-behavioral formulation of their health anxiety.

Psychoeducation differs from the provision of reassurance in that the patient is presented with new information. By comparison, the provision of reassurance involves the repeated presentation of old information (e.g., reminding the patient each week that he or she is healthy, or repeatedly performing medical tests to placate the patient). Coping strategies (e.g., relaxation training) are also often used in psychoeducation, but systematic exposure exercises are usually not included.

Explanatory Therapy. Kellner's (1979) explanatory therapy includes a number of interventions intended to persuade patients that there is nothing wrong with their physical health. Treatment involves repeated physical examinations, performed whenever the patient requests one, or when new symptoms emerge. Patients are also repeatedly told that there is nothing physically wrong with them, and are sometimes given anxiolytic medication if they remain anxious. Explanatory therapy is, therefore, based primarily on reassurance and psychoeducation.

A major concern with explanatory therapy has to do with its use of reassurance. Kellner (1992) advocated the use of reassurance (including repeated physical examinations) because it was considered to be a form of cognitive restructuring. However, we along with many others consider it counterproductive to repeatedly tell the patient that there is nothing wrong (e.g., Barsky, 1996; Warwick & Salkovskis,

1985). Patients with hypochondriasis typically fail to benefit from reassurance (APA, 2000). Another concern with persistently giving reassurance is that it may encourage the patient to be dependent on the advice of the therapist. It would be preferable to teach patients to assure themselves about the significance of their bodily sensations or changes. Studies using single-case designs have shown that hypochondriasis persists when patients receive reassurance and abates when reassurance-seeking is discouraged (Salkovskis & Warwick, 1986). Given these concerns, it is not surprising that explanatory therapy is not widely used today as a treatment for hypochondriasis.

Exposure and Response Prevention. Common features of hypochondriasis include fear and avoidance of stimuli that the person associates with disease. Accordingly, clinicians have combined various forms of exposure therapy to reduce hypochondriasis: in vivo exposure (e.g., exposure to hospitals, doctors), interoceptive exposure (e.g., physical exercise to induce rapid heartbeat), and imaginal exposure (e.g., imagining that one has developed cancer). Exposure is conducted within treatment sessions and as homework assignments. Response prevention is often combined with exposure in order to encourage the patient to delay or refrain from bodily checking and from seeking medical reassurance.

CBT and Behavioral Stress Management (BSM). These interventions contain many of the interventions discussed above, with the exception of the provision of reassurance (also see Table 2). Both types of intervention begin with psychoeducation. The "noisy body" analogy is a useful psychoeducational tool for introducing patients to a cognitive-behavioral approach. Here, troubling sensations are relabeled as harmless "bodily noise" rather than indications of physical dysfunction. Cognitive behavioral therapy also involves cognitive restructuring and behavioral exercises. Cognitive restructuring might be used, for example, to examine beliefs about the meaning of bodily sensations. Behavioral exercises are used to further test beliefs and to examine the effects of hypochondriacal behavior patterns. For example, to test the effects of reassurance-seeking, the patient could be encouraged to refrain from this behavior for a period of time. Often, patients discover that reassurance-seeking drives their disease fears and feelings of vulnerability. Once patients refrain from reassurance-seeking they often find that they are less preoccupied with their health, and feel less vulnerable, because they are not exposed to daily reminders of morbidity and mortality.

Behavioral stress management emphasizes the role of stress in producing harmless, but unpleasant bodily sensations. The patient is encouraged to practice various stress management exercises (e.g., relaxation training, time management, problem solving) as a means of managing stress. This reduces the bodily sensations that fuel hypochondriacal concerns and increases sense of well-being. It was originally developed as a control condition (controlling, for example, nonspecific treatment factors) in a randomized controlled study comparing CBT, BSM, and waitlist control (Clark et al., 1998). Although planned as a control condition, BSM also proved to be effective at reducing health anxiety. This serendipitous result has led to the use of BSM in the treatment of hypochondriasis (for detailed descriptions of BSM and CBT, see Taylor & Asmundson, 2004).

Some patients may be more likely to adhere to, and benefit from, BSM, and others from CBT. The former might be particularly useful for patients with comorbid disorders, such as hypochondriasis co-occurring with a mood disorder, anxiety disorder, or a behavioral medicine problem (e.g., recurrent tension headaches). Like hypochondriasis, these comorbid conditions can to be exacerbated by stress. Consequently, by providing strategies for effective coping, BSM may have a nonspecific, beneficial effect on a person's overall symptom profile. If BSM is used, it is important that patients understand that the rationale for using stress management is to reduce unpleasant but *harmless* bodily sensations. Stress management interventions would be misused if the patient used them to avoid sensations that she or he believed to be dangerous (Taylor & Asmundson, 2004).

Pharmacotherapies

The two most widely used medications in the treatment of hypochondriasis include tricyclic antidepressants and selective serotonin reuptake inhibitors. These are administered in the context of good clinical management, including nonspecific treatment factors (e.g., therapist attention and empathy) and psychoeducation (see Table 2). In clinical studies these medications are typically administered over a period of 12 weeks, although they may be taken over a much longer period (e.g., years) in routine clinical practice, in order to prevent relapse. The doses of these agents, as used in clinical studies of hypochondriasis, are as follows: clomipramine (25–225 mg/day), imipramine (125–150 mg/day), fluoxetine (20–80 mg/day), fluvoxamine (300 mg/day), paroxetine (up to 60 mg/day), and nefazodone (200–500 mg/day), which was pulled from the market in 2003 due to heightened risk of liver failure.

Review of Treatment Research

In this section we review the evidence for the treatments described above. We do so using both narrative and meta-analytic methods.

Narrative Review of Findings

Psychoeducation. Three studies have examined the merits of group psychoeducation as the main component of treatment (Avia et al., 1996; Bouman, 2002; Lidbeck, 1997). Findings suggest that psychoeducation is associated with significant reductions in hypochondriasis, superior to waitlist control, with gains maintained at follow-ups of up to a year. Bouman (2002) found that psychoeducation was associated with mean reduction of 40% in the frequency of medical service utilization (as indicated by comparing the frequency of doctor visits 6 months before versus 6 months after treatment). Participants reported that they valued the opportunity to share their concerns during the psychoeducational program, and most were relieved to learn that they were not the only ones suffering from excessive health anxiety.

Explanatory Therapy. A uncontrolled trial and one controlled study suggest that explanatory therapy can reduce hypochondriasis, and is superior to a waitlist control (Fava et al., 2000; Kellner, 1982). Given the questionable value of giving reassurance in explanatory therapy (as discussed above), the benefits of this treatment may be primarily due to the use of psychoeducation and rudimentary cognitive restructuring exercises.

Exposure and Response Prevention. Uncontrolled trials indicated that exposure and response prevention tends to be successful in reducing features of hypochondriasis (e.g., Logsdail et al., 1991; Visser & Bouman, 1992). In a controlled study, Visser and Bowman (2001) found this treatment to be effective, and superior to a waitlist control, with gains maintained at 7-month follow-up.

CBT and BSM. Many uncontrolled trials have suggested that a course of CBT can effectively reduce hypochondriasis (e.g., Martinez & Botella, 2005; Stern & Fernandez, 1991). Trials comparing CBT to waitlist controls or other treatment conditions have also produced results suggesting the superiority of CBT (e.g., Clark et al., 1998; Warwick et al., 1996). Therapists in most CBT studies have implemented treatment on an individual (one-to-one) basis, although Stern and Fernandez (1991) found that group treatment was also effective. In addition to being economical, group treatment for hypochondriasis can foster a sense of acceptance and social support (Bouman, 2002). Barsky and Ahern's (2004) randomized controlled study indicates that CBT is more efficacious than the usual medical care offered to these patients by primary care physicians (Barsky & Ahern, 2004). Clark et al. (1998) found that both BSM and CBT were effective, compared to the waitlist group. At posttreatment, CBT tended to be more effective than BSM, although there was little difference between the two at 12-month follow-up.

Pharmacotherapies

Case studies and a small number of trials suggest that the following medications can be helpful in reducing hypochondriasis: clomipramine (Kamlana & Gray, 1988; Stone, 1993), imipramine (Lippert, 1986; Wesner & Noyes, 1991), fluoxetine (e.g., Fallon et al., 1996; Viswanathan & Paradis, 1991), fluvoxamine (e.g., Fallon et al., 2003), paroxetine (Oosterbaan et al., 2001), and nefazodone (Kjernisted et al., 2002). These medications can reduce all aspects of hypochondriasis, including disease fears and beliefs, pervasive anxiety, somatic symptoms, avoidance, and reassurance-seeking (Fallon, 2001; Wesner & Noyes, 1991). Little is known about the long-term effects.

There has been only one placebo-controlled pharmacotherapy study (Fallon et al., 1996). Results indicated that there was no significant difference in the proportion of responders in either condition, although there were trends favoring fluoxetine (for patients completing 12 weeks of treatment, 80% of fluoxetine patients were classified as responders, compared to 60% of placebo patients). More recent results, based on an increased sample size, apparently indicate that fluoxetine is superior to placebo, both in terms of outcome after 12 weeks and at 9-month follow-up (B. A. Fallon, personal communication, September 10, 2002).

Despite the promising effects of these drugs, there are several problems in using pharmacotherapy to treat hypochondriasis. There are numerous case reports of health-anxious patients failing to benefit from one or more of these drugs (e.g., Stone, 1993; Viswanathan & Paradis, 1991). Even for short (8–12 week) trials using drugs with few side effects, 13%–21% of patients drop out of treatment (Taylor et al., 2005). Some patients become preoccupied with side

effects (e.g., Stone, 1993; Wesner & Noyes, 1991). In some cases, hypochondriacal symptoms worsen during drug treatment, as patients become alarmed by side effects like gastrointestinal discomfort (Fallon, 2001; Oosterbaan et al., 2001).

Meta-Analytic Review

A preliminary meta-analysis of psychosocial and pharmacological studies was recently conducted by Taylor et al. (2005). A total of 25 trials from 15 studies contained sufficient data for the purpose of computing pre-post effect sizes (Cohen's d for treatment completers) on self-report measures of hypochondriasis and/or for assessing the proportion of treatment dropouts. Participants in these studies had either full or abridged hypochondriasis. Patients in drug trials were on medication at the time of the posttreatment assessment. Treatment durations were typically between 6–12 weeks, and psychosocial treatments typically involved around 12 hours of therapy contact.

Table 2 summarizes the main results for each of the treatments included in the meta-analysis (further details appear in Taylor et al., 2005). The results in the table are limited to studies of full hypochondriasis. The effect sizes for the treatments listed in the table were all larger than the effect size for waitlist control. The latter was 0.29. It was found that CBT and fluoxetine tended to yield the largest effects, and these were broadly similar to one another. Cognitive therapy, CBT, and BSM tended to have the lowest proportions of dropouts. For studies using mixed samples of full and abridged hypochondriasis, the results (not shown in the table) suggested that psychoeducation and CBT had similar effect sizes (0.74 versus 0.51), which were larger than waitlist (0.19) and medical care from a primary care physician (0.20). Psychoeducation tended to have a lower proportion of dropouts than CBT (2% versus 13%). Other treatments were not examined for these mixed samples. Pretreatment to follow-up effect sizes for measures of hypochondriasis could not be calculated for drug studies because follow-ups were not conducted. For studies reporting follow-up data (3–12-month follow-up), results indicated that CBT had the largest effect sizes in studies of full hypochondriasis, and psychoeducation and CBT had the largest effects in studies of mixed full and abridged hypochondriasis. The findings suggest that CBT and fluoxetine are the most efficacious interventions for full hypochondriasis, whereas psychoeducation is most efficacious for mild samples (i.e., patients with abridged hypochondriasis).

Predictors of Treatment Outcome

The research reviewed in the previous section suggests that for mild or short-lived forms of hypochondriasis, psychoeducation may be sufficient, delivered either by the primary care physician or in the form of educational courses. If that does not prove effective, or if the patient has full hypochondriasis, then more intensive interventions could be considered, such as CBT or serotonergic medications.

Not all patients with full hypochondriasis benefit equally from a given form of therapy. Regardless of the type of treatment, the following are the most reliably identified predictors of good outcome, as obtained from a variety of sources (e.g., APA, 2000; Barsky et al., 1998; Hiller et al., 2002): hypochondriasis that is mild, short-lived, and not associated with complicating factors such as personality disorders, comorbid general medical conditions, or contingencies ("secondary gains") that reinforce health anxiety or sick-role behavior. In other words, a good prognosis is associated with the milder forms of full hypochondriasis and the absence of complicating factors. Such findings suggest that it is important to find ways of improving treatment outcome for severe cases. (See Taylor & Asmundson, 2004, for a detailed review.)

Research is also needed to determine if a patient is more likely to benefit more from one treatment (e.g., pharmacotherapy) than another (e.g., CBT). If a patient has a strong preference for one type of treatment, then that patient may be more likely to drop out allocated to a nonpreferred treatment. Evidence so far suggests that no form of treatment is inherently more acceptable to patients than other treatments. Walker and colleagues (1999) presented written descriptions of CBT and pharmacotherapy for "intense illness worries" to a community-based sample of 23 treatment-seeking people with hypochondriasis. The descriptions outlined the time commitment and the major advantages and disadvantages of each treatment. Most (74%) preferred CBT and almost half said they would only accept this treatment. Given that CBT and some medications may be roughly equivalent in efficacy, at least in the short term (Table 2), and that there is no evidence that one treatment works any faster than another, patient preferences and the availability of suitably qualified practitioners are important considerations in selecting treatment. Patients failing to benefit from one intervention can then be placed on another.

Improving Treatment Outcome

There are numerous directions for future research that will improve our understanding of the mechanisms that underlie hypochondriasis and thereby facilitate our ability to provide accurate assessment and effective intervention. Some of the most important issues, presented in greater detail elsewhere (Taylor & Asmundson, 2004), include (1) better understanding of the causal relationship between hypochondriasis and individual difference factors that increase vulnerability to psychopathology (e.g., neuroticism), (2) better understanding of environmental and genetic influences on preoccupation with disease-related fears and beliefs, (3) exploring physiological mechanisms that may be involved in hypochondriasis, (4) establishing whether there are subtypes of hypochondriasis that differ in phenomenology, mechanisms, and response to treatments, and (5) resolving debate regarding whether hypochondriasis should remain a somatoform disorder or be reclassified as an anxiety disorder.

Despite decades of research, it still remains for researchers to firmly demonstrate that psychosocial or pharmacologic treatments are superior to credible placebos. There has only been one placebo-controlled psychosocial intervention, in which the so-called placebo (BSM) appeared to be an active treatment, with gains evident at 12-month follow-up (Clark et al., 1998). However, the benefits of CBT are apparent at follow-ups ranging from 3 to 12 months (Taylor et al., 2005) and the maintenance of such gains would not be expected if CBT was simply a placebo. The only placebo-controlled pharmacologic study suggests that fluvoxamine may be more effective than placebo (B. A. Fallon, personal communication, September 10, 2002).

Additional research on the efficacy of various treatment strategies, alone and in combination, is also required. In addition to further studies of cognitive-behavioral and serotonergic treatments, researchers could also evaluate novel treatments for hypochondriasis. Interpersonal psychotherapy has been shown to be effective in treating other disorders, such as major depression and bulimia nervosa (Nathan & Gorman, 2002). Stuart and Noyes (2005) suggest that this type of therapy may be effective for hypochondriasis, with a focus on the interpersonal consequences of health preoccupation. Methods from motivational enhancement therapy, which have been shown to be effective in treating substance use disorders (Miller & Rollnick, 2002), have been increasingly used in anxiety disorders, and may be usefully integrated into cognitive-behavioral treatment for hypochondriasis (see Taylor & Asmundson, 2004, for details). The merits of such possibilities remain to be empirically investigated.

Pharmacologic treatments also need to be further investigated. For example, studies of medications that show promise for enhancing the effects of behavioral treatment for anxiety disorders, such as D-cycloserine (Ressler et al., 2004), or augmenting strategies (e.g., combining serotonergic medications with atypical antipsychotics such as risperidone; Cottraux et al., 2005) are warranted. Likewise, further controlled trials of self-help approaches are warranted. We have recently written a cognitive-behavioral guidebook for people with health anxiety (Asmundson & Taylor, 2005). Research is currently underway to determine whether this book can be successfully used as bibliotherapy.

Another important area for improving treatment outcome involves treatment acceptability. Results from Barsky and Ahern's (2004) comparison of CBT versus treatment as usual suggests that there is much room for improvement in this regard.

> The treatment offered in this study was not attractive to many hypochondriacal patients, and only 30% of those eligible entered the trial. Hypochondriacal individuals are by definition convinced of the medical nature of their condition and therefore psychosocial treatment seems nonsensical to them. Although a major problem, this should not detract from the fact that those patients who did undergo treatment benefited from it. And since hypochondriasis is a prevalent problem in ambulatory medical practice . . . this fraction of hypochondriacal patients still represents a sizeable population. The treatment must be made more attractive in the future by seamlessly integrating it into the primary care process and conducting it in the medical setting (as our treatment was not). (pp. 1469–1470)

Consistent with some of these recommendations, preliminary research suggests that CBT for hypochondriasis may be more acceptable for patients if it is delivered in a medical, rather than mental health, setting (Tyrer et al., 1999).

Little is known about how treatment protocols need to be adapted or modified for special populations of health-anxious people, such as particular age groups, cultural groups, or groups with severe general medical conditions. Such individuals need to be considered on a case-by-case basis. For children with elevated health anxiety, interventions should be consistent with the child's developmental level (e.g., cognitive restructuring exercises would be simplified or omitted). For cognitively impaired (e.g., dementing) patients, simple contingency management programs that reinforce (reward) adaptive behaviors (e.g., engaging in health activities, talking about topics other than their health) but not maladaptive ones (e.g., complaining about symptoms) might be most effective (Williamson, 1984). For the cognitively intact elderly it is our impression, and that of others (e.g., Monopoli, 2005), that cognitive-behavioral interventions can be useful; however, formal research trials need to be done to confirm this.

Summary and Conclusions

Excessive health anxiety occurs in various different disorders as a secondary condition. As a primary condition, it occurs in the full and abridged forms of hypochondriasis. Etiologic research suggests that genetic factors play a modest role, and that learning experiences regarding health, disease, and medical treatment play an important role. These experiences appear to give rise to maladaptive beliefs which, in turn, lead to behaviors such as persistent reassurance-seeking and other forms of checking, which can perpetuate health anxiety.

When conducting an assessment for the purpose of treatment planning, it is first important to rule out general medical conditions that could account for the patient's presenting problems and to rule in a *DSM–IV–TR* diagnosis of hypochondriasis. Other useful assessment methods include structured clinical interviews, self-report questionnaires, and prospective monitoring methods. For milder (abridged) forms of hypochondriasis, psychoeducation may be sufficient. For more severe conditions, such as full-blown hypochondriasis, cognitive-behavioral methods and serotonergic medications are both promising. Numerous controlled studies support the long-term efficacy of CBT for full-blown hypochondriasis. Serotonergic medications, such as fluoxetine and fluvoxamine, have shown promise in preliminary short-term studies, although most of these studies have been uncontrolled. It is unclear whether the gains from medications are maintained when drugs are discontinued. Research suggests that the gains from psychosocial treatments tend to be maintained at follow-up periods of a year or more.

Although the current psychosocial and pharmacologic treatments are often effective, they are far from completely efficacious. Further research is needed to develop ways of improving patient adherence and increasing treatment efficacy. Much also remains to be learned about the mechanisms of action of these treatments. It is possible that many psychosocial and drug treatments work in much the same way—by reducing the strength of dysfunctional beliefs about bodily changes and symptoms.

References

American Psychiatric Association. (2000). *Diagnostic and statistical manual of mental disorders* (4th ed., text revision). Washington, DC: Author.

Asmundson, G.J.G., & Taylor, S. (2005). *It's not all in your head: How worrying about your health could be making you sick—and what you can do about it.* New York: Guilford Press.

Avia, M. D., Ruiz, M. A., Olivares, M. E., Crespo, M., Guisado, A. B., Sanchez, A., et al. (1996). The meaning of psychological symptoms: Effectiveness of a group intervention with hypochondriacal patients. *Behaviour Research and Therapy, 34,* 23–31.

Barsky, A. J. (1996). Hypochondriasis: Medical management and psychiatric treatment. *Psychosomatics, 37,* 48–56.

Barsky, A. J., & Ahern, D. K. (2004). Cognitive behavior therapy for hypochondriasis: A randomized controlled trial. *Journal of the American Medical Association, 291,* 1464–1470.

Barsky, A. J., Brener, J., Coeytaux, R. R., & Cleary, P. D. (1995). Accurate awareness of heartbeat in hypochondriacal and non-hypochondriacal patients. *Journal of Psychosomatic Research, 39,* 489–497.

Barsky, A. J., Cleary, P. D., Sarnie, M. K., & Klerman, G. L. (1993). The course of transient hypochondriasis. *American Journal of Psychiatry, 150,* 484–488.

Barsky, A. J., Ettner, S. L., Horsky, J., & Bates, D. W. (2001). Resource utilization of patients with hypochondriacal health anxiety and somatization. *Medical Care, 39,* 705–715.

Barsky, A. J., Fama, J. M., Bailey, E. D., & Ahern, D. K. (1998). A prospective 4- to 5-year study of DSM–III–R hypochondriasis. *Archives of General Psychiatry, 55,* 737–744.

Barsky, A. J., & Klerman, G. L. (1983). Overview: Hypochondriasis, bodily complaints, and somatic styles. *American Journal of Psychiatry, 140,* 273–283.

Bouman, T. K. (2002). A community-based psychoeducational group approach to hypochondriasis. *Psychotherapy and Psychosomatics, 71,* 326–332.

Brown, H. D., Kosslyn, S. M., Delamater, B., Fama, J., & Barsky, A. J. (1999). Perceptual and memory biases for health-related information in hypochondriacal individuals. *Journal of Psychosomatic Research, 47,* 67–78.

Clark, D. M., Salkovskis, P. M., Hackmann, A., Wells, A., Fennell, M., Ludgate, J., et al. (1998). Two psychological treatments for hypochondriasis: A randomised controlled trial. *British Journal of Psychiatry, 173,* 218–225.

Cottraux, J., Bouvard, M. A., & Milliery, M. (2005). Combining pharmacotherapy with cognitive-behavioral interventions for obsessive-compulsive disorder. *Cognitive Behaviour Therapy, 34,* 185–192.

Creed, F., & Barsky, A. (2004). A systematic review of the epidemiology of somatization disorder and hypochondriasis. *Journal of Psychosomatic Research, 56,* 391–408.

Ditto, P. H., Jemmott, J. B., & Darley, J. M. (1988). Appraising the threat of illness: A mental representational approach. *Health Psychology, 7,* 183–201.

Easterling, D. V., & Leventhal, H. (1989). Contribution of concrete cognition to emotion: Neutral symptoms as elicitors of worry about cancer. *Journal of Applied Psychology, 74,* 787–796.

Fallon, B. A. (2001). Pharmacologic strategies for hypochondriasis. In V. Starcevic & D. R. Lipsett (Eds.), *Hypochondriasis: Modern perspectives on an ancient malady* (pp. 329–351). New York: Oxford University Press.

Fallon, B. A., Qureshi, A. I., Schneier, F. R., Sanchez-Lacay, A., Vermes, D., Feinstein, R., et al. (2003). An open trial of fluvoxamine for hypochondriasis. *Psychosomatics, 44,* 298–303.

Fallon, B. A., Schneier, F. R., Marshall, R., Campeas, R., Vermes, D., Goetz, D., et al. (1996). The pharmacotherapy of hypochondriasis. *Psychopharmacology Bulletin, 32,* 607–611.

Fava, G. A., Grandi, S., Rafanelli, C., Fabbri, S., & Cazzaro, M. (2000). Explanatory therapy in hypochondriasis. *Journal of Clinical Psychiatry, 61,* 317–322.

Fink, P., Ornbol, E., Toft, T., Sparle, K. C., Frostholm, L., & Olesen, F. (2004). A new, empirically established hypochondriasis diagnosis. *American Journal of Psychiatry, 161,* 1680–1691.

First, M. B., Spitzer, R. L., Gibbon, M., & Williams, J.B.W. (1996). *Structured Clinical Interview for DSM–IV.* New York: New York State Psychiatric Institute, Biometrics Research Department.

Gureje, O. (2004). What can we learn from a cross-national study of somatic distress? *Journal of Psychosomatic Research, 56,* 409–412.

Hadjistavropoulos, H. D., Frombach, I. K., & Asmundson, G.J.G. (1999). Exploratory and confirmatory factor analytic investigations of the Illness Attitudes Scale in a non-clinical sample. *Behaviour Research and Therapy, 37,* 671–684.

Haenen, M. A., de Jong, P. J., Schmidt, A.J.M., Stevens, S., & Visser, L. (2000). Hypochondriacs' estimation of negative outcomes: Domain-specificity and responsiveness to reassuring and alarming information. *Behaviour Research and Therapy, 38,* 819–833.

Haenen, M. A., Schmidt, A.J.M., Schoenmakers, M., & van den Hout, M. A. (1998). Quantitative and qualitative aspects of cancer knowledge: Comparing hypochondriacal subjects and healthy controls. *Psychology and Health, 13,* 1005–1014.

Hiller, W., Leibbrand, R., Rief, W., & Fichter, M. M. (2002). Predictors of course and outcome in hypochondriasis after cognitive-behavioral treatment. *Psychotherapy and Psychosomatics, 71,* 318–325.

Kamlana, S. H., & Gray, P. (1988). Fear of AIDS. *British Journal of Psychiatry, 15,* 1291.

Kellner, R. (1979). Psychotherapeutic strategies in the treatment of psychophysiologic disorders. *Psychotherapy and Psychosomatics, 32*(Suppl. 4), 91–100.

Kellner, R. (1982). Psychotherapeutic strategies in hypochondriasis: A clinical study. *American Journal of Psychotherapy, 36,* 146–157.

Kellner, R. (1986). *Somatization and hypochondriasis.* New York: Praeger.

Kellner, R. (1992). The treatment of hypochondriasis: To reassure or not to reassure? *International Review of Psychiatry, 4,* 71–75.

Kjernisted, K. D., Enns, M. W., & Lander, M. (2002). An open-label clinical trial of nefazodone in hypochondriasis. *Psychosomatics, 43,* 290–294.

Ladee, G. A. (1966). *Hypochondriacal syndromes.* Amsterdam: Elsevier.

Lautenbacher, S., Pauli, P., Zaudig, M., & Burbaumer, N. (1998). Attentional control of pain perception: The role of hypochondriasis. *Journal of Psychosomatic Research, 44,* 251–259.

Leonhard, K. (1961). On the treatment of ideohypochondriac and sensohypochondriac neuroses. *International Journal of Social Psychiatry, 7,* 123–133.

Lesse, S. (1967). Hypochondriasis and psychosomatic disorders masking depression. *American Journal of Psychotherapy, 21,* 607–620.

Lidbeck, J. (1997). Group therapy for somatization disorders in general practice: Effectiveness of a short cognitive-behavioural treatment model. *Acta Psychiatrica Scandinavica, 96,* 14–24.

Lippert, G. P. (1986). Excessive concern about AIDS in two bisexual men. *Canadian Journal of Psychiatry, 31,* 63–65.

Logsdail, S., Lovell, K., Warwick, H. M., & Marks, I. (1991). Behavioural treatment of AIDS-focused illness phobia. *British Journal of Psychiatry, 159,* 422–425.

Longley, S. L., Watson, D., & Noyes, R. (2005). Assessment of the hypochondriasis domain: The multidimensional inventory of hypochondriacal traits (MIHT). *Psychological Assessment, 17,* 3–14.

Lucock, M. P., White, C., Peake, M. D., & Morley, S. (1998). Biased perception and recall of reassurance in medical patients. *British Journal of Health Psychology, 3,* 237–243.

Marcus, D. K. (1999). The cognitive-behavioral model of hypochondriasis: Misinformation and triggers. *Journal of Psychosomatic Research, 47,* 79–91.

Martinez, M. P., & Botella, C. (2005). An exploratory study of the efficacy of a cognitive-behavioral treatment for hypochondriasis using different measures of change. *Psychotherapy Research, 15,* 392–408.

Mayou, R., Kirmayer, L. J., Simon, G., Kroenke, K., & Sharpe, M. (2005). Somatoform disorders: Time for a new approach in DSM–V. *American Journal of Psychiatry, 162,* 847–855.

Miller, W. R., & Rollnick, S. (2002). *Motivational interviewing: Preparing people for change* (2nd ed.). New York: Guilford Press.

Monopoli, J. (2005). Managing hypochondriasis in elderly clients. *Journal of Contemporary Psychotherapy, 35,* 285–300.

Nathan, P. E., & Gorman, J. M. (2002). *A guide to treatments that work* (2nd ed.). New York: Oxford University Press.

Oosterbaan, D. B., van Balkom, A.J.L.M., van Boeijen, C. A., de Meij, T.G.J., & van Dyck, R. (2001). An open study of paroxetine in hypochondriasis. *Progress in Neuro-Psychopharmacology and Biological Psychiatry, 25,* 1023–1033.

Owens, K.M.B., Asmundson, G.J.G., Hadjistavropoulos, T., & Owens, T. J. (2004). Attentional bias toward illness threat in individuals with elevated health anxiety. *Cognitive Therapy and Research, 28,* 57–66.

Pauli, P., & Alpers, G. W. (2002). Memory bias in patients with hypochondriasis and somatoform pain disorder. *Journal of Psychosomatic Research, 52,* 45–53.

Pennebaker, J. W. (1982). *The psychology of physical symptoms.* New York: Springer.

Pilowsky, I. (1967). Dimensions of hypochondriasis. *British Journal of Psychiatry, 113,* 89–93.

Ressler, K. J., Rothbaum, B. O., Tannenbaum, L., Anderson, P., Graap, K., Zimand, E., et al. (2004). Cognitive enhancers as adjuncts to psychotherapy: Use of D-cycloserine in phobic individuals to enhance extinction of fear. *Archives of General Psychiatry, 61,* 1136–1144.

Rief, W., Hiller, W., & Margraf, J. (1998). Cognitive aspects of hypochondriasis and the somatization syndrome. *Journal of Abnormal Psychology, 107,* 587–595.

Robbins, J. M., & Kirmayer, L. J. (1996). Transient and persistent hypochondriacal worry in primary care. *Psychological Medicine, 26,* 575–589.

Salkovskis, P. M., & Warwick, H. M. (1986). Morbid preoccupations, health anxiety and reassurance: A cognitive-behavioural approach to hypochondriasis. *Behaviour Research and Therapy, 24,* 597–602.

Salkovskis, P. M., Warwick, H. M., & Deale, A. C. (2003). Cognitive-behavioral treatment for severe and persistent health anxiety (hypochondriasis). *Brief Treatment and Crisis Intervention, 3,* 353–367.

Stern, R., & Fernandez, M. (1991). Group cognitive and behavioural treatment for hypochondriasis. *British Medical Journal, 303,* 1229–1231.

Stone, A. B. (1993). Treatment of hypochondriasis with clomipramine. *Journal of Clinical Psychiatry, 54,* 200–201.

Stuart, S., & Noyes, R. (2005). Treating hypochondriasis with interpersonal psychotherapy. *Journal of Contemporary Psychotherapy, 35,* 269–283.

Taylor, S., & Asmundson, G.J.G. (2004). *Treating health anxiety: A cognitive-behavioral approach.* New York: Guilford Press.

Taylor, S., Asmundson, G.J.G., & Coons, M. J. (2005). Current directions in the treatment of hypochondriasis. *Journal of Cognitive Psychotherapy, 19,* 291–310.

Taylor, S., Thordarson, D. S., Jang, K. L., & Asmundson, G.J.G. (2006). Genetic and environmental origins of health anxiety: A twin study. *World Psychiatry, 5,* 47–50.

Tyrer, P., Seivewright, N., & Behr, G. (1999). A specific treatment for hypochondriasis? *Lancet, 353,* 672–673.

Visser, S., & Bouman, T. K. (1992). Cognitive-behavioural approaches in the treatment of hypochondriasis: Six single case cross-over studies. *Behaviour Research and Therapy, 30,* 301–306.

Visser, S., & Bouman, T. K. (2001). The treatment of hypochondriasis: Exposure plus response prevention vs. cognitive therapy. *Behaviour Research and Therapy, 39,* 423–442.

Viswanathan, R., & Paradis, C. (1991). Treatment of cancer phobia with fluoxetine. *American Journal of Psychiatry, 148,* 1090.

Walker, J., Vincent, N., Furer, P., Cox, B., & Kjernisted, K. (1999). Treatment preference in hypochondriasis. *Journal of Behavior Therapy and Experimental Psychiatry, 30,* 251–258.

Warwick, H. M., Clark, D. M., Cobb, A. M., & Salkovskis, P. M. (1996). A controlled-trial of cognitive-behavioural treatment of hypochondriasis. *British Journal of Psychiatry, 169,* 189–195.

Warwick, H. M., & Salkovskis, P. M. (1985). Reassurance. *British Medical Journal, 290,* 1028.

Wells, A., & Hackmann, A. (1993). Imagery and core beliefs in health anxiety: Contents and origins. *Behavioural and Cognitive Psychotherapy, 21,* 265–273.

Wesner, R. B., & Noyes, R. (1991). Imipramine: An effective treatment for illness phobia. *Journal of Affective Disorders, 22,* 43–48.

Whitehead, W. E., Crowell, M. D., Heller, B. R., Robinson, J. C., Schuster, M. M., & Horn, S. (1994). Modeling and reinforcement of the sick role during childhood predicts adult illness behavior. *Psychosomatic Medicine, 56,* 541–550.

Williamson, P. N. (1984). An intervention for hypochondriacal complaints. *Clinical Gerontologist, 3,* 64–68.

Body Dysmorphic Disorder

David Veale

Abstract

Body dysmorphic disorder (BDD) is characterized by a preoccupation with an imagined defect in one's appearance. Alternatively, there may be a minor physical abnormality, but the concern is regarded as grossly excessive. It must also cause significant distress or handicap. This chapter reviews comorbidity, demographics, risk factors, and the role of cosmetic procedures in BDD. A cognitive behavioral model is described and the therapy outlined. The chapter also describes the use of pharmacotherapy and treatment guidelines.

Keywords: body dysmorphic disorder, BDD, cognitive behavioral therapy, cosmetic surgery, pharmacotherapy

Body dysmorphic disorder (BDD) is classified as a somatoform disorder in *DSM–IV–TR* (American Psychiatric Association [APA], 2000). However, at the core of BDD is an anxiety disorder characterized by a preoccupation with an imagined defect in one's appearance. Alternatively there may be a minor physical abnormality, but the concern is regarded as grossly excessive. To receive the diagnosis, the person must also either be significantly distressed or handicapped such as in his or her ability to work or to interact socially. Lastly it may not be better accounted for by another mental disorder such as anorexia nervosa (APA, 2000).

History

Body dysmorphic disorder was previously known as dysmorphophobia. An Italian psychiatrist, Morselli, first coined the term in 1886, but it is used less often nowadays probably because *ICD-10* (World Health Organization, 1992) has subsumed dysmorphophobia under hypochondriacal disorder.

One of Freud's patients (Freud, 1959) who was subsequently analyzed by Brunswick (1971) was known as the "Wolf Man" and was preoccupied with imagined defects on his nose. Brunswick wrote: "He neglected his daily life and work because he was engrossed, to the exclusion of all else, with the state of his nose. On the street he looked at himself in every shop window; he carried a pocket mirror, which he took out at every few minutes. First he would powder his nose; a moment later he would inspect it and remove the powder. He would then examine the pores, to see if they were enlarging, to catch the hole, as it were in its moment of growth and development. Then he would again powder his nose, put away the mirror, and a moment later begin the process anew."

Psychopathology

There is frequent comorbidity in BDD, especially for depression, social phobia, and obsessive-compulsive disorder (OCD) (Neziroglu et al., 1996;

Phillips & Diaz, 1997; Veale et al., 1996). There is also heterogeneity in the presentation of BDD, from individuals with borderline personality disorder and self-harming behaviors to those with muscle dysmorphia (Pope et al., 1997) who are less handicapped. Individuals with BDD are preoccupied with the notion that one or more features of their appearance is unattractive, ugly, or deformed. Any part of the body may be involved, though the preoccupation most commonly centers on skin, hair, or facial features—eyes, eyelids, nose, lips or mouth, jaw, or chin. The preoccupation is often focused on several parts of the body simultaneously (Phillips et al., 1993). The typical complaint involves flaws on the face (whether perceived or actual), asymmetry, body features felt to be out of proportion, incipient baldness, acne, wrinkles, vascular markings, scars, or extremes of complexion, ruddiness, or pallor. While some complaints are specific in the extreme, others are vague or amount to no more than a general perception of ugliness. The nature of the preoccupation may change over time, and this may explain why, after cosmetic surgery, the patient's focus may shift to another area of the body. Beliefs about defects in appearance usually carry strong personal meanings. A belief that his nose was too big caused one patient to feel that he would end up alone and unloved and that he might look like a crook. Another, preoccupied with flaws in her skin, found them disgusting and thought of her skin as "dirty." Patients such as these tend to have little if any insight (Phillips, 2004; Phillips et al., 1994). On the contrary, they are likely to display delusions of reference, believing that the people around them notice their "defect" and evaluate them negatively or humiliate them as a consequence of their ugliness. A further aspect of BDD is the time-consuming behaviors adopted to examine the "defect" repeatedly or to disguise or improve it. Examples include gazing into the mirror to compare particular features with those of others, excessive grooming, which can be quite deleterious especially where the skin is concerned, camouflaging the "defect" with clothes or make-up, skin picking, reassurance seeking, dieting, and pursuing dermatological treatment or cosmetic surgery.

Cosmetic Procedures in BDD

There are two retrospective surveys that have reported the outcome of cosmetic surgery in BDD patients seen in a psychiatric clinic. Phillips et al. (2001) reported the outcomes of 58 BDD patients seeking cosmetic surgery. A large majority (82.6%) reported that symptoms of BDD were the same or worse after cosmetic surgery. Veale (2000) reported on 25 BDD patients in a psychiatric clinic in the United Kingdom who had had a total of 46 procedures. Repeated surgery tended to lead to increasing dissatisfaction. Some operations, such as rhinoplasty, appear to be associated with higher degrees of dissatisfaction. Mammaplasty and pinnaplasty tended to have relatively higher satisfaction ratings. These operations tend to be unambiguous in that patients can usually describe the problem that concerns them and their desired outcome, and the cosmetic surgeon can understand their expectations. Most of the patients in the study had multiple concerns about their appearance and, after 50% of the procedures, reported that the preoccupation and other symptoms of BDD transferred to another area of the body. When patients were dissatisfied with their operation, they often felt guilty or angry with themselves or the surgeon at having made their appearance worse, thus further fuelling their depression at a failure to achieve their ideal. This in turn tended to increase mirror gazing and a craving for more surgery. The main weakness of studies in psychiatric clinics is that the data are retrospective, and there is a selection bias of patients in favor of treatment failures. Mental health practitioners are unlikely to be consulted if patients are satisfied with their cosmetic surgery and their symptoms of BDD improve.

Body dysmorphic disorder is not uncommon in cosmetic surgery clinics. Studies have found that between 5% and 15% of patients in cosmetic surgery clinics have BDD (Ishigooka et al., 1998; Sarwer et al., 1998) and an incidence of 12% has been reported from a dermatology clinic in the United States (Phillips et al., 2000). Only one study has followed up on patients with a diagnosis of BDD pre-operatively (Tignol et al., 2007) evaluated the effect of cosmetic surgery in 30 patients with a minimal defect in appearance (of whom 12 had BDD and 18 non-BDD) 5 years after their request for cosmetic surgery. Of the 30, it was possible to re-evaluate 24 (80%) by telephone interview (10 with BDD and 14 non-BDD). Seven participants with BDD had undergone cosmetic surgery versus 8 non-BDD. Patient satisfaction with the surgery was high in both groups. Nevertheless, at follow-up, 6 of the 7 operated BDD patients still had a diagnosis of BDD and exhibited higher levels of handicap and psychiatric comorbidity compared to people without BDD. Moreover, 3 non-BDD patients had developed BDD after surgery. Patient satisfaction with surgery may contribute to explaining why some plastic surgeons continue to operate.

The major questions are what predicts satisfaction with cosmetic surgery and can some patients with BDD be satisfied with the procedure (but continue to be preoccupied and distressed)? A recent study examined the differences between 23 individuals without BDD in a cosmetic surgery clinic who were satisfied with their rhinoplasties and 16 patients in a psychiatric clinic diagnosed with BDD (Veale et al., 2003). The BDD patients were selected because they craved rhinoplasty but for various reasons had not obtained it; for example, they could not afford it or had a fear of the operation failing. The BDD patients were significantly younger than the rhinoplasty patients, but there was no significant difference in sex. As expected, the BDD patients had greater psychological morbidity than the rhinoplasty patients. The BDD patients had higher scores on the Yale-Brown Obsessive Compulsive Scale modified for BDD (Phillips et al., 1997) and for anxiety and depression on the Hospital Anxiety and Depression Scale (Zigmond & Snaith, 1983). The mean scores of the BDD patients were all in the clinical range, while those of the rhinoplasty patients were not. Individuals with BDD were more distressed and reported much greater interference in their social and occupational functioning and in intimate relationships because of their nose. They were more socially anxious and more likely to avoid situations because of their nose. They were more likely to check their nose in mirrors or to feel it with their fingers. These patients were more likely to believe that cosmetic surgery would significantly change their life (e.g., help them to obtain a new partner or job) and were significantly more likely to be dissatisfied with other areas of their body. They were likely to have attempted do-it-yourself (DIY) surgery in the past. (Examples of DIY surgery included using a pair of pliers in an attempt to make the nose thinner, using sticky tape to flatten the nose, and placing tissue up one side of the nose to try to make it look more curved.)

In summary, BDD patients who desire cosmetic rhinoplasty are quite a different population from those patients who obtain routine cosmetic rhinoplasty. A number of clues from this study could be used in the development of a short screening questionnaire or structured interview to help cosmetic surgeons to identify individuals with BDD who are unsuitable for cosmetic surgery. We do not yet know whether the diagnosis of BDD by itself is a contraindication to surgery. Additional factors such as an unrealistic psychosocial outcome may be more important. However good the interview, patients may be economical with the truth, and, even when a surgeon identifies possible symptoms of BDD, the patient may not agree to a referral to a mental health practitioner and may merely go to another surgeon. Prospective outcome studies are required to identify BDD patients and when, if ever, a cosmetic procedure is indicated in BDD.

Comorbidity and Handicap

Body dysmorphic disorder is associated with a high rate of depression and suicide and with DIY cosmetic surgery (Veale, 2000), and in comparison with all other body image disorders, these patients are the most distressed and handicapped by their condition. Phillips et al. (2000) used a quality of life measure and found a degree of distress worse than that of depression, diabetes, or bipolar disorder. Almost all patients with BDD suffer social handicap, avoiding social situations where they may feel self-conscious or that may lead to dating or intimacy. Strategies for enduring such situations include the use of alcohol, illegal substances, or safety behaviors similar to those seen in social phobia. Body dysmorphic disorder can disrupt study and employment. Patients may become effectively housebound. All these factors can and frequently do lead to discord within the family if other members cannot empathize with the sufferer's situation.

Demographics

The prevalence of BDD in the community has been reported as 0.7% in two studies (Faravelli et al., 1997; Otto et al., 2001) with a higher prevalence of milder cases in adolescents and young adults (Bohne et al., 2002). Most surveys of BDD patients attending a psychiatric clinic tend to show an equal sex incidence. They are usually single or separated and unemployed (Neziroglu & Yaryura-Tobias, 1993; Phillips & Diaz, 1997; Phillips et al., 1993; Veale et al., 1996). It is possible that, in the community, more women are affected overall, with a greater proportion experiencing milder symptoms. No cross-cultural studies in BDD have been done except for a small survey of German and American students (Bohne et al., 2002). However, case studies suggest that the clinical presentation of BDD is similar across all cultures. Some cultures may, however, place more emphasis on the importance of appearance, resulting in higher rates of BDD and cosmetic surgery.

Presentation

Although the age of onset of BDD is during adolescence, patients are most likely to present to cosmetic surgeons, dermatologists, ear, nose, and throat surgeons. They are usually not formally diagnosed by mental health professionals until 10–15 years after the onset (Phillips, 1991; Veale et al., 1996). Body dysmorphic disorder may also present in children with symptoms of refusing to attend school and planning suicide (Albertini & Phillips, 1999). Body dysmorphic disorder patients generally feel misunderstood and are secretive about their symptoms because they think they will be viewed as vain or narcissistic. They may indeed be stigmatized by health professionals who view only true disfigurement as worthy of their attention or who confuse BDD with body dissatisfaction (Carter, 2001). Therefore, when they do present to health professionals, patients are more likely to complain of depression or social anxiety unless they are specifically questioned about symptoms of BDD.

Even when BDD is finally diagnosed, patients are often treated inappropriately with antipsychotic medication (Phillips, 1998) or by a therapist who has little experience in treating BDD patients or lacks an effective treatment model. There is, therefore, an unmet need for the diagnosis and effective treatment of BDD. However, promising results have been obtained by cognitive behavioral therapy and the use of serotonin reuptake inhibitors, which are discussed at the end of this chapter.

Risk Factors

As yet, only limited data are available on risk factors for the development of BDD. The research agenda is to distinguish between risk factors that are specific to BDD and those that predispose to other disorders. Various risk factors are hypothesised for the development of BDD (Veale, 2004). These include a genetic predisposition, shyness, perfectionism, an anxious temperament, childhood adversity such as teasing or bullying (about either appearance or competence), poor peer relationships, social isolation or lack of support in the family, sexual abuse, a history of dermatological or other physical stigmata (e.g., acne) as an adolescent (since resolved), and being more aesthetically sensitive than average. Aesthetic sensitivity can be defined as an awareness and appreciation of beauty and harmony. This results in a greater emotional response to more attractive individuals and placing a greater value on the importance of appearance in their identity. This would manifest in an increased likelihood of seeking education or training in art and design (Veale et al., 1996; Veale & Lambrou, 2002; Veale et al., 2002). Aesthetic sensitivity may have three components: (1) perceptual (the ability to differentiate variations in aesthetic proportions); (2) emotional (the degree of emotion experienced when presented with beauty or ugliness); and (3) evaluative (aesthetic values, standards, and identity). Lambrou (2006) found that individuals with BDD have problems in the emotional and evaluative processing when viewing their self-image, rather than in their perceptual processing. Using a comparative group design, 50 BDD individuals were compared with two nonclinical control groups; 50 art and design controls and 50 nonart controls. A digital facial photograph of each participant was manipulated using computer graphic techniques to create a symmetry continuum consisting of 9 images (1 real image and 8 manipulated images). Presented with the symmetry continuum on a computer, participants were required to select and rate facial images representing actual self, ideal self, idea of perfect, most physically attractive, most pleasure, and most disgust. Applying the same methodology, symmetry continua were created for two control conditions, a standardized other face and a building, to illustrate the hypothesised emotional/evaluative disturbance in BDD individuals would be specific to their own face. The difference in BDD individuals was in their emotional and evaluative processing when viewing their own self-image, rather than in their perceptual processing. The art and design group had similar perceptual skills to the BDD group, which were more accurate than the controls.

The onset of BDD is in adolescence, and therefore, particular attention will need to be given to identifying risk factors preceding the onset. For example, teasing about appearance is commonplace among children, yet comparatively few go on to develop BDD. One aim of future research is to determine which factors (or combination of factors) predict future persistence of extreme self-consciousness so that interventions may be devised for those at risk. Compared with other body image disorders, such as eating disorders or anxiety disorders, BDD is greatly underresearched and is only now beginning to attract interest. Many of the suggested risk factors remain speculative.

Cognitive Behavioral Model of BDD

A cognitive behavioral model has been described that emphasizes the maintenance of symptoms (Veale, 2004; Veale et al., 1996). It is proposed that the cycle begins when an external representation of the person's appearance (e.g., looking in a mirror) activates a mental image. The process of selective attention increases awareness of the image and of specific features within the image. The image is used to construct how the person looks in the mirror and provides information about how he or she appears to others from an observer perspective and is fused with reality.

The evidence for imagery in BDD so far comes from a descriptive study that compared 18 BDD patients with 18 healthy controls using a semi-structured interview and questionnaires (Osman et al., 2004). The BDD patients and controls were equally likely to experience spontaneous images of their appearance. However, BDD patients were likely to rate the images as significantly more negative, recurrent, and vivid than normal controls. Images in BDD patients were more distorted, and the "defective" features took up a greater proportion of the whole image. They typically reported visual images, which were sometimes associated with other sensations (e.g., organic sensations of hunger or fatigue). Of particular significance is that the images were more likely to be viewed from an observer perspective than from a field perspective, similar to a finding in social phobia (Hackmann et al., 1998). An observer perspective consists of the individual looking at himself or herself from another person's perspective. A field perspective consists of an individual looking out from his or her own body. It is proposed that activation of imagery is associated with an increased self-focused attention directed toward specific features of an image, leading to a heightened awareness and a relative magnification of certain aspects, which contributes to the development of a distorted body image. Furthermore, any image becomes "fused" with reality, as in the concept of thought-action fusion (Rachman, 1993) or cognitive fusion (Hayes et al., 1999).

The next step in the model is the negative appraisal and aesthetic judgment of the image, by the activation of assumptions and values about the importance of appearance. In BDD, appearance has become overidentified with the self and at the center of a "personal domain" (Veale, 2002). Typical assumptions include: "If I am unattractive, then life is not worth living," "If I am defective, then I will be alone all my life," or "I can only do something when I feel comfortable about my appearance" (Veale et al., 1996). Individuals value the importance of appearance in defining their self or identity, although this may have occurred as a consequence

of feeling ugly (and would not be present if they did not have a preoccupation with their features). Individuals with BDD may also lack a self-serving bias that occurs in normal individuals as has been found in eating disorders (Jansen et al., 2006). This has been described as losing the rose-tinted glasses that normally occurs in individuals without a body image disorder.

The preoccupation is maintained by various safety seeking or "submissive" behaviors, such as mirror checking or camouflaging to reduce scrutiny by others or to enhance appearance. However, these tend to increase the doubts and reinforce the behavior in a further vicious circle. The preoccupation is further reinforced by ruminations (e.g., "Why am I so ugly?"; "If only I was born with a different nose"), which leads to a further deterioration in mood and further questions that cannot be answered. Alternatively individuals are trying to solve a nonexistent problem or hypothetical catastrophes ("What if someone humiliates me?"), which lead to further questions, similar to a process of worry.

Cognitive Behavioral Therapy (CBT)

The efficacy of CBT for BDD has recently been reviewed (Williams et al., 2006) and CBT is included in the clinical guidelines on treating OCD and BDD from the National Institute of Clinical Excellence (NICE) in the UK (National Collaborating Centre for Mental Health, 2006). There are only two randomized controlled studies, both of which used a waitlist comparison group (Rosen et al., 1995; Veale et al., 1996). One of the criticisms of the study by Rosen et al. (1995) is that their patients were not representative as the sample contained only women, several of whom who had disordered eating and they were less handicapped than those seen in other centers. Both studies did not conduct a long-term follow-up and neither study measured delusionality. There are also case-control studies (Geremia & Neziroglu, 2001) and several case series (e.g., Wilhelm, Otto, Lohr, & Deckersbach, 1999). A randomized controlled trial is now required that compares later versions of CBT against an attentional control treatment with equal credibility and a selective serotonin reuptake inhibitor (SSRI). Randomized controlled trials (RCTs) are also required for the use of CBT in adolescents. Key components of CBT include engagement and helping patients to develop a good psychological understanding of the factors that maintain BDD.

Engagement in CBT is helped by the credibility of a clinician who has treated other patients and can talk about the disorder knowledgeably. It is important to validate the patient's beliefs and not discount or trivialize them (Linehan, 1993) (e.g., "What you feel about your appearance is very understandable given that you were bullied as a child").The clinician should search for and reflect upon the evidence collected by patients for their beliefs (rather than seek evidence against the belief they are defective) and the factors that have contributed to the development of those beliefs. The aim is then to normalize their experience and help them to understand what the problem is. Therapists should avoid repeatedly reassuring patients that they look "all right" as it does not fit with their experience and they have heard it many times. They may be recommended a psychoeducational book about BDD that is written for sufferers (Phillip, 1996; Wilhelm, 2006; Veale, Willson, & Clarke, 2008) or to meet other patients in a support group or national charity.

Patients assume a model of "What you see is what you get" in front of a mirror. An alternative model of "What you see is what you feel" is presented because of selective attention to the "picture in their mind" and the emotional component of body image. Body image will depend more upon their mood, early memories, the meaning that they attach to their appearance and the expectations that they bring to a mirror. This leads to a description of a cognitive behavioral model for BDD and how a person with BDD becomes excessively aware of his or her appearance and to giving examples of selective attention in everyday life. It is important not to refer to a "distorted" body image as there is emerging evidence that BDD sufferers may be more accurate in their aesthetic sensitivity (Lambrou, 2006). Instead they may lack the self-serving bias that occurs in healthy individuals, similar to a process in patients with eating disorders (Jansen et al., 2006). The therapist might ask the patient to suspend judgment about his or her appearance and to test out the alternative cognitive behavioral model for the period of therapy. This might lead to a discussion of the prejudice model of information processing and how this may affect their judgment (Padesky, 1993).

Another method of engagement in CBT is similar to that described for hypochondriasis (Clark et al., 1998). A patient is presented with two alternative theories to test out in therapy. The first theory (that the patient has been following) is that he is defective and ugly and he has tried very hard to camouflage or change his appearance. The alternative theory to

be tested during therapy is that the problem is being excessively self-focused on a picture in his mind and making his appearance the most important aspect of his identity. Patients are asked to suspend judgment for the duration of therapy in order to test out whether their experience in various behavioral experiments best fits with that of Theory A or Theory B. An idiosyncratic version of the model is drawn that identifies the various factors that increase an individual's preoccupation and distress with his or her appearance (Veale, 2004). Some patients are impossible to engage in either CBT or pharmacotherapy and have to go through a long career of unnecessary surgery, beauty therapies, dermatological treatment, or suicide attempts before seeking help for their BDD from a mental health professional. Patients will, however, often discount the experience of other BDD patients and the results of studies on cosmetic surgery as they see themselves as ugly and not suffering from BDD.

Once a patient is engaged in therapy and willing to test out alternatives, the therapist can chose from a variety of strategies depending on the formulation and presenting problems. These include (1) behavioral experiments to test out the effect of increasing or decreasing self-focused attention or other safety behaviors, (2) self-monitoring and response prevention for behaviors such as mirror gazing, (3) self-monitoring with a tally counter and habit reversal for behaviors such as skin-picking, (4) task concentration training to help refocus attention away from the self and an observer perspective, and (5) functional analysis on the effect of comparing or ruminating.

An early goal is to improve function with behavioral activation to overcome social withdrawal as depressed mood and isolation reinforces rumination (Martell, et al., 2001). A functional analysis may be conducted on the effect of rumination and whether it increases preoccupation and distress and further avoidance of one's valued directions in life. Problems of being critical and attacking self and shame may be assisted by a "two-chair technique" and compassionate mind training (Gilbert, 2005). Beliefs about being ugly or defective (e.g., "My nose is too crooked") are not directly challenged. However, the meaning of being defective and the importance of appearance to the person's identity may be tackled. Values are best challenged by questioning the functional costs and by reducing the importance of the value to the self in small degrees on a continuum similar to motivational interviewing of anorexia nervosa (Treasure & Ward, 1997). A fundamental thinking error is personalization, in which a patient identifies his or her "self" through his or her appearance and all the other values and selves are diminished. In this regard, a patient may be helped by the concept of "Big I" and "little I," whereby the self or "Big I" is defined by thousands of "little i's" in the form of beliefs, values, likes and dislikes, and characteristics since birth (Dryden, 1998; Lazarus, 1977). Patients are therefore encouraged to focus on all the other characteristics of the self to develop a more functional view and to pursue their valued directions in life despite their preoccupation and distress. Reverse role-play can also be used to strengthen an alternative belief in which patients can practice arguing the case for their alternative belief while the therapist argues the case for the old beliefs or values. Newel & Shrubb (1994) have described this in BDD but have focused on patients' beliefs about their "defect." If I use reverse role-play then it is more likely to be on (1) the meaning or assumptions about being defective or ugly, and (2) the values (e.g., about the importance of appearance and identification with self).

Social Anxiety

The cognitive model of social phobia (Clark & Wells, 1995) can be adapted to BDD to derive an idiosyncratic version of patients' experience in a recent social situation. Patients will need to expose themselves to social situations but with experiments in shifting attentional focus away from the self and the dropping of safety behaviors. Attentional shifting to external cues (whether in social situations or not) may be helped by Task Concentration Training (Bogels, Mulkens, & De Jong, 1997).

Mirror Gazing

Mirror gazing is an early target for intervention as it feeds the selective attention on appearance. Some patients try to cover up or take down mirrors (or a previous therapist may have encouraged this). However, in our experience, this can lead to a different set of problems of mirror avoidance. In this scenario, a patient is likely to maintain his or her distorted body image and symptoms of BDD. Furthermore, he or she will be overwhelmed by a reflection that he or she accidentally catches when he or she passes a mirror. It may be better that patients learn to use mirrors in a healthy way with time limits depending on the activity (e.g., using a limited amount of make-up). Patients (whether they are gazing or avoiding) may need some guidance on their use of mirrors (for examples, see Table 1). In general, patients are encouraged to be aware of their

Table 1. Goals for Mirror Use

1. To use mirrors at a slight distance that are large enough to show most of my body.
2. To focus attention on my reflection in the mirror rather than an internal impression of how I feel.
3. To use a mirror only for an agreed function (e.g., shaving, putting on make-up) and for a limited period.
4. To suspend judgment and rating of my appearance in the mirror.
5. Not to use mirrors that magnify my reflection.
6. To use a variety of different mirrors and lights rather than sticking to one that I "trust."
7. To focus attention on the whole of my face rather than selected areas.
8. Not to use ambiguous reflections (e.g., windows, the backs of CDs, or cutlery).
9. Not to use a mirror whenever I feel I have to know what I look like, but to try to delay the response and do other activities until the urge has diminished.

appearance in the external reflection of a mirror but to suspend judgment (similar to "mindfulness") (Linehan, 1993). Some patients benefit from video feedback if it is possible to test out specific hypotheses by making various predictions (e.g., that their face is a particular shade of red) before the feedback.

Pharmacotherapy

The neurobiology of BDD is speculative. For example, there are case reports of the worsening of BDD with serotonin antagonists. Others have found impaired executive functioning, which implies fronto-striatal dysfunction and an excessive input of anxiety. Body dysmorphic disorder is conceptualised as being on the spectrum of OCD, which may preferentially respond to a potent or selective serotonergic reuptake inhibitor (SSRI) rather than a noradrenergic reuptake inhibitor (for which there is equal efficacy in the treatment of depression). There is evidence for the modest benefit of SSRI antidepressants in two randomized controlled trials and several case series. Phillips et al. (2002) conducted an RCT of the SSRI fluoxetine, which demonstrated fluoxetine was more effective than a placebo. Of note is that patients with and without a delusional disorder did equally well with fluoxetine. In a second study, Hollander et al. (1999) conducted a crossover RCT of clomipramine versus desipramine. It demonstrated greater effectiveness for clomipramine (a potent serotonergic reuptake inhibitor) than desipramine (a potent noradrenergic inhibitor). Expert opinion is that before concluding that an SSRI is ineffective, the maximum tolerated dose must be taken for at least 12–16 weeks (similar to OCD).

There is no evidence for the benefit of antipsychotic medication alone in BDD or as an augmentation agent. Phillips et al. (2005) has demonstrated that adding an antipsychotic, pimozide, to an SSRI was no more effective than adding a placebo to patients who had not responded to an SSRI alone. Lastly Phillips (2005) reported on adding olanzapine to fluoxetine in six patients with BDD. Symptoms were only minimally improved in two patients and unchanged in four. There are no published RCTs on an SSRI in children and adolescents with BDD.

The Future

There is an unmet need for the early detection, diagnosis, and effective treatment of BDD. The gaps in our knowledge are recognized in the National Institute of Health and Clinical Excellence (NICE) guidelines on OCD and BDD, which identified as a research priority the assessment of "the acute and long-term efficacy, acceptability and the cost effectiveness of CBT and SSRIs, alone and in combination, compared with each other and with appropriate control treatments for both the psychological and pharmacological conditions. The trials should be powered to examine the effect of treatment for combined versus single-strand treatments and involve a follow-up of 1, 2 and 5 years" (National Collaborating Centre for Mental Health, 2006, p. 245). It further recommends "appropriately designed studies should be conducted to compare validated screening instruments for the detection of OCD and BDD. For BDD, specific populations would include young people or adults who consult in dermatology or plastic surgery and those with other psychiatric disorders" (p. 246). Much research is therefore required before BDD can catch up on other anxiety disorders, but results of existing studies are promising.

References

Albertini, R. S., & Phillips, K. A. (1999). Thirty-three cases of body dysmorphic disorder in children and adolescents. *Journal of the American Academy of Child and Adolescent Psychiatry, 38,* 453–459.

American Psychiatric Association. (2000). *Diagnostic and statistical manual of mental disorder* (4th ed., text revision). Washington, DC: Author.

Bogels, S. M., Mulkens, S., & De Jong, P. J. (1997). Task concentration training and fear of blushing. *Clinical Psychology and Psychotherapy, 4,* 251–258.

Bohne, A., Keuthen, N. J., Wilhelm, S., Deckersbach, T., & Jenike, M. A. (2002). Prevalence of symptoms of body dysmorphic disorder and its correlates: A cross-cultural comparison. *Psychosomatics, 43,* 486–490.

Bohne, A., Wilhelm, S., Keuthen, N. J., Florin, I., Baer, L., & Jenike, M. A. (2002). Prevalence of body dysmorphic disorder in a German college student sample. *Psychiatry Research, 109,* 101–104.

Brunswick, R. M. (1971). Pertaining to the wolf man: A supplement to Freud's "The history of an infantile neurosis." *Rev Psicoanal, 35,* 5–46.

Carter, L. (2001, June 11). *Body dysmorphia.* Electronic response to "BDD in men" by K. A. Phillips and D. J. Castle; http://bmj.com/cgi/eletters/323/7320/1015#17324

Clark, D. M., Salkovskis, P. M., Hackmann, A., Wells, A., Fennel, M., Ludgate, J., et al. (1998). Two psychological treatments for hypochondriasis: A randomised controlled trial. *British Journal of Psychiatry, 173,* 218–225.

Clark, D. M., & Wells, A. (1995). A cognitive model of social phobia. In R. G. Heimberg, M. R. Liebowitz, D. Hope, & F. T. Schneier (Eds.), *Social phobia: Diagnosis, assessment, and treatment* (pp. 69–93). New York: Guilford Press.

Dryden, W. (1998). *Developing self-acceptance.* Chichester, England: Wiley.

Faravelli, C., Salvatori, S., Galassi, F., Aiazzi, L., Drei, C., & Cabras, P. (1997). Epidemiology of somatoform disorders: A community survey in Florence. *Social Psychiatry and Psychiatric Epidemiology, 32,* 24–29.

Freud, S. (1959). *Three case histories: The wolf man, the rat man, and the psychotic doctor.* London: Schreber.

Geremia, G. M., & Neziroglu, F. (2001). Cognitive therapy in the treatment of body dysmorphic disorder. *Clinical Psychology and Psychotherapy, 8,* 243–251.

Gilbert, P. (Ed.). (2005). *Compassion: Conceptualizations, research and use in psychotherapy.* Hove, England: Routledge.

Hackmann, A., Surawy, C., & Clark, D. M. (1998). Seeing yourself through other's eyes: A study of spontaneously occurring images in social phobia. *Behavioural and Cognitive Psychotherapy, 26,* 3–12.

Hayes, S. C., Strosahl, K. D., & Wilson, K. G. (1999). *Acceptance and commitment therapy: An experiential approach to behavior change.* New York: Guilford Press.

Hollander, E., Allen, A., Kwon, J., Aronowitz, B., Schmeidler, J., Wong, C., et al. (1999). Clomipramine vs. desipramine crossover trial in body dysmorphic disorder: Selective efficacy of a serotonin reuptake inhibitor in imagined ugliness. *Archives of General Psychiatry, 56,* 1033–1042.

Ishigooka, J., Iwao, M., Suzuki, M., Fukayama, Y., Murasaki, M., & Miura, S. (1998). Demographic features of patients seeking cosmetic surgery. *Psychiatry and Clinical Neurosciences, 52,* 283–287.

Jansen, A., Smeets, T., Martijn, C., & Nederkoorn, C. (2006). I see what you see: The lack of self-serving body-image bias in eating disorders. *British Journal of Clinical Psychology, 45,* 123–135.

Lambrou, C. (2006). *The role of aesthetic sensitivity in body dysmorphic disorder.* Unpublished doctoral dissertation, London University.

Lazarus, A. (1977). Towards an egoless state of being. In A. Ellis & R. Grieger (Eds.), *Handbook of rational-emotive therapy* (Vol. 1, pp. 133–138). New York: Springer.

Linehan, M. M. (1993). *Skills training manual.* New York: Guilford Press.

Martell, C. R., Addis, M. E., & Jacobson, N. S. (2001). *Depression in context: Strategies for guided action.* New York: Norton.

National Collaborating Centre for Mental Health. (2006). *Obsessive compulsive disorder: The management of obsessive compulsive disorder and body dysmorphic disorder in children and adults in primary and secondary care.* London: British Psychological Society and Royal College of Psychiatrists.

Newell, R., & Shrubb, S. (1994). Attitude change and behaviour therapy in body dysmorphic disorder: Two case reports. *Behavioural and Cognitive Psychotherapy, 22,* 163–169.

Neziroglu, F., & Khemlani-Patel, S. (2002). A review of cognitive and behavioral treatment for body dysmorphic disorder. *CNS Spectrums, 7,* 464–471.

Neziroglu, F., McKay, D., Todaro J., & Yayura-Tobias, J. A. (1996). Effects of cognitive behavior therapy on persons with body dysmorphic disorder and comorbid axis II diagnoses. *Behavior Therapy, 27,* 67–77.

Neziroglu, F., & Yaryura-Tobias, J. A. (1993). Body dysmorphic disorder: Phenomenology and case descriptions. *Behavoural Psychotherapy, 21,* 27–36.

Osman, S., Cooper, M., Hackmann, M., & Veale, D. (2004). Spontaneously occurring images and early memories in people with body dysmorphic disorder. *Memory, 12,* 428–436.

Otto, M. W., Wilhelm, S., Cohen, L. S., & Harlow, B. L. (2001). Prevalence of body dysmorphic disorder in a community sample of women. *American Journal of Psychiatry, 158,* 2061–2063.

Padesky, C. A. (1993). Schema as self-prejudice. *International Cognitive Therapy Newsletter, 5/6,* 16–17.

Phillips, K. A. (1991). Body dysmorphic disorder: The distress of imagined ugliness. *American Journal of Psychiatry, 148,* 1138–1149.

Phillips, K. A. (1996). *The Broken Mirror: Understanding and treating body dysmorphic disorder.* New York: Oxford University Press.

Phillips, K. A. (1998). Body dysmorphic disorder: Clinical aspects and treatment strategies. *Bulletin of the Menninger Clinic, 62*(4 Suppl. A), A33–A48.

Phillips, K. A. (2000). Quality of life for patients with body dysmorphic disorder. *Journal of Nervous and Mental Disease, 188,* 170–175.

Phillips, K. A. (2002). Pharmacologic treatment of body dysmorphic disorder: Review of the evidence and a recommended treatment approach. *CNS Spectrums, 7,* 453–463.

Phillips, K. A. (2004). Psychosis in body dysmorphic disorder. *Journal of Psychiatric Research, 38,* 63–72.

Phillips, K. A. (2005). Olanzapine augmentation of fluoxetine in body dysmorphic disorder [letter]. *American Journal of Psychiatry, 162,* 1022–1023.

Phillips, K. (2005). Placebo-controlled study of pimozide augmentation of fluoxetine in body dysmorphic disorder. *American Journal of Psychiatry, 162,* 377- 379.

Phillips, K. A., Albertini, R. S., & Rasmussen, S. A. (2002). A randomized placebo-controlled trial of fluoxetine in body dysmorphic disorder. *Archives of General Psychiatry, 59,* 381–388.

Phillips, K. A., & Diaz, S. F. (1997). Gender differences in body dysmorphic disorder. *Journal of Nervous and Mental Disease, 185,* 570–577.

Phillips, K. A., Dufresne, R. G. Jr., Wilkel, C. S., & Vittorio, C. C. (2000). Rate of body dysmorphic disorder in dermatology patients. *Journal of the American Academy of Dermatology, 42,* 436–444.

Phillips, K. A., Grant, J., Siniscalchi, J., Albertini, R. S. (2001). Surgical and nonpsychiatric medical treatment of patients with body dysmorphic disorder. *Psychosomatics, 42,* 504–510.

Phillips, K. A., Hollander, E., Rasmussen, S. A., Aronowitz, B. R., De Caria, C., & Goodman, W. K. (1997). A severity rating scale for body dysmorphic disorder: Development of reliability and validity of a modified version of the Yale-Brown Obsessive Compulsive Scale. *Psychopharmacology Bulletin, 33,* 17–22.

Phillips, K. A., McElroy, L., Keck, P. E., Hudson, J. I., & Pope, H. G. (1994). A comparison of delusional and non-delusional body dysmorphic disorder in 100 cases. *Psychopharmacology Bulletin, 30,* 179–186.

Phillips, K. A., McElroy, L., Keck, P. E., Pope, H. G., & Hudson, J. I. (1993). Body dysmorphic disorder: Thirty cases of imagined ugliness. *American Journal of Psychiatry, 150,* 302–308.

Pope, H. G., Jr., Gruber, A. J., Choi, P., Olivardia, R., & Phillips, K. A. (1997). Muscle dysmorphia: An underrecognized form of body dysmorphic disorder. *Psychosomatics, 38,* 548–557.

Rachman, S. (1993). Obsessions, responsibility, and guilt. *Behaviour Research and Therapy, 31,* 149–154.

Rosen, J. C., Reiter, J., & Orosan, P. (1995). Cognitive-behavioral body image therapy for body dysmorphic disorder. *Journal of Consulting and Clinical Psychology, 63,* 263–269.

Sarwer, D. B., Wadden, T. A., Pertschuk, M. J., & Whitaker, L. A. (1998). Body image dissatisfaction and body dysmorphic disorder in 100 cosmetic surgery patients. *Plastic and Reconstructive Surgery, 101,* 1644–1649.

Tignol, J., Biraben-Gotzamanis, L., Martin-Guehl, C., Grabot, D., & Aouizerate, B. (2007). Body dysmorphic disorder and cosmetic surgery: evolution of 24 subjects with a minimal defect in appearance 5 years after their request for cosmetic surgery. *European Psychiatry, 22*(8), 520–524.

Treasure, J. L., & Ward, A. (1997). A practical guide to the use of motivational interviewing. *European Eating Disorders Review, 5,* 102–114.

Veale, D. (2000). Outcome of cosmetic surgery and "DIY" surgery in patients with body dysmorphic disorder. *Psychiatric Bulletin, 24,* 218–221.

Veale, D. (2002). Overvalued ideas: A conceptual analysis. *Behaviour Research and Therapy, 40,* 383–400.

Veale, D. (2004). Advances in a cognitive behavioural understanding of body dysmorphic disorder. *Body Image, 1,* 113–125.

Veale, D., Boocock, A., Gournay, K., Dryden, W., Shah, F., Wilson, R., et al. (1996). Body dysmorphic disorder: A survey of fifty cases. *British Journal of Psychiatry, 169,* 196–201.

Veale, D., De Haro, L., & Lambrou, C. (2003). Cosmetic rhinoplasty in body dysmorphic disorder. *British Journal of Plastic Surgery, 56,* 546–551.

Veale, D., Ennis, M., & Lambrou, C. (2002). Possible association of body dysmorphic disorder with an occupation or education in art and design. *American Journal of Psychiatry, 159,* 1788–1790.

Veale, D., Gournay, K., Dryden, W., Boocock, A., Shah, F., Willson, R., et al. (1996). Body dysmorphic disorder: A cognitive behavioural model and pilot randomised controlled trial. *Behaviour Research and Therapy, 34,* 717–729.

Veale, D. M., & Lambrou, C. (2002). The importance of aesthetics in body dysmorphic disorder. *CNS Spectrums, 7,* 429–431.

Veale, D. M., Willson, R., & Clarke, A. (2008). *Overcoming body image problems*. London: Constable Robinson.

Wilhelm, S. (2006). *Feeling good about the way you look: A program for overcoming body image problems*. New York: Guilford Press.

Wilhelm, S., Otto, M. W., Lohr, B., & Deckersbach, T. (1999). Cognitive behavior group therapy for body dysmorphic disorder: A case series. *Behaviour Research and Therapy, 37,* 71–75.

Williams, J., Hadjistavropoulous, T., & Sharpe, D. (2006). A meta-analysis of psychological and pharmacological treatments for body dysmorphic disorder. *Behaviour Research and Therapy, 44,* 99–111.

World Health Organization. (1992). *International statistical classification of diseases and related health problems* (10th rev.). Geneva: Author.

Zigmond, A., & Snaith, R. P. (1983). The Hospital Anxiety and Depression Scale. *Acta Psychiatrica Scandinavica, 67,* 361–370.

Gordon J. G. Asmundson *and* R. Nicholas Carleton

Abstract

Fear of pain is a construct that denotes both pain-related fear and pain-related anxiety. The construct and associated fear-anxiety-avoidance models have stimulated considerable research and the development of an effective treatment known as graded exposure in vivo. This chapter has several purposes. After providing a theoretical overview, descriptive and diagnostic issues pertinent to fear of pain are described. Several conceptual controversies are also discussed, including the differential role of fear and anxiety in pain-related avoidance, and whether fear of pain is best conceptualized as a simple phobia or a fundamental predilection to be fearful of anxiety symptoms. Assessment and treatment options for elevated fear of pain are described in detail and with reference to relevant empirical literature. The chapter concludes with suggested avenues for future research.

Keywords: anxiety, assessment, fear, in vivo exposure, kinesiophobia, pain, treatment

Theoretical Overview

Current theory, based largely on elaboration of the Gate Control Theory of Pain (Melzack & Wall, 1965), holds that pain comprises sensory as well as cognitive, affective, behavioral, and social components (Bonica, 1990; Melzack & Wall, 1988). Thus, pain can be viewed as both a sensory and emotional experience. Pain is ubiquitous, typically occurring in response to actual or potential tissue damage as a motivator to withdraw from the source of pain and promote recuperative behavior. In the short-term, pain has survival value; however, when it becomes chronic (i.e., persists for 3 months or more) (International Association for the Study of Pain, 1986), it loses its adaptive qualities. Many people with chronic pain make frequent physician visits, sometimes undergo inappropriate medical evaluations, and often miss work and other important activities because of their symptoms (e.g., Spengler, Bigos, & Martin, 1986). They are also at increased risk for comorbid psychiatric conditions, particularly

depression and anxiety disorders (e.g., Asmundson, Coons, Taylor, & Katz, 2002). Estimates from the United States indicate that 7% of the population has experienced chronic pain in the past 12 months (McWilliams, Cox, & Enns, 2003) at an annual cost exceeding $100 billion (Strassels, 2006; Weisberg & Vaillancourt, 1999).

Relative to the emotional context of pain, the constructs of fear and anxiety have recently garnered considerable theoretical, empirical, and practical attention. Observations regarding the relationship between fear, anxiety, and pain are, however, not new. More than 2,000 years ago Aristotle wrote, "Let fear, then, be a kind of pain or disturbance resulting from the imagination of impending danger, either destructive or painful." Early empirical efforts revealed an association between pain and significant degrees of anxiety (Paulett, 1947; Rowbotham, 1946), viewing the latter as a product of intractable forms of the former. Rooted in these early observations, contemporary *fear-anxiety-avoidance models* of chronic pain are based primarily on the writings of several groups (Asmundson, Norton, & Norton, 1999; McCracken, Zayfert, & Gross, 1992; Vlaeyen, Kole-Snijders, Boeren, & van Eek, 1995; Waddell, Newton, Henderson, Sommerville, & Main, 1993). It is beyond the scope of this chapter to review the seminal works that provided the foundation on which the contemporary models are based, although comprehensive overviews are available (e.g., Asmundson, Norton, & Vlaeyen, 2004; Vlaeyen & Linton, 2000).

While each of the aforementioned groups of researchers has provided slightly different conceptualizations of the role of fear and anxiety in perpetuating pain (discussed in more detail below), the main ideas of each are captured in the model proposed by Vlaeyen and Linton (2000). This model (see Figure 1), focusing specifically on patients with idiopathic (i.e., in the absence of identifiable injury or organic pathology) chronic musculoskeletal pain but also applicable to those with other pain conditions, can be summarized as follows:

• When pain is perceived, a judgment of the meaning or purpose of the pain is placed on the experience (Pain Experience).

• For most people, pain is judged to be undesirable and unpleasant, but not catastrophic or suggestive of a major calamity (No Fear). Typically, the person engages in appropriate behavioral restriction followed by graduated increases in activity (Confrontation) until healing has occurred (Recovery).

• Conversely, for a significant minority of people, a catastrophic meaning is placed on the experience of pain (Pain Catastrophizing). Catastrophizing, influenced by predispositional and current psychological factors, leads to fear of pain (and/or reinjury) and thereafter spirals into a vicious and self-perpetuating cycle that promotes and maintains avoidance, activity limitations, disability, pain, catastrophizing, and so forth.

The fear-anxiety-avoidance models have garnered considerable empirical support, as evidenced

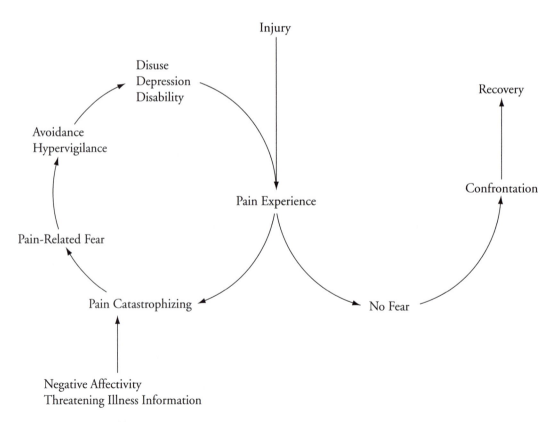

Fig. 1 Fear-avoidance model.

From "Fear-Avoidance and Its Consequences in Chronic Musculoskeletal Pain: A State of the Art," by J.W.S. Vlaeyen and S. J. Linton, 2000, *Pain, 85,* p. 329. Copyright 2000. Reprinted with kind permission from the International Association for the Study of Pain, 909 NE 43rd Ave, Suite 306, Seattle, WA.

by recent reviews (Asmundson et al., 1999; Vlaeyen & Linton, 2000) and an edited book on the topic (Asmundson, Vlaeyen, & Crombez, 2004), and have stimulated development and implementation of tailored assessment and treatment strategies.

Diagnostic and Descriptive Features

Pain can arise from physical injury, progression of disease, muscle tension, indigestion, eye strain, congested sinuses, menstruation, inactivity, and a wide array of other identifiable and unidentifiable sources. Most people do not become overly alarmed by pain; however, as noted above, for some it can provoke clinically significant and debilitating fear and anxiety. There is neither a current diagnostic entity nor are there diagnostic criteria for pathological levels of pain-related fear and anxiety. The *DSM–IV–TR* includes a diagnosis of Pain Disorder in its Somatoform Disorder section for which unspecified psychological factors (among other factors) are identified as diagnostic; yet, many researchers and clinicians who work with chronic pain patients find the *DSM–IV–TR* criteria for pain disorder to be problematic and of limited practical utility. These problems and limitations are succinctly outlined by Fishbain (1995) and Sharp (2004). Likewise, while conceptually similar to the *DSM–IV–TR* specific phobias (see below), this is not typically a diagnosis that is applied in research or clinical practice to those with high pain-related fear and anxiety. Indeed, contrary to the *DSM–IV–TR* diagnostic criteria for specific phobia, most pain patients with high pain-related fear and anxiety are convinced that their fears, anxieties, and related avoidance behavior have a protective function and are in no way excessive or irrational (Vlaeyen, de Jong, Leeuw, & Crombez, 2004).

Fear of pain is a phrase used in the literature to describe both pain-related fear and pain-related anxiety. Hereafter, we use the phrase *fear of pain* in reference to both of these constructs, except in instances where discussing important conceptual distinctions between fear and anxiety. The structure of fear of pain has been assumed to be multidimensional (i.e., comprising cognitive, behavioral, and physiological components) (McCracken, Zayfert, & Gross, 1993) and continuous (i.e., occurring along a continuum ranging from low to high) (Asmundson et al., 2004), and there is recent preliminary evidence from clinical samples to support this (Asmundson, Collimore, Bernstein, Zvolensky, & Hadjistavropoulos, 2007). But, what constitutes high fear of pain? Various measures for assessing fear

of pain exist (see "Assessment"). Space constraints do not permit a comprehensive review of the ways in which scores on each measure can be interpreted to inform the decision of whether an individual's fear of pain is high; however, for illustrative purposes we present how the 40-item *Pain Anxiety Symptoms Scale* (PASS) (McCracken et al., 1992) can be used to make this determination.

The PASS is the most prominent fear of pain measure currently in use, with a total score ranging from 0 to 200. Although definitive cut-off scores for high fear of pain have yet to be established, precedent recommendations are available. High fear of pain has been defined by some researchers using PASS total scores between 94 and 100, or about the 50th percentile (de Gier, Peters, & Vlaeyen, 2003; Staats, Staats, & Hekmat, 2001). A brief review of research using the PASS suggests lower total scores may denote pathological fear of pain. Pooled means from studies with large samples (Hadjistavropoulos, Asmundson, & Kowalyk, 2004; Martin, Hadjistavropoulos, & McCreary, 2005; McCracken, Vowles, & Eccleston, 2005; McCracken et al., 1993; Roelofs et al., 2004) indicate chronic pain patients report higher PASS total scores (M = 76.68, SD = 20.85) than studies evaluating pain-free control participants (M = 59.37, SD = 18.89), $t(1726)$ = 17.70, $p < .001$, r^2 = .15) (Asmundson, Wright, & Hadjistavropoulos, 2005; Muris, Vlaeyen, & Meesters, 2001; Osman, Barrios, Osman, Schneekloth, & Troutman, 1994; Roelofs, Peters, Deutz, Spijker, & Vlaeyen, 2005). Given that approximately 30% of patients with chronic pain have high fear of pain (Asmundson, Norton, & Allerdings, 1997), a PASS total score of approximately 85 (i.e., pooled sample M plus .5 SD) may represent an optimal cut-off, at least in clinical samples. Future efforts to determine definitive cut-off scores for clinical and nonclinical samples using empirical methods are needed to further facilitate identification of, and treatment planning for, pathological fear of pain.

Conceptual Controversies

There is an implicit presupposition in some iterations of the contemporary fear-anxiety-avoidance models that a direct link exists from fear of pain to avoidance behavior when, in fact, anxiety serves as an important intervening variable. To account for this, Asmundson et al. (2004) have proposed a revised model (see Figure 2) wherein catastrophic (mis)interpretation produces a fear-based emotional state designed to protect against perceived

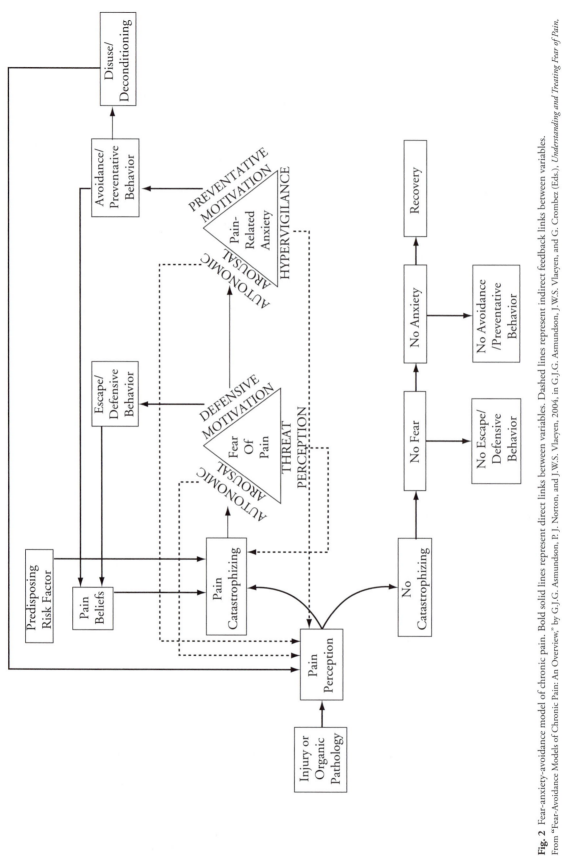

Fig. 2 Fear-anxiety-avoidance model of chronic pain. Bold solid lines represent direct links between variables. Dashed lines represent indirect feedback links between variables. From "Fear-Avoidance Models of Chronic Pain: An Overview," by G.J.G. Asmundson, P.J. Norton, and J.W.S. Vlaeyen, 2004, in G.J.G. Asmundson, J.W.S. Vlaeyen, and G. Crombez (Eds.), *Understanding and Treating Fear of Pain*, p. 15. Copyright 2004. Reprinted with kind permission from Oxford University Press.

pain-related threat (i.e., fear of pain) by motivating escape behaviors and, in some cases, promoting the onset of anxiety. In this model it is anxiety regarding future encounters with pain-related threat that is most important to the development and maintenance of chronicity because it promotes avoidance and other preventative behaviors. Further empirical scrutiny of the distinction between pain-related fear and anxiety and the potentially divergent implications of these constructs for maintaining pain and disability over time is needed.

There are also different views regarding the nature of fear of pain. One view is that fear of pain is similar in many ways to specific phobias (e.g., fear of spiders), wherein fear of nociception (i.e., pain sensations) arising from work or leisure activity is at the root of avoidance and other negative pain-related behaviors. Within this general view there are differing amounts of emphasis on whether the fear is of painful sensations per se (Letham, Slade, Troup, & Bentley, 1983; Vlaeyen & Linton, 2000), the activities that are associated with those sensations (e.g., Waddell et al., 1993), or of painful reinjury (Kori, Miller, & Todd, 1990). Another view is that fear of pain is a manifestation of a fundamental predilection to be generally fearful of anything that produces anxiety symptoms, including pain and its consequences; that is, fear of pain is believed to be a manifestation of anxiety sensitivity (Asmundson et al., 1999; Greenberg & Burns, 2003). Most recently it has been suggested that fear of pain may be a manifestation of a more general predilection to appraisals of illness and injury as indicative of catastrophe (e.g., see Carleton, Asmundson, & Taylor, 2005; Carleton, Park, & Asmundson, 2006; Vancleef, Peters, Roelofs, & Asmundson, 2006).

These conceptual distinctions are particularly important to understanding the mechanisms that underlie the experience and maintenance of idiopathic chronic pain and ongoing pain-related disability. Consequently, they warrant attention in future empirical efforts. They also need to be taken into consideration during assessment and treatment planning.

Assessment
Assessment Rationale and Targets

There are three important first steps in the assessment of a patient with high fear of pain. First, it is critical to rule out existing medical conditions that might account for complaints of pain and functional limitations. Why? It is necessary to determine

whether empirically supported treatments for fear of pain, comprising varying combinations of cognitive and behavioral strategies involving exposure to feared sensations and activities, are indicated. To illustrate, the approach to treating a person with a ruptured intervertebral spinal disc—causing back pain, leg pain, and weakness of the lower extremity muscles—accompanied by high fear of pain would be substantially different from the graded exposure in vivo approach (see below) that might be used for a person with idiopathic low back pain and high fear of pain.

Second, it is necessary to clearly identify the object of fear and anxiety—whether it is actual pain sensations, certain activities that are associated with pain or injury, bodily sensations (mis)interpreted as signs of disease, concerns regarding abilities to pay bills or remain active in professional and leisure pursuits, and so forth. This may sound like a simpler task than it is. Many patients will be reluctant to accept that their pain and functional limitations have anything to do with fear or anxiety, instead attributing them to a physical cause. Most will fear pain sensations, but some may not. Instead, their fear may be more specifically related to the consequences associated with pain, such as permanent disability. In many cases there may be more than one object that warrants consideration in treatment.

Finally, it is necessary to determine why a patient is seeking treatment. Some patients present for treatment not because they believe it will help but, instead, because they have been pressured to do so by their doctor, family, or friends. If not identified and addressed (e.g., by motivational interviewing strategies; see Taylor & Asmundson, 2004), these negative beliefs can interfere with treatment adherence and outcome.

Assessment Methods

There are several assessment methods that are useful in treatment planning for patients with high fear of pain, including self-report, observation (e.g., of facial expressions, protective behaviors, avoidance behaviors), and physiological monitoring (e.g., of heart rate variability, magnitude of startle in response to potentially threatening stimuli). Despite theoretical importance (e.g., Norton & Asmundson, 2003) and practical utility (e.g., Hadjistavropoulos & Craig, 2002) of the observational and physiological methods, it is self-report that is the most often used method for assessing fear of pain. We refer the interested reader to McNeil and Vowles (2004) for further details regarding the observational and physiological monitoring methods. Below we summarize the most often used self-report measures of fear of pain and provide a brief overview of semi-structured interview techniques.

Pain Anxiety Symptoms Scale (PASS) (McCracken et al., 1992). The PASS is, as noted above, the most prominent of the fear of pain measures. It comprises 40 items distributed equally on four 10-item sub-scales that measure factorially distinct dimensions of fear of pain, including cognitive interference related to pain, fearful appraisals of pain, escape and avoidance behavior in response to activities associated with pain, and physiological symptoms arising from pain (Larsen et al., 1997; McCracken et al., 1992; Osman et al., 1994). Each item (e.g., *Pain seems to cause my heart to pound or race*) is responded to using a 6-point scale anchored from 0 (*never*) to 5 (*always*). The PASS has demonstrated good to excellent reliability and validity (McCracken & Gross, 1995). The PASS total score is positively correlated with general anxiety, pain, and self-reported disability (Crombez, Vlaeyen, Heuts, & Lysens, 1999; McCracken & Gross, 1995), nonspecific physical complaints (McCracken, Faber, & Janeck, 1998), and physical capacity (Burns, Mullen, Higdon, Wei, & Lansky, 2000).

Fear of Pain Questionnaire-III (FPQ-III) (McNeil & Rainwater, 1998). The FPQ-III is a 30-item measure intended to assess fears about pain in relation to specific pain-causing stimuli. Each item is responded to using a 5-point Likert scale ranging from 1 (*not at all*) to 5 (*extreme*). The FPQ-III consists of three fac-torially distinct subscales, each related to a specific type of pain: Severe pain (e.g., *having someone slam a heavy car door on your hand*), minor pain (e.g., *biting your tongue while eating*), and medical pain (e.g., *having one of your teeth drilled*). Recent confirmatory factor analyses support the three-factor structure (Albaret, Sastre, Cottensin, & Mullet, 2004), and there is evidence of good test-retest reliability and internal consistency (McNeil & Rainwater, 1998; Osman, Breitenstein, Barrios, Gutierrez, & Kopper, 2001). Correlational analyses indicate that the FPQ-III is moderately positively associated with the PASS (r = .45; Osman et al., 2001), suggesting that these measures may be assessing distinct (e.g., situational versus trait) fear-based constructs.

Fear-Avoidance Beliefs Questionnaire (FABQ) (Waddell et al., 1993). The FABQ is a 16-item measure assessing pain-related beliefs about possible harm from physical activities. Each item (e.g., *Physical activity might harm my back*) is re-sponded to using a 5-point Likert scale ranging

from 0 (*completely disagree*) to 6 (*completely agree*). There are two factorially distinct subscales, one focusing on work-related beliefs and the other on physical activity beliefs. The FABQ and its subscales have good validity, reliability, and internal consis-tency (Crombez et al., 1999; Waddell et al., 1993). Waddell et al. (1993) reported that the subscale scores are moderately related to pain intensity and, even after controlling for pain intensity, that the work-related beliefs subscale is strongly correlated with measures of disability and work loss.

Tampa Scale of Kinesiophobia (TSK) (Kori et al., 1990). The TSK is a 17-item measure designed to tap fears of movement (i.e., kinesiophobia) based on a perceived vulnerability to pain or reinjury. Each item (e.g., *Pain always means I have injured my body*) is responded to using a 4-point Likert scale ranging from 1 (*strongly disagree*) to 4 (*strongly agree*). Factor analyses suggest a two-factor model, measuring harm and fear avoidance, respectively (Goubert et al., 2004; Swinkels-Meewisse, Roelofs, Verbeek, Oostendorp, & Vlaeyen, 2003). The TSK has good reliability and validity (Swinkels-Meewisse et al., 2003; Vlaeyen et al., 1995). The TSK total score is positively correlated with self-reported dis-ability and negatively correlated with performance on a back flexion and extension task (Crombez et al., 1999).

Anxiety Sensitivity Index (ASI) (Peterson & Reiss, 1992). The ASI is a 16-item measure designed to assess fear of anxiety signs and symptoms based on the belief that they may have harmful consequences. Each item (e.g., *Unusual body sensations scare me*) is responded to using a 5-point Likert scale rang-ing from 0 (*agree very little*) to 4 (*agree very much*). The ASI has good validity, reliability, and internal consistency (Deacon & Valentiner, 2001; Peterson & Reiss, 1992) and has been shown to be concep-tually distinct from trait anxiety (McNally, 1996). It is associated with, and predictive of, fear of pain (Asmundson & Norton, 1995; Asmundson & Taylor, 1996; Greenberg & Burns, 2003). These and other recent findings (Zvolensky, Goodie, McNeil, Sperry, & Sorrell, 2001) support the view that fear of pain may be a manifestation of anxiety sensitivity (Carleton, Asmundson, Collimore, & Ellwanger, 2006).

Other Self-Report Measures. There are other mea-sures (see McNeil & Vowles, 2004) that can be used to assess fear of pain. Short forms for several of the aforementioned measures have also been created. These include the PASS-20 (McCracken & Dhingra, 2002) and a 13-item TSK (Clark, Kori,

& Brockel, 1996). Finally, related measures, such as the Pain Catastrophizing Scale (PCS) (Sullivan, Bishop, & Pivik, 1995) and the revised Illness/Injury Sensitivity Index (ISI-R) (Carleton, Park, et al., 2006), also warrant consideration when assessing patients with pain-related fear and anxiety.

Semistructured Interviews. Use of semistructured interview can provide a wealth of information regarding origins of fear of pain, its impact on current beliefs and assumptions, its impact on behavior, as well as ancillary complications (e.g., marital conflict, depression). Therapist-guided inquiries that purposefully avoid direct mention of pain-related fear and anxiety (e.g., *What do you think is the cause of your pain? Why do you think _____ might further harm your back? If the pain is left untreated, what do you think will happen?*) may facilitate identification of the patient's conceptualization of his or her problem. Specific questions (e.g., *What makes your pain worse? What activities does pain stop you from doing?*) can provide invaluable information regarding pain triggers, patterns of avoidance, and the patient's treatment goals (Vlaeyen et al., 2004). The information derived from these questions can also be used in conjunction with the Photograph Series of Daily Activities (PHODA) (Kugler, Wijn, Geilen, de Jong, & Vlaeyen, 1999)—a series of 98 photographs depicting various activities and movements of daily life—for developing a hierarchy of the patient's pain-related fears and anxieties.

Description of Treatments
Overview

The development of chronic pain treatments that focus on the emotional aspects of pain is increasingly pertinent. Indeed, recent review of physical treatments of chronic musculoskeletal pain concluded that, though potentially therapeutic, there is little empirical evidence supporting their effectiveness (Wright & Sluka, 2001). In contrast, a recent meta-analysis (Morley, Eccleston, & Williams, 1999) of randomized controlled trials of cognitive behavior therapy (CBT) for the treatment of chronic pain (excluding headache) concluded that CBT, compared to other treatments and a waitlist control, produced significantly greater improvements in pain, pain behavior, activity levels, affect, and ability to cope effectively. Thus, CBT appears to be an effective treatment for chronic pain. The specific application of CBT for reduction of pain-related fear and anxiety is still in its infancy but is, nonetheless, very promising.

Features of Treatment

There are several approaches—each with varying degrees of empirical support—that we recommend for treating a patient with idiopathic chronic pain accompanied by pain-related fear and anxiety. The first is a variant on CBT for health anxiety as described in Chapter 40 (also see Taylor & Asmundson, 2004). This empirically supported approach can be particularly effective in cases where the patient (mis)interprets pain sensations as being symptomatic of an underlying disease state and is more fearful of the disease and its consequences than of the pain per se. The second, based on the view that fear of pain is a manifestation of anxiety sensitivity, is the application of exposure to anxiety-provoking bodily sensations (i.e., interoceptive exposure); however, while empirically supported for panic and other anxiety disorders (see Taylor, 2000), this approach remains to be systematically evaluated in the context of fear of pain and is not further discussed here. The third, rooted in observed similarities in behavior between chronic pain patients with high fear of pain and patients with specific phobias and various other anxiety disorders, involves the application of graded exposure in vivo. This approach is well suited for patients who avoid activities based on the belief that being active will provoke further pain and, possibly, reinjury. The components and process of this approach are outlined below. More detailed explanations are available elsewhere (e.g., see Vlaeyen et al., 2004).

• Assessment is conducted as described earlier. Care should be taken to facilitate the development of a strong therapeutic relationship (for suggestions specific to patients with high fear of pain, see Hadjistavropoulos & Kowalyk, 2004).

• Psychoeducation is used to help the patient reformulate his or her view of pain as a signal of impending catastrophe (e.g., permanent disability, disease, reinjury) to one of pain as a common experience that can be self-managed. This is accomplished through careful explanation of the fear-anxiety-avoidance model using simplified versions of Figures 1 and 2, adapted to the specific characteristics of the patient's presenting symptoms, behaviors, and beliefs. Appreciation of the premise that *hurt does not always equal harm,* along with a basic understanding of the typical course of pain (and, if appropriate, healing), can ameliorate fear of pain and thereby encourage activity participation.

• Exposure is based on an individualized hierarchy that begins with activities rated as minimally fear- and anxiety-provoking to those rated as highly fear- and anxiety-provoking. The hierarchy can be derived using ratings of movements and activities from the PHODA.

• After obtaining the patient's agreement to perform certain movements and activities, the therapist models each activity in order to demonstrate the correct ergonomic method of performance and to clearly illustrate that he or she does not find it to be threatening. The therapist may also provide assistance as the patient begins performing the activity; however, to promote independence (and reduce probability of becoming a safety signal), the therapist should gradually withdraw from assisting as therapy progresses.

• Prior to each exposure, current and expected levels of pain and anxiety about performing the movement or activity are rated. Ten point visual analog scales, with 0 = *no pain/anxiety* and 10 = *most pain/anxiety possible,* are useful for this purpose. Following each exposure, levels of actual pain and anxiety are rated on similar 10-point scales. This information can be used to monitor and illustrate for the patient changes in pain and anxiety across repeated exposures and tasks.

• Behavioral tests are performed for each movement and activity on the hierarchy in order to challenge expectations (e.g., *I am going to be severely reinjured if I attempt this activity*) and provide evidence for alternatives (e.g., *I can do this activity without harming myself*). Patients repetitively perform each movement or activity, working their way up the hierarchy as expectations that it is harmful are disconfirmed.

• Exposure exercises are conducted first within treatment sessions under therapist supervision and thereafter as homework assignments to promote independence. The number and duration of treatment sessions reported in the literature varies considerably, ranging from as many as 30 1.5 hour sessions delivered 3 times per week to as few as eight 40 minute sessions delivered 2 times per week.

Narrative Overview of Empirical Findings of Graded Exposure in Vivo

Uncontrolled trials indicate that graded exposure in vivo is successful in reducing fear of pain as well as pain severity. To illustrate, Vlaeyen, de Jong, Geilen, Heuts, and van Breukelen (2001) randomly assigned four individuals with high scores on the TSK to receive graded exposure in vivo followed by graded activity (i.e., graduated increases in general activity levels despite pain), or the same treatments in reverse order. Fear of pain, catastrophizing, perceived life control, and functional disability were measured before and after the treatment, with pain-related fearful appraisals assessed daily (using 11 questions adapted from the PASS, TSK, and PCS). A time-series analysis of the daily measures revealed that pain-related fearful appraisals reduced only with the graded exposure in vivo, and not with graded activity, regardless of the treatment order. Furthermore, pre- to posttreatment analysis demonstrated that reductions in pain-related fear corresponded with increases in function and were *followed by* reductions in pain intensity. These findings have subsequently been replicated in a number of case studies of patients with chronic musculoskeletal pain (Boersma et al., 2004; Linton, Overmeer, Janson, Vlaeyen, & de Jong, 2002; Vlaeyen, de Jong, Onghena, Kerckhoffs-Hanssen, & Kole-Snijders, 2002) and complex regional pain syndrome (de Jong et al., 2005). More recently, Woods and Asmundson (2008) completed the first randomized controlled trial, comparing 15 patients receiving graded exposure in vivo to 13 patients receiving graded activity and 16 patients placed on a waitlist. All patients had idiopathic chronic low back pain. Results indicated significantly greater pre- to posttreatment reductions in fear of pain and self-reported disability for patients receiving graded exposure in vivo compared to those in the other conditions. These results, while encouraging, warrant replication.

Outstanding Issues and Conclusion

The fear of pain concept and associated fear-anxiety-avoidance models of chronic pain have stimulated considerable amounts or research over the past two decades and, importantly, have stimulated the development of effective treatments for pain conditions associated with high personal and social costs. Notwithstanding, there are numerous questions that require further conceptual development and empirical evaluation. For example, is fear of pain best conceptualized as a continuous entity and, if so, at what point does it become maladaptive? Or, is fear of pain taxonic, having normative and pathological forms that are qualitatively distinct? Are pain sensations the primary object of fear of pain? Or, is fear of pain a manifestation of a more fundamental fear, perhaps of anxiety symptoms or of disease? Do these differing views hold important implications for effective intervention? What are the basic emotional, environmental, cultural, biological, and genetic influences on fear of pain? Are the subtle nuances between pain-related fear and pain-related anxiety important to assessment and treatment planning? Is graded exposure in vivo the most effective treatment, or are there equally effective pharmacological and psychosocial interventions? For what pain conditions are these interventions indicated? Evidence-based answers to these questions will aid in refining the currently promising interventions that are available to therapists treating chronic pain patients with high fear of pain.

References

Albaret, M-C., Sastre, M.T.M., Cottensin, A., & Mullet, E. (2004). The Fear of Pain Questionnaire: Factor structure in samples of young, middle-aged and elderly European people. *European Journal of Pain, 8*, 273–281.

Asmundson, G.J.G., Collimore, K. C., Bernstein, A., Zvolensky, M. J., & Hadjistavropoulos, H. D. (2007). Is the latent structure of fear of pain continuous or discontinuous: A taxometric analysis of the Pain Anxiety Symptoms Scale. *The Journal of Pain, 8*, 387–395.

Asmundson, G.J.G., Coons, M. J., Taylor, S., & Katz, J. (2002). PTSD and the experience of pain: Research and clinical implications of shared vulnerability and mutual maintenance models. *Canadian Journal of Psychiatry, 47*, 930–937.

Asmundson, G.J.G., & Norton, G. R. (1995). Anxiety sensitivity in patients with physically unexplained chronic back pain: A preliminary report. *Behaviour Research and Therapy, 33*, 771–777.

Asmundson, G.J.G., Norton, G. R., & Allerdings, M. D. (1997). Fear and avoidance in dysfunctional chronic back pain patients. *Pain, 69*, 231–236.

Asmundson, G.J.G., Norton, P. J., & Norton, G. R. (1999). Beyond pain: The role of fear and avoidance in chronicity. *Clinical Psychology Review, 19*, 97–119.

Asmundson, G.J.G., Norton, P. J., & Vlaeyen, J.W.S. (2004). Fear-avoidance models of chronic pain: An overview. In G.J.G. Asmundson, J.W.S. Vlaeyen, & G. Crombez (Eds.), *Understanding and treating fear of pain* (pp. 3–24). Oxford, England: Oxford University Press.

Asmundson, G.J.G., & Taylor, S. (1996). Role of anxiety sensitivity in pain-related fear and avoidance. *Journal of Behavioral Medicine, 19*, 577–586.

Asmundson, G.J.G., Vlaeyen, J.W.S., & Crombez, G. (Eds.). (2004). *Understanding and Treating Fear of Pain*. Oxford, England: Oxford University Press.

Asmundson, G.J.G., & Wright, K. D. (2004). Biopsychosocial approaches to pain. In T. Hadjistavropoulos & K. D. Craig (Eds.), *Pain: Psychological perspectives* (pp. 13–34). Mahwah, NJ: Erlbaum.

Asmundson, G.J.G., Wright, K. D., & Hadjistavropoulos, H. D. (2005). Hypervigilance and attentional fixedness in chronic musculoskeletal pain: Consistency of findings across modified stroop and dot-probe tasks. *Journal of Pain, 6*, 497–506.

Boersma, K., Linton, S., Overmeer, T., Jansson, M., Vlaeyen, J.W.S., & de Jong, J. (2004). Lowering fear-avoidance and enhancing function through exposure in vivo: A multiple baseline study across six patients with back pain. *Pain, 108*, 8–16.

Bonica, J. J. (1990). Evolution and current status of pain programs. *Journal of Pain and Symptom Management, 5*, 368–374.

Burns, J. W., Mullen, J. T., Higdon, L. J., Wei, J. M., & Lansky, D. (2000). Validity of the Pain Anxiety Symptoms Scale (PASS): Prediction of physical capacity variables. *Pain, 84*, 247–252.

Carleton, R. N., Asmundson, G.J.G., Collimore, K. C., & Ellwanger, J. (2006). Strategic and automatic threat processing in patients with chronic musculoskeletal pain: A startle probe investigation. *Cognitive Behaviour Therapy, 35*, 236–247.

Carleton, R. N., Asmundson, G.J.G., & Taylor, S. (2005). Fear of physical harm: Factor structure and psychometric properties of the Injury/Illness Sensitivity Index. *Journal of Psychopathology and Behavioral Assessment, 27*, 235–241.

Carleton, R. N., Park, I., & Asmundson, G.J.G. (2006). The Illness/Injury Sensitivity Index: An examination of construct validity. *Depression and Anxiety, 23*, 340–346.

Clark, M. E., Kori, S. H., & Brockel, J. (1996, November). *Kinesiophobia and chronic pain: Psychometric characteristics and factor analysis of the Tampa Scale.* Paper presented at the 15th Annual Scientific Meeting of the American Pain Society, Washington, DC.

Crombez, G., Vlaeyen, J.W.S., Heuts, P.H.T.G., & Lysens, R. (1999). Pain-related fear is more disabling than pain itself: Evidence on the role of pain-related fear in chronic back pain disability. *Pain, 80*, 329–339.

Deacon, B. J., & Valentiner, D. P. (2001). Dimensions of anxiety sensitivity and their relationship to nonclinical panic. *Journal of Psychopathology and Behavioral Assessment, 23*, 25–33.

De Gier, M., Peters, M. L., & Vlaeyen, J.W.S. (2003). Fear of pain, physical performance, and attentional processes in patients with fibromyalgia. *Pain, 104*, 121–130.

De Jong, J. R., Vlaeyen, J.W.S., Onghena, P., Cuypers, C., den Hollander, M., & Ruijgrok, J. (2005). Reduction of pain-related fear in complex regional pain syndrome type I: The application of graded exposure in vivo. *Pain, 116*, 264–275.

Fishbain, D. (1995). *DSM–IV*: Implications and issues for the pain clinician. *American Pain Society Bulletin, 6*, 6–18.

Goubert, L., Crombez, G., Van Damme, S., Vlaeyen, J.W.S., Bijttebier, P., & Roelofs, J. (2004). Confirmatory factor analysis of the Tampa Scale for Kinesiophobia: Invariant two-factor model across low back pain patients and fibromyalgia. *Clinical Journal of Pain, 20*, 103–110.

Greenburg, J., & Burns, J. W. (2003). Pain anxiety among chronic pain patients: Specific phobia or manifestation of anxiety sensitivity? *Behaviour Research and Therapy, 41*, 223–240.

Hadjistavropoulos, H. D., Asmundson, G.J.G., & Kowalyk, K. M. (2004). Measures of anxiety: Is there a difference in their ability to predict functioning at three-month follow-up among pain patients? *European Journal of Pain, 8*, 1–11.

Hadjistavropoulos, H. D., & Kowalyk, K. M. (2004). Patient-therapist relationships among patients with pain-related fear. In G.J.G. Asmundson, J.W.S. Vlaeyen, & G. Crombez (Eds.), *Understanding and treating fear of pain* (pp. 237–266). Oxford, England: Oxford University Press.

Hadjistavropoulos, T., & Craig, K. D. (2002). A theoretical framework for understanding self-report and observational measures of pain: A communications model. *Behaviour Research and Therapy, 40*, 551–570.

International Association for the Study of Pain. (1986). Classification of chronic pain: Descriptions of chronic pain syndromes and definitions of pain terms. *Pain* (Suppl. 3), S1–S226.

Kori, S. H., Miller, R. P., & Todd, D. D. (1990). Kinesiophobia: A new view of chronic pain behavior. *Pain Management, 3,* 35–43.

Kugler, K., Wijn, J., Geilen, M., de Jong, J., & Vlaeyen, J.W.S. (1999). *The Photograph Series of Daily Activities (PHODA).* Heerlen, the Netherlands: Institute for Rehabilitation Research and School for Physiotherapy.

Larsen, D. K., Taylor, S., & Asmundson, G.J.G. (1997). Exploratory factor analysis of the pain anxiety symptoms scale in patients with chronic pain complaints. *Pain, 69,* 27–34.

Lethem, J., Slade, P. D., Troup, J.D.G., & Bentley, G. (1983). Outline of a fear-avoidance model of exaggerated pain perception. I. *Behaviour Research and Therapy, 21,* 401–408.

Linton, S. J., Overmeer, T., Janson, M., Vlaeyen, J.W.S., de Jong, J. R. (2002). Graded in-vivo exposure treatment for fear-avoidant pain patients with functional disability: A case study. *Cognitive Behaviour Therapy, 31,* 49–58.

Martin, R. R., Hadjistavropoulos, T., & McCreary, D. R. (2005). Fear of pain and fear of falling among younger and older adults with musculoskeletal pain conditions. *Pain Research and Management, 10,* 211–218.

McCracken, L. M., & Dhingra, L. (2002). A short version of the Pain Anxiety Symptoms Scale (PASS-20): Preliminary development and validity. *Pain Research and Management, 7,* 45–50.

McCracken, L. M., Faber, S. D., & Janeck, A. S. (1998). Pain-related anxiety predicts non-specific physical complaints in persons with chronic pain. *Behaviour Research and Therapy, 36,* 621–630.

McCracken, L., & Gross, R. T. (1995). The Pain Anxiety Symptoms Scale (PASS) and the assessment of emotional responses to pain. In L. van de Creek, S. Knapp, T. L. Jackson (Eds.), *Innovations in clinical practice: A source book* (Vol. 14, pp. 309–321). Sarasota, FL: Professional Resource Press/Professional Resource Exchange.

McCracken, L. M., Vowles, K. E., & Eccleston, C. (2005). Acceptance-based treatment for persons with complex, long standing chronic pain: A preliminary analysis of treatment outcome in comparison to a waiting phase. *Behaviour Research and Therapy, 43,* 1335–1346.

McCracken, L. M., Zayfert, C., & Gross, R. T. (1992). The pain anxiety symptoms scale: Development and validation of a scale to measure fear of pain. *Pain, 50,* 67–73.

McCracken, L. M., Zayfert, C., & Gross, R. T. (1993). The Pain Anxiety Symptoms Scale (PASS): A multimodal measure of pain specific anxiety symptoms. *The Behavior Therapist, 16,* 183–184.

McNally, R. J. (1996). Anxiety sensitivity is distinguishable from trait anxiety. In R. M. Rapee (Ed.), *Current controversies in the anxiety disorders.* New York: Guilford Press.

McNeil, D. W., & Rainwater, A. J. (1998). Development of the Fear of Pain Questionnaire-III. *Journal of Behavioral Medicine, 21,* 389–410.

McNeil, D. W., & Vowles, K. E. (2004). Assessment of fear and anxiety associated with pain: conceptualisation, methods and measures. In G.J.G. Asmundson, P. J. Norton, & J.W.S. Vlaeyen (Eds.), *Understanding and treating fear of pain* (pp. 198–212). Oxford, England: Oxford University Press.

McWilliams, L. A., Cox, B. J., & Enns, M. W. (2003). Mood and anxiety disorders associated with chronic pain: An examination in a nationally representative sample. *Pain, 106,* 127–133.

Melzack, R., & Wall, P. D. (1965). Pain mechanisms: A new theory. *Science, 150,* 971–979.

Melzack, R., & Wall, P. D. (1988). *The challenge of pain* (2nd ed.). London: Penguin.

Morley, S., Eccleston, C., & Williams, A. (1999). Systematic review and meta-analysis of randomized controlled trials of cognitive behaviour therapy and behaviour therapy for chronic pain in adults, excluding headache. *Pain, 80,* 1–13.

Muris, P., Vlaeyen, J.W.S., & Meesters, C. (2001). The relationship between anxiety sensitivity and fear of pain in healthy adolescents. *Behaviour Research and Therapy, 39,* 1357–1368.

Norton, P. J., & Asmundson, G.J.G. (2003). Amending the fear-avoidance model of chronic pain: What is the role of physiological arousal? *Behavior Therapy, 34,* 17–30.

Osman, A., Barrios, F. X., Osman, J. R., Schneekloth, R., & Troutman, J. A. (1994). The Pain Anxiety Symptoms Scale: Psychometric properties in a community sample. *Journal of Behavioral Medicine, 17,* 511–522.

Osman, A., Breitenstein, J. L., Barrios, F. X., Gutierrez, P. M., & Kopper, B. A. (2001). The fear of pain questionnaire-III: Further reliability and validity with nonclinical samples. *Journal of Behavioral Medicine, 25,* 155–173.

Paulett, J. D. (1947). Low back pain. *Lancet, 253,* 272–276.

Peterson, R. A., & Reiss, S. (1992). *The Anxiety Sensitivity Index manual* (2nd ed.). Worthington, OH: International Diagnostic Systems.

Roelofs, J., McCracken, L. M., Peters, M. L., Crombez, G., van Breukelen, G., & Vlaeyen, J.W.S. (2004). Psychometric evaluation of the Pain Anxiety Symptoms Scale (PASS) in chronic pain patients. *Journal of Behavioral Medicine, 27,* 167–183.

Roelofs, J., Peters, M. L., Deutz, J., Spijker, C., & Vlaeyen, J.W.S. (2005). The Fear of Pain Questionnaire (FPQ): Further psychometric examination in a non-clinical sample. *Pain, 116,* 339–346.

Rowbotham, G. F. (1947). Pain and its underlying pathology. *Journal of Mental Science, 92,* 595–604.

Sharp, T. J. (2004). The prevalence of post-traumatic stress disorder in chronic pain patients. *Current Pain and Headache Reports, 8,* 111–115.

Spengler, D. M., Bigos, S. J., Martin, N. A., Zeh, J., Fisher, L., & Nachemson, A. (1986). Back injuries in industry: A retrospective study. *Spine, 11,* 241–245.

Staats, P. S., Staats, A., & Hekmat, H. (2001). The additive impact of anxiety and a placebo on pain. *Pain Medicine, 2,* 267–279.

Strassels, S. A. (2006). After all, pain is a complex sensory and emotional experience (IASP, 1994): Clinical economics and the treatment of persistent pain. *The Journal of Pain, 7,* 802–803.

Sullivan, M. J., Bishop, S. R., & Pivik, J. (1995). The Pain Catastrophising Scale: Development and validation. *Psychological Assessment, 7,* 524–532.

Swinkels-Meewisse, I.E.J., Roelofs, J., Verbeek, A.L.M., Oostendorp, R.A.B., & Vlaeyen, J.W.S. (2003). Fear of movement/(re)injury, disability and participation in acute low back pain. *Pain, 105,* 371–379.

Taylor, S. (2000). *Understanding and treating panic disorder: Cognitive-behavioural approaches.* New York: Wiley.

Taylor, S., & Asmundson, G.J.G. (2004). *Treating health anxiety: A cognitive-behavioral approach.* New York: Guilford Press.

Vancleef, L.M.G., Peters, M. L., Roelofs, J., & Asmundson, G.J.G. (2006). Do fundamental fears differentially contribute to pain-related fear and pain catastrophizing? An evaluation of the sensitivity index. *European Journal of Pain, 10,* 527–536.

Vlaeyen, J.W.S., de Jong, J., Geilen, M., Heuts, P.H.T.G., & van Breukelen, G. (2001). Graded exposure in vivo in the treatment of pain-related fear: A replicated single-case experimental design in four patients with chronic low back pain. *Behaviour Research and Therapy, 39,* 151–166.

Vlaeyen, J.W.S., de Jong, J., Leeuw, M., & Crombez, G. (2004). Fear reduction in chronic pain: Graded exposure in vivo with behavioural experiments. In G.J.G. Asmundson, J.W.S. Vlaeyen, & G. Crombez (Eds.), *Understanding and treating fear of pain* (pp. 313–346). Oxford, England: Oxford University Press.

Vlaeyen, J.W.S., de Jong, J. R., Onghena, P., Kerckhoffs-Hanssen, M., & Kole-Snijders, A.M.J. (2002). Can pain-related fear be reduced? The application of cognitive-behavioural exposure in vivo. *Pain Research and Management, 7,* 144–153.

Vlaeyen, J.W.S., Kole-Snijders, A.M. J., Boeren, R.G.B., & van Eek, H. (1995). Fear of movement/(re)injury in chronic low back pain and its relation to behavioral performance. *Pain, 62,* 363–372.

Vlaeyen, J.W.S., & Linton, S. J. (2000). Fear-avoidance and its consequences in chronic musculoskeletal pain. *Pain, 85,* 317–332.

Waddell, G., Newton, M., Henderson, I., Somerville, D., & Main, C.J. (1993). A fear-avoidance beliefs questionnaire (FABQ) and the role of fear-avoidance beliefs in chronic low back pain and disability. *Pain, 52,* 157–168.

Weisberg, J. N., & Vaillancourt, P. D. (1999). Personality factors and disorders in chronic pain. *Seminars in Clinical Neuropsychiatry, 4,* 156–166.

Woods, M., & Asmundson, G.J.G. (2008). Randomized, controlled trial of exposure in vivo versus graded activity and waitlist in treatment of chronic back pain with high fear of pain. *Pain, 136,* 271–280.

Wright, A., & Sluka, K. A. (2001). Nonpharmacological treatments for musculoskeletal pain. *Clinical Journal of Pain, 17,* 33–46.

Zvolensky, M. J., Goodie, J. L., McNeil, D. W., Sperry, J. A., & Sorrell, J. T. (2001). Anxiety sensitivity in the prediction of pain-related fear and anxiety in a heterogeneous chronic pain population. *Behaviour Research and Therapy, 39,* 683–696.

PART 7

Comorbidity and Relationships With Other Conditions

Anxiety Disorders and Substance Use Disorder Comorbidity

Marc Zahradnik *and* Sherry H. Stewart

Abstract

This chapter on comorbid anxiety disorders (ADs) and substance use disorders (SUDs) reviews the literature on the epidemiology, theories of comorbidity, and recent treatment approaches for these concurrent problems. It reviews research on the comorbidity of SUDs within the context of the following five ADs: panic disorder (PD), social phobia (SP), obsessive-compulsive disorder (OCD), generalized anxiety disorder (GAD), and posttraumatic stress disorder (PTSD). The term *SUDs* include both abuse and dependence, and though this review often focuses on alcohol use disorders, other less commonly studied SUDs in relation to AD comorbidity are also covered. Each section of the chapter ends with a concise summary of the issues that are most salient to that specific area.

Keywords: anxiety disorders, epidemiology, substance use disorders, theories of comorbidity, treatment approaches

The purposes of this chapter on comorbid anxiety disorders (ADs) and substance use disorders (SUDs) are to summarize the literature on the epidemiology of their co-occurrence, theories of interrelation, and to provide a review of recent treatment approaches for these concurrent problems. This chapter defines comorbidity as having clinically significant symptoms of both disorders at some time across the lifespan, though not necessarily concurrently (see Kushner, Abrams, & Borchardt, 2000). This chapter covers the comorbidity of SUDs with the following five ADs: panic disorder (PD), social phobia (SP), obsessive-compulsive disorder (OCD), generalized anxiety disorder (GAD), and posttraumatic stress disorder (PTSD).[1] Furthermore, SUD includes both abuse and dependence, and though this review often focuses on alcohol use disorders, other less-commonly studied SUDs in relation to AD comorbidity (e.g., cocaine, tobacco disorders) are also covered. The breadth of coverage is intended to introduce the novice reader to this area; the better-acquainted reader will benefit from being directed to literature on topics that are of specific interest.

Epidemiology of Comorbidity

Epidemiological studies on comorbidity typically attempt to ascertain the probability that having symptoms of disorder X (e.g., an AD) will increase the risk for developing symptoms of disorder Y (e.g., an SUD). The order of X and Y can either be arbitrary—as in a cross-sectional study where information about disorders X and Y is collected at one time—or fixed, as in a prospective study where measurement of X at time 1 is used as a predictor of the change in risk for developing the outcome Y at time 2 (Kushner, Krueger, Frye, & Peterson, 2008). The typical output unit of an epidemiological study is the odds ratio. An odds ratio of 1.0 would indicate a chance relationship between X and Y, such that the chance of developing Y is the same regardless of whether or not X is present. An odds ratio that differs significantly from 1.0 indicates that the covariance between the two disorders cannot be attributed to chance alone. An odds ratio greater than 1.0 indicates that having one of the disorders creates a greater risk for having the other disorder and an odds ratio lesser than 1.0 indicates that having one of the disorders creates a lowered risk for having the other disorder.

Individuals with more than one disorder are more likely to seek or be referred to treatment, thereby inflating comorbidity estimates among clinical samples (Berkson, 1949); therefore, studies in community samples are generally held to reflect more accurate rates of comorbidity (Kushner et al., 2008). We will focus on the latter type of study in this chapter. The three largest community-based epidemiological studies that have provided researchers with presumably the most accurate information on the comorbidity of ADs and SUDs are the Epidemiological Catchment Area (ECA) (e.g., Regier et al., 1990) survey, the National Comorbidity Survey (NCS) (e.g., Kessler et al., 1996) and its replication (Kessler, Berglund, Demler, Jin, & Walters, 2005), and the National Epidemiological Survey on Alcohol and Related Conditions (NESARC) (e.g., Grant et al., 2004).

Substance Use Disorders (SUD)

The *Diagnostic and Statistical Manual of Mental Disorders* (fourth edition, text revision) defines substance abuse as "a maladaptive pattern of substance use leading to clinically significant impairment or distress . . . occurring within a 12 month period" (American Psychiatric Association [APA], 2000, p. 199); this definition focuses on the harmful consequences of repeated use (APA, 2000). A diagnosis of substance dependence, in contrast, includes the symptoms of tolerance, withdrawal, or a pattern of compulsive use (APA, 2000). A diagnosis of substance dependence, which also requires symptoms to have occurred for a 12-month period, is more severe than a diagnosis of substance abuse and always overrides the latter.

Prevalence Rates and Odds Ratios for AD–SUD Comorbidity

Prevalence rates and odds ratios for each *DSM* AD both with and without a comorbid SUD—including alcohol abuse, alcohol dependence, drug abuse, and drug dependence—are presented in Table 1. Four general patterns are evident (see Table 1). First, in

almost all cases, the prevalence rates for an AD co-occurring with a specific SUD are almost always greater than the prevalence rates for an AD without a specific SUD. For example, in the ECA (Regier et al., 1990) the lifetime prevalence rate for PD with alcohol abuse is 7.0% but without alcohol abuse it is only 5.4% (an odds ratio of 1.3). Second, although specific phobias tend to be one of the more prevalent ADs, the five other ADs tend to pose a greater risk factor for comorbid SUD as demonstrated by the higher odds ratios for the five other ADs (mean odds ratio = 2.9) compared to those odds ratios associated with specific phobia (mean odds ratio = 1.8). Third, odds ratios tend to be higher for ADs with alcohol and drug *dependence* (mean odds ratio = 3.9) than for ADs with alcohol and drug *abuse* (mean odds ratio = 1.5). And finally, odds ratios tend to be higher for *drug* use disorders (mean odds ratio = 3.4) than for *alcohol* use disorders (mean odds ratio = 2.0). A more thorough review of the epidemiologic literature on AD–SUD comorbidity can be found in Kushner et al. (2008).

Conclusion

Our review of the epidemiological literature on AD–SUD comorbidity highlights several key issues. While specific phobias tend to be quite prevalent in the population, they tend to be less predictive of a co-occurring SUD than the other five ADs, especially GAD, PD, SP, and PTSD, though the field presently lacks definitive epidemiological data on OCD–SUD comorbidity (see review by Klostermann & Fals-Stewart, 2008). Prior to the *DSM–IV* (APA, 1994), when assessing AD–SUD comorbidity, no distinction was made between having a substance-induced AD and having an independent but comorbid AD–SUD condition (see Grant et al., 2004). Future epidemiological comorbidity studies will benefit from following the lead of the NESARC by accounting for the difference between independent and substance-induced comorbidity ADs, although NESARC data strongly suggest that substance-induced AD comorbidity is actually very rare (Grant et al., 2004). Presently, the data suggest that drug use disorders pose a greater risk for comorbidity than alcohol use disorders. Future epidemiological studies could move the field forward by further categorizing drug use disorders by specific substances (e.g., cocaine versus benzodiazepine) instead of lumping all of these into one homogenous category of drug use disorder; presumably, comorbidity rates with the various ADs could be very different across the various categories of

Table 1. Twelve-Month and Lifetime Prevalence Rates and Odds Ratios for Comorbid ADs and SUDs

AD by Community Survey	% w/out Al A	% with Al A	OR Al A	% w/out Al D	% with Al D	OR Al D	% w/out Dr A	% with Dr A	OR Dr A	% w/out Dr D	% with Dr D	OR Dr D
PD												
ECA	5.4	7.0	1.3	6.6	21.7	3.3	2.4	3.4	1.4	3.0	13.3	4.4
NCS	2.8	1.4	0.5	4.4	7.4	1.7	1.0	0.2	0.2	1.6	7.4	4.7
NESARC												
with ag	0.6	0.8	1.4	0.5	1.8	3.6	0.5	1.9	3.5	0.5	5.4	10.5
w/out ag	1.5	1.2	0.8	1.4	4.7	3.4	1.5	2.4	1.6	1.4	10.3	7.6
SP												
ECA	—	—	—	—	—	—	—	—	—	—	—	—
NCS	2.3	5.2	2.3	3.8	10.5	2.8	0.7	1.3	1.8	1.5	4.8	3.2
NESARC	2.9	2.6	0.9	2.5	6.3	2.5	2.6	5.2	2.0	2.4	13.0	5.4
OCD												
ECA	5.4	7.0	1.3	6.8	17.0	2.5	2.3	7.4	3.2	3.1	11.0	3.6
NCS	—	—	—	—	—	—	—	—	—	—	—	—
NESARC	—	—	—	—	—	—	—	—	—	—	—	—
GAD												
ECA	—	—	—	—	—	—	—	—	—	—	—	—
NCS	2.8	1.1	0.4	3.5	16.2	4.6	0.8	1.3	1.7	1.8	3.2	1.8
NESARC	2.1	1.9	0.9	1.8	5.7	3.1	2.0	4.2	2.1	1.7	17.2	10.4
PTSD												
ECA	—	—	—	—	—	—	—	—	—	—	—	—
NCS	2.0	3.7	1.5	4.0	8.8	2.2	0.7	1.1	1.5	1.5	6.5	4.2
NESARC	—	—	—	—	—	—	—	—	—	—	—	—
Specific Phobia												
ECA	5.3	5.8	1.1	7.2	11.5	1.6	2.2	4.7	2.1	3.0	6.5	2.2
NCS	2.6	3.1	1.2	3.9	8.6	2.2	0.9	0.6	0.7	1.7	3.1	1.8
NESARC	6.9	7.6	1.1	6.3	13.9	2.2	6.9	11.0	1.6	5.9	22.3	3.8

Note. w/out = without; AD = anxiety disorder; PD = panic disorder; ag = agoraphobia; SP = social phobia; OCD = obsessive-compulsive disorder; GAD = generalized anxiety disorder; PTSD = posttraumatic stress disorder; Al A = alcohol abuse; Al D = alcohol dependence; Dr A = drug abuse; Dr D = drug dependence; OR = odds ratio; ECA = Epidemiological Catchment Area Survey; NCS = National Comorbidity Survey; NESARC = National Epidemiological Survey on Alcohol and Related Conditions. ECA (Regier et al., 1990) data reflect lifetime prevalence for a sample of $n = 20,291$. NCS (Kessler et al., 1996) data reflect 12-month prevalence for a subsample ($n = 5,877$) of individuals who screened positive for any lifetime diagnosis from the original total ($n = 8,098$); furthermore, all NCS *% w/out* figures for this table were calculated by the first author. NESARC (Grant et al., 2004) data reflect 12-month prevalence for a sample of $n = 43,093$; for confidence intervals of OR see Grant et al. (2004).

drug use disorder. And finally, the fact that dependence is more predictive of AD–SUD comorbidity than abuse suggests that AD comorbidity is more likely among those with the more severe form of SUD. In an attempt to understand why this may be so, we will now turn our attention to the various theoretical accounts of AD–SUD comorbidity.

Theories Accounting for the Comorbidity of AD and SUD

The three most researched explanations that account for comorbidity between AD and SUD are as follows: substance-induced anxiety, self-medication, and third variables. The first two are causal theories (i.e., SUD → AD; AD → SUD, respectively) and require that order of onset is consistent with the direction of causation (Chilcoat & Breslau, 1998). Each of these explanations is reviewed and their supporting evidence examined.

Substance-Induced Anxiety

The substance-induced anxiety model suggests that anxiety symptoms are a biopsychosocial consequence of chronic substance use (see Kushner et al., 2000). On the one hand, anxiety symptoms can be a direct physiological response to either substance intoxication or withdrawal (e.g., Schuckit & Hesselbrock, 1994). On the other hand, anxiety symptoms can occur through more indirect means such as via guilt regarding the consequences of one's SUD.

The Self-Medication Hypothesis

The *self-medication hypothesis* finds its origin in Conger's (e.g., 1956) *tension-reduction theory,* which suggested that substances have tension-reducing effects and that people learn to administer substances for these effects. In the more refined *stress-response dampening model* (Sher & Levinson, 1982), substance-induced stress-response dampening is defined as a reduction of psychophysiological and behavioral responses to threat. From these origins, the self-medication hypothesis was formalized by Khanztian (1985). The three main conditions of the self-medication hypothesis, as applied to AD–SUD comorbidity are that: (1) the AD develops prior to the SUD; (2) the substance provides relief from the AD symptoms; and (3) substance use for relief from the AD symptoms continues as problematic use (see Chutuape & de Witt, 1995).

Third Variable

Third Variable explanations of AD–SUD comorbidity posit that the two disorders are not causally related to one another. Rather, a third variable or common underlying factor is thought to explain their overlap. The Third Variable hypothesis is the most heterogeneous of the hypotheses because there are so many possible underlying factors that could account for comorbidity. Some examples are individual differences such as anxiety sensitivity (in the cases of PD–, SP–, and PTSD–SUD comorbidity; e.g., Stewart & Kushner, 2001), exposure to non-biological environmental factors such as trauma (in the case of PTSD–SUD comorbidity; e.g., Stewart, 1996), or a genetic factor that predisposes individuals to both disorders (e.g., Merikangas, Stevens, & Fenton, 1996).

Weighing the Evidence

Order of Onset. Order of onset information is necessary but not sufficient for evaluating the two hypotheses proposing direct causal links between the disorders (i.e., self-medication hypothesis and substance-induced anxiety) (Chilcoat & Breslau, 1998). Kushner and colleagues (2008) tabulated the results of eight community-based epidemiological studies of comorbidity (e.g., NCS & ECA) and concluded that for individuals with both an AD and substance dependence, the AD came first 77% of the time. Thus, for 77% of individuals with a comorbid substance dependence disorder and AD, the AD could *not* have been substance-induced. These results suggest that both self-medication and third variables are tenable explanations for the majority of comorbid individuals, whereas the substance-induced anxiety hypothesis is not a likely explanation for most such cases. However, a look into the family studies literature tempers this supposition.

Family History. Family studies on comorbidity, which include twin studies, examine the specific patterns of transmission across families by gathering information on both the individual with the disorder(s), called a *proband,* and their family members (Merikangas et al., 1996). These patterns of familial transmission can then be used to provide evidence for or against the aforementioned hypotheses: if two disorders have a causal relationship, the relatives of probands with the causal disorder (e.g., an AD) will manifest an increased risk for the pure form of the causal disorder (AD) and for the combination of both disorders (AD + SUD), but not for the pure form of the comorbid disorder (SUD) (Merikangas et al., 1996). But, if the two disorders share a common etiology (i.e., third variable explanation) then the relatives of probands will be at equal risk for the pure form of either disorder.

In their review, Kushner and colleagues (2000) conclude that there is evidence to suggest that, to some extent, either disorder can cause the other, but at present, the evidence for a common etiology hypothesis (known as cross-transmission) is scant (Kushner et al., 2000). However, there is a growing body of evidence that one particular psychological variable, namely, anxiety sensitivity, may be a third variable that contributes to both the development of ADs and SUDs and thus helps explain their comorbidity.

Anxiety Sensitivity. Anxiety sensitivity is a cognitive, individual difference variable in which individuals fear those bodily sensations most associated with anxiety, such as racing heartbeat, trembling, and dizziness (Stewart & Kushner, 2001). Anxiety sensitivity has been linked to both ADs, SUDs, and, more recently, to comorbid ADs and SUDs, suggesting its possible role as a third variable (see Stewart & Kushner, 2001, for a review). But, consistent with the self-medication hypothesis, anxiety sensitivity might instead act as a *mediator* (an intervening, explanatory variable) between AD symptoms and substance misuse if it amplifies an individual's preexisting AD symptoms (Reiss, 1991) and compels that individual to increase behaviors such as substance abuse that help reduce his or her AD symptoms. Alternatively, consistent with the substance-induced anxiety model, anxiety sensitivity might mediate the causal relation between substance misuse and AD. Substance withdrawal symptoms (e.g., tachycardia) should be experienced as extremely aversive to individuals with high anxiety sensitivity, thereby increasing the chances that arousal-related withdrawal symptoms would spiral into a full-blown AD (Norton, Norton, Cox, & Belik, 2008; Zvolensky, Schmidt, & Stewart, 2003). Although it is clear that anxiety sensitivity plays an important role in the comorbidity between ADs and SUDs, it is not yet clear as to which etiological model the anxiety sensitivity data most strongly support.

While the information presented so far tends to suggest that of the three theories discussed, the self-medication hypothesis may explain the relationship between AD and SUD in the greatest number of cases (order of onset and family studies are both consistent with this position), recent work suggests that the self-medication hypothesis can be better understood by examining the unique contribution of individual difference variables like anxiety sensitivity. However, both the order of onset and the biopsychosocial mechanisms that influence order of

onset appear to be specific to the unique interaction between certain ADs and certain substances of abuse. We will examine this issue most closely in the case of PD, where variability across substances has been most extensively studied. We also examine other factors that may influence order of onset rates across other ADs comorbid with SUDs.

The complicated relationship between PD and various SUDs is a good example of how an AD may come before or after an SUD, depending on which substance is consumed. A longitudinal study of German adolescents and young adults—evaluated for alcohol use disorders, PD, and other ADs, according to *DSM–IV–TR* (APA, 2000) criteria— followed approximately 3,000 participants over a 4-year period. It found that PD but not other ADs at baseline predicted alcohol use disorder (both abuse and dependence) 4 years later (Zimmermann et al., 2003). However, the fact that PD tends to precede alcohol use disorder seems to be unique to alcohol, as dependence on other substances like cocaine (e.g., O'Brien, Wu, & Anthony, 2005) and cigarettes (e.g., Breslau & Klein, 1999) tends to precede the onset of PD (see Norton et al., 2008, for a review). For example, in examining the Epidemiological Study of Young Adults ($n = 1,007$) and the NCS ($n = 4,411$) data, Breslau and Klein (1999) report that longitudinal measurements showed that daily smokers were 13 times more likely than nonsmokers to develop PD over time. Furthermore, when Breslau and Klein compared individuals who had quit smoking to those that had never smoked, there was no difference in panic attacks between quitters and nonsmokers, suggesting that it is exposure to the drug itself rather than some preexisting characteristic of people susceptible to tobacco that causes the increased risk for PD. While the temporal relationship between PD and SUD depends on the type of substance involved (i.e., PD preceding SUD in the case of drugs with anxiolytic properties such as alcohol, and SUD preceding PD in the case of drugs with stimulant properties such as tobacco and cocaine), the relationship between SP and SUD is equally complicated.

Studies on SP and alcohol use and abuse sometimes show a positive relationship (e.g., Abrams, Kushner, Medina, & Voight, 2001), sometimes show a negative relationship (e.g., Holle, Heimberg, Sweet, & Holt, 1995), and sometime show no relationship at all (e.g., Ham & Hope, 2005). However, a review by Morris, Stewart, and Ham (2005) concludes that those studies that fail to find a positive relationship between SP and alcohol use or abuse tend not to use undergraduate samples and tend *not* to measure the fear-of-negative-evaluation aspect of SP, which typically demonstrates a positive relationship to alcohol problems (see Stewart, Morris, Mellings, & Komar, 2006). Furthermore, drinking problems as opposed to drinking levels, per se, tend to be positively linked to social anxiety (Stewart et al., 2006). The literature that does show evidence of a positive relationship between SP and alcohol use disorder not only indicates that the SP developed before the alcohol use disorder but that substances are generally used to self-medicate (see Carrigan & Randall, 2003, for a review). In particular, there is evidence to suggest that individuals with comorbid SP and alcohol use disorder tend to hold more positive expectancies about alcohol's social assertiveness qualities, general tension reduction properties, and its ability to reduce anxiety in social situations (see Tran & Smith, 2008).

The data on order of onset in cases of PTSD–SUD comorbidity suggest that in most cases both the trauma and PTSD precede the SUD (e.g. Chilcoat & Menard, 2003), and that the subsequent SUD is often the result of attempts to self-medicate (Chilcoat & Breslau, 1998; Stewart, 1996). For example, Chilcoat and Breslau's (1998) 5-year prospective study found that individuals with a baseline history of PTSD were at four times increased risk for abusing substances, over time. Based on neurobiological evidence (see De Bellis, 2002), the self-medication hypothesis suggests that individuals with PTSD misuse central nervous system depressants like alcohol, cannabis, opioids, and benzodiazepines to attenuate certain fear and startle responses as well as the intrusive memories that are characteristic of this AD (Jacobsen, Southwick, & Kosten, 2001). Furthermore, there is growing evidence to suggest that the general tension-relieving properties of substances such as alcohol are expected and sought after by individuals with PTSD (e.g., Simpson, 2003), but not necessarily in a manner that suggests intended relief from specific PTSD symptoms, per se (Ulman, Filipas, & Townsend, 2005). However, there is some evidence to support the substance-induced anxiety model. Under certain conditions, substance misuse may predispose an individual to PTSD either through living the more dangerous lifestyle associated with drug abusers—the *High-risk hypothesis*—or because of physiological and neurochemical changes that can make an individual more susceptible to developing PTSD following trauma exposure—the *Susceptibility hypothesis* (Brown & Wolfe, 1994). In a study examining longitudinal

predictors of risk for traumatization and PTSD, Acierno, Resnick, Kilpatrick, Saunders, and Best (1999) demonstrated that lifetime alcohol use was prospectively linked to developing PTSD following sexual assault, consistent with the susceptibility hypothesis. However, they did not find support for the high-risk hypothesis, as lifetime alcohol use was not associated with increased risk for sexual assault. Therefore, although the self-medication hypothesis is the predominant explanatory model for PTSD–SUD comorbidity, it is clear that other models such as the susceptibility model may also be at play.

Unfortunately, the literature that sets out to explain the theoretical mechanisms that are driving the comorbidity between SUD and either GAD or OCD is less well developed than the literature on comorbid SUD and PD, SP, and PTSD. There are some preliminary clinical outcome data on comorbid SUD and OCD, which helps clarify the theoretical mechanisms that may govern their relationship across time (see Klostermann & Fals-Stewart, 2008). In contrast, for GAD and SUDs there is presently little more than prevalence data available, albeit prevalence data that suggest a meaningful relationship of some kind.

Conclusion

Taken as a whole, the literature tends to support that the self-medication hypothesis often explains AD–SUD comorbidity better than substance-induced anxiety or third variable explanations, especially when individuals *expect* the substance to have a dampening effect on their anxiety; however, there are notable exceptions for specific combinations of comorbid ADs–SUDs (e.g., cigarette smoking appears to predict the later onset of PD). Furthermore, research on the effects of individual difference variables like anxiety sensitivity offers compelling evidence that certain factors might serve as third variables in AD–SUD comorbidity, or might mediate the causal relation between the two disorders. However, many researchers recognize that while the self-medication hypothesis can often explain the onset of comorbidity, it may be overly simplistic (e.g., Stewart, 1996). Once both disorders set in, they typically maintain each other in a process known as *mutual maintenance*. For example, in the case of an SUD with comorbid PTSD, though anxiolytic substances like alcohol can offer dose-dependent relief from certain PTSD symptoms (e.g., hyperarousal), those symptoms not only return once the alcohol has worn off, but may return with even greater severity (Jacobsen et al., 2001), promoting escalating substance abuse and culminating in a vicious cycle where each disorder serves to maintain the other.

Recent Treatment Approaches for AD–SUD Comorbidity

It is widely documented that AD–SUD comorbidity often results in less effective treatment for either disorder and higher rates of relapse to substance misuse (e.g., Bruce et al., 2005; Kushner et al., 2000). A challenge inherent to the treatment of comorbid ADs–SUDs is whether the individual will receive sequential, parallel, or integrated treatment. In sequential treatment, the client is treated for one disorder and then the other in discrete stages. The order of treatment is typically determined by whether the client presents at mental health or addiction services (Randall, Book, Carrigan, & Thomas, 2008). However, treatment of the SUD most commonly precedes treatment of the AD, given beliefs among practitioners that mental health issues cannot be addressed until substance misuse is under control (Riggs & Foa, 2008). The advantage of sequential treatment is that, in some cases, the secondary disorder will remediate after successful treatment of the first disorder, eliminating the necessity of treating the comorbid disorder. Parallel treatment ensures that the client is treated for both disorders at the same time, but typically not by the same treatment provider, and perhaps not even in the same treatment facility; furthermore, there is no guarantee that any coordination or communication will exist between treatment providers (Randall et al., 2008). Integrated models of treatment for comorbid ADs and SUDs recognize the complex interrelation between the two disorders and the possibility of mutual maintenance (Randall et al., 2008) and therefore attempt to create a hybrid treatment that combines the major elements from those treatment protocols/standards that have proven to be effective in treating each disorder independently. Truly integrated treatments also explicitly address the reciprocal relations between the disorders within the treatment strategies. Although sequential and parallel treatments appear to be the default standards, this typically speaks more to systemic issues in health care delivery (e.g., lack of integrated health services; see Weiss, Najavits, & Hennessy, 2004) than to an empirically derived gold standard for treating comorbidity between ADs and SUDs (Toneatto & Rector, 2008). In fact, integrated treatments are the recommended treatment of choice in recent best practice guidelines for comorbid mental health and substance use disorders (Health Canada, 2002). Below we briefly review some of the more promising treatment models for ADs with comorbid SUDs.

Treatment for Comorbid PD and SUDs

A review of the most recent treatment literature on PD and (alcohol use disorder) AUD comorbidity by Toneatto and Rector (2008) reports findings that consistently demonstrate efficacy for various types of sequential treatment but no clear superiority over alcohol treatment alone. For example, in an unpublished trial cited by Toneatto and Rector (2008), there were no treatment group differences between a group that received sequential cognitive behavioral therapy (CBT) for both PD and alcohol use disorder and a group that only received alcohol specific CBT; however, both groups showed a reduction in both alcohol use and anxiety symptoms. So far, the only study to report superiority for a combined PD–alcohol use disorder intervention is one by Kushner et al. (2006) in which a truly integrated model was used. In their pilot treatment protocol, Kushner and colleagues combined key elements—Alcoholics Anonymous and family therapy—of the treatment as usual approach for alcoholism with three key elements—psychoeducation, cognitive restructuring, and cue exposure—from a standard CBT protocol for PD (i.e., Barlow, Craske, Cerny, & Klosko, 1989). After 2 weeks of treatment, the integrated treatment group compared to the treatment as usual control group showed less panic symptoms and demonstrated less severity in alcohol consumption after a relapse. Moreover, the treatment as usual control group showed a higher number of individuals with a diagnosis of alcohol dependence at follow-up. Although it is too early to suggest that their protocol will consistently demonstrate such positive findings across independent replications that include methodological improvements such as random assignment to treatment groups, their findings do suggest that integrated treatment approaches show promise for this form of comorbidity.

Treatment for Comorbid SP and SUDs

Randall, Thomas, and Thevos (2001) were the first group to empirically test a simultaneous treatment model for SP–AUD comorbidity. In a randomized clinical trial, participants were assigned to either an alcohol treatment only group (CBT), or a combined social anxiety (CBT) and alcohol treatment group (CBT). The combined treatment group received treatment for both disorders by the same therapist in the same session, though the treatments were distinct (CBT specific to alcohol versus CBT specific to social anxiety). Thus, the combined treatment would be best described as parallel rather than truly integrated treatment. Contrary to expectation, there were no differences between groups in remediation of social anxiety, and, even more surprisingly, the combined treatment group faired *worse* on 3 of 4 alcohol-related outcome variables (Randall et al., 2001).

Randall et al. (2008) have reasoned that standard alcohol use outcome variables (e.g., quantity and frequency) may not have been suitable indices of improvement in this population, since individuals with attenuated social anxiety are less likely to avoid social situations, which, in turn, increases the likelihood that alcohol might be consumed. It remains unclear what factors contributed to the combined treatment group not showing improvement in social anxiety, though Conrod and Stewart (2005) have reasoned that this may be more indicative of overload on the patients due to the complexity of the combined treatment than of failure of the model, per se. They point to very high dropout rates across studies of combined treatments to date as evidence for the possibility that such treatments are often too demanding for comorbid AD–SUD clients.

Treatment for Comorbid OCD and SUDs

In a randomized clinical trial, Fals-Stewart and Schafer (1992) demonstrated that parallel treatment for both OCD and SUD resulted in greater OCD symptom reduction, lower dropout rates, and higher rates of abstinence from substances at 12-month follow-up compared to either treatment as usual for the SUD (e.g., Alcoholics Anonymous) or treatment as usual plus muscle relaxation. Based on this controlled trial, Klostermann and Fals-Stewart (2008) have identified several key issues in the treatment of OCD and SUDs. They suggest that given the wealth of empirical evidence supporting the use of Exposure and Response Prevention (ERP) in the treatment of OCD (e.g., Jenike, 2004), ERP should be the intervention of choice for the treatment of OCD symptoms in comorbid clients. They also recommend that because ERP and SUD treatments are quite dissimilar, the combined treatment should be delivered in separate, but approximately equal, sessions for both disorders (i.e., parallel treatment).

Treatment for Comorbid PTSD and SUDs

Combined treatment for AD–SUD comorbidity is probably most advanced in the case of PTSD–SUD comorbidity. In their review of this literature,

Riggs and Foa (2008) suggest that treatment programs for comorbid PTSD and SUDs, although differing with respect to their specifics, typically incorporate techniques that promote effective coping skills, focus on both substance relapse prevention and reducing PTSD symptoms, and provide education about the links between SUD and PTSD. Brady, Dansky, Back, Foa, and Carroll (2001) report that their Concurrent Treatment of PTSD and Cocaine Dependence (CTPCD) program (combining coping skills training and exposure into an integrated treatment) can reduce cocaine use by 60% and PTSD symptoms by between 30% and 70%. Unfortunately, their study had a limited sample size and did not include a control group; however, those participants who began but didn't finish the treatment showed no improvement compared to treatment completers (see also review by Riggs & Foa, 2008).

Foa and colleagues (Riggs, Rukstalis, Volpicelli, Kalmanson, & Foa, 2003) have presented preliminary data from an ongoing clinical trial that is the first controlled outcome study of a parallel treatment for PTSD and alcohol dependence. Participants in the combined treatment group receive prolonged exposure (Foa & Rothbaum, 1998) for PTSD, and a combination of pharmacotherapy (naltrexone) and CBT for their alcohol dependence, from different therapists. Preliminary analyses on the first 70 participants in the study show that 12-week dropout rates were not different across groups and comparable to other 12-week programs for SUD alone (Riggs & Foa, 2008). Furthermore, outcome analyses on the first 40 participants to complete treatment reported that those participants who received prolonged exposure (combined group) showed a greater reduction relative to other groups in both PTSD symptoms and cravings for alcohol, and that these reductions were stable across 6 months (Riggs & Foa, 2008).

Based on the best available research to date (e.g., studies using a randomized controlled trial design with large samples), parallel treatment for PTSD with a specific substance disorder (e.g., Riggs et al., 2003) seems promising. Riggs and Foa (2008) also review three different programs that attempt to address comorbid PTSD and substance misuse more generally: Substance Dependence PTSD Therapy (SDPT) (Triffleman, Carroll, & Kellogg, 1999), Project Transcend (Donovan, Padin-Rivera, & Kowaliw, 2001), and Seeking Safety (Najavits, 2004). Unfortunately, it is difficult to compare these programs with the substance-specific treatments for comorbidity mentioned above because these three programs include either a less structured version of imaginal exposure therapy (e.g., Donovan et al., 2001) or no prolonged imaginal exposure at all (Triffleman et al., 1999). The general conclusion that can be drawn is that the treatment efficacy of each program tends to either be no different from an alternative treatment (e.g. Najivits, 2004) or to produce only slight clinical gains (e.g., Donovan et al., 2001). At present, those treatments (e.g., Riggs et al., 2003) that target a specific substance, offer parallel or integrated treatment, and include a component of exposure therapy, seem to hold the most promise, though results are only preliminary at this time.

Conclusion

In summary, additional research is needed to improve standard treatment outcome measures so they can offer a more accurate depiction of positive change over time for individuals with AD–SUD comorbidity, especially with respect to SP (e.g., inclusion of changes in drinking to cope). Integrated and parallel treatments seem to be more promising than sequential treatments; studies should investigate whether integrated treatments offer advantages over parallel treatments as theory might predict. Comorbid treatments that contain elements of the gold standard treatments (e.g., ERP for OCD, prolonged exposure for PTSD) for the AD tend to perform better than those that do not. Finally, though the treatment literature on AD–SUD comorbidity is still in its infancy, the preliminary results in this burgeoning area of AD research seem very encouraging.

Note

1. This review does include some epidemiological data on specific phobia–SUD comorbidity, but only to demonstrate the relatively low frequency of co-occurrence.

References

Abrams, K., Kushner, M., Medina, K., & Voight, A. (2001). The pharmacologic and expectancy effects of alcohol on social anxiety in individuals with social phobia. *Drug and Alcohol Dependence, 64,* 219–231.

Acierno, R., Resnick, H., Kilpatrick, D. G., Saunders, B., & Best, C. L. (1999). Risk factors for rape, physical assault, and posttraumatic stress disorder in women: Examination of differential multivariate relationships. *Journal of Anxiety Disorders, 13,* 541–563.

American Psychiatric Association. (1994). *Diagnostic and statistical manual of mental disorders* (4th ed.). Washington, DC: Author.

American Psychiatric Association. (2000). *Diagnostic and statistical manual of mental disorders* (4th ed., text revision). Washington, DC: Author.

Barlow, D. H., Craske, M. G., Cerny, J. A., & Klosko, J. S. (1989). Behavioral treatment of panic disorder. *The Behavior Therapist, 20,* 261–282.

Berkson. J. (1949). Limitations of the application of four-fold tables to hospital data. *Biological Bulletin, 2,* 47–53.

Brady, K. T., Dansky, B. S., Back, S. E., Foa, E. B., & Carroll, K. M. (2001). Exposure therapy in the treatment of PTSD among cocaine-dependent individuals: Preliminary findings. *Journal of Substance Abuse Treatment, 21,* 47–54.

Breslau, N., & Klein, D. F. (1999). Smoking and panic attacks: An epidemiologic investigation. *Archives of General Psychiatry, 56,* 1141–1147.

Brown, P. J., & Wolfe, J. (1994). Substance abuse and posttraumatic stress disorder comorbidity. *Drug and Alcohol Dependence, 35,* 51–59.

Bruce, S. E., Yonkers, K. A., Otto, M. W., Eisen, J. L., Weisberg, R. B., Pagano, M., et al. (2005). Influence of psychiatric comorbidity on recovery and recurrence in generalized anxiety disorder, social phobia, and panic disorder: A 12-year prospective study. *American Journal of Psychiatry, 162,* 1179–1187.

Carrigan, M. H., & Randall, C. L. (2003). Self-medication in social phobia: A review of the alcohol literature. *Addictive Behaviors, 28,* 269–284.

Chilcoat, H. D., & Breslau, N. (1998). Posttraumatic stress disorder and drug disorders: Testing causal pathways. *Archives of General Psychiatry, 55,* 913–917.

Chilcoat, H. D., & Menard, C. (2003). Epidemiological investigations: Comorbidity of posttraumatic stress disorder and substance use disorder. In P. Ouimette & P. J. Brown (Eds.), *Trauma and substance abuse: Causes, consequences, and treatment of comorbid disorders* (pp. 9–28). Washington, DC: American Psychological Association.

Chutuape, M., & de Wit, H. (1995). Preferences for ethanol and diazepam in anxious individuals: An evaluation of the self-medication hypothesis. *Psychopharmacology, 121,* 91–103.

Conger, J. (1956). Reinforcement theory and the dynamics of alcoholism. *Quarterly Journal of Studies on Alcohol, 17,* 296–305.

Conrod, P. J., & Stewart, S. H. (2005). A critical look at dual-focused cognitive behavioral treatments for comorbid substance use and psychiatric disorders: Strengths, limitations, and future directions. *Journal of Cognitive Psychotherapy, 19,* 261–284.

De Bellis, M. D. (2002). Developmental traumatology: A contributory mechanism for alcohol and substance use disorders. *Psychoneuroendorcrinology, 27,* 155–170.

Donovan, B., Padin-Rivera, E., & Kowaliw, S. (2001). "Transcend": Initial outcomes from a posttraumatic stress disorder/substance abuse treatment program. *Journal of Traumatic Stress, 14,* 757–772.

Fals-Stewart, W., & Schafer, J. (1992). The treatment of substance abusers with obsessive-compulsive disorder: An outcome study. *Journal of Substance Abuse Treatment, 9,* 365–370.

Foa, E. B., & Rothbaum, B. O. (1998). *Treating the trauma of rape: Cognitive–behavioral therapy for PTSD.* New York: Guilford Press.

Grant, B. F., Stinson, F. S., Dawson, D. A., Chou, P., Dufour, M. C., Compton, W., et al. (2004). Prevalence and co-occurrence of substance use disorders and independent mood and anxiety disorders. *Archives of General Psychiatry, 61,* 807–816.

Ham, L. S., & Hope, D. A. (2005). Incorporating social anxiety into a model of college problematic drinking. *Addictive Behaviors, 30,* 127–150.

Health Canada. (2002). *Best practices: Concurrent mental health and substance use disorders* (Prepared by the Centre for Addiction and Mental Health). Ottawa, ON: Author.

Holle, C., Heimberg, R., Sweet, R., & Holt, C. (1995). Alcohol and caffeine use by social phobics: An initial inquiry into drinking patterns and behavior. *Behaviour Research and Therapy, 33,* 561–566.

Jacobsen, L. K., Southwick, S. M., & Kosten, T. R. (2001). Substance use disorders in patients with posttraumatic stress disorder: A review of the literature. *American Journal of Psychiatry, 158,* 1184–1190.

Jenike, M. A. (2004). Obsessive-compulsive disorder. *New England Journal of Medicine, 350,* 259–265.

Kessler, R. C., Berglund, P., Demler, O., Jin, R., & Walters, E. E. (2005). Lifetime prevalence and age-of-onset distributions of *DSM–IV* disorders in the National Comorbidity Survey Replication. *Archives of General Psychiatry, 62,* 593–602.

Kessler, R. C., Nelson, C. B., McGonagle, K. A., Edlund, M. J., Frank, R. G., & Leaf, P. J. (1996). The epidemiology of co-occurring addictive and mental disorders. *American Journal of Orthopsychiatry, 66,* 17–31.

Khantzian, E. (1985). The self-medication hypothesis of addictive disorders: Focus on heroin and cocaine dependence. *American Journal of Psychiatry, 142,* 1259–1264.

Klostermann, K. C., & Fals-Stewart, W. (2008). Treatment of co-morbid obsessive-compulsive disorder and substance use disorders. In S. H. Stewart & P. J. Conrod (Eds.), *Anxiety and substance use disorders: The vicious cycle of comorbidity* (pp. 101–117). New York: Springer.

Kushner, M. G., Abrams, K. & Borchardt, C. (2000). The relationship between anxiety disorders and alcohol use disorders: A review of major perspectives and findings. *Clinical Psychology Review, 20,* 149–171.

Kushner, M., Donahue, C., Sletten, S., Thuras, P., Abrams, K., Peterson, J., et al. (2006). Cognitive behavioral treatment of comorbid anxiety disorder in alcoholism treatment patients: Presentation of a prototype program and future directions. *Journal of Mental Health, 15,* 697–707.

Kushner, M., Krueger, R., Frye, B., & Peterson, J. (2008). Epidemiological perspectives on co-occurring anxiety disorder and substance use disorder. In S. H. Stewart & P. J. Conrod (Eds.), *Anxiety and substance use disorders: The vicious cycle of comorbidity* (pp. 3–17). New York: Springer.

Merikangas, K. A., Stevens, D., & Fenton, B. (1996). Comorbidity of alcoholism and anxiety disorders. *Alcohol Health and Research World, 20,* 100–105.

Morris, E. P., Stewart, S. H., & Ham, L. S. (2005). The relationship between social anxiety disorder and alcohol use disorders: A critical review. *Clinical Psychology Review, 25,* 734–760.

Najavits, L. M. (2004). Treatment of posttraumatic stress disorder and substance abuse: Clinical guidelines for implementing "Seeking Safety" therapy. *Alcoholism Treatment Quarterly, 22,* 43–62.

Norton, G. R., Norton, P. J., Cox, B. J., & Belik, S. (2008). Panic spectrum disorders and substance use. In S. H. Stewart & P. J. Conrod (Eds.), *Anxiety and substance use disorders: The vicious cycle of comorbidity* (pp. 81–98). New York: Springer.

O'Brien, M. S., Wu, L. T., & Anthony, J. C. (2005). Cocaine use and the occurrence of panic attacks in the community: A case-crossover approach. *Substance Use and Misuse, 40,* 285–297.

Randall, C. L., Book, S.W., Carrigan, M. H., & Thomas, S. E. (2008). Treatment of co-occurring alcoholism and social anxiety disorder. In S. H. Stewart & P. J. Conrod (Eds.), *Anxiety and substance use disorders: The vicious cycle of comorbidity* (pp. 139–155). New York: Springer.

Randall, C. L., Thomas, S., & Thevos, A. K. (2001). Concurrent alcoholism and social anxiety disorder: A first step toward developing effective treatments. *Alcoholism: Clinical and Experimental Research, 25,* 210–220.

Regier, D. A., Farmer, M. E., Rae, D. S., Locke, B. Z., Keith, S. J., Judd, L. L., et al. (1990). Comorbidity of mental disorders with alcohol and other drug abuse: Results from the Epidemiologic Catchment Area (ECA) study. *Journal of the American Medical Association, 264,* 2511–2518.

Reiss, S. (1991). Expectancy model of fear, anxiety, and panic. *Clinical Psychology Review, 11,* 141–153.

Riggs, D. S., & Foa, E. B. (2008). Treatment for comorbid posttraumatic stress disorder and substance use disorders. In S. H. Stewart & P. J. Conrod (Eds.), *Anxiety and substance use disorders: The vicious cycle of comorbidity* (pp. 119–137). New York: Springer.

Riggs, D. S., Rukstalis, M., Volpicelli, J. R., Kalmanson, D., & Foa, E. B. (2003). Demographic and social adjustment characteristics of patients with comorbid posttraumatic stress disorder and alcohol dependence: Potential pitfalls of PTSD treatment. *Addictive Behaviors, 28,* 1717–1730.

Schuckit, M. A., & Hesselbrock, V. (1994). Alcohol dependence and anxiety disorders: What is the relationship? *American Journal of Psychiatry, 151,* 1723–1734.

Sher, K. J., & Levenson, R. (1982). Risk for alcoholism and individual differences in the stress-response-dampening effect of alcohol. *Journal of Abnormal Psychology, 91,* 350–367.

Simpson, T. L. (2003). Childhood sexual abuse, PTSD, and the functional roles of alcohol use among women drinkers. *Substance Use and Misuse, 38,* 249–270.

Stewart, S. H. (1996). Alcohol abuse in individuals exposed to trauma: A critical review. *Psychological Bulletin, 120,* 83–112.

Stewart, S. H., & Kushner, M. G. (2001). Introduction to the special issue on "Anxiety sensitivity and addictive behaviors." *Addictive Behaviours, 26,* 775–785.

Stewart, S. H., Morris, E. P., Mellings, T., & Komar, J. A. (2006). Relations of social anxiety variables to drinking motives, drinking quantity and frequency, and alcohol-related problems in undergraduates. *Journal of Mental Health, 15,* 671–682.

Toneatto, T., & Rector, N. A. (2008). Treating co-morbid panic disorder and substance use disorder. In S. H. Stewart & P. J. Conrod (Eds.), *Anxiety and substance use disorders: The vicious cycle of comorbidity* (pp. 157–175). New York: Springer.

Tran, G. Q., & Smith, J. P. (2008). Comorbidity of social phobia and alcohol use disorders: A review of psychopathology research findings. In S. H. Stewart & P. J. Conrod (Eds.), *Anxiety and substance use disorders: The vicious cycle of comorbidity* (pp. 59–79). New York: Springer.

Trifleman, E., Carroll, K., & Kellogg, S. (1999). Substance dependence posttraumatic stress disorder therapy: An integrated cognitive-behavioral approach. *Journal of Substance Abuse Treatment, 17,* 3–14.

Ullman, S. E., Filipas, H. H., & Townsend, S. M. (2005). Trauma exposure, posttraumatic stress disorder and problem drinking in sexual assault survivors. *Journal of Studies on Alcohol, 66,* 610–619.

Weiss, R. D., Najavits, L. M., & Hennessy, G. (2004). Overview of treatment modalities for dual-diagnosis patients: Pharmacotherapy, psychotherapy, and 12-step programs. In H. R. Kranzler & B. J. Rounsaville (Eds.), *Dual diagnosis and psychiatric treatment: Substance abuse and comorbid disorders* (2nd ed., pp. 103–128). New York: Marcel Dekker.

Zimmermann, P., Wittchen, H.-U., Hofler, M., Pfister, H., Kessler, R. C., & Leib, R. (2003). Primary anxiety disorders and the development of subsequent alcohol use disorders: A 4-year community study of adolescents and young adults. *Psychological Medicine, 33,* 1211–1222.

Zvolensky, M. J., Schmidt, N. B., & Stewart, S. H. (2003). Panic disorder and smoking. *Clinical Psychology: Science and Practice, 10,* 29–51.

Anxiety Disorders and Depression Comorbidity

Jonathan D. Huppert

Abstract

The chapter reviews cross-sectional and longitudinal epidemiological studies related to the co-occurrence of anxiety disorders and depression. Results suggest that anxiety disorders and depression tend to co-occur in 20% to 40% of patients. Explanations for increased co-occurrence considered include overlapping diagnostic criteria, genetics, neurophysiology, neurochemistry, negative affect/ temperament, perceived control, interpersonal mechanisms, and biases in information processing. According to most levels of analysis, there is more overlap with GAD and depression while specific phobias have the least overlap. Finally, data on the impact of depression on pharmacological and psychological treatments for anxiety disorders are reviewed. More work is needed to clarify the multiple interactive processes likely at play in the co-occurrence of anxiety and mood disorders and their treatment.

Keywords: anxiety, comorbidity, depression, neurophysiology, phenomenology, psychopathology, treatment

Prevalence of Comorbidity

Individuals with anxiety disorders and comorbid depression have more chronic and severe anxiety symptoms, are more impaired, are at greater risk for suicide, and utilize more services than those without depression (de Graaf et al., 2004). Not only is the impact on the individual significant, but the prevalence of comorbid anxiety and mood disorders is very high. Given the impact on patients and the health care system, it is essential to understand the nature of this comorbidity. One of the core questions is whether anxiety and depression are separate entities or better subsumed under the rubric of negative affect or neuroticism (see Mineka, Watson, & Clark, 1998; Wittchen et al., 2000). Significant efforts have been made to understand the similarities and differences between anxiety and depression at the symptom and affect (Mineka et al., 1998),

cognitive (Mathews & MacLeod, 2005), behavioral genetic (Middeldorp et al., 2005), specific genetic (Leonardo & Hen, 2006), psychophysiological (McNaughton & Corr, 2004), and neurochemical levels (Heim & Nemeroff, 2001). This chapter reviews the research on comorbid anxiety disorders and depression, while raising some methodological and clinical issues relevant to future research.

Prior to examining various approaches to understand the comorbidity of anxiety and depression, it is useful to examine the actual rates of comorbidity among anxiety and depressive disorders in clinical and epidemiological studies (for an earlier review, see also Mineka et al., 1998). While the emphasis of this chapter is depression occurring in the context of primary anxiety disorders, it is also useful to consider the prevalence of anxiety disorders in the context of depression. Lifetime diagnoses fail to distinguish co-occurring diagnoses from the history of a resolved diagnosis and the presence of an additional diagnosis later in life, leading to potentially inflated estimates (also see Kraemer, Wilson, & Hayward, 2006, regarding "pseudo-comorbidity" in lifetime diagnoses). Therefore, this chapter focuses on rates of concurrent comorbidity. The National Comorbidity Survey (NCS) (Kessler, 2006a; Kessler et al., 1994) and the National Comorbidity Survey Replication (NCS-R) (Kessler et al., 2005) in the United States, as well as two large clinical studies (Brown et al., 2001; Rush et al., 2005) provide exemplary data on the prevalence of major depressive disorder (MDD) or dysthymia in anxiety disorders and the prevalence of anxiety disorders in MDD or dysthymia (see Table 1). Most data on the NCS and NCS-R were examined through analysis of the original datasets (Kessler, 2006a, 2006b) for the purposes of this chapter. Given NCS base rates of current MDD in the general population of 4.9%,

and of dysthymia of 1.5%, the risk for a depressive disorder in the context of an anxiety disorder ranges from 5 to 8 times greater than the general population (all $ps < .01$). In addition, the NCS (Kessler, 2006a) reported 1-month prevalence rates of anxiety disorders as follows: 5.5% for specific phobia (SP), 1.4% for panic disorder (PD), 4.5% for social anxiety disorder (SAD), 1.6% for generalized anxiety disorder (GAD), and 2.1% for posttraumatic stress disorder (PTSD). The NCS-R yielded similar results (Kessler, 2006b): The base rates of current major depressive episode in the general population were 3.1%, and dysthymia was 1.2%, and the 1-month prevalence rates of anxiety disorders as follows: 6.3% for SP, 1.0% for PD, 3.5% for SAD, 1.6% for GAD, and 1.7% for PTSD. Risk for depression in the context of anxiety disorders were similar to the NCS (all $ps < .01$). Including the 12-month prevalence of obsessive-compulsive disorder (OCD) from the NCS-R of 1.0% (Kessler et al., 2005) as a proxy for

Table 1. Prevalence of Co-occurring Anxiety Disorders and Depressive Disorders in Epidemiological and Clinical Samples

	Specific Phobia	Panic Disorder	Social Anxiety Disorder	Generalized Anxiety Disorder	OCD	PTSD
% MDD in Anxiety Disorders						
NCS	26%	40%	24%	39%	N/A	36%
NCS-R	14%	34%	20%	35%	N/A	27%
Brown et al.	21%	30%	32%	29%	35%	65%
% Anxiety Disorders in MDD						
NCS	29%	12%	22%	12%	N/A	15%
NCS-R	28%	11%	23%	17%	N/A	14%
Brown et al.	17%	46%	43%	57%	18%	10%
STAR*D	N/A	9%	29%	21%	13%	19%
% Dysthymia in Anxiety Disorders						
NCS	7%	12%	5%	22%	N/A	13%
NCS-R	8%	19%	11%	17%	N/A	16%
Brown et al.	12%	9%	17%	6%	11%	20%
% Anxiety Disorder in Dysthymia						
NCS	25%	12%	16%	24%	N/A	19%
NCS-R	39%	16%	31%	22%	N/A	22%
Brown et al.	23%	34%	56%	50%	14%	8%

Note. MDD = Major Depressive Disorder; OCD = Obsessive-Compulsive Disorder; PTSD = Posttraumatic Stress Disorder; NCS = National Comorbidity Study (Kessler, 2006a); NCS-R = National Comorbidity Study-Replication (Kessler, 2006b); STAR*D (Rush et al., 2005); Brown et al., 2001; N/A = not available. Hierarchical exclusion criteria for GAD and depression were not utilized to obtain these estimates.

current OCD, there appears to be a 3 to 20 times increased risk of having an anxiety disorder if one has a mood disorder (all $ps < .01$).

Given the increased risk for comorbidity of mood and anxiety disorders, there are a number of explanations of why mood and anxiety disorders may co-occur (cf., Middeldorp et al., 2005). These include (1) overlapping diagnostic criteria, (2) one disorder being an epiphenomenon of the other, (3) the disorders are different phases of an underlying disorder, (4) one disorder is a risk factor for the other, (5) there are overlapping genetic and etiological processes, and (6) reciprocal causation. In the rest of the chapter, these possibilities are considered and the potential processes or causes for each possibility are discussed, followed by treatment implications.

Phenomenological/Descriptive Overlap and Distinguishing Features

One reason that depressive disorders may co-occur frequently with anxiety disorders is the overlap in symptoms as defined by the text revision of the fourth edition of the *Diagnostic and Statistical Manual of Mental Disorders (DSM–IV–TR)* (American Psychiatric Association, 2000). There are symptom criteria for GAD, SAD, and PTSD that are also symptom criteria for MDD or dysthymia. There are fewer symptom criteria that overlap with PD, OCD, and SP. The common and distinct features are considered separately for each of the anxiety disorders.

GAD

Brown et al. (2001) reported that approximately 50% of patients with current dysthymia meet criteria for GAD if rule-out criteria are ignored. Symptom criteria that overlap between depressive disorders and GAD include fatigue, sleep disturbance, and poor concentration. These three symptoms are sufficient to meet physiological symptom criteria for the diagnosis of GAD. If an individual feels down and worries most of the time, and has these three other symptoms, he or she would potentially meet criteria for both GAD and dysthymia. In addition, uncontrollable worries may significantly overlap with depressive rumination, although one can distinguish between depressive rumination and anxious worry in that rumination is usually past-focused while worry is usually future-focused (Watkins et al., 2005). However, it may be the case that uncontrollable negative thoughts about past and future are driven by similar processes and are therefore highly likely to co-occur (Watkins et al.,

2005). The considerable overlap of the symptoms of these disorders is taken into account in *DSM–IV–TR* through the exclusion criteria for GAD, which exclude the diagnosis if it occurs exclusively during the course of an MDD.

Despite the significant symptom overlap between GAD and depressive disorders, there are features that distinguish the two. Patients with GAD are likely to experience muscle tension and are not required to exhibit depressive affect; in fact, these patients report lower levels of depression than individuals who meet criteria for MDD (Brown et al., 1997). Uncontrollable worry is also a cardinal feature of GAD, while it is not a criterion for depressive disorders. Furthermore, there are cognitive phenomena such as estimation of impending threats or "loomingness" (Riskind & Williams, 2005), attentional biases toward threat (Mathews & MacLeod, 2005), and intolerance of uncertainty (Dugas, Schwartz, & Francis, 2004) that apply primarily to GAD. Similarly, certain cognitive styles or attitudes are particular to depression such as a personal, permanent, pervasive attribution of negative events combined with a sense of hopelessness (e.g., Alloy et al., 2006), and negative thinking styles (Dugas et al., 2004).

PTSD

Like GAD, PTSD also has many overlapping symptoms with depressive disorders. Some researchers (e.g., McWilliams, Cox, & Asmundson, 2005) have reported data supporting four symptom classes for PTSD, one being dysphoria (reexperiencing, avoidance, and hyperarousal are the others). The symptoms of dysphoria that overlap with depression include loss of interest, foreshortened future, feeling distant from others, irritability, and decreased concentration. In fact, the overlapping symptoms of both GAD and PTSD with depression have led Watson et al. (2005) to recommend a recategorization of the mood disorders to include both PTSD and GAD under the rubric of distress disorders. The fact that PTSD may lead to depression is consistent with psychological models of MDD, including helplessness/hopelessness (Alloy et al., 2006) and interpersonal models (Joiner & Coyne, 1999).

As with GAD, there are features of PTSD that distinguish it from depressive disorders. While trauma is common in depression and may even lead to MDD more frequently than to PTSD (McQuaid et al., 2001), it is not a necessary feature of depression, as it is for PTSD. Additionally, the reexperiencing, hyperarousal, and avoidance criteria are distinct from MDD. Furthermore, individuals with

PTSD have different characteristics, including cognitive processes (Harvey et al., 2004), and cortisol responses to stress (Heim & Nemeroff, 2001).

SAD

With SAD and MDD there is less immediate apparent overlap in diagnostic criteria, but there is considerable overlap in the characteristics not depicted as part of the diagnostic criteria. Depression has a strong interpersonal component (Joiner & Coyne, 1999). In addition, social anxiety and depression both tend to have lower levels of positive affect (see Watson et al., 2005). Finally, interpersonal rejection sensitivity, a characteristic of atypical depression, is clearly also an important aspect of SAD (see Schneier et al., 2003). In fact, Parker et al. (2002) have argued that atypical depression is not a distinct phenomenon, but rather is comorbid MDD and SAD.

A number of factors help differentiate SAD and MDD. Phenomenologically, most SAD patients avoid social situations for fear of negative feedback from others, while depressed individuals are more concerned with negative self-evaluations. Furthermore, individuals with SAD become anxious when experiencing symptoms of arousal or blushing, while these are not major concerns with patients with MDD. Individuals with SAD can show interest in many topics and do not necessarily exhibit elevated levels of sadness or hopelessness. In addition, social anxiety is characterized by thoughts of negative evaluation, embarrassment, criticism, and rejection, while depression is characterized by thoughts of loss, deprivation, pessimism, guilt, worthlessness, and failure (e.g., Cho & Telch 2005). And SAD is uniquely characterized by overestimated probabilities and costs of negative social events, and underestimation of social competence (Harvey et al., 2004). Furthermore, there are multiple studies suggesting early biased attention to threat in social anxiety, but not in depression (Harvey et al., 2004). In fact, depression may even reduce the presence of earlier biases in patients with SAD (Harvey et al., 2004).

PD

Like SAD, PD does not have symptom criteria that explicitly overlap with depressive disorders. One factor that can complicate the differentiation of MDD and PD is that patients with MDD are at risk of having panic attacks during depressive episodes, without meeting criteria for PD. For example, among individuals in the NCS who did not have lifetime panic disorder, 6% of patients with a 1-year diagnosis of MDD reported having had panic attacks in the last 6 months, compared to only 1.3% of individuals without MDD. In addition, panic attacks have been shown to be a risk factor for the later development of MDD (e.g., Bittner et al., 2004). These issues notwithstanding, the distinction between PD and MDD is typically straightforward. In addition to symptom criteria, there are distinctions in PD compared with MDD in the types of thoughts and cognitive processes that occur (Woody et al., 1998), responses to panic challenges (e.g., Kent et al., 2001), and HPA axis responses (e.g., Kellner & Yehuda, 1999).

OCD

Obsessive-compulsive disorder, like panic disorder, is typically quite distinct from depressive disorders, even though there are high rates of comorbidity. There are neurobiological data suggesting that selective serotonin reuptake inhibitors (SSRIs) may act in different, specific areas of the brain in OCD compared with depression (Saxena et al., 2002). In addition, depression responds to non-SRI tricylic antidepressants whereas OCD does not (McNaughten & Coor, 2004). Two characteristics of MDD may be confused with OCD symptoms. First, depressive rumination may be confused with obsessions. This confusion is partially a semantic issue—colloquially, many individuals describe repeated thoughts as "obsessing," and therefore a depressed patient may describe being obsessed about the past. However, in order for guilt or past deeds to meet the criteria of obsessions, they should be consistent, repetitive thoughts, possibly followed by compulsions. In addition, OCD patients with thoughts of harming themselves or others may be considered depressed and suicidal. While many of these individuals are depressed about having these thoughts, there is no necessary relationship between self-harm obsessions and depressive thoughts.

SP

Typically thought to have the least overlap with depression, specific phobia is a fear disorder that does not usually include nonspecific levels of anxiety that are commonly related also to depression. Little research has been conducted examining the commonalities and distinctions in SP and MDD. However, cognitive processes in SP are similar to those in other anxiety disorders (Harvey et al., 2004), and some of these processes such as early attention to threat are not found in depressed individuals. In addition, SSRIs are not effective for SP whereas benzodiazepines, which are sometimes used clinically for specific phobias, are not effective for MDD (McNaughten & Coor, 2004).

Overall, it seems that symptom overlap may account for part of the prevalence of comorbidity in GAD, PTSD, and SAD, but it is less likely to account for comorbidity in PD, OCD, and SP. Anxiety disorders are characterized by apprehension about and hypervigilance for physical or social threat, cognitive biases toward these threats, response to benzodiazepines, SSRIs, and medications that act on multiple neurotransmitter systems (e.g., norepinephrine, serotonin), some differential metabolic changes when administered SSRIs, and certain differences in HPA-Axis responses. Thus, most levels of analysis suggest that while anxiety disorders and depression co-occur, they are distinct disorders.

Time Course of Comorbid Anxiety Disorders and Depression

Many discussions of comorbidity of anxiety disorders and depression have examined the temporal relationship between the two and have concluded that anxiety disorders frequently precede depression (e.g., Andrade et al., 2003; Mineka et al., 1998). It is important to note that these data are necessary but not sufficient to suggest causality. It is likely that many factors play a role in the temporal relationship of the disorders, including the age of onset. For example, Brown and colleagues (2001) found that in 68% of SAD, 64% of SP, 62% of GAD, 36% of PTSD, 49% of OCD, and 31% of PD patients, the onset of MDD occurred after the onset of the anxiety disorder. However, the average age of onset of MDD was 26.4, and average age of onset for anxiety disorders ranged from 15.7 (SAD) to 26.0 (PD). The correlation between age of onset of the anxiety disorder and the percentage of comorbid individuals for whom anxiety preceded depression is $r = -.83$ ($p < .05$), suggesting that age of onset itself strongly influences temporal relationships. Of course, these data need to be taken in the context of the significantly increased risk of depression in anxiety, which increases the likelihood of a true association (though causality requires further evidence). An additional analysis to examine the directionality of the impact of depression and anxiety is to determine whether the onset of depression is earlier for individuals with lifetime histories of anxiety disorders, suggesting that anxiety disorders influence the course of depression. A reexamination of data from the NCS (Kessler, 2006a) for the purpose of this chapter found that age of onset for MDD was typi-

cally 1 to 2 years earlier in patients with comorbid MDD and anxiety disorders except for GAD, for which the age of onset for MDD was the same for patients with and without GAD (all other $ps < .001$). Average age of onset for MDD without an anxiety disorder was approximately 24 years old, but compared with MDD and a comorbid anxiety disorder was as follows: SP = 22.0 +/– 9.6, PD = 21.7 +/– 8.9, SAD = 21.9 +/– 9.8, PTSD = 21.0 +/– 9.8, GAD 23.2 +/– 8.9. On the other hand, lifetime MDD did not affect the age of onset for SAD or PTSD ($ps > .05$), though it did affect GAD ($p < .01$), SP ($p < .05$), and PD ($p < .05$), although the latter effect sizes were extremely small.

In addition to affecting age of onset, do anxiety disorders constitute an increased risk for onset of MDD longitudinally, and if so, what are the aspects of anxiety disorders that lead to the onset of depression? In a retrospective analysis, Zisook et al. (2004) found that individuals with an age of onset of MDD before 18 were more likely to have OCD or PTSD than those with MDD onset after age 18. Goodwin (2002) examined the risk of onset of MDD from the first to second waves of the Epidemiological Catchment Area (ECA) study. Each of the anxiety disorders examined (OCD, SP, agoraphobia, and panic attacks) all independently contributed to the onset of MDD in the second wave of the ECA, even when adjusting for other mental illness and demographic factors. Merikangas et al. (2003) found individuals with anxiety disorders were at increased risk of developing comorbid depressive disorders or depressive disorders alone. In addition, they found that individuals with comorbid anxiety and depressive disorders were very likely to be stable over time. Bittner et al. (2004) found that each of the anxiety disorders created increased risk for onset of a depressive disorder even when controlling for other disorders, except that SP alone did not confer an increased risk. Aspects of anxiety disorders that led to increased risk for development of depression included the number of anxiety disorders, severity of impairment, frequency of avoidance, and presence of panic attacks (Bittner et al., 2004; Wittchen et al., 2000). In contrast to these findings, Pine et al. (1998) found that SP and SAD did not confer elevated risk of onset of depression, but depression did confer an increased risk for later onset of GAD.

A few longitudinal, epidemiological studies have examined other characteristics that may lead to the development of comorbid anxiety and depression. Wittchen et al. (2000) found that additional risk factors, including low school attainment, poor intimate relationships, overprotective family, early separation from a parent, chronic stress, temperament, and parental history of mental disorders, all contributed to the onset of comorbid anxiety and MDD. De Graaf et al. (2004) examined 3-year follow-up data from an epidemiological study and determined risk factors for development of comorbid mood and anxiety disorders beyond either a pure mood or pure anxiety disorder. Risk factors for the development of a mood disorder in the anxiety disorder group included childhood trauma, negative life events, and physical functioning.

Theories of Comorbidity

Given the evidence that individuals with anxiety disorders often have co-occurring depression, that this co-occurrence does not appear to be solely due to symptom overlap, and that the onset of anxiety disorders typically precedes the onset of depression, it is worth examining possible reasons for comorbidity. Approaches to understanding comorbidity have attempted to understand symptom and syndrome overlap on different explanatory levels, from biology to personality characteristics, cognitions, and behaviors. These approaches are not necessarily contradictory. Most of these explanations assume common underlying predispositions to both anxiety and depression.

Genetics

Twin and family studies that examine heritability of depression and anxiety have implicated specific genes in comorbidity. However, there is consensus that there is not a single gene that is involved in the development of comorbidity, but rather a series of polygene-environment interactions.

Family and twin studies have found different degrees of relationship between each of the anxiety disorders and major depression. The strongest evidence exists between GAD and MDD (see Middeldorp et al., 2005, for a review), though reasonable evidence exists for the genetic risk for comorbidity of anxiety disorders and depression overall. Some studies suggest that this underlying vulnerability may lie predominantly in personality traits such as neuroticism, while others suggest that anxiety disorders increase the risk for depression (and possibly that MDD increases the risk for GAD). After a thorough review of the literature on twin and family studies, Middeldorp et al. (2005) concluded that anxiety disorders and MDD are distinct entities, but that neuroticism appears to be a common

underlying vulnerability, and that it is possible that neural interconnections that are not involved in neuroticism may play a role in comorbidity.

One of the genes that has received particular emphasis is the serotonin-related gene (5-HT1A and 5-HTT; see Leonardo & Hen, 2006, for a review of these and others, including TPH; see also McNaughton & Corr, 2004). Polymorphisms in the 5-HT1A gene have been related to presence of anxiety and depression, and the 5-HTT gene is implicated in the mediating effects of SSRIs, which are generally effective for both mood and anxiety symptoms. In addition, a polymorphism in the 5-HTT gene (the double short version) has been related to the development of depression under stress (Caspi et al., 2003), and to a number of personality and psychological variables related to anxiety and depression such as anxiety sensitivity, harm avoidance, and neuroticism (see Leonardo & Hen, 2006, for a review). Finally, individuals with this gene also show greater amygdala activation under stress, and a disconnection between the amygdala and cingulate (Hariri et al., 2005), two areas implicated in anxiety and depression.

Neurophysiology

The prefrontal cortex, amygdala, and anterior cingulate have been implicated in both anxiety and depressive disorders (see Chapter 9; Liotti, & Mayberg, 2001). The amygdala is implicated as the emotional center of the brain and has been shown to play an important role in both anxiety and depression. Similarly, the prefrontal cortex appears to be generally underactive in anxiety and depression, though it may be overactive during rumination, obsessions, and worry (Chapter 9). There are also data showing decreased hippocampal volumes in individuals with PTSD and individuals with MDD (Heim, & Nemeroff, 2001).

Neurochemistry

In addition to a hypothesized overlap of serotonin deficiency in anxiety and mood disorders (McNaughton & Corr, 2004), there are other neurotransmitters and factors that are implicated in comorbidity. Similar to the work on genetics, the neurochemistry of mood and anxiety disorders is also increasingly based on interactions with the environment. For example, cholecystokinin (CCK) and endogenous opioids interact to relate to depression and anxiety (Hebb et al., 2005). In addition, significant emphasis has been placed on stress during early development and its relationship to the dysregulation of the hypothalamic pituitary adrenocortical (HPA) axis (see Heim & Nemeroff, 2001). There have been certain aspects of the HPA axis that distinguish anxiety disorders (especially PTSD) from depression such as response to dexamethasone suppression tests, circadian plasma cortisol, overall cortisol levels, and glucocorticoid receptor binding (Kellner et al., 1999). However, increased release of corticotrophin releasing factor (CRF) and decreased adrenocorticotropic hormone (ACTH) responses to CRF are similar in anxiety and depression. The majority of studies have examined the HPA axis in relation to PTSD and major depression (for a review on the role of hormonal factors in anxiety disorders, see Chapter 10).

Neuroticism/Extraversion, Negative and Positive Affect, and Temperament

One of the most common explanations for the overlap of anxiety disorders and depression is the common underlying personality trait of neuroticism. Significant research has been conducted showing that individuals with elevated neuroticism are at greater risk for both anxiety and mood disorders (e.g., Weinstock & Whisman, 2006). Another common personality construct is that of introversion/extraversion, which has been related more to depression and social anxiety, but not to other anxiety disorders. Personality researchers have increasingly compared the traits of neuroticism and introversion/extraversion to the constructs of negative and positive affect (Watson et al., 2005). Multiple reports have suggested that negative affect is common to both anxiety disorders and depression while lack of positive affect is related more specifically to SAD and depression (Watson et al., 2005). Some epidemiological and genetic studies have begun to investigate whether the co-occurrence of anxiety disorders and depression is accounted for by neuroticism (e.g., Middeldorp et al., 2005). These studies suggest that neuroticism clearly contributes to comorbidity, but that there continues to be increased risk for co-occurrence even after controlling for neuroticism. Overall, the data support the view that neuroticism or negative affect is an important component of the commonalities among the anxiety disorders and depression. More research is needed to determine the role of other factors such as anxiety sensitivity.

Within the sphere of developmental and personality theories, behavioral inhibition and behavioral activation have also been examined within the context of understanding comorbidity (Clark, 2005). Specifically, behavioral inhibition is suggested to be an early determinant of neuroticism and negative affect. Examinations of behaviorally inhibited children suggest they are at risk for later developing social anxiety (see Chapter 11). While some data do not support the notion of behavioral inhibition as a risk factor for depression, other research has suggested that a similar construct is related to anxiety and depression (Neal et al., 2002). It is likely that a global construct of behavioral inhibition is related to most anxiety disorders and to depression (Clark, 2005; McNaughton & Corr, 2004).

Perceived Control

Barlow and colleagues (2002) have noted that anxiety disorders commonly precede depressive disorders, and that lack of perceived control over threat leads to a feeling of helplessness and hopelessness (see Chapter 13). Similarly, Alloy et al. (2006) have noted as part of the helplessness/hopelessness model of depression that anxiety often precedes depression. They propose that underlying comorbid anxiety and depression is a lack of certainty about negative outcomes (leading to anxiety) and a feeling of being unable to control the outcome (helplessness leading to depression).

Interpersonal Mechanisms

As noted earlier, childhood trauma and adversity are risk factors for the development of anxiety and depression. In fact, one study found that approximately 30% of the overlap of anxiety and depression could be accounted for by childhood adversity (Brown, Harris, & Eales, 1996). Research on the development of social anxiety has suggested that parental hostility may be related to both negative social interpretations in social anxiety, and is a risk factor for depression (Taylor & Alden, 2005). It is likely that similar aspects of family function or (perceived criticism, hostility, etc.) play a role in most anxiety disorders (e.g., Chambless et al., 2001). Similarly, interpersonal interactions have been implicated in the maintenance of depression (Joiner & Coyne, 1999), GAD (Borkovec et al., 2002), PD (Carter et al., 1994), SAD (Taylor & Alden, 2005), and PTSD (Riggs et al., 1998). Whether the disturbances in interpersonal functioning are a consequence of neuroticism/behavioral inhibition or interact with such traits requires further examination. Regardless of whether interpersonal factors are common underlying features related to mood and anxiety disorders, their roles in maintenance and treatment are extremely important.

Information Processing Models

Information processing models also suggest that there are commonalities between anxiety disorders and MDD (see Mathews & MacLeod, 2005, for a review). Individuals with anxiety disorders and MDD tend to be more self-focused (Harvey et al., 2004), have recurrent negative memories, intrusive thoughts, selective attention to emotionally congruent stimuli, biased interpretations of ambiguous scenarios, and negative expectancies (Mathews & MacLeod, 2005). Thus, it is likely that there are underlying cognitive processes that are related to the manifestation of depression and anxiety. More recently, studies have begun to show that these cognitive biases may be predictive of or even causal in terms of their relationship to anxiety and depression (see Mathews & MacLeod, 2005).

Treating Comorbid Anxiety Disorders and Depression

Depression as a Predictor of Treatment Response

In general, patients with comorbid anxiety and depression have more severe anxiety symptoms. Severity of symptoms is usually a predictor of treatment outcome, and data do not consistently support the notion that depression affects treatment outcome above and beyond the increased severity of anxiety symptoms. However, a naturalistic study examining the course of anxiety disorders (SAD, PD, and GAD) found that presence of comorbid depression was a factor in decreasing the likelihood of remission of each of the disorders (Bruce et al., 2005).

Treating Comorbid Anxiety Disorders and Depression

Studies have suggested that medications such as SSRIs (e.g., Sonawalla et al., 2002) and venlafaxine (De Nayer et al., 2002) are effective in the treatment of both anxiety and depression. Psychosocial treatments, especially cognitive behavioral therapies (CBT), have also shown promise. However, CBT is usually more symptom-focused than medications and may require focus on both anxious and depressive symptoms to have a full effect (see Joorman et al., 2005). The following sections summarize the treatment outcome literature for each of the individual anxiety disorders.

Panic Disorder. The literature on panic and depression is much more fully developed than that for the other anxiety disorders (see Mennin & Heimberg, 2000). Many recent studies have not found major negative effects of depression on outcome in panic disorder (e.g., Barlow et al., 2000), and Tsao et al. (2005) found that depression decreases even when the focus of treatment is solely on panic.

Social Anxiety Disorder. The largest randomized controlled studies of treatments of SAD have excluded patients with comorbid depression (see Ledley et al., 2005). Given the high rates of co-occurrence, more information is needed on the treatment of individuals with comorbid SAD and MDD. Data from noncontrolled trials suggest that depression adversely impacts outcomes in that patients either have less symptom change (Chambless et al., 1997) or remain more symptomatic and impaired (Erwin et al., 2002), even if they do experience change at similar rates to nondepressed patients (i.e., they started worse, had similar amounts of change, and ended treatment worse off than nondepressed patients). In addition, depressive symptoms may impact outcome and attrition, even if the patient does not meet the threshold for MDD per se (Ledley et al., 2005). In one of the few studies examining medication treatment for comorbid SP and MDD, Schneier et al. (2003) found that citalopram was an effective treatment for both anxiety and depressive symptoms in this population. More research in this area is required to determine the best treatment strategies for patients with comorbid SAD and MDD.

OCD. The literature on treatment of OCD and comorbid depression also suggests that only severe depression may negatively impact the course of treatment and outcome of CBT (Abramowitz, 2004), and that depression does decrease with CBT. Similar results have been found with medication treatments. However, it may be that combined medication and CBT is the best option for comorbid OCD and MDD patients. More research is needed in this area.

GAD and PTSD. Given the diagnostic overlap of depression and GAD and depression and PTSD, relatively few studies have examined the impact of MMD as a predictor of outcome on these disorders. In fact, a review of the literature found only case studies. However, symptoms of depression have not been found to be a predictor of treatment outcome in either medication or psychosocial treatments, and many studies have found that depression is significantly reduced with treatment (e.g., Borkovec et al., 2002; Foa et al., 2005). There have been open label pharmacological studies of comorbid depression and GAD suggesting efficacy (Perugi et al., 2002), but there are no reports on psychosocial treatments for comorbid MDD and GAD or PTSD. However, both medication and psychosocial treatments show that treatment reduces both anxiety and depressive symptoms in patients with GAD or PTSD. Research regarding optimal treatment strategies (combined treatments, monotherapy, sequential treatments) for comorbid anxiety disorders and depression is required.

Summary and Conclusions

Overall, both MDD and dysthymia commonly co-occur with the anxiety disorders, affecting 20% to 40% of anxious patients. The pattern of comorbidity is somewhat different across the spectrum of anxiety disorders, with a particularly strong and distinct relationship between GAD and depression from phenomenological, epidemiological, genetic, and cognitive perspectives. Most other anxiety disorders show similar patterns, with the possibility that SP is most unique from MDD. Data are generally consistent with Barlow's hierarchical model of the anxiety disorders (see Mineka et al., 1998; Chapter 13), in which each of the anxiety disorders and depression contain unique components, but also common underlying negative affect. An integrative biopsychosocial model suggests that there are genetic commonalities between anxiety disorders and depressive disorders, with support from genetic data (e.g., 5-HTT) and twin/family studies. Psychosocial stressors such as early trauma impact upon these predisposing factors, and may lead to disrupted neuroendocrine functioning and prefrontal-cingulate-amygdala circuitry. These processes are potentially reflected by affective, cognitive, and behavioral responses that include early behavioral inhibition, increased negative affect, tendencies to interpret ambiguous scenarios negatively, avoidance, and impairment in many areas of functioning. Much work needs to be done to clarify the interplay of these various processes. Finally, current treatments for comorbid anxiety and mood disorders include SSRIs or atypical antidepressants, CBT, or their combination. However, randomized controlled trials examining the optimal treatments for these comorbid disorders have not been conducted, nor is it known whether combined treatments are necessary, or how to most effectively combine treatments (e.g., simultaneous versus sequential treatments).

References

Abramowitz, J. S. (2004). Treatment of obsessive-compulsive disorder in patients who have comorbid major depression. *Journal of Clinical Psychology, 60,* 1133–1141.

Alloy, L. B., Abramson, L. Y., Whitehouse, W. G., Hogan, M. E., Panzarella, C., & Rose, D. T. (2006). Prospective incidence of first onsets and recurrences of depression in individuals at high and low cognitive risk for depression. *Journal of Abnormal Psychology, 115,* 145–156.

American Psychiatric Association. (2000). *Diagnostic and statistical manual of mental disorders* (4th ed., text revision). Washington, DC: Author.

Andrade, L. H., Caraveo-Aduaga, J. J., Berglund, P., Bijl, R. V., de Graaf, R., Vollebergh, W., et al. (2003). The epidemiology of major depressive episodes: Results from the ICPE surveys. *International Journal of Methods in Psychiatric Research, 12,* 3–21.

Barlow, D. H. (2002). Anxiety and its disorders: The nature and treatment of anxiety and panic. 2nd ed. New York, Guilford Press.

Barlow, D. H., Gorman, J. M., Shear, M. K., & Woods, S. W. (2000). Cognitive-behavioral therapy, imipramine, or their combination for panic disorder: A randomized controlled trial. *Journal of the American Medical Association, 283,* 2529–2536.

Bittner, A., Goodwin, R. D., Wittchen, H., Beesdo, K., Höfler, M., & Lieb, R. (2004). What characteristics of primary anxiety disorders predict subsequent major depressive disorder? *Journal of Clinical Psychiatry, 65,* 618–626.

Borkovec, T. D., Newman, M. G., Pincus, A. L., & Lytle, R. (2002). A component analysis of cognitive-behavioral therapy for generalized anxiety disorder and the role of interpersonal problems. *Journal of Consulting and Clinical Psychology, 70,* 288–298.

Brown, G. W., Harris, T. O., & Eales, M. J. (1996). Social factors and comorbidity of depressive and anxiety disorders. *British Journal of Psychiatry, 168*(Suppl. 30), 50–57.

Brown, T. A., Campbell, L. A., Lehman, C. L., Grisham, J. R., & Mancill, R. B. (2001). Current and lifetime comorbidity of the *DSM–IV* anxiety and mood disorders in a large clinical sample. *Journal of Abnormal Psychology, 110,* 585–599.

Brown, T. A., Korotitsch, W., Chorpita, B. F. & Barlow, D. H. (1997). Psychometric properties of the Depression Anxiety Stress Scales (DASS) in clinical samples. *Behaviour Research and Therapy, 35,* 79–89.

Bruce, S. E., Yonkers, K. A., Otto, M. W., Eisen, J. L., Weisberg, R. B., Pagano, M., et al. (2005). Influence of psychiatric comorbidity on recovery and recurrence in generalized anxiety disorder, social phobia, and panic disorder: A 12-year prospective study. *American Journal of Psychiatry, 162,* 1179–1187.

Carter, M. M., Turovsky, J., & Barlow, D. H. (1994). Interpersonal relationships in panic disorder with agoraphobia: A review of empirical evidence. *Clinical Psychology: Science and Practice, 1,* 25–34.

Caspi, A., Sugden, K., Moffitt, T. E., Taylor, A., Craig, I. W., Harrington, H., et al. (2003). Influence of life stress on depression: Moderation by a polymorphism in the 5-HTT gene. *Science, 301,* 386–389.

Chambless, D. L., Bryan, A. D., Aiken, L. S., Steketee, G., & Hooley, J. M. (2001). Predicting expressed emotion: A study with families of obsessive-compulsive and agoraphobic outpatients. *Journal of Family Psychology, 15,* 225–240.

Chambless, D. L., Tran, G. Q., & Glass, C. R. (1997). Predictors of response to cognitive-behavioral group therapy for social phobia. *Journal of Anxiety Disorders, 11,* 221–240.

Cho, Y., & Telch, M. J. (2005). Testing the cognitive content-specificity hypothesis of social anxiety and depression: An application of structural equation modeling. *Cognitive Therapy and Research, 29,* 399–416.

Clark, L. A. (2005). Temperament as a unifying basis for personality and psychopathology. *Journal of Abnormal Psychology, 114,* 505–521.

De Graaf, R., Bijl, R. V., ten Have, M., Beekman, A.T.F., & Vollebergh, W.A.M. (2004). Pathways to comorbidity: The transition of pure mood, anxiety and substance use disorders into comorbid conditions in a longitudinal population-based study. *Journal of Affective Disorders, 82,* 461–467.

De Nayer, A., Geerts, S., Ruelens, L., Schittecatte, M., De Bleeker, E., & Van Eeckhoutte, I., et al. (2002). Venlafaxine compared with fluoxetine in outpatients with depression and concomitant anxiety. *International Journal of Neuropsychopharmacology, 5,* 115–120.

Dugas, M. J., Schwartz, A., & Francis, K. (2004). Intolerance of uncertainty, worry, and depression. *Cognitive Therapy and Research, 28,* 835–842.

Erwin, B. A., Heimberg, R. G., Juster, H., & Mindlin, M. (2002). Comorbid anxiety and mood disorders among persons with social anxiety disorder. *Behaviour Research and Therapy, 40,* 19–35.

Foa, E. B., Hembree, E. A., Cahill, S. P., Rauch, S.A.M., Riggs, D. S., Feeny, N. C., et al. (2005). Randomized trial of prolonged exposure for posttraumatic stress disorder with and without cognitive restructuring: Outcome at academic and community clinics. *Journal of Consulting and Clinical Psychology, 73,* 953–964.

Goodwin, R. D. (2002). Anxiety disorders and the onset of depression among adults in the community. *Psychological Medicine, 32,* 1121–1124.

Hariri, A. R., Drabant, E. M., Munoz, K. E., Kolachana, B. S., Mattay, V. S., Egan, M. F., et al. (2005). A susceptibility gene for affective disorders and the response of the human amygdala. *Archives of General Psychiatry, 62,* 146–152.

Harvey, A., Watkins, E., Mansell, W., & Shafran, R. (2004). *Cognitive behavioural processes across psychological disorders.* New York: Oxford University Press.

Hebb, A.L.O., Poulin, J., Roach, S. P., Zacharko, R. M., & Drolet, G. (2005). Cholecystokinin and endogenous opioid peptides: Interactive influence on pain, cognition, and emotion. *Progress in Neuropsychopharmacology and Biological Psychiatry, 29,* 1225–1238.

Heim, C., & Nemeroff, C. B. (2001). The role of childhood trauma in the neurobiology of mood and anxiety disorders: Preclinical and clinical studies. *Biological Psychiatry, 49,* 1023–1039.

Joiner, T., & Coyne, J. C. (Eds.). (1999). *The interactional nature of depression: Advances in interpersonal approaches.* Washington, DC: American Psychological Association.

Joormann, J., Kosfelder, J., & Schulte, D. (2005). The impact of comorbidity of depression on the course of anxiety treatments. *Cognitive Therapy and Research, 29,* 569–591.

Kellner, M., & Yehuda, R. (1999). Do panic disorder and posttraumatic stress disorder share a common psychoneuroendocrinology? *Psychoneuroendocrinology, 24,* 485–504.

Kent, J. M., Papp, L. A., Martinez, J. M., Browne, S. T., Coplan, J. D., Klein, D. F., et al. (2001). Specificity of panic response to CO_2 inhalation in panic disorder: A comparison with major depression and premenstrual dysphoric disorder. *American Journal of Psychiatry, 158,* 58–67.

Kessler, R. C. (2006a). *National Comorbidity Survey: Baseline* [Computer file]. Conducted by University of Michigan, Survey Research Center. ICPSR06693-v4. Ann Arbor, MI: Inter-university Consortium for Political and Social Research.

Kessler, R. C. (2006b). *National Comorbidity Survey: Replication (NCS-R), 2001–2003* [Computer file]. Conducted by Harvard Medical School, Department of Health Care Policy/University of Michigan, Survey Research Center. ICPSR04438-v3. Ann Arbor, MI: Inter-university Consortium for Political and Social Research.

Kessler, R. C., Chiu, W. T., Demler, O., & Walters, E. E. (2005). Prevalence, severity, and comorbidity of 12-month *DSM–IV* disorders in the National Comorbidity Survey Replication. *Archives of General Psychiatry, 62,* 617–627.

Kessler, R. C., McGonagle, K. A., Zhao, S., & Nelson, C. B. (1994). Lifetime and 12-month prevalence of *DSM–III–R* psychiatric disorders in the United States: Results from the National Comorbidity Study. *Archives of General Psychiatry, 51,* 8–19.

Kraemer, H. C., Wilson, K. A., & Hayward, C. (2006). Lifetime prevalence and pseudocomorbidity in psychiatric research. *Archives of General Psychiatry, 63,* 604–608.

Ledley, D. R., Huppert, J. D., Foa, E. B., Davidson, J.R.T., Keefe, F. J., & Potts, N.L.S. (2005). Impact of depressive symptoms on the treatment of generalized social anxiety disorder. *Depression and Anxiety, 22,* 161–167.

Leonardo, E. D., & Hen, R. (2006). Genetics of affective and anxiety disorders. *Annual Review of Psychology, 57,* 117–137.

Liotti, M., & Mayberg, H. S. (2001). The role of functional neuroimaging in the neuropsychology of depression. *Journal of Clinical and Experimental Neuropsychology, 23,* 121–136.

Mathews, A., & MacLeod, C. (2005). Cognitive vulnerability to emotional disorders. *Annual Review of Clinical Psychology, 1,* 167–195.

McNaughton, N., & Corr, P. J. (2004). A two-dimensional neuropsychology of defense: Fear/anxiety and defensive distance. *Neuroscience and Biobehavioral Reviews, 28,* 285–305.

McQuaid, J. R., Pedrelli, P., McCahill, M. E., & Stein, M. B. (2001). Reported trauma, post-traumatic stress disorder and major depression among primary care patients. *Psychological Medicine, 31,* 1249–1257.

McWilliams, L. A., Cox, B. J., & Asmundson, G.J.G. (2005). Symptom structure of posttraumatic stress disorder in a nationally representative sample. *Journal of Anxiety Disorders, 19,* 626–641.

Mennin, D. S., & Heimberg, R. G. (2000). The impact of comorbid mood and personality disorders in the cognitive-behavioral treatment of panic disorder. *Clinical Psychology Review, 20,* 339–357.

Merikangas, K. R., Zhang, H., Avenevoli, S., Acharyya, S., Neuenschwander, M., & Angst, J. (2003). Longitudinal trajectories of depression and anxiety in a prospective community study. *Archives of General Psychiatry, 60,* 993–1000.

Middeldorp, C. M., Cath, D. C., Van Dyck, R., & Boomsma, D. I. (2005). The co-morbidity of anxiety and depression in the perspective of genetic epidemiology: A review of twin and family studies. *Psychological Medicine, 35,* 611–624.

Mineka, S., Watson, D., & Clark, L. A. (1998). Comorbidity of anxiety and unipolar mood disorders. *Annual Review of Psychology, 49,* 377–412.

Neal, J. A., Edelmann, R. J., & Glachan, M. (2002). Behavioural inhibition and symptoms of anxiety and depression: Is there a specific relationship with social phobia? *British Journal of Clinical Psychology, 41,* 361–374.

Parker, G., Roy, K., Mitchell, P., Wilhelm, K., Malhi, G., & Hadzi-Pavlovic, D. (2002). Atypical depression: A reappraisal. *American Journal of Psychiatry, 159,* 1480–1481.

Perugi, G., Frare, F., Toni, C., Ruffolo, G., & Torti, C. (2002). Open-label evaluation of venlafaxine sustained release in outpatients with generalized anxiety disorder with comorbid major depression or dysthymia: Effectiveness, tolerability and predictors of response. *Neuropsychobiology, 46,* 145–149.

Pine, D. S., Cohen, P., Gurley, D., Brook, J., & Ma, Y. (1998). The risk for early-adulthood anxiety and depressive disorders in adolescents with anxiety and depressive disorders. *Archives of General Psychiatry, 55,* 56–64.

Riggs, D. S., Byrne, C. A., Weathers, F. W., & Litz, B. T. (1998). The quality of the intimate relationships of male Vietnam veterans: Problems associated with posttraumatic stress disorder. *Journal of Traumatic Stress, 11,* 87–101.

Riskind, J. H., & Williams, N. L. (2005). The looming cognitive style and generalized anxiety disorder: Distinctive danger schemas and cognitive phenomenology. *Cognitive Therapy and Research, 29,* 7–27.

Rush, A. J., Zimmerman, M., Wisniewski, S. R., Fava, M., Hollon, S. D., Warden, D., et al. (2005). Comorbid psychiatric disorders in depressed outpatients: Demographic and clinical features. *Journal of Affective Disorders, 87,* 43–55.

Saxena, S., Brody, A. L., Ho, M. L., Alborzian, S., Maidment, K. M., Zohrabi, N., et al. (2002). Differential cerebral metabolic changes with paroxetine treatment of obsessive-compulsive disorder vs. major depression. *Archives of General Psychiatry, 59,* 250–261.

Schneier, F. R., Blanco, C., Campeas, R., Lewis-Fernandez, R., Lin, S., Marshall, R., et al. (2003). Citalopram treatment of social anxiety disorder with comorbid major depression. *Depression and Anxiety, 17,* 191–196.

Sonawalla, S. B., Farabaugh, A., Johnson, M. W., Morray, M., Delgado, M. L., Pingol, M. G., et al. (2002). Fluoxetine treatment of depressed patients with comorbid anxiety disorders. *Journal of Psychopharmacology, 16,* 215–219.

Taylor, C. T., & Alden, L. E. (2005). Social interpretation bias and generalized social phobia: The influence of developmental experiences. *Behaviour Research and Therapy, 43,* 759–777.

Tsao, J.C.I., Mystkowski, J. L., Zucker, B. G., & Craske, M. G. (2005). Impact of cognitive-behavioral therapy for panic disorder on comorbidity: A controlled investigation. *Behaviour Research and Therapy, 43,* 959–970.

Watkins, E., Moulds, M., & Mackintosh, B. (2005). Comparisons between rumination and worry in a non-clinical population. *Behaviour Research and Therapy, 43,* 1577–1585.

Watson, D., Gamez, W., & Simms, L. J. (2005). Basic dimensions of temperament and their relation to anxiety and depression: A symptom-based perspective. *Journal of Research in Personality, 39,* 46–66.

Weinstock, L. M., & Whisman, M. A. (2006). Neuroticism as a common feature of the depressive and anxiety disorders: A test of the revised integrative hierarchical model in a national sample. *Journal of Abnormal Psychology, 115,* 68–74.

Wittchen, H., Kessler, R. C., Pfister, H., & Lieb, M. (2000). Why do people with anxiety disorders become depressed? A prospective-longitudinal community study. *Acta Psychiatrica Scandinavica, 102,* 14–23.

Woody, S. R., Taylor, S., McLean, P. D., & Koch, W. J. (1998). Cognitive specificity in panic and depression: Implications for comorbidity. *Cognitive Therapy and Research, 22,* 427–443.

Zisook, S., Rush, A. J., Albala, A., Alpert, J., Balasubramani, G. K., Fava, M., et al. (2004). Factors that differentiate early vs. later onset of major depression disorder. *Psychiatry Research, 129,* 127–140.

Anxiety Disorders and Personality Disorders Comorbidity

Mina Brandes *and* O. Joseph Bienvenu

Abstract

Symptoms of all the major personality disorder (PD) clusters have been noted in higher than expected numbers in patients with anxiety disorders; however, Cluster C characteristics appear particularly common. High neuroticism and some personality disorder traits predict later onset of anxiety disorders; conversely, anxiety disorders in adolescence appear to predict onset of PDs by adulthood. Temperament/personality traits such as behavioral inhibition, neuroticism, and Cluster C characteristics also appear to relate to anxiety disorders familially/genetically, and it remains unclear whether inherited personality traits are causal risk factors versus markers of susceptibility for anxiety disorders. Patients with comorbid anxiety and PDs, including Cluster B disorders, appear to have more functional impairment and suicidality. Patients with anxiety disorders and PDs appear to be more ill than those without PDs, but both groups generally respond to treatment. In fact, successful treatment of panic disorder often results in partial "normalization" of personality.

Keywords: anxiety disorders, comorbidity, personality, personality disorders

Anxiety disorders are strongly related to normal personality traits, as well as personality disorder traits. In this chapter, we examine the evidence for ways in which particular personality traits may relate to anxiety disorders, as well as clinical implications of particular personality profiles in patients with anxiety disorders. In this endeavor, we mainly focus on the recent literature. This is not meant to be an exhaustive review; rather, it is meant to illustrate issues of importance to this field using selected examples.

Theoretical and Practical Issues
Dimensions Versus Categories in Personality Disorder Assessment

Leaders in the personality/personality disorders field have continued to emphasize the relevance of considering personality in dimensional terms (i.e., less versus more of a trait), rather than categorical terms (i.e., presence or absence of so-called disorder)

(Widiger, Simonsen, Krueger, Livesley, & Verheul, 2005). It is likely that the next version of the *Diagnostic and Statistical Manual of Mental Disorders (DSM)* will reflect this change. As we shall outline, personality disorder dimensions *and* normal personality dimensions are important to consider in patients with anxiety disorders.

Two normal or general personality dimensions that appear in most personality taxonomies, and seem particularly relevant to the anxiety disorders, are neuroticism and extraversion. *Neuroticism* (also known as *negative affectivity* or *negative emotionality*) refers to one's tendency to experience *negative* emotions and cope poorly with stress. Persons high in neuroticism tend to feel transiently anxious, sad, angry, self-conscious, and vulnerable more often than persons who are low in neuroticism, who might be considered relatively "unflappable." *Extraversion,* on the other hand, refers to a person's tendency to be venturesome, energetic, assertive, sociable, and experience *positive* emotions (e.g., joy). Persons high in extraversion tend to be warm, gregarious, active, excitement-seeking, and emotionally bright compared to more introverted persons. Neuroticism and extraversion tend to be normally distributed in the population, like height or intelligence. These characteristics are also relatively independent of each other; one can be high in neuroticism and extraversion, high in one but not the other, or low in both.

Relationships Between Personality Disorder Traits and "Normal" or "General" Personality Traits

It is worth keeping in mind how personality disorder traits and normal personality traits relate. In a recent meta-analysis, Saulsman and Page noted that high neuroticism and disagreeableness (antagonism) were associated with *each* of the personality disorders. Borderline and dependent traits correlated particularly strongly with neuroticism, while avoidant traits correlated strongly with both neuroticism and introversion. Schizotypal traits also correlated relatively strongly with neuroticism and introversion (Saulsman & Page, 2004).

Generalized Anxiety Disorder as a Dimensional Construct

Some authors have suggested that generalized anxiety disorder (GAD) is better understood as a dimensional construct, as opposed to a categorical illness (Akiskal, 1998). Similar to the usual conception of personality traits, GAD is often described as "lifelong." That is, having a tendency toward high levels of stress and anxiety seems to describe what many patients with GAD are "like," rather than what they "have." It is important to note that GAD is not completely unique in this respect, as the same could be said about some patients with social

phobia (who report early pervasive distress in the context of social evaluation).

Comorbidity as Artifact: Overlapping Criteria and Constructs

Some authors have noted that strong associations between certain personality traits and anxiety disorders could be explained, at least in part, by overlap in criteria/constructs. For example, neuroticism and GAD, and avoidant personality disorder and social phobia, resemble one another to a great extent. Hettema and colleagues (Hettema, Prescott, & Kendler, 2004) have pointed out that some criteria for GAD (irritability, worrying, and nervousness) overlap with questions assessing neuroticism in the Eysenck Personality Questionnaire (Eysenck & Eysenck, 1975). Similarly, the *DSM–IV* (American Psychiatric Association, 1994) diagnostic criteria for avoidant personality disorder and social phobia are not identical, but do overlap in content (see Table 1). Though psychoanalytic writings sometimes mentioned obsessive-compulsive personality traits as being on a continuum with obsessive-compulsive disorder (OCD), it is notable that the current diagnostic criteria do not overlap, with one exception (hoarding). Though hoarding is not mentioned as a specific example of an OCD symptom in the *DSM–IV,* the associated mental phenomena and behaviors often appear to meet OCD criteria.

Relations Between Personality Traits and Anxiety Disorders
Normal Personality Traits and Anxiety Disorders: A Descriptive Summary

There are fairly consistent relationships between the general personality traits, neuroticism and extraversion, and anxiety disorders, in both clinical and nonclinical samples (Bienvenu & Stein, 2003). For instance, Bienvenu and colleagues studied the

Table 1. Overlapping *DSM–IV* Criteria for Social Phobia and Avoidant Personality Disorder

Social Phobia	Avoidant Personality Disorder
• Fear of social or performance situations in which the person is exposed to unfamiliar people or to possible scrutiny by others. The individual fears that he or she will act in a way that will be humiliating or embarrassing.	• Is preoccupied with being criticized or rejected in social situations. • Is unusually reluctant to take personal risks or to engage in any new activities because they may prove embarrassing.
• Feared situations are avoided or endured with anxiety or distress.	• Avoids occupational activities that involve significant interpersonal contact, because of fears of criticism, disapproval, or rejection.

distribution of normal personality traits in persons with and without lifetime anxiety disorders in the general population of east Baltimore (Bienvenu et al., 2004). Although the study group was oversampled for psychopathology, neuroticism and extraversion factor T-scores (mean = 50, standard deviation = 10) were fairly normally distributed in the sample and similar to external population norms (see Figure 1—center). Persons with specific phobia had neuroticism and extraversion scores that were similar to those of subjects without anxiety or depressive disorders (Figure 1—bottom right). In contrast, persons with social phobia or agoraphobia tended to be quite high in neuroticism, introverted, or both (Figure 1—right). Finally, persons with panic disorder, OCD, or GAD tended to be high in neuroticism and average, overall, in extraversion (Figure 1—left). Notably, there was substantial personality variability in each diagnostic group; for example, there were subjects with panic disorder who were not high in neuroticism, and there were individuals with social phobia who were not particularly high in neuroticism or low in extraversion.

Comorbidity among Axis I conditions is associated with greater treatment-seeking (Andrews, Slade, & Issakidis, 2002). Comorbidity among these conditions is also associated with high neuroticism (Andrews et al., 2002; Bienvenu et al., 2001), which may also relate to treatment-seeking.

Personality Disorder Traits and Anxiety Disorders in Clinical Settings: A Descriptive Summary

Symptoms of all of the major personality disorder groupings (i.e., odd, dramatic, and anxious clusters) have been noted in higher than expected numbers in patients with anxiety disorders (Bienvenu & Stein, 2003). In a large sample of outpatients with a primary diagnosis of anxiety disorder, Sanderson et al. found that at least one personality disorder was present in 35% (Sanderson, Wetzler, Beck, & Betz, 1994). By far, the most common personality disorders were from Cluster C (the "anxious/fearful" cluster), and patients with specific phobia had the lowest rates of personality disorders. In another fairly large sample comprising inpatients and outpatients with anxiety disorders, Skodol et al. found that 62% had at least one personality disorder (Skodol et al., 1995). Panic disorder was associated with borderline, avoidant, and dependent personality disorders; social phobia was associated with avoidant personality disorder; obsessive-compulsive disorder was associated with avoidant and obsessive-compulsive personality disorders; and specific phobia was not associated with any personality disorder. In the Harvard/Brown Anxiety Research Project, 24% of the patients had at least one personality disorder. Avoidant, obsessive-compulsive, dependent, and borderline were the most common.

The Collaborative Longitudinal Personality Disorders Study (CLPS) assessed comorbidity in patients selected for personality disorders. In this study, there were particularly high rates of posttraumatic stress disorder (PTSD) in patients with borderline personality disorder (46.9%), and there were particularly high rates of social phobia in patients with avoidant personality disorder (38.2%) (McGlashan et al., 2000). However, several other findings deserve mention. For example, 40.7% of patients with schizotypal personality disorder had panic disorder, and 33.7% had PTSD. Also, 29.4% of patients with obsessive-compulsive personality disorder had GAD.

Personality Disorder Traits and Anxiety Disorders in Community Settings: A Descriptive Summary

Until recently, there were few general population studies of personality disorder/anxiety disorder comorbidity, with a few exceptions. For example, Nestadt et al. found that compulsive personality traits were strongly related to GAD in the Baltimore Epidemiologic Catchment Area study (Nestadt, Romanoski, Samuels, Folstein, & McHugh, 1992).

In the recent National Epidemiologic Survey on Alcohol and Related Conditions (NESARC), personality disorders and Axis I conditions were assessed in a very large U.S. sample. Though some personality disorders were not assessed in the first wave (i.e., borderline, narcissistic, and schizotypal), this study provides a remarkable opportunity to assess personality/anxiety disorder comorbidity, unbiased by treatment-seeking behavior. In the NESARC, anxious cluster personality traits (i.e., avoidant, dependent, and, to a lesser extent, obsessive-compulsive) appear particularly common in general population subjects with anxiety disorders (Grant et al., 2005a). Avoidant and dependent traits were associated, in particular, with GAD and social phobia (Grant et al., 2005b). Similar to results in clinical samples, avoidant personality disorder was more strongly associated with social phobia than any other personality disorder (Grant et al., 2005c). Epidemiologic studies like the NESARC employ nonclinician interviewers and fully structured interviews, as opposed to clinicians and semistructured interviews (with "cross-examination" to establish the presence

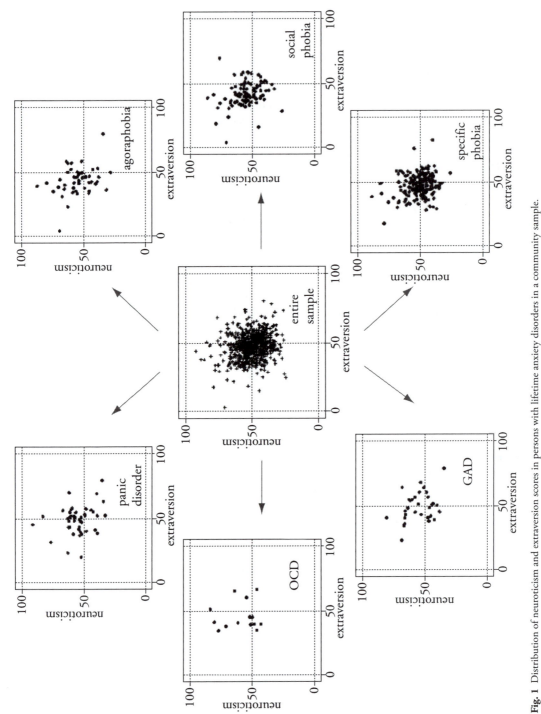

Fig. 1 Distribution of neuroticism and extraversion scores in persons with lifetime anxiety disorders in a community sample.

Note: OCD = obsessive-compulsive disorder; GAD = generalized anxiety disorder. Anxiety disorder diagnoses are not mutually exclusive, and the panel depicting the entire sample includes persons with anxiety disorders.

or absence of given criteria). Nevertheless, the very large sample size and rigorous survey methodology provide the field with important information.

In sum, anxiety disorders appear most strongly associated with Cluster C traits in both clinical and community samples. It will be interesting to determine whether borderline and schizotypal traits are also associated with anxiety disorders in the general population, or whether this comorbidity in clinical samples is due to Berkson's bias (Berkson, 1946).

Possible Causal Relationships

The associations outlined earlier lead to important questions regarding *why* personality traits relate to anxiety disorders. We review the evidence in response to 3 questions: (1) Are personality traits risk factors for anxiety disorders? (2) Are personality traits shaped by the experience of having an anxiety disorder? (3) Are personality traits and anxiety disorders manifestations of the same causes?

Are Personality Traits Risk Factors for Anxiety Disorders? Whether personality traits act as risk factors for anxiety disorders can be addressed by examining personality traits and anxiety disorders longitudinally.

Krueger examined general personality traits and anxiety disorders longitudinally in a cohort of young people in Dunedin, New Zealand. High baseline negative emotionality (an analogue of neuroticism) in late adolescence predicted onset of anxiety disorders by young adulthood (Krueger, 1999). Bramsen and colleagues measured predeployment personality traits in individuals involved in United Nations peacekeeping activities in the former Yugoslavia, using a short form of the Dutch Minnesota Multiphasic Personality Inventory (Bramsen, Dirkzwager, & van der Ploeg, 2000). *Psychoneuroticism* was a very strong predictor of onset of PTSD symptoms, second only to traumatic event exposure in predictive strength. Fauerbach and colleagues examined personality traits in survivors of severe burns. Higher baseline neuroticism and lower baseline extraversion predicted onset of PTSD during the following year in this group (Fauerbach, Lawrence, Schmidt, Munster, & Costa, 2000). Hayward and colleagues, in their 4-year, prospective study of high school students, found that high negative affectivity (another analogue of neuroticism) was a risk factor for 4-symptom panic attacks during adolescence (Hayward, Killen, Kraemer, & Taylor, 2000).

What about personality disorder traits? The Children in the Community Study provided evidence that schizotypal, antisocial, borderline, histrionic, and dependent personality traits present in adolescence and early adulthood (between ages 14 and 22) were associated with increased risk of having an anxiety disorder by middle adulthood (mean age of 33), controlling for baseline anxiety disorders (Johnson, Cohen, Kasen, & Brook, 2006). Bachar and colleagues showed that, among patients who presented to an emergency room following traumatic events, having a high narcissistic vulnerability at 1 week postevent was related to developing PTSD at 1 and 4 months postevent (Bachar, Hadar, & Shalev, 2005).

These studies show that personality traits prospectively predict the onset of anxiety disorders; however, it is important to consider that these studies do not fully elucidate some possible causal mechanisms involved. For example, personality traits could, in these cases, be (earlier) manifestations of genetic and/or environmental influences that also affect risk for anxiety disorders. It is also possible that personality traits are, in some cases, prodromal symptoms of anxiety disorders.

Are Personality Disorder Traits Consequences of Anxiety Disorders? It is commonly believed that personality is still being formed during childhood, adolescence, and perhaps young adulthood. Thus, it may be that personality traits are shaped by the experience of having (or having had) an anxiety disorder, at least in adolescence. We know of no studies, at present, that have assessed this possibility for normal personality traits.

Lewinsohn and colleagues followed subjects recruited from representative schools in western Oregon and found that adolescent anxiety disorders predicted schizotypal, schizoid, borderline, avoidant, and dependent personality traits in early adulthood, controlling for other adolescent Axis I disorders (Lewinsohn, Rohde, Seeley, & Klein, 1997). Unfortunately, Lewinsohn and colleagues did not assess the possibility that these personality traits might have already been present in adolescence. Kasen and colleagues took this area of research a step further in similar analyses of data from the Children in the Community Study (Kasen et al., 2001). They found that adolescent anxiety disorders predicted Cluster A ("odd cluster") and Cluster C personality disorders in young adulthood (when controlling for adolescent personality disorders and several other potentially relevant variables). In a further analysis of the data from the Children in the Community Study, Goodwin and colleagues found that having panic attacks during adolescence was associated with higher prevalence of having any personality disorder during young adulthood and more than threefold increased risk of having a Cluster C personality disorder, after adjusting for adolescent personality disorders (Goodwin, Brook, & Cohen, 2005).

However, the caveat about the possibility of personality traits and anxiety disorders having common etiologies still holds, in this case with personality traits being the later manifestations.

Are Personality Disorder Traits and Anxiety Disorders Manifestations of a Common Etiologic Process? Family studies suggest that personality traits may represent at least part of what is inherited in anxiety disorders. For example, a series of studies has related anxiety disorders to Kagan and colleagues' "behavioral inhibition to the unfamiliar" (Kagan, Reznick, & Snidman, 1987). Behaviorally inhibited children are cautious, quiet, introverted, and shy in unfamiliar situations. Rosenbaum and colleagues have shown that, when parents with panic disorder and agoraphobia were compared to control parents, the former group had higher rates of behaviorally inhibited children. In addition, when behaviorally inhibited children were compared with control children, the former group had higher rates of familial anxiety disorders (Rosenbaum et al., 1993). Similarly, Reich found that avoidant and dependent personality traits were more common in first-degree relatives of patients with panic disorder compared with relatives of controls (Reich, 1991). Also, Samuels and colleagues found that obsessive-compulsive personality traits and neuroticism were elevated in first-degree relatives of patients with OCD, compared with relatives of controls (Samuels et al., 2000). In addition, Stein and colleagues found that trait anxiety and harm avoidance (related to neuroticism and introversion) were elevated in relatives of probands with generalized social phobia, compared with relatives of control probands (Stein, Chartier, Lizak, & Jang, 2001). Finally, in a study of the Swedish general population, Tillfors et al. found that the risks for both social phobia and avoidant personality disorder were elevated if the subjects' parents had excessive social anxiety. The authors concluded that the two disorders reflect dimensions in a spectrum of social anxiety (Tillfors, Furmark, Ekselius, & Fredrikson, 2001). A caveat when considering family study results is that these designs do not differentiate genetic from common environmental effects.

In the past two decades, researchers have begun to use twin designs to determine whether genetic factors may help explain why personality traits are so strongly related to most anxiety disorders. For example, Jardine and colleagues used an Australian twin sample and found that genetic variation in *symptoms* of anxiety was largely dependent on the same factors that affected the neuroticism trait (Jardine, Martin, & Henderson, 1984). Similarly, Hettema and colleagues, using data from the Virginia Twin Registry, found cross-sectional evidence that the genes that influence neuroticism also influence risk for a variety of anxiety disorders (Hettema, Neale, Myers, Prescott, & Kendler, 2006).

Genetically informative longitudinal studies (e.g., twin studies) would be useful in ultimately determining whether inherited personality traits are themselves true risk factors for anxiety disorders, or whether personality traits are simply markers of an inherited spectrum that includes anxiety disorders (Bienvenu & Stein, 2003).

Clinical Course in Patients With Anxiety Disorders and Comorbid Personality Disorders
Effect of Comorbidity on Clinical Features and Severity of Anxiety Disorders

Patients with comorbid anxiety and personality disorders appear to suffer more functional impairment and have increased risk for suicidality. Dammen et al. found that panic disorder patients with personality disorders reported higher psychological distress and suicidal ideation, relative to individuals with panic disorder and no personality disorder (Dammen, Ekeberg, Arnesen, & Friis, 2000). Iketani and colleagues found that, in panic disorder patients seeking outpatient treatment, all who had made serious suicide attempts had a comorbid personality disorder. In particular, there was a significant association between suicide attempts and comorbid Cluster B ("dramatic cluster") personality disorders, especially borderline or histrionic (Iketani et al., 2004). Ozkan and Altindag found that panic disorder patients with comorbid personality disorders had lower Global Assessment of Functioning (GAF) scores. In addition, the presence of comorbid paranoid or borderline personality disorder predicted suicide attempts, and avoidant personality disorder predicted suicidal ideation (Ozkan & Altindag, 2005). Tenney and colleagues studied patients with OCD and found that those with a comorbid personality disorder had higher overall levels of functional impairment, as indicated by lower GAF scores (Tenney, Schotte, Denys, van Megen, & Westenberg, 2003). Baseline data from the CLPS showed that females with both borderline personality disorder and PTSD had lower GAF scores, and a higher percentage of them had more than one lifetime hospitalization than those with either disorder alone. Among women with PTSD, an additional diagnosis of borderline personality disorder was associated with greater suicide proneness (Zlotnick et al., 2003). Goodwin and Hamilton found that individuals with an anxiety disorder and antisocial personality disorder had more suicidal ideation and suicide attempts, compared to those with either disorder alone (Goodwin & Hamilton, 2003). Similarly, in two community surveys (the National Comorbidity Survey and the Ontario Health Survey), individuals with comorbid anxiety and antisocial behavior were found to have poorer quality of life and increased suicidal ideation compared to those with either syndrome alone (Sareen, Stein, Cox, & Hassard, 2004).

Effect of Comorbidity on Prognosis of Anxiety Disorders

Personality disorder traits have often been noted to predict worse treatment outcomes in patients with Axis I conditions (Reich & Vasile, 1993). In a review of factors that predict nonresponse to pharmacotherapy in panic disorder patients, Slaap and den Boer concluded that comorbid personality disorder traits were among the strongest predictors of nonresponse to pharmacotherapy, in both short-term and long-term studies (Slaap & den Boer, 2001). Massion et al. found that patients with GAD and comorbid avoidant or dependent personality disorders had a lower probability of remission at 5 years than those without personality disorders (Massion et al., 2002). In a treatment study of patients with panic disorder, Berger et al. found that comorbid personality disorders, particularly avoidant, were associated with a delayed response to treatment (Berger et al., 2004). Prasko et al. found that, in the short-term, the combination of cognitive behavioral therapy and pharmacotherapy were more effective in patients with panic disorder and/or agoraphobia without personality disorders, compared to those with a comorbid personality disorder (Prasko et al., 2005).

Encouragingly, as noted by Dreessen and Arntz, when baseline severity of illness is taken into account, patients with substantial personality disorder traits and anxiety disorders often seem to improve as much with treatment as patients without substantial personality pathology (Dreessen & Arntz, 1998). That is, there appears to be "parallel" improvement. It seems likely that such patients will need more therapeutic attention, such as intensive and individualized cognitive behavioral interventions, and

perhaps additional medications, in order to experience relief from their anxiety symptoms (Berger et al., 2004; Reich, 2003).

Special Considerations Regarding Obsessive-Compulsive Disorder With Schizotypal Personality Disorder. Patients with OCD and substantial schizotypal personality traits frequently seem to have poorer responses to treatment (Dreessen & Arntz, 1998). While schizotypal personality disorder may not be particularly common among patients with OCD (Samuels et al., 2000), its relationship to poor treatment outcome is fairly consistent (Fricke et al., 2005). Results of a recent study by Moritz and colleagues suggest that it may be the so-called positive schizotypal symptoms (e.g., unusual perceptual experiences) that predict failure of traditional treatments (e.g., serotonin reuptake inhibitors and behavioral therapy) (Moritz et al., 2004). These positive symptoms appear discontinuous from normal personality traits, unlike the avoidant and dependent personality traits that are so common among persons with anxiety disorders. As Moritz and colleagues suggest, patients with positive schizotypal symptoms and OCD may respond better to low-dose atypical neuroleptics and specifically tailored behavioral interventions.

Impact of Treatment of Anxiety Disorders on Comorbid Personality Disorders

There is evidence to suggest that, in individuals with comorbid panic and personality disorders, successful treatment of the anxiety disorder results in at least partial "normalization" of personality traits.

Using the data from the CLPS, Shea and colleagues found that borderline personality disorder patients whose panic disorder was unremitting were less likely to remit from borderline personality disorder (Shea et al., 2004). Marchesi and colleagues, in their 1-year prospective, controlled pharmacotherapy study of patients with panic disorder, found that, after treatment, the rate of comorbid personality disorder decreased from 60% to 43% (Marchesi, Cantoni, Fonto, Giannelli, & Maggini, 2005). This was mainly accounted for by the reduction in the rate of paranoid, avoidant, and dependent traits. In fact, a decrease in avoidant traits was observed only in patients who remitted from panic disorder.

It should be noted that the results of these studies do not necessarily indicate that personality changes with successful treatment result in a return to *premorbid* function. For example, it may be that pharmacologic and psychotherapeutic interventions have effects on personality traits themselves (presumably temporary, in the pharmacologic case) (Jorm, 1989; Knutson et al., 1998). Interestingly, although these patients' personalities normalize to some extent with successful treatment, there is some evidence that their personalities remain differentiable from normal controls (Reich, Noyes, Hirschfeld, Coryell, & O'Gorman, 1987). It is impossible to tell without truly prospective designs whether these differences from controls are "scar" effects of having had an episode of panic disorder.

Conclusion

Personality traits and most anxiety disorders are strongly related. Personality traits may be risk factors for anxiety disorders, consequences of anxiety disorders, or may share common underlying etiologies with anxiety disorders. Future work should further clarify causal relationships. Personality traits also appear to affect the clinical severity and prognosis of anxiety disorders, and vice versa.

References

Akiskal, H. S. (1998). Toward a definition of generalized anxiety disorder as an anxious temperament type. *Acta Psychiatrica Scandinavica, 98*(Suppl. 393), 66–73.

American Psychiatric Association. (1994). *Diagnostic and statistical manual of mental disorders* (4th ed.). Washington, DC: Author.

Andrews, G., Slade, T., & Issakidis, C. (2002). Deconstructing current comorbidity: Data from the Australian National Survey of Mental Health and Well-Being. *British Journal of Psychiatry, 181*, 306–314.

Bachar, E., Hadar, H., & Shalev, A. Y. (2005). Narcissistic vulnerability and the development of PTSD: A prospective study. *Journal of Nervous and Mental Disease, 193*, 762–765.

Berger, P., Sachs, G., Amering, M., Holzinger, A., Bankier, B., & Katschnig, H. (2004). Personality disorder and social anxiety predict delayed response in drug and behavioral treatment of panic disorder. *Journal of Affective Disorders, 80*, 75–78.

Berkson, J. (1946). Limitations of the application of the fourfold table analysis to hospital data. *Biometrics Bulletin, 2*, 47–53.

Bienvenu, O. J., Brown, C., Samuels, J. F., Liang, K. Y., Costa, P. T., Eaton, W. W., et al. (2001). Normal personality traits and comorbidity among phobic, panic and major depressive disorders. *Psychiatry Research, 102*, 73–85.

Bienvenu, O. J., Samuels, J. F., Costa, P. T., Reti, I. M., Eaton, W. W., & Nestadt, G. (2004). Anxiety and depressive disorders and the five-factor model of personality: A higher- and lower-order personality trait investigation in a community sample. *Depression and Anxiety, 20*, 92–97.

Bienvenu, O. J., & Stein, M. B. (2003). Personality and anxiety disorders: A review. *Journal of Personality Disorders, 17*, 139–151.

Bramsen, I., Dirkzwager, A. J., & van der Ploeg, H. M. (2000). Predeployment personality traits and exposure to trauma as predictors of posttraumatic stress symptoms: A prospective study of former peacekeepers. *American Journal of Psychiatry, 157*, 1115–1119.

Dammen, T., Ekeberg, O., Arnesen, H., & Friis, S. (2000). Personality profiles in patients referred for chest pain: Investigation with emphasis on panic disorder patients. *Psychosomatics, 41*, 269–276.

Dreessen, L., & Arntz, A. (1998). The impact of personality disorders on treatment outcome of anxiety disorders: Best-evidence synthesis. *Behaviour Research and Therapy, 36*, 483–504.

Eysenck, H. J., & Eysenck, S.B.G. (1975). *Eysenck Personality Questionnaire Manual.* London: Hodder and Stoughton.

Fauerbach, J. A., Lawrence, J. W., Schmidt, C. W., Jr., Munster, A. M., & Costa, P. T., Jr. (2000). Personality predictors of injury-related posttraumatic stress disorder. *Journal of Nervous and Mental Disease, 188*, 510–517.

Fricke, S., Moritz, S., Andresen, B., Jacobsen, D., Kloss, M., Rufer, M., et al. (2005). Do personality disorders predict negative treatment outcome in obsessive-compulsive disorders? A prospective 6-month follow-up study. *European Psychiatry, 21*, 319–324.

Goodwin, R. D., Brook, J. S., & Cohen, P. (2005). Panic attacks and the risk of personality disorder. *Psychological Medicine, 35*, 227–235.

Goodwin, R. D., & Hamilton, S. P. (2003). Lifetime comorbidity of antisocial personality disorder and anxiety disorders among adults in the community. *Psychiatry Research, 117*, 159–166.

Grant, B. F., Hasin, D. S., Blanco, C., Stinson, F. S., Chou, S. P., Goldstein, R. B., et al. (2005c). The epidemiology of social anxiety disorder in the United States: Results from the National Epidemiologic Survey on Alcohol and Related Conditions. *Journal of Clinical Psychiatry, 66*, 1351–1361.

Grant, B. F., Hasin, D. S., Stinson, F. S., Dawson, D. A., Patricia Chou, S., June Ruan, W., et al. (2005a). Co-occurrence of 12-month mood and anxiety disorders and personality disorders in the U.S.: Results from the national epidemiologic survey on alcohol and related conditions. *Journal of Psychiatric Research, 39*, 1–9.

Grant, B. F., Hasin, D. S., Stinson, F. S., Dawson, D. A., June Ruan, W., Goldstein, R. B., et al. (2005b). Prevalence, correlates, co-morbidity, and comparative disability of *DSM–IV* generalized anxiety disorder in the USA: Results from the National Epidemiologic Survey on Alcohol and Related Conditions. *Psychological Medicine, 35*, 1747–1759.

Hayward, C., Killen, J. D., Kraemer, H. C., & Taylor, C. B. (2000). Predictors of panic attacks in adolescents. *Journal of the American Academy of Child and Adolescent Psychiatry, 39*, 207–214.

Hettema, J. M., Neale, M. C., Myers, J. M., Prescott, C. A., & Kendler, K. S. (2006). A population-based twin study of the relationship between neuroticism and internalizing disorders. *American Journal of Psychiatry, 163*, 857–864.

Hettema, J. M., Prescott, C. A., & Kendler, K. S. (2004). Genetic and environmental sources of covariation between generalized anxiety disorder and neuroticism. *American Journal of Psychiatry, 161*, 1581–1587.

Iketani, T., Kiriike, N., Stein, M. B., Nagao, K., Minamikawa, N., Shidao, A., et al. (2004). Patterns of axis II comorbidity in early-onset versus late-onset panic disorder in Japan. *Comprehensive Psychiatry, 45*, 114–120.

Jardine, R., Martin, N. G., & Henderson, A. S. (1984). Genetic covariation between neuroticism and the symptoms of anxiety and depression. *Genetic Epidemiology, 1*, 89–107.

Johnson, J. G., Cohen, P., Kasen, S., & Brook, J. S. (2006). Personality disorders evident by early adulthood and risk for anxiety disorders during middle adulthood. *Journal of Anxiety Disorders, 20,* 408–426.

Jorm, A. F. (1989). Modifiability of trait anxiety and neuroticism: A meta-analysis of the literature. *Australian and New Zealand Journal of Psychiatry, 23,* 21–29.

Kagan, J., Reznick, J. S., & Snidman, N. (1987). The physiology and psychology of behavioral inhibition in children. *Child Development, 58,* 1459–1473.

Kasen, S., Cohen, P., Skodol, A. E., Johnson, J. G., Smailes, E., & Brook, J. S. (2001). Childhood depression and adult personality disorder: Alternative pathways of continuity. *Archives of General Psychiatry, 58,* 231–236.

Knutson, B., Wolkowitz, O. M., Cole, S. W., Chan, T., Moore, E. A., Johnson, R. C., et al. (1998). Selective alteration of personality and social behavior by serotonergic intervention. *American Journal of Psychiatry, 155,* 373–379.

Krueger, R. F. (1999). Personality traits in late adolescence predict mental disorders in early adulthood: A prospective-epidemiological study. *Journal of Personality, 67,* 39–65.

Lewinsohn, P. M., Rohde, P., Seeley, J. R., & Klein, D. N. (1997). Axis II psychopathology as a function of Axis I disorders in childhood and adolescence. *Journal of the American Academy of Child and Adolescent Psychiatry, 36,* 1752–1759.

Marchesi, C., Cantoni, A., Fonto, S., Giannelli, M. R., & Maggini, C. (2005). The effect of pharmacotherapy on personality disorders in panic disorder: A one year naturalistic study. *Journal of Affective Disorders, 89,* 189–194.

Massion, A. O., Dyck, I. R., Shea, M. T., Phillips, K. A., Warshaw, M. G., & Keller, M. B. (2002). Personality disorders and time to remission in generalized anxiety disorder, social phobia, and panic disorder. *Archives of General Psychiatry, 59,* 434–440.

McGlashan, T. H., Grilo, C. M., Skodol, A. E., Gunderson, J. G., Shea, M. T., Morey, L. C., et al. (2000). The Collaborative Longitudinal Personality Disorders Study: Baseline Axis I/II and II/II diagnostic co-occurrence. *Acta Psychiatrica Scandinavica, 102,* 256–264.

Moritz, S., Fricke, S., Jacobsen, D., Kloss, M., Wein, C., Rufer, M., et al. (2004). Positive schizotypal symptoms predict treatment outcome in obsessive-compulsive disorder. *Behaviour Research and Therapy, 42,* 217–227.

Nestadt, G., Romanoski, A. J., Samuels, J. F., Folstein, M. F., & McHugh, P. R. (1992). The relationship between personality and *DSM–III* Axis I disorders in the population: Results from an epidemiologic survey. *American Journal of Psychiatry, 149,* 1228–1233.

Ozkan, M., & Altindag, A. (2005). Comorbid personality disorders in subjects with panic disorder: do personality disorders increase clinical severity? *Comprehensive Psychiatry, 46,* 20–26.

Prasko, J., Houbova, P., Novak, T., Zalesky, R., Espa-Cervena, K., Paskova, B., et al. (2005). Influence of personality disorder on the treatment of panic disorder—comparison study. *Neuro Endocrinology Letters, 26,* 667–674.

Reich, J. (1991). Avoidant and dependent personality traits in relatives of patients with panic disorder, patients with dependent personality disorder, and normal controls. *Psychiatry Research, 39,* 89–98.

Reich, J. (2003). The effect of Axis II disorders on the outcome of treatment of anxiety and unipolar depressive disorders: A review. *Journal of Personality Disorders, 17,* 387–405.

Reich, J., Noyes, R., Jr., Hirschfeld, R., Coryell, W., & O'Gorman, T. (1987). State and personality in depressed and panic patients. *American Journal of Psychiatry, 144,* 181–187.

Reich, J. H., & Vasile, R. G. (1993). Effect of personality disorders on the treatment outcome of axis I conditions: An update. *Journal of Nervous and Mental Disease, 181,* 475–484.

Rosenbaum, J. F., Biederman, J., Bolduc-Murphy, E. A., Faraone, S. V., Chaloff, J., Hirshfeld, D. R., et al. (1993). Behavioral inhibition in childhood: A risk factor for anxiety disorders. *Harvard Review of Psychiatry, 1,* 2–16.

Samuels, J., Nestadt, G., Bienvenu, O. J., Costa, P. T., Jr., Riddle, M. A., Liang, K. Y., et al. (2000). Personality disorders and normal personality dimensions in obsessive-compulsive disorder. *British Journal of Psychiatry, 177,* 457–462.

Sanderson, W. C., Wetzler, S., Beck, A. T., & Betz, F. (1994). Prevalence of personality disorders among patients with anxiety disorders. *Psychiatry Research, 51,* 167–174.

Sareen, J., Stein, M. B., Cox, B. J., & Hassard, S. T. (2004). Understanding comorbidity of anxiety disorders with antisocial behavior: Findings from two large community surveys. *Journal of Nervous and Mental Disease, 192,* 178–186.

Saulsman, L. M., & Page, A. C. (2004). The five-factor model and personality disorder empirical literature: A meta-analytic review. *Clinical Psychology Review, 23,* 1055–1085.

Shea, M. T., Stout, R. L., Yen, S., Pagano, M. E., Skodol, A. E., Morey, L. C., et al. (2004). Associations in the course of personality disorders and Axis I disorders over time. *Journal of Abnormal Psychology, 113,* 499–508.

Skodol, A. E., Oldham, J. M., Hyler, S. E., Stein, D. J., Hollander, E., Gallaher, P. E., et al. (1995). Patterns of anxiety and personality disorder comorbidity. *Journal of Psychiatric Research, 29,* 361–374.

Slaap, B. R., & den Boer, J. A. (2001). The prediction of non-response to pharmacotherapy in panic disorder: A review. *Depression and Anxiety, 14,* 112–122.

Stein, M. B., Chartier, M. J., Lizak, M. V., & Jang, K. L. (2001). Familial aggregation of anxiety-related quantitative traits in generalized social phobia: Clues to understanding "disorder" heritability? *American Journal of Medical Genetics, 105,* 79–83.

Tenney, N. H., Schotte, C. K., Denys, D. A., van Megen, H. J., & Westenberg, H. G. (2003). Assessment of *DSM–IV* personality disorders in obsessive-compulsive disorder: Comparison of clinical diagnosis, self-report questionnaire, and semi-structured interview. *Journal of Personality Disorders, 17,* 550–561.

Tillfors, M., Furmark, T., Ekselius, L., & Fredrikson, M. (2001). Social phobia and avoidant personality disorder as related to parental history of social anxiety: A general population study. *Behaviour Research Therapy, 39,* 289–298.

Widiger, T. A., Simonsen, E., Krueger, R., Livesley, W. J., & Verheul, R. (2005). Personality disorder research agenda for the *DSM–V. Journal of Personal Disorders, 19,* 315–338.

Zlotnick, C., Johnson, D. M., Yen, S., Battle, C. L., Sanislow, C. A., Skodol, A. E., et al. (2003). Clinical features and impairment in women with borderline personality disorder (BPD) with post-traumatic stress disorder (PTSD), BPD without PTSD, and other personality disorders with PTSD. *Journal of Nervous and Mental Disease, 191,* 706–713.

46 Anxiety Disorders and Physical Comorbidity

Shay-Lee Belik, Jitender Sareen *and* Murray B. Stein

Abstract

Comorbidity of anxiety disorders and physical illnesses is common, and has the potential to negatively impact the individual. Nevertheless, anxiety often remains undetected in medical settings. The aim of this chapter is to explore these comorbidities with respect to a number of physical conditions and their specific associations with anxiety disorders. Several studies have illustrated an association between anxiety and physical conditions. The physical conditions demonstrating the strongest findings of an association with anxiety disorders have been with asthma, gastrointestinal problems, chronic pain conditions, and cardiac disorders. Among the anxiety disorders, posttraumatic stress disorder and panic disorder seem to have the greatest evidence for association with several physical conditions. Mechanisms and clinical implications are discussed.

Keywords: autoimmune disorders, cancer, cardiac disorders, chronic pain, comorbidity, gastrointestinal disorders, medical, metabolic disorders, neurologic disorders, respiratory disorders

In recent years there has been an expanding body of literature around the association between anxiety disorders and physical illnesses, particularly due to the fact that anxious patients have increasingly sought mental health treatment in primary and general health care settings (e.g., Regier et al., 1993; Young, Klap, Sherbourne, & Wells, 2001). Evidence for the common co-occurrence of anxiety and general medical conditions comes from two main settings: (1) general medical or specialty clinical samples, and (2) community/epidemiologic samples. In particular, a number of clinical studies of individuals with specific physical illnesses (e.g., Ginzburg, Solomon, & Bleich, 2002; Goodwin et al., 2003b; Heszen-Niejodek, Gottschalk, & Januszek, 1999; Paterniti et al., 1999; Simon et al., 2002; Thomas, Jones, Scarinci, & Brantley, 2003) have noted higher than expected levels of anxiety disorders among patients seeking treatment for physical conditions. Similarly, large-scale epidemiologic studies have found a

positive association between the presence of an anxiety disorder and presence of a physical illness (e.g., Goodwin, Jacobi, & Thefeld, 2003a; Goodwin & Stein, 2002; Honda & Goodwin, 2004; Huovinen, Kaprio, & Koskenvuo, 2001). It is unclear, however, whether the strength of the association between anxiety disorders and physical conditions can be attributed to an increased frequency of treatment-seeking or reporting of somatic symptoms among those with such comorbidity.

The association between anxiety disorders and physical illness deserves attention as it has been linked to a range of negative outcomes, including increased nonsuicide related mortality (Kawachi et al., 1994) and disability. A recent study by Sareen et al. (2006) explored the relationship between physical disorders and anxiety disorders using the German Health Survey, a nationally representative sample of individuals aged 18–65 years from the noninstitutionalized German population ($n = 4,181$). This was the first study to systematically evaluate the association between anxiety disorders and physical conditions in a large epidemiologic sample that included standardized physician-based diagnosis of physical health conditions. Table 1 identifies the main findings of this study. Sareen et al. (2006) demonstrated that the presence of one or more anxiety disorders was uniquely associated with a broad range of physician-diagnosed physical conditions and that comorbidity of anxiety disorders with physical conditions was associated with increased likelihood of poor quality of life and disability compared to a physical condition alone.

The comorbidity between anxiety disorders and physical conditions has been the focus of a number of investigations; however, the underlying causal pathways remain unknown and may be the result of a variety of factors. In the context of a physical condition, the anxiety disorder could be a pathophysiologic consequence of the metabolic or physiologic effects of the physical disorder, a psychological reaction to the experience of having a serious medical illness, or a side effect of the treatment of a medical condition. Previous work has suggested that the anxiety disorder may, in many instances, precede the onset of medical conditions among individuals with comorbidity (Sareen et al., 2006). For example, the presence of an anxiety disorder may increase the likelihood of physical illness through biological mechanisms (e.g., changes in the hypothalamic-pituitary axis system), or as a consequence of a substance use disorder that has developed as a result of the anxiety disorder. Shared risk factors, including environmental, personality, or genetic factors, may predispose individuals to both physical illness and anxiety disorders. Research has indicated that childhood adversity (Levitan, Rector, Sheldon, & Goering, 2003), socioeconomic disadvantage, and some personality variables (Goodwin, Cox, & Clara, 2006) may lead individuals to be at greater risk of both anxiety disorders and physical illness. An important caveat in considering this review is that the vast majority of studies in this area are cross-sectional and thus preclude any causal inferences.

The aim of this chapter is to explore these comorbidities with respect to a number of physical illnesses and their specific associations with anxiety disorders. Although some disorders may fit under multiple headings equally well (e.g., migraine may fit within chronic pain or neurologic disorders), we have chosen to place them where they appear to be most similar to other disorders under that heading.

Inclusion of previous studies is selective, not exhaustive, with our main focus being to include data of the highest quality for each physical condition. We included peer-reviewed literature that has been published over the last 20 years and relevant publications from earlier years. We used a PubMed search that included search terms related to anxiety disorders, anxiety, medical conditions, physical conditions, the names of the disorder groupings discussed below, and the names of individual physical conditions within these categories.

Cardiac Disorders

Among the physical conditions, there is a strong body of literature suggesting a link between anxiety disorders and cardiac conditions. Increasing evidence from a number of prospective longitudinal studies has implicated high levels of chronic phobic anxiety as a risk factor for fatal coronary heart disease (CHD) sudden cardiac death (SCD) among both men and women (Albert, Chae, Rexrode, Manson, & Kawachi, 2005; Kawachi et al., 1994; Kubzansky, Kawachi, Weiss, & Sparrow, 1998). In three prospective cohort studies involving men (Haines, Imeson, & Meade, 1987; Kawachi et al., 1994; Kawachi, Sparrow, Vokonas, & Weiss, 1994) and one prospective cohort involving women (Albert et al., 2005), high levels of phobic anxiety, as measured by a score of 4 or greater on the Crown-Crisp index at baseline, were associated with an elevated risk of SCD and fatal CHD during 2-year follow-up. This association remained significant in models that adjusted for age and a broad range of major cardiovascular risk factors, such as cigarette smoking, alcohol intake, and body mass index. Additionally, higher levels of phobic anxiety have been shown to be related to a higher resting heart rate and lower heart rate variability (Kawachi et al., 1994). These results suggest an association between phobic anxiety and altered cardiac autonomic control and may predispose individuals to increased risk of sudden cardiac death.

The onset of a life-threatening disease, such as myocardial infarction (MI), has been demonstrated to be associated specifically with posttraumatic stress symptoms (Bennett, Conway, Clatworthy, Brooke, & Owen, 2001; Ginzburg et al., 2002). A longitudinal study of posttraumatic stress disorder (PTSD) among MI patients found that 7 months post-MI, 16% of the patients were identified with PTSD (Ginzburg, 2006). Above-threshold PTSD symptoms have been shown to have a negative effect on adherence to medications 6 months to 1 year

Table 1. Summary of Findings of Sareen et al. (2006)

	Cardiac	Gastrointestinal	Respiratory	Metabolic	Chronic Pain	Any Physical Illness
Prevalence (past month) of anxiety disorders in those with physical illness	–13% of individuals with a cardiac disease had an anxiety disorder –8.9% of individuals with hypertension had an anxiety disorder	–18.8% of individuals with a gastrointestinal disease had an anxiety disorder	–15.2% of individuals with respiratory diseases had an anxiety disorder –12.0% of individuals with allergic conditions had an anxiety disorder	–10.6% of individuals with diabetes had an anxiety disorder –14.8% of individuals with thyroid disease had an anxiety disorder	–10.7% of individuals with arthritic conditions had an anxiety disorder –20.3% of individuals with migraine headache had an anxiety disorder	–10.3% of individuals with any physical illness had an anxiety disorder
Association[a] of anxiety and physical illness	–no significant association noted for cardiac diseases or hypertension	–presence of an anxiety disorder was associated with past-month gastrointestinal disorders (OR = 2.10)	–presence of an anxiety disorder was associated with past-month respiratory disorders (OR = 1.71) –no significant association with allergic conditions	–presence of an anxiety disorder was associated with past-month thyroid disorders (OR = 1.59) –no significant association noted with diabetes	–presence of an anxiety disorder was associated with past-month arthritic conditions (OR = 1.66) –presence of an anxiety disorder was associated with past-month migraine headaches (OR = 2.12)	–presence of an anxiety disorder was associated with any past-month physical condition (OR = 1.70)

	Cardiovascular	Gastrointestinal	Respiratory/Allergic	Metabolic/Endocrine	Arthritic/Migraine	Overall
Temporal sequence of onset	–an anxiety disorder preceded hypertension in 72.0% of comorbid cases –an anxiety disorder preceded cardiac disease in 69.7% of comorbid cases	–an anxiety disorder preceded gastrointestinal diseases in 58.8% of comorbid cases	–an anxiety disorder preceded respiratory disorders and allergic conditions in 61.8% of comorbid cases	–an anxiety disorder preceded diabetes in 73.6% of comorbid cases –an anxiety disorder preceded thyroid disorders in 64.3% of comorbid cases	–an anxiety disorder preceded arthritic conditions in 73.4% of comorbid cases –an anxiety disorder preceded migraine headache in 63.7% of comorbid cases	
Quality of Life/Impairment	–not examined	–no significant effect on SF-36 physical component scores –no significant effect on number of disability days	–comorbid cases had significantly lower mean physical component scores on the SF-36 –no significant effect on number of disability days	–no significant effect on SF-36 physical component scores –no significant effect on number of disability days	–comorbid cases had significantly lower mean physical component scores on the SF-36 –comorbid cases with arthritic conditions had increased odds of disability days (OR = 1.66)	–comorbid cases had significantly lower mean physical component scores on the SF-36 –comorbid cases had increased odds of disability days (OR = 1.69)

Note. Cancer, autoimmune, and neurologic disorders were not included in this study.

[a]Association when adjusting for sociodemographic factors and presence of a past-month mood or substance use disorder.

Adapted from "Disability and Poor Quality of Life Associated With Comorbid Anxiety Disorders and Physical Conditions," by J. Sareen, F. Jacobi, B. J. Cox, S. L. Belik, I. Clara, and M. B. Stein, 2006, *Archives of Internal Medicine, 166,* pp. 2109–2116, using the German Health Survey, a nationally representative sample of individuals aged 18–65 years from the noninstitutionalized German population (*n* = 4,181).

post-MI, which predicts adverse outcome during the first year after an acute MI (Shemesh et al., 2004). Treatment of PTSD may prove to be an important step in improving adherence and outcomes.

Hypertension. The prevalence of current and lifetime panic attacks in primary care patients with hypertension has been noted to be significantly higher than in normotensive patients (current prevalence: 17% versus 11%, lifetime prevalence: 35% versus 22%; Davies et al., 1999). Findings on the relationship between anxiety disorders and hypertension have been mixed. Some studies have found an association (Davies et al., 1999). However, a recent study in a large community sample did not find an association between anxiety disorders and hypertension as measured by a physician (Sareen et al., 2006). This discrepancy in the literature might be due to differences in methodology of assessment of hypertension or differences in samples (i.e., treatment-seeking sample versus epidemiologic sample).

Mitral Valve Prolapse. Mitral valve prolapse is a common cardiac condition that shares many symptoms common to panic disorder (Margraf, Ehlers, & Roth, 1988). Since Pariser et al. (1978) suggested a relationship between these two disorders, this association has received considerable attention. The prevalence of mitral valve prolapse in patients with panic disorder has been reported to range from 5% to 50%, depending on the diagnostic methods and the selection criteria used (Katerndahl, 1993). Despite early studies reporting an association, no definite causal association has been proven (Dager, Cowley, & Dunner, 1987).

A number of mechanisms have been proposed to explain the association between anxiety and cardiac disorders. These mechanisms include the direct effects of phobic anxiety on arrhythmogenesis, through proarrhythmic processes such as alterations in autonomic tone, rather than on atherogenesis. Possible mechanisms could also include indirect effects, wherein anxiety may lead to physical illness (e.g., diabetes, hypertension) or unhealthy lifestyle habits (e.g., smoking [Kubzansky et al., 1998], obesity [Simon et al., 2006]), which may increase the risk of CHD.

Gastrointestinal Disorders

The association between gastrointestinal (GI) symptoms and emotional factors, such as anger, fear, or anxiety, is well established; however, the exact nature of this relationship remains unclear. Previous work in this area has illustrated that individuals with panic disorder have a higher rate of endorsing gastrointestinal symptoms (Lydiard et al., 1994). Lydiard et al. (1994) assessed the prevalence of GI symptoms in individuals with panic disorder and other psychiatric disorders in a national community survey of 13,537 respondents. Individuals with panic disorder had the highest rate of unexplained GI symptoms (7.2%) compared with other diagnostic categories.

Irritable Bowel Syndrome. Irritable bowel syndrome (IBS) constitutes the largest group of diagnoses seen by gastroenterologists, with worldwide prevalence rates ranging from 9% to 23% (Drossman, Whitehead, & Camilleri, 1997). From 50% to 90% of patients with IBS who seek medical attention have psychiatric comorbidity, most commonly major depression, panic disorder, social phobia, generalized anxiety disorder (GAD), and PTSD (Drossman et al., 1988; Irwin et al., 1996; Walker et al., 1990). Psychiatric patients with anxiety also have a significantly increased prevalence of IBS (Kaplan, Masand, & Gupta, 1996; Lydiard, 1997).

Panic disorder and IBS coexist frequently in both psychiatric and IBS patient populations (Kaplan et al., 1996; Lydiard et al., 1994). Few studies, however, have looked directly at this relationship. A recent study looking at the prevalence of IBS in outpatients seeking treatment for panic disorder determined that 46.3% of patients with panic disorder met criteria for IBS, in contrast to 2.5% of patients in the control group who were seeking treatment in a general physician's office for other medical illnesses (Kaplan et al., 1996). One study noted nearly equal likelihood of IBS prior to panic disorder and panic disorder followed by IBS, at 42.1% and 52.6%, respectively (Kaplan et al., 1996).

Peptic Ulcer Disease. Peptic ulcer disease (PUD) occurs more frequently than would be expected among individuals with anxiety disorders (Rogers et al., 1994). Recent work by Goodwin and Stein (2002) using the National Comorbidity Survey indicated that GAD was associated with a significantly increased risk of self-reported PUD (odds ratio [OR] = 2.8) after adjusting for sociodemographic factors, comorbid mental disorders, and physical morbidity. Additionally, analyses revealed a dose-response relationship between number of GAD symptoms and increased risk of self-reported PUD.

The high prevalence of anxiety disorders in GI disorders patients could reflect shared risk or pathophysiological factors, or could simply reflect increased anxiety related to unexplained abdominal pain. There may also exist a circular effect of the interaction of these disorders, such that anxiety symptoms increase the severity of GI symptoms, while chronic GI symptoms increase anxiety.

Respiratory Disorders

There has been an expanding body of literature on the relationship between asthma and anxiety disorders. Previous data from clinical and community settings suggest that asthma and anxiety disorders co-occur more often than would be expected by chance. Several studies have found elevated rates of anxiety disorders, including panic attacks and GAD, among clinical samples of patients with asthma (Nascimento et al., 2002; Perna, Bertani, Politi, Columbo, & Bellodi, 1997). In fact, the prevalence of panic disorder in studies of asthmatic patients is three to ten times higher than that seen in the general population (Karajgi, Rifkin, Doddi, & Kolli, 1990; Van Peski-Oosterbaan, Spinhoven, Van der Does, Willems, & Sterk, 1996). Several studies have also noted elevated rates of asthma among anxiety disorder patients (Koltek, Wilkes, & Atkinson, 1998; Pollack et al., 1996).

Further, epidemiological studies among adults and youth have found linkages between asthma and anxiety disorders (Goodwin & Eaton, 2003; Goodwin, Fergusson, & Horwood, 2004; Goodwin, Pine, & Hoven, 2003). Recent findings from a cross-sectional study of 4,181 community-dwelling adults, which used physician-diagnosed asthma and standardized measures of mental disorders, indicated an association between current severe asthma and any anxiety disorder (OR = 2.65), specific phobia (OR = 4.78), panic disorder (OR = 4.61), and panic attacks (OR = 4.12) (Goodwin et al., 2003a).

Three longitudinal studies have been done looking at the association between panic and asthma (Goodwin et al., 2004; Hasler et al., 2005; Jonas, Wagener, Lando, & Feldman, 1999). Findings illustrate that active asthma predicts subsequent panic disorder or panic attacks (ORs ranging from 1.9–4.5) (Goodwin et al., 2004; Hasler et al., 2005). It is interesting that the presence of panic disorder also predicted subsequent asthma symptoms in one study (OR = 6.3) (Hasler et al., 2005).

Panic disorder patients with asthma may have difficulty differentiating symptoms of asthma from those related to panic attacks. Thus, they may not be clear about whether to take medications for their physical illness or to take medications for their anxiety. In the specific example of comorbidity of panic disorder with asthma, patients often encounter difficulties knowing whether to utilize asthma treatment medications (i.e., beta-agonists) or anxiolytic medications. If they misinterpret a panic attack for an asthma attack, they may find that utilizing a beta-agonist likely worsens the panic attack symptoms. On the other hand, an asthma attack that is interpreted as being a panic attack would be unlikely to resolve with an anxiolytic medication.

Metabolic Disorders

Thyroid. Panic attacks have classically been associated with hyperthyroidism (Katerndahl & Vande Creek, 1983). This is understandable when considering the symptom overlap of the two conditions, namely tremulousness, palpitations, diaphoresis, and general agitation. Panic has also been associated with hypothyroidism, with one study demonstrating a direct relationship between panic attack severity and thyroid stimulating hormone (TSH) levels (Kikuchi et al., 2005). The prevalence of thyroid disease history among individuals with panic disorder ranges from 5% to 23% (Noyes, Jr. et al., 1992; Orenstein, Peskind, & Raskind, 1988). When considering both a history of thyroid disease as well as abnormal thyroid testing, a rate of 6.7% has been reported in panic disorder (Simon et al., 2002). The presence of thyroid peroxidase autoantibodies (TPOAb) is common in the community even in individuals with normal TSH and without a history of thyroid disorder: 14.2% of women and 4.3% of men have TPOAb (Engum, Bjoro, Mykletun, & Dahl, 2005). These individuals have elevated rates of generalized anxiety disorder (GAD), social phobia, and anxiety disorder not otherwise specified in some studies (Carta et al., 2004, 2005), but not in others (Engum et al., 2005).

Diabetes. Depressive and anxiety disorders have been reported in 36% of individuals with Type 2 diabetes in a clinical sample (Thomas et al., 2003). Most epidemiologic studies have also found higher prevalence rates of anxiety disorders in people with diabetes compared with the general population (Lustman, 1988; Peyrot & Rubin, 1997). A recent study by Kruse and colleagues (2003), in an epidemiologic cross-sectional study, found that people with diabetes were significantly more likely to have an anxiety disorder compared to individuals without diabetes when controlling for age, sex, marital status, and socioeconomic status (OR = 2.05). Interestingly, people with diabetes and anxiety more frequently had adequate glycemic control compared to their counterparts without mental disorders. Regarding specific anxiety disorders, GAD seems most prevalent in people with diabetes, with lifetime rates up to 20.5% (Grigsby, Anderson, Freedland, Clouse, & Lustman, 2002). Other anxiety disorders with elevated rates in the diabetic population include agoraphobia (10.2%) and simple phobia (24.8%).

Chronic Pain Conditions

Previous studies looking at the relationship between anxiety disorders and chronic pain conditions have indicated that the prevalence of anxiety disorders is higher in individuals with a chronic pain condition than in the general population. McWilliams et al. (2004) utilized a large, nationally representative survey from the United States to examine the relationship between two anxiety-based problems (GAD and panic attacks) and three chronic pain conditions (arthritis, migraine, and back pain). Prevalence of GAD in individuals with chronic pain ranged from 5.6% in those with arthritis to 9.1% in those with migraine. Similarly, prevalence of panic attacks was higher in those with chronic pain, with estimates ranging between 11.2% and 17.4%. Even after adjusting for the effects of sociodemographics and presence of another self-report chronic pain condition, panic attacks and GAD were more than twice as likely in those with one of the three chronic pain conditions examined (ORs ranging from 2.09–3.86). Sareen et al. (2005) recently demonstrated the strongest association with arthritis to exist with PTSD and panic attacks. The association between chronic pain and PTSD has been hypothesized to be related to mutual maintenance. This model suggests that pain serves as a reminder of the traumatic event, and, conversely, that arousal triggered by the reminder promotes avoidance of pain-related situations (Asmundson, Coons, Taylor, & Katz, 2002).

To date, one study has prospectively investigated the relationship between migraine and anxiety disorders. Swartz and colleagues looked at new onset migraines in a community sample of 1,343 adults at-risk of developing migraine. In logistic regression models adjusting for age, sex, and psychiatric illness at baseline, only phobia was predictive of incident migraines (OR = 1.70). This is contrary to findings from cross-sectional studies indicating a strong relationship between migraine and anxiety disorders. Results implicate that a third factor may be involved in this relationship, which might increase the risk of both migraine and anxiety.

The majority of research in this area has been limited by the fact that identification of painful conditions has been by self-report. Presence of an anxiety disorder may lead to a bias in self-reported chronic pain conditions, such that individuals with an anxiety disorder may report painful conditions more frequently. One exception is the study by Sareen and colleagues (2006), discussed earlier, in which painful conditions were diagnosed by physicians. Findings from this investigation reflect an important step forward in this domain, adding integrity to the diagnosis of chronic pain conditions.

Cancer

The majority of patients with cancer will understandably undergo some degree of emotional distress, particularly on initial diagnosis. Current estimates have suggested that approximately 25% of cancer patients meet diagnostic criteria for major depression or anxiety disorders (Derogatis et al., 1983; van't Spijker, Trijsburg, & Duivenvoorden, 1997). While the association between depression and cancer diagnosis is well documented in cancer patients (Kerrihard, Breitbart, Dent, & Strout, 1999), the association between cancer and other mental disorders, in particular anxiety disorders, is largely unknown.

The prevalence of anxiety disorders among cancer patients varies widely in the literature. Most studies estimate the current prevalence of any anxiety disorder among individuals with cancer within a range of 15% and 28% (Kessler et al., 1994). One study, by Honda and Goodwin (2004), examined the U.S. National Comorbidity Survey and found an association between cancer and simple phobia (OR = 2.5) and agoraphobia (OR = 3.3), even after adjusting for demographic factors. Another study, using a Danish sample of 61,709 women with breast cancer, illustrated that psychiatric admission with anxiety disorders were significantly more common among breast cancer patients than among the general female population (standardized incidence ratio = 1.25) (Hjerl, Andersen, Keiding, Mortensen, & Jorgensen, 2002).

A particular area of interest in cancer patients has been PTSD. Life-threatening illness has recently been recognized as a stressor that can precipitate PTSD (Andrykowski, Cordova, Studts, & Miller, 1998; Jacobsen et al., 1998). Therefore, the question has been raised as to whether PTSD diagnosis secondary to cancer is applicable to the psychological reaction related to being diagnosed with cancer. The prevalence of cancer-related PTSD ranges from 0% to 32% (Mundy et al., 2000), depending on the method used to assess PTSD (i.e., SCID, PCL-C, or CAPS-I). Most studies calculated their prevalence rates based on retrospectively asking patients if they have experienced PTSD symptoms at any time since their diagnosis. However, one study by Mundy and colleagues (2000) reported the highest incidence for lifetime cancer-related PTSD within their sample (35%), despite reporting no patients who met PTSD criteria at least 3 months following treatment completion.

Although research has been conducted to establish the prevalence of anxiety disorder in cancer patients, work looking at other anxiety disorders specifically has been limited. In particular, panic attack and panic disorder have been less well studied. A review of cases reported that approximately 20% of all psychiatric consultations at a regional cancer center within a 2-year period directly related to panic disorder and panic attacks (Thomas, Glynne-Jones, Chait, & Marks, 1997), suggesting that panic is a more common problem for cancer patients than has been previously reported.

To date, most studies in this field have noted that anxiety is commonly undiagnosed and untreated in cancer patients, resulting in a significant negative impact on quality of life, social support, health care utilization, and even disease outcome (Jones, 2001). Reasons for the underdiagnosis of anxiety disorders in cancer patients may be related to a lack of time during a doctor visit, misinterpretation of anxiety as expected "normal" reaction to cancer, the symptoms of anxiety being attributed to the cancer, or a focus on medical problems (McDaniel, Musselman, Porter, Reed, & Nemeroff, 1995; Sellick & Crooks, 1999).

The mechanism of the relationship between cancer and anxiety disorders is not known. Similar to depressive symptoms, it could be that anxiety symptoms may be a predisposing factor for cancer through potential biological pathways. Alternatively, anxiety disorders may develop in those diagnosed with cancer from a number of causes—the emotional impact of diagnosis, coping with treatment, concerns regarding relapse, and facing the possibility of death. As well, cancer treatment can often make the patient feel worse, particularly in young people who may have felt physically fit and healthy before starting treatment. The pattern of remission followed by relapse, frequently seen in cancer patients, may also contribute to subsequent psychopathology. In fact, psychiatric disorders may be apparent long after initial diagnosis of cancer, with up to 30% of long-term survivors of cancer reported to suffer chronic, clinical anxiety (van't Spijker et al., 1997). However, a meta-analysis reviewing 58 studies indicated that cancer patients are no more burdened by anxiety disorders than people in the general population (Fann, Katon, Uomoto, & Esselman, 1995). Further studies are needed to delineate the effect of anxiety disorders on those individuals diagnosed with cancer.

Neurologic Disorders

Neurologic diseases cause damage to nervous structures that control personality organization. Therefore, it may be particularly difficult to differentiate anxiety from personality correlates or reactive tendencies in patients with these disorders.

Traumatic Brain Injuries. Psychiatric disorders are a major source of disability among individuals who have experienced a traumatic brain injury (Deb, Lyons, Koutzoukis, Ali, & McCarthy, 1999; Van Reekum, Bolago, Finlayson, Garner, & Links, 1996). The rates of lifetime anxiety disorders in patients with traumatic brain injury range from 1% to 28% depending on the particular anxiety disorder (i.e., GAD, panic disorder, phobic disorder, OCD, or PTSD) (Koponen et al., 2002). Recent experience in the U.S. military with returnees from conflicts in Iraq and Afghanistan suggest that TBI and PTSD may frequently co-occur (Warden, 2006).

Restless Legs Syndrome. The co-occurrence of restless legs syndrome (RLS) and anxiety has been noted in a few studies (Winkelmann et al., 2005). A recent study looking at this relationship (Kahn-Greene, Killgore, Kamimori, Balkin, & Killgore, 2007) determined that patients with RLS had an increased risk of having lifetime and past 12-month anxiety disorders when compared to controls with somatic morbidity of other types, with particularly strong associations with panic disorder (OR = 4.7) and GAD (OR = 3.5). In these cases, RLS occurred as the primary condition, indicating that mental disorder symptoms may be caused by their RLS symptoms. For example, sleep deprivation and sleep disturbances as a result of RLS could increase the risk of psychiatric disorders in the individual (Janssens et al., 2003).

Multiple Sclerosis. Anxiety disorders are quite common and frequently overlooked in patients with multiple sclerosis (MS), likely due to the difficulty in differentiating anxiety symptoms from neurologic symptoms associated with the disorder. One study indicated that 34% of patients recently diagnosed with MS had clinically relevant levels of anxiety (score ≥8 on the *Hospital Anxiety and Depression Scale;* Galeazzi et al., 2005), whereas another indicated that 36% of patients with MS had a lifetime anxiety disorder (as measured using the

Structured Clinical Interview for DSM–IV) (Galeazzi et al., 2005). The rates of lifetime anxiety disorders in patients with MS as measured in one study are 10% for OCD, 4% for GAD, 6% for panic disorder, 12% for specific phobia, 8% for agoraphobia, and 2% for social phobia (Chalfant, Bryant, & Fulcher, 2004). However, this study was limited to a sample size of 50 patients with MS and a 50-person healthy control comparison group. The modest sample size meant that the study was lacking in power to detect individual anxiety disorders as more common in the MS group when compared to the controls; however, an elevated rate of any anxiety disorder was apparent in patients with MS (OR = 3.46).

Parkinson's Disease. Anxiety occurs in about 65% of patients with Parkinson's disease and is often more severe than in elderly people who are equally physically disabled with other chronic physical illnesses (Lamberg, 2001). Few studies have looked directly at this association. One study by Stein et al. (1990) systematically evaluated 24 patients with Parkinson's disease, concluding that 38% had a clinically significant current anxiety disorder. Of these, 22% had the onset of the anxiety disorder before the diagnosis of Parkinson's disease and 78% had the onset of anxiety after the diagnosis of Parkinson's disease. It has been hypothesized that the onset of motor arrests, or freezing, may cause a person to become distressed and may trigger or worsen anxiety symptoms, such as panic attacks. In one prospective study, phobic anxiety was noted to be a risk factor for the subsequent onset of Parkinson's disease (Weisskopf, Chen, Schwarzschild, Kawachi, & Ascherio, 2003).

Vestibular Disturbance and Dizziness. Dizziness is one of the most common presenting symptoms in primary care (Frommberger, Tettenborn, Buller, & Benkert, 1994; Stein, Asmundson, Ireland, & Walker, 1994). Many patients with "unexplained" dizziness have psychiatric disorders, particularly panic disorder, with rates ranging from 14% to 41% (Kessler et al., 1994), 5 to 15 times higher than in the general population (Simpson, Nedzelski, Barber, & Thomas, 1988). In one pilot study of 17 nonrandom patients with dizziness, 76% had panic disorder and/or agoraphobia, compared to 8% of 24 patients presenting with tinnitus (Yardley, Luxon, & Haacke, 1994). Another 24% percent reported phobias and 6% had GAD.

Studies of dizzy patients reveal that severity of dizziness complaints correlated with psychological distress, phobic and somatic anxiety traits, avoidance, autonomic arousal, and social anxiety

(Brandt, 1996). Brandt defined a clinical entity called phobic postural vertigo (PPV), a syndrome of subjective unsteadiness caused by stress, perceptual stimuli, or social situations that bring on dizziness, and that result in subsequent avoidance (Yardley, 1994; Yardley et al., 1994). The behavioral restriction and avoidance due to fear of dizziness in patients with PPV are quite similar to the phobic avoidance in patients with panic disorder, as defined in the fourth edition of the *Diagnostic and Statistical Manual of Mental Disorders (DSM-IV)* (American Psychiatric Association, 1994). As well, the overlap between PPV and panic disorder is observed in the *DSM–IV* criteria for panic disorder in that three symptoms of panic disorder are commonly seen in individuals with PPV—sweating, nausea, and dizziness (Aronson & Logue, 1988; Cox et al., 1993). In fact, approximately 50% to 90% of panic disorder patients report experiencing dizziness (Yardley, Masson, Verschuur, Haacke, & Luxon, 1992). As well, both vestibular symptoms and panic disorder are associated with some form of catastrophic cognitions (Sullivan, Clark, & Katon, 1993).

In general, patients presenting with dizziness have high rates of panic disorder in most studies, through the contribution of actual vestibular dysfunction is not clear. One study of 75 patients with dizziness reported that those without actual vestibular dysfunction had a significantly higher lifetime incidence of panic disorder (21%) and agoraphobia (24%) than did patients with vestibular abnormalities (5% panic disorder, 13% agoraphobia) (Hoffman, O'Leary, & Munjack, 1994). These findings may reflect a measure of somatization in those with complaints of dizziness without an objective measure of vestibular abnormality. In contrast, studies examining vestibular dysfunction in patients presenting with panic disorder have reported significant dysfunction, especially among panic disorder patients with moderate to severe agoraphobia (Robinson, 1997).

Stroke. Few studies on stroke have focused on its association with anxiety disorders. Some studies have reported a prevalence of anxiety disorders ranging from 3% to 28% in stroke patients (Starkstein et al., 1990). Other studies have noted that 20% to 30% of patients in the chronic phase of stroke have anxiety disorders, independent of stroke severity (Leppavuori, Pohjasvaara, Vataja, Kaste, & Erkinjuntti, 2003). This high variability in prevalence rates may be related to selection of patient populations, the criteria used to diagnose the anxiety disorder, and the time that has elapsed since the stroke.

Leppavuori and colleagues examined the prevalence of poststroke GAD in a large sample of stroke patients (n = 277; Leppavuori et al., 2003). They identified 20.6% of the patients to have GAD, either due to a general medical condition or not. Within these individuals, there were those who had GAD as a primary diagnosis (11.2%) and those that were diagnosed with GAD due to stroke (9.4%). This is much higher than the prevalence of GAD in the general population, which has been found to be 5.7% (Kessler, Chiu, Demler, & Walters, 2005). Generally, the individuals diagnosed with either form of GAD had had a more severe stroke and were more impaired in psychosocial functioning and activities of daily living.

More recently, PTSD-related symptoms were found to be present in 31% of patients 1 year after a nonsevere stroke (Bruggimann et al., 2006). These symptoms were independent of neurologic impairment, peristroke amnesia, long-term memory impairment, nosognosia, hypochondriac preoccupations, and physical pain. The presence of such symptoms was, however, associated with the subjective intensity of the traumatic experience. Contrary to previous literature illustrating that depression was most frequent following stroke (Starkstein et al., 1990), this study illustrated poststroke anxiety symptoms to be more common (Bruggimann et al., 2006).

Current theories regarding this association have implicated specific neurochemical and neuropeptide systems, as well as lesions in specific brain areas, for this comorbidity. As well, medications (i.e., corticosteroids) that are traditionally used to treat individuals with some neurologic conditions can produce psychiatric side effects; in particular, anxiety symptoms.

Autoimmune Disorders

PANDAS and Pediatric OCD. Childhood-onset OCD was once considered to be exclusively a psychological disorder, but is now also known to be a neurobiological disorder. Studies in this area have led to the identification of a subgroup of children with OCD and Tourette's syndrome in whom symptom exacerbations were temporally related to a group-A beta-hemolytic streptococcal (GABHS) infections (Allen, Leonard, & Swedo, 1995; Swedo et al., 1998). Group-A beta-hemolytic *Streptococcus pyogenes* is a bacterium responsible for numerous human maladies. Pediatric autoimmune neuropsychiatric disorders associated with streptococcal infection (PANDAS) are a relatively new entity im-

plicating autoimmune processes in the pathophysiology of obsessive-compulsive disorder (OCD) and tic disorders. Antibodies produced against group-A beta-hemolytic *Streptococcus pyogenes* cross-react with autoantigens in the basal ganglia and produce symptoms seen in OCD. These autoantibodies also produce symptoms of Sydenham's Chorea, as well as cause rheumatic fever in certain individuals. The relative frequency of cells bearing this marker is an inherited characteristic.

There is evidence that both supports and counters the validity of PANDAS as a distinct subgroup of persons with OCD and tic disorders. Evidence supporting the role of autoantibodies as etiological agents includes elevated levels of antineuronal antibodies in children with PANDAS. In one study, antibasal ganglia antibodies were found in 42% of children with OCD, whereas they were present in under 10% of controls (Rauch & Jenike, 1993). Since the basal ganglia is a major brain region associated with OCD pathophysiology (Mell, Davis, & Owens, 2005), it is understandable that antibodies targeting those structures could affect the symptoms of the disorder.

The criterion describing a temporal relation to symptom exacerbation and GABHS infection is more controversial. Recent findings from a population-based case-control study indicated that children with a new diagnosis of OCD, Tourette's syndrome, or tic disorder were more than twice as likely as controls to have had at least 1 streptococcal infection in the 3 months before disease onset (OR = 2.22) and almost twice as likely to have had at least 1 streptococcal infection in the 12 months before onset (OR = 1.91; Luo et al., 2004). Conversely, another study found no significant association between OCD and tic exacerbations and GABHS infections (Loiselle, Wendlandt, Rohde, & Singer, 2003). And although cross-reactive autoantibodies are not universally present in children with poststreptococcal tics or OCD (Murphy et al., 2004), children with large symptom fluctuations were demonstrated to have a positive correlation between streptococcal titres and obsessive and compulsive symptom severity levels (Hoekstra & Minderaa, 2005).

Evidence exists that is suggestive of an autoimmune etiology in a subgroup of OCD and tic disorder patients, but causal inferences cannot be drawn at this time (Sheps & Sheffield, 2001). The prevalence of PANDAS, either among children with streptococcal infection or among children with OCD or tics, remains unclear. Although data support the existence of PANDAS, the hypothesis that streptococcal infection directly leads to OCD or tic disorders in children is yet unproven.

Summary and Conclusions

Comorbidity of anxiety disorders and physical illnesses is common, and has the potential to negatively impact the individual. Nevertheless, anxiety often remains undetected in medical settings (Kroenke, Spitzer, Williams, Monahan, & Lowe, 2007). Clinicians need to be aware that a general physical illness may be accounting for, or worsening symptoms, among patients who are refractory to initial treatment for anxiety disorders. It is also likely that anxiety disorders influence patient compliance with physician-prescribed medication and advice that might lead to healthy behaviors, such as adherence to diet and exercise, and could affect patient outcomes. On the other hand, psychiatric disorders could amplify severity and number of physical symptoms and increase the likelihood that an individual will present to a health care provider (Vineis, 2002).

Although there is mounting evidence that anxiety disorders are often comorbid with physical illness, four specific limitations of the current literature on this topic exist. First, the association between anxiety disorders and physical illness found in clinical samples may be limited by sampling biases (Sareen et al., 2006). Second, although epidemiologic samples reduce the likelihood of sampling bias, most of these studies have utilized self-report diagnosis of physical illnesses, with the exception of one (Sareen et al., 2006). Since individuals with anxiety disorders are more likely to report physical symptoms (Sareen et al., 2006), it is possible that there may be a self-report bias of physical illness among individuals with anxiety disorders. Third, most epidemiologic studies have utilized lay interviewers to diagnose mental disorders rather than trained health professionals. Fourth, there have been discrepant findings on the relationship between comorbidity of anxiety disorders and physical conditions with disability and quality of life. Some primary care sample studies have found that anxiety symptoms and anxiety disorders are associated with excess disability among primary care patients suffering with physical health problems (Nisenson, Pepper, Schwenk, & Coyne, 1998), while others have found that the associated disability was either minimal (Jacobi et al., 2004), or due to comorbidity with other mental disorders. Finally, it will be important to discern in future studies the specific mechanisms that lead to functional impairment (i.e., reduced quality of life and increased disability) among those with comorbid anxiety and physical disorders.

Note

Preparation of this article was supported by (1) a CIHR Canada Graduate Scholarship—Master's Award awarded to Ms. Belik; (2) a Western Regional Training Centre studentship funded by Canadian Health Services Research Foundation, Alberta Heritage Foundation for Medical Research, and Canadian Institutes of Health Research awarded to Ms. Belik; (3) a CIHR New Investigator grant awarded to Dr. Sareen; and (4) a Career Development (K24) Award from the National Institutes of Health (MH64122) to Dr. Stein.

References

Albert, C. M., Chae, C. U., Rexrode, K. M., Manson, J. E., & Kawachi, I. (2005). Phobic anxiety and risk of coronary heart disease and sudden cardiac death among women. *Circulation, 111,* 480–487.

Allen, A. J., Leonard, H., & Swedo, S. E. (1995). Current knowledge of medications for the treatment of childhood anxiety disorders. *Journal of the American Academy of Child and Adolescent Psychiatry, 34,* 976–986.

American Psychiatric Association. (1994). *Diagnostic and statistical manual for mental disorders* (4th ed.). Washington, DC: American Psychiatric Press.

Andrykowski, M. A., Cordova, M. J., Studts, J. L., & Miller, T. W. (1998). Posttraumatic stress disorder after treatment for breast cancer: Prevalence of diagnosis and use of the PTSD Checklist-Civilian Version (PCL-C) as a screening instrument. *Journal of Consulting and Clinical Psychology, 66,* 586–590.

Aronson, T. A., & Logue, C. M. (1988). Phenomenology of panic attacks: A descriptive study of panic disorder patients' self-reports. *Journal of Clinical Psychiatry, 49,* 8–13.

Asmundson, G.J.G., Coons, M. J., Taylor, S., & Katz, J. (2002). PTSD and the experience of pain: Research and clinical implications of shared vulnerability and mutual maintenance models. *Canadian Journal of Psychiatry, 47,* 930–937.

Bennett, P., Conway, M., Clatworthy, J., Brooke, S., & Owen, R. (2001). Predicting post-traumatic symptoms in cardiac patients. *Heart and Lung, 30,* 458–465.

Brandt, T. (1996). Phobic postural vertigo. *Neurology, 46,* 1515–1519.

Bruggimann, L., Annoni, J. M., Staub, F., von, S. N., Van der, L. M., & Bogousslavsky, J. (2006). Chronic posttraumatic stress symptoms after nonsevere stroke. *Neurology, 66,* 513–516.

Carta, M. G., Hardoy, M. C., Carpiniello, B., Murru, A., Marci, A. R., Carbone, F. et al. (2005). A case control study on psychiatric disorders in Hashimoto disease and Euthyroid Goitre: Not only depressive but also anxiety disorders are associated with thyroid autoimmunity. *Clinical Practice and Epidemiology in Mental Health, 10,* 1–23.

Carta, M. G., Loviselli, A., Hardoy, M. C., Massa, S., Cadeddu, M., Sardu, C. et al. (2004). The link between thyroid autoimmunity (antithyroid peroxidase autoantibodies) with anxiety and mood disorders in the community: A field of interest for public health in the future. *BMC Psychiatry, 18,* 25.

Chalfant, A. M., Bryant, R. A., & Fulcher, G. (2004). Posttraumatic stress disorder following diagnosis of multiple sclerosis. *Journal of Traumatic Stress, 17,* 423–428.

Cox, B. J., Hasey, G., Swinson, R. P., Kuch, K., Cooke, R., Warsh, J. et al. (1993). The symptom structure of panic attacks in depressed and anxious patients. *Canadian Journal of Psychiatry, 38,* 181–184.

Dager, S. R., Cowley, D. S., & Dunner, D. L. (1987). Biological markers in panic states: Lactate-induced panic and mitral valve prolapse. *Biological Psychiatry, 22,* 339–359.

Davies, S. J., Ghahramani, P., Jackson, P. R., Noble, T. W., Hardy, P. G., Hippisley-Cox, J. et al. (1999). Association of panic disorder and panic attacks with hypertension. *American Journal of Medicine, 107,* 310–316.

Deb, S., Lyons, I., Koutzoukis, C., Ali, I., & McCarthy, G. (1999). Rate of psychiatric illness 1 year after traumatic brain injury. *American Journal of Psychiatry, 156,* 374–378.

Derogatis, L. R., Morrow, G. R., Fetting, J., Penman, D., Piasetsky, S., Schmale, A. M., et al. (1983). The prevalence of psychiatric disorders among cancer patients. *Journal of the American Medical Association, 249,* 751–757.

Drossman, D. A., McKee, D. C., Sandler, R. S., Mitchell, C. M., Cramer, E. M., Lowman, B. C., et al. (1988). Psychosocial factors in the irritable bowel syndrome: A multivariate analysis of patients and nonpatients with irritable bowel syndrome. *Gastroenterology, 95,* 701–708.

Drossman, D. A., Whitehead, W. E., & Camilleri, M. (1997). Irritable bowel syndrome: A technical review for practice guideline development. *Gastroenterology, 112,* 2120–2137.

Engum, A., Bjoro, T., Mykletun, A., & Dahl, A. A. (2005). Thyroid autoimmunity, depression and anxiety; are there any connections? An epidemiological study of a large population. *Journal of Psychosomatic Research, 59,* 263–268.

Fann, J. R., Katon, W. J., Uomoto, J. M., & Esselman, P. C. (1995). Psychiatric disorders and functional disability in outpatients with traumatic brain injuries. *American Journal of Psychiatry, 152,* 1493–1499.

Frommberger, U. H., Tettenborn, B., Buller, R., & Benkert, O. (1994). Panic disorder in patients with dizziness. *Archives of Internal Medicine, 154,* 590–591.

Galeazzi, G. M., Ferrari, S., Giaroli, G., Mackinnon, A., Merelli, E., Motti, L., et al. (2005). Psychiatric disorders and depression in multiple sclerosis outpatients: Impact of disability and interferon beta therapy. *Neurology and Science, 26,* 255–262.

Ginzburg, K. (2006). Comorbidity of PTSD and depression following myocardial infarction. *Journal of Affective Disorders, 94,* 135–143.

Ginzburg, K., Solomon, Z., & Bleich, A. (2002). Repressive coping style, acute stress disorder, and posttraumatic stress disorder after myocardial infarction. *Psychosomatic Medicine, 64,* 748–757.

Goodwin, R. D., Cox, B. J., & Clara, I. (2006). Neuroticism and physical disorders among adults in the community: Results from the National Comorbidity Survey. *Journal of Behavioral Medicine, 29,* 229–238.

Goodwin, R. D., & Eaton, W. W. (2003). Asthma and the risk of panic attacks among adults in the community. *Psychological Medicine, 33,* 879–885.

Goodwin, R. D., Fergusson, D. M., & Horwood, L. J. (2004). Asthma and depressive and anxiety disorders among young persons in the community. *Psychological Medicine, 34,* 1465–1474.

Goodwin, R. D., Jacobi, F., & Thefeld, W. (2003a). Mental disorders and asthma in the community. *Archives of General Psychiatry, 60,* 1125–1130.

Goodwin, R. D., Olfson, M., Shea, S., Lantigua, R. A., Carrasquilo, O., Gameroff, M. J., et al. (2003b). Asthma and mental disorders in primary care. *General Hospital Psychiatry, 25,* 479–483.

Goodwin, R. D., Pine, D. S., & Hoven, C. W. (2003). Asthma and panic attacks among youth in the community. *Journal of Asthma, 40,* 139–145.

Goodwin, R. D., & Stein, M. B. (2002). Generalized anxiety disorder and peptic ulcer disease among adults in the United States. *Psychosomatic Medicine, 64,* 862–866.

Grigsby, A. B., Anderson, R. J., Freedland, K. E., Clouse, R. E., & Lustman, P. J. (2002). Prevalence of anxiety in adults with diabetes: A systematic review. *Journal of Psychosomatic Research, 53,* 1053–1060.

Haines, A. P., Imeson, J. D., & Meade, T. W. (1987). Phobic anxiety and ischaemic heart disease. *British Medical Journal, 295,* 297–299.

Hasler, G., Gergen, P. J., Kleinbaum, D. G., Ajdacic, V., Gamma, A., Eich, D., et al. (2005). Asthma and panic in young adults. *American Journal of Respiratory and Critical Care Medicine, 171,* 1224–1230.

Heszen-Niejodek, I., Gottschalk, L. A., & Januszek, M. (1999). Anxiety and hope during the course of three different medical illnesses: A longitudinal study. *Psychotherapy and Psychosomatics, 68,* 304–312.

Hjerl, K., Andersen, E. W., Keiding, N., Mortensen, P. B., & Jorgensen, T. (2002). Increased incidence of affective disorders, anxiety disorders, and non-natural mortality in women after breast cancer diagnosis: A nation-wide cohort study in Denmark. *Acta Psychiatrica Scandinavica, 105,* 258–264.

Hoekstra, P. J., & Minderaa, R. B. (2005). Tic disorders and obsessive-compulsive disorder: Is autoimmunity involved? *International Review of Psychiatry, 17,* 497–502.

Hoffman, D. L., O'Leary, D. P., & Munjack, D. J. (1994). Autorotation test abnormalities of the horizontal and vertical vestibulo-ocular reflexes in panic disorder. *Otolaryngology—Head and Neck Surgery, 110,* 259–269.

Honda, K., & Goodwin, R. D. (2004). Cancer and mental disorders in a national community sample: Findings from the National Comorbidity Survey. *Psychotherapy and Psychosomatics, 73,* 235–242.

Huovinen, E., Kaprio, J., & Koskenvuo, M. (2001). Asthma in relation to personality traits, life satisfaction, and stress: A prospective study among 11,000 adults. *Allergy, 56,* 971–977.

Irwin, C. I., Falsetti, S. A., Lydiard, R. B., Ballenger, J. C., Brock, C. D., & Brener, W. (1996). Comorbidity of posttraumatic stress disorder and irritable bowel syndrome. *Journal of Clinical Psychiatry, 57,* 576–578.

Jacobi, F., Wittchen, H.-U., Holting, C., Hofler, M., Pfister, H., Muller, N., et al. (2004). Prevalence, co-morbidity and correlates of mental disorders in the general population: Results from the German Health Interview and Examination Survey (GHS). *Psychological Medicine, 34,* 597–611.

Jacobsen, P. B., Widows, M. R., Hann, D. M., Andrykowski, M. A., Kronish, L. E., & Fields, K. K. (1998). Posttraumatic stress disorder symptoms after bone marrow transplantation for breast cancer. *Psychosomatic Medicine, 60,* 366–371.

Janssens, A. C., van Doorn, P. A., de Boer, J. B., Kalkers, N. F., van der Meche, F. G., Passchier, J., et al. (2003). Anxiety and depression influence the relation between disability status and quality of life in multiple sclerosis. *Multiple Sclerosis, 9,* 397–403.

Jonas, B., Wagener, D., Lando, J., & Feldman, J. (1999). Symptoms of anxiety and depression as risk factors for development of asthma. *Journal of Applied Biobehavioral Research, 4,* 91–119.

Jones, R. D. (2001). Depression and anxiety in oncology: The oncologist's perspective. *Journal of Clinical Psychiatry, 62*(Suppl. 8), 52–55.

Kahn-Greene, E. T., Killgore, D. B., Kamimori, G. H., Balkin, T. J., & Killgore, W. D. (2007). The effects of sleep deprivation on symptoms of psychopathology in healthy adults. *Sleep Medicine, 8,* 215–221.

Kaplan, D. S., Masand, P. S., & Gupta, S. (1996). The relationship of irritable bowel syndrome (IBS) and panic disorder. *Annals of Clinical Psychiatry, 8,* 81–88.

Karajgi, B., Rifkin, A., Doddi, S., & Kolli, R. (1990). The prevalence of anxiety disorders in patients with chronic obstructive pulmonary disease. *American Journal of Psychiatry, 147,* 200–201.

Katerndahl, D. A. (1993). Panic and prolapse: Meta-analysis. *Journal of Nervous and Mental Disease, 181,* 539–544.

Katerndahl, D. A., & Vande Creek, L. (1983). Hyperthroidism and panic attacks. *Psychosomatics, 24,* 491–496.

Kawachi, I., Colditz, G. A., Ascherio, A., Rimm, E. B., Giovannucci, E., Stampfer, M. J., et al. (1994). Coronary heart disease/myocardial infarction: Prospective study of phobic anxiety and risk of coronary heart disease in men. *Circulation, 89,* 1992–1997.

Kawachi, I., Sparrow, D., Vokonas, P. S., & Weiss, S. T. (1994). Coronary heart disease/myocardial infarction: Symptoms of anxiety and risk of coronary heart disease: The Normative Aging Study. *Circulation, 90,* 2225–2229.

Kerrihard, T., Breitbart, W., Dent, R., & Strout, D. (1999). Anxiety in patients with cancer and human immunodeficiency virus. *Seminars in Clinical Neuropsychiatry, 4,* 114–132.

Kessler, R. C., Chiu, W. T., Demler, O., & Walters, E. E. (2005). Prevalence, severity, and comorbidity of 12-month *DSM–IV* disorders in the National Comorbidity Survey Replication. *Archives of General Psychiatry, 62,* 617–627.

Kessler, R. C., McGonagle, K. A., Zhao, S., Nelson, C. B., Hughes, M., Eshleman, S., et al. (1994). Lifetime and 12-month prevalence of psychiatric disorders in the United States: Results from the National Comorbidity Survey. *Archives of General Psychiatry, 51,* 8–19.

Kikuchi, M., Komuro, R., Oka, H., Kidani, T., Hanaoka, A., & Koshino, Y. (2005). Relationship between anxiety and thyroid function in patients with panic disorder. *Progress in Neuro-psychopharmacology and Biological Psychiatry, 29,* 77–81.

Koltek, M., Wilkes, T. C., & Atkinson, M. (1998). The prevalence of posttraumatic stress disorder in an adolescent inpatient unit. *Canadian Journal of Psychiatry, 43,* 64–68.

Koponen, S., Taiminen, T., Portin, R., Himanen, L., Isoniemi, H., Heinonen, H., et al. (2002). Axis I and II psychiatric disorders after traumatic brain injury: A 30-year follow-up study. *American Journal of Psychiatry, 159,* 1315–1321.

Kroenke, K., Spitzer, R. L., Williams, J. B., Monahan, P. O., & Lowe, B. (2007). Anxiety disorders in primary care: Prevalence, impairment, comorbidity, and detection. *Annals of Internal Medicine, 146,* 317–325.

Kruse, J., Schmitz, N., & Thefeld, W. (2003). On the association between diabetes and mental disorders in a community sample: Results from the German National Health Interview and Examination Survey. *Diabetes Care, 26,* 1841–1846.

Kubzansky, L. D., Kawachi, I., Weiss, S. T., & Sparrow, D. (1998). Anxiety and coronary heart disease: A synthesis of epidemiological, psychological, and experimental evidence. *Annals of Behavioral Medicine, 20,* 47–58.

Lamberg, L. (2001). Psychiatric symptoms common in neurological disorders. *Journal of the American Medical Association, 286,* 154–156.

Leppavuori, A., Pohjasvaara, T., Vataja, R., Kaste, M., & Erkinjuntti, T. (2003). Generalized anxiety disorders three to four months after ischemic stroke. *Cerebrovascular Disease, 16,* 257–264.

Levitan, R. D., Rector, N. A., Sheldon, T., & Goering, P. (2003). Childhood adversities associated with major depression and/or anxiety disorders in a community sample of Ontario: Issues of comorbidity. *Depression and Anxiety, 17,* 34–42.

Loiselle, C. R., Wendlandt, J. T., Rohde, C. A., & Singer, H. S. (2003). Antistreptococcal, neuronal, and nuclear antibodies in Tourette syndrome. *Pediatric Neurology, 28,* 119–125.

Luo, F., Leckman, J. F., Katsovich, L., Findley, D., Grantz, H., Tucker, D. M., et al. (2004). Prospective longitudinal study of children with tic disorders and/or obsessive-compulsive disorder: Relationship of symptom exacerbations to newly acquired streptococcal infections. *Pediatrics, 113,* e578–e585.

Lustman, P. J. (1988). Anxiety disorders in adults with diabetes mellitus. *Psychiatric Clinics of North America, 11,* 419–432.

Lydiard, R. B. (1997). Anxiety and the irritable bowel syndrome: Psychiatric, medical, or both? *Journal of Clinical Psychiatry, 58*(Suppl. 3), 51–58.

Lydiard, R. B., Greenwald, S., Weissman, M. M., Johnson, J., Drossman, D. A., & Ballenger, J. C. (1994). Panic disorder and gastrointestinal symptoms: Findings from the NIMH Epidemiologic Catchment Area project. *American Journal of Psychiatry, 151,* 64–70.

Margraf, J., Ehlers, A., & Roth, W. T. (1988). Mitral valve prolapse and panic disorder. *Psychosomatic Medicine, 50,* 93–113.

McDaniel, J. S., Musselman, D. L., Porter, M. R., Reed, D. A., & Nemeroff, C. B. (1995). Depression in patients with cancer: Diagnosis, biology, and treatment. *Archives of General Psychiatry, 52,* 89–99.

McWilliams, L. A., Goodwin, R. D., & Cox, B. J. (2004). Depression and anxiety associated with three pain conditions: Results from a nationally representative sample. *Pain, 111,* 77–83.

Mell, L. K., Davis, R. L., & Owens, D. (2005). Association between streptococcal infection and obsessive-compulsive disorder, Tourette's syndrome, and tic disorder. *Pediatrics, 116,* 56–60.

Mundy, E. A., Blanchard, E. B., Cirenza, E., Gargiulo, J., Maloy, B., & Blanchard, C. G. (2000). Posttraumatic stress disorder in breast cancer patients following autologous bone marrow transplantation or conventional cancer treatments. *Behaviour Research and Therapy, 38,* 1015–1027.

Murphy, T. K., Sajid, M., Soto, O., Shapira, N., Edge, P., Yang, M., et al. (2004). Detecting pediatric autoimmune neuropsychiatric disorders associated with streptococcus in children with obsessive-compulsive disorder and tics. *Biological Psychiatry, 55,* 61–68.

Nascimento, I., Nardi, A. E., Valenca, A. M., Lopes, F. L., Mezzasalma, M. A., Nascentes, R., et al. (2002). Psychiatric disorders in asthmatic outpatients. *Psychiatry Research, 110,* 73–80.

Nisenson, L. G., Pepper, C. M., Schwenk, T. L., & Coyne, J. C. (1998). The nature and prevalence of anxiety disorders in primary care. *General Hospital Psychiatry, 20,* 21–28.

Noyes, R., Jr., Woodman, C., Garvey, M. J., Cook, B. L., Suelzer, M., Clancy, J., et al. (1992). Generalized anxiety disorder vs. panic disorder: Distinguishing characteristics and patterns of comorbidity. *Journal of Nervous and Mental Disease, 180,* 369–379.

Orenstein, H., Peskind, A., & Raskind, M. A. (1988). Thyroid disorders in female psychiatric patients with panic disorder or agoraphobia. *American Journal of Psychiatry, 145,* 1428–1430.

Pariser, S., Pinta, E., & Jones, B. (1978). Mitral valve prolapse and anxiety neurosis/panic disorder. *American Journal of Psychiatry, 135,* 240–241.

Paterniti, S., Alperovitch, A., Ducimetiere, P., Dealberto, M. J., Lepine, J. P., & Bisserbe, J. C. (1999). Anxiety but not depression is associated with elevated blood pressure in a community group of French elderly. *Psychosomatic Medicine, 61,* 77–83.

Perna, G., Bertani, A., Politi, E., Columbo, G., & Bellodi, L. (1997). Asthma and panic attacks. *Biological Psychiatry, 42,* 625–630.

Peyrot, M., & Rubin, R. R. (1997). Levels and risks of depression and anxiety symptomatology among diabetic adults. *Diabetes Care, 20,* 585–590.

Pollack, M. H., Kradin, R., Otto, M. W., Worthington, J., Gould, R., Sabatino, S. A., et al. (1996). Prevalence of panic in patients referred for pulmonary function testing at a major medical center. *American Journal of Psychiatry, 153,* 110–113.

Rauch, S. L., & Jenike, M. A. (1993). Neurobiological models of obsessive-compulsive disorder. *Psychosomatics, 34,* 20–32.

Regier, D. A., Narrow, W. E., Rae, D. S., Manderscheid, R. W., Locke, B. Z., & Goodwin, F. K. (1993). The de facto U.S. mental and addictive disorders service system: Epidemiologic Catchment Area prospective 1-year prevalence rates of disorders and services. *Archives of General Psychiatry, 50,* 85–94.

Robinson, R. G. (1997). Neuropsychiatric consequences of stroke. *Annual Review of Medicine, 48,* 217–229.

Rogers, M. P., White, K., Warshaw, M. G., Yonkers, K. A., Rodriguez-Villa, F., Chang, G., et al. (1994). Prevalence of medical illness in patients with anxiety disorders. *International Journal of Psychiatry in Medicine, 24,* 83–96.

Sareen, J., Cox, B. J., Clara, I., & Asmundson, G.J.G. (2005). The relationship between anxiety disorders and physical disorders in the U.S. National Comorbidity Survey. *Depression and Anxiety, 21,* 193–202.

Sareen, J., Jacobi, F., Cox, B. J., Belik, S. L., Clara, I., & Stein, M. B. (2006). Disability and poor quality of life associated with comorbid anxiety disorders and physical conditions. *Archives of Internal Medicine, 166,* 2109–2116.

Sellick, S. M., & Crooks, D. L. (1999). Depression and cancer: An appraisal of the literature for prevalence, detection, and practice guideline development for psychological interventions. *Psycho-Oncology, 8,* 315–333.

Shemesh, E., Yehuda, R., Milo, O., Dinur, I., Rudnick, A., Vered, Z., et al. (2004). Posttraumatic stress, nonadherence, and adverse outcome in survivors of a myocardial infarction. *Psychosomatic Medicine, 66,* 521–526.

Sheps, D. S., & Sheffield, D. (2001). Depression, anxiety, and the cardiovascular system: The cardiologist's perspective. *Journal of Clinical Psychiatry, 62*(Suppl. 8), 12–16.

Simon, G. E., Von Korff, M., Saunders, K., Miglioretti, D. L., Crane, P. K., van Belle, G., et al. (2006). Association between obesity and psychiatric disorders in the U.S. adult population. *Archives of General Psychiatry, 63,* 824–830.

Simon, N. M., Blacker, D., Korbly, N. B., Sharma, S. G., Worthington, J. J., Otto, M. W., et al. (2002). Hypothyroidism and hyperthyroidism in anxiety disorders revisited: New data and literature review. *Journal of Affective Disorders, 69,* 209–217.

Simpson, R. B., Nedzelski, J. M., Barber, H. O., & Thomas, M. R. (1988). Psychiatric diagnoses in patients with psychogenic dizziness or severe tinnitus. *Journal of Otolaryngology, 17,* 325–330.

Starkstein, S. E., Cohen, B. S., Fedoroff, P., Parikh, R. M., Price, T. R., & Robinson, R. G. (1990). Relationship between anxiety disorders and depressive disorders in patients with cerebrovascular injury. *Archives of General Psychiatry, 47,* 246–251.

Stein, M. B., Asmundson, G.J.G., Ireland, D., & Walker, J. R. (1994). Panic disorder in patients attending a clinic for vestibular disorders. *American Journal of Psychiatry, 151,* 1697–1700.

Stein, M. B., Heuser, I. J., Juncos, J. L., & Uhde, T. W. (1990). Anxiety disorders in patients with Parkinson's disease. *American Journal of Psychiatry, 147,* 217–220.

Sullivan, M. D., Clark, M. R., & Katon, W. J. (1993). Psychiatric and otologic diagnoses in patients complaining of dizziness. *Archives of Internal Medicine, 153,* 1479–1484.

Swedo, S. E., Leonard, H. L., Garvey, M., Mittleman, B., Allen, A. J., Perlmutter, S., et al. (1998). Pediatric autoimmune neuropsychiatric disorders associated with streptococcal infections: Clinical description of the first 50 cases. *American Journal of Psychiatry, 155,* 264–271.

Thomas, J., Jones, G., Scarinci, I., & Brantley, P. (2003). A descriptive and comparative study of the prevalence of depressive and anxiety disorders in low-income adults with type 2 diabetes and other chronic illnesses. *Diabetes Care, 26,* 2311–2317.

Thomas, S. F., Glynne-Jones, R., Chait, I., & Marks, D. F. (1997). Anxiety in long-term cancer survivors influences the acceptability of planned discharge from follow-up. *Psycho-Oncology, 6,* 190–196.

Van Peski-Oosterbaan, A., Spinhoven, P., Van der Does, A., Willems, L. N., & Sterk, P. J. (1996). Is there a specific relationship between asthma and panic disorder? *Behaviour Research and Therapy, 34,* 333–340.

Van Reekum, R., Bolago, I., Finlayson, M.A.J., Garner, S., & Links, P. S. (1996). Psychiatric disorders after traumatic brain injury. *Brain Injury, 10,* 319–327.

Van't Spijker, A., Trijsburg, R. W., & Duivenvoorden, H. J. (1997). Psychological sequelae of cancer diagnosis: A meta-analytical review of 58 studies after 1980. *Psychosomatic Medicine, 59,* 280–293.

Vineis, P. (2002). History of bias. *Soz Praventivmed, 47,* 156–161.

Walker, E. A., Roy-Byrne, P. P., Katon, W. J., Li, L., Amos, D., & Jiranek, G. (1990). Psychiatric illness and irritable bowel syndrome: A comparison with inflammatory bowel disease. *American Journal of Psychiatry, 147,* 1656–1661.

Warden, D. (2006). Military TBI during the Iraq and Afghanistan wars. *Journal of Head Trauma Rehabilitation, 21,* 398–402.

Weisskopf, M. G., Chen, H., Schwarzschild, M. A., Kawachi, I., & Ascherio, A. (2003). Prospective study of phobic anxiety and risk of Parkinson's disease. *Movement Disorders, 18,* 646–651.

Winkelmann, J., Prager, M., Lieb, R., Pfister, H., Spiegel, B., Wittchen, H.-U., et al. (2005). Depression and anxiety disorders in patients with restless legs syndrome. *Journal of Neurology, 252,* 67–71.

Yardley, L. (1994). Prediction of handicap and emotional distress in patients with recurrent vertigo: Symptoms, coping strategies, control beliefs and reciprocal causation. *Social Science and Medicine, 39,* 573–581.

Yardley, L., Luxon, L. M., & Haacke, N. P. (1994). A longitudinal study of symptoms, anxiety and subjective well-being in patients with vertigo. *Clinical Otolaryngology, 19,* 109–116.

Yardley, L., Masson, E., Verschuur, C., Haacke, N., & Luxon, L. (1992). Symptoms, anxiety and handicap in dizzy patients: Development of the vertigo symptom scale. *Journal of Psychosomatic Research, 36,* 731–741.

Young, A. S., Klap, R., Sherbourne, C. D., & Wells, K. B. (2001). The quality of care for depressive and anxiety disorders in the United States. *Archives of General Psychiatry, 58,* 55–61.

Anxiety and Sleep

Allison G. Harvey, Ilana S. Hairston, June Gruber *and* Anda Gershon

Abstract

Sleep disturbances in the form of insomnia, nightmares, or nocturnal panic attacks are prominent features across the anxiety disorders. The first aim of this chapter is to highlight the potential importance of sleep in individuals with anxiety disorders. It is argued that sleep is important not only because disturbed sleep impairs the quality of a patient's life, but also because it likely contributes to the maintenance of the anxiety disorder. The second aim is to review the evidence base for treating patients who suffer from comorbid insomnia and an anxiety disorder. Research attention and clinical intervention for sleep disturbance among individuals with anxiety disorders is a critical domain for future research.

Keywords: anxiety, insomnia, nightmares, nocturnal panic, sleep

Insomnia, nightmares, or nocturnal panic attacks are prominent features of sleep disturbance that spans across many anxiety disorders. In a meta-analysis of 177 studies, Benca and colleagues (1992) reported that individuals with an anxiety disorder take longer to get to sleep at the beginning of the night, experience more awakenings during the night, obtain less sleep overall, and exhibit poorer sleep efficiency, relative to nonpatients. More recently, a review of the literature by Papadimitriou and Linkowski (2005) suggests that the major findings reported by Benca et al. have held over the ensuing decade. Moreover, Papadimitriou and Linkowski (2005) found an especially strong association between sleep disturbance and several anxiety disorders, including panic disorder, generalized anxiety disorder (GAD), obsessive-compulsive disorder, and posttraumatic stress disorder (PTSD). Although most of the evidence to date is based on samples of adults in their middle years, there is also evidence of an association between sleep disturbance and anxiety disorders in children and adolescence (Forbes et al., 2006), as

well as among older adults (Spira, Friedman, Flint, & Sheikh, 2005).

The first aim of this chapter is to highlight the potential importance of sleep problems in individuals with anxiety disorders. We argue that disturbed sleep not only impairs the quality of a patient's life but may also contribute to the maintenance of the anxiety disorder. Our second aim is to review the evidence base for treating patients who suffer from comorbid sleep disturbance and anxiety disorder. As will become evident throughout the chapter, there is a dearth of evidence that specifically delineates the relationship between sleep disturbance and anxiety disorder and thus several of our proposals are based on evidence from healthy nonpatients or patients with other clinical disorders. We raise this caveat at the outset as an important limitation to the conclusions that we draw. We turn now to begin this chapter by offering an overview of concepts that are basic to understanding human sleep; this knowledge is important for clinicians treating individuals who suffer from sleep disturbance.

A Brief Primer on Human Sleep

Human sleep can be divided into nonrapid eye movement (or NREM) sleep, which can be subdivided into four stages (Stages 1, 2, 3, and 4), through which sleep progressively deepens, followed by rapid eye movement (or REM) sleep. Each NREM–REM cycle spans 70 to 120 minutes (Shneerson, 2000). Rapid eye movement sleep is most commonly associated with dreaming, although dreaming is known to occur during NREM sleep as well. This link between REM sleep and dreaming will be discussed in more detail below.

Sleep Assessment

In recognition of the complex issues involved in assessing sleep (Smith, Nowakowski, Soeffing, Orff, & Perlis, 2003), a combination of objective and subjective methods, as well as retrospective and prospective methods, are typically employed. The gold standard measure of sleep is polysomnography (PSG), used to classify sleep into the aforementioned sleep stages according to standardized markers (Rechtschaffen & Kales, 1968). It involves placing surface electrodes on the scalp and face to measure electrical brain activity (electroencephalogram, EEG), eye movement (electro-oculogram, EOG), and muscle tone (electromyogram, EMG). The data obtained are used to classify each epoch of data by sleep stage and in terms of sleep cycles (NREM and REM). Actigraphy is a less expensive and more consumer-friendly alternative means of providing an objective estimate of sleep. Actigraphs are small, wrist-worn, devices that sample physical motion. Because the body becomes more quiescent during sleep, actigraphy can easily differentiate between periods of wakefulness and periods of sleep (Sadeh, Alster, Urbach, & Lavie, 1989).

Subjective reports of sleep quantity and quality are additional important measures. Sleep diaries, completed by the individual immediately on waking, are highly correlated with objective measures of sleep (Wilson, Watson, & Currie, 1998). Also, the individuals' perception of their own sleep (i.e., how they *believe* or *feel* they have slept) has been shown to affect their daytime functioning (Neitzert Semler & Harvey, 2005). A sleep diary includes questions that enable the calculation of the following global measures: sleep onset latency (i.e., time from lights out to falling asleep at the beginning of the night), number and duration of awakenings, total sleep time, and a rating of sleep quality. Several questionnaire measures have been validated to index the presence of sleep disturbance (e.g., Pittsburgh Sleep Quality Index; Buysse, Reynolds, Monk, Berman, & Kupfer, 1989), insomnia (e.g., Insomnia Severity Index; Bastien, Vallieres, & Morin, 2001), and daytime sleepiness (e.g., Stanford Sleepiness Scale; Hoddes, Zarcone, Smythe, Phillips, & Dement, 1973). A combination of one or more of these questionnaires along with a 7-day sleep diary (completed immediately on waking) provides an excellent basic assessment of sleep (Morin & Espie, 2003; Perlis, Smith, Jungquist, & Posner, 2005).

Sleep Across the Lifespan

Sleep patterns change enormously across the life cycle. In newborns, average total sleep time typically ranges between 16–18 hours, organized into 3- to 4-hour sleep periods across the 24-hour cycle. The average amount of sleep per 24-hour period obtained by a 5-year-old is 11.1 hours and 10.2 hours in a 9-year-old (Hoban, 2004). In adolescence, nighttime sleep decreases from an average of 9 hours at age 13 years to 7.9 hours at age 16 years (Hoban, 2004). In young adults, average nighttime sleep varies between 7–9 hours and in the middle adult years between 6–8 hours. Nocturnal sleep is further reduced in older adults, where there is an increase in daytime napping (Shneerson, 2000).

Accompanying these changes in the amount of sleep are alterations in sleep architecture over the course of development. Newborn infants are thought to start sleep with REM and then move into NREM, with each REM-NREM cycle lasting about 50 minutes (Carskadon & Dement, 2005). In newborns REM and NREM phases are called "active" and "quiet" sleep, respectively, because of the absence of prototypical PSG markers in infancy. Whereas at birth approximately 50% of sleep is spent in active sleep, once a child is 2 years of age this percentage has reduced to 20%–30% of total sleep time. Between the ages of 6 and 11, the amount of Stages 3 and 4 sleep reduces and Stage 2 sleep increases (Hoban, 2004). Across the adolescent years, the adult sleep cycle length becomes established, with Stages 3 and 4 further decreasing in length, accompanied by increases in Stage 2 sleep (Carskadon & Dement, 2005).

Why Is Sleep Important in the Anxiety Disorders?
Sleep Disturbance Impairs Quality of Life

Although not specifically examined in patients with anxiety disorders, there is substantial evidence that sleep disturbance impairs quality of life and incurs great costs due to economic and social disability.

For example, the consequences of insomnia are well documented and include functional impairment, work absenteeism, impaired concentration and memory, and increased use of medical services (Roth & Ancoli-Israel, 1999) and a doubled risk of work-related and driving accidents (Ohayon, Caulet, Philip, Guilleminault, & Priest, 1997). Moreover, we know from sleep deprivation studies in nonpatient samples that inadequate sleep has a dose-response relationship with performance on tasks of cognitive function (Dinges, Rogers, & Baynard, 2005). In sum, sleep disturbance has wide-ranging and serious adverse effects on the affected individual's quality of life.

A Bi-Directional Relationship Between Sleep Disturbance and Anxiety: The Case for Mutual Maintenance

In the past it has been assumed that insomnia is a symptom, or epiphenomenon, of the psychiatric disorders with which it is commonly comorbid, including the anxiety disorders. However, evidence is steadily accruing to suggest that there is a bidirectional relationship between insomnia and other psychiatric disorders (as depicted in Figure 1). We turn to review evidence that lends preliminary support to this proposal in the anxiety disorders.

Epidemiological Data. Based on a large cross-sectional study (Ohayon & Roth, 2003), it was concluded that a history of psychiatric illness is closely related to the severity and chronicity of current insomnia; namely, that the likelihood of a previous psychiatric disorder was 6 times higher in individuals with severe insomnia and 4 times higher in individuals with moderate insomnia. Where insomnia and anxiety disorder were comorbid, 18% exhibited insomnia prior to the onset of an anxiety disorder, in 39% of the cases the two appeared simultaneously, and in 43% the anxiety appeared before the insom-

nia. Since these prevalence rates were obtained using cross-sectional assessments with retrospective reporting, it is not possible to determine the temporal relationship between the onset of anxiety disorders and disturbances in sleep. There is, however, prospective evidence showing that persistent insomnia is associated with an increased risk of developing an anxiety disorder (Breslau, Roth, Rosenthal, & Andreski, 1996; Ford & Kamerow, 1989). Together, these findings have been interpreted as suggesting that insomnia and anxiety disorders may interact in multiple ways: as a risk for, as a symptom of, and as a mutual maintainer (Ohayon & Roth, 2003).

Evidence That Daytime Anxiety Contributes to Sleep Disturbance (depicted in Figure 1 with a dashed line). The basis of the proposal that daytime anxiety contributes to sleep disturbance includes the premise that worry and physiological arousal are core features of anxiety (Barlow, 2002). Taking worry first, experimental manipulations that *reduce* worry in individuals with insomnia are associated with a *reduction* in sleep impairment (Harvey & Payne, 2002; Haynes, Adams, & Franzen, 1981) and experimental manipulations that *increase* worry in normal sleepers are associated with an *increase* in sleep impairment (Gross & Borkovec, 1982; Hall, Buysse, Reynolds, Kupfer, & Baum, 1996; Tang & Harvey, 2004). Similarly, in the case of physiological arousal, experimental manipulations that *increase* physiological arousal (e.g., caffeine intake) are associated with an *increase* in sleep disturbance (Bonnet & Arand, 1992; Tang & Harvey, 2004).

Evidence That Sleep Disturbance Contributes to Daytime Anxiety (depicted in Figure 1 with a dotted line). In this section we suggest that there are at least two ways in which sleep disturbance may contribute to daytime anxiety. These will now be described.

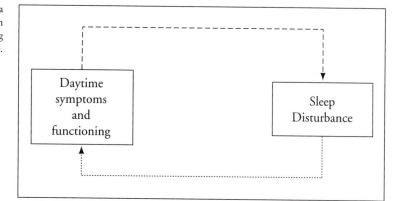

Fig. 1 Graphical depiction of a bidirectional relationship between daytime symptoms and functioning and sleep disturbance.

Effects of Sleep Disturbance on Daytime Mood Regulation. Problems of mood regulation are defined by Hyman (Hyman, 2000) as "the failure to recover a moderate affective state after a highly pleasant or unpleasant emotional experience" (p. 437). There is accruing evidence that sleep has an important role in mood regulation. In nonpatient samples, Pilcher and Huffcutt (1996) conducted a meta-analysis of 19 studies conducted from 1984 to 1992 of short-term total sleep deprivation (less than or equal to 45 hours), long-term total sleep deprivation (greater than 48 hours), or partial sleep deprivation (sleep period of less than 5 hours in a 24-hour period). The results indicated that among healthy nonpatient samples, mood was adversely affected by sleep deprivation (effect size of −3.16). This finding has been replicated in more recent studies. For example, Dinges et al. (1997) restricted the sleep of healthy nonpatient participants to 5 hours per night for 1 week. The results indicated that mood progressively declined as sleep deprivation accumulated throughout the week. Moreover, Drake et al. (2001) allocated healthy participants to three schedules of sleep loss: slow (6 hours time in bed for four nights), intermediate (4 hours time in bed for two nights), and rapid (0 hours time in bed for one night). A control group who obtained 8 hours time in bed over the same time period was also included. A dose-response relationship between mood and sleep was observed such that greater mood impairment was evident in the rapid sleep loss group as opposed to the slow, cumulative sleep loss, who experience more impairment relative to the control group. Hence, a large body of literature provides evidence that sleep disturbance causes mood disturbance the following day in healthy participants. The implications of these data have started to be worked out for children and adolescents (Dahl, 2002) and for individuals with major depressive disorder (Cartwright, Baehr, Kirkby, Pandi-Perumal, & Kabat, 2003) and bipolar disorder (Harvey, Mullin, & Hinshaw, 2006). However, the applicability to individuals with anxiety disorders has yet to be delineated. It is certainly tempting, given the strength of the available evidence in both healthy nonpatients and in patients diagnosed with mood disorders, to speculate that sleep disturbances may contribute directly to anxious mood.

Effects of Sleep Disturbance on Emotional Processing. Rachman (1980) defines emotional processing as "a process whereby emotional disturbances are absorbed and decline to the extent that other experiences and behaviour can proceed without

disruption." It is thought that REM sleep plays an important role in emotional processing (Cartwright, Luten, Young, Mercer, & Bears, 1998; Cartwright, Young, Mercer, & Bears, 1998; Perlis & Nielsen, 1993). Perlis and Nielson (1993) summarized three lines of empirical support for this hypothesis. First, abnormal REM sleep can be observed across various groups of individuals diagnosed with a psychiatric disorder, including those diagnosed with schizophrenia, major depression, borderline personality disorder, and eating disorder. Of course, causal relations are impossible to discern from such associations, though it seems that disruptions in REM sleep may be associated in more than a casual fashion with important psychiatric conditions.

Second, presleep mood and stress appear to influence the content of dreaming, the emotion within a dream, and latency to REM as well as REM density (e.g., Breger, Hunter, & Lane, 1971; Cartwright, Bernick, Borowitz, & Kling, 1969; De Koninck & Brunette, 1991). In other words, stress, mood, and emotion appear to be linked directly to important sleep parameters.

Third, both REM sleep and dreaming have been shown to influence daytime mood. Evidence for this linkage can be derived from REM deprivation studies that showed that individuals deprived of REM experienced greater anxiety, irritability, and reduced adaptability the following day (see Perlis & Nielsen, 1993, for a review of these studies). Evidence from prospective studies also implicate REM sleep in emotional processing (Cartwright, Young, et al., 1998).

An additional line of evidence to emerge more recently is from the neuroscience literature. For example, evidence from fMRI studies demonstrates the presence of amygdala activity during REM sleep but not NREM sleep (e.g., Maquet et al., 1996). As the amygdala is implicated in the acquisition of emotional memories, this observation is also consistent with the possibility that REM sleep has a role in the processing of emotional information.

These findings implicating REM sleep in emotional processing may well be relevant to the anxiety disorders, particularly to PTSD, which has been conceptualized as a disorder of failed emotional processing (Foa & Kozak, 1986). Comparisons between individuals with PTSD and controls have consistently yielded reports of increased REM density in PTSD patients relative to healthy nonpatients. REM density refers to the frequency of eye movements within REM periods. A polysomnographic study of sleep in a community sample found that most sleep parameters in PTSD were within normal limits, though an increased number of brief arousals from REM sleep was detected in subjects with PTSD (Breslau et al., 2004). Findings regarding other aspects of REM sleep (e.g., amount of REM, reduced latency to REM, and awakenings from REM) in PTSD and in other anxiety disorders remain mixed (see Harvey, Jones, & Schmidt, 2003; Papadimitriou & Linkowski, 2005).

Summary. Taken together, there is fairly robust evidence that core features of the anxiety disorders, namely worry and physiological arousal, likely contribute to sleep disturbance. Prospective research suggests that sleep disturbance is a risk factor for developing an anxiety disorder. Two pathways by which sleep disturbance may serve to mutually maintain anxiety disorders have been presented; sleep disturbance may impair mood regulation ability and sleep disturbance may impair emotional processing. While these hypotheses require testing in samples of anxious individuals, supportive evidence is derived from studies of healthy nonpatients and patients diagnosed with schizophrenia, major depression, borderline personality disorder, and eating disorder. If future research confirms the applicability of these findings to the anxiety disorders, the bidirectional relationship between anxiety during the day and sleep disturbance at night (depicted in Figure 1) will be supported.

Treatment of Sleep Disturbance Comorbid with Anxiety Disorder

Given the evidence reviewed that sleep disturbance appears to be a risk factor for developing an anxiety disorder (Breslau et al., 1996; Ford & Kamerow, 1989), along with the possibility that sleep disturbance may serve to mutually maintain anxiety disorders, it is important to be able to offer clients a treatment that effectively alleviates the sleeping difficulty.

Cognitive Behavioral Therapy for Insomnia (CBT-I)

This multicomponent treatment typically involves one or more of the following components: stimulus control, sleep restriction, sleep hygiene, paradoxical intention, relaxation therapy, imagery training, and cognitive restructuring for unhelpful beliefs about sleep (see Table 1 for a description of each component; for a detailed clinician's guide, see Morin & Espie [2003] and Perlis, Junquist, Smith, & Posner, [2005]). The components of CBT-I are administered over 4–10 weekly sessions in either

individual (e.g., Edinger, Wohlgemuth, Radtke, Marsh, & Quillian, 2001) or group (e.g., Espie, Inglis, Tessier, & Harvey, 2001; Morin, Colecchi, Stone, Sood, & Brink, 1999) format. CBT-I has been shown to be a highly effective treatment as indicated by a review conducted by the Standards of Practice Committee of the American Academy of Sleep Medicine (Morin, Hauri, et al., 1999), which has been recently updated (Morin et al., 2006). The positive effects of the treatment are known to be sustained well beyond the end of treatment (e.g., Edinger et al., 2001; Espie et al., 2001; Morin et al., 2004).

CBT-I for Sleep Disturbance in the Anxiety Disorders

There is encouraging evidence from a large clinical replication series ($n = 100$) that individuals with insomnia and comorbid anxiety and/or depression respond to CBT-I for insomnia in a comparable fashion to individuals with insomnia alone (Morin, Stone, McDonald, & Jones, 1994). In this study the participants were grouped according to their primary sleep diagnosis as follows: psychophysiological/primary insomnia ($n = 31$), insomnia associated with psychopathology ($n = 22$; comprising individuals with an anxiety disorder and/or depression), drug-dependent insomnia ($n = 21$), and others ($n = 26$). Regardless of diagnosis, the treatment produced substantial reductions in total wake time, sleep-onset latency, wake after sleep onset, and early-morning awakening. In other words, preliminary evidence suggests that CBT-I may be an effective intervention for the treatment of sleep disturbances in individuals with anxiety disorders.

Targeting Cognitive Processes and a Transdiagnostic Approach

To briefly mention a new direction that is relevant in the context of the anxiety disorders, over the past 7 years our group has been developing and evaluating an approach to treating insomnia that aims to reverse five cognitive processes shown to be involved in the maintenance of insomnia, including (1) worry and rumination, (2) attentional bias toward, and monitoring for, sleep-related threat, (3) misperception of sleep and daytime functioning, (4) unhelpful beliefs about sleep, and (5) use of safety behaviors that maintain unhelpful beliefs about sleep (Harvey, 2005).

Several of these maintaining processes are "transdiagnostic" in that they are processes that are in common *across* insomnia and the anxiety disorders

Table 1. Description of CBT-I Treatment Components

Treatment Component	Description
Stimulus control	Patient is asked to go to bed only when tired or sleepy, limit bedroom activities to sleep and sex, leave the bedroom if unable to fall asleep within 15–20 minutes, rise at the same time each morning, and to limit daytime napping.
Sleep restriction	Curtailing time in bed to the actual time slept. The patient is prescribed a specific amount of time in bed (sleep window) that is not to be exceeded. Initially, sleep window is equal to the patient's subjective estimation of sleep time, and then adjusted weekly based upon sleep efficiency for the previous week.
Sleep hygiene	The patient is educated about behaviors known to interfere with sleep (e.g., caffeine intake, alcohol and nicotine use, daytime napping, variable sleep schedule, physical exercise within 4 hrs. of bedtime, etc.). These behaviors are then monitored on a daily basis.
Paradoxical intention	The patient is instructed to try to stay awake when in bed, thus reducing the anxiety associated with trying to fall asleep.
Relaxation therapy	The patient is educated about techniques aimed at reducing psychophysiological arousal (e.g., progressive muscle relaxation, diaphragmatic breathing, autogenic training, biofeedback, meditation, yoga, and hypnosis).
Cognitive restructuring	Patient's irrational beliefs about sleep are identified and corrected with accurate alternative beliefs by education and discussion about sleep requirements, the biological clock, and the effects of sleep loss on sleep-wake functions.

(Harvey, Watkins, Mansell, & Shafran, 2004). This raises two clinical implications. First, directly targeting treatment to the shared or transdiagnostic processes may provide a way forward for efficiently and effectively treating comorbid cases (Harvey et al., 2004). Second, the current approach to treating comorbid cases would be to apply CBT-I sequentially with the evidence-based intervention for the anxiety disorder. For example, if a patient presents with anxiety and insomnia, the sequential approach would involve treating the anxiety first and then moving on to treat the insomnia, or vice versa. This approach perhaps makes the most sense if the co-occurring disorders are independent and additive. But if the disorders mutually maintain each other, the sequential approach may not be maximally efficient (Westen, Novotny, & Thompson-Brenner, 2004). Given increasingly compelling evidence for mutual maintenance between insomnia and its commonly comorbid disorders, it may be more efficient to treat comorbid disorders simultaneously. One way this might be achieved is by treating maintaining mechanisms that are shared by the insomnia and the comorbid disorder (i.e., the transdiagnostic processes).

Pharmacological Approaches

Several classes of medications are used for treating insomnia. When insomnia is comorbid with an anxiety disorder, benzodiazepine receptor agonists are the most popular pharmacological choices (Nutt, 2005). However, to the best of our knowledge, there are no controlled trials of sleep medications for individuals with anxiety disorders. For the treatment of individuals with insomnia we know that controlled clinical trials have shown that all benzodiazepines are more effective than placebo for improving sleep measures (Holbrook, Crowther, Lotter, Cheng, & King, 2000; Kupfer & Reynolds, 1997). In a meta-analysis of 22 placebo-controlled hypnotic trials ($n = 1,894$), benzodiazepines and zolpidem (a nonbenzodiazepine hypnotic) were found to produce reliable improvements in sleep (Nowell et al., 1997). As the median treatment duration in those studies was only 1 week (range of 4–35 days), the efficacy of these hypnotic agents beyond the acute treatment phase remains largely unknown. Thus, hypnotic medications are effective for the short-term management of insomnia. Interestingly, two recent trials raise the possibility that longer-term treatment may also be effective for some individuals (Krystal et al., 2003; Perlis, McCall, Krystal, & Walsh, 2004), although neither study included a follow-up to evaluate whether the benefits to sleep were sustained after treatment ceased. Also, we note that all hypnotic medications carry some risks of daytime residual effects, as well as risks of tolerance and dependence. When used on a regular and prolonged basis, rebound insomnia is a common problem associated with discontinuation, particularly after prolonged usage. In general, the newer medications (e.g., zolpidem and eszopiclone) produce fewer withdrawal symptoms (i.e., rebound insomnia) upon discontinuation (Morin & Espie, 2003). In summary, hypnotic medications are efficacious and clinically indicated in some selected situations (e.g., acute insomnia), but their role in the management of chronic insomnia is not well documented and remains more controversial and use in anxious individuals with insomnia has not yet been studied. See Stein and Mellman (2005) for additional discussion of this topic.

Special Topics

In this section we review two areas relevant to the topic of sleep and anxiety: one is nocturnal panic, a common feature of panic disorder, and one is nightmares, a common feature of PTSD. We are addressing these separately as the evidence that has accrued to date suggests they may require more specialized interventions.

Nocturnal Panic

Nocturnal panic is defined as an abrupt awakening from sleep without an identifiable trigger during which the individual experiences intense fear or discomfort, accompanied by cognitive and physiological arousal (American Psychiatric Association, 2000). This can include shortness of breath, increased heart rate, depersonalization or derealization, chest pressure, nausea, and a fear of dying. Nocturnal panic typically occurs during late Stage 2 or early Stage 3 sleep and lasts between 2 and 8 minutes. Following a nocturnal panic, individuals often report difficulty returning to sleep.

Nocturnal panic is distinct from night terrors that occur predominantly in Stage 4 sleep and are characterized by absence of memory of the event, while individuals are able to vividly recall nocturnal panics. Sleep apnea is distinguishable from nocturnal panic in that it occurs during Stage 1, 2, and REM sleep and typically occurs repeatedly during the night, compared to the single occurrence of nocturnal panic per night. In contrast to sleep pa-

ralysis, nocturnal panic is not associated with the inability to move one's body. Finally, unlike nightmares that occur during REM sleep, nocturnal panic is exclusive to non-REM sleep (for a more detailed review of the differences between nocturnal panic and other sleep disorders, see Papadimitriou & Linkowski, 2005). Nocturnal panic, however, is identical in symptom quality, duration, and severity to waketime panic attacks. In fact, 30%–45% of individuals with panic disorder experience recurrent nocturnal panics (Craske & Tsao, 2005). Some researchers have speculated that nocturnal panic may actually represent a more severe form of panic disorder rather than a distinct diagnostic category (Craske, 2002).

Cognitive behavioral therapy for nocturnal panic targets misappraisals of anxiety sensations. This is based on a cognitive model of nocturnal panic (Craske, 2002) in which individuals misappraise subtle interoceptive changes (e.g., increase in heart rate) as a sign of catastrophe (Craske, 2001). This misappraisal often leads to heightened arousal, reinforcing the belief that something catastrophic is happening, spiraling into nocturnal panic. Over time, the physiological sensations of nocturnal panic are feared, leading individuals to avoid situations that are associated with nocturnal panic (i.e., sleeping). Thus, individuals with nocturnal panic often become fearful of sleep and may deliberately avoid sleep onset. Avoidance of sleep results in sleep deprivation, putting the individual at risk for more nocturnal panics as well as preventing the acquisition of disconfirming evidence that nocturnal panics are not harmful or catastrophic (Craske & Tsao, 2005). The CBT treatment for nocturnal panic focuses on providing accurate information about panic attacks, with an emphasis on the harmless nature of physiological fluctuations during sleep. Specific misappraisals are categorized as probability overestimations or catastrophizations and are evaluated in session using a hypothesis testing approach (e.g., "What is the evidence for . . . ?). The therapist works with the patient to gather data, explore alternative explanations (e.g., heart rate increases attributable to normal physiological changes during sleep), and examining realistic consequences of these beliefs (e.g., "What would the worse case be if I woke up during a panic episode? How would I cope?"). Exposure therapy is an important component and takes the form of inducing physical sensations associated with panic (e.g., heart increase, hyperventilzation, dizziness) in order to help the patient weaken associations between internal physiological cues and the typical panic response (Craske & Tsao, 2005).

Research supports the efficacy of CBT for nocturnal panic, with marked reductions in the severity and frequency of nocturnal panic during treatment, with effects lasting through a 9-month follow-up (Craske, 2005). Nocturnal panic symptom improvement was also associated with decreased physiological reactivity to laboratory stressors. By contrast, pharmacological treatments have received little empirical attention. While extant research shows promising results for benzodiazepines and antidepressants in the reduction, these studies have been limited to uncontrolled single-case trials (Mellman & Uhde, 1990).

Nightmares

Nightmare disorder, or dream anxiety disorder, is a parasomnia characterized by the repeated occurrence of frightening dreams, usually during the second half of the night, and most commonly associated with rapid-eye movement sleep (REM). Nightmares are vivid and complex dreams, and upon wakening there is good recall of their content (Kramer, 2000). Waking from the nightmare is a sufficient, but not necessary, criteria for nightmare disorder (Zadra & Donderi, 2000). When waking from the nightmare occurs, it is complete and usually accompanied by physiological symptoms of anxiety or fear, although these symptoms are not as severe as observed in night terrors. Due to the anxiety and cognitive clarity achieved upon waking, returning to sleep after a nightmare is often difficult. In addition to reducing total sleep time, recurring nightmares may create anxiety about falling asleep (Nielsen, 2005). As a result, nightmare disorder is often associated with increased sleep onset latency and cognitive and emotional impairment similar to insomnia (Ohayon, Morselli, & Guilleminault, 1997).

The prevalence rate of nightmare disorder, as a primary disorder in adults, ranges from 2%–10% (Belicki & Belicki, 1982; Nielsen & Zadra, 2000). Nightmare disorder is also comorbid with several psychiatric disorders, including GAD and PTSD (Krakow et al., 2002). In the latter, nightmares have been conceptualized as a signal of failed emotional processing (Rachman, 1980).

Krakow and colleagues have developed an approach for treating nightmares called imagery rehearsal therapy. To date, this intervention has mainly been used for PTSD individuals who experience frequent nightmares (Krakow & Zadra,

2006). Imagery rehearsal therapy is a two-tier process wherein first the client is introduced to the notion that nightmares are an acquired behavior, sustained by habit; second, the client learns to consciously manipulate the imagery of the nightmare, and rehearses the manipulated version of the dream. Subjects who receive imagery rehearsal therapy report significant reduction in the frequency of their nightmares, as well in the severity of their PTSD symptoms (Krakow & Zadra, 2006). The apparent success of imagery rehearsal therapy in reducing overall PTSD severity underscores the importance of addressing the disorder-related sleep problem in the general treatment regimen.

Summary and Conclusions

The overall aim of this chapter has been to highlight the potential importance of sleep problems in individuals with anxiety disorders. We have argued that research attention and clinical intervention for sleep disturbance among individuals with anxiety disorders is important for two main reasons: (1) Sleep disturbance will adversely affect quality of life, and (2) there may be a bidirectional vicious cycle relationship between sleep disturbance and anxiety disorders such that anxiety symptoms during the day increase sleep disturbance, and sleep disturbance increases anxiety symptoms during the next day. In support, we presented evidence that core symptoms experienced by anxious individuals during the daytime (worry and physiological arousal) contribute to sleep disturbance. Moreover, we presented evidence that the role of sleep may include mood regulation and emotional processing. As such, we suggest that sleep disturbance is one possible variable of considerable influence in the complex set of processes that serve to maintain anxiety disorders. Given this, investigations of sleep among anxious individuals is a critical domain for future research. One goal of research will be to maximally inform intervention. It seems easy to imagine that a high-quality psychological intervention for sleep disturbance, or perhaps a transdiagnostic treatment that targets the processes that are common to the insomnia and anxiety disorder, will be an important component of a comprehensive intervention for individuals with anxiety disorders. The psychological intervention approach for treating sleep disturbance (CBT-I) is emphasized here given the strong evidence that has accrued for its effectiveness in treating insomnia and the preliminary evidence for its effectiveness treating insomnia that is comorbid with an anxiety disorder.

References

American Psychiatric Association. (2000). *Diagnostic and statistical manual of mental disorders* (4th ed., text revision). Washington, DC: Author.

Barlow, D. H. (2002). *The origins of anxious apprehension, anxiety disorders, and related emotional disorders* (2nd ed.). New York: Guilford Press.

Bastien, C. H., Vallieres, A., & Morin, C. M. (2001). Validation of the Insomnia Severity Index as an outcome measure for insomnia research. *Sleep Medicine, 2*, 297–307.

Belicki, K., & Belicki, D. (1982). Nightmare in a university population. *Sleep Research, 11*, 116–119.

Benca, R. M., Obermeyer, W. H., Thisted, R. A., & Gillin, J. C. (1992). Sleep and psychiatric disorders: A meta-analysis. *Archives of General Psychiatry, 49*, 651–668.

Bonnet, M. H., & Arand, D. L. (1992). Caffeine use as a model of acute and chronic insomnia. *Sleep, 15*, 526–536.

Breger, L., Hunter, I., & Lane, R. W. (1971). The effect of stress on dreams. *Psychological Issues, 7*, 1–213.

Breslau, N., Roth, T., Burduvali, E., Kapke, A., Schultz, L., & Roehrs, T. (2004). Sleep in lifetime posttraumatic stress disorder: A community-based polysomnographic study. *Archives of General Psychiatry, 61*, 508–516.

Breslau, N., Roth, T., Rosenthal, L., & Andreski, P. (1996). Sleep disturbance and psychiatric disorders: A longitudinal epidemiological study of young adults. *Biological Psychiatry, 39*, 411–418.

Buysse, D. J., Reynolds, C. F., Monk, T. H., Berman, S. R., & Kupfer, D. J. (1989). The Pittsburgh Sleep Quality Index: A new instrument for psychiatric practice and research. *Psychiatry Research, 28*, 193–213.

Carskadon, M. A., & Dement, W. C. (2005). Normal human sleep: An overview. In M. H. Kryger, T. Roth, & W. C. Dement (Eds.), *Principles and practice of sleep medicine* (4th ed., pp. 13–23). Philadelphia: Elsevier Saunders.

Cartwright, R., Baehr, E., Kirkby, J., Pandi-Perumal, S. R., & Kabat, J. (2003). REM sleep reduction, mood regulation and remission in untreated depression. *Psychiatry Research, 121*, 159–167.

Cartwright, R., Luten, A., Young, M., Mercer, P., & Bears, M. (1998). Role of REM sleep and dream affect in overnight mood regulation: A study of normal volunteers. *Psychiatry Research, 81*, 1–8.

Cartwright, R., Young, M. A., Mercer, P., & Bears, M. (1998). Role of REM sleep and dream variables in the prediction of remission from depression. *Psychiatry Research, 80*, 249–255.

Cartwright, R. D., Bernick, N., Borowitz, G., & Kling, A. (1969). Effect of an erotic movie on the sleep and dreams of young men. *Archives of General Psychiatry, 20*, 262–271.

Craske, M. G., Lang, A. J., Aikins, D., & Mystkowski, J. L. (2005). Cognitive behavioral therapy for nocturnal panic. *Journal of Clinical Psychiatry, 51*, 513–516.

Craske, M. G., Lang, A. J., Aikins, D., Mystkowski, J. L., & Rowe, M. K. (2001). Reactivity to interoceptive cues in nocturnal panic. *Journal of Behavioral Therapy and Experimental Psychiatry, 32*, 173–190.

Craske, M. G., Lang, A. J., Rowe, M. A., DeCola, J. P., Simmons, J., Mann, C., et al. (2002). Presleep attributions about arousal during sleep: Nocturnal panic. *Journal of Abnormal Psychology, 111*, 53–62.

Craske, M. G., & Tsao, J. C. (2005). Assessment and treatment of nocturnal panic attacks. *Sleep Medicine Reviews, 9*, 173–184.

Dahl, R. E. (2002). The regulation of sleep-arousal, affect, and attention in adolescence: Some questions and speculations. In M. A. Carskadon (Ed.), *Adolescent sleep patterns: Biological, social and psychological influences* (pp. 269–284). Cambridge: Cambridge University Press.

De Koninck, J., & Brunette, R. (1991). Presleep suggestion related to a phobic object: Successful manipulation of reported dream affect. *Journal of General Psychology, 118*, 185–200.

Dinges, D. F., Pack, F., Williams, K., Gillen, K. A., Powell, J. W., Ott, G. E., et al. (1997). Cumulative sleepiness, mood disturbance, and psychomotor vigilance performance decrements during a week of sleep restricted to 4–5 hours per night. *Sleep, 20*, 267–267.

Dinges, D. F., Rogers, N. L., & Baynard, M. D. (2005). Chronic sleep deprivation. In M. H. Kryger, T. Roth, & W. C. Dement (Eds.), *Principles and practice of sleep medicine* (4th ed., pp. 67–76). Philadelphia: Elsevier Saunders.

Drake, C. L., Roehrs, T. A., Burduvali, E., Bonahoom, A., Rosekind, M., & Roth, T. (2001). Effects of rapid versus slow accumulation of eight hours of sleep loss. *Psychophysiology, 38*, 979–987.

Edinger, J. D., Wohlgemuth, W. K., Radtke, R. A., Marsh, G. R., & Quillian, R. E. (2001). Cognitive behavioral therapy for treatment of chronic primary insomnia: A randomized controlled trial. *Journal of the American Medical Association, 285*, 1856–1864.

Espie, C. A., Inglis, S. J., Tessier, S., & Harvey, L. (2001). The clinical effectiveness of cognitive behaviour therapy for chronic insomnia: Implementation and evaluation of a sleep clinic in general medical practice. *Behaviour Research and Therapy, 39*, 45–60.

Foa, E. B., & Kozak, M. J. (1986). Emotional processing of fear: Exposure to corrective information. *Psychological Bulletin, 99*, 20–35.

Forbes, E. E., Williamson, D. E., Ryan, N. D., Birmaher, B., Axelson, D. A., & Dahl, R. E. (2006). Peri-sleep-onset cortisol levels in children and adolescents with affective disorders. *Biological Psychiatry, 59*, 24–30.

Ford, D. E., & Kamerow, D. B. (1989). Epidemiologic study of sleep disturbances and psychiatric disorders: An opportunity for prevention? *Journal of the American Medical Association, 262*, 1479–1484.

Gross, R. T., & Borkovec, T. D. (1982). Effects of a cognitive intrusion manipulation on the sleep-onset latency of good sleepers. *Behavior Therapy, 13*, 112–116.

Hall, M., Buysse, D. J., Reynolds, C. F., III, Kupfer, D. J., & Baum, A. (1996). Stress-related intrusive thoughts disrupt sleep onset and continuity. *Sleep Research, 25*, 163.

Harvey, A. G. (2005). A cognitive theory of and therapy for chronic insomnia. *Journal of Cognitive Psychotherapy, An International Quarterly, 19*, 41–60.

Harvey, A. G., Jones, C., & Schmidt, D. A. (2003). Sleep and posttraumatic stress disorder: A review. *Clinical Psychology Review, Special issue on Post Traumatic Stress Disorder, 23*, 377–407.

Harvey, A. G., Mullin, B. C., & Hinshaw, S. P. (2006). Sleep and circadian rhythms in children and adolescents with bipolar disorder. *Development and Psychopathology, 18*, 1147–1168.

Harvey, A. G., & Payne, S. (2002). The management of unwanted pre-sleep thoughts in insomnia: Distraction with imagery versus general distraction. *Behaviour Research and Therapy, 40*, 267–277.

Harvey, A. G., Watkins, E., Mansell, W., & Shafran, R. (2004). *Cognitive behavioural processes across psychological disorders: A* transdiagnostic approach to research and treatment. Oxford, England: Oxford University Press.

Haynes, S. N., Adams, A., & Franzen, M. (1981). The effects of presleep stress on sleep-onset insomnia. *Journal of Abnormal Psychology, 90,* 601–606.

Hoban, T. F. (2004). Sleep and its disorders in children. *Seminars in Neurology, 24,* 327–340.

Hoddes, E., Zarcone, V., Smythe, H., Phillips, R., & Dement, W. C. (1973). Quantification of sleepiness: A new approach. *Psychophysiology, 10,* 431–436.

Holbrook, A. M., Crowther, R., Lotter, A., Cheng, C., & King, D. (2000). The diagnosis and management of insomnia in clinical practice: A practical evidence-based approach. *Canadian Medical Association Journal, 162,* 216–220.

Hyman, S. E. (2000). Goals for research on bipolar disorder: The view from NIMH. *Biological Psychiatry, 48,* 436–441.

Krakow, B., Schrader, R., Tandberg, D., Hollifield, M., Koss, M. P., Yau, C. L., et al. (2002). Nightmare frequency in sexual assault survivors with PTSD. *Journal of Anxiety Disorders, 16,* 175–190.

Krakow, B., & Zadra, A. (2006). Clinical management of chronic nightmares: Imagery rehearsal therapy. *Behavioral Sleep Medicine, 4,* 45–70.

Kramer, M. (2000). Dreams and psychopathology. In M. H. Kryger, T. Roth, & W. Dement (Eds.), *Principles and practices of sleep medicine* (3rd ed., pp. 511–519). Philadelphia: Elsevier Saunders.

Krystal, A. D., Walsh, J. K., Laska, E., Caron, J., Amato, D. A., Wessel, T., et al. (2003). Sustained efficacy of eszopiclone over 6 nights of nightly treatment: Results of a randomized, double-blind, placebo-controlled study in adults with chronic insomnia. *Sleep, 26,* 793–799.

Kupfer, D. J., & Reynolds, C. F., III. (1997). Management of insomnia. *New England Journal of Medicine, 336,* 341–346.

Maquet, P., Peters, J., Aerts, J., Delfiore, G., Degueldre, C., Luxen, A., et al. (1996). Functional neuroanatomy of human rapid-eye-movement sleep and dreaming. *Nature, 383,* 163–166.

Mellman, T. A., & Uhde T. W. (1989). Electroencephalographic sleep in panic disorder: A focus on sleep-related panic attacks. *Archives of General Psychiatry, 46,* 178–184.

Mellman, T. A., & Uhde, T. W. (1990). Patients with frequent sleep panic: Clinical findings and response to medication treatment. *Journal of Clinical Psychiatry, 51,* 513–516.

Morin, C. M., Bastien, C., Guay, B., Radouco-Thomas, M., Leblanc, J., & Vallieres, A. (2004). Randomized clinical trial of supervised tapering and cognitive behavior therapy to facilitate benzodiazepine discontinuation in older adults with chronic insomnia. *American Journal of Psychiatry, 161,* 332–342.

Morin, C. M., Bootzin, R. R., Buysse, D. J., Edinger, J. D., Espie, C. A., & Lichstein, K. L. (2006). Psychological and behavioral treatment of insomnia: An update of recent evidence (1998–2004). *Sleep, 29,* 1396–1406.

Morin, C. M., Colecchi, C., Stone, Sood, R., & Brink, D. (1999). Behavioral and pharmacological therapies for late-life insomnia. *Journal of the American Medical Association, 281,* 991–999.

Morin, C. M., & Espie, C. A. (2003). *Insomnia: A clinical guide to assessment and treatment.* New York: Kluwer Academic/Plenum.

Morin, C. M., Hauri, P. J., Espie, C. A., Spielman, A. J., Buysse, D. J., & Bootzin, R. R. (1999). Nonpharmacologic treatment of chronic insomnia: An American Academy of Sleep Medicine review. *Sleep, 22,* 1134–1156.

Morin, C. M., Stone, J., McDonald, K., & Jones, S. (1994). Psychological management of insomnia: A clinical replication series with 100 patients. *Behavior Therapy, 25,* 291–309.

Neitzert Semler, C., & Harvey, A. G. (2005). Misperception of sleep can adversely affect daytime functioning in insomnia. *Behaviour Research and Therapy, 43,* 843–856.

Nielsen, T. A. (2005). Chronobiology of dreaming. In M. H. Kryger, T. Roth, & W. Dement (Eds.), *Principles and practices of sleep medicine* (4th ed., pp. 535–550). Philadelphia: Elsevier Saunders.

Nowell, P. D., Mazumdar, S., Buysse, D. J., Dew, M. A., Reynolds, C. F., III, & Kupfer, D. J. (1997). Benzodiazepines and zolpidem for chronic insomnia: A meta-analysis of treatment efficacy. *Journal of the American Medical Association, 278,* 2170–2177.

Nutt, D. J. (2005). Overview of diagnosis and drug treatments of anxiety disorders. *CNS Spectrums, 10,* 49–56.

Ohayon, M. M., Caulet, M., Philip, P., Guilleminault, C., & Priest, R. G. (1997). How sleep and mental disorders are related to complaints of daytime sleepiness. *Archives of Internal Medicine, 157,* 2645–2652.

Ohayon, M. M., Morselli, P. L., & Guilleminault, C. (1997). Prevalence of nightmares and their relationship to psychopathology and daytime functioning in insomnia subjects. *Sleep, 20,* 340–348.

Ohayon, M. M., & Roth, T. (2003). Place of chronic insomnia in the course of depressive and anxiety disorders. *Journal of Psychiatric Research, 37,* 9–15.

Papadimitriou, G. N., & Linkowski, P. (2005). Sleep disturbance in anxiety disorders. *International Review of Psychiatry, 17,* 229–236.

Perlis, M., Smith, M., Jungquist, C., & Posner, D. (Eds.). (2005). *The cognitive-behavioral treatment of insomnia: A session by session guide.* New York: Springer.

Perlis, M. L., McCall, W. V., Krystal, A.D., & Walsh, J. K. (2004). Long-term, non-nightly administration of zolpidem in the treatment of patients with primary insomnia. *Journal of Clinical Psychiatry, 65,* 1128–1137.

Perlis, M. L., & Nielsen, T. A. (1993). Mood regulation, dreaming and nightmares: Evaluation of a desensitization function for REM sleep. *Dreaming, 3,* 243–257.

Pilcher, J. J., & Huffcutt, A. I. (1996). Effects of sleep deprivation on performance: A meta-analysis. *Sleep, 19,* 318–326.

Rachman, S. (1980). Emotional processing. *Behaviour Research and Therapy, 18,* 51–60.

Rechtschaffen, A., & Kales, A. (1968). *A manual of standardized terminology, techniques and scoring system for sleep stages of human subjects.* Bethesda, MD: U.S. Department of Health, Education and Welfare.

Roth, T., & Ancoli-Israel, S. (1999). Daytime consequences and correlates of insomnia in the United States: Results of the 1991 National Sleep Foundation Survey. II. *Sleep, 22,* S354–S358.

Sadeh, A., Alster, J., Urbach, D., & Lavie, P. (1989). Actigraphically based automatic bedtime sleep-wake scoring: Validity and clinical applications. *Journal of Ambulatory Monitoring, 2,* 209–216.

Shneerson, J. M. (2000). *Handbook of sleep medicine.* Oxford, England: Blackwell Science.

Smith, L. J., Nowakowski, S., Soeffing, J. P., Orff, H. J., & Perlis, M. L. (2003). The measurement of sleep. In M. L. Perlis &

K. L. Lichstein (Eds.), *Treating sleep disorders: Principles and practice of behavioral sleep medicine* (pp. 29–73). New York: Wiley.

Spira, A. P., Friedman, L., Flint, A., & Sheikh, J. I. (2005). Interaction of sleep disturbances and anxiety in later life: Perspectives and recommendations for future research. *Journal of Geriatric Psychiatry and Neurology, 18,* 109–115.

Stein, M. B., & Mellman, T. A. (2005). Anxiety disorders. In M. H. Kryger, T. Roth, & W. C. Dement (Eds.), *Principles and practice of sleep medicine* (4th ed., pp. 1297–1310). Philadelphia: Elsevier Saunders.

Tang, N. K., & Harvey, A. G. (2004). Effects of cognitive arousal and physiological arousal on sleep perception. *Sleep, 27,* 69–78.

Westen, D., Novotny, C. M., & Thompson-Brenner, H. (2004). The empirical status of empirically supported psychotherapies: Assumptions, findings, and reporting in controlled clinical trials. *Psychological Bulletin, 130,* 631–663.

Wilson, K. G., Watson, S. T., & Currie, S. R. (1998). Daily diary and ambulatory activity monitoring of sleep in patients with insomnia associated with chronic musculoskeletal pain. *Pain, 75,* 75–84.

Zadra, A., & Donderi, D.C. (2000). Nightmares and bad dreams: Their prevalence and relationship to well-being. *Journal of Abnormal Psychology, 109,* 273–281.

PART 8

Anxiety in Specific Populations

Anxiety Disorders and Hoarding in Older Adults

Catherine R. Ayers, Steven R. Thorp *and* Julie Loebach Wetherell

Abstract

This chapter focuses on anxiety disorders in later life. Anxiety disorders are relatively common in older adulthood, with prevalence rates as high as 15%. The assessment of late-life anxiety is complicated due to the unique presentation, medical comorbidities, psychiatric comorbidities, and other diagnostic considerations in an older population. Self-report and clinician-rated scales have been validated for use with older adults. Research suggests the benefit of both pharmacological treatments and psychotherapy for late-life anxiety disorders. GAD has received most of the scant research attention devoted to anxiety in older adults; late-life PTSD, OCD, agoraphobia, and hoarding are understudied areas. Directions for future research include long-term management of anxiety symptoms and psychotherapy-pharmacotherapy combination treatment.

Keywords: anxiety, assessment, comorbidity, evidence-based practices, hoarding, elderly, late onset, older adults, treatment

This chapter focuses on the unique nature and presentation of anxiety disorders in later life. The bulk of the available research examines generalized anxiety disorder (GAD) in older persons. Available research on other anxiety disorders such as obsessive-compulsive disorder (OCD), posttraumatic stress disorder (PTSD), and phobias is limited. A review of treatment outcome studies is provided. Given the link between hoarding and OCD in younger populations, hoarding behaviors in late life are also reviewed. Finally, recommendations for future research are discussed.

Presentation of Anxiety in Later Life
Prevalence Rates of Anxiety Disorders

The National Comorbidity Study Replication (NCS-R) found that anxiety disorders were the most common mental disorders, with 12-month prevalence rates of 18.1%, compared to 9.5% for mood disorders (Kessler, Chiu, et al., 2005). Among adults aged 60 or older, the average lifetime preva-

lence rate of any anxiety disorder was 15.3%, and lifetime rates for specific disorders in this older adult population were 2.0% for panic disorder, 1.0% for agoraphobia without panic, 7.5% for specific phobia, 6.6% for social phobia, 3.6% for generalized anxiety disorder, 2.5% for posttraumatic stress disorder, and 0.7% for obsessive-compulsive disorder (Kessler, Berglund, et al., 2005).

Approximately one-quarter (24%) of medically ill older adults have anxiety disorders (Tolin, Robison, Gaztambide, & Blank, 2005). Homebound elderly (Bruce & McNamara, 1992) and nursing home residents (Junginger, Phelan, Cherry, & Levy, 1993) have even higher rates. Moreover, Himmelfarb and Murrell (1984) indicate that as many as 20% of older adults suffer from significant anxiety symptoms, although they do not meet full diagnostic criteria. Evidence suggests that late-life anxiety is associated with disability, impairment in quality of life, and increased mortality rates (De Beurs et al., 1999; van Hout et al., 2004; Wetherell et al., 2004).

Further, geriatric anxiety is associated with more visits to primary care providers and increased average length of visits (van Hout et al., 2004).

The relatively small amount of published research on geriatric anxiety is alarming, especially when compared to the much larger late life depression literature base. Epidemiological evidence suggests that anxiety is more common than depression in older adults (Beekman et al., 1998; Regier, Boyd, Burke, & Rae, 1988). Additionally, almost twice as many mental health Medicare claims are filed for anxiety disorders (38%) than for affective disorders (21%; Ettner, 1997). Anxiety disorders often precede mood disorders. The NCS-R researchers (Kessler, Berglund, et al., 2005) found that the median age of onset for anxiety disorders was 11 years, as compared to 20 years for substance use disorders and 30 years for mood disorders.

Comparison to General Adult Population

The following section addresses the differences and similarities in the presentation of anxiety disorders in the general adult population (age 18–64) and the older adult population (ages 65 and older). In a community sample, anxiety symptoms did not vary with age, and the levels of anxiety remained constant across young and old age groups (Fuentes & Cox, 2000). Worry, the hallmark of GAD, appears to be different between younger and older adults. Work and interpersonal matters appear to be salient worry themes for younger individuals (Roemer, Molina, & Borkovec, 1997), while older adults appear to worry more about health than other topics (Hunt, Wisocki, & Yanko, 2003). Diefenbach and colleagues (2001) found older adult groups with and without GAD reported that family and other interpersonal areas were the most frequent types of worries, followed by miscellaneous categories and illness/health/injury. However, Wetherell and colleagues (2003) found differences in worry between GAD and non-GAD patients related to minor matters, finances, social/interpersonal issues, and personal health. The authors suggested that worry about others may be normal, whereas excessive worry about oneself may be pathological.

Among OCD patients, older persons had more concerns about hand washing and fear of having sinned but fewer problems with regard to symmetry, need to know, and counting rituals (Kohn, Westlake, Rasmussen, Marsland, & Norman, 1997). Recent research has shown that cognitive concerns, obsessional beliefs, and OCD symptoms are similar in both ages groups with the exception of increased subjective cognitive concerns in older people (Teachman, 2007). Panic among older adults is characterized by lower levels of arousal and severity, fewer panic symptoms, and less depression compared to younger age groups (Sheikh, Swales, Carlson, & Lindley, 2004). In a study of PTSD across the lifespan, patients in the elderly group had more social dysfunction than the younger patients, and a "powerful other" locus of control belief in these older patients was associated with more avoidance, social dysfunction, and depression (Chung, Preveza, Papandreou, & Prevezas, 2006).

Early Onset Versus Late Onset

As noted earlier, the NCS-R researchers (Kessler, Berglund, et al., 2005) discovered that the median age of onset is much earlier for anxiety disorders (11 years) than for substance abuse (20 years) or mood disorders (30 years). Results from a longitudinal study showed that persons high in the personality trait neuroticism, women, and those experiencing stressful life events (including having a partner who developed a major illness) were most at risk for becoming anxious in late life (De Beurs, Beekman, Deeg, Van Dyck, & Van Tilburg, 2000; De Beurs et al., 2001).

In a younger adult population with GAD, Hoehn-Saric and colleagues (1993) found that anxiety state measures did not differentiate between early and late onset GAD patients. Although many older GAD patients report an onset in childhood or adolescence, approximately half develop the disorder in late life (Le Roux, Gatz, & Wetherell, 2005). Older adults with an early onset of GAD appear to have a more severe course characterized by pathological worry than those with a later onset. This may suggest a breakdown in coping skills for those who developed the disorder later in life versus those who have an inherent vulnerability to GAD. Role disability (e.g., coping with radical changes in identity and/or income) may be a risk factor for onset of GAD in late life (Le Roux et al., 2005).

There is evidence that the onset of PTSD may be delayed until later life, or that PTSD symptoms may reemerge in late life (Port, Endahl, & Frazier, 2001). It is possible that the exacerbation of symptoms in late life may be due to increased cognitive impairment, more social isolation, or decrements in health status. Age-related decreases in attention, working memory, explicit memory, and prospective memory may result in the recurrence of PTSD in late life (Floyd, Rice, & Black, 2002). It is also possible that individuals can suppress PTSD symptoms with high levels of activity (e.g., working multiple jobs, focusing on family duties) until disease, injury, or personal loss results in diminished activity and the reemergence of severe PTSD symptoms (Lipton & Shaffer, 1988).

Medical Comorbidity

Medical comorbidity can complicate the assessment of anxiety in older persons. It is difficult for clinicians to discriminate between physical deterioration due to the aging process or disease verses increased morbidity due to anxiety. Anxiety has been associated with medical conditions related to cardiovascular, respiratory, gastrointestional, and endocrine systems (Small, 1997; Wise and Rieck, 1993). Physical concerns that typically occur in conjunction with anxiety (such as headaches, diarrhea, and muscle aches) are also symptoms of common medical conditions. For example, Wetherell and colleagues (2003) found that sleep disturbance and muscle tension were more commonly reported in GAD patients compared to non-GAD controls. Also, PTSD is associated with many physical health problems (Rodgers, Norman, Thorp, Lebeck, & Lang, 2005). Somatic symptoms are often reported to primary care physicians and treated as a medical rather than psychiatric condition.

Psychiatric Comorbidity

Depression and other psychiatric disorders are commonly found in conjunction with anxiety (Kessler, Chiu, et al., 2005; van Balkom et al., 2000). Thirty-five percent of older people with depression have at least one anxiety-related problem throughout their lifetime and 23% have current diagnoses (Lenze et al., 2000). Further, anxiety often leads to depression (e.g. Lenze et al., 2005). One study found that 10% of community-dwelling older adults suffered from two or more anxiety diagnoses, and 12% had chronic somatic diseases (van Balkom et al., 2000). Little research has been completed on the comorbidity of substance use and abuse and anxiety in late life. It has been suggested that sleeping medications, alcohol, and antianxiety drugs may be misused by older adults to treat their anxiety symptoms (Fingerhood, 2000). However, preliminary research shows that excessive alcohol intake was not significantly associated with any late life anxiety disorder (van Balkom et al., 2000).

Assessment of Anxiety

One of the primary challenges to the empirical literature is that many studies use instruments and diagnostic criteria that have not been validated with older adults (Fuentes & Cox, 1997). Most of the anxiety assessment instruments used in research were initially developed for use with a general adult population. An advantage for using these instruments is that it allows for the examination of age differences. However, the measures may not be picking up the subtle differences in the presentation of late life anxiety. While there is some assessment research and normative data for late life GAD and PTSD, there is very limited information on late life panic disorder, agoraphobia, specific phobias, social phobia, and OCDs.

Self-Report Measures

The most frequently used self-report instruments for late life anxiety include the Beck Anxiety Inventory (BAI) (Beck, Epstein, Brown & Steer, 1988), State-Trait Anxiety Inventory (STAI) (Spielberger, Gorsuch, Lushene, Vagg, & Jacobs, 1983), and Penn State Worry Questionnaire (PSWQ) (Meyer, Miller, Metzger, & Borkovec, 1990). Research on the BAI suggests that symptoms associated with medical illness may inflate scores (Wetherell & Gatz, 2005). However, the constellations of symptoms represented in the BAI appears to be similar across age groups, as indicated by factor analysis (Wetherell & Arean, 1997). Research on the STAI indicates a lack of discriminate validity with measures of depression (Kabacoff, Segal, Hersen, & Van Hasselt, 1997). Additionally, the factor structure of the STAI was not confirmed for older adults. The PSWQ may be less sensitive to worry over a short period of time, and the reverse scored items may be difficult for older adults to decipher (Hopko et al, 2003). In addition, while the PSWQ has been shown to have high internal consistency, there is minimal evidence of construct validity and modest concurrent validity (Beck, Stanley, & Zebb, 1995). Hopko and colleagues (2003) found that the data fit poorly with well-established models for younger adults. Thus, although these measures are often used with older adults populations, they may lack sensitivity.

Other researchers have significantly modified existing measures for use with an older population or developed new ones. Lowe and Reynolds (2000) have expanded on the Adult Manifest Anxiety Scale to develop a parallel measure for older persons (Adult Manifest Anxiety Scale—Elderly; AMAS-E). Sinoff, Ore, Zlotogorsky, and Tamir (1999) have developed the Short Anxiety Screening Test (SAST), which has demonstrated adequate sensitivity and specificity for older adults. The Worry Scale (WS) (Wisocki, Handen, & Morse, 1986) was specifically designed to measure worry in an older adult population and appears to have adequate psychometric properties (Stanley et al., 1996).

Van Zelst et al. (2003) presented the Self-Rating Inventory for Posttraumatic Stress Disorder (SRIP), which was designed for use with community dwelling older adults. A cut-off score was selected to optimize the balance of sensitivity and specificity, but this score resulted in missed "true" diagnoses over one-quarter of the time. Nonetheless, the SRIP may be useful as a brief screening instrument for PTSD among older adults in the community. Summers, Hyer, Boyd, & Boudewyns (1996) found that the Mississippi Scale for Combat Related PTSD (Keane et al., 1988) and the MMPI-PK subscale (MMPI-2) (Keane et al., 1984) could correctly classify PTSD when lower cut-off scores were used for older veterans. Similarly, Summers and colleagues (1996) found that the Mississippi Scale, the MMPI-PK subscale, the Impact of Event Scale (IES) (Horowitz et al., 1979), and the SCL-90-R (Derogatis, 1977) PTSD scale could reliably discriminate between older combat veterans with and without PTSD if cut-off scores are lower than those used for younger veterans.

Clinician Rating Scales

Clinician rating scales have also been examined for use with an older population. The most commonly used scales, the Anxiety Disorders Interview Schedule (ADIS-R) (DiNardo, Moras, Barlow, Rapee, & Brown, 1993) and Hamilton Anxiety Rating Scale (HARS) (Hamilton, 1959) have high interrater agreement in older adults (Beck, Stanley, & Zebb, 1995, 1999). Segal and colleagues (1993) found adequate reliability for the general category of anxiety disorders and interrater reliability on the Structured Clinical Interview for the *DSM* in older adults (SCID *DSM–III–R*, Axis I version) (Spitzer, Williams, & Gibbon, 1987). Although the versions of the ADIS and SCID that were used in these studies are based on *DSM–III–R* criteria, *DSM–IV* versions exist for each of these interviews (Di Nardo, Brown, & Barlow, 1994; First, Spitzer, Gibbon, & Williams, 1996).

Since its introduction in 1990, the Clinician-Administered PTSD Scale (CAPS) (Blake et al., 1990; Weathers, Keane, & Davidson, 2001) has become the gold standard for assessing PTSD in the general population due to its flexibility and good psychometric properties. Hyer, Summers, Boyd, Litaker, and Boudewyns (1996) examined the use of the CAPS in a sample of older combat veterans, and found that the scale was appropriate for use in this population based on its high internal consistency (alphas of .87 and .88 for the three PTSD symptom clusters and .95 for PTSD symptoms overall) and good validity, sensitivity, efficiency, and agreement.

Assessment Considerations

Regardless of the assessment approach, there are several special considerations involved in the assessment of older persons. When examining the older anxiety patient, it is important to keep in mind possible declines in sensory and cognitive abilities. Assessors may need to provide accommodations such as stronger lighting, larger font sizes on printed material, and the use of visual aides. In addition, the accuracy of reporting symptoms should be considered. Wetherell and colleagues (2003) found evidence that older people have particular problems with the accurate identification of their own anxiety symptoms. Interviewers may need to use cohort appropriate language (e.g. "wound up" instead of "tension") and less psychologically oriented terms.

Treatment of Anxiety in Later Life

For additional reviews of evidence-based treatment of geriatric anxiety disorders, please refer to Ayers et al. (2007) and Wetherell and colleagues (2005).

Cognitive Behavioral Therapy

Cognitive behavioral therapy (CBT) protocols include education about anxiety, self-monitoring, relaxation training, exposure to anxiety-provoking thoughts and situations, and cognitive restructuring. A few treatments have added problem solving skills training, behavioral activation, sleep hygiene, reflective listening, life review, and memory aids. Group treatment is more common than individually administered formats. CBT has been successful when compared to a waiting list (WL) or other minimal contact control (MCC) conditions (e.g., Stanley et al., 2003; Wetherell, Gatz, & Craske, 2003). One study included memory aids and strategies such as between-session telephone calls to increase homework compliance (Mohlman et al., 2003). This study produced higher effect sizes than other CBT studies, suggesting that memory aides may result in better outcomes for late life GAD. Another investigation compared CBT directly to supportive therapy (Stanley, Beck, & Glassco, 1996). Both treatments were effective for reducing anxiety and depressive symptoms. Wetherell and colleagues (2003) compared CBT and a discussion group to WL. It was found that CBT and the discussion group were similarly efficacious (and both outperformed WL), though CBT was superior to the discussion group on one measure of worry frequency at posttreatment.

One investigation found that CBT significantly reduced symptoms in a mixed anxiety sample, relative to a waiting list, although sertraline appeared to perform better than CBT (Schuurmans et al., 2006). Radley and colleagues (1997) and King and Barrowclough (1991) likewise found efficacy for CBT in small samples of patients with mixed anxiety disorders. Barrowclough et al. (2001) used a home-based individual format to address anxiety symptoms, and demonstrated significant effects for CBT relative to supportive therapy.

Some research suggests the effectiveness of CBT for other specific anxiety disorders. One noncontrolled study produced promising results demonstrating the effectiveness of CBT in older panic disorder (PD) patients (Swales, Solfvin, & Sheikh, 1996). However, there have been no randomized controlled psychosocial interventions conducted exclusively with older adults with PD. A retrospective chart review of older inpatients with OCD, treated with exposure and response prevention (a type of CBT), and other interventions (e.g., pharmacotherapy), showed improvements in self-reported symptoms (Carmin, Pollard, & Ownby, 1998).

Remarkably, only a small number of case studies on the psychological treatment of trauma or PTSD in older adults have been published to date (e.g., Maercker, 2002; Russo, Hersen, & Van Hasselt, 2001), and the largest of these is based on only three cases. These studies use CBT and a mixture of other interventions. The studies lack well-defined assessment and treatment procedures; they are underpowered due to small sample sizes; and they provide no control or comparison groups.

Relaxation

Several studies provide evidence for the efficacy of relaxation training for subjective anxiety symptoms (e.g., Scogin, Rickard, Keith, Wilson, & McElreath, 1992). Relaxation training typically includes some combination of progressive muscle relaxation, breathing retraining, meditation, and education about tension and stress. Most studies have found support for relaxation training compared to a waitlist or pseudorelaxation placebo control condition. However, Sallis and colleagues (1983) actually found an increase in anxiety symptoms following relaxation training, and relaxation training did more poorly than supportive therapy. One important finding emphasizes that continued practice of relaxation skills is needed in order to maintain benefits (De Berry, 1981–1982). Imaginal relaxation, in which participants are taught to imagine tensing various muscle groups rather than actually tense them, appears to be as effective as standard progressive muscle relaxation with the tension component, and may be of particular benefit to older adults with musculoskeletal conditions or injuries that make tensing painful (Scogin et al., 1992).

Pharmacological Treatments

Anxiolytic or antidepressant medications are prescribed to approximately one-half of the patients who are assigned an anxiety disorder diagnosis in primary care settings (Stanley, Roberts, Bourland, & Novy, 2001). Benzodiazepines are the most common treatment for late-life anxiety (e.g., Klap, Unroe, & Unützer, 2003). Benzodiazepines do relieve short-term symptoms from anxiety disorders (e.g., Frattola et al., 1992), but limited and short-term use of benzodiazepines is recommended given the possible negative consequences (Sheikh & Cassidy, 2000). Benzodiazepine use is associated with hip fracture and accidents requiring medical attention (e.g., Allain, Bentue-Ferrer, Polard, Akwa, & Patat, 2005) as well as psychomotor retardation and cognitive impairment and decline (Longo & Johnson, 2000; Paterniti, Dufouil, & Alperovitch, 2002). These medications can also cause tolerance, withdrawal, and toxicity (Krasucki, Howard, & Mann, 1999).

Several pharmacotherapy studies of late-life anxiety disorders have tested antidepressant medications with a variety of anxiety-related conditions. Sheikh and Swales (1999) found promising results when comparing the efficacy of imipramine, alprazolam, and placebo in patients with PD. A follow-up to this study demonstrated improvement in anxiety symptoms in patients with PD using sertraline (Sheikh, Lauderdale, & Cassidy, 2004). A sample with mixed anxiety disorders showed high response rates to fluvoxamine (Wylie et al., 2000). Katz and colleagues (2002) demonstrated the efficacy of venlafaxine for GAD. Lenze and colleagues (2005) found citalopram superior to placebo in the only prospective, randomized trial to date of a serotonergic antidepressant. Gains were maintained at 32-week follow-up for patients who continued taking the medication (Blank et al., 2006). Gorenstein et al. (2005) found that medication management (MM) plus CBT did not yield greater reductions in worry, state, or trait anxiety than MM alone, although CBT did show an advantage over MM on some SCL-90 subscales.

Selective serotonin reuptake inhibitors (SSRIs) have been recommended as a first-line pharmaceutical intervention for PTSD for the general population (Friedman, Davidson, Mellman, & Southwick, 2000). Peskind, Bonner, Hoff, & Raskind (2003) conducted an open-label trial of prazosin (a CNS active, lipophilic alpha-1 adrenergic antagonist) in nine older men with PTSD symptoms. After 8 weeks of treatment, eight of the nine participants experienced more than a 50% reduction in nightmares (based on a single item from the CAPS) and demonstrated at least moderate improvement on overall PTSD symptomatology (as assessed by the Clinical Global Impression scale). However, side effects (episodic urinary incontinence, transient lightheadedness, and dizziness) were reported by one-third of the participants, and blood pressure decreased in most participants. Suppression of trauma-related nightmares continued for up to 18 months for some participants, but one-third of the patients who discontinued prazosin during maintenance treatment had a strong reemergence of nightmares. This suggests that the medication does not permanently change the pathophysiology of chronic PTSD, and prazosin would need to be continued to maintain treatment gains.

Hoarding in Later Life
Characteristics/Prevalence Rates

Hoarding is defined as in inability to discard worthless objects that take up an excessive amount of space and interfere with functioning (Frost & Hartl, 1996). Hoarding is classified as a symptom of obsessive-compulsive personality disorder in the *DSM–IV–TR* (American Psychiatric Association, 2000), and many researchers regard hoarding as a symptom or subtype of OCD. Some have argued that compulsive hoarding is a discrete clinical syndrome characterized by indecisiveness, perfectionism, procrastination, difficulty organizing tasks, and avoidance (e.g., Frost & Hartl, 1996).

To date, there have not been any large-scale epidemiological studies of hoarding. Prevalence rates are often derived from adult protective service cases in the community or clinical research on OCD and dementia. Steketee and Frost (2003) estimate a lifetime prevalence rate of 1%–2%. There is some evidence that hoarding behaviors increase or got worse with age. In an examination of OCD in younger and older age groups, higher levels of hoarding were reported in the older age group (Teachman, 2007).

Other findings and anecdotal evidence from community service providers have found a significant number of older adult hoarders (e.g., Kim, Frost, & Steketee, 2001). Additionally, more than 40% of elder service agency complaints to health departments involve hoarding (Frost, Steketee, & Williams, 2000).

The onset of hoarding appears to start in childhood or adolescence (Grisham, Frost, Steketee, Kim, & Hood, 2006). The course tends to be chronic, with severe levels of hoarding starting in the mid-30s. The question remains as to why so many older adult cases are reported to community service agencies. It is likely that there is a mixture of both chronic and late-onset hoarding behaviors. For late-onset cases, age-related physical and cognitive changes, medical conditions, and life events have been thought to exacerbate symptoms. However, these relationships have not been thoroughly examined.

Elderly hoarders are typically female, unmarried, and living alone (Kim et al., 2001). Individuals who have never married are at greater risk for impairment. The amount of material is often so great that it interferes with normal maneuvering through the home, cooking, and grooming. For example, in 45% of cases in one sample, hoarders could not use their refrigerators and freezers, 42% could not use their kitchen sink, 42% could not use their bathtub, 20% could not use their bathroom sink, and 10% could not use their toilet (Kim et al., 2001).

Hoarding and Comorbidity

Hoarding is a complex behavior that has been found in relatively healthy populations (e.g., Marx & Cohen-Mansfield, 2003), but it is also linked to many psychiatric symptoms. In general adult populations, hoarding has been associated with OCD (Frost, Steketee, Williams, & Warren 2000), depression (Steketee et al., 2000), and schizophrenia (Luchins, Goldman, Lieb, & Hanrahan, 1992). Late-life hoarding has been found to be associated with dementia (e.g., Greenberg, Witztum, & Levy, 1990). Hwang and colleagues (1998) found 22.6% of patients with a dementia diagnosis (e.g., dementia of the Alzheimer's Type, vascular dementia, and dementia not otherwise specified) displayed hoarding behaviors. This finding was echoed in an investigation of nursing home patients with dementia (Rabinowitz et al., 2005). Hoarding behaviors appeared to increase with severity of dementia, but it was not clear whether this behavior is a manifestation of dementia or these patients had a premorbid history of hoarding.

Health Risks and Consequences of Hoarding

Hoarding causes significant impairment and poses a serious health risk for older people. Direct consequences include fire hazards and food contamination while indirect consequences include decreased social support, anxiety, and depression (Frost & Gross, 1993). One study found that in 81% of hoarding cases, the service providers viewed hoarding as a significant health threat (Kim et al., 2001). Hoarding is one of the few psychiatric symptoms that can have an almost direct link to morbidity and mortality. One report showed that out of 58 cases of hoarding, there were five house fires and three fatalities directly resulting from the fires (Frost, Steketee, & Williams, 2000). Fifty percent of hoarding cases in this investigation resulted in evictions and approximately one-third were placed in nursing homes.

Hoarding Interventions

To date, treatment response to older adults with compulsive hoarding has not been examined. Most elderly hoarders deny, minimize, or rationalize their problems. Often, hoarders will not allow service providers into their homes. Interventions are typically handled by adult protective services and not mental health agencies. In a community sample, only 24% of elderly hoarders were receiving mental health treatment. In fact, the typical community intervention included either full or partial cleaning out of the home, which often leads to recluttering (Kim et al., 2001).

Prior to treatment a thorough assessment of the amount of clutter, beliefs about possessions, information processing deficits, avoidance behaviors, daily functioning, medication compliance, level of insight, and social/occupational functioning is recommended (Saxena and Maidment, 2004). Neurocognitive status, anxiety symptoms, and disability level should be assessed. After the initial assessment, a combination of psychotherapy, medication management, and medical and social services is warranted.

Studies utilizing a CBT approach have demonstrated efficacy in mid-life samples (e.g., Tolin, Frost, & Steketee, 2007). This CBT-based model developed by Hartl and Frost (1999) is directed toward decreasing clutter, improving decision making and organizational skills, and strengthening resistance to urges to save. This model includes exposure and response prevention, decision-making training, motivational interviewing, and cognitive restructuring. Given that hoarding behaviors increase with age, it is imperative that treatment response in older adults is examined.

Summary and Conclusions

The assessment of late-life anxiety is a complex process. Self-report and clinician ratings have been validated for anxious older adults. Data suggest the potential utility of both pharmacological and psychotherapeutic treatments for late-life anxiety disorders. The CBT literature has demonstrated the effectiveness of CBT compared to no treatment, but evidence does not consistently support an advantage of CBT relative to other psychosocial treatment options (e.g., supportive therapy). Pharmacological treatment is more effective than placebo in the treatment of late-life anxiety, and some evidence suggests that it is more effective than CBT (Schuurmans et al., 2006). Psychotherapy and pharmacotherapy combinations have not yet been tested with anxious older adults. More research is needed to determine whether medication is an effective long-term management strategy for geriatric anxiety. Hoarding in late life is a significant social service and psychiatric problem and can lead to severe impairment and even death. Further research in the psychiatric characterization and treatment of late life hoarding is needed. Assessment of psychiatric comorbidity, including hoarding, will aid in the development of effective and practical interventions for late-life anxiety disorders. Long-term follow-up of patients and creative methods for the dissemination of treatments remain important goals for future research.

References

Allain, H., Bentue-Ferrer, D., Polard, E., Akwa, Y., & Patat, A. (2005). Postural instability and consequent falls and hip fractures associated with use of hypnotics in the elderly: A comparative review. *Drugs and Aging, 22,* 749–765.

American Psychiatric Association. (2000). *Diagnostic and statistical manual of mental disorders* (4th ed. text revision). Washington, DC: Author.

Ayers, C. R., Sorrell, J. T., Thorp, S. R., Wetherell, J. L. (2007). Evidence-based psychological treatment for late-life anxiety. *Psychology and Aging, 22,* 8–17.

Barrowclough, C., King, P., Colville, J., Russell, E., Burns, A., & Tarrier, N. (2001). A randomized trial of the effectiveness of cognitive-behavioral therapy and supportive counseling for anxiety symptoms in older adults. *Journal of Consulting and Clinical Psychology, 69,* 756–762.

Beck, A. T., Epstein, N., Brown, G., & Steer, R. A. (1988). An inventory for measuring clinical anxiety: Psychometric properties. *Journal of Consulting and Clinical Psychology, 56,* 893–897.

Beck, J. G., Stanley, M. A., & Zebb, B. J. (1995). Psychometric properties of the Penn State Worry Questionnaire in older adults. *Journal of Clinical Geropsychology, 1,* 33–42.

Beck, J. G., Stanley, M. A., & Zebb, B. J. (1999). Effectiveness of the Hamilton Anxiety Scale with older generalized anxiety disorder patients. *Journal of Clinical Geropsychology, 5,* 281–290.

Beekman, A.T.F., Bremmer, M. A., Deeg, D.J.H., van Balkom, A.J.L.M., Smit, J. H., de Beurs, E., et al. (1998). Anxiety disorders in later life: A report from the longitudinal aging study Amsterdam. *International Journal of Geriatric Psychiatry, 13,* 717–726.

Blake, D. D., Keane, T. M., Wine, P. R., Mora, C., Taylor, K. L., & Lyons, J. A. (1990). Prevalence of PTSD symptoms in combat veterans seeking medical treatment. *Journal of Traumatic Stress, 3,* 15–27.

Blank, S., Lenze, E. J., Mulsant, B. H., Amanda, D. W., Karp, J. F., Shear, M. K., et al. (2006). Outcomes of late-life anxiety disorders during 32 weeks of citalopram treatment. *Journal of Clinical Psychiatry, 67,* 468–472.

Blazer, D., George, L. K., & Hughes, D. (1991). The epidemiology of anxiety disorders: An age comparison. In C. Salzman & B. D. Lebowitz (Eds.), *Anxiety in the elderly: Theory and research* (pp. 17–30). New York: Springer.

Bruce, M. L., & McNamara, R. (1992). Psychiatric status among the homebound elderly: An epidemiologic perspective. *Journal of the American Geriatrics Society, 40,* 561–566.

Carmin, C. N., Pollard, C. A., & Ownby, R. L. (1998). Obsessive-compulsive disorder: Cognitive behavioral treatment of older versus younger adults. *Clinical Gerontologist, 19,* 77–81.

Chung, M. C., Preveza, E., Papandreou, K., & Prevezas, N. (2006). Spinal cord injury, posttraumatic stress, and locus of control among the elderly: a comparison with young and middle-aged patients. *Psychiatry, 69,* 69–80.

DeBerry, S. (1981–1982). An evaluation of progressive muscle relaxation on stress related symptoms in a geriatric population. *International Journal of Aging and Human Development, 14,* 255–269.

De Beurs, E., Beekman, A.T.F., Deeg, D.J.H., Dyck, R. V., & Tilburg, W. V. (2000). Predictors of change in anxiety symptoms of older persons: Results from the longitudinal aging study Amsterdam. *Psychological Medicine, 30,* 515–527.

De Beurs, E., Beekman, A., Geerlings, S., Deeg, D., Van Dyck, R., & Van Tilburg, W. (2001). On becoming depressed or anxious in late life: Similar vulnerability factors but different effects of stressful life events. *British Journal of Psychiatry, 179,* 426–431.

De Beurs, E., Beekman, A.T.F., van Balkom, A.J.L.M., Deeg, D.J.H., van Dyck, R., & van Tilburg, W. (1999). Consequences of anxiety in older persons: Its effect on disability, well-being and use of health services. *Psychological Medicine, 29,* 583–593.

Derogatis, L. R. (1977). *SCL-90 administration, scoring, and procedures manual I for the r(evised) version.* Baltimore, MD: Johns Hopkins University School of Medicine.

Diefenbach, G. J., Stanley, M. A., & Beck, J. G. (2001). Worry content reported by older adults with and without generalized anxiety disorder. *Aging and Mental Health, 5,* 269–274.

Di Nardo, P., Brown, T. A., & Barlow, D. H. (1994). *Anxiety Disorders Interview Schedule for DSM–IV.* New York: Oxford University Press.

Di Nardo, P. A., Moras, K., Barlow, D. H., & Rapee, R. M. (1993). Reliability of *DSM–III–R* anxiety disorder categories: Using the anxiety disorders interview schedule-revised (ADIS–R). *Archives of General Psychiatry, 50,* 251–256.

Eisen, J. L., Beer, D. A., Pato, M. T., & Venditto, T. A. (1997). Obsessive-compulsive disorder in patients with schizophrenia or schizoaffective disorder. *American Journal of Psychiatry, 154,* 271–273.

Ettner, S. L. (1997). Mental health services under Medicare: The influence of economic incentives. *Harvard Review of Psychiatry, 4,* 283–286.

Fingerhood, M. (2000). Substance abuse in older people. *Journal of the American Geriatrics Society, 48,* 985–995.

First, M. B., Spitzer, R. L., Gibbon, M., & Williams, J.B.W. (1996). *Structured Clinical Interview for DSM–IV Axis I disorders—Patient edition (SCID-I/P, Version 2.0).* New York: Biometrics Research Department, New York State Psychiatric Institute.

Floyd, M., Rice, J., & Black, S. R. (2002). Recurrence of post-traumatic stress disorder in late life: A cognitive aging perspective. *Journal of Clinical Geropsychology, 8,* 303–311.

Friedman, M. J., Davidson, J.R.T., Mellman, T. A., & Southwick, S. M. (2000). Pharmacotherapy. In E. B. Foa, T. M. Keane, & M. J. Friedman (Eds.), *Effective treatments for PTSD: Practice guidelines from the international society for traumatic stress studies* (pp. 326–329). New York: Guilford Press.

Franks, M., Lund, D. A., Poulton, D., & Caserta, M. S. (2004). Understanding hoarding behavior among older adults: A case study approach. *Journal of Gerontological Social Work, 42,* 77–107.

Frattola, L., Piolti, R., Bassi, S., & Albizzati, M. G. (1992). Effects of alpidem in anxious elderly outpatients: A double-blind, placebo-controlled trial. *Clinical Neuropharmacology, 15,* 477–487.

Frost, R. O., & Gross, R. C. (1993). The hoarding of possessions. *Behaviour Research and Therapy, 31,* 367–381.

Frost, R. O., & Hartl, T. L. (1996). A cognitive-behavioral model of compulsive hoarding. *Behaviour Research and Therapy, 34,* 341–350.

Frost, R.O., Steketee, G., & Williams, L. (2000). Hoarding: A community health problem. *Health and Social Care in the Community, 8,* 229–234.

Frost, R. O., Steketee, G., Williams, L. F., & Warren, R. (2000). Mood, personality disorder symptoms and disability in obsessive compulsive hoarders: A comparison with clinical and nonclinical controls. *Behaviour Research and Therapy, 38,* 1071–1081.

Fuentes, K., & Cox, B. (2000). Assessment of anxiety in older adults: A community-based survey and comparison with younger adults. *Behaviour Research and Therapy, 38,* 297–309.

Gorenstein, E. E., Kleber, M. S., Mohlman, J., DeJesus, M., Gorman, J. M., & Papp, L. A. (2005). Cognitive-behavioral therapy for management of anxiety and medication taper in older adults. *American Journal of Geriatric Psychiatry, 13,* 901–909.

Greenberg, D., Witztum, E., & Levy, A. (1990). Hoarding as a psychiatric symptom. *Journal of Clinical Psychiatry, 51,* 417–421.

Grisham, J. R., Frost, R. O., Steketee, G., Kim, H., & Hood, S. (2006). Age of onset of compulsive hoarding. *Journal of Anxiety Disorders, 20,* 675–686.

Gross, J. J., Carstensen, L. L., Pasupathi, M., Tsai, J., Götestam Skorpen, C., & Hsu, A.Y.C. (1997). Emotion and aging: Experience, expression, and control. *Psychology and Aging, 12,* 590–599.

Hamilton, M. (1959). The assessment of anxiety states by rating. *British Journal of Medical Psychology, 32,* 50–55.

Hartl, T. L., & Frost, R. O. (1999). Cognitive-behavioral treatment of compulsive hoarding: A multiple baseline experimental case study. *Behaviour Research and Therapy, 37,* 451–461.

Himmelfarb, S., & Murrell, S. A. (1984). The prevalence and correlates of anxiety symptoms in older adults. *Journal of Psychology: Interdisciplinary and Applied, 116,* 159–167.

Hoehn-Saric, R., Hazlett, R. L., & McLeod, D. R. (1993). Generalized anxiety disorder with early and late onset of anxiety symptoms. *Comprehensive Psychiatry, 34,* 291–298.

Hopko, D. R., Reas, D. L., Beck, J. G., Stanley, M. A., Wetherell, J. L., Novy, D. M., et al. (2003). Assessing worry in older adults: Confirmatory factor analysis of the Penn State Worry Questionnaire and psychometric properties of an abbreviated model. *Psychological Assessment, 15,* 173–183.

Horowitz, M. J., Wilner, N., & Alvarez, W. (1979). Impact of Event Scale: A measure of subjective distress. *Psychosomatic Medicine, 41,* 209–218.

Hunt, S., Wisocki, P., & Yanko, J. (2003). Worry and use of coping strategies among older and younger adults. *Journal of Anxiety Disorders, 17,* 547–560.

Hwang, J., Tsai, S., Yang, C., Liu, K., & Lirng, J. (1998). Hoarding behavior in dementia: A preliminary report. *American Journal of Geriatric Psychiatry, 6,* 285–289.

Hyer, L., Summers, M. N., Boyd, S., Litaker, M., & Boudewyns, P. (1996). Assessment of older combat veterans with the Clinician-Administered PTSD Scale: Psychometric properties, correct classification rations, and best items. *Journal of Traumatic Stress, 9,* 587–595.

Junginger, J., Phelan, E., Cherry, K., & Levy, J. (1993). Prevalence of psychopathology in elderly persons in nursing homes and in the community. *Hospital and Community Psychiatry, 44,* 381–383.

Kabacoff, R. I., Segal, D. L., Hersen, M., & Van Hasselt, V. B. (1997). Psychometric properties and diagnostic utility of the Beck Anxiety Inventory and the State-Trait Anxiety Inventory with older adult psychiatric outpatients. *Journal of Anxiety Disorders, 11,* 33–47.

Katz, I. R., Reynolds, C. F., III, Alexopoulos, G. S., & Hackett, D. (2002). Venlafaxine ER as a treatment for generalized anxiety disorder in older adults: Pooled analysis of five randomized placebo-controlled clinical trials. *Journal of the American Geriatrics Society, 50,* 18–25.

Keane, T. M., Caddell, J. M., & Taylor, J. L. (1988). The Mississippi Scale for Combat-Related Posttraumatic Stress Disorder: Three studies in reliability and validity. *Journal of Consulting and Clinical Psychology, 56,* 85–90.

Keane, T. M., Malloy, P. F., & Fairbank, J. A. (1984). Empirical development of an MMPI subscale for the assessment of combat-related post-traumatic stress disorder. *Journal of Consulting and Clinical Psychology, 52,* 888–891.

Kessler, R. C., Berglund, P., Demler, O., Jin, R., Merikangas, K. R., & Walters, E. E. (2005). Lifetime prevalence and age-of-onset distributions of *DSM–IV* disorders in the National Comorbidity Survey Replication. *Archives of General Psychiatry, 62,* 617–627.

Kessler, R. C., Chiu, W. T., Demler, O., & Walters, E. E. (2005). Prevalence, severity, and comorbidity of 12-month *DSM–IV* disorders in the National Comorbidity Survey Replication. *Archives of General Psychiatry, 62,* 617–627.

Kim, H., Steketee, G., & Frost, R. O. (2001). "Hoarding by elderly people": Erratum. *Health and Social Work, 26,* 234.

King, P., & Barrowclough, C. (1991). A clinical pilot study of cognitive-behavioural therapy for anxiety disorders in the elderly. *Behavioural Psychotherapy, 19,* 337–345.

Klap, R., Unroe, K. T., & Unützer, J. (2003). Caring for mental illness in the United States: A focus on older adults. *American Journal of Geriatric Psychiatry, 11,* 517–524.

Kohn, R., Westlake, R. J., Rasmussen, S. A., & Marsland, R. T. (1997). Clinical features of obsessive-compulsive disorder in elderly patients. *American Journal of Geriatric Psychiatry, 5,* 211–215.

Krasucki, C., Howard, R., & Mann, A. (1999). Anxiety and its treatment in the elderly. *International Psychogeriatrics, 11,* 25–45.

Lau, A. W., Edelstein, B. A., & Larkin, K. T. (2001). Psychophysiological arousal in older adults: A critical review. *Clinical Psychology Review, 21,* 609–630.

Lawton, M. P., Kleban, M. H., & Dean, J. (1993). Affect and age: Cross-sectional comparisons of structure and prevalence. *Psychology and Aging, 8,* 165–175.

Lenze, E. J., Mulsant, B. H., Mohlman, J., Shear, M. K., Dew, M. A., & Schulz, R., et al. (2005). Generalized anxiety disorder in late life: Lifetime course and comorbidity with major depressive disorder. *American Journal of Geriatric Psychiatry, 13,* 77–80.

Lenze, E. J., Mulsant, B. H., Shear, M. K., Dew, M. A., Miller, M. D., & Pollock, B. G., et al. (2005). Efficacy and tolerability of citalopram in the treatment of late-life anxiety disorders: Results from an 8-week randomized, placebo-controlled trial. *American Journal of Psychiatry, 162,* 146–150.

Lenze, E. J., Mulsant, B. H., Shear, M. K., Schulberg, H. C., Dew, M. A., Begley, et al. (2000). Comorbid anxiety disorders in depressed elderly patients. *American Journal of Psychiatry, 157,* 722–728.

Le Roux, H., Gatz, M., & Wetherell, J. L. (2005). Age at onset of generalized anxiety disorder in adults. *American Journal of Psychiatry, 13,* 23–30.

Lipton, M. I., & Shaffer, W. R. (1988). Physical symptoms related to post-traumatic stress disorder (PTSD) in an aging population. *Military Medicine, 153,* 316–318.

Longo, L. P., & Johnson, B. (2000). Addiction: Part I. Benzodiazepines—side effects, abuse risk and alternatives. *American Family Physician, 61,* 2121–2128.

Lowe, P. A., & Reynolds, C. R. (2000). Exploratory analyses of the latent structure of anxiety among older adults. *Educational and Psychological Measurement, 60,* 100–116.

Luchins, D. J., Goldman, M. B., Lieb, M., & Hanrahan, P. (1992). Repetitive behaviors in chronically institutionalized schizophrenic patients. *Schizophrenia Research, 8,* 119–123.

Maercker, A. (2002). Life-review technique in the treatment of PTSD in elderly patients: Rationale and three single case studies. *Journal of Clinical Geropsychology, 8,* 239–249.

Marx, M. S., & Cohen-Mansfield, J. (2003). Hoarding behavior in the elderly: A comparison between community-dwelling persons and nursing home residents. *International Psychogeriatrics, 15,* 289–306.

Meyer, T. J., Miller, M. L., Metzger, R. L., & Borkovec, T. D. (1990). Development and validation of the Penn State Worry Questionnaire. *Behaviour Research and Therapy, 28,* 487–495.

Mohlman, J., Gorenstein, E. E., Kleber, M., de Jesus, M., Gorman, J. M., & Papp, L. A. (2003). Standard and enhanced cognitive-behavior therapy for late-life generalized anxiety disorder: Two pilot investigations. *American Journal of Geriatric Psychiatry, 11,* 24–32.

Paterniti, S., Dufouil, C., & Alperovitch, A. (2002). Long-term benzodiazepine use and cognitive decline in the elderly: the Epidemiology of Vascular Aging Study. *Journal of Clinical Psychopharmacology, 22,* 285–293.

Peskind, E. R., Bonner, L. T., Hoff, D. J., & Raskind, M. A. (2003). Prazosin reduces trauma-related nightmares in older men with chronic posttraumatic stress disorder. *Journal of Geriatric Psychiatry and Neurology, 16,* 165–171.

Port, C. L., Endahl, B., & Frazier, P. (2001). A longitudinal and retrospective study of PTSD among older prisoners of war. *American Journal of Psychiatry, 158,* 1474–1479.

Poyurovsky, M., Bergman, J., & Weizman, R. (2006). Obsessive-compulsive disorder in elderly schizophrenia patients. *Journal of Psychiatric Research, 40,* 189–191.

Rabinowitz, J., Davidson, M., De Deyn, P. P., Katz, I., Brodaty, H., & Cohen-Mansfield, J. (2005). Factor analysis of the Cohen-Mansfield Agitation Inventory in three large samples of nursing home patients with dementia and behavioral disturbance. *American Journal of Geriatric Psychiatry, 13,* 991–998.

Radley, M., Redston, C., Bates, F., & Pontefract, M. (1997). Effectiveness of group anxiety management with elderly clients of a community psychogeriatric team. *International Journal of Geriatric Psychiatry, 12,* 79–84.

Regier, D. A., Boyd, J. H., Burke, J. D., & Rae, D. S. (1988). One-month prevalence of mental disorders in the United States: Based on five Epidemiologic Catchment Area sites. *Archives of General Psychiatry, 45,* 977–986.

Rodgers, C. S., Norman, S. B., Thorp, S. R., Lebeck, M. M., & Lang, A. J. (2005). Trauma exposure, posttraumatic stress disorder and health behaviors: Impact on special populations. In T. A. Corales (Ed.), *Focus on post-traumatic stress disorder research* (pp. 203–224). Hauppauge, NY: Nova Science Publishers.

Roemer, L., Molina, S., & Borkovec, T. D. (1997). An investigation of worry content among generally anxious individuals. *Journal of Nervous and Mental Disease, 185,* 314–319.

Russo, S. A., Hersen, M., & van Hasselt, V. B., (2001). Treatment of reactivated post-traumatic stress disorder: Imaginal exposure in an older adult with multiple traumas. *Behavior Modification, 25,* 94–115.

Sallis, J. F. (1983). Anxiety and depression management for the elderly. *International Journal of Behavioral Geriatrics, 1,* 3–12.

Saxena, S., & Maidment, K. M. (2004). Treatment of compulsive hoarding. *Journal of Clinical Psychology, 60,* 1143–1154.

Schuurmans, J., Comijs, H., Emmelkamp, P.M.G., Gundy, C.M.M., Weijnen, I., & Van Den Hout, M., et al. (2006). A randomized, controlled trial of the effectiveness of cognitive-behavioral therapy and sertraline versus a waitlist control group for anxiety disorders in older adults. *American Journal of Geriatric Psychiatry, 14,* 255–263.

Scogin, F., Rickard, H. C., Keith, S., & Wilson, J. (1992). Progressive and imaginal relaxation training for elderly persons with subjective anxiety. *Psychology and Aging, 7,* 419–424.

Segal, D. L., Hersen, M., Van Hasselt, V. B., & Kabacoff, R. I. (1993). Reliability of diagnosis in older psychiatric patients using the structured clinical interview for *DSM–III–R. Journal of Psychopathology and Behavioral Assessment, 15,* 347–356.

Sheikh, J. I., & Cassidy, E. L. (2000). Treatment of anxiety disorders in the elderly: Issues and strategies. *Journal of Anxiety Disorders, 14,* 173–190.

Sheikh, J. I., Lauderdale, S. A., & Cassidy, E. L. (2004). Efficacy of sertraline for panic disorder in older adults: A preliminary open-label trial. *American Journal of Geriatric Psychiatry, 12,* 230.

Sheikh, J. I., & Swales, P. J. (1999). Treatment of panic disorder in older adults: A pilot study comparison of alprazolam, imipramine and placebo. *International Journal of Psychiatry in Medicine, 29,* 107–117.

Sheikh, J. I., Swales, P. J., Carlson, E. B., & Lindley, S. E. (2004). Aging and panic disorder: Phenomenology, comorbidity, and risk factors. *American Journal of Geriatric Psychiatry, 12,* 102–109.

Sinoff, G., Ore, L., Zlotogorsky, D., & Tamir, A. (1999). Short anxiety screening test: A brief instrument for detecting anxiety in the elderly. *International Journal of Geriatric Psychiatry, 14,* 1062–1071.

Small, G. W. (1997). Recognizing and treating anxiety in the elderly. *Journal of Clinical Psychiatry, 58,* 41–50.

Speilberger, C. D., Gorsuch, R. L., Lushene, R., Vagg, P. R., & Jacobs, G. A. (1983). *Manual for the State-Trait Anxiety Inventory.* Palo Alto, CA: Consulting Psychologists Press.

Spitzer, R. L., & Williams, J.B.W. (1987). *Revising DSM–III: The process and major issues.* New York: Cambridge University Press.

Stanley, M. A., Beck, J. G., & Glassco, J. D. (1996). Treatment of generalized anxiety in older adults: A preliminary comparison of cognitive-behavioral and supportive approaches. *Behavior Therapy, 27,* 565–581.

Stanley, M. A., Beck, J. G., & Zebb, B. J. (1996). Psychometric properties of four anxiety measures in older adults. *Behaviour Research and Therapy, 34,* 827–838.

Stanley, M. A., Roberts, R. E., Bourland, S. L., & Novy, D. M. (2001). Anxiety disorders among older primary care patients. *Journal of Clinical Geropsychology, 7,* 105–116.

Steketee, G., & Frost, R. (2003). Compulsive hoarding: Current status of the research. *Clinical Psychology Review, 23,* 905–927.

Steketee, G., Frost, R. O., Wincze, J., Greene, K.A.I., & Douglass, H. (2000). Group and individual treatment of compulsive hoarding: A pilot study. *Behavioural and Cognitive Psychotherapy, 28,* 259–268.

Steketee, G., Henninger, N. J., & Pollard, C. A. (2000). Predicting treatment outcomes for obsessive-compulsive disorder: Effects of comorbidity. In W. K. Goodman, M. V. Rudorfer, & J. D. Maser (Eds.), *Obsessive-compulsive disorder: Contemporary issues in treatment* (pp. 257–274). Mahwah, NJ: Erlbaum.

Summers, M. N., Hyer, L., Boyd, S., & Boudewyns, P. A. (1996). Diagnosis of later-life PTSD among elderly combat veterans. *Journal of Clinical Geropsychology, 2,* 103–115.

Swales, P. J., Solfvin, J. F., & Sheikh, J. I. (1996). Cognitive-behavioral therapy in older panic disorder patients. *American Journal of Geriatric Psychiatry, 4,* 46–60.

Teachman, B. A. (2007). Linking obsessional beliefs to OCD symptoms in older and younger adults. *Behavior Research and Therapy, 45,* 1671–1681.

Tolin, D. F., Robison, J. T., Gaztambide, S., & Blank, K. (2005). Anxiety disorders in older Puerto Rican primary care patients. *American Journal of Geriatric Psychiatry, 13,* 150–156.

Tolin, D., Frost, R. O., & Steketee, G. (2007). An open trial of cognitive behavioral therapy for compulsive hoarding. *Behaviour Research and Therapy, 45,* 1461–1470.

van Balkom, A.J.L.M., Beekman, A.T.F., de Beurs, E., Deeg, D.J.H., van Dyck, R., & van Tilburg, W. (2000). Comorbidity of the anxiety disorders in a community-based older population in the Netherlands. *Acta Psychiatrica Scandinavica, 101,* 37–45.

Van Hout, H.P.J., Beekman, A.T.F., De Beurs, E., Comijs, H., Van Marwijk, H., De Haan, M., et al. (2004). Anxiety and the risk of death in older men and women. *British Journal of Psychiatry, 185,* 399–404.

Van Zelst, W. H., de Beurs, E., Beekman, A.T.F., Deeg, D.J.H., & van Dyck, R. (2003). Prevalence and risk factors of posttraumatic stress disorder in older adults. *Psychotherapy and Psychosomatics, 72,* 333–342.

Weathers, F. W., Keane, T. M., & Davidson, J. R. (2001). Clinician-administered PTSD scale: A review of the first ten years of research. *Depression and Anxiety, 13,* 132–156.

Wetherell, J. L., & Areán, P. A. (1997). Psychometric evaluation of the Beck Anxiety Inventory with older medical patients. *Psychological Assessment, 9,* 136–144.

Wetherell, J. L., & Gatz, M. (2005). The Beck Anxiety Inventory in older adults with generalized anxiety disorder. *Journal of Psychopathology and Behavioral Assessment, 27,* 17–24.

Wetherell, J. L., Gatz, M., & Craske, M. G. (2003). Treatment of generalized anxiety disorder in older adults. *Journal of Consulting and Clinical Psychology, 71,* 31–40.

Wetherell, J. L., Lenze, E. J., & Stanley, M. A. (2005). Evidence-based treatment of geriatric anxiety disorders. *Psychiatric Clinics of North America, 28,* 871–896.

Wetherell, J. L., Le Roux, H., & Gatz, M. (2003). *DSM–IV* criteria for generalized anxiety disorder in older adults: Distinguishing the worried from the well. *Psychology and Aging, 18,* 622–627.

Wetherell, J. L., Thorp, S. R., Patterson, T. L., Golshan, S., Jeste, D. V., & Gatz, M. (2004). Quality of life in geriatric generalized anxiety disorder: A preliminary investigation. *Journal of Psychiatric Research, 38,* 305–312.

Wise, M. G., & Rieck, S. O. (1993). Diagnostic considerations and treatment approaches to underlying anxiety in the medically ill. *Journal of Clinical Psychiatry, 54,* 22–26.

Wisocki, P. A., Handen, B., & Morse, C. K. (1986). The worry scale as a measure of anxiety among homebound and community active elderly. *The Behavior Therapist, 9,* 91–95.

Wylie, M. E., Miller, M. D., Shear, K., Little, J. T., Mulsant, B. H., Pollock, B. G., et al. (2000). Fluvoxamine pharmacotherapy of anxiety disorders in later life: Preliminary open-trial data. *Journal of Geriatric Psychiatry and Neurology, 13,* 43–48.

Anxiety Disorders in Children and Adolescents

Jami M. Furr, Shilpee Tiwari, Cynthia Suveg *and* Philip C. Kendall

Abstract

Maladaptive anxiety in youth occurs when the fear associated with a situation or object is disproportionate in the level and duration of distress experienced and to what is developmentally appropriate. This chapter provides an overview of how anxiety in youth is expressed with respect to cognition, physiological arousal, and emotion dysregulation. Next, this chapter reviews the specific symptoms and diagnostic criteria for each of the anxiety disorders that often onset during childhood. It also describes the epidemiology of, and risk factors associated with, anxiety in youth, and reviews the empirical literature on the assessment and treatment of anxiety in youth. Finally, this chapter highlights areas in need of further empirical attention.

Keywords: assessment, child anxiety, cognitive behavioral therapy, epidemiology, treatment

Anxiety, an emotional state linked with fear, occurs in association with the perception of threat or danger (Barlow, 1991; Spielberger, 1972, 1983). Fear can be adaptive, as is the case when an individual experiences a *fight-or-flight* response in the presence of a truly dangerous situation. However, maladaptive anxiety occurs when the fear associated with a situation or object is disproportionate in the level and duration of distress experienced. In the case of youth, this determination is made in relation to normal development. This chapter provides an overview of how anxiety in youth is expressed with respect to cognition, physiological arousal, and emotion dysregulation. It also describes the epidemiology of and the risk factors associated with, anxiety in youth, and reviews the empirical literature on the assessment and treatment of anxiety in youth. Finally, this chapter highlights areas in need of further empirical attention.

Descriptive Features of Anxiety
General Features of Anxiety in Youth

Cognitive, somatic, and emotional features are central to understanding anxiety in youth (Chorpita, 2002; Clark & Watson, 1991). Each of these is discussed in this section.

COGNITIVE DISTORTIONS

Cognition plays a key role in anxiety in youth. Cognition refers to the thoughts one has about a situation, and includes the incorporation of input from multiple sources, selection of an adequate plan, and activation of additional systems (e.g., physiological). Cognitive schemas refer to core assumptions or beliefs about the self and the world (Beck, Emery, & Greenberg, 1985), whereas automatic thoughts may be distorted thoughts or images about one's ability to manage or function, or one's capacity to handle the consequences that occur from a given situation (Ingram & Kendall, 1987).

Depending on their thoughts, people act according to what they believe will result from their behavior (Prins, 1986). Accordingly, debilitating anxiety can result from a persistent overestimation of the likelihood of threat and the response to protect one's self from perceived harm (Beck, 1976; Beck et al., 1985; Kendall, 1984; Treadwell & Kendall, 1996). These cognitive distortions promote anxiety and are based on false, unchallenged, negative, and automatic predictions (Suarez & Bell-Dolan, 2001). In anxious youth, these negative self-statements may focus on future-oriented questioning that relates to danger, harm, or threat, and have been found to be predictive of anxiety severity (Kendall, 1985; Kendall & Chansky, 1991; Treadwell & Kendall, 1996). Anxious self-statements in youth were also found to mediate treatment outcome, by decreasing the number of negative self-statements and subsequently anxiety severity (Treadwell & Kendall, 1996). If cognitive distortions go unchallenged, they contribute to the maintenance of anxiety disorders and increased impairment (Dumas & Nilsen, 2003).

SOMATIC SYMPTOMS

Anxiety in youth is also associated with various physical symptoms, including stomachaches, headaches, muscle tension, and increased heart rate, that stem from an aroused autonomic nervous system (American Psychological Association [APA], 1994). Children with anxiety disorders have greater levels of somatic complaints than children (1) with no anxiety diagnoses (Dorn et al., 2003; Hofflich, Hughes, & Kendall, 2006; Kendall & Pimentel, 2003) and (2) with other psychiatric disorders (e.g., panic disorder) (Masi, Favilla, Millepiedi, & Mucci, 2000). Specifically, studies find increased reports of headaches, stomachaches, and musculoskeletal pains among anxious children (Bernstein et al., 1997; Egger, Costello, Erkanli, & Angold, 1999). Children with anxiety can experience increased physiological arousal that may present as sleep difficulties or fidgetiness. Consistent with these data, several anxiety disorders in the fourth edition of the *Diagnostic and Statistical Manual of Mental Disorders (DSM-IV)* (APA, 1994) require somatic symptoms to be present for a diagnosis. Although *DSM–IV* criteria and research findings highlight the heightened presence of stomachaches and headaches in separation anxiety disorder (SAD), youth with SAD are also more likely to report racing heart, shakiness, restlessness, and feelings of "being sick" than children with no anxiety disorder (Hofflich et al., 2006). However,

these somatic complaints are not specific to SAD; children with generalized anxiety disorder (GAD) and social phobia (SOP) are also more likely to experience several of these complaints. For example, children with GAD are more likely than children with no anxiety disorder to report chest pain, weird or unreal feelings, racing heart, headaches, or feeling sick to their stomachs (Egger et al., 1999; Kendall & Pimentel, 2003). Children with SOP endorse feeling shaky, trembling, sweating, and heart palpitations (Hofflich et al., 2006). Thus, it appears that somatic complaints are reported by anxiety-disordered youth, but may not indicate a particular anxiety disorder. Somatic symptoms are stable over time and may predict future psychological problems (Dhossche, Ferdinand, van der Ende, & Verhulst, 2001).

From cognitive theory, the hypersensitivity to and catastrophic interpretation of such internal sensations may heighten sensitivity to changes in carbon dioxide levels in the blood and shortness of breath in panic disorder (PD) (Barlow, 1988; Carter, Hollon, Carson, & Shelton, 1995; Clark, 1986). This misinterpretation in which children have heightened sensitivity to and negatively interpret their somatic symptoms may increase the level of fear they experience and subsequently their level of avoidance (Clark & Watson, 1991). Thus, cognitive misinterpretations that focus the child's attention on the meaning of his or her physical symptoms can increase the autonomic response, avoidance behavior, and vigilance (Musa & Lepine, 2000; Sweeny & Pine, 2004). This sensitivity to physiology has been viewed as a risk factor for anxiety disorders (Silverman & Weems, 1999; Stein, Jang, & Livesley, 1999). For example, youth with PD vigilantly scan themselves for physiological signs and their environment for potential anxiety triggers, which can lead to avoidance of the feared situations or objects.

EMOTIONAL FUNCTIONING

High negative affect has been found to be associated with anxiety disorders and anxiety in general. Negative affect (Clark & Watson, 1991) is associated with behavioral inhibition, neuroticism, and apprehension (Barlow, 2002), and can be characterized by distress, anger, fear, and disgust. A diminished sense of control and heightened hopelessness are also associated with anxiety (Mineka, Watson, & Clark, 1998), and these processes can be linked to a child's ability to regulate emotions. Youth with anxiety may have difficulty knowing how to adjust their emotional reactions so that an appropriate level of emotion is exhibited (Southam-Gerow & Kendall, 2000). Anxious youth may experience emotions with high intensity and limited sense of control (Suveg & Zeman, 2004). In addition, children with anxiety have emotional expression problems, such as inhibited expression, nonnormative expression, or lack of control of their emotions (Allesandri & Lewis, 1996; Thompson & Calkins, 1996).

Children with anxiety disorders have limited understanding of emotion regulation (e.g., hiding or changing feelings) and causes of emotion, but are similar to children without anxiety disorders in their ability to use cues to understand emotions and the existence of multiple emotions (Southam-Gerow & Kendall, 2000; Zeman, Shipman, & Suveg, 2002). An inability to identify emotional states, to regulate anger and sadness, and to express anger has been found to predict internalizing symptoms (Zeman et al., 2002), suggesting that a focus on the emotion of anxiety rather than avoiding this experience may be beneficial in treatment (Safran & Greenberg, 1989).

Aspects of Anxiety Disorders in Youth

Based on the *DSM–IV*, the only anxiety disorder that must (by definition) begin in childhood or adolescence is SAD. Separation anxiety disorder is referred to as developmentally inappropriate and excessive anxiety about separating from home or a caregiver (e.g., parent, loved one) that causes significant distress or impairment in the child's academic, social, or other general functioning. The onset of SAD occurs before the age of 18 and this disorder is not typically assigned in adults. Youth with SAD often have difficulty or distress about separating or anticipating separation from their caregiver, worry about harm befalling their caregiver or themselves so that the caregiver is never seen again, reluctance or refusal to go places without their caregiver (e.g., entering another room in the house alone, attending a birthday party or sleepover), and physical complaints (e.g., headaches, nausea, stomachaches) when away from their caregiver.

Although other anxiety disorders are often diagnosed in both adults and youth, some include slightly different diagnostic criteria when diagnosing the problem in children or adolescents. Social Phobia (SOP) is an excessive fear of one or more social or performance situations in which the person could be exposed to unfamiliar people or possible scrutiny by others (APA, 1994). Most persons with SOP have anxiety that they might do something em-barrassing or humiliating in front of others. When SOP is diagnosed in childhood, these children must demonstrate the capacity for developmentally appropriate social relationships with familiar people and anxiety in peer settings, not only in situations with adults. Although some children may have the capacity to recognize their social fears as excessive or unreasonable, this specific SOP criterion need not be present in youth. Criteria for SOP must be met for 6 months for the disorder to be diagnosed in a child or adolescent (there is no duration requirement for adults with SOP).

Generalized anxiety disorder in *DSM–IV* is excessive anxiety and worry (apprehensive expectation) regarding events or activities in one's daily life (i.e., school performance) that is difficult to control, and that lasts for at least 6 months. For a diagnosis of GAD in childhood, the child must experience at least one associated symptom (e.g., restlessness, irritability, muscle tension, sleep disturbance), and significant impairment or distress must be present in the child's social, academic, and general functioning.

Another anxiety disorder that can arise during childhood is obsessive-compulsive disorder (OCD), which is defined by having either obsessions or compulsions, or a combination of the two, causing significant distress or impairment (APA, 1994). *Obsessions* are recurrent, persistent, intrusive, and inappropriate thoughts, images, or impulses that extend beyond real-life concerns. Typically, a person will try to ignore, suppress, or neutralize the thoughts or images with a different thought or action, but is able to recognize the thoughts or images as a product of his or her own mind (rather than from thought insertion). *Compulsions* are repetitive behaviors (e.g., hand washing, ordering, checking) or mental rituals (e.g., praying, counting, repeating words silently) that the person feels driven to perform as a response to an obsession, to reduce anxiety, or to prevent something bad from happening. Individuals with OCD often show evidence of thought-action fusion (TAF), which refers to the belief that thinking about a feared event increases the likelihood of the event actually occurring or that thinking about performing an unacceptable behavior is just as bad as actually engaging in that behavior (Rassin, Merckelbach, Muris, & Spaan, 1999; Shafran, Thordarson, & Rachman, 1996). However, Comer, Kendall, Franklin, Hudson, and Pimentel (2004) caution that at earlier stages of cognitive development, *all* children may exhibit high levels of TAF, and that instances of magical thinking in youth should not automatically be considered as evidence of OCD. The OCD criterion requiring that an individual recognize the obsessions or compulsions as excessive or unreasonable is not required or expected of children.

Increasing debate has occurred about whether posttraumatic stress disorder (PTSD) should be diagnosed in children due to numerous discrepancies between the criteria required for adults and children (Ziksook, Chentsoven-Dutton, & Shuchter, 1998). The *DSM–IV* defines a trauma as having experienced or witnessed an event that involved actual or threatened death, serious injury, or a physical threat, accompanied by feelings of fear, helplessness, or horror (APA, 1994). Children may respond with disorganized or agitated behavior as well as intense fear or horror. To receive a PTSD diagnosis, children must express reexperiencing of the event, avoidance of reminders of the trauma, numbing of general responsiveness, and increased arousal when reminded of the trauma (e.g., hypervigilance, exaggerated startle response). The avoidance and arousal criteria for a PTSD diagnosis in children are similar to those for adults, though some have questioned the developmental appropriateness of applying the reexperiencing criteria to children with PTSD (Carrion, Weems, Ray, & Reiss, 2002). In young children, repetitive play reflecting themes related to the trauma may be expressed rather than intrusive and recurrent thoughts, images, or perceptions. Children may also experience distressing dreams without recognizable content. Flashbacks of the event (where one feels as though the trauma is recurring at the present time) often do not present in children, yet children may reenact trauma-specific behavior.

A specific phobia (SP) is a marked and persistent fear that is cued by the presence of or anticipation of a specific object or situation (e.g., flying, heights, animals, injections), and that is excessive and unreasonable (APA, 1994). Upon exposure to the feared stimuli, children respond with anxiety. Children may be unable to recognize that their fear is unreasonable or excessive. Five main types of SP are defined in *DSM–IV*: animal type, natural environment type (e.g., heights, thunderstorms), blood-injection-injury type (e.g., receiving an injection or medical procedure), situational type (e.g., public transportation, bridges, elevators, flying), and other type (e.g., choking, vomiting, space).

Panic disorder with or without agoraphobia (PDA/PD) is typically not diagnosed until adolescence or young adulthood (Biederman et al., 1997). Core features of PD include the presence of recurrent unexpected panic attacks (discrete periods of intense fear or discomfort including at least 4 out of 13 associated symptoms [mostly physical symptoms of arousal] that develop abruptly and peak within 10 minutes), as well as having persistent concern about having additional panic attacks, worrying about the implications or consequences of the attack, or a significant change in behavior (that lasts at least 1 month) associated with the attacks (APA, 1994). The diagnosis of PDA is given when the PD symptoms are experienced in conjunction with anxiety about being in places or situations from which escape might be difficult or embarrassing or in which help is unavailable if a panic attack occurs. The situations in which a panic attack may occur are often avoided or endured with marked distress and may require the presence of a companion (or safety person). A diagnosis of PD or PDA can be difficult among school-aged youth as it overlaps with other anxiety diagnoses and with school refusal.

In summary, there are a number of diagnostic features that are unique to childhood anxiety disorders. For example, the criteria for several disorders recognize that children may not recognize that their fear is excessive or unrealistic. In addition, children may respond to feared situations in ways that adults typically do not, including crying, freezing, or clinging. Several disorders also require that symptoms be present for a full 6 months, in recognition of the fact that children often have transient periods of anxiety that are developmentally normal, and that clear up without treatment.

Epidemiology
Risk Factors

A number of risk factors may predispose a child to developing an anxiety disorder, including biological factors (e.g., genetics, neurochemistry), psychological factors (e.g., emotional regulation), family and peer influences (e.g., parenting strategies), sociocultural influences (e.g., life events), and historical factors (e.g., cohort effects). A variety of risk factors interact and can result in the onset of an anxiety disorder in childhood, either by acting directly on the child or indirectly through a parent or caregiver. A diathesis-stress model, taking into account both vulnerabilities of the child as well as environmental risk factors, is the most common approach to understanding the development and maintenance of anxiety disorders in youth.

BIOLOGICAL FACTORS

The brain is always adjusting and changing in response to a child's experiences. Neurons become more and more specialized with development, and the brain is especially plastic in the early years—making childhood a time for considerable neural change, and leading to an increased potential for the development of anxiety disorders (Nelson, 1999). Anxiety disorders appear to involve a variety of neurotransmitters, and changes in the ways these neurotransmitters are processed and absorbed can influence behavior and mood. Specifically, the neurotransmitters serotonin, norepinephrine, and gamma-amino-butyric acid (GABA) have been identified in the development of anxiety disorders. Serotonin is related to behavioral control and emotional expression, whereas norepinephrine plays a role in the processing of information in the environment and in the *fight-or-flight* response to danger. And GABA prevents neurons from firing and thus can help control fear and other emotions. Hormones may also contribute to anxiety disorders. In particular, low levels of cortisol can affect the ability to manage stress effectively and can alert a child to possible threat when actual danger is not present.

Genetics also contribute to anxiety disorders. However, it is assumed that genes typically do not determine behavior directly (Dumas & Nilsen, 2003). Rather, genetics are believed to influence the manner in which the nervous system develops and functions, and how this system interacts with and responds to the surrounding environment. Genes establish a range for one's behavior: a genetic vulnerability, where multiple genes are acting in concert to increase the probability of an anxiety disorder (Andrews, Stewart, Allen, & Henderson, 1990; Torgersen, 1983).

PSYCHOLOGICAL FACTORS

Temperament and personality influence the development of anxiety disorders in youth (Biederman et al., 1993; Kagan, Reznik, & Snidman, 1988). Behavioral inhibition (BI) is the tendency for young children to become withdrawn, nervous, and avoidant when faced with new or unfamiliar stimuli (Kagan, Reznick, Clarke, Snidman, & Garcia-Coll, 1984). These stimuli may include unfamiliar people or environments, or even new toys. Behaviorally inhibited children rarely engage with unknown adults or children and are limited in their exploration of their environment. Infants as young as 4 months have displayed aspects of BI, and it has been suggested that as many as 10%–20% of young children can be classified as behaviorally inhibited (Kagan, 1989). Although BI is linked to

infancy or young childhood, evidence suggests that BI often persists through middle childhood (Kagan, Reznick, Snidman, Gibbons, & Johnson, 1988). Longitudinal research suggests that BI is associated with later anxiety disorders (e.g., Chorpita & Barlow, 1998; Gest, 1997; Kagan, 1997). For example, Prior, Smart, Sanson, and Oberklaid (2000) found that shy or inhibited children were more likely to have anxiety problems in adolescence and later life than children not rated as shy.

Behavioral explanations, such as the two-factor model of anxiety (Mowrer, 1960), apply principles of classical and operant conditioning and suggest that anxiety develops after an event or object is associated with unconditioned fearful emotions. Once fearful, the person avoids the feared situation or object so as not to experience the overwhelming feelings. Each time the feared situation or object is avoided, the fear and avoidance is reinforced—a pattern that can lead to an anxiety disorder. Modeling of anxious and avoidant behavior are also influential (Gerull & Rapee, 2002). Children who experience uncontrollable stimuli or stress often demonstrate low perceived control and inhibition in other situations (Chorpita & Barlow, 1998), which can contribute to tension, increased agitation, and the facilitation of cognitive distortions linked to anxiety.

Cognitive behavioral theory helps explain how a child interprets evidence from an event or an encounter with fearful stimuli as either contradicting a schema about being safe or confirming a schema that the world is dangerous and unsafe (e.g., Foa & Kozak, 1986; Janoff-Bulman, 1995). Given that youth are forming their identity, self-esteem, and coping strategies (Kirk & Madden, 2003), they may be more vulnerable to shifts in their schemas (Pynoos, Steinberg, & Piacentini, 1999; Steinberg & Avenevoli, 2000), and may be encouraged not to approach related situations (Meiser-Stedman, 2002).

Stressful life events or traumatic events are also related to anxiety disorders (e.g., PTSD). Although many children who experience a stressful or threatening event do not develop an anxiety disorder, a considerable proportion of youth later develop an anxiety disorder following the traumatic event. Specifically, life-threatening events (i.e., threat of losing a loved one, physical trauma) best predict high levels of anxiety symptoms in children (Eley & Stevenson, 2000). Conditions of chronic stress (i.e., lack of resources, community violence) can also lead to anxiety. This is particularly relevant given that one study found that nearly 25% of children have experienced a traumatic event (Costello, Erkanli, Fairbank, & Angold, 2002). Thus, traumatic events can impact children's sense of safety and their beliefs about the danger present in their everyday world (Brown, Harris, & Eales, 1993).

FAMILIAL FACTORS

Parental psychopathology has been found to be a significant risk factor for childhood anxiety disorders (e.g., Last, Hersen, Kazdin, & Orvaschel, 1991; Martin, Cabrol, Bouvard, Lepine, & Mouren-Simeoni, 1999). Anxious children are more likely than nonanxious children to have an anxious parent (Last, Hersen, Kazdin, Francis, & Grubb, 1987; Turner, Beidel, & Costello, 1987). For example, increased prevalence rates of PD and PDA were found among fathers and mothers of school refusers with separation anxiety disorder (Martin et al., 1999). Conversely, parents with psychopathology are more likely to have children with anxiety disorders (Last, Hersen, Kazdin, Francis et al., 1987). Specifically, one study found nearly half of the offspring of parents with SOP had at least one anxiety disorder (*DSM–III–R* criteria), including overanxious disorder (OAD) (30%), SOP (23%), and SAD (19%) (Mancini, Van Ameringen, Szatmari, Fugere, & Boyle, 1996). However, other researchers propose that parental anxiety is indirectly associated with child anxiety through genetics and/or the environment (Donovan & Spence, 2000), such that the child's own coping skills become impaired (Ginsburg, Siqueland, Masia-Warner, & Hedtke, 2004).

Available resources, parent psychopathology, and insecure parent-child attachment influence parenting styles and behavior and anxiety in children. Increased levels of parental control and emotional involvement are related to SAD, GAD, and low self-efficacy among children (Hirshfield, Biederman, Brody, Faraone, & Rosenbaum, 1997; Hudson & Rapee, 2001; McClure, Brennan, Hammen, & Le Brocque, 2001). Siqueland, Kendall, and Steinberg (1996) demonstrated that parents of children with anxiety disorders exerted more control and granted less autonomy in dialogues with their children and were rated as generally less accepting by their children than were parents of nonanxious controls. Parents can model or reinforce avoidant behaviors by encouraging less social interaction (Rapee & Melville, 1997), modeling cautious or fearful responses (Silverman, Cerny, Nelles, & Burke, 1988), or displaying their own anxiety about separating from their child (Capps,

Sigman, Sena, & Henker, 1996). Lastly, high levels of marital or family conflict are associated with increased levels of anxiety, disproportionate levels of responsibility for the conflict, and increased internalization of the conflict in youth (Davies & Cummings, 1994, 1998; Grych & Fincham, 1990). In summary, risk factors often act in combination with a vulnerable predisposition to fear in the development of anxiety disorders.

Prevalence of Anxiety Disorders in Youth

Recent data on the prevalence of mental health problems (disorders) in children and adolescents revealed a considerable percentage (36.7%) of youth had at least one disorder at the time of the evaluation (Costello, Mustillo, Erkanli, Keeler, & Angold, 2003), an increase from the 17.6% found nearly 20 years prior (Anderson, Williams, McGee, & Silva, 1987). The extent to which mental health problems are diagnosed and treated in pediatric primary care facilities has increased fourfold since the mid-1980s from 1.1 million visits to 4.5 million visits in the late 1990s (Glied & Cuellar, 2003). The prevalence of any anxiety disorder among children and adolescents in a large community sample was 2.4% and had the highest prevalence in 9- to 10-year-old children (4.6%) (Costello et al., 2003). Prevalence estimates and the average age of onset for specific anxiety diagnoses in youth are described in Table 1 (data summarized from Anderson, 1994; Costello, Egger, & Angold, 2004, 2005; Last et al., 1992).

Comorbidity

Although comorbidity rates differ in clinic-referred and community samples (Angold, Costello, & Erkanli, 1999), comorbid samples are needed to better understand the nature of more complex cases (Caron & Rutter, 1991). Anxiety disorders are highly comorbid with other anxiety disorders, mood disorders, and conduct problems. Research finds strong associations between OAD/GAD and major depression (Last, Hersen, Kazdin, Finkelstein, et al., 1987), suicide attempts and ideation (Brent et al., 1986), and low self-esteem (Strauss, Lease, Last, & Francis, 1988). However, Last, Strauss, and Francis (1987) found that the total number of comorbid diagnoses was similar among children diagnosed with principal OAD, avoidant disorder, SAD, or major depression. Verduin and Kendall (2003) reported that children with principal SAD had the highest number of comorbid diagnoses, including SOP, functional enuresis, and GAD. Both

Table 1. Prevalence Estimates for Anxiety Disorders in Youth

Disorder	Overall	(% range) Clinical/ Community (%/%)	Age of Onset M (years)	M/F (%/%)
SP	0–22	15/3–5	6–8	M < F
SOP	1–13	0–13	7.3	M = F
GAD/OAD	1–4	10–58/1–19	5.8–11.0	M < F (adol)
SAD	1–11	2–5	7	M < F
OCD	0–4	2–4/0–4	10–13	M > F
PTSD	0–7	3.7/0–7	<16	M (4) < F (7)
PD	0–2.5	5–15/0–2.5	13.4	M < F
AG	1–3	1–3	9.5	M < F
Any	2.2–9.9	2.4	9–10	M (8) < F (12)

Note: SP = specific phobias; SOP = social phobia; GAD = generalized anxiety disorder; OAD = overanxious disorder; SAD = separation anxiety disorder; OCD = obsessive-compulsive disorder; PTSD = posttraumatic stress disorder; PD = panic disorder; AG = agoraphobia; Any = any anxiety disorder; M = mean age in years; M/F = male to female sex differences and percentages given if known. Clinical/Community represents the prevalence rates in clinical versus community samples if known. Clinical here refers to findings for "clinical samples" but without differentiating the manner with which "clinical status" was determined. Only one percentage shown represents prevalence in community sample.

OAD/GAD and SAD may raise the risk for developing PD later in life, but more research must be conducted (Aschenbrand, Kendall, Webb, Safford, & Flannery-Schroeder, 2003). In addition, studies report a high percentage of comorbidity of PTSD and near-clinical levels of PTSD with forms of anxiety and depression (Breslau, Chilcoat, Kessler, & Davis, 1999; Mayou, Bryant, & Ehlers, 2001; Pfefferbaum et al., 1999).

Anxiety disorders are most frequently diagnosed concurrently with a depressive disorder, in comparison to attention-deficit/hyperactivity disorder (ADHD), conduct disorder (CD), oppositional defiant disorder (ODD), or substance use disorders (Costello et al., 2003; Curry, March, & Hervey, 2004; Verduin & Kendall, 2003). An average rate of 41% for depression was found among those with anxiety disorders (Kovacs & Devlin, 1998). There has also been extensive literature showing significant comorbidity of ADHD and anxiety as well as a significant overlap (30%–62% occurrence) of anxiety and ODD or CD (Anderson et al., 1987; Angold et al., 1999; Bird, Gould, & Staghezza, 1993). Studies suggest that comorbid anxiety may moderate the negative impact of externalizing disorders (e.g., ODD, CD) in children, as reflected by less fighting, fewer school problems, and fewer problems with the law in children who have comorbid anxiety disorders as well as conduct problems (for a review, see Caron & Rutter, 1991).

Longitudinal Research

Anxiety disorders are among the most common, if not the most common, category of disorders in youth (Bernstein & Borchardt, 1991; Costello et al., 2005). Both lifetime (28.8%; Kessler, Berglund, Demler, Jin, & Walters, 2005) and 12-month prevalence estimates (Kessler, Chiu, Demler, & Walters, 2005) suggest a significant impact of anxiety disorders over the lifespan. Anxious children have been found to experience a variety of difficulties in academic achievement (King & Ollendick, 1989; Van Ameringen, Mancini, & Farvolden, 2003), social and peer relations (Greco & Morris, 2005; Hartup, 1983), and future emotional health (Cantwell & Baker, 1989; Feehan, McGee, & Williams, 1993). Research suggests that most anxiety disorders do not remit with the passage of time (e.g., Pine, Cohen, Gurley, Brook & Ma, 1998), and that childhood GAD/OAD increases vulnerability to developing GAD as well as other anxiety disorders in adulthood. If left untreated, GAD interferes with daily functioning and increases financial costs to the community (Massion, Warshaw, & Keller, 1993; Roy-Byrne & Katon, 1997). Additional research suggests that anxiety disorders in childhood may temporally precede the development of depressive disorders later in life (Biederman, Faraone, Mick, & Lelon, 1995; Brady & Kendall, 1992; Kovacs, Gatsonis, Paulauskas & Richards, 1989).

Other sequelae of anxiety disorders in youth include an increased odds ratio for substance use problems (see Clark & Neighbors, 1996; Clark & Winters, 2002; Costello et al., 2003), and specifically, youth with OCD have higher rates of alcohol and marijuana dependence later in life (Douglass et al., 1995). For example, those who were less successfully treated for anxiety as youth (at a 7.4-year follow-up; Kendall, Safford, Flannery-Schroeder, & Webb, 2004) were more likely to have more drinking days per month, to use marijuana, to have unwanted social or interpersonal consequences from drug use, to give up activities because of drug use, to have unsuccessful attempts to control drug use, and to have used larger amounts than those successfully treated. The presence of an anxiety disorder, with increased age, has also been associated with an increase in the likelihood of a depressive disorder (Brady & Kendall, 1992; Costello et al., 2003; Pine et al., 1998).

Retrospective reports from anxiety-disordered adults identify difficulties with anxiety in childhood (Abe, 1972; Öst, 1987). For example, 68% of children with OCD were likely to meet diagnostic criteria for that disorder 7 years later (Flament et al., 1990). And PTSD may become chronic when trauma continues over an extended period of time (e.g., war; Beitchman et al., 1992), but is likely to improve after a single traumatic incident (Shannon et al., 1994). Aschenbrand et al. (2003) found that youth with SAD were more likely to meet criteria for anxiety disorders generally than were youth who had GAD or SOP.

Assessment

Given that anxiety is multifaceted, often occurring through a complex interaction of cognitive, behavioral, and physiological factors, the accurate assessment of anxiety disorders requires the use of instruments that measure symptomatology across a variety of response systems. The assessment of anxiety disorders in youth can be particularly challenging given developmental changes in cognitive ability and emotional expressivity, and biological changes that occur throughout development. Anxiety itself may hinder accurate reporting due to the child's concerns about being evaluated, increasing the likelihood of socially desirable responses and compromising valid self-reports (Comer & Kendall, 2004).

A multimethod approach is recommended. Multimethod assessment involves the collection of information from parents, children, and teachers, as well as from a variety of settings, including school,

home, and peer interactions (Achenbach, McConaughy, & Howell, 1987). A multimethod approach is commonly preferred and practiced (Jensen et al., 1999), and involves structured diagnostic interviews and the use of parent, child, and teacher reports. Family assessment, physiological recordings, and structured behavioral observations are used less frequently. This section provides an overview of the instruments currently available for the assessment of anxiety disorders in youth; it is recommended that a combination of instruments be used to increase accuracy and overcome the challenges posed by the assessment of this population.

Clinical Interviews

Semistructured interviews for the assessment of anxiety disorders in youth provide a structured interviewing format while also allowing for elaboration from informants as judged appropriate by a diagnostician. The *Anxiety Disorders Interview Schedule for Children—Parent and Child Versions for DSM-IV* (ADIS-C/P) (Silverman & Albano, 1997) is a semistructured diagnostic interview, administered separately to parents and children, which primarily assesses anxiety disorders in youth. The ADIS-C/P also assesses mood disorders, externalizing disorders, and pervasive developmental disorders, providing information on possible comorbid conditions. Based on the symptoms, distress, and interference reported during child and parent interviews, the diagnostician assigns a final, composite clinician severity rating (CSR) ranging from 0–8: CSRs of 0 indicate that no symptoms are present; CSRs between 1 and 3 indicate subclinical levels of impairment; and CSRs between 4 and 8 indicate a clinically significant level of distress and impairment. The ADIS-C/P has demonstrated favorable psychometric properties, including excellent retest reliability (Silverman, Saavedra, & Pina, 2001), excellent convergent validity (March, Parker, Sullivan, Stallings, & Conners, 1997; Wood, Piacentini, Bergman, McCracken, & Barrios, 2002), and good interrater reliability (Rapee, Barrett, Dadds, & Evans, 1994). The ADIS-C/P has also been demonstrated to be sensitive to treatment-related changes (Kendall et al., 1997; Silverman, Kurtines, Ginsburg, Weems, Lumpkin, et al., 1999).

The *Schedule for Affective Disorders and Schizophrenia in School-Age Children* (K-SADS) (Puig-Antich & Chambers, 1978) is another commonly used semistructured interview. Similar to the ADIS-C/P, the K-SADS involves parent and child interviews by a common diagnostician, with final diagnoses being derived from information collected from both informants. The measure assesses both current and past anxiety disorders, mood disorders, psychotic disorders, behavioral disorders, and substance use disorders, and contains "skip-out" criteria for entry into each diagnostic area, eliminating the need to inquire about all symptoms in each domain. Newer versions of the K-SADS allow for assessment of current symptomatology, such as during the week preceding the interview (K-SADS-P) (Ambrosini, Metz, Prabucki, & Lee, 1989), as well as lifetime symptoms (K-SADS-P/L) (Kaufman et al., 1997). All versions of the K-SADS have demonstrated adequate psychometric properties (for a review, see Ambrosini, 2000). In addition to the ADIS-C/P and the K-SADS, the *Diagnostic Interview for Children and Adolescents* (DICA) (Herjanic & Reich, 1982) and the *National Institute of Mental Health (NIMH) Diagnostic Interview Schedule for Children* (DISC) (Shaffer et al., 1996) are other structured interviews that may be used to assess anxiety disorders in youth.

Although the use of semistructured interviews is beneficial for diagnosing anxiety disorders in youth, the lack of concordance between informants remains a limitation (Choudhury, Pimentel, & Kendall, 2003; DiBartolo, Albano, Barlow, & Heimberg, 1998). Specifically, research has shown that parent-child agreement on observable, nonschool-based symptoms is higher than that for unobservable, school-based symptoms (Comer & Kendall, 2004; Herjanic & Reich, 1982), most likely due to parents having increased access to the former. In addition, parent-child agreement may also be affected by age, as the reliability of child reports tends to increase with age, and the reliability of parents' reports tends to decrease as the child ages (Edelbrock, Costello, Duncan, Kalas, & Conover, 1985). To help overcome limitations associated with discrepancies in responding between informants, the use of semistructured interviews as part of a multimethod assessment is suggested.

Child Self-Report Measures

Several self-report measures are available to assess anxiety in youth (newer and common measures are briefly reviewed). These include the *Multidimensional Anxiety Scale for Children* (MASC) (March et al., 1997), *Screen for Child Anxiety and Related Emotional Disorders* (SCARED) (Birmaher et al., 1997), *State-Trait Anxiety Inventory for Children* (STAIC) (Spielberger, 1973), *Negative Affectivity Self-Statement Questionnaire* (NASSQ) (Ronan,

Kendall, & Rowe, 1994), and *Coping Questionnaire* (CQ) (Kendall, 1994). The strengths and weaknesses associated with this particular methodology are also reviewed.

The MASC is a 39-item self-report inventory that assesses four factors: physical symptoms (tense/restless and somatic/autonomic symptoms), social anxiety (humiliation/rejection and public performance), harm avoidance (anxious coping and perfectionism), and separation/panic anxiety. In terms of psychometric properties, 3-week retest reliability for the MASC has been shown in past studies to be .79 in clinical (March et al., 1997) and .88 in school-based samples (March & Sullivan, 1999), and good 3-month retest reliability has also been demonstrated (March & Albano, 1998).

The SCARED is a 41-item child self-report inventory that assesses symptoms of panic, separation anxiety, social phobia, and generalized anxiety disorder and symptoms of school refusal. The SCARED has shown good psychometric properties in two different clinical samples (Birmaher et al., 1997, 1999), and a community sample (Muris et al., 1998).

The STAIC consists of two separate 20-item inventories: (1) the state scale, designed to assess present state and situation-specific anxiety, and (2) the trait scale, designed to assess stability in anxiety across situations. Findings regarding the reliability and validity of the STAIC are mixed, and suggest this measure may best be used as a general screening instrument for anxiety (Barrios & Hartmann, 1988).

The NASSQ examines cognitive content in anxious children by measuring self-statements associated with negative affect. Specifically, it measures the frequency of occurrence of negative self-statements on a 5-point scale and consists of separate items for younger and older children. Overall, the measure has demonstrated good retest and internal reliability and is sensitive to changes in treatment (Kendall et al., 1997).

The CQ also assesses cognitive content by measuring the child's perception of his or her ability to cope in stressful, anxiety-provoking situations, using three child-generated situations. It has been used in a number of controlled cognitive behavioral therapy (CBT) trials for childhood anxiety and has been found to be sensitive to treatment effects (Kendall, 1994; Kendall et al., 1997).

Self-report methodology allows for an inexpensive, cost-effective examination of anxiety symptomatology in youth. However, child self-reports must be interpreted with caution for several reasons: (1) they may not adequately capture idiosyncratic fears that are specific to a particular child (Kendall & Ronan, 1990), and in such cases may not be useful for planning treatment; and (2) they do not account for developmental variability in comprehension. As such, younger children may not be able to understand the questions posed or their corresponding response scales, leading to an invalid assessment. Anxious children may respond in a socially desirable manner due to fear of being negatively evaluated, calling into question the validity of their responses. In general, despite the appeal of expediency, the use of brief self-report instruments alone to diagnose children (in the absence of a structured diagnostic interview) may be misguided, especially in the absence of documentation that the instrument distinguishes among diagnostic groups (e.g., Comer & Kendall, 2005; Kendall & Flannery-Schroeder, 1995).

Parent and Other-Report Measures

In addition to the parental counterparts of the child self-report measures just described (e.g., MASC-Parent, CQ-Parent), the impact of the child's anxiety symptoms on daily functioning can be assessed using the *Child Anxiety Impact Scale-Parent Version* (CAIS-P) (Langley, Bergman, McCracken, & Piacentini, 2004). The CAIS-P measures functioning in a variety of domains and comprises three subscales: school, social, and home/family. The CAIS-P has demonstrated good internal consistency and construct validity; and results have indicated that it is a reliable and valid measure for the assessment of the impact of anxiety on child and adolescent functioning (Langley et al., 2004).

The *Child Behavior Checklist* (CBCL) (Achenbach & Edelbrock, 1983) is another rating scale that is widely used with parents of anxious youth. The CBCL is a 118-item inventory that assesses behavioral problems and social and academic competence. Although the CBCL does not differentiate between specific anxiety disorders, it effectively discriminates between externalizing and internalizing disorders (Seligman, Ollendick, Langley, & Baldacci, 2004) and provides information on the child's participation in social activities and peer interaction, which may be useful in evaluating treatment effects.

The *Teacher Report Form* (TRF) (Achenbach, 1991) is a version of the CBCL designed for completion by teachers. The TRF allows for assessment of the child's classroom functioning and may be useful for contrasting the child's behavior at home and at school, and for assessing children whose primary concerns include social interaction or evaluation by peers. The TRF does not provide diagnostic clarity with regard to specific anxiety disorders, but does provide a general measure of internalizing symptomatology.

As with child self-reports, the use of parent-report or other-report measures has limitations. For example, parents or teachers may not be fully aware of the extent of the child's anxiety symptoms, given their internalizing nature (Comer & Kendall, 2004). In addition, most observable anxiety symptoms occur outside of parents' visibility (e.g., at school or during interactions with peers). Parents who are prone to anxiety may also be more likely to over-report their child's anxiety symptoms (e.g., Frick, Silverthorn, & Evans, 1994). Conversely, some parents may be likely to underreport symptoms either because they are unaware of the extent of the child's anxiety symptoms or because they are concerned with providing socially desirable responses. Thus, the use of self-report measures with parents and teachers should be part of a multimethod assessment to increase accuracy and better inform treatment planning.

Treatment
Psychological Treatments

Several approaches to psychologically treat anxiety in youth are available; however, behavioral and cognitive behavioral approaches have undergone the greatest amount of empirical evaluation. Using criteria set forth by the American Psychological Association Task Force on the Promotion and Dissemination of Psychological Procedures (1995; see also Ollendick, King, & Chorpita, 2006), cognitive behavioral treatments (with and without a family component) are deemed "probably efficacious" when treating anxiety in youth.

Although some treatment outcome trials have examined single anxiety disorders (reviewed later), several studies have included youth with GAD, SAD, and/or SOP. Kendall and colleagues' program of treatment outcome research has included all three disorders and has not found differential treatment effects by diagnosis (Kendall, 1994; Kendall, et al., 1997). In the first randomized clinical trial, 47 9- to 13-year-old anxiety-disordered youth were randomly assigned to either CBT or a waitlist condition (Kendall, 1994). Outcome was evaluated using structured diagnostic interviews, child self-reports, parent and teacher reports, child self-talk, and behavioral observations. The CBT (see therapist manual; Kendall & Hedtke, 2006a) included identifying somatic reactions to anxiety, challenging anxious cognitions, developing a plan to cope with anxiety-provoking situations, engaging in exposure tasks, evaluating efforts at managing anxiety, administering self-reward as appropriate, and using the *Coping Cat Workbook* (see Kendall & Hedtke, 2006b). Modeling, imaginal and in vivo exposures, role-play, and relaxation exercises were implemented. The child was also encouraged to practice the coping skills that were learned in session during anxiety-provoking situations that arose when at home or in school (for a practical discussion of exposure tasks, see Kendall et al., 2005). Throughout treatment, therapists rewarded the children for their efforts at coping. Improvements were found on self-report measures of coping and symptomatology, parent ratings of behavior, behavioral observations, and on diagnostic status (64% of children no longer met criteria for an anxiety disorder). A 3.5-year follow-up revealed maintenance of the positive treatment gains (Kendall & Southam-Gerow, 1996). A second randomized controlled trial by Kendall et al. (1997) that used similar methodology as the 1994 trial also indicated similar positive treatment effects at posttreatment, 1-year, and 7.4-year (Kendall et al., 2004) follow-up.

Several adaptations of CBT have also been developed and evaluated, with generally positive outcomes. For example, in a multiple-baseline design, Suveg, Kendall, Comer, and Robin (2006) examined the effectiveness of an emotion-focused CBT treatment. The treatment maintained all of the empirically supported treatment components of CBT (e.g., modeling, exposure tasks), but also targeted deficits in emotional functioning (e.g., emotion understanding and emotion regulation) that were identified through basic research (e.g., Suveg & Zeman, 2004). The initial results were promising—children exhibited a decrease in anxiety symptoms and improvements in emotional functioning. Other research teams have found empirical support for a variety of CBT approaches, such as family-based (e.g., see Barmish & Kendall, 2005, for a review), family-based group (Shortt, Barrett, & Fox, 2001), group (e.g., Flannery-Schroeder & Kendall, 2000; Silverman, Kurtines, Ginsburg, Weems, Lumpkin et al., 1999), and school-based group (Ginsburg & Drake, 2002).

Importantly, CBT appears comparably effective for children with comorbid externalizing problems (e.g., Berman, Weems, Silverman, & Kurtines, 2000; Flannery-Schroeder, Suveg, Kendall, Safford, & Webb, 2004; Rapee, 2000; Southam-Gerow, Kendall, & Weersing, 2001). Few studies have examined the impact of depression on treatment outcome, though Berman et al. (2000) found depression was a negative predictor of treatment outcome.

Variants of CBT have also been developed for the treatment of specific anxiety disorders. For example, Social Effectiveness Therapy for Children (SET-C) is designed for children with social phobia (Beidel, Turner, & Morris, 2000; see also Beidel & Roberson-Nay, 2005). Although many of the components of SET-C are similar to other CBT programs (e.g., education, exposure tasks), SET-C differentiates itself with the inclusion of a social skills training component and the lack of cognitive restructuring. In a study comparing SET-C and a nonspecific intervention, children participated in twice-weekly treatment for 12 weeks. Parts were conducted in a group format (e.g., social skills training) whereas other parts were conducted individually (e.g., in vivo exposure). Results indicated that 67% of children in the SET-C condition, compared to 5% in the nonspecific intervention condition no longer met criteria for SOP at posttreatment and a 6-month follow-up revealed maintenance of the treatment gains. Other versions of CBT have also been shown to reduce social anxiety symptoms (e.g., Hayward et al., 2000; Masia, Klein, Storch, & Corda, 2001; Spence, Donovan, & Brechman-Toussaint, 2000).

A variant of CBT, exposure and response prevention (ERP), has been studied for treating pediatric OCD (March & Leonard, 1998). This therapy consists of (1) exposing the child to feared stimuli and situations and (2) preventing the child from engaging in rituals that serve to decrease anxiety (albeit temporarily) associated with exposure to the feared stimuli. To facilitate success, children are also taught skills similar to those in typical CBT programs, such as differentiating levels of fear, identifying and challenging negative cognitions, and utilizing coping thoughts (see March, Franklin, & Foa, 2005; March & Mulle, 1998). Findings are emerging to support the use of ERP in the treatment of OCD in youth. In addition to open trials (e.g., Franklin et al., 1998; March, Mulle, & Herbel, 1994), 3 controlled trials provide support for the use of ERP in the treatment of OCD in youth (Barrett, Healy-Farrell, & March, 2004; de Haan, Hoogduin, Buitelaar, & Keijsers, 1998; Pediatric OCD Treatment Study Team, 2004).

Variants of CBT have been widely researched for the treatment of PTSD in youth, including psychoeducation, problem solving, challenging cognitive distortions, relaxation training, and exposure. Cognitive behavioral and behavioral treatments have been examined in victims exposed to war (Saigh,

1989), child sexual abuse (CSA) (Cohen, Deblinger, Mannarino, & Steer, 2004), violence (Stein et al., 2003), and single-incident disasters (March, Amaya-Jackson, Murray, & Shulte, 1998), among others. Unfortunately, many studies have had small sample sizes, no control group or random assignment, or nonstandardized assessments (see Feeny, Foa, Treadwell, & March, 2004). With randomized clinical trials, the literature with CSA victims is perhaps the most developed.

Cohen and colleagues (2004) examined the efficacy of CBT in the treatment of CSA (although some children were also exposed to other traumas including domestic or community violence, physical abuse). Treatment included typical CBT components (e.g., psychoeducation, relaxation training, cognitive restructuring, gradual exposure), and parents were taught skills to manage the children's difficult behaviors. The trauma-focused therapy (TF-CBT) was compared to a nondirective supportive therapy (NST), standard community care (SCC), and child-centered therapy (CCT). The results were promising, with TF-CBT evidencing greater improvement in symptomatology than SCC (Deblinger, Lippman, & Steer, 1996), NST (Cohen & Mannarino, 1998), and CCT (Cohen et al., 2004). Cohen et al. (2004) also found that TF-CBT was superior to CCT for alleviating parental distress and increasing positive parenting.

Several behavioral and cognitive behavioral interventions have empirical support for the treatment of specific phobias. Much of the earlier research examining the treatment of SP focused on imaginal and in vivo desensitization (e.g., Mann & Rosenthal, 1969) and participant modeling (e.g., Bandura, Blanchard, & Ritter, 1969), whereas more recent research has examined CBT (e.g., Silverman, Kurtines, Ginsburg, Weems, Rabian, et al., 1999). Although treatment generally involves gradual exposure to the feared stimulus over the course of several weeks or months, more recently, researchers have begun to examine the effectiveness of one-session treatment approaches (e.g., Muris, Merckelbach, Van Haaften, & Mayer, 1997; Öst, Svensson, Hellström, & Kindwall, 2001). In the study by Öst et al. (2001), phobic youth between the ages of 7 and 17 were randomly assigned to a one-session exposure treatment with or without the parent present, or to a waitlist. Treatment consisted of a 3-hour graduated exposure session to the feared stimuli. Assessments included independent assessor ratings and self-reports of anxiety. The two treatment groups did not differ from each other

on these ratings, although the child alone group did better than the parent group on the behavioral approach test. The positive treatment gains were maintained at follow-up.

Pharmacological Treatments

Part of the rationale for pharmacological treatments for anxiety in youth stems from their use with anxiety- or mood-disordered adults who have shown responsiveness to tricyclic antidepressants (TCAs), monoamine oxidase inhibitors (MAOIs), and more recently, selective serotonin reuptake inhibitors (SSRIs). The focus of recent research with anxious youth has been on SSRIs; this is likely due to the research establishing SSRIs as safe and effective and first-line pharmacological treatments for anxiety in adults (e.g., Ball, Kuhn, Wall, Shekhar, & Goddard, 2005; Greist, Jefferson, Kobak, Katzelnick, & Serlin, 1995; Salzman, Goldenberg, Bruce, & Keller, 2001).

Numerous open trials examining the efficacy of SSRIs with anxiety-disordered youth initially showed the SSRIs to be safe and effective for childhood OCD (March, Biederman, et al., 1998), SOP, SAD, OAD (Birmaher et al., 1994), and selective mutism (Dummitt, Klein, Tancer, Asche, & Martin, 1996). Based on the preliminary research, NIMH's Research Units on Pediatric Psychopharmacology (RUPP) initiative launched a multisite, randomized, placebo-controlled trial examining the efficacy of fluvoxamine for the treatment of SAD, SOP, and GAD (RUPP Anxiety Group, 2001). The study examined 128 children between the ages of 6 and 17 who met diagnostic criteria for SOP, SAD, or GAD, as determined by the K-SADS. The decision to study this cluster of disorders was based on their high comorbidity rate (Gould, Buckminster, Pollack, Otto, & Yap, 1997; Kendall & Brady, 1995). Participants were randomly assigned to receive fluvoxamine or pill placebo for 8 weeks of double-blind treatment. Assessment consisted of self- and parent-report measures, as well as clinician ratings on anxiety symptoms and measures of global improvement. The results indicated that fluvoxamine was superior to placebo on measures of symptom reduction and global improvement. Specifically, 76% of children assigned to receive fluvoxamine showed considerable improvement, as compared to 29% of children assigned to receive placebo. Additionally, fluvoxamine was generally well tolerated and considered to be safe, with only 8% of children in the fluvoxamine group discontinuing due to side effects.

Researchers have examined the use of other SSRIs (as well as the serotonin norepinephrine reuptake inhibitor, venlafaxine) for the treatment of child anxiety. To date, fluoxetine (Clark et al., 2005; Fairbanks et al., 1997), sertraline (Compton et al., 2001; Rynn, Siqueland, & Rickels, 2001), paroxetine (Wagner et al., 2004), and venlafaxine (Khan, Kunz, Nicolacopoulos, Jenkins, & Yeung, 2002) have been deemed safe and efficacious as pharmacological treatments for anxiety disorders in youth. Although the majority of studies examined a cluster of anxiety disorders (e.g., SOP, SAD, GAD), some studies have focused on a particular anxiety disorder. Rynn et al. (2001) examined the safety and efficacy of sertraline in a sample of 22 children aged 5–17 with GAD and found that sertraline was superior to placebo in symptom reduction after 9 weeks of double-blind treatment. Similarly, both paroxetine (Wagner et al., 2004) and sertraline (Compton et al., 2001) have been found to be safe and efficacious for the treatment of youth with SOP. Wagner et al. (2004) conducted a multisite, randomized, placebo-controlled trial evaluating the efficacy and tolerability of paroxetine for socially phobic youth, using a sample of 322 children between the ages of 12 and 17. Following 16 weeks of treatment, 77.6% of the participants assigned to the paroxetine group showed clinician-rated improvement and were considered responders to treatment, as compared to 38.3% of participants in the placebo group. Additionally, 34.6% of the participants assigned to the paroxetine group met remission criteria, compared to only 8% of participants assigned to the placebo group. Regarding side effects, the authors reported that the majority of adverse events (AEs) ranged from mild to moderate in intensity, with the most common AEs being insomnia, decreased appetite, and vomiting. Although an exact figure was not provided, the authors also stated that withdrawal from the study due to AEs in the paroxetine group was low. Taken together, these results suggest that paroxetine is generally well tolerated by this age group, and similar to the other SSRIs, can be a safe and effective treatment for anxiety-disordered youth.

Studies examining the safety and efficacy of the SSRIs in youth with OCD constitute the bulk of research addressing medications with a single anxiety disorder. March, Biederman, et al. (1998) examined the efficacy of sertraline in 187 children (ages 6–17) with OCD. Participants were randomized to receive either sertraline (n = 92) or pill placebo (n = 95) for a duration of 12 weeks. Participants in the sertraline group showed greater improvement on 3 out of 4 outcome measures, including clinician-rated improvement and symptom reduction. All AEs associated with sertraline use were mild to moderate in nature, and the most frequently observed AEs included nausea, insomnia, drowsiness, decreased libido, and diarrhea. Sertraline and other SSRIs (e.g., fluoxetine) have been approved by the United States Food and Drug Administration (FDA) for use with children and adolescents with OCD. The SSRIs, according to the American Academy of Child and Adolescent Psychiatry (AACAP, 1998) are generally considered first-line agents for the treatment of pediatric OCD.

Although the SSRIs, as a whole, have a more favorable side-effect profile in youth than other pharmacological agents, several side effects require consideration and should be monitored closely. As reviewed in Yörbik and Birmaher (2003), the most common side effects associated with SSRI use in pediatric populations include gastrointestinal difficulties (abdominal distress, nausea, diarrhea, vomiting, or decreased appetite) and central nervous system effects, such as increased motor activity, disinhibition or behavioral activation, headaches, insomnia, or drowsiness. Other side effects that have been reported include weight increase or decrease, tremor, restlessness, sexual side effects, vivid dreams, apathy, akathisia, and allergies.

Although the majority of AEs reported in the trials reviewed have been mild to moderate, close monitoring of side effects is essential during treatment with SSRIs. Given cautions regarding suicidal ideation or behavior in youth receiving antidepressant medication—particularly those with comorbid major depression—the FDA mandates monitoring of patients receiving SSRIs. In October 2004, these concerns prompted the FDA to issue a black box warning mandating the documentation of suicidal risk associated with antidepressant use in youth to be provided to parents with each prescription. In addition, manufacturers must now include a warning statement in product labeling that recommends the close monitoring of individuals receiving SSRI treatment. As a result of this warning, the FDA has only approved the use of SSRIs in pediatric populations for the treatment of OCD.

A limitation of the research on SSRIs for anxiety in youth is the lack of data on long-term outcomes. As described in the AACAP practice parameters (1998), the optimal time to maintain an individual who has responded to treatment with SSRIs on medication is unclear. Such long-term research is important, given that participants may remain symptomatic at the end of shorter treatment periods (Birmaher et al., 2003). The RUPP Anxiety Group (2002) ran a 6-month open treatment follow-up: after 6 months with fluvoxamine, 94% of initial responders either retained their therapeutic response or showed additional improvement. A 1-year follow-up (Clark et al., 2005) revealed that continued fluoxetine may be beneficial. Participants receiving fluoxetine treatment showed greater improvement according to clinician ratings and parent and child reports than those receiving no medication. Among those receiving fluoxetine, only 5% were considered to have shown no improvement, in contrast to 30% of those not taking medication.

A concern for research on pharmacological treatment of anxious youth is generalizability. Do the inclusion criteria limit the generalizability of the results? As suggested in the AACAP's practice parameters for the treatment of OCD (1998), the use of antidepressants may actually alleviate other difficulties, such as irritability, depressive symptoms, or impulsivity, implying that SSRIs may improve comorbidities. As noted, the use of SSRIs in youth with comorbid anxiety and depression should involve careful monitoring of suicidal impulses or behavior.

Despite some limitations, research on pharmacological agents in youth supports the use of SSRIs for treating anxiety. The choice of agent is generally based on considerations of side effects, suicide risk, medical issues, concomitant medications, comorbid disorders, and previous trials with different agents—decisions made on an individual patient basis. Additionally, AACAP practice parameters (1998) advise that individually based decisions determine whether the use of SSRIs should be combined with psychological treatment.

Combined Psychological and Pharmacological Treatments

Research examining the potentially additive effect of combined medication and psychological interventions is still relatively scarce. In a multisite study of 112 youth ages 7 to 17, participants with a primary diagnosis of OCD were randomized to receive a 12-week manualized treatment of CBT, sertraline, a combination of CBT and sertraline, or placebo (Pediatric OCD Treatment Study Team [POTS], 2004). Using the Children's Yale-Brown Obsessive Compulsive Scale (CY-BOCS) (Goodman, Price, Rasmussen, Riddle, & Rapoport, 1991) as a measure of improvement, results utilizing the intent-to-treat sample indicated that CBT, sertra-

line, and their combination were superior to placebo. There were no significant differences between CBT and sertraline, although a combination of the therapies was superior to either monotherapy. When CY-BOCS scores were dichotomized into those less than or equal to 10 and those greater than 10 (indicating "clinical remission"; POTS, 2004), the combined treatment and CBT did not differ from each other, but were significantly different from placebo. Combined treatment (but not CBT alone) was superior to medication alone; and medication only did not differ from placebo. Site effects indicated that CBT alone and medication only conditions differed by site. Another study from our Center at Temple University and five other sites (the Child and Adolescent Anxiety Multimodal Treatment Study or CAMS) is currently comparing CBT, sertraline, their combination, and pill placebo with anxious youth (i.e., GAD, SOP, SAD) aged 7–17. It is hoped that the results of the CAMS study will address a major gap in the treatment outcome literature for anxious youth.

Summary and Conclusions

Advances have certainly been made in the treatment of anxiety in youth. Yet, several avenues of future research may prove significant and useful in advancing our understanding of successful treatment of anxiety in youth. For example, research needs to examine whether CBT approaches are superior to other types of psychosocial interventions. Second, research needs to examine the relative efficacy of psychological treatments, pharmacological approaches, and their combination. Such studies may also help provide practitioners with information on which treatments may be better for children with particular characteristics. Although the treatments are helpful in alleviating anxious symptoms within a research context, we also need to know more about how the treatments work in community settings.

References

Abe, K. (1972). Phobias and nervous symptoms in childhood and maturity: Persistence and associations. *British Journal of Psychiatry, 120,* 275–283.

Achenbach, T. M. (1991). *Integrative guide for the 1991 CBCL/4–18, YSR, and TRF.* Burlington: University of Vermont.

Achenbach, T. M., & Edelbrock, C. (1983). *Manual for the Child Behavior Checklist and Revised Child Behavior Profile.* Burlington: University of Vermont, Associates in Psychiatry.

Achenbach, T. M., McConaughy, S. H., & Howell, C. T. (1987). Child/adolescent behavioral and emotional problems: Implications of cross-informant correlations for situational specificity. *Psychological Bulletin, 101,* 213–232.

Allesandri, S. M., & Lewis, M. (1996). Development of the self-conscious emotions in maltreated children. In M. Lewis & M. W. Sullivan (Eds.), *Emotional development in atypical children* (pp. 185–201). Mahwah, NJ: Erlbaum.

Ambrosini, P. J. (2000). Historical development and present status of the Schedule for Affective Disorders and Schizophrenia for School-Age Children (K-SADS). *Journal of the American Academy of Child and Adolescent Psychiatry, 39,* 49–58.

Ambrosini, P. J., Metz, C., Prabucki, K., & Lee, J. C. (1989). Videotape reliability of the third revised edition of the K-SADS. *Journal of the American Academy of Child and Adolescent Psychiatry, 28,* 723–728.

American Academy of Child and Adolescent Psychiatry. (1998). Practice parameters for the assessment and treatment of children and adolescents with obsessive-compulsive disorder. *Journal of the American Academy of Child and Adolescent Psychiatry, 37,* 27S–45S.

American Psychiatric Association. (1994). *Diagnostic and statistical manual of mental disorders* (4th ed.). Washington, DC: Author.

American Psychological Association Task Force on Promotion and Dissemination of Psychological Procedures. (1995). Training in and dissemination of empirically-validated psychological treatments: Report and recommendations. *The Clinical Psychologist, 48,* 3–24.

Anderson, J. C. (1994). Epidemiological issues. In T. H. Ollendick, N. J., King, & W. Yule (Eds.), *International handbook of phobic and anxiety disorders in children and adolescents* (pp. 43–65). New York: Plenum.

Anderson, J. C., Williams, S., McGee, R., & Silva, P. A. (1987). DSM–III disorders in preadolescent children. *Archives of General Psychiatry, 44,* 69–76.

Andrews, G., Stewart, G., Allen, R., & Henderson, A. S. (1990). The genetics of six anxiety disorders: A twin study. *Journal of Affective Disorders, 19,* 23–29.

Angold, A., Costello, E., & Erkanli, A. (1999). Comorbidity. *Journal of Child Psychology and Psychiatry and Allied Disciplines, 40,* 57–87.

Aschenbrand, S. G., Kendall, P. C., Webb, A., Safford, S. M., & Flannery-Schroeder, E. (2003). Is childhood separation anxiety disorder a predictor of adult panic disorder and agoraphobia? A seven-year longitudinal study. *Journal of the American Academy for Child and Adolescent Psychiatry, 42,* 1478–1485.

Ball, S. G., Kuhn, A., Wall, D., Shekhar, A., & Goddard, A. W. (2005). Selective serotonin reuptake inhibitor treatment for generalized anxiety disorder: A double-blind, prospective comparison between paroxetine and sertraline. *Journal of Clinical Psychiatry, 66,* 94–99.

Bandura, A., Blanchard, E. B., & Ritter, B. (1969). Relative efficacy of desensitization and modeling approaches for inducing behavioral, affective, and attitudinal changes. *Journal of Personality and Social Psychology, 13,* 173–199.

Barlow, D. H. (1988). *Anxiety and its disorders: The nature and treatment of anxiety and panic.* New York: Guilford Press.

Barlow, D. H. (1991). Disorders of emotion. *Psychological Inquiry, 2,* 58–71.

Barlow, D. H. (2002). *Anxiety and its disorders: The nature and treatment of anxiety and panic* (2nd ed.). New York: Guilford Press.

Barmish, A., & Kendall, P. C. (2005). Should parents be co-clients in CBT with anxious youth? *Journal of Clinical Child and Adolescent Psychology, 34,* 569–581.

Barrett, P., Healy-Farrell, L., & March, J. (2004). Cognitive-behavioral family treatment of childhood obsessive-compulsive disorder: A controlled trial. *Journal of the American Academy of Child and Adolescent Psychiatry, 43,* 46–62.

Barrios, B. A., & Hartmann, D. B. (1988). Fears and anxieties. In E. J. Mash & L. G. Terdal (Eds.), *Behavioral assessment of childhood disorders* (2nd ed., pp. 196–264). New York: Guilford Press.

Beck, A. (1976). *Cognitive therapy and the emotional disorders.* New York: International Universities Press.

Beck, A. T., Emery, G., & Greenberg, R. L. (1985). *Anxiety disorders and phobias: A cognitive perspective.* New York: Basic Books.

Beidel, D. C., & Roberson-Nay, R. (2005). Social effectiveness therapy for children. In E. D. Hibbs & P. S. Jensen (Eds.), *Psychosocial treatments for child and adolescent disorders: Empirically based strategies for clinical practice* (2nd ed., pp. 75–96). Washington, DC: American Psychological Association.

Beidel, D. C., Turner, S. M., & Morris, T. L. (2000). Behavioral treatment of childhood social phobia. *Journal of Consulting and Clinical Psychology, 6,* 1072–1080.

Beitchman, J. H., Zucker, K. J., Hood, J. E., DaCosta, G. A., Akman, D., & Cassavia, E. (1992). A review of the long-term effects of child sexual abuse. *Child Abuse and Neglect, 16,* 101–118.

Berman, S. L., Weems, C. F., Silverman, W. K., & Kurtines, W. M. (2000). Predictors of outcome in exposure-based cognitive and behavioral treatments for phobic and anxiety disorders in children. *Behavior Therapy, 31,* 713–731.

Bernstein, G. A., & Borchardt, C. M. (1991). Anxiety disorders of childhood and adolescents: A review. *Journal of the American Academy of Child and Adolescent Psychiatry, 30,* 519–532.

Bernstein, G. A., Massie, E. D., Thuras, P. D., Perwien, A. R., Borchardt, C. M., & Crosby, R. D. (1997). Somatic symptoms in anxious-depressed school refusers. *Journal of the American Academy of Child and Adolescent Psychiatry, 36,* 661–668.

Biederman, J., Faraone, S., Mick, E., & Lelon, E. (1995). Psychiatric comorbidity among referred juveniles with major depression: Fact or artifact? *Journal of the American Academy of Child and Adolescent Psychiatry, 34,* 579–590.

Biederman, J., Faraone, S. V., Marrs, A., Moore, P., Garcia, J., Ablon, S., et al. (1997). Panic disorder and agoraphobia in consecutively referred children and adolescents. *Journal of the American Academy of Child and Adolescent Psychiatry, 36,* 214–223.

Biederman, J., Rosenbaum, J. F., Bolduc-Murphy, E. A., Faraone, S. V., Charloff, J., Hirshfeld, D. R., et al. (1993). A 3-year follow-up of children with and without behavioral inhibition. *Journal of the American Academy of Child and Adolescent Psychiatry, 32,* 814–821.

Bird, H. R., Gould, M. S., & Staghezza, B. M. (1993). Patterns of diagnostic comorbidity in a community sample of children aged 9 through 16 years. *Journal of the American Academy of Child and Adolescent Psychiatry, 32,* 361–368.

Birmaher, B., Axelson, D. A., Monk, K., Kalas, C., Clark, D. B., Ehmann, M., et al. (2003). Fluoxetine for the treatment of childhood anxiety disorders. *Journal of the American Academy of Child and Adolescent Psychiatry, 42,* 415–423.

Birmaher, B., Brent, D. A., Chiappetta, L., Bridge, J., Monga, S., & Baugher, M. (1999). Psychometric properties of the Screen for Child Anxiety Related Emotional Disorders Scale (SCARED): A replication study. *Journal of the American Academy of Child and Adolescent Psychiatry, 38,* 1230–1236.

Birmaher, B., Khetarpal, S., Brent, D. A., Cully, M., Balach, L., Kaufman, J., et al. (1997). The Screen for Child Anxiety Related Emotional Disorders (SCARED): Scale construction and psychometric characteristics. *Journal of the American Academy of Child and Adolescent Psychiatry, 36*, 545–553.

Birmaher, B., Waterman, G. S., Ryan, N., Cully, M., Balach, L., Ingram, J., et al. (1994). Fluoxetine for childhood anxiety disorders. *Journal of the American Academy of Child and Adolescent Psychiatry, 33*, 993–999.

Brady, E., & Kendall, P. (1992). Comorbidity of anxiety and depression in children and adolescents. *Psychological Bulletin, 111*, 244–255.

Brent, D. A., Kalas, R., Edelbrock, C., Costello, A. J., Dulcan, M. K., & Conover, N. (1986). Psychopathology and its relationship to suicidal ideation in childhood and adolescence. *Journal of the American Academy of Child and Adolescent Psychiatry, 25*, 666–673.

Breslau, N., Chilcoat, H. D., Kessler, R. C., & Davis, G. C. (1999). Previous exposure to trauma and PTSD effects of subsequent trauma: Results from the Detroit area survey of trauma. *American Journal of Psychiatry, 156*, 902–907.

Brown, G. W., Harris, T. O., & Eales, M. J. (1993). Etiology of anxiety and depressive disorders in an inner-city population: 2. Comorbidity and adversity. *Psychological Medicine, 23*, 155–165.

Cantwell, D. P., & Baker, L. (1989). Stability and natural history of *DSM–III* childhood diagnoses. *Journal of the American Academy of Child and Adolescent Psychiatry, 28*, 691–700.

Capps, L., Sigman, M., Sena, R., & Henker, B. (1996). Fear, anxiety, and perceived control in children of agoraphobic parents. *Journal of Child Psychology and Psychiatry, 37*, 445–452.

Caron, C., & Rutter, M. (1991). Comorbidity in child psychopathology: Concepts, issues and research strategies. *Journal of Child Psychology and Psychiatry and Allied Disciplines, 32*, 1063–1080.

Carrion, V. G., Weems, C. F., Ray, R., & Reiss, A. L. (2002). Toward an empirical definition of pediatric PTSD: The phenomenology of PTSD symptoms in youth. *Journal of the American Academy of Child and Adolescent Psychiatry, 41*, 166–172.

Carter, M. M., Hollon, S. D., Carson, R., & Shelton, R. C. (1995). Effects of a safe person on induced distress following a biological challenge in panic disorder with agoraphobia. *Journal of Abnormal Psychology, 104*, 156–163.

Chorpita, B. F. (2002). The tripartite model and dimensions of anxiety and depression: An examination of structure in a large school sample. *Journal of Abnormal Child Psychology, 30*, 177–190.

Chorpita, B. F., & Barlow, D. H. (1998). The development of anxiety: The role of control in the family environment. *Psychological Bulletin, 124*, 3–21.

Choudhury, M. S., Pimentel, S. S., & Kendall, P. C. (2003). Childhood anxiety disorders: Parent-child (dis)agreement using a structured interview for the *DSM–IV. Journal of the American Academy of Child and Adolescent Psychiatry, 42*, 957–964.

Clark, D., & Winters, K. (2002). Measuring risks and outcomes in substance use disorders prevention research. *Journal of Consulting and Clinical Psychology, 70*, 1207–1223.

Clark, D. B., Birmaher, B., Axelson, D., Monk, K., Kalas, C., Ehmann, M., et al. (2005). Fluoxetine for the treatment of childhood anxiety disorders: Open-label, long-term extension to a controlled trial. *Journal of the American Academy of Child and Adolescent Psychiatry, 44*, 1263–1270.

Clark, D. M. (1986). A cognitive approach to panic. *Behaviour Research and Therapy, 24*, 461–470.

Clark, L., & Watson, D. (1991). Tripartite model of anxiety and depression: Psychometric evidence and taxonomic implications. *Journal of Abnormal Psychology, 100*, 316–336.

Clark, L. A., & Neighbors, B. (1996). Adolescent substance abuse and internalizing disorders. *Child and Adolescent Psychiatric Clinics of North America, 5*, 45–55.

Cohen, J. A., Deblinger, E., Mannarino, A. P., & Steer, R. A. (2004). A multi-site, randomized controlled trial for children with sexual abuse-related PTSD symptoms. *Journal of the American Academy of Child and Adolescent Psychiatry, 43*, 393–402.

Cohen, J. A., & Mannarino, A. P. (1998). Interventions for sexually abused children: Initial treatment findings. *Child Maltreatment, 3*, 17–26.

Comer, J. S., & Kendall, P. C. (2004). A symptom-level examination of parent-child agreement in the diagnosis of anxious youths. *Journal of the American Academy of Child and Adolescent Psychiatry, 43*, 878–886.

Comer, J. S., & Kendall, P. C. (2005). High-end specificity of the children's depression inventory in a sample of anxiety-disordered youth. *Depression and Anxiety, 22*, 11–19.

Comer, J. S., Kendall, P. C., Franklin, M. E., Hudson, J. L., & Pimentel, S. S. (2004). Obsessing/worrying about the overlap between obsessive-compulsive disorder and generalized anxiety disorder in youth. *Clinical Psychology Review, 24*, 663–683.

Compton, S. N., Grant, P. J., Chrisman, A. K., Gammon, P. J., Brown, V. L., & March, J. S. (2001). Sertraline in children and adolescents with social anxiety disorder: An open trial. *Journal of the American Academy of Child and Adolescent Psychiatry, 40*, 564–571.

Costello, E. J., Egger, H. L., & Angold, A. (2004). Developmental epidemiology of anxiety disorders. In T. H. Ollendick & J. S. March (Eds.), *Phobic and anxiety disorders in children and adolescents: A clinician's guide to effective psychosocial and pharmacological interventions* (pp. 61–91). New York: Oxford University Press.

Costello, E. J., Egger, H. L., & Angold, A. (2005). 10-year research update review: The epidemiology of child and adolescent psychiatric disorders: I. Methods and public health burden. *Journal of the American Academy of Child and Adolescent Psychiatry, 44*, 972–986.

Costello, E. J., Erkanli, A., Fairbank, J. A., & Angold, A. (2002). The prevalence of potentially traumatic events in childhood and adolescence. *Journal of Traumatic Stress, 15*, 99–112.

Costello, E. J., Mustillo, S., Erkanli, A., Keeler, G., & Angold, A. (2003). Prevalence and development of psychiatric disorders in childhood and adolescence. *Archives of General Psychiatry, 60*, 837–844.

Curry, J. F., March, J. S., & Hervey, A. S. (2004). Comorbidity of childhood and adolescent anxiety disorders: Prevalence and implications. In T. H. Ollendick & J. S. March (Eds.), *Phobic and anxiety disorders in children and adolescents: A clinician's guide to effective psychosocial and pharmacological interventions* (pp. 119–140). New York: Oxford University Press.

Davies, P. T., & Cummings, E. M. (1994). Marital conflict and child adjustment: An emotional security hypothesis. *Psychological Bulletin, 116*, 387–411.

Davies, P. T., & Cummings, E. M. (1998). Exploring children's emotional security as a mediator of the link between marital relations and child adjustment. *Child Development, 69,* 124–139.

Deblinger, E., Lippmann, J., & Steer, R. (1996). Sexually abused children suffering posttraumatic stress symptoms: Initial treatment outcome findings. *Child Maltreatment, 1,* 310–321.

De Haan, E., Hoogduin, K. A., Buitelaar, J., & Keijsers, G. (1998). Behavior therapy versus clomipramine for the treatment of obsessive-compulsive disorder. *Journal of the American Academy of Child and Adolescent Psychiatry, 37,* 1022–1029.

Dhossche, D., Ferdinand, R., van der Ende, J., & Verhulst, F. (2001). Outcome of self-reported functional-somatic symptoms in a community sample of adolescents. *Annals of Clinical Psychiatry, 13,* 191–199.

DiBartolo, P. M., Albano, A. M., Barlow, D. H., & Heimberg, R. G. (1998). Cross-informant agreement in the assessment of social phobia in youth. *Journal of Abnormal Child Psychology, 26,* 213–220.

Donovan, C. L., & Spence, S. H. (2000). Prevention of childhood anxiety disorders. *Clinical Psychology Review, 20,* 509–531.

Dorn, L. D., Campo, J. C., Thato, S., Dahl, R. E., Lewin, S., Chandra, R., et al. (2003). Psychological comorbidity and stress reactivity in children and adolescents with recurrent abdominal pain and anxiety disorders. *Journal of the American Academy of Child and Adolescent Psychiatry, 42,* 66–75.

Douglass, H. M., Moffitt, T. E., Dar, R., McGee, R., & Silva, P. (1995). Obsessive-compulsive disorder in a birth cohort of 18-year-olds: Prevalence and predictors. *Journal of the American Academy of Child and Adolescent Psychiatry, 34,* 1424–1431.

Dumas, J. E., & Nilsen, W. J. (2003). *Abnormal child and adolescent psychology.* Boston: Allyn and Bacon.

Dummitt, E. S., III, Klein, R. G., Tancer, N. K., Asche, B., & Martin, J. (1996). Fluoxetine treatment of children with selective mutism: An open trial. *Journal of the American Academy of Child and Adolescent Psychiatry, 35,* 615–621.

Edelbrock, C., Costello, A. J., Duncan, M. K., Kalas, R., & Conover, N. C. (1985). Age differences in the reliability of the psychiatric interview of the child. *Child Development 56,* 265–275.

Egger, H. L., Costello, E. J., Erkanli, A., & Angold, A. (1999). Somatic complaints and psychopathology in children and adolescents: Stomach aches, musculoskeletal pains, and headaches. *Journal of the American Academy of Child and Adolescent Psychiatry, 38,* 852–860.

Eley, T. C., & Stevenson, J. (2000). Specific life events and chronic experiences differentially associated with depression and anxiety in young twins. *Journal of Abnormal Child Psychology, 28,* 383–394.

Fairbanks, J. M., Pine, D. S., Tancer, N. K., Dummitt, E. S., III, Kentgen, L. M., Martin, J., et al. (1997). Open fluoxetine treatment of mixed anxiety disorders in children and adolescents. *Journal of Child and Adolescent Psychopharmacology, 7,* 17–29.

Feehan, M., McGee, R., & Williams, S. (1993). Mental health disorders from age 15 to age 18 years. *Journal of the American Academy of Child and Adolescent Psychiatry, 32,* 1118–1126.

Feeny, N. C., Foa, E. B., Treadwell, K.R.H., & March, J. (2004). Posttraumatic stress disorder in youth: A critical review of the cognitive and behavioral treatment outcome literature. *Professional Psychology: Research and Practice, 35,* 466–476.

Flament, M. F., Koby, E., Rapoport, J. L., Berg, C. J., Zahn, T., Cox, C., et al. (1990). Childhood obsessive-compulsive disorder: A prospective follow-up study. *Journal of Child Psychology and Psychiatry, 31,* 363–380.

Flannery-Schroeder, E., & Kendall, P. C. (2000). Group and individual cognitive-behavioral treatments for youth with anxiety disorders: A randomized clinical trial. *Cognitive Therapy and Research, 24,* 251–278.

Flannery-Schroeder, E., Suveg, C., Kendall, P. C., Safford, S., & Webb, A. (2004). Effect of comorbid externalizing disorders on child anxiety treatment outcomes. *Behaviour Change, 21,* 14–25.

Foa, E. B., & Kozak, M. J. (1986). Emotional processing of fear: Exposure to corrective information. *Psychological Bulletin, 99,* 20–35.

Franklin, M. E., Kozak, M. J., Cashman, L. A., Coles, M. E., Rheingold, A. A., & Foa, E. B. (1998). Cognitive-behavioral treatment of pediatric obsessive-compulsive disorder: An open clinical trial. *Journal of the American Academy of Child and Adolescent Psychiatry, 37,* 412–419.

Frick, P. J., Silverthorn, P., & Evans, C. (1994). Assessment of childhood anxiety using structured interviews: Patterns of agreement among informants and association with maternal anxiety. *Psychological Assessment, 6,* 372–379.

Gerull, F. C., & Rapee, R. M. (2002). Mother knows best: Effects of maternal modeling on the acquisition of fear and avoidance behaviour in toddlers. *Behaviour Research and Therapy, 40,* 279–287.

Gest, S. D. (1997). Behavioral inhibition: Stability and associations with adaptation from childhood to early adulthood. *Journal of Personality and Social Psychology, 72,* 467–475.

Ginsburg, G. S., & Drake, K. L. (2002). School-based treatment for anxious African-American adolescents: A controlled pilot study. *Journal of the American Academy of Child and Adolescent Psychiatry, 41,* 768–775.

Ginsburg, G. S., Siqueland, L., Masia-Warner, C., & Hedtke, K. A. (2004). Anxiety disorders in children: Family matters. *Cognitive and Behavioral Practice, 11,* 28–43.

Glied, S., & Cuellar, A. E. (2003). Trends and issues in child and adolescent mental health. *Health Affairs, 22,* 39–50.

Goodman, W., Price, L., Rasmussen, S., Riddle, M., & Rapoport, J. (1991). *Children's Yale-Brown Obsessive Compulsive Scale (CY-BOCS).* New Haven, CT: Yale University.

Gould, R. A., Buckminster, S., Pollack, M. H., Otto, M. W., & Yap, L. (1997). Cognitive-behavioral and pharmacological treatment for social phobia: A meta-analysis. *Clinical Psychology: Science and Practice, 4,* 291–306.

Greco, L., & Morris, T. (2005). Factors influencing the link between social anxiety and peer acceptance: Contributions of social skills and close friendships during middle childhood. *Behavior Therapy, 36,* 197–205.

Greist, J. H., Jefferson, J. W., Kobak, K. A., Katzelnick, D. J., & Serlin, R. C. (1995). Efficacy and tolerability of serotonin transport inhibitors in obsessive-compulsive disorder: A meta-analysis. *Archives of General Psychiatry, 52,* 53–60.

Grych, J. H., & Fincham, F. D. (1990). Marital conflict and children's adjustment: A cognitive-contextual framework. *Psychological Bulletin, 108,* 267–290.

Hartup, W. W. (1983). Peer relations. In P. Mussen (Ed.), *Handbook of Child Psychology* (pp. 103–196). New York: Wiley.

Hayward, C., Varady, S., Albano, A. M. Thienemann, M. Henderson, L., & Schatzberg, A. F. (2000). Cognitive-behavioral group therapy for social phobia in female adolescents: Results of a pilot study. *Journal of the American Academy of Child and Adolescent Psychiatry, 39,* 721–734.

Herjanic, B., & Reich, W. (1982). Development of a structured psychiatric interview for children: Agreement between child and parent on individual symptoms. *Journal of Abnormal Child Psychology, 10,* 307–324.

Hirschfield, D. R., Biederman, J., Brody, L., Faraone, S. V., & Rosenbaum, J. F. (1997). Expressed emotion toward children with behavioral inhibition: Associations with maternal anxiety disorder. *Journal of the American Academy of Child and Adolescent Psychiatry, 36,* 910–917.

Hofflich, S. A., Hughes, A. A., & Kendall, P. C. (2006). Somatic complaints and childhood anxiety disorders. *International Journal of Clinical and Health Psychology, 6,* 229–242.

Hudson, J. L., & Rapee, R. M. (2001). Parent-child interactions in clinically anxious children and their siblings. *Journal of Clinical Child and Adolescent Psychology, 31,* 548–555.

Ingram, R. E., & Kendall, P. C. (1987). The cognitive side of anxiety. *Cognitive Therapy and Research, 11,* 523–536.

Janoff-Bulman, R. (1995). Victims of violence. In G. S. Everly, Jr., & J. M. Lating (Eds.), *Psychotraumatology: Key papers and core concepts in post-traumatic stress* (pp. 73–86). New York: Plenum.

Jensen, P. S., Rubio-Stipec, M., Canino, G., Bird, H. R., Dulcan, M. K., Schwab-Stone, M. E., et al. (1999). Parent and child contributions to diagnosis of mental disorder: Are both informants always necessary? *Journal of the American Academy of Child and Adolescent Psychiatry, 38,* 1569–1579.

Kagan, J. (1989). Temperamental contributions to social behavior. *American Psychologist, 44,* 668–674.

Kagan, J. (1997). Temperament and the reactions to unfamiliarity. *Child Development, 68,* 139–143.

Kagan, J., Reznick, J. S., Clarke, C., Snidman, N., & Garcia-Coll, C. (1984). Behavioral inhibition to the unfamiliar. *Child Development, 55,* 2212–2225.

Kagan, J., Reznik, J. S., & Snidman, N. (1988). Biological bases of childhood shyness. *Science, 240,* 167–173.

Kagan, J., Reznick, J. S., Snidman, N., Gibbons, J., & Johnson, M. O. (1988). Childhood derivatives of inhibition and lack of inhibition to the unfamiliar. *Child Development, 59,* 1580–1589.

Kaufman, J., Birmaher, B., Brent, D., Rao, U., Flynn, C., Moreci, P., et al. (1997). Schedule for Affective Disorders and Schizophrenia for School Age Children-Present and Lifetime Version (K-SADS-PL): Initial reliability and validity data. *Journal of the American Academy of Child and Adolescent Psychiatry, 36,* 980–988.

Kendall, P. C. (1984). Behavioral assessment and methodology. In G. T. Wilson, C. M. Franks, K. D. Braswell, & P. C. Kendall (Eds.), *Annual review of behavior therapy: Theory and practice* (Vol. 9, pp. 39–94). New York: Guilford Press.

Kendall, P. C. (1985). Toward a cognitive-behavioral model of child psychopathology and a critique of related interventions. *Journal of Abnormal Child Psychology, 13,* 357–372.

Kendall, P. C. (1994). Treating anxiety disorders in children: Results of a randomized clinical trial. *Journal of Consulting and Clinical Psychology, 62,* 100–110.

Kendall, P. C. & Brady, E. U. (1995). Comorbidity in the anxiety disorders of childhood: Implications for validity and clinical significance. In K. D. Craig & K. S. Dobson (Eds.), *Anxiety and depression in adults and children: Banff international behavioral science series* (pp. 3–36). Thousand Oaks, CA: Sage.

Kendall, P. C., & Chansky, T. E. (1991). Considering cognitions in anxiety-disordered children. *Journal of Anxiety Disorders, 5,* 167–185.

Kendall, P. C., & Flannery-Shroeder, E. C. (1995). Rigor, but not rigor mortis, in depression research. *Journal of Personality and Social Psychology, 68,* 892–894.

Kendall, P. C., Flannery-Schroeder, E., Panichelli-Mindel, S. M., Southam-Gerow, M., Henin, A., & Warman, M. (1997). Therapy for youths with anxiety disorders: A second randomized clinical trial. *Journal of Consulting and Clinical Psychology, 65,* 366–380.

Kendall, P. C., & Hedtke, K. A. (2006a). *Cognitive-behavioral therapy for anxious children: Therapist manual* (3rd ed.). Ardmore, PA: Workbook Publishing.

Kendall, P. C., & Hedtke, K. A. (2006b). *Coping cat workbook* (2nd ed.). Ardmore, PA: Workbook Publishing.

Kendall, P. C., & Pimentel, S. (2003). On the physiological symptom constellation in youth with generalized anxiety disorder (GAD). *Journal of Anxiety Disorders, 17,* 211–221.

Kendall, P. C., Robin, J. A., Hedtke, K. A., Suveg, C., Flannery-Schroeder, E., & Gosch, E. (2005). Considering CBT with anxious youth? Think exposures. *Cognitive and Behavioral Practice, 12,* 136–150.

Kendall, P. C., & Ronan, K. R. (1990). Assessment of childhood anxieties, fears, and phobias: Cognitive-behavioral models and methods. In C. R. Reynolds & R. W. Kamphaus (Eds.), *Handbook of psychological and educational assessment of children: Personality, behavior, and context* (pp. 223–244). New York: Guilford Press.

Kendall, P. C., Safford, S., Flannery-Schroeder, E., & Webb, A. (2004). Child anxiety treatment: Outcomes in adolescence and impact on substance use and depression at 7.4-year follow-up. *Journal of Consulting and Clinical Psychology, 72,* 276–287.

Kendall, P., & Southam-Gerow, M. (1996). Long-term follow-up of treatment for anxiety disordered youth. *Journal of Consulting and Clinical Psychology, 65,* 883–888.

Kessler, R., Berglund, P., Demler, O., Jin, R., & Walters, E. (2005). Lifetime prevalence and age-of-onset distributions of *DSM–IV* disorders in the national comorbidity survey replication. *Archives of General Psychiatry, 62,* 593–602.

Kessler, R., Chiu, W., Demler, O., & Walters, E. (2005). Prevalence, severity, and comorbidity of 12-month *DSM–IV* disorders in the national comorbidity survey replication. *Archives of General Psychiatry, 62,* 617–627.

Khan, A., Kunz, N. R., Nicolacopoulos, E., Jenkins, L., & Yeung, P. P. (2002, May). *Venlafaxine extended release for the treatment of children and adolescents with generalized anxiety disorder.* Paper presented at the American Psychiatric Association 155th Annual Meeting, Philadelphia, PA.

King, N. J., & Ollendick, T. H. (1989). Children's anxiety and phobic disorders in school settings: Classification, assessment, and intervention issues. *Review of Educational Research, 59,* 431–470.

Kirk, A. B., & Madden, L. L. (2003). Trauma related critical incident debriefing for adolescents. *Child and Adolescent Social Work Journal, 20,* 123–134.

Kovacs, M., & Devlin, B. (1998). Internalizing disorders in childhood. *Journal of Child Psychology and Psychiatry and Applied Disciplines, 39,* 47–63.

Kovacs, M., Gatsonis, C., Paulauskas, S., & Richards, C. (1989). Depressive disorders in childhood: IV. A longitudinal study of comorbidity with and risk for anxiety disorders. *Archives of General Psychiatry, 46,* 776–782.

Langley, A. K., Bergman, R. L., McCracken, J., & Piacentini, J. C. (2004). Impairment in childhood anxiety disorders: Preliminary examination of the Child Anxiety Impact Scale-Parent version. *Journal of Child and Adolescent Psychopharmacology, 14,* 105–114.

Last, C. G., Hersen, M., Kazdin, A. E., Finkelstein, R., & Strauss, C. C. (1987). Comparison of *DSM–III* separation anxiety and overanxious disorders: Demographic characteristics and patterns of comorbidity. *Journal of the American Academy of Child and Adolescent Psychiatry, 26,* 527–531.

Last, C. G. Hersen, M., Kazdin A., Francis, G., & Grubb, H. (1987). Disorders in mothers of anxious children. *American Journal of Psychiatry, 144,* 1580–1583.

Last, C. G., Hersen, M., Kazdin, A., & Orvaschel, H. (1991). Anxiety disorders in children and their families. *Archives of General Psychiatry, 48,* 928–934.

Last, C. G., Perrin, S., Hersen, M., & Kazdin, A. E. (1992). *DSM–III–R* anxiety disorders in children: Sociodemographic and clinical characteristics. *Journal of the American Academy of Child and Adolescent Psychiatry, 31,* 1070–1076.

Last, C. G., Strauss, C. C., & Francis, G. (1987). Comorbidity among childhood anxiety disorders. *Journal of Nervous and Mental Disease, 175,* 726–730.

Mancini, C., Van Ameringen, M., Szatmari, P., Fugere, C., & Boyle, M. (1996). A high-risk pilot study of the children of adults with social phobia. *Journal of the American Academy of Child and Adolescent Psychiatry, 35,* 1511–1517.

Mann, J., & Rosenthal, T. L. (1969). Vicarious and direct counterconditioning of test anxiety through individual and group desensitization. *Behavior Research and Therapy, 7,* 359–367.

March, J. S., & Albano, A. M. (1998). Advances in the assessment of pediatric anxiety disorders. *Advances in Clinical Child Psychology, 20,* 213–241.

March, J. S., Amaya-Jackson, L., Murray, M. C., & Shulte, A. (1998). Cognitive-behavioral psychotherapy for children and adolescents with post-traumatic stress disorder following a single-incident stressor. *Journal of the American Academy of Child and Adolescent Psychiatry, 37,* 585–593.

March, J. S., Biederman, J., Wolkow, R., Safferman, A., Mardekian, J., Cook, E. H., et al. (1998). Sertraline in children and adolescents with obsessive-compulsive disorder: A multicenter randomized controlled trial. *Journal of the American Medical Association, 280,* 1752–1756.

March, J. S., Franklin, M., & Foa, E. (2005). Cognitive-behavioral psychotherapy for pediatric obsessive-compulsive disorder. In E. D. Hibbs & P. S. Jensen (Eds.), *Psychosocial treatments for child and adolescent disorders: Empirically based strategies for clinical practice* (2nd ed.). Washington, DC: American Psychological Association.

March, J. S., & Leonard, H. (1998). Obsessive-compulsive disorder in children and adolescents. In R. Swinson, M. Antony, J. Rachman, & M. Richter (Eds.), *Obsessive compulsive disorder: Theory, research and treatment* (pp. 367–397). New York: Guilford Press.

March, J. S., & Mulle, K. (1998). *OCD in children and adolescents: A cognitive-behavioral treatment manual.* New York: Guilford Press.

March, J. S., Mulle, K., & Herbel, B. (1994). Behavioral psychotherapy for children and adolescent with obsessive-compulsive disorder: An open trial of a new protocol-driven treatment package. *Journal of the American Academy of Child and Adolescent Psychiatry, 33,* 333–341.

March, J. S., Parker, J., Sullivan, K., Stallings, P., & Conners, C. (1997). The multidimensional anxiety scale for children (MASC): Factor structure, reliability, and validity. *Journal of the American Academy of Child and Adolescent Psychiatry, 36,* 554–565.

March, J. S., & Sullivan, K. (1999). Test-retest reliability of the Multidimensional Anxiety Scale for Children. *Journal of Anxiety Disorders, 13,* 349–358.

Martin, C., Cabrol, S., Bouvard, M. P., Lepine, J. P., & Mouren-Simeoni, M. C. (1999). Anxiety and depressive disorders in father and mothers of anxious school-refusing children. *Journal of the American Academy of Child and Adolescent Psychiatry, 38,* 916–922.

Masi, G., Favilla, L., Millepiedi, S., & Mucci, M. (2000). Panic disorder in clinically referred children and adolescents. *Child Psychiatry and Human Development, 31,* 139–151.

Masia, C. L., Klein, R. G., Storch, E. A., & Corda, B. (2001). School-based behavioral treatment social anxiety disorder in adolescents: Results of a pilot study. *Journal of the American Academy of Child and Adolescent Psychiatry, 40,* 780–786.

Massion, A. O., Warshaw, M. G., & Keller, M. B. (1993). Quality of life and psychiatric morbidity in panic disorder and generalized anxiety disorder. *American Journal of Psychiatry, 150,* 600–607.

Mayou, R., Bryant, B., & Ehlers, A. (2001). Prediction of psychological outcomes one year after a motor vehicle accident. *American Journal of Psychiatry, 158,* 1231–1238.

McClure, E. B., Brennan, P., Hammen, C., & Le Brocque, R. M. (2001). Parental anxiety disorders, child anxiety disorders, and the perceived parent-child relationship in an Australian high-risk sample. *Journal of Abnormal Child Psychology, 29,* 1–10.

Meiser-Stedman, R. (2002). Towards a cognitive-behavioral model of PTSD in children and adolescents. *Clinical Child and Family Psychology Review, 5,* 217–232.

Mineka, S., Watson, D., & Clark, L. A. (1998). Comorbidity of anxiety and unipolar mood disorders. *Annual Review of Psychology, 49,* 377–412.

Mowrer, O. H. (1960). *Learning theory and behavior.* New York: Wiley.

Muris, P., Merckelbach, H., Mayer, B., van Brakel, A., Thissen, S., Moulaert, V., et al. (1998). The Screen for Child Anxiety Related Emotional Disorders (SCARED) and traditional childhood anxiety measures. *Journal of Behavior Therapy and Experimental Psychiatry, 29,* 327–339.

Muris, P., Merckelbach, H., van Haaften, H., & Mayer, B. (1997). Eye movement desensitization and reprocessing versus exposure in vivo: A single-session cross-over study of spider-phobic children. *British Journal of Psychiatry, 171,* 82–86.

Musa, C. Z., & Lepine, J. P. (2000). Cognitive aspects of social phobia: A review of theories and experimental research. *European Psychiatry, 15,* 59–66.

Nelson, C. A. (1999). Neural plasticity and human development. *Current Directions in Psychological Science, 8,* 42–45.

Ollendick, T. H., King, N. J., & Chorpita, B. F. (2006). Empirically supported treatments for children and adolescents. In P. C. Kendall (Ed.), *Child and adolescent therapy: Cognitive-behavioral procedures* (pp. 492–520). New York: Guilford Press.

Öst, L. G. (1987). Age of onset of different phobias. *Journal of Abnormal Psychology, 96,* 223–229.

Öst, L. G., Svensson, L., Hellström, K., & Kindwall, R. (2001). One-session treatment of specific phobias in youths: A randomized clinical trial. *Journal of Consulting and Clinical Psychology, 69,* 814–824.

Pediatric OCD Treatment Study Team. (2004). Cognitive-behavioral therapy, sertraline, and their combination for children and adolescents with obsessive-compulsive disorder: The Pediatric OCD Treatment Study (POTS) randomized controlled trial. *Journal of the American Medical Association, 292,* 1969–1976.

Pfefferbaum, B., Nixon, S. J., Tucker, P. M., Tivis, R. D., Moore, V. L., Gurwitch, R. H., et al. (1999). Posttraumatic stress responses in bereaved children after the Oklahoma City bombing. *Journal of the American Academy of Child and Adolescent Psychiatry, 38,* 1372–1379.

Pine, D., Cohen, P., Gurley, D., Brook, J., & Ma, Y. (1998). Risk for early-adulthood anxiety and depressive disorders in adolescents with anxiety and depressive disorders. *Archives of General Psychiatry, 55,* 56–64.

Prins, P.J.M. (1986). Children's self-speech and self-regulation during a fear-provoking behavioral task. *Behaviour Research and Therapy, 24,* 181–191.

Prior, M., Smart, D., Sanson, A., & Oberklaid, F. (2000). Does shy-inhibited temperament in childhood lead to anxiety problems in adolescence? *Journal of the American Academy of Child and Adolescent Psychiatry, 39,* 461–468.

Puig-Antich, J., & Chambers, W. (1978). *The Schedule for Affective Disorders and Schizophrenia for School-Age Children (Kiddie-SADS).* New York: New York State Psychiatric Institute.

Pynoos, R. S., Steinberg, A. M., & Piacentini, J. C. (1999). A developmental psychopathology model of childhood traumatic stress and intersection with anxiety disorders. *Biological Psychiatry, 46,* 1542–1554.

Rapee, R. M. (2000). Group treatment of children with anxiety disorders: Outcome and predictors of treatment response. *Australian Journal of Psychology, 52,* 125–130.

Rapee, R. M., Barrett, P. M., Dadds, M. R., & Evans, L. (1994). Reliability of the *DSM–III–R* childhood anxiety disorders using structured interview: Interrater and parent-child agreement. *Journal of the American Academy of Child and Adolescent Psychiatry, 33,* 984–992.

Rapee, R. M., & Melville, L. F. (1997). Retrospective recall of family factors in social phobia and panic disorder. *Depression and Anxiety, 5,* 7–11.

Rassin, E., Merckelbach, H., Muris, P., & Spaan, V. (1999). Thought-action fusion as a causal factor in the development of intrusions. *Behaviour Research and Therapy, 37,* 231–237.

The Research Units on Pediatric Psychopharmacology Anxiety Study Group. (2001). Fluvoxamine for the treatment of anxiety disorders in children and adolescents. *New England Journal of Medicine, 344,* 1279–1285.

The Research Units on Pediatric Psychopharmacology Anxiety Study Group. (2002). Treatment of pediatric anxiety disorders: An open-label extension of the Research Units on Pediatric Psychopharmacology anxiety study. *Journal of Child and Adolescent Psychopharmacology, 12,* 175–188.

Ronan, K., Kendall, P., & Rowe, M. (1994). Negative affectivity in children: Development and validation of a questionnaire. *Cognitive Therapy and Research, 18,* 509–528.

Roy-Byrne, P. P., & Katon, W. (1997). Generalized anxiety disorder in primary care: The precursor/modifier pathway to increased health care utilization. *Journal of Clinical Psychiatry, 58,* 34–38.

Rynn, M. A., Siqueland, L., & Rickels, K. (2001). Placebo-controlled trial of sertraline in the treatment of children with generalized anxiety disorder. *American Journal of Psychiatry, 158,* 2008–2014.

Safran, J. D., & Greenberg, L. S. (1989). The treatment of anxiety and depression: The process of affective change. In P. C. Kendall, & D. Watson (Eds.), *Anxiety and depression: Distinctive and overlapping features* (pp. 455–489). New York: Academic Press.

Saigh, P. A. (1989). The use of in vitro flooding in the treatment of traumatized adolescents. *Journal of Developmental and Behavioral Pediatrics, 10,* 17–21.

Salzman, C., Goldenberg, I., Bruce, S. E., & Keller, M. B. (2001). Pharmacologic treatment of anxiety disorders in 1989 versus 1996: Results from the Harvard/Brown Anxiety Disorders Research Program. *Journal of Clinical Psychiatry, 62,* 149–152.

Seligman, L. D., Ollendick, T. H., Langley, A. K., & Baldacci, H. B. (2004). The utility of measures of child and adolescent anxiety: A meta-analytic review of the Revised Children's Anxiety Scale, the State-Trait Anxiety Inventory for Children, and the Child Behavior Checklist. *Journal of Clinical Child and Adolescent Psychology, 33,* 557–565.

Shaffer, D., Fisher, P., Dulcan, M. K., Davis, D., Piacentini, J., Schwab-Stone, M., et al. (1996). The NIMH Diagnostic Interview Schedule for Children, Version 2.3. (DISC 2.3): Description, acceptability, prevalence rates, and performance in the MECA study. *Journal of the American Academy of Child and Adolescent Psychiatry, 49,* 865–877.

Shafran, R., Thordarson, D. S., & Rachman, S. (1996). Thought-action fusion in obsessive compulsive disorder. *Journal of Anxiety Disorders, 10,* 379–391.

Shannon, M. P., Lonigan, C. J., Finch, A. J., & Taylor, C. M. (1994). Children exposed to disaster: I. Epidemiology of posttraumatic symptoms and symptom profiles. *Journal of the American Academy of Child and Adolescent Psychiatry, 33,* 80–93.

Shortt, A. L., Barrett, P. M., & Fox, T. L. (2001). Evaluating the FRIENDS program: A cognitive-behavioral group treatment for anxious children and their parents. *Journal of Clinical Child Psychology, 30,* 525–535.

Silverman, W. K., & Albano, A. M. (1997). *Anxiety Disorders Interview Schedule for DSM–IV: Child and Parent Versions.* San Antonio, TX: Psychological Corporation.

Silverman, W. K., Cerny, J. A., Nelles, W. B., & Burke, A. E. (1988). Behavior problems in children of parents with anxiety disorders. *Journal of the American Academy of Child and Adolescent Psychiatry, 27,* 779–784.

Silverman, W. K., Kurtines, W., Ginsburg, G., Weems, C., Lumpkin, P., & Carmichael, D. (1999). Treating anxiety disorders in children with group cognitive-behavioral therapy: A randomized clinical trial. *Journal of Consulting and Clinical Psychology, 67,* 995–1003.

Silverman, W. K., Kurtines, W. M., Ginsburg, G. S., Weems, C. F., Rabian, B., & Serafini, L. T. (1999). Contingency management, self-control, and education support in the treatment of childhood phobic disorders: A randomized clinical trial. *Journal of Consulting and Clinical Psychology, 5,* 675–687.

Silverman, W. K., Saavedra, L. M., & Pina, A. A. (2001). Test-retest reliability of anxiety symptoms and diagnoses with anxiety disorders interview schedule for *DSM–IV*: Child and parent versions. *Journal of the American Academy of Child and Adolescent Psychiatry, 40,* 937–944.

Silverman, W. K., & Weems, C. F. (1999). Anxiety sensitivity in children. In S. Taylor (Ed.), *Anxiety sensitivity: Theory, research, and treatment of the fear of anxiety* (pp. 239–268). Mahwah, NJ: Erlbaum.

Siqueland, L., Kendall, P. C., & Steinberg, L. (1996). Anxiety in children: Perceived family environments and observed family interaction. *Journal of Clinical Child Psychology, 25,* 225–237.

Southam-Gerow, M. A., & Kendall, P. C. (2000). A preliminary study of the emotion understanding of youth referred for treatment of anxiety disorders. *Journal of Clinical Child Psychology, 29,* 319–327.

Southam-Gerow, M. A., Kendall, P. C., & Weersing, V. R. (2001). Examining outcome variability: Correlates of treatment response in a child and adolescent anxiety clinic. *Journal of Clinical Child Psychology, 30,* 422–436.

Spence, S. H., Donovan, C., & Brechman-Toussaint, M. (2000). The treatment of childhood social phobia: The effectiveness of a social skills training-based, cognitive-behavioural intervention, with and without parent involvement. *Journal of Child Psychology and Psychiatry and Allied Disciplines, 41,* 713–726.

Spielberger, C. (1973). *STAI manual for the State-Trait Anxiety Inventory.* Florida: Psychological Assessment Resources.

Spielberger, C. D. (1972). *Anxiety: Current trends in theory and research: I.* New York: Academic Press.

Spielberger, C. D. (1983). *Manual for the State-Trait Anxiety Inventory (STAI).* Palo Alto, CA: Consulting Psychologists Press.

Stein, B. D., Jaycox, L. H., Kataoka, S. H., Wong, M., Tu, W., Elliott, M. N., et al. (2003). A mental health intervention for school children exposed to violence. *Journal of the American Medical Association, 290,* 603–611.

Stein, M. B., Jang, K. L., & Livesley, W. J. (1999). Heritability of anxiety sensitivity: A twin study. *American Journal of Psychiatry, 156,* 246–251.

Steinberg, L., & Avenevoli, S. (2000). The role of context in the development of psychopathology: A conceptual framework and some speculative propositions. *Child Development, 71,* 66–74.

Strauss, C. C., Lease, C. A., Last, C. G., & Francis, G. (1988). Overanxious disorder: An examination of developmental differences. *Journal of Abnormal Child Psychology, 16,* 433–443.

Suarez, L., & Bell-Dolan, D. (2001). The relationship of child worry to cognitive biases: Threat interpretation and likelihood of event occurrence. *Behavior Therapy, 32,* 425–442.

Suveg, C., Kendall, P. C., Comer, J. C., & Robin, J. A. (2006). Emotion-focused CBT for anxious youth: A multiple-base-line evaluation. *Journal of Contemporary Psychotherapy, 36,* 77–85.

Suveg, C., & Zeman, J. (2004). Emotion regulation in children with anxiety disorders. *Journal of Clinical Child and Adolescent Psychology, 33,* 750–759.

Sweeny, M., & Pine, D. (2004). Etiology of fear and anxiety. In T. H. Ollendick & J. S. March (Eds.), *Phobic and anxiety disorders in children and adolescents: A clinician's guide to effective psychosocial and pharmacological interventions* (pp. 34–60). New York: Oxford University Press.

Thompson, R. A., & Calkins, S. D. (1996). The double-edged sword: Emotional regulation for children at risk. *Development and Psychopathology, 8,* 163–182.

Torgersen, S. (1983). Genetic factors in anxiety disorders. *Archives of General Psychiatry, 40,* 1085–1089.

Treadwell, K.R.H., & Kendall, P. C. (1996). Self-talk in youth with anxiety disorders: States of mind, content specificity, and treatment outcome. *Journal of Consulting and Clinical Psychology, 64,* 941–950.

Turner, S. M., Beidel, D. C., & Costello, A. (1987). Psychopathology in the offspring of anxiety disordered parents. *Journal of Consulting and Clinical Psychology, 55,* 229–235.

Van Ameringen, M., Mancini, C., & Farvolden, P. (2003). The impact of anxiety disorders on educational achievement. *Journal of Anxiety Disorders, 17,* 561–571.

Verduin, T. L., & Kendall, P. C. (2003). Differential occurrence of comorbidity within childhood anxiety disorders. *Journal of Clinical Child and Adolescent Psychology, 32,* 290–295.

Wagner, K. D., Berard, R., Stein, M. B., Wetherhold, E., Carpenter, D. J., Perera, P., et al. (2004). A multicenter, randomized, double-blind, placebo-controlled trial of paroxetine in children and adolescents with social anxiety disorder. *Archives of General Psychiatry, 61,* 1153–1162.

Wood, J. J., Piacentini, J. C., Bergman, R. L., McCracken, J., & Barrios, V. (2002). Concurrent validity of the anxiety disorders section of the Anxiety Disorders Interview Schedule for *DSM–IV:* Child and parent versions. *Journal of Clinical Child and Adolescent Psychology, 31,* 335–342.

Yörbik, Ö., & Birmaher, B. (2003). Pharmacological treatment of anxiety disorders in children and adolescents. *Bulletin of Clinical Psychopharmacology, 13,* 133–141.

Zeman, J., Shipman, K., & Suveg, C. (2002). Anger and sadness regulation: Prediction to internalizing and externalizing symptoms in children. *Journal of Clinical Child and Adolescent Psychology, 31,* 393–398.

Ziksook, S., Chentsoven-Dutton, Y., & Shuchter, S. R. (1998). PTSD following bereavement. *Annals of Clinical Psychiatry, 10,* 157–163.

Anxiety and Culture

Laila Asmal *and* Dan J. Stein

Abstract

The intersection between anxiety and culture, which forms the subject of this chapter, has been approached using various theoretical frameworks. This chapter outlines a clinical approach, which emphasizes the universality of biomedical disorders, and an anthropological approach, which emphasizes that the expression and experience of illness differs from time to time and place to place. It is argued that an integrated approach, which combines the strengths of the clinical and anthropological approaches, recognizing both disease mechanisms and illness experiences, is possible. An integrated approach proves useful not only in conceptualizing cross-cultural data on anxiety disorders, but also in everyday clinical practice.

Keywords: anthropology, cross-cultural, culture

This chapter examines the relationship between anxiety and culture. It begins by outlining three approaches to conceptualizing the intersection of anxiety and culture—a clinical approach, an anthropological approach, and an integrated approach. This is followed by an overview of the *DSM–IV* perspective on anxiety disorders and culture. We then consider each of the major anxiety disorders—panic disorder, obsessive-compulsive disorder, social anxiety disorder, posttraumatic stress disorder, and generalized anxiety disorder—using the perspective of the integrated approach, arguing that although some psychobiological mechanisms underlying the anxiety disorders are universal, perception and experience of these disorders may vary significantly across different cultural groups.

Conceptualizing Anxiety and Culture

There are a number of ways to consider the intersection of culture and anxiety (Friedman, 1994; Ballenger et al., 2001). We have previously suggested

a heuristic framework that contrasts three approaches, namely a clinical approach, an anthropological approach, and a clinical anthropological (integrated) approach (Stein, 1991; Stein & Williams, 2002). Such a division is theoretically derived and may be overly simplistic for describing the views of any single anthropologist or clinician. Nevertheless, this framework may serve as a useful way to explore the strengths and weaknesses of key debates within anthropology and medicine, and their application to anxiety and its disorders.

Clinical Approach

The clinical position is based on a Western, scientific approach to mental illness. Science draws upon evidence from observation and experimentation in order to explain the world and the individuals that exist within society. Conclusions drawn from this empirically based approach allow for the application of a frame of reference to different settings and populations. The *DSM,* for example, allows for the extension of a Western-based model to non-Western settings. The clinical approach argues for the universality of anxiety disorders, emphasizing that culture influences the content rather than the form of a disorder. Proponents of this position may suggest that the neurobiological substrates of anxiety disorders are universal and that psychosocial factors influence symptom manifestation. Thus, for example, the form of obsessions and compulsions in OCD is universal, but their content may vary, with increased prevalence of obsessions centered on religious content in areas where religious concerns are dominant (de Bilbao & Ginnakopoulos, 2005).

Anthropological Approach

Anthropologists argue that the scientific process of observation and evaluation takes place within the paradigm of a community of scientists and is itself therefore a social construct. The anthropological approach emphasizes that psychopathology can only be assessed by understanding the patient's cultural context and by acknowledging possibly disparate cultural backgrounds of clinician and patient. Proponents of this position may argue, for example, that one could erroneously diagnose agoraphobia without understanding the cultural beliefs of certain ethnic groups that restrict the participation of women in public life. The anthropological approach further suggests that the *DSM* system is itself a social construct, based on a Western framework that reflects Western values (such as individualism) (Cooper, 2004).

In an early review of the anxiety disorders, Good and Kleinman (1985) applied a number of lesions from the anthropological approach to the anxiety disorders, and argued that:

1. Anxiety disorders are disorders of the interpretive process and not just culturally varying presentations of underlying universal psychopathology.

2. There are vast differences cross-culturally in the experience and expression of symptoms of anxiety, as well as in the roots of anxiety.

3. Collation of data on anxiety disorders using Western rating scales entails key methodological problems, and runs the risk of reifying Western constructs.

Integrated (Clinical Anthropological) Approach

An integrated approach combines the strengths of the clinical and anthropological approaches. It suggests that all psychiatric disorders comprise psychopathology that is produced by both biological and psychosocial processes. No one psychiatric disorder is more "biological" than another and no disorder or categorization is free from psychosocial and cultural influence. An integrated approach acknowledges that science is culturally based, but believes that science allows for progress in the understanding of the psychobiological mechanisms underpinning psychopathology. At that same time, an integrated approach accepts that disorders are expressed and experienced differently in different sociocultural settings. The next section contrasts the concepts of *disease* and *illness* and may be helpful in demonstrating the integrated approach to anxiety and culture.

Disease Versus Illness

The distinction between the concepts of *disease* and *illness* may be useful in formulating an integrated approach to understanding the anxiety disorders. Disease refers to a biomedical state that is objectively recognizable across cultures, for example, tachycardia, or shortness of breath. Illness, on the other hand, refers to the subjective experience of the relevant biomedical states, and the meaning a person places on that experience (Kleinman, 1988).

According to the clinical anthropological (integrated) perspective, a comprehensive understanding of anxiety disorders requires an understanding of both disease states (the objectively recognizable aspects of the anxiety disorders), as well as of the relevant subjective illness (the expression and experience of these conditions). From a research perspective, an integrated approach attempts to explore the psychobiological mechanisms that produce both the objective and subjective aspects of anxiety disorders. From a clinical perspective, the patient's perception of a disorder effects both course and outcome, and the ability of the clinician to understand the patient's experience forms that basis for a collaborative approach toward a management plan.

The *DSM*, Anxiety, and Culture

The *DSM–IV* considers the influence of culture on all psychiatric disorders, including anxiety disorders, in three ways:

1. Under specific disorders *DSM–IV* provides a subtext on culture, for example, there is a discussion on how culture can impact on the clinical presentation of different anxiety disorders.

2. *DSM–IV* provides an appendix of culture-bound syndromes. Some of these are characterized

by significant symptoms of anxiety, for example, ataque de nervios, brain fag, and Dhat syndrome.

3. *DSM–IV* includes an appendix outlining a structured cultural formulation designed for use on individual patients to determine diagnosis and management. This is detailed below.

Culture-Bound Syndromes

The expression *culture-bound syndrome* is used to describe a collection of signs and symptoms restricted to a limited number of cultures primarily by reason of certain psychosocial features (Prince & Tcheng-Laroche, 1987). *DSM–IV* has incorporated 25 culture-bound syndromes into its classification system, including at least 15 that may be considered to be part of the anxiety disorders spectrum. *DSM–IV* notes there is rarely a direct correlation between a single culture-bound syndrome and a particular *DSM* diagnosis.

Labeling a particular disorder as "culture-bound" has been criticized insofar as this runs the risk of losing sight of the cultural underpinnings of all psychiatric disorders. A consequence may be that cultural context is not fully assessed and considered in patients presenting with symptoms of a "straight-forward" *DSM* diagnosis. Conversely, by focusing on the "otherness" of culture-bound syndromes one may place insufficient emphasis on the possible neurobiological substrates of these syndromes.

A further criticism of the term *culture-bound* is that many of these syndromes may not be as unique as once thought, both epidemiologically and phenomenologically. An example is Dhat syndrome, regarded as a culture-bound syndrome prevalent in India and characterized by semen-loss and anxiety. Not only is semen-loss anxiety seen in other parts of Southern Asia, but similar anxieties centered around semen-loss are well documented in 18th- and 19th-century European, American, and Australian medical literature (Sumathipala et al., 2004).

Cultural Formulation According to the DSM–IV

It has been argued that if clinicians use a multiaxial assessment with consideration of cultural factors influencing etiology and management for each patient, the term *culture-bound syndrome* may become redundant (Sumathipala et al., 2004). The cultural formulation recommended in Appendix 1 of the *DSM–IV* is one way of comprehensively assessing cultural influences on symptoms, diagnosis, and management.

The formulation considers the influence of culture under four divisions:

1. Cultural identity of the individual.
2. Cultural explanations of the individual's illness.
3. Cultural factors related to the psychosocial environment (e.g., social stressors, support) and levels of functioning.
4. Cultural elements of the relationship between the individual and the clinician.

Further discussion under each heading may include information regarding the patient's cultural reference group, idioms of distress for that group, comparisons of patient's symptoms to norms of that group, social stressors and support, language ability and preference, immigrant and minority status, and social and cultural disparity of patient and clinician.

The following sections will consider each of the major anxiety disorders, using an integrated approach, and examining both disease and illness.

Panic Disorder

There is considerable evidence that panic disorder exists across different cultural groups:

1. Epidemiological studies suggest that, although there are some differences between population groups, prevalence rates for panic disorders are rather similar internationally (Aoki et al., 1994; Kessler et al., 2006).
2. Epidemiological and clinical studies report similar age of onset, gender ratios, and outcomes of panic disorder in different settings (Wittchen & Essau, 1993).
3. There is growing evidence detailing the specific psychobiological mechanisms that produce the symptoms of panic disorder (Gorman et al., 2000).

Although some psychobiological underpinnings of panic disorder may be universal, expression and experience of the disorder varies across different cultural groups. Agoraphobia, for example, commonly presents in Western settings with driving avoidance, but Simons et al. (1985) relate a case report of an Inuk where agoraphobia manifested as kayaking avoidance. In the Muslim community in Qatar, fear of the after-death experience rather than a fear of dying itself appears to dominate panic attacks (el Islam, 1994).

Ataque de nervios can be thought of as an idiom of distress; used most commonly by Hispanic individuals to describe patterns of loss of emotional control consonant with panic disorder, affective disorders, or other anxiety disorders (Hinton et al., in press; Liebowitz et al., 1998). Up to 80% of patients with ataque de nervios meeting the criteria for panic disorder describe their panic attacks as *ataques* and report feelings of suffocating, fear of dying, and increased fearfulness during these *ataques*.

Course and prognosis of panic disorder appears to be influenced by perception of panic symptoms by both patient and clinician. It is not uncommon for patients presenting with panic attacks in Western settings to be misdiagnosed with medical disorders such as angina. Ataque de nervios may be suboptimally managed when self-treated; in a prospective study, Salman et al. (1997) noted that many patients took medication only when they felt it was necessary.

Social and cultural factors shaping gender roles may increase agoraphobia among females. A Yugoslavian study described women with agoraphobia as being more likely to stay at home and require a companion when going outdoors compared to men with agoraphobia (Starcevic et al., 1998). Further research is needed, however, to determine whether agoraphobia is related to sociocultural gender norms.

Social Anxiety Disorder

There is growing understanding of the universal psychobiological mechanisms that underlie social anxiety disorder:

1. Epidemiological studies suggest social anxiety disorder is prevalent across a range of diverse cultures, and that the symptoms of this condition are fairly invariate (Weissman et al., 1996).
2. Animal models suggest that phenomena analogous to social anxiety occur in a range of species, and that similar psychobiological mechanisms may underpin processes such as social submission (Gilbert, 2001; Stein & Bouwer, 1997).
3. A range of biological research, including functional and molecular imaging studies, has contributed to understanding the specific neurocircuitry and neurochemistry of social anxiety disorder (Mathew et al., 2001).

Although similar psychobiological mechanisms may be responsible for social anxiety disorder in different settings, the expression and experience of this condition may differ from time to time, and from place to place. It is notable that, although SAD is more common in females, in the West, men are more likely to present for clinical treatment. The reason

for this discrepancy is unclear but could be related to perceived gender roles—whereas males may be socially expected to be dominant, the behavior of a woman who is shy or spends little time outside her home may be normalized. Western studies also show an increased incidence of social anxiety disorders in lower socioeconomic groups (Schneier et al., 1992) and a higher risk of performance anxiety in immigrant groups and in those having to use a second language to communicate (Stein et al., 1998).

Taijin kyofusho syndrome (TKS) is well described in Japanese and other Eastern cultures (Matsunaga et al., 2001). The *DSM–IV* describes TKS as "an individual's intense fear that his or her body, its parts or its functions, displease, embarrass, or are offensive to other people in appearance, odor, facial expressions, or movements." There are a number of phenomenological similarities between TKS and social anxiety disorder; both disorders involve social anxiety and subsequent social avoidance. It has been argued that individuals with social anxiety disorder characteristically fear situations where they may embarrass themselves in contrast to TKS patients who fear offending or embarrassing others (Kleinknecht et al., 1994). However, it has been demonstrated that patients with SAD may in fact also fear offending others and conversely patients with TKS may present with typical SAD symptoms such as blushing (Choy et al., in press). Additionally, patients with TKS appear to be responsive to both SSRIs (Matsunaga et al., 2001) and Morita therapy, which has elements comparable to behavior therapy (Gibson, 1974).

Obsessive-Compulsive Disorder

There is convincing evidence that OCD is underpinned by some universal psychobiological mechanisms:

1. Epidemiological studies suggest that OCD has a similar prevalence across a broad range of countries (Matsunaga & Seedat, 2007).
2. There is growing data from neurogenetics and neuroimaging research that specific neurocircuitry and neurotransmitters are involved in the pathogenesis of OCD (Friedlander & Desrocher, 2006).
3. Epidemiological and clinical studies indicate that demographic factors such as age and gender ratios, and subtypes of OCD (e.g., OCD with comorbid tics) are similar in different countries.

Nonetheless, the variability of symptom expression in different settings suggests cultural factors may affect the expression and experience of OCD. This may contribute to differences in prevalence of OCD spectrum disorders, such as body dysmorphic disorder, which is seen more often in a Western context (Lochner & Stein, 2006), and differences in obsessional concerns (e.g., fear of bewitchment, spirit possession, or having neglected a ritual remains a common cause of intense anxiety in a number of cultures (Lambo, 1962; Lemelson, 2003)).

Posttraumatic Disorder (PTSD)

There is substantial evidence for the universality of PTSD across different social and cultural contexts:

1. Epidemiological studies confirm the existence of PTSD in a range of countries, and show that it is more likely to occur after severe trauma (Kessler et al., 2006).
2. PTSD is characterized by specific neuroanatomical and neurochemical changes that differ from those seen during a normal stress response (Nemeroff et al., 2005).
3. There is considerable evidence that phenomena reminiscent of PTSD exists across cultures as well as in different historical eras (Jones et al., 2002; Marsella et al., 1996).

Although some psychobiological mechanisms underpinning PTSD appear to be universal, there are differences in the expression and experience of symptoms across cultures (Friedman & Jaranson, 2004). A review by Jones et al. (2002) of servicemen records of the Boer War, World Wars I and II, the Korean and Malaysian conflict, and the Gulf war demonstrated that postcombat syndromes have arisen after all of the last century's major wars but symptom form is influenced by the nature of the war and by medical interpretation of symptoms.

Epidemiological studies have found marginalized populations to be at greater risk of PTSD (Keane et al., 1990). It has been argued that some of the predictors of PTSD may also be predictors of trauma exposure itself, such as age, gender, minority grouping, and socioeconomic status (Halligan et al., 2000). Women, for example, have a higher proportional lifetime risk of PTSD than men, with case reports suggesting women are afflicted with a greater symptom load, longer course of illness, and worse quality-of-life outcomes than men (Olff et al., 2007; Seedat et al., 2005). A higher incidence of PTSD was also noted in Black and Hispanic war veterans in the National Vietnam Veterans Readjustment Study (NVVRS, 1988).

Cultural rituals and community support appear to play a role in reducing PTSD symptoms (Shay, 1994). Conversely, a negative or condemning social environment in the aftermath of trauma may be associated with increased incidence of PTSD such as in cases of combat (Kaniasty, 2005). The South African Truth and Reconciliation Commission (TRC) was assembled to bear witness to and document gross human rights abuses under apartheid; a study of the relationship between testifying before the TRC and psychiatric status suggested that, although such a process might be useful for society as a whole, it was not a substitute for an individual therapeutic program for survivors of human rights abuse (Kaminer et al., 2001).

Generalized Anxiety Disorder (GAD)

There is growing awareness of the importance of GAD in primary care settings, with increasing evidence that specific underlying psychobiological mechanisms mediate this disorder:

1. Cross-cultural epidemiological studies demonstrate that a substantial proportion of patients presenting to primary health care settings have generalized anxiety disorder (Goldberg et al., 1995; Kroenke et al., 2007).
2. Animal studies have contributed to understanding the molecular basis for differences in avoidance behavior across different individuals, and across different inbred strains (Golden & Hen, 2005).
3. Although the neurobiological processes of GAD remain to be fully delineated, there is evidence that specific neuroanatomical pathways and neurotransmitter systems underpin particular GAD symptoms, for example, fatigue (Jetty et al., 2001).

A constellation of comorbid anxiety-depressive-somatic symptoms appears to be common throughout the world. Nevertheless, idioms of distress may differ. In Western settings, distress can be expressed both in psychological ways (e.g., worrying in GAD) and in somatic terms. In some settings, idioms of distress more commonly focus on somatic symptoms. A number of studies in Africa, for example, have reported the sensation of an insect crawling in the head or other part of the body as a principal symptom of an anxiety-depressive-somatic syndrome known as brain fag (Ebigbo, 1986; Peltzer et al., 1998).

Neurasthenia, a clinical entity included in the *ICD–10,* shows significant concordance with shenjing shuairuo, a disorder common in China characterized by fatigue, poor concentration, dizziness, headaches, insomnia, memory loss, autonomic and somatic complaints including pain, gastrointestinal problems, and sexual dysfunction (DSM–IV). The experience of anxiety in terms of shenjing shuairuo or brain fag is likely informed by explanatory models that emphasize somatic symptoms.

The expression and experience of anxiety may differ from time to time and place to place (Roy-Byrne & Wagner, 2004) and may reflect culturally shaped beliefs regarding notions of disease etiology and treatment as well as what is deemed culturally appropriate help-seeking behavior. The explanatory model a patient uses may therefore show crucial differences from that of the clinician (Kleinman, 1988) and careful negotiation about these models is needed to allow the clinician to justify treatment choices in a way that the patient experiences as empathic and which improves adherence.

Summary and Conclusions

There is a good deal of evidence that universal psychobiological mechanisms underlie anxiety disorders. It is, however, crucial to consider ethnic, gender, and social factors that may influence the expression and experience of anxiety disorders in fundamental ways.

Women are at greater risk of developing anxiety disorders than men, although the social and biological factors mediating this increase in risk necessitate further research. There is an inverse and causal relationship between socioeconomic status and mental health (Dohrenwend, 1992; Yu & Williams, in press), with individuals from lower socioeconomic groups and low education at greater risk of developing anxiety disorders. Further studies are needed to determine how socioeconomic factors influence the pathogenesis of anxiety disorders and how preventative interventions may be effective in forestalling these conditions (Stein & Williams, 2002).

Ethnicity and gender also have a significant influence on pharmacological treatment and psychotherapeutic management. The last decade has seen considerable progress in research focusing on the biological mechanisms responsible for ethnic variations in psychotropic medication metabolism and effects. Nonetheless, a great challenge remains in the evaluation of the extent to which cultural factors (such as patient expectations and clinician-patient interaction) influence biological factors (Lin et al., 2001).

A comprehensive assessment of the impact of culture on symptom expression, diagnosis, and management is suggested on all patients regardless of background. Further research is clearly indicated to understand health-seeking behavior in patients with anxiety disorders and the beliefs that prevent individuals from seeking medical care. From a clinical perspective, understanding the patient's explanatory model fosters trust and encourages a collaborative treatment plan (Kleinman, 1978).

References

American Psychiatric Association. (2000). *Diagnostic and statistical manual of mental disorders* (4th edition, text revision), Washington, DC: Author.

Aoki, Y., Fujihara, S., & Kitamura, T. (1994). Panic attacks and panic disorder in Japanese non-patient population: Epidemiology and psychosocial correlates. *Journal of Affective Disorders, 32,* 51–59.

Ballenger, J. C., Davidson, J. R., Lecrubier, Y., Nutt, D. J., Kirmayer, L. J., Lepine, J. P., et al. (2001). Consensus statement on transcultural issues in depression and anxiety from the International Consensus Group on Depression and Anxiety. *Journal of Clinical Psychiatry, 62*(Suppl. 13), 47–55.

Brown, D. R., Eaton, W. W., & Sussman, L. (1990). Racial differences in prevalence of phobic disorders. *Journal of Nervous and Mental Disease, 178,* 434–441.

Chang, D. F., Myers, H. F., Yeung, A., Zhang, Y., Zhao, J., & Yu, S. (2005). Shenjing shuairuo and the *DSM–IV*: Diagnosis, distress, and disability in a Chinese primary care setting. *Transcultural Psychiatry, 42,* 204–218.

Choy, Y., Schneier, F. R., Heimberg, R. G., Oh, K. S., & Liebowitz, M. R. (2008). Features of the offensive subtype of Taijin-Kyofu-Sho in U.S. and Korean patients with *DSM–IV* social anxiety disorder. *Depression and Anxiety, 42,* 230–240.

Clarvit, S. R., Schneier, F. R., & Liebowitz, M. R. (1996). The offensive subtype of taijin-kyofu-sho in New York City: The phenomenology and treatment of a social anxiety disorder. *Journal of Clinical Psychiatry, 57,* 523–527.

Cooper, R. (2004). What is wrong with the *DSM? History of Psychiatry, 15,* 5–25.

De Bilbao, F., & Giannakopoulos, P. (2005). Effect of religious culture on obsessive-compulsive disorder symptomatology: A transcultural study in monotheistic religions. *Revue Medicale Suisse, 30,* 2818–2821.

Dohrenwend, B. P., Levav, I., Shrout, P. E., Schwartz, S., Naveh, G., & Link, B. G. (1992). Socioeconomic status and psychiatric disorders: The causation-selection issue. *Science, 255,* 946–952.

El-Islam, M. F. (1994). Cultural aspects of morbid fears in Qatari women. *Social Psychiatry and Psychiatric Epidemiology, 29,* 137–140.

Fontenelle, L. F., Mendlowicz, M. V., Marques, C., & Versiani, M. (2004). Trans-cultural aspects of obsessive-compulsive disorder: A description of a Brazilian sample and a systematic review of international clinical studies. *Journal of Psychiatric Research, 38,* 403–411.

Friedlander, L., & Desrocher, M. (2006). Neuroimaging studies of obsessive-compulsive disorder in adults and children. *Clinical Psychology Review, 26,* 32–49.

Friedman, M .J., & Jaranson, J. M. (1994). The applicability of the PTSD concept to refugees. In A. J. Marsella, T. H. Borneman, S. Ekblad, & J. Orley (Eds.), *Amidst peril and pain: The mental health and well-being of the world's refugees* (pp. 207–227). Washington, DC: American Psychological Association.

Friedman, S. (Ed.). (1997). *Cultural issues in the treatment of anxiety.* New York: Guilford Press.

Gibson, H. B. (1974). Morita therapy and behaviour therapy. *Behaviour Research and Therapy, 12,* 347–353.

Gilbert, P. (2001). Evolution and social anxiety. The role of attraction, social competition, and social hierarchies. *Psychiatric Clinics of North America, 24,* 723–751.

Goisman, R. M., Goldenberg, I., Vasile, R. G., & Keller, M. B. (1995). Comorbidity of anxiety disorders in a multicenter anxiety study. *Comprehensive Psychiatry, 36,* 303–311.

Goldberg, D. P., & Lecrubier, Y. (1995). Form and frequency of mental disorders across centres. In T. B. Üstün & N. Sartorius (Eds.), *Mental illness in general health care: An international study* (pp. 323–334). Chichester, England: Wiley on behalf of WHO.

Goldenberg, I. M., White, K., Yonkers, K., Reich, J., Warshaw, M. G., Goisman, R. M., et al. (1996). The infrequency of "pure culture" diagnoses among the anxiety disorders. *Journal of Clinical Psychiatry, 57,* 528–533.

Good, B. J., & Kleinman, A. M. (1985). Culture and anxiety: Cross-cultural evidence for the patterning of anxiety disorders. In A. H. Tuma & J. Maser (Eds.), *Anxiety and the anxiety disorders* (pp. 297–324). Hillsdale, NJ: Erlbaum.

Gorman, J. M., Kent, J. M., Sullivan, G. M., & Coplan, J. D. (2000) Neuroanatomical hypothesis of panic disorder, revised. *American Journal of Psychiatry, 157,* 493–505.

Greenberg, D., & Witztum, E. (1994). Cultural aspects of obsessive compulsive disorder. In E. Hollander, J. Zohar, Marazzati, & B. Olivier (Eds.), *Current insights in obsessive compulsive disorder* (pp. 11–21). Chichester, England: Wiley.

Guarnaccia, P. J., & Rogler, L. H. (1999). Research on culture bound syndromes: New directions. *American Journal of Psychiatry, 56,* 1322–1327.

Hahn, R. A., & Kleinman, A. (1983). Biomedical practice and anthropological theory. *Annual Review of Anthropology, 12,* 305–333.

Halligan, S. L., & Yehuda, R. (2000). Risk Factors for PTSD. *PTSD Research Quarterly 11*(3), 1–8.

Hinton, D. E., Chong, R., Pollack, M. H., Barlow, D. H., & McNally, R. J. (in press). Ataque de nervios: Relationship to anxiety sensitivity and dissociation. *Depression and Anxiety.*

Jones, E., Hodgins-Vermaas, R., McCartney, H., Everitt, B., Beech, C., Poynter, D., et al. (2002). Post-combat syndromes from the Boer war to the Gulf war: A cluster analysis of their nature and attribution. *British Medical Journal, 324,* 321–324.

Kaminer, D., Stein, D. J., Mbanga I., & Zungu-Dirwayi, N. (2001). The Truth and Reconciliation Commission in South Africa: Relation to psychiatric status and forgiveness among survivors of human rights abuses. *British Journal of Psychiatry, 178,* 373–377.

Kaniasty, K. (2005, Spring). Social support and traumatic stress. *PTSD Research Quarterly, 16.* Retrieved July 19, 2007, from http://www.ncptsd.va.gov

Keane, M. T. (1990, Fall). The epidemiology of post-traumatic disorder: Some comments and concerns. *PTSD Research Quarterly, 1.* Retrieved July 19, 2007, from http://www.ncptsd.va.gov

Kessler, R. C., Chiu, W. T., Jin, R., Ruscio, A. M., Shear, K., & Walters, E. E. (2006). The epidemiology of panic attacks, panic disorder, and agoraphobia in the National Comorbidity Survey Replication. *Archives of General Psychiatry, 63,* 415–424.

Kirmayer, L. (1991). The place of culture in psychiatric nosology: Taijin kyofusho and *DSM–III–R. Journal of Nervous and Mental Disease, 179,* 19–28.

Kizu, A., Miyoshi, N., Yoshida, Y., & Miyagishi, T. (1994). A case with fear of emitting body odour resulted in successful treatment with clomipramine. *Hokkaido Igaku Zasshi, 69,* 1477–1480.

Klein, D. F. (1993). False suffocation alarms, spontaneous panics, and related conditions: An integrative hypothesis. *Archives of General Psychiatry, 50,* 306–317.

Kleinknecht, R. A., Dinnel, D. L., Tanouye-Wilson, S., & Lonner, W. J. (1994). Cultural variation in social anxiety and phobia: A study of Taijin Kyofusho. *Behavior Therapist, 17,* 175–178.

Kleinman, A. (1977). Depression, somatisation, and the new "cross-cultural psychiatry." *Social Science Medicine, 11,* 3–10.

Kleinman, A. (1980). *Patients and healers in the context of culture: An exploration of the borderland between anthropology, medicine, and psychiatry.* Los Angeles: University of California Press.

Kleinman, A. (1988). *Rethinking psychiatry: From cultural category to personal experience.* New York: Free Press.

Kroenke, K., Spitzer, R. L., Williams, J. B., Monahan, P. O., & Lowe, B. (2007). Anxiety disorders in primary care: Prevalence, impairment, comorbidity, and detection. *Annals of Internal Medicine, 146,* 317–325.

Liebowitz, M. R., Salman, E., Jusino, C. M., Garinkel, R., Street, L., & Cardenas, D. L., et al. (1994). Ataque de nervios and panic disorder. *American Journal of Psychiatry, 151,* 871–875.

Lin, K. M., Smith, M. W., & Ortiz, V. (2001). Culture and psychopharmacology. *Psychiatric Clinics of North America, 24,* 523–538.

Lochner, C., & Stein, D. J. (2006). Does work on obsessive-compulsive spectrum disorders contribute to understanding the heterogeneity of obsessive-compulsive disorder? *Progress in Neuro-Psychopharmacology and Biological Psychiatry, 30,* 353–361.

Marsella, A. J., Friedman, M. J., Gerrity, E. T., & Scurfield, R. M. Ethnocultural aspects of PTSD: Some closing thoughts. In A. J. Marsella, M. J. Friedman, E. T. Gerrity, & R. M. Scurfield (Eds.), *Ethnocultural aspects of posttraumatic stress disorder: Issues, research, and clinical applications.* Washington, DC: American Psychological Association.

Mathew, S. J., Coplan, J. D., & Gorman, J. M. (2001). Neurobiological mechanisms of social anxiety disorder. *American Journal of Psychiatry, 158,* 1558–1567.

Matsunaga, H., Kiriike, N., Matsui, T., Iwasaki, Y., & Stein, D. J. (2001). Taijin kyofusho: A form of social anxiety disorder that responds to serotonin reuptake inhibitors? *International Journal of Neuropsychopharmacology, 4,* 231–237.

Matsunaga, H., & Seedat, S. (2007). Obsessive-compulsive spectrum disorders: Cross-national and ethnic issues. *CNS Spectrums, 12,* 392–400.

Norris, F. H., Murphy, A. D., Baker, C. K., Perilla, J. L., Rodriguez, F. G., & Rodriguez, J. de J. (2003). Epidemiology of trauma and posttraumatic stress disorder in Mexico. *Journal of Abnormal Psychology, 112,* 646–656.

Okasha, A., Saad, A., Khalil, A. H., Seif, El., Dawla, A., & Yehia, N. (1994). Phenomenology of obsessive-compulsive disorder: A transcultural study. *Comprehensive Psychiatry, 35,* 191–197.

Olff, M., Langeland, W., Draijer, N., & Gersons, B. P. (2007). Gender differences in posttraumatic stress disorder. *Psychological Bulletin, 133,* 183–204.

Papp, L. A., Klein, D. F., & Gorman, J. M. (1993). Carbon dioxide hypersensitivity, hyperventilation, and panic disorder. *American Journal of Psychiatry, 150,* 1149–1157.

Peltzer, K., Cherian, V. I., & Cherian, L. (1998). Brain Fag symptoms in rural South African secondary school pupils. *Psychological Reports, 83,* 1187–1196.

Prince, R., & Tcheng-Larouche, F. (1987). Culture-bound syndromes and international disease classifications. *Culture, Medicine, and Psychiatry, 11,* 3–20.

Salman, E., Diamond, K., Jusino, C., Sanchez-LaCay, A., & Liebowitz, M. R. (1997). Hispanic Americans. In S. Friedman (Ed.), *Cultural issues in the treatment of anxiety* (pp. 59–80). New York: Guilford Press.

Schneier, F. R., Johnson, J., Hornig, C. D., Liebowitz, M. R., & Weissman, M. M. (1992). Social phobia: Comorbidity and morbidity in an epidemiologic sample. *Archives of General Psychiatry, 49,* 282–288.

Seedat, S., Stein, D. J., & Carey, P. D. (2005). Post-traumatic stress disorder in women: Epidemiological and treatment issues. *CNS Drugs, 19,* 411–427.

Starcevic, V., Djordjevic, A., Latas, M., & Bobjevic, G. (1998). Characteristics of agoraphobia in women and men with panic disorder with agoraphobia. *Depression and Anxiety, 8,* 8–13.

Stein, D. J. (1993). Cross-cultural psychiatry and the *DSM–IV. Comprehensive Psychiatry, 34,* 322–329.

Stein, D. J., & Bouwer, C. (1997). Blushing and social phobia: A neuroethological speculation. *Medical Hypotheses, 49,* 101–108.

Stein, D. J., Frenkel, M., & Hollander, E. (1991). Classification of Koro. *American Journal of Psychiatry, 148,* 1279–1280.

Stein, D. J., Le Roux, L., Bouwer, C., & van Heerden, B. (1998). Is olfactory reference syndrome on the obsessive-compulsive spectrum? Two cases and a discussion. *Journal of Neuropsychiatry and Clinical Neuroscience, 10,* 96–99.

Stein, D. J., & Rapoport, J. L. (1996). Cross-cultural studies and obsessive-compulsive disorder. *CNS Spectrums, 1,* 42–46.

Stein, D. J., Shoulberg, N., Helton, K., & Hollander, E. (1992). The neuroethological model of obsessive-compulsive disorder. *Comprehensive Psychiatry, 33,* 274–281.

Stein, D. J., van der Linden, G., & Schmidt, A. (1998). Social phobia when using a second language. *South African Medical Journal, 88,* 61.

Stein, D .J., & Williams, D. R. (2002). Cultural and social aspects of anxiety disorders. In D. J. Stein & E. Hollander (Eds.), *Textbook of anxiety disorders* (pp. 463–474). Washington, DC: American Psychiatric Press.

Sumathipala, A., Sisibaddana, S. H., & Bhugra, D. (2004). Culture-bound syndromes: The story of dhat syndrome. *British Journal of Psychiatry, 184,* 200–209.

Weissman, M. M., Bland, R. C., Canino, G. J., Greenwald, S., Lee, C. K., Newman, S. C., et al. (1996). The cross-national epidemiology of social phobia: A preliminary report. *International Clinical Psychopharmacology, 11,* 9–14.

Wittchen, H.-U., & Essau, C. A. (1993). Epidemiology of panic disorder: Progress and unresolved issues. *Journal of Psychiatric Research, 27*(Suppl. 1), 47–68.

Yehuda, R., & McFarlane, A. C. (1995). Conflict between current knowledge about posttraumatic stress disorder and its original conceptual basis. *American Journal of Psychiatry, 152,* 1705–1713.

Yu, Y., & Williams, D. R. (2006). Socioeconomic status and mental health. In C. S. Aneshensel & J. C. Phelan (Eds.), *Handbook of the sociology of mental health* (pp. 151–166). New York: Springer.

PART 9

Future Directions

Future Directions in Anxiety Disorders Research

Martin M. Antony *and* Murray B. Stein

Abstract

This chapter reviews the latest advances in knowledge about anxiety-based problems, and proposes future directions for anxiety disorders research. Areas discussed include diagnostic issues (including proposed changes for *DSM–V*), epidemiology and descriptive psychopathology (e.g., age of onset, patterns of comorbidity, gender, ethnicity, core features), etiology, and treatment.

Keywords: anxiety disorders, etiology, psychopathology, research, treatment

In the past few decades, our knowledge about the nature, causes, and best practices for managing anxiety disorders and related conditions has expanded dramatically. As reviewed throughout this book, advances have been made in the classification and descriptive psychopathology of anxiety disorders, and there is now considerable evidence supporting the roles of both psychological factors (e.g., experiential and situational avoidance, biases in attention and memory, interpretational biases, traumatic experiences, observational learning, verbal transmission of information, family accommodation, personality traits) and biological factors (e.g., genetics, effects of neurotransmitters, endocrine changes, activity in particular brain regions, etc.) in the etiology and maintenance of anxiety disorders. Moreover, as readers will appreciate, the schisms between "psychological" and "biological" factors are disappearing as we understand more about the interactions between the brain and our experiences. In addition, effective psychological and pharmacological treatments now exist for all of the anxiety disorders, several of which were previously considered to be more or less untreatable.

Despite these advances, there remains much to be learned about the nature and causes of anxiety disorders, and about the best ways to assess and treat these conditions in clinical practice. The purpose of this chapter is to review exciting new directions in anxiety disorders research, and to look ahead to areas that remain to be studied in depth.

Future Directions in the Classification of Anxiety Disorders

Although the diagnostic criteria for many of the anxiety disorders have been revised and updated over time, the list of basic anxiety disorders in the *Diagnostic and Statistical Manual of Mental Disorders (DSM)* has mostly remained unchanged since the publication of *DSM–III* (American Psychiatric Association, 1980). An exception was the introduction of acute stress disorder in *DSM–IV* (American Psychiatric Association, 1994), which, it has turned out, has been a controversial diagnosis unlikely to survive into *DSM–V*. The development of *DSM–V* is now moving forward, with a tentative publication date of 2011 (see http://www.dsm5.org/). In the context of the initial planning of *DSM–V*, a number of questions and issues are being raised (Rounsaville et al., 2002), including:

1. What is the most appropriate definition of the term *mental disorder?*

2. What is the best way to establish the validity of psychiatric diagnoses?

3. To what extent should the classification of psychopathology rely on a dimensional approach that describes the severity of symptoms along continuous dimensions, as opposed to the current categorical approach that describes symptoms and syndromes as either present or absent?

4. Is it possible to improve consistency between the *DSM–V* and the next edition of the World Health Organization's *International Classification of Diseases (ICD-11)*?

5. How can *DSM–V* be improved to be more relevant across a wider range of socioeconomic strata and cultures?

6. Is it possible to develop strategies for reducing our reliance on clinical judgment, in favor of increased use of laboratory tests, psychological testing, and standardized self-report rating scales? Such an approach would make it easier to use *DSM–V* in a wider range of nonpsychiatric settings, perhaps for early detection of mental disorders.

Another important question that researchers are now asking concerns the extent to which etiology should be considered in the classification of mental disorders, as it is in many medical conditions (Charney et al., 2002). Starting with the publication of *DSM–III* in 1980, the last few editions of the *DSM* have taken a descriptive and atheoretical approach to classification, purposely avoiding issues of etiology. Are we now at a stage in our understanding of the etiology of anxiety disorders that etiological factors should be considered in classification? Although it may be decades before our knowledge of etiology and pathophysiology is complete enough to adequately inform our classification of mental disorders, some have raised the question of whether our current state of knowledge is advanced enough to have at least some of our nomenclature based on what we know about etiology. In fact, Charney et al. (2002) suggest a possible new multiaxial classification system consisting of five axes:

Axis I: *Genotype* (e.g., identification of genes that relate to risk factors, protective factors, and response to particular treatments)

Axis II: *Neurobiological phenotype* (e.g., identification of particular patterns in neuroimaging, cognitive function, and emotional regulation that relate to genotype and response to particular treatments)

Axis III: *Behavioral phenotype* (e.g., the range and frequency of expressed behaviors that are associated with the genotype, neurobiological phenotype, the environment, in response to particular treatments)

Axis IV: *Environmental modifiers or precipitants* (e.g., environmental variables that affect the behavioral or neurobiological phenotypes)

Axis V: Therapeutic targets and response

Although important decisions remain to be made by those developing *DSM–V,* the outcome of these general discussions could have a considerable impact on how anxiety disorders and other psychological problems are classified. In addition to these general issues, there have also been preliminary discussions about issues that are more specifically relevant to the anxiety disorders. For example, some investigators have argued that OCD should no longer be classified as an anxiety disorder, and instead should be grouped with other conditions commonly referred to as obsessive-compulsive (OC) spectrum disorders (Bartz & Hollander, 2006). Disorders typically included in the OC spectrum include body dysmorphic disorder, hypochondriasis, tic disorders, and others, though there is not complete agreement about which conditions belong. The proposal to group OCD with other OC spectrum disorders is based on the fact that these conditions are associated with OC features and are often similar to OCD with respect to patient characteristics, course, comorbidity, neurobiology, and response to treatment. In a recent survey of 187 OCD experts (108 psychiatrists, 69 psychologists, and 10 others) regarding the proposal to remove OCD from the anxiety disorders and group it with various OC spectrum disorders, 60% agreed and 40% disagreed with the proposal (Mataix-Cols, Pertusa, & Leckman, 2007). There was significantly more support for the proposal among psychiatrists (75%) than among other professionals (40%–45%).

In addition to removing OCD from the anxiety disorders, some researchers have argued that generalized anxiety disorder (GAD) and posttraumatic stress disorder (PTSD) have more in common with depression than they do with other anxiety disorders. For example, Gamez, Watson, and Doebbeling (2007) found that the personality features associated with GAD and PTSD were more similar to those associated with depression than to those associated with other anxiety disorders. Using data from a large epidemiological sample, Slade and Watson (2006) used confirmatory factor analysis to examine the relationships among various mental disorders. The study identified a *distress factor* that included such disorders as major depression, dysthymic disorder, GAD, and PTSD. A separate *fear factor* included disorders such as social phobia, panic disorder, agoraphobia, and OCD. Based on these and other findings, some have argued that GAD and PTSD might be better grouped with depressive disorders, perhaps under the general heading of *distress disorders.*

It is still too early to know how anxiety disorders will be classified in *DSM–V.* Calls will likely be made for all kinds of changes in the ways in which anxiety disorders are organized, as well as for changes in the diagnostic criteria for particular anxiety disorders in the next edition of the *DSM.* Despite the potential benefits of making such changes, revisions to the *DSM* also come with important costs (e.g., training clinicians in the new nomenclature, research based on new diagnostic criteria, impact on insurance companies, legal systems, etc.). Weighing the costs and benefits will be a significant challenge in the process of revising *DSM–IV.*

Epidemiology and Descriptive Psychopathology

Although the literature on the epidemiology and descriptive psychopathology of anxiety disorders is quite advanced, many questions remain to be answered. Some examples are provided in the following sections.

Age of Onset

Many studies have reported on the age of onset for anxiety disorders. However, three issues that limit the conclusions that can be drawn from this literature include (1) the reliance on retrospective reports of questionable validity, (2) the inconsistent manner in which data are coded from individuals who report having had their symptoms for "as long as they can remember," and (3) the fact that age of onset studies have typically failed to distinguish between the age of onset for the *symptoms* of a disorder versus the age of onset for the *syndrome.* An exception is a study on specific phobias by Antony, Brown, and Barlow (1997) that asked about the age of onset for participants' excessive fear, as well as the age at which the fears began to cause significant distress and impairment (i.e., the age at which full diagnostic criteria were met). This study found that the age of onset for the full disorder was on average 9 years later than the age of onset for the initial symptoms (i.e., extreme fear without clinically significant distress or impairment). Future studies will need to distinguish between the onset of anxiety symptoms and the onset of the anxiety disorder.

Gender and Anxiety Disorders

It is well established that anxiety disorders occur more frequently in women than in men, although sex differences are considerably smaller in some anxiety disorders (e.g., social phobia, specific phobias of blood/needles) than in others (e.g., panic disorder, GAD). Although possible reasons for sex differences across anxiety disorders have been identified (e.g., societal expectations, biological differences, etc.), considerable research is still needed to fully understand the reasons for the gender differences that exist. In addition to variations in the presence of anxiety disorders across the sexes, there may also be differences in the ways in which these disorders are expressed (e.g., symptom profile, etc.) across the sexes—an issue for which there is currently very little research available.

Ethnicity and Anxiety Disorders

There are some studies on the effects of culture, religion, and related factors on the prevalence and expression of anxiety disorders, but much of the existing research has simply measured the frequency of anxiety symptoms across different groups. Very little is known about reasons for cultural differences in the expression of anxiety. Nor are there adequate data addressing the expression of anxiety symptoms and syndromes that are different from those described in the *DSM–IV* anxiety disorders section. Better understanding the nature of anxiety disorders across ethnic groups may lead to the development of more culturally appropriate treatments, an issue to which we will return later in this chapter.

Patterns of Comorbidity

Patterns of comorbidity between particular anxiety disorders and other conditions (e.g., other anxiety disorders, mood disorders, substance use disorders, personality disorders, etc.) are well established. However, much less is known about the reasons for comorbidity. For example, are the OCD-like behaviors seen in people with autism, eating disorders, and certain impulse control disorders etiologically related to those observed in people with OCD? Furthermore, what accounts for the high rates of co-occurrence between anxiety disorders and depression? Although researchers have begun to address questions such as these, there is still much more work to be done in this area. Because comorbidity is very common among people with anxiety disorders, and certain types of comorbidity have been found to affect the outcome of treatment, improved outcomes may result from gaining a better understanding of the nature and causes of comorbidity.

Understanding Heterogeneity and Subtypes

It is generally accepted that anxiety disorders are heterogeneous conditions. *DSM–IV* (American Psychiatric Association, 1994) acknowledges heterogeneity within several anxiety disorders, though only to a limited extent. Examples include requiring that a clinician specify which of five types (i.e., animal type, natural environment type, blood-injection-injury type, situational type, other type) best describes a patient's specific phobia, whether a patient's panic disorder is accompanied by agoraphobia, whether a patient's social phobia is *generalized,* whether a patient's OCD is accompanied by *poor insight,* whether a patient's PTSD is *acute* versus *chronic,* and whether the patient's PTSD had a *delayed onset.*

Some investigators have questioned whether these are the best ways to describe the variability that occurs within anxiety disorders. For example, Antony, Brown, and Barlow (1997) questioned the value of including the five specific phobia types in *DSM–IV.* Others have developed alternative ways of describing heterogeneity. For example, Heimberg, Holt, Schneier, Spitzer, and Liebowitz (1993) proposed three subtypes (generalized, nongeneralized, discrete) of social phobia. Similarly, investigators have proposed various ways of capturing heterogeneity in OCD—for example, taking into account the presence versus absence of tics, the specific symptom content (e.g., contamination and washing, doubting and checking, incompleteness concerns, etc.), and other factors (e.g., Leckman et al., 1995; Rasmussen & Eisen, 1992; Rosario-Campos et al., 2006; Summerfeldt, Richter, Antony, & Swinson, 1999). More research is needed to better understand heterogeneity within anxiety disorders and whether different symptom profiles are associated with different responses to treatment.

Core Features of Anxiety Disorders

Investigators are increasingly recognizing that anxiety disorders share various basic core features, and that effective psychological treatments can be developed to target these core dimensions, regardless of the specific diagnosis (see Chapter 33). Transdiagnostic approaches to understanding anxiety disorders can also help to conceptualize patterns of comorbidity that are often observed in patients. Antony (2002) observed a number of dimensions that appear to be relevant to all anxiety disorders. These include the presence of fear, anticipatory anxiety, and worry, situational avoidance, avoidance of thoughts and feelings, interoceptive anxiety (i.e.,

anxiety sensitivity), and overprotective behaviors (e.g., compulsive rituals, safety behaviors, etc.). In addition, it was proposed that these symptoms may be moderated by other factors such as skills deficits, family issues, life stress, and medical complications.

Antony and Rowa (2005) refined this list, suggesting a number of core features that are important to assess and treat: anxiety cues and triggers (including situational cues, interoceptive cues, and cognitive cues), avoidance behaviors (including situational avoidance and experiential avoidance), compulsions and overprotective behaviors (i.e., safety behaviors), physical symptoms and responses, skills deficits, environmental and family factors, and medical and health issues. They suggested that by understanding symptoms associated with these dimensions, individualized treatment protocols can be developed to target these core features, particularly when additional relevant information has been assessed (e.g., associated distress and functional impairment, development and course of the problem, treatment history, and associated problems and comorbidity).

Although the value of considering these core dimensions may be evident when thinking about anxiety disorders from a cognitive behavioral perspective, it is quite possible that clinicians working from a different perspective might identify very different core features. It remains to be determined whether these are in fact the most important dimensions for understanding anxiety disorders, and whether administering individualized treatments based on these assessment data will in fact lead to better outcomes than standardized treatments designed to target particular disorders.

Understanding the Similarities and Differences Among Relevant Constructs

The definitions and boundaries for basic constructs (e.g., fear, anxiety, panic) remain unclear. For example, whereas some investigators argue that fear and anxiety are distinct emotional states (e.g., Barlow, 2002), others do not distinguish between these experiences, arguing that panic is simply an intense form of anxiety (e.g., Clark, 1986; Rapee, 1996). Similarly, whereas some researchers (e.g., Barlow, 2002) have argued that panic and fear are identical states, others (e.g., Klein, 1993) have argued that panic and fear are different, and that they reflect unique pathophysiological processes.

The definition of worry is also in need of refinement, and it needs to be differentiated from other cognitive processes that occur in people with anxiety disorders. Some investigators have proposed that worry is a purposeful activity designed to reduce anxiety by distracting individuals from feared imagery and sensations (e.g., Borkovec, Alcaine, & Behar, 2004). Beck and others (e.g., Beck, Emery, & Greenberg, 1985) have argued that negative thoughts and predictions are responsible for increased anxiety as well as other unpleasant emotions. What remains unclear is the relationship between worry and negative automatic thoughts, and what is actually happening in people's minds when they worry.

Similarly, the relationships among experiences such as worries, obsessions, intrusive memories, depressive ruminations, and other types of distressing cognitive activity are poorly understood, as are the relationships between relevant traits, such as impulsivity and compulsivity. Advances in research on information processing and the pathophysiological underpinnings of these constructs may help to answer questions about the nature of these states, and the boundaries among them.

Etiology of Anxiety Disorders

As reviewed throughout this book, there have been many advances in our understanding of the factors that contribute to the onset and maintenance of anxiety disorders. It is now well established that anxiety disorders stem from a complex interaction between our experiences (e.g., negative experiences, modeling, transmission of information, reinforcement from the environment, parenting, relationships with family and peers, etc.), how we process information (e.g., biases in interpretation, attention, and memory), and other individual differences (e.g., genetics, neuroanatomy, neurotransmitter activity, hormonal activity, personality, etc.). It appears that our genes influence the types of experiences we have, as well as the ways in which we process information. Formally disparate avenues of research are increasingly converging, as investigators try to understand the relationship between biological and psychological processes. Research is ongoing in these areas, and it is almost certain that our understanding of the etiology of anxiety disorders will continue to improve in the future.

Because anxiety disorders often begin early in life, research on children and adolescents will be key to discovering the most important risk factors for developing anxiety disorders. In addition, prospective and longitudinal studies on the development and course of anxiety disorders are greatly needed; retrospective studies have dominated the literature thus far.

Recent Developments in the Treatment of Anxiety Disorders

Effective treatments now exist for all of the anxiety disorders. Nevertheless, some people do not benefit from existing treatments, and those who do respond to treatment often experience only partial improvement. Therefore, the focus on much of the recent treatment research has been on trying to understand the relative effects of various treatment approaches, as well as identifying strategies for improving outcomes with existing treatments (Antony, Ledley, & Heimberg, 2005). Examples of the types of questions addressed in recent studies include:

• Is there an advantage (or disadvantage) of group treatment versus individual treatment for anxiety disorders (Anderson & Rees, 2007; Mörtberg, Clark, Sundin, Åberg, & Wistedt, 2007)?
• Does the frequency (intensity) of sessions affect outcome during psychological treatment of OCD (Abramowitz, Foa, & Franklin, 2003) or panic disorder (Craske et al., 2006)?
• Do medication, cognitive behavioral therapy (CBT), or a combination of these treatments lead to greater improvement (Davidson et al., 2004; Foa et al., 2005)?
• Can CBT be used to help patients discontinue their use of benzodiazepines (Gosselin, Ladouceur, Morin, Dugas, & Baillargeon, 2006)?
• Does social skills training enhance outcomes with CBT for social phobia (Herbert et al., 2005)?
• Does home-based CBT work better than office-based CBT for OCD (Rowa et al., 2007)?
• Does including parents in the treatment of child anxiety disorders lead to better outcomes (Wood, Piacentini, Southam-Gerow, Chu, & Sigman, 2006)?

In addition, there have been several new directions in anxiety disorders treatment research that have generated considerable interest. First, a number of recent studies have found that D-cycloserine (a partial glutamatergic agonist that enhances memory and learning), leads to better treatment outcomes during exposure therapy, relative to exposure alone (Hofmann, 2007). This line of research opens new possibilities for a mechanistically informed combining of pharmacological and psychological treatments. Second, a number of recent studies suggest that "transdiagnostic" psychological treatments that focus on a patient's particular anxiety and mood symptoms, irrespective of diagnosis, can lead to significant improvement (Barlow, Allen, & Choate, 2004; Norton, Hayes, & Hope, 2004). Finally, there has been great interest in mindfulness meditation and acceptance-based approaches to treating anxiety disorders (Orsillo & Roemer, 2005).

Despite the volume of research devoted to developing new treatments and improving upon existing treatments, there is still much that remains unknown. First, there are many issues for which evidence regarding the best ways to administer treatment is contradictory. For example, whereas some studies have shown that adding cognitive strategies to exposure for social phobia leads to improved outcomes (Mattick & Peters, 1988), other studies have found little benefit of combining these approaches over exposure alone (Mersch, 1995). Similarly, whereas some studies have shown that distraction interferes with the effects of exposure for phobias (Kamphuis & Telch, 2000), other studies have found no effects of distraction (Antony, McCabe, Leeuw, Sano, & Swinson, 2001), and some have shown benefits of distraction both within and across sessions (Oliver & Page, 2008). More research is needed to better understand the source of these discrepancies.

There are many treatment approaches for which research is lacking. For example, studies that have investigated the effects of combining medications and CBT for anxiety disorders have almost always studied the effects of concurrent treatments, rather than sequential treatments. Therefore, little is know about the effects of combining treatments sequentially (e.g., CBT followed by medication, medication followed by CBT). Little is known about the best ways to combine psychological treatment strategies as well. For example, should cognitive strategies be taught before exposure strategies? Should interoceptive exposure be taught before or after situational exposure when treating panic disorder? Should patients use cognitive strategies during their exposure practices? When should mindfulness-acceptance based approaches be used?

In addition, there are many popular anxiety treatments for which there is very little research, including insight-oriented psychotherapy, hypnosis, biofeedback, herbal treatments, and various complementary and alternative interventions (e.g., acupuncture). Similarly, very little is known about the effects of lifestyle changes (e.g., changing habits related to exercise, diet, stress management, and sleep) on the course of anxiety disorders. Given the interest of the public in these types of treatments (Roy-Byrne et al., 2005), the lack of empirical evidence about their utility is unfortunate, and must be rectified.

Identifying the Most Important Components of Effective Treatment

Most evidence-based psychological treatments include groups of strategies (e.g., cognitive restructuring, relaxation training, exposure, skills training, psychoeducation, etc.) that in combination have been shown to be effective. However, dismantling studies have often found that some of the strategies used in standard protocols are more important than others. For example, breathing retraining seems to add little to the treatment of panic disorder (Schmidt et al., 2000). The eye movements proposed to be an important component of eye movement desensitization and reprocessing (EMDR) have been found to offer little benefit beyond the effects of the other components of EMDR, such as exposure (Lohr, Tolin, & Lilienfeld, 1998). Finally, among the interoceptive exposure exercises used in the treatment of panic disorder, some (e.g., breathing through a straw, hyperventilating, spinning) have been found to be much more potent for triggering feared sensations than other exercises (e.g., staring at a light and then reading) (Antony, Ledley, Liss, & Swinson, 2006).

There are still many questions about the most important components of standard treatments that remain to be answered. For example, which cognitive strategies (e.g., behavioral experiments, cognitive restructuring, completion of thought records, challenging core beliefs, perspective shifting, etc.) are most effective? Is imaginal exposure useful, and if so, under what conditions? What is the most effective way to administer imaginal exposure? How much time should be devoted to various treatment components? Which methods of relaxation (e.g., progressive muscle relaxation, breathing retraining, imagery) are most effective for treating worry and generalized anxiety? What is the best way to assess whether a particular patient with social phobia is likely to benefit from social skills training in addition to exposure and cognitive restructuring?

Identifying the Mechanisms Through Which Treatment Works

Although much is known about how effective various treatments are, less is known about the mechanisms through which treatments have their effects. Even for well-established strategies such as exposure, cognitive restructuring, and antidepressant medications, there is much work to be done to fully understand why these treatments work. One general approach that may help to uncover the mechanisms underlying effective treatments is to consider anxiety disorders and their treatments from a variety of perspectives. Straube et al. (2006) did just that in a study that examined the effects of CBT on brain activation in specific phobia. In this study, increased activation in the insula and anterior cingulate cortex was associated with specific phobia symptoms, whereas an attenuation of these brain responses was correlated with successful treatment. Further research on the relationships between cognitive behavioral and biological processes during treatment may lead to exciting new advances in our understanding of the processes through which treatments have their effects.

Understanding Predictors of Response

A number of effective treatments exist for people with anxiety disorders, and in many cases, it has been difficult to show consistent advantages of one approach over another across large groups of individuals. For example, there are few differences in outcomes across various effective antidepressants (e.g., paroxetine versus sertraline versus venlafaxine). In addition, there are few differences in the acute effects of medications, CBT, and combined treatments for most anxiety disorders. Group and individual treatments are often equally effective, and various combinations of CBT strategies often work about equally well.

Nevertheless, it is important to recognize that, although various treatments may be equivalent across large groups of patients, that does not meant that they are equally likely to be effective for any one patient. For example, patients with panic disorder who do not respond to medication alone often respond to CBT (Heldt et al., 2006). Although we understand the relative effects of various treatments, much less is known about which treatments work for whom, and under what conditions. A number of studies have investigated various predictors of outcome (e.g., comorbidity, age of onset, severity, compliance with treatment, therapist variables, etc.); nevertheless, there is still almost no research that can help a clinician to choose among various treatment options for a particular patient. Future studies may help to identify symptom profiles, genetic polymorphisms, or other factors that can help clinicians to select treatments with a high likelihood of success and fewer adverse events for a particular individual.

Developing Strategies for Treatment Resistant Cases

There has been increased recognition in recent years in the limitations of evidence-based psycho-logical and pharmacological treatments. Investigators have begun to explore strategies for improving outcomes and for preventing the recurrence of symptoms (e.g., Antony et al., 2005). For example, in the pharmacological literature, investigators have begun to study the effects of augmenting standard pharmacological treatments with other treatments. In recent years, a number of studies have shown that combining atypical antipsychotic medications with antidepressants may lead to improved outcomes for some patients (Pollack et al., 2006). Similarly, combining a benzodiazepine with antidepressant treatment for the first month of treatment may lead to earlier improvements in patients with panic disorder, compared to treatment with an antidepressant alone (Goddard et al., 2001), and combining an SSRI with clonazepam may improve outcomes in patients with generalized social phobia (Seedat & Stein, 2004).

An exciting new development in the psychological treatment of anxiety disorders has been recent research on motivational interviewing. Motivational interviewing is an intervention designed to enhance motivation for treatment, thereby improving outcomes (Arkowitz, Westra, Miller, & Rollnick, 2008; Miller & Rollnick, 2002). Much of the work in this area has been in the fields of addictions and health psychology. However, these strategies have recently been applied with some success to the treatment of anxiety disorders (Westra & Dozois, 2006). Despite these preliminary findings, more research is needed to establish whether motivational interviewing is useful for resolving ambivalence about treatment, enhancing compliance, and improving outcomes.

In addition to developing ways of improving outcomes, there is a great need for research on prevention of relapse and recurrence following treatment of anxiety disorders. For example, little is known about the ideal duration of pharmacological treatment for anxiety disorders, and what the best ways are of dealing with recurrence of symptoms following discontinuation of treatment. Furthermore, although CBT for anxiety disorders often includes some work on strategies for maintaining gains (often at the last session), little is known about whether these strategies are effective, and how to best teach them to patients.

Studying the Effects of Treatment on Particular Groups

Much of the research on anxiety disorders has been based on adults between the ages of 18 and 65 years, primarily from Western cultures. Although there is a considerable literature on anxiety disorders in children, the state of knowledge regarding the treatment of anxiety in children is far behind that in adults. For example, there are relatively few studies of pharmacotherapy for anxious children (compared to studies in adults), and in the literature on psychological treatments, studies have tended to focus on the most basic issues (e.g., establishing the efficacy of treatment strategies).

The literature on treating anxiety disorders in older adults is very small, and most studies have focused on the treatment of generalized anxiety disorder (GAD). Given that studies to date have often not found CBT treatments to be more effective than alternative approaches (e.g., supportive therapies) with older adults suffering from GAD (see Chapter 48), there appears to be room for further development of cognitive behavioral treatments for older adults with GAD. In addition, treatments for older adults with other anxiety disorders need to be developed and tested. With the aging population, this need will only become more pressing in the coming years.

As reviewed earlier, anxiety disorders often occur in the context of other conditions. Most treatment studies include patients with certain types of comorbidity (especially other anxiety disorders), but other types of comorbidity (e.g., cognitive impairment, developmental disabilities, psychotic disorders, substance use disorders) are almost always excluded. Therefore, there is virtually no research on the treatment of anxiety disorders in the context of these other problems. This is an important gap in the literature, leaving clinicians with no empirical basis for how to manage patients suffering from an anxiety disorder as well as cognitive impairment, significant substance use, or serious mental illness.

Finally, there is very little known on how to adapt treatments for people from non-Western cultures. As reviewed by Asmal and Stein (Chapter 50), there are ethnic differences in responses to pharmacological treatments, though the reasons for these difference are poorly understood. In addition, it is not clear whether established psychological treatments for *DSM–IV* anxiety disorders are effective across cultures (or even across socioeconomic strata). Nor have these treatments been adapted for the range of culture-specific anxiety problems that are not represented in *DSM–IV.*

Improving Access to Effective Treatments

Although effective treatments for anxiety disorders are available, few practitioners use them, and few consumers are aware of them. For example, Rowa, Antony, Brar, Summerfeldt, and Swinson (2000) found that only about a third of individuals presenting for treatment at an anxiety disorders specialty clinic had previously received CBT for their anxiety disorder, though the percentage that had tried an evidence-based pharmacological approach was higher. Similarly, a study of patients with anxiety disorders in primary care found that only 25% of individuals had received appropriate medications and fewer than 10% had received an adequate psychological treatment (Stein et al., 2004).

In recent years, a number of measures have been taken to increase awareness of evidence-based treatments. For example, many psychiatry residency programs in the United States and Canada now require training in CBT (Ravitz & Silver, 2004; Sudak, Beck, & Gracely, 2002). Training in evidence-based treatments is now more common in clinical psychology training programs as well, particularly since the Society of Clinical Psychology (Division 12 of the American Psychological Association) published its list of empirically supported treatments and strategies for disseminating them (Chambless et al., 1998; Task Force on Promotion and Dissemination of Psychological Procedures [Division of Clinical Psychology, American Psychological Association], 1995).

A recent article from *The Times* (Hawkes, 2007) reported that in the United Kingdom, the government recently announced a plan to spend £170 million to train 3,600 therapists to deliver CBT, which will allow for almost a million additional people suffering from anxiety disorders and depression to access effective psychological treatment. In fact, the plan is for all primary care practices in the United Kingdom to soon have access to nondrug interventions. Although evidence-based treatments have yet to be supported in the same way elsewhere, attempts to deliver effective treatments for anxiety disorders in primary care settings in the United States are underway (Sullivan et al., 2007), and initial studies have shown that anxiety disorders can be effectively treated in a primary care environment (e.g., Roy-Byrne et al., 2005). There have also been attempts to develop practice-research networks to bridge the gap between science and practice (e.g., Borkovec, 2004). Nevertheless, despite these efforts, there is still much work to be done to disseminate effective treatments to practitioners and to the public.

One of the challenges in disseminating effective treatments is making them affordable and easy to access. In recent years, there has been a considerable amount of work directed toward these goals. Examples include the development of numerous evidence-based self-help books (Redding, Herbert, Forman, & Gaudiano, in press), videoconferencing for treating people in remote areas (e.g., Himle et al., 2006), computerized treatments (e.g., Proudfoot et al., 2004), virtual reality treatments that allow for exposure to feared cues (e.g., flying, storms, heights) in the therapist's office (Parsons & Rizzo, in press), Internet-based treatments (e.g., Carlbring et al., 2007), telephone administered treatments (e.g., Lovell et al., 2006), and brief psychological treatments (e.g., Clark et al., 1999). Although research supports the use of these cost-effective approaches, many of these treatment options are still not widely available.

Conclusion

Over the past few decades, enormous gains have been made in our understanding of the nature, etiology, and treatment of anxiety disorders. Nevertheless, there is still much that we don't understand about these prevalent, often disabling, conditions. Furthermore, although effective interventions exist for all of the anxiety disorders, many people do not receive evidence-based treatments, and among those who do, many continue to experience clinically significant symptoms following treatment. The challenge for anxiety disorders researchers over the next few decades will be to continue to expand our knowledge base, to improve upon current treatments, and to discover ways to ensure that those who need treatment receive it.

References

Abramowitz, J. S., Foa, E. B., & Franklin, M. E. (2003). Exposure and ritual prevention for obsessive-compulsive disorder: Effects of intensive versus twice-weekly sessions. *Journal of Consulting and Clinical Psychology, 71,* 394–398.

American Psychiatric Association. (1980). *Diagnostic and statistical manual of mental disorders* (3rd ed.). Washington, DC: Author.

American Psychiatric Association. (1994). *Diagnostic and statistical manual of mental disorders* (4th ed.). Washington, DC: Author.

Anderson, R. A., & Rees, C. S. (2007). Group versus individual cognitive-behavioural treatment for obsessive-compulsive disorder: A controlled trial. *Behaviour Research and Therapy, 45,* 123–137.

Antony, M. M. (2002). Enhancing current treatments for anxiety disorders: Commentary on Roemer and Orsillo. *Clinical Psychology: Science and Practice, 9,* 91–94.

Antony, M. M., Brown, T. A., & Barlow, D. H. (1997). Heterogeneity among specific phobia types in *DSM–IV. Behaviour Research and Therapy, 35,* 1089–1100.

Antony, M. M., Ledley, D. R., & Heimberg, R. G. (Eds.). (2005). *Improving outcomes and preventing relapse in cognitive behavioral therapy.* New York: Guilford Press.

Antony, M. M., Ledley, D. R., Liss, A., & Swinson, R. P. (2006). Responses to symptom induction exercises in panic disorder. *Behaviour Research and Therapy, 44,* 85–98.

Antony, M. M., McCabe, R. E., Leeuw, I., Sano, N., & Swinson, R. P. (2001). Effect of distraction and coping style on in vivo exposure for specific phobia of spiders. *Behaviour Research and Therapy, 39,* 1137–1150.

Antony, M. M., & Rowa, K. (2005). Evidence-based assessment of anxiety disorders. *Psychological Assessment, 17,* 256–266.

Arkowitz, H., Westra, H. A., Miller, W. R., & Rollnick, S. (2008). *Motivational interviewing in the treatment of psychological problems.* New York: Guilford Press.

Barlow, D. H. (2002). *Anxiety and its disorders: The nature and treatment of anxiety and panic* (2nd ed.). New York: Guilford Press.

Barlow, D. H., Allen, L. B., & Choate, M. L. (2004). Toward a unified treatment for emotional disorders. *Behavior Therapy, 35,* 205–230.

Bartz, J. A., & Hollander, E. (2006). Is obsessive-compulsive disorder an anxiety disorder? *Progress in Neuropsychopharmacology and Biological Psychiatry, 30,* 338–352.

Beck, A. T., Emery, G., & Greenberg, R. L. (1985). *Anxiety disorders and phobias.* New York: Basic Books.

Borkovec, T. D. (2004). Research in training clinics and practice research networks: A route to the integration of science and practice. *Clinical Psychology: Science and Practice, 11,* 212–216.

Borkovec, T. D., Alcaine, O., & Behar, E. (2004). Avoidance theory of worry and generalized anxiety disorder. In R. G. Heimberg, C. L. Turk, & D. S. Mennin (Eds.), *Generalized anxiety disorder: Advances in research and practice* (pp. 77–108). New York: Guilford Press.

Carlbring, P., Gunnarsdóttir, M., Hedensjö, L., Andersson, G., Ekselius, L., & Furmark, T. (2007). Treatment of social phobia: Randomised trial of internet-delivered cognitive-behavioural therapy with telephone support. *British Journal of Psychiatry, 190,* 123–128.

Carson, W. H., Kitagawa, H., & Nemeroff, C. B. (2004). Drug development for anxiety disorders: New roles for atypical antipsychotics. *Psychopharmacology Bulletin, 38,* 38–45.

Chambless, D. L., Baker, M. J., Baucom, D. H., Beutler, L. E., Calhoun, K. S., Crits-Christoph, P., et al. (1998). Update on empirically validated therapies, II. *The Clinical Psychologist, 51*(1), 3–14.

Charney, D. S., Barlow, D. H., Botteron, K., Cohen, J. D., Goldman, D., Gur, R. E., et al. (2002). Neuroscience research agenda to guide development of a pathophysiologically based classification system. In D. J. Kupfer, M. B. First, & D. Regier (Eds.), *A research agenda for DSM–V* (pp. 31–83). Washington, DC: American Psychiatric Press.

Clark, D. M. (1986). A cognitive approach to panic. *Behaviour Research and Therapy, 24,* 461–470.

Craske, M. G., Roy-Byrne, P., Stein, M. B., Sullivan, G., Hazlett-Stevens, H., Bystritsky, A., et al. (2006). CBT intensity and outcome for panic disorder in a primary care setting. *Behavior Therapy, 37,* 112–119.

Davidson, J. R., Foa, E. B., Huppert, J. D., Keefe, F. J., Franklin, M. E., Compton, J. S., et al. (2004). Fluoxetine, comprehensive cognitive behavioral therapy, and placebo in generalized social phobia. *Archives of General Psychiatry, 61,* 1005–1013.

Foa, E. B., Liebowitz, M. R., Kozak, M. J., Davies, S., Campeas, R., Franklin, M. E., et al. (2005). Randomized, placebo-controlled trial of exposure and ritual prevention, clomipramine, and their combination in the treatment of obsessive-compulsive disorder. *American Journal of Psychiatry, 162,* 151–161.

Gamez, W., Watson, D., & Doebbeling, B. N. (2007). Abnormal personality and the mood and anxiety disorders: implications for structural models of anxiety and depression. *Journal of Anxiety Disorders, 21,* 526–539.

Goddard, A. W., Brouette, T., Almai, A., Jetty, P., Woods, S. W., & Charney, D. S. (2001). Early co-administration of clonazepam with sertraline for panic disorder. *Archives of General Psychiatry, 58,* 681–686.

Gosselin, P., Ladouceur, R., Morin, C. M., Dugas, M. J., & Baillargeon, L. (2006). Benzodiazepine discontinuation among adults with GAD: A randomized trial of cognitive-behavioral therapy. *Journal of Consulting and Clinical Psychology, 74,* 908–919.

Hawkes, N. (2007). More talking therapists to help the depressed. *Times Online* (2007, October 11). Retrieved November 4, 2007, from http://www.timesonline.co.uk/tol/news/uk/health/article2633797.ece

Heimberg, R. G., Holt, C. S., Schneier, F. R., Spitzer, R. L., & Liebowitz, M. R. (1993). The issue of subtypes in the diagnosis of social phobia. *Journal of Anxiety Disorders, 7,* 249–269.

Heldt, E., Gus Manfro, G., Kipper, L., Blaya, C., Isolan, L., & Otto, M. W. (2006). One-year follow-up of pharmacotherapy-resistant patients with panic disorder treated with cognitive-behavior therapy: Outcome and predictors of remission. *Behaviour Research and Therapy, 44,* 657–665.

Herbert, J. D., Gaudiano, B. A., Rheingold, A. A., Myers, V. H., Dalrymple, K., & Nolan, E. M. (2005). Social skills training augments the effectiveness of cognitive behavioral group therapy for social anxiety disorder. *Behavior Therapy, 36,* 125–138.

Himle, J. A., Fischer, D. J., Muroff, J. R., Van Etten, M. L., Lokers, L. M., Abelson, J. L., et al. (2006). Videoconferencing-based cognitive-behavioral therapy for obsessive-compulsive disorder. *Behaviour Research and Therapy, 44,* 1821–1829.

Hoffart, A., Due-Madsen, J., Lande, B., Gude, T., Bille, H., & Torgersen, S. (1993). Clomipramine in the treatment of agoraphobic inpatients resistant to behavioral therapy. *Journal of Clinical Psychiatry, 54,* 481–487.

Hofmann, S. G. (2007). Enhancing exposure-based therapy from a translational research perspective. *Behaviour Research and Therapy, 45,* 1987–2001.

Kamphuis, J. H., & Telch, M. J. (2000). Effects of distraction and guided threat reappraisal on fear reduction during exposure-based treatments for specific fears. *Behaviour Research and Therapy, 38,* 1163–1181.

Klein, D. F. (1993). False suffocation alarms, spontaneous panics, and related conditions. *Archives of General Psychiatry, 50,* 306–317.

Leckman, J. F., Grice, D. E., Barr, L. C., deVries, A.L.C., Martin, C., Cohen, D. J., et al. (1995). Tic-related vs. non-tic-related obsessive compulsive disorder. *Anxiety, 1,* 208–215.

Lohr, J. M., Tolin, D. F., & Lilienfeld, S. O. (1998). Efficacy of Eye Movement Desensitization and Reprocessing: Implications for behavior therapy. *Behavior Therapy. 29,* 123–156.

Lovell, K., Cox, D., Haddock, G., Jones, C., Raines, D., Garvey, R., et al. (2006). Telephone administered cognitive behaviour therapy for treatment of obsessive compulsive disorder: Randomised controlled non-inferiority trial. *British Medical Journal, 333,* 1–5. Retrieved December 1, 2007, from http://www.bmj.com/cgi/content/full/333/7574/883

Mataix-Cols, D., Pertusa, A., & Leckman, J. F. (2007). Issues for *DSM-V*: How should obsessive-compulsive and related disorders be classified? *American Journal of Psychiatry, 164,* 1313–1314.

Mattick, R. P., & Peters, L. (1988). Treatment of severe social phobia: Effects of guided exposure with and without cognitive restructuring. *Journal of Consulting and Clinical Psychology, 56,* 251–260.

Means-Christensen, A., Sherbourne, C. D., Roy-Byrne, P., Craske, M. G., Bystritsky, A., & Stein, M. B. (2003). The Composite International Diagnostic Interview (CIDI-Auto): Problems and remedies for diagnosing panic disorder and social phobia. *International Journal of Psychiatric Research, 12,* 167–181.

Mersch, P. P. (1995). The treatment of social phobia: The differential effectiveness of exposure in vivo and an integration of exposure in vivo, rational emotive therapy and social skills training. *Behaviour Research and Therapy, 33,* 259–269.

Miller, W. R., & Rollnick, S. (2002). *Motivational interviewing: Preparing people for change* (2nd ed.). New York: Guilford Press.

Mörtberg, E., Clark, D. M., Sundin, Ö., Åberg, W. A., & Wistedt, A. (2007). Intensive group cognitive treatment and individual cognitive therapy vs. treatment as usual in social phobia: A randomized controlled trial. *Acta Psychiatrica Scandinavica, 115,* 142–154.

Norton, P. J., Hayes, S. A., & Hope, D. A. (2004). Effects of a transdiagnostic group treatment for anxiety on secondary depression. *Depression and Anxiety, 20,* 198–202.

Oliver, N. S., & Page, A. C. (2008). Effects of internal and external distraction and focus during exposure to blood-injury-injection stimuli. *Journal of Anxiety Disorders, 22,* 283–291.

Orsillo, S. M., & Roemer, L. (Eds.). (2005). *Acceptance- and mindfulness-based approaches to anxiety: Conceptualization and treatment.* New York: Springer.

Parsons, T. D., & Rizzo, A. A. (in press). Affective outcomes of virtual reality exposure therapy for anxiety and specific phobias: A meta-analysis. *Journal of Behavior Therapy and Experimental Psychiatry.*

Pollack, M. H., Simon, N. M., Worthington, J. J., Doyle, A. L., Peters, P., Toshkov, F., et al. (2003). Combined paroxetine and clonazepam treatment strategies compared to paroxetine monotherapy for panic disorder. *Journal of Psychopharmacology, 17,* 276–282.

Pollack, M. H., Simon, N. M., Zalta, A. K., Worthington, J. J., Hoge, E. A., Mick, E., et al. (2006). Olanzapine augmentation of fluoxetine for refractory generalized anxiety disorder: A placebo controlled study. *Biological Psychiatry, 59,* 211–215.

Proudfoot, J., Ryden, C., Everitt, B., Shapiro, D. A., Goldberg, D., Mann, A., et al. (2004). Clinical efficacy of computerised cognitive-behavioural therapy for anxiety and depression in primary care: Randomised controlled trial. *British Journal of Psychiatry, 185,* 46–54.

Rapee, R. M. (1996). Information processing views of panic disorder. In R. M. Rapee (Ed.), *Current controversies in the anxiety disorders* (pp. 77–93). New York: Guilford Press.

Rasmussen, S. A., & Eisen, J. L. (1992). The epidemiology and clinical features of obsessive compulsive disorder. *Psychiatric Clinics of North America, 15,* 742–758.

Ravitz, P., & Silver, I. (2004). Advances in psychotherapy education. *Canadian Journal of Psychiatry, 49,* 219–220.

Redding, R. E., Herbert, J. D., Forman, E. M., & Gaudiano, B. A. (in press). Popular self-help books for anxiety, depression, and trauma: How scientifically grounded and useful are they? *Professional Psychology: Research and Practice.*

Rosario-Campos, M. C., Miguel, E. C., Quatrano, S., Chacon, P., Ferrao, Y., Findley, D., et al. (2006). The Dimensional Yale–Brown Obsessive–Compulsive Scale (DY-BOCS): An instrument for assessing obsessive-compulsive symptom dimensions. *Molecular Psychiatry, 11,* 495–504.

Rounsaville, B. J., Alarcón, R. D., Andrews, G., Jackson, J. S., Kendell, R. E., & Kendler, K. (2002). Basic nomenclature issues for *DSM–V.* In D. J. Kupfer, M. B. First, & D. Regier (Eds.), *A research agenda for DSM-V* (pp. 1–29). Washington, DC: American Psychiatric Press.

Rowa, K., Antony, M. M., Brar, S., Summerfeldt, L. J., & Swinson, R. P. (2000). Treatment histories of patients with three anxiety disorders. *Depression and Anxiety, 12,* 92–98.

Rowa, K., Antony, M. M., Summerfeldt, L. J., Purdon, C., Young, L., & Swinson, R. P. (2007). Office-based vs. home-based behavioral treatment for obsessive-compulsive disorder. *Behaviour Research and Therapy, 45,* 1883–1892.

Roy-Byrne, P. P., Bystritsky, A., Russo, J., Craske, M. G., Sherbourne, C. D., & Stein, M. B. (2005). Use of herbal medicine in primary care patients with mood and anxiety disorders. *Psychosomatics, 46,* 117–122.

Roy-Byrne, P., Craske, M., Stein, M., Sullivan, G., Bystritsky, A., Katon, W., et al. (2005). A randomized effectiveness trial of cognitive-behavioral therapy and medication for primary care panic disorder. *Archives of General Psychiatry, 62,* 290–298.

Roy-Byrne, P., Stein, M. B., Russo, J., Mercier, E., Thomas, R., McQuaid, J., et al. (1999). Panic disorder in the primary care setting: comorbidity, disability, service utilization, and treatment. *Journal of Clinical Psychiatry, 60,* 492–499.

Schmidt, N. B., Woolaway-Bickel, K., Trakowski, J., Santiago, H., Storey, J., Koselka, M., et al. (2000). Dismantling cognitive-behavioral treatment for panic disorder: Questioning the utility of breathing retraining. *Journal of Consulting and Clinical Psychology, 68,* 417–424.

Seedat, S., & Stein, M. B. (2004). Double-blind, placebo-controlled assessment of combined clonazepam with paroxetine compared with paroxetine monotherapy for generalized social anxiety disorder. *Journal of Clinical Psychiatry, 65,* 244–248.

Slade, T., & Watson, D. (2006). The structure of common DSM-IV and ICD-10 mental disorders in the Australian general population. *Psychological Medicine, 36,* 1593–1600.

Stein, M. B., Forde, D. R., Anderson, G., & Walker, J. R. (1997). Obsessive-compulsive disorder in the community: An epidemiologic survey with clinical reappraisal. *American Journal of Psychiatry, 154,* 1120–1126.

Stein, M. B., Sherbourne, C. D., Craske, M. G., Means-Christensen, A., Bystritsky, A., Katon, W., et al. (2004). Quality of care for primary care patients with anxiety disorders. *American Journal of Psychiatry, 161,* 2230–2237.

Stein, M. B., Walker, J. R., & Forde, D. R. (1994). Setting diagnostic thresholds for social phobia: Considerations from a community survey of social anxiety. *American Journal of Psychiatry, 151,* 408–412.

Straube, T., Glauer, M., Dilger, S., Mentzel, H. J., & Miltner, W. H. (2006). Effects of cognitive-behavioral therapy on brain activation in specific phobia. *Neuroimage, 29,* 125–135.

Sudak, D. M., Beck, J. S., & Gracely, E. J. (2002). Readiness of psychiatry residency training programs to meet the ACGME requirements in cognitive-behavioral therapy. *Academic Psychiatry, 26,* 96–101.

Sullivan, G., Craske, M. G., Sherbourne, C., Edlund, M. J., Rose, R. D., Golinelli, D., et al. (2007). Design of the Coordinated Anxiety Learning and Management (CALM) study: Innovations in collaborative care for anxiety disorders. *General Hospital Psychiatry, 29,* 379–387.

Summerfeldt, L. J., & Antony, M. M. (2002). Structured and semi-structured diagnostic interviews. In M. M. Antony & D. H. Barlow (Eds.), *Handbook of assessment and treatment planning psychological disorders* (pp. 3–37). New York: Guilford Press.

Summerfeldt, L. J., Richter, M. A., Antony, M. M., & Swinson, R. P. (1999). Symptom structure in obsessive compulsive disorder: A confirmatory factor-analytic study. *Behaviour Research and Therapy, 37,* 297–311.

Task Force on Promotion and Dissemination of Psychological Procedures [Division of Clinical Psychology—American Psychological Association]. (1995). Training in and dissemination of empirically-validated psychological treatments: Report and recommendations. *The Clinical Psychologist, 48*(1), 3–23.

Westra, H. A., & Dozois, D.J.A. (2006). Preparing clients for cognitive behavioral therapy: A randomized pilot study of motivational interviewing for anxiety. *Cognitive Therapy and Research, 30,* 481–498.

Wood, J .J., Piacentini, J. C., Southam-Gerow, M., Chu, B. C., & Sigman, M. (2006). Family cognitive behavioral therapy for child anxiety disorders. *Journal of the American Academy of Child and Adolescent Psychiatry, 45,* 314–321.

INDEX

A

aberrant cognition, 136
acceptance, 476–77
  as change mechanism, 478–80
  GAD treatment and, 370
  open trials, 482–83*t*
acceptance and commitment therapy
    (ACT)
  evolution of, 477
  GAD treatment and, 370
  PDA treatment and, 310
  protocol, 485
  SAD treatment and, 340–41
  trials, 481
acceptance-enhanced cognitive behavioral
    therapy for panic (AE-CBT), PDA
    treatment and, 310
ACC. *See* anterior cingulate cortex
acetylcholine (ACh), 407
ACQ. *See* Agoraphobia Cognitions
    Questionnaire
acrophobia
  DCS and, 329
  VRE and, 329
ACTH. *See* adrenocorticotropic hormone
acupressure, 456
acupuncture, 456
acute reactivity
  PD and, 114
  PTSD and, 116
acute stress disorder (ASD), 6–7, 69
  CBT and, 417
  classical conditioning model for,
    251–52
  early learning theory models of,
    251–52
  external events and, 250
  pharmacotherapy, 407
  PTSD *v.,* 423
  PTSD vulnerability factors and,
    253–54
  treatment
    benzodiazepine and, 407
    beta-blockers and, 407
    psychological, 423–24
ADD. *See* Anxiety and Depression
    Detector
adenosine 2A receptor gene (*ADORA2A*),
    91
ADHD. *See* attention-deficit hyperactivity
    disorder

ADIS-C/P. *See* Anxiety Disorders
    Interview Schedule for Children:
    Parent and Child Versions for
    DSM-IV
ADIS-IV-L. *See* Anxiety Disorders
    Interview Schedule for DSM-IV:
    Lifetime Version
ADIS-R. *See* Anxiety Disorders Interview
    Scale
ADIS. *See* Anxiety Disorders Interview
    Schedule
ADORA2A. See adenosine 2A receptor
    gene
adrenal hypertrophy, 112
adrenocorticotropic hormone (ACTH), 7
  AD-depression comorbidity and, 582
  CRF and, 79
  HPA axis and, 112, 113
  noradrenergic pathways and, 271
  panic attacks and, 118–19
  PD and, 113–14
  PTSD acute reactivity and, 116
  suppression, 114
ADs. *See* anxiety disorders
Adult Manifest Anxiety Scale—Elderly
    (AMAS-E), 627
AE-CBT. *See* acceptance-enhanced
    cognitive behavioral therapy for
    panic
aesthetic sensitivity, 544
affect
  AD-depression comorbidity and, 582
  intensity, 155
age of onset (AOO)
  of BDD, 544
  comorbidity and, 29
  estimating, 20–21
  median, 123–24
  of OCD, 131
  persistence and, 21–22
  refining, 669
  variation of specific phobia, 22
aggression, OCD and, 58–59
agoraphobia (AG), 5, 35–37, 209
  comorbidity in cancer, 602–3
  definition of, 35
  family studies and, 89
  heritability of, 88
  ICD-10 and, 23
  lifetime prevalence of, 23–24
  linkage studies, 89–91, 90

OCD comorbidity in, 61
panic attacks and, 216
perfectionism and, 195
psychodynamic formulations and, 211
PTSD and, 271
standardized measures for, 286
treatment, 182
Agoraphobia Cognitions Questionnaire
    (ACQ), 286
agreeableness
  OCD and, 200
  personality domains and, 190–92
AG. *See* agoraphobia
alarms, 41
alcohol abuse
  panic attacks and, 36
  SAD comorbidity, 341
  SP comorbidity in, 569–70
alcohol use disorder (AUD), 571
allele variation, 159
allostatic load, 70
alprazolam, 300
AM404, 411–12
AMAS-E. *See* Adult Manifest Anxiety
    Scale—Elderly
ambiguity, 142
  modifying interpretive bias and, 146–47
American Academy of Child and
    Adolescent Psychiatry, 648
American Psychiatric Association (APA)
  Clinical and Counseling Division, 489
  OCD guidelines, 380
  PDA treatment guidelines and, 308
  PD treatment guidelines and, 302
  treatment and, 10
American Psychological Association Task
    Force and the Promotion and
    Dissemination of Psychological
    Procedures, 645
AMT. *See* anxiety management training
amygdala, 8. *See also* basolateral nucleus
    of amygdala; central nucleus of
    amygdala
  AD-depression comorbidity and, 581
  exposure treatments and, 473
  fear and, 155
  GAD and, 100
  hyperactivity, 98
  neurocircuitry, 99, 99*f*
  panic and, 127–28
  PD and, 100

amygdala (*continued*)
PTSD and, 66, 99, 406–7
REM sleep and, 614
SAD and, 99–100
SP and, 100
specific genes, 80–81
stress and, 127–28
amyotrophic lateral sclerosis, 360
androgen, 131
anger, social phobia and, 211
animal models
challenges for, 81–82
experimental neurosis in, 160–62
validity of, 75–76
vicarious learning and, 166
ANS. *See* autonomic nervous system
antalarmin, 79
anterior cingulate cortex (ACC), 98–99,
100
OCD and, 104
PD and, 101
PTSD and, 100–101
SAD and, 101
SP and, 101
TENC and, 101
anticonvulsants
for GAD, 353–59
PD treatment and, 301–2
PTSD treatment and, 410–11
for SAD treatment, 324
antidepressants, 11
benzodiazepines and, 301
FDA-approved, 516*t*
for GAD, 352–53
trials for, 354–58*t*
PD treatment and, 296, 297
PTSD treatment and, 408–10
antipsychotics, atypical
for GAD, 359–60
PD treatment and, 301
PTSD treatment and, 411
for SAD treatment, 325
SRI augmentation and, 380
anxieties.com, 494
anxiety. *See also* health anxiety
AS and, 193
affect intensity of, 155
animal models of, 75–76
anthropological approach to, 658
assessments, 627
in youth, 643–45
attention and, 137–39
BNST and, 155
childhood, CBT and, 193
chronic, 154
clinical approach to, 657–58
consequences of, 154–55, 220–21
cues, 154, 280–81
culture and, 657–58
depression *v.*, 162–63
development, 162–63
diathesis-stress model of, 163
experimentally-induced, 159–62

fear *v.*, 153
genetic contribution to, 156–59
geriatric, 626
hypochondriasis and, 525
integrated approach to, 658
interpretive bias and, 142–43
maladaptive, 636
maternal, 176
measures of, for rodents, 76–77
as memory structure, 238
nature of, 153–55
obsessional, 392
origins of, 156–67
overlap, with depression, 268
parental, 175–76
sensitivity, 155
sleep disturbance and, 613
social, 180
catastrophic thinking and, 164
somatization of, 513
stimulus-driven *v.* cognition-driven, 98
substance-induced, 568
symptoms, 513
treatment, in later life, 628–30
vicarious learning of, 165
worry *v.*, 49–50
in youth, 636–38
Anxiety and Depression Detector (ADD),
515
Anxiety Control Questionnaire, 164
anxiety disorder not otherwise specified
(NOS), 265
OCD and, 270–71
prevalence of, 273–74
anxiety disorders (ADs)
aberrant cognition and, 136
adolescent *v.* adult, 125
bias relationship to, 145–47
child, 497
child-adolescent, treatment of, 21
chronic pain and, 551
classification of, 265–66
codification of, 28
cognitions and, 42
cognitive components of, 280
comorbidity in, 28–29, 34, 87, 513–14,
565
comorbidity in autoimmune disorders,
605–6
comorbidity in cancer, 602–3
comorbidity in chronic pain, 602
comorbidity in depression, 576–78
theories, 581–83
time course of, 580–81
comorbidity in GI disorders, 600–601
comorbidity in neurologic disorders,
603–4
comorbidity in personality disorders
prognosis of, 593
treatment of, 593
comorbidity in physical disorders,
596–97
comorbidity in respiratory disorders, 601

comorbidity in sleep disturbance,
615–17
comorbidity in SUD, treatment, 571–73
continuity of, 124–25
co-occurring with depressive disorders,
577*t*
core features of, 670
core pathology conceptualization of, 442
costs of, 514
CSA and, 176
detection, 513
developmental origins of, 125–26
development of, 280
diagnosis, 97–98
discriminating between, 278
DSM classification of, 441
early onset *v.* late onset of, 626–27
ethnicity and, 660
etiology of, 671
functional impact of, 514
gender and, 660
genetic epidemiology of, 87–92
genetic vulnerabilities for, 269
medical comorbidity in, 513
molecular genetics of, 89–92
multiple, 515
neuroendocrinology of, 113–18
neuroticism/extraversion distribution,
590*f*
OCD comorbidity in, 60–61
in older adults, 626
personality disorder traits and,
591–92
common etiology of, 592
personality traits and, 588–92
pharmacological treatment of, 429–30
phenomenology, 97–98
predominant, 278
prevalence of, 512–13
in later life, 625–26
in primary care, 512–13, 515
psychological treatment for, 13*t*
recognition of, 512–13
relationships between, 269–71
severity of, 272
sleep and, 611
social relationships and, 178–82
societal costs of, 29
specific, 515
substance-induced, 265, 566
treatment, 11–12
of comorbid, 443
recent developments in, 671–74
variables contributing to, 159
in youth
aspects of, 638–39
comorbidity of, 641–42
longitudinal research of, 642–43
prevalence of, 641, 642*t*
risk factors, 639–41
treatment, 645–49
Anxiety Disorders Interview Scale
(ADIS-R), 628

Anxiety Disorders Interview Schedule (ADIS), 266
Anxiety Disorders Interview Schedule for Children: Parent and Child Versions for DSM-IV (ADIS-C/P), 643
Anxiety Disorders Interview Schedule for DSM-IV: Lifetime Version (ADIS-IV-L), 266
  diagnostic comorbidity and, 267
anxiety-like behavior
  environment and, 81
  systems modulating, 78–81
anxiety management training (AMT)
  efficacy of, 422
  for GAD, 365
  PTSD treatment and, 418
anxiety sensitivity (AS), 192–95, 203
  AD-SUD comorbidity and, 569
  assessment by, 281–82
  fear of pain and, 558
  as mediator, 569
  misinterpretation of, 215–18
  PTSD and, 198–99
  SAD and, 196–97
  vicarious conditioning and, 213–14
Anxiety Sensitivity Index (ASI), 36, 286
  fear of pain assessment and, 556
  fear-related bodily sensations and, 136
  insula and, 102
  panic onset and, 128
anxiolytics, 81
anxious apprehension model, 226
anxious-misery, 201
AOO. See age-of-onset
APA. See American Psychiatric Association
APD. See avoidant personality disorder
applied relaxation, 337. See also relaxation training
  GAD treatment and, 365
  specific phobia treatment and, 344
applied tension, 12
  specific phobia treatment and, 344
approach behavior, 479–80
arginine vasopressin (AVP), 112
aromatherapy, 455
  massage and, 453–54
arousal, PTSD and, 6
ASD. See acute stress disorder
ASI. See Anxiety Sensitivity Index
AS. See anxiety sensitivity
assessment, 4
  behavioral, 283–85
  diagnostic, 277–80
  diary measures and, 285
  domains of, 280–83
  feedback as, 288
  following treatment, 288
  interoceptive, 284–85
  multimethod, 288
  psychophysiological, 285
  purpose of, 277
  standardized measures for, 285–88

association
  irrelevant, 243
  studies, 91–92
asthma, 601
attachment theory, 163
Attacking Anxiety, 492
attention
  bias, 137–39
  self-focused, 218
  threats and, 154
Attentional Control Training task, 436
attention-deficit hyperactivity disorder (ADHD)
  comorbidity, 642
  continuity of, 125
  OCD and, 131
attributional style, negative, 163
attribution-based models, of PTSD, 256
audio materials, 492
AUD. See alcohol use disorder
augmentation/refractory sample trials, in OCD, 377t
augmentation strategies
  for OCD treatment, 376–78
  for SAD treatment, 328
automaticity, mindfulness and, 479
automatic processes, emotion and, 137
automatic thoughts, 446
autonomic nervous system (ANS), 111
autonomic response, 268–69
  in rodents, 77
autonomy, encouragement of, 163
avoidance behaviors, 281
  assessment by, 281
  situational, 281
  attentional, 138–39
  behavioral assessment and, 284
  CBT targeting, 367
  for GAD, 367
  cognitive-emotional, 234
  conditioning and, 252
  consequences of, 221
  control and, 164
  DTS and, 288
  experiential v. emotional, 478–79
  experimental, 310
  exposure treatments and, 468
  hoarding and, 243
  hypochondriasis and, 526
  IU and, 230
  obsession and, 240
  OCD and, 57
  psychodynamic formulations and, 210
  PTSD and, 6, 66, 67
  in rodents, 76
  specific phobia and, 41
  targeting, 478–79
  worry as, 227
avoidant personality disorder (APD)
  SAD and, 37–38
  SP v., 588t

AVP. See arginine vasopressin
axiogenic beliefs, 218
ayurveda, 456–57
azapirones, 359

B
BAI. See Beck Anxiety Inventory (BAI)
BA/P. See behavioral activation positive affect
Barlow, Carolee, 80
Barlow, D.H., 226
Barlow et al. protocol, 445
  outcome data, 446–47
barriers to care, 519
basal ganglia, 129
basal state studies
  PD, 113
  PTSD, 115–16
basolateral nucleus of amygdala (BLA), 406
BAS. See Behavioral Approach System
BATs. See behavioral approach tests
BDD. See body dysmorphic disorder
BDI. See Beck Depression Index
Beck Anxiety Inventory (BAI), 627
Beck Depression Index (BDI), 401
Beck, J. G., 225–26
bed nucleus of stria terminalis (BNST), 155
behavioral activation, 466
  in BDD treatment, 546
behavioral activation positive affect (BA/P), 157
Behavioral Approach System (BAS), 157
behavioral approach tests (BATs), 284
  progressive v. selective, 284
behavioral assessment, 283–85
behavioral experiments, 466
  OCD and, 395
behavioral genetic studies, 157–59
behavioral inhibition (BI), 89, 214
Behavioral Inhibition System (BIS), 157
behavioral models, 211–15
  cognitive theories and, 215–20
  cultural factors and, 214
  evolutionary theories and, 215
  temperament and, 214
behavioral stress management (BSM), 534–35
  narrative review, 535–36
behavioral theory, of OCD, 129
behavior genetics, 173–74
behavior therapy (BT)
  for GAD, 370
  for OCD, 392–94
    theoretical basis, 392–93
beliefs
  dysfunctional, 526–28, 527f
  erroneous, 395
  hoarding and, 243
  of hypochondriasis, 527t
  modifying, 369
  obsessions and, 241

beliefs (*continued*)
  positive
    GAD and, 231, 233
    motivational interviewing and, 372
    role of, 234
    worry and, 230, 368
  responsibility, 239–40
  worry and, 228–29, 368
benzodiazepines, 11
  for AD-insomnia comorbidity, 616–17
  adverse effects of, 300
  antidepressants and, 301
  ASD treatment and, 407
  CBT and, 300, 434
  for GAD, 359
  for nocturnal panic, 618
  for older adults, 629–30
  PD treatment and, 296, 300–301
  in primary care, 517
  PTSD treatment and, 407–8
  for SAD treatment, 324
  side effects, 517
beta-adrenergic receptor antagonists, 517
beta-blockers
  PD treatment and, 301
  in primary care, 517
  side effects, 517
bias, 136
  attention, 137–39
  covariation, 143–45
  expectancy, 144–45
    eliminating, 145–46
  interpretive, 142–43
  relation to anxiety disorders of, 145–47
  TAF, 241
  telescoping, 20
biofeedback, 454
biological challenge paradigm, 193
biological challenges, 284–85
biologically based practices, 452–53
biological models
  of panic disorder, 36
  of PTSD, 66
biological processes, 7–8
biological treatments, 11
biological vulnerability, 156–59
bipolar disorder
  linkage studies, 91
  OCD comorbidity in, 60–61
BI. *See* behavioral inhibition
BIS. *See* Behavioral Inhibition System
BLA. *See* basolateral nucleus of amygdala
blood-injury phobia, 22
blood pressure, panic attacks and, 36–37
BNST. *See* bed nucleus of stria terminalis
bodily sensations. *See also* anxiety
    sensitivity; physical sensations
  BSM and, 535
  hypervigilance to, 218
  hypochondriasis and, 526
  misinterpretation of, 215–18
body dysmorphic disorder (BDD)
  AOO of, 544

cognitive behavioral model of, 544–45
cosmetic procedures in, 542–43
demographics, 543
effect of, 543
future research in, 548
history, 541
mirror gazing and, 547
NICE and, 548
OCD and, 6, 28
presentation, 544
psychopathology, 541–42
risk factors, 544
social anxiety and, 547
treatment
    CBT and, 545–47
    pharmacotherapy and, 547–48
borderline personality disorder (BPD)
  DBT and, 478
  PTSD comorbidity in, 589
Borkovec, Thomas, 367
Bosnia, PTSD and, 27
Boston University, 164
brain differences, 97
brain imaging studies, 132
breathing retraining, 629
Brief Social Phobia Scale, 322
Brief Symptom Inventory-18 (BSI-18), 515
British Medical Journal, 127
BSM. *See* behavioral stress management
BT. *See* behavior therapy
bupropion
  PD treatment and, 301
  in primary care, 516
  for SAD treatment, 325
buspirone
  PD treatment and, 301
  in primary care, 516–17
  as SRI augmenting agent, 383

C

CAIS-P. *See* Child Anxiety Impact Scale-
    Parent Version
CAM. *See* complementary and/or
    alternative medicine
Canadian Psychiatric Association (CPA),
    308
  treatment and, 10
cancer, 602–3
cannabinoids, 412
capacity consumption, 138
CAPS. *See* Clinician Administered PTSD
    Scale
cardiac disorders, 597–600
catastrophic thinking, 164
catecholamine, 116
catechol-O-methyltransferase *(COMT)*
    gene, 92
CBCL. *See* Child Behavior Checklist
CBGT. *See* cognitive behavioral group
    therapy
CBT. *See* cognitive behavioral therapy
CCAP. *See* Collaborative Care for Anxiety
    and Panic Study

CCK-B agonists, 114
CCK. *See* cholecystokinin
CC. *See* collaborative care
CD. *See* conduct disorder
CeA. *See* central nucleus of amygdala
Centella asiatica. See gotu kola
Center for Anxiety and Related Disorders,
    164
central drive studies
  of PD, 114–15
  PTSD and, 116–17
central nervous system (CNS), 452
central nucleus of amygdala (CeA), 406
cerebrospinal fluid (CSF), CRH in, 113
CGI-I. *See* Clinical Global
    Impression-Improvement
CHD. *See* coronary heart disease
checking rituals, 391
  memory and, 141–42
Child Anxiety Impact Scale-Parent Version
    (CAIS-P), 645
Child Behavior Checklist (CBCL), 645
childhood
  anxiety disorders, 497
    sexual abuse and, 176
  CBT and, 193
  psychodynamic formulations and, 210–11
childhood sexual abuse (CSA), 141
  CBT for, 647
childhood temperament, 9–10
children. *See also* youth
  AD etiology and, 671
  cognitive behavioral model of
    intervention for, 503f
  comorbidity in, 500
  indicated prevention for, 503–4
  internalization and, 180–81
  neglect and, 178–79
  with OCD, 384
  panic attacks in, 127
  panic symptomatology in, 193–94
  parenting style and, 163
  prevention approaches for, 498
  risk factors for, 501–2, 506
  selective prevention for, 504–5
  universal prevention for, 505–7
  untreated, 498
Children's Yale-Brown Obsessive
    Compulsive Scale (CY-BOCS), 649
chiropractic, 453
cholecystokinin (CCK)
  AD-depression comorbidity and,
    581–82
  neurotransmitter system, 91
Christchurch Health and Development
    Study, 124
chromosome linkage studies, 90
chronicity, 21–22
chronic pain, 551–53, 602
  conceptual controversies, 553–55
  diagnostic features of, 553
  fear-anxiety-avoidance model of,
    552–53, 554f

fear-avoidance model of, 552*f*
treatment, 557
CIDI. *See* Composite International
Diagnostic Interview
cingulate cortex, 80
Clark, David, 9, 241–42
classification, 4, 265–66
categorical approach to, 272
dimensional, 271–73
future directions in, 271, 667–69
multiaxial, 668
thresholds, 271
claustrophobia, 219
cleaning, 58–59
Clinical Global Impression-Improvement
(CGI-I), 352
clinical interviews, 279–80
of youth, 643–44
clinical severity rating (CSR), 266
Clinician Administered PTSD Scale
(CAPS), 287–88
older adults and, 628
clinician rating scales, 628
clomipramine, 376
BDD treatment and, 547–48
efficacy studies of, 433
hypochondriasis treatment and, 535
OCD and, 516
clonazepam, 300
OCD treatment and, 378
in primary care, 517
as SRI augmenting agent, 383
clonidine, 407
CLPS. *See* Collaborative Longitudinal
Personality Disorders Study
cluster analysis, of OCSD, 59
cluster C disorders, 61–62
CNS. *See* central nervous system
CO_2 exposure, 480
Cochrane Database, 455
cognition restructuring
guilt feelings and, 421
PE and, 419–20
cognitions
anxiety disorders and, 42
anxiety prevention and, 502
worry and, 51–52
cognitive avoidance model, of GAD, 234
cognitive avoidance theory, 226–28
emotional dysregulation model and, 231
empirical support for, 227
cognitive behavioral group therapy
(CBGT), 335–36
phenelzine *v.*, for SAD treatment, 338
cognitive behavioral interventions
cost-effective, 313
for specific phobias, 343–44
cognitive behavioral model
of BDD, 544–45
for children, 503*f*
of OCD
of Rachman, 240–41
of Salkovski, 239–40

cognitive behavioral therapy (CBT),
12. *See also* cognitive behavioral
therapy for insomnia
access to, 674
AD-depression comorbidity treatment
and, 583
for ADs in youth, 645–47
ADs in youth and, 640–41
AD-SUD comorbidity treatment,
571–73
ASD treatment and, 423–24
availability of, 431–33
in BDD treatment, 546
BDD treatment and, 545–47
benzodiazepines and, 300, 434
BSM and, 534–35
narrative review, 535–36
for children, 497–98
chronic pain treatment and, 557
combined with pharmacotherapy,
429–30
for CSA, 647
DCS and, 435–36
discontinuation, SSRI
discontinuation *v.*, 379
efficacy of, 442–43
for GAD, 370–72
efficacy studies, 433–34
EMDR and, 418–19
emotion-focused, 646
ERP effectiveness and, 396
family-based, 646
family treatment and, 184
fear of pain treatment and, 557
fear reduction and, 461
fluoxetine and, 433
fluvoxamine and, 433–34
GAD treatment and, 365
group-based, 504
GSAD pharmacotherapy and, 329
hypochondriasis treatment and, 531–35
meta-analysis of, 536
TAU v, 538
individual *v.* group, for PDA treatment,
312
integrated models of care and, 518
in later life, 628–29
mechanisms of, 430
medication and, for PDA treatment,
311–12
meta-analyses of, 337–38
models of OCD, 240–43
validation of, 245–46
for nocturnal panic, 617–18
OCD treatment and, 240, 375
efficacy of, 246–47
for older adults, 631
PDA and
effectiveness studies, 312–13
efficacy studies, 311–12
research review, 311–13
PDA treatment and, 308
long-term outcome of, 317

PD treatment and, 303
prevention, 508
in primary care, 517
PTSD treatment and, efficacy of, 419–22
Rachman's cognitive behavioral model of
OCD, 240–41
RCTs of, 497
relationships and, 182–83
response predictors, 673
SAD treatment and, 334–37, 338–39
cognitive change, 343
selective, 505
self-help, 491
social phobia treatment and, 145, 211
targeting avoidance, 367
therapeutic learning and, 430
tolerability of, 430–31
training, 674
cognitive behavioral therapy for insomnia
(CBT-I), 615–17
effectiveness of, 618
treatment components, 616*t*
cognitive biases, 41
cognitive change, 343
cognitive components, 280
cognitive distortions, of youth, 636–37
cognitive processes, 218–20
in PTSD, 255
cognitive processing therapy (CPT),
419–21
cognitive restructuring
Erickson et al. protocol and, 446
exposure treatments plus, for SAD,
335–36
meta-analyses of, 338
Norton and Hope protocol and, 444–45
PDA treatment and, 309
self-help treatment and, 493
specific phobia treatment and, 344
cognitive symptoms
anxiety sensitivity and, 192, 194
scar model and, 195
cognitive theory, 9
behavioral models and, 215–20
of OCD, 129–30
cognitive therapy (CT)
barriers to care in, 519
cortisol levels and, 118
efficacy of, for GAD, 370
with ERP, 398–99
ERP *v.*, 397–98, 398*t*
GAD treatment and, 232, 365
implementation of, 394–95
for OCD, efficacy of, 246–47
OCD and, 394–95
PDA treatment and, 310
PTSD treatment and, 418
efficacy, 420–21
theoretical basis of, 394
collaborative care (CC), 518
Collaborative Care for Anxiety and Panic
study (CCAP), 313, 518
barriers to care and, 519

Collaborative Longitudinal Personality
    Disorders Study (CLPS), 589
combination treatments, 12
    availability of, 431–33
    combination, frontal activation, 436
    with DCS, 435–36
    NMDA and, 435
    for SAD, 326–28, 327t
    sequential, 672
    use of, 434
    for youth, 649
comorbidity, 3–4, 513–14
    AD-depression
        prevalence of, 576–78
        theories, 581–83
        time course of, 580–81
        treatment, 583–84
    AD-personality disorder, 588–91
        causal relationship, 591–92
        clinical course, 592–94
        symptom severity and, 592–93
    AD-physical disorder, 596–97, 598–99t
    of ADs, in youth, 641–42
    AD-SUD
        CBT and, 571–73
        high-risk hypothesis, 570
        lifetime prevalence of, 567t
        susceptibility hypothesis, 570
        theories, 568–71
        third variable for, 568
        treatment, 571–73
    among anxiety disorders, 28–29
    of anxiety disorders, 34
    as artifact, 588
    in BDD, 541
    in cancer, 602–3
    in cardiac disorders, 597–600
    in children, 500
    in chronic pain, 602
    continuity and, 125
    core pathology conceptualization and,
        442
    diagnosing, 267, 278–79
    DSM-IV hierarchical rules and, 272
    epidemiology of, 565–68
    in GAD, 49
    in GI disorders, 600–601
    in hoarding, 630–31
    medical, 513, 627
    in metabolic disorders, 601–2
    in neurological disorders, 603–5
    in OCD, 60–62, 384
    order of onset, 568
    patterns of, 669
    in PDA, 314–15
    PD-SUD, 569
    personality factors and, 203–4
    in physical disorders, 283
    prevalence for AD-SUD, 566
    psychiatric, 513, 627
    in PTSD, 68–69
    PTSD-SUD, 570
    in respiratory disorders, 601

in SAD, 341–42
SP-alcohol abuse, 569–70
in specific phobia, 41
treatment of, 443
compassionate mind training, 546
competence, control and, 160
complementary and/or alternative
    medicine (CAM), 451
    body-based practices, 453
    commonly used, 452t
    with conventional medical treatments,
        457
    future of, 672
    mind-body intervention strategies and,
        454–55
    whole medical systems and, 456–57
compliance. See homework compliance
Composite International Diagnostic
    Interview (CIDI), 20
    prevalence of agoraphobia and, 23
    prevalence of SEPAD and, 25
    prevalence of social phobia and, 24
compulsions
    definition of, 57, 391
    ERP and, 393
    maintaining, 401
    nonclinical, 58
    obsessions v., 129–30
    reassurance-seeking behavior and, 270
    relationship with obsessions, 245
    spontaneous decay of, 392
    in youth, 638
computer-based treatments, 675
COMT gene. See catechol-O-
        methyltransferase gene
Concurrent Treatment of PTSD and
        Cocaine Dependence (CTPCD),
        572
conditioned response (CR), 77
    conditioning model for PTSD and,
        251–52
conditioned stimulus (CS), conditioning
        model for PTSD and, 251–52
conditioned stimulus-unconditioned
        response (CS-US) association, 411
    extinction learning and, 463
conditioning. See also Pavlovian
        conditioning; superconditioning
    avoidance and, 252
    classical models, 8
    dose-dependent response model,
        251–52
    learned fear and, 77
    model for ASD, 251–52
    model for PTSD, 251–52
    PTSD and, 66, 126
    theories, 211
    two-factor theory, 252
    vicarious, 166
        specific phobia and, 213–14
conduct disorder (CD)
    comorbidity, 642
    continuity of, 125

conscientiousness
    OCD and, 200
    personality domains and, 190–92
    PTSD and, 197–98
Consensus Statement on Social Anxiety
    Disorder, 328
construct validity, 75–76
contamination obsessions, 58–59, 391
    psychosocial environment and, 283
context-specificity, 470
continuity, 124–25
    heterotypic, 125
    homotypic, 125
control
    avoidance behavior and, 164
    competence and, 160
    cortisol and, 164–65
    diminished sense of, 156, 159–65
    emotional, 220
    illusion of, 216
    locus of, 162–63
    loss of, HPA axis and, 162
    parental, 174–76
    perceived
        AD-depression comorbidity and, 582
        moderational v. mediational, 164
    social phobia and, 218
Coping Cat, 497, 503
    for ADs in youth, 646
Coping Koala, 503–4
Coping Questionnaire (CQ), 644
coping strategies
    maladaptive, 529
    problem-based v. emotion-based, 502
Coping with Illness Anxiety, 531–34
core pathology conceptualization,
        442–43
    accessibility of, 443–44
    dissemination of, 443–44
coronary heart disease (CHD), 597
correlations, illusory, 144–45
cortico-striatal-thalamic circuit, 98
    OCD and, 99f, 105
corticotropin-releasing factor (CRF),
        7, 154. See also corticotropin-
        releasing hormone
    AD-depression comorbidity and, 582
    anxiety-like behavior modulation and,
        78–79
    early experiences and, 161
    pituitary gland sensitivity and, 161
corticotropin-releasing hormone (CRH).
        See also corticotropin-releasing
        factor
    in CSF, 113
    gene, 92, 158
    HPA axis and, 112, 113
    PD central drive and, 115
    in stress response, 112
cortisol
    cognitive therapy and, 118
    control and, 164–65
    experimental neurosis, 160–61

HPA axis and, 112
panic attacks and, 118–19
PD and
  basal state studies, 113
  central drive, 115
PTSD and, 115–16
SEPAD and, 164
specific phobia and, 118
co-rumination, 181
cosmetic procedures, 542–43
cosmetic surgery, 542–43
costs
  of anxiety disorders, 514
  of chronic pain, 551
  reducing, 674–75
course of illness, 21–22
covariation bias, 143–45
CPA. *See* Canadian Psychiatric Association
CPT. *See* cognitive processing therapy
CQ. *See* Coping Questionnaire
CRF_1 antagonists, 79
CRF. *See* corticotropin-releasing factor
CRH. *See* corticotropin-releasing hormone
cross-cultural factors, PTSD and, 69
CR. *See* conditioned response
CSA. *See* childhood sexual abuse
CSR. *See* clinical severity rating
CS. *See* conditioned stimulus
CS-US association. *See* conditioned
    stimulus-unconditioned response
    association
CTPCD. *See* Concurrent Treatment of
    PTSD and Cocaine Dependence
CT. *See* cognitive therapy
cued recall tests, 139–40
cultural factors, behavioral models and, 214
cultural influences, 10, 181
culture
  anxiety and, 657–58
  formation off, 659
  GAD and, 661–62
  OCD and, 660–61
  PD and, 659–60
  PTSD and, 661
  SAD and, 660
  somatic symptoms and, 661–62
culture-bound syndromes, 10, 659
CY-BOCS. *See* Children's Yale-Brown
    Obsessive Compulsive Scale

D
dACC. *See* dorsal ACC
danger
  learned, 165–67
  somatic symptoms *v.,* 166
DA. *See* dopamine
Davidson Trauma Scale (DTS), 288
DBS. *See* deep brain stimulation
DBT. *See* dialectical behavior therapy
DCS. *See* D-cycloserine
D-cycloserine (DCS)
  acrophobia treatment and, 329
  as augmentation gent, 378

combination treatment with, 435–36
extinction learning mechanisms and,
    466–67
memory consolidation and, 339
PTSD treatment and, 412
SAD treatment and, 325, 339
VRE and, 344
DeCode group, 90
deep brain stimulation (DBS), 378–79
  for OCD, 378–79
defensive startle, 76–77
deficits, 136
dementia, 630
de-methylation, 81
depression
  allele variation and, 159
  anxiety *v.,* 162–63
  BDD comorbidity in, 543
  biochemical processes of, 7–8
  chronic pain and, 551
  comorbidity
    in BDD, 541
    in PDA, 314–15
  comorbidity in ADs, 576–78
    theories, 581–83
    time course of, 580–81
    treatment, 583–84
  GAD *v.,* 48
  genetic studies of, 269
  glutamate and, 360
  helplessness *v.,* 162
  hypochondriasis treatment and, 531
  medical comorbidity in, 513
  OCD treatment and, 401
  OCD *v.,* 579
  overlap, with anxiety, 268
  in primary care, 515
  social phobia and, 269–70
depressive disorders
  co-occurring with ADs, 577*t*
  GAD *v.,* 578
  PTSD *v.,* 578–79
depressive rumination, 52
desensitization, systematic, 461–62
DESNOS. *See* disorders of extreme stress
    not otherwise specified
development processes, 9–10
dexamethasone, 113
dexamethasone suppression test (DST)
  PD and, 114–15
  PTSD and, 114–17
diabetes, 601–2
  OCD treatment and, 385
diagnosis
  establishing, 278–79
  predominant, 278
  validating, 667
*Diagnostic and Statistical Manual of Mental
    Disorders (DSM)*
  anxiety disorder codification and, 28
  anxiety disorders and, 34
  BSI-18 and, 515
  CAM and, 451–52

clinical approach of, 657–58
future direction of, 667–69
OCD and, 28
SAD definition and, 37
*Diagnostic and Statistical Manual of Mental
    Disorders, fifth edition (DSM-V)*
  dimensional classification of, 273
  improvements in, 668
*Diagnostic and Statistical Manual of Mental
    Disorders, fourth edition (DSM-IV)*, 4
  agoraphobia, 36
  anxiety disorder comorbidity and, 28–29
  anxiety disorders in, 441
  APD and, 37–38
  ASD and, 423
  classification system of, 265–66
  continuity of psychiatric disorders and,
    124
  cultural formation and, 659
  culture and, 658–59
  culture-bound syndromes and, 659
  disorder constructs, 267–69
  DSM-III-R v., 267
  GAD classification, 350
  GAD diagnosis and, 48
  GAD diagnostic criteria and, 366
  hierarchical rules, 272
  hierarchy rules, 267
  ICD v., 19
  inconsistency of, 272
  molecular genetics and, 89
  panic attacks and, 41
  panic disorder
    baseline diagnosis of, 36
    definition and, 35
  prevalence of agoraphobia and, 23
  prevalence of GAD and, 25–26
  prevalence of social phobia and, 24
  PTSD diagnosis and, 259
  SAD and, 37–38, 638
  schizo-obsessive disorder and, OCD
    comorbidity with, 61
  somatic symptoms in, 637
  specific phobias and, 5–6, 209
  subtypes of, 39
  TKS and, 660
  trauma definition, 67
*Diagnostic and Statistical Manual of Mental
    Disorders, fourth edition, text
    revision (DSM-IV-TR)*
  ASD and, 250
  BDD and, 541
  chronic pain diagnosis and, 553
  GAD diagnostic criteria and, 48
  hypochondriasis diagnosis in, 529–30
  obsessions and, 51
  OCD classification, 391–92
  OCD features and, 56–57
  prevalence of SEPAD and, 24
  PTSD and, 250
  SUD diagnosis, 566
  symptom criteria, 578
  traumatic stressors and, 251

Diagnostic and Statistical Manual of Mental Disorders, third edition (DSM-III)
  anxiety disorders in, 441
  DSM-IV v., 20
  GAD diagnostic criteria and, 47, 225, 366
  panic disorder definition and, 35
  phobic disorders and, 39
  trauma definition, 66–67
Diagnostic and Statistical Manual of Mental Disorders, third edition, revised (DSM-III-R)
  anxiety disorder comorbidity and, 87
  anxiety disorders in, 441
  DSM-IV v., 267
  GAD diagnostic criteria and, 350, 366
  prevalence of GAD and, 25
diagnostic criteria, 3–4, 19–20
  differences in, 20
Diagnostic Interview for Children and Adolescents (DICA), 644
Diagnostic Interview Schedule, prevalence of agoraphobia and, 23
Diagnostic Interview Schedule (DIS), 19–20
Diagnostic Interview Schedule for Children (DISC), 644
dialectical behavior therapy (DBT), 478
diary measures, 285
DICA. *See* Diagnostic Interview for Children and Adolescents
Dietary Supplement Health and Education Act (DSHEA), 457
difference in patient report, 266
dimensional data, 266
Diogenes' syndrome, 630
discontinuation studies, 379–80
DISC. *See* Diagnostic Interview Schedule for Children
disease, illness *v.,* 658
disgust, OCD and, 105
disorders of extreme stress not otherwise specified (DESNOS), 69–70
DIS. *See* Diagnostic Interview Schedule
distress disorders, 669
  comorbidity in, 28
distress factor, 668–69
dmPFC. *See* dorsal mPFC
dopamine (DA)
  OCD and, 376
  PTSD and, 407
dorsal ACC (dACC), OCD risk factors and, 129
dorsal mPFC (dmPFC), 101–2
dose-dependent response model, 251–52
dosing, single acute *v.* chronic, 82
dot-probe paradigm, 138, 146
doubt, pathological
  OCD and, 57
  triggers, 394
dream anxiety disorder. *See* nightmare disorder

dropout rates, 431*t*
  hypochondriasis treatment and, 536
  self-help treatment and, 491
drug abuse, panic attacks and, 36
DSHEA. *See* Dietary Supplement Health and Education Act
DSM-IV. See Diagnostic and Statistical Manual of Mental Disorders, fourth edition
DSM-IV-TR. See Diagnostic and Statistical Manual of Mental Disorders, fourth edition, text revision
DST. *See* dexamethasone suppression test
dsythemic disorder, diagnostic reliability of, 266
DTS. *See* Davidson Trauma Scale
dual processing models of PTSD, 255–56
duloxetine, for GAD, 353
DUP25, 91
duration (E) criterion, 68
dysmorphophobia. *See* body dysmorphic disorder
dysthymia
  GAD comorbidity and, 49
  prevalence, 577

E
early experiences
  anxiety vulnerability and, 164
  CRF and, 161
early learning theory models, 251–52
eating disorders
  OCD and, 28
  specific phobia *v.,* 6
ECA. *See* Epidemiological Catchment Area
E criterion. *See* duration criterion
ECT. *See* electroconvulsive therapy
EE. *See* expressed emotion
effectiveness studies, of ERP, 396
efficacy studies
  of CBT, 433–34
  of combined treatments, 433–34
  pharmacotherapy, 433–34
EFT. *See* emotion-focused therapy
ego-dystonicity, 241–42
electroconvulsive therapy (ECT), for OCD treatment, 378
EMDR. *See* eye movement desensitization and reprocessing
emotion. *See also* expressed emotion
  automatic processes and, 137
  GAD and, 231–32
  perceptual memory and, 154
emotional attachment problems, hoarding and, 243
emotional disorders, dimensional classification of, 273
emotional dysregulation model, 231–32
emotional functioning, of youth, 637
emotional overinvolvement (EOI), 182
emotional processing
  extinction learning mechanisms and, 465
  sleep disturbance and, 614–15

emotional processing models, for PTSD, 253–58
emotional processing theories
  criticism of, 258
  fear activation and, 471
emotional regulation therapy, for GAD, 233
emotional skills
  facilitation of, 479
  regulation of, 479
emotion-focused therapy (EFT), PDA treatment and, 311
emotion regulation, worry and, 51
emotions, fear of, 478
energy medicine, 455–56
engagement, in BDD treatment, 545–46
environment
  anxiety-like behavior and, 81
  family, 176
  genetics and, 173–74
  psychosocial, assessment by, 282
  twin studies and, 173
EOI. *See* emotional overinvolvement
epidemics, 525
Epidemiological Catchment Area (ECA), 566
  MDD comorbidity and, 580
epidemiological survey, of sleep, 613
epidemiological surveys
  of comorbidity, 555–56
  considerations for, 20–21
  mental disorders in, assessment of, 19–21
epigenetic inheritance, research, 132
equifinality, 181–82
Erickson et al. protocol, 445–46
  outcome data, 446–47
ERK. *See* extracellular signal-regulated kinase
ERP. *See* exposure with response prevention
escitalopram, for SAD treatment, 323
ethics, human experiments and, 166
ethnicity, 660, 662
event-related potential (ERP), 104
evolutionary theories, behavioral models and, 215
expectancy-free living, 367
expectancy violation, extinction learning mechanisms and, 465–66
Expert Consensus Guidelines, 11
Expert Knowledge Systems, 11
explanatory therapy, 534
  narrative review, 535
exposure therapy
  CT and, 421
  models of, 462
  PTSD and, efficacy of, 419–20
  PTSD treatment and, 418
exposure treatments
  context-specificity and, 470
  designing, 467–68
  duration of, 470–71
  fear activation during, 471–72

fear of pain treatment and, 558
　review of, 558
frequency of, 470–71
graduated, 447
history of, 461–62
hypochondriasis treatment and, 534
　narrative review, 535
mechanisms of, 462–64, 467
meta-analyses of, 338
mindfulness and, 479
moderators of, 472
outcome maximizing, 467–72
outcomes, 469–70
pharmacotherapy and, 432–33
plus cognitive restructuring, for SAD,
　335–36
for SAD, 335
social phobia and, 468
specific phobia treatment and, 343
sustained excitation during, 472
exposure with response prevention (ERP),
　238
augmentation, 399–400
CBT model validation and, 245
comorbid OCD-SUD and, 572
CT v., 397–98, 398t
CT with, 398–99
description of, 393
effective studies of, 395–97
effects of, 396t
efficacy of, 395
frequency of, 400
mechanisms of action, 393–94
medication v., 399
for OCD, efficacy of, 246–47
OCD treatment and, 392–93
poor insight and, 400
RET v., 397
for youth, 646
expressed emotion (EE), 182, 401
extinction learning, 463–64
mechanisms of, 464–67
extracellular signal-regulated kinase
　(ERK), 80–81
extraversion
ADs and, 590f
OCD and, 199–200, 201
personality disorder assessment and, 588
personality domains and, 190–92
PTSD and, 197–98
SAD and, 195
eye movement desensitization and
　reprocessing (EMDR), 12
key components n, 672
PTSD treatment and, 417–19
efficacy of, 421–22
relaxation training and, 420
specific phobia treatment, 344
eye tracking, attentional avoidance and, 139

F
FABQ. See Fear-Avoidance Beliefs
　Questionnaire

face recognition, attention and, 138
face validity, 75
FAH. See fear and avoidance hierarchies
fainting, behavioral models for, 212–13
false alarms, 156
nonclinical, 165
False Safety-behavior Elimination Therapy
　(F-SET), 445
familial aggregation, 88–89
Familial Enhancement of Avoidant
　Responding (FEAR), 175
family, 174–78
ADs in youth and, 641
CBT and, 184
discussions, 183
environment, 176
OCD and, 178
treatment, 183–84
family history, AD-SUD comorbidity
　and, 568
family studies, 88–89
faulty inference processes, 242–43
F criterion, 68. See also functional
　impairment
FDA. See Food and Drug Administration
fear. See also fear of pain
acquisition, 8, 462, 464
activation, during exposure treatments,
　471–72
amygdala and, 155
amygdala neurocircuitry and, 99
anxiety v., 153
behavioral assessment and, 284
conditioned, 211
conditioning models, 66
cues
　pharmacotherapy and, 432
　for PTSD, 258
of emotions, 478
enhanced by stress, 81
of fear, 212–13
habituation and, 462–63
learned, 254
　PTSD and, 406
　in rodents, 77
meaning of, 220
as memory structure, 238–39
nature of, 155–56
obsessional, acquisition of, 392
panic attacks v., 41
of physical sensations, 282
reduction, 461, 463
return of, 463
　extinction learning and, 464
situational, exposure treatments and,
　468
social learning and, 180
system, 156
unconditioned, 211
without panic, 216
fear and avoidance hierarchies (FAH), 284
fear-anxiety-avoidance model, of chronic
　pain, 552–53, 554f

Fear-Avoidance Beliefs Questionnaire
　(FABQ), 556
fear-avoidance model, of chronic pain, 552f
fear disorders, comorbidity in, 28
feared stimulus, hypervigilance to, 239
fear factor, 668–69
FearFighter, 492–93
Fear of Negative Evaluation Scale (FNE),
　286
fear of pain, 551–52, 553
anxiety sensitivity and, 558
assessment
　methods, 555–57
　rationale, 555
　questions, 558–59
　specific phobias v., 555
treatment
　features, 557–58
　frequency, 558
　review, 558
Fear of Pain Questionnaire-III (FPQ-III),
　fear of pain assessment and, 556
fear-potentiated startle (FPS), 77
fear-related bodily sensations, 136
fears
learned, 177–78
obsessional, 391
FEAR. See Familial Enhancement of
　Avoidant Responding
fear structures, 226
feedback, 288
feedback inhibition
of PD, 114–15
PTSD and, 116–17
FFM. See five-factor model
FFS. See flight-fight system
fight or flight response, 156
fire, hoarding and, 631
5-HT1A receptor, 78, 360–61
AD-depression comorbidity and, 581
5-HT. See serotonin
5-HTTLPR. See serotonin transporter
　promoter
five-factor model (FFM), 190–92
IHM and, 202–3
OCD and, 200
specific phobias and, 201–2
flashbacks, 98
flight-fight system (FFS), 157
flight or fight response, 41
CRF and, 79
mind-body intervention and, 454
neuroendocrinology of, 113
in youth, 640
flinch response, 76
fluoxetine
BDD treatment and, 547
CBT and, 433
　for SAD treatment, 339
hypochondriasis treatment and, 535
meta-analysis of, 536
PTSD treatment and, 408–9
for SAD treatment, 322–23

fluphenazine, 411
fluvoxamine
    CBT and, 433–34
    hypochondriasis treatment and, 535
    for SAD treatment, 321–22
fMRI. *See* functional magnetic resonance
        imaging
FNE. *See* Fear of Negative Evaluation
        Scale
focus, cultivating, 478
Food and Drug Administration (FDA)
    antidepressants, 515, 516*t*
    GAD medications, 351*t*
    GAD pharmacotherapy and, 350
    SNRIs and, 299
    supplements and, 457
forgetting, directed, 141
FPQ-III Fear of Pain Questionnaire-III
FPS. *See* fear-potentiated startle
free recall tests, 139–40
freezing, 156
    in rodents, 76
Freud, Sigmund, BDD and, 541
FRIENDS program, 504
    effectiveness, 505
        long-term, 507
    universal prevention and, 505–6
frontal activation, 436
Frost, R., 243–44
F-SET. *See* False Safety-behavior
        Elimination Therapy
functional connectivity, 104
functional impairment, 4
    PTSD and, 68
    sleep disturbance and, 613*f*
functional magnetic resonance imaging
        (fMRI)
    combination treatment and, 436
    PD and, 127

G
gabapentin, for SAD treatment, 324
GABA. *See* gamma-aminobutyric acid
GABHS. *See* group-A beta-hemolytic
        streptococcal
GAD-7, 287
    screening, 515
GAD-Q-IV. *See* Generalized Anxiety
        Disorder Questionnaire—IV
GAD. *See* generalized anxiety disorder
GADSS. *See* Generalized Anxiety Disorder
        Severity Scale
GAF. *See* Global Assessment of
        Functioning
gamma-aminobutyric acid (GABA)
    ADs in youth and, 640
    PD treatment and, 297
    PTSD treatment and, 410
gastrin related peptide (GRP), 80
gastrointestinal (GI) disorders, 600–601
gastrointestinal problems, GAD
        comorbidity in, 49
Gate Control Theory of Pain, 551

gatekeepers, 250
gender, 662, 669
gene-by-environment (GxE) interaction, 93
gene-environment intersection, 165
generalized anxiety disorder (GAD), 3–4, 7
    amygdala and, 100
    AOO of, 21
    autonomic arousal and, 268–69
    classification, 350
    clinical features of, 47–49
    cognitive model for, MCT and, 368
    comorbidity in, 49
    comorbidity in asthma, 601
    comorbidity in chronic pain, 602
    comorbidity in depression, treatment,
        583–84
    continuity of, 124
    CT and, 232
    culture and, 661–62
    depression *v.*, 48
    depressive disorders *v.*, 578
    diagnosis, 47–49
        history of, 47–48
    diagnostic criteria, shifting, 366
    as dimensional construct, 577
    dot-probe paradigm and, 138
    dropout rates, 431
    early onset *v.* late onset of, 626–27
    emotional dysregulation model of,
        231–32
    emotional regulation therapy for, 233
    FDA-approved medications, 351*t*
    5-HT1A receptor and, 360–61
    genetic vulnerabilities for, 269
    glutamate and, 360
    heritability of, 88
    heterocyclic antidepressants and, in
        primary care, 516
    ICD-10 and, 48
    integrated models of care and, 518
    interpretive bias in, 142
    intolerance of uncertainty model for,
        230–31
    IU and, 233
    latent factor, 270
    MBSR and, 481
    MCT for, 233–34
    memory bias and, 140
    metacognitive model of, 228–30
    mindfulness and, 481
    model of anxious apprehension for, 226
    models of, 234
    NAC and, 360
    NATs and, 226
    neurocircuitry and, 105
    neuroendocrinology of, 118
    neuroimaging of, 105
    neuroticism and, 202, 589
    nightmare disorder and, 618
    OCD and, 51, 270–71
    OCD comorbidity in, 61
    in older adults, 674
    panic attacks and, 278

pathological worry *v.*, 229
personality factors in, 201
pharmacotherapy for, 350–52
positive beliefs and, 231
prevalence of, 25–26, 48–49
in primary care, 515
quality of life and, 282
reclassification of, 668–69
recurrence of, 25–26
schema theory and, 225–26
sleep and, 611
standardized measures for, 287
SUD comorbidity in, 566
symptom criteria, 578
as syndrome, 231–32
taxonomic development of, 225
TCAs and, in primary care, 516
treatment, 232–33, 364
    ACT and, 370
    anticonvulsants for, 353–59
    antidepressants for, 352–53
    antidepressant trials for, 354–58*t*
    atypical antipsychotics for, 359–60
    azapirones for, 359
    belief modification and, 369
    benzodiazepines for, 359
    CBT and, 365
    CBT targeting avoidance, 367
    CBT targeting IU, 367
    comorbidity in, 443
    disorder-specific, 366–67, 371–72
    early interventions, 364–65
    efficacy, 233–34, 370–72
    experimental therapeutics in, 360
    future of, 372–73
    generalist, 365–66
    Hospital Anxiety and Depression
        Scale and, 359
    integrative psychotherapy and,
        369–70
    motivational interviewing and, 372
    problem solving and, 368
    self-help, 491
    SNRIs for, 353
    TCAs for, 353
    written emotional disclosure and,
        372–73
treatments, psychological, 364–70
worry and, 226
worry in, 49–51
worry *v.*, 48
in youth, 638
Generalized Anxiety Disorder
        Questionnaire—IV (GAD-Q-IV),
        232
Generalized Anxiety Disorder Severity
        Scale (GADSS), 287
generalized psychological vulnerability,
        159–65
generalized social anxiety disorder
        (GSAD)
    pharmacotherapy in, 321–25
    pharmacotherapy of, 329

general neurotic syndrome, 267, 274
genes
  amygdala specific, 80–81
  cingulate cortex specific, 80
  discovery in rodents, 79–80
genetic polymorphism, 87
genetics
  AD-depression comorbidity and, 581
  ADs in youth and, 640
  association studies and, 91–92
  behavior, 173–74
  core pathology conceptualization an, 442
  environment and, 173–74
  epidemiology of anxiety disorders, 87–92
  family studies and, 88–89
  linkage studies and, 89–91
  molecular, of anxiety disorders, 89–92
  PD risk factors and, 128
  studies, 269
  in temperament models, 165
  triple vulnerability theory and, 156–59
  twin studies and, 88
German Health Survey, 596
Global Assessment of Functioning (GAF)
  AD-personality disorder comorbidity and, 592–93
  reliability of, 271
glucocorticoid receptor (GR), 81
glucocorticoids
  dexamethasone and, 113
  effect of, 112
glucose metabolism, 102
glutamate, 360
  OCD and, 375–76
  PTSD treatment and, 411
glycowithanolides (WSG), 456–57
GMP. See good manufacturing practices
good manufacturing practices (GMP), 457
gotu kola, 453
Gray's behavioral inhibition system, 154
group-A beta-hemolytic streptococcal (GABHS), 605
GR. See glucocorticoid receptor
GSAD. See generalized social anxiety disorder
guilt feelings
  PTSD and, 421
  reducing, 422
GxE interaction. See gene-by-environment interaction

H

habituation, 462–63, 465
  emotional processing and, 465
HAM-A. See Hamilton Anxiety Rating Scale
Hamilton Anxiety Rating Scale (HAM-A), 352–53
  benzodiazepines and, 359

Hamilton Anxiety Rating Scale (HARS), 628
HARS. See Hamilton Anxiety Rating Scale
health anxiety, 527t
  dysfunctional beliefs and, 529
  factors involved in, 528f
  hypochondriasis v., 538
  reinforcement of, 529
health care utilization, 4
heart rates, during panic attacks, 36–37
helplessness, moderation of, 162
heritability, 88–89. See also epigenetic inheritance
  family studies and, 89
heterocyclic antidepressants, 516
heterogeneity, 670
high-risk hypothesis, 570
hippocampus, 98–99, 103
  AD-depression comorbidity and, 581
  exposure treatments and, 473
  HPA axis and, 160
  OCD risk factors and, 129
  PTSD and, 407
hoarding, 58–59
  characteristics, 630
  comorbidity, 630–31
  fire and, 631
  health risks, 631
  interventions, 631
  in later life, 630–31
  linkage studies, 91
  model for, 243–44
homeopathy, 456
homework compliance
  PDA treatment and, 316
  SAD treatment and, 342–43
homographs, 143, 146
Hospital Anxiety and Depression Scale
  BDD and, 543
  GAD treatment and, 359
HPA axis. See hypothalamic-pituitary-adrenal axis
human experiments, ethics and, 166
hyperarousal symptoms
  DTS and, 288
  PTSD and, 67–68
Hypericum perforatum. See St. John's wort
hypertension, 600
hyperthyroidism, 601
hyperventilation, 193
hypnosis, 454
hypochondriasis. See also health anxiety
  abridged, 526
  assessment methods, 530–31
  assessment rationale, 529–30
  cognitive-behavioral model of, 526–27
  diagnosis of, 525–26
  dysfunctional beliefs of, 527t
  etiology of, 526–29
  health anxiety v., 538
  OCD and, 6, 28
  prevalence of, 526
  prospective monitoring of, 530–31

specific phobia v., 6
  treatment, 531–35, 532–33t
    CBT and, 531–35
    history of, 531
    improving, 537–38
    meta-analysis, 536
    outcome predictors, 537
    pharmacotherapy and, 535
    review, 535–36
    treatment planning, 529–31
hypothalamic-pituitary-adrenal (HPA) axis, 79, 111
  activation, PD and, 113–14
  acute reactivity, in PTSD, 116
  AD-depression comorbidity and, 581–82
  control, loss of, 162
  description, 111
  dysregulation, 119
  experimental neurosis and, 160
  hippocampus and, 160
  SAD and, 117
  study of, 112–13
hypothesis testing, 466

I

IBA. See inference-based approach
IBS. See irritable bowel syndrome
ICD-10. See International Classification of Diseases, tenth revision
ICD-11. See International Classification of Diseases, eleventh revision
I/EP. See interpersonal/emotional processing
IES. See Impact of Event Scale
IHM. See Integrative Hierarchical Model of Anxiety and Depression
III. See Interpretation of Intrusions Inventory
illness, disease v., 658
imagery, in BDD, 545
imagery rehearsal, GAD treatment and, 365, 367
imagery rehearsal therapy, for nightmare disorder, 518
imipramine
  hypochondriasis treatment and, 535
  panic attacks and, 34
  PD treatment and, 297
Impact of Event Scale (IES), 288, 628
impulsivity, OCSD and, 59
inductive reasoning, OCD control and, 246
inference-based approach (IBA), for OCD, efficacy of, 246–47
inferences, 242–43
information processing
  biased, 234
  distorted, 219
  emotional processing v., 257
  hoarding and, 243
  models, AD-depression comorbidity and, 583
  models for PTSD, 254–57
  theory, ego-dystonicity and, 242

information shock, 256
inhibition, partner support of, 180–81
insight, OCD treatment and, 400
insomnia, 611. *See also* cognitive
    behavioral therapy for insomnia
  consequences of, 613
  pharmacotherapy for, 616
insula, 8, 98–99, 102
  OCD and, 105
  PTSD and, 102–3
  SAD and, 103
  SP and, 103
  TENC and, 102–3
intakes, group treatments and, 444
integrated models of care, 517–19
Integrative Hierarchical Model of Anxiety
    and Depression (IHM), 191–92
  FFM and, 202–3
intended action, 479–80
interference, assessment by, 282
internalization
  children and, 180–81
  disorders, 28
  targeting, 478–79
International Classification of Diseases,
    eleventh revision (ICD-11), 668
International Classification of Diseases,
    tenth revision (ICD-10)
  anxiety disorder codification and, 28
  CAM and, 451–52
  DSM-IV v., 19
  GAD and, 48
  OCD and, 28
  prevalence of agoraphobia and, 23
  prevalence of GAD and, 25
International Consensus Group on
    Depression and Anxiety,
    334–35
Internet
  based treatments, 675
    for PDA, 313
  delivered prevention programs, for
    PDA, 314
  limited access, 492–93
  NIMH and, 489
  open access programs, 494
  self-help treatment and, 492
interoceptive exposure, 309
interpersonal/emotional processing (I/EP),
    369–70
  efficacy of, 371–72
interpersonal mechanisms, 582
interpersonal psychotherapy (IPT), 340
interpretation bias, 142–43
Interpretation of Intrusions Inventory
    (III), 245
interpretive bias, 146–47
intervention continuum, 501*f*
interviews. *See also* clinical interviews
  fear of pain assessment and, 557
  motivational, 372–73, 673
  older adults and, 628
  review questions, lifetime, 20

screening, 514
structured, 279
intolerance of uncertainty (IU)
  CBT targeting, for GAD, 367–68
  GAD treatment and, 233
  model for GAD, 230–31
  model of GAD, features of, 234
intrusions, 288
intrusive thoughts, 394
  significance of, 241
in vivo exposure, 12
  PDA treatment and, 309
IPT. *See* interpersonal psychotherapy
IQ, 126
Iraq, 405
irritable bowel syndrome (IBS)
  comorbidity in, 600
  GAD comorbidity in, 49
IU. *See* intolerance of uncertainty

K

Kandel, Eric, 80
kava, 452
Kendler, Kenneth, 158
K-SADS. *See* Schedule for Affective
    Disorders and Schizophrenia in
    School-Age Children

L

Larkin et al. protocol, 445
  outcome data, 446–47
last observation carried forward analysis
    (LOCF), 322
  anticonvulsants for GAD and, 359
  SSRIs for GAD and, 352
latent class analysis (LCA), 29
latent factor, OCD *v.* GAD, 270
LCA. *See* latent class analysis
LC. *See* locus coeruleus
learning
  anxiety prevention and, 502
  exposure-based, 469–70
  extinction, 463–64
  fear, 254
  prior, 254
  safety, 464
  social, 180
  therapeutic, 430
learning theory, 165–67
  contemporary, 254
  for PTSD, 253–58
  specific phobias and, 177–78
lemon balm, 452–53
levetiracetam, 324
LHPA axis. *See* limbic-hypothalamic-
    pituitary-adrenal axis
Liebowitz Social Anxiety Scale (LSAS), 286
  SAD treatment response and, 328
lifetime prevalence
  for AD-SUD comorbidity, 567*t*
  of agoraphobia, 35
  of agoraphobia without panic disorder,
    23–24

estimating, 20–21
of OCD, 391–92
of panic disorder, 22, 35
persistence and, 21–22
of PTSD, 27–28
of SAD, 38
of specific phobia, 40
limbic-hypothalamic-pituitary-adrenal
    (LHPA) axis, 111
linkage studies, 89–91
LOCF. *See* last observation carried forward
    analysis
locomotor behavior, 76
locus coeruleus (LC), PD and, 296
longitudinal-developmental studies, 123
long-term outcome, of PDA treatment,
    316–17
low excitement seeking, 62
LSAS. *See* Liebowitz Social Anxiety
    Scale
Lumpkin et al. protocol, 446
  outcome data, 446–47

M

magnetic resonance imaging (MRI),
    129
magnetic resonance spectroscopy
    (MRS), 297
magnetic therapy, 456
major depressive disorder (MDD)
  AS and, 194
  ACTH suppression and, 114
  comorbidity, in PDA, 314–15
  comorbidity in OCD, 580
  comorbidity in PTSD, 580
  dimensional ratings of, 271
  OCD comorbidity in, 60
  panic attacks and, 36
  prevalence, 577
  social phobia and, 270
MAOIs. *See* monoamine oxidase
    inhibitors
MAPK. *See* mitogen activated kinase
Marks, Isaac, 37
marriage, social phobia and, 179
MASC. *See* Multidimensional Anxiety
    Scale for Children
massage, 453–54
MBCT. *See* mindfulness-based cognitive
    therapy
MBSR. *See* mindfulness-based stress
    reduction
MCIs. *See* minimal-contact interventions
MDD. *See* major depressive disorder
Meaney, Michael, 81
medial prefrontal cortex (mPFC), 98–99,
    101
  combination treatment and, 436
  PD and, 102
  PTSD and, 101–2
  SAD and, 102
  SP and, 102
  TENC and, 101–2

medical background, assessment by, 283
medical disorders, OCD treatment and, 385
medications, 11. *See also* pharmacotherapy
  CBT and, for PDA treatment, 311–12
  effectiveness, 380
  ERP *v.,* 399
  GMP of, 457
  hypochondriasis, 525
  for OCD, 381*t*
meditation, 629
  OCD and, 455
Mellisa officinalis. See lemon balm
memory. *See also* situationally accessed
      memory; verbally accessed memory
  bias, 139–42
  consolidation, 467
  DCS and, 339
  distrust, 142
  emotional, 465
  exposure, PTSD treatment and, 420
  inhibition, 141
  models, for PTSD, 253–58
  OCD and, 141–42
  PCC and, 103
  perceptual, emotion and, 154
  priming effects on, 141
  PTSD and, 406
  reconsolidation, 406
  structures, 238–39
  tasks, 140–41
  traumatic, recurrence of, 255–56
mental defeat, 256
mental disorders
  definition of, 667
  in epidemiological surveys, assessment
    of, 19–21
mental illness, 657
metabolic disorders, 601–2
metacognitive model of GAD, 228–30
  features of, 234
  treatment and, 233
metacognitive therapy (MCT), for GAD,
    233–34, 368–69, 371–72
metyrapone, 117
Midwest Center for Stress and Anxiety,
    492
mind-body intervention strategies,
    454–55
mindfulness, 476–77
  automaticity and, 479
  case studies, 480–81
  as change mechanism, 478–80
  experiments, 480
  GAD treatment and, 370
  open trials, 482–83*t*
  research, 480–81
  trials, 481
mindfulness-based cognitive therapy
    (MBCT), 477–78
mindfulness-based stress reduction
    (MBSR), 477
  GAD and, 481
  panic and, 481

Mini International Neuropsychiatric
    Interview (MINI), 514
minimal-contact interventions (MCIs),
    PDA treatment and, 313
minimal-contact therapy, 489, 491, 493
minimum contact control (MCC), 628
MINI. *See* Mini International
    Neuropsychiatric Interview
mirror gazing
  BDD and, 547
  goals, 547*t*
mirtazapine, 409
  in primary care, 516
MI. *See* Mobility Inventory for
    Agoraphobia
MI. *See* myocardial infarction
Mississippi Scale for Combat Related
    PTSD, 628
mitogen activated kinase (MAPK), 80
mixed disorders, epidemiology of, 19
MMPI-PK, 628
Mobility Inventory for Agoraphobia (MI),
    286
modifying action tendencies, 445
monoamine oxidase inhibitors (MAOIs)
  ADs in youth and, 648
  ASD treatment and, 407
  CBT and, for SAD treatment, 338
  for GAD, 350
  for GSAD, 321
  monotherapy randomized controlled
    trials, 376
  PD treatment and, 299–300
  for SAD treatment, 323
  side effects, 516
  as SRI replacement, 383
mood disorders
  AD comorbidity in, 578
  OCD comorbidity in, 60–61
mood regulation, sleep disturbance and,
    614
mood stabilizers, PTSD treatment and,
    410–11
morbidity, anxiety disorders and, 87
mPFC. *See* medial prefrontal cortex
MPS. *See* Multidimensional Perfectionism
    Scale
MRI. *See* magnetic resonance imaging
MRS. *See* magnetic resonance
    spectroscopy
MTPM. *See* multilevel trait predictor
    model
Multidimensional Anxiety Scale for
    Children (MASC), 644
Multidimensional Inventory of
    Hypochondrial Traits, 430
Multidimensional Perfectionism Scale
    (MPS), 195
  specific phobias and, 202
multifinality, 181–82
multilevel trait predictor model (MTPM),
    203
multiple sclerosis, 603–4

muscle dysmorphia, 542
music therapy, 454–55
mutual maintenance, 570
myocardial infarction (MI), 597–600
MySelfHelp.com, 494

N
N-acetylcysteine (NAC), 360
NAC. *See* N-acetylcysteine
NA. *See* negative affectivity
NaSSA. *See* noradrenic/specific
    serotonergic antidepressant
National Center for Complementary and
    Alternative Medicine (NCCAM),
    451
National Comorbidity Survey (NCS), 566
  anxious-misery and, 201
  depressive disorders and, 577
  GAD prevalence and, 48–49
  PTSD and, 68–69
  PTSD and PDA and, 271
National Comorbidity Survey Replication
    (NCS-R), 22
  ADs in later life and, 625
  depressive disorders and, 577
  late onset ADs and, 625
  median AOO and, 123–24
  panic disorder prevalence and, 35
  SAD prevalence and, 38
National Epidemiological Survey on
    Alcohol and Related Conditions
    (NESARC), 566
  AD-personality disorder comorbidity, 589
National Institute of Clinical Excellence
    (NICE), 545, 548
National Institute of Mental Health
    (NIMH), Internet and, 489
NATs. *See* negative automatic thoughts
natural disaster, PTSD and, 27
N-BI. *See* neuroticism/behavioral
    inhibition
NCCAM. *See* National Center for
    Complementary and Alternative
    Medicine
NCS-R, anxiety disorder comorbidity
    and, 87
NCS-R. *See* National Comorbidity Survey
    Replication
NCS. *See* National Comorbidity Survey
nefazodone
  in primary care, 516
  for SAD treatment, 323
negative affectivity (NA), 442
  AS and, 194
  in youth, 637
Negative Affectivity Self-Statement
    Questionnaire (NASSQ), 644
Negative Affect Syndrome, Barlow et al.
    protocol and, 445
negative automatic thoughts (NATs), 226
  worry *v.,* 232
negative problem orientation, 230
  worry and, 231

neglect, 178–79
NESARC. *See* National Epidemiological Survey on Alcohol and Related Conditions
NE. *See* norepinephrine
neurasthenia, 661–62
neuroanatomy
  functional, 98
  locations, 98*f*
neurobiology
  extinction learning mechanisms and, 465–66
  of PTSD, 406–7
  triple vulnerability theory and, 156–57
neurochemistry, 581–82
neurocircuitry, 98
  amygdalocentric, 99*f*
  functional connectivity, 104
  GAD and, 105
  OCD and, 104–5
  pertinent, 98–99
neuroendocrine function, 111
  triple vulnerability theory and, 164–65
neuroimaging
  of GAD, 105
  treatment studies, 105–6
neurological disorders, 603–5
neurophysiology, AD-depression comorbidity and, 581
neurosis
  definition of, 265
  experimental, 160–62
neurosurgery, for OCD, 379
neuroticism
  ADs and, 589, 590*f*
  GAD and, 202
  genetic factors for, 128
  OCD and, 199–200, 201
  OCD comorbidity in, 62
  PD and, 192–93
  personality disorder assessment and, 587–88
  personality domains and, 190–92
  PTSD and, 197–98, 202
  self-criticism and, 196
  stability and, 157
neuroticism/behavioral inhibition (N-BI), 157
neuroticism/extraversion, AD-depression comorbidity and, 582
neurotransmitters
  OCD and, 375–76
  PD and, 296
neutralization, OCD and, 130
neutralizing acts, 240, 244
New England Journal of Medicine, PD causes and, 127
New Zealand's National Health Committee, 11
NICE. *See* National Institute of Clinical Excellence
nightmare disorder, 618
  nocturnal, 611

night terrors, 617
NIMH. *See* National Institute of Mental Health
NMDA. *See* N-methyl-D-aspartate
N-methyl-D-aspartate (NMDA), 254
  in combination treatments, 435
  extinction learning mechanisms and, 466
NNT analysis. *See* Number Need to Treat analysis
nondirective supportive therapy (NST), 647
nonrapid eye movement (NREM) sleep, 612
noradrenergic pathways, abnormalities, 271
noradrenic/specific serotonergic antidepressant (NaSSA), 11
norepinephrine (NE)
  antagonists, ASD treatment and, 407
  PD and, 296
  PTSD and, 407
Norton and Hope protocol, 444–45
  outcome data, 446–47
nosology, 125
NOS. *See* anxiety disorder not otherwise specified
NREM sleep. *See* nonrapid eye movement sleep
NST. *See* nondirective supportive therapy
Number Need to Treat (NNT) analysis, SAD treatment efficacy and, 326
numbing symptoms. *See also* avoidance
  DTS and, 288
  PTSD and, 6, 67

O

OASIS. *See* Overall Anxiety Severity and Impairment Scale
OBQ. *See* Obsessive Beliefs Questionnaire
obsessions. *See also* contamination obsessions
  appraisal, 239
  avoidance and, 240
  beliefs and, 241
  catastrophic misinterpretation of, 240
  chronic worry *v.,* 270
  compulsions *v.,* 129–30
  convergence of, 244–45
  definition, 51
  definition of, 56–57, 391
  development of, 401
  disturbance characteristic of, 239
  ego-dystonic, 241–42
  ERP and, 393
  as inference, 242
  nonclinical, 58
  relationship with compulsions, 245
  suppression of, 245–46
  worry and, 51–52
  in youth, 638

Obsessive Beliefs Questionnaire (OBQ), 245
Obsessive-Compulsive Cognitions Working Group (OCCWG), 244–45
obsessive-compulsive disorder (OCD), 3–4, 6, 98
  ADHD and, 131
  androgen and, 131
  anxiety disorder NOS and, 270–71
  AOO of, 21, 131
  association studies of, 92
  augmentation/refractory sample trials in, 377*t*
  avoidance behaviors and, 281k
  behavioral experiments and, 395
  behavioral models for, 392
  behavioral theory of, 129
  CBT and, 240
  characterization of, 391–92
  checking rituals, 141–42
  clinical course of, 131
  clomipramine and, 516
  cognitive models of, 394
  cognitive restructuring, 244
  cognitive theory of, 129–30
  comorbidity, 60–62
    in BDD, 541
  comorbidity in depression, treatment, 583
  comorbidity in MDD, 580
  comorbidity in SUD, treatment, 572
  convergence of models for, 244–45
  cortico-striatal-thalamic circuit and, 98, 99*f*
  covariation with PTSD, 130
  culture and, 660–61
  danger and, 165
  definitions of, 56–57
  depression *v.,* 579
  developmental approach to, 128–31
  development of, 167
  diagnostic features of, 56–57
  diagnostic reliability of, 266
  disgust and, 105
  dropout rates, 431
  family and, 178
  family studies and, 89
  FFM and, 200
  GAD and, 51, 270–71
  heritability of, 88
  heterogeneity of, 130–31
  hoarding model, 243–44
  intrusive thoughts and, 394
  IU and, 231
  latent factor, 270
  lifetime prevalence of, 391–92
  linkage studies, 89–91
  medications, 381*t*
  meditation and, 455
  memory functioning in, 141–42
  mindfulness and, 481
  monotherapy randomized controlled trials for, 376

natural history of, 131
neurobiological risk factors, 129
neurocircuitry and, 104–5
neuroimaging treatment studies and, 106
neuroticism and, 589
neurotransmitters and, 375–76
neutralization and, 130
as OC spectrum disorders, 668
in older adults, 626
PANDAS and, 605–6
pediatric, 646
    SSRIs for, 648
perfectionism and, 195, 200
personality factors in, 199–200
pharmacology, 376–78
prevalence of, 21, 28
psychological approach to, 238
psychological models for, 129–30
psychosocial environment and, 283
psychosocial risk factors, 130
Rachman's cognitive behavioral model
    of, 240–41
research, new, 131
Salkovski's cognitive behavioral model
    of, 239–40
schizotypal personality traits and, 593
standardized measures for, 286–87
subclinical, 131
subtypes, 57t, 130–31
SUD comorbidity in, 566
suppression of, 245–46
symptom criteria, 579
symptom subtypes, 58–59
    approaches to, 59–60
TCAs and, in primary care, 516
Tourette's syndrome comorbidity in,
    129
treatment, 375
    algorithm, 382–83f
    BT and, 392–94
    CBT and, 448
    clinical course, 379
    combined, 433
    with comorbidity, 384
    CT and, 394
    DCS and, 435
    depression and, 401
    discontinuation, 384
    discontinuation studies, 379–80
    dosages, 381t
    EE and, 401
    ERP and, 392–93
    ERP with CT and, 398–99
    ERP with medication and, 398–99
    initial management approaches, 380
    long-term outcome of, 379–80
    motivation to begin, 402
    natural history, 379
    outcome literature, 395–400
    outcome predictors, 400–401
    PDs and, 401
    poor insight and, 400
    relationships and, 182

second-line management approaches,
    380–83
    side effects, 381t
    somatic approach, 378–79
    in special populations, 384
    surgical approach, 378–79
    variations, 400
treatment efficacy, 246–47
Tripartite Model and, 199
in youth, 638–39
Obsessive-Compulsive Inventory (OCI),
    286–87
obsessive-compulsive personality disorder
    (OCPD)
    OCD and, 6
    OCD comorbidity in, 61–62
obsessive-compulsive spectrum disorders
    (OCSD), 6, 59, 668
    OCD comorbidity in, 60
OCCWG. See Obsessive-Compulsive
    Cognitions Working Group
OCD. See obsessive-compulsive disorder
OCI. See Obsessive-Compulsive Inventory
O'Connor, K., 242–43
OCPD. See obsessive-compulsive
    personality disorder
OCSD. See obsessive-compulsive spectrum
    disorders
ODD. See oppositional defiant disorder
OFC. See orbitofrontal cortex
Öhman, Arne, 215
older adults
    ADs in, 626
    benzodiazepine for, 629–30
    CBT for, 631
    GAD in, 674
    OCD in, 626
    PD in, 629
    pharmacotherapy for, 629–30
    self-reporting, 627–28
    SSRIs for, 630
omega-3 fatty acids, 453
oncoprotein 18/stathmin, 80
ondansetron, 325
openness
    OCD and, 199–200
    personality domains and, 190–92
open trials, 482–83t
opposite action tendencies, 466
oppositional defiant disorder (ODD)
    comorbidity, 642
    continuity of, 125
orbitofrontal cortex (OFC), 98
    glucose metabolism and, 102
    OCD and, 104
    OCD risk factors and, 129
ordering, 58–59
order of onset, comorbidity, 568
organization, hoarding model and, 243
Overall Anxiety Severity and Impairment
    Scale (OASIS), 285
overanxious disorder (OAD), 641
    SAD and, 38

overconsolidation model for PTSD, 255
overestimating, 143–44

P

Paced Auditory Serial Attention Task,
    436
Padua Inventory—Washington State
    University Revised (PI-WSUR),
    287
pain. See also chronic pain; fear of pain
    syndromes, 453
Pain Anxiety Symptoms Scale (PASS), 553
    fear of pain assessment and, 556
PANDAS. See pediatric autoimmune
    neuropsychiatric disorders
    associated with streptococcal
    infection
panic
    amygdala and, 127–28
    ASI and, 128
    behavioral models for, 212–13
    cognitive theory of, 215
    fear without, 216
    genetic factors for, 128, 158
    MBSR and, 481
    nature of, 155–56
    nocturnal, 617–18
    nonclinical, 155
    physical conditions and, 283
    spontaneous, 156
    symptomatology, 193–94
Panic Attack Record, 285
panic attacks, 5, 209. See also panic
    disorder
    ACTH and, 118–19
    agoraphobia and, 216
    alarms and, 41
    in children, 127
    comorbidity in asthma, 601
    comorbidity in hyperthyroidism, 601
    cortisol and, 118–19
    cued, 5, 35
    fear v., 41
    GAD and, 278
    imipramine and, 34
    limited symptom, 5
    maintaining factors of, 41–42
    model of, 216f
    nocturnal, 611
    panic disorder v., 22
    parental modeling and, 177
    physiological changes during, 36–37
    social phobia and, 209–10
    symptoms of, 35
    triggers, 36
    uncued, 5
    without panic disorder, 35–36
Paniccenter.net, 494
panic control treatment (PCT), 309–10
panic disorder (PD), 5, 35–37, 98
    AS and, 194
    ACC and, 101
    acute reactivity and, 114

panic disorder (*continued*)
amygdala and, 100
autonomic arousal and, 268
barriers to care, 519
basal state studies, 113
biological models of, 36
causes of, 127
central drive of, 114–15
chronicity of, 35
comorbidity in asthma, 601
comorbidity in depression, treatment, 583
comorbidity in IBS, 600
comorbidity in SUD, 569
treatment, 571
controlled studies of, 296
covariation bias in, 145
culture and, 659–60
definition of, 35
developmental approach to, 127–28
diagnostic reliability of, 266
dropout rates, 431
family studies and, 89
feedback inhibition of, 114–15
fMRI and, 127
heritability of, 88
hippocampus and, 103
HPA activation and, 113–14
HPA axis dysregulation and, 119
IHM and, 192
interpretive bias in, 142
lifetime prevalence of, 22
linkage studies, 89–91
maintenance of, 9
mPFC and, 102
neuroendocrinology of, 113–15
neuroimaging treatment studies and, 106
neuroticism and, 192–93, 589
OCD comorbidity in, 61
OFC glucose metabolism and, 102
in older adults, 629
overview, 295–96
panic attacks *v.*, 22
parental modeling and, 177
PCC and, 104
pharmacotherapy of, 296–302, 298*t*
physical sensations and, 281–82
in primary care, 515
psychological theories of, 36–37
PTSD and, 271
risk factors, 127–28, 295–96
specific phobia *v.*, 6, 39–40
standardized measures for, 286
SUD comorbidity in, 566
symptom criteria, 579
syndrome, 90–91
TCAs and, in primary care, 516
treatment
CBT and, 303
combined, 433–34
duration of, 302
goals of, 296

relationships and, 182
research, 302
in youth, 637, 639
Panic Disorder Severity Scale (PDSS), 286
treatment goals and, 296
panic disorder with agoraphobia (PDA)
CBT and
effectiveness studies, 312–13
efficacy studies, 311–12
research review, 311–13
clinical features of, 314
CT and, 310
medical comorbidity in, 314–15
PCT and, 309–10
prevention research, 313–14
psychiatric comorbidity in, 314–15
PTSD and, 271
standardized measures for, 286
treatment
CBT and, 308
comprehensive, 309
cost-effective, 313
homework compliance and, 316
interpersonal factors in, 315–16
long-term outcome, 316–17
outcome predictors, 314–16
strategies, 308–9
therapist variables and, 316
panic-focused psychodynamic psychotherapy (PFPP), PDA treatment and, 310–11
Parallel Distributed Processing Connectionist Neural Network (PDP-CNN), 466
paraventricular nucleus (PVN), 112
parental modeling, 177–78
parental reporting, 645
parent-child attachment, 9, 176–77
parenting, 174–76
parenting style
ADs in youth and, 641
vicarious learning and, 165–66
parenting styles, 162–63
parents, psychopathology and, 183
parent training, 503–4
paroxetine, 409
hypochondriasis treatment and, 535
for SAD treatment, 322
partner relationships, 178
inhibition and, 180–81
PASS. *See* Pain Anxiety Symptoms Scale
pathoplasty models, 191
in PTSD, 199
Patient Health Questionnaire (PHQ), 514–15
patient retention, 430–31
Pavlovian conditioning, 154
PCC. *See* posterior cingulate cortex
PC. *See* perceived criticism
PCT. *See* panic control treatment
PDP-CNN. *See* Parallel Distributed Processing Connectionist Neural Network

PDs, OCD treatment and, 401
PDSS. *See* Panic Disorder Severity Scale
pediatric autoimmune neuropsychiatric disorders associated with streptococcal infection (PANDAS), 129, 605
pediatric OCD and, 605–6
peer
acceptance, 179
social learning and, 180
victimization, 180
Penn State Worry Questionnaire (PSWQ), 233, 287
older adults and, 627
peptic ulcer disease (PUD), 600–601
perceived criticism (PC), 315
perceptual distortion, 219–20
perfectionism, 195
OCD and, 200
SAD and, 196
persistence, 21–22
personal history, 530
personality disorders, 10–11
assessment, dimensions *v.* categories, 587–88
OCD comorbidity in, 61–62
traits, 588
ADs and, 591–92
personality factors, 202–4
comorbidity and, 203–4
hierarchical organization of, 190–92
personality-psychopathology relationships, 273
personality traits, 10–11
as AD risk factors, 591
ADs in youth and, 640
anxiety disorders and, 588–92
personality disorder traits *v.*, 588
PE-SIT protocol, 421
PE therapy. *See* prolonged exposure therapy
PET. *See* positron-emission tomography
PFPP. *See* panic-focused psychodynamic psychotherapy
pharmacotherapy. *See also* medications
for AD-insomnia comorbidity, 616–17
for ADs in youth, 647–49
ASD, 407
availability of, 431–33
BDD treatment and, 547–48
CBT and, 12
for SAD treatment, 338–39
combined with CBT, 429–30
comorbid PTSD-SUD and, 572
core pathology conceptualization and, 442–43
cost of, 514
efficacy studies, 433–34
exposure treatments and, 432–33
fear cues and, 432
for GAD, 350–52
general considerations, 517
of GSAD, 329

hypochondriasis treatment and,
532–33t, 535
research, 538
review of, 536
mechanisms of, 430
for OCD, 376–78, 380–85
for older adults, 629–30
of panic disorder, 296–302, 298t
patient retention and, 430–31
in primary care, 515–17
PTSD, 407–11
in SAD, 321–25
tolerability of, 430–31
phenelzine
CBGT v., for SAD treatment, 338
PD treatment and, 299–300
social phobia treatment and, 145
phobias. See also specific types
blood, 213
injury, 213
phenomenology of, 98
psychological processes and, 8–9
phobic disorders, 39
PHODA. See Photograph Series of Daily
Activities
Photograph Series of Daily Activities
(PHODA), 557
physical abuse, OCD and, 130
physical disorders
comorbidity in, 283
comorbidity in ADs, 596–97
physical sensations. See also bodily
sensations
assessment by, 281–82
interoceptive assessment and, 284–85
physiological hyperarousal, 268
Piper methysticum. See kava
pituitary gland, sensitivity, CRF and, 161
PI-WSUR. See Padua Inventory—
Washington State University
Revised
placebo, 537
polysomnography (PSG), 612
positron-emission tomography (PET),
PTSD acute reactivity and, 116
posterior cingulate cortex (PCC), 98–99,
103
PD and, 104
PTSD and, 104
SAD and, 104
SP and, 104
post-stress syndromes, other, 70
posttraumatic stress disorder (PTSD), 3, 6
ACC and, 100–101
acute reactivity and, 116
agoraphobia and, 271
allostatic load and, 70
amygdala and, 99
AOO of, 21
ASD v, 69
ASD v., 423
associated features, 68–69
attribution-based models of, 256

avoidant/numbing symptoms, 67
basal state studies, 115–16
biological models of, 66
borderline personality disorder
comorbidity in, 589
CBT and, 417
central drive studies and, 116–17
characteristics of, 405–6
classical conditioning model for, 251–52
clinical interviews and, 279
clinical issues, 70
cognitive processes in, 255
comorbidity in, 68–69
comorbidity in cancer, 602–3
comorbidity in chronic pain, 602
comorbidity in depression, treatment,
583–84
comorbidity in MDD, 580
comorbidity in MI, 597–600
comorbidity in SUD, 570
treatment, 572–73
complex, 69–70
conceptualization of, 259
conceptualized, 406
covariation with OCD, 130
cross-cultural factors and, 69
CSA-related, 141
cultural influences on, 181
culture and, 661
depressive disorders v., 578–79
developmental approach to, 126–27
diagnosis and, DSM-IV, 259
diagnostic criteria, 66–68
directed forgetting and, 141
dropout rates, 431
dual processing models of, 255–56
dual representation model of, 256
early learning theory models of, 251–52
emotional processing models for,
253–58
emotional processing models of, 257–58
epidemiology, 70
external events and, 250
fear cues, 258
feedback inhibition and, 116–17
functional impairment and, 68
hippocampus and, 103
HPA axis dysregulation and, 119
hyperarousal symptoms, 67–68
incubation period, 406
insula and, 102–3
interpretive bias in, 143
lifetime prevalence of, 27–28
memory models for, 253–58
metyrapone and, 117
mPFC and, 101–2
neurobiology of, 406–7
neuroendocrinology of, 115–17
neuroimaging treatment studies and,
105–6
neuroticism and, 202
new learning theory models for, 253–58
nightmare disorder and, 618

ongoing stressors and, 68
overconsolidation model for, 255
overview, 65–66
partial/subsyndromal, 69
pathoplasty models in, 199
PDA and, 271
PD and, 271
persistent symptoms of, 250
personality factors in, 197–99
pharmacotherapy, 407–11
phenomenology, 97–98
preevent risk factors, 253
prevalence of, 26–28
prevention of, 127
in primary care, 515
prior learning and, 254
psychological models of, 65–66
psychotherapy and, 127
reactivation of, 68
reclassification of, 668–69
reexperiencing symptoms, 67
relapse of, 68
REM sleep and, 614–15
risk factors, 70, 126
self-reporting, 628
social support and, 68
standardized measures for, 287–88
stress response theory of, 257
SUD comorbidity in, 566
symptoms
co-occurence of, 259
criteria, 578–79
treatment
AMT efficacy and, 422
anticonvulsants and, 410–11
antidepressants and, 408–10
antipsychotics and, 411
cannabinoids and, 412
comorbidity and, 443
CS-US association and, 411
CT and, 420–21
DCS and, 412, 436
dissemination of, 424–26
efficacy of, 419–22
EMDR and, 421–22
future of, 411–12
manualized, 424–25
mood stabilizers and, 410–11
psychological, 417–19
self-help, 491
self-help and, 491
SSRIs and, 408–10
training, 425
two-factor theory, 252
uncontrollability of, 253
vulnerability factors for, 253–54
vulnerability to, 197–99
written emotional disclosure and, 372–73
in youth, 646
in youth and, 639
prazosin, for older adults, 630
predictive validity, 75
predominantly self-help therapy, 491

prefrontal cortex
  AD-depression comorbidity and, 581
  exposure treatments and, 473
pregabalin, for SAD treatment, 324
pregnancy, OCD treatment and, 384–85
preparedness theory, 40
presence-absence ratings, 266
prevalence. *See also* lifetime prevalence
  of AD-depression comorbidity, 576–78
  of ADs in youth, 641, 642*t*
  for AD-SUD comorbidity, 566
  of anxiety disorders, 512–13
  of GAD, 25–26, 48–49
  of hoarding, in later life, 630
  of hypochondriasis, 526
  of OCD, 28
  of panic disorder, 35
  of PTSD, 26–28
  ratios, 21–22
  of SEPAD, 24–25
  of social phobia, 24
  of specific phobia, 22–23
prevalence rates, 3–4
prevention, 125
  in children, 498
  indicated, 499
    for children, 503–4
    effectiveness of, 507
  multilevel programming, 508
  of PTSD, 127
  research, 507–9
    directions in, 508
    PDA, 313–14
    principles for, 501–2
  selective, 499
    for children, 504–5
    effectiveness of, 507
  strategies, 499–501
  training, 508
  universal, 499–500
    for children, 505–7
    effectiveness of, 507–8
primary care
  anxiety disorders in, 512–13
  barriers to care in, 519
  hypochondriasis treatment and, 531
  integrated models of care, 517–19
  pharmacotherapy, general
    considerations, 517
  psychosocial interventions, 517
  treatment options, 515
Prime-MD, 514
probability estimation, OCD control
    and, 246
proband, 568
problem solving
  GAD treatment and, 368
  negative problem orientation and, 230
  worry and, 50
Project MATCH, SAD comorbidity and,
    341
prolonged exposure (PE) therapy, 419
  dissemination, 425

propranolol, ASD treatment and, 407
PSG. *See* polysomnography
PSWQ. *See* Penn State Worry
    Questionnaire
psychiatric disorders, roots of, 124
psychoanalytic theory, 210–11
psychodynamic theories, 210–11, 220
psychodynamic therapy
  for SAD, 340
  for specific phobia, 344–45
psychoeducation, 534
  in BDD treatment, 545
  fear of pain treatment and, 557
  hypochondriasis treatment and, 531
  narrative review, 535
psychological models
  for OCD, 129–30
  panic disorder and, 36–37
  of PTSD, 65–66
psychological processes, 8–9
psychological treatments, 11–12, 13*t*
  evidence-based, for PDA, 308–11
  for GAD, 364–70
  for PTSD, 417–19
psychoneuroticism, 591
psychopathology
  developmental research and, 132
  dimensional approach to, 668
  dimensional models of, 272
  parental, 183
psychosocial stressors, 10
psychotherapy, 11–12
  hypochondriasis treatment and,
    532–33*t*
  integrative
    efficacy of, 371–72
    for GAD, 369–70
  interpersonal, hypochondriasis
      treatment and, 537
  PTSD and, 127
  supportive, 344–45
PTSD Checklist, 515
PTSD. *See* posttraumatic stress disorder
public health, 514
public speaking, SAD and, 38
PubMed, 597
Purdon, C., 241–42
PVN. *See* paraventricular nucleus

Q
QTLs. *See* quantitative trait loci
quality of life
  comorbidity and, 514
  loss of, 282
  sleep and, 612–13
quantitative trait loci (QTLs), 81
  linkage studies and, 91
questionnaires, 285. *See also* self-reporting
quetiapine, for SAD treatment, 325

R
rACC. *See* rostral ACC
Rachman, S., 240–41

randomized controlled trials (RCTs)
  of CAM, 451–52
  of ERP, 395
rapid eye movement (REM) sleep, 612
  amygdala and, 614
  emotional processing and, 614
  nightmare disorder and, 618
  PTSD and, 614–15
rational emotive therapy (RET), 397
RCTs. *See* randomized controlled trials
reaction time (RT), 138
reactivation, of PTSD, 68
reassurance-seeking behavior
  compulsions and, 270
  hypochondriasis treatment and, 534
reboxetine, 325
reciprocal inhibition, 462
recognition tests, 139–40
reexperiencing symptoms, 6
  PTSD and, 6, 67
reinforcement, patterns of, 283
relapse, of PTSD, 68
relationships, treatment outcome and,
    182–84
relaxation training. *See also* applied
    relaxation
  EMDR and, 420
  exposure treatments and, 462
  GAD treatment and, 232–33
  Larkin et al. protocol and, 445
  for older adults, 629
  PDA treatment and, 309
  in primary care, 517
  for SAD, 337
relevant constructs, 670–71
reliability, 266–67
  structured interviews and, 279
religious obsession, 58–59
REM sleep. *See* rapid eye movement sleep
repetition, 243
repetitive behavior, 58
repetitive thought, 52
research, 125
  development in, 671–74
  GAD-specific, 366
  prevention
    directions in, 508
    principles for, 501–2
respiratory disorders, 213, 601
response, predictors of, 673
response prevention
  ERP and, 393
  hypochondriasis treatment and, 534
  narrative review, 535
responsibility, 239–40
restless leg syndrome (RLS), 603
RET. *See* rational emotive therapy
reversible inhibitors of monoamine
    oxidase-A (RIMAs), 300
  for GSAD, 321
  for SAD treatment, 323–24
reward deficiency, OCSD and, 59
rhesus monkeys, 160

rhinoplasty, 543
riluzole, 360
RIMAs. *See* reversible inhibitors of
    monoamine oxidase-A
risk factors
    for ADs, 591
    for ADs in youth, 639–41
    for BDD, 544
    for children, 501–2, 506
    for OCD, 129
    for PD, 127–28, 295–96
    for PTSD, 70, 126–27
        preevent, 253
risperidone, 411
ritualistic behavior, 58
    ERP and, 393
    faulty inference processes and, 242–43
    obsessional anxiety and, 392
ritual of inaction, 210
RLS. *See* restless leg syndrome
Robillard, S., 242–43
rodents
    gene discovery, 79–80
    measures of anxiety for, 76–77
role-playing, reverse, 547
rostral ACC (rACC), 100–101
    OCD and, 104–5
RT. *See* reaction time
RUPP Anxiety Group, 649

S

SAD. *See* social anxiety disorder
SADS. *See* Social Avoidance and
    Distress Scale
safety
    behaviors, 218–19
        eliminating, 469–70
    precautions, 209
    in PTSD treatment, 70
Salk Institute, 80
Salkovskis, P. M., 239–40
SAM. *See* situationally accessed memory
SAST. *See* Short Anxiety Screening Test
SCARED. *See* Screen for Child Anxiety
    and Related Emotional Disorders
scar model, 191
    of AS, 195
SCA. *See* sudden cardiac arrest
SCC. *See* standard community care
Schedule for Affective Disorders and
    Schizophrenia in School-Age
    Children (K-SADS), 643–44
schema theory, 225–26. *See also* cognitive
    theory
    intolerance of uncertainty model and,
        231
    Salkovski's cognitive behavioral model of
        OCD and, 239
schizo-obsessive disorder, 61
schizophrenia
    Expressed Emotion and, 182
    OCD comorbidity in, 61
schizotypal personality traits, 593

Schmidt protocol, 445
    outcome data, 446–47
SCID. *See* Structured Clinical Interview
    for DSM-IV Axis I Disorders
SCL-90-R
    BSI-18 and, 515
    older adults and, 628
Screen for Child Anxiety and Related
    Emotional Disorders (SCARED),
    644
screening programs, 514–15
SC. *See* supportive counseling
SDPT. *See* Substance Dependence PTSD
    Therapy
selective serotonin reuptake inhibitors
    (SSRIs), 11
    AD-depression comorbidity treatment
        and, 583
    ADs in youth and, 647–49
    alternatives, 376–78
    augmentation, 376–78
    BDD treatment and, 547–48
    CBT and, for SAD treatment, 338
    discontinuation, CBT discontinuation
        v., 379
    for GAD, 350, 352
        in special populations, 352–53
    hypochondriasis treatment and, 535
    neuroimaging treatment studies and, 105
    for OCD, 376–78
        efficacy of, 246–47
    OCD *v.* depression and, 579
    for older adults, 630
    PD treatment and, 297–99
    pregnancy and, 384–85
    in primary care, 515
    PTSD treatment and, 408–10
    SAD treatment and, 321–25
        response, 328–29
    side effects, 515
    TKS and, 660
selegiline, 325
self-administered therapy, 489, 490
self confrontation, 493–94
self-criticism, 196
    PTSD and, 198
self-harm disorders, OCD and, 28
self-help treatments, 488, 675
    ethics of, 494–95
    meta-analysis of, 491
    overview, 490t
    recent studies, 491–94
self-medication hypothesis, 568
self-monitoring forms, 285
self-perception, social phobia and, 217
Self-Rating Inventory for PTSD (SRIP),
    628
self-regulation
    metacognitive model of GAD and, 228
    PTSD risk factors and, 126–27
self-reporting
    for children, 644
    fear of pain assessment and, 556–57

in older adults, 627–28
    scales, 285
    screening, 514–15
sensation-focused intensive therapy
    (SFIT), PDA treatment and, 310
sensitivity
    aesthetic, 544
    parenting style and, 163
    in PTSD treatment, 70
SEPAD. *See* separation anxiety disorder
separation anxiety disorder (SEPAD)
    agoraphobia and, 23
    cortisol and, 164
    developmental approach to, 127
    prevalence of, 24–25
    prevention of, 123–24
serotonin (5-HT), 7–8
    anxiety-like behavior modulation and,
        78
    hypothesis, 376
    PTSD and, 407
serotonin-norepinephrine reuptake
    inhibitors (SNRIs), 11
    CBT and, 429–30
    course of, 280
    etiology of, 7–11
    FDA and, 299
    for GAD, 350, 353
    for GSAD, 321
    introduction to, 4–7
    monotherapy randomized controlled
        trials, 376
    neurobiological approach to, 4
    PD treatment and, 297–99
    psychological approach to, 4
    PTSD treatment and, 410
    for SAD treatment, 323
    side effects, 515
    as SSRI alternative, in OCD treatment,
        378
serotonin reuptake inhibitors (SRIs)
    augmentation, 376–78, 380–83
    replacement, 380–83
serotonin transporter promoter
    (5-HTTLPR), 7–8
    SAD treatment response and, 328–29
sertraline, 409
    for older adults, 629
    for SAD treatment, 322
Sesbania grandiflora, 456
sexual abuse. *See also* childhood sexual
    abuse
    childhood anxiety disorders and, 176
    OCD and, 130
sexual obsession, 58–59
SFIT. *See* sensation-focused intensive
    therapy
shame
    PTSD treatment and, 422
    social phobia and, 211
Short Anxiety Screening Test (SAST),
    627
shyness, 195

sibling relationships, 178
simple phobia. *See also* specific phobia
  family studies and, 89
  linkage studies, 91
SimP. *See* simple phobia
single nucleotide polymorphism (SNP), association studies of, 92
SIT. *See* stress inoculation therapy
situationally accessed memory (SAM), 256
skills deficit, 281
sleep
  ADs and, 611
  age and, 612
  assessment, 612
  deprivation, 614
  disturbance
    anxiety and, 613
    CBT-I for, 615
    comorbid in AD, 615–17
    emotional processing and, 614–15
    functional impairment and, 613*f*
    mood regulation and, 614
  quality of life and, 612–13
SNP. *See* single nucleotide polymorphism
SNRIs. *See* serotonin-norepinephrine reuptake inhibitors
social anxiety
  BDD and, 547
  behavioral models for, 212
social anxiety disorder (SAD). *See also* generalized social anxiety disorder; social phobia
  AS and, 196–97
  ACC and, 101
  alarms and, 41–42
  amygdala and, 99–100
  CBT for, 334–37
  cognitions and, 42
  comorbidity in depression, treatment, 583
  culture and, 660
  definition, 37–38
  dropout rates, 431
  FFM and, 195–97
  hippocampus and, 103
  insula and, 103
  lifetime prevalence of, 38
  mPFC and, 102
  neuroendocrinology of, 117–18
  neuroimaging treatment studies and, 106
  PCC and, 104
  perfectionism and, 196
  personality factors in, 195–97
  phenomenology of, 38–39
  remission, 328
  standardized measures for, 286
  subtypes, 341
  symptom criteria, 579
  treatment
    ACT and, 340–41
    alternate approaches, 340–41
    augmentation strategies, 328
    benzodiazepines and, 324

    CBT *v.* drug, 326
    cognitive change, 343
    combination therapy, 326–28, 327*t*
    drug comparison, 326*t*
    efficacy, 325–26
    efficacy studies, 433
    expectancies, 342
    homework compliance, 342–43
    IPT and, 340
    MAIOs and, 323
    outcome factors, 341–43
    pharmacology and CBT for, 338–39
    psychodynamic therapy and, 340
    relaxation strategies and, 337
    resistance, 328
    response predictors, 328–29
    RIMAs and, 323–24
    SNRIs and, 323
    SSRIs and, 321–25
    SST and, 336–37
    tricyclic antidepressants and, 323
  in youth, 637
Social Avoidance and Distress Scale (SADS), 286
Social Effectiveness Therapy for Children (SET-C), 646
social performance, social skills *v.*, 179
social phobia, 5. *See also* social anxiety disorder
  AOO of, 21
  association studies of, 92
  CBT and, 211
  control and, 218
  cultural influences on, 181
  danger and, 165
  depression and, 269–70
  diagnostic reliability of, 266
  exposure treatments and, 468
  family studies and, 89
  genetic studies of, 269
  heritability of, 88
  linkage studies, 89–91
  marriage and, 179
  model of, 217*f*
  panic attacks and, 209–10
  prevalence of, 24
  quality of life and, 282
  self-perception and, 217
  shame *v.* anger and, 211
  with social skills, 179
  treatment, 145
  triggers, 166–67
social phobia (SOP), in youth, 638
Social Phobia and Anxiety Inventory (SPAI), 286
Social Phobia Inventory (SPIN), 286
  screening, 515
social rejection, 10, 178–79
social relationships, 178–82
social skills
  perceived, 166–67
  SAD and, 38
  social performance *v.*, 179

social skills training (SST), for SAD, 336–37
social support, PTSD and, 68
societal costs, 29
SocP. *See* social phobia
Socratic questioning
  in primary care, 517
  PTSD treatment and, 418
somatic approaches, to OCD treatment, 378–79
somatic clusters, OCSD and, 59
somatic symptoms
  anxiety sensitivity and, 192
  culture and, 661–62
  danger *v.*, 166
  scar model and, 195
  of youth, 637
somatoform disorders, panic attacks and, 36
South African Truth and Reconciliation Commission (TRC), 661
SPAI. *See* Social Phobia and Anxiety Inventory
specificity, 125
specific phobia (SP)
  comorbidity in, 41
  phenomenology of, 40–41
specific phobias (SP), 5–6
  ACC and, 101
  alcohol abuse comorbidity in, 569–70
  amygdala and, 100
  AOO of, 21
  AOO variation of, 22
  APD *v.*, 588*t*
  attentional avoidance and, 139
  behavioral models for, 211–15
  cognitive behavioral interventions for, 343–44
  comorbidity in BDD, 541
  comorbidity in cancer, 602–3
  comorbidity in SUD, treatment, 571–72
  covariation bias and, 144–45
  definition of, 39–40
  developmental approach to, 127–28
  DSM-IV and, 209
  fear of pain *v.*, 555
  FFM and, 201–2
  heritability of, 88
  hippocampus and, 103
  insula and, 103
  learned, 177–78
  lifetime prevalence of, 40
  mPFC and, 102
  MPS and, 202
  neuroendocrinology of, 118
  neuroimaging treatment studies and, 106
  panic disorder *v.*, 39–40
  PCC and, 104
  personality factors in, 201–2
  pharmacological treatment of, 329
  prevalence of, 22–23
  prevention of, 123–24
  in primary care, 515

psychoanalytic theory and, 210–11
self-administered therapy and, 490
skills deficit and, 281
subtypes, 39
SUD comorbidity in, 566
symptom criteria, 579–80
treatment, outcome predictors, 345
twin studies of, 158
vicarious conditioning and, 213–14
vicarious learning and, 166
youth and, 639
speeches
   attention and, 138
   PCC and, 104
   safety behaviors and, 218–19
SPIN. *See* Social Phobia Inventory
SQUID. *See* superconducting quantum
   interference device
SRIP. *See* Self-Rating Inventory for PTSD
SRIs. *See* serotonin reuptake inhibitors
SSRIs. *See* selective serotonin reuptake
   inhibitors
stability, neuroticism and, 157
STAIC. *See* State-Trait Anxiety Inventory
   for Children
STAI. *See* State-Trait Anxiety Inventory
standard community care (SCC), 647
standardized measures, 285–88
startle reflex, 77
State-Trait Anxiety Inventory (STAI), 233
   older adults and, 627
State-Trait Anxiety Inventory for Children
   (STAIC), 644
stathmin, 80
stimulus control, GAD treatment and, 365
St. John's wort
   CAM and, 451
   for SAD treatment, 325
stop, look, and listen state, 154
Streptococcus pyrogenes, 605
stress
   amygdala and, 127–28
   controllable *v.* uncontrollable, 160
   CRF and, 78–79
   fear enhancement by, 81
   nontraumatic, 70
   tolerance, hypochondriasis and, 526
stress-diathesis disorder, 126
stress inoculation therapy (SIT), 418
   PE and, 419–20
stressors
   autonomic response to, in rodents, 77
   ongoing, PTSD and, 68
   PTSD risk factors and, 70, 126
   traumatic, 251
   unpredictable, 160
stress response, CRH in, 112
stress-response dampening models, 568
stress response theory of PTSD, 257
Stroop interference
   attention and, 137
   overriding, 138
structural equation modeling, 88

Structured Clinical Interview for DSM-IV
   Axis I Disorders (SCID), 266
   hypochondriasis assessment and, 530
   older adults and, 628
   proliferation of, 279–80
Substance Dependence PTSD Therapy
   (SDPT), 572
substance use disorders (SUDs)
   comorbid, 565
   comorbidity, 642
   comorbidity in ADs
      lifetime prevalence of, 567*t*
      treatment, 571–73
   comorbidity in OCD, treatment, 572
   comorbidity in PD, 569
      treatment, 571
   comorbidity in PTSD, 570
      treatment, 572–73
   comorbidity in SP, treatment, 571–72
   diagnosis, 566
   in youth, 643
   subtypes, understanding, 670
sudden cardiac arrest (SCA), 597
SUDs. *See* substance use disorders
suicide
   BDD comorbidity in, 543
   risk, 4
superconditioning, 255
superconducting quantum interference
   device (SQUID), 456
supplements, 457
supportive counseling (SC), for ASD,
   423–24
surgery, do-it-yourself, 543
surgical approaches, to OCD treatment,
   378–79
susceptibility hypothesis, 570
sustained excitation, during exposure
   treatments, 472
symmetry, 58–59
symptom induction exercises, 284–85
systematic review, 490–91

T

TAF. *See* thought-action fusion
taijin kyofusho (TK), 39
   cultural influences on, 181
   culture and, 660
Tampa Scale of Kinesiophobia (TSK), 556
Task Force on Promotion and
   Dissemination of Psychological
   Procedures
TAU. *See* treatment as usual
TCAs. *See* tricyclic antidepressants
TCM. *See* traditional Chinese medicine
Teacher Report Form (TRF), 645
telephone-based treatments, 675
temperament
   AD-depression comorbidity and, 582
   ADs in youth and, 640
   behavioral models and, 214
temperament models, 156–57
   genetics in, 165

TENC. *See also* trauma-exposted non-
   PTSD control
   ACC and, 101
   hippocampus and, 103
   insula and, 102–3
   mPFC and, 101–2
tender conscience, 244
tension-reduction theory, 568
TF-CBT. *See* trauma-focused therapy
therapists
   ERP and, 393
   variables, in PDA treatment, 316
thought-action fusion (TAF), 9, 52
   OCD development and, 167
   Rachman's cognitive behavioral model of
      OCD and, 241
   Salkovski's cognitive behavioral model of
      OCD and, 239
   in youth, 638–39
thought control, 241–42
threat(s)
   attention and, 154
   attention bias and, 137–39
   covariation bias and, 145
   directed forgetting and, 141
   domains, 58
   information, 177–78
   interpretive bias for, 143
   memory bias and, 140
   PTSD and, 65–66
thymus hypertrophy, 112
thyroid peroxidase autoantibodies
   (TPOAb), 601
thyroid stimulating hormone (TSH), 601
tiagabine, for GAD, 359
tic disorders, OCD and, 28
The Times, 674
TK. *See* taijin kyofusho
TMS. *See* transcranial magnetic
   stimulation
tonic immobility. *See* freezing
Tourette's syndrome
   OCD and, 6
   OCD comorbidity in, 129
   PANDAS and, 605–6
TPOAb. *See* thyroid peroxidase
   autoantibodies
traditional Chinese medicine (TCM), 456
training
   CBT, 674
   compassionate mind, 546
   prevention, 508
   PTSD treatment, 424–26
trait models, 156–57
transcranial magnetic stimulation (TMS),
   for OCD treatment, 378
transdiagnostic treatment protocols,
   444–46
   case reports, 446–47
   outcome data, 446–47
   quasi-experimental trials, 447
   RCTs, 447
   uncontrolled trials, 447

trauma, 405–6. *See also* PTSD
  ADs in youth and, 640–41
  definition, 66–67
  dosage, 252
  EMDR and, 419
  PTSD prevalence and, 26
  PTSD risk factors and, 126
  specific phobia and, 40
  survivors, 423–24
  treatment dissemination, 424–26
  vulnerability to, 197
trauma-exposed non-PTSD control
    (TENC), amygdala and, 99
trauma-focused therapy (TF-CBT), 647
traumatic brain injuries, 603
TRC. *See* South African Truth and
    Reconciliation Commission
treatment(s)
  access to, 674–75
  algorithm, for OCD, 382–83*f*
  approaches, 4
  assessment following, 288
  availability of, 431
  CAM and, 457
  combination
    availability of, 431–33
    with DCS, 435
    frontal activation, 436
    use of, 434
  of comorbidity, 279
  effects, core pathology conceptualization
    and, 442–43
  frequency, 282
  generalist, 365–66
    efficacy of, 370–71
  group, 444
  history, 282
  key components in, 672
  manualized, 424–25
  mechanisms and, 672–73
  motivation to begin, 402
  neuroimaging, 105–6
  options, 515
  of particular groups, 673–74
  refusal of, 239
  relationships and, 182–84
  resistant cases, 673
  tolerability of, 430–31
  unified models of, 442
treatment as usual (TAU)
  CC *v.*, 518
  hypochondriasis treatment and,
    CBT v, 538
  PDA treatment and, 312–13
TRF. *See* Teacher Report Form
trichotillomania, 6, 28
tricyclic antidepressants (TCAs)
  ADs in youth and, 648
  ASD treatment and, 407
  for GAD, 350, 353
  hypochondriasis treatment and, 535
  monotherapy randomized controlled
    trials, 376

PD treatment and, 299
pregnancy and, 384–85
in primary care, 516
for SAD treatment, 323
side effects, 516
Tridimensional Personality Questionnaire
    Harm Avoidance Scale, family
    studies and, 89
triggers, 280–81
  of doubt, 394
Tripartite Model, 191–92
  OCD and, 199
  SAD and, 195–97
  validity of, 268
triple vulnerability theory, 153,
    156–67
trust, in PTSD treatment, 70
TSH. *See* thyroid stimulating hormone
TSK. *See* Tampa Scale of Kinesiophobia
twin studies, 88
  environment and, 173
  of hypochondriasis, 527–28
  of specific phobia, 158
two-factor theory, 252

U

UCR. *See* unconditioned response
UCS. *See* unconditioned stimulus
uncertainty, 230. *See also* intolerance of
    uncertainty
unconditioned response (UCR), 251–52
unconditioned stimulus (UCS), 251–52
University of Manchester, 491
unreliability, diagnostic, 266
U.S. Air Force, 193
U.S. National Comorbidity Survey
    Replication, 28–29

V

valerian, 452–53
Valeriana officinalis. See valerian
VAM. *See* verbally accessed memory
venlafaxine
  AD-depression comorbidity treatment
    and, 583
  for GAD, 353
  for SAD treatment, 323
ventral mPFC (vmPFC), 101–2
verbally accessed memory (VAM), 256
vicarious learning, 165–66
Vietnam, 405
Vietnam Era Twin Registry data, 88
violence
  PTSD epidemiology and, 70
  PTSD prevalence and, 27
Virginia Adult Twin Study of Psychiatric
    and Substance Use Disorders, 158
virtual reality exposure (VRE), 675
  acrophobia treatment and, 329
  specific phobia treatment and, 343–44
vitamins, 453
vmPFC. *See* ventral mPFC
VRE. *See* virtual reality exposure

vulnerabilities
  model for, 191–92
  specific, 165–67

W

waitlist control, 246
  BSM *v.*, 535
WDQ. *See* Worry Domains Questionnaire
Weekly Record of Anxiety and
    Depression, 285
Wells, Adrian, 368
WGAS. *See* whole genome association study
whole genome association study (WGAS),
    93
whole medical systems, 456–57
WHO. *See* World Health Organization
Withania somnifera, 456
WMH. *See* World Mental Health Survey
    Initiative
word-stem completion, 140–41
World Health Organization (WHO)
  CIDI and, 20
  OCD and, 56
World Mental Health (WMH) Survey
    Initiative, 20
  comorbidity and, 29
  prevalence of SEPAD and, 24–25
  SEPD and, 23
worry, 4
  anxiety and, 155
  anxiety *v.,* 49–50
  as avoidance behavior, 227
  beliefs about, 368
  chronic, obsessions *v.,* 270
  cognitive avoidance theory of, 226–28
  as coping strategy, 227
  definitions of, 49–50
  depressive rumination and, 52
  effects of, 50
  GAD and, 49–51, 226, 366, 578
  GAD *v.,* 48
  metacognitive model of, 228–30
  NATs *v.,* 232
  negative beliefs and, 228–29
  negative problem orientation and, 231
  normal *v.* pathological, 50–51
  obsessions and, 51–52
  in older adults, 626
  pathological, 229
  positive beliefs and, 230, 368
  reduced-concreteness theory of, 227
  related cognition phenomena and, 51–52
  triggers, 228
  Type 1 *v.* Type 2, 228–29
  usefulness of, 233
  verbal component of, 227
  work of, 228
Worry Domains Questionnaire (WDQ),
    287
Worry Scale (WS), 627
written emotional disclosure, 372–73
WSG. *See* glycowithanolides
WS. *See* Worry Scale

Y

Yale-Brown Obsessive Compulsive Scale
(Y-BOCS), 287
  ERP efficacy and, 395
  ERP with CT and, 398–99
  neuroimaging treatment studies and, 106
  OCD treatment and, 380
Y-BOCS. *See* Yale-Brown Obsessive
  Compulsive Scale
yoga, 455
yohimbine hydrochloride, 436

youth. *See also* children
  ADs in
    aspects of, 638–39
    comorbidity of, 641–42
    prevalence of, 641, 642*t*
    risk factors, 639–41
    treatment, 645–49
  anxiety assessment in, 643–45
  anxiety disorders in, longitudinal
    research of, 642–43
  anxiety in, 636–38

  clinical interviews of, 643–44
  cognitive distortions of,
    636–37
  combination treatment for,
    649
  emotional functioning of, 637
  GAD in, 638
  OCD in, 638–39
  PTSD and, 639
  SOP in, 638
  SP and, 639